The Constitutional
Rights of Women

NEW EDITION,

REVISED AND UPDATED

The Constitutional Rights of Women

Cases in Law
and
Social Change

Leslie Friedman Goldstein

The University

of Wisconsin Press

Published 1988

The University of Wisconsin Press
114 North Murray Street
Madison, Wisconsin 53715

The University of Wisconsin Press, Ltd.
1 Gower Street
London WC1E 6HA, England

Second edition

Printed in the United States of America

For LC CIP information see the colophon

ISBN 0-299-11240-3 cloth; 0-299-11244-6 paper

This book is dedicated to my past and
future students of women and the
law. They continue to inspire and
refresh my interest in the subject.

Contents

Introduction   xi

1. Ancient History: Early Interpretations of Due Process and
   Equal Protection   3

   Due Process and Equal Protection Clauses: The *Slaughter-House
   Cases* (1873) discussion   /   3

   Legislation Protective of Women and the Due Process Clause   /   8

   Substantive Due Process   /   8
      Lochner v. New York (1905)   /   8

   Protection for Women and the Decline of Economic
   Substantive Due Process   /   19
      Muller v. Oregon (1908)   /   19
      Bunting v. Oregon (1917)   /   23
      Adkins v. Children's Hospital (1923)   /   24
      Radice v. New York (1924)   /   37
      West Coast Hotel Company v. Parrish (1937)   /   41
      United States v. Darby (1941), excerpt   /   48

   The Pregnancy Leave Issue: Old Wine in New Bottles   /   49
      California Federal Savings and Loan v. Guerra (1987)   /   49
      Wimberly v. Labor and Industrial Relations Commission
      (1987), discussion   /   65

2. The Equal Protection Clause and Gender Discrimination: 1868–1975   66

   Dead-End Road to Equality: The Privileges or
   Immunities Clause   /   66

   Access to the Bar: *Myra Bradwell v. State of Illinois* (1873)   /   66
      Brief of Bradwell's Counsel, excerpt   /   67
      Bradwell v. Illinois (1873)   /   70

   Early Struggle for the Ballot   /   73
      Minor v. Happersett (1875)   /   73

   The Ballot Through Constitutional Amendment: Women Take to
   the Streets   /   83

   Introduction to the Equal Protection Clause   /   88

Suspect Classification / 88
McLaughlin v. Florida (1964), excerpt / 90
Ordinary Equal Protection Scrutiny / 92
Sex as a Classification: A Century of "Ordinary Scrutiny" / 95
Discrimination Against Men / 95
Quong Wing v. Kirkendall (1912) / 95
Breedlove v. Suttles (1937) / 99
Discrimination Against Women / 101
Goesaert v. Cleary (1948) / 101
Hoyt v. Florida (1961) / 104
Ballard v. United States (1946), discussion / 105
Sex as a Semisuspect Classification / 109
Reed v. Reed (1971) / 112
Frontiero v. Richardson (1973) / 115
Kahn v. Shevin (1974) / 127
Schlesinger v. Ballard (1975) / 133
Taylor v. Louisiana (1975) / 140
Weinberger v. Wiesenfeld (1975) / 152
Stanton v. Stanton (1975) / 159

3. Gender and "More Rigid Scrutiny"   165
New Rule / 165
Craig v. Boren (1976) / 165
Craig Rule in Operation / 179
Califano v. Goldfarb (1977) / 179
Califano v. Webster (1977) / 192
Wengler v. Druggists Mutual Insurance (1980), discussion / 195

Fathers' Rights and Equal Protection / 196
Stanley v. Illinois (1972) / 196
Fiallo v. Bell (1977), discussion / 205
Quilloin v. Walcott (1978), discussion / 207
Caban v. Mohammed (1979) / 208
Parham v. Hughes (1979), discussion / 221
Lehr v. Robertson (1983) / 222

Revolutionizing Marriage / 232
Orr v. Orr (1979) / 233
Kirchberg v. Feenstra (1981), discussion / 240

Defining Discrimination: The Question of Impact / 240
Personnel Administrator v. Feeney (1979) / 240

The Military / 249
Rostker v. Goldberg (1981) / 249

Rape / 267
Michael M. v. Sonoma County (1981) / 267

Separate But Equal / 282
    Williams v. McNair (1971), discussion / 284
    Vorchheimer v. Philadelphia (1977), discussion / 285
    Mississippi University for Women v. Hogan (1982) / 286

4. Women, Procreation, and the Right of Privacy   298
    Substantive Due Process and Implied Rights / 298
    Sterilization / 302
        Buck v. Bell (1927) / 303
        Skinner v. Oklahoma (1942) / 305
    Contraception / 310
        Griswold v. Connecticut (1965) / 310
        Eisenstadt v. Baird (1972) / 323
        Carey v. Population Services International (1977), discussion / 333
    Abortion / 334
        Roe v. Wade and *Doe v. Bolton* (1973) / 336
    Restrictions on Abortion / 360
        Planned Parenthood v. Danforth (1976) / 361
        Bellotti v. Baird (1976), discussion / 373
        H.L. v. Matheson (1981), discussion / 374
        Colautti v. Franklin (1979), discussion / 374
        City of Akron v. Akron Center for Reproductive Health (1983) / 374
        Planned Parenthood v. Ashcroft and *Simopoulos v. Virginia*
            (1983), discussion / 395
        Thornburgh v. ACOG (1986) / 395
    Money for Abortions / 413
        Beal v. Doe (1977) / 413
        Maher v. Roe (1977) / 420
        Poelker v. Doe (1977) / 434
        Harris v. McRae (1980) / 437
    Penalties on Pregnancy / 455
        Cleveland Board of Education v. LaFleur (1974) / 455
        Turner v. Department of Employment (1975), discussion / 464
        Geduldig v. Aiello (1974) / 464
        General Electric v. Gilbert (1976) / 469
        Nashville Gas v. Satty (1977) / 480
        Newport News Shipbuilding v. EEOC (1983) / 488

5. Congressional Enforcement of Equal Protection   498
    Employment / 498
        The First Decade of Judicial Implementation / 498
            Phillips v. Martin-Marietta Corporation (1971) / 498
            Corning Glass Works v. Brennan (1974), discussion / 501
            Dothard v. Rawlinson (1977) / 504

Pensions / 513
Los Angeles Department of Water and Power v. Manhart
(1978) / 513
Arizona Governing Committee v. Norris (1983) / 523
Note on Comparable Worth / 537
County of Washington v. Gunther (1981), discussion / 537
First Amendment Rights vs. Anti-Discrimination Law / 539
Pittsburgh Press v. Human Relations Commission (1973),
discussion / 539
Hishon v. King & Spaulding (1984), discussion / 539
Roberts v. U.S. Jaycees (1984), discussion / 540
Hudnut v. American Booksellers' Association (1986),
discussion / 541
Education / 542
Grove City College v. Bell (1984) / 542
Sexual Harassment / 552
Meritor Savings Bank v. Vinson (1986) / 552
Affirmative Action / 562
Johnson v. Transportation Agency (1987) / 562

Epilogue   585

Notes   589

Timetable of Women's Rights Cases   601

Appendix A: How the Supreme Court Operates   613

Appendix B: The Constitution of the United States   617

Case Index   631

Introduction

Several good reasons can be stated for studying women's rights from the perspective of American constitutional law. For one, it is an area of law in which rapid and substantial change has taken place within the quite recent past. The U.S. Supreme Court has flatly reversed itself, explicitly altering the meaning of the national Constitution within a mere fourteen-year time span (*Hoyt v. Florida,* 1961, was overruled by *Taylor v. Louisiana,* 1975). The Court has initiated profound and controversial social change by announcing that a woman's right to have an abortion is a right secured to her by the Constitution (*Roe v. Wade* and *Doe v. Bolton,* 1973). And the Court has grappled with the dilemma of knowing that while a particular constitutional amendment (the Equal Rights Amendment) had been overwhelmingly adopted by Congress and appeared for ten years to be in the process of obtaining state ratification, several members of the Court believed that the content of the new amendment already was implicit in the Constitution. Thus, the arena of women's rights provides a nearly ideal laboratory for examining the way the Supreme Court of the United States, as interpreter of the fundamental law of the land, both initiates and responds to social change. The role that legal argument plays in this process, the role of changing societal mores and assumptions, and perhaps even the role of political pressures, can all be explored by analyzing these cases.

These cases provide, in addition, a stage on which abstract legal terms such as "suspect classification," "minimum rationality scrutiny," and "substantive due process" take on concrete meaning, as readers see them applied to live controversies of topical interest. Moreover, readers will be able to trace the roots of these doctrines back into their legal-historical origins; they can witness the twists and turns of the substantive due process doctrine, for example, as it evolves from the solid roots of *Lochner v. New York* to apparent withering in *West Coast Hotel v. Parrish* and *United States v. Darby,* and then to the surprise sprouting of a vigorous new branch in *Griswold v. Connecticut.*

Of course, even more pressing, albeit mundane, reasons emerge for studying these cases: there is value in simply knowing what is the standing law of the land, especially on important questions of public policy. Knowledge of the existing constitutional law is an essential prerequisite for deciding, for example, whether the Equal Rights Amendment needs to be added to the Constitution.

Such knowledge will also be a valuable tool in assessing the probable legal impact of that amendment. Acquaintance with present law is indispensable for evaluating the need for future law.

Finally, as is true of any study of constitutional law (i.e., of law presumed to be in some sense "higher than the product of mere legislative majorities"), these cases provide an opportunity for the reader to ponder serious and perennial normative questions, questions ultimately linked to the core issue of what constitutes the good society. Some of the questions relate particularly to women's rights as such. For example, is it permissible, and not a violation of the idea of fairness implied in the phrase "equal protection of the law," for society to provide a special tax advantage to widows that it denies to widowers? (See *Kahn v. Shevin.*) If it is permissible to have special protective legislation for women, where is the line to be drawn between protecting women, on the one hand, and cutting women off from important legal and political rights, on the other? (See *Bradwell v. Illinois, Hoyt v. Florida, Taylor v. Louisiana.*) And at what point does well-intentioned protective legislation for women become unfair discrimination against men? (Compare *Kahn v. Shevin* to *Weinberger v. Wiesenfeld.*)

Other normative questions arising out of these cases reach far beyond women's issues as such. The *Adkins v. Children's Hospital/West Coast Hotel v. Parrish* line of cases presents the eternally problematic question of how far an individual's liberty may be hindered for the sake of societal welfare. A great many of these cases pose the general question of whether some sectors of society may be singled out by the law for special treatment, and the subsidiary but more difficult question of how to decide at what point such special treatment becomes unjust to the rest of society. Of particular importance to the American regime, but also of importance to all other would-be democratic regimes, is the question posed with particular force by the abortion cases: Even as a body of nonaccountable decision makers, set purposefully above political pressures because of their assumed superior wisdom on the law, just how far can the Supreme Court distance itself from prevailing public opinion? Does too much distance tend to the destruction of the very democratic quality that makes the Constitution worth protecting in the first place?

Throughout this book, the questions asked at the end of each case have attempted to stimulate the exploration of some of these issues. But, as another constitutional casebook once pointed out, the most important question in every case has actually been omitted: How would you have decided this case?*

Before proceeding to a discussion of actual cases, it may be helpful to define what I mean by "women's rights." The term actually has three different usages in this text. First, it refers to women's right to be treated equally with men. Portions

*Walter F. Barnes, *Constitutional Cases in American Government* vi (New York: Thomas Y. Crowell, 1963).

of chapters 1 through 3 deal with women's rights in this sense. Women have a right to "equal protection of the law," and equal treatment of them in this sense is commanded by the Constitution. In other words, statutes denying this kind of equality of treatment are directly proscribed by the Constitution.

Second, the term can refer to women's right to be treated unequally from men, in other words, favored or "protected" by the law. When used in this sense, the word "right" does not mean that the Constitution requires such treatment (*contra* the first usage), but it does mean that the Constitution permits such difference of treatment. Another way of stating this idea is to say that men's right to "equal protection of the law" does not mean they shall in every way be treated the same as women. The courts recognize that not all groups in society are "similarly situated" and that to compensate for dissimilar societal situations, it may be appropriate to allow unequal treatment by the law in order to attain "equal protection of the law." The Fourteenth Amendment has been read as sometimes permitting (but not as commanding) such unequal treatment of women. Other portions of chapters 1 through 3 deal with this development.

Finally, "women's rights" can refer to rights that are common to all American citizens but affect women in particularly strong ways, or affect only women, for reasons that are biological rather than legal. The constitutional right to privacy in matters as personal as birth control and abortion is in a real sense a woman's right because women are the ones who give birth and have abortions. (Of course, men share in the right to use birth control, and in a certain sense share in the right to terminate a pregnancy involving their own offspring. Clearly, however, the potential mother is the more drastically and directly affected by the denial or the granting of these rights.) Chapter 4 deals with women's rights in this third sense of the term.

Although women's rights under the law in fact vary from state to state, since we live under fifty different state legal systems, this text treats only national-level women's rights. When Congress exercises its power to enforce the Fourteenth Amendment (see section 5 of that amendment) by passing statutes that assure women equal treatment within particular contexts (e.g., hiring and firing for jobs in the private sector), Congress is rendering such treatment a legal right of women that applies nationwide. Similarly, any Supreme Court interpretation of women's rights under the Constitution applies nationwide. By contrast, judicial or legislative interpretations, issued by state authorities, of rights under state constitutions, although they may affect in significant ways the lives of millions of people, are limited in their impact to the jurisdiction of that one state. Consequently they are not treated in this book. The same applies to rulings of particular federal district or circuit courts; their interpretations of federal law are binding only within their own district or circuit. Thus, they are omitted from this book, despite their importance in affecting the lives of many people.

The Constitutional
Rights of Women

CHAPTER 1

Ancient History: Early Interpretations of Due Process and Equal Protection

The Due Process and Equal Protection Clauses: The Slaughter-House Cases (1873)

Contemporary Americans have a tendency to assume that any statute that they do not like must be somehow unconstitutional; indeed, their chances of convincing federal judges on the point have increased dramatically over the past three decades. That recent increase would not have been possible without three specific developments of the nineteenth century: the Thirteenth, Fourteenth, and Fifteenth amendments to the U.S. Constitution. Before those amendments were adopted, although the federal government was hemmed in by various clauses, including the famous Bill of Rights (the first ten amendments to the Constitution), state governments were left almost entirely unfettered by the Constitution.[1] Most of the legislation affecting our daily lives is state legislation, and state governments were originally free to infringe on freedom of speech, to establish religions, to try people without giving them lawyers, and to treat various groups of persons—including women—as unequally as they pleased. During the nineteenth century state governments did all these things and many others that seem equally shocking to us in our twentieth century notions of the Constitution.

The post–Civil War amendments changed this situation, placing the shield of the national Constitution between the basic citizen rights of the individual and the potentially tyrannical government of his or her own state. The Thirteenth Amendment freed the slaves, and the Fifteenth Amendment prohibited states from depriving persons of the right to vote on the grounds of race or previous condition of servitude. The Fourteenth Amendment cast its net more broadly, encompassing what might be viewed as the fundamental rights of citizenship, or even the fundamental rights of life within a free and just society. It contains three clauses that have together shouldered the burden of most of the important constitutional litigation of the twentieth century.

1. No state shall make or enforce any law which shall abridge the privileges or immunities of citizens of the United States;

2. nor shall any state deprive any person of life, liberty, or property without due process of law;

3. nor deny to any person within its jurisdiction the equal protection of the laws.

Reference is made to these three clauses so frequently that they are called simply (1) the privileges or immunities clause, (2) the due process clause, and (3) the equal protection clause. Although the privileges or immunities clause seems to sweep the most broadly of the three, its efficacy was drastically undermined in early Fourteenth Amendment litigation. This development left to the two remaining clauses the job of protecting civil rights and civil liberties against state governmental interference. Indeed, the task of protecting women's rights, as well as of protecting virtually all other constitutional rights, has fallen upon the due process clause and the equal protection clause.

Women's rights litigation is about as old as Fourteenth Amendment litigation. The first women's rights case (*Bradwell v. State of Illinois*, see chapter 2) was decided by the Supreme Court in 1873 on the day after the Court had handed down its first Fourteenth Amendment decision in the *Slaughter-House Cases*. (Incidentally, the *Bradwell* arguments were presented to the Court two weeks before those of the *Slaughter-House Cases*.) In the *Slaughter-House Cases*, the Supreme Court laid down the basic rules of the game for future Fourteenth Amendment litigation, rules effective, to some extent, today. The basic impact of those cases was to decimate the privileges or immunities clause as a potential grounds for attacking state statutes.

The cases arose out of challenges by a number of butchers to a Louisiana statute that granted to a single corporation located in a prescribed area a twenty-five-year monopoly for maintaining "slaughterhouses, landings for cattle and stockyards" within the metropolitan area surrounding and including New Orleans. Under this 1869 statute, butchers who wanted to continue to carry on their trade in the New Orleans area had to rent facilities from the monopoly at rates regulated by the state. Louisiana's rationale for passing the law was to protect the general population from the unpleasant fumes, sounds, and other disturbances associated with the slaughtering of animals by limiting those activities to a single, narrowly circumscribed area of town. The butchers argued that this law should be voided on several constitutional grounds; they claimed that it established "involuntary servitude" in violation of the Thirteenth Amendment, and that in violation of the Fourteenth Amendment it abridged their "privileges or immunities" of American citizenship, took their liberty and property without due process of law, and denied them equal protection of law.

In response to the Thirteenth Amendment argument, the Supreme Court said simply that it was not plausible to claim that a law restricting the slaughtering of cattle to a single part of the city, even if it did grant monopoly privileges to some, was somehow placing the nonmonopolists in a state of servitude. The Thirteenth Amendment argument was just too far-fetched to be convincing.

To answer the Fourteenth Amendment privileges or immunities argument, the Court had to dig a little harder, because there was a precedent interpreting the phrase "privileges and immunities" rather broadly, although the precedent involved not the Fourteenth Amendment but the privileges and immunities clause of Article IV (the one that calls for granting to out-of-staters "the privileges and immunities of citizens of the several states"). This precedent, *Corfield v. Coryell* (a non-Supreme Court case of 1823) had established that the phrase referred to

> those privileges and immunities which are fundamental; which belong of right to the citizens of all free governments, and which have at all times been enjoyed by citizens of the several states which compose this Union, from the time of their becoming free, independent, and sovereign. What these fundamental principles are, it would be more tedious than difficult to enumerate. They may all, however, be comprehended under the following general heads: protection by the government, with the right to acquire and possess property of every kind, and to pursue and obtain happiness and safety, subject nevertheless, to such restraints as the government may prescribe for the general good of the whole; the right of a citizen of one State to pass through, or reside in, any other State for purposes of trade, agriculture, professional pursuits, or otherwise; to claim the benefit of the writ of habeas corpus; to institute and maintain actions of any kind in the courts of the State; to take, hold, and dispose of property, either real or personal; and an exemption from higher taxes or impositions than are paid by the other citizens of the State, may be mentioned as some of the particular privileges and immunities of citizens which are clearly embraced by the general description of privileges deemed to be fundamental.[2]

As the four dissenters argued, this precedent and the Supreme Court precedents that had followed its line of argument seemed to establish that one's right to pursue a livelihood, and all other privileges which are so basic that they "belong of right to the citizens of all free governments," were now to be shielded by the Fourteenth Amendment from any harm one's own state government might attempt upon them. In other words, all those protections that the Article IV privileges and immunities clause created for citizens traveling into new states, the Fourteenth Amendment privileges or immunities clause now seemed to provide for citizens vis-à-vis their home-state governments. State governments would no longer be allowed to create and abolish civil rights according to their whims; civil rights of Americans would become truly nationalized. The Fourteenth Amendment thus wrought a radical shift in the governmental structure of the United States (although its being radical is not surprising if one recalls that the country had just fought a protracted and bloody Civil War over the states' rights question). It was such a radical shift that the Supreme Court majority in the *Slaughter-House Cases* refused to acknowledge that it had taken place.

Justice Miller wrote for the majority that the language of the Fourteenth Amendment privileges and immunities clause was not so clearly and emphatically radical in intent that he could accept the idea that the clause was designed to bring about such a drastic change.

> When, as in the case before us, these consequences are so serious, so far-reaching and pervading, so great a departure from the structure and spirit of our institutions; when the effect is to fetter and degrade the state governments . . . in the exercise of powers heretofore universally conceded to them of the most ordinary and fundamental character; when in fact it radically changes the whole theory of the relations of the State and Federal governments to each other and of both these governments to the people; . . . in the absence of language which expresses such a purpose too clearly to admit of doubt we must reject the "radical" interpretation.[3]

What then did Justice Miller make of the privileges and immunities clause? The answer is a simple one: not much. He argued that the Fourteenth Amendment phrase "privileges and immunities of citizens *of the United States*" meant something different from the notion of fundamental civic rights expressed in the Article IV phrase "privileges and immunities of citizens *of the several states.*" The Fourteenth Amendment, he maintained, safeguarded only the rights of national citizenship (a collection he very narrowly circumscribed). The basic civil rights described in *Corfield v. Coryell* he placed in the category of state citizenship rights, and these, he claimed, lay out of reach of the Fourteenth Amendment.

As for the content of those national citizenship rights, he explained that they were the special rights accruing to Americans by virtue of our living in a single united nation under a national constitution. For example, as national citizens we have a right of free access to all American seaports. This right derives from the clause that gives to Congress (rather than to the states) authority to regulate foreign commerce. The strange thing about Justice Miller's interpretation is that all the rights he places under the shield of the Fourteenth Amendment privileges or immunities clause were already protected by the national Constitution before the Fourteenth Amendment was adopted. He rendered the privileges or immunities clause a virtual nullity. And such it has remained to this day.

What did not endure from Justice Miller's *Slaughter-House Cases* opinion was the limited scope that he also tried to impose on the due process and equal protection clauses. In answer to the argument that a lawfully adopted statute regulating the property of butchers could be viewed as having deprived them of "property with due process of law," Miller took his bearings by the well-established meaning of the due process clause of the Fifth Amendment, which restrained the national government in words identical to those restraining the states in the Fourteenth. Miller said simply that "under no construction of that provision that we have ever seen, or any that we deem admissable" could such a property regulation be viewed as unlawful. Justice Miller was following the well-entrenched tradition that viewed the phrase "due process of law" as an obvious reference to the proper legal procedures or processes that had to accompany any taking of life, liberty, or property. He could not treat seriously enough even to design a counterargument, the claim that the due process clause regulated the substantive qualities of laws. He did not frame any real response to the novel viewpoint of dissenters Swayne and Bradley that if a law, in its substance, took away liberty or property to a degree that was not "fair" or "just,"[4] it violated the due process clause. As the next section of this chapter reveals, it took roughly thirty years for what was a new viewpoint in 1873 to become the official law of the land.

Finally, Justice Miller's majority opinion disposed of the equal protection clause argument with two sentences:

> We doubt very much whether any action of a State not directed by way of discrimination against the Negroes as a class, or on account of their race, will ever be held to come within the purview of this provision. It is so clearly a provision for that race and that emergency, that a strong case would be necessary for its application to any other.[5]

Miller did not unconditionally reject the possibility that the equal protection clause might be used to protect nonracial groups, such as women, but he expressed deep skepticism that a strong enough case would ever be presented to convince the Court to depart from the specific historical intention of the Fourteenth Amendment.

Miller's predictions concerning the restricted application of the equal protection clause proved considerably more durable than his expectations on the due process clause.[6] Although the reach of the clause fairly quickly stretched beyond "Negroes as a class" to strike down legislation that discriminated against Chinese/Orientals,[7] the clause did remain, until the mid-twentieth century, almost exclusively a prohibition on racial discrimination. This exclusive application, although not following the strict words of Miller's *Slaughter-House Cases* opinion, certainly seems to have been guided by its spirit of a narrow interpretation based on specific historic intent.

The only extension beyond the racial-discrimination concept of the equal protection clause that the Supreme Court ventured before the 1940s occurred in an area closely related to that of racial discrimination; in 1915 the Court used the equal protection clause to strike down a law that blatantly discriminated against aliens.[8] Alienage, of course, is closely tied conceptually to race. The logical heritage, then, from the *Slaughter-House Cases* version of the equal protection clause endured more or less intact well into the twentieth century.

Nevertheless, it should be noted that this narrow application of the Fourteenth Amendment was accompanied historically by a series of cases that gave lip service, but only lip service, to an equal protection standard of much more far-reaching potential. That standard was the rule that whenever the law "classified" different groups of persons, or treated them unequally, the classification had to have some "reasonable" relationship to promoting the public good. In other words, laws could treat people unequally if (but only if) there was some reasonable basis for doing so. In practice, however, this standard was all bark and no bite. An honest acknowledgment of its toothlessness is provided in one of the Court opinions from this period: "A classification may not be merely arbitrary, but necessarily there must be great freedom of discretion, even though it results in 'ill-advised, *unequal and oppressive* legislation'."[9]

In summary, then, the legacy of the *Slaughter-House Cases*, the first Supreme Court interpretation of the Fourteenth Amendment, was as follows: (1) the privileges or immunities clause was emptied of any real meaning; (2) the idea that the due process clause might create a limit on the substance of legislation, requiring that the mandate of a statute be "fair," was summarily rejected—so summarily that the majority opinion devoted virtually no discussion to determining what the due process clause did mean; (3) the equal protection clause was interpreted to focus narrowly on the evil of racial discrimination. Although the Court soon began to give lip service to the idea that the equal protection clause had a considerably more general impact, in practice it continued to follow the lead of the *Slaughter-House Cases* until the mid-twentieth century.

Legislation Protective of Women and the Due Process Clause

Substantive Due Process: *Lochner v. New York* (1905)

As they had for the butchers in Louisiana, corporate lawyers continued for years to hammer away at state economic regulations, using the Fourteenth Amendment as their principal weapon. The most effective part of that weapon proved to be the due process clause, interpreted so as to limit the substance of legislation (not just the procedures by which the legislation was adopted or enforced). Toward the end of the nineteenth century, the Court turned away from the deferential attitude toward state legislative authority that had characterized the *Slaughter-House Cases* and started declaring various pieces of state economic legislation unconstitutional on the grounds that such legislation clashed with the due process clause. The first peak of this new trend was reached in *Lochner v. New York*

(1905).[10] The Court saw itself in this era as protecting the citizen rights of the individual against government power; the civil "rights" that they defended were economic or "property" rights. As the following sections show, the particular economic "right" receiving attention in *Lochner* is one that the Court dubbed "freedom of contract."

Ironically, this first protection of citizen rights, in one sense, evolved into an inhibition of women's rights, in a second sense. As indicated in the discussion of the various meanings of "women's rights" in the Introduction, "rights" can refer to a "thou-shalt-not-infringe" statement to the legislature, but the term can also refer to a "thou-may-provide-special-protection-for" statement to the legislature. The economic rights (in the thou-shalt-not sense) of the individual that the Supreme Court enshrined in *Lochner v. New York* eventually (in *Adkins v. Children's Hospital*, 1923) were applied so as to undercut women's rights to be accorded special protection in economics legislation.

This abstract discussion of concepts of rights will take on some concrete meaning with an examination of the circumstances of the *Lochner v. New York* case. As a public welfare measure, the state of New York had enacted a statute that prohibited bakers from working any longer than a ten-hour day or a sixty-hour week. While many of us might think of this statute in terms of the public's (or legislature's) "right" to protect its health by regulating labor conditions in food-producing establishments, and while some of us might conceptualize it in terms of the right of the economically powerless to be protected by special legislation, the Supreme Court viewed it differently. They focused on the individual's right to be "free" (in the sense of unrestrained by regulatory legislation) in deciding how long to employ, or be employed by, another individual. In other words, while the Supreme Court majority saw themselves as guarding the workingman's "right" to work as long as he "wanted," many people viewed the Court as destroying the workingman's "right" to protect himself, by legislation, against demands from his employer that he work cruelly long hours. The Supreme Court was reading the due process clause as though it commanded the legislature: Thou shalt not interfere with the right of freedom of contract on the mere pretext that workers need protection against their bosses. Only very special circumstances, such as widespread agreement that particular forms of labor are extraordinarily unhealthy (e.g., coal mining), can justify interference with liberty of contract.

The following excerpts from the majority and dissenting opinions elucidate the majority's justification for this "reading" of the due process clause and the dissenters' attacks on that argument.

Lochner v. New York, 198 U.S. 45 (1905)*

MR. JUSTICE PECKHAM delivered the opinion of the Court.

The indictment, it will be seen, charges that the plaintiff in error violated . . . the labor law of the State of New York, in that he wrongfully and unlawfully required and permitted an employee working for him to work more than sixty hours in one week. There is nothing in any of the opinions delivered in this case, either in the Supreme Court or the Court of Appeals of the State, which construes the section, in using the word "required," as referring to any physical force being used to obtain the labor of an employee. It is assumed that the word means nothing more than the requirement arising from voluntary contract for such labor in excess of the number of hours specified in the statute. . . .

The employee may desire to earn the extra money, which would arise from his working more than the prescribed time, but this statute forbids the employer from permitting the employee to earn it.

The statute necessarily interferes with the right of contract between the employer and employees, concerning the number of hours in which the latter may labor in the bakery of the employer. The general right to make a contract in relation to his business is part of the liberty of the individual protected by the Fourteenth Amendment of the Federal Constitution. *Allgeyer v. Louisiana*, 165 U.S. 578. Under that provision no State can deprive any person of life, liberty or property without due process of law. The right to purchase or to sell labor is part of the liberty protected by this amendment, unless there are circumstances which exclude the right. There are, however, certain powers, existing in the sovereignty of each State in the Union, somewhat vaguely termed police powers, the exact description and limitation of which have not been attempted by the courts. Those powers, broadly stated and without, at present, any attempt at a more specific limitation, relate to the safety, health, morals and general welfare of the public. Both property and liberty are held on such reasonable conditions as may be imposed by the governing power of the State in the exercise of those powers, and with such conditions the Fourteenth Amendment was not designed to interfere. *Mugler v. Kansas*, 123 U.S. 623; *In re Kemmler*, 136 U.S. 436; *Crowley v. Christensen*, 137 U.S. 624.

The State, therefore, has power to prevent the individual from making certain kinds of contracts, and in regard to them the Federal Constitution offers no protection. If the contract be one which the State, in the legitimate exercise of its police power, has the right to prohibit, it is not prevented from prohibiting it by the Fourteenth Amendment. Contracts in violation of a statute, either of the Federal or state

---

*The reader unfamiliar with the court system and legal citation and terminology may find it helpful to read Appendix A before starting the main body of the text. Regarding the sections of the case decisions which appear, certain editorial alterations have been made:

All omitted text has been marked with ellipses.

In a few instances some repetitious citations and note numbers have been silently omitted.

The style of the cases has been altered to generally conform with the suggestions of *A Uniform System of Citation*, fourteenth edition.

No change has been made in the content of the cases themselves. Within judicial opinions brackets indicate material added by the author of this book unless the brackets appear within quotations or parentheses internal to the opinion.

government, or a contract to let one's property for immoral purposes, or to do any other unlawful act, could obtain no protection from the Federal Constitution, as coming under the liberty of person or of free contract. Therefore, when the State, by its legislature, in the assumed exercise of its police powers, has passed an act which seriously limits the right to labor or the right of contract . . . it becomes of great importance to determine which shall prevail—the right of the individual to labor for such time as he may choose, or the right of the State to prevent the individual from laboring or from entering into any contract to labor beyond a certain time prescribed by the State.

This court has recognized the existence and upheld the exercise of the police powers of the States in many cases which might fairly be considered as border ones. . . . Among the later cases where the state law has been upheld by this court is that of *Holden v. Hardy*, 169 U.S. 366. A provision in the act of the legislature of Utah was there under consideration, the act limiting the employment of workmen in all underground mines or workings, to eight hours per day. . . . The act was held to be a valid exercise of the police powers of the State. . . . It was held that the kind of employment, mining, smelting, etc., and the character of the employees in such kinds of labor, were such as to make it reasonable and proper for the State to interfere to prevent the employees from being constrained by the rules laid down by the proprietors in regard to labor. . . . There is nothing in *Holden v. Hardy* which covers the case now before us.

It must, of course, be conceded that there is a limit to the valid exercise of the police power by the State. There is no dispute concerning this general proposition. Otherwise the Fourteenth Amendment would have no efficacy and the legislatures of the States would have unbounded power, and it would be enough to say that any piece of legislation was enacted to conserve the morals, the health or the safety of the people; such legislation would be valid, no matter how absolutely without foundation the claim might be. The claim of the police power would be a mere pretext—become another and delusive name for the supreme sovereignty of the State to be exercised free from constitutional restraint. This is not contended for. In every case that comes before this court, therefore, where legislation of this character is concerned and where the protection of the Federal Constitution is sought, the question necessarily arises: Is this a fair, reasonable and appropriate exercise of the police power of the State, or is it an unreasonable, unnecessary and arbitrary interference with the right of the individual to his personal liberty or to enter into those contracts in relation to labor which may seem to him appropriate or necessary for the support of himself and his family? . . .

This is not a question of substituting the judgment of the court for that of the legislature. If the act be within the power of the State it is valid, although the judgment of the court might be totally opposed to the enactment of such a law. But the question would still remain: Is it within the police power of the State? and that question must be answered by the court.

The question whether this act is valid as a labor law, pure and simple, may be dismissed in a few words. There is no reasonable ground for interfering with the liberty of person or the right of free contract, by determining the hours of labor, in the occupation of a baker. There is no contention that bakers as a class are not equal in intelligence and capacity to men in other trades or manual occupations, or that they are not able to assert their rights and care for themselves without the protecting arm of the State, interfering with their independence of judgment and of action. They are in no sense wards of the State. Viewed in the light of a purely labor law, with no reference whatever to the question of health, we think that a law like the one before us involves neither the safety, the morals nor the welfare of the public, and that the interest of the public is not in the slightest degree affected by such an act. The law must be upheld, if at all, as a law pertaining to the health of the individual engaged in the occupation of a baker. It does not affect any other portion of the public than those who are engaged in that occupation. Clean and wholesome bread does not depend upon whether the baker works but ten hours per day or only sixty hours a week. The limitation of the hours of labor does not come within the police power on that ground.

It is a question of which of two powers or rights shall prevail—the power of the State to legislate or the right of the individual to liberty of person and freedom of contract. The mere assertion that the subject relates though but in a remote degree to the public health does not necessarily render the enactment valid. The act must have a more direct relation, as a means to an end, and the end itself must be appropriate and legitimate, before an act can be held to be valid which interferes with the general right of an individual to be free in his person and in his power to contract in relation to his own labor.

. . . One of the judges of the Court of Appeals, in upholding the law, stated that, in his opinion, the regulation in question could not be sustained unless they were able to say, from common knowledge, that working in a bakery and candy factory was an unhealthy employment. The judge held that, while the evidence was not uniform, it still led him to the conclusion that the occupation of a baker or confectioner was unhealthy and tended to result in diseases of

the respiratory organs. Three of the judges dissented from that view, and they thought the occupation of a baker was not to such an extent unhealthy as to warrant the interference of the legislature with the liberty of the individual.

We think the limit of the police power has been reached and passed in this case. There is, in our judgment, no reasonable foundation for holding this to be necessary or appropriate as a health law to safeguard the public health or the health of the individuals who are following the trade of a baker. If this statute be valid, . . . there would seem to be no length to which legislation of this nature might not go. . . .

We think that there can be no fair doubt that the trade of a baker, in and of itself, is not an unhealthy one to that degree which would authorize the legislature to interfere with the right to labor, and with the right of free contract on the part of the individual, either as employer or employee. In looking through statistics regarding all trades and occupations, it may be true that the trade of a baker does not appear to be as healthy as some other trades, and is also vastly more healthy than still others. To the common understanding the trade of a baker has never been regarded as an unhealthy one. Very likely physicians would not recommend the exercise of that or of any other trade as a remedy for ill health. Some occupations are more healthy than others, but we think there are none which might not come under the power of the legislature to supervise and control the hours of working therein, if the mere fact that the occupations not absolutely and perfectly healthy is to confer that right upon the legislative department of the Government. It might be safely affirmed that almost all occupations more or less affect the health. There must be more than the mere fact of the possible existence of some small amount of unhealthiness to warrant legislative interference with liberty. It is unfortunately true that labor, even in any department, may possibly carry with it the seeds of unhealthiness. But are we all, on that account, at the mercy of legislative majorities? A printer, a tinsmith, a locksmith, a carpenter, a lawyer's or a physician's clerk, or a clerk in almost any kind of business, would all come under the power of the legislature, on this assumption. No trade, no occupation, no mode of earning one's living, could escape this all-pervading power, and the acts of the legislature in limiting the hours of labor in all employments would be valid, although such limitation might seriously cripple the ability of the laborer to support himself and his family. In our large cities there are many buildings into which the sun penetrates for but a short time in each day, and these buildings are occupied by people carrying on the business of bakers, brokers, lawyers, real estate, and many other kinds of business, aided by many clerks, messengers, and other employees. Upon the assumption of the validity of this act under review, it is not possible to say that an act, prohibiting lawyers' or bank clerks, or others, from contracting to labor for their employers more than eight hours a day, would be invalid. It might be said that it is unhealthy to work more than that number of hours in an apartment lighted by artificial light during the working hours of the day; that the occupation of the bank clerk, the lawyer's clerk, the real estate clerk, or the broker's clerk in such offices is therefore unhealthy, and the legislature in its paternal wisdom must, therefore, have the right to legislate on the subject. . . .

It is also urged, pursuing the same line of argument, that it is to the interest of the State that its population should be strong and robust, and therefore any legislation which may be said to tend to make people healthy must be valid as health laws, enacted under the police power. If this be a valid argument and a justification for this kind of legislation, it follows that the protection of the Federal Constitution from undue interference with liberty of person and freedom of contract is visionary, wherever the law is sought to be justified as a valid exercise of the police power. Scarcely any law but might find shelter under such assumptions, and conduct, properly so called, as well as contract, would come under the restrictive sway of the legislature. Not only the hours of employees, but the hours of employers, could be regulated, and doctors, lawyers, scientists, all professional men, as well as athletes and artisans, could be forbidden to fatigue their brains and bodies by prolonged hours of exercise, lest the fighting strength of the State be impaired. We mention these extreme cases because the contention is extreme. We do not believe in the soundness of the views which uphold this law. On the contrary, we think that such a law as this, although passed in the assumed exercise of the police power, and as relating to the public health, or the health of the employees named, is not within that power, and is invalid. The act is not, within any fair meaning of the term, a health law, but is an illegal interference with the rights of individuals, both employers and employees, to make contracts regarding labor upon such terms as they may think best, or which they may agree upon with the other parties to such contracts. Statutes of the nature of that under review, limiting the hours in which grown and intelligent men may labor to earn their living, are mere meddlesome interferences with the rights of the individual, and they are not saved from condemnation by the claim that they are passed in the exercise of the police power and upon the subject of the health of the individual whose rights are interfered with, unless there be some fair ground, reasonable in and of itself, to say that there is material danger to the public health or to the health of the employees, if the hours of labor are not curtailed. If this be not clearly the case the individuals . . . are under the protection of the Federal Constitution regarding their liberty . . . and the legislature of the State has no power to limit their right as proposed in this statute. . . . A prohibition to enter into any contract of labor in a bakery for more than a certain number of hours a week, is, in our judgment, so wholly beside the matter of a proper, reasonable and fair provision, as to run counter to that liberty of person and of free contract provided for in the Federal Constitution.

It was further urged on the argument that restricting the hours of labor in the case of bakers was valid because it tended to cleanliness on the part of the workers, as a man was more apt to be cleanly when not overworked, and if cleanly then his "output" was also more likely to be so. What has already been said applies with equal force to this contention. We do not admit the reasoning to be sufficient to justify the claimed right of such interference. The State in that case would assume the position of a supervisor, or *pater familias*, over every act of the individual. . . . In our judgment it is not possible in fact to discover the connection between the number of hours a baker may work in the bakery and the healthful quality of the bread made by the workman. The connection, if any exists, is too shadowy and thin to build any argument for the interference of the legislature. If the man works ten hours a day it is all right, but if ten and a half or eleven his health is in danger and his bread may be unhealthful, and, therefore, he shall not be permitted to do it. This, we think, is unreasonable and entirely arbitrary. When assertions such as we have adverted to become necessary in order to give, if possible, a plausible foundation for the contention that the law is a "health law," it gives rise to at least a suspicion that there was some other motive dominating the legislature than the purpose to subserve the public health or welfare.

This interference on the part of the legislatures of the several States with the ordinary trades and occupations of the people seems to be on the increase. . . .

It is impossible for us to shut our eyes to the fact that many of the laws of this character, while passed under what is claimed to be the police power for the purpose of protecting the public health or welfare, are, in reality, passed from other motives. We are justified in saying so when, from the character of the law and the subject upon which it legislates, it is apparent that the public health or welfare bears but the most remote relation to the law. The purpose of a statute must be determined from the natural and legal effect of the language employed; and whether it is or is not repugnant to the Constitution of the United States must be determined from the natural effect of such statutes when put into operation, and not from their proclaimed purpose. *Minnesota v. Barber*, 136 U.S. 313; *Brimmer v. Rebman*, 138 U.S. 78.

It is manifest to us that the limitation of the hours of labor as provided for in this section of the statute under which the indictment was found, and the plaintiff in error convicted, has no such direct relation to and no such substantial effect upon the health of the employe, as to justify us in regarding the section as really a health law. It seems to us that the real object and purpose were simply to regulate the hours of labor between the master and his employees. Under such circumstances the freedom of master and employee to contract with each other in relation to their employment, and in defining the same, cannot be prohibited or interfered with, without violating the Federal Constitution.

. . .

Reversed.

MR. JUSTICE HARLAN, with whom MR. JUSTICE WHITE and MR. JUSTICE DAY concurred, dissenting.

While this court has not attempted to mark the precise boundaries of what is called the police power of the State, the existence of the power has been uniformly recognized, both by the Federal and state courts.

All the cases agree that this power extends at least to the protection of the lives, the health and the safety of the public against the injurious exercise by any citizen of his own rights. . . .

[This court said] in *Barbier v. Connolly,* 113 U.S. 27: "But neither the [Fourteenth] Amendment—broad and comprehensive as it is—nor any other Amendment was designed to interfere with the power of the State, sometimes termed its police power, to prescribe regulations to promote the health, peace, morals, education, and good order of the people."

Speaking generally, the State in the exercise of its powers may not unduly interfere with the right of the citizen to enter into contracts that may be necessary and essential in the enjoyment of the inherent rights belonging to every one, among which rights is the right "to be free in the enjoyment of all his faculties; to be free to use them in all lawful ways; to live and work where he will; to earn his livelihood by any lawful calling; to pursue any livelihood or avocation." This was declared in *Allgeyer v. Louisiana,* 165 U.S. 578, 589. But in the same case it was conceded that the

right to contract in relation to persons and property or to do business, within a State, may be "regulated and sometimes prohibited, when the contracts or business conflict with the policy of the State as contained in its statutes" (p. 591).

So, as said in *Holden v. Hardy,* 169 U.S. 366, 391:

This right of contract, however, is itself subject to certain limitations which the State may lawfully impose in the exercise of its police powers. While this power is inherent in all governments, it has doubtless been greatly expanded in its application during the past century, owing to an enormous increase in the number of occupations which are dangerous, or so far detrimental to the health of the employees as to demand special precautions for their well-being and protection, or the safety of adjacent property. While this court has held, notably in the cases of *Davidson v. New Orleans,* 96 U.S. 97, and *Yick Wo v. Hopkins,* 118 U.S. 356, that the police power cannot be put forward as an excuse for oppressive and unjust legislation, it may be lawfully resorted to for the purpose of preserving the public health, safety or morals, or the abatement of public nuisances, and a large discretion "is necessarily vested in the legislature to determine not only what the interests of the public require, but what measures are necessary for the protection of such interests." (*Lawton v. Steele,* 152 U.S. 133, 136.)

Referring to the limitations placed by the State upon the hours of workmen, the court in the same case said (p. 395): "These employments, when too long pursued, the legislature has judged to be detrimental to the health of the employees, and, so long as there are reasonable grounds for believing that this is so, its decision upon this subject cannot be reviewed by the Federal courts."

Granting then that there is a liberty of contract which cannot be violated even under the sanction of direct legislative enactment, but assuming, as according to settled law we may assume, that such liberty of contract is subject to such regulations as the State may reasonably prescribe for the common good and the well-being of society, what are the conditions under which the judiciary may declare such regulations to be in excess of legislative authority and void? Upon this point there is no room for dispute; for, the rule is universal that a legislative enactment, Federal or state, is never to be disregarded or held invalid unless it be, beyond question, plainly and palpably in excess of legislative power. In *Jacobson v. Massachusetts*, 197 U.S. 11, we said that the power of the courts to review legislative action in respect of a matter affecting the general welfare exists only "when that which the legislature has done comes within the rule that if a statute purporting to have been enacted to protect the public health, the public morals or the public safety, has no real or substantial relation to those objects, or is beyond all question, a plain, palpable invasion of rights secured by the fundamental law"—citing *Mugler v. Kansas*, 123 U.S. 623, 661; *Minnesota v. Barber*, 136 U.S. 313, 320; *Atkin v. Kansas*, 191 U.S. 207, 223. If there be doubt as to the validity of the statute, that doubt must therefore be resolved in favor of its validity, and the courts must keep their hands off, leaving the legislature to meet the responsibility for unwise legislation. If the end which the legislature seeks to accomplish be one to which its power extends, and if the means employed to that end, although not the wisest or best, and yet not plainly and palpably unauthorized by law, then

the court cannot interfere. In other words, when the validity of a statute is questioned, the burden of proof, so to speak, is upon those who assert it to be unconstitutional. *McCulloch v. Maryland*, 4 Wheat. 316, 421.

. . .

It is plain that this statute was enacted in order to protect the physical well-being of those who work in bakery and confectionery establishments. It may be that the statute had its origin, in part, in the belief that employers and employees in such establishments were not upon an equal footing, and that the necessities of the latter often compelled them to submit to such exactions as unduly taxed their strength. Be this as it may, the statute must be taken as expressing the belief to the people of New York that, as a general rule, and in the case of the average man, labor in excess of sixty hours during a week in such establishments may endanger the health of those who thus labor. Whether or not this be wise legislation it is not the province of the court to inquire. Under our systems of government the courts are not concerned with the wisdom or policy of legislation. So that in determining the question of power to interfere with liberty of contract, the court may inquire whether the means devised by the State are germane to an end which may be lawfully accomplished and have a real or substantial relation to the protection of health, as involved in the daily work of the persons, male and female, engaged in bakery and confectionery establishments. But when this inquiry is entered upon I find it impossible, in view of common experience, to say that there is here no real or substantial relation between the means employed by the State and the end sought to be accomplished by its legislation. *Mugler v. Kansas, supra.* . . . Therefore I submit that this court will transcend its functions if it assumes to annul the statute of New

York. It must be remembered that this statute does not apply to all kinds of business. It applies only to work in bakery and confectionery establishments, in which, as all know, the air constantly breathed by workmen is not as pure and healthful as that to be found in some other establishments or out of doors.

Professor Hirt in his treatise on the "Diseases of the Workers" has said:

> The labor of the bakers is among the hardest and most laborious imaginable, because it has to be performed under conditions injurious to the health of those engaged in it. It is hard, very hard work, not only because it requires a great deal of physical exertion in an overheated workshop and during unreasonably long hours, but more so because of the erratic demands of the public, compelling the baker to perform the greater part of his work at night, thus depriving him of an opportunity to enjoy the necessary rest and sleep, a fact which is highly injurious to his health.

Another writer says: "The constant inhaling of flour dust causes inflammation of the lungs and of the bronchial tubes. . . ." [Other scientific references were cited here.]

We judicially know that the question of the number of hours during which a workman should continuously labor has been, for a long period, and is yet, a subject of serious consideration among civilized peoples, and by those having special knowledge of the laws of health. Suppose the statute prohibited labor in bakery and confectionery establishments in excess of eighteen hours each day. No one, I take it, could dispute the power of the State to enact such a statute. But the statute before us does not embrace extreme or exceptional cases. It may be said to occupy a middle ground in respect of the hours of labor. What is the true ground for the State to take between legitimate protection, by legislation, of the public health and liberty of contract is not a question easily solved, nor one in respect of which there is or can be absolute certainty. . . .

We also judicially know that the number of hours that should constitute a day's labor in particular occupations involving the physical strength and safety of workmen has been the subject of enactments by Congress and by nearly all the States. Many, if not most, of those enactments fix eight hours as the proper basis of a day's labor.

I do not stop to consider whether any particular view of this economic question presents the sounder theory. . . . It is enough for the determination of this case, and it is enough for this court to know, that the question is one about which there is room for debate and for an honest difference of opinion. There are many reasons of a weighty, substantial character, based upon the experience of mankind, in support of the theory that, all things considered, more than ten hours' steady work each day, from week to week, in a bakery or confectionery establishment, may endanger the health, and shorten the lives of the workmen, thereby diminishing their physical and mental capacity to serve the State, and to provide for those dependent upon them.

If such reasons exist that ought to be the end of this case, for the State is not amenable to the judiciary, in respect of its legislative enactments, unless such enactments are plainly, palpably, beyond all questions, inconsistent with the Constitution of the United States. We are not to presume that the State of New York has acted in bad faith. Nor can we assume that its legislature acted without due deliberation, or that it did not determine this question upon the fullest attainable information, and for the common good. We cannot say that the State has acted without reason nor ought we to proceed upon the theory that its action is a mere sham. . . . Let the State alone in the management of its purely domestic affairs, so long as it does not appear beyond all question that it has violated the Federal Constitution. This view necessarily results from the principle that the health and safety of the people of a State are primarily for the State to guard and protect.

· · ·

The responsibility therefor rests upon legislators, not upon the courts. No evils arising from such legislation could be more far-reaching than those that might come to our system of government if the judiciary, abandoning the sphere assigned to it by the fundamental law, should enter the domain of legislation, and upon grounds merely of justice or reason or wisdom annul statutes that had received the sanction of the people's representatives. . . . (*Atkin v. Kansas*, 191 U.S. 207, 223.)

The judgment in my opinion should be affirmed.

MR. JUSTICE HOLMES dissenting.

I regret sincerely that I am unable to agree with the judgment in this case, that I think it my duty to express my dissent.

This case is decided upon an economic theory which a large part of the country does not entertain. If it were a question whether I agreed with that theory, I should desire to study it further and long before making up my mind. But I do not conceive that to be my duty, because I strongly believe that my agreement or disagreement has nothing to do with the right of a majority to embody their opinions in law. It is

settled by various decisions of this court that state constitutions and state laws may regulate life in many ways which we as legislators might think as injudicious or if you like as tyrannical as this, and which equally with this interfere with the liberty to contract. Sunday laws and usury laws are ancient examples. A more modern one is the prohibition of lotteries. The liberty of the citizen to do as he likes so long as he does not interfere with the liberty of others to do the same, which has been a shibboleth for some well-known writers, is interfered with by school laws, by the Post Office, by every state or municipal institution which takes his money for purposes thought desirable, whether he likes it or not. The Fourteenth Amendment does not enact Mr. Herbert Spencer's Social Statics. The other day we sustained the Massachusetts vaccination law. *Jacobson v. Massachusetts*, 197 U.S. 11. United States and state statutes and decisions cutting down the liberty to contract by way of combination are familiar to this court. *Northern Securities Co. v. United States*, 193 U.S. 197. Two years ago we upheld the prohibition of sales of stock on margins or for future delivery in the constitution of California. *Otis v. Parker*, 187 U.S. 606. The decision sustaining an eight-hour law for miners is still recent. *Holden v. Hardy*, 169 U.S. 366. Some of these laws embody convictions or prejudices which judges are likely to share. Some may not. But a constitution is not intended to embody a particular economic theory, whether of paternalism and the organic relation of the citizen of the State or of *laissez faire*.

. . . Every opinion tends to become a law. I think that the word liberty in the Fourteenth Amendment is perverted when it is held to prevent the natural outcome of a dominant opinion, unless it can be said that a rational and fair man necessarily would admit that the statute proposed would infringe fundamental principles as they have been understood by the traditions of our people and our law. It does not need research to show that no such sweeping condemnation can be passed upon the statute before us. A reasonable man might think it a proper measure on the score of health. Men whom I certainly could not pronounce unreasonable would uphold it as a first instalment of a general regulation of the hours of work. Whether in the latter aspect it would be open to the charge of inequality I think it unnecessary to discuss.

CASE QUESTIONS

1. How convincing are the following assertions from the majority opinion?
   a) "This is not a question of substituting the judgment of the court for that of the legislature."
   b) "Clean and wholesome bread does not depend upon whether the baker works but ten hours per day or sixty hours per week."
   c) "There is . . . no reasonable foundation for holding this to be necessary or appropriate as a health law to safeguard the public health or the health of individuals who are following the trade of a baker."

2. The "police power" (general legislating power) of the state is, as the Court puts it, the power to promote "the safety, health, morals, and general welfare of the public." Even if one concedes that this is not a "health" regulation, is it plausible to argue that maximum-hours labor regulations do not have a "direct relation, as a means to an end," to any of the other goals within the police power?

3. The majority builds part of its case on the premise that bakers are "able to assert their rights and care for themselves without the protecting arm of the State, interfering with their independence of judgment and of action. They are in no sense wards of the State." If the Supreme Court would permit ten-hour-day legislation for women workers only if the Court were convinced that women do need to be, in a sense, wards of the state, should women forgo the legislation rather than stoop to such an argument?

Protection for Women and the Decline of Economic Substantive Due Process

In 1908, a young lawyer named Louis D. Brandeis (the same Brandeis who later became a Supreme Court justice), presented to the Court a radically new form of legal argument. The case of *Muller v. Oregon* involved a challenge to an Oregon maximum-hours statute proscribing the employment of women in factories, laundries, or other "mechanical establishments" for any longer than ten hours a day. In response to the *Lochner* majority's assertion that it was not "reasonable" to believe that maximum-hours legislation promoted public health, Oregon's lawyer, Brandeis, devoted over one hundred pages of his brief to subject matter that theretofore had not been viewed as part of a "legal" argument: a heavily statistical discussion of the relationship between hours of labor and the health and morals of women, including cross-cultural analysis of American and European factory legislation. (The actual research of gathering these statistics was performed by prominent women reformists, Josephine Goldmark and Florence Kelly.) Only two pages of the brief followed the traditional pattern of explaining American legal precedents as they related to the case.

Brandeis's new approach was a huge success. He won a unanimous opinion in behalf of the statute's constitutionality. As the following excerpt reveals, however, the assumptions about the "nature" of women that brought about this "victory" may leave some contemporary feminists more than a little uncomfortable.

Muller v. Oregon, 208 U.S. 412 (1908)

MR. JUSTICE BREWER wrote for the Court.

The single question is the constitutionality of the statute under which the defendant was convicted, so far as it affects the work of a female in a laundry. . . .

It is the law of Oregon that women, whether married or single, have equal contractual and personal rights with men. . . .

It thus appears that, putting to one side the elective franchise, in the matter of personal and contractual rights they stand on the same plane as the other sex. Their rights in these respects can no more be infringed than the equal rights of their brothers. We held in *Lochner v. New York*, 198 U.S. 45, that a law providing that no laborer shall be required or permitted to work in bakeries more than sixty hours in a week or ten hours in a day was not, as to men, a legitimate exercise of the police power of the state, but an unreasonable, unnecessary, and arbitrary interference with the right and liberty of the individual to contract in relation to his labor, and as such was in conflict with, and void under

[the Fourteenth Amendment of] the Federal Constitution. That decision is invoked by plaintiff in error as decisive of the question before us. But this assumes that the difference between the sexes does not justify a different rule respecting a restriction of the hours of labor.

In patent cases counsel are apt to open the argument with a discussion of the state of the art. It may not be amiss, in the present case, before examining the constitutional question, to notice the course of legislation, as well as expressions of opinion from other than judicial sources. In the brief filed by Mr. Louis D. Brandeis for the defendant in error is a very copious collection of all these matters, an epitome of which is found in the margin.*

*[Here followed a footnote by the Court citing sections of the statutory codes of nineteen states that contained restrictions on women's labor and references to similar statutes in the laws of seven European nations. The Court concluded its summary of the brief as follows:] . . . Then follow extracts from over ninety reports of committees, bureaus of statistics, commissioners of hygiene, inspectors of factories, both in this country and

The legislation and opinions referred to in the margin may not be, technically speaking, authorities, and in them is little or no discussion of the constitutional question presented to us for determination, yet they are significant of a widespread belief that woman's physical structure, and the functions she performs in consequence thereof, justify special legislation restricting or qualifying the conditions under which she should be permitted to toil. Constitutional questions, it is true, are not settled by even a consensus of present public opinion, for it is the peculiar value of a written constitution that it places in unchanging form limitations upon legislative action, and thus gives a permanence and stability to popular government which otherwise would be lacking. At the same time, when a question of fact is debated and debatable, and the extent to which a special constitutional limitation goes is affected by the truth in respect to that fact, a widespread and long-continued belief concerning it is worthy of consideration. We take judicial cognizance of all matters of general knowledge.

It is undoubtedly true, as more than once declared by this court, that the gen-

---

in Europe, to the effect that long hours of labor are dangerous for women, primarily because of their special physical organization. The matter is discussed in these reports in different aspects, but all agree as to the danger. . . . Following them are extracts from similar reports discussing the general benefits of short hours from an economic aspect of the question. . . . Perhaps the general scope and character of all these reports may be summed up in what an inspector for Hanover says: "The reasons for the reduction of the working day to ten hours—(a) the physical organization of women, (b) her maternal functions, (c) the rearing and education of the children, (d) the maintenance of the home—are all so important and so far-reaching that the need for such reduction need hardly be discussed."

eral right to contract in relation to one's business is part of the liberty of the individual, protected by the Fourteenth Amendment to the Federal Constitution; yet it is equally well settled that this liberty is not absolute and extending to all contracts, and that a state may, without conflicting with the provisions of the Fourteenth Amendment, restrict in many respects the individual's power of contract. Without stopping to discuss at length the extent to which a state may act in this respect, we refer to the following cases in which the question has been considered: *Allgeyer v. Louisiana*, 165 U.S. 578, *Holden v. Hardy*, 169 U.S. 366, *Lochner v. New York, supra.*

That woman's physical structure and the performance of maternal functions place her at a disadvantage in the struggle for subsistence is obvious. This is especially true when the burdens of motherhood are upon her. Even when they are not, by abundant testimony of the medical fraternity continuance for a long time on her feet at work, repeating this from day to day, tends to injurious effects upon the body, and, as healthy mothers are essential to vigorous offspring, the physical well-being of woman becomes an object of public interest and care in order to preserve the strength and vigor of the race.

Still again, history discloses the fact that woman has always been dependent upon man. He established his control at the outset by superior physical strength, and this control in various forms, with diminishing intensity, has continued to the present. As minors, though not to the same extent, she has been looked upon in the courts as needing especial care that her rights may be preserved. Education was long denied her, and while now the doors of the schoolroom are opened and her opportunities for acquiring knowledge are great, yet even with that and the consequent increase of capacity for business affairs it is still true that in the struggle for subsistence she is not an equal competitor with her brother. Though limitations upon personal and contractual rights may be removed by legislation, there is that in her disposition and habits of life which will operate against a full assertion of those rights. She will still be where some legislation to protect her seems necessary to secure a real equality of right. Doubtless there are individual exceptions, and there are many respects in which she has an advantage over him; but looking at it from the viewpoint of the effort to maintain an independent position in life, she is not upon an equality. Differentiated by these matters from the other sex, she is properly placed in a class by herself, and legislation designed for her protection may be sustained, even when like legislation is not necessary for men, and could not be sustained. It is impossible to close one's eyes to the fact that she still looks to her brother and depends upon him. Even though all restrictions on political, personal, and contractual rights were taken away, and she stood, so far as statutes are concerned, upon an absolutely equal plane with him, it would still be true that she is so constituted that she will rest upon and look to him for protection: that her physical structure and a proper discharge of her maternal functions—having in view not merely her own health, but the well-being of the race—justify legislation to protect her from the greed as well as the passion of man. The limitations which this statute places upon her contractual powers, upon her right to agree with her employer as to the time she shall labor, are not imposed solely for her benefit, but also largely for the benefit of all. Many words cannot make this plainer. The two sexes differ in structure of body, in the functions to be performed by each, in the amount of physical strength, in the capacity for long-continued labor, particularly when done standing, the influence of vigorous health upon the future well-being of the race, the self-reliance which enables one to assert full rights, and in the capacity to maintain the struggle for subsistence. This difference justifies a difference in legislation, and upholds that which is designed to compensate for some of the burdens which rest upon her.

We have not referred in this discussion to the denial of the elective franchise in the state of Oregon, for while that may disclose a lack of political equality in all things with her brother, that is not of itself decisive. The reason runs deeper, and rests in the inherent difference between the two sexes, and in the different functions in life which they perform.

For these reasons, and without questioning in any respect the decision in *Lochner v. New York*, we are of the opinion that it cannot be adjudged that the act in question is in conflict with the Federal Constitution, . . . and the judgment of the Supreme Court of Oregon is *Affirmed.*

CASE QUESTIONS

1. If *Lochner* had really established a constitutional right to "freedom of contract," does *Muller v. Oregon* amount to a statement that women have fewer constitutional rights than men?

2. Does this decision hinge on women's physical weakness? Could an employer who tests all his women employees for physical endurance before hiring them claim that he should be exempted from the statute?

3. Does this decision hinge on women's supposed psychological dependence on men? On women's unique capacity to bear future generations? If physical weakness and psychological dependence were scientifically disproved, would women's birth-giving role continue to justify special treatment by society?

The Supreme Court could not for long endure the logical tension created by their position that maximum-hours legislation as a health measure was wholly irrational for men, whereas the same legislation was entirely rational for women. In 1917, in the case of *Bunting v. Oregon,* the Supreme Court reversed itself, upholding a ten-hour-day statute that applied to workers in milling or manufacturing establishments of any kind.

By the time this case was argued, Brandeis had already been nominated to the Supreme Court (although he did not take his seat in time to participate in the decision). Oregon's counsel this time was another future Supreme Court justice, Felix Frankfurter, who again presented what was by now called a "Brandeis brief" to defend the rationality of the statute. The case for the rationality of maximum-hours legislation as a health measure was so obvious that the Supreme Court devoted most of its argument to an ancillary part of the statute that dealt with overtime pay requirements—to rebutting the contention that this law was a wage regulation in disguise. They tersely laid to rest the somewhat decayed corpse of the *Lochner* approach to hours legislation, giving the whole subject no more than one paragraph (reprinted below), and managing to avoid any explicit reference to *Lochner.*

Bunting v. Oregon, 243 U.S. 426 (1917)

MR. JUSTICE McKENNA delivered the opinion of the court.

The consonance of the Oregon law with the Fourteenth Amendment is the question in the case, and this depends upon whether it is a proper exercise of the police power of the state, as the supreme court of the state decided that it is.

That the police power extends to health regulations is not denied, but it is denied that the law has such purpose or justification. . . .

Section 1 of the law expresses the policy that impelled its enactment to be the interest of the state in the physical well-being of its citizens and that it is injurious to their health for them to work "in any mill, factory or manufacturing establishment" more than ten hours in any one day. . . .

There is a contention made that the law, even regarded as regulating hours of service, is not either necessary or useful "for preservation of the health of employees in mills, factories, and manufacturing establishments." The record contains no facts to support the contention, and against it is the judgment of the legislature and the supreme court, which said: "In view of the well-known fact that the custom in our industries does not sanction a longer service than ten hours per day, it cannot be held, as a matter of law, that the legislative requirement is unreasonable or

arbitrary as to hours of labor. Statistics show that the average daily working time among workingmen in different countries, is, in Australia, 8 hours; in Britain, 9; in the United States, 9¾; in Denmark, 9¾; in Norway, 10; Sweden, France, and Switzerland, 10½; Germany, 10¼; Belgium, Italy, and Austria, 11; and in Russia, 12 hours.["]

Further discussion we deem unnecessary.

Judgment affirmed.

The CHIEF JUSTICE, MR. JUSTICE VAN DEVANTER, and MR. JUSTICE McREYNOLDS, dissent [without written opinion].

By this time, the strategy for liberals who wanted social welfare legislation seemed obvious. They needed only to restrict their social welfare legislation at first to women, use the weaker-sex rationale to convince the Court to accept the protective legislation as "reasonable," and then, having obtained this concession, enact the same reasonable measures to protect the men of the community as well. Nevertheless, at the next plateau of social welfare legislation, minimum-wage statutes, this three-step strategy collapsed on step two.

The first minimum-wage case settled by the Supreme Court was *Adkins v. Children's Hospital* (1923).[11] It involved a District of Columbia statute that created a minimum-wage board with authority to set minimum wages for child labor and to establish for women workers minimum wages geared to "the necessary cost of living" and adequate to maintain those workers "in good health and to protect their morals." Although this case presented a usual challenge, one from a thwarted employer, the Children's Hospital, the Court's opinion also contained the decision for an unusual companion case, *Adkins v. Lyons*, in which objection to the minimum-wage law came from a dissatisfied female employee. This woman worked at the Congress Hall Hotel for $35 a month and two free meals a day. She claimed that these wages were the best she was capable of earning, and if she were not permitted to settle for these, she would have to go without work. In other words, she believed that her labor skills were not worthy of the minimum wage, and that if the law were enforced she would be fired and would not be able to find a new job.

Once again, Felix Frankfurter argued the case for the statute, and once again Justice Brandeis refrained from participating in the decision. Justice Brandeis's daughter Elizabeth was secretary of the District of Columbia Minimum Wage Board, and the appearance of conflict of interest had to be avoided.

Because the case came from the District rather than from a state, the constitutional clause at issue was the Fifth Amendment due process clause, which commands the federal government, rather than the Fourteenth Amendment due process clause, which is addressed to the states. Because the two clauses contain identical wording, however, what the Court said about the due process clause here also applied to the states. And what they said was that minimum-wage laws constitute "undue" interferences with the "liberty of contract."

Justice Sutherland's majority opinion (the Court divided 5–3) contained a number of surprises. One was that he relied heavily on the *Lochner v. New York* precedent even though that case had appeared to have been silently overruled by *Bunting v. Oregon.* (With an uncanny ability to look in two opposite directions at once, Sutherland faced *Bunting* long enough to admit that it established the constitutionality of maximum-hours legislation—just what *Lochner* had denied— and simultaneously looked to *Lochner* to find the precedent that created and rendered virtually inviolable the right to freedom of contract.)

A second surprise was Sutherland's assertion that the Nineteenth Amendment (giving women the vote) nullified the constitutional basis to single out women for special protection; Americans had transcended the myth of "the ancient inequality of the sexes" and had brought the "civil and political" differences between the sexes "to the vanishing point," he claimed. Sutherland's argument was that although hours legislation properly took gender into account, because of women's physical weakness, wage legislation was premised on an assumption of woman's incapacity to fend for herself in the economy. Now that women had the vote, as well as the legal right to make contracts, Sutherland believed that there was no longer any justification for putting further "restrictions" on women's "freedom." He made these assertions notwithstanding the undisputed evidence that then, as now, women's earnings were, on the average, at the bottom of the pay scale (e.g., women earn less per year than black men, and black men earn less than white men).

It is worth noting that Sutherland's views did have contemporaneous support from an unexpected quarter. Alice Paul, leader of the decidedly militant branch of the women's suffragist movement, had been rallying her forces, since 1913, behind the slogan "Equality Not Protection." Not satisfied with the success of the suffrage amendment effort in 1920, Ms. Paul and her Women's Party within three years had drafted and submitted to Congress the Equal Rights Amendment. That was the same year that *Adkins v. Children's Hospital* was handed down.

Adkins v. Children's Hospital, 261 U.S. 525 (1923)

MR. JUSTICE SUTHERLAND wrote for the Court:

. . . The judicial duty of passing upon the constitutionality of an act of Congress is one of great gravity and delicacy. The statute here in question has successfully borne the scrutiny of the legislative branch of the government, which, by enacting it, has affirmed its validity; and that determination must be given great weight. This Court, by an unbroken line of decisions from Chief Justice Marshall to the present day, has steadily adhered to the rule that every possible presumption is in favor of the validity of an act of Congress until overcome beyond rational doubt. But if by clear and indubitable demonstration a statute be opposed to the Constitution we have no choice but to say so. The Constitution, by its own terms, is the supreme law of the land, emanating from the people, the repository of ultimate sovereignty under our form of government. A congressional statute, on the other hand, is the act of an agency of this sovereign authority and if it conflict with the Constitution must fall; for that which is not supreme must yield to that which is. To hold it invalid (if it be invalid) is a plain exercise of the judicial power— that power vested in courts to enable them to administer justice according to law. From the authority to ascertain and determine the law in a given case, there necessarily results, in case of conflict, the duty to declare and enforce the rule of the supreme law and reject that of an inferior act of legislation which, transcending the Constitution, is of no effect and binding on no one. This is not the exercise of a substantive power to review and nullify acts of Congress, for no such substantive power exists. It is simply a necessary concomitant of the power to hear and dispose of a case or controversy properly before the court, to the determination of which must be brought the test and measure of the law.

The statute now under consideration is attacked upon the ground that it authorizes an unconstitutional interference with the freedom of contract included within the guaranties of the due process clause of the Fifth Amendment. That the right to contract about one's affairs is a part of the liberty of the individual protected by this clause, is settled by the decisions of this Court and is no longer open to question. *Allgeyer v. Louisiana*, 165 U.S. 578, 591; *New York Life Insurance Co. v. Dodge*, 246 U.S. 357, 373–374; *Coppage v. Kansas*, 236 U.S. 1, 10, 14; *Adair v. United States*, 208 U.S. 161; *Lochner v. New York*, 198 U.S. 45; *Butchers' Union Co. v. Crescent City Co.*, 111 U.S. 746; *Muller v. Oregon*, 208 U.S. 412, 421. Within this liberty are contracts of employment of labor. In making such contracts, generally speaking, the parties have an equal right to obtain from each other the best terms they can as the result of private bargaining. . . .

In *Coppage v. Kansas, supra* (p. 14), this Court, speaking through Mr. Justice Pitney, said:

Included in the right of personal liberty and the right of private property—partaking of the nature of each—is the right to make contracts for the acquisition of property. Chief among such contracts is that of personal employment, by which labor and other services are exchanged for money or other forms of property. If this right be struck down or arbitrarily interfered with, there is a substantial impairment of liberty in the long-established constitutional sense. The right is as essential to the laborer as to the capitalist, to the poor as to the rich; for the vast majority of persons have no other honest way to begin to acquire property, save by working for money.

An interference with this liberty so serious as that now under consideration, and so disturbing of equality of right, must be deemed to be arbitrary, unless it be supportable as a reasonable exercise of the police power of the State.

There is, of course, no such thing as absolute freedom of contract. It is subject to a great variety of restraints. But freedom of contract is, nevertheless, the general rule and restraint the exception; and the exercise of legislative authority to abridge it can be justified only by the existence of exceptional circumstances. Whether these circumstances exist in the present case constitutes the question to be answered. It will be helpful to this end to review some of the decisions where the interference has been upheld and consider the grounds upon which they rest.

1. *Those dealing with statutes fixing rates and charges to be exacted by businesses impressed with a public interest.* There are many cases, but it is sufficient to cite *Munn v. Illinois,* 94 U.S. 113. . . . In the case at bar the statute does not depend upon the existence of a public interest in any business to be affected, and this class of cases may be laid aside as inapplicable.

2. *Statutes relating to contracts for the performance of public work. Atkin v. Kansas,* 191 U.S. 207; *Heim v. McCall,* 239 U.S. 175; *Ellis v. United States,* 206 U.S. 246. These cases sustain such statutes as depending, not upon the right to condition private con-

tracts, but upon the right of the government to prescribe the conditions upon which it will permit work of a public character to be done for it. . . . We may, therefore, . . . dismiss these decisions from consideration as inapplicable.

3. *Statutes prescribing the character, methods and time for payment of wages.* . . . In none of the statutes thus sustained, was the liberty of employer or employee to fix the amount of wages the one was willing to pay and the other willing to receive interfered with. Their tendency and purpose was to prevent unfair and perhaps fraudulent methods in the payment of wages and in no sense can they be said to be, or to furnish a precedent for, wage-fixing statutes.

4. *Statutes fixing hours of labor.* It is upon this class that the greatest emphasis is laid in argument and therefore, and because such cases approach most nearly the line of principle applicable to the statute here involved, we shall consider them more at length. In some instances the statute limited the hours of labor for men in certain occupations and in others it was confined in its application to women. No statute has thus far been brought to the attention of this Court which by its terms, applied to all occupations. . . . [The statute in *Holden v. Hardy,* 169 U.S. 366] was sustained as a legitimate exercise of the police power, on the ground that the legislature had determined that these particular employments, when too long pursued, were injurious to the health of the employees, and that . . . there were reasonable grounds for supporting this determination. . . .

That this constituted the basis of the decision is emphasized by the subsequent decision in *Lochner v. New York,* 198 U.S. 45, reviewing a state statute which restricted the employment of all persons in bakeries to ten hours in any one day. The Court referred to *Holden v. Hardy, supra,* and, declaring it to be inapplicable, held the statute unconstitutional as an unreasonable, unnecessary and arbitrary interference with the liberty of contract and therefore void under the Constitution.

[Here followed two full pages of lengthy quotes from *Lochner* to the effect that legislative interferences with liberty of contract may not be "arbitrary" or "unreasonable."]

Subsequent cases in this Court have been distinguished from that decision, but the principles therein stated have never been disapproved.

In *Bunting v. Oregon*, 243 U.S. 426, a state statute forbidding the employment of any person in any mill, factory or manufacturing establishment more than ten hours in any one day, and providing payment for overtime not exceeding three hours in any one day at the rate of time and a half of the regular wage, was sustained on the ground that, since the state legislature and State Supreme Court had found such a law necessary for the preservation of the health of employees in these industries, this Court would accept their judgement, in the absence of facts to support the contrary conclusion. The law was . . . sustained as a reasonable regulation of hours of service. . . .

In the *Muller* case the validity of an Oregon statute, forbidding the employment of any female in certain industries more than ten hours during any one day was upheld. The decision proceeded upon the theory that the difference between the sexes may justify a different rule respecting hours of labor in the case of women than in the case of men. It is pointed out that these consist in differences of physical structure, especially in respect of the maternal functions, and also in the fact that historically woman has always been dependent upon man, who has established his control by superior physical strength. . . . But the ancient inequality of the sexes, otherwise

than physical, as suggested in the *Muller* case (p. 421) has continued "with diminishing intensity." In view of the great—not to say revolutionary—changes which have taken place since that utterance, in the contractual, political and civil status of women, culminating in the Nineteenth Amendment, it is not unreasonable to say that these differences have now come almost, if not quite, to the vanishing point. In this aspect of the matter, while the physical differences must be recognized in appropriate cases, and legislation fixing hours or conditions of work may properly take them into account, we cannot accept the doctrine that women of mature age, *sui juris*, require or may be subjected to restrictions upon their liberty of contract which could not lawfully be imposed in the case of men under similar circumstances. To do so would be to ignore all the implications to be drawn from the present day trend of legislation, as well as that of common thought and usage, by which woman is accorded emancipation from the old doctrine that she must be given special protection or be subjected to special restraint in her contractual and civil relationships. In passing, it may be noted that the instant statute applies in the case of the woman employer contracting with a woman employee as it does when the former is a man.

The essential characteristics of the statute now under consideration, which differentiate it from the laws fixing hours of labor, will be made to appear as we proceed. It is sufficient now to point out that the latter . . . deal with incidents of the employment having no necessary effect upon the heart of the contract, that is, the amount of wages to be paid and received. A law forbidding work to continue beyond a given number of hours leaves the parties free to contract about wages and thereby equalize whatever additional burdens may be imposed upon the employer as a result of the restrictions as to hours, by an adjustment in respect of the amount of wages. Enough has been said to show that the authority to fix hours of labor cannot be exercised except in respect of those occupations where work of long continued duration is detrimental to health. This Court has been careful in every case where the question has been raised, to place its decision upon this limited authority of the legislature to regulate hours of labor and to disclaim any purpose to uphold the legislation as fixing wages, thus recognizing an essential difference between the two. It seems plain that these decisions afford no real support for any form of law establishing minimum wages.

. . . [This] is simply and exclusively a price-fixing law, confined to adult women (for we are not now considering the provisions relating to minors), who are legally as capable of contracting for themselves as men. It forbids two parties having lawful capacity—under penalties as to the employer—to freely contract with one another in respect of the price for which one shall render service to the other in a purely private employment where both are willing, perhaps anxious, to agree, even though the consequence may be to oblige one to surrender a desirable engagement and the other to dispense with the services of a desirable employee.[1] The price fixed by the board need have no relation to the capacity or earning power of the employee, the number of hours which may happen to constitute the day's work, the character of the place where the work is to be done, or the circumstances or surroundings of the employment; and, while it has no other basis to support its validity than the assumed necessities of the employee, it takes no account of any independent resources

she may have. It is based wholly on the opinions of the members of the board and their advisers—perhaps an average of their opinions, if they do not precisely agree—as to what will be necessary to provide a living for a woman, keep her in health and preserve her morals. It applies to any and every occupation in the District, without regard to its nature or the character of the work.

The standard furnished by the statute for the guidance of the board is so vague as to be impossible of practical application with any reasonable degree of accuracy. What is sufficient to supply the necessary cost of living for a woman worker and maintain her in good health and protect her morals is obviously not a precise or unvarying sum—not even approximately so. The amount will depend upon a variety of circumstances: the individual temperament, habits of thrift, care, ability to buy necessaries intelligently, and whether the woman lives alone or with her family. To those who practice economy, a given sum will afford comfort, while to those of contrary habit the same sum will be wholly inadequate. The cooperative economies of the family group are not taken into account though they constitute an important consideration in estimating the cost of living, for it is obvious that the individual expense will be less in the case of a member of a family than in the case of one living alone. The relation between earnings and morals is not capable of standardization. It cannot be shown that well paid women safeguard their morals more carefully than those who are poorly paid. Morality rests upon other considerations than wages; and there is, certainly, no such prevalent connection between the two as to justify a broad attempt to adjust the latter with reference to the former. As a means of safe-guarding morals the attempted classification, in our opinion, is without reasonable basis. No dis-

---

1. This is the exact situation in the *Lyons* case. . . .

tinction can be made between women who work for others and those who do not; nor is there ground for distinction between women and men, for, certainly, if women require a minimum wage to preserve their morals men require it to preserve their honesty. For these reasons, and others which might be stated, the inquiry in respect of the necessary cost of living and of the income necessary to preserve health and morals, presents an individual and not a composite question, and must be answered for each individual considered by herself and not by a general formula prescribed by a statutory bureau.

. . .

The law takes account of the necessities of only one party to the contract. It ignores the necessities of the employer by compelling him to pay not less than a certain sum, not only whether the employee is capable of earning it, but irrespective of the ability of his business to sustain the burden, generously leaving him, of course, the privilege of abandoning his business as an alternative for going on at a loss. Within the limits of the minimum sum, he is precluded, under penalty of fine and imprisonment, from adjusting compensation to the differing merits of his employees. It compels him to pay at least the sum fixed in any event, because the employee needs it, but requires no service of equivalent value from the employee. It therefore undertakes to solve but one-half of the problem. The other half is the establishment of a corresponding standard of efficiency, and this forms no part of the policy of the legislation, although in practice the former half without the latter must lead to ultimate failure, in accordance with the inexorable law that no one can continue indefinitely to take out more than he puts in without ultimately exhausting the supply. The law is not confined to the great and powerful employers but embraces those whose bargaining power may be as weak as that of the employee. It takes no account of periods of stress and business depression, of crippling losses, which may leave the employer himself without adequate means of livelihood. To the extent that the sum fixed exceeds the fair value of the services rendered, it amounts to a compulsory exaction from the employer for the support of a partially indigent person, for whose condition there rests upon him no peculiar responsibility, and therefore, in effect, arbitrarily shifts to his shoulders a burden which, if it belongs to anybody, belongs to society as a whole.

The feature of this statute which, perhaps more than any other, puts upon it the stamp of invalidity is that it exacts from the employer an arbitrary payment for a purpose and upon a basis having no causal connection with his business, or the contract or the work the employee engages to do. The declared basis, as already pointed out, is not the value of the service rendered, but the extraneous circumstance that the employee needs to get a prescribed sum of money to insure her subsistence, health and morals. The ethical right of every worker, man or woman, to a living wage may be conceded. One of the declared and important purposes of trade organizations is to secure it. And with that principle and with every legitimate effort to realize it in fact, no one can quarrel; but the fallacy of the proposed method of attaining it is that it assumes that every employer is bound at all events to furnish it. The moral requirement implicit in every contract of employment, viz, that the amount to be paid and the service to be rendered shall bear to each other some relation of just equivalence, is completely ignored. The necessities of the employee are alone considered and these arise outside of the employment, are the same when there is no employment, and as great in one occupation as in another. Certainly the employer by paying a fair equivalent for the service rendered, though not sufficient to support the employee, has neither caused nor contributed to her poverty. On the contrary, to the extent of what he pays he has relieved it. In principle, there can be no difference between the case of selling labor and the case of selling goods. If one goes to the butcher, the baker or grocer to buy food, he is morally entitled to obtain the worth of his money but he is not entitled to more. . . . A statute requiring an employer to pay in money, to pay at prescribed and regular intervals, to pay the value of the services rendered, even to pay with fair relation to the extent of the benefit obtained from the service, would be understandable. But a statute which prescribes payment without regard to any of these things and solely with relation to circumstances apart from the contract of employment, the business affected by it and the work done under it, is so clearly the product of a naked, arbitrary exercise of power that it cannot be allowed to stand under the Constitution of the United States.

We are asked, upon the one hand, to consider the fact that several States have adopted similar statutes, and we are invited, upon the other hand, to give weight to the fact that three times as many States presumably as well informed and as anxious to promote the health and morals of their people, have refrained from enacting such legislation. We have also been furnished with a large number of printed opinions approving the policy of the minimum wage, and our own reading has disclosed a large number to the contrary. These are all proper enough for the consideration of the lawmaking bodies, since their tendency is to establish the desirability or undesirability of the legislation; but they reflect no legitimate light upon the question of its validity, and that is what we are called upon to decide. The elucidation of that question cannot be aided by counting heads.

It is said that great benefits have resulted from the operation of such statutes, not alone in the District of Columbia but in the several States, where they have been in force. A mass of reports, opinions of special observers and students of the subject, and the like, has been brought before us in support of this statement, all of which we have found interesting but only mildly persuasive. That the earnings of women now are greater than they were formerly and that conditions affecting women have become better in other respects may be conceded, but convincing indications of the logical relation of these desirable changes to the law in question are significantly lacking. They may be, and quite probably are, due to other causes. We cannot close our eyes to the notorious fact that earnings everywhere in all occupations have greatly increased—not alone in States where the minimum wage law obtains but in the country generally—quite as much or more among men as among women and in occupations outside the reach of the law as in those governed by it. No real test of the economic value of the law can be had during periods of maximum employment, when general causes keep wages up to or above the minimum; that will come in periods of depression and struggle for employment when the efficient will be employed at the minimum rate while the less capable may not be employed at all.

Finally, it may be said that if, in the interest of the public welfare, the police power may be invoked to justify the fixing of a minimum wage, it may, when the public welfare is thought to require it, be invoked to justify a maximum wage. The power to fix high wages connotes, by like course of reasoning, the power to fix low wages. If, in the face of the guaranties of the Fifth Amendment, this form of legislation shall be legally justified, the field for the operation of the police power will have been widened to a great and dangerous degree. . . . A wrong decision does not end with itself: it is a precedent, and, with the swing of sentiment, its bad influence may run from one extremity of the arc to the other.

It has been said that legislation of the kind now under review is required in the interest of social justice, for whose ends freedom of contract may lawfully be subjected to restraint. The liberty of the individual to do as he pleases, even in innocent matters, is not absolute. It must frequently yield to the common good, and the line beyond which the power of interference may not be pressed is neither definite nor unalterable but may be made to move, within limits not well defined, with changing need and circumstance. Any attempt to fix a rigid boundary would be unwise as well as futile. But, nevertheless, there are limits to the power, and when these have been passed, it becomes the plain duty of the courts in the proper exercise of their authority to so declare. To sustain the individual freedom of action contemplated by the Constitution, is not to strike down the common good but to exalt it; for surely the good of society as a whole cannot be better served than by the preservation against arbitrary restraint of the liberties of its constituent members.

It follows from what has been said that the act in question passes the limit prescribed by the Constitution, and, accordingly, the decrees of the court below are

Affirmed.

Mr. Chief Justice Taft, dissenting.

I regret much to differ from the Court in these cases.

The boundary of the police power be-

yond which its exercise becomes an invasion of the guaranty of liberty under the Fifth and Fourteenth Amendments to the Constitution is not easy to mark. Our Court has been laboriously engaged in pricking out a line in successive cases. We must be careful, it seems to me, to follow that line as well as we can and not to depart from it by suggesting a distinction that is formal rather than real.

Legislatures in limiting freedom of contract between employee and employer by a minimum wage proceed on the assumption that employees, in the class receiving least pay, are not upon a full level of equality of choice with their employer and in their necessitous circumstances are prone to accept pretty much anything that is offered. They are peculiarly subject to the overreaching of the harsh and greedy employer. The evils of the sweating system and of the long hours and low wages which are characteristic of it are well known. Now, I agree that it is a disputable question in the field of political economy how far a statutory requirement of maximum hours or minimum wages may be a useful remedy for these evils, and whether it may not make the case of the oppressed employee worse than it was before. But it is not the function of this Court to hold congressional acts invalid simply because they are passed to carry out economic views which the Court believes to be unwise or unsound.

Legislatures which adopt a requirement of maximum hours or minimum wages may be presumed to believe that when sweating employers are prevented from paying unduly low wages by positive law they will continue their business, abating that part of their profits, which were wrung from the necessities of their employees, and will concede the better terms required by the law; and that while in individual cases hardship may result, the restriction will enure to the benefit of the general class of employees in whose interest the law is passed and so to that of the community at large.

The right of the legislature under the Fifth and Fourteenth Amendments to limit the hours of employment on the score of the health of the employee, it seems to me, has been firmly established. As to that, one would think, the line had been pricked out so that it has become a well formulated rule. In *Holden v. Hardy,* 169 U.S. 366, it was applied to miners and rested on the unfavorable environment of employment in mining and smelting. In *Lochner v. New York,* 198 U.S. 45, it was held that restricting those employed in bakeries to ten hours a day was an arbitrary and invalid interference with the liberty of contract secured by the Fourteenth Amendment. Then followed a number of cases beginning with *Muller v. Oregon,* 208 U.S. 412, sustaining the validity of a limit on maximum hours of labor for women to which I shall hereafter allude, and following these cases came *Bunting v. Oregon,* 243 U.S. 426. In that case, this Court sustained a law limiting the hours of labor of any person, whether man or woman working in any mill, factory or manufacturing establishment to ten hours a day with a proviso as to further hours to which I shall hereafter advert. The law covered the whole field of industrial employment and certainly covered the case of persons employed in bakeries. Yet the opinion in the *Bunting* case does not mention the *Lochner* case. No one can suggest any constitutional distinction between employment in bakery and one in any other kind of a manufacturing establishment which should make a limit of hours in the one invalid, and the same limit in the other permissible. It is impossible for me to reconcile the *Bunting* case and the *Lochner* case and I have always supposed that the *Lochner* case was thus overruled *sub silentio.* Yet the opinion of the Court herein in support of its conclusion quotes from the opinion in the *Lochner* case as one which has been sometimes distinguished but never

overruled. Certainly there was no attempt to distinguish it in the *Bunting* case.

However, the opinion herein does not overrule the *Bunting* case in express terms, and therefore I assume that the conclusion in this case rests on the distinction between a minimum of wages and a maximum of hours in the limiting of liberty to contract. I regret to be at variance with the Court as to the substance of this distinction. In absolute freedom of contract the one term is as important as the other, for both enter equally into the consideration given and received, a restriction as to one is not any greater in essence than the other, and is of the same kind. One is the multiplier and the other the multiplicand.

If it be said that long hours of labor have a more direct effect upon the health of the employee than the low wage, there is very respectable authority from close observers, disclosed in the record and in the literature on the subject quoted at length in the briefs, that they are equally harmful in this regard. Congress took this view and we can not say it was not warranted in so doing.

With deference to the very able opinion of the Court and my brethren who concur in it, it appears to me to exaggerate the importance of the wage term of the contract of employment as more inviolate than its other terms. Its conclusion seems influenced by the fear that the concession of the power to impose a minimum wage must carry with it a concession of the power to fix a maximum wage. This, I submit, is a *non sequitur.* A line of distinction like the one under discussion in this case is, as the opinion elsewhere admits, a matter of degree and practical experience and not of pure logic. Certainly the wide difference between prescribing a minimum wage and a maximum wage could as a matter of degree and experience be easily affirmed.

Moreover, there are decisions by this Court which have sustained legislative limitations in respect to the wage term in contracts of employment. . . . While these did not impose a minimum on wages, they did take away from the employee the freedom to agree as to how they should be fixed, in what medium they should be paid, and when they should be paid, all features that might affect the amount or the mode of enjoyment of them. . . . In *Bunting v. Oregon, supra,* employees in a mill, factory or manufacturing establishment were required if they worked over a ten hours a day to accept for the three additional hours permitted not less than fifty per cent more than their usual wage. This was sustained as a mild penalty imposed on the employer to enforce the limitation as to hours; but it necessarily curtailed the employee's freedom to contract to work for the wages he saw fit to accept during those three hours. I do not feel, therefore, that either on the basis of reason, experience or authority, the boundary of the police power should be drawn to include maximum hours and exclude a minimum wage.

Without, however, expressing an opinion that a minimum wage limitation can be enacted for adult men, it is enough to say that the case before us involves only the application of the minimum wage to women. If I am right in thinking that the legislature can find as much support in experience for the view that a sweating wage has as great and as direct a tendency to bring about an injury to the health and morals of workers, as for the view that long hours injure their health, then I respectfully submit that *Muller v. Oregon,* 208 U.S. 412, controls this case. The law which was there sustained forbade the employment of any female in any mechanical establishment or factory or laundry for more than ten hours. This covered a pretty wide field in women's work and it would not seem that any sound distinction between that case and this can be built up on the fact that the law before us applies to all occupations of women with

power in the board to make certain exceptions. Mr. Justice Brewer, who spoke for the Court in *Muller v. Oregon,* based its conclusion on the natural limit to women's physical strength and the likelihood that long hours would therefore injure her health, and we have had since a series of cases which may be said to have established a rule of decision. *Riley v. Massachusetts,* 232 U.S. 671; *Miller v. Wilson,* 236 U.S. 373; *Bosley v. McLaughlin,* 236 U.S. 385. The cases covered restrictions in wide and varying fields of employment. . . .

I am not sure from a reading of the opinion whether the court thinks the authority of *Muller v. Oregon* is shaken by the adoption of the Nineteenth Amendment. The Nineteenth Amendment did not change the physical strength or limitations of women upon which the decision in *Muller v. Oregon* rests. The Amendment did give women political power and makes more certain that legislative provisions for their protection will be in accord with their interests as they see them. But I don't think we are warranted in varying constitutional construction based on physical differences between men and women, because of the Amendment.

But for my inability to agree with some general observations in the forcible opinion of Mr. Justice Holmes who follows me, I should be silent and merely record my concurrence in what he says. It is perhaps wiser for me, however, in a case of this importance, separately to give my reasons for dissenting.

I am authorized to say that Mr. Justice Sanford concurs in this opinion.

Mr. Justice Holmes, dissenting.

The question in this case is the broad one, Whether Congress can establish minimum rates of wages for women in the District of Columbia with due provision for special circumstances, or whether we must say that Congress has no power to meddle with the matter at all. To me, notwithstanding the deference due to the prevailing judgment of the Court, the power of Congress seems absolutely free from doubt. The end, to remove conditions leading to ill health, immorality and the deterioration of the race, no one would deny to be within the scope of constitutional legislation. The means are means that have the approval of Congress, of many States, and of those governments from which we have learned our greatest lessons. When so many intelligent persons, who have studied the matter more than any of us can, have thought that the means are effective and are worth the price, it seems to me impossible to deny that the belief reasonably may be held by reasonable men. If the law encountered no other objection than that the means bore no relation to the end or that they cost too much I do not suppose that anyone would venture to say that it was bad. I agree, of course, that a law answering the foregoing requirements might be invalidated by specific provisions of the Constitution. For instance it might take private property without just compensation. But in the present instance the only objection that can be urged is found within the vague contours of the Fifth Amendment, prohibiting the depriving any person of liberty or property without due process of law. To that I turn.

The earlier decisions upon the same words in the Fourteenth Amendment began within our memory and went no farther than an unpretentious assertion of the liberty to follow the ordinary callings. Later that innocuous generality was expanded into the dogma, Liberty of Contract. Contract is not specially mentioned in the text that we have to construe. It is merely an example of doing what you want to do, embodied in the word liberty. But pretty much

all law consists in forbidding men to do some things that they want to do, and contract is no more exempt from law than other acts. Without enumerating all the restrictive laws that have been upheld I will mention a few that seem to me to have interfered with liberty of contract quite as seriously and directly as the one before us. Usury laws prohibit contracts by which a man receives more than so much interest for the money that he lends. Statutes of frauds restrict many contracts to certain forms. Some Sunday laws prohibit practically all contracts during one-seventh of our whole life. Insurance rates may be regulated. *German Alliance Insurance Co. v. Lewis*, 233 U.S. 389. [Several precedents on contractual regulations follow.] Finally women's hours of labor may be fixed; *Muller v. Oregon*, 208 U.S. 412; *Riley v. Massachusetts*, 232 U.S. 671, 679; *Hawley v. Walker*, 232 U.S. 718; *Miller v. Wilson*, 236 U.S. 373; *Bosley v. McLaughlin*, 236 U.S. 385; and the principle was extended to men with the allowance of a limited overtime to be paid for "at the rate of time and one-half of the regular wage," in *Bunting v. Oregon*, 243 U.S. 426.

I confess that I do not understand the principle on which the power to fix a minimum for the wages of women can be denied by those who admit the power to fix a maximum for their hours of work. I fully assent to the proposition that here as elsewhere the distinctions of the law are distinctions of degree, but I perceive no difference in the kind or degree of interference with liberty, the only matter with which we have any concern, between the one case and the other. The bargain is equally affected whichever half you regulate. . . . It will need more than the Nineteenth Amendment to convince me that there are no differences between men and women, or that legislation cannot take those differences into account. I should not hesitate to take them into account if I thought it necessary to sustain this act. *Quong Wing v. Kirkendall,* 233 U.S. 59, 63. But after *Bunting v. Oregon,* 243 U.S. 426, I had supposed that it was not necessary, and that *Lochner v. New York,* 198 U.S. 45, would be allowed a deserved repose.

 This statute does not compel anybody to pay anything. It simply forbids employment at rates below those fixed as the minimum requirement of health and right living. It is safe to assume that women will not be employed at even the lowest wages allowed unless they earn them, or unless the employer's business can sustain the burden. In short the law in its character and operation is like hundreds of so-called police laws that have been upheld. . . . The fact that the statute warrants classification, which like all classifications may bear hard upon some individuals . . . is no greater infirmity than is incident to all law. . . .

The criterion of constitutionality is not whether we believe the law to be for the public good. We certainly cannot be prepared to deny that a reasonable man reasonably might have that belief in view of the legislation of Great Britain, Victoria and a number of States of this Union. The belief is fortified by a very remarkable collection of documents submitted on behalf of the appellants material here, I conceive, only as showing that the belief reasonably may be held. . . . If a legislature should adopt . . . the doctrine that "freedom of contract is a misnomer as applied to a contract between an employer and an ordinary individual employee," 29 Harv. L. Rev. 13, 25, I could not pronounce an opinion with which I agree impossible to be entertained by reasonable men. . . .

 I am of opinion that the statute is valid and that the decree should be reversed.

CASE QUESTIONS

1. When the Court majority say that the minimum-wage statute is "arbitrary," what do they mean by that term? That it is irrational to think that a minimum wage will raise living standards (and thereby improve health)? That it is irrational to think that a woman's earning power affects her "morals" (i.e., sexual behavior)? That it is unfair to employers? Does the due process clause seem to prohibit taking property or liberty by "unfair" laws?

2. The dissenters here attack not only Sutherland's treatment of the precedents but also his analysis of the "woman question." Is there some third position on the woman question that would allow protective legislation for women and yet not assume some sort of psychological inferiority of women?

3. Everyone on the Court except Holmes (and Brandeis, who was silent) assumes that a maximum-wage law would be clearly unconstitutional. Would it?

The case of *Radice v. New York,* decided only months after *Adkins,* illustrates more clearly than the latter why Alice Paul and her followers opposed legislation aimed at protecting women in the economic arena. Although laws limiting the number of hours an employee could work per day or week have a readily discernible relationship to public health (in that they prevent people of either sex from being overworked to the point of weakened health), the relationship to public health or welfare of the statute challenged by Mr. Radice, a Buffalo, New York, restaurateur, was not all that obvious.

The part of the New York statute that Radice was contesting prohibited employing women between the hours of 10 P.M. and 6 A.M. in restaurants or "in connection with any restaurant" in large cities. (Other parts of the statute, not under challenge, established maxima of the nine-hour day and a fifty-four-hour week for women in restaurant work.) The statute was riddled with exceptions: it did not apply to restaurants in small cities or towns, it did not apply to "singers and performers of any kind," it did not apply to cloakroom and restroom attendants, it did not apply to hotel-related restaurants and their kitchens, and it did not apply to employees-only eating establishments operated by employers for their workers. In short, it meant that women in major cities could not work as waitresses or cooks or hostesses in most restaurants after ten o'clock at night. But they could work in the same restaurants in other capacities, and they could even work as waitresses, cooks, or hostesses in a select few restaurants.

Although the statute was challenged by an employer, it is not hard to see that this law had the impact of stamping certain jobs as "men only." These were the same jobs that women were permitted to do during daylight hours or in smaller towns.

How did nine Supreme Court justices convince themselves that this complex combination of permissions and prohibitions was "reasonably" related to the promotion of public health or welfare? They simply "assumed" certain beliefs to be facts—beliefs about the "more delicate organism" of women, which were alleged in the state's defense of its statute. Justice Sutherland's opinion provides no really satisfactory explanation why the Court continued to assume that beliefs alleged by legislatures in behalf of wage legislation (such as the law voided in *Adkins*) had no basis in reality, but that beliefs alleged in relation to what hour of the night a person worked did have such a basis.

Another curious aspect of Sutherland's opinion is the disparity in his treatment of the due process challenge to the statute and the equal protection challenge to it. Supposedly, "reasonableness" was to be the test for applying either clause. Just as liberty was not to be limited unless that limitation bore a rational relationship to promoting public welfare, so statutory classifications differentiating groups of people were to be based on a reasonable connection to the public good. Although he claims to be following this guideline, Sutherland actually proffers no reason why working at night as a waitress in a hotel-related restaurant would have a less harsh impact on women's health or welfare than working at the same job in a nonhotel restaurant. (For a fuller discussion of the equal protection clause, see chapter 2.)

Radice had been convicted of the crime of employing a woman in his restaurant after 10 P.M. In his defense he had argued that the law violated both the due process and the equal protection clauses of the Fourteenth Amendment. The Court of Appeals of New York had upheld his conviction without writing any opinion, and this case came to the Supreme Court from there. Here is how Justice Sutherland answered Radice's two constitutional arguments:

Radice v. New York, 264 U.S. 292 (1924)

MR. JUSTICE SUTHERLAND delivered the opinion of the Court.

. . .

The validity of the statute is challenged upon the ground that it contravenes the provisions of the Fourteenth Amendment, in that it violates (1) the due process clause, by depriving the employer and employee of their liberty of contract, and (2) the equal protection clause, by an unreasonable and arbitrary classification.

1. The basis of the first contention is that the statute unduly and arbitrarily interferes with the liberty of two adult persons to make a contract of employment for themselves. The answer of the State is that night work of the kind prohibited, so injuriously affects the physical condition of women, and so threatens to impair their peculiar and natural functions, and so exposes them to the dangers and menaces incident to night life in large cities, that a statute prohibiting such work falls within the police power of the State to preserve and promote the public health and welfare.

The legislature had before it a mass of information from which it concluded that night work is substantially and especially detrimental to the health of women. We

cannot say that the conclusion is without warrant. The loss of restful night's sleep can not be fully made up by sleep in the day time, especially in busy cities, subject to the disturbances incident to modern life. The injurious consequences were thought by the legislature to bear more heavily against women than men, and, considering their more delicate organism, there would seem to be good reason for so thinking. The fact, assuming it to be such, properly may be made the basis of legislation applicable only to women. Testimony was given upon the trial to the effect that the night work in question was not harmful; but we do not find it convincing. Where the constitutional validity of a statute depends upon the existence of facts, courts must be cautious about reaching a conclusion respecting them contrary to that reached by the legislature; and if the question of what the facts establish be a fairly debatable one, it is not permissible for the judge to set up his opinion in respect of it against the opinion of the lawmaker. The state legislature here determined that night employment of the character specified, was sufficiently detrimental to the health and welfare of women engaging in it to justify its suppression; and, since we are unable to say that the finding is clearly unfounded, we are precluded from reviewing the legislative determination. *Holden v. Hardy*, 169 U.S. 366, 395. The language used by this Court in *Muller v. Oregon*, 208 U.S. 412, 422, in respect of the physical limitations of women, is applicable and controlling:

> The limitations which this statute places upon her contractual powers, upon her right to agree with her employer as to the time she shall labor, are not imposed solely for her benefit, but also largely for the benefit of all. Many words cannot make this plainer. The two sexes differ in structure of body, in the functions to be performed by each, in the amount of physical strength, in the capacity for long-continued labor, particularly when done standing, the influence of vigorous health upon the future well-being of the race, the self-reliance which enables one to assert full rights, and in the capacity to maintain the struggle for subsistence. This difference justifies a difference in legislation and upholds that which is designed to compensate for some of the burdens which rest upon her.

Adkins v. Children's Hospital, 261 U.S. 525, is cited and relied upon; but that case presented a question entirely different from that now being considered. The statute in the *Adkins* case was a wage-fixing law, pure and simple. It had nothing to do with the hours or conditions of labor. We held that it exacted from the employer "an arbitrary payment for a purpose and upon a basis having no causal connection with his business, or the contract or the work" of the employee; but, referring to the *Muller* case, we said (p. 553) that "the physical differences [between men and women] must be recognized in appropriate cases, and

legislation fixing hours or conditions of work may properly take them into account." *See also Riley v. Massachusetts*, 232 U.S. 671; *Miller v. Wilson*, 236 U.S. 373; *Bosley v. McLaughlin*, 236 U.S. 385; and *compare Truax v. Raich*, 239 U.S. 33, 41, and *Coppage v. Kansas*, 236 U.S. 1, 18–19.

2. Nor is the statute vulnerable to the objection that it constitutes a denial of the equal protection of the laws. The points urged under this head are (a) that the act discriminates between cities of the first and second class and other cities and communities; and (b) excludes from its operation women employed in restaurants as singers and performers, attendants in ladies' cloak rooms and parlors, as well as those employed in dining rooms and kitchens of hotels and in lunch rooms or restaurants conducted by employers solely for the benefit of their employees.

The limitation of the legislative prohibition to cities of the first and second class does not bring about an unreasonable and arbitrary classification. *Packard v. Banton*, 264 U.S. 140; *Hayes v. Missouri*, 120 U.S. 68. Nor is there substance in the contention that the exclusion of restaurant employees of a special kind, and of hotels and employees' lunch rooms, renders the statute obnoxious to the Constitution. The statute does not present a case where some persons of a class are selected for special restraint from which others of the same class are left free (*Connolly v. Union Sewer Pipe Co.*, 184 U.S. 540, 564); but a case where all in the same class of work, are included in the restraint. Of course, the mere fact of classification is not enough to put a statute beyond the reach of the equality provision of the Fourteenth Amendment. Such classification must not be "purely arbitrary, oppressive or capricious." *American Sugar Refining Co. v. Louisiana*, 179 U.S. 89, 92. But the mere production of inequality is not enough. Every selection of persons for regulation so results, in some degree. The inequality produced, in order to encounter the challenge of the Constitution, must be "actually and palpably unreasonable and arbitrary." *Arkansas Natural Gas Co. v. Railroad Commission*, 261 U.S. 379, 384, and cases cited. . . . Directly applicable are recent decisions of this Court sustaining hours of labor for women in hotels but omitting women employees of boarding houses, lodging houses, etc., *Miller v. Wilson, supra*, at 382; and limiting the hours of labor of women pharmacists and student nurses in hospitals but excepting graduate nurses. *Bosley v. McLaughlin, supra*, at 394–96. The opinion in the first of these cases was delivered by Mr. Justice Hughes, who, after pointing out that in hotels women employees are for the most part chambermaids and waitresses; that it cannot be said that the conditions of work are the same as those which obtain in the other establishments; and that it is not beyond the power of the legislature to recognize the differences, said (pp. 383–84):

The contention as to the various omissions which are noted in the objections here urged ignores the well-established principle that the legislature is not bound, in order to support the constitutional validity of its regula-

tion, to extend it to all cases which it might possibly reach. Dealing with practical exigencies, the legislature may be guided by experience. *Patsone v. Pennsylvania*, 232 U.S. 138, 144. It is free to recognize degrees of harm, and it may confine its restrictions to those classes of cases where the need is deemed to be clearest. As has been said, it may "proceed cautiously, step by step," and "if an evil is specially experienced in a particular branch of business" it is not necessary that the prohibition "should be couched in all-embracing terms." *Carroll v. Greenwich Insurance Co.*, 199 U.S. 401, 411. If the law presumably hits the evil where it is most felt, it is not to be overthrown because there are other instances to which it might have been applied. *Keokee Coke Co. v. Taylor*, 234 U.S. 224, 227. Upon this principle which has had abundant illustration in the decisions cited below, it cannot be concluded that the failure to extend the act to other and distinct lines of business, having their own circumstances and conditions, or to domestic service, created an arbitrary discrimination as against the proprietors of hotels.

The judgment below is *Affirmed*.

CASE QUESTIONS

1. On the whole, do laws like the one at issue here, benefit women?

2. Can a viable case be made for claiming, as the Court does, that hours legislation is more directly related to public welfare than wage legislation?

3. As noted above, Justice Sutherland does not explain the reason why working in hotel restaurants would be less deleterious to women's health than working in other restaurants. Suppose the "reason" for this exception in the statute was that hotels had a powerful lobby in Albany,

and that without this exception, therefore, this legislation could not have garnered enough votes to pass. Would that constitute a "reasonable" basis for the statutory classification? If so, what meaning does the equal protection clause have?

Despite its concessions for hours legislation, the Court continued its opposition to minimum-wage legislation through the Great Depression and through the first administration of Franklin D. Roosevelt. As late as 1936, the Court invalidated a women's minimum-wage law of the state of New York,[12] again essentially on the grounds that the due process clause forbids laws that in their substance constitute unfair (in the Court's eyes) regulations of property. (This notion has come to be known as the doctrine of "economic substantive due process.") Using its own versions of various other legal doctrines, the Court also invalidated a great many other social welfare measures, including the bulk of Roosevelt's New Deal. Naturally, this infuriated FDR, and after his overwhelming electoral victory of 1936, he introduced into Congress his famous (or notorious) Court-packing plan. By adding six judges to the Court, all his own appointments, FDR would have been able to transform the 6–3 and 5–4 decisions against his programs into, at worst, 6–9 decisions in his favor.

Just as the debate on this plan was taking place in Congress, the Supreme Court dramatically reversed itself on a number of legal issues, including minimum wages for women and various central planks of the New Deal platform. This reversal has been called "the switch in time that saved nine." Although there is now evidence that the crucial "swing" judge (Roberts) had changed his mind about the minimum-wage issue some months before the impending threat of the Court-packing plan, as far as the American public of 1937 knew, the switches were all of a parcel. Although Roosevelt lost his Court-packing plan, he "won the war." After the crucial doctrinal switch in 1937, Roosevelt had the opportunity to appoint seven new justices in the period between 1937 and 1941. By the time Roosevelt died, he had appointed eight of the nine justices on the Court (the ninth was Roberts).

The Court's reversal on minimum wages for women occurred in the case of *West Coast Hotel v. Parrish*. At issue was a statute of the state of Washington that paralleled in every major respect the District of Columbia statute that the Supreme Court had voided in *Adkins*. It created a board to establish minimum wages for women and children workers, specifying that in the case of women workers, the wage be adequate "for the decent maintenance of women" and "not detrimental to health and morals." One interesting variation in this case involves the original plaintiff. The person who initiated the lawsuit was Elsie Parrish, an employee who, unlike the woman employee in the companion case to *Adkins v. Children's Hospital*, wanted this law enforced. Elsie Parrish was suing her employer, the West Coast Hotel, for back pay owed her to bring her wages up to the legal minimum of $14.50 a week (for forty-eight hours' work).

The following case shows one of the rare occasions when the Supreme Court openly and explicitly overruled one of its own precedents.

West Coast Hotel Company v. Parrish, 300 U.S. 379 (1937)

MR. CHIEF JUSTICE HUGHES delivered the opinion of the Court.

. . .

We think that the question [whether to overrule *Adkins v. Children's Hospital*] which was not deemed to be open in the *Morehead* case [decided in 1936] is open and is necessarily presented here. The Supreme Court of Washington has upheld the minimum wage statute of that State. It has decided that the statute is a reasonable exercise of the police power of the State. In reaching that conclusion the state court has invoked principles long established by this Court in the application of the Fourteenth Amendment. The state court has refused to regard the decision in the *Adkins* case as determinative and has pointed to our decisions both before and since that case as justifying its position. We are of the opinion that this ruling of the state court demands on our part a reexamination of the *Adkins* case. The importance of the question, in which many States having similar laws are concerned, the close division by which the decision in the *Adkins* case was reached, and the economic conditions which have supervened, and in the light of which the reasonableness of the exercise of the protective power of the State must be considered, make it not only appropriate, but we think imperative, that in deciding the present case the subject should receive fresh consideration.

The principle which must control our decision is not in doubt. The constitutional provision invoked is the due process clause of the Fourteenth Amendment governing the States, as the due process clause invoked in the *Adkins* case governed Congress. In each case the violation alleged by those attacking minimum wage regulation for women is deprivation of freedom of contract. What is this freedom? The Constitution does not speak of freedom of contract. It speaks of liberty and prohibits the deprivation of liberty without due process of law. In prohibiting that deprivation the Constitution does not recognize an absolute and uncontrollable liberty. Liberty in each of its phases has its history and connotation. But the liberty safeguarded is liberty in a social organization which requires the protection of law against the evils which menace the health, safety, morals and welfare of the people. Liberty under the Constitution is thus necessarily subject to the restraints of due process, and regulation which is reasonable in relation to its subject and is adopted in the interests of the community is due process.

This essential limitation of liberty in general governs freedom of contract in particular. More than twenty-five years ago we set forth the applicable principle in these words. . . .

There is no absolute freedom to do as one wills or to contract as one chooses. The guaranty of liberty does not withdraw from legislative supervision that wide department of activity which consists of the making of contracts, or deny to government the power to provide restrictive safeguards. Liberty implies the absence of arbitrary restraint, not immunity from reasonable regulations and prohibitions imposed in the interests of the community. (*Chicago, B.&Q. R. Co. v. McGuire*, 219 U.S. 549, 567.)

This power under the Constitution to restrict freedom of contract has had many illustrations. [Here the Court footnoted 22 different precedents.] That it may be exercised in the public interest with respect to contracts between employer and employee is undeniable. Thus statutes have been sustained limiting employment in underground mines and smelters to eight hours a day (*Holden v. Hardy*, 169 U.S. 366); . . . in limiting hours of work of employees in manufacturing establishments (*Bunting v. Oregon*, 243 U.S. 426); and in maintaining workmen's compensation laws (*New York Central R. Co. v. White*, 243 U.S. 188; *Mountain Timber Co. v. Washington*, 243 U.S. 219). In dealing with the relation of employer and employed, the legislature has necessarily a wide field of discretion in order that there may be suitable protection of health and safety, and that peace and good order may be promoted through regulations designed to insure wholesome conditions of work and freedom from oppression. *Chicago B.&Q. R. Co. v. McGuire, supra* (p. 570).

The point that has been strongly stressed that adult employees should be deemed competent to make their own contracts was decisively met nearly forty years ago in *Holden v. Hardy, supra*, where we pointed out the inequality in the footing of the parties. We said (*id.*, 397):

The legislature has also recognized the fact, which the experience of legislators in many States has corroborated, that the proprietors of these establishments and their operatives do not stand upon an equality, and that their interests are, to a certain extent, conflicting. The former naturally desire to obtain as much labor as possible from their employees, while the latter are often induced by the fear of discharge to conform to regulations which their judgment, fairly exercised, would pronounce to be detrimental to their health or strength. In other words, the proprietors lay down the rules and the laborers are practically constrained to obey them. In such cases self-interest is often an unsafe guide, and the legislature may properly interpose its authority.

And we added that the fact "that both parties are of full age and competent to contract does not necessarily deprive the State of the power to interfere where the parties do not stand upon an equality, or where the public health demands that one party to the contract shall be protected against himself." "The State still retains an interest in his welfare, however reckless he may be. The whole is no greater than the sum of all the parts, and when the individual health, safety and welfare are sacrificed or neglected, the State must suffer."

It is manifest that this established principle is peculiarly applicable in relation to the employment of women in whose protection the State has a special interest. That phase of the subject received elaborate consideration in *Muller v. Oregon*, 208 U.S. 412 (1908), where the constitutional authority of the State to limit the working hours of women was sustained. We emphasized the consideration that "woman's physical structure and the performance of maternal functions place her at a disadvantage in the struggle for subsistence" and that her physical well being "becomes an object of public interest and care in order to preserve the strength and vigor of the race." We emphasized the need of protecting women against oppression despite her possession of contractual rights. We said that "though limitations upon personal and contractual rights may be removed by legislation, there is that in her disposition and habits of life which will operate against a full assertion of those rights. She will still be where some legislation to protect her seems necessary to secure a real equality of right." Hence she was "properly placed in a class by herself, and legislation designed for her protection may be sustained even when like legislation is not necessary for men and could not be sustained." We concluded that the limitations which the statute there in question "placed upon her contractual powers, upon her right to agree with her employer as to the time she shall labor" were "not imposed solely for her benefit, but also largely for the benefit of all." Again, *Quong Wing v. Kirkendall*, 233 U.S. 59, 63, in referring to a differentiation with respect to the employment of women, we said that the Fourteenth Amendment did not interfere with state power by creating a "fictitious equality." We referred to recognized classifications on the basis of sex with regard to hours of work and in other matters, and we observed that the particular points at which that difference shall be enforced by legislation were largely in the power of the State. In later rulings this Court sustained the regulation of hours of work of women employees in *Riley v. Massachusetts*, 232 U.S. 671 (factories), *Miller v. Wilson*, 236 U.S. 373 (hotels), and *Bosley v. McLaughlin*, 236 U.S. 385 (hospitals).

This array of precedents and the principles they applied were thought by the dissenting Justices in the *Adkins* case to demand that the minimum wage statute be sustained. The validity of a distinction . . . between a minimum wage and a maximum

of hours in limiting liberty of contract was especially challenged. 261 U.S., p. 564. That challenge persists and is without any satisfactory answer. As Chief Justice Taft observed: "In absolute freedom of contract the one term is as important as the other, for both enter equally into the consideration given and received, a restriction as to the one is not greater in essence than the other and is of the same kind. One is the multiplier and the other the multiplicand." And Mr. Justice Holmes, while recognizing that "the distinctions of the law are distinctions of degree," could "perceive no difference in the kind or degree of interference with liberty, the only matter with which we have any concern, between the one case and the other. The bargain is equally affected whichever half you regulate." *Id.*, p. 569.

. . . We are unable to conclude that in its minimum wage requirement the State has passed beyond the boundary of its broad protective power.

. . . The statement of Mr. Justice Holmes in the *Adkins* case is pertinent: "This statute does not compel anybody to pay anything. It simply forbids employment at rates below those fixed as the minimum requirement of health and right living. It is safe to assume that women will not be employed at even the lowest wages allowed unless they earn them, or unless they can sustain the burden. In short the law in its character and operation is like hundreds of so-called police laws that have been upheld." 261 U.S., p. 570. And Chief Justice Taft forcibly pointed out the consideration which is basic in a statute of this character:

> Legislatures which adopt a requirement of maximum hours or minimum wages may be presumed to believe than when sweating employers are prevented from paying unduly low wages by positive law they will con-

tinue their business, abating that part of their profits, which were wrung from the necessities of their employees, and will concede the better terms required by the law; and that while in individual cases hardship may result, the restriction will enure to the benefit of the general class of employees in whose interest the law is passed and so to that of the community at large. (*Id.*, p. 563.)

We think that the views thus expressed are sound and that the decision in the *Adkins* case was a departure from the true application of the principles governing the regulation by the State of the relation of employer and employed. Those principles have been reenforced by our subsequent decisions. . . .

With full recognition of the earnestness and vigor which characterize the prevailing opinion in the *Adkins* case, we find it impossible to reconcile that ruling with these well-considered declarations. What can be closer to the public interest than the health of women and their protection from unscrupulous and overreaching employers? And if the protection of women is a legitimate end of the exercise of state power, how can it be said that the requirement of the payment of a minimum wage fairly fixed in order to meet the very necessities of existence is not an admissible means to that end? The legislature of the State was clearly entitled to consider the situation of women in employment, the fact that they are in the class receiving the least pay, that their bargaining power is relatively weak, and that they are the ready victims of those who would take advantage of their necessitous circumstances. The legislature was entitled to adopt measures to reduce the evils of the "sweating system," the exploiting of workers at wages so low as to be insufficient to meet the bare cost of living,

thus making their very helplessness the occasion of a most injurious competition. The legislature had the right to consider that its minimum wage requirements would be an important aid in carrying out its policy of protection. The adoption of similar requirements by many States evidences a deep-seated conviction both as to the presence of the evil and as to the means adopted to check it. Legislative response to that conviction cannot be regarded as arbitrary or capricious, and that is all we have to decide. Even if the wisdom of the policy be regarded as debatable and its effects uncertain, still the legislature is entitled to its judgment.

There is an additional and compelling consideration which recent economic experience has brought into a strong light. The exploitation of a class of workers who are in an unequal position with respect to bargaining power and are thus relatively defenseless against the denial of a living wage is not only detrimental to their health and well being but casts a direct burden for their support upon the community. What these workers lose in wages the taxpayers are called upon to pay. The bare cost of living must be met. We may take judicial notice of the unparalleled demands for relief which arose during the recent period of depression and still continue to an alarming extent despite the degree of economic recovery which has been achieved. It is unnecessary to cite official statistics to establish what is of common knowledge through the length and breadth of the land. The community is not bound to provide what is in effect a subsidy for unconscionable employers. The community may direct its law-making power to correct the abuse which springs from their selfish disregard of the public interest. The argument that the legislation in question constitutes an arbitrary discrimination, because it does not extend to men, is unavailing.

This Court has frequently held that the legislative authority, acting within its proper field, is not bound to extend its regulation to all cases which it might possibly reach. The legislature "is free to recognize degrees of harm and it may confine its restrictions to those classes of cases where the need is deemed to be clearest." If "the law presumably hits the evil where it is most felt, it is not to be overthrown because there are other instances to which it might have been applied." There is no "doctrinaire requirement" that the legislation should be couched in all embracing terms. *Carroll v. Greenwich Insurance Co.*, 199 U.S. 401, 411; *Patsone v. Pennsylvania*, 232 U.S. 138, 144; *Keokee Coke Co. v. Taylor*, 234 U.S. 224, 227; *Sproles v. Binford*, 286 U.S. 374, 396; *Semler v. Oregon Board*, 294 U.S. 608, 610, 611. This familiar principle has repeatedly been applied to legislation which singles out women, and particular classes of women, in the exercise of the State's protective power. *Miller v. Wilson, supra*, p. 384; *Bosley v. McLaughlin, supra*, pp. 394, 395; *Radice v. New York, supra*, pp. 295–98. Their relative need in the presence of the evil, no less than the existence of the evil itself, is a matter for the legislative judgment.

Our conclusion is that the case of *Adkins v. Children's Hospital, supra,* should be, and it is, overruled. The judgment of the Supreme Court of the State of Washington is

Affirmed.

Mr. Justice Sutherland, dissenting:

Mr. Justice Van Devanter, Mr. Justice McReynolds, Mr. Justice Butler and I think the judgment of the court below should be reversed.

The principles and authorities relied upon to sustain the judgment, were considered in *Adkins v. Children's Hospital*, 261 U.S. 525, and *Morehead v. New York ex rel. Tipaldo*, 298 U.S. 587; and their lack of application to cases like the one in hand was pointed out. A sufficient answer to all that is now said will be found in the opinions of the court in those cases. Nevertheless, in the circumstances, it seems well to restate our reasons and conclusions.

. . .

If the Constitution, intelligently and reasonably construed . . . stands in the way of desirable legislation, the blame must rest upon that instrument, and not upon the court for enforcing it according to its terms. The remedy in that situation—and the only true remedy—is to amend the Constitution.

. . . "What a court is to do, therefore, is *to declare the law as written,* leaving it to the people themselves to make such changes as new circumstances may require. The meaning of the constitution is fixed when it is adopted, and it is not different at any subsequent time when a court has occasion to pass upon it."

. . .

Coming, then, to a consideration of the Washington statute, it first is to be observed that it is in every substantial respect identical with the statute involved in the *Adkins* case. Such vices as existed in the latter are present in the former. And if the *Adkins* case was properly decided, as we who join in this opinion think it was, it necessarily follows that the Washington statute is invalid. . . .

In the *Adkins* case we . . . said that while there was no such thing as absolute freedom of contract, but that it was subject to a great variety of restraints, nevertheless, freedom of contract was the general rule and restraint the exception; and that the power to abridge that freedom could only be justified by the existence of exceptional circumstances. . . .

The Washington statute, like the one for the District of Columbia, fixes minimum wages for adult women. Adult men and their employers are left free to bargain as they please; and it is a significant and an important fact that all state statutes to which our attention has been called are of like character. The common-law rules restricting the power of women to make contracts have, under our system, long since practically disappeared. Women today stand upon a legal and political equality with men. There is no longer any reason why they should be put in different classes in respect of their legal right to make contracts; nor should they be denied, in effect, the right to compete with men for work paying lower wages which men may be willing to accept. And it is an arbitrary exercise of the legislative power to do so. . . . An appeal to the principle that the legislature is free to recognize degrees of harm and confine its restrictions accordingly, is but to beg the question, which is—since

the contractual rights of men and women are the same, does the legislation here involved, by restricting only the rights of women to make contracts as to wages, create an arbitrary discrimination? We think it does. Difference of sex affords no reasonable ground for making a restriction applicable to the wage contracts of all working women from which like contracts of all working men are left free. Certainly a suggestion that the bargaining ability of the average woman is not equal to that of the average man would lack substance. The ability to make a fair bargain, as everyone knows, does not depend upon sex.

If, in the light of the facts, the state legislation, without reason or for reasons of mere expediency, excluded men from the provisions of the legislation, the power was exercised arbitrarily. On the other hand, if such legislation in respect of men was properly omitted on the ground that it would be unconstitutional, the same conclusion of unconstitutionality is inescapable in respect of similar legislative restraint in the case of women, 261 U.S. 553. . . .

CASE QUESTIONS

1. Both the majority and minority opinions claim that their own position is the one that really supports women's rights. Which position is correct?

2. Does the majority opinion rest on the grounds that "the protection of women is a legitimate exercise of state power" because women "are the ready victims of those who would take advantage of their necessitous circumstances"? If so, what is the import of the majority's later statement that "the legislative authority,

acting *within its proper field,* is not bound to extend its regulation to all cases where it might possible reach"? (Emphasis added.) Does the majority opinion offer independent justification for minimum-wage laws to protect workers *qua* workers?

3. Is the minority correct in its assertion that the majority argument about degrees of harm "begs the question" concerning arbitrary discrimination between men and women?

4. Consider the minority's rule of constitutional interpretation: "The meaning of the constitution is fixed when it is adopted, and it is not different at any subsequent time." If one opts for the idea of an "evolving" constitution, does the idea that the government is limited by the fundamental law still retain any meaning?

5. Would the Equal Rights Amendment render this women's minimum-wage law unconstitutional?

Although the *West Coast* majority opinion did not present an unambiguous answer to the question of the constitutionality of potential minimum-wage laws that would apply to workers in general—a question lurking in the shadows of that case—it was not too long before the Court squarely faced that question. In the 1941 case of *United States v. Darby*, the Court confronted the issue of the constitutionality of the national Fair Labor Standards Act (or Wages and Hours Act). This act establishes minimum wages and maximum hours for all workers producing goods intended for interstate commerce. As in *Adkins v. Children's Hospital*, the Court here dealt with the Fifth Amendment due process clause (because national legislation was involved) but presented arguments that applied equally to the Fourteenth Amendment due process clause.

The parallels between the *West Coast Hotel Co. v. Parrish/United States v. Darby* pattern and the earlier *Muller v. Oregon/Bunting v. Oregon* pattern are striking. Most obvious, of course, is the central fact that, as with the hours legislation acceptance pattern, this minimum-wage-law chronology presented a piece of general welfare legislation to the Supreme Court within a few years after the same kind of legislation on a protection-of-women basis had been acknowledged as reasonable by that Court. The proponents of social welfare legislation, once again having used the need to protect women as the cutting edge of their argument, were widening its wedge so as to shelter all members of society behind the same rationale.

The second striking similarity between the two patterns involves the relative amounts of attention devoted to due process clause arguments between the first and the second cases in each series. Like *Muller v. Oregon*, *West Coast Hotel v. Parrish* was entirely devoted to the due process question, and the weight of the argument in both cases rested largely on the assumption of the special needs and/or weaknesses of women. Similarly, like the *Bunting* sequel to *Muller*, the *Darby* sequel to *West Coast Hotel* spent only one paragraph on the due process question, devoting all the rest of a rather lengthy opinion to other legal issues. (In *Darby*, those questions involved the constitutional relationship between national and state legislative power.) In other words, once the constitutionality of women's legislation had been seriously debated, the due process question for similar legislation of *general* applicability was again simply assumed to have been already settled. Here is all the Court had to say about the due process challenge in *Darby*:

United States v. Darby, 312 U.S. 100 (1941), excerpt

Validity of the wage and hour provisions under the Fifth Amendment.

. . .

Since our decision in *West Coast Hotel Co. v. Parrish*, 300 U.S. 379, it is no longer open to question that the fixing of a minimum wage is within the legislative power and that the bare fact of its exercise is not a denial of due process under the Fifth more than under the Fourteenth Amendment. Nor is it any longer open to question that it is within the legislative power to fix maximum hours. *Holden v. Hardy*, 169 U.S. 366; *Muller v. Oregon*, 208 U.S. 412; *Bunting v. Oregon*, 243 U.S. 426; *Baltimore & Ohio R. Co. v. Interstate Commerce Comm'n*, 221 U.S. 612. Similarly the statute is not objectionable because applied alike to both men and women. Cf. *Bunting v. Oregon*, 243 U.S. 426.

The repeated success of the *Muller/Bunting* and the *West Coast Hotel/Darby* approach to obtaining societal acceptance of social welfare legislation via the women-and-children-first technique, renders understandable why veterans of social welfare legislation battles, such as the AFL-CIO, for years (prior to the mid-1960s) opposed the Equal Rights Amendment. Those groups were reluctant to discard an old and trustworthy weapon of past wars. For those supporters of the ERA who also value the legislation gained by weapons the ERA would probably forbid, certain questions arise: Is the women-and-children-first path to the acceptance of progressive legislation obsolete? If so, why? Changes in societal attitudes? Changes in women? Changes in the composition of the Supreme Court? If the technique is not obsolete, of course, a far more ponderous question must be addressed: Are the societal gains to be obtained by the ERA worth the cost of this particular political weapon?

The Pregnancy Leave Issue: Old Wine in New Bottles

As the most prominent women activists of the early twentieth century were divided over whether the Constitution should permit legislatures to single out women employees for special protection, a similar controversy has erupted in the late 1980s. In the 1920s the pro-special-treatment women's activists had more prestige, numbers, and political influence. In the 1980s the balance of power among feminist leaders is reversed; the equal-treatment feminists are predominant. But influential feminist advocates of special treatment are making their voices heard, as new cases present in new contexts this old issue.

While this book was in preparation, the U.S. Supreme Court decided a case that pitted certain self-proclaimed feminists (including some attorneys) against such feminist strongholds as the National Organization for Women, the National Women's Political Caucus, the American Civil Liberties Union, and the League of Women Voters. The case, *California Federal Savings & Loan v. Guerra*, 55 U.S.L.W. 4077, began when Lillian Garland attempted after four months maternity leave in 1982 to return to the receptionist job that she had held for several years. The bank refused to rehire her, relying on its stated policy reserving such right of refusal for any employee on a leave of absence. California's Fair Employment and Housing Act, § 12945(b)(2) required employers to grant pregnancy disability leave of up to four months. Specifically, the law said:

> It shall be an unlawful employment practice unless based upon a bona fide occupational qualification:
>
>   . . .
>
>   (b) For any employer to refuse to allow a female employee affected by pregnancy, childbirth, or related medical conditions. . . .
>
>   . . .
>
>   (2) To take a leave on account of pregnancy for a reasonable period of time; provided, such period shall not exceed four months. . . . Reasonable period of time means that period during which the female employee is disabled on account of pregnancy, childbirth, or related medical conditions. . . .
>   An employer may require any employee who plans to take a leave pursuant to this section to give reasonable notice of the date such leave shall commence and the estimated duration of such leave.

Federal law (always supreme in case of a conflict, according to Article VI, § 2 of the Constitution) forbids employers to discriminate on the basis of sex and states in the Pregnancy Discrimination Act ("PDA") (42 U.S.C. § 2000e[k]):

> The terms . . . "on the basis of sex" include, but are not limited to, because of or on the basis of pregnancy, childbirth, or related medical conditions; and women affected by pregnancy, childbirth, or related medical conditions, shall be treated the same for all employment-related purposes, including receipt of benefits under fringe benefit programs, as other persons not so affected but similar in their ability or inability to work, and nothing in section 2000e–2(h) of this title shall be interpreted to permit otherwise.

The district court judge felt that this federal law negated California's law and he so declared. The federal circuit court of appeals reversed, stating that the federal law was intended to enhance, not diminish, women's employment opportunities. That court interpreted the PDA as intended "to construct a floor beneath which pregnancy disability benefits may not drop—not a ceiling above which they may not rise" (758 F.2d, at 396). The Supreme Court took the appeal from this decision and a number of interest groups submitted additional *amicus* briefs. The American Civil Liberties Union's brief, submitted on the side of the bank, argues:

> Protectionist laws reflect an ideology which values women most highly for their childbearing and nurturing roles. Such laws reinforce stereotypes about women's inclinations and abilities; they deter employers from hiring women of child-bearing age or funnel them into less responsible positions; and they make women *appear* to be more expensive, less reliable employees.

Prof. Lucinda Finley of Yale Law School has argued publicly to the contrary: "Pretending men and women are the same is not equality. . . . The equal treatment argument, carried to the extreme, tries to defy social reality, particularly among poor women. The social reality is that there are a lot of women out there in need." The news article from which these quotes are taken[13] points out that related potential future legislation that might be barred by an overly rigid approach to equality includes requirements of paid maternity leave or time off during the workday for breastfeeding. It also notes that women are currently 45 percent of the U.S. workforce and 90 percent of them have or will have children. More than 60 percent of these women workers have no guarantees that the job they leave for childbirth will be available to them when they are ready to return to work.

The Supreme Court decided this case on January 13, 1987. It is the first of the cases in this text to be decided by the newly composed Court: Justice Rehnquist replaced Burger as the Chief Justice and the vacancy left by Burger's retirement has been filled by Justice Scalia, who sides here with the majority of six, but for reasons of his own, which he explains below.

Justice Stevens, too, departs from the majority reasoning in part. He is very much influenced by a 1979 precedent, *United Steelworkers v. Weber*, 443 U.S. 193, that had upheld private employer affirmative action programs for black employees. The particular program upheld there had set aside 50 percent of the slots in an inplant craft training program for qualified black workers. This program was upheld by the Court against a challenge by a white worker shut out of the program despite his seniority (the basic qualifying factor), which was superior to that of many of the accepted blacks. He based his challenge on Title VII of the Civil Rights Act, which prohibited, among other things:

> any employer, labor organization, or joint labor-management committee [to] discriminate against any individual because of his race, color, religion, sex, or national origin in admission [to] any program established to provide apprenticeship or other training.

Neither the other majority justices, nor the dissenters, made any mention of this precedent that Justice Stevens found so compelling.

California Federal Savings and Loan Association v. Mark Guerra, Director, Department of Fair Employment and Housing, 55 U.S.L.W. 4077 (1987)

JUSTICE MARSHALL delivered the opinion of the Court.

The question presented is whether Title VII of the Civil Rights Act of 1964, as amended by the Pregnancy Discrimination Act of 1978, pre-empts a state statute that requires employers to provide leave and reinstatement to employees disabled by pregnancy.

I

. . . Respondent Fair Employment and Housing Commission, the state agency authorized to interpret the FEHA, has construed § 12945(b)(2) to require California employers to reinstate an employee returning from such pregnancy leave to the job she previously held, unless it is no longer available due to business necessity. In the latter case, the employer must make a reasonable, good faith effort to place the employee in a substantially similar job. The statute does not compel employers to provide *paid* leave to pregnant employees. Accordingly, the only benefit pregnant workers actually derive from § 12945(b)(2) is a qualified right to reinstatement.

Title VII of the Civil Rights Act of 1964, 42 U.S.C. § 2000e *et seq.*, also prohibits various forms of employment discrimination, including discrimination on the basis of sex. However, in *General Electric Co. v. Gilbert*, 429 U.S. 125 (1976), this Court ruled that discrimination on the basis of pregnancy was not sex discrimination under Title VII.* In response to the *Gilbert* decision, Congress passed the Pregnancy Discrimination Act of 1978 (PDA), 42 U.S.C. § 2000e(k). The PDA specifies that sex discrimination includes discrimination on the basis of pregnancy.[6]

II

Petitioner California Federal Savings and Loan Association (Cal. Fed.) is a federally chartered savings and loan association based in Los Angeles; it is an employer covered by both Title VII and § 12945(b)(2). Cal. Fed. has a facially neutral leave policy that permits employees who have com-

*This case is included in chapter 4—Au.

6. The PDA added subsection (k) to § 701, the definitional section of Title VII. Subsection (k) provides, in relevant part:

"The terms 'because of sex' or 'on the basis of sex' include, but are not limited to, because of or on the basis of pregnancy, childbirth, or related medical conditions; and women affected by pregnancy, childbirth, or related medical conditions shall be treated the same for all employment-related purposes, including receipt of benefits under fringe benefit programs, as other persons not so affected but similar in their ability or inability to work, and nothing in section 703(h) of this title shall be interpreted to permit otherwise."

The legislative history of the PDA reflects Congress' approval of the views of the dissenters in *Gilbert*. See *Newport News Shipbuilding & Dry Dock Co. v. EEOC*, 462 U.S. 669, 678–79, and nn.15–17 (1983) (citing legislative history).

pleted three months of service to take unpaid leaves of absence for a variety of reasons, including disability and pregnancy.
Although it is Cal. Fed.'s policy to try to
provide an employee taking unpaid leave
with a similar position upon returning,
Cal. Fed. expressly reserves the right to
terminate an employee who has taken a
leave of absence if a similar position is not
available.

. . .

. . . [W]e now affirm [the Court of
Appeals ruling].

III

A

In determining whether a state statute
is pre-empted by federal law and therefore
invalid under the Supremacy Clause of the
Constitution, our sole task is to ascertain
the intent of Congress. *See Shaw v. Delta Air
Lines, Inc.*, 463 U.S. 85, 95 (1983); *Malone v.
White Motor Corp.*, 435 U.S. 497, 504 (1978).
Federal law may supersede state law in
several different ways. First, when acting
within constitutional limits, Congress is
empowered to pre-empt state law by so stating in express terms. *E.g., Jones v. Rath
Packing Co.*, 430 U.S. 519, 525 (1977). Second, congressional intent to pre-empt state
law in a particular area may be inferred
where the scheme of federal regulation is
sufficiently comprehensive to make reasonable the inference that Congress "left
no room" for supplementary state regulation. *Rice v. Santa Fe Elevator Corp.*, 331 U.S.
218, 230 (1947). Neither of these bases for
pre-emption exists in this case. . . .

As a third alternative, in those areas
where Congress has not completely dis-
placed state regulation, federal law may
nonetheless pre-empt state law to the extent it actually conflicts with federal law.
Such a conflict occurs either because "com-

pliance with both federal and state regulations is a physical impossibility," *Florida
Lime & Avocado Growers, Inc. v. Paul*, 373
U.S. 132, 142–143 (1963), or because the
state law stands "as an obstacle to the accomplishment and execution of the full
purposes and objectives of Congress."
Hines v. Davidowitz, 312 U.S. 52, 67 (1941).
[Other citations omitted.] Nevertheless,
pre-emption is not to be lightly presumed.
See Maryland v. Louisiana, 451 U.S. 725, 746
(1981).

This third basis for pre-emption is at
issue in this case. In two sections of the
1964 Civil Rights Act, §§ 708 and 1104,
Congress has indicated that state laws will
be pre-empted only if they actually conflict
with federal law. Section 708 of Title VII
provides:

> Nothing in this title shall be
> deemed to exempt or relieve any per-
> son from any liability, duty, penalty, or
> punishment provided by any present
> or future law of any State or political
> subdivision of a State, other than any
> such law which purports to require or
> permit the doing of any act which
> would be an unlawful employment
> practice under this title. (§ 2000e–7.)

Section 1104 of Title XI, applicable to all
titles of the Civil Rights Act, establishes the
following standard for pre-emption:

> Nothing contained in any title of
> this Act shall be construed as indicat-
> ing an intent on the part of Congress
> to occupy the field in which any such
> title operates to the exclusion of State
> laws on the same subject matter, nor
> shall any provision of this Act be con-
> strued as invalidating any provision of
> State law unless such provision is in-
> consistent with any of the purposes of
> this Act, or any provision thereof.
> (§ 2000h–4.)

Accordingly, there is no need to infer congressional intent to pre-empt state laws from the substantive provisions of Title VII; these two sections provide a "reliable indicium of congressional intent with respect to state authority" to regulate employment practice. *Malone v. White Motor Corp., supra,* at 505.

Sections 708 and 1104 severely limit Title VII's pre-emptive effect. Instead of pre-empting state fair employment laws, § 708 "'simply left them where they were before the enactment of title VII.'" *Shaw v. Delta Air Lines, Inc., supra,* at 103, n.24. Similarly, § 1104 was intended primarily to "assert the intention of Congress to preserve existing civil rights laws." 110 Cong. Rec. 2788 (1964) (remarks of Rep. Meader). *See also* H.R. Rep. No. 914, 88th Cong., 1st Sess., 59 (1963) (additional views of Rep. Meader).[12] The narrow scope of pre-emption available under §§ 708 and 1104 reflects the importance Congress attached to state antidiscrimination laws in achieving Title VII's goal of equal employment opportunity. [Citations omitted.] The legislative history of the PDA also supports a narrow interpretation of these provisions, as does our opinion in *Shaw v. Delta Air Lines, Inc., supra.*[15]

In order to decide whether the California statute requires or permits employers to violate Title VII, as amended by the PDA, or is inconsistent with the purposes of the statute, we must determine whether the PDA prohibits the States from requiring employers to provide reinstatement to pregnant workers, regardless of their policy for disabled workers generally.

B

Petitioners argue that the language of the federal statute itself unambiguously rejects California's "special treatment" approach to pregnancy discrimination, thus rendering any resort to the legislative history unnecessary. They contend that the second clause of the PDA forbids an employer to treat pregnant employees any differently than other disabled employees. Because "[t]he purpose of Congress is the ultimate touchstone" of the pre-emption inquiry, *Malone v. White Motor Corp.,* 435 U.S., at 504 however, we must examine the PDA's language against the background of its legislative history and historical context. As to the language of the PDA, "[i]t is a 'familiar rule, that a thing may be within the letter of the statute and yet not within the statute, because not within its spirit, nor within the intention of its makers.'" *Steelworkers v. Weber,* 443 U.S. 193, 201 (1979) (quoting *Church of the Holy Trinity v. United States,* 143 U.S. 457, 459 [1892]). *See Train v. Colorado Public Interest Research Group, Inc.,* 426 U.S. 1, 10 (1976); *United States v. Ameri-*

12. Representative Meader, one of the sponsors of the 1964 Civil Rights Act, proposed the precursor to § 1104 as an amendment to the Civil Rights Act, *see* 110 Cong. Rec. 2788 (1964), because he feared that § 708 and similar provisions in other titles were "wholly inadequate to preserve the validity and force of State laws aimed at discrimination." H.R. Rep. No. 914, 88th Cong., 1st Sess., 59 (1963) (additional views of Rep. Meader). His version provided that state laws would not be pre-empted "except to the extent that there is a direct and positive conflict between such provisions so that the two cannot be reconciled or consistently stand together." 110 Cong. Rec. 2787 (1964). The version ultimately adopted by Congress was a substitute offered by Rep. Mathias without objection from Rep. Meader. *Id.* at 2789. There is no indication that this substitution altered the basic thrust of § 1104.

15. In *Shaw v. Delta Air Lines, Inc.,* 463 U.S. 85, 100 (1983), we concluded that Title VII did not pre-empt a New York statute which proscribed discrimination on the basis of pregnancy as sex discrimination at a time when Title VII did not equate the two.

can Trucking Assns., 310 U.S. 534, 543–44 (1940).

It is well established that the PDA was passed in reaction to this Court's decision in *General Electric Co. v. Gilbert*, 429 U.S. 125 (1976). . . . *Newport News Shipbuilding & Dry Dock Co. v. E.E.O.C.* 462 U.S. 669, at 678 (1983).* By adding pregnancy to the definition of sex discrimination prohibited by Title VII, the first clause of the PDA reflects Congress' disapproval of the reasoning in *Gilbert. Newport News*, at 678–79, and n.17 (citing legislative history). Rather than imposing a limitation on the remedial purpose of the PDA, we believe that the second clause was intended to overrule the holding in *Gilbert* and to illustrate how discrimination against pregnancy is to be remedied. *Cf.* 462 U.S., at 678, n.14 ("The meaning of the first clause is not limited by the specific language in the second clause, which explains the application of the general principle to women employees"); *see also id.* at 688 (REHNQUIST, J., dissenting).[16] Accordingly, subject to certain limitations,[17] we agree with the Court of Appeals' conclusion that Congress intended the PDA to be "a floor beneath which pregnancy disability benefits may not drop—not a ceiling above which they may not rise." 758 F. 2d, at 396.

The context in which Congress considered the issue of pregnancy discrimination supports this view of the PDA. Congress

*This case appears in chapter 4.—Au.

16. Several commentators have construed the second clause of the PDA in this way. *See, e.g.,* Note, *Employment Equality Under The Pregnancy Discrimination Act of 1978*, 94 Yale L. J. 929, 937 (1985); Note, *Sexual Equality Under the Pregnancy Discrimination Act*, 83 Colum. L. Rev. 690, 696, and n.26 (1983).

17. For example, a State could not mandate special treatment of pregnant workers based on stereotypes or generalizations about their needs and abilities. *See infra.*

had before it extensive evidence of discrimination *against* pregnancy, particularly in disability and health insurance programs like those challenged in *Gilbert* and *Nashville Gas Co. v. Satty*, 434 U.S. 136 (1977).[18] The reports, debates, and hearings make abundantly clear that Congress intended the PDA to provide relief for working women and to end discrimination against pregnant workers.[19] In contrast to the thorough account of discrimination against pregnant workers, the legislative history is devoid of any discussion of preferential treatment of pregnancy,[20] beyond acknowledgments of

18. *See Discrimination on the Basis of Pregnancy, 1977, Hearings on S. 995 before the Subcommittee on Labor of the Senate Committee on Human Resources,* 95th Cong., 1st Sess., 31–33 (1977) (statement of Vice Chairman, Equal Employment Opportunity Commission, Ethel Bent Walsh); *id.* at 113–117 (statement of Wendy W. Williams); *id.* at 117–121 (statement of Susan Deller Ross); *id.* at 307–10 (statement of Bella S. Abzug). *See also Legislation to Prohibit Sex Discrimination on the Basis of Pregnancy, Hearings on H.R. 5055 and H.R. 6075 before the Subcommittee on Employment Opportunities of the House Committee on Education and Labor,* 95th Cong., 1st Sess. (1977).

19. *See, e.g.,* 123 Cong. Rec. 8144 (1977) (remarks of Sen. Bayh) (legislation "will end employment discrimination against pregnant workers"); 124 Cong. Rec. 21440 (1978) (remarks of Rep. Chisholm) (bill "affords some 41 percent of this Nation's labor force some greater degree of protection and security without fear of reprisal due to their decision to bear children"); *id.* at 21442 (remarks of Rep. Tsongas) (bill "would put an end to an unrealistic and unfair system that forces women to choose between family and career—clearly a function of sex bias in the law"); *id.* at 36818 (remarks of Sen. Javits) (the "bill represents only basic fairness for women employees"); *id.* at 38574 (remarks of Rep. Sarasin) (subcommittee "learned of the many instances of discrimination against pregnant workers, as we learned of the hardships this discrimination brought to women and their families").

20. The statement of Senator Brooke, quoted

the existence of state statutes providing for such preferential treatment. *See infra.* Opposition to the PDA came from those concerned with the cost of including pregnancy in health and disability benefit plans and the application of the bill to abortion,[21] not from those who favored special accommodation of pregnancy.

In support of their argument that the PDA prohibits employment practices that favor pregnant women, petitioners and several *amici* cite statements in the legislative history to the effect that the PDA does not *require* employers to extend any benefits to pregnant women that they do not already provide to other disabled employees. For example, the House Report explained that the proposed legislation "does not require employers to treat pregnant employees in any particular manner. . . . H.R. 6075 in no way requires the institution of any new programs where none currently exist."[22] We do not interpret these references to support petitioners' construction of the statute. On the contrary, if Congress had intended to *prohibit* preferential treatment, it would have been the height of understatement to say only that the legislation would not *require* such conduct. It is hardly conceivable that Con-

gress would have extensively discussed only its intent not to require preferential treatment if in fact it had intended to prohibit such treatment.

We also find it significant that Congress was aware of state laws similar to California's but apparently did not consider them inconsistent with the PDA. In the debates and reports on the bill, Congress repeatedly acknowledged the existence of state antidiscrimination laws that prohibit sex discrimination on the basis of pregnancy.[23] Two of the States mentioned then required employers to provide reasonable leave to pregnant workers.[24] After citing these state laws, Congress failed to evince the requisite "clear and manifest purpose" to supersede them. *See Pacific Gas & Electric Co. v. State Energy Resources Conservation*

---

in the dissent, *post,* merely indicates the Senator's view that the PDA does not *itself* require special disability benefits for pregnant workers. It in no way supports the conclusion that Congress intended to prohibit the *States* from providing such benefits for pregnant workers. *See* n.29, infra.

21. *See, e.g.,* S. Rep. No. 95–331, at 9 (1977), Leg. Hist. 46 (discussing cost objections); H.R. Conf. Rep. No. 95–1786, at 3–4 (1978), Leg. Hist. 196–97 (application of the PDA to abortion).

22. H.R. Rep. No. 95–948, at 4 (1978), Leg. Hist. 150. *See also* S. Rep. No. 95–331, *supra,* at 4, Leg. Hist. 41; 123 Cong. Rec. 7540 (1977) (remarks of Sen. Williams); *id.* at 10582 (remarks of Rep. Hawkins); *id.* at 29387 (remarks of Sen. Javits); *id.* at 29664 (remarks of Sen. Brooke).

23. *See, e.g., id.* at 29387 (remarks of Sen. Javits), Leg. Hist. 67 ("several state legislatures . . . have chosen to address the problem by mandating certain types of benefits for pregnant employees"). *See also* S. Rep. No. 95–331, *supra,* at 3, Leg. Hist. 40; H.R. Rep. No. 95–948, *supra,* at 10–11, Leg. Hist. 156–157; 123 Cong. Rec. 29648 (1977) (list of States that require coverage for pregnancy and pregnancy-related disabilities); *id.* at 29662 (remarks of Sen. Williams).

24. *See, e.g.,* Conn. Gen. Stat. § 31–126(g) (1977), now codified at § 46a–60(a)(7) (1985); Mont. Rev. Codes § 41–2602 (Smith Supp. 1977), now codified at Mont. Code Ann. §§ 49–2–310 and 49–2–311 (1986). . . .

. . . *See also* Mass. Gen. Laws ch. 149, § 105D (1985) (providing up to eight weeks maternity leave).

The dissent suggests that the references to the Connecticut and Montana statutes should be disregarded, because Congress did not expressly state that it understood that "these statutes required anything more than equal treatment." *Post.* However, we are not as willing as the dissent to impute ignorance to Congress. Where Congress has cited these statutes in the House and Senate Reports on the PDA, we think it fair to assume that it was aware of their substantive provisions.

and Development Comm'n, 461 U.S. 190, 206 (1983). To the contrary, both the House and Senate Reports suggest that these laws would continue to have effect under the PDA.[25]

Title VII, as amended by the PDA, and California's pregnancy disability leave statute share a common goal. The purpose of Title VII is "to achieve equality of employment opportunities and remove barriers that have operated in the past to favor an identifiable group of . . . employees over other employees." *Griggs v. Duke Power Co.*, 401 U.S. 424, 429–30 (1971). [Additional citations omitted.] Rather than limiting existing Title VII principles and objectives, the PDA extends them to cover pregnancy. As Senator Williams, a sponsor of the Act, stated: "The entire thrust . . . behind this legislation is to guarantee women the basic right to participate fully and equally in the workforce, without denying them the fundamental right to full participation in family life." 123 Cong. Rec. 29658 (1977).

Section 12945(b)(2) also promotes equal employment opportunity. By requiring employers to reinstate women after a reasonable pregnancy disability leave, § 12945(b)(2) ensures that they will not lose their jobs on account of pregnancy disability.[27] California's approach is consistent with the dissenting opinion of JUSTICE BRENNAN in *General Electric Co. v. Gilbert*, which Congress adopted in enacting the PDA. Referring to *Lau v. Nichols*, 414 U.S. 563 (1974), a Title VII decision, JUSTICE BRENNAN stated:

> [D]iscrimination is a social phenomenon encased in a social context and, therefore, unavoidably takes its meaning from the desired end products of the relevant legislative enactment, end products that may demand due consideration of the uniqueness of the 'disadvantaged' individuals. A realistic understanding of conditions found in today's labor environment warrants taking pregnancy into account in fashioning disability policies. (429 U.S., at 159 [footnote omitted].)

By "taking pregnancy into account," California's pregnancy disability leave statute allows women, as well as men, to have families without losing their jobs.

We emphasize the limited nature of the benefits § 12945(b)(2) provides. The statute is narrowly drawn to cover only the period of *actual physical disability* on account of pregnancy, childbirth, or related medical conditions. Accordingly, unlike the protective labor legislation prevalent earlier in this century, § 12945(b)(2) does not reflect archaic or stereotypical notions about pregnancy and the abilities of pregnant workers. A statute based on such stereotypical assumptions would, of course, be inconsistent with Title VII's goal of equal employment opportunity. *See, e.g., Los Angeles Dept. of Water and Power v. Manhart*, 435 U.S. 702, 709 (1978); *Phillips v. Martin Marietta Corp.*, 400 U.S. 542, 545 (1971) (MARSHALL, J., concurring).*

---

25. For example, the Senate Report states: "Since title VII does not preempt State laws which would not require violating title VII, . . . these States would continue to be able to enforce their State laws if the bill were enacted." S. Rep. No. 95-331, *supra*, at 3, n.1, Leg. Hist. 40.

27. As authoritatively construed by respondent Commission, the provision will "insure that women affected by pregnancy, childbirth, or related medical conditions have equal employment opportunities as persons not so affected." California Fair Employment and Housing Commission's Proposed Regulation, *see* App. 49.

*These cases appear chapter 5.—Au.

C

Moreover, even if we agreed with petitioners' construction of the PDA, we would nonetheless reject their argument that the California statute requires employers to violate Title VII.[29] Section 12945(b)(2) does not prevent employers from complying with both the federal law (as petitioners construe it) and the state law. This is not a case where "compliance with both federal and state regulations is a physical impossibility," *Florida Lime & Avocado Growers, Inc. v. Paul*, 373 U.S. 132, 142–43 (1963), or where there is an "inevitable collision between the two schemes of regulation." *Id.* at 143.[30] Section 12945(b)(2) does not compel California employers to treat pregnant workers *better* than other disabled employees; it merely establishes benefits that employers must, at a minimum, provide to pregnant workers. Employers are free to give comparable benefits to other disabled employees, thereby treating "women affected by pregnancy" no better than "other persons not so affected but similar in their ability or inability to work." Indeed, at oral argument, petitioners conceded that compliance with both statutes "is theoretically possible." Tr. of Oral Arg. 6.

Petitioners argue that "extension" of the state statute to cover other employees would be inappropriate in the absence of a clear indication that this is what the California Legislature intended. They cite cases in which this Court has declined to rewrite underinclusive state statutes found to violate the Equal Protection Clause. *See, e.g., Wengler v. Druggists Mutual Insurance Co.*, 446 U.S. 142, 152–53 (1980); *Caban v. Mohammed*, 441 U.S. 380, 392–93, n.13 (1979). This argument is beside the point. Extension is a remedial option to be exercised by a court once a statute is found to be invalid.[31] *See, e.g., Califano v. Wescott*, 443 U.S. 76, 89 (1979).*

IV

Thus, petitioners' facial challenge to § 12945(b)(2) fails. The statute is not preempted by Title VII, as amended by the PDA, because it is not inconsistent with the purposes of the federal statute, nor does it

---

29. Petitioners assert that even if § 12945(b)(2) does not *require* employers to treat pregnant employees differently from other disabled employees, it *permits* employers to do so because it does not specifically prohibit different treatment. Of course, since the PDA does not itself prohibit different treatment, it certainly does not require the States to do so. Moreover, if we were to interpret the term "permit" as expansively as petitioners suggest, the State would be required to incorporate every prohibition contained in Title VII into its state law, since it would otherwise be held to "permit" any employer action it did not expressly prohibit. We conclude that "permit" in § 708 must be interpreted to preempt only those state laws that expressly *sanction* a practice unlawful under Title VII; the term does not pre-empt state laws that are silent on the practice.

30. Indeed, Congress and the California Legislature were each aware in general terms of the regulatory scheme adopted by the other when they enacted their legislation. California recognized that many of its provisions would be preempted by the PDA and, accordingly, exempted employers covered by Title VII from all portions of the statute except those guaranteeing unpaid leave and reinstatement to pregnant workers. Congress was aware that some state laws mandated certain benefits for pregnant workers, but did not indicate that they would be pre-empted by federal law. *See supra.*

---

31. We recognize that, *in cases where a state statute is otherwise invalid*, the Court must look to the intent of the state legislature to determine whether to extend benefits or nullify the statute. By arguing that extension would be inappropriate in this case, however, *post*, and citing this as a basis for pre-emption, the dissent simply ignores the prerequisite of invalidity.

*The three cases in this paragraph are treated in chapter 3.—Au.

require the doing of an act which is unlawful under Title VII.[32]

The judgment of the Court of Appeals
is

Affirmed.

JUSTICE STEVENS, concurring in part,
and concurring in the judgment.

The Pregnancy Discrimination Act of
1978 (PDA) does not exist in a vacuum. As
JUSTICE WHITE recognizes in his dissent,
Congress did not intend to "put pregnancy
in a class by itself within Title VII," and the
enactment of the PDA "did not mark a departure from Title VII principles." *Post*. But
this realization does not lead me to support
JUSTICE WHITE's position; rather, I believe
that the PDA's posture as part of Title VII
compels rejection of his argument that the
PDA mandates complete neutrality and forbids all beneficial treatment of pregnancy.[1]

In *Steelworkers v. Weber*, 443 U.S. 193
(1979), the Court rejected the argument

that Title VII prohibits all preferential treatment of the disadvantaged classes that the
statute was enacted to protect. The plain
words of Title VII, which would have led to
a contrary result, were read in the context
of the statute's enactment and its purposes.[2] In this case as well, the language of
the Act seems to mandate treating pregnant employees the same as other employees. I cannot, however, ignore the fact
that the PDA is a definitional section of
Title VII's prohibition against gender-based
discrimination. Had *Weber* interpreted Title
VII as requiring neutrality, I would agree
with JUSTICE WHITE that the PDA should
be interpreted that way as well. But since
the Court in *Weber* interpreted Title VII to
draw a distinction between discrimination
against members of the protected class and
special preference *in favor of* members of
that class, I do not accept the proposition
that the PDA requires absolute neutrality.

I therefore conclude that JUSTICE MAR-
SHALL's view, which holds that the PDA
allows some preferential treatment of pregnancy, is more consistent with our inter-

32. Because we conclude that in enacting the
PDA Congress did not intend to prohibit all
favorable treatment of pregnancy, we need not
decide and therefore do not address the question whether § 12945(b)(2) could be upheld as a
legislative response to leave policies that have a
disparate impact on pregnant workers.

1. . . .I do not reach the question whether
§ 1104 of the Civil Rights Acts of 1964 is applicable to Title VII. . . . Even if § 1104 applies, the
California statute would not be pre-empted in
this case. Since Section IIIA of JUSTICE MAR-
SHALL's opinion does not make it clear whether
it decides this issue, or whether it only assumes
for the purposes of the decision that § 1104 applies, I do not join that section. I do, however,
join the remainder of the Court's opinion.

. . . I have . . . concluded that I should choose
between the conflicting views of the PDA expressed by JUSTICE MARSHALL and JUSTICE
WHITE, even though JUSTICE SCALIA may be correct in arguing that this case could be decided
without reaching that issue.

2. There is a striking similarity between the
evidence about the enactment of Title VII that
was available in *Steelworkers v. Weber*, 443 U.S.
193 (1979), and the evidence available regarding
the enactment of the PDA. First, the plain language in both cases points to neutrality, *see* 443
U.S., at 201, although, if anything, that language
was even less equivocal in *Weber* than it is here.
See ante. Second, in both cases the records are replete with indications that Congress' goal was to
bar discrimination against the disadvantaged
class or classes at issue. *See* 443 U.S., at 201–4.
Third, in neither case was there persuasive evidence that Congress considered the ramifications of a rule mandating complete neutrality.
See 443 U.S., at 204. Finally, there were statements in the legislative histories of both provisions stressing that Congress did not intend to
require preferential treatment, statements that
undermine the conclusion that Congress indeed
intended to *prohibit* such treatment. *See* 443 U.S.,
at 204–6.

pretation of Title VII than JUSTICE WHITE's view is. This is not to say, however, that all preferential treatment of pregnancy is automatically beyond the scope of the PDA.[3] Rather, as with other parts of Title VII, preferential treatment of the disadvantaged class is only permissible so long as it is consistent with "accomplish[ing] the goal that Congress designed Title VII to achieve." *Weber, supra,* at 204. That goal has been characterized as seeking "to achieve equality of employment opportunities and to remove barriers that have operated in the past to favor an identifiable group of . . . employees over other employees." *Griggs v. Duke Power Co.,* 401 U.S. 424, 429–30 (1971).

It is clear to me . . . that the California statute meets this test. Thus, I agree that a California employer would not violate the PDA were it to comply with California's statute without affording the same protection to men suffering somewhat similar disabilities.

JUSTICE SCALIA, concurring in the judgment.

The only provision of the Civil Rights Act of 1964 whose effect on pre-emption need be considered in the present case is § 708 of Title VII, 42 U.S.C. § 2000e–7. Although both that section and § 1104, 42 U.S.C. § 2000h–4, are described by the majority as pre-emption provisions, they are more precisely *antipre-emption* provisions, prescribing that nothing in Title VII (in the case of § 708) and nothing in the entire

3. I do not read the Court's opinion as holding that Title VII presents no limitations whatsoever on beneficial treatment of pregnancy. Although the opinion does make some mention of the "floor" but "not a ceiling" language employed by the Court of Appeals, the Court also points out that there are limitations on what an employer can do, even when affording "preferential" treatment to pregnancy. *See ante,* at n.17 [and last paragraph of IIIB].

Civil Rights Act (in the case of § 1104) shall be deemed to pre-empt state law unless certain conditions are met. The exceptions set forth in the general § 1104 ban on pre-emption ("inconsisten[cy] with any of the purposes of this Act, or any provision thereof") are somewhat broader than the single exception set forth in the Title VII § 708 ban. Because the Pregnancy Disability Act (PDA) is part of Title VII, the more expansive prohibition of pre-emption particularly applicable to that Title applies. If that precludes pre-emption of Cal. Gov't Code Ann. § 12945(b)(2) (West 1980), it is unnecessary to inquire whether § 1104 would do so.

Section 708 narrows the pre-emptive scope of the PDA so that it pre-empts only laws which "purpor[t] to require or permit the doing of any act which would be an unlawful employment practice" under the title. 42 U.S.C. § 2000e–7. Thus, whether or not the PDA prohibits discriminatorily favorable disability treatment for pregnant women, § 12945(b)(2) of the California Code cannot be pre-empted, since it does not remotely purport to require or permit any refusal to accord federally mandated equal treatment to others similarly situated. No more is needed to decide this case.

. . .

I am fully aware that it is more convenient for the employers of California and the California Legislature to have us interpret the PDA prematurely. It has never been suggested, however, that the constitutional prohibition upon our rendering of advisory opinions is a doctrine of convenience. I would affirm the judgment of the Court of Appeals on the ground that § 12945(b)(2) of the California Code does not purport to require or permit any act that would be an unlawful employment practice under any conceivable interpretation of the PDA, and therefore, by virtue of § 708, cannot be pre-empted.

JUSTICE WHITE, with whom THE CHIEF JUSTICE and JUSTICE POWELL join, dissenting.

I disagree with the Court that § 12945(b)(2) is not pre-empted by the Pregnancy Discrimination Act of 1978 (PDA) and § 708 of Title VII. Section 703(a) of Title VII forbids discrimination in the terms of employment on the basis of race, color, religion, sex, or national origin. The PDA gave added meaning to discrimination on the basis of sex:

> The terms "because of sex" or "on the basis of sex" [in section 703(a) of this title] include, but are not limited to, because of or on the basis of pregnancy, childbirth or related medical conditions; and women affected by pregnancy, childbirth, or related medical conditions shall be treated the same for all employment-related purposes, including receipt of benefits under fringe benefit programs, as other persons not so affected but similar in their ability or inability to work. . . ." (§ 2000e[k].)

The second clause quoted above could not be clearer: it mandates that pregnant employees "shall be treated the same for all employment-related purposes" as non-pregnant employees similarly situated with respect to their ability or inability to work. This language leaves no room for preferential treatment of pregnant workers. The majority would avoid its plain meaning by misapplying our interpretation of the clause in *Newport News Shipbuilding & Dry Dock Co. v. EEOC*, 462 U.S. 669, 678, n.14 (1983). The second clause addresses only female employees and was not directly implicated in *Newport News* because the pregnant persons at issue in that case were spouses of male employees. . . .

Contrary to the mandate of the PDA,

California law requires every employer to have a disability leave policy for pregnancy even if it has none for any other disability. An employer complies with California law if it has a leave policy for pregnancy but denies it for every other disability. On its face, § 12945(b)(2) is in square conflict with the PDA and is therefore pre-empted. Because the California law permits employers to single out pregnancy for preferential treatment and therefore to violate Title VII, it is not saved by § 708 which limits pre-emption of state laws to those that require or permit an employer to commit an unfair employment practice.[1]

The majority nevertheless would save the California law on two grounds. First, it holds that the PDA does not require disability from pregnancy to be treated the same as other disabilities; instead, it forbids less favorable, but permits more favorable, benefits for pregnancy disability. The express command of the PDA is unambiguously to the contrary, and the legislative history casts no doubt on that mandate.

The legislative materials reveal Congress' plain intent not to put pregnancy in a class by itself within Title VII, as the majority does with its "floor . . . not a ceiling" approach. The Senate Report clearly stated:

> By defining sex discrimination to include discrimination against pregnant women, the bill rejects the view that employers may treat pregnancy and its incidents as *sui generis*, without regard to its functional comparability to other

1. The same clear language preventing preferential treatment based on pregnancy forecloses respondents' argument that the California provision can be upheld as a legislative response to leave policies that have a disparate impact on pregnant workers. Whatever remedies Title VII would otherwise provide for victims of disparate impact, Congress expressly ordered pregnancy to be treated in the same manner as other disabilites.

conditions. Under this bill, the treatment of pregnant women in covered employment must focus not on their condition alone but on the actual effects of that condition on their ability to work. Pregnant women who are able to work must be permitted to work on the same conditions as other employees; and when they are not able to work for medical reasons, they must be accorded the same rights, leave privileges and other benefits, as other workers who are disabled from working.[2]

The House Report similarly stressed that the legislation did not mark a departure from Title VII principles:

It must be emphasized that this legislation, *operating as part of Title VII*, prohibits only discriminatory treatment. Therefore, it does not require employers to treat pregnant employees in any particular manner with respect to hiring, permitting them to continue working, providing sick leave, furnishing medical and hospital benefits, providing disability benefits, or any other matter. H.R. 6075 in no way requires the institution of any new programs where none currently exist. The bill would simply require that pregnant women be treated the same as other employees on the basis of their ability or inability to work.[3]

The majority correctly reports that Congress focused on discrimination against, rather than preferential treatment of, pregnant workers. There is only one direct reference in the legislative history to preferential treatment. Senator Brooke stated during the Senate debate: "I would emphasize most strongly that S. 995 in no way provides special disability benefits for working women. They have not demanded, nor asked, for such benefits. They have asked only to be treated with fairness, to be accorded the same employment rights as men."[4] Given the evidence before Congress of the widespread discrimination against pregnant workers, it is probable that most Congresspersons did not seriously consider the possibility that someone would want to afford preferential treatment to pregnant workers. The parties and their *amici* argued vigorously to this Court the policy implications of preferential treatment of pregnant workers. In favor of preferential treatment it was urged with conviction that preferential treatment merely enables women, like men, to have children without losing their jobs. In opposition to preferential treatment it was urged with equal conviction that preferential treatment represents a resurgence of the 19th century protective legislation which perpetuated sex-role stereotypes and which impeded women in their efforts

2. S. Rep. No. 95–331, at 4 (1977), Legislative History of the Pregnancy Discrimination Act of 1978 for the Senate Committee on Labor and Human Resources 41 (1980) (Leg. Hist.)

3. H.R. Rep. No. 95–948, at 4 (1978), Leg. Hist. 150 (emphasis added). The same theme was also expressed repeatedly in the floor debates. Senator Williams, for example, the Chairman of the Senate Committee on Labor and Human Resources and a sponsor of the Senate bill,

described the bill as follows in his introduction of the bill to the Senate:
"The central purpose of the bill is to require that women workers be treated equally with other employees on the basis of their ability or inability to work. The key to compliance in every case will be equality of treatment. In this way, the law will protect women from the full range of discriminatory practices which have adversely affected their status in the work force." 123 Cong. Rec. 29385 (1977), Leg. Hist. 62–63.

4. 123 Cong. Rec. 29664 (1977), Leg. Hist. 135.

to take their rightful place in the work-place. *See, e.g., Muller v. Oregon,* 208 U.S. 412, 421–23 (1908); *Bradwell v. Illinois,* 16 Wall. 130, 141 (1873) (Bradley, J., concurring). It is not the place of this Court, however, to resolve this policy dispute. Our task is to interpret Congress' intent in enacting the PDA. Congress' silence in its consideration of the PDA with respect to preferential treatment of pregnant workers cannot fairly be interpreted to abrogate the plain statements in the legislative history, not to mention the language of the statute, that equality of treatment was to be the guiding principle of the PDA.

Congress' acknowledgment of state antidiscrimination laws does not support a contrary inference. The most extensive discussion of state laws governing pregnancy discrimination is found in the House Report.[5] It was reported that six States, Alaska, Connecticut, Maryland, Minnesota, Oregon and Montana, and the District of Columbia specifically included pregnancy in their fair employment practices laws. [Here follow details on additional state laws that the House Report discussed.—Au.] . . . The Report did not in any way set apart the Connecticut and Montana statutes, on which the majority relies, from the other state statutes. The House Report gave no indication that these statutes required anything more than equal treatment. Indeed, the state statutes were considered, not in the context of pre-emption, but in the context of a discussion of health insurance costs. . . .

Nor does anything in the legislative history from the Senate side indicate that it carefully considered the state statutes, including those of Connecticut and Montana, and expressly endorsed their provisions. The Senate Report noted that "25 States presently interpret their own fair employment practices laws to prohibit sex discrimination based on pregnancy and childbirth," and Senator Williams presented during the Senate debate a list of States which required coverage for pregnancy and pregnancy-related disabilities, but there was no analysis of their provisions.[7] . . .

Passing reference to state statutes without express recognition of their content and without express endorsement is insufficient in my view to override the PDA's clear equal-treatment mandate, expressed both in the statute and its legislative history.

The Court's second, and equally strange, ground is that even if the PDA does prohibit special benefits for pregnant women, an employer may still comply with both the California law and the PDA: it can adopt the specified leave policies for pregnancy and at the same time afford similar benefits for all other disabilities. This is untenable. California surely had no intent to require employers to provide general disability leave benefits. It intended to prefer pregnancy and went no farther. Extension of these benefits to the entire work force would be a dramatic increase in the scope of the state law and would impose a significantly greater burden on California employers. That is the province of the California Legislature. *See Wengler v. Druggists Mutual Insurance Co.,* 446 U.S. 142, 152–53 (1980); *Caban v. Mohammed,* 441 U.S. 380, 392–93, n.13 (1979); *Craig v. Boren,* 429 U.S. 190, 210, n.24 (1976).* Nor can § 12945(b)(2) be saved by applying Title VII in tandem with it, such that employers would be required to afford reinstatement rights to pregnant workers as a matter of state law

---

5. H.R. Rep. No. 95–948, at 10–11 (1978), Leg. Hist. 156–57.

7. S. Rep. No. 95–331, at 3, Leg. Hist. 40; 123 Cong. Rec. 29648 (1977), Leg. Hist. 91.

* *Craig* appears in chapter 3.—Au.

but would be required to afford the same rights to all other workers as a matter of federal law. The text of the PDA does not speak to this question but it is clear from the legislative history that Congress did not intend for the PDA to impose such burdens on employers. As recognized by the majority, opposition to the PDA came from those concerned with the cost of including pregnancy in health and disability benefit plans. *Ante.* The House Report acknowledged these concerns and explained that the bill "in no way requires the institution of any new programs where none currently exist."[9] The Senate Report gave a similar assurance.[10] In addition, legislator after legislator stated during the floor debates that the PDA would not require an employer to institute a disability benefits program if it did not already have one in effect.[11] Congress intended employers to be free to provide any level of disability benefits they wished—or none at all—as long as pregnancy was not a factor in allocating such benefits. The conjunction of § 12945(b)(2)

9. H.R. Rep. No. 95–948, at 4 (1978), Leg. Hist. 150.

10. S. Rep. No. 95–331, at 4 (1977), Leg. Hist. 41.

11. 123 Cong. Rec. 7541 (1977), Leg. Hist. 8 (remarks of Sen. Brooke) ("[T]he bill being introduced would not mandate compulsory disability coverage"); *id.* at 8145, Leg. Hist. 19 (remarks of Sen. Bayh) ("Under the provisions of our legislation, only those companies which already voluntarily offer disability coverage would be affected."); *id.* at 10582, Leg. Hist. 25 (remarks of Rep. Hawkins) ("[A]n employer who does not now provide disability benefits to his employees will not have to provide such benefits to women disabled due to pregnancy or childbirth"); *id.* at 29386, Leg. Hist. 64 (remarks of Sen. Williams) ("[T]his legislation does not require that any employer begin to provide health insurance where

and the PDA requires California employers to implement new minimum disability leave programs. Reading the state and federal statutes together in this fashion yields a result which Congress expressly disavowed.

In sum, preferential treatment of pregnant workers is prohibited by Title VII, as amended by the PDA. Section 12945(b)(2) of the California Gov't. Code, which extends preferential benefits for pregnancy, is therefore pre-empted. It is not saved by § 708 because it purports to authorize employers to commit an unfair employment practice forbidden by Title VII.[12]

---

it is not presently provided"); *id.* at 29388, Leg. Hist. 71 (remarks of Sen. Kennedy) ("This amendment does not require all employers to provide disability insurance plans; it merely requires that employers who have disability plans for their employees treat pregnancy-related disabilities in the same fashion that all other temporary disabilities are treated with respect to benefits and leave policies."); *id.* at 29663, Leg. Hist. 131 (remarks of Sen. Cranston) ("[S]ince the basic standard is comparability among employees, an employer who does not provide medical benefits at all, would not have to pay the medical costs of pregnancy or childbirth"); *id.* Leg. Hist. 133 (remarks of Sen. Culver) ("The legislation before us today does not mandate compulsory disability coverage").

12. Section 12945(b)(2) does not *require* employers to treat pregnant employees better than other disabled employees; employers are free voluntarily to extend the disability leave to all employees. But if this is not a statute which "purports to . . . permit the doing of any act which would be an unlawful employment practice" under Title VII, I do not know what such a statute would look like.

Neither is § 12945(b)(2) saved by § 1104 of the Civil Rights Act since it is inconsistent with the equal-treatment purpose and provisions of Title VII.

CASE QUESTIONS

1. The dissenters in n.3 cite a statement from the PDA's sponsor to the effect that "the key to compliance . . . will be equality of treatment."

   The majority argue that § 12945(b)(2) promotes equality because: "By taking pregnancy into account, California's pregnancy disability leave statute allows women, as well as men, to have families without losing their jobs."

   Which side has the sounder comprehension of "equality"? Which side gives the more persuasive account of Congressional intent? Should the latter be the decisive criterion?

2. Is Justice Stevens convincing in arguing that the *Weber* precedent should settle this case? Why might the other justices be ignoring that precedent?

Wimberly v. Labor and Industrial Relations Commission (1987), discussion

One week later the Supreme Court added a coda to the *Guerra* reasoning by an 8–0 decision in the *Wimberly v. Labor and Industrial Relations Commission*, 55 U.S.L.W. 4146. There, in an opinion by Justice O'Connor, the Court affirmed a ruling of the Missouri Supreme Court to the effect that there was no conflict between Missouri's law that denied unemployment benefits to all workers who leave their jobs voluntarily and the 1976 Federal Unemployment Compensation Amendments which provided that states may not deny unemployment compensation "solely on the basis of pregnancy or termination of pregnancy." Justice O'Connor ruled that when Missouri, pursuant to its statute, denied unemployment compensation to a woman who left work to have a baby, and who then could not get her job back when she tried three months later, the state did not transgress the federal law. This was because Missouri imposed only a "neutral rule" that treated pregnancy the same as other voluntary reasons for leaving work including "other types of temporary disabilities." The federal rule prohibiting discrimination against pregnancy here was read as not *requiring* preferential treatment of pregnancy. In *Guerra* a similar rule was read as not *forbidding* preferential treatment.

Meanwhile, Congress currently debates the Family and Medical Leave Act, mandating that employers permit unpaid leave of up to 18 weeks to any parent for birth or adoption or serious illness of a child, and up to 26 weeks leave for medical disability including pregnancy. This bill is being intensely opposed by business organizations and by some states' rights advocates (since these issues are generally left to state law.)[14] Whether Congress will move more forthrightly to forbid state laws requiring special benefits for women who are giving birth or lactating remains an open question.

CHAPTER 2

The Equal Protection Clause and Gender Discrimination: 1868–1975

Dead-End Road to Equality: The Privileges or Immunities Clause

Access to the Bar: *Myra Bradwell v. State of Illinois* (1873)

The first case challenging a sex classification as a violation of the Fourteenth Amendment was *Myra Bradwell v. State of Illinois* (1873).[1] In fact, *Bradwell v. Illinois* was probably the first Supreme Court case to present a Fourteenth Amendment challenge to any legislation. By a quirk of history, although *Bradwell* was argued at the Supreme Court a couple of weeks before the *Slaughter-House Cases* were argued, the Supreme Court handed down the *Slaughter-House Cases* decision one day in advance of the *Bradwell* decision. This timing rendered the *Slaughter-House Cases* the historic first official interpretation of the Fourteenth Amendment. For that reason, the Court presented much more thorough and detailed arguments in the *Slaughter-House Cases* than they presented in the *Bradwell* decision. In deciding Myra Bradwell's fate, they could simply announce, in effect, that they were following the Fourteenth Amendment principles they had explicated the day before. By this twist of fate, a case involving a few butchers who resented geographic limitations on their trade became the "landmark" constitutional law case—included in virtually every Constitutional Law course and casebook—whereas the case of Myra Bradwell, who was forbidden to practice law for no reason other than that she was a married woman, and who actually reached the Court first with the same arguments—gathers dust in the proverbial bin of history.

Calling it fate, as I have done, may give a distorted picture of the Court's motivation for reversing the order of the cases. Illinois officials apparently considered Myra Bradwell's petition so trivial that they did not even send a lawyer to the Supreme Court to present their side of the case. Thus, the Supreme Court opinion contains this complaint, "The record [of what transpired at Myra Bradwell's earlier hearing in the Illinois Supreme Court] is not very perfect." The lack of a detailed record of prior judicial proceedings may partially explain why the Supreme Court did not wish to use Myra Bradwell's case for making constitutional history.

Myra Bradwell had trained for the Illinois bar under the tutelage of her husband, an attorney. By the time she passed the state bar exam, she had already attained widespread respect in legal circles for her editorship of *The Chicago Legal News*, a journal that provided up-to-date case summaries of current legal developments. Her application to the Illinois bar was not totally unprecedented—in 1869 the Iowa judiciary admitted Arabella Mansfield, who had passed the bar exam with high honors, to the bar of that state, despite an explicit reference to males in the Iowa statutes on bar eligibility.[2]

Mrs. Bradwell's lawyer's arguments are in fact more interesting than the Supreme Court's opinion. He must grapple seriously with the meaning of the Fourteenth Amendment because the *Slaughter-House Cases*, explicating the clauses of that amendment, had yet to be handed down. Apparently Bradwell's lawyer viewed the equal protection and due process clauses as clauses about the way laws should be applied rather than about limits upon the content of laws. He viewed the privileges and immunities clause as the really forceful clause of the Fourteenth Amendment, as the one that shields the basic civil rights of Americans against potentially oppressive state legislation. On reading the three important clauses of the Fourteenth Amendment, it is difficult to disagree with his implicit ranking of them. After the Supreme Court had disagreed with him, however, knocking all meaning out of the privileges and immunities clause in their *Slaughter-House Cases* decision,[3] the very claims that Bradwell's lawyer made about the privileges or immunities clause were eventually applied to the equal protection clause. His argument serves as a model for future equal protection litigation. Here is the relevant portion of it:

Brief of Bradwell's Counsel for Bradwell v. Illinois (1873), excerpt

The conclusion is irresistible that the professon of the law, like the clerical profession and that of medicine, is an avocation open to every citizen of the United States. And while the legislature may prescribe qualifications for entering upon this pursuit, it cannot, under the guise of fixing qualifications, exclude a class of citizens from admission to the bar. The legislature may say at what age candidates shall be admitted; may elevate or depress the standard of learning required. But a qualification to which a whole class of citizens can never attain is not a regulation of admission to the bar, but is, as to such citizens, a prohibition. For instance, a state legislature could not, in enumerating the qualifications, require the candidate to be a white citizen. I presume it will be admitted that such an act would be void. The only provision in the Constitution of the United States which secures to colored male citizens the privilege of admission to the bar, or the pursuit of the other ordinary avocations of life is the provision that "No state shall make or enforce any law which shall abridge the privileges or immunities of the citizens." If this provision protects the colored citizen, then it protects every citizen, black or white, male or female.

Why may a colored citizen buy, hold and sell land in any state of the Union? Because he is a citizen of the United States, and that is one of the privileges of a citizen. Why may a colored citizen be admitted to the bar? Because he is a citizen, and that is one of the avocations open to every citizen, and no state can abridge his right to pursue it. Certainly no other reason can be given.

Now, let us come to the case of Myra Bradwell. She is a citizen of the United States and of the state of Illinois, residing therein. She has been judicially ascertained to be of full age, and to possess the requisite character and learning. Indeed, the court below in its opinion found in the record says: "Of the ample qualifications of the applicant we have no doubt." Still, admission to the bar was denied the petitioner; not upon the ground that she was not a citizen; not for . . . reasonable regulations prescribed by the legislature; but upon the sole ground that inconvenience would result from permitting her to enjoy her legal rights in this, to wit: that her clients might have difficulty in enforcing the contracts they might make with her as their attorney, because of her being a married woman.

Now, with entire respect to that court, it is submitted that this argument *ab inconvenienti*, which might have been urged with whatever force belongs to it against adopting the Fourteenth Amendment in the full scope of its language, is utterly futile to resist its full and proper operation, now that it has been adopted.

I maintain that the Fourteenth Amendment opens to every citizen of the United States, male or female, black or white, married or single, the honorable professions as well as the servile employments of life; and that no citizen can be excluded from any one of them. Intelligence, integrity and honor are the only qualifications that can be prescribed as conditions precedent to an entry upon any honorable pursuit or profitable avocation, and all the privileges and immunities which I vindicate to a colored citizen, I vindicate to our mothers, our sisters and our daughters.

Of a bar composed of men and women of equal integrity and learning, women might be more or less frequently retained as the taste or judgment of clients might dictate; but the broad shield of the Constitution is over all, and protects each in that measure of success which his or her individual merits may secure.

Justice Miller in the Supreme Court opinion below does not address the arguments of Bradwell's counsel at all. Relying on the distinction drawn in his *Slaughter-House Cases* opinion, Miller simply asserts that the opportunity to enter the legal profession, if it is a "privilege or immunity" of citizenship, pertains only to state citizenship. As he explained in *Slaughter-House*, the Fourteenth Amendment protects only the privileges and immunities of national citizenship, and because the opportunity to become a lawyer does not fall into that category (except for practice in the federal courts, which was not directly at issue here),[4] Mrs. Bradwell's plight is unaffected by the Fourteenth Amendment.

As is also evident, the Court's opinion is totally silent concerning the equal protection clause. That is at least a bit puzzling in the light of the combination of Miller's statements in *Slaughter-House* and the Bradwell attorney's argument here. Miller made clear in his *Slaughter-House Cases* opinion that he agrees with Bradwell's counsel in the conclusion that anti-Negro legislation is prohibited by the Fourteenth Amendment. Whereas the lawyer finds that prohibition in the privileges or immunities clause, Miller finds it in the equal protection clause. The counsel's argument, then, has not been met: he claims, in effect, that if the generally worded commands of the Fourteenth Amendment prohibit discrimination on account of race, they implicitly prohibit it on account of sex. Since the equal protection clause contains the same degree of generality in its wording as does the privileges and immunities clause, the lawyer's argument, as it would apply to the equal protection clause, seems to deserve a response. Justice Miller's *Slaughter-House Cases* opinion reveals that he believes that the equal protection clause applies only to racial discrimination and not to other forms of discrimination. He does not repeat the point here, but perhaps he believed that his reference to his *Slaughter-House Cases* opinion of the preceding day was adequate explanation.

The four judges who dissented on the preceding day in the *Slaughter-House Cases* do take counsel's arguments more seriously than Miller does, apparently because they take the privileges or immunities clause itself more seriously. Only Chief Justice Chase, however, was willing to accept the full implications of the views on the privileges or immunities clause with which he had aligned himself the day before. He dissents here without opinion, but the lines of his reasoning are not difficult to surmise. He had concurred with the dissent in the *Slaughter-House Cases* that had argued that "equality of right, among citizens in the pursuit of the ordinary avocations of life . . . with exemption from all disparaging and partial enactments . . . is the distinguishing privilege of citizens of the United States."[5] Because the first clause of the Fourteenth Amendment granted citizenship to "all persons" born in the United States, and because women were clearly persons, the validity of Mrs. Bradwell's claim would seem to be the obvious conclusion.

Justice Bradley views it differently; he explains on behalf of the two other dissenters of yesterday why they now concur with Justice Miller. Justice Bradley's own *Slaughter-House Cases* dissent, just twenty-four hours earlier, had included the following statement:

> If my views are correct with regard to what are the privileges and immunities of citizens, it follows conclusively that any law . . . depriving a large class of citizens of the privilege of pursuing a lawful employment does abridge the privileges of those citizens.[6]

Is his explanation here in *Bradwell v. Illinois* a convincing explanation for treating women as a "peculiar" case?

Myra Bradwell v. State of Illinois, 83 U.S. (16 Wall.) 130 (1873)

Mr. Justice Miller delivered the opinion of the court.

The supreme court denied the application apparently upon the ground that it was a woman who made it.

In regard to [the Fourteenth] Amendment counsel for the plaintiff in this court truly says that there are certain privileges and immunities which belong to a citizen of the United States as such; otherwise it would be nonsense for the Fourteenth Amendment to prohibit a state from abridging them, and he proceeds to argue that admission to the bar of a state, of a person who possesses the requisite learning and character, is one of those which a state may not deny.

In this latter proposition we are not able to concur with counsel. We agree with him that there are privileges and immunities belonging to citizens of the United States, in that relation and character, and that it is these and these alone which a state is forbidden to abridge. But the right to admission to practice in the courts of a state is not one of them. This right in no sense depends on citizenship of the United States. It has not, as far as we know, ever been made in any state or in any case to depend on citizenship at all. Certainly many prominent and distinguished lawyers have been admitted to practice, both in the state and Federal courts, who were not citizens of the United States or of any state. But, on whatever basis this right may be placed, so far as it can have any relation to citizenship at all, it would seem that, as to the courts of

the state, it would relate to citizenship of the state, and as to Federal courts, it would relate to citizenship of the United States.

The opinion just delivered in the *Slaughter-House Cases*, from Louisiana, *ante*, 394, renders elaborate argument in the present case unnecessary; for, unless we are wholly and radically mistaken in the principle on which those cases are decided, the right to control and regulate the granting of license to practice law in the courts of a state is one of those powers which are not transferred for its protection to the Federal government, and its exercise is in no manner governed or controlled by citizenship of the United States in the party seeking such license.

It is unnecessary to repeat the argument on which the judgment in those cases is founded. It is sufficient to say, they are conclusive of the present case.

The judgment of the State Court is, therefore *Affirmed*.

Mr. Justice Bradley:

I concur in the judgment of the Court in this case, by which the judgment of the supreme court of Illinois is affirmed, but not for the reasons specified in the opinion just read.

The claim of the plaintiff, who is a married woman, to be admitted to practice as an attorney and counselor at law, is based upon the supposed right of every person, man or woman, to engage in any lawful employment for a livelihood. The supreme court of Illinois denied the application on the ground that, by the common law, which is the basis of the laws of Illinois, only men were admitted to the bar, and the legislature had not made any change in this respect, but had simply provided that no person should be admitted to practice as attorney or counselor without having previously obtained a license for that purpose from two justices of the supreme court, and that no person should receive a license without first obtaining a certificate from the court of some county of his good moral character. In other respects it was left to the discretion of the court to establish the rules by which admission to the profession should be determined. The court, however, regarded itself as bound by at least two limitations. One was that it should establish such terms of admission as would promote the proper administration of justice, and the other that it should not admit any persons or class of persons not intended by the legislature to be admitted, even though not expressly excluded by statute. In view of this latter limitation the court felt compelled to deny the application of females to be admitted as members of the bar. Being contrary to the rules of the common law and the usages of Westminster Hall from time immemorial, it could not be supposed that the legislature had intended to adopt any different rule.

It certainly cannot be affirmed, as a historical fact, that this has ever been established as one of the fundamental privileges and immunities of the sex. On the contrary, the civil law, as well as nature herself, has always recognized a wide difference in the respective spheres and destinies of man and woman. Man is, or should be, woman's protector and defender. The natural and proper timidity and delicacy which belongs to the female sex evidently unfits it for many of the occupations of civil life. The constitution of the family organization, which is founded in the divine ordinance, as well as in the nature of things, indicates the domestic sphere as that which properly belongs to the domain and functions of womanhood. The harmony, not to say identity, of interests and views which belong or should belong to the family institution, is repugnant to the idea of a woman adopting a distinct and independent career from that of her husband. So firmly fixed was this sentiment in the founders of the common law that it became a maxim of that system of jurisprudence that a woman had no legal existence separate from her husband, who was regarded as her head and representative in the social state; and, notwithstanding some recent modification of this civil status, many of the special rules of law flowing from and dependent upon this cardinal principle still exist in full force in most states. One of these is, that a married woman is incapable, without her husband's consent, of making contracts which shall be binding on her or him. This very incapacity was one circumstance which the supreme court of Illinois deemed important in rendering a married woman incompetent fully to perform the duties and trusts that belong to the office of an attorney and counselor.

It is true that many women are unmarried and not affected by any of the duties, complications, and incapacities arising out of the married state, but these are exceptions to the general rule. The paramount destiny and mission of woman are to fulfill the noble and benign offices of wife and mother. This is the law of the Creator. And the rules of civil society must be adapted to the general constitution of things, and cannot be based upon exceptional cases.

The humane movements of modern society, which have for their object the multiplication of avenues for woman's advancement, and of occupations adapted to her condition and sex, have my heartiest concurrence. But I am not prepared to say that it is one of her fundamental rights and privileges to be admitted into every office and position, including those which require highly special qualifications and demanding special responsibilities. In the nature of things it is not every citizen of every age, sex, and condition that is qualified for every calling and position. It is the prerogative of the legislator to prescribe regulations founded on nature, reason, and experience for the due admission of qualified persons to professions and callings demanding special skill and confidence. This fairly belongs to the police power of the state; and, in my opinion in view of the peculiar characteristics, destiny, and mission of woman, it is within the province of the legislature to ordain what offices positions, and callings shall be filled and discharged by men, and shall receive the benefits of those energies and responsibilities, and that decision and firmness which are presumed to predominate in the sterner sex.

For these reasons I think that the laws of Illinois now complained of are not obnoxious to the charge of abridging any of the privileges and immunities of citizens of the United States.

Mr. Justice Field and Mr. Justice Swayne:

We concur in the opinion of Mr. Justice Bradley.

Dissenting, Mr. Chief Justice Chase.

CASE QUESTIONS

1. Is Justice Miller admitting that the opportunity to enter the bar for federal courts is a privilege or immunity of "citizens of the United States" and that therefore states may not abridge that opportunity on the basis of gender?

2. Although Miller refused in the *Slaughter-House Cases* to define "the privileges and immunities of the citizens of the United States," he did characterize them there as rights "which owe their existence to the Federal government, its National charac-

ter, its Constitution, or its laws." Since the 1870s, women have not used the privileges or immunities clause for challenges to gender-based discrimination. Are there arguments that might render the clause useful in such challenges?

3. Bradwell's lawyer argued, in effect, for a "reasonableness" test as a standard for the privileges or immunities clause. Had he convinced the court as to the standard, would Mrs. Bradwell have won a favorable result?

CASENOTE

The legal disabilities of married women referred to by Justice Miller prevailed in every state of the union as of 1848. Married women had no legal capacity to earn money, make contracts, or buy or sell property. Anglo-American common law defined the marital couple as legally "one," and viewed the husband as the personification of the unit. The women's rights movement succeeded in attaining legislative elimination of the vast majority of these legal disabilities in the 1850–1900 period. For a discussion of Supreme Court amelioration of late twentieth-century remnants of them, see discussion of *Orr v. Orr*, and *Kirchberg v. Feenstra* in chapter 3.

Early Struggle for the Ballot: *Virginia Minor v. Reese Happersett* (1875)

Bradwell v. Illinois predated the era of women's litigation under the equal protection clause; for Bradwell's lawyer clearly believed that the privileges or immunities clause was the only one that limited the content of legislation, and the Court majority of 1873, even as they opened their eyes to the power of the equal protection clause to limit statutory content, refused to extend their vision beyond the racial impact of the equal protection clause. Women were to make one more stab at obtaining citizen equality via privileges or immunities clause litigation before they finally turned their efforts toward the eventually more fruitful equal protection clause. This second stab came at the hands of Virginia Minor, president of the Missouri Woman Suffrage Association. Her immediate target was the right to vote.

Virginia Minor was not alone in her attack on the American status quo. Although her name is the one placed in Supreme Court records, she was in fact only one among some one-hundred-fifty members of the National Woman's Suffrage Association who engaged in a widespread campaign of mild civil disobedience during the elections of 1872. They attempted to register and vote in ten different states where it was illegal for women to vote, claiming that the Fourteenth Amendment conferred suffrage upon them as one of the privileges or immunities of national citizenship.[7] Mrs. Minor lost her case in court. But her story, the story of women's effort to obtain a constitutional right of suffrage, began long before 1872 and was to continue long after 1875.

Although it is widely known that the Woman's Suffrage Association[8] traces its origins to a loosely structured group that began in 1848 during the first Women's Rights Convention in Seneca Falls, New York, it is not generally known that both the exercise of women's suffrage in America and political efforts by women to obtain voting rights, predate the 1848 convention by two full centuries. The first (and only) recorded instance of a demand for women's suffrage in the American colonies occurred in January 1648. A Mrs. Margaret Brent, who had the power of attorney as executor of the estate of the deceased governor Calvert of Maryland, petitioned the Maryland assembly (a gathering of all "freemen," in which persons could also cast delegated "proxy" votes of freemen unable to attend) for a vote in their proceedings. The assembly was willing to let Mrs. Brent participate as one who would cast a proxy vote in her role as attorney (evidently for the Calvert heirs), but this decision was vetoed by the governor. Mrs. Brent thereupon lodged an official protest against all proceedings of the assembly.[9]

Another fragment of evidence indicates that even in the 1600s not all women in the colonies were forced to watch the political game from the sidelines, as it were, "under protest." In 1640, in the colony of Rhode Island, records indicate that women who had attained the status of property owner via widowhood did participate in the political proceedings by which property owners *qua* citizens gave their consent to certain decisions of governing officials.[10] And in the records of the colony of New Netherland (New York) is found the clearest evidence that women property owners participated in the suffrage. In 1655, on Long Island, a Lady Deborah Moody definitely participated in the town-meeting selection process whereby magistrates for the town were nominated.[11]

The extent to which these were rare and exceptional practices in the American colonies remains unknown, as does why, how, and when the exceptional practices vanished altogether. But certainly by the time of the American Revolution, despite Abigail Adam's private remonstrances to her husband, John,[12] women were excluded from the suffrage, either by the reference to "men" in the statutes or by use of the pronoun "he," in every colony except New Jersey.

In New Jersey all gender references were omitted from suffrage statutes; as of July 2, 1776, suffrage was extended to "all inhabitants" who fulfilled certain wealth and residency requirements. Evidently, however, for the first fourteen years of the statute's duration most people, and all the women, interpreted "inhabitants" to mean "men." In 1790, an important change occurred. A member of the state legislature's committee on revising the election laws, Joseph Cooper, was an active member of the (Quaker) Society of Friends. Quakers allowed their women members complete voting equality within the church organization, and Mr. Cooper argued that according to both principles of justice and the principles of the U.S. Constitution, the government should do the same. To placate Cooper, the committee inserted the crucial phrase "he or she" into those parts of the statute that referred to voter eligibility requirements.[13]

For a while the custom of nonvoting among New Jersey women persisted despite this change in the statute, but the politicians' lust for electoral victory eventually broke through the restraints of community habit. In a closely contested state legislative race in 1797, the challenge of the rapidly growing Jeffersonian party evidently frightened the usually status quo-oriented Federalists into the radical tactic of bringing some seventy-five women to the polls in one district. By the time of the presidential election of 1800, women were voting throughout New Jersey.

This early heyday of women's suffrage lasted only until 1807. In that year the all-male, all-white legislature of New Jersey deliberately inserted into their suffrage requirements the phrase "white, male" and with these two small words snatched the ballot out of the hands of all those New Jersey citizens who happened to be female or black. The rationale proffered for this "reform" by the legislature will puzzle modern-day readers. The argument was that allowing women to vote produced a massive amount of voting fraud. It is not clear from the historical record why women were supposed to have been more successful than men in fraudulent claims about their economic eligibility to vote. Nor is it clear whether women actually did disguise themselves (as was alleged) in different costumes so that they could vote more than once, nor whether (as the women suffragists later argued) these frauds were in fact perpetrated by men disguised as women. What is clear is that voter fraud was so rampant by 1807 that the state legislature declared the results of a particular county election void because of fraud. By November of that year the legislature responded to the problem with the explanation that "doubts have been raised . . . in regard to the admission of aliens, females, and persons of color, or negroes to vote in elections." Arguing that it was "highly necessary to the safety, quiet good order and dignity of the state to clear up said doubts," the legislature proceeded to take the vote away from every woman and every black in the state. Thus ended the earliest statewide experiment with women suffrage in America.

Forty-one years later, when the women's rights movement formally began, women were, at least in one part of the country, trying to get back rights that had once belonged to them. Strangely enough, just ten years before the organized effort began in Seneca Falls, New York, women were actually granted a very limited role in the election process in Kentucky. In 1838 that state legislature bestowed upon certain women the right to vote for school trustees; these lucky few were widows with school-age children who happened to live in districts so sparsely populated that they had no incorporated towns or villages.[14] This limited generosity probably existed because some rural school districts were so sparsely populated that no, or very few, fathers of school-age children lived in them. Still, even this limited practice exemplified the germ of the principle that undergirded the entire women's suffrage effort: those persons who are affected by laws ought to have some say in the making of those laws.

The then-prevailing notion that matters concerning children had a particularly strong impact on women enabled women to make a couple of other early major advances on that sector of the suffrage front related to public education. Kansas, when it entered the Union in 1861, had a constitutional provision (adopted by the Kansas territory in 1859) granting to all women full and equal rights of participation on all questions "pertaining to the organization and conduct of the public schools."[15] The idea of granting "school suffrage" to women, however, did not exactly catch on like wildfire. Although in several states it eventually constituted women's first inroad into the male bastion of suffrage, by 1870 only one other state, Michigan (in 1867), had granted even school suffrage to women.[16]

The first areas in which the movement for general suffrage rights attained success were far away from that original scene of women's suffrage in New Jersey: the (nonstate) territories of Utah and Wyoming. This development occurred in the winter of 1869–1870, apparently for reasons having little to do with the growth of an egalitarian women's rights ideology. Evidently, in both territories women voters were perceived as an element that would strengthen the political hand of the established status quo in the face of a growing element of frontier "drifters."[17] Aside from the question of motivation, these developments in the far West were the beginnings of a substantial shift in the political treatment of women. But the limited size of that beginning in the territories did not alter one bit from 1870 to the presidential election of 1872, when Virginia Minor and her 149 fellow suffragists decided to take matters into their own hands.

At that time not a single state allowed women to vote in general elections. The suffragists launched their peaceable assault at the ballot boxes of ten states and the District of Columbia. Although four women succeeded in having their votes counted,[18] many of the women were arrested for their efforts and subjected to fines or jail or both.[19] Virginia Minor was simply refused the opportunity to register by the St. Louis registrar, Reese Happersett. Her husband, a lawyer named Francis Minor, pressed the suit in the civil courts on her behalf. By March 1875, when the case was finally settled by the Supreme Court, the women's suffrage effort had still made absolutely no advances since the Utah-Wyoming territories gains of 1869–1870.[20] Not one justice on the Supreme Court was inclined to demand a change in the laws of every single state of the Union by adopting a daring reinterpretation of the Fourteenth Amendment.

Minor v. Happersett, 88 U.S. (21 Wall.) 162 (1875)

Mr. Chief Justice Waite delivered the opinion of the Court.

The question is presented in this case, whether, since the adoption of the Fourteenth Amendment, a woman, who is a citizen of the United States and of the State of Missouri, is a voter in that State, notwithstanding the provision of the constitution and laws of the States, which confine the right of suffrage to men alone. . . .

It is contended that the provisions of the Constitution and laws of the State of Missouri which confine the right of suffrage and registration therefor to men, are in violation of the Constitution of the United States and, therefore, void. The argument is, that as a woman, born and naturalized in the United States and subject to the jurisdiction thereof, is a citizen of the United States and of the State in which she resides, she has the right of suffrage as one of the privileges and immunities of her citizenship, which the State cannot by its laws or Constitution abridge.

There is no doubt that women may be

citizens. They are persons, and by the Fourteenth Amendment "All persons born or naturalized in the United States and subject to the jurisdiction thereof" are expressly declared to be "citizens of the United States and of the State wherein they reside." But, in our opinion, it did not need this Amendment to give them that position. Before its adoption, the Constitution of the United States did not in terms prescribe who should be citizens of the United States or of the several States, yet there were necessarily such citizens without such provision. There cannot be a nation without a people. The very idea of a political community, such as a nation is, implies an association of persons for the promotion of their general welfare. Each one of the persons associated becomes a member of the nation formed by the association. He owes it allegiance and is entitled to its protection. Allegiance and protection are, in this connection, reciprocal obligations. The one is a compensation for the other; allegiance for protection and protection for allegiance.

For convenience it has been found necessary to give a name to this membership. The object is to designate by a title the person and the relation he bears to the nation. For this purpose the words "subject," "inhabitant," and "citizen" have been used, and the choice between them is sometimes made to depend upon the form of the government. Citizen is now more commonly employed, however, and as it has been considered better suited to the description of one living under a republican government, it was adopted by nearly all of the States upon their separation from Great Britain, and was afterwards adopted in the Articles of Confederation and in the Constitution of the United States. When used in this sense it is understood as conveying the idea of membership of a nation, and nothing more.

To determine, then, who were citizens of the United States before the adoption of the Amendment, it is necessary to ascertain what persons originally associated themselves together to form the nation, and what were afterwards admitted to membership.

Looking at the Constitution itself, we find that it was ordained and established by "the people of the United States" (Preamble), and then going further back, we find that these were the people of the several States that had before dissolved the political bands which connected them with Great Britain, and assumed a separate and equal station among the powers of the earth (Dec. of Ind.), and that had by Articles of Confederation and Perpetual Union, in which they took the name of "the United States of America," entered into a firm league of friendship with each other for their common defense, the security of their liberties and their mutual and general welfare, binding themselves to assist each other against all force offered to or attack made upon them, or any of them, on account of religion, sovereignty, trade, or any other pretense whatever.

Whoever, then, was one of the people of either of these States when the Constitution of the United States was adopted, became *ipso facto* a citizen—a member of the nation created by its adoption. He was one of the persons associating together to form the nation, and was, consequently, one of its original citizens. . . .

Additions might always be made to the citizenship of the United States in two ways: first, by birth and second, by naturalization. This is apparent from the Constitution itself, for it provides, art. II, § 1, that "no person except a natural born citizen, or a citizen of the United States at the time of the adoption of the Constitution, shall be eligible to the office of President," and, art. I, § 8, that Congress shall have power "to establish a uniform rule of naturalization." Thus new citizens may be born or they may be created by naturalization.

The Constitution does not, in words, say who shall be natural born citizens. Resort must be had elsewhere to ascertain that. At common law, with the nomenclature of which the framers of the Constitution were familiar, it was never doubted that all children born in a country of parents who were its citizens became themselves, upon their birth, citizens also. These were natives, or natural-born citizens, as distinguished from aliens or foreigners. . . . It is sufficient for everything we have now to consider that all children born of citizen parents within the jurisdiction are themselves citizens. The words "all children" are certainly as comprehensive, when used in this connection, as "all persons," and if females are included in the last they must be in the first. That they are included in the last is not denied. In fact the whole argument of the plaintiff proceeds upon that idea.

Under the power to adopt a uniform system of naturalization, Congress, as early as . . . 1804 . . . enacted . . . that when any alien who had declared his intention to become a citizen in the manner provided by law died before he was actually naturalized, his widow and children should be considered as citizens of the United States, and entitled to all rights and privileges as such upon taking the necessary oath, 2 Stat. 292; and in 1855 it was further provided that any woman who might lawfully be naturalized under the existing laws, married or who should be married to a citizen of the United States should be deemed and taken to be a citizen. 10 Stat. 604.

From this it is apparent that, from the commencement of the legislation upon this subject, alien women and alien minors could be made citizens by naturalization. . . .

But if more is necessary to show that women have always been considered as citizens the same as men, abundant proof is to be found in the legislative and the judicial history of the country. Thus, by the Constitution, the judicial power of the United States is made to extend to controversies between citizens of different States. Under this it has been uniformly held that the citizenship necessary to give the courts of the United States jurisdiction of a cause must be affirmatively shown on the record. . . . Notwithstanding this the records of the courts are full of cases in which the jurisdiction depends upon the citizenship of women, and not one can be found, we think, in which objection was made on that account. Certainly none can be found in which it has been held that women could not sue or be sued in the courts of the United States. Again; at the time of the adoption of the Constitution, in many of the States (and in some probably now) aliens could not inherit or transmit inheritance. There are a multitude of cases to be found in which the question has been presented whether a woman was or was not an alien, and as such capable or incapable of inheritance, but in no one has it been insisted that she was not a citizen because she was a woman. On the contrary, her right to citizenship has been in all cases assumed. The only question has been whether, in the particular case under consideration, she had availed herself of the right.

In the Legislative Department of the Government, similar proof will be found. Thus, in the preemption laws, 5 Stat. 455, § 10, a widow, "being a citizen of the United States," is allowed to make settlement on the public lands and purchase upon the terms specified, and women, "being citizens of the United States," are permitted to avail themselves of the benefit of the homestead law. 12 Stat. 392.

. . . [S]ex has never been made one of the elements of citizenship in the United States. In this respect men have never had an advantage over women. The same laws precisely apply to both. The Fourteenth Amendment did not affect the citizenship of women any more than it did of men. In this particular, therefore, the rights of Mrs. Minor do not depend upon the Amendment. She has always been a citizen from her birth, and entitled to all the privileges and immunities of citizenship. The Amendment prohibited the State, of which she is a citizen from abridging any of her privileges and immunities as a citizen of the United States; but it did not confer citizenship on her. That she had before its adoption.

If the right of suffrage is one of the necessary privileges of the citizen of the United States, then the Constitution and laws of Missouri confining it to men are in violation of the Constitution of the United States, as amended, and consequently void. The direct question is, therefore, presented whether all citizens are necessarily voters.

The Constitution does not define the privileges and immunities of citizens. For that definition we must look elsewhere. In this case we need not determine what they are, but only whether suffrage is necessarily one of them.

It certainly is nowhere made so in express terms. The United States has no voters in the States of its own creation. The elective officers of the United States are all elected directly or indirectly by state voters. The members of the House of Representatives are to be chosen by the people of the States, and the electors in each State must have the qualifications requisite for electors of the most numerous branch of the State Legislature. Const. art. I, § 2. Senators are to be chosen by the Legislatures of the States, and necessarily the members of the Legislature required to make the choice are elected by the voters of the State. Const. art. I, § 3. Each State must appoint in such manner as the Legislature thereof may direct, the electors to elect the President and Vice-President. Const. art. II, § 2. The times, places and manner of holding elections for Senators and Representatives are to be prescribed in each State by the Legislature thereof: but Congress may at any time, by law, make or alter such regulations, except as to the place of choosing Senators. Const. art. I, § 4. It is not necessary to inquire whether this power of supervision thus given to Congress is sufficient to authorize any interference with the state laws prescribing the qualifications of voters, for no such interference has ever been attempted. The power of the State in this particular is certainly supreme until Congress acts.

The Amendment did not add to the privileges and immunities of a citizen. It simply furnished an additional guaranty for the protection of such as he already had. [Emphasis added.] No new voters were necessarily made by it. Indirectly it may have had that effect, because it may have increased the number of citizens entitled to suffrage under the Constitution and laws of the States, but it operates for this purpose, if at all, though the States and the state laws, and not directly upon the citizen.

It is clear, therefore, we think, that the Constitution has not added the right of suffrage to the privileges and immunities of citizenship as they existed at the time it was adopted. This makes it proper to inquire whether suffrage was co-extensive with the citizenship of the States at the time of its adoption. If it was, then it may with force be argued that suffrage was one of the rights which belonged to citizenship, and in the enjoyment of which every citizen must be protected. But if it was not, the contrary may with propriety be assumed.

When the Constitution of the United States was adopted, all the several States, with the exception of Rhode Island, had Constitutions of their own. Rhode Island continued to act under its charter from the Crown. Upon an examination of those Constitutions we find that in no State were all citizens permitted to vote. Each State determined for itself who should have that power. [Here followed the suffrage requirements of the first thirteen states.]

In this condition of the law in respect to suffrage in the several states, it cannot for a moment be doubted that if it had been intended to make all citizens of the United States voters, the framers of the Constitution would not have left it to implication. So important a change in the condition of citizenship as it actually existed, if intended, would have been expressly declared.

But if further proof is necessary to show that no such change was intended, it can easily be found both in and out of the Constitution. By Article IV, § 2, it is provided that "The citizens of each State shall be entitled to all the privileges and immunities of citizens in the several States." If suffrage is necessarily a part of citizenship, then the citizens of each State must be entitled to vote in the several States precisely as their citizens are. This is more than asserting that they may change their residence and become citizens of the State and thus be voters. It goes to the extent of insisting that while retaining their original citizenship they may vote in any State. This, we think, has never been claimed. And again, by the very terms of the Amendment we have been considering (the Fourteenth), "Representatives shall be apportioned among the several States according to their respective numbers, counting the whole number of persons in each State, excluding Indians not taxed. But when the right to vote at any election for the choice of electors for President and Vice-President

of the United States, representatives in Congress, the executive and judicial officers of a State, or the members of the Legislature thereof, is denied to any of the male inhabitants of such State, being twenty-one years of age and citizens of the United States, or in any way abridged, except for participation in the rebellion, or other crimes, the basis of representation therein shall be reduced in the proportion which the number of such male citizens shall bear to the whole number of male citizens twenty-one years of age in such State." Why this, if it was not in the power of the Legislature to deny the right of suffrage to some male inhabitants? And if suffrage was necessarily one of the absolute rights of citizenship to male inhabitants? Women and children are, as we have seen, "persons." They are counted in the enumeration upon which the appropriation is to be made, but if they were necessarily voters because of their citizenship unless clearly excluded, why inflict the penalty for the exclusion of males alone? Clearly, no such form of words would have been selected to express the idea here indicated, if suffrage was the absolute right of all citizens.

And still again; after the adoption of the Fourteenth Amendment, it was deemed necessary to adopt a fifteenth, as follows: "The right of citizens of the United States to vote shall not be denied or abridged by the United States, or by any State, on account of race, color or previous condition of servitude." The Fourteenth Amendment had already provided that no State should make or enforce any law which should abridge the privileges or immunities of citizens of the United States. If suffrage was one of these privileges or immunities, why amend the Constitution to prevent its being denied on account of race, etc? Nothing is more evident than that the greater must include the less, and if all were already protected, why go through with the form of amending the Constitution to protect a part?

It is true that the United States guaranties to every State a republican form of government. Const. art. IV, § 4. It is also true that no State can pass a bill of attainder*, Const. art. I, § 10, and that no person can be deprived of life, liberty or property without due process of law. Const. amend. V. All these several provisions of the Constitution must be construed in connection with the other parts of the instrument, and in the light of the surrounding circumstances.

The guaranty is of a republican form of government. No particular government is designated as republican, neither is the exact form to be guarantied, in any manner especially designated. Here, as in other parts of the instrument, we are compelled to resort elsewhere to ascertain what was intended.

The guaranty necessarily implies a duty on the part of the States themselves to provide such a government. All the States had governments when the Constitution was adopted. In all, the people participated to some extent, through their representatives elected in the manner specially provided. These governments the Constitution did not change. They were accepted precisely as they were, and it is, therefore, to be presumed that they were such as it was the duty of the States to provide. Thus we have unmistakable evidence of what was republican in form, within the meaning of that term as employed in the Constitution.

As has been seen, all the citizens of the States were not invested with the right of suffrage. In all, save perhaps New Jersey,

*Bill of Attainder: Statute that imposes a penalty on all members of a named group; statute that declares guilt on the basis of who people are rather than on what acts they have committed.—Au.

this right was only bestowed upon men and not upon all of them. Under these circumstances it is certainly now too late to contend that a government is not republican, within the meaning of this guaranty in the Constitution, because women are not made voters.

The same may be said of the other provisions just quoted. Women were excluded from suffrage in nearly all the States by the express provision of their Constitution and laws. If that had been equivalent to a bill of attainder, certainly its abrogation would not have been left to implication. Nothing less than express language would have been employed to effect so radical a change. So, also, of the Amendment which declares that no person shall be deprived of life, liberty or property without due process of law, adopted as it was as early as 1791. If suffrage was intended to be included within its obligations language better adapted to express that intent would most certainly have been employed. The right of suffrage, when granted, will be protected. He who has it can only be deprived of it by due process of law, but in order to claim protection he must first show that he has the right.

But we have already sufficiently considered the proof found upon the inside of the Constitution. That upon the outside is equally effective. The Constitution was submitted to the States for adoption in 1787, and was ratified by nine States in 1790. Vermont was the first new State admitted to the union, and it came in under a Constitution which conferred the right of suffrage only upon men of the full age of twenty-one years, having resided in the State for the space of one whole year next before the election, and who were of quiet and peaceable behavior. This was in 1791. [The Court gave two more, similar examples.] But we need not particularize further. No new State has ever been admitted to the Union which has conferred the right of suffrage upon women, and this has never been considered a valid objection to her admission. . . . Since then the governments of the insurgent States have been reorganized under a requirement that before their representatives could be admitted to seats in Congress they must have adopted new Constitutions, republican in form. In no one of these Constitutions was suffrage conferred upon women, and yet the States have all been restored to their original position as States in the Union.

Besides this, citizenship has not in all cases been made a condition precedent to the enjoyment of the right of suffrage. Thus, in Missouri, persons of foreign birth, who have declared their intention to become citizens of the United States, may under certain circumstances vote. The same provision is to be found in the Constitutions of Alabama, Arkansas, Florida, Georgia, Indiana, Kansas, Minnesota and Texas.

Certainly, if the courts can consider any question settled, this is one. For nearly ninety years the people have acted upon the idea that the constitution, when it conferred citizenship, did not necessarily confer the right of suffrage. If uniform practice, long continued, can settle the construction of so important an instrument as the Constitution of the United States confessedly is, most certainly it has been done here. Our province is to decide what the law is, not to declare what it should be.

We have given this case the careful consideration its importance demands. If the law is wrong, it ought to be changed; but the power for that is not with us. The arguments addressed to us bearing upon such a view of the subject may, perhaps be sufficient to induce those having the power to make the alteration but they ought not to be permitted to influence our judgment in determining the present rights of the parties now litigating before us. Nor argument as to woman's need of suffrage can be considered. We can only act upon her rights as they exist. It is not for us to look at the hardship of withholding. Our duty is at an end if we can find it is within the power of a State to withhold.

Being unanimously of the opinion that the Constitution of the United States does not confer the right of suffrage upon anyone, and that the Constitutions and laws of the several States which commit that important trust to men alone are not necessarily void, we *Affirm* the judgment of the court below.

CASE QUESTIONS

1. Does it seem puzzling that persons not allowed to vote could be considered "citizens"? Are American-born persons under the age of eighteen considered "citizens"?

2. What portion of the "citizen" privileges cited by Justice Waite are what could be called economic, as distinguished from political or legal, rights? Is a certain level of economic participation implied by the word "citizen"?

3. In the light of the italicized statements about the privileges and immunities clause (in the eighteenth paragraph) can one conclude that the Court believed that the clause added nothing to the

Constitution? (N.B. the phrase "additional guaranty.")

4. The members of the Court say that their "province is to decide what the law is, not to declare what it should be." Do they always follow this maxim? Should they?

The Supreme Court's rejection of the Minors' privileges or immunities clause argument in this case had two decisive effects on the women's movement. First, the Court's emphatic denial that the privileges or immunities clause added any new civil rights to the Constitution (see italicized sentences) motivated women's rights litigants to turn their attention to other clauses of the Constitution in subsequent cases. Second, this decision made it clear that an additional constitutional amendment would be required if women were ever to gain nationwide suffrage at a single stroke. Litigation efforts on the basis of the existing Constitution offered no hope for the suffragists. Within three years the eventual Nineteenth Amendment was introduced into Congress for the first time by Senator Aaron Sargent of California.[21] It was to be forty-two years before that amendment obtained ratification.

The Ballot Through Constitutional Amendment: Women Take to the Streets

While most books on constitutional law do not discuss the political process by which formal constitutional amendments are obtained, a discussion of women's constitutional rights would be incomplete without the story of the successful battle for the Nineteenth Amendment. That account has meaning not only because it fills in the picture of the costs of Virginia Minor's failure at the Supreme Court but also because a second constitutional amendment to expand the legal rights of women recently came within inches of ratification. If women's equal rights advocates begin to lose consistently in the halls of the Supreme Court, they will have no choice but to renew their political campaign for the ERA. It is possible that women today will find it necessary to follow the lessons of those who in the past labored for decades to gain in the Constitution's own words what one of their allies failed to gain by judicial interpretation.

In the aftermath of the Minors' failure at the Supreme Court, it was not immediately obvious to the suffragists that amending the national Constitution was the surest route to victory. At that time there were two nationwide suffragist organizations: the American Woman Suffrage Association, led by Susan B. Anthony and Elizabeth Cady Stanton, and the National Woman Suffrage Association, led by Lucy Stone and Julia Ward Howe. The former lobbied Congress steadily from 1878 to 1893 for passage of what came to be known as the Anthony Amendment.[22] The latter, for decades, focused its efforts on persuading the states, on a one-by-one basis, to grant women the vote. The suffragists' variegated and often uncoordinated efforts were summed up by one of the veterans of the campaign as follows:

> To get the word "male" in effect out of the Constitution cost the women of the country fifty-two years of pauseless campaign. . . . During that time they were forced to conduct 56 campaigns of referenda to male voters; 480 campaigns to get [state] legislatures to submit suffrage amendments to voters; 47 campaigns to get state constitutional conventions to write woman suffrage into state constitutions; 277 campaigns to get state party conventions to include woman suffrage planks; 30 campaigns to get presidential party conventions to adopt woman suffrage planks in party platforms, and 19 campaign with 19 successive Congresses.[23]

In short, it was a long and arduous struggle, in which millions of dollars and millions of hours of labor were expended on many fronts: in political organizing, propagandizing, petitioning, speech making, parading, lobbying, and picketing. The story includes a cast ranging from prominent socialites to immigrant factory workers. Before it ended, it was also to include mob violence, jail sentences, hunger strikes in jail accompanied by brutal forced feedings, and legislative votes so close that partisans were carried in on stretchers.[24]

In 1893 the two suffragist armies decided to combine forces into a single National American Woman Suffrage Association. Despite the protestations of Susan B. Anthony, the NAWSA decided to deemphasize the lobbying effort for a constitutional amendment. As a result of this decision, the amendment stopped receiving favorable committee reports in Congress in 1893, and after 1896 it did not even manage to get out of committee for a floor vote. The amendment remained a dead issue until it was stirred back into life by a new women's suffrage group that formed under the leadership of Alice Paul in 1913.

During the period from 1893 to 1913, the NAWSA exhausted its energies in hundreds of state campaigns. By 1910 it had won only four victories: Wyoming (in 1890) and Utah (in 1896) each entered the Union retaining the women's suffrage they had adopted while still territories, and Colorado (in 1893) and Idaho (in 1896) each adopted women's suffrage in state referenda. All four states were sparsely populated and lacked significant political impact.

Toward the end of this period, from 1910 to 1913, NAWSA efforts did take on some added vigor. The association was stimulated by newly forming suffrage groups led by women who had participated in the more militant British suffragist movement; these groups introduced more flamboyant tactics into the American campaign. This period added outdoor ("protest") meetings, street parades, automobile tours, and trolley tours to the women's movement. Also, the new groups introduced the political organizing tactics often associated with political party machines: the keeping of file cards on all voters on a precinct basis, careful voter canvassing, and the appointment of thousands of election district "captains" whose job it was to mobilize voters in their own district.[25] With this new style of campaigning, by 1911 the NAWSA managed to win victories in state referenda in two western states: Washington and California. In 1912, they brought in three more victories in Arizona, Kansas, and Oregon.

Although by this time women had the vote in nine states with a total of forty-five electoral votes, a very discouraging pattern was emerging. Women were winning in some state referenda, but they were losing in many others. And the ones in which they lost were the more industrialized, more populated, more politically powerful states of the Midwest and East. Liquor interests, fearing that women would favor Prohibition, and other conservative business interests funded massive antisuffrage campaigns, which included the plying of legislators with liquor and blatant frauds at the ballot box. It was apparent by 1913 that the bigger and more important the state, the more impressive the antisuffrage campaign would be. This pattern continued through 1915. Out of a total of eleven state referenda, in 1914 and 1915, the suffragists managed to win only in the two least populated states; Montana and Nevada. They lost both of the Dakotas, Nebraska, Missouri, Ohio, New York, Pennsylvania, New Jersey, and Massachusetts.[26]

The period 1913–1915, however, brought a number of crucial changes to the American women's suffrage effort. The first was the rise to prominence of Alice Paul. Ms. Paul had worked in the militant British suffrage movement, had returned to the United States in 1910, and began chairing the NAWSA's Congressional Committee in 1912. For her first major contribution, Ms. Paul organized a suffrage parade; five thousand women marched through Washington, D.C., on the day before Woodrow Wilson's inauguration in 1913. The paraders were physically harassed by crowds of hostile onlookers, and for some reason the police ignored the problem. Along parts of the route full-scale rioting broke out, and the National Guard was finally called in to restore order.[27] This incident produced tremendous press publicity and stimulated a variety of prosuffrage pilgrimages to Washington. In April 1913, Ms. Paul organized the Congressional Union (soon to become the Women's Party), which aimed at a single-minded campaign for a constitutional amendment. Within the year, Ms. Paul left the NAWSA, whose leadership still felt that the time was not ripe for an all-out drive for the federal amendment.[28]

The next two important changes involved the leadership of the NAWSA. In late 1914 it received two million dollars in the form of a personal bequest from Mrs. Frank Leslie (a wealthy publisher) to Carrie Chapman Catt with instructions that the money be used "to the furtherance of the cause of woman suffrage."[29] Then, in December 1915, Ms. Catt was drafted for the presidency of the NAWSA. The combination of Ms. Catt's organizational genius, the NAWSA's new-found prosperity, the militant tactics of the Congressional Union, and the undeniably major role that women played in the World War I economy eventually proved too powerful even for the wealthy antisuffrage forces.

The lobbying pressures of the Congressional Union brought the suffrage amendment to the floor of Congress for the first time since 1896. It was voted down in the Senate in March 1914 and in the House in January 1915.[30] Whereas the Congressional Union took the approach of castigating "the party in power" for failure to pass the amendment, the NAWSA developed close ties to President Wilson, inviting him to their 1916 convention, where their leaders believed he was converted to their cause. At that same convention, Carrie Chapman Catt propounded a secret plan for a concerted six-year drive for the federal amendment.[31] It succeeded in four.

The drama of the long quest for women's suffrage reached its climax in the thirteen-month stretch from January 1917 through January 1918. In January 1917 Alice Paul's organization, now called the Women's Party, initiated a new tactic: they stationed silent pickets outside the White House, as a constant reminder of women's demands. The picket signs and banners carried messages that grew more strident as the United States entered World War I. When American "patriots" saw such statements as "Democracy Should Begin at Home" and derogatory refrences to "Kaiser Wilson," fights broke out between onlookers and the women picketers. Beginning in June, the police started arresting pickets for obstructing the sidewalks. (Their attackers were never arrested.) At their trials the women refused to address the charges against them; they either stood mute or delivered speeches for the suffrage cause. They also refused to pay fines, claiming that such payment would imply admission of guilt. When given the "option," they chose jail as against paying fines. One spokeswoman described their feelings as follows: "As long as the government and the representatives of the government prefer to send women to jail on petty and technical charges, we will go to jail. Persecution has always advanced the cause of justice."[32]

The earliest arrestees were dismissed without jail sentences. As the picketing and violence continued, jail sentences of a few days, then a few weeks, and finally six months were imposed. By the time the first session of Congress ended, a total of 218 women from 26 states had been arrested, and 97 women had gone to prison.[33]

Once in prison, these women drew added attention to their cause by demanding to be treated as political prisoners rather than as common criminals. To dramatize this complaint the women went on hunger strikes. Police administrators resorted to brutal forced feedings. This sequence of events drew continuous and nationwide media attention. The forced feedings, in particular, produced newspaper stories replete with gory details. The public outcry grew so intense that the Wilson administration ordered unconditional release of all picketers on November 27 and 28.[34]

Although it publicly disavowed any connection with the militant picketers, the NAWSA took advantage of the sympathetic atmosphere generated by the intense publicity about the women prisoners. The NAWSA membership campaigned tirelessly all around the country, buttonholing legislators, canvassing precincts, petitioning congressmen. Major political successes finally began to accumulate. In 1917 the first congresswoman took her seat, Jeannette Rankin of Montana. In New York, women finally won a referendum for suffrage in a heavily populated eastern state. Six state legislatures avoided the difficulties of a referendum by taking advantage of Article II, section 1, of the Constitution, which states that presidential electors are to be appointed "in such manner as the Legislature thereof may direct." Thus North Dakota, Ohio, Indiana, Rhode Island, Nebraska, and Michigan joined Illinois (who had done so in 1913) in granting women presidential suffrage. And the Arkansas state legislature, in March 1917, granted women the primary vote, which in the then one-party Democratic South was as meaningful as the vote in northern general elections.[35]

In December 1917, just two weeks after the picketers had been released from jail, the House of Representatives set January 10, 1918, as the date for voting on the suffrage amendment. The drama of that vote was unsurpassed by any in American history. Women in the galleries watched anxiously as four of the determining votes for the amendment came in literally from sickbeds. Congressman T. W. Sims of Tennessee had a broken arm and shoulder but refused to have them set, lest he miss the crucial vote. Despite the excruciating pain, he stayed on to the end, trying to persuade those colleagues who were ambivalent. The Republican House Leader, James Mann of Illinois, deathly pale and barely able to stand, came to the session straight from a six-month stint in the hospital. Representative Robert Crosser of Ohio also came in ill. And Henry Barnhart of Indiana was literally carried in on a stretcher for the last roll call. One congressman, Frederick Hicks of New York, actually left his wife's deathbed to come to Washington for the vote. Mrs. Hicks, a dedicated suffragist, died just before he left; after the vote, he returned home for her funeral. The amendment passed the House with no votes to spare; it attained exactly the number needed for the required two-thirds majority, 274–136.[36]

Although the amendment just missed the needed two-thirds majority in the Senate that year, and although in 1918 there were more pickets, more jailings, and more hunger strikes,[37] the tide really had turned. The later stages of victory were somewhat anticlimactic. Steady campaigning by the NAWSA and their allies increased the prosuffrage majority in the Senate to within one vote of two-thirds in the February 1919 (lame-duck) session. The newly elected sixty-sixth Congress finally passed the amendment in May 1919 by exactly two-thirds in the Senate and by 304–89 in the House.[38] Ratification in three-fourths of the state legislatures came remarkably quickly. By August 26, 1920, American women had obtained the vote as a matter of explicit constitutional right.

Introduction to the Equal Protection Clause

Suspect Classification: *McLaughlin v. Florida* (1964)

After women's rights litigants were twice rebuffed in pleas based on the privileges or immunities clause, they proceeded to focus their attention on the Fourteenth Amendment's equal protection clause. An overview of the equal protection clause itself may prove useful as an introduction to the cases involving women's equal protection litigation.

That "no state shall deny to any person within its jurisdiction the equal protection of the law" is a command, like most of those in the Constitution, with more than one possible interpretation. Obviously, it means at least that all shall be equal "in the eyes of the law," that is, that the law as written shall be applied evenhandedly to all persons without regard to wealth or station. Although even that minimal meaning of the clause establishes a worthy (but, sadly, too often unattained) goal for the legal system, judges and legislators recognized from the start that the clause surely requires something more. That extra something in the way of "equal protection" refers to a certain measure of equality in the content of the laws themselves.

All laws treat different people differently. A person who kills another under circumstances of self-defense may go free; a person who kills without those circumstances must go to prison. A murderer with a history of three prior criminal convictions receives a more severe penalty than a murderer with no prior convictions. Fifteen-year-olds who commit murder receive a lesser sentence than thirty-year-olds who commit the same act. Persons who are certifiably insane and commit murder are sent to a hospital; sane murderers (if one can use that term) are sent to prison. All these inequalities of treatment are mandated by statute law, and none of them violates the equal protection clause. But certain kinds of legal categorizations do violate that clause, as that clause has always been understood.

It is much easier to itemize the classifications forbidden by the equal protection clause than it is to explicate the principle underlying that prohibition. Everyone understood, as shown in the *Slaughter-House Cases*, that the equal protection clause was intended to outlaw the Black Codes, or Slave Codes, which then prevailed throughout the South. These codes prohibited all blacks or all persons who had once been slaves from owning property, from entering certain occupations, from attending schools, and so forth. In the phrase "equal protection of the law," Congress and the states that ratified the amendment[39] were announcing the rule that laws denying rights on the basis of race or previous condition of servitude were henceforth unconstitutional. While this is not a suitable context for exploring the anomalies of the separate-but-equal approach to this rule, which distorted it from 1896 to 1954, it is nonetheless true that laws depriving blacks of rights granted to nonblacks were widely understood to have been rendered unconstitutional by the equal protection clause. Thus, as early as 1880, a law excluding blacks from jury duty was declared invalid by the Supreme Court.[40]

As explained in chapter 1, this prohibition on racial discrimination by overt legal mandate was soon broadened to cover the example of a law that, as applied, resulted in excluding virtually all persons of Chinese origin from entering certain occupations.[41] Not long after that, the prohibition was further extended to cover the case of laws that discriminated against aliens without good reason.[42] This sort of race or nationality discrimination, when it has no other basis than majority dislike of a minority group, is termed "invidious discrimination" by the Supreme Court and is banned by the equal protection clause.

Not every racial classification in laws is banned, however. To complicate matters further, certain deprivations of rights on bases other than race or nationality—for example, the deprivation of the vote on the basis of poverty—have also been declared "invidious" by the modern Supreme Court. Instead of creating a ban on racial classifications, the equal protection clause imposes a heavy burden of justification on those classifications. In situations of extreme public need, where a "compelling" or "overriding" governmental need can be demonstrated, the Court *will* permit legislative lines to be drawn on the basis of race. The busing of schoolchildren and the racially oriented gerrymandering of school district lines for desegregation are recent examples of these justified exceptions. Instead of being forbidden classifications, then, race and nationality are said to be "suspect classifications." They are suspected (or assumed) to be "invidious" (based on unreasoning group antagonisms) until proven to be justified by a "compelling legislative purpose."

The historical circumstances surrounding the adoption of the Fourteenth Amendment provide a ready explanation for labeling racial classifications as "suspect" by virtue of the equal protection clause. When one recognizes that the cases extending the "suspect classification" shadow to cover nationality and alienage were both cases involving Chinese/Orientals,[43] the conceptual connection between racial and nationality classifications takes on an even more concrete reality. The transformation of other sorts of classifications, such as poverty, from acceptable to "suspect" is not as readily explainable. That process did not really begin until the mid-twentieth century (during the tenure of many judges appointed by Franklin Roosevelt),[44] but it is solidly entrenched now.[45] By 1969, Chief Justice Warren made reference to lines "drawn on the basis of wealth or race" as involving "two factors which independently render a classification highly suspect."[46] What characteristics race, nationality, and poverty have in common that would render them equally suspect as "invidious" are not easy to determine.[47] But whatever those characteristics are, other discriminated-against groups have been trying to claim a share in them so as to gather shelter from the suspect classification umbrella. Most prominent among such groups[48] have been women.

An understanding of the way that the suspect classification doctrine operates is absolutely crucial for understanding how the U.S. Constitution will protect (and create) women's rights. There are two reasons for this. The first is that gender may yet be declared a suspect classification under the existing Fourteenth Amendment equal protection clause. In 1973, as will become apparent below, in the case of *Frontiero v. Richardson*[49] the Court came bewilderingly close to doing just that. Although at present it looks as if the Court will refrain from taking that step for reasons related to the ERA campaign, the possibility nonetheless remains that if the ERA becomes a totally dead issue, the Court will declare gender to be a suspect classification on the basis of the equal protection clause alone.

Second, if the Equal Rights Amendment does succeed in gaining ratification, the need to understand the legal ramifications of suspect classifications will no longer rest on a hypothetical possibility. For it is certain that, just as the historical circumstances surrounding the adoption of the equal protection clause rendered it a pronouncement that racial classifications in the law would be "suspect," so the wording of the ERA will cause it to be interpreted as rendering sex classifications "suspect." This point is worth reemphasis, for fairly widespread confusion surrounds the potential impact of the ERA. Just as racial classifications are not *absolutely* banned under the Fourteenth Amendment, there is no reason to believe that gender classifications would be absolutely barred by the ERA. Instead, as with the former, the latter would simply be strongly disfavored (or, to use the technical term, suspect). An examination of a sample of the Court's treatment of racial classifications will thus provide an accurate estimate of the degree of justification that would be required before a gender classification could be upheld under the ERA.

One typical recent treatment of a racial classification occurred in the case of *McLaughlin v. Florida* in 1964.[50] The case involved a Florida statute making it a crime for a biracial couple to "occupy in the nighttime the same room." If a "Negro man and a white woman or a white man and Negro woman" lived in the same room, both members of the couple could receive up to one year in jail. No proof of fornication was required to prove guilt. Florida had *additional* statutes punishing fornication, adultery, and "lewd cohabitation," all of which required proof of sexual intercourse to determine guilt; so this statute clearly concerned a "crime" based solely on the race of the "offenders." Florida argued that this law's purpose derived from its support for another of their statutes—an antimiscegenation law. (Miscegenation is marriage between members of two different races.) The Supreme Court's unanimous reply was that even *assuming* for the sake of argument that the antimiscegenation statute was constitutional (three years later, they were to make clear that it was not),[51] and that this statute in fact aided its enforcement, such justification was simply not enough. Here are their own words concerning the degree of justification needed to support racial classification in the law:

McLaughlin v. Florida, 379 U.S. 184 (1964), excerpt

We deal here with a classification based upon the race of the participants, which must be viewed in light of the historical fact that the central purpose of the Fourteenth Amendment was to eliminate racial disrimination emanating from official sources in the States. This strong policy renders racial classifications "constitutionally suspect." *Bolling v. Sharpe,* 347 U.S. 497, 499; and subject to the "most rigid scrutiny." *Korematsu v. United States,* 323 U.S. 214, 216; and "in most circumstances irrelevant" to any constitutionally acceptable legislative purpose, *Hirabayashi v. United States,* 320 U.S. 81, 100. Thus it is that racial classifications have been held invalid in a variety of contexts. *See, e.g., Virginia Board of Elections v. Hamm,* 379 U.S. 19 (designation of race in voting and property records); *Anderson v. Martin,* 375 U.S. 399 (designation of race on nomination papers and ballots); *Watson v. City of Memphis,* 373 U.S. 526 (segregation in public parks and playgrounds); *Brown v. Board of Education,* 349 U.S. 294 (segregation in public schools).

We deal here with a racial classification embodied in a criminal statute. In this context, where the power of the State weighs most heavily upon the individual or the group, we must be especially sensitive to the policies of the Equal Protection Clause which, as reflected in congressional enactments dating from 1870, were intended to secure "the full and equal benefit of all laws and proceedings for the security of persons and property" and to subject all persons "to like punishment, pains, penalties, taxes, licenses, and exactions of every kind, and to no other." R.S. § 1977, 42 U.S.C. § 1981 (1958 ed.).

Our inquiry, therefore, is whether there clearly appears in the relevant materials *some overriding statutory purpose* requiring the proscription of the specified conduct when engaged in by a white person and a Negro, but not otherwise. Without such justification the racial classification contained in § 798.05 is reduced to an invidious discrimination forbidden by the Equal Protection Clause.

That a general evil be partially corrected may at times, and without more, serve to justify the limited application of a criminal law; but legislative discretion to employ the piecemeal approach stops short of permitting a State to narrow statutory coverage to focus on a racial group. Such classifications *bear a far heavier burden of justification.*

. . .

There is involved here an exercise of the state police power which trenches upon the constitutionally protected freedom from invidious official discrimination based on race. Such a law, even though [we might assume that it was] enacted pursuant to a valid state interest, *bears a heavy burden of justification,* as we have said, and will be upheld only if it is *necessary, and not merely rationally related, to* the accomplishment of *a permissible state policy.* [All emphases added to text.]

As the Court stated in *McLaughlin,* and as emphasized by my italics, the constitutional test for any suspect classification is that it must be proved to be necessary for the accomplishment of some overriding legislative purpose. What, then, is an "overriding" purpose? It means, in general, a weighty or important purpose, so important as to outweigh the constitutional condemnation of racial discrimination; sometimes the adjective "compelling" has been used by the Court in place of "overriding." Two overriding purposes held adequate to justify racial classifications were (1) national defense during wartime, which was used to justify the mass incarceration of Japanese-Americans on the West Coast during World War II;[52] and (2) the need to eliminate de jure school segregation in communities where decades of governmentally forced segregation have had an inevitable and enduring effect on shaping neighborhood residential patterns.

The Court not only permits racial classifications to be used for desegregation purposes, but has declared unconstitutional a law forbidding such classifications. The North Carolina Anti-Busing Law stated, "No student shall be assigned or compelled to attend any school on account of race, creed, color, or national origin." In 1971, the Supreme Court unanimously struck down the statute, explaining that "state policy must give way when it operates to hinder vindication of federal constitutional guarantees."[53] The constitutional guarantee of which they were speaking was the fundamental right of children (under earlier decisions interpreting the equal protection clause) to equal educational opportunity. If any community had a "dual," or two-race, school system in the past, its constitutional obligation was to disestablish, or desegregate, that dual system to provide equal educational opportunity. For this reason, racial classifications were not only permitted but even required:

> Just as the race of students must be considered in determining whether a constitutional violation has occurred, so also must race be considered in formulating a remedy. To forbid, at this stage, all assignments made on the basis of race would deprive school authorities of the *one tool absolutely essential to fulfillment of their constitutional obligation* to eliminate existing dual school systems. (Emphasis added.)[54]

If gender were to become officially a suspect classification, some circumstances, would surely arise, parallel to those of the busing situation, that still required gender distinctions in the law. This matter receives further consideration in the Casenote following *Frontiero v. Richardson* below.

Ordinary Equal Protection Scrutiny

As noted in chapter 1, because the equal protection clause was stated in general terms without specific mention of race, at least in *principle* the clause soon acquired a general content with implications reaching far beyond its specific prohibition (or near-prohibition) of racial (or suspect) classifications. These implications constitute an alternative constitutional doctrine of which women's rights litigants may avail themselves as long as the "suspect classification" label continues to elude their grasp. It is important to examine this alternative equal protection approach in order both to understand the legal context that stimulated the ERA campaign of the 1970s and to grasp the significance of the changes in constitutional law wrought by the Supreme Court since that campaign began.[55] This general approach, or "ordinary" equal protection scrutiny, in the century before 1970 presented a partly cloudy/partly sunny picture of opportunity for litigants attacking sex discrimination.

The clouds in this picture were the first part to develop. The *Slaughter-House Cases,* with the statement that the equal protection clause probably applied only to racial discrimination, created the first major roadblock (as explained in chapter 1), and the Supreme Court made only minor dents in that block until the mid-twentieth century. Those minor dents were shaped by broad statements of principle that the Court applied with such a light touch that for the first fifty years the impact of these statements was barely perceptible. Still, they did create at least a small bright spot in the precedent law to which later litigants could eventually appeal with much more noticeable success.

By 1886 the Supreme Court had acknowledged that "the equal protection of the laws is a pledge of the protection of equal laws."[56] "Equal laws," however, did not mean laws that affected all members of society equally. As explained above, all laws affect different people with differing impacts. What "equal laws" did mean was that the equal protection clause, in addition to denoting racial classifications suspect, created a certain standard of fairness against which all legislative classifications would have to be measured.

At first that standard of fairness was stated only in the vaguest, and therefore most unenforceable, of terms. In 1885 the Court explained the equal protection clause as though it were little (if anything) more than a guideline of legislative convenience:

> Special burdens are often necessary for general benefits. . . . Regulations for these purposes may press with more or less weight upon one than upon another, but they are designed, not to impose unequal or *unnecessary* restrictions upon any one, but to promote, with *as little inconvenience as possible*, the general good. (Emphasis added.)[57]

By "unnecessary" here the Court meant utterly groundless. Thus they read the equal protection clause as stating that legislatures could not penalize particular groups of people in whimsical or "purely arbitrary" ways. Equal protection required that there be some point to any classification that a legislature enacted into law. But what legislature would bother to enact a law that had absolutely no purpose? If this seems an exaggerated depiction of the turn-of-the-century Court's nonrule of equal protection, consider the following explanation of it in the Court's own words in a 1911 case:

1. The equal protection clause of the Fourteenth Amendment does not take from the State the power to classify in the adoption of police laws, but admits of a wider scope of discretion in that regard, and avoids what is done *only when* it is without *any* reasonable basis and therefore is *purely arbitrary.* 2. A classification having *some* reasonable basis does not offend against the clause merely because it is not made with mathematical nicety or because in practice it results in some inequality. 3. When the classification in such a law is called in question, *if any state of facts reasonably can be conceived that would sustain it, the existence of the state of facts must be assumed.* 4. One who assails the classification in such a law must carry the *burden of showing that it does not rest upon any reasonable basis but is essentially arbitrary.* (Emphasis added.)[58]

This italicization, of course, stresses the interpretation compatible with my point, and it is worth noting that the requirement that classifications have a "reasonable" basis is one of the most accordionlike standards of the American legal system. Thus the Court's oft-quoted 1920 statement that equal protection required that classifications "be reasonable, not arbitrary and . . . rest upon some ground of difference having a fair and substantial relation to the object of the legislation, so that all persons similarly circumstanced shall be treated alike,"[59] can be read in a variety of ways. It looks like it means that legislative classifications must be in fact sensibly related to the public welfare purpose at which the law is aiming. This fullblown version would stress the "fair and substantial relation" phrase in the standard. Nevertheless, if the Court wanted to stress the word "some" (reading, "classifications . . . must rest upon *some* ground of difference") and wanted to interpret "object of the legislation" in a narrow way, they could collapse the reasonableness accordion into almost invisible size.

For example, a law that prohibited women from entering the state bar to become lawyers, by the expanded, or rigorous, reasonableness standard could be said to have no "fair and substantial" relation to the legislative objective of providing well-qualified lawyers to serve the public (the broad objective of bar admissions standards). But, of the same law, using the same 1920 statement as a guide, the Court could say that there is some ground for excluding women from the bar and that the (narrow) legislative objective of keeping women at home to care for their children does have a reasonable relationship to the legislative practice of excluding them from all paid professions.

To alter the metaphor, then, the "reasonableness" standard for the equal protection clause provided the Court with a hammer that it could wield with whatever strength it desired. Wielded by a strong arm, the hammer could be used to strike down much, even most, legislation—depending on how substantial the "substantial relation" had to be and the breadth of the "object of the legislation" on which the Court chose to focus. Wielded by a gentle hand, the reasonableness hammer could strike so lightly as to make no impression. Not needing the equal protection hammer for striking down economic legislation—the task that preoccupied the Court in the first few decades of this century and for which the sledgehammer of economic substantive due process was more than adequate—the Supreme Court allowed the equal protection hammer to lie dormant, wielding it with only the gentlest of kid gloves during this period. *Radice v. New York* (see chapter 1) provides a good period example of the Court's disparate treatment of these two clauses.

Thus, for several decades this "reasonableness" equal protection principle received no more than lip service from the Court. They openly admitted that the principle, as they interpreted it, permitted laws to be "ill-advised, unequal," and even "oppressive." [60] In other words they were willing to view as "reasonable" any law for which the legislature, or legislature's counsel, could conjure up any rationale, even if unpersuasive or implausible.

This accordionlike "reasonableness" test for applying the equal protection clause, because it is the one applied in the common case—as contrasted with the "suspect classification" approach, which occurs only in the rare case—is often called the "ordinary scrutiny" approach to equal protection. Ordinarily, when a particular legislative classification is challenged as a denial of equal protection of the laws, the Supreme Court justices simply ask themselves whether this classification bears some "reasonable" relationship to some valid legislative purpose. In *McLaughlin v. Florida*, above, the Court referred to the need to subject suspect classifications, not to "ordinary scrutiny," but rather to "the most rigid scrutiny." The general rule then, is that suspect classifications receive "strict scrutiny" (i.e., must be shown to be necessary for the attainment of a compelling governmental interest), whereas all other classifications receive merely "ordinary scrutiny" or—because the accordion is generally kept in its collapsed state—"minimal scrutiny" (i.e., need only to bear some logical or "rational" relationship to some legitimate governmental purpose). [61]

The direction of, as well as the obstacles along, women's alternative to the suspect classification route should now be clear. Women's rights litigants could venture along the ordinary scrutiny path in challenging sex-discriminatory legislation as a violation of equal protection of the laws. To reach their goal of having those laws declared void, the litigants would have to surmount the obstacle of having to demonstrate that the laws had no rational relationship to promoting a valid legislative purpose. That task of demonstration would vary in difficulty according to the rigor with which the Court chose to apply the reasonableness test.

Sex as a Classification: A Century of "Ordinary Scrutiny"

Discrimination Against Men

By the early 1900s, the principle that the equal protection clause broadly limited the content of legislation, according to the rationality standard described in the preceding section, was firmly established. As long as the Court followed the four guidelines for applying the reasonableness test that were quoted above, the chances were almost nil that a challenger could successfully prove that a law embodied an "unreasonable" classification. In short, as applied during the early twentieth century, the rule simply accorded every conceivable benefit of doubt to the side of the statute under attack.

The earliest equal protection clause challengers to gender discrimination were men rather than women. And they were attacking legislation that singled out women for special benefit. Whether legislation ostensibly protective of women helps them more than it hurts them is, of course, a subject of considerable controversy.[62] But that it hurts men is often intuitively obvious, and "men's rights" advocates were quick to assert their claim in court.

In 1908, in *Muller v. Oregon,* which is treated in chapter 1, the Supreme Court conceded that although they still viewed a general ten-hour-day law as an "unreasonable" restraint on freedom, a "reasonable" basis in public health considerations might exist to justify a ten-hour-day rule for the weaker sex— women. The parties challenging the law in *Muller* had not claimed that the law was unfair in excluding men from its coverage; rather, they had tried to argue that it was never reasonable to limit any adult's freedom to work more than ten hours a day in ordinary jobs. In other words, the *Muller* litigants were challenging the principle of protective legislation per se; the fact that the law applied to women was, from their point of view (although not from the Court's), incidental.

Within a few years, the Supreme Court received a case that challenged on sex discrimination grounds a law providing special economic benefits to women. Quong Wing, a male Chinese-American[63] who operated a hand laundry in Lewis and Clark County, Montana, challenged a Montana law that imposed a ten-dollar "license tax" on all operators of hand laundries. The statute explicitly exempted steam laundries from this tax, and it also exempted women who ran laundries employing no more than two women. Quong Wing challenged both exemptions as a violation of the equal protection clause of the Fourteenth Amendment.

The Supreme Court's response to Quong Wing's challenge is illustrative of two prevalent tendencies in equal protection clause analysis of this early period. First, it illustrates in stark colors the Court's willingness to swallow any argument in defense of legislation providing special treatment to women. Justice Oliver Wendell Holmes devotes all of one sentence to the matter of the "reasonableness" of this sex-based occupational tax. Second, the Holmes majority opinion illustrates the bifurcated approach to equal protection scrutiny that had already developed by this time. Racial discrimination was scrutinized with far more care than "ordinary" classifications were. Justice Holmes indicates the Court's grounds for suspecting that this sex discrimination law may be a race discrimination law in disguise. If it were a matter of race discrimination, Justice

Holmes admits, it "would be a discrimination that the Constitution does not allow." Holmes's defense of the constitutionality of this law offers no hints why the equal protection clause would forbid the same discrimination against Chinese-American men that it would permit against men in general.

The local district court in Quong Wing's home county, incidentally, had agreed with Mr. Wing. He had won a declaration that the law was unconstitutional, only to have that decision reversed by the Montana Supreme Court. Justice Holmes, then, was responding to a decision that had upheld the statute.

Quong Wing v. Kirkendall, 223 U.S. 62 (1912)

MR. JUSTICE HOLMES delivered the opinion of the Court.

. . . The only question is whether this is an unconstitutional discrimination, depriving the plaintiff of the equal protection of the laws. U.S. Const. amend. XIV.

The case was argued upon the discrimination between the instrumentalities employed in the same business and that between men and women. One like the former was held bad in *In re Yot Sang*, 75 Fed. 983, and while the latter was spoken of by the supreme court of the state as an exemption of one or two women, it is to be observed that in 1900, the census showed more women than men engaged in hand laundry work in that state. Nevertheless we agree with the supreme court of the state so far as these grounds are concerned. A state does not deny the equal protection of the laws merely by adjusting its revenue laws and taxing system in such a way as to favor certain industries or forms of industry. Like the United States, although with more restriction and in less degree, a state may carry out a policy, even a policy with which we might disagree. *McLean v. Arkansas*, 211 U.S. 539, 547; *Armour Packing Co. v. Lacy*, 200 U.S. 226, 235; *Connolly v. Union Sewer Pipe Co.*, 184 U.S. 540, 562. It may make discriminations, if founded on distinctions that we cannot pronounce unreasonable and purely arbitrary, as was illustrated in *American Sugar Ref. Co. v. Louisiana*, 179 U.S. 89, 92, 95; *Williams v. Fears*, 179 U.S. 270, 276; *W.W. Cargill Co. v. Minnesota*, 180 U.S. 452, 469. . . . If the state sees fit to encourage steam laundries and discourage hand laundries, that is its own affair. And if, again, it finds a ground of distinction in sex, that is not without precedent. It has been recognized with regard to hours of work. *Muller v. Oregon*, 208 U.S. 412.

It is recognized in the respective rights of husband and wife in land during life, in the inheritance after the death of the spouse. Often it is expressed in the time fixed for coming of age. If Montana deems it advisable to put a lighter burden upon women than upon men with regard to an employment that our people commonly regard as more appropriate for the former, the Fourteenth Amendment does not interfere by creating a fictitious equality where there is a real difference. The particular points at which that difference shall be emphasized by legislation are largely in the power of the state.

Another difficulty suggested by the statute is that it is impossible not to ask whether it is not aimed at the Chinese, which would be a discrimination that the Constitution does not allow. *Yick Wo v.*

Hopkins, 118 U.S. 356. It is a matter of common observation that hand laundry work is a widespread occupation of Chinamen in this country, while, on the other hand, it is so rare to see men of our race engaged in it that many of us would be unable to say that they ever had observed a case. But this ground of objection was not urged, and rather was disclaimed when it was mentioned from the bench at the argument. It may or may not be that if the facts were called to our attention in a proper way the objection would prove to be real. . . . It rests with counsel to take the proper steps, and if they deliberately omit them, we do not feel called upon to institute inquires on our own account. Laws frequently are enforced which the court recognizes as possibly or probably invalid if attacked by a different interest or in a different way. Therefore, without prejudice to the question that we have suggested, when it shall be raised, we must conclude that so far as the present case is concerned, the judgment must be affirmed.

Judgment Affirmed.

Mr. Justice Hughes concurs in the result.

Mr. Justice Lamar, dissenting:

I dissent from the conclusions reached in the first branch of the opinion, because, in my judgment, the statute, which is not a police but a revenue measure, makes an arbitrary discrimination. It taxes some and exempts others engaged in identically the same business. It does not graduate the license, so that those doing a large volume of business pay more than those doing less. On the contrary, it exempts the large business and taxes the small. It exempts the business that is so large as to require the use of steam, and taxes that which is so small that it can be run by hand. Among these small operators there is a further discrimination, based on sex. It would be just as competent to tax the property of men and exempt that of women. The individual characteristics of the owner do not furnish a basis on which to make a classification for purposes of taxation.

It is the property or the business which is to be taxed, regardless of the qualities of the owner. A discrimination founded on the personal attributes of those engaged in the same occupation, and not on the value or the amount of the business, is arbitrary. "A classification must always rest upon some difference which bears a reasonable and just relation to the act in respect to which the classification is proposed." *Connolly v. Union Sewer Pipe Co.* 184 U.S. 560.

CASE QUESTIONS

1. Does Justice Holmes suggest any *reason* why it might be "advisable to put a lighter burden upon women than upon men with regard to an employment that our people commonly regard as more appropriate for the former"? Does he seem to think the "reason" is obvious? What reasons might he have had in

mind? A legislative goal of encouraging women to pursue domestic arts? A legislative goal of keeping men from competing with women in the hand laundry business because, as a result of economic discrimination, there were so few businesses in which women could earn a living that some had to be "protected" for them? The same legislative goal of inhibiting male competition, but based on the conclusion that, since most of the one or two person, female-run laundry operations were not really "businesses" but were just efforts by women to earn a bit of extra money by "taking in laundry," such operations should not be taxed on the same basis as businesses run by men?

Are all these potential reasons for the statute equally "reasonable"? Should the equal protection clause permit some of them but not others? Should the constitutionality of a statute hinge on the motivation or intention of the legislature?

2. Suppose that legislative debate preceding the adoption of this statute had focused on the economic discrimination argument; in other words, suppose there was good reason to believe that this statute aimed at equalizing the competitive disadvantage that women face as a result of private economic discrimination by potential employers and clients. Then suppose further that, two years later, the legislature also excluded all nonwhite males from the license tax, because they too suffer economic discrimination. Would the latter statute be constitutional? Would the Holmes Supreme Court have thought so?

The Supreme Court's cavalier approach to male complaints about sex discrimination continued long after Justice Holmes left the Court. In 1937, the Court again, and this time unanimously, rejected the constitutional arguments of a man complaining about sex-based discrimination in tax laws.

The state of Georgia required all males (except the blind) between the ages of twenty-one and sixty to pay a one-dollar annual tax. This tax was called a "poll tax," evidently because it was collected when people tried to register to vote, and because they were not allowed to vote if their poll taxes were not paid in full. Despite the label, however, alien males, who were not permitted to vote, had to pay the tax, and elderly males who did vote were excused from the tax on the basis of age. Women in the twenty-one to sixty age group, regardless of their marital status, had to pay the tax *only* if they registered to vote.

A twenty-eight year old man named Nolan Breedlove tried to register to vote without having paid his poll taxes. When the registrars turned him away, he initiated a suit in the local courts to have these tax laws declared unconstitutional on the grounds that they conflicted with the equal protection clause, the privileges and immunities clause, and the Nineteenth Amendment. The county court and the state supreme court both rejected his claims, and Breedlove appealed to the U.S. Supreme Court.

The Supreme Court paid little attention to Breedlove's privileges and immunities argument. Justice Butler's opinion followed the old *Minor v. Happersett* ruling that the right to vote was not a privilege of national citizenship.

The Court opinion took the Nineteenth Amendment argument only slightly more seriously. Because members of both sexes, if they wanted to vote, had to pay the tax, the Court saw no plausibility in the claim that this tax tended to abridge the right to vote "on account of sex." The Court buttressed this reasoning with the observation that requiring "the payment of poll taxes as a prerequisite to voting" was a widely accepted practice in the American states. (Eventually, in 1966, the Supreme Court did declare poll taxes a violation of equal protection of the laws.)[64]

The Court gave the most weight to Breedlove's equal protection argument. Beginning with the reminder "The equal protection clause does not require absolute equality," Justice Butler first justified exempting minors and the elderly from the tax. The young, of course, do not generally support themselves, so taxing them would usually result just in extra taxes on their parents. And the old are excused from a variety of public duties, such as jury duty and service in the militia. Justice Butler reasoned that this tax exemption did not differ to a "substantial" degree from those other exemptions for the elderly.

His arguments aimed at justifying the tax discrimination between non-voting women and non-voting men are reprinted in full.

Breedlove v. Suttles, Tax Collector, 302 U.S. 277 (1937)

MR. JUSTICE BUTLER delivered the opinion of the Court.

The tax being upon the persons, women may be exempted on the basis of special considerations to which they are naturally entitled. In view of burdens necessarily borne by them for the preservation of the race, the State reasonably may exempt them from poll taxes. *Cf. Muller v. Oregon*, 208 U.S. 412, 421 *et seq.; Quong Wing v. Kirkendall*, 223 U.S. 59, 63; *Riley v. Massachusetts*, 232 U.S. 671, *Miller v. Wilson*, 236 U.S. 373; *Bosley v. McLaughlin*, 236 U.S. 385. The laws of Georgia declare the husband to be the head of the family and the wife to be subject to him. To subject her to the levy would be to add to his burden. Moreover, Georgia poll taxes are laid to raise money for education purposes, and it is the father's duty to provide for education of the children.

Discrimination in favor of all women being permissible, appellant may not complain because the tax is laid only upon some or object to registration of women without payment of taxes for previous years. *Aetna Ins. Co. v. Hyde*, 275 U.S. 440, 447; *Rosenthal v. New York*, 226 U.S. 260, 270. . . .

CASE QUESTIONS

1. Is there any part of Justice Butler's reasoning that justifies exempting unmarried women from this tax?

2. Consider Justice Butler's claim that women bear the burden of preserving the human race, and therefore deserve "special consideration." Is he implying that mothers must be home rearing children and therefore cannot earn money for paying taxes? What of women with no children and women whose children have grown up and left home?

3. Would Justice Butler's conclusion have been more plausible if he had premised it on the general social fact that the majority of adult women in Georgia were not financially self-sufficient, and relied on their husbands or fathers for support? If he had premised it on the social fact that women on the average earned less than men?

4. If the statute authorized a one dollar per year payment to every woman 21–60 who refrained from voting, would the Court have treated it differently? If it authorized payment to non-voting blacks?

Discrimination Against Women

When legislation purporting to protect women blatantly cut them off from certain job opportunities, they, too, took complaints to court. As the *Radice v. New York* (1924) case (chapter 1) made evident, due process challenges to such laws generally foundered on the *Muller v. Oregon* (1908) precedent. Eventually, women tried asserting their rights under the equal protection clause. Operating under the shadow of the Court's any-rationalization-is-reasonable approach to "ordinary scrutiny," these women fared no better than the men's rights litigants.

The 1948 case of *Goesaert v. Cleary*[65] provides a typical sampling of the Court's approach to "ordinary" equal protection scrutiny. Like *Bradwell v. Illinois*, it involved a statute restricting women's access to a bar. Ms. Goesaert was challenging a Michigan statute that prohibited a woman from serving liquor as a bartender unless she was "the wife or daughter of the male owner" of a licensed liquor establishment. In marked historical contrast to the *Bradwell* case, Ms. Goesaert's case was argued at the Supreme Court by a woman lawyer. Nevertheless, Ms. Goesaert fared no better than Myra Bradwell had.

Justice Frankfurter, who writes the majority opinion here, had served as lawyer on the *Bunting v. Oregon* and the *Adkins v. Children's Hospital* cases, in which he argued that the Fourteenth Amendment does not prohibit states from enacting social welfare legislation that gives special protection to women. While his conclusions in *Goesaert v. Cleary* are obviously consistent with his previous advocacy role, one can argue that he did not take seriously the question whether a *principled* distinction can be drawn between hours and wage legislation protective of women, on the one hand, and legislation barring some women from certain trades, on the other. What is the answer to that question?

Goesaert v. Cleary, Liquor Control Commission of Michigan, 335 U.S. 464 (1948)

MR. JUSTICE FRANKFURTER delivered the opinion of the Court.

. . . The claim, denied below, one judge dissenting. 74 F. Supp. 735, and renewed here, is that Michigan cannot forbid females generally from being barmaids and at the same time make an exception in favor of the wives and daughters of the owners of liquor establishments. Beguiling as the subject is, it need not detain us long. To ask whether or not the Equal Protection of the Laws Clause of the Fourteenth Amendment barred Michigan from making the classification the State has made between wives and daughters of owners of liquor places and wives and daughters of nonowners, is one of those rare instances where to state the question is in effect to answer it.

We are, to be sure, dealing with a historic calling. We meet the alewife, sprightly and ribald, in Shakespeare, but centuries before him she played a role in the social life in England. See, e.g., Jusserand, English Wayfaring Life in the Middle Ages, 133, 134, 136–37 (1889). The Fourteenth Amendment did not tear history up by the roots, and the regulation of the liquor traffic is one of the oldest and most untrammeled of legislative powers. Michigan could, beyond question, forbid all women from working behind a bar. This is so despite the vast changes in the social and legal position of women. The fact that women may now have achieved the virtues that men have longed claimed as their prerogatives and

now indulge in vices that men have long practiced, does not preclude the States from drawing a sharp line between the sexes, certainly in such matters as the regulation of the liquor traffic. See the Twenty-first Amendment and Carter v. Virginia, 321 U.S. 131. The Constitution does not require legislatures to reflect sociological insight, or shifting social standards, any more than it requires them to keep abreast of the latest scientific standards.

While Michigan may deny to all women opportunities for bartending, Michigan cannot play favorites among women without rhyme or reason. The Constitution in enjoining the equal protection of the laws upon States precludes irrational discrimination as between persons or groups of persons in the incidence of a law. But the Constitution does not require situations "which are different in fact or opinion to be treated in law as though they were the same." Tigner v. Texas, 310 U.S. 141, 147. Since bartending by women may, in the allowable legislative judgment, give rise to moral and social problems against which it may devise preventive measures, the legislature need not go to the full length of prohibition if it believes that as to a defined group of females other factors are operating which either eliminate or reduce the moral and social problems otherwise calling for prohibition. Michigan evidently believes that the oversight assured through ownership of a bar by a barmaid's husband or father minimizes hazards that may confront a barmaid without such protecting oversight. This Court is certainly not in a position to gainsay such belief by the Michigan legislature. If it is entertainable, as we think it is, Michigan has not violated its duty to afford equal protection of its laws. We cannot cross-examine either actually or argumentatively the mind of Michigan legislators nor question their motives. Since the line they have drawn is not without a basis in reason, we cannot give ear to the suggestion that the real impulse behind this legislation was an unchivalrous desire of male bartenders to try to monopolize the calling.

It would be an idle parade of familiar learning to review the multitudinous cases in which the constitutional assurance of the equal protection of the laws has been applied. The generalities on this subject are not in dispute; their application turns peculiarly on the particular circumstances of a case. . . .

Nor is it unconstitutional for Michigan to withdraw from women the occupation of bartending because it allows women to serve as waitresses where liquor is dispensed. The District Court has sufficiently indicated the reasons that may have influenced the legislature in allowing women to be waitresses in a liquor establishment over which a man's ownership provides control. Nothing need be added to what was said below as to the other grounds on which the Michigan law was assailed.

Judgment Affirmed

MR. JUSTICE RUTLEDGE, with whom MR. JUSTICE DOUGLAS and MR. JUSTICE MURPHY join, dissenting.

While the equal protection clause does not require a legislature to achieve "abstract symmetry" or to classify with "mathematical nicety," that clause does require lawmakers to refrain from invidious distinctions of the sort drawn by the statute challenged in this case.

The statute arbitrarily discriminates between male and female owners of liquor establishments. A male owner, although he himself is always absent from his bar, may employ his wife and daughter as barmaids. A female owner may neither work as a barmaid herself nor employ her daughter in that position, even if a man is always present in the establishment to keep order. This inevitable result of the classification belies the assumption that the statute was motivated by a legislative solicitude for the moral and physical well-being of women who, but for the law, would be employed as barmaids. Since there could be no other conceivable justification for such discrimination against women owners of liquor establishments, the statute should be held invalid as a denial of equal protection.

CASE QUESTIONS

1. To what extent does Justice Frankfurter's opinion rely on the Twenty-first Amendment? In *California v. LaRue*, 410 US. 948 (1972) the Supreme Court held that a state's right to regulate liquor traffic under the Twenty-first Amendment over-

rode even some of the rights of free expression implied by the First Amendment. If the ERA were to be ratified, would the Twenty-first Amendment nonetheless keep this Michigan statute constitutional?

2. Just what is the "basis in reason" that Frankfurter finds for keeping women from behind the bar? For making an exception of wives and daughters of male bar owners? For not making an additional exception for female owners and their daughters "even if a man is always present . . . to keep order"?

3. Frankfurter, for part of his opinion, relies on the lower court's rationale for allowing women to be waitresses but not bartenders "where a man's ownership provides control." That rationale was the following:

> . . . the Legislature may also have reasoned that a *graver responsibility* attaches to the bartender who has control of the liquor supply than to the waitress who merely receives prepared orders of liquor . . . [or] that the presence of female waitresses does not constitute a serious social problem where a male bartender is *in charge* of the premises, or where a male licensee bears *the ultimate responsibility* for the operations . . . [or that it was] necessary to have *male control of and responsibility* for the supply of liquor . . . but not necessarily to regulate the routine tasks of the waitresses.[66] (Emphasis added.)

Do these "reasons" imply any unusual ideas about women's ability to bear responsibility?

4. If the Michigan legislature altered the statute to comply with the dissenters' objections concerning an exemption for female bar-owners, would the law still violate the equal protection clause? Would it violate the ERA?

As may be evident by this point in the story, the Supreme Court for a long time allowed the flimsiest of "reasons" to support statutes challenged as denials of equal protection in those contexts where race ("strict scrutiny") was not at issue. This pattern continued to cloud the efforts of women's rights litigants even into the 1960s, a period when the Court was thought of as generally "liberal."

A 1960s example of the Court's acceptance of unreasoned "reasons" for denials to women of equal treatment involved neither type of bar but rather an incident taking place within that sanctuary of family life, the home. One Mrs. Hoyt of Florida assaulted and killed her husband with a baseball bat during a "marital upheaval," as the Court put it. Mrs. Hoyt not only suspected her husband of adultery but had the further motivation that he rejected her when she said she was willing to take him back. She pleaded "temporary insanity" and was convicted of second-degree murder by an all-male jury.

Florida law provided that no female could serve on a jury unless she had personally made a trip down to the circuit court office and specifically requested to be put on the jury list. Because men did not have to make these efforts, the law naturally produced an enormous disproportion of male to female jurors, which resulted in many all-male juries, like Mrs. Hoyt's. (Of ten thousand persons on her local jury list of eligibles, only ten were women.) Mrs. Hoyt claimed that this statute denied her equal protection of the law because "women jurors would have been more understanding or compassionate than men in assessing the quality of [her] act and her defense of 'temporary insanity'."

In deciding *Hoyt*, as is often the situation, the Court had available to it alternative lines of precedents that pointed in opposed directions. On one hand (against Mrs. Hoyt) were the equal protection cases presented above. On the other hand, were a line of trial-by-jury cases that *might* have been used to infer the rule that impartiality in jury trials was a necessary element of equal protection, and that impartiality required a fair cross section of the community.

In its role as supervisor of the federal courts, in the 1940s the U.S. Supreme Court had outlawed the systematic exclusion of daily wage-earners from federal juries with the following reasoning:

> The American tradition of trial by jury, considered in connection with either criminal or civil proceedings necessarily contemplates an impartial jury drawn from a cross-section of the community. . . . This does not mean, of course, that every jury must contain representatives of all the economic, social, religious, racial, political and geographical groups of the community; frequently such complete representation would be impossible. But it does mean that prospective jurors shall be selected by court officials without systematic and intentional exclusion of any of these groups. Recognition must be given to the fact that those eligible for jury service are to be found in every stratum of society. Jury competence is an individual rather than a group or class matter. That fact lies at the very heart of the jury system. To disregard it is to open the door to class distinctions and discriminations which are abhorrent to the democratic ideals of trial by jury. (*Thiel v. Southern Pacific*, 328 U.S. 217, 220.)

Ballard v. United States (1946), discussion

The Court had also ruled in the 1946 case, *Ballard v. U.S.* (329 U.S. 187), that three elements of the Congressional statute governing federal jury selection (Judicial Code § 275, 28 U.S.C. § 411) "reflect a design to make the jury 'a cross-section of the community' and truly representative of it." Those three elements in the statute were (a) a prohibition on racial exclusion, (b) a command that jurors be chosen "without regard to party affiliation," and (c) a rule that jurors be selected from such parts of the district as to make most likely an impartial jury and not unduly burden the citizens of any one part of the district. (Note that it is not at all obvious that these three rules imply more strongly than does the phrase "equal protection of the laws" the rule that juries must be chosen from a representative cross-section of the community.) Having arrived at the representative cross-section rule in *Ballard*, the Court then used it to guide the interpretation of the federal statute requiring that jurors in federal trials be chosen according to state juror selection rules. California in 1946 (unlike 40 percent of the states) did make women eligible for jury duty. But as a matter of state practice women were not called to serve. Federal courts in California, in a good faith effort to obey federal law, had been following state practice rather than the letter of state statute. The Supreme Court in *Ballard* held this federal practice in the particular state of California to be a "departure from the federal scheme Congress adopted" and to be an error to be corrected by the Court's power "over the administration of justice in the federal courts." In ordering this correction the Supreme Court reasoned:

> It is said, however, that an all male panel drawn from the various groups within a community will be as truly representative as if women were included. The thought is that the factors which tend to influence the action of women are the same as those which influence the action of men—personality, background, economic status—and not sex. Yet it is not enough to say that women when sitting as jurors neither act nor tend to act as a class. Men likewise do not act as a class. But, if the shoe were on the other foot, who would claim that a jury was truly representative of the community if all men were intentionally and systematically excluded from the panel? The truth is that the two sexes are not fungible; a community made up exclusively of one is different from a community composed of both; the subtle interplay of influence one [has] on the other is among the imponderables. To insulate the courtroom from either may not in a given case make an iota of difference. Yet a flavor, a distinct quality is lost if either sex is excluded. The exclusion of one may indeed make the jury less representative of the community than would be true if an economic or racial group were excluded.

It was Justice Douglas who wrote these words in 1946 regarding federal trials in one state. In *Hoyt v. Florida,* a case concerning state trials in a different state fifteen years later, he shows no sign of remembering his own arguably relevant logic.

Hoyt v. Florida, 368 U.S. 57 (1961)

Mr. Justice Harlan delivered the opinion of the Court.

. . . Of course [Mrs. Hoyt's] premises misconceive the scope of the right to an impartially selected jury assured by the Fourteenth Amendment. That right does not entitle one accused of crime to a jury tai-lored to the circumstances of the particular case, whether relating to the sex or other condition of the defendant, or to the nature of the charges to be tried. It requires only that the jury be indiscriminately drawn from among those eligible in the community for jury service, untrammelled by any arbitrary and systematic exclusions. See

Fay v. New York, 332 U.S. 261, 284–85, and the cases cited therein. The result of this appeal must therefore depend on whether such an exclusion of women from jury service has been shown.

I

We address ourselves first to appellant's challenge to the statute on its face.

Several observations should initially be made. We of course recognize that the Fourteenth Amendment reaches not only arbitrary class exclusions from jury service based on race or color, but also all other exclusions which "single out" any class of persons "for different treatment not based on some reasonable classification." *Hernandez v. Texas,* 347 U.S. 475, 478. We need not, however, accept appellant's invitation to canvass in this case the continuing validity to this Court's dictum in *Strauder v. West Virginia,* 100 U.S. 303, 310, to the effect that a State may constitutionally "confine" jury duty "to males." This constitutional proposition has gone unquestioned for more than eighty years in the decisions of the Court, *see Fay v. New York, supra,* at 289–90, and had been reflected, until 1957, in congressional policy respecting jury service in the federal courts themselves.[2] Even were it to be assumed that this question is still

2. From the First Judiciary Act of 1789, § 29, 1 Stat. 73, 88, to the Civil Rights Act of 1957, 71 Stat. 634, 638, 28 U.S.C. § 1861—a period of 168 years—the inclusion or exclusion of women on federal juries depended upon whether they were eligible for jury service under the law of the State where the federal tribunal sat.

By the Civil Rights Act of 1957 Congress made eligible for jury service "Any citizen of the United States," possessed of specified qualifications, 28 U.S.C. § 1861, thereby for the first time making . . . women eligible for federal jury service even though ineligible under state law. There is no indication that such congressional action was impelled by constitutional consideration.

open to debate, the present case tenders narrower issues.

Manifestly, Florida's § 40.1(1) does not purport to exclude women from state jury service. Rather, the statute "gives to women the privilege to serve but does not impose service as a duty." . . . This is not to say, however, that what in form may be only an exemption of a particular class of persons can in no circumstances be regarded as an exclusion of that class. Where, as here, an exemption of a class in the community is asserted to be in substance an exclusionary device, the relevant inquiry is whether the exemption itself is based on some reasonable classification and whether the manner in which it is exercisable rests on some rational foundation.

In the selection of jurors Florida has differentiated between men and women in two respects. It has given women an absolute exemption from jury duty based solely on their sex, no similar exemption obtaining as to men. And it has provided for its effectuation in a manner less onerous than that governing exemptions exercisable by men: women are not to be put on the jury list unless they have voluntarily registered for such service; men, on the other hand, even if entitled to an exemption, are to be included on the list unless they have [annually] filed a written claim of exemption. . . .

In neither respect can we conclude that Florida's statute is not "based on some reasonable classification," and that it is thus infected with unconstitutionality. Despite the enlightened emancipation of women from the restrictions and protections of bygone years, and their entry into many parts of community life formerly considered to be reserved to men, woman is still regarded as the center of home and family life. We cannot say that it is constitutionally impermissible for a State, acting in pursuit of the general welfare, to conclude that a woman should be relieved from the civic duty of jury service unless she herself determines that such service is consistent with her own special responsibilities.

Florida is not alone in so concluding. Women are now eligible for jury service in all but three States of the Union. Of the forty-seven States where women are eligible, seventeen besides Florida, as well as the District of Columbia, have accorded women an absolute exemption based solely on their sex, exercisable in one form or another. In two of these states, as in Florida, the exemption is automatic, unless a woman volunteers for such service. It is true, of course, that Florida could have limited the exemption, as some other States have done, only to women who have family responsibilities. But we cannot regard it as irrational for a state legislature to consider preferable a broad exemption, whether born of the State's historic public policy or of a determination that it would not be administratively feasible to decide in each individual instance whether the family responsibilities of a prospective female juror were serious enough to warrant an exemption.

Likewise we cannot say that Florida could not reasonably conclude that full effectuation of this exemption made it desirable to relieve women of the necessity of affirmatively claiming it, while at the same time requiring of men an assertion of the exemptions available to them. Moreover, from the standpoint of its own administrative concerns the State might well consider that it was "impractical to compel large numbers of women, who have an absolute exemption, to come to the clerk's office for examination since they so generally assert their exemption."

Appellant argues that whatever may have been the design of this Florida enactment, the statute in practical operation results in an exclusion of women from jury service, because women, like men, can be expected to be available for jury serice only under compulsion. . . .

This argument, however, is surely beside the point. Given the reasonableness of the classification involved in § 40.01(1), the relative paucity of women jurors does not carry the constitutional consequence appellant would have it bear. "Circumstances or chance may well dictate that no persons in a certain class will serve on a particular jury or during some particular period." *Hernandez v. Texas, supra*, at 482.

We cannot hold this statute as written offensive to the Fourteenth Amendment.

II

Appellant's attack on the statute as applied in this case fares no better. . . .

This case in no way resembles those involving race or color in which the circumstances shown were found by this Court to compel a conclusion of purposeful discriminatory exclusions from jury service. *E.g., Hernandez v. Texas, supra; Norris v. Alabama,* 294 U.S. 587; *Smith v. Texas,* 311 U.S. 128; *Hill v. Texas,* 316 U.S. 400; *Eubanks v. Louisiana,* 356 U.S. 584. There is present here neither the unfortunate atmosphere of ethnic or racial prejudices which underlay the situations depicted in those cases, nor the long course of discriminatory administrative practice which the statistical showing in each of them evinced.

In the circumstances here depicted, it indeed "taxes our credulity," *Hernandez v. Texas, supra,* at 482, to attribute to these administrative officials a deliberate design to exclude the very class whose eligibility for jury service the state legislature, after many years of contrary policy, had declared only a few years before. [Women became "eligible" for Florida juries in 1948.]

. . . We must sustain the judgment of the Supreme Court of Florida.

The Chief Justice, Mr. Justice Black and Mr. Justice Douglas, concurring.

We cannot say from this record that Florida is not making a good faith effort to have women perform jury duty without discrimination on the ground of sex. Hence we concur in the result, for the reasons set forth in part II of the Court's opinion.

CASE QUESTIONS

1. What "reason" justifies excluding single women from jury duty?

2. Should the fact that a particular classification appears in the statutes of a large number of states be treated as evidence that there is a reasonable basis for the classification?

3. Does the three-judge concurring opinion imply that those judges would view an across-the-board ineligibility for women jurors as unconstitutional?

4. Is it likely that an all-male jury has certain biases not shared by women? That persons who earn less than 10,000 dollars a year have biases not shared by those who earn over 20,000 dollars? That Democrats have biases not shared by Republicans? That persons over 60 have biases not shared by persons under 35? Should communities be required to have laws that do not produce systematic jury bias in any of these directions?

CASENOTE

As recently as 1968 the Court refused to reconsider the issue settled in *Hoyt* (*State v. Hall*, 385 U.S. 98).

Sex as a Semisuspect Classification

Hoyt v. Florida was the last case involving women's rights that the Supreme Court decided by the traditional "ordinary equal protection scrutiny" approach. It is true that the Court followed its old-fashioned minimal scrutiny standard even as late as 1969, in a case involving prisoners' rights; in that instance they announced that statutory classifications challenged under the equal protection clause need bear no more than "some rational relationship to a legitimate state end and will be set aside as violative of the Equal Protection Clause only if based on reasons *totally unrelated* to the pursuit of that goal . . . *only if no grounds can be conceived* to justify them." (Emphasis added.)[67] It is also true, however, that by 1969 old-fashioned ordinary equal protection scrutiny was, if not consistently rejected, disregarded with increasing frequency at the Supreme Court level. By the end of the 1960s the Court had transformed the equal protection clause from a toothless restraint on state legislation into one with considerable bite.

The transformation of the equal protection clause into a more potent weapon for litigants challenging discriminatory statutes developed along two different doctrinal paths. The first was the suspect classification/strict scrutiny path already described. The Court not only expanded the suspect classification category beyond its traditional race-nationality-alienage bounds so that poverty was often treated as a suspect basis of discrimination,[68] but also extended the strict scrutiny approach, formerly reserved to those classifications, to another kind of discrimination: discrimination involving restraints on fundamental rights.

Like the designation of poverty as a "suspect classification," the extension of the rigid scrutiny approach to infringements of "fundamental rights" had its roots in the 1940s FDR-appointed Supreme Court and did not attain its growth into a fullblown statement of constitutional principle until the Warren Court of the 1960s. The Court first used "fundamental rights" language to strike down a statute under an equal protection challenge back in 1942. They declared a sterilization statute unconstitutional, saying that it affected "one of the basic civil rights of man" and that therefore it must be subjected to "strict scrutiny."[69] By the end of the 1960s, other fundamental rights had joined procreation in the equal protection/strict scrutiny arsenal[70]—including the right to vote[71] and the right to travel freely among the states.[72]

If discriminated-against groups could neither gain the designation of "suspect" nor find a "fundamental right" that had been infringed, to invoke the strict scrutiny test by which to invalidate a statute, they still did not need to despair. For in the late 1960s a second doctrinal path opened up to them. In two cases involving laws that penalized illegitimate children,[73] the Court took a very unusual step, a step that broke through the block previously hampering ordinary scrutiny equal protection challenges. The Court used ordinary equal protection reasonableness language but applied it with bite.[74] Thus, instead of asking, "Is there any *conceivable* reason for this classification?" the Court began asking, "Now, is this classification *really* reasonable?" Naturally, nuances of the latter question are much more likely than those of the former to result in holdings that particular classifications are "unreasonable." Thus the Court majority argued in these two decisions that there was "no possible rational basis" for the statutes, even though three Supreme Court justices, in dissent, argued that reasoned justification for the statutes was "obvious." Unless one concludes that three Supreme Court justices can be viewed as wholly irrational, one must acknowledge that something very new indeed was happening.

Although still speaking in terms of ordinary versus strict scrutiny, the Court was beginning to use a third standard of equal protection scrutiny, looser than that in suspect classification/fundamental rights cases, but stricter than that of minimal ordinary scrutiny. The Court in these "third standard" cases continued to insist that it looks merely for some reasonable basis for the statute, but its practice belied its words. Once the Court began applying scrutiny that was semistrict in practice though "ordinary" in label, the future prospects of women's rights litigants became much sunnier. By 1971, perhaps influenced by certain political developments, and under the leadership of Chief Justice Warren Burger, the Supreme Court added women to illegitimates, as groups for whom the statutory denial of benefits would be treated as at least semisuspect. The Court, however, did not admit it was using this new doctrine for gender discrimination until December of 1976, in the case of *Craig v. Boren;*[75] there the Court claimed in retrospect that this doctrine had governed the gender discrimination precedents over the previous six years.

The Supreme Court's 1971 enforcement of the reasonableness standard·"with bite" for women's equal protection challenges initiated a new epoch in women's rights litigation. No single cause can explain why the justices began to apply this new form of equal protection scrutiny to women's rights cases within a decade of their blithe dismissal of the women's discrimination claim in *Hoyt v. Florida.* A multiplicity of political and societal changes took place in the intervening decade, which supplemented the impact of the legal developments in the equal protection doctrine summarized at the end of the preceding section.

In 1961 President Kennedy, at the suggestion of Esther Peterson, director of the Women's Bureau, established a national Commission on the Status of Women. In partial response to the commission's report, fifty such state commissions were formed in 1963. In July 1962, President Kennedy by executive order barred sex discrimination within the federal civil service. Also in 1963, Betty Friedan's *The Feminine Mystique,* was published—calling for drastic changes in societal roles for women. The scientific development and subsequent widespread popularity of the birth-control pill further contributed to demographic and cultural changes during the decade. Increasing numbers of women were attending college and entering the labor force. The draining of young men from the labor force that resulted from the Vietnam War substantially increased job opportunities for women. The percentage of working women in the United States by the 1970s doubled that of the 1920s. By the end of the 1960s a genuine "women's movement" flourished along two fronts: (1) national organizations appealing, in general, to middle-class professional women, such as the National Organization for Women (formed in 1966), the National Federation of Business and Professional Women,[76] the National Women's Political Caucus, and the Women's Equity Action League; and (2) hundreds of small, ill-organized, more self-proclaimedly radical groups, with a generally younger clientele than the national organizations, seeming to draw in women who were veterans of, but frustrated by the sexism within, the civil rights and antiwar movements.[77]

Meanwhile, legislative changes took place, but for reasons that varied substantially as the decade wore on. In 1963 Congress passed the Equal Pay Act, requiring equal pay for equal work. Evidently a response to some findings of blatantly antifemale discrimination revealed in the report of the Commission on the Status of Women, the act nonetheless bore important signs of being tokenism. The act contained no viable enforcement mechanisms; moreover, its reach excluded executive, administrative, and professional employees. In 1964, Title VII was included in the 1964 Civil Rights Act, barring sex discrimination in employment. However, many of the votes that helped gain the section's inclusion on the bill were those of southern opponents to the bill who viewed Title VII as a combination joke and political tactic designed to ensure the Civil Rights Act's failure. Although both Title VII and the rest of the bill successfully passed into law, its enforcement agency (Equal Employment Opportunity Commission) was for several years given no power beyond that of conciliation (bringing employer and discriminated-against employee together to talk). By 1967, however, women began to make substantial advances on the enforcement front. In that year President Johnson (in Executive Order 11375) prohibited sex discrimination by employers under federal contract or subcontract. In 1972, in a continuation of this trend, the Equal Employment Opportunity Commission acquired the power to sue discriminating employers in federal courts.

Finally, trends within the legal profession during this decade created certain pressures upon the Court. By 1971 a number of law school journals had published articles or even symposia on women's rights questions.[78] In May 1971 the California Supreme Court jumped the gun on the U.S. Supreme Court, declaring sex classifications to be "suspect" and to require, therefore, "compelling justification."[79]

Perhaps most significant, the House of Representatives voted for the Equal Rights Amendment in August, 1970 by a margin of greater than ten to one: 350–15. The Senate did not vote on it during that session. In the new Congress, in October 1971 the House again overwhelmingly endorsed the ERA, 354–24. *Reed v. Reed* was handed down on November 22, 1971. (In March, 1972 the Senate was to vote for the ERA with near-unanimity, 84–8.)

I recapitulate these events leading up to the Court's shift of approach, if not of language, in *Reed v. Reed* in November 1971, not as a way of implying that the Court succumbed to political pressure. Possibly the shift would have occurred simply on the basis of the late-1960s shifts in constitutional doctrine outlined in the preceding section. Nevertheless, the Supreme Court does not operate in a political vacuum. Congress was exhibiting overwhelming support for the ERA by 1971, the President was issuing executive orders barring sex discrimination, and the Supreme Court moved in the same direction. This combination was probably not pure coincidence.

For whatever reason, the Court definitely did begin a new wave in interpretations of the equal protection clause vis-à-vis women with the 1971 case of *Reed v. Reed*. That case and the women's rights cases that followed in its wake establish a pretty firm impression that the Court is not about to return to the any-rationalization-is-reasonable approach of *Hoyt v. Florida.*

Reed v. Reed again took the Supreme Court into the precincts of a marital dispute. Mr. and Mrs. Reed, who were divorced, were competing for the legal appointment as administrator of their deceased son's estate. According to Idaho statute § 15–314, if other qualifications for being administrator of a particular estate are equal (such as, here, the qualification of being a parent), then "males must be preferred to females." The probate judge appointed Cecil Reed the administrator, citing no grounds other than the command of this statute. Sally Reed appealed the decision. The district court held that to follow § 15–314 would be an unconstitutional denial of equal protection of the laws; and the Idaho Supreme Court, on further appeal, upheld Cecil Reed's appointment, reasoning that the statute was not a violation of equal protection. In a unanimous opinion the U.S. Supreme Court held that, although both the Idaho legislature and the Idaho Supreme Court believed that it was reasonable to classify women in this way, it was nonetheless "arbitrary" and thus not reasonable. Here is how the U.S. Supreme Court explained its conclusions:

Reed v. Reed, 404 U.S. 71 (1971)

MR. CHIEF JUSTICE BURGER delivered the opinion of the Court.

. . . Having examined the record and considered the briefs and oral arguments of the parties, we have concluded that the arbitrary preference established in favor of males by § 15–314 of the Idaho Code cannot stand in the face of the Fourteenth Amendment's command that no state deny the equal protection of the laws to any person within its jurisdiction.

Idaho does not, of course, deny letters of administration to women altogether. Indeed, under § 15–312, a woman whose spouse dies intestate has a preference over a son, father, brother, or any other male relative of the decedent. Moreover, we can judicially notice that in this country, presumably due to the greater longevity of women, a large proportion of estates, both intestate and under wills of decedents, are administered by surviving widows.

Section 15–314 is restricted in its operation to those situations where competing applications for letters of administration have been filed by both male and female members of the same entitlement class established by § 15-312. In such situations, § 15-314 provides that different treatment be accorded to the applicants on the basis of their sex; it thus establishes a classification subject to scrutiny under the Equal Protection Clause.

In applying that clause, this Court has consistently recognized that the Fourteenth Amendment does not deny to States the power to treat different classes of persons in different ways. *Barbier v. Connolly,* 113 U.S. 27 (1885); *Lindsley v. Natural Carbonic Gas Co.,* 220 U.S. 61 (1911); *Railway Express Agency v. New York,* 336 U.S. 106 (1949); *McDonald v. Board of Election Commissioners,* 394 U.S. 802 (1969). The Equal Protection Clause of that amendment does, however, deny to States the power to legislate that different treatment be accorded to persons placed by a statute into different classes on the basis of criteria wholly unrelated to the objective of that statute. A classification "must be reasonable, not arbitrary, and must rest upon some ground of difference having a fair and substantial relation to the object of the legislation, so that all persons similarly circumstanced shall be treated alike." *Royster Guano Co. v. Virginia,* 253 U.S. 412, 415 (1920). The question presented by this case, then, is whether a difference in the sex of competing applicants for letters of administration bears a rational relationship to a state objective that is sought to be advanced by the operation of §§ 15–312 and 15–314.

In upholding the latter section, the Idaho Supreme Court concluded that its objective was to eliminate one area of controversy when two or more persons, equally entitled under § 15–312, seek letters of administration and thereby present the probate court "with the issue of which one should be named." The court also concluded that where such persons are not of the same sex, the elimination of females from consideration "is neither an illogical nor arbitrary method devised by the legislature to resolve an issue that would otherwise require a hearing as to the relative merits . . . of the two or more petitioning relatives. . . ." 93 Idaho, at 514, 465 P.2d, at 638.

Clearly the objective of reducing the workload on probate courts by eliminating one class of contests is not without some legitimacy. The crucial question, however, is whether § 15–314 advances that objective in a manner consistent with the command of the Equal Protection Clause. We hold that it does not. To give a mandatory preference to members of either sex over members of the other, merely to accomplish the elimination of hearings on the merits, is to make the very kind of arbitrary legislative choice forbidden by the Equal Protection Clause of the Fourteenth Amendment; and whatever may be said as to the positive values of avoiding intrafamily controversy, the choice in this context may not lawfully be mandated solely on the basis of sex.

We note finally that if § 15–314 is viewed merely as a modifying appendage to § 15–312 and as aimed at the same objective, its constitutionality is not thereby saved. The objective of § 15–312 clearly is to establish degrees of entitlement of various classes of persons in accordance with their varying degrees and kinds of relationship to the intestate. Regardless of their sex, persons within any one of the enumerated classes of that section are similarly situated with respect to that objective. By providing dissimilar treatment for men and women who are thus similarly situated, the challenged section violates the Equal Protection Clause. *Royster Guano Co. v. Virginia, supra.*

The judgment of the Idaho Supreme Court is reversed and the case remanded for further proceedings not inconsistent with this opinion.

Reversed and remanded.

CASE QUESTIONS

1. Is it fair to say that a preference for males over females as estate administrators is an "arbitrary legislative choice"? More arbitrary than, say, spouse over father?

2. Was it unreasonable in 1971 to believe that, as a general category, men would be more competent than women as a general category in the task of administering an estate?

3. Recall the language of *Hoyt v. Florida* where the Court justified a jury exemption for all women on the grounds that some have special family responsibilities:

> But we cannot regard it as irrational for a state legislature to consider preferable a broad exemption [even if it were] . . . born of a determination that *it would not be administratively feasible* to decide in each individual instance whether the family responsibilities of a prospective juror were serious enough to warrant an exemption. (Emphasis added.)

Has the Court's rejection in *Reed* of the administrative convenience rationale for sex-based classifications indicated that the rule of *Hoyt* would no longer be good law?

During the year and a half that elapsed between *Reed v. Reed* and the next case that involved discrimination against women, *Frontiero v. Richardson*, the Equal Rights Amendment to the Constitution made considerable progress through the legislative labyrinth. Introduced in every session of Congress since 1923, it finally won the needed two-thirds majority in each house on March 22, 1972 (four months after *Reed*[80] was decided). The amendment's language is brief and to the point:

> Equality of rights under the law shall not be denied or abridged by the United States or by any state on account of sex. The Congress shall have the power to enforce, by appropriate legislation, the provisions of this article. The amendment shall take effect two years after the date of ratification.

By January 1973, when Sharron Frontiero's lawyers were presenting her case to the Supreme Court, twenty-two state legislatures of the thirty-two that had held sessions after the ERA was proposed had ratified it.

As explained earlier, the ERA would render sex-based classifications in laws constitutionally suspect. Sally Reed's lawyers had argued that the equal protection clause of the Fourteenth Amendment on its own rendered sex classifications suspect, but Justice Burger's brief opinion sidestepped her argument and instead used language of the ordinary scrutiny arbitrariness-versus-reasonableness approach. The justices' opinions in the *Frontiero* decision bring into the foreground of attention the suspect classification approach urged by Sally Reed's lawyers and then again by Sharron Frontiero's and the pending ERA, which would have written that approach into the Constitution. Notice, however, that the Court splits almost in half over the question of what should be the Court's response to congressional ratification of the ERA. Justice Brennan cites it as grounds for treating sex as a suspect classification; Justice Powell, for doing the contrary. Both justices, writing for a total of seven of the nine, indicate the view that the ERA would make gender classifications suspect.

Sharron Frontiero and her husband, Joseph, were pressing a claim under the due process clause of the Fifth Amendment, rather than the Fourteenth Amendment. The two clauses are identical except that the Fifth applies to the federal government (as do all parts of the Constitution that do not explicitly mention the states) whereas the Fourteenth applies to state governments. The Frontieros' arguments referred to the Fifth Amendment because their complaint involved a federal statute, but the Court was fully aware that whatever it said about the due process clause of the Fifth would also apply to the due process clause of the Fourteenth and thereby limit all the state governments. Furthermore, it was a longstanding rule that the due process clause of the Fifth implied the command of "equal protection of the law" spelled out in the Fourteenth.[81] Thus, equal protection arguments figured prominently in this decision. The parties involved realized that equal protection precedents established in this case would apply to state laws in future cases.

Joseph Frontiero was a veteran receiving a monthly GI benefit of $205 while he attended college full-time. Sharron Frontiero was a lieutenant in the U.S. Air Force. Under federal law,[82] males who were members of the "uniformed services" (army, navy, air force, marine corps, coast guard, Environmental Science Services Administration, and the public health services) *automatically* received an extra housing allowance and extra medical benefits if they had a wife. To receive the same housing and medical benefits for a husband, a woman who worked in the same uniformed services had to prove that she paid more than one-half of her husband's living costs. Joseph Frontiero's living costs were $354 a month. Because his veteran's benefits were $205 a month, Sharron Frontiero could claim to be paying no more than three sevenths of his living costs—just under half. Thus, she could not obtain the extra spouse benefits that would have been automatically available to any male in her position.

Eight of the nine justices agreed that this situation was so unfair that it violated "due process of law." But they agreed on the basis of differing reasons, and those differences were of decisive importance for future women's rights litigants. There is no majority agreement on a legal rationale here, and thus no "Court opinion," only a number of opinions expressing the respective views of various fractions of the Court.

Sharron and Joseph Frontiero v. Elliot Richardson, Secretary of Defense, 411 U.S. 677 (1973)

MR. JUSTICE BRENNAN announced the judgment of the Court and an opinion in which MR. JUSTICE DOUGLAS, MR. JUSTICE WHITE, and MR. JUSTICE MARSHALL join.

. . . Thus, the question for decision is whether this difference in treatment constitutes an unconstitutional discrimination against servicewomen in violation of the

Due Process Clause of the Fifth Amendment. A three-judge District Court for the Middle District of Alabama, one judge dissenting, rejected this contention and sustained the constitutionality of the provisions of the statutes making this distinction. 341 F. Supp. 201 (1972). . . . We reverse.

I

. . . Appellants [contend] that, by making this distinction, the statutes unreasonably discriminate on the basis of sex in violation of the Due Process Clause of the Fifth Amendment.[5] In essence, appellants asserted that the discriminatory impact of the statutes is two-fold: first, as a procedural matter, a female member is required to demonstrate her spouse's dependency, while no such burden is imposed upon male members; and second, as a substantive matter, a male member who does not provide more than one-half of his wife's support receives benefits, while a similarly situated female member is denied such benefits. Appellants therefore sought a permanent injunction against the continued enforcement of these statutes and an order directing the appellees to provide Lieutenant Frontiero with the same housing and medical benefits that a similarly situated male member would receive.

Although the legislative history of these statutes sheds virtually no light on the purposes underlying the differential treatment accorded male and female members, a majority of the three-judge District Court surmised that Congress might reasonably have concluded that, since the

husband in our society is generally the "breadwinner" in the family—and the wife typically the "dependent" partner—"it would be more economical to require married female members claiming husbands to prove actual dependency than to extend the presumption of dependency to such members." 341 F. Supp., at 207. Indeed, given the fact that approximately 99 percent of all members of the uniformed services are male, the District Court speculated that such differential treatment might conceivably lead to a "considerable saving of administrative expense and manpower."

II

At the outset, appellants contend that classifications based upon sex, like classifications based upon race, alienage, and national origin are inherently suspect and must therefore be subjected to close judicial scrutiny. We agree and, indeed, find at least implicit support for such an approach in our unanimous decision only last Term in *Reed v. Reed*, 404 U.S. 71 (1971).

In *Reed*, the Court considered the constitutionality of an Idaho statute providing that, when two individuals are otherwise equally entitled to appointment as administrator of an estate, the male applicant must be preferred to the female. . . .

The Court noted that the Idaho statute "provides that different treatment be accorded to the applicants on the basis of their sex; it thus establishes a classification subject to scrutiny under the Equal Protection Clause." 404 U.S., at 75. Under "traditional" equal protection analysis, a legislative classification must be sustained unless it is "patently arbitrary" and bears no rational relationship to a legitimate governmental interest. *See Jefferson v. Hackney*, 406 U.S. 535, 546 (1972); *Richardson v. Belcher* 404 U.S. 78, 81 (1971); *Flemming v. Nestor*, 363 U.S. 603, 611 (1960); *McGowan v. Maryland*, 366 U.S. 420, 426 (1961); *Dandridge v. Williams*, 397 U.S. 471, 485 (1970).

5. "[W]hile the Fifth Amendment contains no equal protection clause, it does forbid discrimination that is 'so unjustifiable as to be violative of due process.'" *Schneider v. Rusk*, 377 U.S. 163, 168 (1964); *see Shapiro v. Thompson*, 304 U.S. 618, 641–42 (1969); *Bolling v. Sharpe*, 347 U.S. 497 (1954).

In an effort to meet this standard, appellee contended that the statutory scheme was a reasonable measure designed to reduce the workload on probate courts by eliminating one class of contests. Moreover, appellee argued that the mandatory preference for male applicants was in itself reasonable since "men [are] as a rule more conversant with business affairs than . . . women." Indeed, appellee maintained that "it is a matter of common knowledge, that women still are not engaged in politics, the professions, business or industry to the extent that men are." And the Idaho Supreme Court, in upholding the constitutionality of this statute, suggested that the Idaho Legislature might reasonably have "concluded that in general men are better qualified to act as an administrator than are women."

Despite these contentions, however, the Court held the statutory preference for male applicants unconstitutional. In reaching this result, the court implicitly rejected appellee's apparently rational explanation of the statutory scheme, and concluded that, by ignoring the individual qualifications of particular applicants, the challenged statute provided "dissimilar treatment for men and women who are . . . similarly situated." *Reed v. Reed, supra,* at 77. The Court therefore held that, even though the State's interest in achieving administrative efficiency "is not without some legitimacy," "[t]o give a mandatory preference to members of either sex over members of the other, merely to accomplish the elimination of hearings on the merits, is to make the very kind of arbitrary legislative choice forbidden by the [Constitution] . . ." *Id.* at 76. This departure from "traditional" rational basis analysis with respect to sex-based classifications is clearly justified.

There can be no doubt that our Nation has had a long and unfortunate history of sex discrimination. Traditionally, such discrimination was rationalized by an attitude of "romantic paternalism" which, in practical effect, put women not on a pedestal, but in a cage. Indeed, this paternalistic attitude became so firmly rooted in our national consciousness that, exactly 100 years ago, a distinguished member of this Court was able to proclaim:

Man is, or should be, woman's protector and defender. The natural and proper timidity and delicacy which belongs to the female sex evidently unfits it for many of the occupations of civil life. The constitution of the family organization, which is founded in the divine ordinance, as well as in the nature of things, indicates the domestic sphere as that which properly belongs to the domain and functions of womanhood. The harmony, not to say identity, of interests and views which belong, or should belong to the family institution is repugnant to the ideas of a woman adopting a distinct and independent career from that of her husband. . . .

. . . The paramount destiny and mission of woman are to fulfill the noble and benign offices of wife and mother. This is the law of the Creator. (*Bradwell v. Illinois,* 83 U.S. [16 Wall.] 130, 141 [1873] [Bradley, J., concurring].)

As a result of notions such as these, our statute books gradually became laden with gross, stereotypical distinctions between the sexes and, indeed, throughout much of the 19th century the position of women in our society was, in many respects, comparable to that of blacks under the pre-Civil War slave codes. Neither slaves nor women could hold office, serve on juries, or bring suit in their own names, and married women traditionally were denied the legal capacity to hold or convey property or to serve as legal guardians of their own children. *See generally* L. Kanowitz, *Women and the Law: The Unfinished Revolution* 5–6 (1969); G. Myrdal, *An American Dilemma* 1073 (2d ed. 1962). And although blacks were guaranteed the right to vote in 1870, women were denied even that right— which is itself "preservative of other basic civil and political rights"—until adoption of the Nineteenth Amendment half a century later.

It is true, of course, that the position of women in America has improved markedly in recent decades. Nevertheless, it can hardly be doubted that, in part because of the high visibility of the sex characteristic,[16] women still face pervasive, although at times more subtle, discrimination in our educational institutions, on the job market and, perhaps most conspicuously, in the political arena.[17] *See generally* K. Amundsen, *The Silenced Majority: Women and American Democracy* (1971); The President's Task Force on Women's Rights and Responsibilities, *A Matter of Simple Justice* (1970).

Moreover, since sex, like race and national origin, is an immutable character-

istic determined solely by the accident of birth, the imposition of special disabilities upon the members of a particular sex because of their sex would seem to violate "the basic concept of our system that legal burdens should bear some relationship to individual responsibility. . . ." *Weber v. Aetna Casualty & Surety Co.*, 406 U.S. 164, 175 (1972). And what differentiates sex from such nonsuspect statutes as intelligence or physical disability, and aligns it with the recognized suspect criteria, is that the sex characteristic frequently bears no relation to ability to perform or contribute to society. As a result, statutory distinctions between the sexes often have the effect of invidiously relegating the entire class of females to inferior legal status without regard to the actual capabilities of its individual members.

We might also note that, over the past decade, Congress has itself manifested an increasing sensitivity to sex-based classifications. In Title VII of the Civil Rights Act of 1964, for example, Congress expressly declared that no employer, labor union, or other organization subject to the provisions of the Act shall discriminate against any individual on the basis of "race, color, religion, sex, or national origin." Similarly, the Equal Pay Act of 1963 provides that no employer covered by the Act "shall discriminate . . . between employees on the basis of sex." And § 1 of the Equal Rights Amendment, passed by Congress on March 22, 1972, and submitted to the legislatures of the States for ratification, declares that [e]quality of rights under the law shall not be denied or abridged by the United States or by any State on account of sex."[21] Thus,

16. *See, e.g.*, Note, Sex Discrimination and Equal Protection: Do We Need a Constitutional Amendment?, 84 *Harv. L. Rev.* 1499, 1507 (1971).

17. It is true, of course, that when viewed in the abstract, women do not constitute a small and powerless minority. Nevertheless, in part because of past discrimination, women are vastly underrepresented in this nation's decisionmaking councils. There has never been a female President, nor a female member of this Court. Not a single woman presently sits in the United States Senate, and only fourteen women hold seats in the House of Representatives. And, as appellants point out, this underrepresentation is present throughout all levels of our State and Federal government. *See* Joint Reply Brief of Appellants and American Civil Liberties Union (*Amicus Curiae*) 9.

21. H.R.J. Res. No. 208, 92nd Cong., 2d Sess. (1972). In conformity with these principles, Congress in recent years has amended various statutory schemes similar to those presently under consideration so as to eliminate the differ-

Congress has itself concluded that classifications based upon sex are inherently invidious, and this conclusion of a coequal branch of Government is not without significance to the question presently under consideration.

With these considerations in mind, we can only conclude that classifications based upon sex, like classification based upon race, alienage, or national origin, are inherently suspect, and must therefore be subjected to strict judicial scrutiny. Applying the analysis mandated by that stricter standard of review, it is clear that the statutory scheme now before us is constitutionally invalid.

III

The sole basis of the classification established in the challenged statutes is the sex of the individuals involved. Thus, under 37 U.S.C. §§ 401, 403, and 10 U.S.C. §§ 2072, 2076, a female member of the uniformed services seeking to obtain housing and medical benefits for her spouse must prove his dependency in fact, whereas no such burden is imposed upon male members. In addition, the statutes operates so as to deny benefits to a female member, such as appellant Sharron Frontiero, who provides less than one-half of his [sic] spouse's support. Thus, to this extent at least, it may fairly be said that these statutes command "dissimilar treatment for men and women who are . . . similarly situated." *Reed v. Reed, supra,* at 77.

Moreover, the Government concedes that the differential treatment accorded men and women under these statutes serves no purpose other than mere "administra-

tive convenience." In essence, the Government maintains that, as an empirical matter, wives in our society frequently are dependent upon their husbands, while husbands rarely are dependent upon their wives. Thus, the Government argues that Congress might reasonably have concluded that it would be both cheaper and easier simply conclusively to presume that wives of male members are financially dependent upon their husbands, while burdening female members with the task of establishing dependency in fact.[22]

The Government offers no concrete evidence, however, tending to support its view that such differential treatment in fact saves the Government any money. In order to satisfy the demands of strict judicial scrutiny, the Government must demonstrate, for example, that it is actually cheaper to grant increased benefits with respect to all male members, than it is to determine which male members are in fact entitled to such benefits and to grant increased benefits only to those members whose wives actually meet the dependency requirement. Here, however, there is substantial evidence that, if put to the test, many of the wives of male members would fail to qualify for benefits.[23] And in light of

22. It should be noted that these statutes are not in any sense designed to rectify the effects of past discrimination against women. On the contrary, these statutes seize upon a group—women—who have historically suffered discrimination in employment, and rely on the effects of this past discrimination as a justification for heaping on additional economic disadvantages. Cf. *United States v. Gaston County,* 395 U.S. 285, 296–97 (1969).

23. In 1971, 43 percent of all women over the age of 16 were in the labor force, and 18 percent worked full-time 12 months per year. See U.S. Women's Bureau, Dept. of Labor, *Highlights of Women's Employment & Education* 1 (W.B. Pub. No. 71–191, March 1972). Moreover, 41.5 percent of all married women are employed. See

ential treatment of men and women. See 5 U.S.C. § 2108, as amended, 85 Stat. 644; 5 U.S.C. § 7152, as amended, 85 Stat. 644; 5 U.S.C. § 8341, as amended, 84 Stat. 1961; 38 U.S.C. § 102(b), as amended, 86 Stat. 1074.

the fact that the dependency determination with respect to the husbands of female members is presently made solely on the basis of affidavits, rather than through the more costly hearing process the Government's explanation of the statutory scheme is, to say the least, questionable.

In any case, our prior decisions make clear that, although efficacious administration of governmental programs is not without some importance, "the Constitution recognizes higher values than speed and efficiency." *Stanley v. Illinois,* 405 U.S. 645, 656 (1972). And when we enter the realm of "strict judicial scrutiny," there can be no doubt that "administrative convenience" is not a shibboleth, the mere recitation of which dictates constitutionality. *See Shapiro v. Thompson,* 394 U.S. 618 (1969); *Carrington v. Rash,* 380 U.S. 89 (1965). On the contrary, any statutory scheme which draws a sharp line between the sexes, *solely* for the purpose of achieving administrative convenience, necessarily commands "dissimilar treatment for men and women who are . . . similarly situated," and therefore involves the "very kind of arbitrary legislative choice forbidden by the [Constitution]. . . ." *Reed v. Reed, supra,* at 77, 76. We therefore conclude that, by according differential treatment to male and female members of the uniformed services for the sole purpose of achieving administrative convenience, the challenged statutes violate the Due Process Clause of the Fifth Amendment insofar as they require a female member to prove the dependency of her husband.

Reversed.

U.S. Bureau of Labor Statistics, Dept. of Labor; *Work Experience of the Population in 1971* 4 (Summary Special Labor Force Report, August 1972). . . .

MR. JUSTICE STEWART concurs in the judgment, agreeing that the statutes before us work an invidious discrimination in violation of the Constitution. *Reed v. Reed,* 404 U.S. 71.

MR. JUSTICE POWELL, with whom THE CHIEF JUSTICE and MR. JUSTICE BLACKMUN join, concurring in the judgment.

I agree that the challenged statutes constitute an unconstitutional discrimination against service women in violation of the Due Process Clause of the Fifth Amendment, but I cannot join the opinion of MR. JUSTICE BRENNAN, which would hold that all classifications based upon sex, "like classifications based upon race, alienage, and national origin," are "inherently suspect and must therefore be subject to close judicial scrutiny." *Supra.*

It is unnecessary for the Court in this case to characterize sex as a suspect classification, with all of the far-reaching implications of such a holding. *Reed v. Reed,* 404 U.S. 71 (1971), which abundantly supports our decision today, did not add sex to the narrowly limited group of classifications which are inherently suspect. In my view, we can and should decide this case on the authority of *Reed* and reserve for the future any expansion of its rationale.

There is another, and I find compelling, reason for deferring a general categorizing of sex classifications as invoking the strictest test of judicial scrutiny. The Equal Rights Amendment, which if adopted will resolve the substance of this precise question, has been approved by the Congress and submitted for ratification by the States. If this amendment is duly adopted, it will represent the will of the people accomplished in the manner prescribed by the Constitution. By acting prematurely and unnecessarily, as I view it, the Court has assumed a decisional responsibility at the very time when state legislatures, functioning within the traditional democratic process, are debating the proposed Amendment. It seems to me that this reaching out to pre-empt by judical action a major political decision which is currently in process of resolution does not reflect appropriate respect for duly prescribed legislative processes.

There are times when this Court, under our system, cannot avoid a constitutional decision on issues which normally should be resolved by the elected representatives of the people. But democratic institutions are weakened, and confidence in the restraint of the Court is impaired, when we appear unnecessarily to decide sensitive issues of broad social and political importance at the very time they are under consideration within the prescribed constitutional processes.

Mr. Justice Rehnquist dissents for the reasons stated by Judge Rives in his opinion for the District Court, *Frontiero v. Laird*, 341 F. Supp. 201 (1972).

[Those reasons from Judge Rives' opinion are excerpted below:]

. . . Plaintiffs point out that a male member may claim his wife without proving her actual dependency, while a female member must prove such in order to claim her husband. At first blush, then, the statute seems to draw a classification entirely on the basis of sex. Such is not the case. Rather than focus attention solely to the different treatment afforded male and female members claiming their respective spouses, we must examine the over-all statutory scheme. A conclusive presumption of dependency is extended in the following instances:

1. *To male members* claiming spouses and unmarried, legitimate, minor children; and

2. *to female members* claiming unmarried, legitimate, minor children for purposes of medical and dental benefits.

On the other hand, dependency in fact must be shown:

1. *By male members* claiming adult children, parents, and parents-in-law; and

2. *by female members* claiming anyone other than an unmarried, legitimate, minor child for medical and dental benefits.

Thus, on the whole the availability of the presumption does not turn exclusively on the basis of the member's sex but rather on the nature of the relationship between the member and the claimed dependent.[1] . . .

Yet even if we were to view this case in the narrow context invited by plaintiffs' approach, viz., the different treatment accorded a male member claiming his wife as a dependent and a female member claiming her husband, we would uphold the statute. Before moving to that discussion however, it is necessary to clarify the standards by which we judge the statute.

An Act of Congress carries with it a strong presumption of constitutionality and places the burden upon the challenging party to prove the unconstitutionality of the statute at issue. . . . The Due Process Clause of the Fifth Amendment, on which this challenge is based, bars federal legislation embodying a baseless classification.

1. We have concluded that Congress chose to employ a presumption of dependency in certain instances for reasons of administrative and economic convenience. That such a justification is sound is treated *infra*.

. . . Undoubtedly there is much similarity between the equal protection test which courts employ in determining the validity of a state statute and the due process test which is utilized in evaluating a federal statute.

Thus, in determining the constitutionality of the statutory scheme which plaintiffs attack, this Court must ask whether the classification established in the legislation is reasonable and not arbitrary and whether there is a rational connection between the classification and a legitimate governmental end.[2] In making that judgment, the statute must be upheld "if any state of facts rationally justifying it is demonstrated to *or perceived by* the courts." (*United States v. Maryland Savings-Share Insurance Corp.*, 400 U.S. 4 [1970] [challenge to a federal tax statute]. [Emphasis supplied.])

The Supreme Court has recently enunciated the test for determining whether a classification squares with the Equal Protection Clause of the Fourteenth Amendment:

In the area of economics and social welfare, a State does not violate the Equal Protection Clause merely because the classifications made by its laws are imperfect. If the classification has some "reasonable basis," it does not offend the Constitution simply because the classification "is not made with mathematical nicety or because in practice it results in some inequality." . . . "The prob-

lems of government are practical ones and may justify, if they do not require, rough accommodations—illogical, it may be, and unscientific." . . . "A statutory discrimination will not be set aside if any state of facts reasonably may be conceived to justify it. . . ." (*Dandridge v. Williams*, 397 U.S. 471, 485 [1970].)

In summary, the law is well-settled that a statutory classification, challenged as an unlawful discrimination, should be upheld if it has a rational basis.

The defendants contend that the statutory provisions here at issue do no more than establish a conclusive presumption that a married male member of the uniformed services has a dependent wife while requiring a married female member of the uniformed services to prove the dependence of her husband, a distinction which, they say, does no more than take account of facts which the courts and statistical studies evidence in no way discriminate against females, as such. It seems clear that the reason Congress established a conclusive presumption in favor of married service men was to avoid imposing on the uniformed services a substantial administrative burden of requiring actual proof from some 200,000 male officers and over 1,000,000 enlisted men that their wives were actually dependent upon them. The question presented here then is whether the price for enjoying this administrative benefit fails to justify the different treatment of married service women.

. . . The classification which establishes a conclusive presumption in favor of married service men claiming wives allows the uniformed services to carry out the statutory purposes with a considerable saving of administrative

---

2. In *Reed v. Reed* 404 U.S. 71 (1971), the Supreme Court was faced with a challenge to a state law which allegedly discriminated on the basis of sex. In stating the test by which to judge that statute the Court did not require that it meet the compelling interest test, see *Shapiro v. Thompson* 394 U.S. 618 (1969), but rather that it satisfy the rational connection standard. Similarly in this case we would be remiss in applying the compelling interest test.

expense and manpower. Congress apparently reached the conclusion that it would be more economical to require married female members claiming husbands to prove actual dependency than to extend the presumption of dependency to such members.[3] Such a presumption made to facilitate administration of the law does not violate the equal protection guarantee of the Constitution if it does not unduly burden or oppress one of the classes upon which it operates. *See Adams v. City of Milwaukee*, 228 U.S. 572. (1913). "[L]egislation may impose special burdens upon defined classes in order to achieve permissible ends." *Rinaldi v. Yeager*, 384 U.S. 305, 309 (1966) (dictum). Nothing in the instant statutory classification jeopardizes the ability of a female member to obtain the benefits intended to be bestowed upon her by the statutes. The classification is burdensome for a female member who is not actually providing over one-half the support for her claimed husband only to the extent that were she a man she could receive dependency benefits in spite of the fact that her spouse might not be actually dependent, as that term has been defined by Congress. In other words, the alleged injustice of the distinction lies in the possibility that some married service men are getting "windfall" payments, while married service women are denied them. Sharron Frontiero is one

3. It should be remembered that for purposes of medical and dental benefits the presumption of dependency is extended to a female member claiming any unmarried minor, legitimate children. And on the other hand a male member must prove actual dependency when he claims adult children, parents, or parents-in-law who by reason of incapacity are unable to support themselves.

of the service women thus denied a windfall.

. . . [W]e are of the opinion that the incidental bestowal of some undeserved benefits on male members of the uniformed services does not so unreasonably burden female members that the administrative classification should be ruled unconstitutional. Under . . . a contrary finding . . . [t]he Court would be faced with a Hobson-like choice in fashioning a remedy: either strike down the conclusive presumption in favor of married service men, forcing the services to invest the added time and expense necessary to administer the law accurately, or require the presumption to be applied to both male and female married members, thereby abandoning completely the concept of dependency in fact upon which Congress intended to base the extension of benefits.

. . .

This is not to say that if plaintiffs could prove that the rational basis—administrative and economic convenience—did not exist due process would nevertheless be satisfied. (*Tot v. United States*, 319 U.S. 463 [1943].) But the plaintiffs here have not come close to proving such a state of facts. There is no evidence before this Court proving that so many male members are in fact dependent on their wives as to make it advisable to deny male members the presumption of dependency. Nor is there proof that so many female members have dependent husbands as to justify extending the benefit of the presumption to them. . . .

Moreover, the result we here reach is clearly in harmony with . . . *Reed v. Reed*, 404 U.S. 71 (1971), [striking] down, as violative of the Equal Protection Clause of the Fourteenth Amendment, an Idaho statute which discriminated against women. The statute there in question established a conclusive presumption that the father of a deceased child is more suitable than the mother to serve as administrator of the child's estate. The Supreme Court held that such a classification had no lawful justification:

Clearly the objective of reducing the workload on probate courts by eliminating one class of contests is not without some legitimacy. The crucial question, however, is whether § 15–314 advances that objective in a manner consistent with the command of the Equal Protection Clause. We hold that it does not. To give a mandatory preference to members of either sex over members of the other, merely to accomplish the elimination of hearings on the merits, is to make the very kind of arbitrary legislative choice forbidden by the Equal Protection Clause of the Fourteenth Amendment; and whatever may be said as to the positive values of avoiding intrafamily controversy the choice in this context may not lawfully be mandated *solely* on the basis of sex. (*Id.* at 76.)

As we have noted the classification here at issue is not drawn solely on the basis of sex, as was the case in *Reed*. Second, while there is arguably some similarity between the administrative advantage of avoiding probate hearing and the administrative benefit of not having to determine the actual dependency of over a million service wives, there is a significant qualitative distinction. In *Reed* there was a statutory presumption which had no relation to the statutory purpose of selecting the best qualified administrator. The effect was to exclude certain qualified females from serving as administrators, whereas the classification presented here does not exclude qualified female members. They merely have to show actual dependency.

This Court would be remiss if it failed to notice, lurking behind the scenes, a subtler injury purportedly inflicted on service women as a subclass under these statutes. That is the indignity a woman may feel, as a consequence of being the one left out of the windfall, of having to traverse the added red tape of proving her husband's dependency, and most significantly, of being treated differently. The Court is not insensitive to the seriousness of these grievances, but it is of the opinion that they are mistaken wrongs, the result of a misunderstanding of the statutory purpose. The classifications established by these statutes are purely administrative and economic ones, which are only based in part on sex. There is no reason to believe that the Congress would not respond to a significant change in the practical circumstances presumed by the statutory classification or that the present statutory scheme is merely a child of Congress' "romantic paternalism" and "Victorianism."

CASE QUESTIONS

1. How many of the nine justices conclude that sex classifications in statutes are inherently suspect and can be constitutional only when they are supported by

"compelling justification"? How many judges conclude that sex classifications can be constitutional only when they are simply not "arbitrary" or "invidious"—i.e., as long as they bear some "rational" relation to a valid legislative purpose? As of 1973, is sex a suspect classification?

2. Does the four-judge Brennan opinion rely primarily on case precedents (previous Supreme Court statements about the meaning of the Constitution) or on other sources? What other kinds of authority besides legal precedents appear in Brennan's reasoning? Are there particular strengths or weaknesses inherent in the use of these kinds of authority by Supreme Court judges?

3. Does Brennan's opinion imply that he and those who concur with him de-

ceived the American public in the *Reed v. Reed* case? That they did not realize what they were saying? Is either a desirable implication?

4. After comparing the opinions of the Court majority to those of the Judge Rives opinion, which Justice Rehnquist endorsed, does it seem convincing that the discrimination in this statute "bears no rational relationship to a legitimate governmental interest"?

5. Whose version of *Reed v. Reed* is most convincing: Brennan's, Powell's, or Rives'?

6. Notice that in note 22 Brennan distinguishes this statute from laws *protective* of women. Does his general line of reasoning suggest that he would uphold such legislation?

CASENOTE

While seven justices indicated here that the ERA would make gender a suspect classification and the other two express no disagreement on the point, it is worth noting that the amendment's legal impact was explained somewhat differently both by official Congressional reports and by an influential *Yale Law Journal* article often cited by ERA proponents. Both of the latter stated that the ERA would ban all legislative sex discrimination except for two kinds: (1) laws designed to take into account actual physiological differences of reproductive function, such as laws involving separate bathrooms, rape, wet-nurses, spermdonors, costs of giving birth, or determinations of paternity;[83] and (2) laws designed to com-

pensate women for the impact of societal discrimination against them.[84]

The Supreme Court never specifically endorsed this two-exceptions-only approach to either the ERA or the equal protection clause, but it is not difficult to assimilate the two-exceptions approach to the compelling interest approach. The Court could simply let the concerns for recognizing actual physiological difference and for compensating women for societal discrimination guide its understanding of what constitutes a compelling governmental interest. In fact both of these concerns very much shaped the kind of exceptions to the rule of gender equality that the Supreme Court was willing to permit after 1971.

In a sense, *Frontiero* brought the principle that sex is a semisuspect classification out of the closet. The frank admission by four justices that the *Reed* result would have been different if the Supreme Court had followed the reasonableness test it was espousing indicated that the Court was examining sex classifications with something other than the traditional minimal scrutiny. The implicit claim by Justices Stewart, Powell, Blackmun, and Burger that the armed forces' denial of spouse benefits to women like Sharron Frontiero was arbitrary and had no reasonable basis, in the face of Judge Rives' elaborate defense of the reasons underlying the statute, amounts to a similar admission couched in different terms. What they seem to be saying is this: When it comes to sex discrimination in the law, not just *any* reason, such as administrative convenience, will pass the "reasonableness" test. There has to be a pretty good reason before the Court will hold that sex discrimination is justified, although the Court is not willing at this time to go so far as to say that it must be a "compelling" reason.

The justices soon revealed that they could in fact be convinced of the existence of such a "pretty good" justification. They did so in a case involving a women's-right-to-special-benefit or, conversely, a men's rights case, *Kahn v. Shevin.* *Kahn v. Shevin* presented a challenge by Mr. Kahn, a widower, to a Florida statute that gave to widows an automatic 500 dollars annual property-tax exemption. The statute provided no parallel benefits to widowers. The Dade County Circuit Court had agreed with Mr. Kahn's argument that this statute denied him equal protection of the laws. The Florida Supreme Court had reversed, persuaded by the argument of Florida's Attorney General Shevin that this statute met the test propounded in Reed: "a fair and substantial relation to the [valid] object of the legislation."

Mr. Kahn appealed that decision to the U.S. Supreme Court, where his case was presented by two well-known women's rights attorneys, Ruth Bader Ginzburg and Melvin Wulf, the same attorneys who had worked on the Court briefs for the successful *Reed v. Reed* and *Frontiero v. Richardson* plaintiffs.[85] In *Kahn v. Shevin,* they were not so successful. The U.S. Supreme Court upheld the Florida Supreme Court.

The grounds on which the Court did so, however, are difficult to locate. First, the Court majority recapitulated the "fair and substantial" language of *Reed* and stated that this statute met that standard. As already indicated; this language, at least in *Reed* and *Frontiero,* was used to connote a somewhat stiffer test than the old minimal scrutiny "reasonableness" test from which it originated. Then the Court majority went on to say that in matters of tax legislation the "reasonableness" test is the one that should apply, and that this law was "well within" the bounds of reasonableness. Most puzzling, Justice Douglas, who had been a member of the four-judge group in *Frontiero* that had argued that sex classifications are suspect and therefore should require compelling justification, authored the *Kahn* majority opinion in support of the reasonableness test. (His three former allies from *Frontiero* did have the consistency to dissent in this case.) Here follows Douglas's explanation and his former allies' critique of it:

Kahn v. Shevin, Attorney General of Florida, 416 U.S. 351 (1974)

MR. JUSTICE DOUGLAS delivered the opinion of the Court.

. . .

Since at least 1885, Florida has provided for some form of property tax exemption for widows. . . . The Florida Supreme Court [found the widow/widower] . . . classification valid because it has a "'fair and substantial relation to the object of the legislation,'" that object being the reduction of "the disparity between the economic capabilities of a man and a woman." . . . We affirm.

There can be no dispute that the financial difficulties confronting the lone woman in Florida or in any other State exceed those facing the man. Whether from overt discrimination or from the socialization process of a male-dominated culture, the job market is inhospitable to the woman seeking any but the lowest paid jobs.[4] . . .

[D]ata compiled by the Women's Bureau of the United States Department of Labor show that in 1972 a woman working full time had a median income which was only 57.9 percent of the median for males—a figure actually six points lower than had been achieved in 1955.[5] Other data point in

the same direction.[6] The disparity is likely to be exacerbated for the widow. While the widower can usually continue in the occupation which preceded his spouse's death, in many cases the widow will find herself suddenly forced into a job market with which she is unfamiliar, and in which, because of her former economic dependency, she will have fewer skills to offer.

Year	Median earnings		Women's median earnings as percent of men's
	Women	Men	
1972	$5,903	$10,202	57.9
1971	5,593	9,399	59.5
1970	5,323	8,966	59.4
1969	4,977	8,227	60.5
1968	4,457	7,664	58.2
1967	4,150	7,182	57.8
1966	3,973	6,848	58.0
1965	3,823	6,375	60.0
1964	3,690	6,195	59.6
1963	3,561	5,978	59.6
1962	3,446	5,794	59.5
1961	3,351	5,644	59.4
1960	3,293	5,417	60.8
1959	3,193	5,209	61.3
1958	3,102	4,927	63.0
1957	3,008	4,713	63.8
1956	2,827	4,466	63.3
1955	2,719	4,252	63.9

4. In 1970 while 40 percent of males in the work force earned over $10,000 and 70 percent over $7,000, 45 percent of women working full time earned less than $5,000, and 73.9 percent earned less than $7,000. U.S. Bureau of The Census: *Current Population Reports*, Series P–60, No. 80.

5. The Women's Bureau provides the following data:

6. For example, in 1972 the median income of women with four years of college was $8,736— exactly $100 more than the median income of men who had never even completed one year of high school. Of those employed as managers or administrators, the women's median income was only 53.2 percent of the men's, and in the professional and technical occupations the figure was 67.5 percent. . . .

There can be no doubt, therefore, that Florida's differing treatment of widows and widowers "'rest[s] upon some ground of difference having a fair and substantial relation to the object of the legislation.'" *Reed v. Reed,* 404 U.S. 71, 76, quoting *Royster Guano....*

This is not a case like *Frontiero v. Richardson,* 411 U.S. 677, where the Government denied its female employees both substantive and procedural benefits granted males "*solely* . . . for administrative convenience." *Id.* at 690. (Emphasis in original.)[8] We deal here with a state tax law reasonably designed to further the state policy of cushioning the financial impact of spousal loss upon the sex for which that loss imposes a disproportionately heavy burden. We have long held that "[w]here taxation is concerned and no specific federal right, apart from equal protection, is imperiled, the States have large leeway in making classifications and drawing lines which in their judgment produce reasonable systems of taxation." *Lehnhausen v. Lake Shore Auto Parts Co.,* 410 U.S. 356, 359. A state tax law is not arbitrary although it "discriminate[s] in favor of a certain class . . . if the discrimination is founded upon a reasonable distinction, or difference in state policy," not in conflict with the Federal Constitution. *Allied Stores v. Bowers,* 358 U.S. 522, 528. This principle has weathered nearly a century of Supreme Court adjudication, and it applies here as

well. The statute before us is well within those limits.[10]

Affirmed.

MR. JUSTICE BRENNAN, with whom MR. JUSTICE MARSHALL joins, dissenting.

. . . In my view . . . a legislative classification that distinguishes potential beneficiaries solely by reference to their gender-based status as widows or widowers, like classifications based upon race, alienage, and national origin, must be subjected to close judicial scrutiny, because it focuses upon generally immutable characteristics over which individuals have little or no control, and also because gender-based classifications too often have been inex-

---

8. And in *Frontiero* the plurality opinion also noted that the statutes there were "not in any sense designed to rectify the effects of past discrimination against women. On the contrary, these statutes seize upon a group—women—who have historically suffered discrimination in employment, and [heap] . . . on additional economic disadvantages." 411 U.S., at 689 n.22 (citations omitted).

10. The dissents argue that the Florida legislature could have drafted the statute differently, so that its purpose would have been accomplished more precisely. But the issue, of course, is not whether the statute could have been drafted more wisely, but whether the lines chosen by the Florida Legislature are within constitutional limitations. The dissents would use the Equal Protection Clause as a vehicle for reinstating notions of substantive due process that have been repudiated. "We have returned to the original constitutional proposition that courts do not substitute their social and economic beliefs for the judgment of legislative bodies, [which] are elected to pass laws." *Ferguson v. Skrupa,* 372 U.S. 726, 730.

Gender has never been rejected as an impermissible classification in all instances. Congress has not so far drafted women into the Armed Services, 50 U.S.C. App. § 454. The famous Brandeis Brief in *Muller v. Oregon,* 208 U.S. 412, on which the Court specifically relied, *id.* at 419–20, emphasized that the special physical structure of women has a bearing on the "conditions under which she should be permitted to toil." *Id.* at 420. These instances are pertinent to the problem in the tax field which is presented by this present case. . . .

cusably utilized to stereotype and stigmatize politically powerless segments of society. *See Frontiero v. Richardson*, 411 U.S. 677 (1973). The Court is not, therefore, free to sustain the statute on the ground that it rationally promotes legitimate governmental interests; rather, such suspect classifications can be sustained only when the State bears the burden of demonstrating that the challenged legislation serves overriding or compelling interest that cannot be achieved either by a more carefully tailored legislative classification or by the use of feasible, less drastic means. While, in my view, the statute serves a compelling governmental interest by "cushioning the financial impact of spousal loss upon the sex for which that loss imposes a disproportionately heavy burden," I think that the statute is invalid because the State's interest can be served equally well by a more narrowly drafted statute.

Gender-based classifications cannot be sustained merely because they promote legitimate governmental interests, such as efficacious administration of government. *Frontiero v. Richardson, supra; Reed v. Reed*, 404 U.S. 71 (1971). For "when we enter the realm of 'strict judicial scrutiny,' there can be no doubt that 'administrative convenience' is not a shibboleth, the mere recitation of which dictates constitutionality. *See Shapiro v. Thompson*, 394 U.S. 618 (1969); *Carrington v. Rash*, 380 U.S. 89 (1965). On the contrary, any statutory scheme which draws a sharp line between the sexes, solely for the purpose of achieving administrative convenience, necessarily commands 'dissimilar treatment for men and women who are . . . similarly situated,' and therefore involves the 'very kind of arbitrary legislative choice forbidden by the [Constitution]. . . .' *Reed v. Reed*, 404 U.S., at 77, 76." *Frontiero v. Richardson, supra*, at 690. But Florida's justification of § 196.191(7) is not that it serves administrative conve-

nience or helps to preserve the public fisc. Rather, the asserted justification is that § 196.191(7) is an affirmative step toward alleviating the effects of past economic discrimination against women.

I agree that, in providing special benefits for a needy segment of society long the victim of purposeful discrimination and neglect, the statute serves the compelling state interest of achieving equality for such groups.[5] No one familiar with this country's history of pervasive sex discrimination against women can doubt the need for remedial measures to correct the resulting economic imbalances. Indeed, the extent of the economic disparity between men and women is dramatized by the data cited by the Court, *ante*. By providing a property tax exemption for widows, § 196.191(7) assists in reducing that economic disparity for a class of women particularly disadvantaged by the legacy of economic discrimination. In that circumstance, the purpose and effect of the suspect classification are ameliorative; the statute neither stigmatizes nor denigrates widowers not also benefited by the legislation. Moreover, inclusion of needy widowers within the class of beneficiaries would not further the State's overriding interest in remedying the economic effects of past sex discrimination for needy victims of that discrimination. While doubtless some widowers are in financial need, no one suggests that such need results from sex discrimination as in the case of widows.

The statute nevertheless fails to satisfy the requirements of equal protection,

---

5. Significantly, the Florida statute does not compel the beneficiaries to accept the State's aid. The taxpayer must file for the tax exemption. This case, therefore, does not require resolution of the more difficult questions raised by remedial legislation which makes special treatment mandatory. . . .

since the State has not borne its burden of proving that its compelling interest could not be achieved by a more precisely tailored statute or by use of feasible, less drastic means. § 196.191(7) is plainly overinclusive, for the $500 property tax exemption may be obtained by a financially independent heiress as well as by an unemployed widow with dependent children. The State has offered nothing to explain why inclusion of widows of substantial economic means was necessary to advance the State's interest in ameliorating the effects of past economic discrimination against women.

Moreover, alternative means of classification, narrowing the class of widow beneficiaries, appear readily available. The exemption is granted only to widows who complete and file with the tax assessor a form application establishing their status as widows. By merely redrafting that form to exclude widows who earn annual incomes, or possess assets, in excess of specified amounts, the State could readily narrow the class of beneficiaries to those widows for whom the effects of past economic discrimination against women have been a practical reality.

Mr. Justice White, dissenting.

The Florida tax exemption at issue here is available to all widows but not to widowers. The presumption is that all widows are financially more needy and less trained or less ready for the job market than men. It may be that most widows have been occupied as housewife, mother, and homemaker and are not immediately prepared for employment. But there are many rich widows who need no largess from the State; many others are highly trained and have held lucrative positions long before the death of their husbands. At the same time, there are many widowers who are needy and who are in more desperate financial straits and have less access to the job market than many widows. Yet none of them qualifies for the exemption.

I find the discrimination invidious and violative of the Equal Protection Clause. There is merit in giving poor widows a tax break, but gender-based classifications are suspect and require more justification than the State has offered.

I perceive no purpose served by the exemption other than to alleviate current economic necessity, but the State extends the exemption to widows who do not need the help and denies it to widowers who do. It may be administratively inconvenient to make individual determinations of entitlement and to extend the exemption to needy men as well as needy women, but administrative efficiency is not an adequate justification for discriminations based purely on sex. *Frontiero v. Richardson*, 411 U.S. 677 (1973); *Reed v. Reed*, 404 U.S. 71 (1971).

It may be suggested that the State is entitled to prefer widows over widowers because their assumed need is rooted in past and present economic discrimination against women. But this is not a credible explanation of Florida's tax exemption; for if the State's purpose was to compensate for past discrimination against females, surely it would not have limited the exemption to women who are widows. Moreover, even if past discrimination is considered to be the criterion for current tax exemption, the State nevertheless ignores all those widowers who have felt the effects of economic discrimination, whether as a member of a racial group or as one of the many who cannot escape the cycle of poverty. It seems to me that the State in this case is merely conferring an economic benefit in the form of a tax exemption and has not adequately explained why women should be treated differently from men.

I dissent.

CASE QUESTIONS

1. Does the majority's footnote 8 imply that the standard of scrutiny applied to statutes that hurt women should differ from the standard applied to laws that help women?

2. Does the majority's approving citation of *Muller v. Oregon* and of that case's reliance on the unique physical structure of women indicate a turning away from the logic of *Reed* and *Frontiero?*

3. Why is the assumption that wives are frequently economically dependent on their husbands valid when Florida makes it about widows but invalid when the U.S. Army makes it about army officers? (See *Frontiero v. Richardson.*)

4. Justice White suggests that it might be acceptable for the state to make special restitution to women as a group to compensate for past discrimination but not acceptable for the state to single out widows for help. Is it unreasonable for the state to assume that among women who pay property tax, widows as a group are most likely to need compensatory help for the harm done by societal patterns of sex discrimination, since they have lost a family member with adult learning power? Does White seem to prefer a special income-tax break for all females? Would such a tax structure be good public policy?

5. Would it be unconstitutional for the government to provide a special tax benefit to all blacks, Chicanos, Puerto Ricans, and Native Americans because they suffer economic discrimination? Unwise?

6. Why is it a "plus" that this statute does not force women to take the tax exemption? (See Brennan's footnote 5.)

7. Justice Brennan would accept this statute if it helped only poor widows rather than all widows. Is it unreasonable for the legislature to assume that all women would probably more affluent if not for the widespread sex discrimination constricting their opportunities both through overt job discrimination and also, more subtly, through the entire socialization process? If that is a reasonable assumption, don't all women, rich and poor, deserve compensation?

The Court majority's repeated use in *Kahn* of such terms as "reasonably," "reasonable," and "not arbitrary" seemed to imply that the "fair and substantial relationship" test of *Reed* had been reduced back down to its earlier meaning as a mere synonym for "reasonableness." Such a change, of course, would have undercut the momentum of the *Reed* and *Frontiero* steps toward declaring sex classifications suspect. It did not become clear until later cases whether that was what was happening in *Kahn,* or whether the Court was simply carving out a special exception for taxing and welfare policy, or whether the Court majority believed that laws discriminating against men were not as "suspect" as laws discriminating against women.

By a change of his vote in the next antimale discrimination case, Justice Douglas, at least, seemed to demonstrate that the middle of these three possibilities best explained his own view of the *Kahn v. Shevin* decision. Even without his vote, however, the *Kahn* majority held five votes, and these produced the majority in *Schlesinger v. Ballard* (1975) to uphold the antimale discrimination at issue there.

Schlesinger (then Secretary of Defense James Schlesinger) was appealing a U.S. district court decision that naval regulations 10 U.S.C. § 6382(a) and 10 U.S.C. § 6401 were unconstitutional as violations of the concept of equal protection implied by the Fifth Amendment due process clause. Section 6382(a) mandated that any lieutenant in the U.S. Navy or captain in the U.S. Marine Corps who is twice passed over for promotion shall receive an honorable discharge in the year of his second failure to be promoted. The section did not apply to women officers. Women navy lieutenants and marine captains were given a minimum of thirteen years of officer service duty according to § 6401, before they could be forced out of the corps by such a discharge.

Lieutenant Robert Ballard had initiated this lawsuit bcause, pursuant to § 6382(a), he was ordered discharged from the navy after only nine years of service as an officer. He contended that this rule amounted to sheer sex discrimination because, had he been female, he would have been allowed thirteen years of service. In his particular case, this time disparity had substantial financial repercussions; if he were allowed to stay in the service for four more years, he would have been entitled to a lifetime pension (since he had put in seven additional years as an enlisted man).

The district court had issued an injunction forbidding the navy to discharge Ballard until he had accumulated thirteen years of commissioned service, on the grounds that *Frontiero* had prohibited legislation treating differently "men and women who are similarly situated." In its reasoning, the district court had asserted that fiscal and administrative convenience was not a constitutionally adequate grounds to justify this sex-based discrimination (citing *Reed* and *Frontiero*).

The Supreme Court, however, lifted the injunction and declared the statutory scheme constitutional. The five-justice majority found that the statutes promoted more substantial goals than administrative or fiscal convenience. This majority employed the language of a "rationality" test in discussing this particular sex discrimination, yet their acknowledgments that "administrative convenience" and "archaic generalizations" would be inadequate to justify sex discrimination hinted, at least, of a test stiffer than the mere "rationality" test. In short, *Schlesinger v. Ballard* did little to clarify the doctrinal confusion wrought by *Reed*, *Frontiero*, and *Kahn*. Here is the Court's explanation:

Schlesinger v. Ballard, 419 U.S. 498 (1975)

MR. JUSTICE STEWART delivered the opinion of the Court.

. . .

I

At the base of the system governing the promotion and attrition of male line officers in the Navy is a congressional designation of the authorized number of the Navy's enlisted personnel, and a correlated limitation upon the number of active line officers as a percentage of that figure. Congress has also established the ratio of distribution of line officers in the several grades above lieutenant in fixed proportions to the total number of line officers.

. . .

Because the Navy has a pyramidal organizational structure, fewer officers are needed at each higher rank than were needed in the rank below. In the absence of some mandatory attrition of naval officers, the result would be stagnation of promotion of younger officers and disincentive to naval service. If the officers who failed to be promoted remained in the service, the promotion of younger officers through the ranks would be retarded. Accordingly, a basic "up or out" philosophy was developed to maintain effective leadership by heightening competition for the higher ranks while providing junior officers with incentive and opportunity for promotion. It is for this reason, and not merely for administrative or fiscal policy considerations, that § 6382(a) requires that lieutenants be discharged when they are "considered as having failed of selection for promotion to the grade of lieutenant commander . . . for the second time." Similar selection-out rules apply to officers in different ranks who are twice passed over for promotion.

. . . Section 6401 was initially intended approximately to equate the length of service of women officers before mandatory discharge for want of promotion with that of male lieutenants discharged under § 6382(a).[9] Subsequently, however, Congress specifically recognized that the provisions of § 6401 would probably result in longer tenure for women lieutenants than for male lieutenants under § 6382. When it enacted legislation eliminating many of the former restrictions on women officers' participation in the naval service in 1967, Congress expressly left undisturbed the 13-year tenure provision of § 6401. And both the House and Senate Reports observed that the attrition provisions governing women line officers would parallel "present provisions with respect to male officers except that the *discharge of male officers probably occurs about 2 years earlier.*" S. Rep. No. 676, [90th Cong., 1st Sess.,] at 12; H.R. Rep. No. 216, 90th Cong., 1st Sess., at 17. (Emphasis added.)

II

It is against this background that we must decide whether, agreeably to the Due Process Clause of the Fifth Amendment, the Congress may accord to women naval officers a 13-year tenure of commissioned service under § 6401 before mandatory discharge for want of promotion, while requiring under § 6382(a) the mandatory discharge of male lieutenants who have been

---

9. . . . [A] male line officer who had achieved the rank of lieutenant would typically have completed 12 years of service before being considered for the rank of lieutenant commander, and would have completed 13 years of service before being passed over twice for promotion to the grade of lieutenant commander.

twice passed over for promotion but who, like Ballard, may have had less than 13 years of commissioned service. In arguing that Congress has acted unconstitutionally, the appellee relies primarily upon the Court's recent decisions in *Frontiero v. Richardson*, 411 U.S. 677, and *Reed v. Reed*, 404 U.S. 71. . . .

In both *Reed* and *Frontiero* the challenged classifications based on sex were premised on overbroad generalizations that could not be tolerated under the Constitution. In *Reed*, the assumption underlying the Idaho statute was that men would generally be better estate administrators than women. In *Frontiero*, the assumption underlying the federal armed services benefit statutes was that female spouses of servicemen would normally be dependent upon their husbands, while male spouses of servicewomen would not.

In contrast, the different treatment of men and women naval officers under §§ 6401 and 6382 reflects, not archaic and overbroad generalization, but, instead, the demonstrable fact that male and female line officers in the Navy are not similarly situated with respect to opportunities for professional service. The appellee has not challenged the current restrictions on women officers' participation in combat and in most sea duty. Specifically, "women may not be assigned to duty in aircraft that are engaged in combat missions nor may they be assigned to duty on vessels of the Navy other than hospital ships and transports." 10 U.S.C. § 6015. Thus, in competing for promotion, female lieutenants will not generally have compiled records of seagoing service comparable to those of male lieutenants. In enacting and retaining § 6401, Congress may thus quite rationally have believed that women line officers had less opportunity for promotion than did their male counterparts, and that a longer period of tenure for women officers would,

therefore, be consistent with the goal to provide women officers with "fair and equitable career advancement programs." H.R. Rep. No. 216, *supra*, at 5. *Cf. Kahn v. Shevin*, 416 U.S. 351.[12]

The complete rationality of this legislative classification is underscored by the fact that in corps where male and female lieutenants are similarly situated, Congress has not differentiated between them with

12. The dissenting opinion argues that, in retaining § 6401 in 1967, Congress may not have intended to give a longer tenure to women line officers than to their male counterparts, because "it is plausible to conclude that Congress continued to believe, as it had in 1948, that the separation provisions for men and women would, given the opportunity to work properly, result in equal average tenure for both sexes." This conclusion cannot, however, be reconciled with Congress' recognition that mandatory retirement provisions for women line officers "parallel present provisions with respect to male officers *except that the discharge of male officers probably occurs about 2 years earlier.*" . . . A major factor prompting the 1967 amendments was Congress' express concern that unless restrictions on promotions of women naval officers were lifted, the operation of § 6401 would cause excessive forced retirement of women lieutenants. In discussing the problem, the House Report explicitly described the 13-year provision:

"A particularly severe problem of promotion stagnation exists among WAVE officers in the Navy. The present grade limitations on promotion of WAVE officers to the grades of commander-lieutenant commander have so reduced the vacancies that the Navy will be forced to discharge most regular WAVE lieutenants when they reach their 13th year of service if relief is not provided." H.R. Rep. No. 216, *supra*, at 8.

It is thus clear that Congress in 1967 [after "relief" was provided by expanding the promotional opportunities available to women] intentionally retained the 13-year tenure provision of § 6401, and did so with specific knowledge that it gave women line officers a longer tenure than their male counterparts.

respect to tenure. . . . These include officers in the medical, dental, judge advocate general, and medical service corps. Conversely, active male lieutenants who are members of the Nurse Corps, like female lieutenants in that corps, are within the ambit of . . . a 13-year tenure provision like § 6401.

In both *Reed* and *Frontiero* the reason asserted to justify the challenged gender-based classifications was administrative convenience, and that alone. Here, on the contrary, the operation of the statutes in question results in a flow of promotions commensurate with the Navy's current needs and serves to motivate qualified commissioned officers to so conduct themselves that they may realistically look forward to higher levels of command. . . . The responsibility for determining how best our armed forces shall attend to th[eir] business rests with Congress, *see* U.S. Const. art. I, § 8, cls. 12–14, and with the President. *See* U.S. Const. art II, § 2, cl. 1. We cannot say that, in exercising its broad constitutional power here, Congress has violated the Due Process Clause of the Fifth Amendment.[13]

The judgment is *Reversed.*

---

13. We observe that because of the restrictions that were removed from women officers' participation in naval service in 1967, *see* Act of November 8, 1967, 81 Stat. 374, S. Rep. No. 676, [*supra*], more opportunity has become available for women officers. We are told by the Solicitor General that since 1967, the Secretary of the Navy has implemented a program for acceleration of women officers' promotion and that today women are being considered for promotion within the same time periods as are men. Apparently believing that the need for a tenure differential has subsided, the Department of Defense has submitted a bill to Congress that would substitute for § 6401 the same rule that governs male lieutenants. . . .

Mr. Justice Brennan, with Mr. Justice Douglas and Mr. Justice Marshall, dissenting.

The Court concludes that the statutory scheme which results in different periods of tenure for male and female line lieutenants of the Navy does not contravene the Due Process Clause of the Fifth Amendment because "Congress may . . . quite rationally have believed that women line officers had less opportunity for promotion than did their male counterparts, and that a longer period of tenure for women officers would, therefore, be consistent with the goal to provide woman officers with "fair and equitable career advancement programs.'" *Ante.* I believe, however, that a legislative classification that is premised solely upon gender must be subjected to close judicial scrutiny. *Frontiero v. Richardson,* 411 U.S. 677 (1973); *Kahn v. Shevin,* 416 U.S. 351 (1974) (Brennan, J., dissenting). Such suspect classifications can be sustained only if the Government demonstrates that the classification serves compelling interests that cannot be otherwise achieved. Here, the Government as much as concedes that the gender-based distinctions in separation provisions for Navy officers fulfill no compelling purpose.

Further, the Court goes far to conjure up a legislative purpose which *may* have underlay the gender-based distinction here attacked. I find nothing in the statutory scheme or the legislative history to support the supposition that Congress intended, by assuring women but not men line lieutenants in the Navy a 13-year tenure, to com-

---

These developments no more than reinforce the view that it is for Congress, and not for the courts, to decide when the policy-goals sought to be served by § 6401 are no longer necessary to the Navy's officer promotion and attrition program.

pensate women for other forms of disadvantage visited upon them by the Navy.[1] Thus, the gender-based classification of which respondent complains is not related, rationally or otherwise, to any legitimate legislative purpose fairly to be inferred from the statutory scheme of its history, and cannot be sustained.

I

. . . Congress' original purpose in enacting slightly different separation provisions for men and women is quite certain—to create the *same* tenure in years for women lieutenants as for the average male lieutenant before involuntary separation was permitted.

However, for reasons not entirely clear upon the record in this case, the promotion zone system for men did not, as administered by the Navy, result in the normal 13-year tenure for men before involuntary separation. . . . Rather, in 1967 the normal tenure for men seems to have been about 11 years, and in 1972, when respondent was due for discharge, it was eight or nine years.

In 1967, Congress decided to eliminate many of the provisions restricting career opportunities for women. In doing so it wished, as the Court notes, to provide women with "fair and equitable career advancement programs." H.R. Rep. No. 216, *supra*, at 5. However, contrary to the Court's

assumption, Congress determined to achieve this goal not by providing special compensatory treatment for women, but by removing most of the restrictions upon them and then subjecting them to the same provisions generally governing men. H.R. Rep. No. 216, *supra*, at 3; S. Rep. No. 676, *supra*, at 2.

First, the entire structure of the 1967 Act is directed toward assimilating as much as possible the promotion structure for women line officers to that of men. . . . These additions make the retention of thirteen year tenure for women line lieutenants somewhat anomalous, since [certain phrases in them now] . . . appear to have no function. . . . Thus, as the hesitant language the Court uses in describing Congress' possible compensatory purpose recognizes, it is impossible to divine from the structure of the Act itself a reason for retaining the 13-year tenure for women but not for men.

Second, the legislative history of the 1967 Act makes quite clear that Congress' purpose in retaining the 13-year tenure for women line lieutenants was not to take account of the limited opportunities available to women in the Navy. Congress explicitly recognized that in some instances involuntary retirement and separation provisions "permit women to remain on active duty for longer periods than male officers." It believed that "[u]nder current circumstances, *there is no logical basis for these differences.*" S. Rep. No. 216, *supra*, at 2 (Emphasis supplied.) *See* H.R. Report 216, *supra*, at 2–3; *Hearings, Senate Committee on Armed Services on H.R. 4772, 4903, 5894,* 90th Cong., 1st Sess. 41 (1967). The 1967 Act was to "apply the standard attrition provisions of male officers promotion and retirement laws to women officers. The *only* exception to this would be the selective continuation of nurses." H.R. Rep. No. 216, *supra*, at 3. (Emphasis supplied.) *See* S.

---

1. Indeed, I find quite troublesome the notion that a gender-based difference in treatment can be justified by another, broader, gender-based difference in treatment imposed directly and currently by the Navy itself. While it is true that the restrictions upon women officers' opportunities for professional service are not here directly under attack, they are obviously implicated on the Court's chosen ground for decision, and the Court ought at least to consider whether they may be valid before sustaining a provision it conceives to be based upon them.

Rep. No. 676, *supra*, at 2. In light of these statements, Congress could not have had the purpose of compensating women line officers for their inferior position in the Navy by retaining longer tenure periods for women.

Moreover, the legislative history is replete with indications of a decision not to give women any special advantage. "The purpose of the legislation has been limited to the removal of arbitrary restrictions. No effort has been made to provide special assurances to women officers, and none is recommended." Letter from General Counsel, Department of Defense, in S. Rep. No. 676, *supra*, at 5; H.R. Rep. No. 216, *supra*, at 5. "The purpose of the bill is to create *parity* only in respect to recognizing merit and performance." H.R. Rep. No. 216, *supra*, at 9. *See* S. Rep. No. 676, *supra*, at 3. (Emphasis supplied.)

To infer a determination purposely to perpetuate a longer retention period for women line officers is, therefore, entirely to misconceive Congress' perception of the problem and of the proper solution. While the reason for the failure to revise §§ 6382 and 6401 is not clear, it is certainly plausible to conclude that Congress continued to believe, as it had in 1948, that the separation provisions for men and women would, given the opportunity to work properly, result in equal average tenure for both sexes.

II

Given this analysis of the relationship between § 6382 and § 6401, the difference in tenure which resulted . . . from the operation of these sections manifestly serves no overriding or compelling governmental interest. Indeed, the Government concedes as much in discussing proposed H.R. 12405, 93rd Cong., 2d Sess., §§ 2(5) and 4(18), to which the Court refers: "The Department of Defense considers that the separate rule for women, while serving a *le-*

gitimate governmental purpose . . . is on balance no longer *needed* as a matter of military personnel policy." Brief for Appellant, at 18. (Emphasis supplied.) Since the executive department most intimately concerned with the promotion policy in the Navy can perceive no need for the gender-based classification under attack, the interest served by the classification, if any, can hardly be overriding or compelling.

Further, while I believe that "[p]roviding special benefits for a needy segment of society long the victim of discrimination and neglect" can serve "the compelling . . . interest of achieving equality for such groups," *Kahn v. Shevin, supra,* 416 U.S., at 358–59 (BRENNAN, J., dissenting), I could not sustain this statutory scheme even if I accepted the Court's supposition that such a purpose lay behind this classification. Contrary to the Court's intimation, *ante,* women do not compete directly with men for promotion in the Navy. Rather, selection boards for women are separately convened, 10 U.S.C. § 5704, the number of women officers to be selected for promotion is separately determined, 10 U.S.C. § 5760, promotion zones for women are separately designated, 10 U.S.C. § 5764, and women's fitness for promotion is judged as compared to other women, 10 U.S.C. § 5707. In this situation, it is hard to see how women are disadvantaged . . . for promotion by the fact that their duties in the Navy are limited, or how increasing their tenure before separation for non-promotion is necessary to compensate for other disadvantage.

III

The Court suggests no purpose other than compensation for disadvantages of women which might justify this gender-based classification. I agree that the "up and out" philosophy "was developed to maintain effective leadership by heightening competition for the higher ranks while providing junior officers with incentive and opportunity for promotion." *Ante.* But the purpose behind the "up and out" philosophy applies as well to women as to men. The issue here is not whether the treatment accorded either women or men under the statutory scheme would, if applied even-handedly to both sexes, forward a legitimate or compelling state interest, but whether the *differences* in the provisions applicable to men and women can be justified by a governmental purpose.

For this same reason, the invocation of the deference due Congress in determining how best to assure the readiness of our Armed Forces for battle cannot settle the issue before us. As *Frontiero v. Richardson, supra,* illustrates, the fact that an equal protection claim arises from statutes concerning military personnel policy does not itself mandate deference to the congressional determination, at least if the sex-based classification is not relevant to and justifed by the military purposes.

Thus, the validity of the statutory scheme must stand or fall upon the Court's asserted compensatory goal. Yet, as the analysis in part I, *supra,* demonstrates, this purpose was not in fact behind either the original enactment of § 6401 or its retention in 1967. . . . Never, to my knowledge, have we endeavored to sustain a statute upon a supposition about the legislature's purpose in enacting it when the asserted justification can be shown conclusively not to have underlay the classification in any way.[11] . . .

MR. JUSTICE WHITE, dissenting.

Agreeing for the most part with MR. JUSTICE BRENNAN's dissenting opinion, I also dissent from the judgment of the Court.

---

11. Indeed, to do so is to undermine the very premises of deference to legislative determination. If a legislature, considering the competing factors, determines that it is wise policy to treat two groups of people differently in pursuit of a certain goal, courts often defer to that legislative determination. But when a legislature has decided not to pursue a certain goal, upholding a statute on the basis of that goal is not properly deference to a legislative decision at all; it is deference to a decision which the legislature could have made but did not.

CASE QUESTIONS

1. Justice Brennan points out that in competitions for promotions, women officers compete only with other women, and he concludes from this that the navy has no need to provide compensatory time for women to accumulate promotion-worthy career records. Even if women are being compared only with other women, would it not be true that naval officers who are denied combat-duty opportunities take a longer time to accumulate a record of notable achievements? Is this irrelevant, since a fixed number of women officers (those who have the best records as compared with other women) is promoted, regardless of their absolute level of achievement? Might the navy have a legitimate interest in assuring that its noncombat officers who are promoted do receive ade-

quate time to build up respectable ca- reer records, which appear worthy of promotion?

2. Brennan persuasively uses the state- ment by a congressional committee that *"under current circumstances,* there is no logical basis for these differences" (1967), and the statement by the De- fense Department (1975) that the sepa- rate treatment of women serves a *"legiti- mate"* purpose but *"is on balance no longer*

needed." (Emphasis added.) Could the 1967 statement have referred to the an- ticipated changes to be derived from the law then being enacted? Might Con- gress also have believed in 1974–1975 that the residuum of the past restric- tions on women naval officers' oppor- tunities for promotion had not yet been fully obliterated by the 1967 changes, despite the Defense Department's asser- tions? (See also footnote 13 of the major- ity opinion.)

A week after the *Schlesinger* decision, the Court produced a reexamination of the issue it had dealt with in *Hoyt v. Florida.* This time the state involved was Louisiana and the person complaining about the no-women jury was a man, Billy Taylor; but the state law at issue was identical to the one that the Supreme Court had upheld only fourteen years earlier in *Hoyt.* An all-male jury had found Billy Taylor guilty of aggravated kidnapping. Every woman in Louisiana was excluded from jury duty unless she filed a written affidavit declaring her desire to serve. As of 1970, Louisiana was the only state that still retained this kind of statute; Florida abandoned its "volunteers only" approach to jury duty for women back in 1967.[86]

Only three years earlier, in 1972, the Supreme Court had refused to recon- sider the *Hoyt* precedent in a Louisiana case similar to Taylor's; at that time they had explained, "Nothing in past adjudication [indicates] that [a male] petitioner has been denied equal protection by the alleged exclusion of women from grand jury service."[87] The *Frontiero* decision, however, made it much more difficult for the Court to ignore the implications of *Reed.* So in *Taylor* the Court admits that "past adjudications" had indeed wrought significant changes since 1961.

Interestingly, while the Court solidified in its opposition to sex discrimina- tion in the law, the public sentiment against such discrimination seemed to be softening. The political momentum of the ERA had slowed to a crawl by Janu- ary 1975.

At the end of 1973, in a mere nineteen months, the ERA had been ratified by thirty states. During the year that elapsed from then until *Taylor v. Louisiana* was handed down in January 1975, the pro-ERA forces garnered only three of the eight more states needed for ratification.[88] And in 1973 and 1974 two state legis- latures voted to rescind their earlier ratification. Although the legal force of such rescissions is likely to be nil, the mood of the country seemed to be shifting. The passage of the ERA looked far less certain in early 1975 than it had in January

1973 (the time of *Frontiero*). Nonetheless, the Supreme Court's mood remained steady. Just as they had in *Frontiero*, the Supreme Court in *Taylor v. Louisiana* rejected by an 8–1 vote the statutory sex discrimination under challenge. (Justice Rehnquist once again was the lone dissenter.)

It may seem strange that a man would complain about the absence of women on a jury, and, indeed, it would seem stranger to people familiar with the law than to laypeople. For there is a fixed principle of law that only parties who have a personal stake in the outcome of a particular decision—who actually stand to gain or lose, depending on what the judge says—are allowed to challenge laws in the federal courts. This status of having a stake in the decision is called "standing," and one might well wonder whether Billy Taylor had standing, as a man, to challenge the exclusion of women from juries.

Fortunately for Billy Taylor, a couple of years before his case reached the Supreme Court, the Court had held that a white man had standing to challenge the exclusion of blacks from juries. Still, the message of that precedent, *Peters v. Kiff*,[89] as it would apply to males challenging female jury exclusion was not clear; the six-judge majority of *Peters* had split in half over the reasons why a white could challenge the exclusion of blacks from juries. Three of the justices[90] based their decision on the narrow grounds that it was a federal crime for any official, even a state or local one, to exclude blacks from juries; they concluded, therefore, that to convict anyone in such an illegal trial procedure would violate "due process of law." Because no comparable statute made it a crime to exclude women from juries, this line of reasoning would help neither the women of Louisiana nor Billy Taylor. The other three justices of the *Peters* majority, however, the ones whose views constituted the "Court" opinion,[91] espoused a line of reasoning that directly and explicitly applied to people in Billy Taylor's situation.

When the Court majority divides into two plurality opinions, as it did in *Peters* the Court opinion does not have the same binding force that it would if a majority of justices concurred in it. Still, the reasoning provides a line of argument that can be cited by future courts who want to hark back to it for the tone of legitimacy it provides. And the *Taylor v. Louisiana* majority cites the three-justice Court opinion from *Peters* more than once.

The opinion from *Peters*, authored by Justice Marshall, announced an all but open break with the viewpoint of the *Hoyt* decision. Marshall stated, first, that "the exclusion of a discernible class from jury service injures not only those defendants who belong to the excluded class, but other defendants as well, in that it destroys the possibility that the jury will reflect a representative cross section of the community."[92] He went on to argue that the Fourteenth Amendment's guarantee of due process of law includes trial by a competent and impartial tribunal.[93] This protection is so important that even the appearance of bias or partiality in the tribunal is forbidden.[94] This list of premises laid the groundwork for Marshall's conclusion (reprinted at length in footnote 12 of the *Taylor* decision) that the systematic exclusion of a "substantial and identifiable class of citizens" from jury service creates so much appearance of bias and probability of bias that such exclusion is forbidden by the due process clause.

The requirement that trials be decided impartially was a longstanding aspect of due process. One additional change since the *Hoyt* decision was that, whereas Hoyt had challenged all-male juries with the claim that such juries conflicted with the generally worded guarantees of "due process of law" and "equal protection of the law," a 1968 case, *Duncan v. Louisiana*,[95] had established that "due process of law" itself implies the *specific* idea of the right to trial by an impartial jury in any criminal prosecution. (This idea is spelled out in the Sixth Amendment, but as written there it applies only to the federal government.) In the 1975 case of *Taylor v. Louisiana*, then, the Supreme Court was interpreting not just the general phrases "due process" and "equal protection" but also the more precise term "an impartial jury." Whether this difference was substantial enough to explain the Court's explicit overruling of *Hoyt* is a question better addressed after a reading of the Court's discussion of it.

Another remarkable aspect of this decision is the Court's surprising rediscovery of *Ballard v. United States*.[96] That case predated *Hoyt* by fifteen years and was completely ignored by all the *Hoyt* justices. Suddenly, it has been unearthed to become a major building-block in Marshall's reasoning, and used to establish that juries cannot be representative cross-sections of the community if women are excluded from them.

Billy Taylor's appeal of his conviction on the grounds that the Louisiana jury system was unconstitutional had been rejected by two state courts before it reached the U.S. Supreme Court.

Billy Taylor v. Louisiana, 419 U.S. 522 (1975)

MR. JUSTICE WHITE delivered the opinion of the Court.

. . . [T]he Louisiana Code of Criminal Procedure provided that a woman should not be selected for jury service unless she had previously filed a written declaration of her desire to be subject to jury service. The constitutionality of these provisions is the issue of this case.

I

. . . [T]he Louisiana jury selection system deprived appellant of his Sixth and Fourteenth Amendment right to an impartial jury trial. . . . In consequence, appellant's conviction must be reversed.

II

The Louisiana jury selection system does not disqualify women from jury service, but in operation its conceded systematic impact is that only a very few women, grossly disproportionate to the number of eligible women in the community, are called for jury service. In this case, no women were on the venire from which the petit jury was drawn. The issue we have, therefore, is whether a jury selection system which operates to exclude from jury service an identifiable class of citizens constituting 53 percent of eligible jurors in the community comports with the Sixth and Fourteenth Amendments.

. . . Taylor's claim is that he was constitutionally entitled to a jury drawn from a venire constituting a fair cross section of the community and that the jury that tried him was not such a jury by reason of the exclusion of women. Taylor was not a member of the excluded class; but there is no rule that claims such as Taylor presents may be made only by those defendants who are members of the group excluded from jury service. *Peters v. Kiff*, 407 U.S. 493 (1972). . . .

III

The background against which this case must be decided includes our holding in *Duncan v. Louisiana*, 391 U.S. 145 (1968), that the Sixth Amendment's provision for jury trial is made binding on the States by virtue of the Fourteenth Amendment. Our inquiry is whether the presence of a fair cross section of the community on venires, panels or lists from which petit juries are drawn is essential to the fulfillment of the Sixth Amendment's guarantee of an impartial jury trial in criminal prosecutions.

The Court's prior cases are instructive. Both in the course of exercising its supervisory powers over trials in federal courts and *in the constitutional context, the Court has unambiguously declared that the American concept of the jury trial contemplates a jury drawn from a fair cross section of the community.* [Emphasis added.] A unanimous Court stated in *Smith v. Texas*, 311 U.S. 128, 130 (1940), that "[i]t is part of the established tradition in the use of juries as instruments of public justice that the jury be a body truly representative of the community." To exclude racial groups from jury service was said to be

"at war with our basic concepts of a democratic society and a representative government." A state jury system that resulted in systematic exclusion of Negroes as jurors was therefore held to violate the Equal Protection Clause of the Fourteenth Amendment. *Glasser v. United States*, 315 U.S. 60, 85 (1942), in the context of a federal criminal case and the Sixth Amendment's jury trial requirement, stated that "our notions of what a proper jury is have developed in harmony with our basic concepts of a democratic system and representative government," and repeated the Court's understanding that the jury "be a body truly representative of the community . . . and not the organ of any special group or class."

A federal conviction by a jury from which women had been excuded, although eligible for service under state law, was reviewed in *Ballard v. United States*, 329 U.S. 187 (1946). Noting the federal statutory "design to make a jury a cross section of the community" and the fact that women had been excluded, the Court exercised its supervisory powers over the federal courts and reversed the conviction. In *Brown v. Allen*, 344 U.S. 443, 474 (1953), the Court declared that "[o]ur duty to protect the federal constitutional rights of all does not mean we must or should impose on states our conception of the proper source of jury lists, so long as the source reasonably reflects a cross-section of the population suitable in character and intelligence for that civic duty."

Some years later in *Carter v. Jury Comm'n*, 396 U.S. 320, 330 (1970), the Court observed that the exclusion of Negroes from jury service because of their race "contravenes the very idea of a jury—'a body truly representative of the community. . . .'" (Quoting from *Smith v. Texas, supra*.) At about the same time it was contended that the use of six-man juries in noncapital criminal cases violated the Sixth

Amendment for failure to provide juries drawn from a cross section of the community, *Williams v. Florida*, 399 U.S. 78 (1970). In the course of rejecting that challenge, we said that the number of persons on the jury should "be large enough to promote group deliberation, free from outside attempts at intimidation, and to provide a fair possibility for obtaining a representative cross-section of the community." *Id.* at 100. In like vein, in *Apodaca v. Oregon*, 406 U.S. 404, 410–11 (1970) (plurality opinion), it was said that "a jury will come to such a [commonsense] judgment as long as it consists of a group of laymen representative of a cross section of the community who have the duty and the opportunity to deliberate . . . on the question of a defendant's guilt." Similarly, three Justices in *Peters v. Kiff*, 407 U.S., at 500, observed that the Sixth Amendment comprehended a fair possibility for obtaining a jury constituting a representative cross section of the community.

The unmistakable import of this Court's opinions, at least since 1941, *Smith v. Texas, supra* and not repudiated by intervening decisions, is that the selection of a petit jury from a representative cross section of the community is an essential component of the Sixth Amendment right to a jury trial. [Emphasis added.] Recent federal legislation governing jury selection within the federal court system has a similar thrust. . . . Committee Reports of both the House and the Senate recognized that the jury plays a political function in the administration of the law and that the requirement of a jury's being chosen from a fair cross section of the community is fundamental to the American system of justice. Debate on the floors of the House and Senate on the Act invoked the Sixth Amendment, the Constitution generally, and prior decisions of this Court in support of the Act.

We accept the fair cross-section re-

quirement as fundamental to the jury trial guaranteed by the Sixth Amendment and are convinced that the requirement has solid foundation. The purpose of a jury is to guard against the exercise of arbitrary power—to make available the common-sense judgment of the community as a hedge against the overzealous or mistaken prosecutor and in preference to the professional or perhaps over-conditioned or biased response of a judge. *Duncan v. Louisiana*, 391 U.S., at 155–56. This prophylactic vehicle is not provided if the jury pool is made up of only special segments of the populace or if large, distinctive groups are excluded from the pool. Community participation in the administration of the criminal law, moreover, is not only consistent with our democratic heritage but is also critical to public confidence in the fairness of the criminal justice system. Restricting jury service to only special groups or excluding identifiable segments playing major roles in the community cannot be squared with the constitutional concept of jury trial. "Trial by jury presupposes a jury drawn from a pool broadly representative of the community as well as impartial in a specific case. . . . The broad representative character of the jury should be maintained, partly as assurance of a diffused impartiality and partly because sharing in the administration of justice is a phase of civic responsibility." *Thiel v. Southern Pacific Co.*, 328 U.S. 217, 227 (1946) (Frankfurter, J., dissenting).

IV

We are also persuaded that the fair cross section requirement is violated by the systematic exclusion of women, who in the judicial district involved here amounted to 53 percent of the citizens eligible for jury service. This conclusion necessarily entails the judgment that women are sufficiently numerous and distinct from men that if they are systematically eliminated from jury panels, the Sixth Amendment's fair cross section requirement cannot be satisfied. This very matter was debated in *Ballard v. United States, supra*. Positing the fair cross-section rule—there said to be a statutory one—the Court concluded that the systematic exclusion of women was unacceptable. The dissenting view that an all-male panel drawn from various groups in the community would be as truly representative as if women were included, was firmly rejected:

> The thought is that the factors which tend to influence the action of women are the same as those which influence the action of men—personality, background, economic status—and not sex. Yet it is not enough to say that women when sitting as jurors neither act nor tend to act as a class. . . . [I]f the shoe were on the other foot, who would claim that a jury was truly representative of the community if all men were intentionally and systematically excluded from the panel? The truth is that the two sexes are not fungible; a community made up exclusively of one is different from a community composed of both; the subtle interplay of influence one on the other is among the imponderables. To insulate the courtroom from either may not in a given case make an iota of difference. Yet a flavor, a distinct quality is lost if either sex is excluded. The exclusion of one may indeed make the jury less representative of the community than would be true if an economic or racial group were excluded. (329 U.S., at 193–94[12].)

12. Compare the opinion of MARSHALL, J., joined by DOUGLAS and STEWART, JJ., in *Peters v. Kiff*, 407 U.S. 493, 502–4 (1972): "These principles compel the conclusion that a State cannot,

In this respect, we agree with the Court in *Ballard*: If the fair cross-section rule is to govern the selection of juries, as we have concluded it must, women cannot be systematically excluded from jury pan-

---

consistent with due process, subject a defendant to indictment or trial by a jury that has been selected in an arbitrary and discriminatory manner, in violation of the Constitution and laws of the United States. Illegal and unconstitutional jury selection procedures cast doubt on the integrity of the whole judicial process. They create the appearance of bias . . . , and they increase the risk of actual bias as well.

. . .

"But the exclusion from jury service of a substantial and identifiable class of citizens has a potential impact that is too subtle and too pervasive to admit of confinement to particular issues or particular cases.

. . .

"Moreover, we are unwilling to make the assumption that the exclusion of Negroes has relevance only for issues involving race. When any large and identifiable segment of the community is excluded from jury service, the effect is to remove from the jury room qualities of human nature and varieties of human experience, the range of which is unknown and perhaps unknowable. It is not necessary to assume that the excluded group will consistently vote as a class in order to conclude, as we do, that its exclusion deprives the jury of a perspective on human events that may have unsuspected importance in any case that may be presented." (Footnote omitted.)

Controlled studies of the performance of women as jurors conducted subsequent to the Court's decision in *Ballard* have concluded that women bring to juries their own perspectives and values that influence both jury deliberation and result. *See generally* Rudolph, *Women on Juries—Voluntary or Compulsory?*, 44 J. Amer. Jud. Soc. 206 (1961); 55 J. Sociology & Social Research 442 (1971); 3 J. Applied Soc. Psych. 267 (1973); 19 Sociometry 3 (1956).

els from which petit juries are drawn. This conclusion is consistent with the current judgment of the country, now evidenced by legislative or constitutional provisions in every State and at the federal level qualifying women for jury service.[13]

V

There remains the argument that women as a class serve a distinctive role in society and that jury service would so substantially interfere with that function that the State has ample justification for excluding women from service unless they volunteer, even though the result is that almost all jurors are men. It is true that *Hoyt v. Florida*, 368 U.S. 57 (1961), held that such a system did not deny due process of law or equal protection of the laws because there was a sufficiently rational basis for such an exemption.[15] But *Hoyt* did not involve a de-

fendant's Sixth Amendment right to a jury drawn from a fair cross section of the community and the prospect of depriving him of that right if women as a class are systematically excluded. The right to a proper jury cannot be overcome on merely rational grounds.[16] There must be weightier reasons if a distinctive class representing 53 percent of the eligible jurors is for all practical purposes to be excluded from jury service. No such basis has been tendered here.

The States are free to grant exemptions from jury service to individuals in case of special hardship or incapacity and to those engaged in particular occupations the uninterrupted performance of which is critical to the community's welfare. *Rawlins v. Georgia*, 201 U.S. 638 (1906). It would not appear that such exemptions would pose substantial threats that the remaining pool of jurors would not be representative of the community. A system excluding all women, however, is a wholly different matter. It is untenable to suggest these days that it would be a special hardship for each and every woman to perform jury service or that society cannot spare any women from their present duties.[17] This may be the

---

13. This is a relatively modern development. Under the English common law, women, with the exception of the trial of a narrow class of cases, were not considered to be qualified for jury service by virtue of the doctrine of *propter defectum sexus*, a "defect of sex." 3 W. Blackstone, *Commentaries* 362 (Lewis ed. 1897). This common law rule was made statutory by Parliament in 1870 . . . , and then rejected by Parliament in 1919. . . . In this country women were disqualified by state law to sit as jurors until the end of the 19th century. They were first deemed qualified for jury service by a State in 1898. 35 Utah Rev. Stat. Ann. § 1297. Today, women are qualified as jurors in all the States. The jury service statutes and rules of most States do not on their face extend to women the type of exemption presently before the Court, although the exemption provisions of some States do appear to treat men and women differently in certain respects.

15. The state interest, as articulated by the Court, was based on the assumption that "woman is still regarded as the center of home and family life." *Hoyt v. Florida*, 368 U.S., at 62. Louisiana makes a similar argument here, stating that its grant of an automatic exemption from

jury service to females involves only the State's attempt "to regulate and provide stability to the state's own idea of family life."

16. In *Hoyt*, the Court determined both that the underlying classification was rational and that the State's proffered rationale for extending this exemption to females without family responsibilities was justified by administrative convenience. 386 U.S., at 62–63.

17. In *Hoyt v. Florida, supra*, the Court placed some emphasis on the notion, advanced by the State there and by Louisiana here in support of the rationality of its statutory scheme, that "woman is still regarded as the center of home and family life." 368 U.S., at 62. Statistics compiled by the Department of Labor indicate that in October 1974, 54.2 percent of all woman between 18 and 64 years of age were in the labor

case with many, and it may be burdensome to sort out those who should not be exempted from those who should serve. But that task is performed in the case of men, and the administrative convenience in dealing with women as a class is insufficient justification for diluting the quality of community judgment represented by the jury in criminal trials.

VI

Although this judgment may appear a foregone conclusion from the pattern of some of the Court's cases over the past 30 years, as well as from legislative developments at both federal and state levels, it is nevertheless true that until today no case had squarely held that the exclusion of women from jury venires deprives a criminal defendant of his Sixth Amendment right to trial by an impartial jury drawn from a fair cross section of the community. It is apparent that the first Congress did not

perceive the Sixth Amendment as requiring women on criminal jury panels; for the direction of the First Judiciary Act of 1789 was that federal jurors were to have the qualifications required by the States in which the federal court was sitting and at the time women were disqualified under state law in every State. Necessarily, then, federal juries in criminal cases were all-male, and it was not until the Civil Rights Act of 1957, 71 Stat. 634, 638, 28 U.S.C. § 1861, that Congress itself provided that all citizens, with limited exceptions, were competent to sit on federal juries. Until that time, federal courts were required by statute to exclude women from jury duty in those States where women were disqualified. Utah was the first State to qualify women for juries; it did so in 1898, n.13, *supra*. Moreover, *Hoyt v. Florida* was decided and has stood for the proposition that, even if women as a group could not be constitutionally disqualified from jury service, there was ample reason to treat all women differently from men for the purpose of jury service and to exclude them unless they volunteered.[19]

---

force. United States Dept. of Labor, *Women in the Labor Force* (Oct. 1974). Additionally, in March 1974, 45 percent of women with children under the age of 18 were in the labor force; with respect to families containing children between the ages of six and 17, 67.3 percent of mothers who were widowed, divorced or separated were in the work force, while 51.2 percent of the mothers whose husbands were present in the household were in the work force. Even in family units in which the husband was present and which contained a child under three years old, 31 percent of the mothers were in the work force. United States Dept. of Labor, *Marital and Family Characteristics of the Labor Force,* Table F (March 1974). While these statistics perhaps speak more to the evolving nature of the structure of the family unit in American society than to the nature of the role played by women who happen to be members of a family unit, they certainly put to rest the suggestion that all women should be exempt from jury service based solely on their sex and the presumed role in the home.

19. *Hoyt v. Florida,* as had *Fay v. New York,* 322 U.S. 261, 289–90 (1947), also referred to the historic view that jury service could constitutionally be confined to males: "We need not, however, accept appellant's invitation to canvass in this case the continuing validity of this Court's dictum in *Strauder v. West Virginia,* 100 U.S. 303, 310, to the effect that a State may constitutionally 'confine' jury duty 'to males.' This constitutional proposition has gone unquestioned for more than eighty years in the decisions of the Court, *see Fay v. New York, supra,* at 289–90, and had been reflected, until 1957, in congressional policy respecting jury service in the federal courts themselves." . . . *See also Glasser v. United States,* 315 U.S., at 60, 64–65, 85–86 (1942).

It is most interesting to note that *Strauder v. West Virginia* itself stated that "the constitution of juries is a very essential part of the protection

Accepting as we do, however, the view that the Sixth Amendment affords the defendant in a criminal trial the opportunity to have the jury drawn from venires representative of the community, we think it is no longer tenable to hold that women as a class may be excluded or given automatic exemptions based solely on sex if the consequence is that criminal jury venires are almost totally male. To this extent we cannot follow the contrary implications of the prior cases, including *Hoyt v. Florida*. If it was ever the case that women were unqualified to sit on juries or were so situated that none of them should be required to perform jury service, that time has long since passed. If at one time it could be held that Sixth Amendment juries must be drawn from a fair cross section of the community but that this requirement permitted the almost total exclusion of women, this is not the case today. Communities differ at different times and places. What is a fair cross section at one time or place is not necessarily a fair cross section at another time or a different place. Nothing persuasive has been presented to us in this case suggesting that all-male venires in the parishes involved here are fairly representative of the local population otherwise eligible for jury service.

VII

Our holding does not augur or authorise the fashioning of detailed jury selection codes by federal courts. The fair cross-section principle must have much leeway in application. The States remain free to prescribe relevant qualifications for

their jurors and to provide reasonable exemptions so long as it may be fairly said that the jury lists or panels are representative of the community. . . .

It should also be emphasized that in holding that petit juries must be drawn from a source fairly representative of the community we impose no requirement that petit juries actually chosen must mirror the community and reflect the various distinctive groups in the population. Defendants are not entitled to a jury of any particular composition, *Fay v. New York*, 332 U.S. 261, 284 (1947); *Apodaca v. Oregon*, 406 U.S., at 413 (plurality opinion); but the jury wheels, pools of names, panels or venires from which juries are drawn must not systematically exclude distinctive groups in the community and thereby fail to be reasonably representative thereof.

The judgment of the Louisiana Supreme Court is *reversed* and the case remanded to that court for further proceedings not inconsistent with this opinion.

Mr. Justice Rehnquist, dissenting.

The Court's opinion reverses a conviction without a suggestion, much less a showing, that the appellant has been unfairly treated or prejudiced in any way by the manner in which his jury was selected. In so doing, the Court invalidates a jury selection system which it approved by a substantial majority only 12 years ago. I disagree with the Court and would affirm the judgment of the Supreme Court of Louisiana.

The majority opinion canvasses various of our jury trial cases, beginning with *Smith v. Texas*, 311 U.S. 128 (1940). Relying on carefully chosen quotations, it concludes that the "unmistakable import" of our cases is that the fair cross section requirement "is an essential component of the Sixth Amendment right to a jury trial." I disagree. Fairly read, the only "un-

---

such a mode of trial is intended to secure. The very idea of a jury is a body of men composed of the peers or equals of the person whose rights it is selected or summoned to determine; that is, of his neighbors, fellows, associates, persons having the same legal status as that which he holds." 100 U.S., at 308.

mistakable import" of those cases is that due process and equal protection prohibit jury selection systems which are likely to result in biased or impartial [sic] juries. *Smith v. Texas, supra,* concerned the equal protection claim of a Negro who was indicted by a grand jury from which Negroes had been systematically excluded. *Glasser v. United States,* 315 U.S. 60 (1942), dealt with allegations that the only women selected for jury service were members of a private organization which had conducted pro-prosecution classes for prospective jurors. *Brown v. Allen,* 344 U.S. 443 (1953), rejected the equal protection and due process contentions of several black defendants that members of their race had been discriminatorily excluded from their juries. *Carter v. Jury Comm'n,* 396 U.S. 320 (1970), similarly dealt with equal protection challenges to a jury selection system, but the persons claiming such rights were blacks who had sought to serve as jurors.

In *Hoyt v. Florida,* 368 U.S. 57 (1961), this Court gave plenary consideration to contentions that a system such as Louisiana's deprived a defendant of equal protection and due process. These contentions were rejected, despite circumstances which were much more suggestive of possible bias and prejudice than are those here— the defendant in *Hoyt* was a woman whose defense to charges of murdering her husband was that she had been driven temporarily insane by his suspected infidelity and by his rejection of her efforts at reconciliation. 368 U.S., at 58–59. The complete swing of the judicial pendulum 12 [sic] years later must depend for its validity on the proposition that during those years things have changed in constitutionally significant ways. I am not persuaded of the sufficiency of either of the majority's proffered explanations as to intervening events.

The first determinative event, in the Court's view, is *Duncan v. Louisiana,* 391

U.S. 145 (1968). Because the Sixth Amendment was there held applicable to the States, the Court feels free to dismiss *Hoyt* as a case which dealt with entirely different issues—even though in fact it presented the identical problem. But *Duncan's* rationale is a good deal less expansive than is suggested by the Court's present interpretation of that case. *Duncan* rests on the following reasoning.

The test for determining whether a right extended by the Fifth and Sixth Amendments with respect to federal criminal proceedings is also protected against state action by the Fourteenth Amendment has been phrased in a variety of ways in the opinions of this Court. The question has been asked whether a right is among those "fundamental principles of liberty and justice which lie at the base of all our civil and political institutions," *Powell v. Alabama,* 287 U.S. 45, 67 (1932); whether it is "basic in our system of jurisprudence," *In re Oliver,* 333 U.S. 257, 273 (1948); and whether it is "a fundamental right, essential to a fair trial," *Gideon v. Wainwright,* 372 U.S. 335, 342–44 (1963); *Malloy v. Hogan,* 378 U.S. 1, 6 (1964); *Pointer v. Texas,* 380 U.S. 400, 403 (1965). . . . *Because we believe that trial by jury in criminal cases is fundamental to the American scheme of justice,* we hold that the Fourteenth Amendment guarantees a right of jury trial in all criminal cases. . . . (391 U.S., at 148–49. Emphasis added.)

[This] is a sturdy test, one not readily satisfied by every discrepancy between federal and state practice. . . .

In explaining the conclusion that a jury trial is fundamental to our scheme of justice, and therefore should be required of the States, the Court pointed out that jury trial was designed to be a defense "against arbitrary law enforcement," 391 U.S., at 156, and "to prevent oppression by the Government." *Id.* at 155. The Court stated its belief that jury trial for serious offenses is "essential for preventing miscarriages of justice and for assuring that fair trials are provided for all defendants." *Id.* at 158.

I cannot conceive that today's decision is necessary to guard against oppressive or arbitrary law enforcement, or to prevent miscarriages of justice and to assure fair trials. Especially is this so when the criminal defendant involved makes no claims of prejudice or bias. The Court does accord some slight attention to justifying its ruling in terms of the basis on which the right to jury trial was read into the Fourteenth Amendment. It concludes that the jury is not effective, as a prophylaxis against arbitrary prosecutorial and judical power, if the "jury pool is made up of only special segments of the populace or if large, distinctive groups are excluded from the pool." It fails, however, to provide any satisfactory explanation of the mechanism by which the Louisiana system undermines the prophylactic role of the jury, either in general or in this case. The best it can do is to posit "a flavor, a distinct quality," which allegedly is lost if either sex is excluded. However, this "flavor" is not of such importance that the Constitution is offended if any given petit jury is not so enriched. This smacks more of mysticism than of law. The Court does not even purport to practice its mysticism in a consistent fashion— presumably doctors, lawyers, and other groups, whose frequent exemption from jury service is endorsed by the majority, also offer qualities as distinct and important as those at issue here.

In *Hoyt*, this Court considered a stronger due process claim than is before it today, but found that fundamental fairness had not been offended. I do not understand how our intervening decision in *Duncan* can support a different result. After all, *Duncan* imported the Sixth Amendment into the Due Process Clause only because, and only to the extent that, this was perceived to be required by fundamental fairness.

The second change since *Hoyt* that appears to undergird the Court's turnabout is societal in nature, encompassing both our higher degree of sensitivity to distinctions based on sex, and the "evolving nature of the structure of the family unit in American society." Op., at n.17. These are matters of degree, and it is perhaps of some significance that in 1962 Mr. Justice Harlan saw fit to refer to the "enlightened emancipation of women from the restrictions and protections of bygone years, and their entry into many parts of community life formerly considered to be reserved to men." *Hoyt, supra* 368 U.S., at 61–62. Nonetheless, it may be fair to conclude that the Louisiana system is in fact an anachronism, inappropriate at this "time or place." But surely constitutional adjudication is a more canalized function than enforcing as against the States this Court's perception of modern life.

Absent any suggestion that appellant's trial was unfairly conducted, or that its result was unreliable, I would not require Louisiana to retry him (assuming the State can once again produce its evidence and witnesses) in order to impose on him the sanctions which its laws provide.

CASE QUESTIONS

1. Is Justice White being accurate when he says that the Court's prior cases have *unambiguously* declared that a jury trial requires a "fair cross-section of the community," and that this is the *unmistakable import* of past cases? (See italicized passages of section III.) How did Justice Rehnquist manage to "mistake" their import? What motivation might White have for exaggeration?

2. White, in attempting to distinguish this case from *Hoyt*, states that "the right to a proper jury cannot be overcome on merely rational grounds." Had *Hoyt* held that the right to equal protection of the laws could be "overcome" on merely rational grounds? Is White implying that constitutional rights can be "overcome" whenever the reason is weighty enough? If not, what is he implying? If constitutional rights can be overridden whenever the government finds it necessary, what is the value of a written constitution?

3. In that part of his opinion accompanying footnote 17, White points out that it would be untenable to claim that "society cannot spare any women from their present duties" (since over 54 percent of women of working age were in the labor force in 1974). Had *Hoyt* rested on that now-untenable assumption? (In 1960 the portion in the labor force of women 16 to 65 was 38 percent.)

4. Which of the following changes since *Hoyt* seem to have most influenced the Court's turnabout?
   a) The enlarged portion of women in the labor force.
   b) The abandonment of automatic jury exemptions for women by all state legislatures by 1975.
   c) The decision in *Duncan v. Louisiana* that the right to trial by jury is a required part of "due process."
   d) The *Frontiero* and *Reed* decisions (which the Court does not mention).
   e) Changed attitudes toward women on the part of Supreme Court justices.

5. Does White imply (in the text of footnote 19) that the Court in *Hoyt* took seriously the possibility that "women as a group could not be constitutionally disqualified from jury service?" Does that seem an accurate characterization of *Hoyt?*

6. Is Justice Rehnquist persuasive in his suggestion that exempting lawyers and doctors from juries removes a "distinct quality" or "flavor" from jury deliberations in the same way that exempting women does? Does that argument tend to undermine the majority's claim in section VII of their opinion?

Although the Court in *Taylor* did not even mention whether sex is a suspect classification, and although it did not mention the *Reed* or *Frontiero* precedents, two aspects of the Court's *Taylor* opinion place it within the line of cases developing the doctrine that sex classifications in the law would be examined with something more than the closed-eyes' scrutiny of the "reasonableness" approach.

First, the Court said openly that this particular sex classification (the jury duty exemption) could not be upheld on the basis of reasonableness. The justices demanded of this classification a "weightier justification"—a standard that looks very similar to the "compelling interest" test. Their reason for applying the compelling interest/strict scrutiny approach was not a "suspect classification" one; rather, it was that the right to trial by an impartial jury is a "fundamental right" and that therefore any limit on the right would be subjected to strict scrutiny.[97] Nevertheless, *Taylor v. Louisiana* marks the first time that a clear majority explicitly subjected legislative discrimination against women to rigid scrutiny, and the first time that a clear majority stated that the concededly "reasonable" grounds of administrative convenience was not enough to justify such a sex classification.

Second, in scrutinizing the proffered justification for the statute, the Court emphatically rejected the woman's-place-is-in-the-home rationale of *Hoyt*. Instead of simply saying that the woman's-place argument was not compelling enough for this situation, the justices said that in this day and age the argument was not even a "reasonable" one. To assume that all women fit a mold that applied now only to a minority was, to use their word, "untenable."

This shift was a major one, indeed. The kinds of justifications for depriving women of legal rights that had been found "reasonable" in such cases as *Bradwell*, *Goesaert*, and *Hoyt* had always relied almost entirely on the premise that there is "a wide difference in the respective spheres and destinies of man and woman."[98] The rejection of this premise in *Taylor v. Louisiana* had to mean that the "reasonableness" test as applied to sex-based discrimination would look different from its 1961 *Hoyt v. Florida* configuration. Perhaps the change wrought by *Taylor* was to lay bare the unwritten premise that had been silently undergirding the majority justices' reasoning ever since the 1971 *Reed v. Reed* case. Finally it was clear why the Court majority had viewed the statutes of *Reed* and *Frontiero* as unreasonable: those statutes made assumptions about all women that were true of only about half or even fewer than half—no longer reasonable assumptions.[99]

Only two months after the *Schlesinger v. Ballard* decision, in March 1975, the Supreme Court for the first time declared void (strictly on the grounds of gender discrimination) a statute arguably discriminating against males. The case was *Casper Weinberger v. Stephen Wiesenfeld*; and as in *Reed v. Reed*, the first case to strike down antifemale sex discrimination, the result was a unanimous one (although Justice Douglas did not participate.) *Weinberger* was the first unanimous decision declaring void a sex discrimination statute since Justice Rehnquist joined the Court (He joined after *Reed* and dissented in *Frontiero*, and *Taylor*.) Once again the case was argued by the two specialists in women's rights law, Ruth Bader Ginzburg and Melvin Wulf. *Weinberger v. Wiesenfeld* added one more to their string of victories against sex discrimination, which had begun with *Reed* and *Frontiero*.[100]

In drafting the Court opinion, Justice Brennan sidestepped the doctrinal rift between the reasonableness faction of Justice Stewart, Blackmun, Powell, Burger, and Rehnquist, and the compelling-interest faction of White, and Marshall and himself. Justice Douglas, a usual member of the latter faction (except in the *Kahn* decision), was severely ill during this period, and would officially retire in November 1975, replaced in December by Justice Stevens. Brennan managed to bind seven of the eight justices to his majority opinion[101] by avoiding any references to either a reasonableness test or to an "overriding interest" test for sex discrimination.[102] Instead, he termed the discrimination "unjustifiable" and "irrational" in relation to the government's professed versus actual purpose for it. His conclusion was based on the long-standing but conveniently vague rule (also cited in *Reed* and *Frontiero*) that legislation may not provide "dissimilar treatment for men and women who are . . . similarly situated."[103]

Although the plaintiff against the law was male here, the case was analyzed by both the federal district court and the U.S. Supreme Court as a discrimination against women wage-earners. The ambiguity arises because the Social Security statute under challenge discriminated against male (husband) beneficiaries of the Social Security contributions of deceased female workers. From the perspective that looks at who earned the benefits being denied, the law discriminates against women. But from the perspective that looks at who actually suffers by failure to receive benefits—benefits that would be received, were he a woman—the victim of the discrimination is male—the surviving husband.

This case was initiated on the complaint of Stephen C. Wiesenfeld. He married Paula Polatschek, a schoolteacher, in 1970. She had been working full-time for five years by then, and she continued to work after their marriage. In each of these years, the maximum Social Security percentage was deducted from her income. During the two and one-half years of their married life, Paula was the main economic supporter of the couple. In 1970 and 1971, she earned about $10,000 a year to Stephen's $2000–$3000 a year. In 1972, she earned $7000 a year to Stephen's $2500. On June 5, 1972, she died in childbirth, leaving an infant son, Jason.

After her death, Stephen applied for Social Security benefits for his son and himself. For his son, he received about $250 a month.[104] For himself, he received nothing, even though statute 42 U.S.C. § 402(g), would have awarded him $250 a month for himself had he been an unemployed female. Had he been a woman and chosen to go to work under these circumstances, he would have lost, out of the $3000 a year, $1 for every $2 earned above $2400 a year (widows with dependent children received no personal annuity if they earned over $8400 annually). The district court decided, in Stephen Wiesenfeld's favor, that the statutory scheme violated the rule of equal protection implied by the Fifth Amendment due process clause. Then Casper Weinberger, Secretary of the Department of Health, Education, and Welfare, appealed the case to the Supreme Court.

Weinberger v. Wiesenfeld, 420 U.S. 636 (1975)

Mr. Justice Brennan delivered the opinion of the court.

II

The gender-based distinction made by § 402(g) is indistinguishable from that invalidated in *Frontiero v. Richardson*, 411 U.S. 677 (1973). *Frontiero* involved statutes which provided the wife of a male serviceman with dependents' benefits but not the husband of a servicewoman unless she proved that she supplied more than one-half of her husband's support. The Court held that the statutory scheme violated the right to equal protection secured by the Fifth Amendment. . . . A virtually identical "archaic and overbroad" generalization "not . . . tolerated under the Constitution" underlies the distinction drawn by § 402(g), namely, that male workers' earnings are vital to the support of their families, while the earnings of female wage-earners do not significantly contribute to their families' support.[11]

· · ·

Underlying the 1939 scheme [of the original Social Security Act] was the principle that "under a social-insurance plan, the primary purpose is to pay benefits in accordance with the *probable needs of beneficiaries rather than to make payments to the estate of a deceased person regardless of whether or*

not he leaves dependents." H.R. Rep. No. 728, *supra*, at 7. (Emphasis supplied.) It was felt that "[t]he payment of these survivorship benefits and supplements for the wife of an annuitant are . . . in keeping with the principle of social insurance. . . ." Thus, the framers of the Act legislated on the "then generally accepted presumption that a man is responsible for the support of his wife and child." *Hoskins and Bixby, Women and Social Security-Law and Policy in Five Countries,* Social Security Administration Research Report No. 42, 77 (1973).

Obviously, the notion that men are more likely than women to be the primary supporters of their spouses and children is not entirely without empirical support. *See Kahn v. Shevin*, 416 U.S. 351, 354 n.7 (1974). But such a gender-based generalization cannot suffice to justify the denigration of the efforts of women who do work and whose earnings contribute significantly to their families' support.

Section 402(g) clearly operates, as did the statutes invalidated by our judgment in *Frontiero*, to deprive women of protection for their families which men receive as a result of their employment. Indeed, the classification here is in some ways more pernicious. First, it was open to the servicewoman under the statutes invalidated in *Frontiero* to prove that her husband was in fact dependent upon her. Here, Stephen Wiesenfeld was not given the opportunity to show, as may well have been the case, that he was dependent upon his wife for his support, or that, had his wife lived, she would have remained at work while he took over the care of the child. Second, in this case social security taxes were deducted from Paula's salary during the years in which she worked. Thus, she not only failed to receive for her family the same

11. See the observations in *Frontiero*, 411 U.S. at 689, n.23, that in view of the large percentage of married women working (41.5 percent in 1971), the presumption of complete dependency of wives upon husbands has little relationship to present reality. In the same vein, *Taylor v. Louisiana*, (1975), observed that current statistics belie "the presumed role in the home" of contemporary women, n.17.

protection which a similarly situated male worker would have received, but she also was deprived of a portion of her own earnings in order to contribute to the fund out of which benefits would be paid to others. Since the Constitution forbids the gender-based differentiation premised upon assumptions as to dependency made in the statutes before us in *Frontiero*, the Constitution also forbids the gender-based differentiation that results in the efforts of women workers required to pay social security taxes producing less protection for their families than is produced by the efforts of men.

III

The Government seeks to avoid this conclusion with two related arguments. First, it claims that because social security benefits are not compensation for work done, Congress is not obligated to provide a covered female employee with the same benefits as it provides to a male. Second, it contends that § 402(g) was "reasonably designed to offset the adverse economic situation of women by providing a widow with financial assistance to supplement or substitute for her own efforts in the marketplace," Brief for Appellants, 14, and therefore does not contravene the equal protection guarantee.

A

. . . The Government apparently contends that since benefits derived from the social security program do not correlate necessarily with contributions made to the program, a covered employee has no right whatever to be treated equally with other employees as regards the benefits which flow from his or her employment.

We do not see how the fact that social security benefits are "noncontractual" can sanction differential protection for covered employees which is solely gender-based.

From the outset, social security old age, disability, and survivors' (OASDI) benefits have been "afforded as a matter of right, related to past participation in the productive processes of the country." Final Report of the Advisory Council on Social Security 17 (1938). It is true that social security benefits are not necessarily related directly to tax contributions, since the OASDI system is structured to provide benefits in part according to presumed need. . . . But the fact remains that the statutory right to benefits is directly related to years worked and amount earned by a covered employee, and not to the need of the beneficiaries directly. Since OASDI benefits do depend significantly upon the participation in the work force of a covered employee, and since only covered employees and not others are required to pay taxes toward the system, benefits must be distributed according to classifications which do not without sufficient justification differentiate among covered employees solely on the basis of sex.

B

The Government seeks to characterize the classification here as one reasonably designed to compensate women beneficiaries as a group for the economic difficulties which still confront women who seek to support themselves and their families. The Court held in *Kahn v. Shevin, supra*, 416 U.S., at 355, that a statute "reasonably designed to further a state policy of cushioning the financial impact of spousal loss upon that sex for which that loss imposes a disproportionately heavy burden" can survive an equal protection attack. *See also Schlesinger v. Ballard*. But the mere recitation of a benign, compensatory purpose is not an automatic shield which protects against any inquiry into the actual purposes underlying a statutory scheme. Here, it is apparent both from the statutory scheme itself and from the legislative history of § 402(g) that Congress' purpose in providing benefits to young widows with children was not to provide an income to women who were, because of economic discrimination, unable to provide for themselves. Rather, § 402(g), linked as it is directly to responsibility for minor children, was intended to permit women to elect not to work and to devote themselves to the care of children. Since this purpose in no way is premised upon any special disadvantages of women, it cannot serve to justify a gender-based distinction which diminishes the protection afforded to women who do work.

That the purpose behind § 402(g) is to provide children deprived of one parent with the opportunity for the personal attention of the other could not be more clear in the legislative history. The Advisory Council on Social Security, which developed the 1939 amendments, said explicitly that "[s]uch benefits [§ 402(g)] are intended as supplements to the orphans' benefits *with the purpose of enabling the widow to remain at home and care for the children.*" Final Report of the Advisory Council on Social Security 31 (1938). (Emphasis supplied.) In 1971, a new Advisory Council, considering amendments to eliminate the various gender-based distinctions in the OASDI structure, reiterated this understanding: "Present law provides benefits for the mother of young . . . children . . . if she chooses to stay home and care for the children instead of working. In the Council's judgment, it is desirable to allow a woman who is left with the children the *choice* of whether to stay at home to care for the children or to work." Advisory Council on Social Security, *Reports on the Old-Age, Survivors, and Disability Insurance and Medicare Programs* 30 (1971) (hereinafter *1971 Reports*). (Emphasis added.)

. . . Congress decided not to provide

benefits to all widows even though it was recognized that some of them would have serious problems in the job market. Instead, it provided benefits only to those women who had responsibility for minor children, because it believed that they should not be required to work.

The whole structure of survivors' benefits conforms to this articulated purpose. . . . If Congress were concerned with providing women with benefits because of economic discrimination, it would be entirely irrational to except those women who had spent many years at home rearing children [but whose children are grown], since those women are most likely to be without the skills required to succeed in the job market. . . .

Given the purpose of enabling the surviving parent to remain at home to care for a child, the gender-based distinction of § 402(g) is entirely irrational. The classification discriminates among surviving children solely on the basis of the sex of the surviving parent. Even in the typical family hypothesized by the Act, in which the husband is supporting the family and the mother is caring for the children, this result makes no sense. The fact that a man is working while there is a wife at home does not mean that he would, or should be required to, continue to work if his wife dies. It is no less important for a child to be cared for by its sole surviving parent when that parent is male rather than female. And a father, no less than a mother, has a constitutionally protected right to the "companionship, care, custody, and management" of "the children he has sired and raised, [which] undeniably warrants deference and, absent a powerful countervailing interest, protection." *Stanley v. Illinois*, 405 U.S. 645, 651 (1972).* Further, to the extent that women who work when they have sole

* This case appears in chapter 3.—Au.

responsibility for children encounter special problems, it would seem that men with sole responsibility for children will encounter the same child-care related problems. Stephen Wiesenfeld, for example, found that providing adequate care for his infant son impeded his ability to work.

Finally, to the extent that Congress legislated on the presumption that women as a group would choose to forego work to care for children while men would not,[20] the statutory structure, independent of the gender-based classification, would deny or reduce benefits to those men who conform to the presumed norm and are not hampered by their child-care responsibilities. Benefits under § 402(g) decrease with increased earnings.

According to the Government, "the bulk of male workers would receive no benefits in any event," Brief for Appellant, because they earn too much. Thus, the gender-based distinction is gratuitous; without it, the statutory scheme would only provide benefits to those men who are in fact similarly situated to the women the statute aids.

20. Precisely this view was expressed by the 1971 Advisory Council on Social Security, whose recommendations upon which gender-based distinctions in the OASDI system to retain and which to discard were followed in the 1972 Social Security Amendments: "The Council believes that it is unnecessary to offer the same choice [whether to work or care for surviving children] to a man. Even though many more married women work today than in the past, so that they are both workers and homemakers, very few men adopt such a dual role; the customary and predominant role of the father is not that of a homemaker but rather that of the family breadwinner. A man generally continues to work to support himself and his children after the death or disability of his wife. The Council therefore does not recommend that benefits be provided for a young father who has children in his care." 1971 Reports, supra, at 30.

Since the gender-based classifications of § 402(g) cannot be explained as an attempt to provide for the special problems of women, it is indistinguishable from the classification held invalid in Frontiero. Like the statutes there, "[b]y providing dissimilar treatment for men and women who are . . . similarly situated, the challenged section violates the . . . Clause." Reed v. Reed, 404 US. 71, 77 (1971).

Affirmed.

Mr. Justice Powell, with whom The Chief Justice joins, concurring.

I concur in the judgment and generally in the opinion of the Court. But I would identify the impermissible discrimination effected by § 402(g) somewhat more narrowly than the Court does. Social Security is designed, certainly in this context, for the protection of the family. Although it lacks the contractual attributes of insurance or an annuity, Flemming v. Nestor, 363 U.S. 603 (1960), it is a contributory system and millions of wage earners depend on it to provide basic protection for their families in the event of death or disability.

Many women are the principal wage earners for their families, and they participate in the Social Security system on exactly the same basis as men. When the mother is a principal wage earner, the family may suffer as great an economic deprivation upon her death as would occur upon the death of a father wage earner. It is immaterial whether the surviving parent elects to assume primary child care responsibility rather than work, or whether other arrangements are made for child care. The statutory scheme provides benefits both to a surviving mother who remains at home and to one who works at low wages. A surviving father may have the same need for benefits as a surviving mother.* The statutory scheme therefore impermissibly discriminates against a female wage earner because it provides her family less protection than it provides that of a male wage earner, even though the family needs may be identical. I find no legitimate governmental interest that supports this gender classification.

Mr. Justice Douglas took no part in the consideration or decision of this case.

Mr. Justice Rehnquist, concurring in the result.

Part IIIB of the Court's opinion contains a thorough examination of the legislative history and statutory context which define the role and purpose of § 402(g). I believe the Court's examination convinc-

* I attach less significance to the view emphasized by the Court that a purpose of the statute is to enable the surviving parent to remain at home to care for a child. In light of the long experience to the contrary, one may doubt that fathers generally will forego work and remain at home to care for children to the same extent that mothers may make this choice. Under the current statutory program, however, the payment of benefits is not conditioned on the surviving parent's decision to remain at home [but rather on the meagerness or absence of wages].

ingly demonstrates that the only purpose of § 402(g) is to make it possible for children of deceased contributing workers to have the personal care and attention of a surviving parent, should that parent desire to remain in the home with the child. Moreover, the Court's opinion establishes that the Government's proffered legislative purpose is so totally at odds with the context and history of § 402(g) that it cannot serve as a basis for judging whether the Statutory distinction between men and women rationally serves a valid legislative objective.

This being the case, I see no necessity for reaching the issue of whether the statute's purported discrimination against female workers violates the Fifth Amendment as applied in *Frontiero v. Richardson*, 411 U.S. 677 (1973). I would simply conclude, as does the Court in its part IIIB, that the restriction of § 402(g) benefits to surviving mothers does not rationally serve any valid legislative purpose including that for which § 402(g) was obviously designed. This is so because it is irrational to distinguish between mothers and fathers when the sole question is whether a child of a deceased contributing worker should have the opportunity to receive the full-time attention of the only parent remaining to it. To my mind, that should be the end of the matter. I therefore concur in the result.

CASE QUESTIONS

1. Suppose Congress were to re-pass this identical statute with a new statement of purpose that—
   a) recognized that widows with dependent children bear a double burden of child support and self-support,

   b) recognized that widows with dependent children, as a statistical group, are much less likely than widowers to earn a large enough salary to be able both to support a family and to pay for the child care arrangements,

c) asserted the goal of the statute to be easing the financial burden on these hard-pressed widows.

How would such a statute differ in principle from the one that the Court upheld one year earlier in *Kahn v. Shevin?*

Does *Weinberger* undermine the foundations of *Kahn?*

2. In what respects does Justice Rehnquist differ from the majority opinion? Why is he so reluctant to use the *Frontiero* precedent?

Within one month of Justice Rehnquist's acknowledgment of the irrationality of sex discrimination in one parent-child context (in *Weinberger*), the Court handed down a decision that again dealt with sex discrimination in a parent-child context. The case was *Thelma Stanton v. James Stanton.* This time Justice Rehnquist was not so willing to declare the discrimination irrational, but he did not claim it was rational either. He wanted the Court to avoid deciding the merits of the case. The rest of the Court, as usual, was more willing than he to strike down the sex discrimination at issue. Unlike *Taylor* (involving trial by jury) or *Weinberger* (involving the companionship of one's children) this case involved no established fundamental right. Thus it presented a direct equal protection challenge to a gender-based discrimination in Utah law.

Thelma Stanton divorced her husband, James, in Utah in 1960. Their two children remained with Thelma, and James was ordered to pay child support for them on a monthly basis. When the daughter, Sherri (the elder child), reached eighteen, her father halted his support payments for her. When Thelma sued for the money in court, she was told that because her daughter, according to Utah statutes, lost her legal status as a "minor" when she turned eighteen, the father no longer had to support her. He would have to support Sherri's younger brother, Rick, until Rick turned twenty-one, because under Utah law males kept their minor status until the age of twenty-one. Thelma claimed that this arrangement denied Sherri equal protection of the laws, because it cost her three years of support from her father, money she would have received had she been male.

Stanton v. Stanton, 421 U.S. 7 (1975)

MR. JUSTICE BLACKMUN delivered the opinion of the Court.

This case presents the issue whether a state statute specifying for males a greater age of majority than it specifies for females denies, in the context of a parent's obligation for support payments for his children, the equal protection of the laws guaranteed by § 1 of the Fourteenth Amendment.

I

. . . The appellant appealed to the Supreme Court of Utah. She contended, among other things, that § 15–2–1, Utah Code Ann. 1953, to the effect that the period of minority for males extends to age 21 and for females to age 18, is invidiously discriminatory and serves to deny due process and equal protection of the laws, in violation of the Fourteenth Amendment and of the corresponding provisions of the Utah Constitution. . . . On this issue, the Utah court affirmed [the divorce court's rejection of Thelma's claim]. The court acknowledged, "There is no doubt that the questioned statute treats men and women differently," but said that people may be treated differently "so long as there is a reasonable basis for the classification, which is related to the purposes of the act, and it applies equally and uniformly to all persons within the class." 30 Utah 2d., at 318, 517 P.2d, at 1012. The court referred to what it called some "old notions," namely, "that generally it is the man's primary responsibility to provide a home and its essentials," *id.;* that "it is a salutary thing for him to get a good education and/or training before he undertakes those responsibilities," 30 Utah 2d. at 319, 517 P.2d, at 1012; that "girls tend generally to mature physically, emotionally and mentally before boys"; and that "they generally tend to marry earlier," *id.* It concluded that

> it is our judgment that there is no basis upon which we would be justified in concluding that the statute is so beyond a reasonable doubt in conflict with constitutional provisions that it should be stricken down as invalid. (517 P.2d, at 1013.)

If such a change were desirable, the court said, "that is a matter which should commend itself to the attention of the legislature." 517 P.2d, at 1013. The appellant, thus, was held not entitled to support for Sherri for the period after she attained 18, but was entitled to support for Rick "during his minority" unless otherwise ordered by the trial court. 517 P.2d, at 1014. . . .

III

We turn to the merits. The appellant argues that Utah's statutory prescription establishing different ages of majority for males and females denies equal protection; that it is a classification based solely on sex and affects a child's "fundamental right" to be fed, clothed, and sheltered by its parents; that no compelling state interest supports the classification; and that the statute can withstand no judicial scrutiny, "close" or otherwise, for it has no relationship to any ascertainable legislative objective. The appellee contends that the test is that of rationality and that the age classification has a rational basis and endures any attack based on equal protection.

We find it unnecessary in this case to decide whether a classification based on sex is inherently suspect. *See Weinberger v. Wiesenfeld* (1975); *Schlesinger v. Ballard* (1975); *Geduldig v. Aiello* (1974); *Kahn v. Shevin* (1974); *Frontiero v. Richardson* (1973); *Reed v. Reed* (1971) [citation nos. omitted].

Reed, we feel, is controlling here. That case presented an equal protection challenge to a provision of the Idaho probate code which gave preference to males over females when persons otherwise of the same entitlement applied for appointment as administrator of a decedent's estate. No regard was paid under the statute to the applicants' respective individual qualifications. In upholding the challenge, the Court reasoned that the Idaho statute accorded different treatment on the basis of sex and that it "thus establishes a classification subject to scrutiny under the Equal Protection Clause." *Id.* at 75. The clause, it was said, denies to States "the power to legislate that different treatment be accorded to persons placed by a statute into different classes on the basis of criteria wholly unrelated to the objective of that statute." *Id.* at 75–76. "A classification 'must be reasonable, not arbitrary, and must rest upon some ground of difference having a fair and substantial relation to the object of the legislation, so that all persons similarly circumstanced shall be treated alike.' *Royster Guano Co. v. Virginia,* 253 U.S. 412, 415 (1920)." *Id.* at 76. It was not enough to save the statute that among its objectives were the elimination both of an area of possible family controversy and of a hearing on the comparative merits of petitioning relatives.

The test here, then, is whether the difference in sex between children warrants the distinction in the appellee's obligation to support that is drawn by the Utah statute. We conclude that it does not. It may be true, as the Utah court observed and as is argued here, that it is the man's primary responsibility to provide a home and that it is salutary for him to have education and training before he assumes that responsibility; that girls tend to mature earlier than boys; and that females tend to marry earlier than males. The last mentioned factor, however, under the Utah statute loses whatever weight it otherwise might have, for the statute states that "all minors obtain their majority by marriage"; thus minority, and all that goes with it, is abruptly lost by marriage of a person of either sex at whatever tender age the marriage occurs.

Notwithstanding the "old notions" to which the Utah court referred, we perceive nothing rational in the distinction drawn by § 15–2–1 which, when related to the divorce decree, results in the appellee's liability for support for Sherri only to age 18 but for Rick to age 21. This imposes "criteria wholly unrelated to the objective of that statute." A child, male or female, is still a

child. No longer is the female destined solely for the home and the rearing of the family, and only the male for the marketplace and the world of ideas. *See Taylor v. Louisiana,* n.17 (1975). Women's activities and responsibilities are increasing and expanding. Coeducation is a fact, not a rarity. The presence of women in business, in the professions, in government and, indeed, in all walks of life where education is a desirable, if not always a necessary antecedent, is apparent and a proper subject of judicial notice. If a specified age of minority is required for the boy in order to assure him parental support while he attains his education and training, so, too, it is for the girl. To distinguish between the two on educational grounds is to be self-serving: if the female is not to be supported so long as the male, she hardly can be expected to attend school as long as he does, and bringing her education to an end earlier coincides with the role-typing society has long imposed. And if any weight remains in this day in the claim of earlier maturity of the female, with a concomitant inference of absence of need for support beyond 18, we fail to perceive its unquestioned truth or its significance, particularly when marriage, as the statute provides, terminates minority for a person of either sex.

Only Arkansas, so far as our investigation reveals, remains with Utah in fixing the age of majority for females at 18 and for males at 21. . . . Furthermore, Utah itself draws the 18–21 distinction only in § 15–2–1 defining minority, and in § 30–1–9 relating to marriage without the consent of parent or guardian. See also § 30–1–2(4) making void a marriage where the male is under 16 or the female under 14. Elsewhere, in the State's present constitutional and statutory structure, the male and the female appear to be treated alike. [Here the Court cites many Utah statutes and sections of the state constitution.] . . .

This is not to say that § 15–2–1 does

not have important effect in application. A "minor" may disaffirm his contracts. § 15–2–2. An "infant" must appear in court by guardian or guardian *ad litem*. Rule 17(b), Utah Rules of Civ. P. A parent has a right of action for injury to, or wrongful death of, "a minor child." § 78–11–6. A person "[u]nder the age of majority" is not competent or entitled to serve as an administrator of a decedent's estate, § 75–4–4. . . . The statute of limitations is tolled while a person entitled to bring an action is "[u]nder the age of majority." § 78–12–36. Thus, the distinction drawn by § 15–2–1 affects other rights and duties. It has pervasive effect. . . .

We therefore conclude that under any test—compelling state interest, or rational basis, or something in between—§ 15–2–1, in the context of child support, does not survive an equal protection attack. In that context, no valid distinction between male and female may be drawn.

IV

Our conclusion that in the context of child support the classification effectuated by § 15–2–1 denies the equal protection of the laws, as guaranteed by the Fourteenth Amendment, does not finally resolve the controversy as between this appellant and this appellee. With the age differential held invalid, it is not for this Court to determine when the appellee's obligation for his children's support, pursuant to the divorce decree, terminates under Utah law. The appellant asserts that with the classification eliminated, the common law applies and that at common law the age of majority for both males and females is 21. The appellee claims that any unconstitutional inequality between males and females is to be remedied by treating males as adults at age 18, rather than by withholding the privileges of adulthood from women until they reach 21. This plainly is an issue of state law to be resolved by the Utah courts on remand; the

issue was noted, incidentally, by the Supreme Court of Utah. 517 P.2d, at 1013. The appellant, although prevailing here on the federal constitutional issue, may or may not ultimately win her law suit. . . .

The judgment of the Supreme Court of Utah is reversed and the case is remanded for further proceedings not inconsistent with this opinion.

It is so ordered.

Mr. Justice Rehnquist, dissenting.

The Court views this case as requiring a determination of whether the Utah statute specifying that males must reach a higher age than females before attaining their majority denies females the equal protection of the laws guaranteed by § 1 of the Fourteenth Amendment to the United States Constitution. The Court regards the constitutionality of § 15–2–1, Utah Code Ann. (1953), as properly at issue because of the manner in which the Supreme Court of Utah approached and decided the case. But this Court is subject to constraints with respect to constitutional adjudication which may well not bind the Supreme Court of Utah. This Court is bound by the rule, "to which it has rigidly adhered . . . never to formulate a rule of constitutional law broader than is required by the precise facts to which it is to be applied." *Liverpool N.Y. & Phil. S.S. Co. v. Commissioners of Emigration,* 113 U.S. 33, 39 (1885), and we try to avoid deciding constitutional questions which "come to us in highly abstract form." *Rescue Army v. Municipal Court,* 331 U.S. 549, 575 (1947). Fidelity to these longstanding rules dictates that we have some regard for the factual background of this case, as fully outlined in the Court's opinion, before deciding the constitutional question that has been tendered to us.

The Utah statute which the Court invalidates "in the context of child support," does not by its terms define the age at which the obligation of a divorced parent to support a child ceases. The parties concede that the Stantons could have provided in their property settlement agreement that appellee's obligation to support Sherri and Rick would terminate when both turned 18, when both turned 21, or when one turned 18 and the other turned 21. This case arises only because appellant and appellee made no provision in their property settlement agreement fixing the age at which appellee's obligation to support his son or daughter would terminate. The Supreme Court of Utah, faced with the necessity of filling in this blank, referred to the State's general age of majority statute in supplying the terms which the parties had neglected to specify themselves.

Had the Supreme Court of Utah relied upon the statute only insofar as it cast light on the intention of the parties regarding the child support obligations contained in the divorce decree, there would be no basis for reaching the constitutionality of the statute. In supplying the missing term in an agreement executed between two private parties, a court ordinarily looks to the customs, mores, and practice of the parties in an attempt to ascertain what was intended. If, upon consideration of these factors, including the age of majority statutes, the Utah Supreme Court had concluded that the Stantons intended to bestow more of their limited resources upon a son than a daughter, perhaps for the reasons stated in the opinion of the Supreme Court of Utah, that strikes me as an entirely permissible basis upon which to construe the property settlement agreement.

On the other hand, the Supreme Court of Utah may have concluded that, the par-

ties having failed to specify this term of the agreement, the question became one of Utah statutory law rather than one of determining the intent of the parties. If that were its determination, the constitutionality of § 15–2–1, Utah Code Ann. (1953), would indeed be implicated in this case.

I do not think it possible to say with confidence which of these two approaches was taken by the Supreme Court of Utah in this case. In addition to this difficulty, there is another element of attentuation between the claim asserted on behalf of Sherri to be treated like her brother for purposes of child support, and the actual case before us. Utah has a comprehensive scheme dealing with child support in its Uniform Civil Liability for Support Act, § 78–45–1 *et. seq.*, Utah Code Ann. (Supp. 1973). Under that Act, "child" is defined as "a son or daughter under the age of twenty-one years," § 78–45–2(4). Thus for . . . any direct claim by Sherri against appellee, Utah law treats her precisely as it does her brother. The claim asserted in the case is not by Sherri, but by her mother, and the source of any claim which the mother has against appellee necessarily arises out of the voluntary property settlement agreement which they executed at the time of their divorce.

These factors lead me to conclude that the issue which the Court says is presented by this case, and which it decides, cannot properly be decided on these facts if we are to adhere to our established policy of avoiding unnecessary constitutional adjudication. I would dismiss the appeal for that reason. *Rescue Army v. Municipal Court, supra; Socialist Labor Party v. Gilligan* 406 U.S. 583 (1972).

CASE QUESTIONS

1. How relevant is it, in setting the age of majority, whether females mature earlier than males? Would the answer vary by whether the Court is using the "reasonable basis" test, compelling interest, or something in between? What is the "legislative objective" of a law setting the age of adulthood? Is this statute still valid in contexts other than child support?

2. How important to this decision was the fact that forty-eight other states do not make a sex distinction in defining minors? the fact that Utah does not make the distinction in several related contexts? that, as noted in *Taylor,* women's societal role has changed in recent decades? How important should each of these be in interpreting the equal protection clause?

3. How plausible is Justice Rehnquist's suggestion that this different treatment of the children resulted from an earlier voluntary agreement by both parents?

CHAPTER 3

Gender and
"More Rigid Scrutiny"

New Rule: Craig v. Boren

By the end of the 1976, the death knell of the ERA could be heard. The rush of its early popularity continued until March 22, 1973, the anniversary of Congressional adoption. During January, February, and March of 1973, eight additional states ratified. Then, however, the pace dramatically slowed. Three more ratifications came in 1974, bringing the total to 33 (66 percent), and one more in 1975. March of 1976 was the fourth anniversary of Congressional action, and no previous successful Constitutional amendment had taken longer than four years for ratification.[1] By the end of 1976 no additional states ratified. (One more ratification came in 1977, and it was to be the last, bringing the total to 35 [70 percent], three states short.) As of December 1976, more than two-thirds of the states had ratified an amendment proposed by near-unanimity in each house of Congress. And surveys of public opinion showed majorities favoring the amendment even in the non-ratifying states. But the ratification process seemed to have become derailed. At this point the U.S. Supreme Court abandoned its reticence about the principles that had been guiding its thinking on sex discrimination since *Reed*.

In the case of *Craig v. Boren*, in December 1976, a majority of the Supreme Court for the first time announced openly that gender-based discriminations were quasisuspect. The Court finally laid its doctrinal cards on the table with a frank announcement that to comport with the constitutional requirement of equal protection, "classifications by gender must serve important governmental objectives and must be substantially related to achievement of those objectives." Justice Brennan's opinion, which announced this rule, had the adherence of five other justices, for a total majority of six. This decision marked the first time since *Reed v. Reed* (1971) that any more than four justices had agreed on a general standard for judging the constitutionality of sex-based discriminations.

As often happens in constitutional adjudication, the seed for this momentous decision sprouted in the soil of a trivial set of facts. Two young Oklahoma men, Mark Walker and Curtis Craig, objected to a state law permitting 18–20-year-old women to purchase beer containing 3.2 percent alcohol but prohibiting men of that age from making such purchases. Because of the risk that they would reach age twenty-one before the federal courts completed their case and that this would cause them to lose standing,* Mr. Walker and Mr. Craig joined with a woman who had a beer-vending license, Carolyn Whitener, in taking their suit to court. Ms. Whitener's complaint against the statute, of course, was that it cost her the business of 18–20-year-old males who might purchase beer.

Both men did turn twenty-one before the Court decided the case (Curtis Craig, the younger one, just three months before the December 1976 decision), so the standing issue focused on Ms. Whitener's complaint. Because there is no constitutional right to sell beer, nor to buy and sell generally in freedom from government regulations, Ms. Whitener's objection to the statute had to rest on the constitutional right of equal protection asserted by Craig and Walker (even though her standing derived from the financial cost imposed on her by the statute). When one person in court makes a legal argument asserting the claims of another person, this is called "third-party standing," or "*jus tertii* standing." (The "second" party is the person in favor of the statute—in this case, Governor Boren.) Allowing this kind of standing is viewed by the Court as somewhat optional.

Oklahoma, in response to the Supreme Court's *Reed v. Reed* decision and to a federal court decision relying upon it, had eliminated most of the sex differences in the state's age-of-majority statutes. Before 1972, for example, girls but not boys had been held criminally responsible for crimes as "adults" once they turned sixteen. All such differences in both civil law and criminal law were eliminated in 1972, except for the age difference for legal permission to buy "3.2 beer."

Oklahoma defended its beer rules with an argument based on traffic safety. The state presented documents in Court proving that (1) more than ten times as many males as females between the ages of eighteen and twenty were arrested for drunk driving; (2) roughly ten times as many males as females in that age bracket were arrested for public drunkenness; (3) a slightly greater percentage (84 percent as against 77 percent) of male drivers than female drivers under age twenty-one preferred beer to other alcoholic beverages. The federal district court found these documents adequate to establish constitutionality under the *Reed* precedent. The U.S. Supreme Court, agreed that "*Reed* . . . is controlling" but, disagreed with the lower court as to whether this law met the standard establishment by *Reed*. The Supreme Court's description of *Reed*, however, is somewhat new:

Craig v. Boren, 429 U.S. 190 (1976)

Mr. Justice Brennan delivered the opinion of the Court.

. . . The question to be decided is whether such a gender-based differential

* "Standing" is explained in the introduction to *Taylor v. Louisiana* in chapter 2.

constitutes a denial to males 18–20 years of age of the Equal Protection of the Laws in violation of the Fourteenth Amendment. . . .

I

We first address a preliminary question of standing. Appellant Craig attained the age of 21 after we noted probable jurisdiction. Therefore, since only declaratory and injunctive relief against enforcement of the gender-based differential is sought, the controversy has been rendered moot as to Craig. *See, e.g., DeFunis v. Odegaard*, 416 U.S. 312 (1972). The question thus arises whether appellant Whitener, the licensed vendor of 3.2 percent beer, who has a live controversy against enforcement of the statute, may rely upon the equal protection objections of males 18–20 years of age to establish her claim of unconstitutionality of the age-sex differential. We conclude that she may.

Initially, it should be noted that, despite having had the opportunity to do so, appellees never raised before the District Court any objection to Whitener's reliance upon the claimed unequal treatment to 18–20-year-old males as the premise of her equal protection challenge to Oklahoma's 3.2 beer law. *See* 399 F. Supp., at 1306 n.1. Indeed, at oral argument Oklahoma acknowledged that appellees always "presumed" that the vendor, subject to sanctions and loss of license for violation of the statute, was a proper party-interest to object to the enforcement of the sex-based regulatory provision. Tr., at 41. While such a concession certainly would not be controlling upon the reach of this Court's constitutional authority to exercise jurisdiction under Article III, our decisions have settled that limitations on a litigant's assertion of *jus tertii* are not constitutionally mandated, but rather stem from a salutary "rule of self-restraint" designed to minimize unwarranted intervention into contro-

versies where the applicable constitutional questions are ill-defined and speculative. *See, e.g., Barrows v. Jackson*, 346 U.S. 249, 255, 257 (1953); *see also Singleton v. Wulff*, (1976) (POWELL, J., dissenting). These prudential objectives thought to be enhanced by restrictions on third-party standing cannot be furthered here, where the lower court already has entertained the relevant constitutional challenge and the parties have sought—or at least have never resisted—an authoritative constitutional determination. In such circumstances, a decision by us to forego consideration of the constitutional merits in order to await the initiation of a new challenge to the statute by injured third parties would be impermissibly to foster repetitive and time-consuming litigation under the guise of caution and prudence. . . .

In any event, we conclude that appellant Whitener has established independently her claim to assert *jus tertii* standing. The operation of §§ 241 and 245 plainly have inflicted "injury in fact" upon appellant sufficient to guarantee her "concrete adverseness," *Baker v. Carr*, 369 U.S. 186, 204 (1962), and to satisfy the constitutional-based standing requirements imposed by Article III. The legal duties created by the statutory sections under challenge are addressed directly to vendors such as appellant. She is obliged either to heed the statutory discrimination, thereby incurring a direct economic injury. . . , or to disobey the statutory command and suffer, in the words of Oklahoma's Assistant Attorney General, "sanctions and perhaps loss of license." Tr., at 41. This Court repeatedly has recognized that such injuries establish the threshold requirements of a "case or controversy" mandated by Article III. [Citation omitted.]

As a vendor with standing to challenge the lawfulness of §§ 241 and 245, appellant is entitled to assert those concomitant rights of third parties that would be "diluted or adversely affected" should her constitutional challenge fail and the statues remain in force. *Griswold v. Connecticut*, 381 U.S. 479, 481 (1965); *see* Note, *Standing to assert Constitutional* Jus Tertii, 88 Harv. L. Rev. 423, 432 (1974). Otherwise, the threatened imposition of governmental sanctions might deter appellant and other similarly situated vendors from selling 3.2 beer to young males, thereby ensuing that "enforcement of the challenged restriction against the [vendor] would result indirectly in the violation of third parties' rights." *Warth v. Seldin*, 422 U.S. 490, 510 (1975). Accordingly, vendors and those in like positions have been uniformly permitted to resist efforts at restricting their operations by acting as advocates for the rights of third parties who seek access to their market or function. *See, e.g., Eisenstadt v. Baird*, 405 U.S. 438 (1972); *Sullivan v. Little Hunting Park*, 396 U.S. 229 (1969); *Barrows v. Jackson*. . . .

II

A

. . . Analysis may appropriately begin with the reminder that *Reed v. Reed*, emphasized that statutory classifications that distinguish between males and females are "subject to scrutiny under the Equal Protection Clause." 404 U.S., at 75. To withstand constitutional challenge, previous cases establish that classifications by gender must serve important governmental objectives and must be substantially related to achievement of those objectives. Thus, in *Reed*, the objectives of "reducing the workload on probate courts," *id.* at 76, and "avoiding intrafamily controversy," *id.* at 77, were deemed of insufficient importance to sustain use of an overt gender criterion in the appointment of intestate administrators. Decisions following *Reed* similarly have rejected administrative ease and con-

venience as sufficiently important objectives to justify gender-based classifications. *See, e.g., Stanley v. Illinois*, 405 U.S. 645, 656 (1972); *Frontiero v. Richardson*, 411 U.S. 677, 690 (1973); *cf. Schlesinger v. Ballard*, 419 U.S. 498, 506–7 (1975). And only two Terms ago, *Stanton v. Stanton*, 421 U.S. 7 (1975), expressly stating that *Reed v. Reed* was "controlling," *id.* at 13, held that *Reed* required invalidation of a Utah differential age-of-majority statute, notwithstanding the statute's coincidence with and furtherance of the State's purpose of fostering "old notions" of roletyping and preparing boys for their expected performance in the economic and political worlds. *Id.* at 14–15.[6]

Reed v. Reed has also provided the underpinning for decisions that have invalidated statutes employing gender as an inaccurate proxy for other, more germane bases of classification. Hence, "archaic and overbroad" generalizations, *Schlesinger v. Ballard*, 419 U.S., at 508, concerning the financial position of servicewomen, *Frontiero v. Richardson*, 411 U.S., at 689 n.3, and working women *Weinberger v. Wiesenfeld*, 420 U.S. 636, 643 (1975), could not justify use of a gender line in determining eligibility for certain governmental entitlements. Similarly increasingly outdated misconceptions concerning the role of females in the home rather than in the "marketplace and world of ideas" were rejected as loose-fitting characterizations incapable of supporting state statutory schemes that were premised upon their accuracy. *Stanton v.*

---

6. *Kahn v. Shevin*, 416 U.S. 351 (1974) and *Schlesinger v. Ballard*, 419 U.S. 498 (1975), upholding the use of gender-based classifications, rested upon the Court's perception of the laudatory purposes of those laws as remedying disadvantageous conditions suffered by women in economic and military life. *See* 416 U.S., at 353–54; 419 U.S., at 508. Needless to say, in this case [such compensation is not at issue]. . . .

Stanton; Taylor v. Louisiana, 419 U.S. 522, 535 n.17 (1975). In light of the weak congruence between gender and the characteristic or trait that gender purported to represent, it was necessary that the legislatures choose either to realign their substantive laws in a gender-neutral fashion, or to adopt procedures for identifying those instances where the sex-centered generalization actually comported to fact. *See, e.g., Stanley v. Illinois,* 405 U.S., at 658; *cf. Cleveland Board of Educ. v. LaFleur,* 414 U.S. 632, 650 (1974).

In this case too, "*Reed* we feel, is controlling. . . ." *Stanton v. Stanton* 421 U.S., at 13. We turn then to the question whether, under *Reed,* the difference between males and females with respect to the purchase of 3.2 percent beer warrants the differential in age drawn by the Oklahoma Statute. We conclude that it does not.

B

The District Court recognized that *Reed v. Reed* was controlling. In applying the teachings of that case, the Court found the requisite important governmental objective in the traffic-safety goal proffered by the Oklahoma Attorney General. It then concluded that the statistics introduced by the appellees established that the gender-based distinction was substantially related to achievement of that goal.

C

We accept for purposes of discussion the District Court's identification of the objective underlying §§ 241 and 245 as the enhancement of traffic safety. Clearly, the protection of public health and safety represents an important function of state and local governments. However, appellees' statistics in our view cannot support the conclusion that the gender-based distinction closely serves to achieve that objective and therefore the distinction cannot under

Reed withstand equal protection challenge.

The appellees introduced a variety of statistical surveys.

. . .

Even were this statistical evidence accepted as accurate, it nevertheless offers only a weak answer to the equal protection question presented here. The most focused and relevant of the statistical surveys, arrests of 18–20-year-olds for alcohol-related driving offenses, exemplifies the ultimate unpersuasiveness of this evidentiary record. Viewed in terms of the correlation between sex and the actual activity that Oklahoma seeks to regulate—driving while under the influence of alcohol—the statistics broadly establish that .18 percent of females and 2 percent of males in that age group were arrested for that offense. While such a disparity is not trivial in a statistical sense, it hardly can form the basis for employment of a gender line as a classifying device. Certainly if maleness is to serve as a proxy for drinking and driving, a correlation of 2 percent must be considered an unduly tenuous "fit." Indeed, prior cases have consistently rejected the use of sex as a decision making factor even though the statutes in question certainly rested on far more predictive empirical relationships than this.[13]

Moreover, the statistics exhibit a va-

13. For example, we can conjecture that in *Reed,* Idaho's apparent premise that women lacked experience in formal business matters (particularly compared to men) would have proved to be accurate in substantially more than 2 percent of all cases. And in both *Frontiero* and *Wiesenfeld,* we expressly found the government's empirical defense of mandatory dependency tests for men but not women to be unsatisfactory, even though we recognized that husbands still are far less likely to be dependent on their wives than vice versa. *See, e.g.,* 411 U.S., at 688–90.

riety of other shortcomings. . . . Setting aside the obvious methodological problems,[14] the surveys do not adequately justify the salient features of Oklahoma's gender-based traffic-safety law. None purports to measure the use and dangerousness of 3.2 percent beer as opposed to alcohol generally, a detail that is of particular importance since, in light of its low alcohol level, Oklahoma apparently considers the 3.2 percent beverage to be "nonintoxicating." 37 Okla. Stat. § 163.1 (1971 ; *see State ex rel. Springer v. Bliss*, 185 P.2d 220 (1947). . . .

There is no reason to belabor this line of analysis. It is unrealistic to expect either members of the judiciary or state officials to be well versed in the rigors of experimental or statistical technique. But this merely illustrates that, proving broad sociological propositions by statistics is a dubious business, and one that inevitably is in tension with the normative philosophy that underlies the Equal Protection Clause. Suffice to say that the showing offered by the appellees does not satisfy us that sex represents a legitimate, accurate proxy for the regulation of drinking and driving. In fact, when it is further recognized that Oklahoma's statute prohibits only the selling of

3.2 percent beer to young males and not their drinking the beverage once acquired (even after purchase by their 18–20-year-old female companions), the relationship between gender and traffic safety becomes far too tenuous to satisfy *Reed*'s requirement that the gender-based difference be substantially related to achievement of the statutory objective.

We hold, therefore, that under *Reed*, Oklahoma's 3.2 percent beer statute invidiously discriminates against males 18–20 years of age.

D

[Discussion of Twenty-first Amendment omitted.]

We conclude that the gender-based differential contained in 37 Okla. Stat. § 245 constitutes a denial of the Equal Protection of the Laws to males aged 18–20[23] and *Reverse* the judgment of the District Court.

MR. JUSTICE BLACKMUN, concurring.

I join the Court's opinion except part IID thereof. I agree, however, that the Twenty-first Amendment does not save the challenged Oklahoma statute.

MR. JUSTICE POWELL, concurring.

I join the opinion of the Court as I am in general agreement with it. I do have reservations as to some of the discussion con-

14. The very social stereotypes that find reflection in age differential laws, *see Stanton v. Stanton,* 421 U.S., at 114–15, are likely substantially to distort the accuracy of these comparative statistics. Hence "reckless" young men who drink and drive are transformed into arrest statistics, whereas their female counterparts are chivalrously escorted home. *See, e.g.,* W. Reckless & B. Kay, *The Female Offender* 4, 7, 13, 16–17 (*Report to Pres. Comm'n on Law Enforcement & Admin. of Justice, 1967*). Moreover, the Oklahoma surveys, gathered under a regime where the age-differential law in question has been in effect, are lacking in controls necessary for appraisal of the actual effectiveness of the male 3.2 percent beer prohibition. . . .

23. Insofar as *Goesaert v. Cleary,* 335 U.S. 464 (1948), may be inconsistent, that decision is disapproved. Undoubtedly reflecting the view that *Goesaert's* Equal Protection analysis no longer obtains, the District Court made no reference to that decision in upholding Oklahoma's statute. Similarly, the opinions of the federal and state courts cited earlier in the text invalidating gender lines with respect to alcohol regulation uniformly disparaged the contemporary vitality of *Goesaert.*

cerning the appropriate standard for equal protection analysis and the relevance of the statistical evidence. Accordingly, I add this concurring statement.

With respect to the equal protection standard, I agree that *Reed v. Reed*, is the most relevant precedent. But I find it unnecessary, in deciding this case, to read that decision as broadly as some of the Court's language may imply. *Reed* and subsequent cases involving gender-based classifications make clear that the Court subjects such classifications to a more critical examination than is normally applied when "fundamental" constitutional rights and "suspect classes" are not present. *

I view this as a relatively easy case. No one questions the legitimacy or importance of the asserted governmental objective: the promotion of highway safety. . . . [T]he case turns on whether the state legislature, by the classification it has chosen, has adopted a means that bears a "fair and substantial relation" to this objective. *Reed v.*

---

*As is evident from our opinion, the Court has had difficulty in agreeing upon a standard of equal protection analysis that can be applied consistently to the wide variety of legislative classifications. There are valid reasons for dissatisfaction with the "two-tier" approach that has been prominent in the Court's decisions in the past decade. Although viewed by many as a result-oriented substitute for more critical analysis, that approach—with its narrowly limited "upper-tier"—now has substantial precedential support. As has been true of *Reed* and its progeny, our decision today will be viewed by some as a "middle-tier" approach. While I would not endorse that characterization and would not welcome a further subdividing of equal protection analysis, candor compels the recognition that the relatively deferential "rational basis" standard of review normally applied takes on a sharper focus when we address a gender-based classification. So much is clear from our recent cases. . . .

Reed, 404 U.S., at 76, quoting *Royster Guano.*

It seems to me that the statistics offered by the State and relied upon by the District Court do tend generally to support the view that young men drive more, possibly are inclined to drink more, and—for various reasons—are involved in more accidents than young women. Even so, I am not persuaded that these facts and the inferences fairly drawn from them justify this classification based on a three-year age differential between the sexes, and especially one that is so easily circumvented as to be virtually meaningless. Putting it differently, this gender-based classification does not bear a fair and substantial relation to the object of the legislation.

Mr. Justice Stevens, concurring.

There is only one Equal Protection Clause. It requires every State to govern impartially. It does not direct the courts to apply one standard of review in some cases and a different standard in other cases. Whatever criticism may be levelled at a judicial opinion implying that there are at least three such standards applies with the same force to a double standard.

I am inclined to believe that what has become known as the two-tiered analysis of equal protection claims does not describe a completely logical method of deciding cases, but rather is a method the Court has employed to explain decisions that actually apply a single standard in a reasonably consistent fashion. I also suspect that a careful explanation of the reasons motivating particular decisions may contribute more to an identification of that standard than an attempt to articulate it in all-encompassing terms. It may therefore be appropriate for me to state the principal reasons which persuaded me to join the Court's opinion.

In this case, the classification is not as obnoxious as some the Court has condemned,[1] nor as inoffensive as some the Court has accepted. It is objectionable because it is based on an accident of birth,[2] because it is a mere remnant of the now almost universally rejected tradition of discriminating against males in this age bracket,[3] and because, to the extent it reflects any physical difference between males and females, it is actually perverse.[4] The question then is whether the traffic safety justification put forward by the State is sufficient to make an otherwise offensive classification acceptable.

The classification is not totally irrational. For the evidence does indicate that there are more males than females in this age bracket who drive and also more who drink. Nevertheless, there are several reasons why I regard the justification as unacceptable. It is difficult to believe that the statute was actually intended to cope with the problem of traffic safety,[5] since it has

1. Men as a general class have not been the victims of the kind of historic, pervasive discrimination that has disadvantaged other groups.

2. "[S]ince sex, like race and national origin, is an immutable characteristic determined solely by the accident of birth, the imposition of special disabilities upon the members of a particular sex because of their sex would seem to violate 'the basic concept of our system that legal burdens should bear some relationship to individual responsibility. . . ' *Weber v. Aetna Casualty & Surety Co.*, 406 U.S. 164." *Frontiero v. Richardson*, 411 U.S. 677, 686.

3. Apparently Oklahoma is the only State to permit this narrow discrimination to survive the elimination of the disparity between the age of majority for males and females.

4. Because males are generally heavier than females, they have a greater capacity to consume alcohol without impairing their driving ability than do females.

5. There is no legislative history to indicate that this was the purpose, and several features of the statutory scheme indicate the contrary. The statute exempts license holders who dispense

only a minimal effect on access to a not-very-intoxicating beverage and does not prohibit its consumption. Moreover, the empirical data submitted by the State accentuates the unfairness of treating all 18–21-year-old males as inferior to their female counterparts. The legislation imposes a restraint on one hundred percent of the males in the class allegedly because about 2 percent of them have probably violated one or more laws relating to the consumption of alcoholic beverages. It is unlikely that this law will have a significant deterrent effect either on that 2 percent or on the law-abiding 98 percent. But even assuming some such slight benefit, it does not seem to me that an insult to all of the young men of the State can be justified by visiting the sins of the 2 percent on the 98 percent.

MR. JUSTICE STEWART, concurring [in the judgment].

I agree that the appellant Whitener has standing to assert the equal protection

3.2 beer to their own children, and a related statute makes it unlawful for 18-year old men (but not women), to work in establishments in which 3.2 beer accounts for over 25 percent of gross sales. 37 Okla. Stat. § 241, 243, 245.

There is, of course, no way of knowing what actually motivated this discrimination, but I would not be surprised if it represented nothing more than the perpetuation of a stereotyped attitude about the relative maturity of the members of the two sexes in this age bracket. If so, the following comment is relevant: "[A] traditional classification is more likely to be used without pausing to consider its justification than is a newly created classification. Habit, rather than analysis, makes it seem acceptable and natural to distinguish between male and female, alien and citizen, legitimate and illegitimate; for too much of our history there was the same inertia in distinguishing between black and white. But that sort of stereotyped reaction may have no rational

claims of males between 18 and 20 years old. [Citations omitted.] I also concur in the Court's judgment on the merits of the constitutional issue before us.

Every State has broad power under the Twenty-first Amendment to control the dispensation of alcoholic beverages within its borders. *E.g., California v. LaRue*, 409 U.S. 109; *Seagram & Sons v. Hostetter*, 384 U.S. 35; *Hostetter v. Idlewild Bon Voyage Liquor Corp.*, 377 U.S. 324, 330; *Mahoney v. Joseph Triner Corp.*, 304 U.S. 401; *State Board of Equalization v. Young's Market Co.*, 299 U.S. 59. But "[t]his is not to say that the Twenty-first Amendment empowers a State to act with total irrationality or invidious discrimination in controlling the dispensation of liquor. . . ." *California v. LaRue*, at 120 n.* (concurring opinion).

The disparity created by these Oklahoma statutes amounts to total irrationality. For the statistics upon which the state now relies, whatever their other shortcomings, wholly fail to prove or even suggest that 3.2 beer is somehow more deleterious when it comes into the hands of a male aged 18–20 than of a female of like age. The disparate statutory treatment of the sexes here, without even a colorably valid justification or explanation, thus amounts to invidious discrimination. *See Reed v. Reed*, 404 U.S. 71.

MR. CHIEF JUSTICE BURGER, dissenting.

I am in general agreement with MR. JUSTICE REHNQUIST's dissent, but even at the risk of compounding the obvious confusion created by those voting to reverse the District Court, I will add a few words.

At the outset I cannot agree that appellant Whitener has standing arising from

---

relationship—other than purely prejudicial discrimination—to the stated purpose for which the classification is being made." *Mathews v. Lucas* (STEVENS, J., dissenting).

her status as a saloonkeeper to assert the constitutional rights of her customers. In this Court "a litigant may only assert his own constitutional rights or immunities." *United States v. Raines*, 362 U.S. 17, 21 (1960). There are a few, but strictly limited exceptions to that rule; despite the most creative efforts, this case fits within none of them.

This is not *Sullivan v. Little Hunting Park*, 396 U.S. 229 (1969), or *Barrows v. Jackson*, 346 U.S. 249 (1953), for there is here no barrier whatever to Oklahoma males 18–20 years of age asserting, in an appropriate forum, any constitutional rights they may claim to purchase 3.2 percent beer. Craig's successful litigation of this very issue was prevented only by the advent of his 21st birthday. There is thus no danger of interminable dilution of those rights if appellant Whitener is not permitted to litigate them here. *Cf. Eisenstadt v. Baird*, 405 U.S. 438, 445–46 (1972).

Nor is this controlled by *Griswold v. Connecticut*, 381 U.S. 479 (1965). It borders on the ludicrous to draw a parallel between a vendor of beer and the intimate professional physician-patient relationship which undergirded relaxation of standing rules in that case.

Even in *Eisenstadt*, the Court carefully limited its recognition of third party standing to cases in which the relationship between the claimant and the relevant third party "was not simply the fortuitous connection between a vendor and potential vendees, but the relationship between one who acted to protect the rights of a minority and the minority itself." 405 U.S., at 445. This is plainly not the case here. . . .

In sum, permitting a vendor to assert the constitutional rights of vendees whenever those rights are arguably infringed introduces a new concept of constitutional standing to which I cannot subscribe.

On the merits . . . [t]hough today's decision does not go so far as to make gender-based classifications "suspect," it makes gender a disfavored classification. Without an independent constitutional basis supporting the right asserted or disfavoring the classification adopted, I can justify no substantive constitutional protection other than the normal *McGowan v. Maryland*, 366 U.S. 420, at 425–26, protection afforded by the Equal Protection Clause.

The means employed by the Oklahoma Legislature to achieve the objectives sought may not be agreeable to some judges, but since eight members of the Court think the means not irrational, I see no basis for striking down the statute as violative of the Constitution simply because we find it unwise, unneeded, or possibly even a bit foolish.

With MR. JUSTICE REHNQUIST, I would *Affirm* the judgment of the District Court.

MR. JUSTICE REHNQUIST, dissenting.

The Court's disposition of this case is objectionable on two grounds. First is its conclusion that men challenging a gender-based statute which treats them less favorably than women may invoke a more stringent standard of judicial review than pertains to most other types of classifications. Second is the Court's enunciation of this standard, without citation to any source, as being that "classifications by gender must serve *important* governmental objectives and must be *substantially* related to achievement of those objectives." (Emphasis added.) The only redeeming feature of the Court's opinion, to mind, is that it apparently signals a retreat by those who joined the plurality opinion in *Frontiero v. Richardson*, 411 U.S. 677 (1973), from their view that sex is a "suspect" classification for purposes of equal protection analysis. I think the Oklahoma statute challenged here need pass only the "rational basis"

equal protection analysis expounded in cases such as *McGowan v. Maryland*, 366 U.S. 420 (1961), and *Williamson v. Lee Optical Co.*, 348 U.S. 483 (1955), and I believe it is constitutional under that analysis.

In *Frontiero v. Richardson*, the opinion for the plurality sets forth the reasons of four Justices for concluding that sex should be regarded as a suspect classification for purposes of equal protection analysis. These reasons center on our Nation's "long and unfortunate history of sex discrimination," *id.* at 684, which has been reflected in a whole range of restrictions on the legal rights of women, not the least of which have concerned the ownership of property and participation in the electoral process. Noting that the pervasive and persistent nature of the discrimination experienced by women is in part the result of their ready identifiability, the plurality rested its invocation of strict scrutiny largely upon the fact that "statutory distinctions between the sexes often have the effect of invidiously relegating the entire class of females to inferior legal status without regard to the actual capabilities of its individual members." *Id.* at 686–687. *See Stanton v. Stanton*, 421 U.S. 7, 14–15 (1975).

Subsequent to *Frontiero*, the Court has declined to hold that sex is a suspect class, *Stanton v. Stanton*, at 13, and no such holding is imported by the Court's resolution of this case. However, the Court's application here of an elevated or "intermediate" level scrutiny, like that invoked in cases dealing with discrimination against females, raises the question of why the statute here should be treated any differently than countless legislative classifications unrelated to sex which have been upheld under a minimum rationality standard. *Jefferson v. Hackney*, 406 U.S. 535, 546–47 (1972); *Richardson v. Belcher*, 404 U.S. 78, 81–84 (1971); *Dandridge v. Williams* 397 U.S. 471, 484–85 (1970); [additional citations omitted].

Most obviously unavailable to support any kind of special scrutiny in this case, is a history or pattern of past discrimination, such as was relied on by the plurality in *Frontiero* to support its invocation of strict scrutiny. There is no suggestion in the Court's opinion that males in this age group are in any way peculiarly disadvantaged, subject to systematic discriminatory treatment, or otherwise in need of special solicitude from the courts.

. . .

There is, in sum, nothing about the statutory classification involved here to suggest that it affects an interest, or works against a group, which can claim under the Equal Protection Clause that it is entitled to special judicial protection.

It is true that a number of our opinions contain broadly phrased dicta implying that the same test should be applied to all classifications based on sex, whether affecting females or males. *E.g., Frontiero v. Richardson*, at 688; *Reed v. Reed*, 404 U.S. 71, 76. However, before today, no decision of this Court has applied an elevated level of scrutiny to invalidate a statutory discrimination harmful to males, except where the statute impaired an important personal interest protected by the Constitution.[1] There

being no such interest here, and there being no plausible argument that this is a discrimination against females,[2] the Court's reliance on our previous sex-discrimination cases is ill-founded. It treats gender classification as a talisman which—without regard to the rights involved or the person affected—calls into effect a heavier burden of judicial review.

The Court's conclusion that a law which treats males less favorably than females "must serve important governmental objectives and must be substantially related to achievement of those objectives" apparently comes out of thin air. The Equal Protection Clause contains no such language, and none of our previous cases adopt that standard, I would think we have had enough difficulty with the two standards of review which our cases have recognized— the norm of "rational basis," and the "compelling state interest" required where a "suspect classification" is involved—so as to counsel weightily against the insertion

---

1. In *Stanley v. Illinois*, 405 U.S. 645 (1972), the Court struck down a statute allowing separation of illegitimate children from a surviving father but not a surviving mother, without any showing of parental unfitness. The Court stated that "the interest of a parent in the companionship, care, custody, and management of his or her children 'come[s] to this Court with a momentum for respect lacking when appeal is made to liberties which derive merely from shifting economic arrangements.'"

In *Kahn v. Shevin*, 416 U.S. 351 (1974), the Court upheld Florida's $500 property tax exemption for widows only. The opinion of the Court appears to apply a rational basis test, and is so

understood by the dissenters. *Id.* at 355, 357.

In *Weinberger v. Wiesenfeld*, 420 U.S. 636 (1975), the Court invalidated § 202(g) of the Social Security Act, which allowed benefits to mothers but not fathers of minor children, who survive the wage earner. This statute was treated, in the opinion of the Court, as discrimination against female wage earners, on the ground that it minimizes the financial security which their work efforts provide for their families. *Id.* at 645.

2. I am not unaware of the argument from time to time advanced, that all discriminations between the sexes ultimately redound to the detriment of females, because they tend to reinforce "old notions" restricting the roles and opportunities of women. As a general proposition. . . , I believe that this argument was implicitly found to carry little weight in our decisions upholding [antimale] gender-based differences. *See Schlesinger v. Ballard; Kahn v. Shevin.* Seeing no assertion that it has special applicability to the situation at hand, I believe it can be dismissed as an insubstantial consideration.

of still another "standard" between those two. How is this Court to divine what objectives are important? How is it to determine whether a particular law is "substantially" related to the achievement of such objective, rather than related in some other way to its achievement? Both of the phrases used are so diaphanous and elastic as to invite subjective judicial preferences or prejudices relating to particular types of legislation, masquerading as judgments whether such legislation, is directed at "important" objectives or, whether the relationship to those objectives is "substantial" enough.

I would have thought that if this Court were to leave anything to decision by the popularly elected branches of the Government, where no constitutional claim other than that of equal protection is invoked, it would be the decision as to what governmental objectives to be achieved by law are "important," and which are not. As for the second part of the Court's new test, the Judicial Branch is probably in no worse position than the Legislative or Executive Branches to determine if there is any rational relationship between a classification and the purpose which it might be thought to serve. But the introduction of the adverb "substantially" requires courts to make subjective judgments as to operational effects, for which neither their expertise nor their access to data fits them. And even if we manage to avoid both confusion and the mirroring of our own preferences in the development of this new doctrine, the thousands of judges in other courts who must interpret the Equal Protection Clause may not be so fortunate.

II

. . . Our decisions indicate that the application of the Equal Protection Clause in a context not justifying an elevated level of scrutiny does not demand "mathematical nicety" or the elimination of all inequality. Those cases recognize that the practical problems of government may require rough accommodations of interests, and hold that such accommodations should be respected unless no reasonable basis can be found to support them. *Dandridge v. Williams*, at 485. Whether the same ends might have been better or more precisely served by a different approach is no part of the judicial inquiry under the traditional minimum rationality approach. *Richardson v. Belcher*, at 84.

The Court "accept[s] for purposes of discussion" the District Court's finding that the purpose of the provisions in question was traffic safety, and proceeds to examine the statistical evidence in the record in order to decide if "the gender-based distinction *closely* serves to achieve that objective." (Emphasis added.) (Whether there is a difference between laws which "closely serve" objectives and those which are only "substantially related" to their achievement, we are not told.) I believe that a more traditional type of scrutiny is appropriate in this case, and I think that the Court would have done well here to heed its own warning that "[i]t is unrealistic to expect . . . members of the judiciary . . . to be well versed in the rigors of experimental or statistical technique." One need not immerse oneself in the fine-points of statistical analysis, however, in order to see the weaknesses in the Court's attempted denigration of the evidence at hand.

One survey of arrest statistics assembled in 1973 indicated that males in the 18–20 age group were arrested for "driving under the influence" almost 18 times as often as their female counterparts, and for "drunkenness" in a ratio of almost ten-to-one. Accepting, as the Court does, appellants comparison of the total figures with 1973 Oklahoma census data, this survey indicates a 2 percent arrest rate among males in the age group, as compared to a .18 percent rate among females.

Other surveys indicated (1) that over the five-year period from 1967 to 1972, nation-wide arrests for drunken driving increased 138 percent, and that 93 percent of all persons arrested for drunken driving were male; (2) that youths in the 17–21 age group were overrepresented among those killed or injured in Oklahoma traffic accidents, that male casualties substantially exceeded female, and that deaths in this age group continued to rise while overall traffic deaths declined; (3) that over ¾ of the drivers under 20 in the Oklahoma City area are males, and that each of them, on average, drives half again as many miles per year as their female counterpart; (4) that ⅘ of male drivers under 20 in the Oklahoma City area state a drink preference for beer, while about ⅗ of female drivers of that age state the same preference; and (5) that the percentage of male drivers under 20 admitting to drinking within two hours of driving was half again larger than the percentage for females, and that the percentage of male drivers of that age group with a blood alcohol content greater than .01 percent was almost half again larger than for female drivers.

The Court's criticism of the statistics relied on by the District Court conveys the impression that a legislature in enacting a new law is to be subjected to the judicial equivalent of a doctoral examination in statistics. Legislatures . . . are entitled to draw factual conclusions on the basis of the determination of probable cause which an arrest by a police officer normally represents. In this situation, they could reasonably infer that the incidence of drunk driving is a good deal higher than the incidence of arrest.

And while, as the Court observes . . . such statistics may be distorted as a result of stereotyping, the legislature is not re-

quired to prove before a court that its statistics are perfect. In any event, if stereotypes are as pervasive as the Court suggests, they may in turn influence the conduct of the men and women in question, and cause the young men to conform to the wild and reckless image which is their stereotype.

. . . [T]he State of Oklahoma—and certainly this Court for purposes of equal protection review—can surely take notice of the fact that drunkenness is a significant cause of traffic casualties, and that youthful offenders have participated in the increase of the drunk driving problem. On this latter point, the survey data indicating increased driving casualties among 18–21-year-olds, while overall casualties dropped, is not irrelevant.

Nor is it unreasonable to conclude from the expressed preference for beer by ⅘ of the age group males that that beverage was a predominant source of their intoxication-related arrests. . . . [T]he state could reasonably bar those males from any purchases of alcoholic beer, including that of the 3.2 percent variety. This Court lacks the expertise or the data to evaluate the intoxicating properties of that beverage, and in that posture our only appropriate course is to defer to the reasonable inference supporting the statute—that taken in sufficient quality this beer has the same effect as any alcoholic beverage.

. . . [T]he Court appears to hold that that evidence, on its face, fails to support the distinction drawn in the statute. The Court notes that only 2 percent of males (as against .18 percent of females) in the age group were arrested for drunk driving, and that this very low figure establishes "an unduly tenuous 'fit'" between maleness and drunk driving in the 18–20-year-old group. On this point the Court misconceives the nature of the equal protection inquiry.

The rationality of a statutory classification for equal protection purposes does not depend upon the statistical "fit" between the class and the trait sought to be singled out. It turns on whether there may be a sufficiently higher incidence of the trait within the included class than in the excluded class to justify different treatment. Therefore the present equal protection challenge to this gender-based discrimination poses only the question whether the incidence of drunk driving among young men is sufficiently greater than among young women to justify differential treatment. Notwithstanding the Court's critique of the statistical evidence, that evidence suggests clear differences between the drinking and driving habits of young men and women. Those differences are grounds enough for the State reasonably to conclude that young males pose by far the greater drunk driving hazard, both in terms of sheer numbers and in terms of hazard on a per-driver basis. The gender-based difference in treat-ment in this case is therefore not irrational.

The Court's argument that a 2 percent correlation between maleness and drunk driving is constitutionally insufficient therefore does not pose an equal protection issue concerning discrimination between males and females. The clearest demonstration of this is the fact that the precise argument made by the Court would be equally applicable to a flat bar on such purchases by *anyone*, male or female, in the 18–20 age group. . . . The statistics indicate that about 1 percent of the age group population as a whole is arrested. Under the appropriate rational basis test for equal protection, it is neither irrational nor arbitrary to bar [18–20-year-old males] from making purchases of 3.2 beer, which purchases might in many cases be made by a young man who immediately returns to his vehicle with the beverage in his possession.

CASE QUESTIONS

1. Justice Rehnquist charges that the new *Craig v. Boren* rule that gender classifications "must serve important governmental objectives and must be substantially related to the achievement of those objectives" does not come from any precedential source and was pulled "out of thin air." The Court majority claims that this rule that was in fact guiding the Court's thinking in sex discrimination cases dating back to 1971. Who is right?

2. Does Brennan's footnote 23 finally overrule *Goesaert v. Cleary?*

3. Rehnquist insists that the new *Craig* standard is more likely than the old "ra-tional basis" test to invite the imposition of "subjective judicial preferences or prejudices." Yet even using the rational-basis test, Justice Stewart cannot agree with Justices Burger and Rehnquist on the rationality of this statute. Does this tend to refute Rehnquist's claim or not?

4. Justice Stevens maintains that despite its language of "strict scrutiny" and "ordinary scrutiny" and "suspect classifications" and "fundamental rights," the Court has all along been employing one basic guideline: that states must govern impartially. Does his description fit the sex discrimination cases up to 1976?

5. Justice Burger argues that the Supreme Court should never have taken jurisdiction of this case because Ms. Whitener cannot press the constitutional claims of eighteen-year-old males. The Court majority claims to the contrary that *Eisenstadt v. Baird* established a clear precedent for granting standing to Ms. Whitener. Bill Baird (of the *Eisenstadt* case) was a birth-control advocate who handed a package of Emko vaginal foam to a young unmarried woman during a pro-birth-control lecture at Boston University. When he was arrested for violating a law against distributing contraceptives to unmarried people, he relied for his legal defense on the constitutional right of single people to use contraceptives. (See chapter 4.)

Does Bill Baird's relationship to that young woman in his audience seem substantially different from Ms. Whitener's relation to her potential customers? If the lower court had *struck down* the statute, would Burger have been so anxious to deny standing?

6. Does Rehnquist seem to concede that where statutes clearly discriminate against women the precedents now demand that those statutes be subjected to something stricter than ordinary scrutiny? Is this concession compatible with his dissents in *Taylor v. Louisiana* and *Stanton v. Stanton?* Does *Craig* indicate his movement in a new direction?

Craig *Rule in Operation*

Within three months, *Craig v. Boren* was followed by two more social security cases in quick succession. The first, *Califano v. Goldfarb,* presented a challenge by Leon Goldfarb, a seventy-two-year-old widower, to those parts of the Social Security Act that made him ineligible for old-age survivors' benefits from his deceased wife's Social Security payments. If he had been the widow of a worker who had paid Social Security taxes, he would have been eligible to receive benefits. (Widows who would not receive Social Security retirement benefits from their *own* earnings that were as great as those accruing from their husband's earnings were automatically eligible for spouse benefits.) The law that he challenged required a widower to prove that his deceased wife had actually provided "at least one-half of his support" before he could receive old age surviving-spouse benefits from her Social Security taxes. Leon Goldfarb's wife had paid Social Security taxes for twenty-five years on her salary as a full-time secretary. Leon Goldfarb had also worked full-time (as a federal employee, exempted from the Social Security system) and could not prove "actual dependency" in the terms of the law. Had he been a woman in the identical situation, he would have received the benefits.

 The District Court and then the U.S. Supreme Court were persuaded by Goldfarb's attorneys, Ruth Bader Ginzburg and Melvin Wulf,[2] that this disparity in the treatment of men and women "similarly situated" denied equal protection of the law and thus violated the due process clause of the Fifth Amendment. The Supreme Court majority, however, was itself divided as to *why* this statute violated the rule of equal protection.

Four members of the Court—the four who announced the Court judgment—believed that this statutory scheme discriminated against female wage earners because it gave them less protection for their families than male wage-earners paying the same Social Security taxes. Five members of the Court—Justice Stevens, whose vote against the statute determined the majority, and the four dissenters—believed that this statute discriminated against the male survivors of female workers, specifically against nondependent widowers as compared with nondependent widows. In the opinions for this case, the question of who is being harmed by the statute thus assumes constitutional dimensions.

Joseph Califano, Secretary of HEW, v. Leon Goldfarb, 430 U.S. 199 (1977)

Mr. Justice Brennan announced the judgment of the Court and delivered an opinion in which Mr. Justice White, Mr. Justice Marshall, and Mr. Justice Powell joined.

II

The gender-based distinction drawn by § 402(f)(1)(D)—burdening widower but not a widow with the task of proving dependency upon the deceased spouse—presents an equal protection question indistinguishable from that decided in *Weinberger v. Wiesenfeld*, 420 U.S. 636. That decision and the decision in *Frontiero v. Richardson*, 411 U.S. 677, plainly require affirmance of the judgment of the District Court.[4]

. . . [In *Frontiero*] the Government argued that "as an empirical matter, wives in our society frequently are dependent on their husbands, while husbands are rarely dependent on their wives. Thus, . . . Congress might reasonably have concluded that it would be both cheaper and easier simply conclusively to presume that wives of male members are financially dependent on their husbands, while burdening female members with the task of establishing dependency in fact." 411 U.S., at 688–89. But *Frontiero* concluded that, by according such differential treatment to male and female members of the uniformed services for the sole purpose of achieving administrative convenience, the challenged statute violated the Fifth Amendment. *See Reed v. Reed*, 404 U.S. 71, 76 (1971); *Stanley v. Il-*

4. The dissent maintains that this sentence "overstates [the] relevance" of *Wiesenfeld* and *Frontiero*. It is sufficient to answer that the principal propositions argued by appellant and in the dissent—namely the focus on discrimination between surviving, rather than insured, spouses; the reliance on *Kahn v. Shevin*, 416 U.S. 351 (1974); the argument that the presumption of fe-

male dependence is empirically supportable; and the emphasis on the special deference due to classifications in the Social Security Act—were all asserted and rejected in one or both of those cases as justifications for statutes substantially similar in effect to § 402(f)(1)(D).

linois, 405 U.S. 645, 656–57 (1972); *cf. Schlesinger v. Ballard*, 419 U.S. 498, 506–07 (1975).

Weinberger v. Wiesenfeld, like the instant case, presented the question in the context of the OASDI* program. . . . [There the Court noted that, while]

> the notion that men are more likely than women to be the primary supporters of their spouses and children is not entirely without empirical support, . . . such a gender-based generalization cannot suffice to justify the denigration of the efforts of women who do work and whose earnings contribute significantly to their families' support. . . . (420 U.S., at 645.)

Precisely the same reasoning condemns the gender-based distinction made by § 402(f)(1)(D) in this case. For that distinction too operates "to deprive women of protection for their families which men receive as a result of their employment": social security taxes were deducted from Hannah Goldfarb's salary during the quarter-century she worked as a secretary, yet, in consequence of § 402(f)(1)(D), she also "not only failed to receive for her [spouse] the same protection which a similarly situated male worker would have received [for his spouse] but she also was deprived of a portion of her earnings in order to contribute to the fund out of which benefits would be paid to others." *Wiesenfeld* thus inescapably compels the conclusion reached by the District Court that the gender-based differentiation created by § 402(f)(1)(D)—that results in the efforts of female workers required to pay social security taxes producing less protection for their spouses than is produced by the efforts of men—

*Old Age, Survivors, and Disability Insurance—i.e., social security—Au.

is forbidden by the Constitution, at least when supported by no more substantial justification than "archaic and overbroad" generalizations, *Schlesinger v. Ballard*, 419 U.S., at 508, or "old notions," *Stanton v. Stanton*, 421 U.S. 7, 14 (1975), such as "assumptions as to dependency," *Weinberger v. Wiesenfeld*, at 645, that are more consistent with "the role-typing society has long imposed," *Stanton v. Stanton*, at 15, than with contemporary reality. Thus § 402(f)(1)(D) "[b]y providing dissimilar treatment for men and women who are . . . similarly situated . . . violates the [Fifth Amendment]. *Reed v. Reed*, at 77. . . ." *Wiesenfeld*, at 653.

III

Appellant, however, would focus equal protection analysis not upon the discrimination against the covered wage earning female, but rather upon whether her surviving widower was unconstitutionally discriminated against by burdening him but not a surviving widow with proof of dependency. The gist of the argument is that, analyzed from the perspective of the widower, " . . . the denial of benefits reflected the congressional judgment that aged widowers as a class were sufficiently likely not to be dependent upon their wives, that it was appropriate to deny them benefits unless they were . . . dependent." Appellant's Brief.

But *Weinberger v. Wiesenfeld* rejected the virtually identical argument when appellant's predecessor argued that the statutory classification there attacked should be regarded from the perspective of the prospective beneficiary and not from that of the covered wage earner. The Secretary's Brief in that case argued that " . . . the pattern of legislation reflects the considered judgment of Congress that the 'probable need' for financial assistance is greater in the case of a widow, with young children to maintain, than in the case of similarly situated males." The Court, however analyzed the classification from the perspective of the wage earner and concluded that the classification was unconstitutional because "benefits must be distributed according to classifications which do not without sufficient justification differentiate among covered employees solely on the basis of sex." 420 U.S., at 647. Thus, contrary to appellant's insistence *Wiesenfeld* is "dispositive here."

From its inception, the social security system has been a program of social insurance. Covered employees and their employers pay taxes into a fund administered distinct from the general federal revenues to purchase protection against the economic consequence of old age, disability and death. But under § 402(f)(1)(D) female insureds received less protection for their spouses solely because of their sex. Mrs. Goldfarb worked and paid social security taxes for 25 years at the same rate as her male colleagues, but because of § 402(f)(1)(D) the insurance protection received by the males was broader than hers. Plainly then § 402(f)(1)(D) disadvantages women contributors to the social security system as compared to similarly situated men. The section then "impermissibly discriminates against a female wage earner because it provides her family less protection than it provides that of a male wage earner, even though the family needs may be identical." 420 U.S., at 654–55 (POWELL, J., concurring). In a sense of course both the female wage earner and her surviving spouse are disadvantaged by operation of the statute, but this is because "Social Security is designed . . . for the protection of the *family*," 420 U.S., at 654 (JUSTICE POWELL concurring), and the section discriminates against one particular category of family—that in which the female spouse is a wage earner covered by social security. Therefore decision of the equal protection challenge in

this case cannot focus solely on the distinction drawn between widowers and widows but, as *Wiesenfeld* held, upon the gender-based discrimination against covered female wage earners as well.[8]

IV

Appellant's . . . other arguments . . . have no merit.

A

We accept as settled the proposition argued by appellant that Congress has wide latitude . . . under a social welfare program.

But this "does not, of course, immunize [social welfare legislation] from scrutiny under the Fifth Amendment." *Richardson v. Belcher*, 404 U.S. 78, 81. The Social Security Act is permeated with provisions that draw lines in classifying those who are to receive benefits. Congressional decisions

---

8. In any event, gender-based discriminations against men have been invalidated when they do not "serve important governmental objectives and [are not] substantially related to the achievement of those objectives." *Craig v. Boren*. Neither *Kahn v. Shevin*, nor *Schlesinger v. Ballard*, relied on by appellant, supports a contrary conclusion. The gender-based distinctions in the statutes involved in *Kahn* and *Ballard* were justified because the only discernible purpose of each was the permissible one of redressing our society's longstanding disparate treatment of women. *Craig v. Boren*, at n.6 (1976).

But "the mere recitation of a benign, compensatory purpose is not an automatic shield that protects against any inquiry into the actual purposes underlying a legislative scheme." *Weinberger v. Wiesenfeld*, at 648. That inquiry in this case demonstrates that § 402(f)(1)(D) has no such remedial purpose. *See* part IV–V, *infra*. Moreover, the classifications challenged in *Wiesenfeld* and in this case rather than advantage women to compensate for past wrongs compounds those wrongs by penalizing women "who do work and whose earnings contribute significantly to their families' support." *Wiesenfeld*, at 645.

in this regard are entitled to deference as those of the institution charged under our scheme of government with the primary responsibility for making such judgments in light of competing policies and interests. But "[t]o withstand constitutional challenge, . . . classifications by gender must serve important governmental objectives and must be substantially related to the achievement of those objectives." *Craig v. Boren.*[9] Such classifications, however, have frequently been revealed on analysis to rest only upon "old notions" and "archaic and overboard" generalizations, *Stanton v. Stanton,* 421 U.S., at 14; *Schlesinger v. Ballard,* 419 U.S., at 508; *cf. Mathews v. Lucas,* 427 U.S. 495, 512–13 (1976), and so have been found to offend the prohibitions against denial of equal protection of the law. *Reed v. Reed; Frontiero v. Richardson; Weinberger v. Wiesenfeld; Stanton v. Stanton; Craig. v. Boren. See also Stanley v. Illinois; Taylor v. Louisiana,* 419 U.S. 522 (1975).

Therefore, . . . *Wiesenfeld* held that . . . benefits "directly related to years worked and amount earned by a covered employee, and not to the needs of the beneficiaries directly," like the employment-related benefits in *Frontiero,* "must be distributed according to classifications which do not without sufficient justification differentiate among covered employees solely on the basis of sex." 420 U.S., at 647.

B

Appellant next argues that *Frontiero* and *Wiesenfeld* should be distinguished as involving statutes with different objectives

than § 402(f)(1)(D). Rather than merely enacting presumptions designed to save the expense and trouble of determining which spouses are really dependent, providing benefits to all widows, but only to such widowers as prove dependency, § 402(f)(1)(D), it is argued, rationally defines different standards of eligibility because of the differing social welfare needs of widowers and widows. That is, the argument runs, Congress may reasonably have presumed that nondependent widows, who receive benefits, are needier than nondependent widowers, who do not, because of job discrimination against women (particularly older women), *see Kahn v. Shevin,* 416 U.S. 351, 353–54 (1974), and because they are more likely to have been more dependent on their spouses. *See Wiesenfeld,* at 645; *Kahn v. Shevin,* at 354 n.7.

But "inquiry into the actual purposes" of the discrimination, *Wiesenfeld,* at 648, proves the contrary. First, § 402(f)(1)(D) itself is phrased in terms of *dependency,* not need. Congress chose to award benefits not to widowers who could prove that they are needy, but to those who could prove that they had been dependent on their wives for more than one-half of their support. On the face of the statute, dependency, not need, is the criterion for inclusion.

Moreover, the general scheme of OASDI shows that dependence on the covered wage earner is the critical factor in determining beneficiary categories. . . .

Finally, the legislative history . . . refutes appellant's contention. . . .

We conclude, therefore, that the differential treatment of nondependent widows and widowers results not, as appellant asserts, from a deliberate congressional intention to remedy the arguably greater needs of the former, but rather from an intention to aid the dependent spouses of deceased wage earners, coupled with a presumption that wives are usually dependent. This presents precisely the situation faced in

---

9. Thus, justifications that suffice for non-gender-based classifications in the social welfare area do not necessarily justify gender discriminations . . . [A]dministrative convenience and certainty of result have been found inadequate justifications gender-based classifications. *Reed v. Reed; Frontiero v. Richardson; Stanley v. Illinois. Cf. Mathews v. Lucas,* 427 U.S. 495; 509–10 (1976).

Frontiero and *Wiesenfeld.* The only conceivable justification for writing the presumption of wives' dependency into the statute is the assumption, not verified by the Government in *Frontiero,* 411 U.S., at 689, or here, but based simply on "archaic and overbroad" generalizations, *Schlesinger v. Ballard,* 419 U.S., at 508, that it would save the Government time, money, and effort simply to pay benefits to all widows, rather than to require proof of dependency of both sexes. We held in *Frontiero,* and again in *Wiesenfeld,* and therefore hold again here, that such assumptions do not suffice to justify a gender-based discrimination in the distribution of employment-related benefits.

MR. JUSTICE STEVENS, concurring in the judgment.

Although my conclusion is the same, my appraisal of the relevant discrimination and my reasons for concluding that it is unjustified, are somewhat different from those expressed by MR. JUSTICE BRENNAN.

First, I agree with MR. JUSTICE REHNQUIST that the constitutional question raised by this plaintiff requires us to focus on his claim for benefits rather than his deceased wife's tax obligation. She had no contractual right to receive benefits or to control their payment; moreover, the payments are not a form of compensation for her services.[1] At the same salary level, all workers must pay the same tax, whether they are male or female, married or single, old or young, the head of a large family or a small one. The benefits which may ultimately become payable to them or to a wide variety of beneficiaries—including their families, their spouses, future spouses, and even their ex-wives—vary enormously, but

such variations do not convert a uniform tax obligation into an unequal one. The discrimination against this plaintiff would be the same if the benefits were funded from general revenues. In short, . . . the relevant discrimination in this case is against surviving male spouses, rather than against deceased female wage earners.[2]

Second, I also agree with MR. JUSTICE REHNQUIST that a classification which treats certain aged widows more favorably than their male counterparts is not "invidious." Such a classification does not imply that males are inferior to females, *cf. Mathews v. Lucas* (June 29, 1976) (STEVENS, J., dissenting); does not condemn a large class on the basis of the misconduct of an unrepresentative few, *cf. Craig v. Boren* (December 20, 1976) (STEVENS, J., concurring); and does not add to the burdens of an already disadvantaged discrete minority. *Cf. Hampton v. Mow Sun Wong,* 426 U.S. 88, 102. It does, however, treat similarly situated persons differently solely because they are not of the same sex.

Third, MR. JUSTICE REHNQUIST correctly identifies two hypothetical justifications for this discrimination that are comparable to those the Court found acceptable in *Mathews v. Lucas* (June 29, 1976), and *Kahn v. Shevin.* Neither the "administrative convenience" rationale of *Lucas,* nor the "policy of cushioning the financial impact of spousal loss upon the sex for which that loss imposes a disproportionately heavy burden," *Kahn,* at 355, can be described as wholly irrational. Nevertheless, I find both justifications unacceptable in this case.

The administrative convenience rationale rests on the assumption that the cost of providing benefits to nondependent wid-

---

1. For this reason this case is not controlled by *Frontiero v. Richardson.*

2. The contrary analysis in *Weinberger v. Wiesenfeld,* 420 U.S. 636, 646–47, was not necessary to the decision of that case. *See* REHNQUIST, J., concurring, 420 U.S., at 655.

ows is justified by eliminating the burden of requiring those who are dependent to establish that fact. MR. JUSTICE REHNQUIST's careful analysis of the relevant data, *see post*, at n.7, demonstrates that at present only about 10 percent of the married women in the relevant age bracket are nondependent. Omitting any requirement that widows establish dependency therefore expedites the processing of about 90 percent of the applications. This convenience must be regarded as significant even though procedures could certainly be developed to minimize the burden.[4]

But what is the offsetting cost that Congress imposed on the Nation in order to achieve this administrative convenience? Assuming that Congress intended only to benefit dependent spouses, and that it has authorized payments to nondependent widows to save the cost of administering a dependency requirement for widows, it has paid a truly staggering price for a relatively modest administrative gain: the cost of payments to the hundreds of thousands of widows who are not within the described purpose of the statute is perhaps 750 million dollars a year. The figures for earlier years were presumably smaller, but must still have been large in relation to the possible administrative savings. It is inconceivable that Congress would have authorized such large expenditures for an administrative purpose without the benefit of any cost analysis, or indeed, without even discussing the problem. I am therefore convinced that administrative conve-

nience was not the actual reason for the discrimination.[6]

It is also clear that the disparate treatment of widows and widowers is not the product of a conscious purpose to redress the "legacy of economic discrimination" against females. *Kahn v. Shevin*, at 359. The widows who benefit from the disparate treatment are those who were sufficiently successful in the job market to become nondependent on their husbands. Such a widow is the least likely to need special benefits. The widow most in need is the one who is "suddenly forced into a job market with which she is unfamiliar, and in which, because of her former economic dependency, she will have fewer skills to offer." *Kahn v. Shevin*, at 354. To accept the *Kahn* justification we must presume that Congress deliberately gave a special benefit to those females least likely to have been victims of the historic discrimination discussed in *Kahn*. Respect for the legislative process precludes the assumption that the statutory discrimination is the product of such irrational lawmaking.

4. Dependency in the statutory sense is a clearly defined criterion for eligibility which would have to be applied only once for each applicant. It is a requirement which several other classes of potential beneficiaries are required to meet. Moreover, the requirement would be especially easy to apply since 75 percent of the women over 55 do not work.

6. The Secretary appears to concede . . . this. Appellant's Brief. Moreover, a 1957 amendment to the statute is inconsistent with this justification. Widow's benefits were originally not payable to a widow who had lived apart from her husband unless she had been "receiving regular contributions from him toward her support" or unless a court had ordered him to pay support. . . . The requirement that a widow who had lived separately from her husband receive at least some support from him makes sense if Congress was concerned with the statutory 50 percent test for dependency: such widows are obviously far less likely to meet that test than widows who had lived with their husbands. But Congress deleted the provision in 1957 and extended benefits to all widows, including those who lived apart from their husbands, with no requirement of support. The 1957 amendment is affirmative evidence that Congress intended to provide benefits for all widows regardless of

The step-by-step evolution of this statutory scheme included a legislative decision to provide benefits for all widows and a separate decision to provide benefits for dependent widowers. Admittedly, each of these separate judgments has a rational and benign purpose. But I consider it clear that Congress never focused its attention on the question whether to divide nondependent surviving spouses into two classes on the basis of sex. The history of the statute is entirely consistent with the view that Congress simply assumed that all widows should be regarded as "dependents" in some general sense, even though they could not satisfy the statutory support test later imposed on men.[8] It is fair to infer that habit, rather than analysis or actual reflection, made it seem acceptable to equate the terms "widow" and "dependent surviving spouse." That kind of automatic reflex is far different from either a legislative decision to favor females in order to compensate for past wrongs, or a legislative decision that the administrative savings exceed the cost of extending benefits to nondependent widows.

I am therefore persuaded that this discrimination against a group of males is merely the accidental byproduct of a traditional way of thinking about females. . . . [A] rule which effects an unequal distribution of economic benefits solely on the basis of sex is sufficiently questionable that "due process requires that there be a legitimate basis for presuming that the rule was actually intended to serve [the] interest" put forward by the government as its justification. *See Hampton v. Mow Sun Wong*, 426 U.S. 88, 103.[9] . . . [S]omething more than accident is necessary to justify the disparate treatment of persons who have as strong a claim to equal treatment as do similarly situated surviving spouses.

But if my judgment is correct, what is to be said about *Kahn v. Shevin?* For that case involved a discrimination between surviving spouses which originated in 1885; a discrimination of that vintage cannot reasonably be supposed to have been motivated by a decision to repudiate the nineteenth-century presumption that females are inferior to males.[10] It seems clear, therefore, that the Court upheld the Florida statute on the basis of a hypothetical justification

---

whether they could satisfy the statutory dependency test. It is also noteworthy that elsewhere in the statute, Congress indicated its intention to create a presumption of dependency by stating that certain family members are "deemed dependent" under certain circumstances.

For the reasons stated in part IVB of MR. JUSTICE BRENNAN's opinion, the Secretary's alternative explanation of the statute as being a welfare measure intended to alleviate the poverty of elderly widows is plainly unacceptable.

8. The discriminatory feature of the statute can be said to be the fact that women are given the benefit of a broad, vague definition of "dependent" while men are held to a harsh arithmetic standard. . . . Although plaintiff is not a dependent in the definition applied to widowers, it cannot be said with assurance that he is not a dependent in whatever broad sense Congress had in mind when it classified all widows as dependents.

9. In the absence of evidence to the contrary, we might presume that Congress had such an interest in mind, *see Hampton v. Mow Sun Wong*, at 103, but here that presumption is untenable. Perhaps an actual, considered legislative choice would be sufficient to allow this statute to be upheld, but that is a question I would reserve until such a choice has been made.

10. This presumption was expressly recognized in the literature of the nineteenth century. It was this presumption that Mr. Bumble ridiculed when he disclaimed responsibility for his wife's misconduct. Because a part of his disclaimer is so well known, it may not be inappropriate to quote the entire passage:

"It was all Mrs. Bumble. She would do it,"

for the discrimination which had nothing to do with the legislature's actual motivation. On this premise, I would be required to regard *Kahn* as controlling in this case, were it not for the fact that I believe precisely the same analysis applies to *Weinberger v. Wiesenfeld.*

In *Wiesenfeld*, the Court rejected an attempt to use "mere recitation of a benign, compensatory purpose" as "an automatic shield," 420 U.S., at 648, for a statute which was actually based on "'archaic and overboard' generalization[s]." (*Id.* at 643.) In *Wiesenfeld*, as in this case, the victims of the statutory discrimination were widowers. They were totally excluded from eligibility for benefits available to similarly situated widows, just as in this case nondependent widowers are totally excluded from eligibility for benefits payable to nondependent widows. The exclusion in *Wiesenfeld* was apparently the accidental byproduct of the same kind of legislative process that gave rise to *Kahn* and to this case. If there is inconsistency between *Kahn* and *Wiesenfeld*, as I believe there is, it is appropriate to follow the later unanimous holding rather than the earlier, sharply divided decision. And if the cases are distinguishable, *Wiesenfeld* is closer on its facts to this case than is *Kahn.*

---

urged Mr. Bumble; first looking round to ascertain that his partner had left the room.

"That is no excuse." replied Mr. Brownlow. "You were present on the occasion of the destruction of these trinkets, and, indeed, are the more guilty of the two, in the eye of the law: *for the law supposes that your wife acts under your direction.*

"If the law supposes that," said Mr. Bumble, squeezing his hat emphatically in both hands, "the law is a ass—a idiot. If that's the eye of the law, the law's a bachelor; and the worst I wish the law is, that his eye may be opened by experience—by experience." C. Dickens, *The Adventures of Oliver Twist*, c. LI. (Emphasis added.)

For these reasons, and on the authority of the holding in *Wiesenfeld*, I concur in the Court's judgment.

Mr. Justice Rehnquist, with whom The Chief Justice, Mr. Justice Stewart, and Mr. Justice Blackmun join, dissenting.

In the light of this Court's recent decisions beginning with *Reed v. Reed*, one cannot say that there is no support in our cases for the result reached by the Court. One can, however, believe as I do that careful consideration of these cases affords more support for the opposite result than it does for that reached by the Court. Indeed, it seems to me that principles . . . which may be deduced from these cases . . . indicate that the Court has reached the wrong result.

The first of these principles is that cases requiring heightened levels of scrutiny for particular classifications under the Equal Protection Clause, which have originated in areas of the law outside of the field of social insurance legislation, will not be uncritically carried over into that field. This does not mean that the word "social insurance" is some sort of magic phrase which automatically mutes the requirements of the Equal Protection component of Fifth Amendment. But it does suggest that in a legislative system which distributes benefit payments among literally millions of people there are at least two characteristics which are not found in many other types of statutes. The first is that the statutory scheme will typically have been expanded by amendment over a period of years so that it is virtually impossible to say that a particular amendment fits with mathematical nicety into a carefully conceived overall plan for payment of benefits. The second is that what in many other areas of the law will be relatively low-level considerations of "administrative convenience" will in this area of the law be a much more vital relation to the overall legislative plan because of congressional concern for certainty in determination of entitlement and promptness in payment of benefits.

The second principle upon which I believe this legislative classification should be sustained is that set forth in our opinion in *Kahn v. Shevin.* The effect of the statutory scheme is to make it easier for widows to obtain benefits than it is for widowers, since the former qualify automatically while the latter must show proof of need. Such a requirement in no way perpetuates or exacerbates the economic disadvantage which has led the Court to conclude that gender-based discrimination must meet a different test than other types of classifications. It is, like the property tax exemption to widows in *Kahn,* a differing treatment which "'rest[s] upon some ground of difference having a fair and substantial relation to the object of the legislation.'" *Id.* at 355.

I

Both *Weinberger v. Wiesenfeld* and *Frontiero v. Richardson* are undoubtedly relevant to the decision of this case, but the plurality overstates that relevance when it says that these two cases "plainly require affirmance of the judgment of the District Court." The disparate treatment of widows and widowers by this Act is undoubtedly a gender-based classification, but this is the beginning and not the end of the inquiry. In the case of classifications based on legitimacy, and in the case of irrebuttable presumptions, constitutional doctrine which would have invalidated the same distinctions in other contexts has been held not to require that result when they were used within comprehensive schemes for social insurance. The same result should obtain in the case of constitutional principles dealing with gender-based distinctions. . . .

Two observations about *Wiesenfeld* are

pertinent. First, the provision of the Social Security Act held unconstitutional there flatly denied surviving widowers the possibility of obtaining benefits no matter what showing of need might be made. The section under attack in the instant case does not totally foreclose widowers, but simply requires from them a proof of dependency which is not required from similarly situated widows. Second, *Wiesenfeld* was decided before [recent cases which] . . . refused uncritically to extend into the field of social security law constitutional proscriptions against distinctions based on illegitimacy and irrebuttable presumptions which had originated in other areas of the law. While the holding of *Wiesenfeld* is not inconsistent with [those cases] . . . its reasoning is not in complete harmony with the recognition in those cases of the special characteristics of social insurance plans.

II

Those special characteristics arise from the nature of the legislative problem which numerous sessions of Congress have had to face in defining the coverage of the Social Security Act. The program has been participatory from the outset, in the sense that benefits have not been extended to persons without at least a close relationship to a person paying into the system during his working life. But Congress did not legislate with the idea that it was fulfilling any narrow contractual obligation owed to the program participant. On the contrary, Congress has continually increased the amounts of benefits paid, and expanded the pool of eligible recipients by singling out additional, identifiable groups having both the requisite relationship to the contributing worker and a degree of probable need. . . . It is not difficult to predict some traits of the system emerging from this sort of step-by-step legislative expansion.

One is that the resulting statute, like

the process which produced it, extends benefits in a piecemeal fashion. There will be some individuals with needs demonstrably as great as those within a class of qualifying beneficiaries who will nonetheless be treated less favorably than that class. This is because these classes, formulated and reformulated over a period of decades, could not perfectly mirror the abstract definition of equality of need unless Congress were to burden the system with numerous individualized determinations which might frustrate the primary purposes of the Act.

Another characteristic of the Social Security statute which is predictable from the manner of its enactment, is the balance between a desire that payments correlate with degree of need and a recognition that precise correlation is unattainable given the administrative realities of the situation. No one would contend, for example, that all wives of program participants, who are over 62 and entitled to old-age or disability insurance benefits in their own right equal to no more than one-half of their husband's primary amount, are needy. Nonetheless the administrative problems of determining actual need have led Congress to employ these and factors like them as the determinants of eligibility. . . . The over-inclusiveness of such categorizations is, in many cases, not only tolerable but Solomonic. For had Congress attempted to distribute program funds in precise accordance with a purpose to alleviate need, it could very well have created a procedural leviathan consuming substantial amounts of those funds in case-by-case determinations. . . .

The provisions at issue in this case, relating to widows' and widowers' benefits, display all the earmarks of their origins in the oft-repeated process of legislative reconsideration and expansion of beneficiary groups. . . . I agree with the plurality's statement that "[t]here is no indication whatever in any of the legislative history that Congress gave any attention to the specific case of nondependent widows, and found that they were in need of benefits despite their lack of dependency. . . ." *Ante.* But neither is there any reason to doubt that it singled out the group of aged widows for especially favorable treatment because it saw prevalent throughout that group a characteristically high level of need.

. . . The present statutory treatment of widows and widowers would seem to reflect a pair of legislative judgments about the needs of those two groups. The first is that the persons qualifying for spousal benefits are likely to have even more substantial needs after the passing of their spouse. . . .

The second legislative judgment implicit in the widow's and widower's provisions is that widows, as a practical matter, are much more likely to be without adequate means of support than are widowers. The plurality opinion makes much of establishing this point, that the absence of any dependency prerequisite to the award of widow's benefits reflects a judgment, resting on "administrative convenience," that dependence among aged widows is frequent enough to justify waiving the requirement entirely. I differ not with the recognition of this administrative convenience purpose, but with the conclusion that such a purpose necessarily invalidates the resulting classification. Our decisions dealing with social welfare legislation indicate that our inquiry must go further. For rational classifications aimed at distributing funds to beneficiaries under social insurance legislation weigh a good deal more heavily on the governmental interest side of the equal protection balance than they may in other legislative contexts. The "administrative convenience" which is afforded by such classifications in choosing [an estate] administrator. . . , *see Reed*, is significantly less important than is the "convenience" afforded by classifications in administering an Act designed to provide benefits to millions upon millions of beneficiaries with promptness and certainty. For this reason, the plurality errs in merely dispatching this statute with an incantation of "administrative convenience." It should go further and consider the governmental interest . . . in a social insurance statute such as this, in the light of the claimed injury to appellee.

III

Whatever his actual needs, Goldfarb would, of course, have no complaint if Congress had chosen to require proof of dependence by widows as well as widowers, or if it had simply refrained from making any provision whatever for benefits to surviving spouses. "A legislature may address a problem 'one step at a time,' or even 'select one phase of one field and apply a remedy there, neglecting others.' *Williamson v. Lee Optical Co.*, 348 U.S. 483, 489 (1955)." *Jefferson v. Hackney*, 406 U.S. 535, 546 (1972) [additional citations omitted]. Any claim which he has must therefore turn upon the alleged impropriety of giving benefits to widows without requiring them to make the same proof of dependence required of widowers. Yet, in the context of the legislative purpose, this amounts not to exclusion but to overinclusiveness for reasons of administrative convenience which, if reasonably supported by the underlying facts, is not offensive to the Equal Protection Clause in social welfare cases. . . . Here the dependence test was not imposed upon widows, apparently on a . . . belief that the actual rate of dependence was sufficiently high that a requirement of proof would create more ad-

ministrative expense than it would save in the award of benefits.[7]

IV

Perhaps because the reasons asserted for "heightened scrutiny" of gender-based distinctions are rooted in the fact that *women* have in the past been victims of unfair treatment, *see Frontiero*, at 684–88, the plurality says that the difference in treatment here is not only between a widow and a widower, but between the respective deceased spouses of the two. It concludes that wage earning wives are deprived "of protection for their families which men receive as a result of their employment."

But this is a questionable . . . analysis which can be used to prove virtually anything. It might just as well have been urged in *Kahn v. Shevin*, where we upheld a Florida property tax exemption redounding to the benefit of widows but not widowers, that the real discrimination was between the deceased spouses of the respective widow and widower, who had doubtless

---

7. There is substantial . . . evidence indicating that the differential treatment of widows and widowers is economically justifiable on the basis of administrative convenience. There is good reason to suppose that few enough aged widows are not . . . dependent at the time of their husband's death that the costs of administering the test would exceed the savings resulting from its application.

. . . . [The evidence] suggests that the number of married women over 55 who would satisfy the dependence test is something like 88.5 percent—the 77 percent who do not work, plus half of the remaining 23 percent who do. This $^9/_{10}$ correlation appears sufficiently high to justify extension of benefits to the other $^1/_{10}$ for reasons of administrative convenience.

On the side of widower's benefits, . . . the incidence of dependent husbands among all married couples is approximately 1 percent. . . .

by their contributions to the family or marital community helped make possible the acquisition of the property which was now being disparately taxed. . . .

In *Weinberger v. Wiesenfeld*, the Court again invalidated OASDI provisions which denied one group any opportunity to show themselves proper beneficiaries given the apparent statutory purpose. . . . The defect of that statute was its conclusive exception of widowers from the benefited class, solely on the basis of their sex, and in contravention of the legislative purpose to allow parents with deceased spouses to provide personal parental care. There is no plausible claim to be made here that a statutory objective is being thwarted by under-inclusiveness of the class of beneficiaries.

This case is also distinguishable from *Frontiero v. Richardson*, in the sense that social insurance differs from compensation for work done. While there is no basis for assessing the propriety of a given allocation of funds within a social insurance program apart from an identifiable legislative purpose, a compensatory scheme may be evaluated under the principle of equal pay for equal work done. This case is therefore unlike *Frontiero*. . . .

These compensatory fringe benefits were available to male employees as a matter of course, but were unavailable to females except on proof that their husbands depended on them for over one-half of their support. Since males got such compensatory benefits even though their wives were not so dependent, females with non-

dependent husbands were effectively denied equal compensation for equal efforts. The same is not true here, where the benefit payments to survivors are neither contractual nor compensatory for work done, and where there is thus no comparative basis for evaluating the propriety of a given benefit apart from the legislative purpose.

V

The very most that can be squeezed out of the facts of this case in the way of cognizable "discrimination" is a classification which favors aged widows. Quite apart from any considerations of legislative purpose and "administrative convenience" which may be advanced to support the classification, this is scarcely an invidious discrimination. Two of our recent cases have rejected efforts by men to challenge similar classifications. We have held that it is not improper for the military to formulate "up-or-out" rules taking into account sex-based differences in employment opportunities in a way working to the benefit of women. *Schlesinger v. Ballard*, or to grant solely to widows a property tax exemption in recognition of their depressed plight. *Kahn v. Shevin*. A waiver of the dependency prerequisite for benefits, in the case of this same class of aged widows, under a program explicitly aimed at the assistance of needy groups, appears to be well within the holding of the *Kahn* case, which upheld a flat $500 exemption to widows, without any consideration of need. . . .

CASE QUESTIONS

1. In a sense the result in this case depends on the opinion of Justice Stevens, whose vote makes or breaks the majority. His vote in turn seems to depend on his perception of the *actual* (as contrasted with a "possible" or "hypothetical") legislative purpose behind this statute. If Congress were to reenact this statute with a preamble explicitly recognizing that widows (even those whose husbands contributed less than half their support) are more likely to be impoverished in old age than are widowers, would Stevens then vote to uphold it? (See especially his footnote 9.)

2. Does Stevens misconceive the question when he suggests the absurdity of presuming that Congress "deliberately gave a special benefit to those females least likely to have been victims of the historic discrimination"? Should he focus on the comparative advantage between nondependent widows and nondependent widowers instead of the comparative advantage of nondependent widows over dependent widows?

3. Stevens suggests that *Weinberger v. Weisenfeld* (won by the Ginzburg-Wulf attorney team) is not compatible with *Kahn v. Shevin* (lost by the same team). Should an attorney advising a client who now wanted to challenge a *Kahn*-type discrimination encourage him to go to court?

4. Did this statute discriminate against males or against females? Does it matter?

5. If Congress now excludes nondependent widows in Goldfarb's position from eligibility for spouse survival benefits, will this decision have helped or hurt women? Men?

6. Justice Rehnquist's dissenting opinion characterizes this law as requiring "proof of need," when what the statute actually required was proof of "dependency." Is the shift significant?

7. Does the *possibility* of demonstrating dependency permitted by this statute substantially differentiate it from the statute invalidated in *Wiesenfeld?* (That statute had not allowed a widower to prove that he needed financial help in supporting his children.)

8. The *Goldfarb* decision was expected to cost the government an estimated $500 million, in contrast to an estimated $20 million cost due to the *Wiesenfeld* decision.[3] Might this fact have influenced the *Goldfarb* dissenters?

In the post-*Craig* era, the Supreme Court did not simply invalidate all sex-based discriminations. Only three weeks after the *Goldfarb* decision the Court issued a brief "per curiam" (unsigned) opinion that upheld a statutory gender discrimination. In *Califano v. Webster*, the Court rejected a challenge to section 215 of the Social Security Act. That section, which applied only to persons retiring before 1975, when a 1972 amendment to the law took effect, permitted women to calculate their "average" monthly earnings by a more generous averaging technique than that granted to men. The district court in this instance had been persuaded by Mr. Webster that the sex discrimination had no "rational basis" and had held it unconstitutional. The Court's reversal was unanimous.

Califano v. Webster, 430 U.S. 313 (1977)

Per Curiam.

To withstand scrutiny under the equal protection component of the Fifth Amendment's Due Process Clause, "classifications by gender must serve important governmental objectives and must be substantially related to achievement of those objectives." *Craig v. Boren*. Reduction of the disparity in economic condition between men and women caused by the long history of discrimination against women has been recognized as such an important governmental objective. *Schlesinger v. Ballard; Kahn v. Shevin*. But "the mere recitation of a benign, compensatory purpose is not an automatic shield that protects against any inquiry into the actual purposes underlying a legislative scheme." *Weinberger v. Wiesenfeld*, at 648 (1975). Accordingly, we have rejected attempts to justify gender classifications when the classifications in fact penalized women wage earners, *Califano v. Goldfarb*, n.8 (1977); *Weinberger v. Wiesenfeld*, at 645, or when its legislative history revealed that the classification was not enacted as compensation for past discrimination. *Califano v. Goldfarb*, (STEVENS, J., concurring in the judgment); *Weinberger v. Wiesenfeld*, at 648.

The statutory scheme involved here is more analogous to those upheld in *Kahn* and *Ballard* than to those struck down in *Wiesenfeld* and *Goldfarb*. The more favorable treatment of the female wage earner enacted here was not a result of "archaic and overbroad generalizations" about women,

Schlesinger v. Ballard, 419 U.S., at 508, or of "the roletyping society has long imposed" upon women, *Stanton v. Stanton*, 421 U.S. 7, 15 (1975), such as casual assumptions that women are "the weaker sex" or are more likely to be childrearers or dependents. Cf. *Califano v. Goldfarb; Weinberger v. Wiesenfeld*. Rather, "the only discernible purpose of [the differing treatment here is] the permissible one of redressing our society's longstanding disparate treatment of women." *Califano v. Goldfarb*, n.8.

The challenged statute operated directly to compensate women for past economic discrimination. Retirement benefits under the Act are based on past earnings. But as we have recognized, "[w]hether from overt discrimination or from the socialization process of a male-dominated culture, the job market is inhospitable to the woman seeking any but the lowest paid jobs." *Kahn v. Shevin*, 416 U.S., at 353. See generally *id*. at 353–54, and nn.4–6. Thus, allowing women, who as such have been unfairly hindered from earning as much as men, to eliminate additional low-earning years from the calculation of their retirement benefits works directly to remedy some part of the effect of past discrimination. Cf. *Schlesinger v. Ballard*, 419 U.S., at 508.

The legislative history of § 215(b)(3) also reveals that Congress directly addressed the justification for differing treatment of men and women in the former version of that section and purposely enacted the more favorable treatment for female wage earners to compensate for past employment discrimination against women. . . .

[T]he legislative history is clear that the differing treatment of men and women in former § 215(b)(3) was not "the accidental byproduct of a traditional way of thinking about females," *Califano v. Goldfarb*, (STEVENS, J., concurring in result), but rather was deliberately enacted to compensate for particular economic disabilities suffered by women.

That Congress changed its mind in 1972 and equalized the treatment of men and women does not, as the District Court concluded, constitute an admission by Congress that its previous policy was invidiously discriminatory. 413 F. Supp., at 129. Congress has in recent years legislated directly upon the subject of unequal treatment of women in the job market. Congress may well have decided that "[t]hese congressional reforms . . . have lessened the economic justification for the more favorable benefit computation formula in § 215(b)(3)." *Kohr v. Weinberger*, 378 F. Supp. 1299, 1305 (1974). . . . Moreover, elimination of the more favorable benefit computation for women wage earners, even in the remedial context, is wholly consistent with those reforms, which require equal treatment of men and women in preference to the attitudes ot "romantic pater-

nalism" that have contributed to the "long and unfortunate history of sex discrimination." *Frontiero v. Richardson*, at 684.

Reversed.

MR. CHIEF JUSTICE BURGER, with whom MR. JUSTICE STEWART, MR. JUSTICE BLACKMUN, and MR. JUSTICE REHNQUIST join, concurring in the judgment.

While I am happy to concur in the Court's judgment, I find it somewhat difficult to distinguish the Social Security provision upheld here from that struck down so recently in *Califano v. Goldfarb*. Although the distinction drawn by the Court between this case and *Goldfarb* is not totally lacking in substance, I question whether certainty in the law is promoted by hinging the validity of important statutory schemes on whether five Justices view them to be more akin to the "offensive" provisions stuck down in *Weinberger v. Wiesenfeld* and *Frontiero v. Richardson*, or more like the "benign" provisions upheld in *Schlesinger v. Ballard* and *Kahn v. Shevin*. I therefore concur in the judgment of the Court for reasons stated by MR. JUSTICE REHNQUIST in his dissenting opinion in *Goldfarb* in which MR. JUSTICE STEWART, MR. JUSTICE BLACKMUN, and I joined.

By the end of the Supreme Court's 1977–1978 term, the impact of the new *Craig v. Boren* rule was not clearly discernible. The Court had taken up two challenges to Social Security System antimale discrimination, and it struck down the first discrimination but unanimously upheld the second. The patterns of precedent into which each of these cases falls had already taken shape before the *Craig v. Boren* decision. *Califano v. Goldfarb* falls easily in line behind *Frontiero* and *Weinberger*, and *Califano v. Webster* fits easily into the slot carved out by *Kahn v. Shevin* and *Schlesinger v. Ballard*. Thus it still seems that when the Supreme Court can be convinced that a particular legislative sex discrimination aims at redressing the economic or other societal disadvantages that confront women, the Court *will* uphold the discrimination, even under the *Craig* rule.

Wengler v. Druggists Mutual Insurance (1980), discussion

One interesting legacy of the *Goldfarb* decision showed up in a 1980 case, *Wengler v. Druggists Mutual Ins.*[4] The legal issue perfectly mirrored those in *Goldfarb,* except that the context was a state workmen's compensation program providing death benefits for surviving spouses, rather than a federal social security program. The influence of *Goldfarb* as a precedent showed up clearly; instead of 5–4 the justices divide 8–1. Rehnquist wrote a dissent in which he said simply that he still believes *Goldfarb* was wrongly decided and that he believes the rule of following precedent (in Latin "stare decisis") applies with less force in constitutional law than elsewhere.

Even Justice Rehnquist, however, in the post-*Craig* period will sometimes vote to strike down gender discrimination. In a 1979 case, he voted with a unanimous Court in declaring unconstitutional the sex discrimination in an AFDC (Aid to Families with Dependent Children) program that awarded funds to families who lost support due to the unemployment of a father, but not for the unemployment of a mother.[5]

Later litigation revealed additional interests (besides compensating for societal sex discrimination) that the Court would consider "important" enough to justify differential treatment of men and women. These included the need to take account of the differences of situation between unwed mothers and unwed fathers (found sometimes important enough but sometimes not), the need to take account of physiological gender differences in the context of statutory rape laws, and the need to give Congress wide latitude in areas of foreign relations and national security. Cases treating these interests are dealt with in remaining portions of this chapter. Also dealt with are cases where the Court refused to find the legislative interest important enough to justify gender discrimination. These included, respectively, the purported state interests (1) in providing women with the educational option of attending an all-women college and (2) in preserving the traditional concept of marriage, in which the husband must be the provider and head of household.

By the end of this chapter, the reader should be able to decide (at least tentatively) whether the *Craig* rule has produced a body of law shaped by discernible and relatively cogent principles, or whether, as Justice Rehnquist predicted, it simply set the Court loose on an uncharted sea of subjective preference.

Fathers' Rights and Equal Protection

As illustrated by *Taylor v. Louisiana* (in chapter 2), in the *Reed-Craig* period the Court sometimes avoided the need to twist the rationality test by invoking, instead, a relevant fundamental constitutional right (such as the right to trial by jury) which would, quite apart from the gender discrimination, trigger the strict-scrutiny/compelling-interest test. (I.e., if the government tries to infringe a fundamental right, it needs to prove a compelling interest in doing so.) Sometimes the right had a textual referent in the Constitution; trial by jury is mentioned both in Article III and in the Sixth Amendment. Other times (as in the now discredited "liberty of contract" cases covered in chapter 1) the Court claimed to locate the fundamental right in American societal and legal traditions. The latter approach was used by the Court to resolve the conflict between Peter Stanley and the State of Illinois in 1972.

Peter Stanley challenged a set of Illinois statutes that discriminated against unwed fathers. According to Illinois law, if the mother of an illegitimate child died, the child automatically became a ward of the state, to be put up for adoption. If, however, the parents were married and one parent died, their children could not be taken away from the living parent without a court hearing proving parental unfitness. Also, if the unmarried father of a child died, the unmarried mother would not lose custody of the child (unless she were proved to be an unfit parent in a child custody proceeding). In short, the statute automatically conferred child custody on a married father and on a mother, married or unmarried, and it automatically denied it to an unmarried father. Clearly, in treating unmarried mothers differently from unmarried fathers, the law was classifying persons on the basis of gender.

Peter Stanley had lived with Joan Stanley intermittently for eighteen years, during which time they had three children. Peter Stanley supported the children. When Joan Stanley died, Illinois declared two of her children[6] wards of the state in a dependency proceeding, and placed them with court-appointed guardians. Peter Stanley appealed the decision, claiming that this process denied him equal protection of the laws in depriving him of a benefit that would be given by law to unmarried mothers or to married fathers. The Illinois Supreme Court rejected his constitutional argument, and he proceeded to the U.S. Supreme Court.

In responding to Stanley's claim, the Court had more to guide it than the early twentieth century precedents that had cavalierly condoned discrimination against men. Besides the very recent *Reed v. Reed* signal that the equal protection clause was more sensitive to sex-based discrimination than had formerly been true, a number of cases involving the constitutional status of family relationships had entered the body of American legal precedent during the half-century preceding 1972.

Two cases in the 1920s[7] had established that the parental right to guide one's child's education is a "fundamental right" of Americans and that the due process clause requires careful scrutiny of laws infringing on that right. One of those cases[8] established that parents may send their children to private schools (subject however to appropriate accreditation requirements of the state), and the other[9] established the parental right to have one's child study a foreign language.

A case in the 1940s[10] had established that the right of procreation is one of the "basic civil rights of man" and a "basic liberty," and that legislative classifications that infringe on it would be subject to "strict scrutiny" under the equal protection clause.[11] In that case the Supreme Court had declared unconstitutional a law that established sterilization as the punishment for certain crimes.

Then, in 1965[12] and 1972[13] (the latter just a couple of weeks before the *Stanley* decision), the Supreme Court had handed down two groundbreaking decisions on questions involving the use of contraceptives. Both decisions, in striking down prohibitions on contraceptive use and distribution, had relied on a "right to privacy," which the Court said was implied by several of the Bill of Rights amendments and by the very idea of due process of law within the American tradition. In describing that right of privacy in the 1972 case, the Court majority had said, "If the right of privacy means anything, it is the right of the *individual*, married or single, to be free from unwarranted governmental intrusion into matters so fundamentally affecting a person as the decision whether to bear or beget a child."[14]

Thus, Peter Stanley, when he came before the Supreme Court, had available to him two separate legal threads out of which his attorneys might weave his case. First, there was the long thread reaching all the way back to the 1920s that delineated the special legal sanctity of the parent-child relationship.[15] Second, there was the shorter but perhaps potentially sturdier thread that had begun in 1971 to shape a pattern of Supreme Court opposition to gender-based discrimination. The Court opinion of Justice White selected the first of these threads for its dominant lines, but the second can be found woven into the background of the pattern, strengthening the dominant theme.[16]

Peter Stanley v. Illinois, 405 U.S. 645 (1972)

Mr. Justice White delivered the opinion of the Court.

. . .

Stanley presses his equal protection claim here. The State continues to respond that unwed fathers are presumed unfit to raise their children and that it is necessary to hold individualized hearings to determine whether particular fathers are in fact unfit parents before they are separated from their children. We granted certiorari, to determine whether this . . . procedure by presumption could be allowed to stand in light of the fact that Illinois allows married fathers—whether divorced, widowed or separated—and mothers—even if unwed—the benefit of the presumption that they are fit to raise their children.

I

At the outset we reject any suggestion that we need not consider the propriety of the dependency proceeding that separated the Stanleys because Stanley might be able to regain custody of his children as a guardian or through adoption proceedings. . . . Surely in the case before us if there is delay between the doing and the undoing, petitioner suffers from the deprivation of his children and the children suffer from uncertainty and dislocation.

. . . Neither can we ignore that in the proceedings from which this action developed, the "probation officer," the assistant state's attorney, and the judge charged with the case, made it apparent that Stanley, unmarried and impecunious as he is, could not now expect to profit from adoption proceedings.

. . . We must therefore examine the question which Illinois would have us avoid: Is a presumption which distinguishes and burdens all unwed fathers constitutionally repugnant? We conclude that as a matter of due process of law, Stanley was entitled to a hearing on his fitness as a parent before his children were taken from him and that by denying him a hearing and extending it to all other parents whose custody of their children is challenged the State denied Stanley the equal protection of the law guaranteed by the Fourteenth Amendment.

II

The State's right—indeed duty—to protect minor children through a judicial determination of their interests in a neglect proceeding is not challenged here. Rather we are faced with a dependency statute which empowers state officials to circumvent neglect proceedings on the theory that an unwed father is not a "parent" whose existing relationship with his children must be considered. "Parents," says the State, "means the father and mother of a legitimate child. . . , or the natural mother of an illegitimate child, and includes any adoptive parent," Ill. Rev. Stat., ch. 37, § 701–14, but the term does not include unwed fathers.

Under Illinois law, therefore, while the children of all parents can be taken from them in neglect proceedings, that is only after notice, hearing, and proof of such unfitness as a parent as amounts to neglect, an unwed father is uniquely subject to the more simplistic dependency proceeding. By use of this proceeding, the State, on showing that the father was not married to the mother, need not prove unfitness in fact, because it is presumed at law. Thus, the unwed father's claim of parental qualification is avoided as "irrelevant."

In considering this procedure under the Due Process clause, we recognize, as we have in other cases, that due process of law does not require a hearing "in every conceivable case of governmental impairment of private interest." *Cafeteria Workers v. McElroy*, 367 U.S. 886, 894 (1961). That case explained that "[t]he very nature of due process negates any concept of inflexible procedures universally applicable to every imaginable situation" and firmly established that "what procedures due process may require under any given set of circumstances must begin with a determination of the precise nature of the government function involved as well as of the private interest that has been affected by governmental action." *Id.* at 895; *Goldberg v. Kelly,* 397 U.S. 254, 263 (1970).

The private interest here, that of a man in the children he has sired and raised, undeniably warrants deference and, absent a powerful countervailing interest, protection. It is plain that the interest of a parent in the companionship, care, custody, and management of his or her children "come[s] to this Court with a momentum for respect lacking when appeal is made to liberties which derive merely from shifting economic arrangements." *Kovacs v. Cooper,* 336 U.S. 77, 95 (1949) (concurring opinion).

The Court has frequently emphasized the importance of the family. The rights to conceive and to raise one's children have been deemed "essential." *Meyer v. Nebraska,* 262 U.S. 390, 399 (1923), "basic civil rights of man," *Skinner v. Oklahoma,* 316 U.S. 535, 541 (1942), and "[r]ights far more precious . . . than property rights." *May v. Anderson,* 345 U.S. 528, 533 (1953). "It is cardinal with us that the custody, care and nurture of the child reside first in the parents, whose primary function and freedom include preparation for obligations the state can neither supply nor hinder." *Prince v. Massachusetts,* 321 U.S. 158, 166 (1944). The integrity of the family unit has found protection in the Due Process Clause of the Fourteenth Amendment, *Meyer v. Nebraska,* at 399, the Equal Protection Clause of the Fourteenth Amendment, *Skinner v. Oklahoma,* at 541, and the Ninth Amendment, *Griswold v. Connecticut,* 381 U.S. 479, 496 (1965) (Goldberg, J., concurring).

Nor has the law refused to recognize those family relationships unlegitimized by a marriage ceremony. The Court has declared unconstitutional a state statute denying natural, but illegitimate, children a wrongful death action for the death of their mother, emphasizing that such children cannot be denied the right of other children because familial bonds in such cases were often as warm, enduring, and important as those arising within a more formally organized family unit. *Levy v. Louisiana,* 391 U.S. 68, 71–72 (1968). "To say that the test of equal protection should be the 'legal' rather than the 'biological' relationship is to avoid the issue. For the Equal Protection Clause necessarily limits the authority of a State to draw such 'legal' lines as it chooses." *Glona v. American Guarantee Co.,* 391 U.S. 73, 75–76 (1968).

These authorities make it clear that, at the least, Stanley's interest in retaining custody of his children is cognizable and substantial.

For its part, the State has made its interest quite plain: Illinois has declared that the aim of the Juvenile Court Act is to protect "the moral, emotional, mental and physical welfare of the minor and the best interests of the community" and to "strengthen the minor's family ties whenever possible, removing him from the custody of his parents only when his welfare or safety or the protection of the public cannot be adequately safeguarded without removal. . . ." Ill. Rev. Stat. c. 37, §701–702. These are legitimate interests well within the power of the State to implement. . . .

But we are here not asked to evaluate the legitimacy of the state ends, but rather to determine whether the means used to achieve these ends are constitutionally defensible. What is the state interest in separating children from fathers without a hearing designed to determine whether the father is unfit in a particular disputed case? We observe that the State registers no gain towards its declared goals when it separates children from the custody of fit parents. Indeed, if Stanley is a fit father, the State spites its own articulated goals when it needlessly separates him from his family.

In *Bell v. Burson,* 402 U.S. 535 (1971), we found a scheme repugnant to the Due Process Clause because it deprived a driver of his license without reference to the very factor (there fault in driving, here fitness as a parent) which the State itself deemed fundamental to its statutory scheme. Illinois [argues] that Stanley and all other unmarried fathers can reasonably be presumed to be unqualified to raise their children.[5]

It may be, as the State insists, that most unmarried fathers are unsuitable and neglectful parents. It may also be that Stanley is such a parent and that his children should be placed in other hands. But all unmarried fathers are not in this category; some are wholly suited to have custody of their children. This much the State readily concedes, and nothing in this record indicates that Stanley is or has been a neglectful father who has not cared for his children. . . .

[It] may be argued that unmarried fathers are so seldom fit that Illinois need not undergo the administrative inconvenience of inquiry in any case, including Stanley's. The establishment of prompt efficacious procedures to achieve legitimate state ends is a proper state interest worthy of cognizance in constitutional adjudication. But the Constitution recognizes higher values than speed and efficiency.[8] Indeed, one might fairly say of the Bill of Rights in general, and the Due Process Clause in particular, that they were designed to protect the fragile values of a vulnerable citizenry from the overbearing concern for efficiency and efficacy which may characterize praiseworthy government officials no less, and perhaps more, than mediocre ones.

Procedure by presumption is always cheaper and easier than individualized determination. But when, as here, the procedure forecloses the determinative issues of competence and care, when it explicitly disdains present realities in deference to past formalities, it needlessly risks running roughshod over the important interests of both parent and child. It therefore cannot stand.

Bell v. Burson held that the State could not, while purporting to be concerned with

---

5. Illinois says in its brief: ". . . In effect Illinois has imposed a statutory presumption that the best interest of a particular group of children necessitates some governmental supervision in certain clearly defined situations. The group of children who are illegitimate are distinguishable from legitimate children not so much by their status at birth as by the factual differences in their upbringing. While a legitimate child usually is raised by both parents with the attendant familial relationships and a firm concept of home and identity, the illegitimate child normally knows only one parent—the mother.

". . . The Petitioner has premised his argument upon particular factual circumstances—a lengthy relationship with the mother . . . a familial relationship with the two children, and a general assumption that this relationship approximates that in which the natural parents are married to each other.

". . . Even if this characterization were accurate (the record is insufficient to support it) it would not affect the validity of the statutory definition of parent. . . ."

Pp. 24–26 (. . . studies are cited in support of the proposition that men are not naturally inclined to child-rearing), and Transcript of Oral Argument, p. 31 ("We submit that both based on history or [sic] culture the very real differences in terms of their interests in children and their legal responsibility for their children, that the statute here fulfills the compelling governmental objective of protecting children. . . .").

8. *Cf. Reed v. Reed,* 404 U.S. 71, 76 (1971). "Clearly the objective of reducing the workload on probate courts by eliminating one class of contests is not without some legitimacy. . . . [But] [T]o give a mandatory preference to members of either sex over members of the other, merely to accomplish the elimination of hearings on the merits, is to make the very kind of arbitrary legislative choice forbidden by the Equal Protection Clause of the Fourteenth Amendment. . . ."

fault in suspending a driver's license, deprive a citizen of his license without a hearing which would assess fault. Absent fault, the State's declared interest was so attenuated that administrative convenience was insufficient to excuse a hearing where evidence of fault could be considered. That drivers involved in accidents, as a statistical matter, might be very likely to have been wholly or partially at fault did not foreclose hearing and proof in specific cases before licenses were suspended.

We think the Due Process Clause mandates a similar result here. The State's interest in caring for Stanley's children is *de minimis* if Stanley is shown to be a fit father. It insists on presuming rather than proving Stanley's unfitness solely because it is more convenient to presume than to prove. Under the Due Process Clause that advantage is insufficient to justify refusing a father a hearing when the issue at stake is the dismemberment of his family.

III

The State of Illinois assumes custody of the children of married parents, divorced parents, and unmarried mothers only after a hearing and proof of neglect. The children of unmarried fathers, however, are declared dependent children without a hearing on parental fitness and without proof of neglect. Stanley's claim in the state courts and here is that failure to afford him a hearing on his parental qualifications while extending it to other parents denied him equal protection of the laws. We have concluded that all Illinois parents are constitutionally entitled to a hearing on their fitness before their children are removed from their custody. It follows that denying such a hearing to Stanley and those like him while granting it to other Illinois parents is inescapably contrary to the Equal Protection Clause.

The judgment of the Supreme Court of Illinois is *Reversed.* . . .

MR. JUSTICE POWELL and MR. JUSTICE REHNQUIST took no part in the consideration or decision of this case.

MR. JUSTICE DOUGLAS joins in parts I and II of this opinion.

MR. CHIEF JUSTICE BURGER with whom MR. JUSTICE BLACKMUN concurs, dissenting.

The only constitutional issue raised and decided in the courts of Illinois in this case was whether the Illinois statute which omits unwed fathers from the definition of "parents" violates the Equal Protection Clause. We granted certiorari to consider whether the Illinois Supreme Court properly resolved that equal protection issue when it unanimously upheld the statute against petitioner Stanley's attack.

No due process issue was raised in the state courts; and no due process issue was decided by any state court. As MR. JUSTICE DOUGLAS said for this Court in *State Farm Mutual Automobile Ins. Co. v. Duel,* 324 U.S. 154, 160 (1945). "Since the [state] Supreme Court did not pass on the question, we may not do so." . . . The Court's method of analysis seems to ignore the[se] strictures. . . , but the analysis is clear: the Court holds *sua sponte* that the Due Process Clause requires that Stanley, the unwed biological father, be accorded a hearing as to his fitness as a parent before his children are declared wards of the state court; the Court then reasons that since Illinois recognizes such rights to due process in married fathers, it is required by the Equal Protection Clause to give such protection to unmarried fathers. This "method of analysis" is, of course, no more or less than the use of the Equal Protection Clause as a shorthand condensation of the entire Constitution: a State may not deny any constitutional right to some of its citizens without violating the Equal Protection Clause through its failure to deny such rights to all of its citizens. The limits on this Court's jurisdiction are not properly expandable by the use of such semantic devices as that.

Not only does the Court today use dubious reasoning in dealing with limitations upon its jurisdiction, it proceeds as well to strike down the Illinois statute here involved by "answering" arguments which are nowhere to be found in the record or in the State's brief—or indeed in the oral argument. . . .

In regard to the only issue which I consider properly before the Court, I agree with the State's argument that the Equal Protection Clause is not violated when Illinois gives full recognition only to those father-child relationships that arise in the context of family units bound together by legal obligations arising from marriage or from adoption proceedings. Quite apart from the religious or quasi-religious connotations which marriage has—and has historically enjoyed—for a large proportion of this Nation's citizens, it is in law an essentially contractual relationship, the parties to which have legally enforceable rights and duties, with respect both to each other and to any children born to them. Stanley and the mother of these children never entered such a relationship. . . .

Where there is a valid contract of marriage, the law of Illinois presumes that the husband is the father of any child born during the marriage; as the father, he has legally enforceable rights and duties with respect to that child. When a child is born to an unmarried woman, Illinois recognizes the readily identifiable mother, but makes no presumptions as to the identity of the biological father. [He may], however, marry the mother and acknowledge the child as his own; this has the legal effect of legitimating the child and gaining for the father full

recognition as a parent. Ill. Rev. Stat., ch. 3, § 12–8.

. . .

The Illinois Supreme Court correctly held that the State may constitutionally distinguish between unwed fathers and unwed mothers. Here, Illinois' different treatment of the two is part of that State's statutory scheme for protecting the welfare of illegitimate children. In almost all cases, the unwed mother is readily identifiable, generally from hospital records and alternatively by physicians or others attending the child's birth. Unwed fathers, as a class, are not traditionally quite so easy to identify and locate. Many of them either deny all responsibility or exhibit no interest in the child or its welfare; and, of course, many unwed fathers are simply not aware of their parenthood.

Furthermore, I believe that a State is fully justified in concluding, on the basis of common human experience, that the biological role of the mother in carrying and nursing an infant creates stronger bonds between her and the child than the bonds resulting from the male's often casual encounter. This view is reinforced by the observable fact that most unwed mothers exhibit a concern for their offspring either permanently or at least until they are safely placed for adoption, while unwed fathers rarely burden either the mother or the child with their attentions or loyalties. Centuries of human experience buttress this view of the realities of human conditions and suggest that unwed mothers of illegitimate children are generally more dependable protectors of their children than are unwed fathers. While these, like most generalizations, are not without exceptions, they nevertheless provide a sufficient basis to sustain a statutory classification whose objective is not to penalize unwed parents but to further the welfare of illegitimate children in fulfillment of the State's obligations as *parens patriae*.[4]

Stanley depicts himself as a somewhat unusual unwed father, namely, as one who has always acknowledged and never doubted his fatherhood of these children. He alleges that he loved, cared for, and supported these children from the time of their birth until the death of their mother. He contends that he consequently must be treated the same as a married father of legitimate children. Even assuming the truth of Stanley's allegations, I am unable to construe the Equal Protection Clause as requiring Illinois to tailor its statutory definition of "parents" so meticulously as to include such unusual unwed fathers, while at the same time excluding those unwed, and generally unidentified, biological fathers who in no way share Stanley's professed desires.

Indeed, the nature of Stanley's own desires is less than absolutely clear from the record in this case. Shortly after the death

4. When the marriage between the parents of a legitimate child is dissolved by divorce or separation, the State, of course, normally awards custody of the child to one parent or the other. This is considered necessary for the child's welfare, since the parents are no longer legally bound together. The unmarried parents of an illegitimate child are likewise not legally bound together. Thus, even if Illinois did recognize the parenthood of both the mother and father of an illegitimate child, it would, for consistency with its practice in divorce proceedings, be called upon to award custody to one or the other of them, at least once it had by some means ascertained the identity of the father.

of the mother, Stanley turned these two children over to the care of a Mr. and Mrs. Ness; he took no action to gain his own recognition as a father, through adoption, or as a legal custodian, through a guardianship proceeding. Eventually it came to the attention of the State that there was no living adult who had any legally enforceable obligation for the care and support of the children; it was only then that the dependency proceeding here under review took place and that Stanley made himself known to the juvenile court in connection with these two children. Even then, however, Stanley did not ask to be charged with the legal responsibility for the children. He asked only that such legal responsibility be given to no one else. He seemed, in particular, to be concerned with the loss of the welfare payments he would suffer as a result of the designation of others as guardians of the children.

Not only, then, do I see no grounds for holding that Illinois' statutory definition of "parents" on its face violates the Equal Protection Clause; I see no ground for holding that any constitutional right of Stanley has been denied in the application of that statutory definition in the case at bar.

As Mr. Justice Frankfurter once observed, "invalidating legislation is serious business. . . ." *Morey v. Doud*, 354 U.S. 457, 474 (1957) (dissenting opinion). The Court today . . . invalidates a provision of critical importance to Illinois' carefully drawn statutory scheme. . . . And in so . . . [doing, it] embarks on a novel concept of the natural law for unwed fathers which could well have strange boundaries as yet undiscernible.

CASE QUESTIONS

1. How relevant is it, to the legal issues at stake, that Peter Stanley is a "welfare father"? Why does Justice Burger mention it?

2. According to this Illinois statute, if Peter Stanley had been married to Joan Stanley at the time of each child's birth, or if he had married her after both births and then acknowledged the children as his own, even if he had divorced Joan Stanley within hours of the marriage and had never made contact with the children again until Joan Stanley's death, the children would have been lawfully his at the time of her death. Burger argues that the marriage ceremony itself indicates a certain level of responsibility and that it is permissible for the law to take that into account. Is it reasonable that the law give *automatic* deference to the combination of a marriage ceremony and official acknowledgment of paternity, but would give no automatic deference to Peter Stanley's living with and supporting the children throughout their lives and to his informal but continuous acknowledgment of paternity?

3. If the state could demonstrate that 99 out of 100 illegitimate fathers abandon their offspring, and that 99 out of 100 illegitimate mothers either raise their offspring responsibly or else give them up properly for lawful adoption, would this legislative classification be "reasonable"? What about 999 out of 1000? Or 9999 out of 10,000? Does the outcome of this case turn on the reasonableness of Illinois's assumption "that most unmarried fathers are unsuitable and neglectful parents"? On the reasonableness of its assumption that unmarried fathers are less suitable parents than unmarried mothers? On the fact that the state had no compelling interest in depriving unmarried fathers of their own children? If it is the last, what about the state interest in providing for the children's welfare?

4. Does this decision mean that unmarried mothers cannot give up their illegitimate children for adoption without the consent of the father? What if the father refuses to acknowledge paternity—must there be a paternity suit before the child can be adopted? Does this decision mean that states may legislate a requirement that no fetus may be aborted without its father's consent? (Soon after *Stanley* these issues reached the Court.)

Stanley v. Illinois established, in effect, that the right of a natural father to care for, and have the companionship of, his own children, legitimate or illegitimate, is fundamental in American society, and that infringements on that right would be subjected to the strict scrutiny test under both the due process clause and the equal protection clause. Under the Constitution, however, two "fundamental" rights may conflict with each other. In those instances, the judicial outcome is not as predictable as when only one fundamental right is at stake. For example, in 1976 in *Planned Parenthood v. Danforth*,[17] the Supreme Court held that a woman's constitutional right to privacy renders void any laws that require her husband's consent as a precondition for allowing her to abort a fetus she is carrying. Although the Court acknowledged that the father's concern for his unborn child is "deep and proper" and that the relationship is one of "importance," nonetheless, the Court held that since the mother carries the fetus within her own body, her right over its fate overrides the father's.

Similarly, certain powers of government may be deemed so fundamental by the judiciary that those powers override rights which are also fundamental. In general these powers are those involving foreign relations[18] or those thought to involve the basic survival of the nation and its constitutional system. During wartime, for example, governmental powers are interpreted very generously by the courts, and citizen rights tend to be constricted accordingly.[19] The American constitutional system does not contain a doctrine of "emergency" powers that would permit open violations of written constitutional limitations; instead, the limitations on certain powers, such as the war power, are simply construed narrowly.[20] In other words, the classic example of a compelling interest that is generally found to satisfy even the strict scrutiny test is the government's need for flexibility in exercising its foreign relations power. The Court soon acknowledged that not even a father's fundamental right to the care and companionship of his children was enough to override this compelling need. And that acknowledgment, in the decision of *Fiallo v. Bell*[21] (1977), provided a fairly unmistakable signal as to how the Court a few years later would treat arguments for gender equality in the military draft. (See "The Military" below.)

Fiallo v. Bell (1977), discussion

The specific issue in *Fiallo v. Bell* concerned the government's power over the immigration of aliens. The power of Congress to exclude foreigners from U.S. shores has, for more than a century and through a long line of judicial precedents, been treated as unlimited by the Constitution. This hands-off approach to immigration law has at least two rationales. First, aliens outside U.S. territory have no rights accorded by the American Constitution. The second reason for according Congress wide latitude over immigration is that it is a subject intrinsically related to basic foreign policy decisions, and thereby to the most fundamental of sovereign powers: the power to assure national survival.

Ramon M. Fiallo, et al. v. Griffin Bell, Attorney of General of the United States presented a direct clash between the fundamental right of paternity and the fundamental government power over immigration. As is sometimes done in immigration cases, the litigants couched their legal argument in terms of their rights as citizens to have certain aliens admitted into the country. Citizens, after all, do have constitutional rights, even if aliens do not.

The litigants were challenging the constitutionality of sections of the Immigration and Nationality Act that gave preferred status as immigrants to "parents" and "children" of U.S. citizens or of lawful permanent residents, if their American child or parent so requested. In defining "parents" and "children," the statute included relationships between parents and unmarried persons under age twenty-one who are their stepchildren, adopted children, legitimate children, and children legitimated before they reached the age of eighteen. It also included natural mothers and their (unmarried under twenty-one) illegitimate children. It did not include natural fathers and their illegitimate children.

This lawsuit was initiated by the American side of three different illegitimate father-son groups: Ramon Martin Fiallo (a five-year-old born in the United States) and his father, Ramon Fiallo-Sone; Cleophus Warner (a naturalized American citizen) and his son, Serge Warner; and Trevor and Earl Wilson (teen-aged permanent American residents whose mother had died) and their father, Arthur Wilson. Like Peter Stanley, these fathers did not fit the stereotype of unwed fathers. Cleophus Warner, for example, had acknowledged his paternity of Serge Warner shortly after Serge's birth in the French West Indies and had registered his name on Serge's birth certificate. Cleophus had supported Serge financially and maintained him since the boy's birth. Serge's mother had abandoned the boy to his father's care and had married another man. That marriage made it impossible for Cleophus to legitimate the boy under French West Indies law. Ironically, although Cleophus did not qualify as Serge's "parent" under the immigration law, if Cleophus were to marry an American woman, she would then qualify under the law as Serge's stepparent.

In bringing this lawsuit, these litigants realized that they confronted a long tradition of judicial laissez-faire on the subject of immigration legislation. But they could look to *Stanley v. Illinois* for the assertion of equal protection rights of unwed fathers. Also in their favor was a growing body of law indicating judicial disapproval of, and applying "strict scrutiny" to, laws that denied benefits to children solely on the grounds of their illegitimacy.[22] Armed with these two legal weapons—one, a precedent to safeguard the rights of the unwed fathers, and the other, a set of precedents to safeguard the rights of the illegitimate children—these litigants went to battle against Attorney General Bell in the precincts of the U.S. Supreme Court. When the dust settled, the winner was again the government's plenary power over immigration policy.

The Supreme Court never even asked the question whether there was compelling justification for this sex discrimination against unwed fathers (as compared to the mother) or for this illegitimacy discrimination against the children. Instead the Court majority simply applied the most minimal of "minimal scrutiny," asserting that Congress may have been motivated by a concern with the problem of proving paternity or that it may have been motivated by a perception that illegitimate fathers usually do not have close ties to their children. Either of these legislative motivations, in this context, struck the Court as reasonable.

Fiallo v. Bell, however, at least in the eyes of the Supreme Court, did not constitute a repudiation of *Stanley v. Illinois*. Despite the arguments of the litigants and of the Marshall dissent, Justice Powell emphasized that this case involved rules over aliens rather than rules over American citizens. He cited with approval the statement that "Congress regularly makes rules [over immigration] that would be unacceptable if applied to citizens."[23]

Quilloin v. Walcott (1978), discussion

Thus, by 1978 the constitutional status of fathers' rights could be described as follows: *Stanley v. Illinois* had posed for the Court the question, "Is a [legal] presumption which distinguishes and burdens all unwed fathers constitutionally repugnant?" The *Stanley* opinion had seemed to answer yes to that question and then the *Planned Parenthood* and *Fiallo* cases had carved out modest exceptions to that answer, changing it to "Yes, except when there is a conflict with other fundamental rights or when the burden is part of a federal immigration law." In January 1978, the Supreme Court further enlarged the category of exceptions to what had seemed to be the rule of *Stanley*. In a unanimous opinion in the case of *Quilloin v. Walcott*,[24] authored by Justice Marshall (who had dissented to the *Fiallo* exceptions), the Court upheld an application of Georgia statutes which unquestionably did "distinguish and burden all unwed fathers."

The burden imposed, however, was far less harsh than the automatic denial of custody which the Court had condemned in *Stanley*. Georgia distinguished unwed fathers from unwed mothers and from divorced fathers in the following way: If a child was born out-of-wedlock, the child's mother was recognized as its only legal parent *unless* the natural father petitioned the local court for a legitimation order. His petition had to state the name, age and sex of the child and the name of the mother. The mother had to be notified, in advance, of the legitimation hearing. If the judge granted the petition, the child would then become "legitimate" and would acquire rights to inherit from its father. Once the child was legitimated, the unwed father then shared with the mother the legal rights of parents. (In contrast, the laws voided in *Stanley* would have required formal adoption proceedings; they technically treated the father as a stranger to the child.)

This requirement that an unwed father go through a legitimation hearing to become a legal parent, where no such requirement was imposed on divorced fathers or unwed mothers, was challenged by Leon Quilloin in an effort to prevent his son from being adopted by the boy's stepfather. The boy had lived for all of his fourteen years with his mother, Ardell Williams Walcott. She had for the past eleven of those years been married to Randall Walcott, the stepfather. When Randall Walcott petitioned to adopt the boy, the State Department of Human Resources notified Leon Quilloin, the boy's father. Since birth, the boy had used Quilloin's last name and Quilloin had let his name be put on the birth certificate as the father. Contacts between father and son had been sporadic: occasional visits and gifts, but financial support (the father's legal obligation) had been only on an "irregular basis." Once notified, Quilloin petitioned for legitimation, visitation rights, and for a veto of the adoption. (The latter, had the boy been legitimated earlier, would have been his legal right.) He did not seek legal custody. At the hearing, the boy indicated a preference to be adopted. The court, claiming to be guided by the standard of the "best interests of the child" ruled against the father's requests. Quilloin appealed to the Georgia Supreme Court and then the U.S. Supreme Court, on both equal protection and due process grounds.

In Quilloin's Jurisdictional Statement, presented to the U.S. Supreme Court, his attorney challenged the state's distinguishing between unwed fathers and divorced fathers. He failed to mention, however, that Quilloin also objected to the statute's distinction between unwed mothers and unwed fathers. After the U.S. Supreme Court accepted jurisdiction, his attorney tried to raise the latter question. In rejecting Quilloin's challenges, Justice Marshall claimed in a footnote that the Court was not addressing the question of gender discrimination.

Justice Marshall's opinion for the Court was cryptically brief, and his rationale for the decision is far from obvious. All that is obvious about his opinion is its emphasis on the specific factual background of this case. His core conclusion was:

> Whatever might be required in other situations, we cannot say that the State was required in this situation to find anything more than that the adoption, and denial of legitimation, was in the "best interests of the child." (At 255.)

Thus, *Quilloin v. Walcott* failed to create any clear precedent on laws that distinguish between unwed mothers and unwed fathers in the context of release of a child for adoption. The Court did seem to create such a precedent one year later in *Caban v. Mohammed*,[25] but that apparent clarity was to become muddied within a few years in the decision of *Lehr v. Robertson*.[26] The genuineness of differences between unwed mothers and unwed fathers appears to cause the Court substantial difficulty in its quest for principled rules of law.

Caban v. Mohammed presented the Court with a factual setting of unusual drama. Abdiel Caban and Maria Mohammed had lived together for five years, representing themselves as husband and wife (although in fact they had never married and for some of the time he had been married to another woman). During those years they had two children, and the four lived as a family. Then Maria moved out with the children and married another man (Kazim Mohammed) but the children saw their father every weekend. The children then visited their maternal grandmother in Puerto Rico for a year, during which their mother wrote them letters and their father communicated with them through his parents who also lived there. In November 1975, Caban abducted his children and took them back to New York. The Mohammeds then sought and obtained legal custody and

Caban, with his new wife Nina, received visitation rights. Then, in January 1976, the Mohammeds petitioned to adopt the children; two months later the Cabans cross-petitioned for the same thing.

Under New York Domestic Relations Law any unwed mother (like any married parent), unless she had abandoned her child or been judged an unfit parent, retained an absolute right to consent to the adoption of her own child. Unwed fathers had no parallel right; they could appear at the adoption hearing and offer evidence that adoption might not accord with the child's "best interest" but (unlike mothers) they could not veto a decision that would be permanently terminating their rights as a parent. Abdiel Caban lost at the hearing and the adoption was ordered. He appealed to the highest court of New York and then to the U.S. Supreme Court. At the adoption hearing the children were ages four and six; by the time the case was resolved, they were seven and eight. Five of the nine Supreme Court justices sided with their father.

Abdiel Caban v. Kazim and Maria Mohammed, 441 U.S. 380 (1979)

MR. JUSTICE POWELL delivered the opinion of the Court.

On appeal to this Court appellant presses [the] claim. . . . that the distinction drawn under New York law between the adoption rights of an unwed father and those of other parents violates the Equal Protection Clause of the Fourteenth Amendment.

. . .

[T]he Surrogate's decision in the present case, affirmed by the New York Court of Appeals, was based upon the assumption that there was a distinctive difference between the rights of Abdiel Caban, as the unwed father of David and Denise, and Maria Mohammed, as the unwed mother of the children: Adoption by Abdiel was held to be impermissible in the absence of Maria's consent, whereas adoption by Maria could be prevented by Abdiel only if he could show that the Mohammeds' adoption of the children would not be in the children's best interests. Accordingly, it is clear that § 111 treats unmarried parents differently according to their sex.

III

Gender-based distinctions "must serve important governmental objectives and must be substantially related to achievement of those objectives" in order to withstand judicial scrutiny under the Equal Protection Clause. *Craig v. Boren,* 429 U.S. 190, 197 (1977). *See also Reed v. Reed,* 404 U.S. 71 (1971). The question before us, therefore, is whether the distinction in § 111 between unmarried mothers and unmarried fathers bears a substantial relation to some important state interest. Appellees assert that the distinction is justified by a fundamental difference between maternal and paternal relations—that "a natural mother, absent special circumstances, bears a closer relationship with her child . . . than a father does." Tr. of Oral Arg., at 41.

Contrary to appellees' argument and to the apparent presumption underlying

§ 111, maternal and paternal roles are not invariably different in importance. Even if unwed mothers as a class were closer than unwed fathers to their newborn infants, this generalization concerning parent-child relations would become less acceptable as a basis for legislative distinctions as the age of the child increased. The present case demonstrates that an unwed father may have a relationship with his children fully comparable to that of the mother. Appellant Caban, appellee Maria Mohammed, and their two children lived together as a natural family for several years. As members of this family, both mother and father participated in the care and support of their children. There is no reason to believe that the Caban children—aged 4 and 6 at the time of the adoption proceedings—had a relationship with their mother unrivaled by the affection and concern of their father. We reject, therefore, the claim that the broad, gender-based distinction of § 111 is required by any universal difference between maternal and paternal relations at every phase of a child's development.

As an alternative justification for § 111, appellees argue that the distinction between unwed fathers and unwed mother is substantially related to the State's interest in promoting the adoption of illegitimate children. Although the legislative history of § 111 is sparse,[8] *In re Malpica-Orsini*, 36 N.Y.2d 568, app. dismissed for want of a substantial federal question *sub nom. Orsini v. Blasi*, 423 U.S. 1042 (1977), the New York Court of Appeals identified as the legislature's purpose in enacting § 111 the furthering of the interests of illegitimate children, for whom adoption often is the best course. The court concluded that,

[t]o require the consent of fathers of children born out of wedlock. . . , or even some of them, would have the overall effect of denying homes to the homeless and of depriving innocent children of the other blessings of adoption. The cruel and undeserved out-of-wedlock stigma would continue its visitations. At the very least, the worthy process of adoption would be severely impeded. (*Id.* at 572.)

The court reasoned that people wishing to adopt a child born out of wedlock would be discouraged, if the natural father could prevent the adoption by the mere withholding of his consent. Indeed, the court went so far as to suggest that "[m]arriages would be discouraged because of the reluctance of prospective husbands to involve themselves in a family situation where they might only be a foster parent and could not adopt the mother's offspring." *Id.* at 573. Finally, the court noted that if unwed fathers' consent were required before adoption could take place, in many instances the adoption would have to be delayed or eliminated altogether, because of the unavailability of the natural father.

The State's interest in providing for the well-being of illegitimate children is an important one. We do not question that the best interests of such children often may require their adoption into new families who will give them the stability of a normal, two-parent home. Moreover, adoption will remove the stigma under which illegitimate children suffer. But the unquestioned right of the State to further these desirable ends by legislation is not in itself sufficient to justify the gender-based distinction of § 111. Rather, under the relevant cases applying to the Equal Protection Clause it must be shown that the distinction is structured reasonably to further these ends. As we repeated in *Reed v. Reed*,

8. Consent of the unmarried father has never been required for adoption under New York law, although parental consent otherwise has been required at least since the late nineteenth century.

at 76, such a statutory "classification 'must be reasonable, not arbitrary, and must rest on some ground of difference having a fair and substantial relation to the object of the legislation, so that all persons similarly circumstanced shall be treated alike.' *Royster Guano Co. v. Virginia*, 253 U.S. 412, 415 (1920)."

We find that the distinction in § 111 between unmarried mothers and unmarried fathers, as illustrated by this case, does not bear a substantial relation to the State's interest in providing adoptive homes for its illegitimate children. It may be that, given the opportunity, some unwed fathers would prevent the adoption of their illegitimate children. This impediment to adoption usually is the result of a natural parental interest shared by both genders alike; it is not a manifestation of any profound difference between the affection and concern of mothers and fathers for their children. Neither the State nor the appellees have argued that unwed fathers are more likely to object to the adoption of their children than are unwed mothers; nor is there any self-evident reason why as a class they would be.

The New York Court of Appeals in *In re Malpica-Orsini* suggested that the requiring of unmarried fathers' consent for adoption would pose a strong impediment for adoption because often it is impossible to locate unwed fathers when adoption proceedings are brought, whereas mothers are more likely to remain with their children. Even if the special difficulties attendant upon locating and identifying unwed fathers at birth would justify a legislative distinction between mothers and fathers of newborns,[11] these difficulties need not per-

sist past infancy. When the adoption of an older child is sought, the State's interest in proceeding with adoption cases can be protected by means that do not draw such an inflexible gender-based distinction as that made in § 111. In those cases where the father never has come forward to participate in the rearing of his child, nothing in the Equal Protection Clause precludes the State from withholding from him the privilege of vetoing the adoption of that child. Indeed, under the statute as it now stands the Surrogate may proceed in the absence of consent when the parent whose consent otherwise would be required never has come forward or has abandoned the child.[13] But in cases such as this, where the father has established a substantial relationship with the child and has admitted his paternity, a State should have no difficulty in identifying the father even of children born out of wedlock.[15] Thus, no showing has been made that the different treatment afforded unmarried fathers and unmarried mothers under § 111 bears a substantial relationship to the proclaimed interest of the State in promoting the adoption of illegitimate children.

---

11. Because the question is not before us, we express no view whether such difficulties would justify a statute addressed particularly to newborn adoptions, setting forth more stringent re-

quirements concerning the acknowledgment of paternity or a stricter definition of abandonment.

13. If the New York Court of Appeals is correct that unmarried fathers often desert their families (a view we need not question), then allowing those fathers who remain with their families a right to object to the termination of their parental rights will pose little threat to the State's ability to order adoption in most cases. For we do not question a State's right to do what New York has done in this portion of § 111: provide that fathers who have abandoned their children have no right to block adoption of those children. . . .

15. States have a legitimate interest, of course, in providing that an unmarried father's right to object to the adoption of a child will be conditioned upon his showing that it is in fact his child.

In sum, we believe that § 111 is another example of "over-broad generalizations" in gender-based classifications. *See Califano v. Goldfarb*, 430 U.S. 199, 211 (1977); *Stanton v. Stanton*, 421 U.S. 7, 14–15 (1975). The effect of New York's classification is to discriminate against unwed fathers even when their identity is known and they have manifested a significant paternal interest in the child. The facts of this case illustrate the harshness of classifying unwed fathers as being invariably less qualified and entitled than mothers to exercise a concerned judgment as to the fate of their children. Section 111 both excludes some loving fathers from full participation in the decision whether their children will be adopted and, at the same time, enables some alienated mothers arbitrarily to cut off the paternal rights of fathers. We conclude that this undifferentiated distinction between unwed mothers and unwed fathers, applicable in all circumstances where adoption of a child of theirs is at issue, does not bear a substantial relationship to the State's asserted interests.

The judgment of the New York Court of Appeals is

Reversed.

Mr. Justice Stewart, dissenting.

For reasons similar to those expressed in the dissenting opinion of Mr. Justice Stevens, I agree that § 111(1)(c) of the New York Domestic Relations Law is not constitutionally infirm. The State's interest in promoting the welfare of illegitimate children is of far greater importance than the opinion of the Court would suggest. Unlike the children of married parents, illegitimate children begin life with formidable handicaps. They typically depend upon the care and economic support of only one parent—usually the mother. And, even in this era of changing mores they still may face substantial obstacles simply because they are illegitimate. Adoption provides perhaps the most generally available way of removing these handicaps. *See* H. Clark, *Law of Domestic Relations* 177 (1968). Most significantly, it provides a means by which an illegitimate child can become legitimate—a fact that the Court's opinion today barely acknowledges.

The New York statute reflects the judgment that, to facilitate this ameliorative change in the child's status, the consent of only one parent should ordinarily be required for adoption of a child born out of wedlock. The mother has been chosen as the parent whose consent is indispensable. A different choice would defy common sense. But the unwed father, if he is the lawful custodian of the child, must under the statute also consent. And, even when he does not have custody, the unwed father who has an established relationship with his illegitimate child is not denied the opportunity to participate in the adoption proceeding. His relationship with the child will be terminated through adoption only if a court determines that adoption will serve the child's best interest. These distinctions represent, I think, a careful accommodation of the competing interests at stake and bear a close and substantial relationship to the State's goal of promoting the welfare of its children. In my view, the Constitution requires no more.

The appellant has argued that the statute, in granting rights to an unwed mother that it does not grant to an unwed father, violates the Equal Protection Clause by discriminating on the basis of gender. And he also has made the argument that the statute, because it withholds from the unwed father substantive rights granted to all other classes of parents, violates both the Equal Protection Clause and the Due Process Clause of the Fourteenth Amendment.

I find the latter contention less troublesome than does my Brother STEVENS, and see no ultimate merit in the former.

A

The appellant relies primarily on *Stanley v. Illinois*, 405 U.S. 646, in advancing the second argument identified above. But it is obvious that the principle established in that case is not offended by the New York law. The Illinois statute invalidated in *Stanley* employed a stark and absolute presumption that the unwed father was not a fit parent.

. . .

In some circumstances the actual relationship between father and child may suffice to create in the unwed father parental interest comparable to those of the married father. *Cf. Stanley v. Illinois.* But here we are concerned with the rights the unwed father may have when his wishes and those of the mother are in conflict, and the child's best interests are served by a resolution in favor of the mother. It seems to me that the absence of a legal tie with the mother may in such circumstances appropriately place a limit on whatever substantive constitutional claims might otherwise exist by virtue of the father's actual relationship with the children.

B

The appellant's equal protection challenge to the distinction drawn between the unwed father and mother seems to me more substantial. Gender, like race, is a highly visible and immutable characteristic that has historically been the touchstone for pervasive but often subtle discrimination. Although the analogy to race is not perfect and the constitutional inquiry therefore somewhat different, gender-based statutory classifications deserve careful constitutional examination because they may reflect or operate to perpetuate mythical or stereotyped assumptions about the proper roles and the relative capabilities of men and women that are unrelated to any inherent differences between the sexes. *Cf. Orr v. Orr*, 440 U.S. 268. Sex-based classifications are in many settings invidious because they relegate a person to the place set aside for the group on the basis of an attribute that the person cannot change. *Reed v. Reed*, 404 U.S. 71; *Stanton v. Stanton*, 421 U.S. 7; *Frontiero v. Richardson*, 411 U.S. 677; *Weinberger v. Wiesenfeld*, 420 U.S. 636; *Orr v. Orr*, supra. Such laws cannot be defended, as can the bulk of the classifications that fill the statute books, simply on the ground that the generalizations they reflect may be true of the majority of members of the class, for a gender-based classification need not ring false to work a discrimination that in the individual case might be invidious. Nonetheless, gender-based classifications are not invariably invalid. When men and women are not in fact similarly situated in the area covered by the legislation in question, the Equal Protection Clause is not violated. *See, e.g., Schlesinger v. Ballard*, 419 U.S. 498.

In my view, the gender-based distinction drawn by New York falls in this latter category. With respect to a large group of adoptions—those of newborn children and infants—unwed mothers and unwed fathers are simply not similarly situated, as my Brother STEVENS has demonstrated. Our law has given the unwed mother the custody of her illegitimate children precisely because it is she who bears the child and because the vast majority of unwed fathers have been unknown, unavailable, or simply uninterested. . . . This custodial preference has carried with it a correlative power in the mother to place her child for adoption or not to do so.

The majority of the States have incorporated these basic common-law rules in their statutes identifying the persons whose participation or consent is requisite to a valid adoption. . . . These common and statutory rules of law reflect the physical reality that only the mother carries and gives birth to the child, as well as the undeniable social reality that the unwed mother is always an identifiable parent and the custodian of the child—until or unless the State intervenes. The biological father, unless he has established a familial tie with the child by marrying the mother, is often a total stranger from the State's point of view. I do not understand the Court to question these pragmatic differences. An unwed father who has not come forward and who has established no relationship with the child is plainly not in a situation similar to the mother's. New York's consent distinctions have clearly been made on this basis, and in my view they do not violate the Equal Protection Clause of the Fourteenth Amendment. *See Schlesinger v. Ballard*, 419 U.S. 498.

In this case, of course, we are concerned not with an unwilling or unidentified father but instead with an unwed father who has established a paternal relationship with his children. He is thus similarly situated to the mother, and his claim is that he thus has parental interests no less deserving of protection than those of the mother. His contention that the New York law in question consequently discriminates against him on the basis of gender cannot be lightly dismissed. For substantially the reasons expressed by MR. JUSTICE STEVENS in his dissenting opinion, I believe, however, that this gender-based distinction does not violate the Equal Protection Clause as applied in the circumstances of the present case.

It must be remembered that here there are not two, but three interests at stake: the mother's, the father's, and the children's. Concerns humane as well as practical abundantly support New York's provision that only one parent need consent to the adoption of an illegitimate child, though it requires both parents to consent to the adoption of one already legitimate. If the consent of both unwed parents were required, and one withheld that consent, the illegitimate child would remain illegitimate. Viewed in these terms the statute does not in any sense discriminate on the basis of sex. The question, then, is whether the decision to select the unwed mother as the parent entitled to give or withhold consent and to apply that rule even when the unwed father in fact has a paternal relationship with his children constitutes invidious sex-based discrimination.

The appellant's argument would be a powerful one were this an instance in which it has been found that adoption by the father would serve the best interests of the children, and in the face of that finding the mother had been permitted to block the adoption. But this is not such a case. As my Brother STEVENS has observed, under a sex-neutral rule—assuming that New York is free to require the consent of but one parent for the adoption of an illegitimate child—the outcome in this case would have been the same. The appellant has been given the opportunity to show that an adoption would not be in his children's best interests. Implicit in the finding made by the New York courts is the judgment that termination of his relationship with the children will in fact promote their well-being—a judgment we are obligated to accept.

That the statute might permit—in a different context—the unwed mother arbitrarily to thwart the wishes of the caring father as well as the best interests of the child is not a sufficient reason to invalidate it as applied in the present case. For here the legislative goal of the statute—to facilitate adoptions that are in the best interests of illegitimate children after consideration of all other interests involved—has indeed been fully and fairly served by this gender-based classification. Unless the decision to require the consent of only one parent is in itself constitutionally defective, which nobody has argued, the same interests that support that decision are sufficiently profound to overcome the appellant's claim that he has been invidiously discriminated against because he is a male.

I agree that retroactive application of the Court's decision today would work untold harm, and I fully subscribe to part III of MR. JUSTICE STEVENS' dissent.

MR. JUSTICE STEVENS, with whom THE CHIEF JUSTICE and MR. JUSTICE REHNQUIST join, dissenting.

Under § 111(1)(c) of the New York Domestic Relations Law, the adoption of a child born out of wedlock usually requires the consent of the natural mother; it does not require that of the natural father unless he has "lawful custody." Appellant, the natural but noncustodial father of two school-aged children born out of wedlock, challenges that provision insofar as it allows the adoption of his natural children by the husband of the natural mother without his consent. Appellant's primary objection is that this unconsented-to termination of his parental rights without proof of unfitness on his part violates the substantive component of the Due Process Clause of the Fourteenth Amendment. Secondarily, he attacks § 111(1)(c)'s disparate treatment of natural mothers and natural fathers as a violation of the Equal Protection Clause of the same Amendment. In view of the Court's disposition, I shall discuss the equal protection question before commenting on appellant's primary contention. I shall then indicate why I think the holding

of the Court, although erroneous, is of limited effect.

I

This case concerns the validity of rules affecting the status of the thousands of children who are born out of wedlock every day.[2] All of these children have an interest in acquiring the status of legitimacy; a great many of them have an interest in being adopted by parents who can give them opportunities that would otherwise be denied; for some the basic necessities of life are at stake. The state interest in facilitating adoption in appropriate cases is strong—perhaps even "compelling."[3]

2. Illegitimate births accounted for an estimated 14.7 percent and 15.5 percent of all births in the United States during the years 1976 and 1977, respectively. . . . In total births, this represents 468,100 and 515,700 illegitimate births, respectively. Although statistics for New York State are not available, the problem of illegitimacy appears to be especially severe in urban areas. For example, in 1975, over 50 percent of all births in the District of Columbia were out of wedlock. . . .

Adoption is an important solution to the problem of illegitimacy. . . .

3. The reason I say "perhaps" is that the word "compelling" can be understood in different ways. If it describes an interest that "compels" a conclusion that any statute intended to foster that interest is automatically constitutional, few if any interests would fit that description. On the other hand, if it merely describes an interest that compels a court, before holding a law unconstitutional, to give thoughtful attention to a legislative judgment that the law will serve that interest, then the State's interest in facilitating adoption in appropriate cases is unquestionably compelling. See Smith v. Organization of Foster Families, 431 U.S. 816, 844, and n.51; id. at 861–62 (STEWART, J., concurring in judgment); Weber v. Aetna Casualty & Surety Co., 406 U.S. 164, 175; Stanley v. Illinois, 405 U.S. 645, 652; Matter of Malpica-Orsini, 36 N.Y.2d 568, 571–574.

Nevertheless, it is also true that § 111(1)(c) gives rights to natural mothers that it withholds from natural fathers. Because it draws this gender-based distinction between two classes of citizens who have an equal right to fair and impartial treatment by their government, it is necessary to determine whether there are differences between the members of the two classes that provide a justification for treating them differently. That determination requires more than merely recognizing that society has traditionally treated the two classes differently. But it also requires analysis that goes beyond a merely reflexive rejection of gender-based distinctions.

Men and women are different, and the difference is relevant to the question whether the mother may be given the exclusive right to consent to the adoption of a child born out of wedlock. Because most adoptions involve newborn infants or very young children,[7] it is appropriate at the outset to focus on the significance of the difference in such cases.

Both parents are equally responsible for the conception of the child out of wedlock. But from that point on through pregnancy and infancy, the differences between the male and the female have an important impact on the child's destiny. Only the mother carries the child; it is she who has the constitutional right to decide whether to bear it or not.[9] In many cases, only the mother knows who sired the child, and it will often be within her power to withhold that fact, and even the fact of her preg-

nancy, from that person. If during pregnancy the mother should marry a different partner, the child will be legitimate when born, and the natural father may never even know that his "rights" have been affected. On the other hand, only if the natural mother agrees to marry the natural father during that period can the latter's actions have a positive impact on the status of the child; if he instead should marry a different partner during that time, the only effect on the child is negative, for the likelihood of legitimacy will be lessened.

These differences continue at birth and immediately thereafter. During that period, the mother and child are together; the mother's identity is known with certainty. The father, on the other hand, may or may not be present; his identity may be unknown to the world and may even be uncertain to the mother.[11] These natural differences between [un]married fathers and mothers make it probable that the mother, and not the father or both parents, will have custody of the newborn infant.

In short, it is virtually inevitable that from conception through infancy the mother will constantly be faced with decisions about how best to care for the child, whereas it is much less certain that the father will be confronted with comparable problems. There no doubt are cases in which the relationship of the parties at birth makes it appropriate for the State to give the father a voice of some sort in the adoption decision.[13] But as a matter of

7. . . . of the children adopted by unrelated parents in New York in 1974 and 1975, respectively, 66 percent and 62 percent were under one year old, and 90 percent and 88 percent were under six years old. In 1974, moreover, the median age of the child at the time of adoption was five months. . . .

9. See *Planned Parenthood v. Danforth*, 428 U.S. 52, 67–75.

11. The Court has frequently noted the difficulty of proving paternity in cases involving illegitimate children. *E.g.*, *Trimble v. Gordon*, 430 U.S. 762, 770–71; *Gomez v. Perez*, 409 U.S. 535, 538. . . .

13. *Cf.* part II, *infra*. Indeed, New York does give unwed fathers some opportunity to participate in adoption proceedings. In this case, for example, appellant appeared at the adoption hearing with counsel, presented testimony, and

equal protection analysis, it is perfectly obvious that at the time and immediately after a child is born out of wedlock differences between men and women justify some differential treatment of the mother and father in the adoptive process.

Most particularly, these differences justify a rule that gives the mother of the newborn infant the exclusive right to consent to its adoption. Such a rule gives the mother, in whose sole charge the infant is often placed anyway, the maximum flexibility in deciding how best to care for the child. It also gives the loving father an in-

---

was allowed to cross-examine the witnesses offered by appellees. As a substantive matter, the natural father is free to demonstrate, as appellant unsuccessfully tried to do in this case, that the best interests of the child favor the preservation of existing parental rights and forestall cutting off those rights by way of adoption. Had appellant been able to make that demonstration, the result would have been the same as that mandated by the Court's insistence upon paternal as well as maternal consent in these circumstances: neither parent could adopt the child into a new family with a step-parent; both would have parental rights (*e.g.*, visitation); and custody would be determined by the child's best interests.

In this case, although the New York courts made no finding of unfitness on appellant's part, there was ample evidence in the record from which they could draw the conclusion that his relationship with the children had been somewhat intermittent, that it fell far short of the relationship existing between the mother and the children (whether measured by the amount of time spent with the children, the responsibility taken for their care and education, or the amount of resources expended on them), and that judging from appellant's treatment of his first wife and his children by that marriage, there was a real possibility that he could not be counted on for the continued support of the two children and might well be a source of friction between them, the mother, and her new husband. . . .

centive to marry the mother,[14] and has no adverse impact on the disinterested father. Finally, it facilitates the interests of the adoptive parents, the child, and the public at large by streamlining the often traumatic adoption process and allowing the prompt, complete and reliable integration of the child into a satisfactory new home at as young an age as is feasible.[15] Put most simply, it permits the maximum participation of interested natural parents without so burdening the adoption process that its attractiveness to potential adoptive parents is destroyed.

This conclusion is borne out by considering the alternative rule proposed by appellant. If the State were to require the consent of both parents, or some kind of hearing to explain why either's consent is unnecessary or unobtainable,[16] it would unquestionably complicate and delay the adoptive process. Most importantly, such a rule would remove the mother's freedom of choice in her own and the child's behalf without also relieving her of the unshakable responsibility for the care of the child. Furthermore, questions relating to the adequacy of notice to absent fathers could invade the mother's privacy,[17] cause the

---

14. Marrying the mother would not only legitimate the child but would also assure the father the right to consent to any adoption.

15. These are not idle interests. A survey of adoptive parents registered on the New York State Adoption Exchange as of January 1975 showed that over 75 percent preferred to adopt children under three years old; over half preferred children under one year old. . . .

16. Although the Court is careful to leave the States free to develop alternative approaches, it nonetheless endorses the procedure described in text for adoptions of older children against the wishes of natural fathers who have established substantial relationships with the children.

17. To be effective, any such notice would probably have to name the mother and perhaps

adopting parents to doubt the reliability of the new relationship, and add to the expense and time required to conclude what is now usually a simple and certain process.[18] While it might not be irrational for a State to conclude that these costs should be incurred to protect the interest of natural fathers, it is nevertheless plain that those costs, which are largely the result of differences between the mother and the father, establish an imposing justification for *some* differential treatment of the two sexes in this type of situation.

With this much the Court does not disagree; it confines its holding to cases such as the one at hand involving the adoption of an *older* child against the wishes of a natural father who previously has participated in the rearing of the child and who admits paternity. The Court does conclude, however, that the gender basis for the classification drawn by § 111(1)(c) makes differential treatment so suspect that the State has the burden not only of showing that the rule is generally justified but also that the justification holds equally true for *all* persons disadvantaged by the rule. In its view, since the justification is not as strong for some indeterminately small part of the disadvantaged class as it is for the class

as a whole, the rule is invalid under the Equal Protection Clause insofar as it applies to that subclass. With this conclusion I disagree.

If we assume, as we surely must, that characteristics possessed by all members of one class and by no members of the other class justify some disparate treatment of mothers and fathers of children born out of wedlock, the mere fact that the statute draws a "gender-based distinction," should not, in my opinion, give rise to any presumption that the impartiality principle embodied in the Equal Protection Clause has been violated. Indeed, if we make the further undisputed assumption that the discrimination is justified in those cases in which the rule has its most frequent application—cases involving newborn infants and very young children in the custody of their natural mothers, *see* nn.7 and 11, *supra*—we should presume that the law is entirely valid and require the challenger to demonstrate that its unjust applications are sufficiently numerous and serious to render it invalid.

In this case, appellant made no such showing; his demonstration of unfairness, assuming he has made one, extends only to himself and by implication to the unknown number of fathers just like him. Further, while appellant did nothing to inform the New York courts about the size of his subclass and the overall degree of its disadvantage under § 111(1)(c), the New York Court of Appeals has previously concluded that the subclass is small and its disadvantage insignificant by comparison to the benefits of the rule as it now stands.[20]

even identify her further, for example by address. Moreover, the terms and placement of the notice in, for example, a newspaper, no matter how discreet and tastefully chosen, would inevitably be taken by the public as an announcement of illegitimate maternity. To avoid the embarrassment of such announcements, the mother might well be forced to identify the father (or potential fathers)—despite her desire to keep that fact a secret.

18. In the opinion upon which it relied in dismissing the appeal in this case, the New York Court of Appeals concluded that the "trauma" that would be added to the adoption process by a paternal consent rule is "unpleasant to envision." *In re Malpica-Orsini,* at 574.

20. "To require the consent of fathers of children born out of wedlock . . . or even some of them, would have the overall effect of denying homes to the homeless and of depriving innocent children of the other blessings of adoption. The cruel and undeserved out-of-wedlock stigma

The mere fact that an otherwise valid general classification appears arbitrary in an isolated case is not a sufficient reason for invalidating the entire rule. Nor, indeed, is it a sufficient reason for concluding that the application of a valid rule in a hard case constitutes a violation of equal

---

would continue its visitations. At the very least, the worthy process of adoption would be severely impeded.

"Great difficulty and expense would be encountered, in many instances, in locating the putative father to ascertain his willingness to consent. Frequently, he is unlocatable or even unknown. Paternity is denied more often than admitted. Some birth certificates set forth the names of the reputed fathers, others do not.

"Couples considering adoptions will be dissuaded out of fear of subsequent annoyance and entanglements. . . .

"Some of the ugliest disclosures of our time involve black marketing of children for adoption. One need not be a clairvoyant to predict that the grant to unwed fathers of the right to veto adoptions will provide a very fertile field for extortion. . . .

"Marriages would be discouraged because of the reluctance of prospective husbands to involve themselves in a family situation where they might only be a foster parent and could not adopt the mother's offspring.

"We should be mindful of the jeopardy to which existing adoptions would be subjected and the resulting chaos by an unadulterated declaration of unconstitutionality. . . . The attendant trauma is unpleasant to envision." *In re Malpica-Orsini*, at 572–74.

To the limited extent that the Court takes cognizance of these findings and conclusions, it does not dispute them. Instead, the Court merely states that many of these findings do not reflect appellant's situation and "need not" reflect the situation of any natural father who is seeking to prevent the adoption of his older children.

Although I agree that the findings of the New York Court of Appeals are more likely to be true of the strong majority of adoptions that involve infants than they are in the present situation (a

protection principles.[22] We cannot test the conformance of rules to the principle of equality simply by reference to exceptional cases.

Moreover, I am not at all sure that § 111(1)(c) is arbitrary even if viewed solely in the light of the exceptional circumstances presently before the Court. This case involves a dispute between natural parents over which of the two may adopt the children. If both are given a veto, as the Court requires, neither may adopt and the children will remain illegitimate. If, instead of a gender-based distinction, the veto were given to the parent having custody of the child, the mother would prevail just as she did in the state court.[23] Whether or not it is wise to devise a special rule to protect

---

conclusion that should be sufficient to justify the classification drawn by § 111[1][c] in *all* situations), I am compelled to point out that the Court marshals not one bit of evidence to bolster its empirical judgment that most natural fathers facing the adoption of their older children will have appellant's relatively exemplary record with respect to admitting paternity and establishing a relationship with his children.

22. Even if the exclusive consent requirement were limited to newborn infants, there would still be an occasional case in which the interests of the child would be better served by a responsible paternal veto than by an irresponsible maternal veto.

23. In fact, although the Court understands it differently, the New York statute apparently does turn consent rights on custody. Thus, § 111(1)(d) gives consent rights to "any person . . . having lawful custody of the adoptive child." . . . In this light, the allegedly improper impact of the gender-based classification in § 111(1)(c) as challenged by appellant is even more attenuated than I have suggested because it only disqualifies those few natural fathers of older children who have established a substantial relationship with the child, have admitted paternity, and who nonetheless do not have custody of the children.

the natural father who (a) has a substantial relationship with his child, and (b) wants to veto an adoption that a court has found to be in the best interest of the child, the record in this case does not demonstrate that the Equal Protection Clause requires such a rule.

I have no way of knowing how often disputes between natural parents over adoption of their children arise after the father "has established a substantial relationship with the child and is willing to admit his paternity," but has previously been unwilling to take steps to legitimate his relationship. I am inclined to believe that such cases are relatively rare. But whether or not this assumption is valid the far surer assumption is that in the more common adoption situations, the mother will be the more, and often the only responsible parent, and that a paternal consent requirement will constitute a hindrance to the adoption process. Because this general rule is amply justified in its normal application, I would therefore require the party challenging its constitutionality to make some demonstration of unfairness in a significant number of situations before concluding that it violates the Equal Protection Clause. That the Court has found a violation without requiring such a showing can only be attributed to its own "stereotyped reaction" to what is unquestionably, but in this case justifiably, a gender-based distinction.

II

Although the substantive due process issue is more troublesome, I can briefly state the reason why I reject it.

I assume that, if and when one develops, the relationship between a father and his natural child is entitled to protection against arbitrary state action as a matter of due process. *See Stanley v. Illinois*, 405 U.S. 645, 651. Although the Court has not decided whether the Due Process Clause pro-

vides any greater substantive protection for this relationship than simply against official caprice, it has indicated that an adoption decree that terminates the relationship is constitutionally justified by a finding that the father has abandoned or mistreated the child. *See id.* at 652. In my view, such a decree may also be justified by a finding that the adoption will serve the best interests of the child, at least in a situation such as this in which the natural family unit has already been destroyed, the father has previously taken no steps to legitimate the child and a further requirement such as a showing of unfitness would entirely deprive the child—and the State—of the benefits of adoption and legitimation. . . .

III

There is often the risk that the arguments one advances in dissent may give rise to a broader reading of the Court's opinion than is appropriate. That risk is especially grave when the Court is embarking on a new course that threatens to interfere with social arrangements that have come into use over long periods of time. Because I consider the course on which the Court is currently embarked to be potentially most serious, I shall explain why I regard its holding in this case as quite narrow.

The adoption decrees that have been entered without the consent of the natural father must number in the millions. An untold number of family and financial decisions have been made in reliance on the validity of those decrees. Because the Court has crossed a new constitutional frontier with today's decision, those reliance interests unquestionably foreclose retroactive application of this ruling. *See Chevron Oil Co. v. Huson*, 404 U.S. 97, 106–7. Families that include adopted children need have no concern about the probable impact of this case on their familial security.

Nor is there any reason why the decision should affect the processing of most future adoptions. The fact that an unusual application of a state statute has been held unconstitutional on equal protection grounds does not necessarily eliminate the entire statute as a basis for future legitimate state action. The procedure to be followed in cases involving infants who are in the custody of their mothers—whether solely or jointly with the father—or of agencies with authority to consent to adoption, is entirely unaffected by the Court's holding or by its reasoning. In fact, as I read the Court's opinion, the statutes now in effect may be enforced as usual unless "the adoption of older children is sought," *ante,* and "the father has established a substantial relationship with the child and is willing to admit his paternity." *Id.* State legislatures will no doubt promptly revise

their adoption laws to comply with the rule of this case, but as long as state courts are prepared to construe their existing statutes to contain a requirement of paternal consent "in cases such as this," *id.,* I see no reason why they may not continue to enter valid adoption decrees in the countless routine cases that will arise before the statutes can be amended."

In short, this is an exceptional case that should have no effect on the typical adoption proceeding. Indeed, I suspect that it will affect only a tiny fraction of the cases covered by the statutes that must now be rewritten. Accordingly, although my disagreement with the Court is as profound as that fraction is small, I am confident that the wisdom of judges will forestall any widespread harm.

I respectfully dissent.

CASE QUESTIONS

1. How should a state legislator, revising adoption provisions to conform to *Caban v. Mohammed,* proceed regarding illegitimate new-borns? Regarding, say, three year olds whose father had signed the birth certificate, visited several times and provided occasional gifts? Regarding the offspring of an unwed mother who wishes to place her child for adoption and who knows but refuses to divulge the name of the child's father? Would a statute requiring adoption consent only from "any natural parent who

has retained sole custody of an illegitimate child since its birth" satisfy the majority's concerns?

2. Stevens' dissent (n.3) indicates that his views would "perhaps" be unchanged even if the constitutional test were "compelling interest" rather than the "important interest" of the *Craig* rule. Is the wording variation between the two tests nothing more than "a distinction without a difference"?

Parham v. Hughes (1979), discussion

The five man majority for the rights of unwed fathers did not endure even for the one day on which *Caban* was handed down. On that same day, the Court divided five to four against an unwed father in the decision of *Parham v. Hughes*.[27] There Justice Powell deserted the fathers' rights bloc to vote to uphold a statute that permitted mothers but not fathers of illegitimates to bring "wrongful death" lawsuits against persons who had killed their children. Even though Lemuel Parham had signed the birth certificate of his son, contributed to his son's support, and visited the boy regularly, five justices rejected his challenge to this gender discrimination. (Both son and mother had been killed in the same car accident.)

Justice Stewart (writing also for Stevens, Burger, and Rehnquist) reasoned that this gender distinction was justified by two state concerns. First, it served as an incentive to an unwed father to legitimate his child (and thereby to take on the legal duty of support): "Legitimation would have removed the stigma of bastardy and allowed the child to inherit from the father in the same manner as if born in lawful wedlock" (441 U.S., at 353). Second, providing an incentive for the father to go through a legitimation hearing while the child, and presumably the child's mother, were still alive was a rational mechanism for (or in Powell's terms "substantially furthered") "dealing with 'the often difficult problem of proving the paternity of illegitimate children'" (at 357). Justice Powell, in his solo but pivotal opinion, put much more emphasis than Stewart on the *Craig* rule, but said that he felt this second state concern did meet the *Craig* test.

White, writing for Brennan, Marshall, and Blackmun, in dissent, insisted that the proof-of-paternity concern was frivolous, since in any wrongful death lawsuit the parent would have to offer proof of parenthood in order to win. Moreover, the dissenters believed that any connection between barring unwed fathers from wrongful death actions and promoting legitimation hearings was "far too tenuous to justify the sex discrimination" (at 363). They did not find it credible that the hope of future recovery in wrongful death actions would actually lure unwed fathers into legitimating their offspring.

While *Parham* made clear that some gender discriminations against unwed fathers would still be tolerated, *Caban* at least had seemed to cast quite a shadow of doubt over their constitutionality in the context of release for adoption. That shadow, however, was partially lifted in the 1983 decision, *Lehr v. Robertson*.[28]

One cannot simply recount the factual background to the Lehr case, because the Court was divided over the very existence of the facts, and the facts in question somewhat determined the justices' differing viewpoints as to the constitutional rights of Jonathan Lehr, the unwed father. Some points were not in dispute. Lehr lived with Lorraine Robertson for two years, at the end of which she gave birth to a daughter, Jessica (on November 9, 1979). Lehr visited mother and daughter at the hospital but his name was not put on the birth certificate. (Robertson never denied that Lehr was the father.) At this point the Supreme Court majority of six, in the voice of Stevens, says, "He did not live with appellee or Jessica after Jessica's birth, he has never provided them with any financial support, and he has never offered to marry appellee" (at 252). Stevens later summarized the facts as follows: "Appellant has never had any significant custodial, personal, or financial relationship with Jessica, and he did not seek to establish a legal tie until after she was two years old" (at 262).

The three dissenters, White, Marshall, and Blackmun, in an opinion by White, detail Lehr's side of the rest of the story, as follows:

> Lehr visited Lorraine and Jessica in the hospital every day during Lorraine's confinement. According to Lehr, from the time Lorraine was discharged from the hospital until August, 1978, she concealed her whereabouts from him. During this time Lehr never ceased his efforts to locate Lorraine and Jessica and achieved sporadic success until August 1977, after which time he was unable to locate them at all. On those occasions when he did determine Lorraine's location, he visited with her and her children to the extent she was willing to permit it. When Lehr, with the aid of a detective agency, located Lorraine and Jessica in August 1978, Lorraine was already married to Mr. Robertson. Lehr asserts that at this time he offered to provide financial assistance and to set up a trust fund for Jessica, but that Lorraine refused. Lorraine threatened Lehr with arrest unless he stayed away and refused to permit him to see Jessica. Thereafter Lehr retained counsel who wrote to Lorraine in early December 1978, requesting that she permit Lehr to visit Jessica and threatening legal action on Lehr's behalf. On December 21, 1978, perhaps as a response to Lehr's threatened legal action, appellees commenced the adoption action at issue here. (At 269.)

The legal procedures that began with the Robertsons' initiating adoption efforts continued as follows: On January 30, 1979 (a month later) Lehr filed a petition in his home county asking for a determination of paternity, a support order, and reasonable visitation privileges. Robertson received notice of that hearing on February 22, 1979. Four days later her attorney informed her home county's court of the paternity proceeding in Lehr's county. Her county judge stayed the paternity proceeding until he could decide whether that hearing should be moved into the county where the Robertsons resided. On March 3, Lehr was served notice of the motion to move the paternity proceeding and thus learned of the pending adoption proceeding. On March 7, Lehr's attorney telephoned the judge in the Robertsons' county to let him know that he was going to request a stay of the adoption proceeding. However, the lawyer was told that earlier that day the judge had signed the adoption order—the judge had signed in full knowledge of the pending paternity proceeding.

The Supreme Court case then arose out of a petition by Lehr to vacate the adoption order as having resulted from a violation of his constitutional rights to due process and equal protection. Two New York appeals courts upheld the adoption order but both in divided votes, with written dissents.

New York state law, revised after *Stanley v. Illinois*, required several categories of potential unwed fathers to be given notice of, and a chance to be heard at, any pending adoption proceeding. These included those who had been adjudicated to be the father; those who lived openly with the child and its mother, holding themselves out as the father; those who had been identified by the mother in a sworn written statement; and those who had married the mother before the child reached six months old. In addition, any male could send a postcard to New York's "putative father registry," indicating intent to claim paternity of a child. This registration was revokable at will and would establish a right to receive notice of that child's adoption proceeding. Lehr had failed to send such a postcard, although his intent to claim paternity was both a matter of public record and known to the judge. The New York courts had upheld the judge's refusal to accord him notice of the hearing terminating his parental rights (i.e., the adoption) because he had followed the wrong legal procedures. The U.S. Supreme Court (with Jessica nearly four years old) affirmed.

The Supreme Court could have relied on a ruling that this case was not covered by *Caban v. Mohammed*, because, as Justice Stevens notes in a footnote omitted in the following case excerpt, the adoption preceded *Caban* by two months. But in the same note Stevens pointedly remarks that *Caban* had not been authoritatively declared non-retroactive. The majority seems to be trying to narrow the future reach of *Caban v. Mohammed*.

Lehr v. Robertson, 463 U.S. 248 (1983)

JUSTICE STEVENS* delivered the opinion of the Court.

The question presented is whether New York has sufficiently protected an unmarried father's inchoate relationship with a child whom he has never supported and rarely seen in the two years since her birth. The appellant, Jonathan Lehr, claims that the Due Process and Equal Protection Clauses of the Fourteenth Amendment, as interpreted in *Stanley v. Illinois*, 405 U.S. 645 (1972), and *Caban v. Mohammed*, 441 U.S. 380 (1979), give him an absolute right to notice and an opportunity to be heard

*Official Court records dropped the usage "Mr. Justice" shortly before Sandra Day O'Connor's accession to the Court.—Au.

before the child may be adopted. We disagree.

. . .

Appellant . . . offers two alternative grounds for holding the New York statutory scheme unconstitutional. First, he contends that a putative father's actual or potential relationship with a child born out of wedlock is an interest in liberty which may not be destroyed without due process of law; he argues therefore that he had a constitutional right to prior notice and an opportunity to be heard before he was deprived of that interest. Second, he contends that the gender-based classification in the statute, which both denied him the right to consent to Jessica's adoption and accorded him fewer procedural rights than her mother, violated the Equal Protection Clause.

The Due Process Claim

The Fourteenth Amendment provides that no State shall deprive any person of life, liberty, or property without due process of law. When that Clause is invoked in a novel context, it is our practice to begin the inquiry with a determination of the precise nature of the private interest that is threatened by the State. *See, e.g., Cafeteria Workers v. McElroy,* 367 U.S. 886, 895–96 (1961). Only after that interest has been identified, can we properly evaluate the adequacy of the State's process. *See Morrissey v. Brewer,* 408 U.S. 471, 482–83 (1972). We therefore first consider the nature of the interest in liberty for which appellant claims constitutional protection and then turn to a discussion of the adequacy of the procedure that New York has provided for its protection.

I

The intangible fibers that connect parent and child have infinite variety. They are woven throughout the fabric of our society, providing it with strength, beauty, and flexibility. It is self-evident that they are sufficiently vital to merit constitutional protection in appropriate cases. In deciding whether this is such a case, however, we must consider the broad framework that has traditionally been used to resolve the legal problems arising from the parent-child relationship.

In the vast majority of cases, state law determines the final outcome. *Cf. United States v. Yazell,* 382 U.S. 341, 351–53 (1966). Rules governing the inheritance of property, adoption, and child custody are generally specified in statutory enactments that vary from State to State. Moreover, equally varied state laws governing marriages and divorce affect a multitude of

parent-child relationships. The institution of marriages has played a critical role both in defining the legal entitlements of family members and in developing the decentralized structure of our democratic society. In recognition of that role, and as part of their general overarching concern for serving the best interests of children, state laws almost universally express an appropriate preference for the formal family.[13]

In some cases, however, this Court has held that the Federal Constitution supersedes state law and provides even greater protection for certain formal family relationships. In those cases, as in the state cases, the Court has emphasized the paramount interest in the welfare of children and has noted that the rights of the parents are a counterpart of the responsibilities they have assumed. Thus, the "liberty" of parents to control the education of their children that was vindicated in *Meyer v. Nebraska,* 262 U.S. 390 (1923), and *Pierce v. Society of Sisters,* 268 U.S. 510 (1925), was described as a "right, coupled with the high duty, to recognize and prepare [the child] for additional obligations." *Id.* at 535. The linkage between parental duty and parental right was stressed again in *Prince v. Massachusetts,* 321 U.S. 158, 166 (1944),

---

13. *See Trimble v. Gordon,* 430 U.S. 762, 769 (1977) ("No one disputes the appropriateness of Illinois' concern with the family unit, perhaps the most fundamental social institution of our society.") A plurality of the Court noted the societal value of family bonds in *Moore v. City of East Cleveland,* 431 U.S. 494, 505 (1977) (Opinion of POWELL, J.): "Out of choice, necessity, or a sense of family responsibility, it has been common for close relatives to draw together and participate in the duties and the satisfactions of a common home. . . . Especially in times of adversity, such as the death of a spouse or economic need, the broader family has tended to come together for mutual sustenance and to maintain or rebuild a secure home life."

when the Court declared it a cardinal principal "that the custody, care and nurture of the child reside first in the parents, whose primary function and freedom include preparation for obligations the state can neither supply nor hinder." *Id.* at 166. In these cases the Court has found that the relationship of love and duty in a recognized family unit is an interest in liberty entitled to constitutional protection. *See also Moore v. City of East Cleveland*, 431 U.S. 494 (1977) (plurality opinion). "[S]tate intervention to terminate [such a] relationship . . . must be accomplished by procedures meeting the requisites of the Due Process Clause." *Santosky v. Kramer*, 455 U.S. 745, 752 (1982).

There are also a few cases in which this Court has considered the extent to which the Constitution affords protection to the relationship between natural parents and children born out of wedlock. . . . This Court has examined the extent to which a natural father's biological relationship with his illegitimate child receives protection under the Due Process Clause in precisely three cases: *Stanley v. Illinois*, 405 U.S. 645 (1972), *Quilloin v. Walcott*, 434 U.S. 246 (1978), and *Caban v. Mohammed*, 441 U.S. 380 (1979). [Summaries of the three followed.]

. . .

[Because in *Caban* this Court upheld the father's] equal protection claim, the majority did not address his due process challenge. The comments on the latter claim by the four dissenting Justices are nevertheless instructive, because they identify the clear distinction between a mere biological relationship and an actual relationship of parental responsibility.

JUSTICE STEWART correctly observed:

Even if it be assumed that each married parent after divorce has some substantive due process right to maintain his or her parental relationship, *cf. Smith v. Organization of Foster Families*, 431 U.S. 816, 862–63 (opinion concurring in judgment), it by no means follows that each unwed parent has any such right. *Parental rights do not spring full-blown from the biological connection between parent and child. They require relationships more enduring.* (441 U.S., at 397 [emphasis added].)

In a similar vein, the other three dissenters in *Caban* were prepared to "assume that, *if and when one develops*, the relationship between a father and his natural child is entitled to protection against arbitrary state action as a matter of due process." *Caban v. Mohammed*, 441 U.S. 380, 414 (emphasis added).

The difference between the developed parent-child relationship that was implicated in *Stanley* and *Caban*, and the potential relationship involved in *Quilloin* and this case, is both clear and significant. When an unwed father demonstrates a full commitment to the responsibilities of parenthood by "com[ing] forward to participate in the rearing of his child," *Caban*, 441 U.S., at 392, his interest in personal contact with his child acquires substantial protection under the due process clause. At that point it may be said that he "act[s] as a father toward his children." *Id.* at 389, n.7. But the mere existence of a biological link does not merit equivalent constitutional protection. The actions of judges neither create nor sever genetic bonds. "[T]he importance of the familial relationship, to the individuals involved and to the society, stems from the emotional attachments that derive from the intimacy of daily association, and from the role it plays in 'promot[ing] a way of life' through the instruction of children as well as from the fact of blood relationship." *Smith v. Organization of Foster Families for Equality and Re-*

form, 431 U.S. 816, 844 (1977) (quoting *Wisconsin v. Yoder,* 406 U.S. 205, 231–233 [1972]).

The significance of the biological connection is that it offers the natural father an opportunity that no other male possesses to develop a relationship with his offspring. If he grasps that opportunity and accepts some measure of responsibility for the child's future, he may enjoy the blessing of the parent-child relationship and make uniquely valuable contributions to the child's development. If he fails to do so, the Federal Constitution will not automatically compel a state to listen to his opinion of where the child's best interests lie.

In this case, we are not assessing the constitutional adequacy of New York's procedures for terminating a developed relationship. Appellant has never had any significant custodial, personal, or financial relationship with Jessica, and he did not seek to establish a legal tie until after she was two years old.[19] We are concerned only with whether New York has adequately protected his opportunity to form such a relationship.

II

The most effective protection of the putative father's opportunity to develop a relationship with his child is provided by the laws that authorize formal marriage and govern its consequences. But the availability of that protection is, of course, dependent on the will of both parents of the child. Thus, New York has adopted a special statutory scheme to protect the unmarried father's interest in assuming a responsible role in the future of his child.

. . . If this scheme were likely to omit many responsible fathers, and if qualification for notice were beyond the control of an interested putative father, it might be thought procedurally inadequate. Yet, as all of the New York courts that reviewed this matter observed, the right to receive notice was completely within appellant's control. By mailing a postcard to the putative father registry, he could have guaranteed that he would receive notice of any proceedings to adopt Jessica. The possibility that he may have failed to do so because of his ignorance of the law cannot be a sufficient reason for criticizing the law itself. The New York legislature concluded that a more open-ended notice requirement would merely complicate the adoption process, threaten the privacy interests of unwed mothers, create the risk of unnecessary controversy, and impair the desired finality of adoption decrees. Regardless of whether we would have done likewise if we were legislators instead of judges, we surely cannot characterize the state's conclusion as arbitrary.[22]

19. . . . In denying the putative father relief in *Quilloin,* we made an observation equally applicable here: "Nor is this a case in which the proposed adoption would place the child with a new set of parents with whom the child had never before lived. Rather, the result of the adoption in this case is to give full recognition to a family unit already in existence, a result desired by all concerned, except appellant. Whatever might be required in other situations, we cannot say that the State was required in this situation to find anything more than that the adoption, and denial of legitimation, were in the best interests of the child.'" 434 U.S., at 255.

22. Nor can we deem unconstitutionally arbitrary the state courts' conclusion that appellant's absence did not distort its analysis of Jessica's best interests. The adoption does not affect Jessica's relationship with her mother. It gives legal permanence to her relationship with her adoptive father, a relationship they had maintained for 21 months at the time the adoption order was entered. Appellant did not proffer any evidence to suggest that legal confirmation of the established relationship would be unwise; he did not even know the adoptive father.

Appellant argues, however, that even if the putative father's opportunity to establish a relationship with an illegitimate child is adequately protected by the New York statutory scheme in the normal case, he was nevertheless entitled to special notice because the court and the mother knew that he had filed an affiliation proceeding in another court. This argument amounts to nothing more than an indirect attack on the notice provisions of the New York statute. The legitimate state interests in facilitating the adoption of young children and having the adoption proceeding completed expeditiously that underlie the entire statutory scheme also justify a trial judge's determination to require all interested parties to adhere precisely to the procedural requirements of the statute. The Constitution does not require either a trial judge or a litigant to give special notice to nonparties who are presumptively capable of asserting and protecting their own rights. Since the New York statutes adequately protected appellant's inchoate interest in establishing a relationship with Jessica, we find no merit in the claim that his constitutional rights were offended because the family court strictly complied with the notice provisions of the statute.

The Equal Protection Claim

The concept of equal justice under law requires the State to govern impartially. *New York Transit Authority v. Beazer*, 440 U.S. 568, 587 (1979). The sovereign may not draw distinctions between individuals based solely on differences that are irrelevant to a legitimate governmental objective. *Reed v. Reed*, 404 U.S. 71, 76 (1971). Specifically, it may not subject men and women to disparate treatment when there is no substantial relation between the disparity and an important state purpose. *Id.*, *Craig v. Boren*, 429 U.S. 190, 197–99 (1976). The legislation at issue in this case,

sections 111 and 111a of the New York Domestic Relations Law, is intended to establish procedures for adoptions. Those procedures are designed to promote the best interests of the child, protect the rights of interested third parties, and ensure promptness and finality.[25] To serve those ends, the legislation guarantees to certain people the right to veto an adoption and the right to prior notice of any adoption proceeding. The mother of an illegitimate child is always within that favored class, but only certain putative fathers are included. Appellant contends that the gender-based distinction is invidious.

As we noted above, the existence or nonexistence of a substantial relationship between parent and child is a relevant criterion in evaluating both the rights of the parent and the best interests of the child. In *Quilloin v. Walcott, supra*, we noted that the putative father, like appellant, "ha[d] never shouldered any significant responsibility with respect to the daily supervision, education, protection, or care of the child. Appellant does not complain of his exemption from these responsibilities. . . ." 434 U.S., at 256. We therefore found that a Georgia statute that always required a mother's consent to the adoption of a child born out of wedlock, but required the father's consent only if he had legitimated the child, did not violate the Equal Protection Clause. Because, like the father in *Quilloin*, appellant has never established a substantial relationship with his daughter, the New York statutes at issue in this case did not operate to deny appellant equal protection.

We have held that these statutes may

25. Appellant does not contest the vital importance of those ends to the people of New York. It has long been accepted that illegitimate children whose parents never marry are "at risk" economically, medically, emotionally, and educationally. . . .

not constitutionally be applied in that class of cases where the mother and father are in fact similarly situated with regard to their relationship with the child. In *Caban v. Mohammed*, 441 U.S. 380 (1979), the Court held that it violated the Equal Protection Clause to grant the mother a veto over the adoption of a four-year-old girl and a six-year-old boy, but not to grant a veto to their father, who had admitted paternity and had participated in the rearing of the children. The Court made it clear, however, that if the father had not "come forward to participate in the rearing of his child, nothing in the Equal Protection Clause [would] preclude[ ] the State from withholding from him the privilege of vetoing the adoption of that child." 441 U.S., at 392.

Jessica's parents are not like the parents involved in *Caban*. . . . If one parent has an established custodial relationship with the child and the other parent has either abandoned or never established a relationship, the Equal Protection Clause does not prevent a state from according the two parents different legal rights.

The judgment of the New York Court of Appeals is

Affirmed.

JUSTICE WHITE, with whom JUSTICE MARSHALL and JUSTICE BLACKMUN join, dissenting.

The question in this case is whether the State may, consistent with the Due Process Clause, deny notice and an opportunity to be heard in an adoption proceeding to a putative father when the State has actual notice of his existence, whereabouts, and interest in the child.

I

It is axiomatic that "[t]he fundamental requirement of due process is the opportunity to be heard 'at a meaningful time and in a meaningful manner.'" *Mathews v. Eldridge*, 424 U.S. 319, 333 (1976), quoting *Armstrong v. Manzo*, 380 U.S. 545, 552 (1965). As Jessica's biological father, Lehr either had an interest protected by the Constitution or he did not. If the entry of the adoption order in this case deprived Lehr of a constitutionally protected interest, he is entitled to notice and an opportunity to be heard before the order can be accorded finality. [Here followed Lehr's version of facts.]

. . .

The majority posits that "[t]he intangible fibers that connect parent and child . . . are sufficiently vital to merit constitutional protection *in appropriate cases*." (Emphasis added.) It then purports to analyze the particular facts of this case to determine whether appellant has a constitutionally protected liberty interest. We have expressly rejected that approach. In *Board of Regents v. Roth*, 408 U.S. 564, 570–71 (1972), we stated that although "a weighing process has long been a part of any determination of the *form* of hearing required in particular situations, . . . to determine whether due process requirements apply in the first place, we must look not to the 'weight' but to the *nature* of the interest at stake . . . to see if the interest is within the Fourteenth Amendment's protection. . . ." See, *e.g.*, *Smith v. Organization of Foster Families*, 431 U.S. 816, 839–42 (1977); *Ingraham v. Wright*, 430 U.S. 651, 672 (1977); *Meachum v. Fano*, 427 U.S. 215, 224 (1976); *Goss v. Lopez*, 419 U.S. 565, 575–76 (1975); *Morrissey v. Brewer*, 408 U.S. 471, 481 (1972).

The "nature of the interest" at stake here is the interest that a natural parent has in his or her child, one that has long been recognized and accorded constitutional protection. We have frequently "stressed the importance of familial bonds, whether or not legitimized by marriage, and accorded them constitutional protection."

Little v. Streater, 452 U.S. 1, 13 (1981). If "both the child and the [putative father] in a paternity action have a compelling interest" in the accurate outcome of such a case, *id.*, it cannot be disputed that both the child and the putative father have a compelling interest in the outcome of a proceeding that may result in the termination of the father-child relationship. "A parent's interest in the accuracy and justice of the decision to terminate his or her parental status is . . . a commanding one." *Lassiter v. Department of Social Services,* 452 U.S. 18, 27 (1981). It is beyond dispute that a formal order of adoption, no less than a formal termination proceeding, operates to permanently terminate parental rights.

Lehr's version of the "facts" paints a far different picture than that portrayed by the majority. . . . Appellant has never been afforded an opportunity to present his case. The legitimation proceeding he instituted was first stayed, and then dismissed, on appellees' motions. Nor could appellant establish his interest during the adoption proceedings, for it is the failure to provide Lehr notice and an opportunity to be heard there that is at issue here. We cannot fairly make a judgment based on the quality or substance of a relationship without a complete and developed factual record. This case requires us to assume that Lehr's allegations are true. . . .

I reject the peculiar notion that the only significance of the biological connection between father and child is that "it offers the natural father an opportunity that no other male possesses to develop a relationship with his offspring." *Ante.* A "mere biological relationship" is not as unimportant in determining the nature of liberty interests as the majority suggests.

"[T]he usual understanding of 'family' implies biological relationships, and most decisions treating the relation between parent and child have stressed this element." *Smith v. Organization of Foster Families, su-*

pra, at 843. The "biological connection" is itself a relationship that creates a protected interest. Thus the "nature" of the interest is the parent-child relationship; how well-developed that relationship has become goes to its "weight," not its "nature."[4] Whether Lehr's interest is entitled to constitutional protection does not entail a searching inquiry into the quality of the relationship but a simple determination of the *fact* that the relationship exists—a fact that even the majority agrees must be assumed to be established.

. . . That is not to say that due process requires actual notice to every putative father or that adoptive parents or the State must conduct an exhaustive search of records or an intensive investigation before a final adoption order may be entered. The procedures adopted by the State, however, must at least represent a reasonable effort to determine the identity of the putative father and to give him adequate notice.

II

In this case, of course, there was no question about either the identity or the location of the putative father. The mother knew exactly who he was and both she and the court entering the order of adoption knew precisely where he was and how to give him actual notice that his parental rights were about to be terminated by an adoption order. Lehr was entitled to due process, and the right to be heard is one of the fundamentals of that right, which "has

4. The majority's citation of *Quilloin* and *Caban* as examples that the Constitution does not require the same procedural protections for the interests of all unwed fathers is disingenuous. Neither case involved notice and opportunity to be heard. In both, the unwed fathers were notified and participated as parties in the adoption proceedings. *See Quilloin v. Walcott,* 434 U.S. 246, 253 (1978); *Caban v. Mohammed,* 441 U.S. 380, 385 n.3 (1979).

little reality or worth unless one is informed that the matter is pending and can choose for himself whether to appear or default, acquiesce or contest." *Schroeder v. City of New York,* 371 U.S. 208, 212 (1962), quoting *Mullane v. Central Hanover Trust Co.,* 339 U.S. 306, 314 (1950).

The State concedes this much but insists that Lehr has had all the process that is due to him. It relies on § 111–a, which designates seven categories of unwed fathers to whom notice of adoption proceedings must be given, including any unwed father who has filed with the State a notice of his intent to claim paternity. The State submits that it need not give notice to anyone who has not filed his name, as he is permitted to do, and who is not otherwise within the designated categories, even if his identity and interest are known or are reasonably ascertainable by the State.

I am unpersuaded by the State's position. In the first place, § 111–a defines six categories of unwed fathers to whom notice must be given even though they have not placed their names on file pursuant to the section. Those six categories, however, do not include fathers such as Lehr who have initiated filiation proceedings, even though their identity and interest are as clearly and easily ascertainable as those fathers in the six categories. Initiating such proceedings necessarily involves a formal acknowledgement of paternity, and requiring the State to take note of such a case in connection with pending adoption proceedings would be a trifling burden, no more than the State undertakes when there is a final adjudication in a paternity action. Indeed, there would appear to be more reason to give notice to those such as Lehr who acknowledge paternity than to those who have been adjudged to be a father in a contested paternity action.

The State asserts that any problem in this respect is overcome by the seventh category of putative fathers to whom notice

must be given, namely those fathers who have identified themselves in the putative father register maintained by the State. Since Lehr did not take advantage of this device to make his interest known, the State contends, he was not entitled to notice and a hearing even though his identity, location and interest were known to the adoption court prior to the entry of the adoption order. I have difficulty with this position. First, it represents a grudging and crabbed approach to due process. The State is quite willing to give notice and a hearing to putative fathers who have made themselves known by resorting to the putative fathers' register. It makes little sense to me to deny notice and hearing to a father who has not placed his name in the register but who has unmistakably identified himself by filing suit to establish his paternity and has notified the adoption court of his action and his interest. I thus need not question the statutory scheme on its face. Even assuming that Lehr would have been foreclosed if his failure to utilize the register had somehow disadvantaged the State, he effectively made himself known by other means, and it is the sheerest formalism to deny him a hearing because he informed the State in the wrong manner.

No state interest is substantially served by denying Lehr adequate notice and a hearing.

. . . As this case well illustrates, denying notice and a hearing to such a father may result in years of additional litigation and threaten the reopening of adoption proceedings and the vacation of the adoption.

Because in my view the failure to provide Lehr with notice and an opportunity to be heard violated rights guaranteed him by the Due Process Clause, I need not address the question whether § 111–a violates the Equal Protection Clause. . . .

Respectfully, I dissent.

CASE QUESTIONS

1. Does the combination of *Stanley, Quilloin, Caban,* and *Lehr* yield the proposition that single mothers who do not want the child's adoption hindered by the father are encouraged to conceal the child from its father until the adoption is complete? If so, is this wise public policy?

2. Does the court majority in cases like this one' and *Quilloin* seem to be largely motivated by desire to refrain from interfering in an ongoing family (rather than by rules found in the Constitution)? Is the Court well-suited to act as a national child welfare agency?

3. Should an unwed mother and an unwed father be given equal veto rights over the adoption of their new-born child? Equal custody rights to the child? Is this a matter of gender discrimination or a matter of dealing with dissimilar situations?

Revolutionizing Marriage

In 1979, the same year in which the Court moved in *Caban* toward equalizing the rights of unwed fathers, the justices handed down a decision that revolutionized the law of marriage. The traditional Anglo-American law of marriage was replete with consequences for women's legal rights.[29] Some of these were touched on in the chapter 1 discussion of Virginia Minor's case. In addition, however, to prohibitions on married women's earning, buying, selling, and contracting (most of which were lifted in late nineteenth-century reform legislation), the law of marriage brought women a variety of ancillary privileges and duties.

For instance, married women were required to take their husband's legal residence and last name. The latter of these, in the context of rules governing names on a driver's license, was upheld by the U.S. Supreme Court as recently as 1972, even after *Reed*, but in a memorandum decision with no written opinion.[30]

In the context of the criminal law, the fiction of the unity of husband and wife meant that the wife could not be charged with a crime of conspiracy with her husband and that the spouses could testify neither for nor against each other. In 1933, in its role as supervisor of the court system for *federal* crimes, the Supreme Court dropped the rule against favorable spousal testimony (*Funk v. U.S.,* 290 U.S. 371). In 1960, in the same role (*U.S. v. Dege,* 364 U.S. 51) the Court dropped the prohibition on criminal conspiracy charges between a wife and a husband. And in 1980 (*Trammel v. U.S.,* 445 U.S. 40), the Court dropped the ban on letting a spouse testify *against* her (or his) marital partner, except regarding matters of private, marital confidences—for these, the accused can bar adverse testimony by a spouse. None of these new rules affected *state* criminal processes; they applied only in the context of trials for federal crimes. For state crimes each state had its own rules in these matters.

These reforms of the federal criminal process were typically accompanied by progressive-sounding rhetoric. Justice Frankfurter, for example, the author of the infamous *Goesaert v. Cleary* opinion (see chapter 2), wrote in *Dege* in 1960 that the idea that, in marital teams committing crimes women act under their husband's direction "implies a view of American womanhood offensive to the ethos of our society." Despite the rich possibilities of such rhetoric, and despite its modest reforms at the edges, the Court did little to alter the traditional institution of marriage in the U.S. until 1979.

In that year, in the case of *Orr v. Orr,*[31] the essence of the marriage institution was transformed. The legal core of marriage in Anglo-American law has been that the wife has the duties of conjugal (i.e., sexual) and domestic (i.e., household) service. The husband has the duty of financial support. These duties were reciprocal rather than equal. Thus, even if a wife came from wealthy parents and the husband did not, it was his duty to support her, and not the reverse. Or if he were a prize-winning chef, it was still her legal duty to (among other things) cook their home meals. Of course, these duties were not typically enforced by the state in ongoing marriages; they became relevant in such contexts as divorce or in lawsuits for loss of wifely services ("consortium") when a wife was seriously injured. (The lawsuit would be against the party causing the injury.) This basic arrangement of the legal structure of marriage was seismically altered in *Orr v. Orr.*

William H. Orr, upon his divorce from Lillian Orr, challenged the rule (at the time, a rule still operative in a substantial number of states) that only husbands and not wives may be ordered to pay alimony. To abrogate this husbands-only rule of alimony seemed to imply the demolishing of the long-standing rule that it was the husband's, and not the wife's, duty to support the family. The Supreme Court, went ahead and abrogated the traditional alimony rule.

Although Mr. Orr had lost at both the trial and appeals levels in Alabama, he won overwhelmingly at the U.S. Supreme Court. No justice dissented on the merits of the case, but three (Rehnquist, Burger and Powell) did dissent on the question of whether the Court should have jurisdiction.

Orr v. Orr, 440 U.S. 268 (1979)

Mr. Justice Brennan delivered the opinion of the Court.

The question presented is the constitutionality of Alabama alimony statutes which provide that husbands, but not wives, may be required to pay alimony upon divorce.

I

We first address three preliminary questions. . . .

The first concerns the standing of Mr. Orr to assert in his defense the unconstitutionality of the Alabama statutes. It appears that Mr. Orr made no claim that he was entitled to an award of alimony from Mrs. Orr, but only that he should not be required to pay alimony if similarly situated wives could not be ordered to pay. It is therefore possible that his success here will not ultimately bring him relief from the judgment outstanding against him, as the State could respond to a reversal by neutrally extending alimony rights to needy husbands as well as wives. In that event, Mr. Orr would remain obligated to his wife. It is thus argued that the only "proper plaintiff" would be a husband who requested alimony for himself, and not one who merely objected to paying alimony.

This argument quite clearly proves too much. In every equal protection attack upon a statute challenged as underinclusive, the State may satisfy the Constitution's commands either by extending benefits to the previously disfavored class or by denying benefits to both parties (*e.g.*, by repealing the statute as a whole). In this case, if held unconstitutional, the Alabama divorce statutes could be validated by, *inter alia*, amendments which either (1) permit awards to husbands as well as wives, (2) deny alimony to both parties. It is true that under the first disposition Mr. Orr might gain nothing from his success in this Court, although the hypothetical "requesting" plaintiff would. However, if instead the State takes the second course and denies alimony to both spouses, it is Mr. Orr and not the hypothetical plaintiff who would benefit. Because we have no way of knowing how the State will in fact respond, unless we are to hold that underinclusive statutes can never be challenged because *any* plaintiff's success can theoretically be thwarted, Mr. Orr must be held to have standing here. . . .

There is no question but that Mr. Orr bears a burden he would not bear were he female. The issue is highlighted although not altered, by transposing it to the sphere of race. There is no doubt that a state law imposing alimony obligations on blacks but not whites could be challenged by a black who was required to pay. The burden alone is sufficient to establish standing.

The holdings of the Alabama courts stand as a total bar to appellant's relief; his constitutional attack holds the only promise of escape from the burden that derives from the challenged statute. He has therefore "alleged such a personal stake in the outcome of the controversy as to assure that concrete adverseness which sharpens the presentation of issues upon which this court so largely depends for illumination of difficult constitutional questions," *Linda R. S. v. Richard D.*, 410 U.S. 614, 616 (1973), quoting *Baker v. Carr*, 369 U.S. 186, 204 (1962). . . .

. . .

[W]e now turn to the merits.

II

In authorizing the imposition of alimony obligations on husbands, but not on wives, the Alabama statutory scheme "provides that different treatment be accorded . . . on the basis of . . . sex; it thus establishes a classification subject to scrutiny under the Equal Protection Clause," *Reed v. Reed*, 404 U.S. 71, 75 (1971). The fact that the classification expressly discriminates against men rather than women does not protect it from scrutiny. *Craig v. Boren*, 429 U.S. 190 (1976). "To withstand scrutiny" under the equal protection clause, "'classifications by gender must serve important governmental objectives and must be substantially related to achievement of those objectives.'" *Califano v. Webster*, 430 U.S. 313, 316–17 (1977). We shall, therefore, examine the three governmental objectives that might arguably be served by Alabama's statutory scheme.

Appellant views the Alabama alimony statutes as effectively announcing the State's preference for an allocation of family responsibilities under which the wife plays a dependent role, and as seeking for their objective the reinforcement of that model among the State's citizens. *Cf. Stern v. Stern*, 165 Conn. 190, 332 A.2d 78 (1973). We agree, as he urges, that prior cases settle that this purpose cannot sustain the statutes.[9] *Stanton v. Stanton*, 421 U.S. 7, 10 (1975), held that the "old notion" that "generally it is the man's primary responsibility to provide a home and its essentials," can no longer justify a statute that discriminates on the basis of gender. "No longer is the female destined solely for the home and the rearing of the family, and only the male for the marketplace and world of ideas," *id*. at 14–15. *See also Craig v. Boren*, 429 U.S., at 198. If the statute is to survive constitutional attack, therefore, it must be validated on some other basis.

The opinion of the Alabama Court of Civil Appeals suggests other purposes that the statute may serve. Its opinion states that the Alabama statutes were "designed" for "the wife of a broken marriage who needs financial assistance," 351 So. 2d, at 905. This may be read as asserting either of two legislative objectives. One is a legislative purpose to provide help for needy spouses, using sex as a proxy for need. The other is a goal of compensating women for past discrimination during marriage, which assertedly has left them unprepared to fend for themselves in the working world following divorce. We concede, of course, that assisting needy spouses is a legitimate and important governmental objective. We have also recognized "[r]eduction of the disparity in economic condition between men and women caused by the long history of discrimination against women . . . as . . . an important governmental objective," *Califano v. Webster*, 430 U.S., at 317. It only remains, therefore, to determine whether the classification at issue here is "substantially related to achievement of those objectives." *Id*.

Ordinarily, we would begin the analysis of the "needy spouse" objective by considering whether sex is a sufficiently "accurate proxy," *Craig v. Boren*, 429 U.S., at 204, for dependency to establish that the gender classification rests "'upon some ground of difference having a fair and substantial relation to the object of the legislation,'" *Reed v. Reed*, 404 U.S., at 76. Similarly, we would initially approach the "compensation" rationale by asking whether women had in fact been significantly discriminated against in the sphere to which the statute applied a sex-based classification, leaving the sexes "*not* similarly situated with respect to opportunities" in that sphere, *Schlesinger v. Ballard*, 419 U.S. 498, 508

9. Appellee attempts to buttress the importance of this objective by arguing that while "[t]he common law stripped the married woman of many of her rights and most of her property, . . . it attempted to partially compensate by giving her the assurance that she would be supported by her husband." This argument, that the "support obligation was imposed by the common law to compensate the wife for the discrimination she suffered at the hands of the common law," reveals its own weakness. At most it establishes that the alimony statutes were part and parcel of a larger statutory scheme which invidiously discriminated against women, removing them from the world of work and property and "compensating" them by making their designated place "secure." This would be reason to invalidate the entire discriminatory scheme—not a reason to uphold its separate invidious parts. But appellee's argument is even weaker when applied to the facts of this case, as Alabama has long ago removed, by statute, the elements of the common law appellee points to as justifying further discrimination. *See* Ala. Const., art. 10, § 209 (married women's property rights).

(1975). Compare *Califano v. Webster*, 430 U.S., at 318, and *Kahn v. Shevin*, 416 U.S. 351, 353 (1974), with *Weinberger v. Wiesenfeld*, 420 U.S. 636, 648 (1975).[11]

But in this case, even if sex were a reliable proxy for need, and even if the institution of marriage did discriminate against women, these factors still would "not adequately justify the salient features of" Alabama's statutory scheme, *Craig v. Boren*, 429 U.S., at 202. Under the statute, individualized hearings at which the parties' relative financial circumstances are considered *already* occur. . . . There is no reason, therefore, to use sex as a proxy for need. Needy males could be helped along with needy females with little if any additional burden on the State. In such circumstances, not even an administrative convenience rationale exists to justify operating by generalization or proxy. Similarly, since individualized hearings can determine which women were in fact discriminated against vis à vis their husbands, as well as which family units defied the stereotype and left the husband dependent on the wife, Alabama's alleged compensatory purpose may be effectuated without placing burdens solely on husbands. Progress toward fulfilling such a purpose would not be hampered, and it would cost the State nothing more, if it were to treat men and women equally by making alimony burdens independent of sex. "Thus, the gender-based distinction is gratuitous; without it the statutory scheme would only provide benefits to those men who are in fact similarly situated to the women the statute aids," *Weinberger v.*

11. We would also consider whether the purportedly compensatory "classifications in fact penalized women," and whether "the statutory structure and its legislative history revealed that the classification was not enacted as compensation for past discrimination." *Califano v. Webster*, 430 U.S. 313, 317 (1977).

Wiesenfeld, 420 U.S., at 653, and the effort to help those women would not in any way be compromised.

Moreover, use of a gender classification actually produces perverse results in this case. As compared to a gender-neutral law placing alimony obligations on the spouse able to pay, the present Alabama statutes give an advantage only to the financially secure wife whose husband is in need. Although such a wife might have to pay alimony under a gender-neutral statute, the present statutes exempt her from that obligation. Thus, "[t]he [wives] who benefit from the disparate treatment are those who were . . . nondependent on their husbands," *Califano v. Goldfarb*, 430 U.S. 199, 221 (1977) (STEVENS, J., concurring). They are precisely those who are not "needy spouses" and who are "least likely to have been victims of . . . discrimination," *id.*, by the institution of marriage. A gender-based classification which, as compared to a gender-neutral one, generates additional benefits only for those it has no reason to prefer cannot survive equal protection scrutiny.

Legislative classifications which distribute benefits and burdens on the basis of gender carry the inherent risk of reinforcing stereotypes about the "proper place" of women and their need for special protection. Cf. *United Jewish Organizations v. Carey*, 430 U.S. 144, 173–74 (1977) (concurring opinion). Thus, even statutes purportedly designed to compensate for and ameliorate the effects of past discrimination must be carefully tailored. Where, as here, the State's compensatory and ameliorative purposes are as well served by a gender-neutral classification as one that gender-classifies and therefore carries with it the baggage of sexual stereotypes, the State cannot be permitted to classify on the basis of sex. And this is doubly so where the choice made by the State appears to redound—if only indirectly—to the benefit of those without need for special solicitude.

III

Having found Alabama's alimony statutes unconstitutional, we reverse the judgment below and remand the cause for further proceedings not inconsistent with this opinion. That disposition, of course, leaves the state courts free to decide any questions of substantive state law not yet passed upon in this litigation. [Citations omitted.] Therefore, it is open to the Alabama courts on remand to consider whether Mr. Orr's stipulated agreement to pay alimony, or other grounds of gender-neutral state law, bind him to continue his alimony payments.

Reversed.

MR. JUSTICE BLACKMUN, concurring.

On the assumption that the Court's language concerning discrimination "in the sphere" of the relevant preference statute, *ante,* does not imply that society-wide discrimination is always irrelevant, and on the further assumption that that language in no way cuts back on the Court's decision in *Kahn v. Shevin,* 416 U.S. 351 (1974), I join the opinion and judgment of the Court.

MR. JUSTICE STEVENS, concurring.

[Brief response to Justice Rehnquist's standing argument is omitted here.]

MR. JUSTICE REHNQUIST, with whom THE CHIEF JUSTICE joins, dissenting.
In Alabama only wives may be awarded alimony upon divorce. In part I of its opinion, the Court holds that Alabama's alimony statutes may be challenged in this Court by a divorced male who has never sought alimony, who is demonstrably not entitled to alimony even if he had, and

who contractually bound himself to pay alimony to his former wife and did so without objection for over two years. I think the Court's eagerness to invalidate Alabama's statutes has led it to deal too casually with the "case and controversy" requirement of Article III of the Constitution.

I

The Architects of our constitutional form of government, to assure that courts exercising the "judicial power of the United States" would not trench upon the authority committed to the other branches of government, consciously limited the Judicial Branch's "right of expounding the Constitution" to "cases of a Judiciary nature"[1]— that is, to actual "cases" and "controversies" between genuinely adverse parties. Central to this Article III limitation on federal judicial power is the concept of standing. The standing inquiry focuses on the party before the Court, asking whether he has "'such a personal stake in the outcome of the controversy' as to warrant *his* invocation of federal-court jurisdiction and to justify exercise of the court's remedial powers on his behalf." *Warth v. Seldin,* 422 U.S. 490, 498–99 (1975) (emphasis in original), quoting *Baker v. Carr,* 369 U.S. 186, 204 (1962). Implicit in the concept of standing, are the requirements of injury in fact and causation. To demonstrate the "personal stake" in the litigation necessary to satisfy Article III, the party must suffer "a distinct and palpable injury." *Warth v. Seldin, supra,* at 501, that bears a "'fairly traceable' causal

1. 2 M. Farrand, *The Records of the Federal Convention of 1787,* at 430 (rev. ed. 1937). Indeed, on four different occasions the Constitutional Convention rejected a proposal, contained in the "Virginia Plan," to associate Justices of the Supreme Court in a counsel of revision designed to render advice on pending legislation. I *id.* at 21. . . .

connection" to the challenged government action. *Duke Power Company v. Carolina Environmental Study Group, Inc.*, 438 U.S. 59 (1978), quoting *Arlington Heights v. Metropolitan Housing Development Corp.*, 429 U.S. 252, 261 (1977). When a party's standing to raise an issue is questioned, therefore, "the relevant inquiry is whether . . . [he] has shown an injury to himself that is likely to be redressed by a favorable decision." *Simon v. Eastern Kentucky Welfare Rights Org.*, 426 U.S. 26, 38 (1976). Stated differently, a party who places a question before a federal court must "stand to profit in some personal interest" from its resolution, else the exercise of judicial power would be gratuitous. *Id.* at 39.

The sole claim before this Court is that Alabama's alimony statutes, which provide that only husbands may be required to pay alimony upon divorce, violate the Equal Protection Clause of the Fourteenth Amendment.

. . .

A

This Court has long held that in order to satisfy the injury in fact requirement of Article III standing, a party claiming that a statute unconstitutionally withholds a particular benefit must be in line to receive the benefit if the suit is successful.

. . .

It is undisputed that the parties now before us are "a needy wife who qualifies for alimony and a husband who has the property and earnings from which alimony can be paid." *Orr v. Orr*, 351 So. 2d 906, 907 (1977) (Jones, J., dissenting). Under the statute pertinent to the Orrs' divorce, alimony may be awarded against the husband only '[i]f the wife has no separate estate or if it be insufficient for her maintenance." Ala. Code § 30–2–51 (1975). At the time of their divorce, Orr made no claim that he was not

in a position to contribute to his needy wife's support, much less that she should be required to pay alimony to him. . . . On the contrary, the amount of alimony awarded by the Alabama trial court was agreed to by the parties, and appellant has never sought a reduction in his alimony obligation on the ground of changed financial circumstances. . . . On these facts, it is clear that appellant is not in a position to benefit from a sex-neutral alimony statute. His standing to raise the constitutional question in this case, therefore, cannot be founded on a claim that he would, but for his sex, be entitled to an award of alimony from his wife under the Alabama statutes.

B

The Court holds that Mr. Orr's standing to raise his equal protection claim lies in the burden he bears under the Alabama statutes. He is required to pay alimony to his needy former spouse while similarly situated women are not. That the State may render Orr's victory in this Court a hollow one by neutrally extending alimony rights to needy husbands does not, according to the Court, destroy his standing, for the State may elect instead to do away with alimony altogether. The possibility that Alabama will turn its back on the thousands of women currently dependent on alimony checks for their support is, as a practical matter, nonexistent. But my conclusion that appellant lacks standing in this Court does not rest on the strong likelihood that Alabama will respond to today's decision by passing a sex-neutral statute. Appellant has simply not demonstrated that either alternative open to the State—even the entire abrogation of alimony—will free him of his burden.

The alimony obligation at issue in this case was fixed by an agreement between the parties, and appellant makes no claim that the contract is unenforceable under state law. Indeed, the Court itself concedes that "despite the unconstitutionality of the alimony statutes. Mr. Orr may have a continuing obligation to his former wife based upon [their] agreement." The Court casually dismisses the matter, however, as one "which we cannot and would not, predict."

I cannot accede to the Court's offhand dismissal of so serious an obstacle to the exercise of our jurisdiction. . . .

. . .

III

Article III courts are not commissioned to roam at large, gratuitously righting perceived wrongs and vindicating claimed rights. They must await the suit of one whose advocacy is inspired by a "personal stake" in victory. The Framers' wise insistence that those who invoke the power of a federal court personally stand to profit from its exercise ensures that constitutional issues are not decided in advance of necessity and that the complaining party stand in the shoes of those whose rights he champions. Obedience to the rules of standing—the "threshold determinates of the propriety of judicial intervention"—is of crucial importance to constitutional adjudication in this Court, for when the parties leave these halls, what is done cannot be undone except by constitutional amendment.

Much as "Caesar had his Brutus, and Charles the First his Cromwell," Congress and the States have this Court to ensure that their legislative acts do not run afoul of the limitations imposed by the United States Constitution. But this Court has neither a Brutus nor a Cromwell to impose a similar discipline on it. While our "right of expounding the Constitution" is confined to "cases of a Judiciary nature," we are empowered to determine for ourselves when the requirements of Article III are satisfied. Thus, "the only check upon our exercise of power is our own sense of self-restraint." *United States v. Butler*, 297 U.S. 1, 78 (Stone, J., dissenting) (1936). I do not think the Court, in deciding the merits of appellant's constitutional claim, has exercised the self-restraint that Article III requires in this case. I would therefore dismiss Orr's appeal. . . .

Mr. Justice Powell, dissenting.

I agree with Mr. Justice Rehnquist that the Court, in its desire to reach the equal protection issue in this case, has dealt too casually with the difficult Article III problems which confront us. Rather than assume the answer to questions of state law on which the resolution of the Article III issue should depend, and which well may moot the equal protection question in this case, I would abstain from reaching either of the constitutional questions at the present time.

. . .

In these circumstances, I find the Court's insistence upon reaching and deciding the merits quite irreconcilable with the long-established doctrine that we abstain from reaching a federal constitutional claim that is premised on unsettled questions of state law without first affording the state courts an opportunity to resolve such questions. I therefore would remand the case to the Supreme Court of Alabama.

CASE QUESTIONS

1. Does the behavior of the Court majority here and in *Craig v. Boren* show the Court reaching out to settle cases with which it need not have dealt? Does the Court appear to be trying to compensate for the demise of the ERA?

2. Has this decision implicitly destroyed the traditional Anglo-American legal requirement of separate marital rules?

Kirchberg v. Feenstra (1981), discussion

Orr was followed by a decision in which even the *Orr* dissenters agreed that a particular statutory privilege for husbands violated the Equal Protection Clause. In the 1981 case of *Kirchberg v. Feenstra*[32] the U.S. Supreme Court unanimously declared unconstitutional a Louisiana statute "that gave a husband, as 'head and master' of property jointly owned with his wife, the unilateral right to dispose of such property without his spouse's consent." Seven justices relied on the logic of *Craig* and its progeny. Justices Stewart and Rehnquist wrote separately to elaborate their own equal protection test; they viewed as decisive the question of dissimilar treatment of persons "similarly situated for all relevant purposes [of the statute]" (rather than the *Craig* "important governmental interest" test). But they agreed on the result, for this discrimination failed even their test.

Defining Discrimination: The Question of Impact

The *Craig* rule could tell the Court how to deal with gender discrimination but it provided no guidelines for deciding whether gender discrimination were present in non-obvious cases. One type of law that gave the Court difficulty in this regard was legislation that disfavored pregnancy. The Court's difficulty with such statutes is detailed in chapter 4. A second type of law where the very presence of gender discrimination was in question was the sort of law that greatly favors one sex over the other in its *impact*, although the statute itself makes no mention of gender. (This silence is referred to as "facial neutrality.") The Court had dealt with similar difficulties in examining laws with racially disproportionate impacts. Although its record in the racial context was not without inconsistency,[33] the Court by 1976, in *Washington v. Davis*[34] had come up with a firm rule: If a law, neutral on its face, had a racially disparate impact, the Court would treat it as racial discrimination (and thus apply strict scrutiny) only if the challenges to the law could prove that some racial discrimination had been *intentional*. In 1979, the

Supreme Court, in *Personnel Administrator v. Feeney*,[35] chose to apply a similar test for deciding whether to invoke *Craig*-level-scrutiny for laws that hurt one sex more than another but are neutral on their face. The justices were unanimous in agreement on the test for locating discrimination in facially neutral statutes—the criterion must be evidence of an intent to discriminate. They disagreed, however, on how this test applied to the facts before them in this case. Seven justices found no purposeful discrimination, whereas two justices claimed to find some. One reason for their differing conclusion is that the majority placed the burden of proof on the plaintiff; the dissenters, on the defendant.

Helen Feeney brought the case to challenge the Massachusetts laws that provided an absolute preference of military veterans for state civil service jobs. Vets who applied for such a job, as long as they passed the civil service exam, automatically received a higher eligibility rank than any non-veteran applicant. (Among competing veterans, those with the higher score obtained the higher rank.) For any particular job the top three ranking candidates were eligible. Helen Feeney, a 12-year civil service employee, competed for a number of jobs, and scored well on the civil service tests (e.g., second or third in the state). But each time several veterans were ranked ahead of her. She initiated the suit in 1975 in Federal District Court. She won a declaration of unconstitutionality there, but the U.S. Supreme Court then had sent the case back down to the district level for reconsideration after *Washington v. Davis*. The District Court reaffirmed its judgment and the case went back to the U.S. Supreme Court, who reversed the District Court's judgment, as they explain below:

Personnel Administrator v. Feeney, 442 U.S. 256 (1979)

MR. JUSTICE STEWART delivered the opinion of the Court.

I

. . .

C

The veterans' hiring preference in Massachusetts, as in other jurisdictions, has traditionally been justified as a measure designed to reward veterans for the sacrifice of military service, to ease the transition from military to civilian life, to encourage patriotic service, and to attract loyal and well-disciplined people to civil service occupations.

. . .

D

The first Massachusetts veterans' preference statute defined the term "veterans" in gender-neutral language. *See* 1896 Mass. Acts, ch. 517, § 2 ("any person" who served in the United States army or navy), and subsequent amendments have followed this pattern, *see, e.g.,* 1919 Mass. Acts, ch. 150, § 1 ("any person" who served . . .); 1954 Mass. Acts, ch. 531, § 1 ("any person, male or female, including a nurse"). Women who have served in official United States military units during wartime, then, have always been entitled to the benefit of the preference. In addition, Massachusetts, through a 1943 amendment to the definition of "wartime service," extended the preference to women who served in unofficial auxiliary woman's units. 1943 Mass. Acts, ch. 194.

. . .

Notwithstanding the apparent attempts by Massachusetts to include as many military women as possible within the scope of the preference, the statute today benefits an overwhelmingly male class. This is attributable in some measure to the variety of federal statutes, regulations, and policies that have restricted the numbers of women who could enlist in the United States Armed forces,[21] and largely to the simple fact that women have never been

21. The Army Nurse Corps, created by Congress in 1901, was the first official military unit for women, but its members were not granted full military rank until 1944. *See* M. Binkin and S. Bach, *Women and the Military* 4–21 (1977) (hereinafter Binkin and Bach); M. E. Treadwell, *The Women's Army Corps* 6 (Dept. of Army, Office of Chief of Military History, 1954) (hereinafter Treadwell). During World War I, a variety of proposals were made to enlist women for work as doctors, telephone operators and clerks, but all were rejected by the War Department. *See id.* The Navy, however, interpreted its own authority broadly to include a power to enlist women as Yeoman F's and Marine F's. About 13,000 women served in this rank, working primarily at clerical jobs. These women were the first in the United States to be admitted to full military rank and status. *See* Treadwell 10.

Official military corps for women were established in response to the massive personnel needs of the Second World War. . . .

The authorizations for the women's units during World War II were temporary. The Women's Armed Services Integration Act of 1948, 62 Stat. 356–375, established the women's services on a permanent basis. Under the Act, women were given regular military status. However, quotas were placed on the numbers who could enlist; 62 Stat. 357, 360–361 (no more than 2 percent of total enlisted strength): eligibility requirements were more stringent than those for men, and career opportunities were limited. Binken and

subjected to a military draft. See *generally* M. Binkin and S. Bach, *Women and the Military* 4–21 (1977).

When this litigation was commenced, then, over 98 percent of the veterans in Massachusetts were male; only 1.8 percent were female. And over one-quarter of the Massachusetts population were veterans. During the decade between 1963 and 1973 when the appellee was actively participating in the State's merit selection system, 47,005 new permanent appointments were made in the classified official service. Forty-three percent of those hired were women, and, 57 percent were men. Of the women appointed, 1.8 percent were veterans, while 54 percent of the men had veteran status. A large unspecified percentage of the female appointees were serving in lower paying positions for which males traditionally had not applied. . . . The impact of the veterans' preference law upon the public employment opportunities of women has thus been severe. This impact lies at the heart of the appellee's federal constitutional claim.

II

The sole question for decision on this appeal is whether Massachusetts, in granting an absolute lifetime preference to veterans, has discriminated against women in violation of the Equal Protection Clause of the Fourteenth Amendment.

Bach 11–12. During the 1950s and 1960s, enlisted women constituted little more than 1 percent of the total force. In 1967, the 2 percent quota was lifted, Act of Nov. 8, 1967, Pub. L. 90–130, § 1(b), 81 Stat. 376, and in the 1970s many restrictive policies concerning women's participation in the military have been eliminated or modified. *See generally* Binken and Bach, *supra.* In 1972, women still constituted less than 2 percent of the enlisted strength. *Id.* at 14. By 1975, when this litigation was commenced, the percentage had risen to 4.0 percent. *Id.*

A

The Equal Protection Guarantee of the Fourteenth Amendment does not take from the States all power of classification. *Massachusetts Bd. of Retirement v. Murgia*, 427 U.S. 307, 314. Most laws classify, and many affect certain groups unevenly, even though the law itself treats them no differently from all other members of the class described by the law. When the basic classification is rationally based, uneven effects upon particular groups within a class are ordinarily of no constitutional concern. . . .

Certain classifications, however, in themselves supply a reason to infer antipathy. Race is the paradigm. A racial classification, regardless of purported motivation, is presumptively invalid and can be upheld only upon an extraordinary justification. *Brown v. Board of Education*, 347 U.S. 483; *McLaughlin v. Florida*, 379 U.S. 184. This rule applies as well to a classification that is ostensibly neutral but is an obvious pretext for racial discrimination. *Yick Wo v. Hopkins*, 118 U.S. 356; *Guinn v. United States*, 238 U.S. 347; *cf. Lane v. Wilson*, 307 U.S. 268; *Gomillion v. Lightfoot*, 364 U.S. 339. But, as was made clear in *Washington v. Davis*, 426 U.S. 229, and *Village of Arlington Heights v. Metropolitan Housing Development Corp.*, 429 U.S. 252, even if a neutral law has a disproportionately adverse effect upon a racial minority, it is unconstitutional under the Equal Protection Clause only if that impact can be traced to a discriminatory purpose.

Classifications based upon gender, not unlike those based upon race, have traditionally been the touchstone for pervasive and often subtle discrimination. *Caban v. Muhammed*, (dissenting opinion). This Court's recent cases teach that such classifications must bear a "close and substantial relationship to important governmental objectives," *Craig v. Boren*, 429 U.S. 190, 197, and are in many settings unconstitutional.

Reed v. Reed, 404 U.S. 71; *Frontiero v. Richardson*, 411 U.S. 677; *Weinberger v. Wiesenfeld*, 420 U.S. 636; *Craig v. Boren, supra; Califrano v. Goldfarb*, 420 U.S. 199; *Orr v. Orr; Caban v. Muhammed.* Although public employment is not a constitutional right, *Massachusetts Bd. of Retirement v. Murgia, supra*, and the States have wide discretion in framing employee qualifications, see *e.g., New York Transit Authority v. Beazor*, 440 U.S. 568, these precedents dictate that any state law overtly or covertly designed to prefer males over females in public employment would require an exceedingly persuasive justification to withstand a constitutional challenge under the Equal Protection Clause of the Fourteenth Amendment.

B

The cases of *Washington v. Davis, supra*, and *Village of Arlington Heights v. Metropolitan Housing Development Corp., supra*, recognize that when a neutral law has a disparate impact upon a group that has historically been the victim of discrimination, an unconstitutional purpose may still be at work. But those cases signalled no departure from the settled rule that the Fourteenth Amendment guarantees equal laws, not equal results. *Davis* upheld a job-related employment test that white people passed in proportionately greater numbers than Negroes, for there had been no showing that racial discrimination entered into the establishment or formulation of the test. *Arlington Heights* upheld a zoning board decision that tended to perpetuate racially segregated housing patterns, since, apart from its effect, the board's decision was shown to be nothing more than an application of constitutionally neutral zoning policy. Those principles apply with equal force to a case involving alleged gender discrimination.

When a statute gender-neutral on its face is challenged on the ground that its effects upon women are disproportionably adverse, a two-fold inquiry is thus appropriate. The first question is whether the statutory classification is indeed neutral in the sense that it is not gender-based. If the classification itself, covert or overt, is not based upon gender, the second question is whether the adverse effect reflects invidious gender-based discrimination. *See Village of Arlington Heights v. Metropolitan Housing Authority, supra,* at 226. In this second inquiry, impact provides an "important starting point" *id.,* but purposeful discrimination is "the condition that offends the Constitution." *Swann v. Board of Education,* 402 U.S. 1, 16.

It is against this background of precedent that we consider the merits of the case before us.

III

A

. . . The appellee has conceded that ch. 31, § 23 is neutral on its face. She has also acknowledged that state hiring preferences for veterans are not *per se* invalid, for she has limited her challenge to the absolute lifetime preference that Massachusetts provides to veterans. The District Court made two central findings that are relevant here: first, that ch. 31, § 23 serves legitimate and worthy purposes; second, that the absolute preference was not established for the purpose of discriminating against women. The appellee has thus acknowledged and the District Court has thus found that the distinction between veterans and nonveterans drawn by ch. 31, § 23 is not a pretext for gender discrimination. The appellee's concesson and the District Court's finding are clearly correct.

. . .

The distinction made by ch. 31, § 23, is, as it seems to be, quite simply between veterans and non-veterans, not between men and women.

B

The dispositive question, then, is whether the appellee has shown that a gender-based discriminatory purpose has, at least in some measure, shaped the Massachusetts veterans' preference legislation. As did the District Court, she points to two basic factors which in her view distinguish ch. 31, § 23 from the neutral rules at issue in the *Washington v. Davis* and *Arlington Heights* cases. The first is the nature of the preference, which is said to be demonstrably gender-biased in the sense that it favors a status reserved under federal military policy primarily to men. The second concerns the impact of the absolute lifetime preference upon the employment opportunities of women, an impact claimed to be too inevitable to have been unintended. The appellee contends that these factors, coupled with the fact that the preference itself has little if any relevance to actual job performance, more than suffice to prove the discriminatory intent required to establish a constitutional violation.

1

The contention that this veterans' preference is "inherently non-neutral" or "gender-biased" presumes that the State, by favoring veterans, intentionally incorporated into its public employment policies the panoply of sex-based and assertedly discriminatory federal laws that have prevented all but a handful of women from becoming veterans. There are two serious difficulties with this argument. First, it is wholly at odds with the District Court's central finding that Massachusetts has not offered a preference to veterans for the purpose of discriminating against women. Second, it cannot be reconciled with the assumption made by both the appellee and the District Court that a more limited hiring preference for veterans could be sustained. Taken together, these difficulties are fatal.

. . .

2

The appellee's ultimate argument rests upon the presumption, common to the criminal and civil law, that a person intends the natural and foreseeable consequences of his voluntary actions. Her position was well stated in the concurring opinion in the District Court:

> Conceding . . . that the goal here was to benefit the veteran, there is no reason to absolve the legislature from awareness that the means chosen to achieve this goal would freeze women out of all those state jobs actively sought by men. To be sure, the legislature did not wish to harm women. But the cutting-off of women's opportunities was an inevitable concomitant of the chosen scheme—as inevitable as the proposition that if tails is up, heads must be down. Where a law's consequences are *that* inevitable, can they meaningfully be described as unintended? (451 F. Supp. 143, 151.)

This rhetorical question implies that a negative answer is obvious, but it is not. The decision to grant a preference to veterans was of course "intentional." So, necessarily, did an adverse impact upon nonveterans follow from that decision. And it cannot seriously be argued that the legislature of Massachusetts could have been unaware that most veterans are men. . . .

"Discriminatory purpose," however, implies more than intent as volition or intent as awareness of consequences. *See United Jewish Organizations v. Carey,* 430 U.S. 144, 179 (concurring opinion).[24] It im-

plies that the decisionmaker, in this case a state legislature, selected or reaffirmed a particular course of action at least in part "because of," not merely "in spite of," its adverse effects upon an identifiable group. Yet nothing in the record demonstrates that this preference for veterans was originally devised or subsequently re-enacted because it would accomplish the collateral goal of keeping women in a stereotypic and predefined place in the Massachusetts Civil Service.

To the contrary, . . . [w]hen the totality of legislative actions establishing and extending the Massachusetts veterans' preference are considered, *see Washington v. Davis, supra,* 426 U.S., at 242, the law remains what it purports to be: a preference for veterans of either sex over nonveterans of either sex, not for men over women.

IV

. . . . The substantial edge granted to veterans by ch. 31, § 23 may reflect unwise policy. The appellee, however, has simply failed to demonstrate that the law in any way reflects a purpose to discriminate on the basis of sex.

The judgment is reversed, and the case is remanded for further proceedings consistent with this opinion.

MR. JUSTICE STEVENS, with whom MR. JUSTICE WHITE joins, concurring.

While I concur in the Court's opinion, I confess that I am not at all sure that there

---

24. Proof of discriminatory intent must necessarily usually rely on objective factors, several of which were outlined in *Village of Arlington Heights v. Metropolitan Housing Authority.* 429 U.S. 252, 266. The inquiry is practical. What a legislature or any official entity is "up to" may be plain from the results its actions achieve, or the results they avoid. Often it is made clear from what has been called, in a different context, "the give and take of the situation" *Cramer v. United States,* 325 U.S. I, 32–33. (Jackson, J.)

is any difference between the two questions posed *ante*. If a classification is not overtly based on gender, I am inclined to believe the question whether it is covertly gender-based is the same as the question whether its adverse effects reflect invidious gender-based discrimination. However the question is phrased, for me the answer is largely provided by the fact that the number of males disadvantaged by Massachusetts' Veterans Preference (1,867,000) is sufficiently large—and sufficiently close to the number of disadvantaged females (2,954,000)—to refute the claim that the rule was intended to benefit males as a class over females as a class.

MR. JUSTICE MARSHALL, with whom MR. JUSTICE BRENNAN joins, dissenting.

Although acknowledging that in some circumstances, discriminatory intent may be inferred from the inevitable or foreseeable impact of a statute, *ante,* the Court concludes that no such intent has been established here. I cannot agree. In my judgment, Massachusetts' choice of an absolute veterans' preference system evinces purposeful gender-based discrimination. And because the statutory scheme bears no substantial relationship to a legitimate governmental objective, it cannot withstand scrutiny under the Equal Protection Clause.

I

The District Court found that the "prime objective" of the Massachusetts Veterans Preference Statute, Mass. Gen. L. ch. 31, § 23, was to benefit individuals with prior military service. 415 F. Supp. 485, 497 (Mass. 1976). *See* 451 F. Supp. 143, 145 (Mass. 1978). Under the Court's analysis, this factual determination "necessarily compels the conclusion that the state intended nothing more than to prefer 'veterans.' Given this finding, simple logic suggests that an intent to exclude women from

significant public jobs was not at work in this law." *Ante.* I find the Court's logic neither simple nor compelling.

That a legislature seeks to advantage one group does not, as a matter of logic or of common sense, exclude the possibility that it also intends to disadvantage another. Individuals in general and lawmakers in particular frequently act for a variety of reasons. . . . Thus, the critical constitutional inquiry is not whether an illicit consideration was the primary or but-for cause of a decision, but rather whether it had an appreciable role in shaping a given legislative enactment. Where there is "proof that *a* discriminatory purpose has been a motivating factor in the decision. . . . judicial deference is no longer justified." *Arlington Heights v. Metropolitan Housing Corp., supra,* at 265–66. (Emphasis added.)

Moreover, since reliable evidence of subjective intentions is seldom obtainable, resort to inference based on objective factors is generally unavoidable. [Citations omitted.] To discern the purposes underlying facially neutral policies, this Court has therefore considered the degree, inevitability, and foreseeability of any disproportionate impact as well as the alternatives reasonably available. *See Monroe v. Board of Commissioners,* 391 U.S. 450, 459 (1968); *Goss v. Board of Education,* 373 U.S. 683, 688–89 (1963); *Gomillion v. Lightfoot,* 364 U.S. 339 (1960); *Griffin v. Illinois,* 351 U.S. 12, 17 n.11 (1956). *Cf. Albermarle Paper Co. v. Moody,* 422 U.S. 405, 425 (1975).

In the instant case, the impact of the Massachusetts statute on women is undisputed. Any veteran with a passing grade on the civil service exam must be placed ahead of a non-veteran, regardless of their respective scores. The District Court found that, as a practical matter, this preference supplants test results as the determinant of upper-level civil service appointments. 415 F. Supp., at 488–89. Because less than 2 percent of the women in Massachusetts are veterans, the absolute preference formula has rendered desirable state civil service employment an almost exclusively male prerogative. 451 F. Supp., at 151 (Campbell, J., concurring).

As the District Court recognized, this consequence followed foreseeably, indeed inexorably, from the long history of policies severely limiting women's participation in the military.[1] Where the foreseeable impact of a facially neutral policy is so disproportionate, the burden should rest on the State to establish that sex-based considerations played no part in the choice of the particular legislative scheme. Cf. *Castaneda v. Partida*, 430 U.S. 482 (1977); *Washington v. Davis*, 426 U.S. 229, 241 (1976); *Alexander v. Louisiana*, 405 U.S. 625, 632 (1972); see generally Brest, *Palmer v. Thompson: An Approach to the Problem of Unconstitutional Legislative Motive*, 1971 Sup. Ct. L. Rev. 95, 123.

Clearly, that burden was not sustained here. The legislative history of the statute reflects the Commonwealth's patent appre-

1. See 415 F. Supp. 485, 490, 495–99 (Mass. 1976); 451 F. Supp. 143, 145, 148 (Mass. 1978). In addition to the 2 percent quota on women's participation in the armed forces, *see ante*, n.21, enlistment and appointment requirements have been more stringent for females than males with respect to age, mental and physical aptitude, parental consent, and educational attainment. M. Binkin and S. Bach, *Women and the Military* (1977) (hereinafter Binkin and Bach); Note, *The Equal Rights Amendment and the Military*, 82 Yale L. J. 1533, 1539 (1973). Until the 1970's, the armed forces precluded enlistment and appointment of women, but not men, who were married or had dependent children. . . .

Thus, unlike the employment examination in *Washington v. Davis*, 426 U.S. 229 (1976), which the Court found to be demonstrably job-related, the Massachusetts preference statute incorporates the results of sex-based military policies irrelevant to women's current fitness for civilian public employment. *See* 415 F. Supp., at 498–99.

ciation of the impact the preference system would have on women, and an equally evident desire to mitigate that impact only with respect to certain traditionally female occupations. Until 1971, the statute and implementing civil service regulations exempted from operation of the preference any job requisitions "especially calling for women." . . . In practice, this exemption, coupled with the absolute preference for veterans, has created a gender-based civil service hierarchy, with women occupying low grade clerical and secretarial jobs and men holding more responsible and remunerative positions. *See* 415 F. Supp., at 488; 451 F. Supp., at 148 n. 9.

Thus, for over 70 years, the Commonwealth has maintained, as an integral part of its veteran's preference system, an exemption relegating female civil service applicants to occupations traditionally filled by women. Such a statutory scheme both reflects and perpetuates precisely the kind of archaic assumptions about women's roles which we have previously held invalid. *See Orr v. Orr*, (1979); *Califano v. Goldfarb*, 430 U.S. 199, 210–211 (1977); *Stanton v. Stanton*, 421 U.S. 7, 14 (1975); *Weinberger v. Wiesenfeld*, 420 U.S. 636, 645 (1975). Particularly when viewed against the range of less discriminatory alternatives available to assist veterans, Massachusetts' choice of a formula that so severely restricts public employment opportunities for women cannot reasonably be thought gender-neutral. Cf. *Albermarle Paper Co. v. Moody*, *supra*, at 425. The Court's conclusion to the contrary—that "nothing in the record" evinces a "collateral goal of keeping women in a stereotypic and predefined place in the Massachusetts Civil Service," *ante*—displays a singularly myopic view of the facts established below.[3]

3. Although it is relevant that the preference statute also disadvantages a substantial group of men, *see ante* (STEVENS, J., concurring), it is equally pertinent that 47 percent of Massachu-

II

To survive challenge under the Equal Protection Clause, statutes reflecting gender-based discrimination must be substantially related to the achievement of important governmental objectives. *See Califano v. Webster,* 430 U.S. 313, 316–17 (1977); *Craig v. Boren,* 429 U.S. 190, 197 (1976); *Reed v. Reed,* 404 U.S. 71, 76 (1971). Appellants here advance three interests in support of the absolute preference system: (1) assisting veterans in their readjustment to civilian life; (2) encouraging military enlistment; and (3) rewarding those who have served their country. Brief for Appellants 24. Although each of those goals is unquestionably legitimate, the "mere recitation of a benign compensatory purpose" cannot of itself insulate legislative classifications from constitutional scrutiny. *Weinberger v. Wiesenfeld, supra,* at 648. And in this case, the Commonwealth has failed to establish a sufficient relationship between its objectives and the means chosen to effectuate them.

With respect to the first interest, facilitating veterans' transition to civilian status, the statute is plainly overinclusive. . . . By conferring a permanent preference, the legislation allows veterans to invoke their advantage repeatedly, without regard to their date of discharge. . . .

Nor is the Commonwealth's second asserted interest, encouraging military service, a plausible justification for this legislative scheme. In its original and subsequent re-enactments, the statute extended benefits retroactively to veterans who had served during a prior specified period. *See ante.* If the Commonwealth's "actual purpose" is to induce enlistment, this legislative design is hardly well-suited to that end. . . . Moreover, even if such influence could be presumed, the statute is still grossly overinclusive in that it bestows benefits on men drafted as well as those who volunteered.

Finally, the Commonwealth's third interest, rewarding veterans, does not "adequately justify the salient features" of this preference system. *Craig v. Boren,* 429 U.S., at 202. *See Orr v. Orr.* Where a particular statutory scheme visits substantial hardship on a class long subject to discrimination, the legislation cannot be sustained unless "carefully tuned to alternative considerations." *Trimble v. Gordon, supra,* at 772. *See Caban v. Mohammed,* 441 U.S. 380, at n.13 (1979); *Mathews v. Lucas,* 427 U.S. 495 (1976). Here, there are a wide variety of less discriminatory means by which Massachusetts could effect its compensatory purposes. For example, a point preference system, such as that maintained by many States and the Federal Government, or an absolute preference for a limited duration, would reward veterans without excluding all qualified women from upper level civil service positions. Apart from public employment, the Commonwealth, can, and does, afford assistance to veterans in various ways, including tax abatements, educational subsidies, and special programs for needy veterans. . . . Unlike these and similar benefits, the costs of which are distributed across the taxpaying public generally, the Massachusetts statute exacts a substantial price from a discrete group of individuals who have long been subject to employment discrimination, and who, "because of circumstances totally beyond their control, have [had] little if any chance of becoming members in the preferred class." 415 F. Supp., at 499. *See* n.1, *supra.*

---

setts men over 18 are veterans, as compared to 0.8 percent of Massachusetts women. App. 83. Given this disparity, and the indicia of intent noted *supra,* the absolute number of men denied preference cannot be dispositive, especially, since they have not faced the barriers to achieving veteran status confronted by women. *See* n.1, *supra.*

Given the range of alternatives available, this degree of preference is not constitutionally permissible.

I would affirm the judgment of the court below.

CASE QUESTIONS

1. Are state legislators likely to admit publicly that they have unconstitutional intentions? How else can their intentions be discovered?

2. Is the fact that the legislature purposely exempted many low-level, clerical type jobs from the veterans' preference, so that women could have them, itself evidence that the legislators intended the veterans' preference to favor males?

The Military

As *Personal Administrator v. Feeney* made evident, the various restrictions on women's participation in the armed forces have a sizable impact on women's civilian job opportunities. For this reason, as well as out of concern for abstract fairness, a number of feminists opposed women's exclusion from the military draft, and from combat requirements (or combat "opportunities," as career military personnel might think of them, since combat enhances promotion. See *Schlesinger v. Ballard*, chapter 2.) The military issue was not feminists' favorite topic,[36] and even the ERA hearings were ambiguous about the combat question under an ERA. The hearings seemed to imply that, with an ERA, women would be drafted but could still fall under a blanket exclusion from combat;[37] although certainly many ERA proponents thought that the amendment would require lifting the ban on women's combat role. Toward the end of the ERA ratification period, with the ERA apparently politically dead, the question of a males-only military draft reached the Supreme Court.

By this time the *Craig* rule for interpreting the Equal Protection Clause was clearly indicated in relevant precedents. On the other hand, *Fiallo v. Bell*[38] served as a signpost toward another route the Court might follow. In *Fiallo*, even in a situation where the fundamental right of fatherhood might have evoked strict scrutiny, because of the foreign relations context the Court had found the need for deference to Congressional flexibility to be compelling (and deference then meant a minimal rationality test.) In this draft case, *Rostker v. Goldberg*,[39] the Court majority followed the same path of yielding to Congress's foreign relations power. However, Rehnquist, writing for the Court obscures this path by, in effect, claiming that it overlaps the *Craig v. Boren* path. In other words Rehnquist, argues *both* that great deference is due to Congress on military matters *and* that this gender-based discrimination survives *Craig*-level scrutiny, because Congressional flexibility in raising armies is an important governmental interest. As in the *Feeney* decision, the Supreme Court justices are divided over how to interpret the factual record, and that division sways the votes of two of the dissenters.

This case had begun in 1971 when several men liable to be drafted into the War in Vietnam had objected to males-only conscription, on the basis of a Fifth Amendment equal protection (Due Process Clause) argument. The case remained in a kind of legal limbo for several years while the draft was discontinued, and then the case was reactivated in 1980 when President Carter re-instituted draft registration. Goldberg acted on behalf of himself and all males similarly situated; Rostker was director of the Selective Service System. A federal district court on July 18, 1980, three days before registration was to begin, declared the Military Selective Service Act (MSSA) unconstitutional on the grounds of its gender discrimination, and the court enjoined the Government from requiring registration under it. Rostker immediately appealed for a stay of the injunction pending appeal, and Justice Brennan granted it. Registration began on time. The Supreme Court handed down this decision a year later.

Rostker v. Goldberg, 453 U.S. 57 (1981)

JUSTICE REHNQUIST delivered the opinion of the Court.

The question presented is whether the Military Selective Service Act, 50 U.S.C. App. § 451 *et seq.*, violates the Fifth Amendment to the United States Constitution in authorizing the President to require the registration of males and not females.

. . .

II

Whenever called upon to judge the constitutionality of an Act of Congress—"the gravest and most delicate duty that this Court is called upon to perform," *Blodgett v. Holden*, 275 U.S. 142, 148 (1927) (Holmes, J.)—the Court accords "great weight to the decisions of Congress." *CBS, Inc. v. Democratic National Committee*, 412

U.S. 94, 102 (1973). The Congress is a co-equal branch of government whose members take the same oath we do to uphold the Constitution of the United States. . . .

The customary deference accorded the judgments of Congress is certainly appropriate when, as here, Congress specifically considered the question of the Act's constitutionality: *See, e.g.*, S. Rep. No. 96–826, 96th Cong., 2d Sess., 159–61 (1980); 126 Cong. Rec. S6531–S6533 (Sen. Warner) (June 10, 1980), S6547 (Sen. Hatfield) (June 10, 1980).

This is not, however, merely a case involving the customary deference accorded congressional decisions. The case arises in the context of Congress' authority over national defense and military affairs, and perhaps in no other area has the Court accorded Congress greater deference. In rejecting the registration of women, Congress explicitly relied upon its constitutional powers under Article I, § 8, cls. 12–14. The "specific findings" section of the Report of the Senate Armed Services Committee, later adopted by both Houses of Congress, began by stating:

> Article I, section 8 of the Constitution commits exclusively to the Congress the powers to raise and support armies, provide and maintain a Navy, and make rules for Government and regulation of the land and naval forces, and pursuant to these powers it lies within the discretion of the Congress to determine the occasions for expansion of our Armed Forces, and the means best suited to such expansion should it prove necessary. (S. Rep. No. 96–826, *supra*, at 160, U.S. Code Cong. & Admin. News 1980, 2650.)

See also S. Rep. No. 96–226, 96th Cong., 1st Sess., 8 (1979). This Court has consistently recognized Congress' "broad constitutional power" to raise and regulate armies and navies, *Schlesinger v. Ballard*, 419 U.S. 498, 510 (1975). As the Court noted in considering a challenge to the selective service laws, "The constitutional power of Congress to raise and support armies and to make all laws necessary and proper to that end is broad and sweeping." *United States v. O'Brien*, 391 U.S. 367, 377, (1968). *See Lichter v. United States*, 334 U.S. 742, 755 (1948).

Not only is the scope of Congress' constitutional power in this area broad, but the lack of competence on the part of the courts is marked. In *Gilligan v. Morgan*, 413 U.S. 1, 10 (1973), the Court noted:

> It is difficult to conceive of an area of governmental activity in which the courts have less competence. The complex, subtle, and professional deci-

sions as to the composition, training, equipping, and control of a military force are essentially professional military judgments, subject always to civilian control of the Legislative and Executive branches.

. . .

None of this is to say that Congress is free to disregard the Constitution when it acts in the area of military affairs. In that area as any other Congress remains subject to the limitations of the Due Process Clause, *see Ex parte Milligan*, 4 Wall. 2 (1866); *Hamilton v. Kentucky Distilleries & Warehouse Co.*, 251 U.S. 146, 156 (1919), but the tests and limitations to be applied may differ because of the military context. We of course do not abdicate our ultimate responsibility to decide the constitutional question, but simply recognize that the Constitution itself requires such deference to congressional choice. *See CBS, Inc. v. Democratic National Committee*, 412 U.S., at 103. In deciding the question before us we must be particularly careful not to substitute our judgment of what is desirable for that of Congress, or our own evaluation of evidence for a reasonable evaluation by the Legislative Branch.

. . . . Appellees . . . stress that this case involves civilians, not the military, and that "the impact of registration on the military is only indirect and attenuated." Brief for Appellees 19. We find these efforts to divorce registration from the military and national defense context, with all the deference called for in that context, singularly unpersuasive. *United States v. O'Brien*, *supra*, recognized the broad deference due Congress in the selective service area before us in this case. Registration is not an end in itself in the civilian world but rather the first step in the induction process into the military one, and Congress specifically linked its consideration of registration to induction, *see, e.g.*, S. Rep. No. 96–826, *supra*, at 156, 160. Congressional judgments concerning registration and the draft are based on judgments concerning military operations and needs, *see, e.g., id.* at 157, U.S. Code Cong. & Admin. News 1980, 2647 ("the starting point for any discussion of the appropriateness of registering women for the draft is the question of the proper role of women in combat"), and the deference unquestionably due the latter judgments is necessarily required in assessing the former as well. . . . It would be blinking reality to say that our precedents requiring deference to Congress in military affairs are not implicated by the present case.[6]

The Solicitor General argues, largely on the basis of the foregoing cases emphasizing the deference due Congress in the area of military affairs and national security, that this Court should scrutinize the MSSA only to determine if the distinction drawn between men and women bears a rational relation to some legitimate government purpose . . . and should not examine the Act under the heightened scrutiny with which we have approached gender-based discrimination, *see Michael M. v. Superior*

Court of Sonoma County, 450 U.S. 464, (1981); *Craig v. Boren; Reed v. Reed*.[7] We do not think that the substantive guarantee of due process or certainty in the law will be advanced by any further "refinement" in the applicable tests as suggested by the Government. Announced degrees of "deference" to legislative judgments, just as levels of "scrutiny" which this Court announces that it applies to particular classifications made by a legislative body, may all too readily become facile abstractions used to justify a result. In this case the courts are called upon to decide whether Congress, acting under an explicit constitutional grant of authority, has by that action transgressed an explicit guarantee of individual rights which limits the authority so conferred. Simply labelling the legislative decision "military" on the one hand or "gender-based" on the other does not automatically guide a court to the correct constitutional result.

No one could deny that under the test of *Craig v. Boren*, the Government's interest in raising and supporting armies is an "important governmental interest." Congress and its committees carefully considered and debated two alternative means of furthering that interest: the first was to register only males for potential conscription, and the other was to register both sexes. Congress chose the former alternative. When that decision is challenged on equal protection grounds, the question a court must decide is not which alternative it would have chosen, had it been the pri-

---

6. Congress recognized that its decision on registration involved judgments on military needs and operations, and that its decisions were entitled to particular deference: "The Supreme Court's most recent teachings in the field of equal protection cannot be read in isolation from its opinions giving great deference to the judgment of Congress and military commanders in dealing with the management of military forces and the requirements of military discipline. The Court has made it unmistakably clear that even our most fundamental constitutional rights must in some circumstances be modified in the light of military needs, and that Congress' judgment as to what is necessary to preserve our national security is entitled to great deference." S. Rep. No. 96–826, *supra*, at 159–60, U.S. Code Cong. & Admin. News 1980, 2649. . . .

7. It is clear that "[g]ender has never been rejected as an impermissible classification in all instances." *Kahn v. Shevin*, 416 U.S. 351, 356, n.10 (1974). In making this observation the Court noted that "Congress has not so far drafted women into the Armed Services, 50 U.S.C. App. § 454."

mary decisionmaker, but whether that chosen by Congress denies equal protection of the laws.

Nor can it be denied that the imposing number of cases from this Court previously cited suggest that judicial deference to such congressional exercise of authority is at its apogee when legislative action under the congressional authority to raise and support armies and make rules and regulations for their governance is challenged. As previously noted, *ante,* deference does not mean abdication. The reconciliation between the deference due Congress and our own constitutional responsibility is perhaps best instanced in *Schlesinger v. Ballard,* 419 U.S., at 510, where we stated:

> This Court has recognized that 'it is the primary business of armies and navies to fight or be ready to fight wars should the occasion arise.' *U.S. ex rel. Toth v. Quarles,* 350 U.S. 11. . . . The responsibility for determining how best our Armed Forces shall attend to that business rests with Congress, *see* U.S. Const., art. I, § 8, cls. 12–14, and with the President. *See* U.S. Const., art. II, § 2, cl. 1. We cannot say that, in exercising its broad constitutional power here, Congress has violated the Due Process Clause of the Fifth Amendment.

. . .

Schlesinger v. Ballard did not purport to apply a different equal protection test because of the military context, but did stress the deference due congressional choices among alternatives in exercisng the congressional authority to raise and support armies and make rules for their governance. In light of the floor debate and the report of the Senate Armed Services Committee

hereinafter discussed, it is apparent that Congress was fully aware not merely of the many facts and figures presented to it by witnesses who testified before its committees, but of the current thinking as to the place of women in the Armed Services. In such a case, we cannot ignore Congress' broad authority conferred by the Constitution to raise and support armies when we are urged to declare unconstitutional its studied choice of one alternative in preference to another for furthering that goal.

III

This case is quite different from several of the gender-based discrimination cases we have considered in that, despite appellees' assertions, Congress did not act "unthinkingly" or "reflexively and not for any considered reason." The question of registering women for the draft not only received considerable national attention and was the subject of wide-ranging public debate, but also was extensively considered by Congress in hearings, floor debate, and in committee. Hearings held by both Houses of Congress in response to the President's request for authorization to register women adduced extensive testimony and evidence concerning the issue. . . .

. . .

The foregoing clearly establishes that the decision to exempt women from registration was not the "accidental by-product of a traditional way of thinking about women." *Califano v. Webster,* 430 U.S. 313, 320 (1977) (quoting *Califano v. Goldfarb,* 430 U.S. 199, [1977] [STEVENS, J., concurring]). In *Michael M.,* at n.6 (plurality), we rejected a similar argument because of action by the California Legislature considering and rejecting proposals to make a statute challenged on discrimination grounds gender-neutral. The cause for rejecting the argument is considerably stronger here. The issue was considered at great length, and Congress clearly expressed its purpose and intent. Contrast *Califano v. Westcott*, 443 U.S. 76, 87 (1979) ("The gender qualification . . . escaped virtually unnoticed in the hearings and floor debate").[11]

For the same reasons we reject appellees' argument that we must consider the constitutionality of the MSSA solely on the basis of the views expressed by Congress in 1948, when the MSSA was first enacted in its modern form. . . . Congress did not change the MSSA in 1980, but it did thoroughly reconsider the question of exempting women from its provisions, and its basis for doing so. The 1980 legislative history is, therefore, highly relevant in assessing the constitutional validity of the exemption.

The MSSA established a plan for maintaining "adequate armed strength . . . to ensure the security of [the] nation." 50 U.S.C. App. § 451(b). Registration is the first step "in a united and continuous process designed to raise an army speedily and efficiently," *Falbo v. United States*, 320 U.S. 549, 553 (1944) . . . and Congress provided for the reactivation of registration in order to "provide the means for the early delivery of inductees in an emergency." S. Rep. No. 96–826, *supra*, at 156, U.S. Code Cong. & Admin. News 1980, 2646. Although the three-judge District Court often tried to sever its consideration of reg-

istration from the particulars of induction, *see, e.g.,* 509 F. Supp., at 604–5, Congress rather clearly linked the need for renewed registration with its views on the character of a subsequent draft. The Senate Report specifically found that "An ability to mobilize rapidly is essential to the preservation of our national security. A functioning registration system is a vital part of any mobilization plan." S. Rep. No. 96–826, *supra*, at 160, U.S. Code Cong. & Admin. News 1980, 2650. As Senator Warner put it, "I equate registration with the draft." *Hearings on S. 2294, supra*, at 1197. *See also id.* at 1195 (Sen. Jepsen), 1671 (Sen. Exon). Such an approach is certainly logical, since under the MSSA induction is interlocked with registration: only those registered may be drafted, and registration serves no purpose beyond providing a pool for the draft. Any assessment of the congressional purpose and its chosen means must therefore consider the registration scheme as a prelude to a draft in a time of national emergency. Any other approach would not be testing the Act in light of the purposes Congress sought to achieve.

Congress determined that any future draft, which would be facilitated by the registration scheme, would be characterized by a need for combat troops. The Senate Report explained, in a specific finding later adopted by both Houses, that "if mobilization were to be ordered in a wartime scenario, the primary manpower need would be for combat replacements." S. Rep. No. 96–826, *supra*, at 160, U.S. Code Cong. & Admin. News 1980, 2650; *see id.* at 158. This conclusion echoed one made a year before by the same Senate Committee, *see* S. Rep. No. 96–226, *supra*, at 2–3, 6. As Senator Jepsen put it, "The shortage would be in the combat arms. That is why you have drafts." *Hearings on S. 2294, supra*, at 1688. *See also id.* at 1195 (Sen. Jepsen); 126

11. Nor can we agree with the characterization of the MSSA in the Brief for Amicus Curiae National Organization of [sic] Women as a law which "co-erce[s] or preclude[s] women as a class from performing tasks or jobs of which they are capable," or the suggestion that this case involves "[t]he exclusion of women from the military." *Id.* at 19–20. Nothing in the MSSA restricts in any way the opportunities for women to volunteer for military service.

Cong. Rec. H2750 (Rep. Nelson) (April 22, 1980). Congress' determination that the need would be for combat troops if a draft took place was sufficiently supported by testimony adduced at the hearings so that the courts are not free to make their own judgment on the question. *See Hearings on S. 2294, supra,* at 1528–29 (Marine Corps Lt. Gen. Bronars); 1395 (Principal Deputy Assistant Secretary of Army Clark); 1391 (Gen. Yerks); 748 (Gen. Meyer; *House Hearings, supra,* J.A., at 224 (Assistant Secretary of Defense for Manpower Pirie).* *See also Hearing on S. 109 and S. 226, supra,* at 24, 54 (Gen. Rogers). The purpose of registration, therefore, was to prepare for a draft *of combat troops.* [Emphasis in original.]

Women as a group, however, unlike men as a group, are not eligible for combat. The restrictions on the participation of women in combat in the Navy and Air Force are statutory. Under 10 U.S.C. § 6015 "women may not be assigned to duty on vessels or in aircraft that are engaged in combat missions," and under 10 U.S.C. § 8549 female members of the Air Force "may not be assigned to duty in aircraft engaged in combat missions." The Army and Marine Corps preclude the use of women in combat as a matter of established policy. Congress specifically recognized and endorsed the exclusion of women from combat in exempting women from registration. In the words of the Senate Report:

> The principle that women should not intentionally and routinely engage in combat is fundamental, and enjoys wide support among our people. It is universally supported by military leaders who have testified before the Committee. . . . Current law and policy ex-

clude women from being assigned to combat in our military forces, and the Comittee reaffirms this policy. (S. Rep. No. 96–826, *supra,* at 157, U.S. Code Cong. & Admin. News 1980, 2641.)

The Senate Report specifically found that "Women should not be intentionally or routinely placed in combat positions in our military services." *Id.* at 160, U.S. Code Cong. & Admin. News 1980, 2650. *See* S. Rep. No. 96–226, *supra,* at 9.[12] The President expressed his intent to continue the current military policy precluding women from combat, *see* Presidential Recommendations for Selective Service Reform, *supra,* J.A. 34, and appellees present their argument concerning registration against the background of such restrictions on the use of women in combat. Consistent with the approach of this Court in *Schlesinger v. Ballard,* we must examine appellees' constitutional claim concerning registration with these combat restrictions firmly in mind.

The existence of the combat restrictions clearly indicates the basis for Congress' decision to exempt women from registration. The purpose of registration was to prepare for a draft of combat troops. Since women are excluded from combat, Congress concluded that they would not be needed in the event of a draft, and therefore decided not to register them. Again turning to the Senate Report:

> In the Committee's view, the starting point for any discussion of the appropriateness of registering women for the draft is the question of the proper role of women in combat. . . . The policy precluding the use of women in combat is, in the Committee's view, the

---

* J. A. refers to Judge Advocate, counsel for the U.S. military—Au.

12. No major country has women in combat jobs in their standing army.

most important reason for not including women in a registration system. (S. Rep. No. 96–826, *supra*, at 157, U.S. Code Cong. & Admin. News 1980, 2647.[14])

The District Court stressed that the military need for women was irrelevant to the issue of their registration. As that court put it: "Congress could not constitutionally require registration under MSSA of only black citizens or only white citizens, or single out any political or religious group simply because those groups contained sufficient persons to fill the needs of the Selective Service System." 509 F. Supp., at 596. This reasoning is beside the point. The reason women are exempt from registration is not because military needs can be met by drafting men. This is not a case of Congress arbitrarily choosing to burden one of two similarly situated groups, such as would be the case with an all-black or all-white, or an all-Catholic or all-Lutheran, or an all-Republican or all-Democratic registration. Men and women, because of the combat restrictions on women, are simply not similarly situated for purposes of a draft or registration for a draft.

Congress' decision to authorize the

registration of only men, therefore, does not violate the Due Process Clause. The exemption of women from registration is not only sufficiently but closely related to Congress' purpose in authorizing registration. *See Michael M.; Craig v. Boren; Reed v. Reed.* The fact that Congress and the Executive have decided that women should not serve in combat fully justifies Congress in not authorizing their registration, since the purpose of registration is to develop a pool of potential combat troops. As was the case in *Schlesinger v. Ballard, supra,* "the gender classification is not invidious, but rather realistically reflects the fact that the sexes are not similarly situated" in this case. *Michael M.* (plurality). The Constitution requires that Congress treat similarly situated persons similarly, not that it engage in gestures of superficial equality.

In holding the MSSA constitutionally invalid the District Court relied heavily on the President's decision to seek authority to register women and the testimony of members of the Executive Branch and the military in support of that decision. *See, e.g.,* 509 F. Supp., at 603–4, and n.30. As stated by the Administration's witnesses before Congress, however, the President's "decision to ask for authority to register women is based on equity." *House Hearings,* J.A. 217 (statement of Assistant Secretary of Defense Pirie and Director of Selective Service System Rostker); *see also* Presidential Recommendations for Selective Service Reform, *supra,* J.A. 35, 59, 60; *Hearings on S. 2294, supra,* at 1657 (statement of Executive Associate Director of Office of Management and Budget Wellford, Director of Selective Service System Rostker, and Principal Deputy Assistant Secretary of Defense Danzig). This was also the basis for the testimony by military officials. *Hearings on S. 2294,* at 710 (Gen. Meyer), 1002 (Gen. Allen). The Senate Report, evaluating the testimony before the Committee, recog-

14. Justice Marshall's suggestion that since Congress focused on the need for combat troops in authorizing male-only registration the Court could "be forced to declare the male-only registration program unconstitutional," *post,* in the event of a peace-time draft misreads our opinion. The perceived need for combat or combat-eligible troops in the event of a draft was not limited to a wartime draft. *See, e.g.,* S. Rep. No. 96–826, *supra,* at 157, U.S. Code & Admin. News 1980, 2647 (considering problems associated with "[r]egistering women for assignment to combat or *assigning women to combat positions in peace-time*") (emphasis supplied); *id.* at 158 (need for rotation between combat and non-combat positions "[i]n peace and war").

nized that "the argument for registration and induction of women . . . is not based on military necessity, but on considerations of equity." S. Rep. No. 96–826, *supra*, at 158, U.S. Code Cong. & Admin. News 1980, 2648. Congress was certainly entitled, in the exercise of its constitutional powers to raise and regulate armies and navies, to focus on the question of military need rather than "equity." [15] As Senator Nunn of the Senate Armed Services Committee put it:

> Our Committee went into very great detail. We found that there was no military necessity cited by any witnesses for the registration of females.
>
> The main point that those who favored the registration of females made was that they were in favor of this because of the equality issue which is, of course, a legitimate view. But as far as military necessity, and that is what we are primarily, I hope, considering in the overall registration bill, there is no military necessity for this. (126 Cong. Rec. S6544).

See also House Hearings, supra, J.A. 230 (Rep. Holt) ("You are talking about equity. I am talking about military.").[16]

15. The grant of constitutional authority is, after all, to Congress and not to the Executive or military officials.

16. The District Court also focused on what it termed Congress' "inconsistent positions" in encouraging women to volunteer for military service and expanding their opportunities in the service, on the one hand, and exempting them from registration and the draft on the other. 509 F. Supp., at 603–4. This reasoning fails to appreciate the different purposes served by encouraging women volunteers and registration for the draft. Women volunteers do not occupy combat positions, so encouraging women to volunteer is

Although the military experts who testified in favor of registering women uniformly opposed the actual drafting of women, *see, e.g., Hearing on S. 109 and S. 226, supra,* at 11 (Gen. Rogers), *there was testimony that in the event of a draft of 650,000 the military could absorb some 80,000 female inductees. Hearings on S. 2294, at 1661, 1828. The 80,000 would be used to fill noncombat positions, freeing men to go to the front.* In relying on this testimony in striking down the MSSA, *the District Court* palpably exceeded its authority when it *ignored Congress' considered response to this line of reasoning.* [Emphasis added.—Au.]

In the first place, assuming that a small number of women could be drafted for noncombat roles, *Congress* simply *did not consider it worth the added burdens* of including women in draft and registration plans. "It has been suggested that all women be registered, but *only a handful actually be inducted* in an emergency. The Committee finds this a confused and ultimately unsatisfactory solution." S. Rep. No. 96–826, *supra,* at 158, U.S. Code Cong. & Admin. News 1980, 2648. As the Senate Committee recognized a year before, "training would be needlessly burdened by women recruits who could not be used in combat." S. Rep. No. 96–226, *supra,* at 9. *See also* S. Rep. No. 96–826, *supra,* at 159, U.S. Code Cong. & Admin. News 1980, 2649 ("Other administrative problems such as housing and different treatment with regard to dependency, hardship and physical standards would also exist.") It is not for this Court to dismiss such problems as insignificant in the context of military preparedness and

not related to concerns about the availability of combat troops. In the event of a draft, however, the need would be for combat troops or troops which could be rotated into combat. *See* 2656–57, *supra.* Congress' positions are clearly not inconsistent.

the exigencies of a future mobilization. [Emphasis added.—Au.]

Congress also concluded that whatever the need for women for noncombat roles during mobilization, whether 80,000 or less, *it could be met by volunteers. See* S. Rep. No. 96–826, *supra,* at 160; *id.* at 158 ("Because of the combat restrictions, the need would be primarily for men, and *women volunteers would fill the requirements for women*"); *House Hearings, supra,* J.A. 227–228 (Rep. Holt) *See also Hearings on S. 2294, supra,* at 1195 (Gen. Rogers). [Emphasis added.—Au.]

Most significantly, Congress determined that staffing non-combat positions with women during a mobilization would be positively detrimental to the important goal of military flexibility.

> There are other military reasons that preclude very large numbers of women from serving. Military flexibility requires that a commander be able to move units or ships quickly. Units or ships not located at the front or not previously scheduled for the front nevertheless must be able to move into action if necessary. In peace and war, significant rotation of personnel is necessary. We should not divide the military into two groups—one in permanent combat and one in permanent support. Large numbers of non-combat positions must be available to which combat troops can return for duty before being redeployed. (S. Rep. No. 96–826, *supra,* at 158, U.S. Code Cong. & Admin. News 1980, 2648.)

The point was repeated in specific findings, *id.* at 160; *see also* S. Rep. No. 96–226, *supra,* at 9. In sum, *Congress* carefully *evaluated the testimony that 80,000 women conscripts could be usefully employed* in the event of a draft *and rejected it* in the permissible exercise of its constitutional responsibility.

See also Hearing on S. 109 and S. 226, supra, at 16 (Gen. Rogers);[17] *Hearings on S. 2294, supra,* at 1682. [Emphasis added.—Au.] The District Court was quite wrong in undertaking an independent evaluation of this evidence, rather than in adopting an appropriately deferential examination of *Congress'* evaluation of that evidence.

In light of the foregoing, we conclude that Congress acted well within its constitutional authority when it authorized the registration of men, and not women, under the Military Selective Service Act. The decision of the District Court holding otherwise is accordingly reversed.

JUSTICE WHITE, with whom JUSTICE BRENNAN joins, dissenting.

I assume what has not been challenged in this case—that excluding women from combat positions does not offend the Con-

---

17. General Rogers' testimony merits quotation:

> General ROGERS. "One thing which is often lost sight of, Senator, is that in an emergency during war, the Army has often had to reach back into the support base, into the supporting elements in the operating base, and pull forward soldiers to fill the ranks in an emergency; that is, to hand them a rifle or give them a tanker suit and put them in the front ranks."
>
> Senator WARNER. "General Patton did that at one time, I believe at the Battle of the Bulge."
>
> General ROGERS. "Absolutely.
>
> "Now, if that support base and that operating base to the rear consists in large measure of women, then we don't have that opportunity to reach back and pull them forward, because women should not be placed in a forward fighting position or in a tank, in my opinion. So that, too, enters the equation when one considers the subject of the utility of women under contingency conditions."

stitution. Granting that, it is self evident that if during mobilization for war, all non-combat military positions must be filled by combat-qualified personnel available to be moved into combat positions, there would be no occasion whatsoever to have any women in the Army, whether as volunteers or inductees. The Court appears to say that Congress concluded as much and that we should accept that judgment even though the serious view of the Executive Branch, including the responsible military services, is to the contrary. The Court's position in this regard is most unpersuasive. I perceive little, if any, indication that Congress itself concluded that every position in the military, no matter how far removed from combat, must be filled with combat-ready men. Common sense and experience in recent wars, where women volunteers were employed in substantial numbers, belie this view of reality. It should not be ascribed to Congress, particularly in the face of the testimony of military authorities, hereafter referred to, that there would be a substantial number of positions in the services that could be filled by women both in peacetime and during mobilization, even though they are ineligible for combat.

I would also have little difficulty agreeing to a reversal if all the women who could serve in wartime without adversely affecting combat readiness could predictably be obtained through volunteers. In that event, the equal protection component of the Fifth Amendment would not require the United States to go through, and a large segment of the population to be burdened with, the expensive and essentially useless procedure of registering women. But again I cannot agree with the Court that Congress concluded or that the legislative record indicates that each of the services could rely on women volunteers to fill all the positions for which they might be eligible in the event of mobilization. On the contrary, *the*

record as I understand it, supports the District Court's finding that the services would have to conscript at least 80,000 persons to fill positions for which combat-ready men would not be required. The consistent position of *the Defense Department* representatives was that their *best estimate of the number of women draftees who could be used productively by the Services in the event of a major mobilization would be approximately 80,000 over the first six months. See Hearings on S. 2294; Hearings before the Committee on Armed Services,* 96th Cong., Sess. (1980), 1681, 1688; *Hearing on H.R. 6569; Hearings before the Military Personnel Subcommittee of the House Committee on Armed Services,* 96th Cong., 2d Sess. (1980), J.A., at 222–23. This *number took into account the estimated number of women volunteers, see* Deposition of Director of Selective Service Bernard Rostker, at 8; Deposition of Principal Deputy Asst. Secretary of Defense Richard Danzig, J.A., at 276. *Except for a single, unsupported, and ambiguous statement in the Senate Report to the effect that "women volunteers would fill the requirements for women," there is no indication that Congress rejected the Defense Department's figures* or relied upon an alternative set of figures. [Emphasis added.—Au.]

Of course, the division among us indicates that the record in this respect means different things to different people, and I would be content to vacate the judgment below and remand for further hearings and findings on this crucial issue. Absent that, however, I cannot agree that the record supports the view that all positions for which women would be eligible in war time could and would be filled by female volunteers.

The Court also submits that because the primary purpose of registration and conscription is to supply combat troops and because the great majority of non-combat positions must be filled by combat-trained men ready to be rotated into combat, the absolute number of positions for which women would be eligible is so small as to be *de minimis* and of no moment for equal protection purposes, especially in light of the administrative burdens involved in registering all women of suitable age. There is some sense to this; but at least on the record before us, the number of women who could be used in the military without sacrificing combat-readiness is not at all small or insubstantial, and administrative convenience has not been sufficient justification for the kind of outright gender-based discrimination involved in registering and conscripting men but no women at all.

As I understand the record, then, in order to secure the personnel it needs during mobilization, the Government cannot rely on volunteers and must register and draft not only to fill combat positions and those noncombat positions that must be filled by combat-trained men, but also to secure the personnel needed for jobs that can be performed by persons ineligible for combat without diminishing military effectiveness. The claim is that in providing for the latter category of positions, Congress is free to register and draft only men. I discern no adequate justification for this kind of discrimination between men and women. Accordingly, with all due respect, I dissent.

JUSTICE MARSHALL, with JUSTICE BRENNAN, dissenting.

The Court todays places its imprimatur on one of the most potent remaining public expressions of "ancient canards about the proper role of women," *Phillips v. Martin-Marietta Corp.*, 400 U.S. 542, 545 (1971) (MARSHALL, J., concurring). It upholds a statute that requires males but not females to register for the draft, and which thereby categorically excludes women from a fundamental civic obligation. Because I believe the Court's decision is inconsistent with the

Constitution's guarantee of equal protection of the laws, I dissent.

I

. . . [T]his case does not involve a challenge to the statutes or policies that prohibit female members of the Armed Forces from serving in combat.[2] It is with this understanding that I turn to the task at hand.

B

By now it should be clear that statutes like the MSSA, which discriminate on the basis of gender, must be examined under the "heightened" scrutiny mandated by *Craig v. Boren*, 429 U.S. 190 (1976).[3] Under this test, a gender-based classification cannot withstand constitutional challenge unless the classification is substantially related to the achievement of an important governmental objective. *Kirchberg v. Feenstra* (1981); *Wengler v. Druggist Mutual Ins. Co.* (1980); *Califano v. Westcott* (1979); *Orr v. Orr* (1979); *Craig v. Boren*. This test applies whether the classification discriminates against males or females. *Caban v. Mohammed* (1979); *Orr v. Orr; Craig v. Boren*. The party defending the challenged classification carried the burden of demonstrating both the importance of the governmental objective it serves and the substantial relationship between the discriminatory means and the asserted end. *See Wengler v. Druggist Mutual Insurance Co.; Caban v. Mohammed; Craig v. Boren.* Consequently,

2. . . . . Appellees do not concede the constitutional validity of these restrictions on women in combat, but they have taken the position that their validity is irrelevant, for purposes of this case.

3. I join the Court in rejecting the Solicitor General's suggestion that the gender-based classification employed by the MSSA should be scrutinized under the "rational relationship" test used in reviewing challenges to certain types of social and economic legislation. . . .

before we can sustain the MSSA, the Government must demonstrate that the gender-based classification it employs bears "a close and substantial relationship to [the achievement of] important governmental objectives." *Personnel Administrator of Massachusetts v. Feeney*, 442 U.S. 256, 273 (1979).

C

The MSSA states that "an adequate armed strength must be achieved and maintained to insure the security of this Nation." 50 U.S.C. App. § 451(b). I agree with the majority that "none could deny that . . . the Government's interest in raising and supporting armies is an 'important governmental interest.'" Consequently, the first part of the *Craig v. Boren* test is satisfied. But the question remains whether the discriminatory means employed itself substantially serves the statutory end. . . .

II

A

The Government does not defend the exclusion of women from registration on the ground that preventing women from serving in the military is substantially related to the effectiveness of the Armed Forces. Indeed, the successful experience of women serving in all branches of the Armed Services would belie any such claim. Some 150,000 women volunteers are presently on active service in the military, and their number is expected to increase to over 250,000 by 1985.

. . . The justification for the MSSA's gender-based discrimination must therefore be found in considerations that are peculiar to the objectives of registration.

The most authoritative discussion of Congress' reasons for declining to require registration of women is contained in the report prepared by the Senate Armed Services Committee on the Fiscal Year 1981

Defense Authorization Bill. S. Rep. No. 96–826, *supra,* at 156–161. The Report's findings were endorsed by the House-Senate Conferees on the Authorization Bill. *See* S. Conf. Rep. No. 96–895, at 100 (1980). Both Houses of Congress subsequently adopted the findings by passing the Conference Report. 126 Cong. Rec. H7800, S11646 (daily ed., Aug. 26, 1980). As the majority notes, the Report's "findings are in effect findings of the entire Congress." The Senate Report sets out the objectives Congress sought to accomplish by excluding women from registration, *see id.* at 157–61, and this Court may appropriately look to the Report in evaluating the justification for the discrimination.

B

According to the Senate Report, "[t]he policy precluding the use of women in combat is . . . the most important reason for not including women in a registration system." S. Rep. No. 96–826, *supra,* at 157, U.S. Code Cong. & Admin. News 1980, 2647; *see also* S. Rep. No. 96–226, *supra,* at 9. . . . But the validity of the combat restrictions is not an issue we need decide in this case. Moreover, since the combat restrictions on women have already been accomplished through statutes and policies that remain in force whether or not women are required to register or be drafted, including women in registration and draft plans will not result in their being assigned to combat roles. Thus, even assuming that precluding the use of women in combat is an important governmental interest in its own right, there can be no suggestion that the exclusion of women from registration and a draft is substantially related to the achievement of this goal.

The Court's opinion offers a different though related explanation of the relationship between the combat restrictions and Congress' decision not to require registration of women. The majority states that "Congress . . . clearly linked the need for renewed registration with its view of the character of a subsequent draft." The Court also states that "Congress determined that any future draft, which would be facilitated by the registration scheme, would be characterized by a need for combat troops." The Court then reasons that since women are not eligible for assignment to combat, Congress' decision to exclude them from registration is not unconstitutional discrimination inasmuch as "[m]en and women, because of the combat restrictions on women, are simply not similarly situated for purposes of a draft or registration for a draft." There is a certain logic to this reasoning, but the Court's approach is fundamentally flawed.

In the first place, . . . [t]he Court essentially reasons that the gender classification employed by the MSSA is constitutionally permissible because nondiscrimination is not necessary to achieve the purpose of registration to prepare for a draft of combat troops. . . .

This analysis, however, focuses on the wrong question. The relevant inquiry under the *Craig v. Boren* test is not whether a *gender-neutral* classification would substantially advance important governmental interests. Rather, the question is whether the gender-based classification is itself substantially related to the achievement of the asserted governmental interest. Thus, the Government's task in this case is to demonstrate that excluding women from registration substantially furthers the goal of preparing for a draft of combat troops.

. . .

In this case, the Government makes no claim that preparing for a draft of combat troops cannot be accomplished just as effectively by *registering* both men and women but *drafting* only men if only men turn out

to be needed.[11] Nor can the Government argue that this alternative entails the additional cost and administrative inconvenience of registering women. This Court has repeatedly stated that the administrative convenience of employing a gender classification is not an adequate constitutional justification under the *Craig v. Boren* test. *See, e.g., Craig v. Boren* at 198; *Frontiero v. Richardson*, at 690–91 (1973).

The fact that registering women in no way obstructs the governmental interest in preparing for a draft of combat troops points up a second flaw in the Court's analysis. The Court essentially reduces the question of the constitutionality of male-only *registration* to the validity of a hypothetical program for *conscripting* only men. The Court posits a draft in which *all* conscripts are either assigned to those specific combat posts presently closed to women or must be available for rotation into such positions. By so doing, the Court is able to conclude that registering women would be no more than a "gestur[e] of superficial equality," since women are necessarily ineligible for every position to be filled in its hypothetical draft. If it could indeed be guaranteed in advance that conscription would be reimposed by Congress only in circumstances where, and in a form under which, all conscripts would have to be trained for and assigned to combat or combat rotation positions from which women are categorically excluded, then it could be argued that registration of women would be pointless.

But of course, no such guarantee is

11. Alternatively, the Government could employ a classification that is related to the statutory objective but is not based on gender, for example, combat eligibility. Under the current scheme, large subgroups of the male population who are ineligible for combat because of physical handicaps or conscientious objector status are nonetheless required to register.

possible. Certainly, nothing about the MSSA limits Congress to reinstituting the draft only in such circumstances. For example, Congress may decide that the All-Volunteer Armed Forces are inadequate to meet the Nation's defense needs even in times of peace and reinstitute peacetime conscription. In that event, the hypothetical draft the Court relied on to sustain the MSSA's gender-based classification would presumably be of little relevance, and the Court could then be forced to declare the male-only registration program unconstitutional. This difficulty comes about because both Congress and the Court have lost sight of the important distinction between *registration* and *conscription*. Registration provides "an inventory of what the available strength is within the military qualified pool in this country." *Reinstitution of Procedures for Registration Under the Military Selective Service Act: Hearing before the Subcommittee on Manpower and Personnel of the Senate Armed Services Committee,* 96th Cong., 1st Sess., 10 (1980) (Selective Service Hearings) (statement of General Rogers). Conscription supplies the military with the personnel needed to respond to a particular exigency. The fact that registration is a first step in the conscription process does not mean that a registration law expressly discriminating between men and women may be justified by a valid conscription program which would, in retrospect, make the current discrimination appear functionally related to the program that emerged.

But even addressing the Court's reasoning on its own terms, its analysis is flawed because the entire argument rests on a premise that is demonstrably false. As noted, the majority simply assumes that registration prepares for a draft in which *every* draftee must be available for assignment to combat. But the majority's draft scenario finds no support in either the testimony before Congress, or more importantly, in the findings of the Senate Report. Indeed, the scenario appears to exist only in the Court's imagination, for even the Government represents only that "in the event of mobilization, *approximately two-thirds* of the demand on the induction system would be for *combat skills.*" Brief for Appellant, at 29. (Emphasis added.) For my part, rather than join the Court in imagining hypothetical drafts, I prefer to examine the findings in the Senate Report and the testimony presented to Congress.

C

Nothing in the Senate Report supports the Court's intimation that women must be excluded from registration because combat eligibility is a prerequisite for *all* the positions that would need to be filled in the event of a draft. The Senate Report concluded only that "[i]f mobilization were to be ordered in a wartime scenario, the *primary* manpower need would be for combat replacements." S. Rep. No. 96–826, *supra,* at 160, U.S. Code Cong. & Admin. News 1980, 2650 (emphasis added). . . .

This review of the findings contained in the Senate Report and the testimony presented at the congressional hearings demonstrates that there is no basis for the Court's representation that women are ineligible for *all* the positions that would need to be filled in the event of a draft. Testimony about personnel requirements in the event of a draft established that women could fill at least 80,000 of the 650,000 positions for which conscripts would be inducted. Thus, with respect to these 80,000 or more positions, the statutes and policies barring women from combat do not provide a reason for distinguishing between male and female potential conscripts; the two groups are, in the majority's parlance, "similarly situated." As such, the combat restrictions cannot by themselves supply the constitutionally required justification for the MSSA's gender-based classification. Since the classification precludes women from being drafted to fill positions for which they would be qualified and useful, the Government must demonstrate that excluding women from those positions is substantially related to the achievement of an important governmental objective.

III

The Government argues, however, that the "consistent testimony before Congress was to the effect that there is *no military need* to draft women." Brief for Appellant, at 31. (Emphasis in original.) . . . In my view, a more careful examination of the concepts of "equity" and "military need" is required.

As previously noted, the Defense Department's recommendation that women be included in registration plans was based on its conclusion that drafting a limited number of women is consistent with, and could contribute to, military effectiveness. It was against this background that the military experts concluded that "equity" favored registration of women. Assistant Secretary Pirie explained:

> Since women have proven that they can serve successfully as volunteers in the Armed Forces, equity suggests that they be liable to serve as draftees if conscription is reinstated. (1980 House Hearings, *supra*, J.A. 217–218.)

By "considerations of equity," the military experts acknowledged that female conscripts can perform as well as male conscripts in certain positions, and that there is therefore no reason why one group should be totally excluded from registration and a draft. Thus, what the majority so blithely dismisses as "equity" is nothing less than the Fifth Amendment's guarantee of equal protection of the laws which "requires that Congress treat similarly situated persons similarly." Moreover, whether Congress could subsume this constitutional requirement to "military need," in part depends on precisely what the Senate Report meant by "military need." . . . Several witnesses testified that because personnel requirements in the event of a mobilization could be met by drafting men, including women on draft plans is not a military necessity. . . .

To be sure, there is no "military need" to draft women in the sense that a war could be waged without their participation. This fact is, however, irrelevant to resolving the constitutional issue. as previously noted, it is not appellees' burden to prove that registration of women substantially furthers the objectives of the MSSA.[17] Rather, because eligibility for combat is not a requirement for some of the positions to be filled in the event of a draft, it is incumbent on the Government to show that excluding women from a draft to fill those positions substantially furthers an important governmental objective.

It may be, however, that the Senate Report's allusion to "military need" is meant to convey Congress' expectation that women volunteers will make it unnecessary to draft any women. The majority apparently accepts this meaning when it states: "Congress also concluded that whatever the need for women for noncombat roles during mobilization, whether 80,000 or less, it could be met by volunteers." But since the purpose of registration is to protect against unanticipated shortages of volunteers, it is difficult to see how excluding women from registration can be justified by conjectures about the expected number

17. If we were to assign appellees this burden, then all of the Court's prior "mid-level" scrutiny equal protection decisions would be drawn into question. . . .

of female volunteers. I fail to see why the exclusion of a pool of persons who would be conscripted only *if needed* can be justified by reference to the current supply of volunteers. In any event, the Defense Department's best estimate is that in the event of a mobilization requiring reinstitution of the draft, there will not be enough women volunteers to fill the positions for which women would be eligible. The Department told Congress:

> If we had a mobilization, our present best projection is that we could use women in some 80,000 of the jobs we would be *inducting* people for. (1980 Senate Hearings, *supra*, at 1688 [Principal Deputy Assistant Secretary of Defense Danzig]. [Emphasis added.])

Thus, however, the "military need" statement in the Senate Report is understood, it does not provide the constitutionally required justification for the total exclusion of women from registration and draft plans.

IV

Recognizing the need to go beyond the "military need" argument, the Court asserts that "Congress determined that staffing noncombat positions with women during a mobilization would be positively detrimental to the important goal of military flexibility." . . . I find nothing in the Senate Report, to provide any basis for the Court's representation that Congress believed this to be the case.

. . .

Similarly, there is no reason why induction of a limited number of female draftees should any more divide the military into "permanent combat" and "permanent support" groups than is presently the case with the All-Volunteer Armed Forces. The combat restrictions that would prevent a fe-male draftee from serving in a combat or combat rotation position also apply to the 150,000–250,000 women volunteers in the Armed Services. If the presence of increasing but controlled numbers of female volunteers has not unacceptably "divide[d] the military into two groups," it is difficult to see how the induction of a similarly limited additional number of women could accomplish this result. In these circumstances, I cannot agree with the Court's attempt to "interpret" the Senate Report's conclusion that drafting *very large numbers* of women would impair military flexibility, as proof that Congress reached the entirely different conclusion that drafting a limited number of women would adversely affect military flexibility.

V

The Senate Report itself recognized that the "military flexibility" objective speaks only to the question whether "very large numbers" of women should be drafted. . . .

The Senate Report simply failed to consider the possibility that a limited number of women could be drafted. . . . Furthermore, the Senate Report's speculation that a statute authorizing differential induction of male and female draftees would be vulnerable to constitutional challenge is unfounded. The unchallenged restrictions on the assignment of women to combat, the need to preserve military flexibility, and the other factors discussed in the Senate Report provide more than ample grounds for concluding that the discriminatory means employed by such a statute would be substantially related to the achievement of important governmental objectives. Since Congress could have amended § 5(a)(1) to authorize differential induction of men and women based on the military's personnel requirements, the Senate Report's discussion about "added burdens" that would result from drafting equal numbers of male and female draftees provides no basis for concluding that the total exclusion of women from registration and draft plans is substantially related to the achievement of important governmental objectives. . . .

In sum, neither the Senate Report itself nor the testimony presented at the congressional hearings provides any support for the conclusion the Court seeks to attribute to the Report—that drafting a limited number of women, with the number and the timing of their induction and training determined by the military's personnel requirements, would burden training and administrative facilities.

VI

After reviewing the discussion and findings contained in the Senate Report, the most I am able to say of the Report is that it demonstrates that drafting *very large numbers* of women would frustrate the achievement of a number of important governmental objectives that relate to the ultimate goal of maintaining "an adequate armed strength . . . to insure the security of this Nation," 50 U.S.C. App. § 451(b). Or to put it another way, the Senate Report establishes that induction of a large number of men but only a limited number of women, as determined by the military's personnel requirements, would be sub-

stantially related to important governmental interests. But the discussion and findings in the Senate Report do not enable the Government to carry its burden of demonstrating that *completely* excluding women from the draft by excluding them from registration substantially furthers important governmental objectives.

In concluding that the Government has carried its burden in this case, the Court adopts "an appropriately deferential examination of *Congress'* evaluation of [the] evidence," *ante*. (Emphasis in the original.) The majority then proceeds to supplement Congress' actual findings with those the Court apparently believes Congress could (and should) have made. . . . Congressional enactments in the area of military affairs must, like all other laws, be *judged* by the standards of the Constitution. For the Constitution is the supreme law of the land and *all* legislation must conform to the principles it lay down. As the Court has pointed out, "the phrase 'war power' cannot be invoked as a talismanic incantation to support any exercise of congressional power which can be brought within its ambit." *United States v. Robel*, 389 U.S., at 263–264.

I would affirm the judgment of the District Court.

CASE QUESTIONS

1. Marshall endorses the option of registering both men and women but drafting only men. Would such a registration be a sensible use of taxpayers' money? Is there a difference between administrative inconvenience and sheer waste? Does such degree of waste arguably im-

pede the effectiveness of the draft he suggests, and thus undercut his own argument? Would such a registration, for such a contemplated draft, arguably *enhance* military flexibility by giving Congress the ready facility to draft women if the need later arose? Should Congress rather than the Court be making these choices?

2. The italicized portion of Rehnquist's majority opinion highlights his disagreement over the factual record as it is described in the italicized portion of the White-Brennan dissent. Should the case have been remanded (sent back) to the lower court for a further investigation of the facts over which there remains this open dispute?

3. Are there hints here that even Brennan, White, and Marshall would uphold the combat restrictions on females? Consider especially section V of the Marshall-Brennan dissent. To what degree do actual differences between men and women justify different rules for requiring combat participation? For permitting combat participation (to volunteers)? Would it deny equal protection to draft males into combat but to permit only females volunteers in combat?

Rape

Rape law has been a section of the criminal code to receive considerable attention from feminists. For these statutes the bulk of feminists' efforts, in contrast to other areas of the law, has not been toward making these laws gender-neutral, but rather toward reforming testimonial aspects of rape law that have rendered rape prosecutions both difficult to win and taxing on the victims. Anglo-American common law long proceeded on the assumption that women might lightly and falsely charge rape. Consequently, many state jurisdictions, even into the 1970s, required that the victim's word alone, unlike the situation with such crimes as robbery or assault, was not adequate to bring rape charges. Instead, the fact of the crime needed independent corroboration, before prosecution could proceed, of three elements of the crime: (1) force, (2) sexual penetration, and (3) the identity of the rapist. Since eye witnesses were rarely available, these requirements drastically reduced the number of prosecutable rapes. The feminist movement successfully reformed most such statutes, and also achieved some success in sensitizing police and prosecutors' offices to the needs of rape victims. Moreover, a number of states have adopted statutes barring testimony about the sexual history of the rape victim. Additional rape law reforms have included (1) a decision by the U.S. Supreme Court that the death sentence is unconstitutionally harsh in rape cases (favored by reformers as making conviction more readily obtainable[40] and (2) laws in a number of states making rape by a husband a punishable offense. (See section, "Revolutionizing Marriage," for the legal context of this reform.)

Some feminists wanted to go beyond these changes and render all rape laws gender-neutral. A likely target of such reformers was "statutory rape" legislation. Most states had laws punishing males for sex with females deemed too young to give informed consent to sexual intercourse. In California the age of such consent was eighteen. A seventeen-and one-half year old male, Michael M., was prosecuted in Sonoma County for sex with a sixteen-and one-half year old female, Sharon, in June 1978. He challenged the proceedings on the grounds that California's statutory rape law denied him equal protection, in violation of the Fourteenth Amendment. The California Supreme Court, using a strict-scrutiny-compelling-interest test, as required by their own reading of their state constitution, nonetheless upheld the law (as had two lower courts). Using the *Craig* test, the U.S. Supreme Court also upheld the law.

Although this case was prosecuted as consensual intercourse, the facts revealed in Justice Blackmun's opinion, indicated that it was arguably a forcible rape (although he seems to think otherwise). Statutory rape laws function not infrequently as a practical, back-up alternative for prosecutors for these cases where forcible rape convictions appear to have uncertain chances of success, and this need comprised one of California's arguments on behalf of the statute.

Michael M. v. Sonoma County, 450 U.S. 464 (1981)

JUSTICE REHNQUIST, announced the judgment of the Court and delivered an opinion in which THE CHIEF JUSTICE, JUSTICE STEWART, and JUSTICE POWELL joined.

The question presented in this case is whether California's "statutory rape" law, §261.5 of the California Penal Code, violates the Equal Protection Clause of the Fourteenth Amendment. Section 261.5 defines unlawful sexual intercourse as "an act of sexual intercourse accomplished with a female not the wife of the perpetrator, where the female is under the age of 18 years." The statute thus makes men alone criminally liable for the act of sexual intercourse.

. . .

. . . Unlike the California Supreme Court, we have not held that gender-based classifications are "inherently suspect" and thus we do not apply so-called "strict scrutiny" to those classifications. *See Stanton v. Stanton*, 421 U.S. 7 (1975). Our cases have held, however, that the traditional minimum rationality test takes on a somewhat "sharper focus" when gender-based classifications are challenged. *See Craig v. Boren*, 429 U.S. 190, 210 n.* (1976) (POWELL, J., concurring). . . . [I]n *Craig v. Boren*, at 197, the Court [stated] the test to require the classification to bear a "substantial relationship" to "important governmental objectives."

Underlying these decisions is the principle that a legislature not "make overbroad generalizations based on sex which are entirely unrelated to any differences between men and women or which demean the ability or social status of the affected class." *Parham v. Hughes*, 441 U.S. 347, 354 (1979) (STEWART, J., plurality). But because the Equal Protection Clause does not "demand that a statute necessarily apply equally to all persons" or require "things which are different in fact . . . to be treated in law as though they were the same," *Rinaldi v. Yeager*, 384 U.S. 305, 309 (1966), *quoting Tigner v. Texas*, 310 U.S. 141, 147 (1940), this

Court has consistently upheld statutes where the gender classification is not invidious, but rather realistically reflects the fact that the sexes are not similarly situated in certain circumstances. *Parham v. Hughes, supra; Califano v. Webster*, 430 U.S. 313 (1977); *Schlesinger v. Ballard*, 419 U.S. 498 (1975); *Kahn v. Shevin*, 416 U.S. 351 (1974). As the Court has stated, a legislature may "provide for the special problems of women." *Weinberger v. Wiesenfeld*, 420 U.S. 636, 653 (1975).

Applying those principles to this case, the fact that the California Legislature criminalized the act of illicit sexual intercourse with a minor female is a sure indication of its intent or purpose to discourage that conduct. Precisely why the legislature desired that result is of course somewhat less clear. . . . Here, for example, the individual legislators may have voted for the statute for a variety of reasons. Some legislators may have been concerned about preventing teenage pregnancies, others about protecting young females from physical injury or from the loss of "chastity," and still others about promoting various religious and moral attitudes towards premarital sex.

The justification for the statute offered by the State, and accepted by the Supreme Court of California, is that the legislature sought to prevent illegitimate teenage pregnancies. That finding, of course, is entitled to great deference. *Reitman v. Mulkey*, 387 U.S. 369, 373–74 (1967). And although our cases establish that the State's asserted reason for the enactment of a statute may be rejected, "if it could not have been a goal of the legislation," *Weinberger v. Wiesenfeld, supra*, at 648, n.16, this is not such a case.

We are satisfied not only that the prevention of illegitimate pregnancy is at least one of the "purposes" of the statute, but that the State has a strong interest in preventing such pregnancy. At the risk of stating the obvious, teenage pregnancies, which have increased dramatically over the last two decades,[3] have significant social, medical and economic consequences for both the mother and her child, and the State.[4] Of particular concern to the State is that approximately half of all teenage pregnancies end in abortion. And of those children who are born, their illegitimacy makes them likely candidates to become wards of the State.[6]

We need not be medical doctors to discern that young men and young women are not similarly situated with respect to the

3. In 1976 approximately one million 15–19 year olds became pregnant, one-tenth of all women in that age group. Two-thirds of the pregnancies were illegitimate. Illegitimacy rates for teenagers (births per 1,000 unmarried females ages) increased 75 percent for 14–17 year olds between 1961 and 1974 and 33 percent for 18–19 year olds. Alan Guttmacher Institute, *11 Million Teenagers* 10, 13 (1976); C. Chilman, *Adolescent Sexuality In A Changing American Society*, 195 (NIH Pub. No. 80–1426, 1980).

4. The risk of maternal death is 60 percent higher for a teenager under the age of fifteen than for a woman in her early twenties. The risk is 13 percent higher for 15–19 year olds. The statistics further show that most teenage mothers drop out of school and face a bleak economic future . . .

6. The policy and intent of the California Legislature evinced in other legislation buttresses our view that the prevention of teenage pregnancy is a purpose of the statute . . .

Subsequent to the decision below, the California Legislature considered and rejected proposals to render § 261.5 gender neutral, thereby ratifying the judgment of the California Supreme Court. That is enough to answer petitioner's contention that the statute was the "accidental by product of a traditional way of thinking about women." *Califano v. Webster*, 430 U.S. 313, 320 (1977) (quoting *Califano v. Goldfarb*, 430 U.S. 199, 223 (1977) (STEVENS, J., concurring)). . . .

problems and the risks of sexual intercourse. Only women may become pregnant and they suffer disproportionately the profound physical, emotional, and psychological consequences of sexual activity. The statute at issue here protects women from sexual intercourse at an age when those consequences are particularly severe.[7]

The question thus boils down to whether a State may attack the problem of sexual intercourse and teenage pregnancy directly by prohibiting a male from having sexual intercourse with a minor female. We hold that such a statute is sufficiently related to the State's objectives to pass constitutional muster.

Because virtually all of the significant harmful and inescapably identifiable consequences of teenage pregnancy fall on the young female, a legislature acts well within

its authority when it elects to punish only the participant who, by nature, suffers few of the consequences of his conduct. It is hardly unreasonable for a legislature acting to protect minor females to exclude them from punishment. Moreover, the risk of pregnancy itself constitutes a substantial deterrence to young females. No similar natural sanctions deter males. A criminal sanction imposed solely on males thus serves to roughly "equalize" the deterrents on the sexes.

We are unable to accept petitioner's contention that the statute is impermissibly underinclusive and must, in order to pass judicial scrutiny, be *broadened* so as to hold the female as criminally liable as the male. It is argued that this statute is not *necessary* to deter teenage pregnancy because a gender-neutral statute, where both male and female would be subject to prosecution, would serve that goal equally well. The relevant inquiry, however, is not whether the statute is drawn as precisely as it might have been, but whether the line chosen by the California Legislature is within constitutional limitations. *Kahn v. Shevin*, 416 U.S., at 356, n.10.

In any event, we cannot say that a gender-neutral statute would be as effective as the statute California has chosen to enact. The State persuasively contends that a gender-neutral statute would frustrate its interest in effective enforcement. Its view is that a female is surely less likely to report violations of the statute if she herself would be subject to criminal prosecution.[9] In an

---

7. Although petitioner concedes that the State has a "compelling" interest in preventing teenage pregnancy, he contends that the "true" purpose of § 261.5 is to protect the virtue and chastity of young women. As such, the statute is unjustifiable because it rests on archaic stereotypes. What we have said above is enough to dispose of that contention. The question for us—and the only question under the Federal Constitution—is whether the legislation violates the Equal Protection Clause of the Fourteenth Amendment, not whether its supporters may have endorsed it for reasons no longer generally accepted. Even if the preservation of female chastity were one of the motives of the statute, and even if that motive be impermissible, petitioner's argument must fail because "it is a familiar practice of constitutional law that this court will not strike down an otherwise constitutional statute on the basis of an alleged illicit legislative motive." *United States v. O'Brien*, 391 U.S. 367, 383 (1968). In *Orr v. Orr*, 440 U.S. 268 (1979), for example, the Court rejected one asserted purpose as impermissible, but then considered other purposes to determine if they could justify the statute. . . .

9. Petitioner contends that a gender-neutral statute would not hinder prosecutions because the prosecutor could take into account the relative burdens on females and males and generally only prosecute males. But to concede this is to concede all. If the prosecutor, in exercising discretion, will virtually always prosecute just the

area already fraught with prosecutorial difficulties, we decline to hold that the Equal Protection Clause requires a legislature to enact a statute so broad that it may well be incapable of enforcement.[10]

We similarly reject petitioner's argument that § 261.5 is impermissibly overboard because it makes unlawful sexual intercourse with prepubescent females, who are, by definiton, incapable of becoming pregnant. Quite apart from the fact that the statute could well be justified on the grounds that very young females are particularly susceptible to physical injury from sexual intercourse, *see Rundlett v. Oliver*, 607 F.2d 495 (CA1 1979), it is ludicrous to suggest that the Constitution requires the California Legislature to limit the scope of its rape statute to older teenagers and exclude young girls.

There remains only petitioner's contention that the statute is unconstitutional as it is applied to him because he, like Sharon, was under eighteen at the time of sexual intercourse. Petitioner argues that the statute is flawed because it presumes that as between two persons under eighteen, the male is the culpable aggressor. We find petitioner's contentions unpersuasive. Contrary to his assertions, the statute does not rest on the assumption that males are generally the aggressors. It is instead an attempt by a legislature to prevent illegitimate teenage pregnancy by providing an additional deterrent for men. The age of the man is irrelevant since young men are as capable as older men of inflicting the harm sought to be prevented.

In upholding the California statute we also recognize that this is not a case where a statute is being challenged on the grounds that it "invidiously discriminates" against females. . . . Nor is this a case where the gender classification . . . rests on "the baggage of sexual stereotypes" as in *Orr v. Orr*, 440 U.S. 268, 283 (1979). As we have held, the statute instead reasonably reflects the fact that the consequences of sexual intercourse and pregnancy fall more heavily on the female than on the male.

Accordingly, the judgment of the California Supreme Court is affirmed.

Affirmed.

JUSTICE STEWART, concurring.

Section 261.5, on its face, classifies on the basis of sex. A male who engages in sexual intercourse with an underage female who is not his wife violates the statute; a female who engages in sexual intercourse with an underage male who is not

---

man and not the woman, we do not see why it is impermissible for the legislature to enact a statute to the same effect.

10. The question whether a statute is *substantially* related to its asserted goals is at best an opaque one. It can be plausibly argued that a gender-neutral statute would produce fewer prosecutions than the statute at issue here. *See* STEWART, J., concurring. The dissent argues, on the other hand, that "even assuming that a gender neutral statute would be more difficult to enforce. . . . Common sense . . . suggests that a gender-neutral statutory rape law is potentially a greater deterrent of sexual activity than a gender-based law, for the simple reason that a gender-neutral law subjects both men and women to criminal sanctions and thus arguably has a deterrent effect on twice as many potential violators." *Post*. Where such differing speculations as to the effect of a statute are plausible, we think it appropriate to defer to the decision of the California Supreme Court, "armed as it was with the knowledge of the facts and the circumstances concerning the passage and potential impact of [the statute], and familiar with the milieu in which that provision would operate." *Reitman v. Mulkey*, 387 U.S. 369, 378–79 (1967). . . .

her husband does not. The petitioner contends that this state law, which punishes only males for the conduct in question, violates his Fourteenth Amendment right to the equal protection of the law. The Court today correctly rejects that contention.

A

At the outset, it should be noted that the statutory discrimination, when viewed as part of the wider scheme of California law, is not as clearcut as might at first appear. Females are not freed from criminal liability in California for engaging in sexual activity that may be harmful. It is unlawful, for example, for any person, of either sex, to molest, annoy, or contribute to the delinquency of anyone under eighteen years of age. All persons are prohibited from committing "any lewd or lascivious act," including consensual intercourse, with a child under fourteen. And members of both sexes may be convicted for engaging in deviant sexual acts with anyone under eighteen. Finally, females may be brought within the proscription of § 261.5 itself, since a female may be charged with aiding and abetting its violation.

Section 261.5 is thus but one part of a broad statutory scheme that protects all minors from the problems and risks attendant upon adolescent sexual activity. To be sure, § 261.5 creates an additional measure of punishment for males who engage in sexual intercourse with females between the ages of fourteen and seventeen. The question then is whether the Constitution prohibits a state legislature from imposing this *additional* sanction on a gender-specific basis.

B

The Constitution is violated when government, state or federal, invidiously classifies similarly situated people on the basis of the immutable characteristics with which they were born. Thus, detrimental racial classifications by government always violate the Constitution, for the simple reason that, so far as the Constitution is concerned, people of different races are always similarly situated. *See Fullilove v. Klutznick,* 448 U.S. 448, (dissenting opinion); *McLaughlin v. Florida,* 379 U.S. 184, 198 (concurring opinion); *Brown v. Board of Educ.,* 347 U.S. 483; *Plessy v. Ferguson,* 163 U.S. 537, 552 (dissenting opinion). By contrast, while detrimental gender classifications by government often violate the Constitution, they do not always do so, for the reason that there are differences between males and females that the Constitution necessarily recognizes. In this case we deal with the most basic of these differences: females can become pregnant as the result of sexual intercourse; males cannot.

As was recognized in *Parham v. Hughes,* 441 U.S. 347, 354, "a State is not free to make overbroad generalizations based on sex which are entirely unrelated to any differences between men and women or which demean the ability or social status of the protected class." . . .

But we have recognized that in certain narrow circumstances men and women are *not* similarly situated, and in these circumstances a gender classification based on clear differences between the sexes is not invidious, and a legislative classification realistically based upon those differences is not unconstitutional. *See Parham v. Hughes, supra; Califano v. Webster,* 430 U.S. 313, 316–17; *Schlesinger v. Ballard,* 419 U.S. 498. . . .

Applying these principles to the classification enacted by the California Legislature, it is readily apparent that § 261.5 does not violate the Equal Protection Clause. Young women and men are not similarly situated with respect to the problems and risks associated with intercourse and pregnancy, and the statute is realistically related to the legitimate state purpose of reducing those problems and risks.

C

As the California Supreme Court's catalogue shows, the pregnant unmarried female confronts problems more numerous and more severe than any faced by her male partner.[7] She alone endures the medical risks of pregnancy or abortion.[8] She suffers disproportionately the social, educational, and emotional consequences of pregnancy. Recognizing this disproportion, California has attempted to protect teenage females by prohibiting males from participating in the act necessary for conception.

The fact that males and females are not similarly situated with respect to the risks of sexual intercourse applies with the same force to males under eighteen as it does to older males. The risk of pregnancy is a significant deterrent for unwed young

---

7. The court noted that from 1971 through 1976, 83.6 percent of the 4,860 children born to girls under fifteen in California were illegitimate, as were 51 percent of those born to girls 15–17. The court also observed that while accounting for only 21 percent of California pregnancies in 1976, teenagers accounted for 34.7 percent of legal abortions.

8. There is also empirical evidence that sexual abuse of young females is a more serious problem than sexual abuse of young males. For example, a review of five studies found that 88 percent of sexually abused minors were female. Jaffe, Dynneson & ten Bensel, *Sexual Abuse of Children*, 129 Amer. J. of Diseases of Children, 689, 690 (1975). Another study, involving admissions to a hospital emergency room over a three-year period, reported that 86 of 100 children examined for sexual abuse were girls. Orr and Prieto, *Emergency Management of Sexually Abused Children*, 133 Ameri. J. of Diseased Children, 630 (1979). . . .

females that is not shared by unmarried males, regardless of their age. Experienced observation confirms the common-sense notion that adolescent males disregard the possibility of pregnancy far more than do adolescent females. And to the extent that § 261.5 may punish males for intercourse with prepubescent females, that punishment is justifiable because of the substantial physical risks for prepubescent females that are not shared by their male counterparts.

. . .

E

In short, the Equal Protection Clause does not mean that the physiological differences between men and women must be disregarded. While those differences must never be permitted to become a pretext for invidious discrimination, no such discriminaion is presented by this case. The Constitution surely does not require a State to pretend that demonstrable differences between men and women do not really exist.

JUSTICE BLACKMUN, concurring in the judgment.

It is gratifying that the plurality recognizes that "[a]t the risk of stating the obvious, teenage pregnancies . . . have increased dramatically over the last two decades" and "have significant social, medical and economic consequences for both the mother and her child, and the State." There have been times when I have wondered whether the Court was capable of this perception, particularly when it has struggled with the different but not unrelated problems that attend abortion issues. *See*, for example, the opinions (and the dissenting opinions) in *Beal v. Doe*, 432 U.S. 438 (1977); *Maher v. Roe*, 432 U.S.

464 (1977); *Poelker v. Doe,* 432 U.S. 519 (1977); *Harris v. McRae,* 448 U.S. 297 (1980); *Williams v. Zbaraz,* 448 U.S. 358 (1980); and today's opinion in *H. L. v. Matheson. . . .*†

I . . . cannot vote to strike down the California statutory rape law, for I think it is a sufficiently reasoned and constitutional effort to control the problem at its inception. For me, there is an important difference between this state action and a State's adamant and rigid refusal to face, or even to recognize, the "significant . . . consequences"—to the woman—of a forced or unwanted conception. I have found it difficult to rule constitutional, for example, state efforts to block, at that later point, a woman's attempt to deal with the enormity of the problem confronting her, just as I have rejected state efforts to prevent women from rationally taking steps to prevent that problem from arising. *See e.g., Carey v. Population Services International,* 431 U.S. 678 (1977). *See also Griswold v. Connecticut,* 381 U.S. 479 (1965). In contrast, I am persuaded that, although a minor has substantial privacy rights in intimate affairs connected with procreation, California's efforts to prevent teenage pregnancy are to be viewed differently. . . .

Craig v. Boren, 429 U.S. 190 (1976), was an opinion which, in large part, I joined, *id.* at 214. The plurality opinion in the present case points out, *ante,* the Court's respective phrasings of the applicable test in *Reed v. Reed,* 404 U.S. 71, 76 (1971), and in *Craig v. Boren,* 429 U.S., at 197. I vote to affirm the judgment of the Supreme Court of California and to uphold the State's gender-based classification on that test and as exemplified by those two cases and by *Schlesinger v. Ballard,* 419 U.S. 498 (1975); *Weinberger v. Wiesenfeld,* 420 U.S. 636 (1975); and *Kahn v. Shevin,* 416 U.S. 351 (1974).

I note, also, that § 261.5 of the Cali-

†See chapter 4 for these cases.—Au.

fornia Penal Code is just one of several California statutes intended to protect the juvenile. JUSTICE STEWART, in his concurring opinion, appropriately observes that § 261.5 is "but one part of a broad statutory scheme that protects all minors from the problems and risks attendant upon adolescent sexual activity." *Ante.*

I think, too, that it is only fair, with respect to this particular petitioner, to point out that his partner, Sharon, appears not to have been an unwilling participant in at least the initial stages of the intimacies that took place the night of June 3, 1978.* Peti-

*Sharon at the preliminary hearing testified as follows:

"Q [by the Deputy District Attorney]. On June the 4th, at approximately midnight—midnight of June the 3rd, were you in Rohnert Park?

"A [by Sharon]. Yes.

. . .

"Q. Now, after you met the defendant, what happened?

"A. We walked down to the railroad tracks.

"Q. What happened at the railroad tracks?

"A. We were drinking at the railroad tracks and we walked over to this bush and he started kissing me and stuff, and I was kissing him back, too, at first. Then, I was telling him to stop—

"Q. Yes.

"A.—and I was telling him to slow down and stop. He said, 'Okay, okay.' But then he just kept doing it. He just kept doing it and then my sister and two other guys came over to where we were and my sister said—told me to get up and come home. And then I didn't—

"Q. Yes.

"A.—and then my sister and—

. . .

"The Witness: Yeah. We was laying there and we were kissing each other, and then he asked me if I wanted to walk him over to the park; so we walked over to the park and we sat down on a bench and then he started kissing me again and we were laying on the bench. And he told me to take my pants off.

"I said, 'No,'" and I was trying to get up and he hit me back down on the bench and then I just said to myself, 'Forget it,' and I let him do what he wanted to do and he took my pants off and he was telling me to put my legs around him and stuff—

. . .

"Q. Did you have sexual intercourse with the defendant?

"A. Yeah.

"Q. He did put his penis into your vagina?

"A. Yes.

"Q. You said that he hit you?

"A. Yeah.

"Q. He slugged me in the face.

"Q. With what did he slug you?

"A. His fist.

"Q. Where abouts in the face?

"A. On my chin.

"Q. As a result of that, did you have any bruises or any kind of an injury?

"A. Yeah.

"Q. What happened?

"A. I had bruises.

"The Court: Did he hit you one time or did he hit you more than once?

"The Witness: He hit me about two or three times.

. . .

"Q. Now, during the course of that evening, did the defendant ask you your age?

"A. Yeah.

"Q. And what did you tell him?

"A. Sixteen.

"Q. Did you tell him you were sixteen?

"A. Yes.

"Q. Now, you said you had been drinking, is that correct?

"A. Yes.

"Q. Would you describe your condition as a result of the drinking?

"A. I was a little drunk." App. 20–23.

CROSS-EXAMINATION

"Q. Did you go off with Mr. M. away from the others?

"A. Yeah.

"Q. Why did you do that?

"A. I don't know. I guess I wanted to.

"Q. Did you have any need to go to the bathroom when you were there.

"A. Yes.

"Q. And what did you do?

"A. Me and my sister walked down the railroad tracks to some bushes and went to the bathroom.

"Q. Now, you and Mr. M., as I understand it, went off into the bushes, is that correct?

"A. Yes.

"Q. Okay. And what did you do when you and Mr. M. were there in the bushes?

"A. We were kissing and hugging.

"Q. Were you sitting up?

"A. We were laying down.

"Q. You were lying down. This was in the bushes?

"A. Yes.

"Q. How far away from the rest of them were you?

"A. They were just bushes right next the railroad tracks. We just walked off into the bushes; not very far.

. . .

"Q. So your sister and the other two boys came over to where you were, you and Michael were, is that right?

"A. Yeah.

"Q. What did they say to you, if you remember?

"A. My sister didn't say anything. She said, 'Come on, Sharon, let's go home.'

"Q. She asked you to go home with her?

"A. (Affirmative nod.)

"Q. Did you go home with her?

"A. No.

"Q. You wanted to stay with Mr. M.?

"A. I don't know.

"Q. Was this before or after he hit you?

"A. Before.

. . .

"Q. What happened in the five minutes that Bruce stayed there with you and Michael?

"A. I don't remember.

"Q. You don't remember at all?

"A. (Negative head shake.)

"Q. Did you have occasion at that time to kiss Bruce?

tioner's and Sharon's nonacquaintance with each other before the incident: their drinking; their withdrawal from the others of the group; their foreplay, in which she willingly participated and seems to have encouraged; and the closeness of their ages (a

---

"A. Yeah.

"Q. You did? You were kissing Bruce at that time?

"A. (Affirmative nod.)

"Q. Was Bruce kissing you?

"A. Yes.

"Q. And were you standing up at this time?

"A. No, we were sitting down.

. . .

"Q. Okay. So at this point in time you had left Mr. *M.* and you were hugging and kissing with Bruce, is that right?

"A. Yeah.

"Q. And you were sitting up.

"A. Yes.

"Q. Was your sister still there then?

"A. No. Yeah, she was at first.

"Q. What was she doing?

"A. She was standing up with Michael and David.

"Q. Yes. Was she doing anything with Michael and David?

"A. No. I don't think so.

"Q. Whose idea was it for you and Bruce to kiss? Did you initiate that?

"A. Yes.

"Q. What happened after Bruce left?

"A. Michael asked me if I wanted to go walk to the park.

"Q. And what did you say?

"A. I said, "Yes."

"Q. And then what happened?

"A. We walked to the park.

. . .

"Q. How long did it take you to get to the park?

"A. About ten or fifteen minutes.

"Q. And did you walk there?

"A. Yes.

"Q. Did Mr. *M.* ever mention his name?

"A. Yes." *Id.* at 27–32.

difference of only one year and 18 days) are factors that should make this case an unattractive one to prosecute at all, and especially to prosecute as a felony, rather than as a misdemeanor chargeable under § 261.5. But the State has chosen to prosecute in that manner, and the facts, I reluctantly conclude, may fit the crime.

JUSTICE BRENNAN, with whom JUSTICES WHITE and MARSHALL join, dissenting.

I

It is disturbing to find the Court so splintered on a case that presents such a straightforward issue: whether the admittedly gender-based classification in Cal. Penal Code § 261.5 bears a sufficient relationship to the State's asserted goal of preventing teenage pregnancies to survive the "mid-level" constitutional scrutiny mandated by *Craig v. Boren*, 429 U.S. 190 (1976). Applying the analytical framework provided by our precedents, I am convinced that there is only one proper resolution of this issue: the classification must be declared unconstitutional. I fear that the plurality and JUSTICES STEWART and BLACKMUN reach the opposite result by placing too much emphasis on the desirability of achieving the State's asserted statutory goal—prevention of teenage pregnancy—and not enough emphasis on the fundamental question of whether the sex-based discrimination in the California statute is *substantially* related to the achievement of that goal.

II

After some uncertainty as to the proper framework for analyzing equal protection challenges to statutes containing gender-based classifications, this Court settled upon the proposition that a statute containing a gender-based classification cannot withstand constitutional challenge unless the classification is substantially related to the achievement of an important governmental objective. *Kirchberg v. Feenstra* (1981); *Wengler v. Druggists Mutual Ins. Co.* (1980); *Califano v. Westcott*; *Caban v. Mohammed* (1979); *Orr v. Orr* (1979); *Califano v. Goldfarb* (1977); *Califano v. Webster* (1977), *Craig v. Boren*. This analysis applies whether the classification discriminates against males or against females. *Caban v. Mohammed* at 394; *Orr v. Orr* at 278–79; *Craig v. Boren* at 204. The burden is on the government to prove both the importance of its asserted objective and the substantial relationship between the classification and that objective. *See Kirchberg v. Feenstra*; *Wengler v. Druggists Mutual Ins. Co.*; *Caban v. Mohammed* at 393; *Craig v. Boren* at 204. And the State cannot meet that burden without showing that a gender-neutral statute would be a less effective means of achieving that goal. *Wengler v. Druggists Mutual Ins. Co.*; *Orr v. Orr* at 281, 283.

The State of California vigorously asserts that the "important governmental objective" to be served by § 261.5 is the prevention of teenage pregnancy. It claims that its statute furthers this goal by deterring sexual activity by males—the class of persons it considers more responsible for causing those pregnancies.[4] But even assuming that prevention of teenage pregnancy is an important governmental objective and that it is in fact an objective of § 261.5. California still has the burden of proving that there are fewer teenage pregnancies under its gender-based statutory rape law than there would be if the law were gender-neutral. To meet this burden, the State must show that because its statutory rape law punishes only males, and not females, it more effectively deters minor females from having sexual intercourse.

The plurality assumes that a gender-neutral statute would be less effective than § 261.5 in deterring sexual activity because a gender-neutral statute would create significant enforcement problems. The plurality thus accepts the State's assertion that . . .

> a female is surely less likely to report violations of the statute if she herself would be subject to criminal prosecution. In an area already fraught with prosecutorial difficulties, we decline to hold that the Equal Protection Clause requires a legislature to enact a statute so broad that it may well be incapable of enforcement. (*Ante.*)

. . . [T]here are a least two serious flaws in the State's assertion that law enforcement problems created by a gender-neutral statutory rape law would make such a statute less effective than a gender-based statute in deterring sexual activity.

First, the experience of other jurisdictions, and California itself, belies the plurality's conclusion that a gender-neutral statutory rape law "may well be incapable of enforcement." There are now at least 37 States that have enacted gender-neutral statutory rape laws. Although most of these laws protect young persons (of either sex) from the sexual exploitation of older individuals, the laws of Arizona, Florida, and Illinois permit prosecution of both minor females and minor males for engaging in mutual sexual conduct. California has introduced no evidence that those

---

4. In a remarkable display of sexual stereotyping, the California Supreme Court stated: "The Legislature is well within its power in imposing criminal sanctions against males, alone, because they are the *only* persons who may physiologically cause the result which the law properly seeks to avoid." 25 Cal. 3d 608, 613 (1979). (Emphasis in original.)

states have been handicapped by the enforcement problems the plurality finds so persuasive.[7] Surely, if those States could provide such evidence, we might expect that California would have introduced it.

. . .

The second flaw in the State's assertion is that even assuming that a gender-neutral statute would be more difficult to enforce, the State has still not shown that those enforcement problems would make such a statute less effective than a gender-based statute in deterring minor females from engaging in sexual intercourse. Common sense, however, suggests that a gender-neutral statutory rape law is potentially a *greater* deterrent of sexual activity than a gender-based law, for the simple reason that a gender-neutral law subjects both men and women to criminal sanctions and thus arguably has a deterrent effect on twice as many potential violators. Even if fewer persons were prosecuted under the gender-neutral law, as the State suggests, it would still be true that twice as many persons would be *subject* to arrest. The State's failure to prove that a gender-neutral law would be a less effective deterrent than a gender-based law, like the State's failure to prove that a gender-neutral law would be difficult to enforce, should have led this Court to invalidate § 261.5.

III

Until very recently, no California court or commentator had suggested that the

7. There is a logical reason for this. In contrast to laws governing forcible rape, statutory rape laws apply to consensual sexual activity. Force is not an element of the crime. Since a woman who consents to an act of sexual intercourse is unlikely to report her partner to the police—whether or not she is subject to criminal sanctions—enforcement would not be undermined if the statute were to be made gender-neutral.

purpose of California's statutory rape law was to protect young women from the risk of pregnancy. Indeed, the historical development of § 261.5 demonstrates that the law was initially enacted on the premise that young women, in contrast to young men, were to be deemed legally incapable of consenting to an act of sexual intercourse. Because their chastity was considered particularly precious, those young women were felt to be uniquely in need of the State's protection.[10] In contrast, young men were assumed to be capable of making such decisions for themselves; the law therefore did not offer them any special protection.

It is perhaps because the gender classification in California's statutory rape law was initially designed to further these outmoded sexual stereotypes, rather than to reduce the incidence of teenage pregnancies, that the State has been unable to demonstrate a substantial relationship between

10. Past decisions of the California courts confirm that the law was designed to protect the State's young females from their own uninformed decisionmaking. . . . As recently as 1964, the California Supreme Court decided *People v. Hernandez, supra,* 393 P.2d, at 674, in which it stated that the under-age female "is presumed too innocent and naive to understand the implications and nature of her act. . . . The law's concern with her capacity or lack thereof to so understand is explained in part by a popular conception of the social, moral and personal values which are preserved by the abstinence from sexual indulgence on the part of a young woman. An unwise disposition of her sexual favor is deemed to do harm both to herself and the social mores by which the community's conduct patterns are established. Hence the law of statutory rape intervenes in an effort to avoid such a disposition."

It was only in deciding *Michael M.* that the California Supreme Court decided, for the first time in the 130-year history of the statute, that pregnancy prevention had become one of the purposes of the statute.

the classification and its newly asserted goal. *Cf. Califano v. Goldfarb, supra*, 430 U.S., at 223 (STEVENS, J., concurring). But whatever the reason, the State has not shown that Cal. Penal Code § 261.5 is any more effective than a gender-neutral law would be in deterring minor females from engaging in sexual intercourse. It has therefore not met its burden of proving that the statutory classification is substantially related to the achievement of its asserted goal.

I would hold that § 261.5 violates the Equal Protection Clause of the Fourteenth Amendment and I would reverse the judgment of the California Supreme Court.

JUSTICE STEVENS, dissenting.

Local custom and belief—rather than statutory laws of venerable but doubtful ancestry—will determine the volume of sexual activity among unmarried teenagers. The empirical evidence cited by the plurality demonstrates the futility of the notion that a statutory prohibition will significantly affect the volume of that activity or provide a meaningful solution to the problems created by it. Nevertheless, as a matter of constitutional power, unlike my Brother BRENNAN at n.5, I would have no doubt about the validity of a state law prohibiting all unmarried teenagers from engaging in sexual intercourse. The societal interests in reducing the incidence of venereal disease and teenage pregnancy are sufficient, in my judgment, to justify a prohibition of conduct that increases the risk of those harms.

My conclusion that a nondiscriminatory prohibition would be constitutional does not help me answer the question whether a prohibition applicable to only half of the joint participants in the risk-creating conduct is also valid. It cannot be true that the validity of a total ban is an adequate justification for a selective pro-

hibition; otherwise, the constitutional objection to discriminatory rules would be meaningless. The question in this case is whether the difference between males and females justifies this statutory discrimination based entirely on sex.[4]

The fact that the Court did not immediately acknowledge that the capacity to become pregnant is what primarily differentiates the female from the male[5] does

4. Equal protection analysis is often said to involve different "levels of scrutiny." It may be more accurate to say that the burden of sustaining an equal protection challenge is much heavier in some cases than in others. Racial classifications, which are subjected to "strict scrutiny," are presumptively invalid because there is seldom, if ever, any legitimate reason for treating citizens differently because of their race. On the other hand, most economic classifications are presumptively valid because they are a necessary component of most regulatory programs. In cases involving discrimination between men and women, the natural differences between the sexes are sometimes relevant and sometimes wholly irrelevant. If those differences are obviously irrelevant, the discrimination should be treated as presumptively unlawful in the same way that racial classifications are presumptively unlawful. *Cf. Califano v. Goldfarb*, 430 U.S. 199, 223 (1977) (STEVENS, J., concurring in the judgment). But if, as in this case, there is an apparent connection between the discrimination and the fact that only women can become pregnant, it may be appropriate to presume that the classification is lawful. This presumption, however, may be overcome by a demonstration that the apparent justification for the discrimination is illusory or wholly inadequate. Thus, instead of applying a "mid-level" form of scrutiny in all sex discrimination cases, perhaps the burden is heavier in some than in others. Nevertheless, as I have previously suggested, the ultimate standard in these, as in all other equal protection cases, is essentially the same. *See Craig v. Boren*, 429 U.S. 190, 211–12 (1976) (STEVENS, J., concurring). . . .

5. *See General Electric Co. v. Gilbert*, 429 U.S. 125, 162 (1976) (STEVENS, J., dissenting). [See chapter 4.—Au.]

not impeach the validity of the plurality's newly-found wisdom. I think the plurality is quite correct in making the assumption that the joint act that this law seeks to prohibit creates a greater risk of harm for the female than for the male. But the plurality surely cannot believe that the risk of pregnancy confronted by the female—any more than the risk of venereal disease confronted by males as well as females—has provided an effective deterrent to voluntary female participation in the risk-creating conduct. Yet the plurality's decision seems to rest on the assumption that the California Legislature acted on the basis of that rather fanciful notion.

In my judgment, the fact that a class of persons is especially vulnerable to a risk that a statute is designed to avoid is a reason for making the statute applicable to that class. The argument that a special need for protection provides a rational explanation for an exemption is one I simply do not comprehend.

In this case, the fact that a female confronts a greater risk of harm than a male is a reason for applying the prohibition to her—not a reason for granting her a license to use her own judgment on whether or not to assume the risk. Surely, if we examine the problem from the point of view of society's interest in preventing the risk-creating conduct from occurring at all, it is irrational to exempt 50 percent of the potential violators. *See* Dissent of JUSTICE BRENNAN, *ante*. And, if we view the government's interest as that of a *parens patriae* seeking to protect its subjects from harming themselves, the discrimination is actually perverse. Would a rational parent making rules for the conduct of twin children of opposite sex simultaneously forbid the son and authorize the daughter to engage in conduct that is especially harmful to the daughter? That is the effect of this statutory classification.

If pregnancy or some other special harm is suffered by one of the two participants in the prohibited act, that special harm no doubt would constitute a legitimate mitigating factor in deciding what, if any, punishment might be appropriate in a given case. But from the standpoint of fashioning a general preventive rule—or, indeed, in determining appropriate punishment when neither party in fact has suffered any special harm—I regard a total exemption for the members of the more endangered class as utterly irrational.

In my opinion, the only acceptable justification for a general rule requiring disparate treatment of the two participants in a joint act must be a legislative judgment that one is more guilty than the other. The risk-creating conduct that this statute is designed to prevent requires the participation of two persons—one male and one female. In many situations it is probably true that one is the aggressor and the other is either an unwilling, or at least a less willing, participant in the joint act. If a statute authorized punishment of only one participant and required the prosecutor to prove that that participant had been the aggressor, I assume that the discrimination would be valid. Although the question is less clear, I also assume, for the purpose of deciding this case that it would be permissible to punish only the male participant, if one element of the offense were proof that he had been the aggressor, or at least in some respects the more responsible participant in the joint act. The statute at issue in this case, however, requires no such proof. The question raised by this statute is whether the State, consistently with the Federal Constitution, may always punish the male and never the female when they are equally responsible or when the female is the more responsible of the two.

It would seem to me that an impartial lawmaker could give only one answer to that question. The fact that the California Legislature has decided to apply its prohibition only to the male may reflect a legislative judgment that in the typical case the male is actually the more guilty party. Any such judgment must, in turn, assume that the decision to engage in the risk-creating conduct is always—or at least typically—a male decision. If that assumption is valid, the statutory classificaton should also be valid. But what is the support for the assumption? It is not contained in the record of this case or in any legislative history or scholarly study that has been called to our attention. I think it is supported to some extent by traditional attitudes toward male-female relationships. But the possibility that such an habitual attitude may reflect nothing more than an irrational prejudice makes it an insufficient justification for discriminatory treatment that is otherwise blatantly unfair. For, as I read this statute, it requires that one, and only one, of two equally guilty wrongdoers be stigmatized by a criminal conviction.

I cannot accept the State's argument that the constitutionality of the discriminatory rule can be saved by an assumption that prosecutors will commonly invoke this statute only in cases that actually involve a forcible rape, but one that cannot be established by proof beyond a reasonable doubt.[8] That assumption implies that a State has a legitimate interest in convicting a defendant on evidence that is constitutionally insufficient. Of course, the State may create a lesser-included offense that would authorize punishment of the more guilty party, but surely the interest in obtaining convictions on inadequate proof cannot justify a statute that punishes one who is equally or less guilty than his partner.[9]

Nor do I find at all persuasive the suggestion that this discrimination is adequately justified by the desire to encourage females to inform against their male partners. Even if the concept of a wholesale informant's exemption were an acceptable enforcement device, what is the justification for defining the exempt class entirely by reference to sex rather than by reference to a more neutral criterion such as relative innocence? Indeed, if the exempt class is to be composed entirely of members of one sex, what is there to support the view that the statutory purpose will be better served by granting the informing license to females rather than to males? If a discarded male partner informs on a promiscuous female, a timely threat of prosecution might well prevent the precise harm the statute is intended to minimize.

Finally, even if my logic is faulty and there actually is some speculative basis for

---

8. According to the State of California:

"The statute is commonly employed in situations involving force, prostitution, pornography or coercion due to status relationships, and the state's interest in these situations is apparent." Brief for the Respondent, at 3. *See also id.* at 23–25. The State's interest in these situations is indeed apparent and certainly sufficient to justify statutory prohibition of forcible rape, prostitution, pornography and nonforcible, but nonetheless coerced, sexual intercourse.

However, it is not at all apparent to me how this state interest can justify a statute not specifically directed to any of these offenses.

9. Both JUSTICE REHNQUIST and JUSTICE BLACKMUN apparently attach significance to the testimony at the preliminary hearing indicating that the petitioner struck his partner. . . . In light of the fact that the petitioner would be equally guilty of the crime charged in the complaint whether or not that testimony is true, it obviously has no bearing on the legal question presented by this case. . . .

treating equally guilty males and females differently, I still believe that any such speculative justification would be outweighed by the paramount interest in even-handed enforcement of the law. A rule that authorizes punishment of only one of two equally guilty wrongdoers violates the essence of the constitutional requirement that the sovereign must govern impartially.

I respectfully dissent.

CASE QUESTIONS

1. If laws against sex with minors were written in a gender neutral way but only males prosecuted, would a defendant be likely to argue that they were unconstitutional *as applied?* If laws against sex with minors were written in such a way as to punish only the aggressor or initiator of the sex act, might courts confront insurmountable problems of proof? (e.g., What act defines the "initiation" of sexual intercourse? Is the definition provable "beyond a reasonable doubt"?)

2. Do laws like this one help or hurt females?

3. What might Justice Stevens have had in mind when he mentions in note 8 "nonforcible but nonetheless coerced, sexual intercourse"?

Separate But Equal

Even when statutes do single out one or another gender, and thus are not facially neutral, it is not always obvious that the singling out amounts to discriminatory treatment. Statutes that separate men from women, for instance, are not necessarily, at least in principle, providing unequal treatment to the two groups. For litigation challenging legally mandated sex segregation under the equal protection clause, courts have to address two distinctive questions. First, does the separation amount to unequal treatment? And, second, if so, is the unequal treatment nonetheless justified under equal protection standards?

The legal assumption that "separate" can be "equal" prevailed in this country in relation to racial segregation from 1896 to 1954. It prevailed despite the universal understanding that the special purpose of the equal protection clause was to prevent unequal treatment of the black race at the hands of southern state governments. The rule of "separate but equal" permitted the system of Jim Crow legislation, which required that blacks be separated from whites in public buildings of all kinds (including schools), in parks, in restrooms, in public restaurants, and public conveyances (trains, buses, etc.). Blacks were even provided with separate drinking fountains.

In practice, albeit not in legal rhetoric, the "but equal" half of "separate but equal" was never enforced. Facilities provided blacks were almost always more limited and more shabby than those provided whites. This situation remained true until about the mid-twentieth century, at which time federal courts began taking a serious look at the "colored" facilities that southern states were claiming to be equal to those they provided "whites."

Most Americans are aware that the *Brown v. Board of Education*[41] decision in 1954 declared that racially "separate" cannot be "equal" in the field of public education, thus ending the official legality[42] of law-imposed racial segregation in schools. Not many people are aware of two 1950 cases that set the stage for the *Brown* decision, establishing the legal doctrine that was to bring about the demise of school segregation by race. Only when this doctrine is fully understood can one critically evaluate what the federal courts have been doing in the area of gender-based school segregation.

The doctrine that killed racial segregation in public education involved something the Supreme Court called "intangible factors." Once the federal courts began to crack down on southern school boards, and to require something approaching a semblance of actual equality of facilities, certain states developed unusual stratagems for handling their black students; these stratagems directed the Supreme Court's attention to the phenomenon of "intangible factors" that affect the quality of education.

The first unusual stratagem was adopted by Texas.[43] Under pressure from the federal courts, Texas opened a separate "college of law" for blacks rather than admit a black to the University of Texas Law School. The state rented a few rooms, ordered ten thousand books, hired a small part-time faculty, and called it equality. In deciding that this treatment was unconstitutional, the Supreme Court, after canvassing the obvious superiority of the University of Texas Law School in such tangible facilities as number of faculty, variety in course offerings, scope of the library, and so forth, stated with considerable emphasis:

> What is more important, the University of Texas Law School possesses to a far greater degree those qualities which are incapable of objective measurement but which make for greatness in a law school. Such qualities, to name but a few include reputation of the faculty, experience of the administration, position and influence of the alumni, standing in the community, traditions and prestige. [Moreover, the law school] . . . cannot be effective in isolation from the individuals and institutions with which the law interacts. Few students and no one who has practiced law would choose to study in an academic vacuum, removed from the interplay of ideas and the exchange of views with which the law is concerned. The law school to which Texas is willing to admit petitioner excludes from its student body members of the racial groups which number 85 percent of

the population of the State and include most of the lawyers, witnesses, jurors, judges and other officials with whom petitioner will inevitably be dealing when he becomes a member of the Texas bar.

The second critical 1950 case[44] involved a black graduate student who was actually admitted into the erstwhile all-white University of Oklahoma graduate school. (Oklahoma provided black four-year colleges but had no black graduate schools.) The black graduate student was admitted, but under certain conditions. He had to sit at a special desk, designated "colored," adjacent to the classroom; he had to eat at a special table in the cafeteria, designated "colored," and had to eat only at specified times; and he had to study at a separate table, designated "colored," outside the library reading room. In declaring that this treatment was unconstitutional, even though the black student had access to the same physical university plant as white students, the Supreme Court reasoned once again that intangible as well as tangible factors must be considered in determining whether equality of educational facilities was being provided by the state. The court held that equal protection of the laws had been denied this black student because of inequality in the intangible factors shaping the education he would receive; those factors included "ability to study, to engage in discussions and exchange views with other students, and in general, to learn his profession."

Once the Supreme Court began to take into account such intangible factors as the reputation of the school, the reputation of the faculty, and opportunity to interact with fellow students from different backgrounds, the handwriting on the wall was written in large and clear letters. State-imposed racial segregation in any public school produced inequality in these factors and thus would have to be judged a denial of "equal protection of the laws." It was—in 1954.

The point of including this elaborate background on racial segregation has not been to explain the evolution of *Brown v. Board of Education* but to provide background for assessing the constitutionality of gender-based segregation. The question that must be asked for that assessment is: "To what extent do the Court's statements about the intangible but real inequality of educational opportunity offered by racially segregated schools apply to sex-segregated schools?"

Williams v. McNair (1971), discussion

The Supreme Court gave a very terse, negative answer to this question, but with no explanatory opinion, in 1971, in *Williams v. McNair*,[45] just eight months before the seminal decision in *Reed v. Reed*. In 1977 the Court took up the question again,[46] but Justice Rehnquist was in the hospital and could not participate. Without him, the Court split 4–4 and consequently issued no resolution at all. Finally, in 1982 the Court did resolve a case dealing with sex-segregated public education, complete with written opinion. The answer the Court gave in 1982, in the case of *Mississippi University for Women v. Hogan* was the opposite of the one it gave in 1971. If one assumes that Justice Rehnquist would have voted consistently between the 1977 and 1982 cases, then one could conclude that between 1977 and 1982 the Court shifted its position on state-sponsored single-sex education. What changed in that five years is that Sandra Day O'Connor joined the Court, replacing Justice Stewart (who apparently had voted with the *Hogan* dissenters in the 1977 case. The Court does not reveal its line-up when there is a tie vote.) Not only was her vote the pivotal one in shaping the five person majority, but also she wrote the majority opinion here, her first Court opinion in her career as a Supreme Court justice.

In the 1971 case, *Williams v. McNair,* the lower court had, as was standard in that pre-*Reed* period, applied the rational basis test and had reasoned that "there is a respectable body of educators who believe that 'a single-sex institution can advance the quality and effectiveness of its instruction by concentrating upon areas of primary interest to only one sex.'" Since the gender discrimination was thus "not wholly wanting in reason," it was upheld. The context was a challenge by a group of males to their exclusion from Winthrop College, an all-women college provided by South Carolina, along with Citadel, an all-male college, and several coed colleges. They had wanted to attend Winthrop for reasons of economy, since they lived near it. The U.S. Supreme Court, without written opinion, affirmed the lower court's denial of their challenge.

Vorchheimer v. Philadelphia (1977), discussion

The 1977 case, *Vorchheimer v. Philadelphia* had been initiated by a girl, Susan Vorchheimer, seeking admission to the highly prestigious all-male Central High School of Philadelphia. Philadelphia provided one all-girl school, Girls' High, and one all-boy, Central, for highly qualified students interested in a college prep program. Admission was by competitive exam. The city provided no comparable, highly selective coed alternative, although it did provide other kinds of coed high schools (e.g., neighborhood high schools.) The federal district court first took up this issue in 1975 (400 F. Supp. 326), after the precedents of *Reed* through *Stanton* had been established by the Supreme Court. District Judge Newcomer noted the disparity between the words of these precedents (the rationality test) and their results (the rejection of arguably rational laws) and then admitted:

> A lower court faced with this line of cases has an uncomfortable feeling, somewhat similar to a man playing a shell game who is not absolutely sure there is a pea.

Newcomer did uphold the single-sex admissions program of Central High, as did the Circuit Court of Appeals. Both reasoned that the education provided at the two prestigious schools was substantially equal and thus could not violate the Equal Protection Clause. This conclusion was in the face of admissions by Newcomer that "Central has a deserved reputation for training men who will become local and national leaders," that its alumni association "is an influential group in Philadelphia," and that "the number of Girls' High graduates who have become influential in business, professional, or academic affairs does not approach the number who have graduated from Central. . . ." Had the federal courts taken these "intangible factors" more seriously, gender segregation in public education might have been prohibited sooner.

While the clarity of the test later produced in *Craig v. Boren* might have eased the perplexity of Judge Newcomer, it did not seem to produce any powerful Supreme Court consensus. Not only is the Court still split 5–4 as of 1982, but Justice O'Connor's opinion explicitly leaves open the possibility that in other circumstances the Court might uphold single-sex education (see her footnotes 1 and 7).

This 1982 case, *Mississippi University for Women v. Hogan*, arose out of a challenge by Joe Hogan, a registered nurse employed in the city where MUW was located, who wished to pursue a B.A. degree in nursing there. Although otherwise qualified, he was refused admission pursuant to the state laws that maintained MUW as an all-women institution (see Justice O'Connor's first foonote). Hogan argued that the single-sex admission policy violated the Equal Protection Clause. A federal district court had rejected his claims in a summary judgment, but a Circuit Court of Appeals had found in his favor under the *Craig* test (646 F.2d 1116). When Mississippi appealed to the U.S. Supreme Court, the justices responded as follows:

Mississippi University for Women v. Joe Hogan, 458 U.S. 718 (1982)

JUSTICE O'CONNOR delivered the opinion of the Court.

This case presents the narrow issue of whether a state statute that excludes males from enrolling in a state-supported professional nursing school violates the Equal Protection Clause of the Fourteenth Amendment.

I

The facts are not in dispute. In 1884, the Mississippi legislature created the Mississippi Industrial Institute and College for the Education of White Girls of the State of Mississippi, now the oldest state-supported all-female college in the United States. 1884 Miss. Gen. Laws, Ch. XXX, § 6. The school, known today as Mississippi University for Women (MUW), has from its inception limited its enrollment to women.[1]

. . .

1. The charter of MUW, basically unchanged since its founding, now provides:
"The purpose and aim of the Mississippi State College for Women is the moral and intellectual advancement of the girls of the state by the maintenance of a first-class institution for their edu-

We . . . now affirm the judgment of the Court of Appeals.[7]

II

We begin our analysis aided by several firmly-established principles. Because the challenged policy expressly discriminates among applicants on the basis of gender, it is subject to scrutiny under the Equal Protection Clause of the Fourteenth Amend-

---

cation in the arts and sciences, for their training in normal school methods and kindergarten, for their instruction in bookkeeping, photography, stenography, telegraphy, and typewriting, and in designing, drawing, engraving, and painting, and their industrial application, and for their instruction in fancy, general, and practical needlework, and in such other industrial branches as experience, from time to time, shall suggest as necessary or proper to fit them for the practical affairs of life." Miss. Code Ann. § 37–117–3 (1972).

Mississippi maintains no other single-sex public university or college. Thus, we are not faced with the question of whether States can provide "separate but equal" undergraduate institutions for males and females. Cf. *Vorchheimer v. School District of Philadelphia*, 532 F.2d 880 (CA3 1975), aff'd by an equally divided court, 430 U.S. 703 (1977).

7. Although some statements in the Court of Appeals' decision refer to all schools within MUW, *see* 646 F.2d, at 1119, the factual underpinning of Hogan's claim for relief involved only his exclusion from the nursing program, Complaint ¶8–10, and the Court of Appeals' holding applies only to Hogan's individual claim for relief. 646 F.2d, at 1119–20. Additionally, during oral argument, counsel verified that Hogan sought only admission to the School of Nursing. Tr. of Oral Arg. 24. Because Hogan's claim is thus limited, and because we review judgments, not statements in opinions, *Black v. Cutter Laboratories*, 351 U.S. 292 (1956), we decline to address the question of whether MUW's admissions policy, as applied to males seeking admission to schools other than the School of Nursing, violates the Fourteenth Amendment.

ment. *Reed v. Reed*, 404 U.S. 71, 75 (1971). That this statute discriminates against males rather than against females does not exempt it from scrutiny or reduce the standard of review.[8] *Caban v. Mohammed*, 441 U.S. 380, 394 (1979); *Orr v. Orr*, 440 U.S. 268, 279 (1979). Our decisions also establish that the party seeking to uphold a statute that classifies individuals on the basis of their gender must carry the burden of showing an "exceedingly persuasive justification" for the classification. *Kirchberg v. Feenstra*, 450 U.S. 455; 461 (1981); *Personnel Administrator of Massachusetts v. Feeney*, 442 U.S. 256, 273 (1979). The burden is met only by showing at least that the classification serves "important governmental objectives and that the discriminatory means employed" are "substantially related to the achievement of those objectives." *Wengler v. Druggists Mutual Insurance Co.*, 446 U.S. 142, 150 (1980).[9]

---

8. Without question, MUW's admissions policy worked to Hogan's disadvantage. Although Hogan could have attended classes and received credit in one of Mississippi's state-supported co-educational nursing programs, none of which was located in Columbus, he could attend only by driving a considerable distance from his home. A similarly situated female would not have been required to choose between foregoing credit and bearing that inconvenience. Moreover, since many students enrolled in the School of Nursing hold full-time jobs, Hogan's female colleagues had available an opportunity, not open to Hogan, to obtain credit for additional training. The policy of denying males the right to obtain credit toward a baccalaureate degree thus imposed upon Hogan "a burden he would not bear were he female." *Orr v. Orr*, 440 U.S. 268, 273 (1979).

9. In his dissenting opinion, JUSTICE POWELL argues that a less rigorous test should apply because Hogan does not advance a "serious equal protection claim. . . ." JUSTICE BLACKMUN, without proposing an alternative test, labels the test applicable to gender-based discrimination

Although the test for determining the validity of gender-based classification is straightforward, it must be applied free of fixed notions concerning the roles and abilities of males and females. Care must be taken in ascertaining whether the statutory objective itself reflects archaic and stereotypic notions. Thus, if the statutory objective is to exclude or "protect" members of one gender because they are presumed to suffer from an inherent handicap or to be innately inferior, the objective itself is illegitimate. *See Frontiero v. Richardson*, 411 U.S. 677, 684–85 (1973) (plurality opinion).[10]

If the State's objective is legitimate and important, we next determine whether the requisite direct, substantial relationship between objective and means is present. The purpose of requiring that close relationship is to assure that the validity of a classification is determined through reasoned analysis rather than through the mechanical application of traditional, often in-

accurate, assumptions about the proper roles of men and women. The need for the requirement is amply revealed by reference to the broad range of statutes already invalidated by this Court, statutes that relied upon the simplistic, outdated assumption that gender could be used as a "proxy for other, more germane bases of classification," *Craig v. Boren*, 429 U.S. 190, 198 (1976), to establish a link between objective and classification.

Applying this framework, we now analyze the arguments advanced by the State to justify its refusal to allow males to enroll for credit in MUW's School of Nursing.

III

A

The State's primary justification for maintaining the single-sex admissions policy of MUW's School of Nursing is that it compensates for discrimination against women and, therefore, constitutes educational affirmative action. Pet. Brief 8.[13] As

---

as "rigid" and productive of "needless conformity." Our past decisions establish, however, that when a classification expressly discriminates on the basis of gender, the analysis and level of scrutiny applied to determine the validity of the classification do not vary simply because the objective appears acceptable to individual members of the Court. While the validity and importance of the objective may affect the outcome of the analysis, the analysis itself does not change.

Thus, we apply the test previously relied upon by the Court to measure the constitutionality of gender-based discrimination. . . .

10. History provides numerous examples of legislative attempts to exclude women from particular areas simply because legislators believed women were less able than men to perform a particular function. In 1872, this Court remained unmoved by Myra Bradwell's argument that the Fourteenth Amendment prohibited a State from classifying her as unfit to practice law simply because she was female. *Bradwell v. Illinois,* 16 Wall. 130 (1872). . . .

13. In its Reply Brief, the State understandably retreated from its contention that MUW was founded to provide opportunities for women which were not available to men. Apparently, the impetus for founding MUW came not from a desire to provide women with advantages superior to those offered men, but rather from a desire to provide white women in Mississippi access to state-supported higher learning. In 1856, Sally Reneau began agitating for a college for white women. Those initial efforts were unsuccessful, and, by 1870, Mississippi provided higher education only for white men and black men and women. In 1882, two years before MUW was chartered, the University of Mississippi opened its doors to women. However, the institution was in those early years not "extensively patronized by females; most of those who come being such as desire to qualify themselves to teach." By 1890, the largest number of women in any class at the University had been 23, while nearly 350 women enrolled in the first session of

applied to the School of Nursing, we find the State's argument unpersuasive.

In limited circumstances, a gender-based classification favoring one sex can be justified if it intentionally and directly assists members of the sex that is disproportionately burdened. *See Schlesinger v. Ballard,* 419 U.S. 498 (1975). However, we consistently have emphasized that "the mere recitation of a benign, compensatory purpose is not an automatic shield which protects against any inquiry into the actual purposes underlying a statutory scheme." *Weinberger v. Wiesenfeld,* 420 U.S. 636, 648 (1975). The same searching analysis must be made, regardless of whether the State's objective is to eliminate family controversy, *Reed v. Reed,* to achieve administrative efficiency, *Frontiero v. Richardson,* or to balance the burdens borne by males and females.

It is readily apparent that a State can evoke a compensatory purpose to justify an otherwise discriminatory classification only if members of the gender benefited by the classification actually suffer a disadvantage related to the classification. We considered such a situation in *Califano v. Webster,* 430 U.S. 313 (1977), which involved a challenge to a statutory classification that allowed women to eliminate more low-earning years than men for purposes of computing Social Security retirement benefits. Although the effect of the classification was to allow women higher monthly benefits than were available to men with the same earning history, we upheld the statutory scheme, noting that it took into ac-

count that women "as such have been unfairly hindered from earning as much as men" and "work[ed] directly to remedy" the resulting economic disparity. *Id.* at 318.

A similar pattern of discrimination against women influenced our decision in *Schlesinger v. Ballard,* 419 U.S. 498 (1975). There, we considered a federal statute that granted female Naval officers a 13-year tenure of commissioned service before mandatory discharge, but accorded male officers only a nine-year tenure. We recognized that, because women were barred from combat duty, they had had fewer opportunities for promotion than had their male counterparts. By allowing women an additional four years to reach a particular rank before subjecting them to mandatory discharge, the statute directly compensated for other statutory barriers to advancement.

In sharp contrast, Mississippi has made no showing that women lacked opportunities to obtain training in the field of nursing or to attain positions of leadership in that field when the MUW School of Nursing opened its door or that women currently are deprived of such opportunities. In fact, in 1970, the year before the School of Nursing's first class enrolled, women earned 94 percent of the nursing baccalaureate degrees conferred in Mississippi and 98.6 percent of the degrees earned nationwide. . . . As one would expect, the labor force reflects the same predominance of women in nursing. When MUW's School of Nursing began operation, nearly 98 percent of all employed registered nurses were female.

Rather than compensate for discriminatory barriers faced by women, MUW's policy of excluding males from admission to the School of Nursing tends to perpetuate the stereotyped view of nursing as an exclusively woman's job.[15] By assuring that

MUW. Because the University did not solicit the attendance of women until after 1920, and did not accept women at all for a time between 1907 and 1920, most Mississippi women who attended college attended MUW. Thus, in Mississippi, as elsewhere in the country, women's colleges were founded to provide some form of higher education for the academically disenfranchised. [Sources omitted.—Au.]

15. Officials of the American Nurses Association have suggested that excluding men from the

Mississippi allots more openings in its state-supported nursing schools to women that it does to men, MUW's admissions policy lends credibility to the old view that women, not men, should become nurses, and makes the assumption that nursing is a field for women a self-fulfilling prophecy. See *Stanton v. Stanton*, 421 U.S. 7 (1975). Thus, we conclude that, although the State recited a "benign, compensatory purpose," it failed to establish that the alleged objective is the actual purpose underlying the discriminatory classification.

The policy is invalid also because it fails the second part of the equal protection test, for the State has made no showing that the gender-based classification is substantially and directly related to its proposed compensatory objective. To the contrary, MUW's policy of permitting men to attend classes as auditors fatally undermines its claim that women, at least those in the School of Nursing, are adversely affected by the presence of men.

MUW permits men who audit to participate fully in classes. Additionally, both men and women take part in continuing education courses offered by the School of Nursing, in which regular nursing students also can enroll. The uncontroverted record reveals that admitting men to nursing classes does not affect teaching style, that the presence of men in the classroom would not affect the performance of the female nursing students, and that men in co-educational nursing schools do not dominate the classroom. In sum, the record in this case is flatly inconsistent with the

claim that excluding men from the School of Nursing is necessary to reach any of MUW's educational goals.

Thus, considering both the asserted interest and the relationship between the interest and the methods used by the State, we conclude that the State has fallen far short of establishing the "exceedingly persuasive justification" needed to sustain the gender-based classification. Accordingly, we hold that MUW's policy of denying males the right to enroll for credit in its School of Nursing violates the Equal Protection Clause of the Fourteenth Amendment.[17]

B

In an additional attempt to justify its exclusion of men from MUW's School of Nursing, the State contends that MUW is the direct beneficiary "of specific congressional legislation which, on its face, permits the institution to exist as it has in the past." Pet. Brief 19. The argument is based upon the language of § 901(a) in Title IX of the Education Amendments of 1972, 20 U.S.C. § 1681(a). Although § 901(a) prohibits gender discrimination in education programs that receive federal financial assistance, subsection 5 exempts the admissions policies of undergraduate institutions "that traditionally and continually from [their] establishment [have] had a policy of admitting only students of one sex" from the general prohibition. Arguing that

field has depressed nurses' wages. *Hearings Before the United States Equal Employment Opportunity Commission on Job Segregation and Wage Discrimination* 510–11, 517–18, 523 (April 1980). To the extent the exclusion of men has that effect, MUW's admissions policy actually penalizes the very class the State purports to benefit. *Cf. Weinberger v. Wiesenfeld, supra.*

17. JUSTICE POWELL's dissent suggests that a second objective is served by the gender-based classification in that Mississippi has elected to provide women a choice of educational environments. Since any gender-based classification provides one class a benefit or choice not available to the other class, however, that argument begs the question. The issue is not whether the benefited class profits from the classification, but whether the State's decision to confer a benefit only upon one class by means of a discriminatory classification is substantially related to achieving a legitimate and substantial goal.

Congress enacted Title IX in furtherance of its power to enforce the Fourteenth Amendment, a power granted by § 5 of that Amendment, the State would have us conclude that § 1681(a)(5) is but "a congressional limitation upon the broad prohibitions of the Equal Protection Clause of the Fourteenth Amendment." Pet. Brief 20.

The argument requires little comment. Initially, it is far from clear that Congress intended, through § 1681(a)(5), to exempt MUW from any constitutional obligation. Rather, Congress apparently intended, at most, to exempt MUW from the requirements of Title IX.

Even if Congress envisioned a constitutional exemption, the State's argument would fail. Section 5 of the Fourteenth Amendment gives Congress broad power indeed to enforce the command of the Amendment and "to secure to all persons the enjoyment of perfect equality of civil rights and the equal protection of the laws against State denial or invasion. . . ." *Ex parte Virginia,* 100 U.S. 339, 346 (1879). Congress' power under § 5, however, "is limited to adopting measures to enforce the guarantees of the Amendment; § 5 grants Congress no power to restrict, abrogate, or dilute these guarantees." *Katzenbach v. Morgan,* 384 U.S. 641, 651 n.10 (1966). . . .

. . .

CHIEF JUSTICE BURGER, dissenting.

I agree generally with JUSTICE POWELL's dissenting opinion. I write separately, however, to emphasize that the Court's holding today is limited to the context of a professional nursing school. *Ante,* at n.7. Since the Court's opinion relies heavily on its finding that women have traditionally dominated the nursing profession, it suggests that a State might well be justified in maintaining, for example, the option of an all-women's business school or liberal arts program.

JUSTICE BLACKMUN, dissenting.

Unless Mississippi University for Women wished to preserve an historical anachronism, one only states the obvious when he observes that the University long ago should have replaced its original statement of purpose and brought its corporate papers into the twentieth century. It failed to do so and, perhaps in partial consequence, finds itself in this litigation, with the Court's opinion, *ante,* at n.1, now taking full advantage of that failure, to MUW's embarrassment and discomfiture.

Despite that failure, times have changed in the intervening 98 years. What was once an "Institute and College" is now a genuine university, with a two-year School of Nursing established 11 years ago and then expanded to a four-year baccalaureate program in 1974. But respondent Hogan "wants in" at this particular location in his home city of Columbus. It is not enough that his State of Mississippi offers baccalaureate programs in nursing open to males at Jackson and at Hattiesburg. Mississippi thus has not closed the doors of its educational system to males like Hogan. Assuming that he is qualified—and I have no reason whatsoever to doubt his qualifications—those doors are open and his maleness alone does not prevent his gaining the additional education he professes to seek.

I have come to suspect that it is easy to go too far with rigid rules in this area of claimed sex discrimination, and to lose—indeed destroy—values that mean much to some people by forbidding the State from offering them a choice while not depriving others of an alternate choice. JUSTICE POWELL in his separate opinion advances this theme well.

While the Court purports to write narrowly, declaring that it does not decide the same issue with respect to "separate but equal" undergraduate institutions for females and males, *ante,* at n.1, or with respect to units of MUW other than its School of Nursing, *ante,* at n.7, there is inevitable spillover from the Court's ruling today. That ruling, it seems to me, places in constitutional jeopardy any state-supported educational institution that confines its student body in any area to members of one sex, even though the State elsewhere provides an equivalent program to the complaining applicant. The Court's reasoning does not stop with the School of Nursing of the Mississippi University for Women.

I hope that we do not lose all values that some think are worthwhile (and are not based on differences of race or religion) and relegate ourselves to needless conformity. The ringing words of the Equal Protection Clause of the Fourteenth Amendment—what JUSTICE POWELL aptly describes as its "liberating spirit,"—do not demand that price.

JUSTICE POWELL, with whom JUSTICE REHNQUIST joins, dissenting.

The Court's opinion bows deeply to conformity. Left without honor—indeed, held unconstitutional—is an element of diversity that has characterized much of American education and enriched much of American life. The Court in effect holds today that no State now may provide even a single institution of higher learning open only to women students. It gives no heed to the efforts of the State of Mississippi to provide abundant opportunities for young men and young women to attend coeducational institutions, and none to the preferences of the more than 40,000 young women who over the years have evidenced their approval of an all-women's college by choosing Mississippi University for Women (MUW) over seven coeducational universities within the State. The Court decides

today that the Equal Protection Clause makes it unlawful for the State to provide women with a traditionally popular and respected choice of educational environment. It does so in a case instituted by one man, who represents no class, and whose primary concern is personal convenience.

It is undisputed that women enjoy complete equality of opportunity in Mississippi's public system of higher education. Of the State's eight universities and 16 junior colleges, all except MUW are coeducational. At least two other Mississippi universities would have provided respondent with the nursing curriculum that he wishes to pursue. No other male has joined in his complaint. The only groups with any personal acquaintance with MUW to file *amicus* briefs are female students and alumnae of MUW. And they have emphatically rejected respondent's arguments, urging that the State of Mississippi be allowed to continue offering the choice from which they have benefited.

Nor is respondent significantly disadvantaged by MUW's all-female tradition. His constitutional complaint is based upon a single asserted harm: that he must *travel* to attend the state-supported nursing schools that concededly are available to him. The Court characterizes this injury as one of "inconvenience." *Ante,* at n.8. This description is fair and accurate, though somewhat embarrassed by the fact that there is, of course, no constitutional right to attend a state-supported university in one's home town. Thus the Court, to redress respondent's injury of inconvenience, must rest its invalidation of MUW's single-sex program on a mode of "sexual stereotype" reasoning that has no application whatever to the respondent or to the "wrong" of which he complains. At best this is anomalous. And ultimately the anomaly reveals legal error—that of applying a heightened equal protection standard, developed in cases of genuine sexual stereotyping, to a narrowly utilized state classification that provides an *additional* choice for women. Moreover, I believe that Mississippi's educational system should be upheld in this case even if this inappropriate method of analysis is applied.

I

Coeducation, historically, is a novel educational theory. From grade school through high school, college, and graduate and professional training, much of the nation's population during much of our history has been educated in sexually segregated classrooms. At the college level, for instance, until recently some of the most prestigious colleges and universities—including most of the Ivy League—had long histories of single-sex education. As Harvard, Yale, and Princeton remained all-male colleges well into the second half of this century, the "Seven Sister" institutions established a parallel standard of excellence for women's colleges. . . . Harvard and Radcliffe maintained separate admissions policies as recently as 1975.[2]

The sexual segregation of students has been a reflection of, rather than an imposition upon, the preference of those subject to the policy. It cannot be disputed, for example, that the highly qualified women attending the leading women's colleges could have earned admission to virtually any college of their choice.[3] Women attending such

colleges have chosen to be there, usually expressing a preference for the special benefits of single-sex institutions. Similar decisions were made by the colleges that elected to remain open to women only.[4]

The arguable benefits of single-sex colleges also continue to be recognized by students of higher education. The Carnegie Commission on Higher Education has reported that it "favor[s] the continuation of colleges for women. They provide an element of diversity . . . and [an environment in which women] generally . . . speak up more in their classes, . . . hold more positions of leadership on campus, . . . and have more role models and mentors among women teachers and administrators." Carnegie Report, *supra,* quoted in K. Davidson, R. Ginsburg, & H. Kay, *Sex-Based Discrimination* 814 (1975 ed.). A 10-year empirical study by the Cooperative Institutional Research Program of the American Counsel of Education and the University of California, Los Angeles also has affirmed the distinctive benefits of single-sex colleges and

---

2. The history, briefly summarized above, of single-sex higher education in the Northeast is duplicated in other States. I mention only my State of Virginia, where even today Hollins College, Mary Baldwin College, Randolph Macon Woman's College, and Sweet Briar College remain all women's. Each has a proud and respected reputation of quality education.

3. It is true that historically many institutions of higher education—particularly in the East and South—were single-sex. To these extents,

choices were by no means universally available to all men and women. But choices always were substantial, and the purpose of relating the experience of our country with single-sex colleges and universities is to document what should be obvious: generations of Americans, including scholars, have thought—wholly without regard to any discriminatory animus—that there were distinct advantages in this type of higher education.

4. In announcing Wellesley's decision in 1973 to remain a women's college, President Barbara Newell said that "[t]he research we have clearly demonstrates that women's colleges produce a disproportionate number of women leaders and women in responsible positions in society; it does demonstrate that the higher proportion of women on the faculty the higher the motivation for women students." Carnegie Report, *supra,* in Babcock *et al., Sex Discrimination and the Law,* at 1014. . . .

universities. As summarized in A. Astin, *Four Critical Years* 232 (1977), the data established that

> [b]oth [male and female] single-sex colleges facilitate student involvement in several areas: academic, interaction with faculty, and verbal aggressiveness. . . . Men's and women's colleges also have a positive effect on intellectual self-esteem. Students at single-sex colleges are more satisfied than students at coeducational colleges with virtually all aspects of college life. . . . The only area where students are less satisfied is social life.

Despite the continuing expressions that single-sex institutions may offer singular advantages to their students, there is no doubt that coeducational institutions are far more numerous. But their numerical predominance does not establish—in any sense properly cognizable by a court—that individual preferences for single-sex education are misguided or illegitimate, or that a State may not provide its citizens with a choice.

II

This issue in this case is whether a State transgresses the Constitution when—within the context of a public system that offers a diverse range of campuses, curricula, and educational alternatives—it seeks to accommodate the legitimate personal preferences of those desiring the advantages of an all-women's college. In my view, the Court errs seriously by assuming—without argument or discussion—that the equal protection standard generally applicable to sex discrimination is appropriate here. That standard was designed to free women from "archaic and overbroad generalizations. . . ." *Schlesinger v. Ballard,* 419 U.S. 498, 508 (1975). In no previous case have we applied it to invalidate state efforts

to *expand* women's choices. Nor are there prior sex discrimination decisions by this Court in which a male plaintiff, as in this case, had the choice of an equal benefit.

The cases cited by the Court therefore do not control the issue now before us. In most of them women were given no opportunity for the same benefit as men. Cases involving male plaintiffs are equally inapplicable. In *Craig v. Boren,* 429 U.S. 190 (1976), a male under 21 was not permitted to buy beer anywhere in the State, and women were afforded no choice as to whether they would accept the "statistically measured but loose-fitting generalities concerning the drinking tendencies of aggregate groups." *Id.* at 209. A similar situation prevailed in *Orr v. Orr,* 440 U.S. 268, 279 (1979), where men had no opportunity to seek alimony from their divorced wives, and women had no escape from the statute's stereotypical announcement of "the State's preference for an allocation of family responsibilities under which the wife plays a dependent role. . . ."

By applying heightened equal protection analysis to this case, the Court frustrates the liberating spirit of the Equal Protection Clause. It forbids the States from providing women with an opportunity to choose the type of university they prefer. And yet it is these women whom the Court regards as the *victims* of an illegal, stereotyped perception of the role of women in our society. The Court reasons this way in a case in which no woman has complained, and the only complainant is a man who advances no claims on behalf of anyone else. His claim, it should be recalled, is not that he is being denied a substantive educational opportunity, or even the right to attend an all-male or a coeducational college. It is *only* that the colleges open to him are located at inconvenient distances.[11]

11. Students in respondent's position, in "being denied the right to attend the State college in

III

The Court views this case as presenting a serious equal protection claim of sex discrimination. I do not, and I would sustain Mississippi's right to continue MUW on a rational basis analysis. But I need not apply this "lowest tier" of scrutiny. I can accept for present purposes the standard applied by the Court: that there is a gender-based distinction that must serve an important governmental objective by means that are substantially related to its achievement. *E.g., Wengler v. Druggists Mutual Ins. Co.*, 446 U.S. 142, 150 (1980). The record in this case reflects that MUW has a historic position in the State's educational system dating back to 1884. More than 2,000 women presently evidence their preference for MUW by having enrolled there. The choice is one that discriminates invidiously against no one. And the State's purpose in preserving that choice is legitimate and substantial. Generations of our finest minds, both among educators and students, have believed that single-sex, college-level institutions afford distinctive benefits. There are many persons, of course, who have different views. But simply because there are these differences is no reason—certainly none of constitutional dimension—to conclude that no substantial state interest is served when such a choice is made available.

In arguing to the contrary, the Court suggests that the MUW is so operated as to "perpetuate the stereotyped view of nursing as an exclusively women's job." But as the Court itself acknowledges, MUW's School of Nursing was not created until 1971—about 90 years after the single-sex campus itself was founded. This hardly supports a link between nursing as a woman's profession and MUW's single-sex admission policy. Indeed, MUW's School of Nursing was not instituted until more than a decade *after* a separate School of Nursing was established at the coeducational University of Mississippi at Jackson. The School of Nursing makes up only one part—a relatively small part—of MUW's diverse modern university campus and curriculum. The other departments on the MUW campus offer a typical range of degrees and a typical range of subjects. There is no indication that women suffer fewer opportunities at other Mississippi state campuses because of MUW's admission policy.

In sum, the practice of voluntarily chosen single-sex education is an honored tradition in our country, even if it now rarely exists in state colleges and universities. Mississippi's accommodation of such student choices is legitimate because it is completely consensual and is important because it permits students to decide for themselves the type of college education they think will benefit them most. Finally, Mississippi's policy is substantially related to its long-respected objective.[17]

their home town, are treated no differently than are other students who reside in communities many miles distant from any State supported college or university. The location of any such institution must necessarily inure to the benefit of some and to the detriment of others, depending upon the distance the affected individuals reside from the institution." *Heaton v. Bristol*, 317 S.W.2d 86, 99 (Tex. Civ. App. 1958), *cert. denied*, 359 U.S. 230 (1959), quoted in *Williams v. McNair*, 316 F. Supp. 134, 137 (DSC 1970), *aff'd mem.*, 401 U.S. 951 (1971).

17. The Court argues that MUW's means are not sufficiently related to its goal because it has allowed men to audit classes. The extent of record information is that men have audited 138 courses in the last 10 years. Brief for Respondent 21. On average, then, men have audited 14 courses a year. MUW's current annual catalog lists 913 courses offered in *one year.*

It is understandable that MUW might believe that it could allow men to audit courses without materially affecting its environment. MUW

IV

A distinctive feature of America's tradition has been respect for diversity. This has been characteristic of the peoples from numerous lands who have built our country. It is the essence of our democratic system. At stake in this case as I see it is the preservation of a small aspect of this diversity. But that aspect is by no means insignificant, given our heritage of available choice between single-sex and coeducational institutions of higher learning. The Court answers that there is discrimination—not just that which may be tolerable, as for example between those candidates for admission able to contribute most to an educational institution and those able to contribute less—but discrimination of constitutional dimension. But, having found "discrimination," the Court finds it difficult to identify the victims. It hardly can claim that women are discriminated against. A constitutional case is held to exist solely because one man found it inconvenient to travel to any of the other institutions made available to him by the State of Mississippi. In essence he insists that he has a right to attend a college in his home community. This simply is not a sex discrimination case. The Equal Protection Clause was never intended to be applied to this kind of case.[18]

to males seeking admission to schools other than the School of Nursing, violates the Fourteenth Amendment." This would be a welcome limitation if, in fact, it leaves MUW free to remain an all-women's university in each of its other schools and departments—which include four schools and more than a dozen departments. The question the Court does not answer is whether MUW may remain a women's university in every respect except its School of Nursing. This is a critical question for this university and its responsible board and officials. The Court holds today that they have deprived Hogan of constitutional rights because MUW is adjudged guilty of sex discrimination. The logic of the Court's entire opinion, apart from its statements mentioned above, appears to apply sweepingly to the entire university. The exclusion of men from the School of Nursing is repeatedly characterized as "gender-based discrimination," subject to the same standard of analysis applied in previous sex discrimination cases of this Court. Nor does the opinion anywhere deny that this analysis applies to the entire university.

The Court nevertheless purports to decide this case "narrow[ly]." Normally and properly we decide only the question presented. It seems to me that in fact the issue properly before us is the single-sex policy of the University, and it is this issue that I have addressed in this dissent. The Court of Appeals so viewed this case, and unambiguously held that a single-sex state institution of higher education no longer is permitted by the Constitution. I see no principled way—in light of the Court's rationale—to reach a different result with respect to other MUW schools and departments. But given the Court's insistence that its decision applies only to the School of Nursing, it is my view that the Board and officials of MUW may continue to operate the remainder of the University on a single-sex basis without fear of personal liability. The standard of such liability is whether the conduct of the official "violate[s] clearly established statutory or constitutional rights of which a reasonable person would have known". *Harlow v. Fitzgerald*, —— U.S. ——, —— (1982). The Court today leaves in doubt the reach of its decision.

---

charges tuition but gives no academic credit for auditing. The University evidently is correct in believing that few men will choose to audit under such circumstances. This deviation from a perfect relationship between means and ends is insubstantial.

18. The Court, in the opening and closing sentences and note 7 of its opinion, states the issue in terms only of a "professional nursing school" and "decline[s] to address the question of whether MUW's admissions policy, as applied

CASE QUESTIONS

1. According to Justice O'Connor, Hogan suffers gender discrimination as compared to others who live in his region because they can pursue a nursing degree at a state college within commuting distance if they are female, but he cannot. According to Justice Powell, he suffers no gender discrimination because many females in the state share with him the dilemma of not living within commuting distance of a state college where they can pursue a nursing degree. Who is correct?

2. Could Mississippi satisfy the Court's objections by still keeping Joe Hogan out of MUW but admitting him to an all-male nursing college set up elsewhere in the state? If not, what is the meaning of O'Connor's footnote 1? If so, would that be a case of two wrongs making a right?

CASENOTE

Shortly after this decision was handed down, a local Philadelphia judge ordered Central High to admit females.

For further discussion of Title IX, the federal statute prohibiting sex discrimination in educational programs that receive federal funds, see *Grove City v. Bell*, in chapter 5.

CHAPTER 4

**Women, Procreation,
and the Right of Privacy**

Substantive Due Process and Implied Rights

What is probably the most hotly debated women's rights issue in America has
nothing to do with gender-based discrimination. The political controversy over a
woman's right to have an abortion did not cease in 1973 when the Supreme Court
"found" that right in the Constitution, and the controversy does not seem to be
waning. The fact that women are lined up on both sides of the abortion issue
does not remove the issue from the category of women's rights. There are women
who oppose the ERA, too.

That the abortion question is a matter of *women's* rights is abundantly demonstrated in the case of *Planned Parenthood v. Danforth* (1976), which addressed
the specific question whether the father of a fetus could stop its mother from
obtaining an abortion. Was the right to abort a right only of the unified parental
couple or a right of the mother? If it were the former, the potential father would
have absolute veto power over the potential mother's decision. The Supreme
Court's answer was clear: freedom to choose an abortion is a woman's right, not
her husband's right.

This right derives from the constitutional right of privacy. One cannot find
"the right of privacy" anywhere in the letter of the Constitution; it is one of a
small group of implied rights that the Supreme Court has found or invented or
inferred or imagined somewhere in the spirit of that document. For the reader to
decide whether the Court should be engaging in this business of inferring or discovering or inventing "constitutional" rights, a review of the history of other implied constitutional rights may be helpful.

Chapter 1 dealt with cases in which a constitutional right called "liberty of
contract" was said to be at issue. "Liberty of contract" is mentioned nowhere in
the Constitution. Nevertheless, conservative Supreme Court majorities, beginning with the *Lochner v. New York* (1905) case, found it lurking somewhere in the
shadows of the due process clauses of the Fifth and Fourteenth Amendments.

Those clauses command that "liberty" shall not be taken "without due process of law." These justices inferred from that brief command that certain specific

liberties, such as the right to contract freely in lawful business matters, were so fundamental to the American way of life that "due process" required extraordinarily strong justification before any restriction on them could be upheld.[1] For example, the dangers to health attendant to working in a coal mine (*Holden v. Hardy* [1898]) constituted strong enough justification to uphold an hours limit on the working day of miners; however, the dangers to health, public or private, attendant to working long hours in a bakery (*Lochner v. New York* [1905]) did not constitute, according to five Supreme Court justices, a "reasonable ground for interfering with . . . the right of free contract" to the extent of imposing a ten-hour day on bakers.

This use of the due process clause to strike down statutes on the basis of *substantive* or *content* considerations (i.e., on the basis of the substantive question of which liberty was being restricted) became known as "substantive due process." Specifically with regard to cases involving liberty of contract, it became known as "economic substantive due process."

Economic substantive due process has been thoroughly discredited since the late 1940s. It is an abandoned doctrine in American law. It was criticized on at least three different grounds. First, liberal partisans condemned it for policy reasons: the doctrine was employed repeatedly to strike down statutes that liberals (as well as legislative majorities and, probably, popular majorities) believed to be in the public interest.

Second, it was condemned because, in introducing the notion of unwritten constitutional rights into American jurisprudence, it turned judges into nonelected legislators, even nonelected Founding Fathers. By releasing the Supreme Court from the written text of the Constitution, the concept of implied rights could inevitably unleash subjective prejudices to reshape the Constitution in whatever direction the prevailing winds of judicial prejudices tended to push it. Justice Holmes expressed this criticism of economic substantive due process as follows:

> A constitution is not intended to embody a particular economic theory, whether of paternalism and the organic relation of the citizen to the State, or of *laissez faire*.[2]

A third criticism was closely related to the second. In implicitly postulating that some rights were more fundamental to the American system than others,[3] economic substantive due process introduced an additional subjective element into American jurisprudence. Who was to decide which parts of "liberty" were fundamental, and by what test? The due process clause mentions "life, liberty, and property"; it does not rank some liberties above others. Yet the Supreme Court majority of the early twentieth century seemed to be engaging in just such a ranking of liberties, and that majority provided no explanation why the "right to labor or the right of contract" happened to rank near the top of their list.

It was during the heyday of economic substantive due process that the Supreme Court began to infer additional substantive liberties into the due process clause—some of which liberties have textual referents in the First Amendment, but others of which can be found nowhere in the text of the Constitution. In 1923, in the *Meyer v. Nebraska* case, the Court majority announced that the word "liberty" in the due process clause

> connotes not merely freedom from bodily restraint but also the right of the individual to contract, to engage in any of the common occupations of life, to acquire useful knowledge, to marry, establish a home and bring up children, to worship God according to the dictates of his own conscience. . . .[4]

This litany of implied rights, according to Justice McReynolds, included the right of pupils "to acquire knowledge" and of parents "to control the education of their own."

In a 1925 case, *Pierce v. Society of Sisters*,[5] in unanimously striking down an Oregon law that required all children to attend public schools, the Supreme Court reaffirmed "the liberty of parents . . . to direct the upbringing and education of children under their control." The Constitution nowhere mentions such a right, and yet not a single justice dissented.[6] By this time both the doctrine of substantive due process and the concept of implied rights were securely fixed in American constitutional firmament.

During the 1920s and 1930s the Supreme Court gradually added to the barrel of substantive-due-process-protected liberties each of the freedoms mentioned in the First Amendment: freedom of speech[7] and of the press,[8] right to peaceable assembly,[9] freedom for free exercise of religion,[10] and freedom from establishment of religion.[11] Nevertheless, during the 1930s and 1940s, the liberty-of-contract apples in that same barrel had begun to smell noticeably rotten. The aforementioned legal criticisms of economic substantive due process were gaining additional adherents under the economic pressures of the Great Depression and the political pressures stemming from electoral victories of the New Dealers.

Although the policy-oriented condemnation of economic substantive due process did not necessarily extend to substantive due process decisions involving civil liberties, the two other criticisms of substantive due process did present problems. In abandoning the old rule that there was a constitutional right to "freedom of contract," the 1937 Court majority said bluntly: "What is this freedom? The Constitution did not speak of freedom of contract."[12] Yet the Court never addressed a similar critique to the other unmentioned freedoms that it had begun to protect: freedom to acquire knowledge, to marry, to establish a home, and to guide the education of one's children. The Supreme Court retained these other implied freedoms even as it abandoned the one no-longer-implied freedom that had carved out the path for these others.

The addition of the specifically itemized First Amendment freedoms (as distinguished from these unmentioned freedoms) into the substantive due process barrel did provide its own answer to the question: Why single out some parts of liberty for special treatment when the Fourteenth Amendment itself refers only to "liberty" in general and subjects all liberty to the same phrase, "due process of law"? The Constitution, after all, had singled out the First Amendment liberties, had included them at the head of the Bill of Rights, and had strengthened them with language among the most emphatic in the Constitution ("Congress shall make no law . . . abridging"). Thus, special protection for *these* freedoms had a textual basis that was lacking in such claims as the assertion that one has a constitutional "right" to work a twelve-hour day.

In an attempt to develop a more comprehensive explanation why the Court should retain the doctrine of substantive due process, and its related strict scrutiny approach, in matters of civil liberties while rejecting them in economic matters, Justice Stone produced the most famous footnote in Supreme Court history. In it he suggested that something more than a "reasonableness" justification was demanded by "due process" (1) when "legislation appears on its face to be within one of the specific prohibitions of the Bill of Rights," and that it also might be demanded (2) when legislation restricts those political processes essential to the functioning of a democratic law-making process (e.g., the right to vote), and (3) when legislation seems to attack "discrete and insular minorities" such as racial or religious groups.[13] To Justice Stone, and to the post–1937 Supreme Court majority, *due process* meant those liberties essential to a *democratic political process*. Stone's explanation made no reference to the marriage and child-rearing rights established in the early 1920s. Whether those were dead letters in American legal history was not to become clear for another few decades.[14]

Before the Supreme Court returned to the matter of constitutional rights involving family life, the Court found a few more implied rights in the Constitution. Some, like the right to vote[15] and the right of political association,[16] were closely linked, or linkable, to specific phrases in the Constitution. One, the right to travel, had no visible basis in the text of the Constitution.

The Articles of Confederation had provided that "the people of each State shall have free ingress and regress to and from any other State," but the Constitution contains no such statement. Nonetheless, in 1868[17] the Supreme Court invalidated a Nevada tax on passengers leaving the state via commercial transportation. Such legislation violated either the implied message of the Commerce Clause[18] that the states may not impose undue burdens on the free flow of commerce among the states or else the implied message of the very national structure of government: that all citizens of the nation may travel freely within the nation.[19] From the perspective of the individual citizen, the implication of these messages was that every person had a right to be free from undue, state-imposed burdens on his or her travel among the states.

In 1941 the Supreme Court based a decision squarely on this implication, when it declared unconstitutional California's anti-Okie law, which barred entry into the state by "indigent" migrants.[20] Four of the justices in that decision, not comfortable with basing a personal right to travel on Congress' power over commerce, urged (in a concurring opinion by Justice Jackson) that the right of free interstate travel should be viewed as one of the privileges and immunities of national citizenship protected by the Privileges or Immunities Clause of the Fourteenth Amendment. Additional indirect textual support for a constitutional right of free interstate travel can be found in the Article IV, section 2, clause 1 command that out-of-state citizens must be entitled to the "privileges and immunities" of in-state citizens upon arriving in a new state.

The Commerce Clause justification for claiming a "right to travel" can restrict state legislation that interferes with travel, but naturally it cannot be the basis for restricting Congress' own power to regulate travel (which is a part of commerce). Nonetheless, the Supreme Court has ruled that even Congress must observe constitutional constraints in regulating the travel of Americans. In 1958, in a case involving the denial of passports to American leftists,[21] the Court announced that the "right to travel" is a "constitutional right" protected not only against state abridgement but also, via the Fifth Amendment due process clause, against congressional abridgement. The Court majority opinion for that case traced the right all the way back to the Magna Carta and asserted that it is "basic in our scheme of values."

In a more fully developed discussion of the right to travel, in a 1964 case[22] the Supreme Court declared that when statutes swept "*unnecessarily* broadly . . . [into] the area of protected freedoms," they must be declared void. (Emphasis added.) The Court thereby struck down a congressional prohibition on foreign travel by American communists. This "necessity" test was just another formulation of the strict scrutiny test: legislation that interferes with a fundamental right, if it is to be upheld, must be necessitated by (not just reasonably related to) an overriding governmental interest. By 1964, then, at least five justices on the Court were still willing to use substantive due process to strike down statutes, and to use it even for *unwritten* "constitutional" rights. The only explanation offered by the Court for according this strong protection to the right to travel was the brief statement that "freedom of travel is a constitutional liberty closely related to rights of free speech and association."[23]

Sterilization

Meanwhile, those other unwritten constitutional rights that had been established in the early 1920s—the right to marry, to establish a home, and to rear children as one sees fit—remained shrouded in silence for a forty-year period.

Even when the Supreme Court handed down two decisions (one in 1927 and one in 1942) that arguably affected the right to marry and bring up children, the judges continued to ignore these early precedents. Both decisions involved compulsory sterilization statutes.

The first of these, *Buck v. Bell* (1927), upheld a Virginia law mandating the sterilization of inmates of state institutions for the feeble-minded. The law itself contained the conclusion that "experience has shown that heredity plays an important part in the transmission of insanity, imbecility, etc." The statute then provided that a superintendent at one of the state institutions for these people, when he or she believed "that it is for the best interests of the patients and of society," could order the sexual sterilization of any inmate who "was afflicted with hereditary forms of insanity, imbecility, etc."

Various procedural "safeguards" were provided in the statute. The superintendent had to petition the board of directors of the hospital or "colony" for permission for the operation. The would-be victim of the sterilization was given notice of the hearing and was permitted to attend it, as was his or her guardian; if the inmate was a minor, his or her parents were also notified of the hearing. All evidence presented at the hearing was to be put in writing and could be made the basis of an appeal to the circuit court of the county. Further appeal, before the operation would take place, was also available to the Virginia Supreme Court of Appeals.

A recent article on the case argues that scholars and reporters who later visited Carrie Buck (the woman whose sterilization was contested) all found her to be of "obviously normal intelligence." A careful study of the commitment hearing transcript revealed that no evidence of feeble-mindedness was even presented. Instead the commitment seems to have been on account of her pregnancy. Carrie Buck, the daughter of a woman who had borne several illegitimate children, was raised by foster parents, apparently raped by a relative of her foster parents, and then "sent away" to have her baby. The only evidence that Carrie Buck's daughter was mentally deficient was that a Red Cross social worker had looked it over at the age of seven months and claimed, "There is a look about it that is not quite normal. . . . It seems very apathetic and not responsive."[24] None of these facts appears in the decision of the appellate courts, nor do they appear to have been considered by the U.S. Supreme Court.

In appealing the decision of Superintendent Bell of the State Colony of Epileptics and Feeble Minded to have her sterilized, Carrie Buck did not contest the procedural arrangements of the statute. Her attorney argued instead that in its substance it violated "her constitutional right of bodily integrity," thereby violating the substantive implications of the due process clause. None of the courts, including the U.S. Supreme Court, were persuaded by these arguments. In an opinion supported by a total of eight Supreme Court justices, here is how Justice Oliver Wendell Holmes responded to Carrie Buck's plea that she not be sterilized:

Buck v. Bell, 274 U.S. 200 (1927)

MR. JUSTICE HOLMES delivered the opinion of the Court.

. . .

Carrie Buck is a feeble minded white woman who was committed to the State Colony above mentioned in due form. She is the daughter of a feeble minded mother in the same institution, and the mother of an illegitimate feeble minded child. She was eighteen years old at the time of the trial of her case in the Circuit Court, in the latter part of 1924.

. . . It seems to be contended that in no circumstances could such an order be justified. It certainly is contended that the order cannot be justified upon the existing grounds. The judgment finds the facts that have been recited and that Carrie Buck "is the probable potential parent of socially inadequate offspring, likewise afflicted, that she may be sexually sterilized without detriment to her general health and that her welfare and that of society will be promoted by her sterilization," and thereupon makes the order. In view of the general declarations of the legislature and the specific findings of the Court, obviously we cannot say as matter of law that the grounds do not exist, and if they exist they justify the result. We have seen more than once that the public welfare may call upon the best citizens for their lives. It would be strange if it could not call upon those who already sap the strength of the State for these lesser sacrifices, often not felt to be such by those concerned, in order to prevent our being swamped with incompetence. It is better for all the world, if instead of waiting to execute degenerate offspring for crime, or to let them starve for their imbecility, society can prevent those who are manifestly unfit from continuing their kind. The principle that sustains compulsory vaccination is broad enough to cover cutting the Fallopian tubes. *Jacobson v. Massachusetts*, 197 U.S. 11. Three generations of imbeciles are enough. . . .

[Holmes then rejected the argument that it denied equal protection to sterilize only feeble-minded inmates of state institutions rather than all feeble-minded persons.]

MR. JUSTICE BUTLER dissents.

[No written opinion.]

CASE QUESTIONS

1. Are there differences of constitutional dimension between a statute that orders smallpox vaccinations and a statute that orders sterilization? Should there be?

2. Could Justice Holmes' reasoning have been used to sustain compulsory sterilization of all persons whose IQ was below 90, because certain scientists have asserted that IQ is largely hereditary? Could it be used to sustain compulsory sterilization of any second-generation "welfare mother"? It is easy to argue that such programs would be morally

wrong (even abhorrent), but is there anything in the Constitution itself that forbids them? Is the phrase "due process of law" really broad enough to forbid all immoral laws? Should the Constitution be amended so that it would expressly forbid involuntarily sterilizations?

3. If a particular form of retardation were known to be 90 percent genetically transmissible, would that justify state sterilization? What about 50 percent?

Once the Supreme Court had declared that the "socially inadequate" could be forcibly sterilized, it certainly seemed plausible to state legislatures that the Court would also uphold forced sterilizations of persons convicted of serious crime. In 1935 Oklahoma adopted the Habitual Criminal Sterilization Act. That act defined "habitual criminals" as person who were convicted three times of "felonies involving moral turpitude" and ordered that such criminals be sexually sterilized on request of the state's attorney general. A court hearing (including the right of jury trial) in advance of the operation was required, but the only "defenses" available to the potential sterilization victim were (1) that his or her "general health" would suffer from the operation or (2) that he or she did not meet the state's legal definition of "habitual criminal." Certain felonies were expressly excluded from the "moral turpitude" category: "offenses arising out of the violation of the prohibitory laws, revenue acts, embezzlement, or political offenses."

Jack T. Skinner was convicted on three different occasions for crimes of "moral turpitude": chicken stealing in 1926, armed robbery in 1929, and armed robbery again in 1934. The state instituted sterilization proceedings against him in 1935, and he appealed the jury's pro-vasectomy decision to the Oklahoma Supreme Court. That court upheld the decision in a 5–4 decision, and he tried again at the U.S. Supreme Court. This time the U.S. Supreme Court (only fifteen years after turning deaf ears to Carrie Buck's pleas) unanimously agreed that the sterilization statute was unconstitutional.

It is worth noting that at the time of the *Skinner v. Oklahoma* (1942) decision, the United States was engaged in a declared war against the combined forces of world fascism. The Court was not unaware of the popularity of eugenics theories among the nation's enemy. However, the Court, despite its kind treatment of Mr. Skinner, did not go so far as to overrule *Buck v. Bell*. Instead, *Buck v. Bell* was still cited as a viable precedent by every justice who authored an opinion in the *Skinner* case.

The Supreme Court's opinion in the *Skinner* case relied not on the morally abhorrent implications of compulsory sterilization but rather on the equal protection problems raised by sterilizing some criminals and not others. It is extremely uncommon for the Court to interfere with state decisions about the severity of criminal penalties, and even less common for the Court to interfere with them on the basis of the equal protection clause. "Equal protection of the laws" has never been read as requiring that all states impose the same sentence on all perpetrators of a particular criminal offense.[25] Yet the basis of this decision was the premise that the equal protection clause forbade Oklahoma to impose substantially different penalties for substantially similar crimes. This level of interference with the state's basic police power is incomprehensible without reference to the Court's obvious revulsion for compulsory sterilization.

That revulsion is evident in both the Douglas majority opinion and the Stone and Jackson concurring opinions. All three imply that laws affecting "one of the basic civil rights of man"—"the right to have offspring"—will be subjected to strict scrutiny (whether under the equal protection clause, the due process clause, or both). Yet none of the opinions suggest any desire to overrule *Buck v. Bell*. Why they do not remains something of a mystery.

Skinner v. Oklahoma, 316 U.S. 535 (1942)

MR. JUSTICE DOUGLAS delivered the opinion of the Court.

This case touches a sensitive and important area of human rights. Oklahoma deprives certain individuals of a right which is basic to the perpetuation of a race—the right to have offspring.
. . . [T]here is a feature of the Act which clearly condemns it. That is, its failure to meet the requirements of the equal protection clause of the Fourteenth Amendment.
We do not stop to point out all of the inequalities in this Act. A few examples will suffice. In Oklahoma, grand larceny is a felony. Okla. Stats. Ann. tit. 21 §§ 1705, 5. Larceny is grand larceny when the property taken exceeds $20 in value. *Id.* § 1704. Embezzlement is punishable "in the manner prescribed for feloniously stealing property of the value of that embezzled." *Id.* § 1462. Hence, he who embezzles property worth more than $20 is guilty of a felony. A clerk who appropriates over $20 from his employer's till (*id.* § 1456) and a stranger who steals the same amount are thus both guilty of felonies. If the latter repeats his act and is convicted three times, he may be sterilized. But the clerk is not subject to the pains and penalties of the Act no matter how large his embezzlement nor how frequent his convictions.
. . . [I]f we had here only a question as to a State's classification of crimes, such as embezzlement or larceny, no substantial federal question would be raised. *See Moore v. Missouri*, 159 U.S. 673; *Hawker v. New York*, 170 U.S. 189; *Finley v. California*, 222 U.S. 28; *Patsone v. Pennsylvania, supra*. For a State is not constrained in the exercise of its police power to ignore experience which marks a class of offenders or a family of offenses for special treatment. Nor is it prevented by the equal protection clause from confining "its restrictions to those classes of cases where the need is deemed to be clearest." *Miller v. Wilson*, 236 U.S. 373, 384. And *see McLean v. Arkansas*, 211 U.S. 539. . . .

But the instant legislation runs afoul of the equal protection clause, though we give Oklahoma that large deference which the rule of the foregoing cases requires. We are dealing here with legislation which involves one of the basic civil rights of man. Marriage and procreation are fundamental to the very existence and survival of the race. The power to sterilize, if exercised, may have subtle, far-reaching and devastating effects. In evil or reckless hands it can cause races or types which are inimical to the dominant group to wither and disappear. There is no redemption for the individual whom the law touches. Any experiment which the State conducts is to his irreparable injury. He is forever deprived of a basic liberty. We mention these matters not to reexamine the scope of the police power of the States. We advert to them merely in emphasis of our view that strict scrutiny of the classification which a State makes in a sterilization law is essential, lest unwittingly, or otherwise, invidious discriminations are made against groups or types of individuals in violation of the constitutional guaranty of just and equal laws. The guaranty of "equal protection of the laws is a pledge of the protection of equal laws." *Yick Wo v. Hopkins*, 118 U.S. 356, 369. When the law lays an unequal hand on those who have committed intrinsically the same quality of offense and sterilizes one and not the other, it has made as invidious a discrimination as if it had selected a particular race or nationality for oppressive treatment. *Yick Wo v. Hopkins, supra; Gaines v. Canada*, 305 U.S. 337. Sterilization of those who have thrice committed grand larceny, with immunity for those who are embezzlers, is a clear, pointed, unmistakable discrimination. Oklahoma makes no attempt to say that he who commits larceny by trespass or trick or fraud has biologically inheritable traits which he who commits embezzlement lacks. . . .

We have not the slightest basis for inferring that line has any significance in eugenics, nor that the inheritability of criminal traits follows the neat legal distinctions which the law has marked between those two offenses. In terms of fines and imprisonment, the crimes of larceny and embezzlement rate the same under the Oklahoma code. Only when it comes to sterilization are the pains and penalties of the law different. The equal protection clause would indeed be a formula of empty words if such conspicuously artificial lines could be drawn. *See Smith v. Wayne Probate Judges*, 231 Mich. 409, 420–21, 204 N.W. 40. In *Buck v. Bell* the Virginia statute was upheld though it applied only to feeble-minded persons in institutions of the State. But it was pointed out that "so far as the operations enable those who otherwise must be kept confined to be returned to the world, and thus open the asylum to others, the equality aimed at will be more nearly reached." 274 U.S., at 208. Here there is no such saving feature. Embezzlers are forever free. Those who steal or take in other ways are not.

Reversed.

MR. CHIEF JUSTICE STONE, concurring:

I concur in the result, but I am not persuaded that we are aided in reaching it by recourse to the equal protection clause.

If Oklahoma may resort generally to the sterilization of criminals on the assumption that their propensities are transmissible to future generations by inheritance, I seriously doubt that the equal protection clause requires it to apply the measure to all criminals in the first instance, or to none. *See Rosenthal v. New York* 226 U.S. 260, 271; *Keokee Coke Co. v. Taylor*, 234 U.S. 224, 227; *Patsone v. Pennsylvania*, 232 U.S. 138, 144.

Moreover, if we must presume that the legislature knows—what science has been unable to ascertain—that the criminal tendencies of any class of habitual offenders are transmissible regardless of the varying mental characteristics of its individuals, I should suppose that we must likewise presume that the legislature, in its wisdom, knows that the criminal tendencies of some classes of offenders are more likely to be transmitted than those of others. And so I think the real question we have to consider is not one of equal protection, but whether the wholesale condemnation of a class to such an invasion of personal liberty without opportunity to any individual to show that his is not the type of case which would justify resort to it, satisfies the demands of due process.

There are limits to the extent to which the presumption of constitutionality can be pressed, especially where the liberty of the person is concerned (*see United States v. Carolene Products Co.*, 304 U.S. 144, 152, n.4) and where the presumption is resorted to only to dispense with a procedure which the ordinary dictates of prudence would seem to demand for the protection of the individual from arbitrary action. Although petitioner here was given a hearing to ascertain whether sterilization would be detrimental to his health, he has given none to discover whether his criminal tendencies are of an inheritable type. Undoubtedly a state may, after appropriate inquiry, constitutionally interfere with the personal liberty of the individual to prevent the transmission by inheritance of his socially injurious tendencies. *Buck v. Bell*, 274 U.S. 200. But until now we have not been called upon to say that it may do so without giving him a hearing and opportunity to challenge the existence as to him of the only facts which could justify so drastic a measure.

Science has found and the law has recognized that there are certain types of mental deficiency associated with delinquency which are inheritable. But the State does not contend—nor can there be any pretense—that either common knowledge or experience, or scientific investigation, has given assurance that the criminal tendencies of any class of habitual offenders are universally or even generally inheritable. In such circumstances, inquiry whether such is the fact in the case of any particular individual cannot rightly be dispensed with. Whether the procedure by which a statute carries its mandate into execution satisfies due process is a matter of judicial cognizance. A law which condemns, without hearing, all the individuals of a class to so harsh a measure as the present because some or even many merit condemnation, is lacking in the first principles of due process. *Morrison v. California*, 291 U.S. 82, 90, and cases cited; *Taylor v. Georgia*, 315 U.S. 25. And so, while the state may protect itself from the demonstrably inheritable tendencies of the individual which are injurious to society, the most elementary notions of due process would seem to require it to take appropriate steps to safeguard the liberty of the individual by affording him, before he is condemned to an irreparable injury in his person, some opportunity to show that he is without such inheritable tendencies. . . .

MR. JUSTICE JACKSON, concurring:

I join the CHIEF JUSTICE in holding that the hearings provided are too limited in the context of the present Act to afford due process of law. I also agree with the opinion of MR. JUSTICE DOUGLAS that the scheme of classification set forth in the Act denies equal protection of the law. I disagree with the opinion of each in so far as it rejects or minimizes the grounds taken by the other. . . .

I also think the present plan to sterilize the individual in pursuit of a eugenic plan to eliminate from the race characteristics that are only vaguely identified and which in our present state of knowledge are uncertain as to transmissibility presents other constitutional questions of gravity. This Court has sustained such an experiment with respect to an imbecile, a person with definite and observable characteristics, where the condition had persisted through three generations and afforded grounds for the belief that it was transmissible and would continue to manifest itself in generations to come. *Buck v. Bell*, 274 U.S. 200.

There are limits to the extent to which a legislatively represented majority may conduct biological experiments at the expense of the dignity and personality and natural powers of a minority—even those who have been guilty of what the majority define as crimes. But this Act falls down before reaching this problem, which I mention only to avoid the implication that such a question may not exist because not discussed. On it I would also reserve judgment.

CASE QUESTIONS

1. If Oklahoma were to reenact this statute after restructuring its criminal penalties so that the jail sentence for grand larceny were twice as long as that for embezzlement, would that vitiate the Court majority's objection to this statute? If Oklahoma were to reenact this statute after removing the exemption clause for tax criminals, prohibition criminals, political criminals, and embezzlers, would that vitiate the majority's objection?

2. Suppose that social scientists concurred that a tendency to commit violent crime was hereditary in this sense: 1 in 1,000 people are convicted of violent crimes; but, 1 in 100 of the offspring of those convicted of violent crimes (even when adopted and raised by non-criminals) eventually are convicted of violent crimes. Is a tendency ten times that of the normal population, but only likely to strike 1 percent of the target population, grounds to prevent the birth of that entire target population?

3. When Justice Douglas refers to "invidious discriminations. . . . against groups or types of individuals" which may be made by sterilization laws, is he suggesting that classifications for the purpose of sterilization have intrinsically racial implications and therefore should be considered "suspect" (because racial classifications are suspect)?

4. When Justice Jackson reserves judgment on the "problem" of how far a legislative majority may go in conducting "biological experiments at the expense of the dignity and personality and natural powers of a minority," is he implying that *Buck v. Bell* may have overstepped the line? That the line is somewhere *Buck v. Bell* and *Skinner v. Oklahoma?*

5. Is it preposterous to suggest that the all-male Supreme Court was more sensitive to the preciousness of the right of procreation when it was a male whose procreative capacities were being threatened?

6. If the right to bear children is a fundamental civil right, should the state not
need more compelling justification for
overriding it than the state had in *Buck
v. Bell?* If so, why does every justice cite
Buck with apparent approval?

Contraception

When the Court ignored the early 1920s *Meyer* and *Pierce* precedents on the
rights of family life in handing down *Buck v. Bell*, the omission may have been
conscious. The results in the former were not entirely compatible with the results in the latter; because of this, silence had certain face-saving functions.[26] The
Court's silence about these precedents in *Skinner* is more difficult to explain:
Meyer's assertion of constitutional safeguards for the right to marry, establish a
home, and rear children would have helped to buttress Justice Douglas' announcement in *Skinner* that the right to procreate is a fundamental civil right,
and yet he fails to draw on that help.

Perhaps the Court's silence in *Skinner* can be explained by the following consideration: the year in which *Skinner* was decided, 1942, was in the midst of the
period when Supreme Court disapproval of economic substantive due process
was at its peak. The Court at this time was dominated by Roosevelt appointees,
for whom such doctrines (because they had been used to thwart liberal economic
programs) were a definite sore point. The historical and doctrinal linkage between the *Meyer* and *Pierce* cases and the economic substantive due process
cases may have rendered these 1920s precedents tainted in the eyes of the 1942
Court. This could explain that Court's silence regarding a precedent whose potential utility seems, at least in retrospect, obvious.

By 1965, however, the judicial practice of using substantive due process to
protect implied liberties was not so tainted in the eyes of liberals as it had once
been. By this time the Supreme Court had established an implied right to travel,
an implied right of association, and an implied right to vote; and the Court had
repeatedly applied a strict scrutiny approach (clearly derivative from substantive
due process) in examining statutory limitations on these rights. Thus, in 1965,
when the Court finally did announce that a right of privacy exists in matters of
marital intimacy, it freely made reference to these 1920s precedents.[27]

The 1965 case that gave birth to this announcement was *Griswold v. Connecticut*. Griswold, executive director of the Planned Parenthood League of Connecticut, and a physician named Buxton, who served as medical director of the
league's public clinic in New Haven, Connecticut, had been arrested in November 1961. Their crime was having given information to married persons about
available contraceptive devices. Connecticut law made it a crime, punishable by
sixty days to one year in jail or a fifty-dollar fine, to use "any drug . . . or instru-

ment for the purpose of preventing conception." To aid, abet, or advise someone else to commit a crime was in Connecticut, as elsewhere, itself a crime (the crime of being an "accessory"). Griswold and Dr. Buxton were each fined $100 as accessories to married couples whom they advised to commit the crime of using birth control. Their conviction had been upheld by two different appeals courts within Connecticut before it reached the U.S. Supreme Court.

On two previous occasions[28] this ridiculous statute had been challenged at the U.S. Supreme Court. Evidently unwilling to provide the "not unconstitutional" stamp of approval, and yet unable to find a specific constitutional clause that condemned the statute, the Court had twice ducked the constitutional issue, using legal technicalities to avoid deciding the cases.[29] The Court's hope was clearly that Connecticut either would choose never to enforce this statute, letting it die a quiet death of disuse, or else would repeal it through the legislative process. The Court did not reckon with the political power of Roman Catholic lobbying groups in Connecticut. Neither of these sensible options carried the day. Instead, *Griswold v. Connecticut* brought this statute, for the third time within eighteen years, back to the Supreme Court. And this time seven members of the Court found something in the Constitution that implied a right to use birth control.

The majority split into three factions over the question of which dark corner of the Constitution had contained this right to use birth control for so many years. One faction (Justices Harlan and White) chose to illuminate the due process clause itself, arguing that it sheltered all the fundamental liberties of Americans, of which the right of marital privacy was certainly one. Another faction (Justices Douglas and Clark) engaged in a valiant effort to find the right of marital privacy in the shadows or "penumbras," as Douglas put it, of various guarantees of the Bill of Rights, which (Douglas implies) are incorporated into the Fourteenth Amendment phrase "due process of law" as restraints upon the state governments.[30] A third faction (Justices Goldberg, Warren, and Brennan) agreed with both groups: several Bill of Rights amendments do imply a right of marital privacy, and even if they did not, the due process clause would imply the right as a basic liberty in American society. This third group specifically addressed the question of the legitimacy of inferring unwritten rights into the Constitution, and they offered the Ninth Amendment as justification for that practice.

In addition, *Griswold v. Connecticut* brings the whole substantive due process question out of the historical closet. Douglas (in the Court opinion) denies that he is using the doctrine; he carefully attempts to dissociate this decision from *Lochner v. New York* (1905) and its economic substantive due process bedfellows. (He does cite both *Meyer* and *Pierce* in defense of his argument. He transforms them, however, to First Amendment incorporation decisions, ignoring the fact that the First Amendment was not mentioned in either of them, and that they were based squarely on the idea that the due process clause protected fundamental unwritten rights.)[31] Harlan, White, and Goldberg (with Brennan and Warren concurring) defend the validity of a substantive due process approach for un-written rights. And Stewart and Black attack the substantive due process approach, with Black noting pointedly that the *Meyer* and *Pierce* precedents, cited by majority justices, were based on "long-discredited decisions." Black fought a career-long war against this approach, but the *Griswold* battle seems to have indicated a decisive turning point in the direction of his opponents' victory in that war.

Griswold v. Connecticut, 381 U.S. 479 (1965)

MR. JUSTICE DOUGLAS delivered the opinion of the Court.

. . .

We think that appellants have standing to raise the constitutional rights of the married people with whom they had a professional relationship. . . . Certainly the accessory should have standing to assert that the offense which he is charged with assisting is not, or cannot constitutionally be, a crime. . . .

Coming to the merits, we are met with a wide range of questions that implicate the Due Process Clause of the Fifth Amendment. Overtones of some arguments suggest that *Lochner v. New York*, 198 U.S. 45, should be our guide. But we decline that invitation as we did in *West Coast Hotel Co. v. Parrish*, 300 U.S. 379; *Olsen v. Nebraska*, 313 U.S. 236; *Lincoln Union v. Northwestern Co.*, 335 U.S. 525; *Williamson v. Lee Optical Co.*, 348 U.S. 483; *Giboney v. Empire Storage Co.*, 336 U.S. 490.* We do not sit as a super-legislature to determine the wisdom, need, and propriety of laws that touch economic problems, business affairs, or social conditions. This law, however, operates directly on an intimate relation of husband and

*All these rejected economic substantive due process arguments.—Au.

wife and their physician's role in one aspect of that relation.

The association of people is not mentioned in the Constitution nor in the Bill of Rights. The right to educate a child in a school of the parent's choice—whether public or private or parochial—is also not mentioned. Nor is the right to study any particular subject or any foreign language. Yet the First Amendment has been construed to include certain of those rights.

By *Pierce v. Society of Sisters*, the right to educate one's children as one chooses is made applicable to the State by the force of the First and Fourteenth Amendments. By *Meyer v. Nebraska*, the same dignity is given the right to study the German language in a private school. In other words, the State may not, consistently with the spirit of the First Amendment, contract the spectrum of available knowledge. The right of freedom of speech and press includes not only the right to utter or to print, but the right to distribute, the right to receive, the right to read (*Martin v. Struthers*, 319 U.S. 141, 143) and freedom of inquiry, freedom of thought, and freedom to teach (*see Wieman v. Updegraff*, 344 U.S. 183, 195)—indeed the freedom of the entire university community. *Sweezy v. New Hampshire*, 354 U.S. 234, 249–50, 261–63; *Barenblatt v. United States*, 360 U.S. 109, 112; *Baggett v. Bullitt*,

377 U.S. 360, 369. Without those peripheral rights the specific rights would be less secure. And so we reaffirm the principle of the *Pierce* and the *Meyer* cases.

In *NAACP v. Alabama*, 357 U.S. 449, 462, we protected the "freedom to associate and privacy in one's associations," noting that freedom of association was a peripheral First Amendment right. . . . In other words, the First Amendment has a penumbra where privacy is protected from governmental intrusion. In like context, we have protected forms of "association" that are not political in the customary sense but pertain to the social, legal, and economic benefit of the members. *NAACP v. Button*, 371 U.S. 415, 430–31. . . .

Those cases involved more than the "right of assembly"—a right that extends to all irrespective of their race or ideology. *De Jonge v. Oregon*, 299 U.S. 353. The right of "association," like the right of belief (*Board of Education v. Barnette*, 319 U.S. 624), is more than the right to attend a meeting; it includes the right to express one's attitudes or philosophies by membership in a group or by affiliation with it or by other lawful means. Association in that context is a form of expression of opinion; and while it is not expressly included in the First Amendment its existence is necessary in making the express guarantees fully meaningful.

The foregoing cases suggest that specific guarantees in the Bill of Rights have penumbras, formed by emanations from those guarantees that help give them life and substance. Various guarantees creates *zones* of privacy. The right of association contained in the penumbra of the First Amendment is one, as we have seen. The Third Amendment in its prohibition against the quartering of soldiers "in any house" in time of peace without the consent of the owner is another facet of that privacy. The Fourth Amendment explicitly affirms the "right of the people to be secure in their persons, houses, papers, and effects, against unreasonable searches and seizures." The Fifth Amendment in its Self-Incrimination Clause enables the citizen to create a zone of privacy which government may not force him to surrender to his detriment. The Ninth Amendment provides: "The enumeration in the Constitution, of certain rights, shall not be construed to deny or disparage others retained by the people."

The Fourth and Fifth Amendments were described in *Boyd v. United States*, 116 U.S. 616, 630, as protection against all governmental invasions "of the sanctity of a man's home and the privacies of life."* We recently referred in *Mapp v. Ohio*, 367 U.S. 643, 656, to the Fourth Amendment as creating a "right to privacy, no less important than any other right carefully and particularly reserved to the people."

We have had many controversies over these penumbral rights of "privacy and repose." *See, e.g., Breard v. Alexandria*, 341 U.S. 622, 626, 644; *Public Utilities Comm'n v. Pollak*, 343 U.S. 451; *Monroe v. Pape*, 365 U.S. 167; *Lanza v. New York* 370 U.S. 139; *Frank v.*

---

*The Court said . . . about this right of privacy: "The principles laid down in this opinion [by Lord Candem in *Entick v. Carrington*, 19 How. St. Tr. 1029] affect the very essence of constitutional liberty and security. They . . . apply to all invasions on the part of the government and its employes of the sanctity of a man's home and the privacies of life. It is not the breaking of his doors, and the rummaging of his drawers, that constitutes the essence of the offence; but it is the invasion of his indefeasible right of personal security, personal liberty and private property, where that right has never been forfeited by his conviction of some public offence,—it is the invasion of this sacred right which underlies and constitutes the essence. . . ."

Maryland, 359 U.S. 360; *Skinner v. Oklahoma,* 316 U.S. 535, 541. These cases bear witness that the right of privacy which presses for recognition here is a legitimate one.

The present case, then, concerns a relationship lying within the zone of privacy created by several fundamental constitutional guarantees. And it concerns a law which, in forbidding the use of contraceptives rather than regulating their manufacture or sale, seeks to achieve its goals by means having a maximum destructive impact upon that relationship. Such a law cannot stand in light of the familiar principle, so often applied by this Court, that a "governmental purpose to control or prevent activities constitutionally subject to state regulation may not be achieved by means which sweep unnecessarily broadly and thereby invade the area of protected freedoms." *NAACP v. Alabama,* 377 U.S. 288, 307. Would we allow the police to search the sacred precincts of marital bedrooms for telltale signs of the use of contraceptives? The very idea is repulsive to the notions of a privacy surrounding the marriage relationship.

We deal with the right of privacy older than the Bill of Rights—older than our political parties, older than our school system. Marriage is a coming together for better or for worse, hopefully enduring, and intimate to the degree of being sacred. It is an association that promotes a way of life, not causes; a harmony in living, not political faiths; a bilateral loyalty, not commercial or social projects. Yet it is an association for as noble a purpose as any involved in our prior decisions.

Reversed.

MR. JUSTICE GOLDBERG, whom THE CHIEF JUSTICE and MR. JUSTICE BRENNAN join, concurring.

I agree with the Court that Connecticut's birth-control law unconstitutionally intrudes upon the right of marital privacy, and I join in its opinion and judgment. Although I have not accepted the view that "due process" as used in the Fourteenth Amendment incorporates all of the first eight Amendments, I do agree that the concept of liberty protects those personal rights that are fundamental, and is not confined to the specific terms of the Bill of Rights. My conclusion that the concept of liberty is not so restricted and that it embraces the right of marital privacy though that right is not mentioned explicitly in the Constitution is supported both by numerous decisions of this Court, referred to in the Court's opinion, and by the language and history of the Ninth Amendment. In reaching the conclusion that the right of marital privacy is protected, as being within the protected penumbra of specific guarantees of the Bill of Rights, the Court refers to the Ninth Amendment, *ante.* I add these words to emphasize the relevance of that Amendment to the Court's holding.

The Court stated many years ago that the Due Process Clause protects those liberties that are "so rooted in the traditions and conscience of our people as to be ranked as fundamental." *Snyder v. Massachusetts,* 291 U.S. 97, 105. . . . And, in *Meyer v. Nebraska,* 262 U.S. 390, 399, the Court, referring to the Fourteenth Amendment, stated:

> While this Court has not attempted to define with exactness the liberty thus guaranteed, the term has received much consideration and some of the included things have been definitely stated. Without doubt, it denotes not merely freedom from bodily restraint but also [for example,] the right . . . to marry, establish a home and bring up children. . . .

This Court, in a series of decisions, has held that the Fourteenth Amendment absorbs and applies to the States those specifics of the first eight amendments which express fundamental personal rights. The language and history of the Ninth Amendment reveal that the Framers of the Constitution believed that there are additional fundamental rights, protected from governmental infringement, which exist alongside those fundamental rights specifically mentioned in the first eight constitutional amendments.

The Ninth Amendment reads, "The enumeration in the Constitution, of certain rights, shall not be construed to deny or disparage others retained by the people." . . . To hold that a right so basic and fundamental and so deep-rooted in our society as the right of privacy in marriage may be infringed because that right is not guaranteed in so many words by the first eight amendments to the Constitution is to ignore the Ninth Amendment and to give it no effect whatsoever. Moreover, a judicial construction that this fundamental right is not protected by the Constitution because it is not mentioned in explicit terms by one of the first eight amendments or elsewhere in the Constitution would violate the Ninth Amendment, which specifically states that "[t]he enumeration in the Constitution, of certain rights, shall not be *construed* to deny or disparage others retained by the people." (Emphasis added.) . . . [T]he Ninth Amendment shows a belief of the Constitution's authors that fundamental rights exist that are not expressly enumerated in the first eight amendments and an intent that the list of rights included there not be deemed exhaustive . . . [and] that other fundamental personal rights should not be denied . . . protection or disparaged in any other way simply because they are not specifically listed in the first eight constitutional amendments. . . . I do not see how this broadens the authority of the Court; rather it serves to support what this Court has been doing in protecting fundamental rights.

Nor am I turning somersaults with history in arguing that the Ninth Amendment is relevant in a case dealing with a *State's* infringement of a fundamental right. While the Ninth Amendment—and indeed the entire Bill of Rights—originally concerned restrictions upon *federal* power, the subsequently enacted Fourteenth Amendment prohibits the States as well from abridging fundamental personal liberties. And, the Ninth Amendment, in indicating that not all such liberties are specifically mentioned in the first eight amendments, is surely relevant in showing the existence of other fundamental personal rights, now protected from state, as well as federal, infringement.

In determining which rights are fundamental, judges are not left at large to decide cases in light of their personal and private notions. Rather, they must look to the "traditions and [collective] conscience of our people" to determine whether a principle is "so rooted [there] . . . as to be ranked as fundamental." *Snyder v. Massachusetts*, 291 U.S. 97, 105. The inquiry is whether a right involved "is of such a character that it cannot be denied without violating those 'fundamental principles of liberty and justice which lie at the base of all our civil and political institutions'. . . ." *Powell v. Alabama*, 287 U.S. 45, 65. . . .

The Connecticut statutes here involved deal with a particularly important and sensitive area of privacy— that of the marital relation and the marital home. This Court recognized in *Meyer v. Nebraska*, *supra*, that the right "to marry, establish a home and bring up children" was an essential part of the liberty guaranteed by the Fourteenth Amendment, 262 U.S., at 399. In *Pierce v. Society of Sisters*, 268 U.S. 510,

under the Due Process Clause. *Zemel v. Rusk*, 381 U.S. 1. . . . [The] State claims but one justification for its anti-use statute. There is no serious contention that Connecticut thinks the use of artificial or external methods of contraception immoral or unwise in itself, or that the anti-use statute is founded upon any policy of promoting population expansion. Rather, the statute is said to serve the State's policy against all forms of promiscuous or illicit sexual relationships, be they premarital or extramarital, concededly a permissible and legitimate legislative goal.

Without taking issue with the premise that the fear of conception operates as a deterrent to such relationships in addition to the criminal proscriptions Connecticut has against such conduct, I wholly fail to see how the ban on the use of contraceptives by married couples in any way reinforces the State's ban on illicit sexual relationships. . . . Perhaps the theory is that the flat ban on use prevents married people from possessing contraceptives and without the ready availability of such devices for use in the marital relationship, there will be no or less temptation to use them in extramarital ones. This reasoning rests on the premise that married people will comply with the ban in regard to their marital relationship, notwithstanding total nonenforcement in this context and apparent nonenforcibility, but will not comply with criminal statutes prohibiting extramarital affairs and the anti-use statute in respect to illicit sexual relationships, a premise whose validity has not been demonstrated and whose intrinsic validity is not very evident. At most the broad ban is of marginal utility to the declared objective. A statute limiting its prohibition on use to persons engaging in the prohibited relationship would serve the end posited by Connecticut in the same way, and with the same effectiveness or ineffectiveness, as the broad anti-use statue under attack in this case. I find nothing in this record justifying the sweeping scope of this statue, with its telling effect on the freedoms of married persons, and therefore conclude that it deprives such persons of liberty without due process of law.

Mr. Justice Black, with whom Mr. Justice Stewart joins, dissenting.

I agree with my Brother Stewart's dissenting opinion. And like him I do not to any extent whatever base my view that this Connecticut law is constitutional on a belief that the law is wise or that its policy is a good one. In order that there may be no room at all to doubt why I vote as I do, I feel constrained to add that the law is every bit as offensive to me as it is to my Brethren of the majority and my Brothers Harlan, White and Goldberg who, reciting reasons why it is offensive to them, hold it unconstitutional. There is no single one of the graphic and eloquent strictures and criticisms fired at the policy of this Connecticut law either by the Court's opinion or by those of my concurring Brethren to which I cannot subscribe—except their conclusion that the evil qualities they see in the law make it unconstitutional.

Had the doctor defendant here, or even the nondoctor defendant, been convicted for doing nothing more than expressing opinions to persons coming to the clinic that certain contraceptive devices, medicines or practices would do them good and would be desirable, or for telling people how devices could be used, I can think of no reasons at this time why their expressions of views would not be protected by the First and Fourteenth Amendments, which guarantee freedom of speech. But speech is one thing; conduct and physical activities are quite another. The two defendants here were active participants in an organization which gave physical examinations to women, advised them what kind of contraceptive devices or medicines would most likely be satisfactory for them, and then supplied the devices themselves, all for a graduated scale of fees, based on the family income. Thus these defendants admittedly engaged with others in a planned course of conduct to help people violate the Connecticut law. Merely because some speech was used in carrying on that conduct—just as in ordinary life some speech accompanies most kinds of conduct—we are not in my view justified in holding that the First Amendment forbids the State to punish their conduct. . . .

The Court talks about a constitutional "right of privacy" as though there is some constitutional provision or provisions forbidding any law ever to be passed which might abridge the "privacy" of individuals. But there is not. There are, of course, guarantees in certain specific constitutional provisions which are designed in part to protect privacy at certain times and places with respect to certain activities. Such, for example, is the Fourth Amendment's guarantee against "unreasonable searches and seizures." But I think it belittles that Amendment to talk about it as though it protects nothing but "privacy." To treat it that way is to give it a niggardly interpretation, not the kind of liberal reading I think any Bill or Rights provision should be given. The average man would very likely not have his feelings soothed any more by having his property seized openly than by having it seized privately and by stealth. He simply wants his property left alone. And a person can be just as much, if not more irritated, annoyed and injured by an unceremonious public arrest by a policeman as he is by a seizure in the privacy of his office or home.

One of the most effective ways of diluting or expanding a constitutionally guaranteed right is to substitute for the crucial word or words of a constitutional guarantee another word or words, more or less flexible and more or less restricted in meaning. This fact is well illustrated by the use of the term "right of privacy" as a comprehensive substitute for the Fourth Amendment's guarantee against "unreasonable searches and seizures." "Privacy" is a broad, abstract and ambiguous concept which can easily be shrunken in meaning but which can also, on the other hand, easily be interpreted as a constitutional ban against many things other than searches and seizures. I have expressed the view many times that First Amendment freedoms, for example, have suffered from a failure of the courts to stick to the simple language of the First Amendment in construing it, instead of invoking multitudes of words substituted for those the Framers used. For these reasons I get nowhere in this case by talk about a constitutional "right of privacy" as an emanation from one or more constitutional provisions. I like my privacy as well as the next one, but I am nevertheless compelled to admit that government has a right to invade it unless prohibited by some specific constitutional provision. For these reasons I cannot agree with the Court's judgment and the reasons it gives for holding this Connecticut law unconstitutional.

This brings me to the arguments made by my Brothers HARLAN, WHITE and GOLDBERG for invalidating the Connecticut law. . . . I think that if properly construed neither the Due Process Clause nor the Ninth Amendment, nor both together, could under any circumstances be a proper basis for invalidating the Connecticut law. I discuss the due process and Ninth Amendment arguments together because on analysis they turn out to be the same thing—merely using different words to claim for this Court and the federal judiciary power to invalidate any legislative act which the judges find irrational, unreasonable or offensive.

The due process argument which my Brothers HARLAN and WHITE adopt here is based, as their opinions indicate, on the premise that this Court is vested with power to invalidate all state laws that it considers to be arbitrary, capricious, unreasonable, or oppressive, or on this Court's belief that a particular state law under scrutiny has no "rational or justifying" purpose, or is offensive to a "sense of fairness and justice." If these formulas based on "natural justice," or others which mean the same thing, are to prevail, they require judges to determine what is or is not constitutional on the basis of their own appraisal of what laws are unwise or unnecessary. The power to make such decisions is of course that of a legislative body. Surely it has to be admitted that no provision of the Constitution specifically gives such blanket power to courts to exercise such a supervisory veto over the wisdom and value of legislative policies and to hold unconstitutional those laws which they believe unwise or dangerous. I readily admit that no legislative body, state or national, should pass laws that can justly be given any of the invidious labels invoked as constitutional excuses to strike down state laws. But perhaps it is not too much to say that no legislative body ever does pass laws without believing that they will accomplish a sane, rational, wise and justifiable purpose. . . . Such an appraisal of the wisdom of legislation is an attribute of the power to make laws, not of the power to interpret them. The use by federal courts of such a formula or doctrine or whatnot to veto federal or state laws simply takes away from Congress and States the power to make laws based on their own judgment of fairness and wisdom and transfers that power to this Court for ultimate determination—

a power which was specifically denied to federal courts by the convention that framed the Constitution.

Of the cases on which my Brothers WHITE and GOLDBERG rely so heavily, undoubtedly the reasoning of two of them supports their result here—as would that of a number of others which they do not bother to name, e.g., *Lochner v. New York*, 198 U.S. 45, *Coppage v. Kansas*, 236 U.S. 1, *Jay Burns Baking Co. v. Bryan*, 264 U.S. 504, and *Adkins v. Children's Hospital*, 261 U.S. 525. [All are economic substantive due process cases.—Au.] The two they do cite and quote from, *Meyer v. Nebraska*, 262 U.S. 390, and *Pierce v. Society of Sisters*, 268 U.S. 510, were both decided in opinions by Mr. Justice McReynolds which elaborated the same natural law due process philosophy found in *Lochner v. New York, supra*, one of the cases on which he relied in *Meyer*, along with such other long-discredited decisions as, e.g., *Adams v. Tanner*, 244 U.S. 590, and *Adkins v. Children's Hospital, supra*. . . . Without expressing an opinion as to whether either of those cases reached a correct result in light of our later decisions applying the First Amendment to the States through the Fourteenth, I merely point out that the reasoning stated in *Meyer* and *Pierce* was the same natural law due process philosophy which many later opinions repudiated, and which I cannot accept. . . . My Brother GOLDBERG . . . states, without proof satisfactory to me, that in making decisions on this basis judges will not consider "their personal and private notions." One may ask how they can avoid considering them. Our Court certainly has no machinery with which to take a Gallup Poll. And the scientific miracles of this age have not yet produced a gadget which the Court can use to determine what traditions are rooted in the "[collective] conscience of our people." . . . [T]his Court does have power, which it should exercise, to hold laws unconstitutional where they are forbidden by the Federal Constitution. My point is that there is no provision of the Constitution which either expressly or impliedly vests power in this Court to sit as a supervisory agency over acts of duly constituted legislative bodies and set aside their laws because of the Court's belief that the legislative policies adopted are unreasonable, unwise, arbitrary, capricious or irrational. The adoption of such a loose, flexible, uncontrolled standard for holding laws unconstitutional, if it is ever finally achieved, will amount to a great unconstitutional shift of power to the courts which I believe and am constrained to say will be bad for the courts and worse for the country. . . .

[W]hat my concurring Brethren urge today . . . would reinstate the *Lochner, Coppage, Adkins, Burns* lines of cases, cases from which this Court recoiled after the 1930s, and which had been I thought totally discredited until now. Apparently my Brethren have less quarrel with state economic regulations than former Justices of their persuasion had. But any limitations upon their using the natural law due process philosophy to strike down any state law, dealing with any activity whatever, will obviously be only self-imposed.

Mr. Justice Stewart, whom Mr. Justice Black joins, dissenting.

Since 1879 Connecticut has had on its books a law which forbids the use of contraceptives by anyone. I think this is an uncommonly silly law. As a practical matter, the law is obviously unenforceable, except in the oblique context of the present case. As a philosophical matter, I believe the use of contraceptives in the relationship of marriage should be left to personal and private choice, based upon each individual's moral, ethical, and religious beliefs. As a matter of social policy, I think professional counsel about methods of birth control should be available to all, so that each individual's choice can be meaningfully made. But we are asked in this case to say whether we think this law is unwise, or even asinine. We are asked to hold that it violates the United States Constitution. And that I cannot do.

In the course of its opinion the Court refers to no less than six Amendments to the Constitution: the First, the Third, the Fourth, the Fifth, the Ninth, and the Fourteenth. But the Court does not say which of these Amendments, if any, it thinks is infringed by this Connecticut law. . . .

What provision of the Constitution, then, does make this state law invalid? The Court says it is the right of privacy "created by several fundamental constitutional guarantees." With all deference, I can find no such general right of privacy in the Bill of Rights, in any other part of the Constitution, or in any case ever before decided by this Court. . . . We are here to decide cases "agreeably to the Constitution and laws of the United States." It is the essence of judicial duty to subordinate our own personal views, our own ideas of what legislation is wise and what is not. If, as I should surely hope, the law before us does not reflect the standards of the people of Connecticut, the people of Connecticut can freely exercise their true Ninth and Tenth Amendment rights to persuade their elected representatives to repeal it. That is the constitutional way to take this law off the books.

CASE QUESTIONS

1. Does the right of privacy protected in this decision apply to unmarried persons? Do any of the justices think so?

2. Did the Supreme Court invent the right of privacy? Is the right to use birth control a reasonable inference from any particular passage of the Constitution? Does "due process of law" imply protection for all rights deemed "basic" by the Supreme Court? How is the Supreme Court to decide which rights are so basic that they justify overriding legislatures' opinions to the contrary?

3. If American "traditions" indicate the direction by which to find those rights that are "basic," how can the Court claim that an eighty-six-year-old statute violates a "basic" (read "traditional") right?

4. Justice Black is willing to accept a substantive due process approach (including its corollary strict scrutiny) to protect the substance of liberties mentioned, or at least alluded to, in the Constitution. He objects, however, to *any* substantive due process approach (whether the minimal "reasonableness" one or a strict scrutiny one) for a specific liberty not at least implicitly protected by some words of the Constitution. Should the phrase "shall not deprive any person of liberty without due process of law" be read as

implying that every law (because all laws infringe on someone's liberty) must bear a reasonable relationship to the public interest? Would any legislative majority adopt a law that did not promote *their* view of the public interest? What justifies the Supreme Court's assumption that it is better able to discern "rationality" than a legislature is?

5. What if Connecticut had proffered the "serious contention that . . . the use of artificial or external methods of contraception [is] immoral . . . in itself"? The principle that states have the power and duty to promote morality is thoroughly accepted in American jurisprudence. Could the Supreme Court announce that Connecticut's view of morality was misguided, and that the judges knew better? Even if one assumes they do know better, is there an important difference between (1) a system in which judges enforce the *written* law of the land (as adopted by the people in the form of the Constitution) and (2) one in which judges enforce the judges' own views of the national moral code? Can the latter system still be considered a democracy? Can it be considered a democracy if the people have purposely delegated that power to judges (through the due process clause, or the privileges or immunities clause)? If the people have unwittingly so delegated it?

Not a single justice of the *Griswold* majority failed to mention the special status of the marriage institution as a sector of our society where the right to privacy has peculiarly strong claims. It is almost impossible to find statements in the *Griswold* opinion with any direct implications that unmarried persons might have a comparable right. In fact, Justices Harlan, White, and Goldberg (the latter in a section omitted from the excerpt) expressly indicated that the suppression of extramarital sexual activity is a legitimate legislative goal. (If Justices Brennan and Warren, who concurred with Goldberg, are included in this group, the *Griswold* majority can be regarded as on record against the extension of the shield of the "right of privacy" to unmarried sexual activities.)

Within seven years, however, when the Court actually confronted, in *Eisenstadt v. Baird*, the question whether unmarried persons have a "right of privacy" that protects the use of birth control, the Court majority had crossed sides on this question. More precisely, Brennan (who had concurred in the Goldberg opinion in *Griswold*) changed sides. Douglas had expressed no view on the subject in *Griswold* (although he, like everyone else, had stressed the importance of the marriage relationship). Stewart had lined up against any right of privacy in *Griswold*, but evidently, when he finally did accept it,[32] he believed it would logically apply to the unmarried as well as the married, for he did side with the majority in *Eisenstadt*. By the time of the *Eisenstadt* decision, Clark, Harlan, Black, Goldberg, and Warren had all left the Court, to be replaced by Burger, Blackmun, Marshall, Powell, and Rehnquist. Because the latter two arrived on the Court too late to participate in *Eisenstadt*, it is the four-judge majority of Brennan, Douglas, Stewart, and Marshall who produced the ground-breaking Court opinion for that case.

That opinion not only extends to unmarried persons a right to use birth control; in fact, it goes considerably further. Brennan's four-justice majority opinion in *Eisenstadt v. Baird* forges the logical link in the chain between a right to use contraceptive devices and a right to have an abortion. Once *Eisenstadt v. Baird* was announced, the abortion decisions of 1973 were a foregone conclusion. The link that clinched the judicial future was forged by a single sentence of Justice Brennan: "if the right of privacy means anything, it is the right of the individual . . . to be free from unwarranted governmental intrusion into *matters so fundamentally affecting a person as the decision whether to bear or beget a child.*" (Emphasis added.)

The situation provoking this statement began when Bill Baird, a pro-birth-control activist, in the midst of a lecture on contraception at Boston University in 1969, handed a package of Emko Vaginal Foam (a spermicidal contraceptive) to an unmarried young woman. He performed this act in deliberate contravention of Massachusetts law, which prohibited the giving away of any contraceptive devices, except by registered physicians prescribing for married persons, or by registered pharmacists filling such prescriptions. This statute, like the *Griswold* statute, did not address the distribution of implements of birth control for the purpose of preventing disease; distributing them for the prevention of conception was the sole target of the statute. In accordance with this law (1) no one could distribute contraceptives except on medical prescriptions, and (2) no one could give even medically prescribed contraceptives to unmarried persons. Either of these acts were punishable by up to five years in prison.

Bill Baird, a nonphysician, was convicted of the felony of distributing a non-prescribed contraceptive. His conviction was sustained upon appeal to the Massachusetts Supreme Court, and his further appeal was dismissed by the federal district court. Then in his final appeal, the circuit court of appeals sided with Baird, ordering him discharged. Eisenstadt, the sheriff of Suffolk County, Massachusetts, then appealed to the U.S. Supreme Court. Their response follows.

Eisenstadt v. Baird, 405 U.S. 438 (1972)

Mr. Justice Brennan delivered the opinion of the Court.

The legislative purposes that the statute is meant to serve are not altogether clear. In *Commonwealth v. Baird*, the Supreme Judicial Court noted only the State's interest in protecting the health of its citizens: "[T]he prohibition in § 21," the court declared, "is directly related to" the State's goal of "preventing the distribution of articles designed to prevent conception which may have undesirable, if not danger-ous, physical consequences." 247 N.E.2d, at 578. In a subsequent decision, *Sturgis v. Attorney General*, 260 N.E.2d 687, 690 (1970), the court, however, found "a second and more compelling ground for upholding the statute"—namely, to protect morals through "regulating the private sexual lives of single persons."[3] The Court of Appeals, for reasons that will appear, did not con-

sider the promotion of health or the protection of morals through the deterrence of fornication to be the legislative aim. Instead, the court concluded that the statutory goal was to limit contraception in and of itself—a purpose that the court held conflicted "with fundamental human rights" under *Griswold v. Connecticut*, 381 U.S. 479 (1965), where this Court struck down Connecticut's prohibition against the use of contraceptives as an unconstitutional infringement of the right of marital privacy. 429 F.2d, at 1401–2.

We agree that the goals of deterring premarital sex and regulating the distribution of potentially harmful articles cannot reasonably be regarded as legislative aims of §§ 21 and 21A. And we hold that the statute, viewed as a prohibition on contraception *per se*, violates the rights of single persons under the Equal Protection Clause of the Fourteenth Amendment.

I

We address at the outset appellant's contention that Baird does not have standing to assert the rights of unmarried persons denied access to contraceptives because he was neither an authorized distributor under § 21A nor a single person unable to obtain contraceptives. There can

3. Appellant suggests that the purpose of the Massachusetts statute is to promote marital fidelity as well as to discourage premarital sex. Under § 21A, however, contraceptives may be made available to married persons without regard to whether they are living with their spouses or the uses to which the contraceptives are to be put. Plainly the legislation has no deterrent effect on extramarital sexual relations.

be no question, of course, that Baird has sufficient interest in challenging the statute's validity to satisfy the "case or controversy" requirement of article III of the Constitution. Appellant's argument, however, is that this case is governed by the Court's self-imposed rules of restraint . . . that a litigant may only assert his own constitutional rights or immunities. *United States v. Raines,* 362 U.S. 17, 21 (1960). . . . [Our] self-imposed rule against the assertion of third-party rights must be relaxed in this case just as in *Griswold v. Connecticut.* . . . [H]ere the relationship between Baird and those whose rights he seeks to assert is not simply that between a distributor and potential distributees, but that between an advocate of the rights of persons to obtain contraceptives and those desirous of doing so. The very point of Baird's giving away the vaginal foam was to challenge the Massachusetts statute that limited access to contraceptives.

In any event, more important than the nature of the relationship between the litigant and those whose rights he seeks to assert is the impact of the litigation on the third party interests. In *Griswold,* 381 U.S., at 481, the Court stated: "The rights of husband and wife, pressed here, are likely to be diluted or adversely affected unless those rights are considered in a suit involving those who have this kind of confidential relation to them." A similar situation obtains here. Enforcement of the Massachusetts statute will materially impair the ability of single persons to obtain contraceptives. In fact, the case for according standing to assert third-party rights is stronger in this regard here than in *Griswold* because unmarried persons denied access to contraceptives in Massachusetts, unlike the users of contraceptives in Connecticut, are not themselves subject to prosecution and, to that extent, are denied a forum in which to assert their own rights. . . .

II

The basic principles governing application of the Equal Protection Clause of the Fourteenth Amendment are familiar. As THE CHIEF JUSTICE only recently explained in *Reed:*

> In applying that clause, this Court has consistently recognized that . . . [a] classification "must be reasonable, not arbitrary, and must rest upon some ground of difference having a fair and substantial relation to the object of the legislation, so that all persons similarly circumstanced shall be treated alike." (*Royster Guano Co. v. Virginia,* 254 U.S. 412, 415 [1920].)

The question for our determination in this case is whether there is some ground of difference that rationally explains the different treatment accorded married and unmarried persons under [these laws].[7] For the reasons that follow, we conclude that no such ground exists.

First . . . The Massachusetts Supreme Judicial Court . . . reiterated in *Sturgis v. Attorney General, supra,* that the object of the legislation is to discourage premarital sexual intercourse. Conceding that the State could, consistently with the Equal Protection Clause, regard the problems of extramarital and premarital sexual rela-

7. Of course, if we were to conclude that the Massachusetts statute impinges upon fundamental freedoms under *Griswold,* the statutory classification would have to be not merely *rationally related* to a valid public purpose but necessary to the achievement of a compelling state interest. *E.g., Shapiro v. Thompson,* 394 U.S. 618 (1969); *Loving v. Virginia,* 388 U.S. 1 (1967). But just as in *Reed v. Reed,* 404 U.S. 71 (1971), we do not have to address the statute's validity under that test because the law fails to satisfy even the more lenient equal protection standard.

tions as "[e]vils . . . of different dimensions and proportions, requiring different remedies," *Williamson v. Lee Optical Co.*, 348 U.S. 483, 489 (1955), we cannot agree that the deterrence of premarital sex may reasonably be regarded as the purpose of the Massachusetts law.

It would be plainly unreasonable to assume that Massachusetts has prescribed pregnancy and the birth of an unwanted child as punishment for fornication, which is a misdemeanor under Massachusetts [law]. Aside from the scheme of values that assumption would attribute to the State, it is abundantly clear that the effect of the ban on distribution of contraceptives to unmarried persons has at best a marginal relation to the proffered objectives. What Mr. Justice Goldberg said in *Griswold v. Connecticut, supra,* at 498 (concurring opinion), concerning the effect of Connecticut's prohibition on the use of contraceptives in discouraging extramarital sexual relations, is equally applicable here. "The rationality of this justification is dubious, particularly in light of the admitted widespread availability to all persons in the State of Connecticut, unmarried as well as married, of birth-control devices for the prevention of disease, as distinguished from the prevention of conception." *See also id.* at 505–7 (WHITE, J., concurring in judgment). Like Connecticut's laws, §§ 21 and 21A do not at all regulate the distribution of contraceptives when they are to be used to prevent, not pregnancy, but the spread of disease. Nor, in making contraceptives available to married persons without regard to their intended use, does Massachusetts attempt to deter married persons engaging in illicit sexual relations with unmarried persons. Even on the assumption that the fear of pregnancy operates as a deterrent to fornication, the Massachusetts statute is thus so riddled with exceptions that deterrence of premarital sex cannot reasonably be regarded as its aim.

Moreover, §§ 21 and 21A on their face have a dubious relation to the State's criminal prohibition on fornication. As the Court of Appeals explained, "Fornication is a misdemeanor [in Massachusetts], entailing a thirty dollar fine, or three months in jail. . . . Violation of the present statute is a felony, punishable by five years in prison. We find it hard to believe that the legislature adopted a statute carrying a five-year penalty for its possible, obviously by no means fully effective, deterrence of the commission of a ninety-day misdemeanor." 429 F.2d, at 1401. . . . [We] cannot believe that in this instance Massachusetts has chosen to expose the aider and abetter who simply gives away a contraceptive to 20 times the 90-day sentence of the offender himself. . . .

Second. . . . If health were the rationale of § 21A, the statute would be both discriminatory and overbroad. If there is need to have a physician prescribe (and a pharmacist dispense) contraceptives, that need is as great for unmarried persons as for married persons. . . .[8] Furthermore, we must join the Court of Appeals in noting that not all contraceptives are potentially dangerous.[9] As a result, if the Massachu-

8. Appellant insists that the unmarried have no right to engage in sexual intercourse and hence no health interest in contraception that needs to be served. The short answer to this contention is that the same devices the distribution of which the State purports to regulate when their asserted purpose is to forestall pregnancy are available without any controls whatsoever so long as their asserted purpose is to prevent the spread of disease. It is inconceivable that the need for health controls varies with the purpose for which the contraceptive is to be used when the physical act in all cases is one and the same.

9. The Court of Appeals stated, 429 F.2d, at 1401: "[W]e must take notice that not all contraceptive devices risk 'undesirable . . . [or] dangerous physical consequences.' It is 200 years since Casanova recorded the ubiquitous article which, perhaps because of the birthplace of

setts statute were a health measure, it would not only invidiously discriminate against the unmarried, but also be overbroad with respect to the married. . . . We conclude, accordingly, that, despite the statute's superficial earmarks as a health measure, health, on the face of the statute, may no more reasonably be regarded as its purpose than the deterrence of premarital sexual relations.

Third. If the Massachusetts statute cannot be upheld as a deterrent to fornication or as a health measure, may it, nevertheless, be sustained simply as a prohibition on contraception? The Court of Appeals analysis "led inevitably to the conclusion that, so far as morals are concerned, it is contraceptives *per se* that are considered immoral—to the extent that *Griswold* will permit such a declaration." 429 F.2d, at 1401–2. The Court of Appeals went on to hold, *id.* at 1402:

> To say that contraceptives are immoral as such, and are to be forbidden to unmarried persons who will nevertheless persist in having intercourse, means that such persons must risk for themselves an unwanted pregnancy, for the child, illegitimacy, and for society, a possible obligation of support. Such a view of morality is not only the very mirror image of sensible legislation; we consider that it conflicts with fundamental human rights. In the absence of demonstrated harm, we hold it is beyond the competency of the state.

----

its inventor, he termed a 'redingote anglais.' The reputed nationality of the condom has now changed; but we have never heard criticism of it on the side of health. We cannot think that the legislature was unaware of it, or could have thought that it needed a medical prescription. We believe the same could be said of certain other products."

We need not and do not, however, decide that important question in this case because, whatever the rights of the individual to access to contraceptives may be, the rights must be the same for the unmarried and the married alike.

If under *Griswold* the distribution of contraceptives to married persons cannot be prohibited, a ban on distribution to unmarried persons would be equally impermissible. It is true that in *Griswold* the right of privacy in question inhered in the marital relationship. Yet the marital couple is not an independent entity with a mind and heart of its own, but an association of two individuals each with a separate intellectual and emotional makeup. If the right of privacy means anything, it is the right of the *individual,* married or single, to be free from unwarranted governmental intrusion into matters so fundamentally affecting a person as the decision whether to bear or beget a child. *See Stanley v. Georgia,* 394 U.S. 557 (1969). *See also Skinner v. Oklahoma,* 316 U.S. 535 (1942); *Jacobson v. Massachusetts,* 197 U.S. 11, 29 (1905).

On the other hand, if *Griswold* is no bar to a prohibition on the distribution of contraceptives, the State could not, consistently with the Equal Protection Clause, outlaw distribution to unmarried but not to married persons. In each case the evil, as perceived by the State, would be identical, and the underinclusion would be invidious. Mr. Justice Jackson, concurring in *Railway Express Agency v. New York,* 336 U.S. 106, 112–13 (1949), made the point:

> The framers of the Constitution knew, and we should not forget today, that there is no more effective practical guaranty against arbitrary and unreasonable government than to require that the principles of law which officials would impose upon a minority must be imposed generally. Conversely, nothing opens the door to ar-

bitrary action so effectively as to allow those officials to pick and choose only a few to whom they will apply legislation and thus to escape the political retribution that might be visited upon them if larger numbers were affected. Courts can take no better measure to assure that laws will be just than to require that laws be equal in operation.

Although Mr. Justice Jackson's comments had reference to administrative regulations, the principle he affirmed has equal application to the legislation here. We hold that by providing dissimilar treatment for married and unmarried persons who are similarly situated, [these statutes] violate the Equal Protection Clause. The judgment of the Court of Appeals is

Affirmed.

Mr. Justice Powell and Mr. Justice Rehnquist took no part in the consideration or decision of this case.

Mr. Justice Douglas, concurring.

While I join the opinion of the Court, there is for me a narrower ground for affirming. . . . This to me is a simple First Amendment case, that amendment being applicable to the State by reason of the Fourteenth. *Stromberg v. California,* 283 U.S. 359.

Baird addressed an audience of students and faculty at Boston University on the subject of birth control and overpopulation. His address was approximately one hour in length and consisted of a discussion of various contraceptive devices; overpopulation in the world; crises throughout the world due to overpopulation; the large number of abortions performed on unwed mothers; and quack abortionists and the potential harm to women resulting from abortions performed by quack abortionists. Baird also urged members of the audience to petition the Massachusetts Legislature and to make known their feelings with regard to birth control laws in order to bring about a change in the laws. At the close of the address Baird invited members of the audience to come to the stage and help themselves to the contraceptive articles. We do not know how many accepted Baird's invitation. We only know that Baird personally handed one woman a package of Emko Vaginal Foam. He was then arrested. . . .

It is said that only Baird's conduct is involved. . . . The distinction between "speech" and "conduct" is a valid one, insofar as it helps to determine in a particular case whether the purpose of the activity was to aid in the communication of ideas, and whether the form of the communication so interferes with the rights of others that reasonable regulations may be imposed. *See Public Utilities Comm'n v. Pollak,* 343 U.S. 451, 467 (Douglas, J., dissenting). . . . But "this Court has repeatedly stated, [First Amendment] rights are not confined to verbal expression. They embrace appropriate types of action. . . ." *Brown v. Louisiana,* 383 U.S. 131, 141–42.

Baird gave an hour's lecture on birth control and as an aid to understanding the ideas which he was propagating he handed out one sample of one of the devices whose use he was endorsing. . . . There is no evidence or finding that Baird intended that the young lady take the foam home with her when he handed it to her or that she would not have examined the article and then returned it to Baird, had he not been placed under arrest immediately upon handing the article over.

. . . Handing out the article was not even a suggestion that the lady use it. At most it suggested that she become familiar with the product line. . . .

Mr. Justice White, with whom Mr. Justice Blackmun joins, concurring in the result.

Appellee Baird was indicted for giving away Emko Vaginal Foam, a "medicine and article for the prevention of conception. . . ." The State did not purport to charge or convict Baird for distributing to an unmarried person. No proof was offered as to the marital status of the recipient. The gravamen of the offense charged was that Baird had no license and therefore no authority to distribute to anyone. As the Supreme Judicial Court of Massachusetts noted, the constitutional validity of Baird's conviction rested upon his lack of status as a "distributor and not . . . the marital status of the recipient." *Commonwealth v. Baird*, 247 N.E.2d 574, 578 (1969). The Federal District Court was of the same view.

I assume that a State's interest in the health of its citizens empowers it to restrict to medical channels the distribution of products whose use should be accompanied by medical advice. I also do not doubt that various contraceptive medicines and articles are properly available only on prescription, and I therefore have no difficulty with the Massachusetts court's characterization of the statute at issue here as expressing "a legitimate interest in preventing the distribution of articles designed to prevent conception which may have undesirable, if not dangerous, physical consequences." 247 N.E.2d, at 578. Had Baird distributed a supply of the so-called "pill," I would sustain his conviction under this statute. Requiring a prescription to obtain potentially dangerous contraceptive material may place a substantial burden upon the right recognized in *Griswold*, but that burden is justified by a strong state interest and does not, as did the statute at issue in *Griswold*, sweep unnecessarily broadly or

seek "to achieve its goals by means having a maximum destructive impact upon" a protected relationship. *Griswold v. Connecticut*, 381 U.S., at 485.

Baird, however, was found guilty of giving away vaginal foam. Inquiry into the validity of this conviction does not come to an end merely because some contraceptives are harmful and their distribution may be restricted. Our general reluctance to question a State's judgment on matters of public health must give way where, as here, the restrictions at issue burdens the constitutional rights of married persons to use contraceptives. In these circumstances we may not accept on faith the State's classification of a particular contraceptive as dangerous to health. Due regard for protecting constitutional rights requires that the record contain evidence that a restriction on distribution of vaginal foam is essential to achieve the statutory purpose, or the relevant facts concerning the product must be such as to fall within the range of judicial notice.

Neither requirement is met here. Nothing in the record even suggests that the distribution of vaginal foam should be accompanied by medical advice in order to protect the user's health. Nor does the opinion of the Massachusetts court or the State's brief filed here marshal facts demonstrating that the hazards of using vaginal foam are common knowledge or so incontrovertible that they may be noticed judicially. On the contrary, the State acknowledges that Emko is a product widely available without prescription. Given *Griswold v. Connecticut, supra,* and absent proof of the probable hazards of using vaginal foam, we could not sustain appellee's conviction had it been for selling or giving away foam to a married person. . . .

That Baird could not be convicted for distributing Emko to a married person disposes of this case. Assuming, *arguendo*, that the result would be otherwise had the recipient been unmarried, nothing has been placed in the record to indicate her marital status. The state has maintained that marital status is irrelevant because an unlicensed person cannot legally dispense vaginal foam either to married or unmarried persons. This approach is plainly erroneous and requires the reversal of Baird's conviction; for on the facts of this case, it deprives us of knowing whether Baird was in fact convicted for making a constitutionally protected distribution of Emko to a married person. . . .

Because this case can be disposed of on the basis of settled constitutional doctrine, I perceive no reason for reaching the novel constitutional question whether a State may restrict or forbid the distribution of contraceptives to the unmarried. Cf. *Ashwander v. Tennessee Valley Authority*, 297 U.S. 288, 345–48 (1936) (Brandeis, J., concurring).

Mr. Chief Justice Burger, dissenting.

The judgment of the Supreme Judicial Court of Massachusetts in sustaining appellee's conviction for dispensing medicinal material without a license seems eminently correct to me and I would not disturb it. It is undisputed that appellee is not a physician or pharmacist and was prohibited under Massachusetts law from dispensing contraceptives to anyone, regardless of marital status. To my mind the validity of this restriction on dispensing medicinal substance is the only issue before the Court, and appellee has no standing to challenge that part of the statute restricting the persons to whom contraceptives are available. There is no need to labor this point, however, for everyone seems to agree that if Massachusetts has validly required, as a health measure, that all contraceptives be dispensed by a physician or pursuant to a physician's prescription, then the statutory

distinction based on marital status has no bearing on this case. *United States v. Raines*, 362 U.S. 17, 21 (1960).

The opinion of the Court today brushes aside appellee's status as an unlicensed layman by concluding that the Massachusetts Legislature was not really concerned with the protection of health when it passed this statute. Mr. Justice White acknowledges the statutory concern with the protection of health, but finds the restriction on distributors overly broad because the State has failed to adduce facts showing the health hazards of the particular substance dispensed by appellee as distinguished from other contraceptives. . . .

[T]he opinion of the Court and that of Mr. Justice White . . . seriously invade the constitutional prerogatives of the States and regrettably hark back to the heyday of substantive due process.

In affirming appellee's conviction, the highest tribunal in Massachusetts held that the statutory requirement that contraceptives be dispensed only through medical channels served the legitimate interest of the State in protecting the health of its citizens. The Court today blithely hurdles this authoritative state pronouncement and concludes that the statute has no such purpose . . . because, "[i]f there is need to have a physician prescribe . . . contraceptives, that need is as great for unmarried persons as for married persons." 247 N.E.2d 574, 581. This argument confuses the validity of the restriction on distributors with the validity of the further restriction on distributees, a part of the statute not properly before the Court. Assuming the legislature too broadly restricted the class of persons who could obtain contraceptives, it hardly follows that it saw no need to protect the health of all persons to whom they are made available.

. . . I do not think it is the proper function of this Court to dismiss as dubious a state court's explication of a state statute absent overwhelming and irrefutable reasons for doing so.

MR. JUSTICE WHITE, while acknowledging a valid legislative purpose of protecting health, concludes that the State lacks power to regulate the distribution of the contraceptive involved in this case as a means of protecting health. The opinion grants that appellee's conviction would be valid if he had given away a potentially harmful substance, but rejects the State's placing this particular contraceptive in that category. So far as I am aware, this Court has never before challenged the police power of a State to protect the public from the risks of possibly spurious and deleterious substances sold within its borders. . . . [T]he opinion invokes *Griswold v. Connecticut*, 381 U.S. 479 (1965), and puts the statutory classification to an unprecedented test: either the record must contain evidence supporting the classification or the health hazards of the particular contraceptive must be judicially noticeable. This is indeed a novel constitutional doctrine and not surprisingly no authority is cited for it.

Since the potential harmfulness of this particular medicinal substance had never been placed in issue in the state or federal courts, the State can hardly be faulted for its failure to build a record on this point. And it totally mystifies me why, in the absence of some evidence in the record, the factual underpinnings of the statutory classification must be "incontrovertible" or a matter of "common knowledge."

The actual hazards of introducing a particular foreign substance into the human body are frequently controverted, and I cannot believe that unanimity of expert opinion is a prerequisite to a State's exercise of its police power, no matter what the subject matter of their regulation. Even assuming no present dispute among medical authorities, we cannot ignore that it has be-

come commonplace for a drug or food additive to be universally regarded as harmless on one day and to be condemned as perilous on the next. It is inappropriate for this Court to overrule a legislative classification by relying on the present consensus among leading authorities. The commands of the Constitution cannot fluctuate with the shifting tides of scientific opinion.

Even if it were conclusively established once and for all that the product dispensed by appellee is not actually or potentially dangerous in the somatic sense, I would still be unable to agree that the restriction on dispensing it falls outside the State's power to regulate in the area of health. The choice of a means of birth control, although a highly personal matter, is also a health matter in a very real sense, and I see nothing arbitrary in a requirement of medical supervisions. It is generally acknowledged that contraceptives vary in degree of effectiveness and potential harmfulness. There may be compelling health reasons for certain women to choose the most effective means of birth control available, no matter how harmless the less effective alternatives. Others might be advised not to use a highly effective means of contraception because of their peculiar susceptibility to an adverse side effect. . . .

It is revealing, I think, that those portions of the majority and concurring opinions rejecting the statutory limitation on distributors rely on no particular provision of the Constitution. I see nothing in the Fourteenth Amendment or any other part of the Constitution that even vaguely suggests that these medicinal forms of contraceptives must be available in the open market. I do not challenge *Griswold v. Connecticut, supra*, despite its tenuous moorings to the text of the Constitution, but I cannot view it as controlling authority for this case. The Court was there confronted with a statute flatly prohibiting the use of contraceptives, not one regulating their distribution. I simply cannot believe that the limitation on the class of lawful distributors has significantly impaired the right to use contraceptives in Massachu- setts. By relying on *Griswold* in the present context, the Court has passed beyond the penumbras of the specific guarantees into the uncircumscribed area of personal predilections. . . .

CASE QUESTIONS

1. Justice Brennan (for the majority) claims to be rejecting this statute not by means of the compelling interest test but rather by means of the reasonableness test. Because the statute does not regulate the uses to which married persons put contraceptives (see footnote 3), he alleges that it cannot reasonably be viewed as a deterrent to fornication. Suppose that Massachusetts *tightened* its regulations on contraceptives, allowing them to be prescribed by physicians only on receiv- ing a signed oath from married persons to the effect that the devices would be used only with the marriage partner. If the state also were to ban all other distri- bution of contraceptives (e.g., for the purpose of preventing disease) and were to bring the penalties for con- traceptive distribution into line with the penalties for fornication, would the court majority's objections to this statute dissolve?

2. The Court majority informs the Ameri- can public that "not all contraceptives are potentially dangerous." Justice Burger objects that judges are not sup- posed to be telling legislatures what ob- jects they may and may not consider dangerous or needful of medical advice. Is the Court overstepping its bounds on this point? Is this decision compre- hensible without reference to the com- pelling interest test? Is that the differ- ence between Justice White's opinion and the majority opinion?

3. Are married and unmarried persons, in fact, "similarly situated" for purposes of this case? Even in the light of the major- ity's concession that a state could con- stitutionally "regard the problems of extramarital and premarital sexual rela- tions as 'evils of different dimensions and proportions'"?

4. Brennan asserts that he does not have to answer the "important question" whether a state may, on the grounds that contraception itself is immoral, consti- tutionally aim to abolish contraceptive practices as such. His reason for this as- sertion is not easy to follow. He seems to say there are two all-inclusive possi- bilities, and either one vitiates the need to answer the question. One is that *Griswold* implicitly prohibited statutes forbidding the distribution (as well as the use) of contraceptives for married persons; and if married persons' "right of privacy" includes the right to receive contraceptives, then unmarried persons must have the same right. His grounds for this conclusion is that the "right of privacy" acknowledged in *Griswold* "is the right of the *individual*, married or single, to be free from unwarranted

governmental intrusion into matters so fundamentally affecting a person as the decision whether to bear or beget a child." Does this conclusion follow from *Griswold?* Does it contradict much of the logic of *Griswold?*

The other possibility, as Brennan sees it, is that the equal protection clause itself bars making such a distinction between the married and the unmarried if contraception *per se* is viewed as an evil. He claims that in the light of the purpose of the statute, such a distinction would be sheerly arbitrary. Is that conclusion really plausible after the Court in *Griswold* asserted that the need for *marital* privacy is what produces the married couple's constitutional right to use birth control?

5. Would Justice Douglas' argument apply equally to a lecturer who, as part of a lecture advocating legalization of all drugs, handed out of a few samples of heroin, cocaine, and amphetamines?

6. Besides contraception and abortion, what other matters are "so fundamentally affecting a person as the decision

whether to bear or beget a child? Would they include the decision to engage in private, consensual sodomy? In a decision handed down on June 30, 1986, *Bowers v. Hardwick,* 54 U.S.L.W. 4919, Justice White writing for a majority of five said that "none of the rights announced in [cases like *Griswold* and *Eisenstadt*] bears any resemblance to the claimed constitutional right of homosexuals to engage in sodomy. . . . [A]ny claim that these cases . . . stand for the proposition that any kind of private sexual conduct between consenting adults is constitutionally insulated from state proscription is insupportable." Justice Blackmun, writing for the four dissenters, asserted to the contrary, "The right of an individual to conduct intimate relationships in the intimacy of his or her own home seems to me to be at the heart of the Constitution's protection of privacy." Which is a more accurate depiction of the theme of these precedents?

7. Does the right to privacy cover commercial prostitution?

Carey v. Population Services International (1977), discussion

In a 1977 case, *Carey v. Population Services International* (431 U.S. 678), the Supreme Court reaffirmed the basic intent of the *Eisenstadt* decision and extended its reasoning to the situation of unmarried minors under the age of sixteen. Justices White and Stevens provided the crucial votes in declaring void a New York statute that prohibited the distribution of contraceptives to single persons under sixteen years of age. Justice Brennan, Stewart, Marshall, and Blackmun would have held the statute void on somewhat more sweeping grounds (and Justice Powell would have concurred on more narrow grounds). But the decisive opinions of White and Stevens maintained that the law was unconstitutional essentially because, as Brennan had put it in *Eisenstadt,* "It would be plainly unreasonable to assume that [the state] has prescribed pregnancy and the birth of an unwanted child as punishment for fornication. . . ." The statute thus failed even the "rationality" test.

Abortion

The years 1971 to 1973 witnessed an explosion of women's rights developments at the Supreme Court level. The year 1971 began slowly with *Ida Phillips v. Martin-Marietta* (see chapter 5) in January. The 1971–1972 term accelerated the pace, with *Reed v. Reed* (chapter 2), *Eisenstadt v. Baird,* and *Stanley v. Illinois* (chapter 3) in quick succession. The 1972–1973 term continued the fast pace as the Court decided *Frontiero v. Richardson* (chapter 2) and two abortion cases, *Roe v. Wade* and *Doe v. Bolton.*

The two abortion cases were handed down together on January 22, 1973. That event was indisputably the most powerful single blast of this series, whether measured by the number of lives affected,[33] the intensity with which they were affected, or the political aftermath of the decision. None of the other women's rights decisions has produced the political backlash that the doublebarreled abortion decision produced. None has aroused a comparable intensity of political debate. None single-handedly invalidated as many state laws.

The judicial decision to legalize abortion did not occur in a political vacuum. Political activism in behalf of the legalization of abortion, spearheaded by such women's rights groups as NOW and the National Women's Political Caucus reached its peak a year before the Supreme Court's flurry of activity in behalf of women began.

The calendar year of 1970 seems to have been both a turning point and a stopping point for the effort to achieve the legalization of abortion by pressing for legislative action. That year witnessed the legalization of abortion in four states (Hawaii, Alaska, New York, and Washington), two of those involving highly dramatic battles in which legalization was nearly defeated. In Alaska, the legislative decision to legalize was vetoed by the governor. His veto was overridden with one vote to spare. In New York State the prolegalization forces, having barely lost in the assembly on previous ballotings, believed that they were facing defeat when an assemblyman named Michaels rose to his feet with the announcement that although he knew this would end his political career, he was going to change his vote from negative to positive.[34] His shift provided the winning margin in the legislature.

In addition to those victories, the prolegalization forces attained a number of near-misses in 1970. The Arizona House approved a legalization statute in February, only to have it defeated in the Arizona Senate. The Maryland legislature approved legalization in April, only to have it vetoed by Governor Mandel in May. And the House in Vermont approved a legalization bill, only to have it rebuffed in the Vermont Senate. Although the legislative effort succeeded in only four states, the impact of those changes should not be underestimated. These four states were breaking radically with a century-old tradition of harshly punitive treatment of abortion. Naturally, such a dramatic break with the past aroused very strong feelings on both sides of the controversy. The issue did not disappear in these four states after legislative decriminalization.

Judicial activity in the direction of legalization of abortion also took a great leap forward around this time. On the basis of *Griswold* the abortion laws of California, Texas, Wisconsin, Georgia, and the District of Columbia were declared unconstitutional in lower courts in late 1969 and in 1970. In 1970 the U.S. Supreme Court refused to accept jurisdiction to review the California and Wisconsin decisions, thereby leaving those states without valid abortion statutes. The Court did agree to review the Washington, D.C., decision, which had ruled that the District of Columbia's statute was void because of vagueness. That statute permitted abortions when the mother's "health" required, and the district court held that the word "health" was so vague that it did not give fair warning to the physician about what was and was not punishable. (Lack of such warning constitutes denial of "due process of law.")

The years 1971 and 1972 saw an acceleration of activity on the judicial front, whereas legislative momentum slowed to a standstill. The latter can perhaps be explained by the fact that the vigorous lobbying activity—picketing, demonstrating, letter writing, testifying—of the prolegalization abortion groups eventually stimulated in equally active counterlobby of antiabortion groups. For example, on April 15, 1972, ten thousand people (mostly women) marched down Fifth Avenue in New York City to demand repeal of New York's permissive abortion law.[35] This counter-lobby succeeded in the New York State legislature, but Governor Rockefeller vetoed their repeal bill.

Meanwhile, the judiciary was proving a more fruitful lobbying target for the proponents of legalization. In January 1971 a federal district court in Illinois declared the state's abortion law to be an unconstitutional invasion of the right to privacy (following *Griswold*). In 1972 the abortion laws of Florida, New Jersey, and Connecticut met a similar fate. The Connecticut case had been launched, in almost classic interest-group fashion, by a total of 838 women of child-bearing age. By the end of 1972 then, eight states had lost their abortion laws at the hands of judges.

The U.S. Supreme Court by this time had entered the fray. In April 1971 they decided the District of Columbia case,[36] but at that point the signals the Court was emitting about its future direction were ambiguous. The Court held that the District of Columbia statute prohibiting abortion except where necessary for the mother's life or "health" was not void for vagueness. In interpreting "health," however, the Court said that the statute obviously included considerations of mental and emotional health. And the Court seemed to imply that the word "necessary" should be read as "medically appropriate" rather than as "essential." Thus, although the Court *did* uphold an antiabortion statute, it did so with an interpretation that substantially liberalized the statutory permission for abortions.

In May 1971 the Supreme Court docketed for the fall calendar the appeals of the 1970 abortion cases from Texas and Georgia (*Roe v. Wade* and *Doe v. Bolton*). In December 1971 it heard the arguments from counsel in those cases. In March 1972 the Supreme Court handed down *Eisenstadt v. Baird* in words, as I have noted, that foreshadowed the legalization of abortion.[37] In June 1972 the Court announced that the abortion cases would be scheduled for reargument the following fall. Because of the loss of Justices Black and Harlan, the Court had had only seven members at the time of the first arguments. In a decision as momentous as the abortion one was going to be, the Court did not want to appear short-handed. With Justices Rehnquist and Powell filling out the Court, the abortion cases were reargued on October 11, 1972.

The two abortion cases treated challenges to anti-abortion statutes by two women using pseudonyms, Jane Roe and Mary Doe. Each challenged the statute on behalf of herself "and others similarly situated"; thus, these were class-action suits.

Jane Roe was an unmarried pregnant woman who desired an abortion in Texas, where all abortions were forbidden except "for the purpose of saving the life of the mother." The majority of states in American had abortion laws that followed the Texas pattern. She initiated her lawsuit in March 1970.

Mary Doe was a twenty-two-year-old married citizen of Georgia who already had three children and was once again pregnant. Because of her poverty and mental instability, two of her children were in foster homes and one had been placed for adoption. She had been a mental hospital patient and had been advised that having another baby would damage her health more than having an abortion would. Georgia law permitted abortions only for Georgia residents, in an accredited hospital, upon the decision of three licensed physicians and a hospital staff abortion committee that either (1) continued pregnancy would endanger the pregnant woman's life or "seriously and permanently" injure her health; (2) the fetus would "very likely be born with a grave, permanent, and irremediable mental or physical defect"; or (3) the pregnancy resulted from rape or incest. This law was modeled after the American Legal Institute's recommended abortion code. Mary Doe failed to obtain the committee's permission at Grady Memorial Hospital of Atlanta in April 1970. She managed to obtain the permission at Georgia Baptist Hospital in May 1970, but the latter did not accept her as a charity patient, and she could not afford to pay for an abortion there. At that point, she, too, initiated a lawsuit.

Both women had prevailed at the district court level against the attorney general of the state in question. The basis of the district courts' decisions had been the *Griswold* right of privacy, and each district court had issued a declaratory judgment to the effect that the statutes in question were unconstitutional. But both women nonetheless appealed to the Supreme Court, because in each case the district court had declared the particular statutes unconstitutional but had refused to grant the women's request that all future criminal sanctions on abortion be enjoined.

By January 1973, when the Supreme Court handed down its decisions, naturally neither woman was still pregnant. For that reason, nothing that the Court could say would change the outcome for them. A situation such as this is ordinarily considered "moot," and the Court, as a rule, refuses to decide moot cases (because they do not present a concrete "controversy" but are closer to disputes of opinion). Here the Supreme Court made an exception and held that both Roe and Doe had standing to challenge the statutes. Justice Blackmun, writing for the majority, explained this decision as follows:

> The usual rule in federal cases is that an actual controversy must exist at stages of appellate or certiorari review, and not simply at the date the action is initiated. [Case citations omitted.]
>
> But when, as here, pregnancy is a significant fact in the litigation, the normal 266-day human gestation period is so short that the pregnancy will come to term before the usual appellate process is complete. If that termination makes a case moot, pregnancy litigation seldom will survive beyond the trial stage and appellate review will be effectively denied. Our law should not be that rigid. Pregnancy often comes more than once to the same woman. . . . Pregnancy provides a classic justification for a conclusion of nonmootness. It truly could be "capable of repetition, yet evading review. . . ." (*Roe v. Wade* 410 U.S. 113, 125.)

Although Blackmun, writing for the Court majority (consisting of Burger, Douglas, Brennan, Stewart, Marshall, Powell, and himself), issued a separate opinion for each of the two cases, Douglas, Burger, and White (the latter dissenting on behalf of Rehnquist and himself) wrote additional opinions that applied to the combination of the two cases. For this reason, the two cases are consolidated here. The two majority opinions appear together first, and these are followed by the concurring opinions and the dissents.

Roe v. Wade, 410 U.S. 113 (1973) and Doe v. Bolton, 410 U.S. 179 (1973)

Mr. Justice Blackmun delivered the opinion of the Court [for *Roe v. Wade*].

. . .

We forthwith acknowledge our awareness of the sensitive and emotional nature of the abortion controversy, of the vigorous opposing views, even among physicians, and of the deep and seemingly absolute convictions that the subject inspires. One's philosophy, one's experiences, one's religious training, one's attitudes toward life and family and their values, and the moral standards one establishes and seeks to observe, are all likely to influence and to color one's thinking and conclusions about abortion.

In addition, population growth, pollution, poverty, and racial overtones tend to complicate and not to simplify the problem.

Our task, of course, is to resolve the issue by constitutional measurement, free of emotion and of predilection. We seek earnestly to do this, and, because we do, we have inquired into, and in this opinion place some emphasis upon, medical and medical-legal history and what that history reveals about man's attitudes toward the abortion procedure over the centuries. . . .

V

The principal thrust of appellant's attack on the Texas statutes is that they improperly invade a right, said to be possessed by the pregnant woman, to choose to terminate her pregnancy. Appellant would discover this right in the concept of personal "liberty" embodied in the Fourteenth Amendment's Due Process Clause; or in personal, marital, familial, and sexual privacy said to be protected by the Bill of Rights or its penumbras, *see Griswold v. Connecticut*, 381 U.S. 479 (1965); *Eisenstadt v. Baird*, 405 U.S. 438 (1972); *id.* at 460 (WHITE, J., concurring in result); or among those rights reserved to the people by the Ninth Amendment, *Griswold v. Connecticut*, 381 U.S., at 486 (Goldberg, J., concurring). Before addressing this claim, we feel it desirable briefly to survey, in several aspects, the history of abortion, for such insight as that history may afford us, and then to examine the state purposes and interests behind the criminal abortion laws.

VI

It perhaps is not generally appreciated that the restrictive criminal abortion laws in effect in a majority of States today are of relatively recent vintage. Those laws,

generally proscribing abortion or its attempt at any time during pregnancy except when necessary to preserve that pregnant woman's life, are not of ancient or even of common-law origin. Instead, they derive from statutory changes effected, for the most part, in the latter half of the nineteenth century.

1. *Ancient attitudes.* These are not capable of precise determination. . . . [A]bortion was practiced in Greek times as well as in the Roman Era,[9] and . . . "it was resorted to without scruple."[10] . . . If abortion was prosecuted in some places, it seems to have been based on a concept of a violation of the father's right to his offspring. Ancient religion did not bar abortion.[12]

2. *The Hippocratic Oath.* What then of the famous Oath that has stood so long as the ethical guide of the medical profession and that bears the name of the great Greek (460?–377? B.C.), who has been described as the Father of Medicine. . . ? The Oath was not uncontested even in Hippocrates' day; only the Pythagorean school of philosophers frowned upon the related act of suicide. Most Greek thinkers, on the other hand, commended abortion, at least prior to viability. *See* Plato, *Republic*, V, 461; Aristotle, *Politics*, VII, 1335b 25. For the

9. J. Ricci, *The Genealogy of Gynaecology*, 52, 84, 113, 149 (2d ed. 1950) (hereinafter Ricci); L. Lader, *Abortion* 75–77 (1966) (hereinafter Lader); K. Niswander, *Medical Abortion Practices in the United States in Abortion and the Law* 37, 38–40 (D. Smith ed. 1967); G. Williams, *The Sanctity of Life and the Criminal Law* 148 (1957) (hereinafter Williams); J. Noonan, "An Almost Absolute Value in History," in *The Morality of Abortion* 1, 3–7 (J. Noonan ed. 1970) (hereinafter Noonan); Quay, *Justifiable Abortion—Medical and Legal Foundations* (pt. 2), 49 Geo. L.J. 395, 406–42 (1961) (hereinafter Quay).

10. L. Edelstein, *The Hippocratic Oath* 10 (1943) (hereinafter Edelstein).

12. Edelstein 13–14.

Pythagoreans, however, it was a matter of dogma. For them the embryo was animate from the moment of conception, and abortion meant destruction of a living being. The abortion clause of the Oath, therefore, "echoes Pythagorean doctrines," and "[i]n no other stratum of Greek opinion were such views held or proposed in the same spirit of uncompromising austerity."[17] . . . But with the end of antiquity a decided change took place. Resistance against suicide and against abortion became common. The Oath came to be popular. The emerging teachings of Christianity were in agreement with the Pythagorean ethic. The Oath "became the nucleus of all medical ethics" and "was applauded as the embodiment of truth."[19] . . .

This . . . enables us to understand, in historical context, a long-accepted and revered statement of medical ethics.

3. *The common law.*[*] It is undisputed that at common law, abortion performed *before* "quickening"—the first recognizable movement of the fetus *in utero*, appearing usually from the 16th to the 18th week of pregnancy—was not an indictable offense. . . . Christian theology and the canon law came to fix the point of animation at 40 days for a male and 80 days for a female, a view that persisted until the 19th century, [but] there was otherwise little agreement about the precise time of formation or animation. There was agreement, however, that prior to this point the fetus was to be regarded as part of the mother, and its destruction, therefore, was not homicide. Due to continued uncertainty about the precise time when animation occurred, to the lack of any empirical basis

for the 40–80-day view, and perhaps to Aquinas' definition of movement as one of the two first principles of life, Bracton focused upon quickening as the critical point. The significance of quickening was echoed by later common-law scholars and found its way into the received common law in this country.

Whether abortion of a *quick* fetus was a felony at common law, or even a lesser crime, is still disputed. . . . A recent review of the common-law precedents argues . . . that those precedents contradict Coke and that even post-quickening abortion was never established as a common-law crime.[26] . . .[I]t now appear[s] doubtful that abortion was ever firmly established as a common-law crime even with respect to the destruction of a quick fetus.

4. *The English statutory law.* England's first criminal abortion statute. Lord Ellenborough's Act, 43 Geo. 3, ch. 58, came in 1803. It made abortion of a quick fetus, § 1, a capital crime, but in § 2 it provided lesser penalties for the felony of abortion before quickening, and thus preserved the "quickening" distinction. . . . [J. Blackmun traces British abortion law up to the present. As of 1967 British law was similar to the Georgia statute treated in *Doe v. Bolton*.]

5. *The American law.* In this country, the law in effect in all but a few States until mid-nineteenth century was the pre-existing English common law. Connecticut, the first State to enact abortion legislation, adopted in 1821 that part of Lord Ellenborough's Act that related to a woman "quick with child." The death penalty was not imposed. Abortion before quickening was made a crime in that State only in 1860. In 1828, New York

---

17. *Id.* at 18; Lader 76.

19. *Id.* at 64.

*Common law is the traditional law of court precedents in the Anglo-American legal system.—Au.

26. Means, *The Phoenix of Abortional Freedom: Is a Penumbral or Ninth-Amendment Right About to Arise from the Nineteenth-Century Legislative Ashes of a Fourteenth-Century Common-Law Liberty?*, 17 N.Y.L.F. 335 (1971) (hereinafter Means II). . . .

enacted legislation that, in two respects, was to serve as a model for early anti-abortion statutes. First, while barring destruction of an unquickened fetus as well as a quick fetus, it made the former only a misdemeanor, but the latter second-degree manslaughter. Second, it incorporated a concept of therapeutic abortion by providing that an abortion was excused if it "shall have been necessary to preserve the life of such mother, or shall have been advised by two physicians to be necessary for such purpose." By 1840, when Texas had received the common law, only eight American States had statutes dealing with abortion. It was not until after the War Between the States that legislation began generally to replace the common law. Most of those initial statutes dealt severely with abortion after quickening but were lenient with it before quickening. Most punished attempts equally with completed abortions. While many statutes included the exception for an abortion thought by one or more physicians to be necessary to save the mother's life, that provision soon disappeared and the typical law required that the procedure actually be necessary for that purpose.

Gradually, in the middle and late nineteenth century the quickening distinction disappeared from the statutory law of most States and the degree of the offense and the penalties were increased. By the end of the 1950s, a large majority of the jurisdictions banned abortion, however and whenever performed, unless done to save or preserve the life of the mother. . . . In the past several years, however, a trend toward liberalization of abortion statutes has resulted in adoption, by about one-third of the States, of less stringent laws, most of them patterned after the ALI Model Penal Code. . . .

It is thus apparent that at common law, at the time of the adoption of our Constitution, and throughout the major portion of the nineteenth century, abortion was viewed with less disfavor than under most American statutes currently in effect. Phrasing it another way, a woman enjoyed a substantially broader right to terminate a pregnancy than she does in most States today. At least with respect to the early stage of pregnancy, and very possibly without such a limitation, the opportunity to make this choice was present in this country well into the nineteenth century. Even later, the law continued for some time to treat less punitively an abortion procured in early pregnancy.

6. *The position of the American Medical Association.* [J. Blackmun recapitulates AMA committee reports of 1857 and 1871 condemning abortion and calling "the attention of the clergy of all denominations to the perverted views of morality entertained by a large class of females—aye, and men also, on this important question," He then describes the liberalization of AMA positions in 1967 and 1970.]

7. *The position of the American Public Health Association.* In October 1970, the Executive Board of the APHA adopted Standards for Abortion Services. These [urged that:]

> Rapid and simple abortion referral must be readily available through state and local public health departments, medical societies, or other nonprofit organizations. . . . (Recommended Standards for Abortion Services, 61 Am. J. Pub. Health 396 [1971].)

. . . It was said that at present abortions should be performed by physicians or osteopaths who are licensed to practice and who have "adequate training." *Id.* at 398.

8. *The position of the American Bar Association.* At its meeting in February 1972 the ABA House of Delegates approved, with 17

opposing votes, the Uniform Abortion Act. . . . We set forth the Act in full in the margin.[40] . . .

40. "UNIFORM ABORTION ACT"
"Section 1. [*Abortion Defined: When Authorized.*]

"(a) 'Abortion' means the termination of human pregnancy with an intention other than to produce a live birth or to remove a dead fetus.

"(b) An abortion may be performed in this state only if it is performed:

"(1) by a physician licensed to practice medicine [or osteopathy] in this state or by a physician practicing medicine [or osteopathy] in the employ of the government of the United States or of this state, [and the abortion is performed [in the physician's office or in a medical clinic, or] in a hospital approved by the [Department of Health] or operated by the United States, this state, or any department, agency, or political subdivision of either;] or by a female upon herself upon the advice of the physician; and

"(2) within [20] weeks after the commencement of the pregnancy [or after [20] weeks only if the physician has reasonable cause to believe (i) there is a substantial risk that continuance of the pregnancy would endanger the life of the mother or would gravely impair the physical or mental health of the mother, (ii) that the child would be born with grave physical or mental defect, or (iii) that the pregnancy resulted from rape or incest, or illicit intercourse with a girl under the age of 16 years].

"Section 2. [*Penalty.*] Any person who performs or procures an abortion other than authorized by this Act is guilty of a [felony] and, upon conviction thereof, may be sentenced to pay a fine not exceeding [$1,000] or to imprisonment [in the state penitentiary] not exceeding [5 years], or both.

"Section 3. [*Uniformity of Interpretation.*] This Act shall be construed to effectuate its general purpose to make uniform the law with respect to the subject of this Act among those states which enact it.

"Section 4. [*Short Title.*] This Act may be cited as the Uniform Abortion Act.

"Section 5. [*Severability.*] If any provision of this Act or the application thereof to any person or circumstance is held invalid, the invalidity

VII

Three reasons have been advanced to explain historically the enactment of criminal abortion laws in the nineteenth century and to justify their continued existence.

It has been argued occasionally that these laws were the product of a Victorian social concern to discourage illicit sexual conduct. Texas, however, does not advance this justification in the present case, and it appears that no court or commentator has taken the argument seriously. The appellants and *amici* contend, moreover, that this is not a proper state purpose at all and suggest that, if it were, the Texas statutes are overbroad in protecting it since the law fails to distinguish between married and unwed mothers.

A second reason is concerned with abortion as a medical procedure. When most criminal abortion laws were first enacted, the procedure was a hazardous one for the woman. This was particularly true prior to the development of antisepsis. Antiseptic techniques . . . were not generally accepted and employed until about the turn of the century. Abortion mortality was high. Even after 1900, and perhaps until as late as the development of antibiotics in the 1940s, standard modern techniques such as dilation and curettage were not nearly so safe as they are today. Thus, it has been argued that a State's real concern in enacting a criminal abortion law was to protect the pregnant woman, that is, to restrain her from submitting to a procedure that placed her life in serious jeopardy.

Modern medical techniques have altered this situation. Appellants and various *amici* refer to medical data indicating that

does not affect other provisions or applications of this Act which can be given effect without the invalid provision or application, and to this end the provisions of this Act are severable.

abortion in early pregnancy, that is, prior to the end of the first trimester, although not without its risk, is now relatively safe. Mortality rates for women undergoing early abortions, where the procedure is legal, appear to be as low or lower than the rates for normal childbirth. Consequently, any interest of the State in protecting the woman from an inherently hazardous procedure, except when it would be equally dangerous for her to forgo it, has largely disappeared. Of course, important state interests in the areas of health and medical standards do remain. The State has a legitimate interest in seeing to it that abortion, like any other medical procedure, is performed under circumstances that insure maximum safety for the patient. This interest obviously extends at least to the performing physician and his staff, to the facilities involved, to the availability of after-care, and to adequate provision for any complication or emergency that might arise. . . . Moreover, the risk to the woman increases as her pregnancy continues. Thus, the State retains a definite interest in protecting the woman's own health and safety when an abortion is proposed at a late stage of pregnancy.

The third reason is the State's interest—some phrase it in terms of duty—in protecting prenatal life. Some of the argument for this justification rests on the theory that a new human life is present from the moment of conception. The State's interest and general obligation to protect life then extends, it is argued, to prenatal life. Only when the life of the pregnant mother herself is at stake, balanced against the life she carries within her, should the interest of the embryo or fetus not prevail. Logically, of course, a legitimate state interest in this area need not stand or fall on acceptance of the belief that life begins at conception or at some other point prior to live birth. In assessing the State's interest, rec-

ognition may be given to the less rigid claim that as long as at least *potential* life is involved, the State may assert interests beyond the protection of the pregnant woman alone.

Parties challenging state abortion laws have sharply disputed in some courts the contention that a purpose of these laws, when enacted, was to protect prenatal life. . . . [and] they claim that most state laws were designed solely to protect the woman. Because medical advances have lessened this concern, at least with respect to abortion in early pregnancy, they argue that with respect to such abortions the laws can no longer be justified by any state interest. There is some scholarly support for this view of original purpose. The few state courts called upon to interpret their laws in the late nineteenth and early twentieth centuries did focus on the State's interest in protecting the woman's health rather than in preserving the embryo and fetus. Proponents of this view point out that in many States, including Texas, by statute or judicial interpretation, the pregnant woman herself could not be prosecuted for self-abortion or for cooperating in an abortion performed upon her by another. They claim that adoption of the "quickening" distinction through received common law and state statutes tacitly recognizes the greater health hazards inherent in the late abortion and impliedly repudiates the theory that life begins at conception. . . .

VIII

The Constitution does not explicitly mention any right of privacy. In a line of decisions, however, going back perhaps as far as *Union Pacific R. Co. v. Botsford*, 141 U.S. 250, 251 (1891), the Court has recognized that a right of personal privacy, or a guarantee of certain areas or zones of privacy, does exist under the Constitution. In varying contexts, the Court or individual

Justices have, indeed, found at least the roots of that right in the First Amendment, *Stanley v. Georgia*, 394 U.S. 557, 564 (1969); in the Fourth and Fifth Amendments, *Terry v. Ohio*, 392 U.S. 1, 8–9 (1968), *Katz v. United States*, 389 U.S. 347, 350 (1967), *Boyd v. United States*, 116 U.S. 616 (1886), *see Olmstead v. United States*, 277 U.S. 438, 478 (1928) (Brandeis, J., dissenting); in the penumbras of the Bill of Rights, *Griswold v. Connecticut*, 381 U.S., at 484–885: in the Ninth Amendment, *id.* at 486 (Goldberg, J., concurring); or in the concept of liberty guaranteed by the first section of the Fourteenth Amendment, *see Meyer v. Nebraska*, 262 U.S. 390, 399 (1923). These decisions made it clear that only personal rights that can be deemed "fundamental" or "implicit in the concept of ordered liberty," *Palko v. Connecticut*, 302 U.S. 319, 325 (1937), are included in this guarantee of personal privacy. They also make it clear that the right has some extension to activities relating to marriage, *Loving v. Virginia*, 388 U.S. 1, 12 (1967); procreation, *Skinner v. Oklahoma*, 316 U.S. 535, 541–42 (1942); contraception, *Eisenstadt v. Baird*, 405 U.S., at 453–54; *id.* at 460, 463–65 (WHITE, J., concurring in result); family relationships, *Prince v. Massachusetts*, 321 U.S. 158, 166 (1944); and child rearing and education, *Pierce v. Society of Sisters*, 268 U.S. 510, 535 (1925), *Meyer v. Nebraska, supra.*

This right of privacy, whether it be founded in the Fourteenth Amendment's concept of personal liberty and restrictions upon state action, as we feel it is, or, as the District Court determined, in the Ninth Amendment's reservation of rights to the people, is broad enough to encompass a woman's decision whether or not to terminate her pregnancy. The detriment that the State would impose upon the pregnant woman by denying this choice altogether is apparent. Specific and direct harm medically diagnosable even in early pregnancy may be involved. Maternity, or additional offspring, may force upon the woman a distressful life and future. Psychological harm may be imminent. Mental and physical health may be taxed by child care. There is also the distress, for all concerned, associated with the unwanted child, and there is the problem of bringing a child into a family already unable, psychologically and otherwise, to care for it. In other cases, as in this one, the additional difficulties and continuing stigma of unwed motherhood may be involved. All these are factors the woman and her responsible physician necessarily will consider in consultation.

On the basis of elements such as these, appellant and some *amici* argue that the woman's right is absolute and that she is entitled to terminate her pregnancy at whatever time, in whatever way, and for whatever reason she alone chooses. With this we do not agree. Appellant's arguments that Texas either has no valid interest at all in regulating the abortion decision, or no interest strong enough to support any limitation upon the woman's sole determination, are unpersuasive. The Court's decisions recognizing a right of privacy also acknowledge that some regulation in areas protected by that right is appropriate. As noted above, a State may properly assert important interests in safeguarding health, in maintaining medical standards, and in protecting potential life. At some point in pregnancy, these respective interests become sufficiently compelling to sustain regulation of the factors that govern the abortion decision. The privacy right involved, therefore, cannot be said to be absolute. In fact, it is not clear to us that the claim asserted by some *amici* that one has an unlimited right to do with one's body as one pleases bears a close relationship to the right of privacy previously articulated in the Court's decisions. The Court has refused to recognize an unlimited right of this kind in the past. *Jacobson v. Massachusetts,* 197 U.S. 11 (1905) (vaccination); *Buck v. Bell,* 274 U.S. 200 (1927) (sterilization).

We, therefore, conclude that the right of personal privacy includes the abortion decision, but that this right is not unqualified and must be considered against important state interests in regulation. . . . [This] right, nonetheless, is not absolute and is subject to some limitations; and . . . at some point the state interests as to protection of health, medical standards, and prenatal life, become dominant. . . .

Where certain "fundamental rights" are involved, the Court has held that regulation limiting these rights may be justified only by a "compelling state interest," *Kramer v. Union Free School District,* 395 U.S. 621, 627 (1969); *Shapiro v. Thompson,* 394 U.S. 618, 634 (1969), *Sherbert v. Verner,* 374 U.S. 398, 406 (1963), and that legislative enactments must be narrowly drawn to express only the legitimate state interests at stake. *Griswold v. Connecticut,* 381 U.S., at 485; *Aptheker v. Secretary of State,* 378 U.S. 500, 508 (1964); *Cantwell v. Connecticut,* 310 U.S. 296, 307–8 (1940); *see Eisenstadt v. Baird,* 405 U.S., at 460, 463–64 (WHITE, J., concurring in result).

In the recent abortion cases, . . . courts have recognized these principles. Those striking down state laws have generally scrutinized the State's interests in protecting health and potential life, and have concluded that neither interest justified broad limitations on the reasons for which a physician and his pregnant patient might decide that she should have an abortion in the early stages of pregnancy. Courts sustaining state laws have held that the State's determinations to protect health or prenatal life are dominant and constitutionally justifiable.

IX

The District Court held that the appellee failed to meet his burden of demonstrating that the Texas statute's infringement upon Roe's rights was necessary to support a compelling state interest, and that, although the appellee presented "several compelling justifications for state presence in the area of abortions," the statutes outstripped these justifications and swept "far beyond any areas of compelling state interest." 314 F. Supp., at 1222–23. Appellant and appellee both contest that holding. Appellant, as has been indicated, claims an absolute right that bars any state imposition of criminal penalties in the area. Appellee argues that the State's determination to recognize and protect prenatal life from and after conception constitutes a compelling state interest. As noted above, we do not agree fully with either formulation.

A. The appellee and certain *amici* argue that the fetus is a "person" within the language and meaning of the Fourteenth Amendment. In support of this, they outline at length and in detail the well-known facts of fetal development. If this suggestion of personhood is established, the appellant's case, of course, collapses, for the fetus' right to life would then be guaranteed specifically by the Amendment . . . [but] no case [can] be cited that holds that a fetus is a person within the meaning of the Fourteenth Amendment.

The Constitution does not define "person" in so many words. Section 1 of the Fourteenth Amendment contains three references to "person." The first, in defining "citizens," speaks of "persons born or naturalized in the United States." . . . "Person" is used in other places in the Constitution. . . . But in nearly all these instances, the use of the word is such that it has application only postnatally. None indicates, with any assurance, that it has any possible pre-natal application.

All this, together with our observation, *supra,* that throughout the major portion of the nineteenth century prevailing legal abortion practices were far freer than they are today, persuades us that the word "person," as used in the Fourteenth Amendment, does not include the unborn. This is in accord with the results reached in those few cases where the issue has been squarely presented. [He cites seven lower court cases and one Supreme Court case of indirect reference, *U.S. v. Vuitch* 402 U.S. 62 (1971).]

B. The pregnant woman cannot be isolated in her privacy. She carries an embryo and, later, a fetus. . . . The situation therefore is inherently different from marital intimacy, or bedroom possession of obscene material, or marriage, or procreation, or education, with which *Eisenstadt* and *Griswold, Stanley, Loving, Skinner,* and *Pierce* and *Meyer* were respectively concerned. As we have intimated above, it is reasonable and appropriate for a State to decide that at some point in time another interest, that of health of the mother or that of potential human life, becomes significantly involved. The woman's privacy is no longer sole and any right of privacy she possesses must be measured accordingly.

Texas urges that, apart from the Fourteenth Amendment, life begins at conception and is present throughout pregnancy, and that, therefore, the State has a compelling interest in protecting that life from and after conception. We need not resolve the difficult question of when life begins. When those trained in the respective disciplines of medicine, philosophy, and theology are unable to arrive at any consensus, the judiciary, at this point in the development of man's knowledge, is not in a position to speculate as to the answer.

It should be sufficient to note briefly the wide divergence of thinking on this most sensitive and difficult question. There has always been strong support for the view that life does not begin until live birth. This was the belief of the Stoics. It appears to be the predominant, though not the unanimous, attitude of the Jewish faith. It may be taken to represent also the position of a large segment of the Protestant community, insofar as that can be ascertained; organized groups that have taken a formal position on the abortion issue have generally regarded abortion as a matter for the conscience of the individual and her family. As we have noted, the common law found greater significance in quickening. Physicians and their scientific colleagues have regarded that event with less interest and have tended to focus either upon conception, upon live birth, or upon the interim point at which the fetus becomes "viable," that is, potentially able to live outside the mother's womb, albeit with artificial aid. Viability is usually placed at about seven months (28 weeks) but may occur earlier, even at 24 weeks. . . . [The Roman Catholic Church] would recognize the existence of life from the moment of conception. . . . As one brief *amicus* discloses, this is a view strongly held by many non-Catholics as well, and by many physicians. Substantial problems for precise definition of this view are posed, however, by new embryological data that purport to indicate that conception is a "process" over time, rather than an event, and by new medical techniques such as menstrual extraction, the "morning-after" pill, implantation of embryos, artificial insemination, and even artificial wombs.

In areas other than criminal abortion, the law has been reluctant to endorse any theory that life, as we recognize it, begins before live birth or to accord legal rights to the unborn except in narrowly defined situations and except when the rights are contingent upon live birth. For example, the traditional rule of tort law denied recovery for prenatal injuries even though the child was born alive. That rule has been changed in almost every jurisdiction. In most States, recovery is said to be permitted only if the fetus is viable, or at least quick, when the injuries were sustained, though few courts have squarely so held. In a recent development, generally opposed by the commentators, some States permit the parents of a stillborn child to maintain an action for wrongful death because of prenatal injuries. Such an action, however, would appear to be one to vindicate the parents' interest and is thus consistent with the view that the fetus, at most, represents only the potentiality of life. . . .

X

In view of all this, we do not agree that, by adopting one theory of life, Texas may override the rights of the pregnant woman that are at stake. We repeat, however, that the State does have an important and legitimate interest in preserving and protecting the health of the pregnant woman, whether she be a resident of the State or a nonresident who seeks medical consultation and treatment there, and that it has still *another* important and legitimate interest in protecting the potentiality of human life. These interests are separate and distinct. Each grows in substantiality as the woman approaches term and, at a point during pregnancy, each becomes "compelling."

With respect the State's important and legitimate interest in the health of the mother, the "compelling" point, in the light of present medical knowledge, is at approximately the end of the first trimester. This is so because of the now-established medical fact, referred to above, that until the end of the first trimester mortality in abortion may be less than mortality in normal childbirth. It follows that, from and after this point, a State may regulate the abortion procedure to the extent that the regulation reasonably relates to the preservation and protection of maternal health. Examples of permissible state regulation in this area are requirements as to the qualifications of the person who is to perform the

abortion; as to the licensure of that person; as to the facility in which the procedure is to be performed, that is, whether it must be a hospital or may be a clinic or some other place of less-than-hospital status; as to the licensing of the facility; and the like.

This means, on the other hand, that, for the period of pregnancy prior to this "compelling" point, the attending physician, in consultation with his patient, is free to determine, without regulation by the State, that, in his medical judgment, the patient's pregnancy should be terminated. If that decision is reached, the judgment may be effectuated by an abortion free of interference by the State.

With respect to the State's important and legitimate interest in potential life, the "compelling" point is at viability. This is so because the fetus then presumably has the capability of meaningful life outside the mother's womb. State regulation protective of fetal life after viability thus has both logical and biological justifications. If the State is interested in protecting fetal life after viability, it may go so far as to proscribe abortion during that period, except when it is necessary to preserve the life or health of the mother.

Measured against these standards, Article 1196 of the Texas Penal Code, in restricting legal abortions to those "procured or attempted by medical advice for the purpose of saving the life of the mother," sweeps too broadly. The statute made no distinction between abortions performed early in pregnancy and those performed later, and it limits to a single reason, "saving" the mother's life, the legal justification for the procedure. The statute, therefore, cannot survive the constitutional attack made upon it here. . . .

XI

To summarize and to repeat:
1. A state criminal abortion statute of the current Texas type, that excepts from

criminality only a *life-saving* procedure on behalf of the mother, without regard to pregnancy stage and without recognition of the other interests involved, is violative of the Due Process Clause of the Fourteenth Amendment.

(a) For the stage prior to approximately the end of the first trimester, the abortion decision and its effectuation must be left to the medical judgment of the pregnant woman's attending physician.

(b) For the stage subsequent to approximately the end of the first trimester, the State, in promoting its interest in the health of the mother, may, if it chooses, regulate the abortion procedure in ways that are reasonably related to maternal health.

(c) For the stage subsequent to viability, the State in promoting its interest in the potentiality of human life may, if it chooses, regulate, and even proscribe, abortion except where it is necessary, in appropriate medical judgment, for the preservation of the life or health of the mother.

2. The State may define the term "physician," as it has been employed in the preceding paragraphs of this part XI of this opinion, to mean only a physician currently licensed by the State, and may proscribe any abortion by a person who is not a physician as so defined.

In *Doe v. Bolton, post*, procedural requirements contained in one of the modern abortion statutes are considered. That opinion and this one, of course, are to be read together. . . .

MR. JUSTICE BLACKMUN delivered the opinion of the Court [for *Doe v. Bolton*].

. . .

IV

The appellants attack on several grounds those portions of the Georgia abortion statutes that remain after the District Court decision: undue restriction of a right to personal and marital privacy; vagueness; deprivation of substantive and procedural due process; improper restriction to Georgia residents; and denial of equal protection.

A. *Roe v. Wade, supra*, sets forth our conclusion that a pregnant woman does not have an absolute constitutional right to an abortion on her demand. What is said there is applicable here and need not be repeated.

B. . . . Appellants argue that the statutes do not adequately protect the woman's right. This is so because it would be physically and emotionally damaging to Doe to bring a child into her poor, "fatherless" family, and because advances in medicine and medical techniques have made it safer for a woman to have a medically induced abortion than for her to bear a child. Thus, "a statute that requires a woman to carry an unwanted pregnancy to term infringes not only on a fundamental right of privacy but on the right to life itself."

The appellants recognize that a century ago medical knowledge was not so advanced as it is today, that the techniques of antisepsis were not known, and that any abortion procedure was dangerous for the woman. To restrict the legality of the abortion to the situation where it was deemed necessary, in medical judgment, for the preservation of the woman's life was only a natural conclusion in the exercise of the legislative judgment of that time. . . .

C. Appellants argue that § 26–1202(a) of the Georgia statutes, as it has been left by the District Court's decision, is unconstitutionally vague. This argument centers on the proposition that, with the District Court's having struck down the statutorily specified reasons, it still remains a crime for a physician to perform an abortion except when, at § 26–1202(a) reads, it is "based upon his best clinical judgment that an abortion is necessary." The appellants contend that the word "necessary" does not warn the physician of what conduct is proscribed; that the statute is wholly without objective standards and is subject to diverse interpretation; and that doctors will choose to err on the side of caution and will be arbitrary.

The net result of the District Court's decision is that the abortion determination, so far as the physician is concerned, is made in the exercise of his professional, that is, his "best clinical," judgment in the light of all the attendant circumstances. He is not now restricted to the three situations originally specified. Instead, he may range farther afield wherever his medical judgment, properly and professionally exercised, so dictates and directs him. . . .

[We conclude] that the term "health" present[s] no problem of vagueness. "Indeed, whether a particular operation is necessary for a patient's physical or mental health is a judgment that physicians are obviously called upon to make routinely whenever surgery is considered." *United States v. Vuitch*, 402 U.S. 62, 72 (1971).

We agree with the District Court, 319 F. Supp., at 1058, that the medical judgment may be exercised in the light of all factors—physical, emotional, psychological, familial, and the woman's age—relevant to the well-being of the patient. All these factors may relate to health. This allows the attending physician the room he needs to make his best medical judgment. And it is room that operates for the benefit, not the disadvantage, of the pregnant woman.

D. The appellants next argue that the District Court should have declared unconstitutional three procedural demands of the Georgia statute: (1) that the abortion be performed in a hospital accredited by the Joint Commission on Accreditation of Hospitals:[11] (2) that the procedure be approved

by the hospital staff abortion committee; and (3) that the performing physician's judgment be confirmed by the independent examinations of the patient by two other licensed physicians. The appellants attack these provisions not only on the ground that they unduly restrict the woman's right of privacy, but also on procedural due process and equal protection grounds. The physician-appellants also argue that, by subjecting a doctor's individual medical judgment to committee approval and to confirming consultations, the statute impermissibly restricts the physician's right to practice his profession and deprives him of due process.

1. *JCAH accreditation.* . . . In Georgia, there is no restriction on the performance of non-abortion surgery in a hospital not yet accredited by the JCAH [Joint Commission on the Accreditation of Hospitals] so long as other requirements imposed by the State, such as licensing of the hospital and of the operating surgeon, are met.

We hold that the JCAH-accreditation requirement does not withstand constitutional scrutiny in the present context. It is a requirement that simply is not "based on differences that are reasonably related to the purposes of the Act in which it is found." *Morey v. Doud*, 354 U.S. 457, 465 (1957).

This is not to say that Georgia may not or should not, from and after the end of the first trimester, adopt standards for licensing all facilities where abortions may be performed so long as those standards are legitimately related to the objective the State seeks to accomplish. The appellants contend that such a relationship would be lacking even in a lesser requirement that an abortion be performed in a licensed hospital, as opposed to a facility, such as a clinic, that may be required by the State to possess

11. We were advised at reargument, Tr. of Oral Rearg. 10, that only 54 of Georgia's 159 counties have a JCAH-accredited hospital.

all the staffing and services necessary to perform an abortion safely (including those adequate to handle serious complications or other emergency, or arrangements with a nearby hospital to provide such services). Appellants and various *amici* have presented us with a mass of data purporting to demonstrate that some facilities other than hospitals are entirely adequate to perform abortions if they possess these qualifications. The State, on the other hand, has not presented persuasive data to show that only hospitals meet its acknowledged interest in insuring the quality of the operation and the full protection of the patient. We feel compelled to agree with appellants that the State must show more than it has in order to prove that only the full resources of a licensed hospital, rather than those of some other appropriately licensed institution, satisfy these health interests. We hold that the hospital requirement of the Georgia law, because it fails to exclude the first trimester of pregnancy, *see Roe v. Wade, ante,* is also invalid. . . .

2. *Committee approval.* The second aspect of the appellants' procedural attack relates to the hospital abortion committee. . . . Viewing the Georgia statute as a whole, we see no constitutionally justifiable pertinence in the structure for the advance approval. . . . We are not cited to any other surgical procedure made subject to committee approval as a matter of state criminal law. The woman's right to receive medical care in accordance with her licensed physician's best judgment and the physician's right to administer it are substantially limited by this statutorily imposed overview.

3. *Two-doctor concurrence.* Appellants' attack centers on the . . . required confirmation by two Georgia-licensed physicians in addition to the recommendation of the pregnant woman's own consultant (making under the statute, a total of six physicians involved, including the three on

the hospital's abortion committee). We conclude that this provision, too, must fall.

The statute's emphasis, as has been repetitively noted, is on the attending physician's "best clinical judgment that an abortion is necessary." . . . Again, no other voluntary medical or surgical procedure for which Georgia requires confirmation by two other physicians has been cited to us. If a physician is licensed by the State, he is recognized by the State as capable of exercising acceptable clinical judgment. If he fails in this, professional censure and deprivation of his license are available remedies. Required acquiescence by copractitioners has no rational connection with a patient's need and unduly infringes on the physician's right to practice. . . .

E. The appellants attack the residency requirement of the Georgia law . . . as violative of the right to travel stressed in *Shapiro v. Thompson,* 394 U.S. 618, 629–31 (1969), and other cases. A requirement of this kind, of course, could be deemed to have some relationship to the availability of post-procedure medical care for the aborted patient.

Nevertheless, we do not uphold the constitutionality of the residence requirement. It is not based on any policy of preserving state-supported facilities for Georgia residents, for the bar also applies to private hospitals and to privately retained physicians. There is no intimation, either, that Georgia facilities are utilized to capacity in caring for Georgia residents. Just as the Privileges and Immunities Clause, Const. art. IV, § 2, protects persons who enter other States to ply their trade, *Ward v. Maryland,* 12 Wall. 418, 430 (1871); *Blake v. McClung,* 172 U.S. 239, 248–56 (1898), so must it protect persons who enter Georgia seeking the medical services that are available there. *See Toomer v. Witsell,* 334 U.S. 385, 396–97 (1948). A contrary holding would mean that a State could limit to its own residents the general medical care available within its borders. This we could not approve. . . .

V

In summary, we hold that the JCAH-accredited hospital provision and the requirements as to approval by the hospital abortion committee, as to confirmation by two independent physicians, and as to residence in Georgia are all violative of the Fourteenth Amendment. . . .

MR. JUSTICE STEWART, concurring [in *Roe v. Wade*].

In 1963, this Court, in *Ferguson v. Skrupa*, 372 U.S. 726, purported to sound the death knell for the doctrine of substantive due process, a doctrine under which many state laws had in the past been held to violate the Fourteenth Amendment. As Mr. Justice Black's opinion for the court in *Skrupa* put it: "We have returned to the original constitutional proposition that courts do not substitute their social and economic beliefs for the judgment of legislative bodies, who are elected to pass laws." *Id.* at 730.[1]

Barely two years later, in *Griswold v. Connecticut*, 381 U.S. 479, the Court held a Connecticut birth control law unconstitutional. In view of what had been so recently said in *Skrupa*, the Court's opinion in *Griswold* understandably did its best to avoid reliance on the Due Process Clause of the Fourteenth Amendment as the ground for decision. Yet, the Connecticut law did not violate any provision of the Bill of Rights, nor any specific provision of the Constitution.[2] So it was clear to me then,

and it is equally clear to me now, that the *Griswold* decision can be rationally understood only as a holding that the Connecticut statute substantively invaded the "liberty" that is protected by the Due Process Clause of the Fourteenth Amendment. As so understood, *Griswold* stands as one in a long line of pre-*Skrupa* cases decided under the doctrine of substantive due process, and I now accept it as such. . . . The Constitution nowhere mentions a specific right of personal choice in matters of marriage and family life, but the "liberty" protected by the Due Process Clause of the Fourteenth Amendment covers more than those freedoms explicitly named in the Bill of Rights. *See Schware v. Board of Bar Examiners*, 353 U.S. 232, 238–39; *Pierce v. Society of Sisters*, 268 U.S. 510, 534–35; *Meyer v. Nebraska*, 262 U.S. 390, 399–400. *Cf. Shapiro v. Thompson*, 394 U.S. 618, 629–30; *United States v. Guest*, 383 U.S. 745, 757–58; *Carrington v. Rash*, 380 U.S. 89, 96; *Aptheker v. Secretary of State*, 378 U.S. 500, 505; *Kent v. Dulles*, 357 U.S. 116, 127; *Bolling v. Sharpe*, 347 U.S. 497, 499–500; *Truax v. Raich*, 239 U.S. 33, 41.

As Mr. Justice Harlan once wrote:

[T]he full scope of the liberty guaranteed by the Due Process Clause cannot be found in or limited by the precise terms of the specific guarantees elsewhere provided in the Constitution.

---

1. Only Mr. Justice Harlan failed to join the Court's opinion, 372 U.S., at 733.

2. There is no constitutional right of privacy, as such. "[The Fourth] Amendment protects individual privacy against certain kinds of governmental intrusion, but its protections go further, and often have nothing to do with privacy at all. Other provisions of the Constitution protect personal privacy from other forms of governmental invasions. But the protection of a person's *general* right to privacy—his right to be let alone by other people—is, like the protection of his property and of his very life, left largely to the law of the individual States." *Katz v. United States*, 389 U.S. 347, 350–51 (footnotes omitted).

This "liberty" is not a series of isolated points pricked out in terms of the taking of property; the freedom of speech, press, and religion; the right to keep and bear arms; the freedom from unreasonable searches and seizures; and so on. It is a rational continuum which, broadly speaking, includes a freedom from all substantial arbitrary impositions and purposeless restraints . . . and which also recognizes, what a reasonable and sensitive judgment must, that certain interests require particularly careful scrutiny of the state needs asserted to justify their abridgment. (*Poe v. Ullman,* 367 U.S. 497, 543 [opinion dissenting from dismissal of appeal] [citations omitted].)

In the words of Mr. Justice Frankfurter, "Great concepts like . . . 'liberty' . . . were purposely left to gather meaning from experience. For they relate to the whole domain of social and economic fact, and the statesmen who founded this Nation knew too well that only a stagnant society remains unchanged." *National Mutual Ins. Co. v. Tidewater Transfer Co.,* 337 U.S. 582, 646 (dissenting opinion). Several decisions of this Court make clear that freedom of personal choice in matters of marriage and family life is one of the liberties protected by the Due Process Clause of the Fourteenth Amendment. *Loving v. Virginia,* 388 U.S. 1, 12; *Griswold v. Connecticut; Pierce v. Society of Sisters; Meyer v. Nebraska. See also Prince v. Massachusetts,* 321 U.S. 158, 166; *Skinner v. Oklahoma,* 316 U.S. 535, 541. As recently as last Term, in *Eisenstadt v. Baird,* 405 U.S. 438, 453, we recognized "the right of the *individual,* married or single, to be free from unwarranted governmental intrusion into matters so fundamentally affecting a person as the decision whether to bear or beget a child." That right necessarily includes the right of a woman to decide whether or not to terminate her pregnancy. "Certainly the interests of a woman in giving of her physical and emotional self during pregnancy and the interests that will be affected throughout her life by the birth and raising of a child are of a far greater degree of significance and personal intimacy than the right to send a child to private school protected in *Pierce v. Society of Sisters,* or the right to teach a foreign language protected in *Meyer v. Nebraska," Abele v. Markle,* 351 F. Supp. 224, 227 (Conn. 1972).

Clearly, therefore, the Court today is correct in holding that the right asserted by Jane Roe is embraced within the personal liberty protected by the Due Process Clause of the Fourteenth Amendment.

It is evident that the Texas abortion statute infringes that right directly. Indeed, it is difficult to imagine a more complete abridgment of a constitutional freedom than that worked by the inflexible criminal statute now in force in Texas. The question then becomes whether the state interests advanced to justify this abridgment can survive the "particularly careful scrutiny" that the Fourteenth Amendment here requires.

The asserted state interests are protection of the health and safety of the pregnant woman, and protection of the potential future human life within her. These are legitimate objectives, amply sufficient to permit a State to regulate abortions as it does other surgical procedures, and perhaps sufficient to permit a State to regulate abortions more stringently or even to prohibit them in the late stages of pregnancy. But such legislation is not before us, and I think the Court today has thoroughly demonstrated that these state interests cannot constitutionally support the broad abridgment of personal liberty worked by the existing Texas law. Accordingly, I join the Court's opinion holding that the law is invalid under the Due Process Clause of the Fourteenth Amendment.

MR. CHIEF JUSTICE BURGER, concurring [for both *Roe* and *Doe*].

I agree that, under the Fourteenth Amendment to the Constitution, the abortion statutes of Georgia and Texas impermissibly limit the performance of abortions necessary to protect the health of pregnant women, using the term health in its broadest medical context. *See United States v. Vuitch*, 402 U.S. 62, 71–72 (1971). I am somewhat troubled that the Court has taken notice of various scientific and medical data in reaching its conclusion; however, I do not believe that the Court has exceeded the scope of judicial notice accepted in other contexts.

In oral argument, counsel for the State of Texas informed the Court that early abortion procedures were routinely permitted in certain cases, such as nonconsensual pregnancies resulting from rape and incest. In the face of a rigid and narrow statute, such as that of Texas, no one in these circumstances should be placed in a posture of dependence on a prosecutorial policy or prosecutorial discretion. Of course, States must have broad power, within the limits indicated in the opinion, to regulate the subject of abortions, but where the consequences of state intervention are so severe, uncertainty must be avoided as much as possible. For my part, I would be inclined to allow a State to require the certification of two physicians to support an abortion, but the Court holds otherwise. I do not believe that such a procedure is unduly burdensome, as are the complex steps of the Georgia statutes, which require as many as six doctors and the use of a hospital certified by the JCAH.

I do not read the Court's holdings today as having the sweeping consequences attributed to them by the dissenting Justices; the dissenting views discount the reality that the vast majority of physicians observe the standards of their profession, and act only on the basis of carefully deliberated medical judgments relating to life and health. Plainly, the Court today rejects any claim that the Constitution requires abortions on demand.

MR. JUSTICE DOUGLAS, concurring [for both *Roe* and *Doe*].

While I join the opinion of the Court, I add a few words.

I

The questions presented in the present cases . . . involved the right of privacy, one aspect of which we considered in *Griswold v. Connecticut*, 381 U.S. 479, 484, when we held that various guarantees in the Bill of Rights create zones of privacy.[2]

The Ninth Amendment obviously does not create federally enforceable rights. It merely says, "The enumeration in the Constitution, of certain rights, shall not be construed to deny or disparage others retained by the people." But a catalogue of these rights includes customary, traditional, and time-honored rights, amenities, privileges,

2. There is no mention of privacy in our Bill of Rights but our decisions have recognized it as one of the fundamental values those amendments were designed to protect. The fountainhead case is *Boyd v. United States*, 116 U.S. 616, holding that a federal statute which authorized a court in tax cases to require a taxpayer to produce his records or to concede the Government's allegations offended the Fourth and Fifth Amendments. Mr. Justice Bradley, for the Court, found that the measure unduly intruded into the "sanctity of a man's home and the privacies of life." *Id.* at 630. Prior to *Boyd*, in *Kilbourn v. Thompson*, 103 U.S. 168, 190, Mr. Justice Miller held for the Court that neither House of Congress "possesses the general power of making inquiry into the private affairs of the citizen." . . .

and immunities that come within the sweep of "the Blessings of Liberty" mentioned in the preamble to the Constitution. Many of them, in my view, come within the meaning of the term "liberty" as used in the Fourteenth Amendment.

First is the autonomous control over the development and expression of one's intellect, interests, tastes, and personality.

These are rights protected by the First Amendment and, in my view, they are absolute, permitting of no exceptions. The right to remain silent as respects one's own beliefs. . . . the privacy of first-class mail, . . . these aspects of the right of privacy are rights "retained by the people" in the meaning of the Ninth Amendment.

Second is freedom of choice in the basic decisions of one's life respecting marriage, divorce, procreation, contraception, and the education and upbringing of children.

These rights, unlike those protected by the First Amendment, are subject to some control by the police power. Thus, the Fourth Amendment speaks only of "unreasonable searches and seizures" and of "probable cause." These rights are "fundamental," and we have held that in order to support legislative action the statute must be narrowly and precisely drawn and that a "compelling state interest" must be shown in support of the limitation. *E.g., Kramer v. Union Free School District; Shapiro v. Thompson; Carrington v. Rash; Sherbert v. Verner; NAACP v. Alabama.*

The liberty to marry a person of one's own choosing, *Loving v. Virginia;* the right of procreation, *Skinner v. Oklahoma;* the liberty to direct the education of one's children, *Pierce v. Society of Sisters,* and the privacy of the marital relation, *Griswold v. Connecticut,* are in this category.[4] . . .

This right of privacy was called by Mr. Justice Brandeis the right "to be let alone." *Olmstead v. United States,* 277 U.S. 438, 478 (dissenting opinion). That right includes the privilege of an individual to plan his own affairs, for, "'outside areas of plainly harmful conduct, every American is left to shape his own life as he thinks best, do what he pleases, go where he pleases.'" *Kent v. Dulles,* 357 U.S. 116, 126.

Third is the freedom to care for one's health and person, freedom from bodily restraint or compulsion, freedom to walk, stroll, or loaf.

These rights, though fundamental, are likewise subject to regulation on a showing of "compelling state interest." We stated in *Papachristou v. City of Jacksonville,* 405 U.S. 156, 164, that walking, strolling, and wandering "are historically part of the amenities of life as we have known them."

---

4. My Brother STEWART, writing in *Roe v. Wade,* says that our decision in *Griswold* reintroduced substantive due process that had been rejected in *Ferguson v. Skrupa,* 372 U.S. 376. *Skrupa* involved legislation governing a business enterprise; and the Court in that case, as had Mr. Justice Holmes on earlier occasions, rejected the idea that "liberty" within the meaning of the Due Process Clause of the Fourteenth Amendment was a vessel to be filled with one's personal choices of values, whether drawn from the *laissez faire* school, from the socialistic school, or from the technocrats. *Griswold* involved legislation touching on the marital relation and involving the conviction of a licensed physician for giving married people information concerning contraception. There is nothing specific in the Bill of Rights that covers that item. Nor is there anything in the Bill of Rights that in terms protects the right of association or the privacy in one's association. Yet we found those rights in the periphery of the First Amendment, *NAACP v. Alabama,* 357 U.S. 449, 462. Other peripheral rights are the right to educate one's children as one chooses, *Pierce v. Society of Sisters,* 268 U.S. 510, and the right to study the German language, *Meyer v. Nebraska,* 262 U.S. 390. These decisions, with all respect, have nothing to do with substantive due process. One may think they are not peripheral to other rights that are expressed in the Bill of Rights. But that is not enough to bring into play the protection of substantive due process. . . .

As stated in *Jacobson v. Massachusetts*, 197 U.S. 11, 29:

> There is, of course, a sphere within which the individual may assert the supremacy of his own will and rightfully dispute the authority of any human government, especially of any free government existing under a written constitution, to interfere with the exercise of that will.

In *Union Pacific R. Co. v. Botsford*, 141 U.S. 250, 252, the Court said, "the inviolability of the person is as much invaded by a compulsory stripping and exposure as by a blow." . . .

The Georgian statute is at war with the clear message of these cases—that a woman is free to make the basic decision whether to bear an unwanted child. Elaborate argument is hardly necessary to demonstrate that childbirth may deprive a woman of her preferred lifestyle and force upon her a radically different and undesired future. For example, rejected applicants under the Georgia statute are required to endure the discomforts of pregnancy; to incur the pain, higher mortality rate, and aftereffects of childbirth; to abandon educational plans; to sustain loss of income; to forgo the satisfactions of careers; to tax further mental and physical health in providing child care; and, in some cases, to bear the lifelong stigma of unwed motherhood, a badge which may haunt, if not deter, later legitimate family relationships.

II

Such reasoning is, however, only the beginning of the problem. The State has interests to protect. Vaccinations to prevent epidemics are one example, as *Jacobson*, holds. The Court held that compulsory sterilization of imbeciles afflicted with hereditary forms of insanity or imbecility is another. *Buck v. Bell*, 274 U.S. 200. Abortion affects another. While childbirth endangers the lives of some women, voluntary abortion at any time and place regardless of medical standards would impinge on a rightful concern of society. The woman's health is part of that concern; as is the life of the fetus after quickening. These concerns justify the State in treating the procedure as a medical one.

One difficulty is that this statute as construed and applied apparently does not give full sweep to the "psychological as well as physical well-being" of women patients which saved the concept "health" from being void for vagueness in *United States v. Vuitch*, 402 U.S., at 72. But, apart from that, Georgia's enactment has a constitutional infirmity because, as stated by the District Court, it "limits the numbers of reasons for which an abortion may be sought. . . . Such action unduly restricts a decision sheltered by the Constitutional right to privacy." 319 F. Supp., at 1056.

The vicissitudes of life produce pregnancies which may be unwanted, or which may impair "health" in the broad *Vuitch* sense of the term, or . . . which in the full setting of the case may create such suffering, dislocations, misery, or tragedy as to make an early abortion the only civilized step to take. . . .

There is no doubt that the State may require abortions to be performed by qualified medical personnel. The legitimate objective of preserving the mother's health clearly supports such laws. Their impact upon the woman's privacy is minimal. But the Georgia statute outlaws virtually all such operations—even in the earliest stages of pregnancy. In light of modern medical evidence suggesting that an early abortion is safer healthwise than childbirth itself, it cannot be seriously urged that so comprehensive a ban is aimed at protecting the woman's health. Rather, this expansive proscription of all abortions along the temporal spectrum can rest only on a public goal of preserving both embryonic and fetal life.

The present statute has struck the balance between the woman's and the State's interests wholly in favor of the latter. I am not prepared to hold that a State may equate, as Georgia has done, all phases of maturation preceding birth. We held in *Griswold* that the states may not preclude spouses from attempting to avoid the joinder of sperm and egg. If this is true, it is difficult to perceive any overriding public necessity which might attach precisely at the moment of conception. . . .

In summary, the enactment is overbroad. It is not closely correlated to the aim of preserving prenatal life. In fact, it permits its destruction in several cases, including pregnancies resulting from sex acts in which females are below the statutory age of consent. At the same time, however, the measure broadly proscribes aborting other pregnancies which may cause severe mental disorders. Additionally, the statute is overbroad because it equates the value of embryonic life immediately after conception with the worth of life immediately before birth.

III

. . .

The right of privacy has no more conspicuous place than in the physician-patient relationship, unless it can be in the priest-penitent relationship. . . .

The right to seek advice on one's health and the right to place reliance on the physician of one's choice are basic to Fourteenth Amendment values. We deal with fundamental rights and liberties, which, as already noted, can be contained or controlled only by discretely drawn legislation that preserves the "liberty" and regulates only those phrases of the problem of compelling legislative concern. The imposition by the State of group controls over the

physician-patient relationship is not made on any medical procedure apart from abortion, no matter how dangerous the medical step may be. The oversight imposed on the physician and patient in abortion cases denies them their "liberty," *viz.*, their right of privacy, without any compelling, discernible state interest. . . .

MR. JUSTICE REHNQUIST, dissenting [in *Roe v. Wade*].

The Court's opinion brings to the decision of this troubling question both extensive historical fact and a wealth of legal scholarship. While the opinion thus commands my respect, I find myself nonetheless in fundamental disagreement with those parts of it that invalidate the Texas statute in question, and therefore dissent.

I

The Court's opinion decides that a State may impose virtually no restriction on the performance of abortions during the first trimester of pregnancy. Our previous decisions indicate that a necessary predicate for such an opinion is a plaintiff who was in her first trimester of pregnancy at some time during the pendency of her lawsuit. While a party may vindicate his own constitutional rights, he may not seek vindication for the rights of others. *Moose Lodge v. Irvis,* 407 U.S. 163 (1972); *Sierra Club v. Morris,* 405 U.S. 727 (1972). The Court's statement of facts in this case makes clear, however, that the record in no way indicates the presence of such a plaintiff. We know only that plaintiff Roe at the time of filing her complaint was a pregnant woman; for aught that appears in this record, she may have been in her *last* trimester of pregnancy as of the date the complaint was filed.

Nothing in the Court's opinion indicates that Texas might not constitutionally apply its proscription of abortion as written to a woman in that stage of pregnancy. Nonetheless, the Court uses her complaint against the Texas statute as a fulcrum for deciding that States may impose virtually no restrictions on medical abortions performed during the *first* trimester of pregnancy. In deciding such a hypothetical lawsuit, the Court departs from the longstanding admonition that it should never "formulate a rule of constitutional law broader than is required by the precise facts to which it is to be applied." *Liverpool, New York & Philadelphia S.S. Co. v. Commissioners of Emigration,* 113 U.S. 33, 39 (1885). *See also Ashwander v. TVA,* 297 U.S. 288, 345 (1936) (Brandeis, J., concurring).

II

Even if there were a plaintiff in this case capable of litigating the issue which the Court decides, I would reach a conclusion opposite to that reached by the Court. I have difficulty in concluding, as the Court does, that the right of "privacy" is involved in this case. Texas, by the statute here challenged, bars the performance of a medical abortion by a licensed physician on a plaintiff such as *Roe.* A transaction resulting in an operation such as this is not "private" in the ordinary usage of the word. Nor is the "privacy" that the Court finds here even a distant relative of the freedom from searches and seizures protected by the Fourth Amendment to the Constitution, which the Court has referred to as embodying a right to privacy. *Katz v. United States,* 389 U.S. 347 (1967).

If the Court means by the term "privacy" no more than that the claim of a person to be free from unwanted state regulation of consensual transactions may be a form of "liberty" protected by the Fourteenth Amendment, there is no doubt that similar claims have been upheld in our earlier decisions on the basis of that liberty. I agree with the statement of Mr.

Justice Stewart in his concurring opinion that the "liberty," against deprivation of which without due process the Fourteenth Amendment protects, embraces more than the rights found in the Bill of Rights. But that liberty is not guaranteed absolutely against deprivation, only against deprivation without due process of law. The test traditionally applied in the area of social and economic legislation is whether or not a law such as that challenged has a rational relation to a valid state objective. *Williamson v. Lee Optical Co.,* 348 U.S. 483, 491 (1955). The Due Process Clause of the Fourteenth Amendment undoubtedly does place a limit, albeit a broad one, on legislative power to enact laws such as this. If the Texas statute were to prohibit an abortion even where the mother's life is in jeopardy, I have little doubt that such a statute would lack a rational relation to a valid state objective under the test stated in *Williamson.* But the Court's sweeping invalidation of any restrictions on abortion during the first trimester is impossible to justify under that standard, and the conscious weighing of competing factors that the Court's opinion apparently substitutes for the established test is far more appropriate to a legislative judgment than to a judicial one. . . .

As in *Lochner* and similar cases applying substantive due process standards to economic and social welfare legislation, the adoption of the compelling state interest standard will inevitably require this Court to examine the legislative policies and pass on the wisdom of these policies in the very process of deciding whether a particular state interest put forward may or may not be "compelling." The decision here to break pregnancy into three distinct terms and to outline the permissible restrictions the State may impose in each one, for example, partakes more of judicial legislation than it does of a determination of the intent of the drafters of the Fourteenth Amendment.

The fact that a majority of the States reflecting, after all, the majority sentiment in those States, have had restrictions on abortions for at least a century is a strong indication, it seems to me, that the asserted right to an abortion is not "so rooted in the traditions and conscience of our people as to be ranked as fundamental," *Snyder v. Massachusetts*, 291 U.S. 97, 105 (1934). Even today, when society's views on abortion are changing, the very existence of the debate is evidence that the "right" to an abortion is not so universally accepted as the appellant would have us believe.

To reach its result, the Court necessarily has had to find within the scope of the Fourteenth Amendment a right that was apparently completely unknown to the drafters of the Amendment. As early as 1821, the first state law dealing directly with abortion was enacted by the Connecticut Legislature. . . . By the time of the adoption of the Fourteenth Amendment in 1868, there were at least 36 laws enacted by state or territorial legislatures limiting abortion. While many States have amended or updated their laws, 21 of the laws on the books of 1868 remain in effect today. . . .

There apparently was no question concerning the validity of this provision or of any of the other state statutes when the Fourteenth Amendment was adopted. The only conclusion possible from this history is that the drafters did not intend to have the Fourteenth Amendment withdraw from the States the power to legislate with respect to this matter.

III

Even if one were to agree that the case that the court decides were here, and that the enunciation of the substantive constitutional law in the Court's opinion were proper, the actual disposition of the case by the Court is still difficult to justify. The Texas statute is struck down in *toto*, even though the Court apparently concedes that at later periods of pregnancy Texas might impose these selfsame statutory limitations on abortion. My understanding of past practice is that a statute found to be invalid as applied to a particular plaintiff, but not unconstitutional as a whole, is not simply "struck down" but is, instead, declared unconstitutional as applied to the fact situation before the Court. *Yick Wo v. Hopkins*, 118 U.S. 356 (1886); *Street v. New York*, 394 U.S. 576 (1969).

For all of the foregoing reasons, I respectfully dissent.

MR. JUSTICE REHNQUIST, dissenting [in *Doe v. Bolton*].

The holding in *Roe v. Wade*, that state abortion laws can withstand constitutional scrutiny only if the State can demonstrate a compelling state interest, apparently compels the Court's close scrutiny of the various provisions in Georgia's abortion statute. Since, as indicated by my dissent in *Wade*, I view the compelling-state-interest standard as a inappropriate measure of the constitutionality of state abortion laws, I respectfully dissent from the majority's holding.

MR. JUSTICE WHITE, with whom MR. JUSTICE REHNQUIST joins, dissenting [for both cases].

At the heart of the controversy in these cases are those recurring pregnancies that pose no danger whatsoever to the life or health of the mother but are, nevertheless, unwanted for any one or more of a variety of reasons—convenience, family planning, economics, dislike of children, the embarrassment of illegitimacy, etc. The common claim before us is that for any one of such reasons, or for no reason at all, and without asserting or claiming any threat to life or health, any woman is entitled to an abortion at her request if she is able to find a medical advisor willing to undertake the procedure.

The Court for the most part sustains this position: During the period prior to the time the fetus becomes viable, the Constitution of the United States values the convenience, whim, or caprice of the putative mother more than the life or potential life of the fetus; the Constitution, therefore, guarantees the right to an abortion as against any state law or policy seeking to protect the fetus from an abortion not prompted by more compelling reasons of the mother.

With all due respect, I dissent. I find nothing in the language or history of the Constitution to support the Court's judgment. The Court simply fashions and announces a new constitutional right for pregnant mothers and, with scarcely any reason or authority for its action, invests that right with sufficient substance to override most existing state abortion statutes. The upshot is that the people and the legislatures of the 50 States are constitutionally disentitled to weigh the relative importance of the continued existence and development of the fetus, on the one hand, against a spectrum of possible impacts on the mother, on the other hand. As an exercise of raw judicial power, the Court perhaps has authority to do what it does today; but in my view its judgment is an improvident and extravagant exercise of the power of judicial review that the Constitution extends to this Court.

The Court apparently values the convenience of the pregnant mother more than the continued existence and development of life or potential life that she carries. Whether or not I might agree with that marshaling of values, I can in no event join the Court's judgment because I find no constitutional warrant for imposing such an order of priorities on the people and legislatures of the States. In a sensitive area such as this, involving as it does issues over which reasonable men may easily and heatedly differ, I cannot accept the Court's exercise of its clear power of choice by interposing a constitutional barrier to state efforts to protect human life and by investing mothers and doctors with the constitutionally protected right to exterminate it. This issue, for the most part, should be left with the people and to the political processes the people have devised to govern their affairs.

It is my view, therefore, that the Texas statute is not constitutionally infirm because it denies abortions to those who seek to serve only their convenience rather than to protect their life or health. Nor is this plaintiff, who claims no threat to her mental or physical health, entitled to assert the possible rights of those women whose pregnancy assertedly implicates their health. This, together with *United States v. Vuitch*, 402 U.S. 62 (1971), dictates reversal of the judgment of the District Court.

Likewise, because Georgia may constitutionally forbid abortions to putative mothers who, like the plaintiff in this case, do not fall within the reach of § 26–1202(a) of its criminal code, I have no occasion, and the District Court had none, to consider the constitutionality of the procedural requirements of the Georgia statute as applied to those pregnancies posing substantial hazards to either life or health. I would reverse the judgment of the District Court in the Georgia case.

CASE QUESTIONS

1. In *Griswold, Eisenstadt,* and the *Roe* and *Doe* cases, the Supreme Court went out of its way to extend standing to the litigants; in *Griswold* and *Eisenstadt* the litigants were permitted to base their case on the constitutional rights of *other* people. In *Roe* and *Doe* the Court overlooked the problem of mootness, because pregnancy is a short-term, easily repeatable condition. The Court could have held to its standing rules and refused to decide these cases. Would that choice have done less harm to democratic processes than these decisions did? Less harm to the constitutional structure? Was the furtherance of the women's cause worth these costs? Are these "costs" imaginary?

2. The appellees in *Roe v. Wade* argued that the Constitution (which says that neither life, liberty, nor property may be taken without due process of law) implies an inviolable "right to be born." What technique did the Court use to decide that the Constitution implies the right to have an abortion, and that it does not imply a right to be born?

3. What does it matter what the Greeks and Romans thought about abortion? What the ABA or the U.S. Public Health Service believes about the ideal abortion statute? Why are these things in Justice Blackmun's opinion?

4. Blackmun cites *Buck v. Bell* as a precedent in section VII of the Court opinion, and Douglas cites it in section II of his concurrence. Is *Buck v. Bell* compatible with this decision? Which invades the dignity of the "person" more: (1) compulsion by the state that forces someone (as a result, granted, of the person's own mistake) to endure nine months of pregnancy and the travail of childbirth, or (2) compulsion by the state that forces someone to undergo a surgical operation that will forever deprive that person of the chance to bear children?

5. The Court grants that a compelling state interest could justify a blanket prohibition on abortions. Would a severe depletion of the population as a result of war constitute a sufficiently compelling interest? What if a state were to outlaw abortions in a statute that contained a preface explaining that the statute aimed at easing the severe shortage of adoptive babies?

6. Medical science may soon attain the capability of very early stage fetal transplants. How will this development affect the Court's statement that states may prohibit abortions of viable fetuses? (I.e., will states be allowed to mandate transplants in lieu of the destruction of transplantable fetuses?)

7. Is Justice Douglas persuasive in his assertion that "the clear message of" the cases he cites requires that a woman be "free to make the basic decision whether to bear an unwanted child"? That procreational freedom is in fact on the periphery of the First Amendment?

8. Is Justice White treating the situation too lightly when he refers to a nine-month pregnancy and the difficulties of bearing a child as interferences with the "convenience" or "whim" of the putative mother? Is the Court majority treating the situation too lightly when it confidently asserts that a six-month or five-month fetus is not "potential life"? Who, within the governmental structure, is best suited to decide these questions?

Restrictions on Abortion

The Right to Life counteroffensive did not lie down and play dead after the enormous setback imposed by this Supreme Court decision. Their immediate strategy was to secure legislation, in as many states as possible, to hem in the impending outbreak of abortions. The basic approach of such legislation was to forbid abortions in a variety of specified circumstances. These efforts achieved success in a great many states, but, most of that success was to be short-lived. In July 1976 the Supreme Court examined one detailed example of such legislation, and the Court declared unconstitutional its most stringent provisions. Both here and in later cases dealing with abortion restrictions, the Court followed the approach it had laid out in *Doe v. Bolton*.

The statute came from Missouri, and its courtroom defender was John C. Danforth, the state's attorney general. Strangely enough, although the appellant whose name forms the other half of the title of the case was the Planned Parenthood of Central Missouri, no court ever decided whether Planned Parenthood, as an interest group, had standing to challenge this law. The reason was that Planned Parenthood brought suit in conjunction with two licensed physicians actively involved in abortion work, David Hall and Michael Freiman. Because Hall and Freiman did have standing to challenge legislative intrusions into the practice of their profession, the question of Planned Parenthood's standing was bypassed by both the district court and the Supreme Court.

The statute at issue contained nine different provisions under attack.

1. The physicians challenged the statute's definition of "viability" as "that stage of fetal development when the life of the unborn child may be continued indefinitely outside the womb by natural or artificial life-supportive systems"; they argued instead for the fixed definition of viability proffered in *Roe v. Wade*— namely, the last three months of fetal life.

2. The physicians challenged the statutory requirement that a woman desiring an abortion must indicate in writing, during the first twelve weeks of pregnancy, that her decision is "informed and freely given and is not the result of coercion." The challenge to this requirement asserted that *Roe* had prohibited *all* restrictions on abortion during that first trimester, and that even this restriction was thereby unconstitutional.

3. On similar grounds, the physicians challenged the requirement that to perform a first-trimester abortion, the physician must obtain written consent of a woman's spouse unless the abortion is needed to save the woman's life.

4. Also on similar grounds, they challenged the requirement that unmarried women under eighteen obtain written consent from their parents for a first trimester abortion.

5. These doctors attacked the mandate that persons who perform abortions shall "exercise that degree of professional skill, care, and diligence to preserve the . . . fetus which such person would be required to exercise . . . to pre-

serve . . . any fetus intended to be born." Because this section did not make an explicit exception for nonviable fetuses, the physicians felt that it violated the law established in *Roe*.

6&7. The statute also ordered that records be kept, for statistical and public health purposes, of every abortion performed in the state, that these records be held for at least seven years. The appellants claimed that these provisions placed an undue burden on their practice of medicine, and they challenged, in particular, the application of these regulations to abortions within the first twelve weeks of pregnancy.

8. The statute flatly prohibited abortion by the technique of saline amniocentesis, the most popular method of post-first-trimester abortions, after the first twelve weeks of pregnancy. (For medical reasons, saline abortions are performed only after the sixteenth week of pregnancy.) This restriction was attacked on the grounds of unreasonableness.

9. The statute declared that an infant who survived an attempted abortion would become an "abandoned" ward of the state and that his natural parents would lose legal rights to him (unless the abortion had been performed to preserve the mother's life or health).

The district court had upheld every provision except the one that required the physician to make an effort to keep alive every aborted fetus. The Supreme Court ruled that the physicians did not have standing to challenge the ninth provision listed above, for it did not affect them directly. Thus, only the first eight challenges listed here were before the Supreme Court. The state prevailed on the requirement of written consent from the would-be mother, on the flexible definition of viability, and on the reporting and record-keeping provisions. The state lost on parental and spousal consent, the prohibition of saline amniocentesis, and the requirement that an effort be made to preserve the life of every fetus.

The Supreme Court justices aligned in a complex variety of groupings on these issues. The following excerpt provides each alignment's explanation of its own position.

Planned Parenthood v. Danforth, 428 U.S. 52 (1976)

MR. JUSTICE BLACKMUN delivered the opinion of the Court.

IV

A

The definition of viability. Section 2(2) of the Act defines "viability" as "that stage of fetal development when the life of the un-born child may be continued indefinitely outside the womb by natural or artificial life-supportive systems." Appellants claim that this definition violates and conflicts with the discussion of viability in our opinion in *Roe*. 410 U.S., at 160, 163. In particular, appellants object to the failure of the definition to contain any reference to a gestational time period, to its failure to incorporate and reflect the three stages of pregnancy, to the presence of the word "indefinitely," and to the extra burden of regulation imposed. It is suggested that the definition expands the Court's definition of viability, as expressed in *Roe*, and amounts to a legislative determination of what is properly a matter for medical judgment. It is said that the "mere possibility of momentary survival is not the medical standard of viability." Brief for Appellants 67.

In *Roe*, we used the term "viable," properly we thought, to signify the point at which the fetus is "potentially able to live outside the mother's womb, albeit with artificial aid," and presumably capable of "meaningful life outside the mother's womb," 410 U.S., at 160, 163. We noted that this point "is usually placed" at about seven months or 28 weeks, but may occur earlier. *Id.* at 160.

We agree with the District Court and conclude that the definition of viability in the Act does not conflict with what was said and held in *Roe*. . . .

B

The woman's consent. Under § 3(2) of the Act, a woman, prior to submitting to an abortion during the first 12 weeks of pregnancy, must certify in writing her consent to the procedure and "that her consent is informed and freely given and is not the result of coercion." Appellants argue that this requirement is violative of *Roe v. Wade*, 410 U.S., at 164–65, by imposing an extra layer and burden of regulation on the abortion decisions. *See Doe v. Bolton*, 410 U.S., at 195–200. Appellants also claim that the provision is overbroad and vague.

. . .

It is true that *Doe* and *Roe* clearly establish that the State may not restrict the decision of the patient and her physician regarding abortion during the first stage of pregnancy. Despite the fact that apparently no other Missouri statute, with [a few very narrow] exceptions . . . requires a patient's written consent to a surgical procedure, the imposition by § 3(2) of such a requirement . . . even during the first stage, in our view, is not in itself an unconstitutional requirement. The decision to abort, indeed, is an important, and often a stressful one, and it is desirable and imperative that it be made with full knowledge of its nature and consequences. The woman is the one primarily concerned, and her awareness of the decision and its significance may be assured, constitutionally, by the State to the extent of requiring her prior written consent.

We could not say that a requirement imposed by the State that a prior written consent for any surgery would be unconstitutional. As a consequence, we see no constitutional defect in requiring it only for some types of surgery as, for example, an intracardiac procedure, or where the surgical risk is elevated above a specified mortality level, or, for that matter, for abortions.

C

The spouse's consent. Section 3(3) requires the prior written consent of the spouse of the woman seeking an abortion during the first 12 weeks of pregnancy, unless "the abortion is certified by a licensed physician to be necessary in order to preserve the life of the mother."

The appellees defend § 3(3) on the ground that it was enacted in the light of the General Assembly's "perception of marriage as an institution," Brief for Appellees 34, and that any major change in family status is a decision to be made jointly by the marriage partners. Reference is made to an abortion's possible effect on the woman's childbearing potential. It is said that marriage always has entailed some legislatively imposed limitations: reference made to adultery and bigamy as criminal offenses; to Missouri's general requirement. . . , that for an adoption of a child born in wedlock the consent of both parents is necessary; to similar joint consent requirements imposed by a number of States with respect to artificial insemination and the legitimacy of children so conceived; to the law of two States requiring spousal consent for voluntary sterilization. . . .

The appellants, on the other hand, contend that § 3(3) obviously is designed to afford the husband the right unilaterally to prevent or veto an abortion, whether or not he is the father of the fetus. . . . We now hold that the State may not unconstitutionally require the consent of the spouse, as is specified under § 3(3) of the Missouri Act, as a condition for abortion during the first 12 weeks of pregnancy. [T]he State cannot "delegate to a spouse a veto power which the state itself is absolutely and totally prohibited from exercising during the first trimester of pregnancy." 393 F. Supp., at 1375. Clearly, since the State cannot regulate or proscribe abortion during the first stage, when the physician and his patient make that decision, the State cannot delegate authority to any particular person, even the spouse, to prevent abortion during the same period.

We are not unaware of the deep and proper concern and interest that a devoted and protective husband has in his wife's pregnancy and in the growth and development of the fetus she is carrying. Neither has this Court failed to appreciate the importance of the marital relationship in our society. *See, e.g., Griswold v. Connecticut,* 381 U.S. 479, 486 (1965); *Maynard v. Hill,* 125 U.S. 190, 211 (1888). Moreover, we recognize that the decision whether to undergo or to forgo an abortion may have profound effects on the future of any marriage, effects that are both physical and mental, and possibly deleterious. Notwith-

standing these factors, we cannot hold that the State has the constitutional authority to give the spouse unilaterally the ability to prohibit the wife from terminating her pregnancy, when the State itself lacks that right. *See Eisenstadt v. Baird,* 405 U.S. 438, 453 (1972).

It seems manifest that, ideally, the decision to terminate a pregnancy should be one concurred in by both the wife and her husband. No marriage may be viewed as harmonious or successful if the marriage partners are fundamentally divided on so important and vital an issue. But it is difficult to believe that the goal of fostering mutuality and trust in a marriage, and of strengthening the marital relationship and the marriage institution, will be achieved by giving the husband a veto power exercisable for any reason whatsoever or for no reason at all. Even if the State had the ability to delegate to the husband a power it itself could not exercise, it is not at all likely that such action would further, as the District Court majority phrased it, the "interest of the state in protecting the mutuality of decisions vital to the marriage relationship." 392 F. Supp., at 1370.

We recognize, of course, that when a woman, with the approval of her physician but without the approval of her husband, decides to terminate her pregnancy, it could be said that she is acting unilaterally. The obvious fact is that when the wife and the husband disagree on this decision, the view of only one of the two marriage partners can prevail. Since it is the woman who physically bears the child and who is the more directly and immediately affected by the pregnancy, as between the two, the balance weighs in her favor. *Cf. Roe v. Wade,* 410 U.S., at 153.

We conclude that § 3(3) of the Missouri Act is inconsistent with the standards enunciated in *Roe v. Wade,* 410, U.S., at 164–65, and is unconstitutional. . . .

D

Parental consent. Section 3(4) requires, with respect to the first 12 weeks of pregnancy, where the woman is unmarried and under the age of eighteen years, the written consent of a parent or person *in loco parentis* unless, again, "the abortion is certified by a licensed physician as necessary in order to preserve the life of the mother." . . .

The appellees defend the statute in several ways. They point out that the law properly may subject minors to more stringent limitations than are permissible with respect to adults. . . . Missouri law, it is said, "is replete with provisions reflecting the interest of the state in assuring the welfare of minors." Certain decisions are considered by the State to be outside the scope of a minor's ability to act in his own best interest or in the interest of the public, citing statutes proscribing the sale of firearms and deadly weapons to minors without parental consent, and other statutes. . . . It is pointed out that the record contains testimony to the effect that children of tender years (even ages ten and eleven) have sought abortions. Thus, a State's permitting a child to obtain an abortion without the counsel of an adult "who has responsibility or concern for the child would constitute an irresponsible abdication of the State's duty to protect the welfare of minors." . . .

We agree with appellants . . . that the State may not impose a blanket provision, such as § 3(4), requiring the consent of a parent or person *in loco parentis* as a condition for abortion of an unmarried minor during the first 12 weeks of her pregnancy. Just as with the requirement of consent from the spouse, so here, the State does not have the constitutional authority to give a third party an absolute, and possibly arbitrary, veto over the decision of the physician and his patient to terminate the patient's pregnancy, regardless of the reason for withholding the consent.

Constitutional rights do not mature and come into being magically only when one attains the state-defined age of majority. Minors, as well as adults, are protected by the Constitution and possess constitutional rights. *See, e.g., Breed v. Jones,* 421 U.S. 519 (1975); *Goss v. Lopez,* 419 U.S. 565 (1975); *Tinker v. Des Moines School District,* 393 U.S. 503 (1969); *In re Gault,* 387 U.S. 1 (1957). The Court indeed, however, long has recognized that the State has somewhat broader authority to regulate the activities of children than of adults. *Prince v. Massachusetts,* 321 U.S., at 170; *Ginsberg v. New York,* 390 U.S. 629 (1968). It remains, then, to examine whether there is any significant state interest in conditioning an abortion on the consent of a parent or person *in loco parentis* that is not present in the case of an adult.

One suggested interest is the safeguarding of the family unit and of parental authority. 392 F. Supp., at 1370. It is difficult, however, to conclude that providing a parent with absolute power to overrule a determination, made by the physician and his minor patient, to terminate the patient's pregnancy will serve to strengthen the family unit. Neither is it likely that such veto power will enhance parental authority or control where the minor and the nonconsenting parent are so fundamentally in conflict and the very existence of the pregnancy already has fractured the family structure. . . .

We emphasize that our holding that § 3(4) is invalid does not suggest that every minor, regardless of age or maturity, may give effective consent for termination of her pregnancy. . . . The fault with § 3(4) is that it imposes a special consent provision, . . . without a sufficient justification for the restriction.

E

Saline amniocentesis. Section 9 of the statute prohibits the use of saline amniocentesis, as a method or technique of abortion, after the first 12 weeks of pregnancy. . . . The statute imposes this proscription on the ground that the technique "is deleterious to maternal health," and places it in the form of a legislative finding. Appellants challenge this provision on the ground that it operates to preclude virtually all abortions after the first trimester. This is so, it is claimed, because a substantial percentage, in the neighborhood of 70 percent according to the testimony, of all abortions performed in the United States after the first trimester are effected through the procedure of saline amniocentesis. . . .

The District Court's majority . . . [r]eferring to such methods as hysterotomy, hysterectomy, "mechanical means of inducing abortion," and prostaglandin injection, . . . said that at least the latter two techniques were safer than saline. Consequently, the majority concluded, the restriction in § 9 could be upheld as reasonably related to maternal health.

We feel that the majority, in reaching its conclusion, failed to appreciate and to consider several significant facts. First, it did not recognize the prevalence, as the record conclusively demonstrates, of the use of saline amniocentesis as an accepted medical procedure in this country; the procedure, as noted above, is employed in a substantial majority (the testimony from both sides ranges from 68 percent to 80 percent) of all post-first trimester abortions. Second, it failed to recognize that at the time of trial, there were severe limitations on the availability of the prostaglandin technique, which, although promising, was used only on an experimental basis until less than two years before. See *Wolf v. Schroering*, 388 F. Supp., at 637, where it was said that at that time (1974), "there are no physicians in Kentucky competent in the technique of prostaglandin amnio infusion." And the State offered no evidence that prostaglandin abortions were available

in Missouri.[12] Third, the statute's reference to the insertion of "a saline or other fluid" appears to include within its proscription the intra-amniotic injection of prostaglandin itself and other methods that may be developed in the future and that may prove highly effective and completely safe. Finally, the majority did not consider the anomaly inherent in § 9 when it proscribes the use of saline but does not prohibit techniques that are many times more likely to result in maternal death. *See* 392 F. Supp., at 1378 n.8 (dissenting opinion).

These unappreciated or overlooked factors place the State's decision to bar use of the saline method in a completely different light. The State, through § 9, would prohibit the use of a method which the record shows is the one most commonly used nationally by physicians after the first trimester and which is safer, with respect to maternal mortality, than even continuation of the pregnancy until normal childbirth. Moreover, as a practical matter, it forces a woman and her physician to ter-

12. In response to MR. JUSTICE WHITE's criticism that the prostaglandin method of inducing abortion was available in Missouri, either at the time the Act was passed or at the time of trial, we make the following observations. First, there is no evidence in the record . . . that demonstrates that the prostaglandin method was or is available in Missouri. Second, the evidence presented to the District Court does not support such a view. Until January 1974 prostaglandin was used only on an experimental basis in a few medical centers. And, at the time the Missouri General Assembly proscribed saline, the sole distributor of prostaglandin "restricted sales to around twenty medical centers from coast to coast." Brief for Appellee *Danforth* 68.

It is clear, therefore, that at the time the Missouri General Assembly passed the Act, prostaglandin was not available in any meaningful sense of that term. Because of this undisputed fact, it was incumbent upon the State to show that at the time of trial in 1974 prostaglandin was available. It failed to do so. . . .

minate her pregnancy by methods more dangerous to her health than the method outlawed.

And so viewed, particularly in the light of the present unavailability—as demonstrated by the record—of the prostaglandin technique, the outright legislative proscription of saline fails as a reasonable regulation for the protection of maternal health. It comes into focus, instead, as an unreasonable or arbitrary regulation designed to inhibit, and having the effect of inhibiting, the vast majority of abortions after the first 12 weeks. As such, it does not withstand constitutional challenge.

F

Recordkeeping. Sections 10 and 11 of the Act impose recordkeeping requirements for health facilities and physicians concerned with abortions irrespective of the pregnancy stage. Under § 10, each such facility and physician is to be supplied with forms "the purpose and function of which shall be the preservation of maternal health and life by adding to the sum of medical knowledge through the compilation of relevant maternal health and life data and to monitor all abortions performed to assure that they are done only under and in accordance with the provisions of the law." The statute states that the information on the forms "shall be confidential and shall be used only for statistical purposes." The "records, however, may be inspected and health data acquired by local, state, or national public health officers." Under § 11 the records are to be kept for seven years in the permanent files of the health facility where the abortion was performed.

Appellants object to these reporting and recordkeeping provisions on the ground that they, too, impose an extra layer and burden of regulation, and that they apply throughout all stages of pregnancy. . . .

Recordkeeping and reporting requirements that are reasonably directed to the preservation of maternal health and that properly respect a patient's confidentiality and privacy are permissible. . . . As to the first stage [of pregnancy], one may argue forcefully that the State should not be able to impose any recordkeeping requirements that significantly differ from those imposed with respect to other, and comparable, medical or surgical procedures. We conclude, however, that the provisions of §§ 10 and 11, while perhaps approaching permissible limits, are not constitutionally offensive in themselves. Recordkeeping of this kind, if not abused or overdone, can be useful to the State's interest in protecting the health of its female citizens, and may be a resource that is relevant to decisions involving medical experience and judgment. The added requirements for confidentiality . . . and for retention for seven years, a period not unreasonable in length, assist and persuade us in our determination of the constitutional limits. And so regarded, we see no legally significant impact or consequence on the abortion decision or on the physician-patient relationship. . . .

G

Standard of care. Appellee Danforth [in a companion case] appeals from the unanimous decision of the District Court that § 6(1) of the Act is unconstitutional. That section provides:

No person who performs or induces an abortion shall fail to exercise that degree of professional skill, care and diligence to preserve the life and health of the fetus which such person would be required to exercise in order to preserve the life and health of any fetus intended to be born and not aborted. Any physician or person assisting in the abortion who shall fail to take such measures to encourage or to sustain the life of the child, and the death of the child results, shall be deemed guilty of manslaughter. . . . Further, such physician or other person shall be liable in an action for damages.

The District Court held that the first sentence was unconstitutionally overbroad because it failed to exclude from its reach the stage of pregnancy prior to viability. 392 F. Supp., at 1371.

The Attorney General argues that the District Court's interpretation is erroneous and unnecessary. He claims that the first sentence of § 6(1) establishes only the general standard of care that applies to the person who performs the abortion, and that the second sentence describes the circumstances when that standard of care applies, namely, when a live child results from the procedure. Thus, the first sentence, it is said, despite its reference to the fetus, has no application until a live birth results. . . .

[W]e are unable to accept the appellee's sophisticated interpretation of the statute. Section 6(1) requires the physician to exercise the prescribed skill, care, and diligence to preserve the life and health of the *fetus*. It does not specify that such care need be taken only after the stage of viability has been reached. As the provision now reads, it impermissibly requires the physician to preserve the life and health of the fetus, whatever the stage of pregnancy. The fact that the second sentence of § 6(1) refers to a criminal penalty where the physician fails "to take such measures to encourage or to sustain the life of the *child*, and the death of the *child* results" (emphasis supplied), simply does not modify the duty imposed by the previous sentence or limit that duty to pregnancies that have reached the stage of viability.

We conclude, as did the District Court, that § 6(1) must stand or fall as a unit. Its provisions are inextricably bound together.

And a physician's or other person's criminal failure to protect a liveborn infant surely will be subject to prosecution in Missouri under the State's criminal statutes.

The judgment of the District Court is affirmed in part and reversed in part.

Mr. Justice Stewart, with whom Mr. Justice Powell joins, concurring.

While joining the Court's opinion, I write separately to indicate my understanding of some of the constitutional issues raised by this case. . . .

I agree with the Court that the patient consent provision in § 3(2) is constitutional. While § 3(2) obviously regulates the abortion decision during all stages of pregnancy, including the first trimester, I do not believe it conflicts with the statement in *Roe v. Wade*, 410 U.S., at 163, that "for the period of pregnancy prior to [approximately the end of the first trimester] the attending physician, in consultation with his patient, is free to determine, without regulation by the state, that, in his medical judgment, the patient's pregnancy should be terminated. If that decision is reached, the judgment may be effectuated by an abortion free of interference by the State." 410 U.S., at 163. That statement . . . was not intended to preclude the State from enacting a provision aimed at ensuring that the abortion decision is made in a knowing, intelligent, and voluntary fashion.

As to the provision of the law that requires a husband's consent to an abortion, § 3(3), the primary issue that it raises is whether the State may constitutionally recognize and give effect to a right on his part to participate in the decision to abort a jointly conceived child. This seems to me a rather more difficult problem than the Court acknowledges. Previous decisions have recognized that a man's right to father children and enjoy the association of his offspring is a constitutionally protected freedom. *See Stanley v. Illinois*, 405 U.S. 645; *Skinner v. Oklahoma*, 316 U.S. 535. But the Court has recognized as well that the Constitution protects "a *woman's* decision whether or not to terminate her pregnancy." 410 U.S., at 153. (Emphasis added.) In assessing the constitutional validity of § 3(3) we are called upon to choose between these competing rights. I agree with the Court, that since "it is the woman who physically bears the child and who is the more directly and immediately affected by the pregnancy . . . the balance weighs in her favor."

With respect to the state law's requirement of parental consent, § 3(4), I think it clear that its primary constitutional deficiency lies in its imposition of an absolute limitation on the minor's right to obtain an abortion . . . [A] materially different constitutional issue would be presented under a provision requiring parental consent or consultation in most cases but providing for prompt (i) judicial resolution of any disagreement between the parent and the minor, or (ii) judicial determination that the minor is mature enough to give an informed consent without parental concurrence or that abortion in any event is in the minor's best interest. Such a provision would not impose parental approval as an absolute condition upon the minor's right but would assure in most instances consultation between the parent and child.

There can be little doubt that the State furthers a constitutionally permissible end by encouraging an unmarried pregnant minor to seek the help and advice of her parents in making the very important decision whether or not to bear a child. That is a grave decision, and a girl of tender years, under emotional stress, may be ill-equipped to make it without mature advice and emotional support. It seems unlikely that she will obtain adequate counsel and support from the attending physician at an abortion clinic, where abortions for pregnant minors frequently take place.

MR. JUSTICE STEVENS, concurring in part and dissenting in part.

With the exception of parts IVD and IVE, I join the Court's opinion. . . .

In my opinion . . . the parental consent requirement is consistent with the holding in *Roe*. The State's interest in the welfare of its young citizens justifies a variety of protective measures. Because he may not foresee the consequences of his decision, a minor may not make an enforceable bargain. He may not lawfully work or travel where he pleases, or even attend exhibitions of constitutionally protected adult motion pictures. Persons below a certain age may not marry without parental consent. Indeed, such consent is essential even when the young woman is already pregnant. The State's interest in protecting a young person from harm justifies the imposition of restraints on his or her freedom even though comparable restraints on adults would be constitutionally impermissible. Therefore, the holding in *Roe v. Wade* that the abortion decision is entitled to constitutional protection merely emphasizes the importance of the decision; it does not lead to the conclusion that the state legislature has no power to enact legislation for the purpose of protecting a young pregnant woman from the consequences of an incorrect decision.

The abortion decision is, of course, more important than the decision to attend or to avoid an adult motion picture, or the decision to work long hours in a factory. It is not necessarily any more important than the decision to run away from home or the decision to marry. But even if it is the most important kind of a decision a young person may ever make, that assumption merely enhances the quality of the State's interest in maximizing the probability that the decision be made correctly and with full understanding of the consequences of either alternative.

The Court recognizes that the State may insist that the decision not be made without the benefit of medical advice. But since the most significant consequences of the decision are not medical in character, it would seem to me that the State may, with equal legitimacy, insist that the decision be made only after other appropriate counsel has been had as well. Whatever choice a pregnant young woman makes—to marry, to abort, to bear her child out of wedlock—the consequences of her decision may have a profound impact on her entire future life. A legislative determination that such a choice will be made more wisely in most cases if the advice and moral support of a parent play a part in the decisionmaking process is surely not irrational. Moreover, it is perfectly clear that the parental consent requirement will necessarily involve a parent in the decisional process.

If there is no parental consent requirement, many minors will submit to the abortion procedure without ever informing their parents. An assumption that the parental reaction will be hostile, disparaging or violent no doubt persuades many children simply to bypass parental counsel which would in fact be loving, supportive and, indeed, for some indispensable. It is unrealistic, in my judgment, to assume that every parent-child relationship is either (a) so perfect that communication and accord will take place routinely or (b) so imperfect that the absence of communication reflects the child's correct prediction that the parent will exercise his or her veto arbitrarily to further a selfish interest rather than the child's interest. A state legislature may conclude that most parents will be primarily interested in the welfare of their children, and further, that the imposition of a parental consent requirement is an appro-

priate method of giving the parents an opportunity to foster that welfare. . . . [E]ven doctors are not omniscient; specialists in performing abortions may incorrectly conclude that the immediate advantages of the procedure outweigh the disadvantages which a parent could evaluate in better perspective. In each individual case factors much more profound than a mere medical judgment may weigh heavily in the scales. The overriding consideration is that the right to make the choice be exercised as wisely as possible.

The Court assumes that parental consent is an appropriate requirement if the minor is not "capable of understanding the procedure and of appreciating its consequences and those of available alternatives." *Ante.* This assumption is, of course, correct and consistent with the predicate which underlies all State legislation seeking to protect minors from the consequences of decisions they are not yet prepared to make. In all such situations chronological age has been the basis for imposition of a restraint on the minor's freedom of choice even though it is perfectly obvious that such a yardstick is imprecise and perhaps even unjust in particular cases. The Court seems to assume that the capacity to conceive a child and the judgment of the physician are the only constitutionally permissible yardsticks for determining whether a young woman can independently make the abortion decision. I doubt the accuracy of the Court's empirical judgment. Even if it were correct, however, as a matter of constitutional law I think a State has power to conclude otherwise and to select a chronological age as its standard.

In short, the State's interest in the welfare of its young citizens is sufficient, in my judgment, to support the parental consent requirement.

[On IVE, Stevens, J., agrees with the Court's result, but he explains the reasons slightly differently.]

Mr. Justice White, with whom The Chief Justice and Mr. Justice Rehnquist join, concurring in the judgment in part and dissenting in part.

. . . [E]ven accepting *Roe v. Wade*, there is nothing in the opinion in that case and nothing articulated in the Court's opinion in this case which justifies the invalidation of [these] five provisions. . . . Accordingly, I dissent, in part.

I

Roe v. Wade, 410 U.S. 113, 163, holds that until a fetus becomes viable, the interest of the State in the life or potential life it represents is outweighed by the interest of the mother in choosing "whether or not to terminate her pregnancy." *Id.* at 153. Section 3(3) of the Act provides that a married woman may not obtain an abortion without her husband's consent. The Court strikes down this statute in one sentence. It says that "since the State cannot . . . proscribe abortion . . . the State cannot delegate authority to any particular person, even the spouse, to prevent abortion. . . ." *Ante.* But the State is not—under § 3(3)—delegating to the husband the power to vindicate the *State's* interest in the future life of the fetus. It is instead recognizing that the husband has an interest of his own in the life of the fetus which should not be extinguished by the unilateral decision of the wife. It by no means follows, from the fact that the mother's interest in deciding "whether or not to terminate her pregnancy" outweighs the *State's* interest in the potential life of the fetus, that the husband's interest is also outweighed and may not be protected by the State. A father's interest in having a child—perhaps his only child—may be unmatched by any other interest in his life. *See Stanley v. Illinois*, 405 U.S. 645, 651, and cases there cited. It is truly surprising that the majority finds in

the United States Constitution, as it must in order to justify the result it reaches, a rule that the State must assign a greater value to a mother's decision to cut off a potential human life by abortion than to a father's decision to let it mature into a live child. Such a rule cannot be found there, nor can it be found in *Roe v. Wade, supra.* These are matters which a State should be able to decide free from the suffocating power of the federal judge, purporting to act in the name of the Constitution.

In describing the nature of a mother's interest in terminating a pregnancy, the Court in *Roe v. Wade* mentioned only the post-birth burdens of rearing a child, *id.* at 153, and rejected a rule based on her interest in controlling her own body during pregnancy. *Id.* at 154. Missouri has a law which prevents a woman from putting a child up for adoption over her husband's objection. . . . This law represents a judgment by the State that the mother's interest in avoiding the burdens of child rearing do not outweigh or snuff out the father's interest in participating in bring up his own child. That law is plainly valid, but no more so than § 3(3) of the Act now before us. . . .

II

Section 3(4) requires that an unmarried woman under eighteen years of age obtain the consent of a parent or a person *in loco parentis* as a condition to an abortion. Once again the Court strikes the provision down in a sentence. . . . [T]he purpose of the parental consent requirement is not merely to vindicate the very right created in *Roe v. Wade, supra,*—the right of the pregnant woman to decide "whether or *not* to terminate her pregnancy." *Id.* at 153. (Emphasis added.) The abortion decision is unquestionably important and has irrevocable consequences whichever way it is made. Missouri is entitled to protect the minor unmarried woman from making the decision in a way which is not in her own best interests, and it seeks to achieve this goal by requiring parental consultation and consent. This is the traditional way by which States have sought to protect children from their own immature and improvident decisions; and there is absolutely no reason expressed by the majority why the State may not utilize that method here.

III

Section 9 of the Act prohibits abortion by the method known as saline amniocentesis—a method used at the time the Act was passed for 70 percent of abortions performed after the first trimester. Legislative history reveals that the Missouri Legislature viewed saline amniocentesis as far less safe a method of abortion than the so-called prostaglandin method. The court below took evidence on the question and summarized it as follows:

The record of trial discloses that use of the saline method exposes a woman to the danger of severe complications, regardless of the skill of the physician or the precaution taken. Saline may cause one or more of the following conditions: Disseminated intravascular coagulation or "consumptive coagulapathy" (disruption of the blood clotting mechanism), which may result in severe bleeding and possibly death; hypernatremia (increase in blood sodium level), which may lead to convulsions and death; and water intoxication (accumulated water in the body tissue which may occur when oxygen is used in conjunction with the injection of saline), resulting in damage to the central nervous system or death. There is also evidence that saline amniocentesis causes massive tissue destruction to

the inside of the uterus. [Citations to transcript pages omitted—Au.]

The District Court also cited considerable evidence establishing that the prostaglandin method is safer. In fact, the Chief of Obstetrics at Yale University, Dr. Anderson, suggested that "physicians should be liable for malpractice if they chose saline over prostaglandin after having been given all the facts on both methods." The Court nevertheless reverses the decision of the District Court sustaining § 9 against constitutional challenge. It does so apparently because saline amniocentesis was widely used before the Act was passed; because the prostaglandin method was seldom used and was not generally available; and because other abortion techniques more dangerous than saline amniocentesis were not banned. At bottom the majority's holding—as well as the concurrence—rests on this *factual* finding that the prostaglandin method is unavailable to the women of Missouri. It therefore concludes that the ban on the saline method is "an unreasonable or arbitrary regulation designed to inhibit, and having the effect of inhibiting, the vast majority of abortions after the first 12 weeks." *Ante.* This factual finding was not made either by the majority or by the dissenting judge below. Appellants have not argued that the record below supports such a finding. In fact the record below does not support such a finding. There is *no* evidence in the record that women in Missouri will be unable to obtain abortions by the prostaglandin method. What evidence there is in the record on this question supports the contrary conclusion.[3] The record discloses

3. The absence of more evidence on the subject in the record seems to be a result of the fact that the claim that the prostaglandin method is unavailable was not part of their litigating strategy below.

that the prostaglandin method of abortion was the country's second most common method of abortion during the second trimester; that although the prostaglandin method had previously been available only on an experimental basis, it was, at the time of trial available in "small hospitals all over the country," Trial Transcript, at 342; that in another year or so the prostaglandin method would become—even in the absence of legislation on the subject—the most prevalent method. Anderson deposition, at 47. Moreover, one doctor quite sensibly testified that if the saline method were banned, hospitals would quickly switch to the prostaglandin method.

The majority relies on the testimony of one doctor that—as already noted—prostaglandin had been available on an experimental basis only until January 1, 1974; and that its manufacturer, the Upjohn Company, restricted its sales to large medical centers for the following six months, after which sales were to be unrestricted. In what manner this evidence supports the proposition that prostaglandin is unavailable to the women of Missouri escapes me. The statute involved in this case was passed on June 14, 1974; evidence was taken in July 1974; the District Court's decree sustaining the ban on the saline method which this Court overturns was entered in January 1975; and this Court declares the statute unconstitutional in July of 1976. There is simply no evidence in the record that prostaglandin was or is unavailable at any time relevant to this case.

In any event, the point of § 9 is to change the practice under which most abortions were performed under the saline amniocentesis method generally available. It promises to achieve that result, if it remains operative, and the evidence discloses that the result is a desirable one or at least that the legislature could have so viewed it.

IV

Section 6(1) of the Act provides:

No person who performs or induces an abortion shall fail to exercise that degree of professional skill, care and diligence to preserve the life and health of the fetus which such person would be required to exercise in order to preserve the life and health of any fetus intended to be born and not aborted. Any physician or person assisting in the abortion who shall fail to take such measures to encourage or to sustain the life of the child, and the death of the child results, shall be deemed guilty of manslaughter. . . . Further, such physician or other person shall be liable in an action for damages.

If this section is read in any way other than through a microscope, it is plainly intended to require that, where a "fetus . . . [may have] the capability of meaningful life outside the mother's womb," *Roe v. Wade*, at 163, the abortion be handled in a way which is designed to preserve that life notwithstanding the mother's desire to terminate it. Indeed, even looked at through a microscope the statute seems to go no further. It requires a physician to exercise "that degree of professional skill . . . to preserve the fetus," which he would be required to exercise if the mother wanted a live child. Plainly, if the pregnancy is to be terminated at a time when there is no chance of life outside the womb, a physician would not be required to exercise any care or skill to preserve the life of the fetus during abortion no matter what the mother's desires. The statute would appear then to operate only in the gray area after the fetus *might* be viable but while the physician is still able to certify "with reasonable medical certainty that the fetus is not viable." See § 5 of the Act which flatly prohibits abortions absent such a certification. Since the State has a compelling interest, sufficient to outweigh the mother's desire to kill the fetus, when the "fetus . . . has the capability of meaningful life outside the mother's womb," *Roe v. Wade,* at 163, the statute is constitutional.

Incredibly, the Court reads the statute instead to require "the physician to preserve the life and health of the fetus, whatever the stage of pregnancy," *ante,* thereby attributing to the Missouri Legislature the strange intention of passing a statute with absolutely no chance of surviving constitutional challenge under *Roe v. Wade.*

. . .

V

I join the judgment of the Court insofar as it upholds the other portions of the Act against constitutional challenge.

CASE QUESTIONS

1. Is this decision consistent with the Court's statement in *Stanley v. Illinois* that a father's right to enjoy the care and comfort of his children is "fundamental" and is protected by the Constitution?

2. Does the fact that Missouri required parental consent and spousal consent *only* for first-trimester abortions support the majority's suspicion that the prohibition on the saline amniocentesis technique was a thinly disguised attempt to prohibit abortions themselves during the post-first-trimester period?

Bellotti v. Baird (1976), discussion

Although the Court majority in *Danforth* rejected Missouri's *absolute* requirement of parental consent for abortions performed on unmarried minors, they did qualify their rejection with the proviso that "not . . . every minor . . . may give effective consent." Justice Stewart (joined by Justice Powell) elaborated this qualification in this concurring opinion: a nonabsolute requirement of parental consent—one that in unusual circumstances could be superseded by a judicial hearing—would, he believed, pass constitutional muster. The Court majority itself, in nonbinding dicta, announced a similar principle in another case handed down on the same day, *Bellotti v. Baird (I).*[38]

Bellotti v. Baird involved a Massachusetts parental consent ordinance. For technical reasons, the Supreme Court did not decide the "merits" of the case but remanded it back to the lower courts for another decision. In so doing, however, the Supreme Court indicated that it *would* uphold the law if Massachusetts were to interpret its statute as imposing only a flexible parental consent requirement—

one permitting a judge to override parental vetoes in cases of mature and "informed" minors or in other cases where the best interest of the minor would be served thereby. Such a statute would encourage parental *consultation* for unmarried minors without endowing those parents with an absolute veto power over their daughter's abortion decision. That seems to be the point at which the Supreme Court has located the balance between the state's concern for the welfare of minor women and the constitutional freedoms of these young women.

H.L. v. Matheson (1981), discussion

In 1981 the Supreme Court clarified a related issue concerning minors' abortion rights. In *H.L. v. Matheson*[39] the Court upheld a statute from Utah that required notification "if possible, [of] the parents or guardian of the woman upon whom the abortion is to be performed, if she is a minor." The plaintiff was a fifteen-year-old minor residing with her parents, and the Court sustained the law specifically with regard to these facts, indicating that its holding would not necessarily apply to a mature or emancipated minor or to one presenting mitigating evidence concerning her relationship with her parents. Justices Blackmun, Brennan, and Marshall dissented.

Colautti v. Franklin (1979), discussion

Another clarification of *Danforth* came about in 1979 with regard to viability. In *Colautti v. Franklin*,[40] the Court declared void for vagueness a Pennsylvania provision that rendered physicians criminally liable if they failed to "exercise that degree of professional . . . diligence to preserve the life and health of the fetus which [they] . . . would be required to exercise [for] . . . any fetus intended to be born," and to choose the abortion technique most likely to produce a live fetus as long as it did not endanger the mother's health. These provisions applied to instances when the fetus was viable or when there was "sufficient reason to believe that the fetus may be viable." Blackmun writing for the majority found the standard of care provision "impermissibly vague" and the section on viability "ambiguous" and lacking in protection for the physician who makes an honest error of judgment. He defined viability as the point "when, in the judgment of the attending physician on the particular facts of the case before him, there is a reasonable likelihood of the fetus' sustained survival outside the womb, with or without artificial support." Justice White wrote a dissent joined by Rehnquist and Burger claiming that the Court was backtracking on permission for abortion-regulations it had granted in *Roe* and *Danforth,* and he emphasized that under *Roe* viability had been defined as *potential* ability to survive outside the womb, as distinguished from *actual* ability to do so. He felt the Court majority was now moving toward the latter definition.

The Court's next major clarification of its guidelines for abortion restrictions was provided in 1983 in *Akron v. Akron Center for Reproductive Health.*[41] The most noteworthy aspect of that decision was the dissent of Justice O'Connor. Her replacement of Justice Stewart on the Court meant that the 6–3 division for striking down abortion restrictions, which had prevailed, could now become a bare 5–4 division against such restrictions. As it happened, in this decision Justice Burger deviated from his *Danforth* and *Colautti* pattern, and voted with the anti-restrictions majority. Perhaps this departure was because of disagreement with Justice O'Connor's frank suggestion that the reasoning of *Roe* be abandoned, even though that issue had not been specifically raised by the parties to the case. Indeed, Justice O'Connor's implicit suggestion that *Roe v. Wade* might be overruled was the most significant aspect of this case: she urged the Court to hold that the state interest in preserving potential life amounts to a compelling interest for prohibiting abortions, not just starting at viability but starting from the time of conception. Justice Powell presents an elaborate rebuttal of her apparent recommendation to overrule *Roe* in his footnote 1.

City of Akron v. Akron Center for Reproductive Health, 462 U.S. 416 (1983)

JUSTICE POWELL delivered the opinion of the Court.

In this litigation we must decide the constitutionality of several provisions of an ordinance enacted by the city of Akron, Ohio, to regulate the performance of abortions. Today we also review abortion regulations enacted by the State of Missouri, *see Planned Parenthood Ass'n of Kansas City, Mo., Inc. v. Ashcroft* and by the State of Virginia, *see Simopoulos v. Virginia.*

These cases come to us a decade after we held in *Roe v. Wade,* 410 U.S. 113 (1973), that the right of privacy, grounded in the concept of personal liberty guaranteed by the Constitution, encompasses a woman's right to decide whether to terminate her pregnancy. Legislative responses to the Court's decision have required us on several occasions, and again today, to define the limits of a State's authority to regulate the performance of abortions. And arguments continue to be made, in these cases as well, that we erred in interpreting the Constitution. Nonetheless, the doctrine of *stare decisis,* while perhaps never entirely persuasive on a constitutional question, is a doctrine that demands respect in a society governed by the rule of law.[1] We respect it today, and reaffirm *Roe v. Wade.*

1. There are especially compelling reasons for adhering to *stare decisis* in applying the principles of *Roe v. Wade.* That case was considered with special care. It was first argued during the 1971 Term, and reargued—with extensive briefing—the following Term. The decision was joined by the Chief Justice and six other Justices. Since *Roe* was decided in February 1973, the Court repeatedly and consistently has accepted and applied the basic principle that a woman has a fundamental right to make the highly personal choice whether or not to terminate her pregnancy. *See Connecticut v. Menillo,* 423 U.S. 9 (1975); *Planned Parenthood of Central Mo. v. Danforth,* 428 U.S. 52 (1976); *Bellotti v. Baird,* 428 U.S.

I

In February 1978 the city counsel of Akron enacted Ordinance No. 160–1978, entitled "Regulation of Abortions." The ordinance sets forth 17 provisions that regu-

132 (1976); *Beal v. Doe*, 432 U.S. 438 (1977); *Maher v. Roe*, 432 U.S. 464 (1977); *Colautti v. Franklin*, 439 U.S. 379 (1979); *Bellotti v. Baird*, 443 U.S. 622 (1979); *Harris v. McRae*, 448 U.S. 297 (1980); *H.L. v. Matheson*, 450 U.S. 398 (1981).

Today, however, the dissenting opinion rejects the basic premise of *Roe* and its progeny. The dissent stops short of arguing flatly that *Roe* should be overruled. Rather, it adopts reasoning that, for all practical purposes, would accomplish precisely that result. The dissent states that "[e]ven assuming that there is a fundamental right to terminate pregnancy in some situations," the State's compelling interests in maternal health and potential human life "are present *throughout* pregnancy." (Emphasis in original.) The existence of these compelling interests turns out to be largely unnecessary, however, for the dissent does not think that even one of the numerous abortion regulations at issue imposes a sufficient burden on the "limited" fundamental right, *post*, at n.10, to require heightened scrutiny. Indeed, the dissent asserts that, regardless of cost, "[a] health regulation, such as the hospitalization requirement, simply does not rise to the level of 'official interference' with the abortion decision." (quoting *Harris v. McRae*, 448 U.S. 297, 328 [1980] [WHITE, J., concurring]). The dissent therefore would hold that a requirement that all abortions be performed in an acute-care, general hospital does not impose an unacceptable burden on the abortion decision. It requires no great familiarity with the cost and limited availability of such hospitals to appreciate that the effect of the dissent's views would be to drive the performance of many abortions back underground free of effective regulation and often without the attendance of a physician.

In sum, it appears that the dissent would uphold virtually any abortion regulation under a rational-basis test. It also appears that even where heightened scrutiny is deemed appropriate, the dissent would uphold virtually any abor-

late the performance of abortions, see Akron Codified Ordinances ch. 1870, five of which are at issue in this case:

(i) Section 1870.03 requires that all abortions performed after the first trimester of pregnancy be performed in a hospital.

(ii) Section 1870.05 sets forth requirements for notification of and consent by parents before abortions may be performed on unmarried minors.

(iii) Section 1870.06 requires that the attending physician make certain specified statements to the patient "to insure that the consent for an abortion is truly informed consent."

(iv) Section 1870.07 requires a 24-hour waiting period between the time the woman signs a consent form and the time the abortion is performed.

(v) Section 1870.16 requires that fetal remains be "disposed of in a humane and sanitary manner."

A violation of any section of the ordinance is punishable as a criminal misdemeanor. § 1870.18. . . .

On April 19, 1978, a lawsuit challenging virtually all of the ordinance's provisions was filed in the District Court for the Northern District of Ohio. The plaintiffs, respondents and cross-petitioners in this Court, were three corporations that operate abortion clinics in Akron and a physician who has performed abortions at one of the clinics. The defendants, petitioners and cross-respondents here, were the city of Akron and three city officials ("Akron"). Two individuals ("intervenors") were permitted to intervene as co-defendants "in their in-

tion-inhibiting regulation because of the State's interest in preserving potential human life (arguing that a 24-hour waiting period is justified in part because the abortion decision "has grave consequences for the fetus"). This analysis is wholly incompatible with the existence of the fundamental right recognized in *Roe v. Wade*.

dividual capacity as parents of unmarried daughters of child-bearing age." . . .

. . . The District Court invalidated four provisions, including § 1870.05 (parental notice and consent), § 1870.06(B) (requiring disclosure of facts concerning the woman's pregnancy, fetal development, the complications of abortion, and agencies available to assist the woman), and § 1870.16 (disposal of fetal remains). The court upheld the constitutionality of the remainder of the ordinance, including § 1870.03 (hospitalization for abortions after the first trimester), § 1870.06(C) (requiring disclosure of the particular risks of the woman's pregnancy and the abortion technique to be employed), and § 1870.07 (24-hour waiting period).

All parties appealed some portion of the District Court's judgment. The Court of Appeals for the Sixth Circuit affirmed in part and reversed in part. 651 F. 2d 1198 (1981). . . .

. . . We now reverse the judgment of the Court of Appeals upholding Akron's hospitalization requirement, but affirm the remainder of the decision invalidating the provisions on parental consent, informed consent, waiting period, and disposal of fetal remains.

II

In *Roe v. Wade*, the Court held that the "right of privacy, . . . founded in the Fourteenth Amendment's concept of personal liberty and restrictions upon state action, . . . is broad enough to encompass a woman's decision whether or not to terminate her pregnancy." 410 U.S., at 153. Although the Constitution does not specifically identify this right, the history of this Court's constitutional adjudication leaves no doubt that "the full scope of the liberty guaranteed by the Due Process Clause cannot be found in or limited by the precise terms of the specific guarantees elsewhere provided in the Constitution." *Poe v. Ullman,* 367 U.S. 497, 543 (1961) (Harlan, J., dissenting from dismissal of appeal). Central among these protected liberties is an individual's "freedom of personal choice in matters of marriage and family life." *Roe,* 410 U.S., at 169 (STEWART, J., concurring). *See, e.g., Eisenstadt v. Baird,* 405 U.S. 438 (1972); *Loving v. Virginia,* 388 U.S. 1 (1967); *Griswold v. Connecticut,* 381 U.S. 479 (1965); *Pierce v. Society of Sisters,* 268 U.S. 510 (1925); *Meyer v. Nebraska,* 262 U.S. 390 (1923). The decision in *Roe* was based firmly on this long-recognized and essential element of personal liberty.

The Court also has recognized, because abortion is a medical procedure, that the full vindication of the woman's fundamental right necessarily requires that her physician be given "the room he needs to make his best medical judgment." *Doe v. Bolton,* 410 U.S. 179, 192 (1973). *See Whalen v. Roe,* 429 U.S. 589, 604–05, n.33 (1977). The physician's exercise of this medical judgment encompasses both assisting the woman in the decisionmaking process and implementing her decision should she choose abortion. *See Colautti v. Franklin,* 439 U.S. 379, 387 (1979).

At the same time, the Court in *Roe* acknowledged that the woman's fundamental right "is not unqualified and must be considered against important state interests in abortion." *Roe,* 410 U.S., at 154. But restrictive state regulation of the right to choose abortion, as with other fundamental rights subject to searching judicial examination, must be supported by a compelling state interest. *Id.* at 155. We have recognized two such interests that may justify state regulation of abortions.[10]

10. In addition, the Court repeatedly has recognized that, in view of the unique status of children under the law, the States have a "significant" interest in certain abortion regulations

First, a State has an "important and legitimate interest in protecting the potentiality of human life." *Id.* at 162. Although this interest exists "throughout the course of the woman's pregnancy," *Beal v. Doe*, 432 U.S. 438, 446 (1977), it becomes compelling only at viability, the point at which the fetus "has the capability of meaningful life outside the mother's womb," *Roe*, 410 U.S., at 163. *See Planned Parenthood of Central Mo. v. Danforth*, 428 U.S. 52, 63–65 (1976). At viability this interest in protecting the potential life of the unborn child is so important that the State may proscribe abortions

altogether, "except when it is necessary to preserve the life or health of the mother." *Roe*, 410 U.S., at 164.

Second, because a State has a legitimate concern with the health of women who undergo abortions, "a State may properly assert important interests in safeguarding health [and] in maintaining medical standards." *Id.* at 154. We held in *Roe*, however, that this health interest does not become compelling until "approximately the end of the first trimester" of pregnancy.[11] *Id.* at 163. Until that time, a preg-

---

aimed at protecting children "that is not present in the case of an adult." *Planned Parenthood of Central Mo. v. Danforth*, 428 U.S. 52, 75 (1976). *See Carey v. Population Services International*, 431 U.S. 678, 693, n.15 (1977) (plurality opinion). The right of privacy includes "independence in making certain kinds of important decisions," *Whalen v. Roe*, 429 U.S. 589, 599–600 (1977), but this Court has recognized that many minors are less capable than adults of making such important decisions. *See Bellotti v. Baird*, 443 U.S. 622, 633–35 (1979) (plurality opinion) (*Bellotti II*); *Danforth, supra*, at 102 (STEVENS, J., concurring in part and dissenting in part.) Accordingly, we have held that the States have a legitimate interest in encouraging parental involvement in their minor children's decision to have an abortion. *See H.L. v. Matheson*, 450 U.S. 398 (1981) (parental notice); *Bellotti II, supra*, at 639, 648 (plurality opinion) (parental consent). A majority of the Court, however, has indicated that these state and parental interests must give way to the constitutional right of a mature minor or of an immature minor whose best interests are contrary to parental involvement. *See e.g., Matheson, supra*, at 420 (POWELL, J., concurring); *id.* at 450–51 (MARSHALL, J., dissenting). The plurality in *Bellotti II* concluded that a State choosing to encourage parental involvement must provide an alternative procedure through which a minor may demonstrate that she is mature enough to make her own decision or that the abortion is in her best interest. *See Bellotti, supra*, at 643–44.

11. *Roe* identified the end of the first trimester as the compelling point because until that time— according to the medical literature available in 1973—"mortality in abortion may be less than mortality in normal childbirth." 410 U.S., at 163. There is substantial evidence that developments in the past decade, particularly the development of a much safer method for performing second-trimester abortions, *see infra*, have extended the period in which abortions are safer than childbirth. *See, e.g.*, LeBolt, *et al.*, *Mortality from Abortion and Childbirth: Are the Populations Comparable?*, 248 J.A.M.A. 188, 191 (1982) (abortion may be safer than childbirth up to gestational ages of 16 weeks).

We think it prudent, however, to retain *Roe*'s identification of the beginning of the second trimester as the approximate time at which the State's interest in maternal health becomes sufficiently compelling to justify significant regulation of abortion. We note that the medical evidence suggests that until approximately the end of the first trimester, the State's interest in maternal health would not be served by regulations that restrict the manner in which abortions are performed by a licensed physician. *See, e.g.*, American College of Obstetricians and Gynecologists (ACOG), Standards for Obstetric-Gynecologic Services 54 (5th ed. 1982) (hereinafter ACOG Standards) (uncomplicated abortions generally may be performed in a physician's office or an outpatient clinic up to 14 weeks from the first day of the last menstrual period); ACOG Technical Bulletin No. 56, Methods of Mid-Trimester Abortion (Dec. 1979) ("Regardless of

nant woman must be permitted, in consultation with her physician, to decide to have an abortion and to effectuate that decision "free of interference by the State."[12] *Id.* at 163.

This does not mean that a State never may enact a regulation touching on the woman's abortion right during the first weeks of pregnancy. Certain regulations that have no significant impact on the woman's exercise of her right may be permissible where justified by important state health objectives. In *Danforth, supra,* we unanimously upheld two Missouri statu-

_____

advances in abortion technology, midtrimester terminations will likely remain more hazardous, expensive, and emotionally disturbing for women than earlier abortions.")

The *Roe* trimester standard thus continues to provide a reasonable legal framework for limiting a State's authority to regulate abortions. Where the State adopts a health regulation governing the performance of abortions during the second trimester, the determinative question should be whether there is a reasonable medical basis for the regulation. *See Roe, supra,* at 163. The comparison between abortion and childbirth mortality rates may be relevant only where the State employs a health rationale as a justification for a complete prohibition on abortions in certain circumstances. *See Danforth,* 428 U.S., at 78–79 (invalidating state ban on saline abortions, a method that was "safer, with respect to maternal mortality, than even continuation of the pregnancy until normal childbirth").

12. Of course, the State retains an interest in ensuring the validity of *Roe's* factual assumption that "the first trimester abortion [is] as safe for the woman as normal childbirth at term," an assumption that "holds true only if the abortion is performed by medically competent personnel under conditions insuring maximum safety for the woman." *Connecticut v. Menillo,* 423 U.S. 9, 11 (1975) (per curiam). On this basis, for example, it is permissible for the State to impose criminal sanctions on the performance of an abortion by a nonphysician. *Id.*

tory provisions, applicable to the first trimester, requiring the woman to provide her informed written consent to the abortion and the physician to keep certain records, even though comparable requirements were not imposed on most other medical procedures. *See* 428 U.S., at 65–67, 79–81. The decisive factor was that the State met its burden of demonstrating that these regulations furthered important health-related State concerns. But even these minor regulations on the abortion procedure during the first trimester may not interfere with physician-patient consultation or with the woman's choice between abortion and childbirth. *See id.* at 81.

From approximately the end of the first trimester of pregnancy, the State "may regulate the abortion procedure to the extent that the regulation reasonably relates to the preservation and protection of maternal health." *Roe,* 410 U.S., at 163. The State's discretion to regulate on this basis does not, however, permit it to adopt abortion regulations that depart from accepted medical practice. We have rejected a State's attempt to ban a particular second-trimester abortion procedure, where the ban would have increased the costs and limited the availability of abortions without promoting important health benefits. *See Danforth,* 428 U.S. at 77–78. If a State requires licensing or undertakes to regulate the performance of abortions during this period, the health standards adopted must be "legitimately related to the objective the State seeks to accomplish." *Doe,* 410 U.S., at 195.

III

Section 1870.03 of the Akron ordinance requires that any abortion performed "upon a pregnant woman subsequent to the end of the first trimester of her pregnancy" must be "performed in a hospital" . . . [and] prevents the performance of abortions in outpatient facilities that are not part of an acute-care, full-service hospital.

In the District Court plaintiffs sought to demonstrate that this hospitalization requirement has a serious detrimental impact on a woman's ability to obtain a second-trimester abortion in Akron and that it is not reasonably related to the State's interest in the health of the pregnant woman. The District Court did not reject this argument, but rather found the evidence "not . . . so convincing that it is willing to discard the Supreme Court's formulation in *Roe*" of a line between impermissible first- trimester regulation and permissible second-trimester regulation. 479 F. Supp., at 1215. The Court of Appeals affirmed on a similar basis. It accepted plaintiffs' argument that Akron's hospitalization requirement did not have a reasonable health justification during at least part of the second trimester, but declined to "retreat from the 'bright line' in *Roe v. Wade*." 651 F.2d, at 1210. We believe that the courts below misinterpreted this Court's prior decisions, and we now hold that § 1870.03 is unconstitutional.

A

In *Roe v. Wade* the Court held that after the end of the first trimester of pregnancy the State's interest becomes compelling, and it may "regulate the abortion procedure to the extent that the regulation reasonably relates to the preservation and protection of maternal health." 410 U.S., at 163. We noted, for example, that States could establish requirements relating "to the facility in which the procedure is to be performed, that is, whether it must be in a hospital or may be a clinic or some other place of less-than-hospital status." *Id.* In the companion case of *Doe v. Bolton* the Court invalidated a Georgia requirement that all abortions be performed in a hospital licensed by the State Board of Health and accredited by the Joint Commission on Accreditation of Hospitals. *See* 410 U.S., at

201. We recognized the State's legitimate health interests in establishing, for second-trimester abortions, "standards for licensing all facilities where abortions may be performed." *Id.* at 195. We found, however, that "the State must show more than [was shown in *Doe*] in order to prove that only the full resources of a licensed hospital, rather than those of some other appropriately licensed institution, satisfy these health interests." *Id.*

We affirm today, *see supra,* n.11, that a State's interest in health regulation becomes compelling at approximately the end of the first trimester. The existence of a compelling state interest in health, however, is only the beginning of the inquiry. The State's regulation may be upheld only if it is reasonably designed to further that state interest. *See Doe,* 410 U.S., at 195. And the Court in *Roe* did not hold that it always is reasonable for a State to adopt an abortion regulation that applies to the entire second trimester. A State necessarily must have latitude in adopting regulations of general applicability in this sensitive area. But if it appears that during a substantial portion of the second trimester the State's regulation "depart[s] from accepted medical practice," *supra,* the regulation may not be upheld simply because it may be reasonable for the remaining portion of the trimester. Rather, the State is obligated to make a reasonable effort to limit the effect of its regulations to the period in the trimester during which its health interest will be furthered.

B

There can be no doubt that § 1870.03's second-trimester hospitalization requirement places a significant obstacle in the path of women seeking an abortion. A primary burden created by the requirement is additional cost to the woman. The Court of Appeals noted that there was testimony that a second-trimester abortion costs more than twice as much in a hospital as in a clinic. Moreover, the court indicated that second-trimester abortions were rarely performed in Akron hospitals. *Id.* (only nine second-trimester abortions performed in Akron hospitals in the year before trial). Thus, a second-trimester hospitalization requirement may force women to travel to find available facilities, resulting in both financial expense and additional health risk. It therefore is apparent that a second-trimester hospitalization requirement may significantly limit a woman's ability to obtain an abortion.

Akron does not contend that § 1870.03 imposes only an insignificant burden on women's access to abortion, but rather defends it as a reasonable health regulation. This position had strong support at the time of *Roe v. Wade,* as hospitalization for second-trimester abortions was recommended by the American Public Health Association (APHA), *see Roe,* 410 U.S., at 143–46, and the American College of Obstetricians and Gynecologists (ACOG), *see* Standards for Obstetric-Gynecologic Services 65 (4th ed. 1974). Since then, however, the safety of second-trimester abortions has increased dramatically.[22] The principal reason is that the D&E [dilation and evacuation] procedure is now widely and successfully used for second-trimester abortions.[23] The Court of Appeals found that there was "an abundance of evidence that D&E is the safest method of performing post-first trimester abortions today."

651 F.2d, at 1209. The availability of the D&E procedure during the interval between approximately 12 and 16 weeks of pregnancy, a period during which other second-trimester abortion techniques generally cannot be used,[24] has meant that women desiring an early second-trimester abortion no longer are forced to incur the health risks of waiting until at least the sixteenth week of pregnancy.

For our purposes, an even more significant factor is that experience indicates that D&E may be performed safely on an outpatient basis in appropriate nonhospital facilities. The evidence is strong enough to have convinced the APHA to abandon its prior recommendation of hospitalization for all second-trimester abortions. . . . Similarly, the ACOG no longer suggests that all second-trimester abortions be performed in a hospital. . . .

These developments, and the professional commentary supporting them, constitute impressive evidence that—at least during the early weeks of the second trimester—D&E abortions may be performed as safely in an outpatient clinic as in a full-service hospital. We conclude, therefore, that "present medical knowledge," *Roe,* 410 U.S., at 163, convincingly undercuts Akron's justification for requiring that *all* second-trimester abortions be performed in a hospital.

Akron nonetheless urges that "[t]he fact that some mid-trimester abortions may be done in a minimally equipped clinic does not invalidate the regulation." It is true that a state abortion regulation is not unconstitutional simply because it does not correspond perfectly in all cases to the

22. The death-to-case ratio for all second-trimester abortions in this country fell from 14.4 deaths per 100,000 abortions in 1972 to 7.6 per 100,000 in 1977. *See* Tyler, *et al., Second-Trimester Induced Abortion in the United States,* published in Second Trimester Abortion 17–20.

23. At the time *Roe* was decided, the D&E procedure was used only to perform first-trimester abortions.

24. Instillation procedures, the primary means of performing a second-trimester abortion before the development of D&E, generally cannot be performed until approximately the 16th week of pregnancy. . . .

asserted state interest. But the lines drawn in a state regulation must be reasonable, and this cannot be said of § 1870.03. By preventing the performance of D&E abortions in an appropriate nonhospital setting, Akron has imposed a heavy, and unnecessary, burden on women's access to a relatively inexpensive, otherwise accessible, and safe abortion procedure.[28] Section 1870.03 has "the effect of inhibiting . . . the vast majority of abortions after the first 12 weeks," *Danforth*, 428 U.S., at 79, and therefore unreasonably infringes upon a woman's constitutional right to obtain an abortion.

IV

We turn next to § 1870.05(B), the provision prohibiting a physician from performing an abortion on a minor pregnant woman under the age of fifteen unless he obtains "the informed written consent of one of her parents or her legal guardian" or unless the minor obtains "an order from a court having jurisdiction over her that the abortion be performed or induced." The District Court invalidated this provision because "[i]t does not establish a procedure by which a minor can avoid a parental veto of her abortion decision by demonstrating that her decision is, in fact, informed. Rather, it requires, in all cases, both the minor's informed consent and either parental consent or a court order." 479 F. Supp., at 1201. The Court of Appeals affirmed on the same basis.

The relevant legal standards are not in dispute. The Court has held that "the State may not impose a blanket provision . . . requiring the consent of a parent or person *in loco parentis* as a condition for abortion of

28. In the United States during 1978, 82.1 percent of all abortions from 13–15 weeks and 24.6 percent of all abortions from 16–20 weeks were performed by the D&E method.

an unmarried minor." *Danforth*, 428 U.S., at 74. In *Bellotti v. Baird*, 443 U.S. 622 (1979) (*Bellotti II*), a majority of the Court indicated that a State's interest in protecting immature minors will sustain a requirement of a consent substitute, either parental or judicial. *See id.* at 640–42 (plurality opinion for four Justices); *id.* at 656–57 (WHITE, J., dissenting) (expressing approval of absolute parental or judicial consent requirement). *See also Danforth*, 428 U.S., at 102–5 (STEVENS, J., concurring in part and dissenting in part). The *Bellotti II* plurality cautioned, however, that the State must provide an alternative procedure whereby a pregnant minor may demonstrate that she is sufficiently mature to make the abortion decision herself or that, despite her immaturity, an abortion would be in her best interests. 443 U.S., at 643–44. Under these decisions, it is clear that Akron may not make a blanket determination that *all* minors under the age of fifteen are too immature to make this decision or that an abortion never may be in the minor's best interests without parental approval.

Akron's ordinance does not create expressly the alternative procedure required by *Bellotti II*. But Akron contends that the . . . [state courts will] construe the ordinance in a manner consistent with the constitutional requirement[s.] . . .

. . . This suit, however, concerns a municipal ordinance that creates no procedures for making the necessary determinations. . . . In these circumstances, we do not think that the Akron ordinance, as applied in Ohio juvenile proceedings, is reasonably susceptible of being construed to create an "opportunity for case-by-case evaluations of the maturity of pregnant minors." *Bellotti II*, 443 U.S., at 643, n.23 (plurality opinion). We therefore affirm the Court of Appeals' judgment that § 1870.05(B) is unconstitutional.

V

The Akron ordinance provides that no abortion shall be performed except "with the informed written consent of the pregnant woman, . . . given freely and without coercion." § 1870.06(A). Furthermore, "in order to insure that the consent for an abortion is truly informed consent," the woman must be "orally informed by her attending physician" of the status of her pregnancy, the development of her fetus, the date of possible viability, the physical and emotional complications that may result from an abortion, and the availability of agencies to provide her with assistance and information with respect to birth control, adoption, and childbirth. § 1870.06(B). In addition, the attending physician must inform her "of the particular risks associated with her own pregnancy and the abortion technique to be employed . . . [and] other information which in his own medical judgment is relevant to her decision as to whether to have an abortion or carry her pregnancy to term." § 1870.06(C).

. . . The Court of Appeals concluded that both provisions were unconstitutional. *See* 651 F.2d, at 1207. We affirm.

A

In *Danforth, supra,* we upheld a Missouri law requiring a pregnant woman to "certif[y] in writing her consent to the abortion and that her consent is informed and freely given and is not the result of coercion." 428 U.S., at 85. . . .

. . . This does not mean, however, that a State has unreviewable authority to decide what information a woman must be given before she chooses to have an abortion. It remains primarily the responsibility of the physician to ensure that appropriate information is conveyed to his patient, depending on her particular circumstances. *Danforth's* recognition of the State's interest in ensuring that this information be given will not justify abortion regulations designed to influence the woman's informed choice between abortion or childbirth.[33]

B

Viewing the city's regulations in this light, we believe that § 1870.06(B) attempts to extend the State's interest in ensuring "informed consent" beyond permissible limits. First, it is fair to say that much of the information required is designed not to inform the woman's consent but rather to persuade her to withhold it altogether. Subsection (3) requires the physician to inform his patient that "the unborn child is a human life from the moment of conception," a requirement inconsistent with the Court's holding in *Roe v. Wade* that a State may not adopt one theory of when life begins to justify its regulation of abortions. *See* 410 U.S., at 159–62. Moreover, much of the detailed description of "the anatomical and physiological characteristics of the particular unborn child" required by subsection (3) would involve at best speculation by the physicians. And subsection (5), that begins with the dubious statement that "abortion is a major surgical procedure" and proceeds to describe numerous possible physical and psychological complications of abortion, is a "parade of horribles" intended to suggest that abortion is a particularly dangerous procedure.

33. A State is not always foreclosed from asserting an interest in whether pregnancies end in abortion or childbirth. In *Maher v. Roe,* 432 U.S. 464 (1977), and *Harris v. McRae,* 448 U.S. 297 (1980), we upheld governmental spending statutes that reimbursed indigent women for childbirth but not abortion. This legislation to further an interest in preferring childbirth over abortion was permissible, however, only because it did not add any "restriction on access to abortion that was not already there." *Maher,* 432 U.S., at 474.

384 The Constitutional Rights of Women

An additional, and equally decisive, objection to § 1870.06(B) is its intrusion upon the discretion of the pregnant woman's physician. This provision specifies a litany of information that the physician must recite to each woman regardless of whether in his judgment the information is relevant to her personal decision. For example, even if the physician believes that some of the risks outlined in subsection (5) are nonexistent for a particular patient, he remains obligated to describe them to her. In *Danforth* the Court warned against placing the physician in just such an "undesired and uncomfortable straitjacket." 428 U.S., at 67, n.8. Consistent with its interest in ensuring informed consent, a State may require that a physician make certain that his patient understands the physical and emotional implications of having an abortion. But Akron has gone far beyond merely describing the general subject matter relevant to informed consent. By insisting upon recitation of a lengthy and inflexible list of information, Akron unreasonably has placed "obstacles in the path of the doctor upon whom [the woman is] entitled to rely for advice in connection with her decision." *Whalen v. Roe*, 429 U.S. 589, 604 n.33 (1977).

C

Section 1870.06(C) presents a different question. Under this provision, the "attending physician" must inform the woman

> of the particular risks associated with her own pregnancy and the abortion technique to be employed including providing her with at least a general description of the medical instructions to be followed subsequent to the abortion in order to insure her safe recovery, and shall in addition provide her with such other information which in his own medical judgment is relevant to her decision as to whether to have

an abortion or carry her pregnancy to term.

The information required clearly is related to maternal health and to the State's legitimate purpose in requiring informed consent. . . .

We are not convinced, however, that there is as vital a state need for insisting that the physician performing the abortion, or for that matter any physician, personally counsel the patient in the absence of a request. The State's interest is in ensuring that the woman's consent is informed and unpressured; the critical factor is whether she obtains the necessary information and counseling from a qualified person, not the identity of the person from whom she obtains it. Akron and intervenors strongly urge that the nonphysician counselors at the plaintiff abortion clinics are not trained or qualified to perform this important function. The courts below made no such findings, however, and on the record before us we cannot say that the woman's consent to the abortion will not be informed if a physician delegates the counseling task to another qualified individual.

In so holding, we do not suggest that the State is powerless to vindicate its interest in making certain the "important" and "stressful" decision to abort "is made with full knowledge of its nature and consequences." *Danforth*, 428 U.S., at 67. Nor do we imply that a physician may abdicate his essential role as the person ultimately responsible for the medical aspects of the decision to perform the abortion. A State may define the physician's responsibility to include verification that adequate counseling has been provided and that the woman's consent is informed. In addition, the State may establish reasonable minimum qualifications for those people who perform the primary counseling function. *See, e.g., Doe*, 410 U.S., at 195 (State may require a medical facility "to possess all the staffing and services necessary to perform an abortion safely"). In light of these alternatives, we believe that it is unreasonable for a State to insist that only a physician is competent to provide the information and counseling relevant to informed consent. We affirm the judgment of the Court of Appeals that § 1870.06 (C) is invalid.

VI

The Akron ordinance prohibits a physician from performing an abortion until 24 hours after the pregnant woman signs a consent form [except in medical emergencies]. § 1870.07. . . .

. . .

We find that Akron has failed to demonstrate that any legitimate state interest is furthered by an arbitrary and inflexible waiting period. There is no evidence suggesting that the abortion procedure will be performed more safely. Nor are we convinced that the State's legitimate concern that the woman's decision be informed is reasonably served by requiring a 24-hour delay as a matter of course. The decision whether to proceed with an abortion is one as to which it is important to "affor[d] the physician adequate discretion in the exercise of his medical judgment." *Colautti v. Franklin*, 439 U.S. 379, 387 (1979). In accordance with the ethical standards of the profession, a physician will advise the patient to defer the abortion when he thinks this will be beneficial to her. But if a woman, after appropriate counseling, is prepared to give her written informed consent and proceed with the abortion, a State may not demand that she delay the effectuation of that decision.

VII

Section 1870.16 of the Akron ordinance requires physicians performing abortions to "insure that the remains of the unborn child are disposed of in a humane and sanitary manner." . . .

Akron contends that the purpose of § 1870.16 is simply "to preclude the mindless dumping of aborted fetuses on garbage piles.'" . . . It is far from clear, however, that this provision has such a limited intent. The phrase "humane and sanitary" does, as the Court of Appeals noted, suggest a possible intent to "mandate some sort of 'decent burial' of an embryo at the earliest stages of formation." 651 F.2d, at 1211. This level of uncertainty is fatal where criminal liability is imposed. See *Colautti v. Franklin*, 439 U.S. 379, 396 (1979). Because § 1870.16 fails to give a physician "fair notice that his contemplated conduct is forbidden," *United States v. Harriss*, 347 U.S. 612, 617 (1954), we agree that it violates the Due Process Clause.

. . .

JUSTICE O'CONNOR, with whom JUSTICE WHITE and JUSTICE REHNQUIST join, dissenting.

In *Roe v. Wade*, 410 U.S. 113, (1973), the Court held that the "right of privacy . . . founded in the Fourteenth Amendment's concept of personal liberty and restrictions upon state action . . . is broad enough to encompass a woman's decision whether or not to terminate her pregnancy." *Id.* at 153. The parties in these cases have not asked the Court to reexamine the validity of that holding and the court below did not address it. Accordingly, the Court does not re-examine its previous holding. Nonetheless, it is apparent from the Court's opinion that neither sound constitutional theory nor our need to decide cases based on the application of neutral principles can accommodate an analytical framework that varies according to the "stages" of pregnancy, where those stages, and their concomitant standards of review, differ according to the level of medical technology available when a particular challenge to state regulation occurs. The Court's analysis of the Akron regulations is inconsistent both with the method of analysis employed in previous cases dealing with abortion, and with the Court's approach to fundamental rights in other areas.

Our recent cases indicate that a regulation imposed on "a lawful abortion 'is not unconstitutional unless it unduly burdens the right to seek an abortion.'" *Maher v. Roe*, 432 U.S. 464, 473 (1977) (quoting *Bellotti v. Baird*, 428 U.S. 132, 147 [1977] [*Bellotti I*]). *See also Harris v. McRae*, 448 U.S. 297, 314 (1980). In my view, this "unduly burdensome" standard should be applied to the challenged regulations throughout the entire pregnancy without reference to the particular "stage" of pregnancy involved. If the particular regulation does not "unduly burden[]" the fundamental right, *Maher*, 432 U.S., at 473, then our evaluation of that regulation is limited to our determination that the regulation rationally relates to a legitimate state purpose. Irrespective of what we may believe is wise or prudent policy in this difficult area, "the Constitution does not constitute us as 'Platonic Guardians' nor does it vest in this Court the authority to strike down laws because they do not meet our standards of desirable social policy, 'wisdom,' or 'common sense.'" *Plyler v. Doe*, 457 U.S. 202, 242, (1982) (Burger, C.J., dissenting).

I

The trimester or "three-stage" approach adopted by the Court in *Roe*, and, in a modified form, employed by the Court to analyze the state regulations in these cases, cannot be supported as a legitimate or useful framework for accommodating the woman's right and the State's interests. The decision of the Court today graphically illustrates why the trimester approach is a completely unworkable method of accommodating the conflicting personal rights and compelling state interests that are involved in the abortion context.

As the Court indicates today, the State's compelling interest in maternal health changes as medical technology changes, and any health regulation must not "depart from accepted medical practice." *Ante.* In applying this standard, the Court holds that "the safety of second-trimester abortions has increased dramatically" since 1973, when *Roe* was decided. *Ante.* Although a regulation such as one requiring that all second-trimester abortions be performed in hospitals "had strong support" in 1973 "as a reasonable health regulation," *id*, this regulation can no longer stand because, according to the Court's diligent research into medical and scientific literature, the dilation and evacuation procedure (D&E), used in 1973 only for first-trimester abortions, "is now widely and successfully used for second trimester abortions." *Id.* Further, the medical literature relied on by the Court indicates that the D&E procedure may be performed in an appropriate non-hospital setting for "at least . . . the early weeks of the second trimester. . . ." *Ante.* The Court then chooses the period of 16 weeks of gestation as that point at which D&E procedures may be performed safely in a non-hospital setting, and thereby invalidates the Akron hospitalization regulation.

It is not difficult to see that despite the Court's purported adherence to the trimester approach adopted in *Roe*, the lines drawn in that decision have now been "blurred" because of what the Court accepts as technological advancement in the safety of abortion procedure. The State may no longer rely on a "bright line" that separates permissible from impermissible regulation, and it is no longer free to consider the second trimester as a unit and weigh the risks posed by all abortion procedures throughout that trimester. Rather, the State must continuously and conscientiously study contemporary medical and scientific literature in order to determine whether the effect of a particular regulation is to "depart from accepted medical practice" insofar as particular procedures and particular periods within the trimester are concerned. Assuming that legislative bodies are able to engage in this exacting task,[4] it is difficult to believe that our Constitution *requires* that they do it as a prelude to protecting the health of their citizens. It is even more difficult to believe that this Court, without the resources available to those bodies entrusted with making legislative choices, believes itself competent to make these inquiries and to revise these standards every time the American College of Obstetricians and Gynecologists (ACOG) or similar group revises its views about what is and what is not appropriate medical procedure in this area. Indeed, the ACOG standards on which the Court relies were changed in 1982 after trial in the present cases. Before ACOG changed its standards in 1982, it recommended that all mid-trimester abortions be performed in a hospital. *See Akron Center for Reproductive Health, Inc. v. City of Akron*, 651 F.2d 1198, 1209 (6th Cir. 1981). As today's decision indicates, medical technology is changing, and this change will necessitate our continued functioning as the nation's "*ex officio* medical board with powers to approve or disapprove medical and operative practices and standards throughout the United States." *Planned Parenthood v. Danforth*, 428 U.S. 52, 99 (1976) (WHITE, J., concurring in part and dissenting in part).

Just as improvements in medical technology inevitably will move *forward* the

point at which the State may regulate for reasons of maternal health, different technological improvements will move *backward* the point of viability at which the State may proscribe abortions except when necessary to preserve the life and health of the mother.

In 1973, viability before 28 weeks was considered unusual. The fourteenth edition of L. Hellman & J. Pritchard, *Williams Obstetrics*, on which the Court relied in *Roe* for its understanding of viability, stated that "[a]ttainment of a [fetal] weight of 1,000 g [or a fetal age of approximately 28 weeks gestation] is . . . widely used as the criterion of viability." *Id.* at 493. However, recent studies have demonstrated increasingly earlier fetal viability.[5] It is certainly

---

4. Irrespective of the difficulty of the task, legislatures, with their superior fact-finding capabilities, are certainly better able to make the necessary judgments than are Courts.

5. One study shows that infants born alive with a gestational age of less than 25 weeks and weight between 500 and 1,249 grams have a 20 percent chance of survival. *See* Phillip, *et al.*, *Neonatal Mortality Risk for the Eighties: The Importance of Birth Weight/Gestational Age Groups*, 68 Pediatrics 122 (1981). Another recent comparative study shows that preterm infants with a weight of 1000 grams or less born in one hospital had a 42 percent rate of survival. Kopelman, *The Smallest Preterm Infants: Reasons for Optimism and New Dilemmas*, 132 Am. J. Diseases Children 461 (1978). An infant weighing 484 grams and having a gestational age of 22 weeks at birth is now thriving in a Los Angeles hospital, and the attending physician has stated that the infant has a "95 percent chance of survival." Washington Post, March 31, 1983, at A2, col. 2. The aborted fetus in No. 81–185, *Simopoulos v. Virginia, post,* weighed 495 grams and was approximately 22 gestational weeks.

Recent developments promise even greater success in overcoming the various respiratory and immunological neonatal complications that stand in the way of increased fetal viability. *See, e.g.,* Beddis, et al., *New Technique for Servo-Control of Arterial Oxygen Tension in Preterm Infants,* 54 Archives of Disease Childhood 278 (1979). "There is absolutely no question that in the current era there has been a sustained and progressive improvement in the outlook for sur-

reasonable to believe that fetal viability in the first trimester of pregnancy may be possible in the not too distant future. Indeed, the Court has explicitly acknowledged that *Roe* left the point of viability "flexible for anticipated advancements in medical skill." *Colautti v. Franklin*, 439 U.S. 379, 387 (1979). "[W]e recognized in *Roe* that viability was a matter of medical judgment, skill, and technical ability, and we preserved the flexibility of the term." *Danforth, supra*, 428 U.S., at 64.

The *Roe* framework, then, is clearly on a collision course with itself. As the medical risks of various abortion procedures decrease, the point at which the State may regulate for reasons of maternal health is moved further forward to actual childbirth. As medical science becomes better able to provide for the separate existence of the fetus, the point of viability is moved further back toward conception. Moreover, it is clear that the trimester approach violates the fundamental aspiration of judicial decision making through the application of neutral principles "sufficiently absolute to give them roots throughout the community and continuity over significant periods of time. . . ." A. Cox, *The Role of the Supreme Court in American Government* 114 (1976). The *Roe* framework is inherently tied to the state of medical technology that exists whenever particular litigation ensues. Although legislatures are better suited to make the necessary factual judgments in this area, the Court's framework forces legislatures, as a matter of constitutional law, to speculate about what constitutes "accepted medical practice" at any given time. Without the necessary expertise or ability, courts must then pretend to act as science review boards and examine those legislative judgments.

_____
vival of small premature infants." Stern, *Intensive Care of the Pre-Term Infant*, 26 Danish Med. Bull. 144 (1979).

The Court adheres to the *Roe* framework because the doctrine of *stare decisis* "demands respect in a society governed by the rule of law." *Ante.* Although respect for *stare decisis* cannot be challenged, "this Court's considered practice [is] not to apply *stare decisis* as rigidly in constitutional as in nonconstitutional cases." *Glidden Company v. Zdanok*, 370 U.S. 530, 543 (1962). Although we must be mindful of the "desirability of continuity of decision in constitutional questions . . . when convinced of former error, this Court has never felt constrained to follow precedent. In constitutional questions, when correction depends on amendment and not upon legislative action this Court throughout its history has freely exercised its power to reexamine the basis of its constitutional decisions." *Smith v. Allwright*, 321 U.S. 649, 665 (1944).

Even assuming that there is a fundamental right to terminate pregnancy in some situations, there is no justification in law or logic for the trimester framework adopted in *Roe* and employed by the Court today on the basis of *stare decisis*. For the reasons stated above, that framework is clearly an unworkable means of balancing the fundamental right and the compelling state interests that are indisputably implicated.

II

The Court in *Roe* correctly realized that the State has important interests "in the areas of health and medical standards" and that "[t]he State has a legitimate interest in seeing to it that abortion, like any other medical procedure, is performed under circumstances that insure maximum safety for the patient." 410 U.S., at 149, 150. The Court also recognized that the State has "*another* important and legitimate interest in protecting the potentiality of human life." *Id.* at 162. (Emphasis in original.) I agree completely that the State has these interests, but in my view, the point at which these interests become compelling does not depend on the trimester of pregnancy. Rather, these interests are present *throughout* pregnancy.

This Court has never failed to recognize that "a State may properly assert important interests in safeguarding health [and] in maintaining medical standards." 410 U.S., at 154. . . . "The mode and procedure of medical diagnostic procedures is not the business of judges." *Parham v. J.R.*, 442 U.S. 584, 607–08 (1979). Under the *Roe* framework, however, the state interest in maternal health cannot become compelling until the onset of the second trimester of pregnancy because "until the end of the first trimester mortality in abortion may be less than mortality in normal childbirth." 410 U.S., at 163. Before the second trimester, the decision to perform an abortion "must be left to the medical judgment of the pregnant woman's attending physician." *Id.* at 164.[6]

The fallacy inherent in the *Roe* framework is apparent: just because the State has a compelling interest in ensuring maternal safety once an abortion may be more dangerous in childbirth, it simply does not follow that the State has *no* interest before that point that justifies state regulation to ensure that first-trimester abortions are performed as safely as possible.[7]

6. Interestingly, the Court in *Danforth* upheld a recordkeeping requirement as well as the consent provision even though these requirements were imposed on first-trimester abortions and although the State did not impose comparable requirements on most other medical procedures. *See Danforth, supra,* 428 U.S., at 65–67, 79–81 (1976). *Danforth,* then, must be understood as a retreat from the position ostensibly adopted in *Roe* that the State had *no* compelling interest in regulation during the first trimester of pregnancy that would justify restrictions imposed on the abortion decision.

7. For example, the 1982 ACOG Standards, on which the Court relies so heavily in its analysis, provide that physicians performing first-trimester abortions in their offices should provide for

The state interest in potential human life is likewise extant throughout pregnancy. In *Roe*, the Court held that although the State had an important and legitimate interest in protecting potential life, that interest could not become compelling until the point at which the fetus was viable. The difficulty with this analysis is clear: *potential* life is no less potential in the first weeks of pregnancy than it is at viability or afterward. At any stage in pregnancy, there is the *potential* for human life. Although the Court refused to "resolve the difficult question of when life begins," *id.* 410 U.S., at 159, the Court chose the point of viability—when the fetus is *capable* of life independent of its mother—to permit the complete proscription of abortion. The choice of viability as the point at which the state interest in *potential* life becomes compelling is no less arbitrary than choosing any point before viability or any point afterward. Accordingly, I believe that the State's interest in protecting potential human life exists throughout the pregnancy.

III

Although the State possesses compelling interests in the protection of potential human life and in maternal health throughout pregnancy, not every regulation that the State imposes must be measured against the State's compelling interests and examined with strict scrutiny. This Court has acknowledged that "the right in *Roe v. Wade* can be understood only by considering both the woman's interest and the nature of the State's interference with it. *Roe* did not declare an unqualified 'constitutional right to an abortion,' . . . Rather, the right protects the woman from unduly burdensome interference with her freedom to decide whether to terminate her pregnancy." *Maher, supra,* 432 U.S., at 473–74, The Court

prompt emergency treatment or hospitalization in the event of any complications. . . .

and its individual Justices have repeatedly utilized the "unduly burdensome" standard in abortion cases.[8]

The requirement that state interference "infringe substantially" or "heavily burden" a right before heightened scrutiny is applied is not novel in our fundamental-rights jurisprudence, or restricted to the abortion context. In *San Antonio Independent School District v. Rodriguez*, 411 U.S. 1, 37, 38 (1973), we observed that we apply "strict judicial scrutiny" only when legislation may be said to have "'deprived,' 'infringed,' or 'interfered' with the free exercise of some such fundamental personal right or liberty." If the impact of the regulation does not rise to the level appropriate for our strict scrutiny, then our inquiry is limited to whether the state law bears "some rational relationship to legitimate state purposes." *Id.* at 40.

. . .

Indeed, the Court today follows this approach. Although the Court does not use the expression "undue burden," the Court recognizes that even a "significant obstacle" can be justified by a "reasonable" regulation. *See ante.*

The "undue burden" required in the abortion cases represents the required threshold inquiry that must be conducted before this Court can require a State to justify its legislative actions under the exacting "compelling state interest" standard. . . .

The "unduly burdensome" standard is particularly appropriate in the abortion context because of the *nature* and *scope* of the right that is involved. The privacy right involved in the abortion context "cannot be said to be absolute." *Roe, supra,* 410 U.S., at 154. "*Roe* did not declare an unqualified 'constitutional right to an abortion.'" *Maher, supra,* 432 U.S., at 473. Rather, the *Roe* right is intended to protect against state action "drastically limiting the availability and safety of the desired service," *id.* at 472, against the imposition of an "absolute obstacle" on the abortion decision, *Danforth, supra,* 428 U.S., at 70–71, n.11, or against "official interference" and "coercive restraint" imposed on the abortion decision, *Harris, supra,* 448 U.S., at 328 (WHITE, J., concurring). That a state regulation may "inhibit" abortions to some degree does not require that we find that the regulation is invalid. *See H.L. v. Matheson,* 450 U.S. 398, 413 (1981).

The abortion cases demonstrate that an "undue burden" has been found for the most part in situations involving absolute

8. *See Bellotti v. Baird,* 428 U.S. 132, 147 (1976) (*Bellotti I*) (State may not "impose undue burdens upon a minor capable of giving informed consent." In *Bellotti I*, the Court left open the question whether a judicial hearing would unduly burden the *Roe* right of an adult woman. *See* 428 U.S., at 147.); *Bellotti v. Baird,* 443 U.S. 622, 640 (1979) (*Bellotti II*) (opinion of JUSTICE POWELL) (State may not "unduly burden the right to seek an abortion"); *Harris v. McRae,* 448 U.S. 297, 314 (1980) *supra,* 448 U.S., at 314 ("The doctrine of *Roe v. Wade,* the Court held in *Maher* 'protects the woman from unduly burdensome interference with her freedom to decide whether to terminate her pregnancy,' [432 U.S., at 473–74], such as the severe criminal sanctions at issue in *Roe v. Wade, supra,* or the absolute requirement of spousal consent for an abortion challenged in *Planned Parenthood of Central Missouri v. Danforth,* 428 U.S. 52"); *Beal v. Doe,* 432 U.S. 438, 446 (1977) (The state interest in protecting potential human life "does not, at least until approximately the third trimester, become sufficiently compelling to justify unduly burdensome state interference. . . .") . . . Even though the Court did not explicitly use the "unduly burdensome" standard in evaluating the informed-consent requirement in *Planned Parenthood v. Danforth,* 428 U.S. 52 (1976), the informed-consent requirement for first trimester abortions in *Danforth* was upheld because it did not "unduly burden[] the right to seek an abortion." *Bellotti I, supra,* 428 U.S. at 147.

obstacles or severe limitations on the abortion decision. In *Roe*, the Court invalidated a Texas statute that criminalized *all* abortions except those necessary to save the life of the mother. In *Danforth, supra,* the Court invalidated a state prohibition of abortion by saline amniocentesis because the ban had "the effect of inhibiting . . . the vast majority of abortions after the first 12 weeks." 428 U.S., at 79. The Court today acknowledges that the regulation in *Danforth* effectively represented "a *complete* prohibition of abortions in certain circumstances." *Ante,* at n.11. (Emphasis added.) In *Danforth, supra,* the Court also invalidated state regulations requiring parental or spousal consent as a prerequisite to a first-trimester abortion because the consent requirements effectively and impermissibly delegated a "veto power" to parents and spouses during the first trimester of pregnancy. In both *Bellotti I, supra,* and *Bellotti v. Baird,* 443 U.S. 622 (1979) (*Bellotti II*), the Court was concerned with effective parental veto over the abortion decision.[9]

In determining whether the State imposes an "undue burden," we must keep in mind that when we are concerned with ex-

9. The only case in which the Court invalidated regulations that were not "undue burdens" was *Doe v. Bolton,* 410 U.S. 179, (1973), which was decided on the same day as *Roe.* In *Doe,* the Court invalidated a hospitalization requirement because it covered first-trimester abortion. The Court also invalidated a hospital accreditation requirement, a hospital-committee approval requirement, and a two-doctor concurrence requirement. The Court clearly based its disapproval of these requirements on the fact that the State did not impose them on any other medical procedure apart from abortion. But the Court subsequent to *Doe* has expressly rejected the view that differential treatment of abortion requires invalidation of regulations. *See Danforth, supra,* 428 U.S., at 67, 80–81; *Maher v. Roe,* 432 U.S. 464, 480, (1977); *Harris, supra,* 448 U.S., at 325. . . .

tremely sensitive issues, such as the one involved here, "the appropriate forum for their resolution in a democracy is the legislature. We should not forget that 'legislatures are ultimate guardians of the liberties and welfare of the people in quite as great a degree as the courts.' *Missouri, K.&T. R. Co. v. May,* 194 U.S. 267, 270 (1904) (Holmes, J.)." *Maher, supra,* 432 U.S., at 479–80. . . .

We must always be mindful that "[t]he Constitution does not compel a state to fine-tune its statutes so as to encourage or facilitate abortions. To the contrary, state action 'encouraging childbirth except in the most urgent circumstances' is 'rationally related to the legitimate government objective of protecting potential life.' *Harris v. McRae,* 448 U.S., at 325. *Accord Maher v. Roe,* at 473–74." *H.L. v. Matheson,* at 413.

IV

A

Section 1870.03 of the Akron ordinance requires that second-trimester abortions be performed in hospitals. The Court holds that this requirement imposes a "significant obstacle" in the form of increased cost and decreased availability of abortions, *ante,* and the Court rejects the argument offered by the State that the requirement is a reasonable health regulation under *Roe, supra,* 410 U.S., at 163.

For the reasons state above, I find no justification for the trimester approach used by the Court to analyze this restriction. I would apply the "unduly burdensome" test and find that the hospitalization requirement does not impose an undue burden on that decision.

The Court's reliance on increased abortion costs and decreased availability is misplaced. As the City of Akron points out, there is no evidence in this case to show that the two Akron hospitals that performed second-trimester abortions denied an abortion to any woman, or that they would not permit abortion by the D&E procedure. In addition, there was no evidence presented that other hospitals in nearby areas did not provide second-trimester abortions. Further, almost *any* state regulation, including the licensing requirements that the Court *would* allow, *see ante,* at n.26, inevitably and necessarily entails increased costs for *any* abortion. In *Simopoulos v. Virginia,* the Court upholds the State's stringent licensing requirements that will clearly involve greater cost because the State's licensing scheme "is not an unreasonable means of furthering the State's compelling interest in" preserving maternal health. *Id.* Although the Court acknowledges this indisputably correct notion in *Simopoulos,* it inexplicably refuses to apply it in this case. A health regulation, such as the hospitalization requirement, simply does not rise to the level of "official interference" with the abortion decision. *See Harris, supra,* 448 U.S., at 328 (WHITE, J., concurring).

. . .

Further, the regulation has a "rational relation" to a valid state objective of ensuring the health and welfare of its citizens. *See Williamson v. Lee Optical Co.,* 348 U.S. 483, 491 (1955).[11]

11. . . . In its decision today, the Court fully endorses the *Roe* requirement that a burdensome health regulation, or as the Court appears to call it, a "significant obstacle," *ante,* be "reasonably related" to the state compelling interest. . . . Nevertheless, the Court fails to apply the "reasonably related" standard. The hospitalization requirement "reasonably relates" to its compelling interest in protection and preservation of maternal health under any normal understanding of what "reasonably relates" signifies.

The Court concludes that the regulation must fall because "it appears that during a substantial portion of the second trimester the State's regu-

B

Section 1870.05(B) of the Akron ordinance provides that no physician shall perform an abortion on a minor under fifteen years of age unless the minor gives written consent, and the physician first obtains the informed written consent of a parent or guardian, or unless the minor first obtains "an order from a court having jurisdiction over her that the abortion be performed or induced." Despite the fact that this regulation has yet to be construed in the state courts, the Court holds that the regulation is unconstitutional because it is not "reasonably susceptible of being construed to create an 'opportunity for case-by-case evaluations of the maturity of pregnant minors.'" *Ante* (quoting *Bellotti II, supra,* 443 U.S., at 643–44, n.23 [plurality opinion]). I believe that the Court should have abstained from declaring the ordinance unconstitutional.

. . .

In light of the Court's complete lack of knowledge about how the Akron ordinance will operate, and how the Akron ordinance and the state juvenile court statute interact, our "'scrupulous regard for the rightful independence of state governments'" counsels against "unnecessary interference by the federal courts with proper and validly administered state concerns, a course so essential to the balanced working

lation 'depart[s] from accepted medical practice,' *supra.*" *Ante.* It is difficult to see how the Court concludes that the regulation "depart[s] from accepted medical practice" during "a substantial portion of the second trimester," *ante,* in light of the fact that the Court concludes that D&E abortions may be performed safely in an outpatient clinic through 16 weeks, or 4 weeks into the second trimester. *Ante.* Four weeks is hardly a "substantial portion" of the second trimester.

of our federal system." *Harrison v. NAACP, supra,* 360 U.S., at 176 (quoting *Matthews v. Rodgers,* 284 U.S. 521, 525 [1932]).

C

The Court invalidates the informed consent provisions of § 1870.06(B) and § 1870.06(C) of the Akron ordinance. Although it finds that subsections (1), (2), (6), and (7) of § 1870.06 (B) are "certainly . . . not objectionable," *ante,* n.37, it refuses to sever those provisions from subsections (3), (4), and (5) because the State requires that the "acceptable" information be provided by the attending physician when "much, if not all of it, could be given by a qualified person assisting the physician," *id.* . . .

. . .

The validity of subsections (3), (4), and (5) are not before the Court because it appears that the City of Akron conceded their unconstitutionality before the court below. . . . In my view, the remaining subsections of § 1870.06(B) are separable from the subsections conceded to be unconstitutional. Section 1870.19 contains a separability clause. . . .

The remainder of § 1870.06(B), and § 1870.06(C), impose no undue burden or drastic limitation on the abortion decision. The City of Akron is merely attempting to ensure that the decision to abort is made in light of that knowledge that the City deems relevant to informed choice. As such, these regulations do not impermissibly affect any privacy right under the Fourteenth Amendment.

D

Section 1870.07 of the Akron ordinance requires a 24-hour waiting period between the signing of a consent form and the actual performance of the abortion, except in cases of emergency. *See* § 1870.12.

The court below invalidated this requirement because it affected abortion decisions during the first trimester of pregnancy. The Court affirms the decision below, not on the ground that it affects early abortions, but because "Akron has failed to demonstrate that any legitimate state interest is furthered by an arbitrary and inflexible waiting period." *Ante.* The Court accepts the arguments made by Akron Center that the waiting period increases the costs of obtaining an abortion by requiring the pregnant woman to make two trips to the clinic, and increases the risks of abortion through delay and scheduling difficulties. The decision whether to proceed should be left to the physician's "'discretion in the exercise of his medical judgment.'" *Ante* (quoting *Colautti, supra,* 439 U.S., at 387).

It is certainly difficult to understand how the Court believes that the physician-patient relationship is able to accommodate any interest that the State has in maternal physical and mental well-being in light of the fact that the record in this case shows that the relationship is non-existent. *See* 651 F.2d, at 1217 (Kennedy, J., concurring in part and dissenting in part). It is also interesting to note that the American College of Obstetricians and Gynecologists recommends that "[p]rior to abortion, the woman should have access to special counseling that explores options for the management of unwanted pregnancy, examines the risks, and allows sufficient time for reflection prior to making an informed decision." 1982 ACOG Standards for Obstetric-Gynecologic Services, at 54.

The waiting period does not apply in cases of medical emergency. Therefore, should the physician determine that the waiting period would increase risks significantly, he or she need not require the woman to wait. The Court's concern in this respect is simply misplaced. Although the waiting period may impose an additional cost on the abortion decision, this increased cost does not unduly burden the availability of abortions or impose an absolute obstacle to access to abortions. Further, the State is not required to "fine-tune" its abortion statutes so as to minimize the costs of abortions. *H.L. v. Matheson, supra,* 450 U.S., at 413.

Assuming *arguendo* that any additional costs are such as to impose an undue burden on the abortion decision, the State's compelling interests in maternal physical and mental health and protection of fetal life clearly justify the waiting period. As we acknowledged in *Danforth, supra,* 428 U.S., at 67, the decision to abort is "a stressful one," and the waiting period reasonably relates to the State's interest in ensuring that a woman does not make this serious decision in undue haste. The decision also has grave consequences for the fetus, whose life the State has a compelling interest to protect and preserve. "No other [medical] procedure involves the purposeful termination of a potential life." *Harris, supra,* 448 U.S., at 325. The waiting period is surely a small cost to impose to ensure that the woman's decision is well-considered in light of its certain and irreparable consequences on fetal life, and the possible effects on her own.

E

Finally, § 1870.16 of the Akron ordinance requires that "[a]ny physician who shall perform or induce an abortion upon a pregnant woman shall insure that the remains of the unborn child are disposed of in a humane and sanitary manner." The Court finds this provision void-for-vagueness. I disagree.

. . .

In the present case, the City of Akron has informed this Court that the intent of the "humane" portion of its statute, as distinguished from the "sanitary" portion, is merely to ensure that fetuses will not be "'dump[ed] . . . on garbage piles.'" Br. for City of Akron in No. 81–746, at 48. In light of the fact that the City of Akron indicates no intent to require that physicians provide "decent burials" for fetuses, and that "humane" is no more vague than the term "sanitary," the vagueness of which Akron Center does not question, I cannot conclude that the statute is void for vagueness.

V

For the reasons set forth above, I dissent. . . .

CASE QUESTIONS

1. If a state's interest in protecting potential life is "compelling" throughout pregnancy could states ban abortions throughout pregnancy? Even an abortion for rape victims? For women whose health is seriously threatened by pregnancy? Abortions for fetuses with diseases that will cause their death within the first year of life? Can the answers to these questions avoid the imposition of "extraconstitutional values"?

2. If the interest is compelling throughout pregnancy, might it be compelling before pregnancy as well—i.e., could states ban the use of contraceptive de-

vices? Intrauterine device contraceptives (IUDs) function by preventing the fertilized egg (after "conception") from nesting in the uterine wall. By Justice O'Connor's "throughout pregnancy" analysis, could IUDs be banned?

3. The majority demands a compelling interest of any restriction that imposes a "significant obstacle" on the freedom to choose abortion. Justice O'Connor argues that this demand should be made only of restrictions that "unduly bur-

den" the abortion choice. Is this a meaningful distinction? If a state imposes a $100 tax on every abortion taking place in a clinic, on the grounds that the revenue is needed to defray costs of extra police protection at such clinics, would that constitute an undue burden in O'Connor's analysis? A $500 tax?

4. Is an inflexible (short of emergencies) waiting period of 24 hours before an abortion reasonable or unreasonable?

Planned Parenthood v. Ashcroft and *Simopoulos v. Virginia* (1983), discussion

On the same day that the Akron case was decided, the Supreme Court handed down *Planned Parenthood v. Ashcroft*, 462 U.S. 476, and *Simopoulos v. Virginia*, 462 U.S. 506. In the latter the Court upheld a rule that all second-trimester abortions be performed in specially licensed clinics. In the former, a majority of five (Burger, Powell, O'Connor, Rehnquist, and White) upheld the requirements of (1) a pathology report for all abortions, (2) the presence of a second physician to care for the fetus during abortions performed after viability, and (3) either parental or judicial consent for abortions on minors. The first was sustained as a minimally burdensome regulation, similar to record-keeping requirements. The second was sustained as closely related to the state's compelling interest in the life of a viable fetus. The third was upheld as compatible with the rules of *Bellotti I* and *II;* judges could consent to the abortion if the minor were mature enough to make the choice or if it were in the minor's best interest. Blackmun wrote the dissent to all three holdings. The group of four dissenters objected to the first on the grounds that pathology reports were not routine practice and could add up to $40 to abortion costs. They objected to the second physician rule because sometimes severe danger to women's health would demand abortion techniques (D&E) that could not result in a live fetus. For these situations the presence of a second physician served no purpose. And they objected to the consent rule for minors because they believed minors should be allowed to make this choice freely and in private. (The four had expressed this view in *Bellotti II*, but they were outnumbered.)

In June of 1986 the Supreme Court handed down the most recent of its decisions dealing with abortion restrictions, *Thornburgh (Governor of Pennsylvania) v. American College of Obstetricians and Gynecologists of Pennsylvania*, 54 U.S.L.W. 4618. The case involved challenges brought by the Pennsylvania section of the

ACOG, plus several other abortion providers and others, to a number of Pennsylvania statutes limiting abortions. The Justice Department under President Reagan had submitted a supplementary brief in the case, as an *amicus curiae*, in order to argue that *Roe* should be overruled. Since Pennsylvania refused to cede to the Justice Department any of its oral argument time, the Supreme Court did not hear any oral argument from the federal government in the case, although they did receive the written brief. In rare cases the Supreme Court does grant permission for extra oral argument time to *amicus* petitioners, and the Justice Department did request this, but the Court refused.

This time the Court did divide 5–4 in its vote to strike down the restrictions. Moreover, Justice Burger, in joining the pro-restriction dissenters, stated that if the Court continued to treat abortion restrictions in this way, he, too, agreed that the Court "should re-examine *Roe*." In addition, O'Connor and White produced dissents, in each of which Rehnquist concurred. White directly urged that *Roe* be overruled, in a very lengthy and carefully reasoned dissent, which finally explained why he distinguished between contraception and abortion in his votes in the right to privacy cases. Justice Stevens was so impressed with his dissent that he wrote a separate opinion solely to rebut its arguments. Excerpts from these opinions follow:

Thornburgh (Governor of Pennsylvania) v. American College of Obstetricians and Gynecologists et al., 54 U.S.L.W. 5416 (1986)

JUSTICE BLACKMUN delivered the opinion of the Court.

IV

This case, as it comes to us, concerns the constitutionality of six provisions of the Pennsylvania Act that the Court of Appeals struck down as facially invalid: § 3205 ("informed consent"); § 3208 ("printed information"); §§ 3214(a) and (h) (reporting requirements); § 3211(a) (determination of viability); § 3210(b) (degree of care required in postviability abortions); and § 3210(c) (second-physician requirement). We have no reason to address the validity of the other sections of the Act challenged in the District Court.

A

Less than three years ago, this Court, in *Akron, Ashcroft,* and *Simopoulos,* reviewed challenges to state and municipal legislation regulating the performance of abortions. In *Akron,* the Court specifically reaffirmed *Roe v. Wade,* 410 U.S. 111 (1973). *See* 462 U.S., at 420, 426–31. Again today, we reaffirm the general principles laid down in *Roe* and in *Akron.*

. . . The States are not free, under the guise of protecting maternal health or potential life, to intimidate women into continuing pregnancies. . . .

B

We turn to the challenged statutes:

1. Section 3205 ("informed consent") and § 3208 (printed information). Section 3205(a) requires that the woman give her "voluntary and informed consent" to an abortion. Failure to observe the provisions of § 3205 subjects the physician to suspension or revocation of his license, and subjects any other person obligated to provide information relating to informed consent to criminal penalties. § 3205(c). A requirement that the woman give what is truly a voluntary and informed consent, as a general proposition, is, of course, proper and is surely not unconstitutional. *See Danforth*, 428 U.S., at 67. But the State may not require the delivery of information designed "to influence the woman's informed choice between abortion or childbirth." *Akron*, 462 U.S., at 443–44.

. . .

. . . Seven explicit kinds of information must be delivered to the woman at least 24 hours before her consent is given, and five of these must be presented by the woman's physician. The five are: (a) the name of the physician who will perform the abortion, (b) the "fact that there may be detrimental physical and psychological effects which are not accurately foreseeable," (c) the "particular medical risks associated with the particular abortion procedure to be employed," (d) the probable gestational age, and (e) the "medical risks associated with carrying her child to term." The remaining two categories are (f) the "fact that medical assistance benefits may be available for prenatal care, childbirth and neonatal care," and (g) the "fact that the father is liable to assist" in the child's support, "even in instances where the father has offered to pay for the abortion." §§ 3205(a)(1) and (2). The woman also must be informed that materials printed and supplied by the Commonwealth that describe the fetus and that list agencies offering alternatives to abortion are available for her review. If she chooses to review the materials but is unable to read, the materials "shall be read to her," and any answer she seeks must be "provided her in her own language." § 3205(a)(2)(iii). She must certify in writing, prior to the abortion, that all this has been done. § 3205(a)(3). The printed materials "shall include the following statement":

> There are many public and private agencies willing and able to help you to carry your child to term, and to assist you and your child after your child is born, whether you choose to keep your child or place her or him for adoption. The Commonwealth of Pennsylvania strongly urges you to contact them before making a final decision about abortion. The law requires that your physician or his agent give you the opportunity to call agencies like these before you undergo an abortion. (§ 3208[a][1].)

The materials must describe the "probable anatomical and physiological characteristics of the unborn child at two-week gestational increments from fertilization to full term, including any relevant information on the possibility of the unborn child's survival." § 3208(a)(2).

. . .

. . . Forcing the physician or counselor to present the materials and the list to the woman makes him or her in effect an agent of the State in treating the woman and places his or her imprimatur upon both the materials and the list. . . . All this is, or comes close to being, state medicine imposed upon the woman, not the professional medical guidance she seeks, and it officially structures—as it obviously was intended to do—the dialogue between the woman and her physician.

. . . Under the guise of informed consent, the Act requires the dissemination of information that is not relevant to such consent, and, thus, it advances no legitimate state interest.

. . . This type of compelled information is the antithesis of informed consent. . . . [Pennsylvania] would require the physician to recite its litany "regardless of whether in his judgment the information is relevant to [the patient's] personal decision." . . . Section 3205's informational requirements therefore are facially unconstitutional.

. . .

2. Sections 3214(a) and (h) (reporting) and § 3211(a) (determination of viability). . . . The report required . . . is detailed and must include, among other things, identification of the performing and referring physicians and of the facility or agency; information as to the woman's political subdivision and State of residence, age, race, marital status, and number of prior pregnancies; the date of her last menstrual period and the probable gestational age; the basis for any determination of nonviability; and the method of payment for the abortion.

. . .

The scope of the information required and its availability to the public belie any assertions by the Commonwealth that it is advancing any legitimate interest.

. . .

Pennsylvania's reporting requirements raise the spectre of public exposure and harassment of women who choose to exercise their personal, intensely private, right,

with their physician, to end a pregnancy. Thus, they pose an unacceptable danger of deterring the exercise of that right, and must be invalidated.

3. Section 3210(b) (degree of care for postviability abortions) and § 3210(c) (second-physician requirement when the fetus is possibly viable). Section 3210(b) sets forth two independent requirements for a postviability abortion. First, it demands the exercise of that degree of care "which such person would be required to exercise in order to preserve the life and health of any unborn child intended to be born and not aborted." Second, "the abortion technique employed shall be that which would provide the best opportunity for the unborn child to be aborted alive unless," in the physician's good-faith judgment, that technique "would present a significantly greater medical risk to the life or health of the pregnant woman." An intentional, knowing, or reckless violation of this standard is a felony of the third degree, and subjects the violator to the possibility of imprisonment for not more than seven years and to a fine of not more than $15,000. See 18 Pa. Cons. Stat. §§ 1101(2) and 1103(3) (1983).

The Court of Appeals ruled that § 3210(b) was unconstitutional because it required a "trade-off" between the woman's health and fetal survival, and failed to require that maternal health be the physician's paramount consideration. . . .

. . . We agree with the Court of Appeals and therefore find the statute to be facially invalid.

Section 3210(c) requires that a second physician be present during an abortion performed when viability is possible. The second physician is to "take control of the child and . . . provide immediate medical care for the child, taking all reasonable steps necessary, in his judgment, to preserve the child's life and health." Violation of this requirement is a felony of the third degree.

In *Planned Parenthood Assn. v. Ashcroft*, 462 U.S. 476 (1983), the Court, by a 5–4 vote, but not by a controlling single opinion, ruled that a Missouri statute requiring the presence of a second physician during an abortion performed after viability was constitutional. JUSTICE POWELL, joined by THE CHIEF JUSTICE, concluded that the State had a compelling interest in protecting the life of a viable fetus and that the second physician's presence provided assurance that the State's interest was protected more fully than with only one physician in attendance. *Id.* at 482–86. JUSTICE POWELL recognized that, to pass constitutional muster, the statute must contain an exception for the situation where the health of the mother was endangered by delay in the arrival of the second physician. Recognizing that there was "no clearly expressed exception" on the face of the Missouri statute for the emergency situation, JUSTICE POWELL found the exception implicit in the statutory requirement that action be taken to preserve the fetus "provided it does not pose an increased risk to the life or health of the woman." *Id.* at 485, n.8.

Like the Missouri statute, § 3210(c) of the Pennsylvania statute contains no express exception for an emergency situation. While the Missouri statute, in the view of JUSTICE POWELL, was worded sufficiently to imply an emergency exception, Pennsylvania's statute contains no such comforting or helpful language and evinces no intent to protect a woman whose life may be at risk. Section 3210(a) provides only a defense to criminal liability for a physician who concluded, in good faith, that a fetus was nonviable "or that the abortion was necessary to preserve maternal life or health." It does not relate to the second-physician requirement and its words are not words of emergency.

It is clear that the Pennsylvania Legislature knows how to provide a medical-emergency exception when it chooses to do so. . . . We necessarily conclude that the legislature's failure to provide a medical-emergency exception in § 3210(c) was intentional. All the factors are here for chilling the performance of a late abortion, which, more than one performed at an earlier date, perhaps tends to be under emergency conditions.

V

Constitutional rights do not always have easily ascertainable boundaries, and controversy over the meaning of our Nation's most majestic guarantees frequently has been turbulent. As judges, however, we are sworn to uphold the law even when its content gives rise to bitter dispute. *See Cooper v. Aaron*, 358 U.S. 1 (1958). We recognized at the very beginning of our opinion in *Roe*, 410 U.S., at 116, that abortion raises moral and spiritual questions over which honorable persons can disagree sincerely and profoundly. But those disagreements did not then and do not now relieve us of our duty to apply the Constitution faithfully.

Our cases long have recognized that the Constitution embodies a promise that a certain private sphere of individual liberty will be kept largely beyond the reach of government. *See, e.g., Carey v. Population Services International*, 431 U.S. 678 (1977); *Moore v. East Cleveland*, 431 U.S. 494 (1977); *Eisenstadt v. Baird*, 405 U.S. 438 (1972); *Griswold v. Connecticut*, 381 U.S. 479 (1965); *Pierce v. Society of Sisters*, 268 U.S. 510 (1925); *Meyer v. Nebraska*, 262 U.S. 390 (1923). *See also Whalen v. Roe*, 429 U.S. 589, 598–600 (1977). That promise extends to women as well as to men. Few decisions are more personal and intimate, more properly private, or more basic to individual dignity and autonomy, than a woman's decision—with the guidance of her physician and within the limits specified in *Roe*—whether to end her pregnancy. A woman's right to make that choice freely is fundamental. Any other result, in our view, would protect inadequately a central part of the sphere of liberty that our law guarantees equally to all.

The Court of Appeals correctly invalidated the specified provisions of Pennsylvania's 1982 Abortion Control Act. Its judgment is affirmed.

It is so ordered.

JUSTICE STEVENS, concurring.

The scope of the individual interest in liberty that is given protection by the Due Process Clause of the Fourteenth Amendment is a matter about which conscientious judges have long disagreed. Although I believe that that interest is significantly broader than JUSTICE WHITE does, I have always had the highest respect for his views on this subject. In this case, although our ultimate conclusions differ, it may be useful to emphasize some of our areas of agreement in order to ensure that the clarity of certain fundamental propositions not be obscured by his forceful rhetoric.

[Here followed summaries of Justice White's reasoning in contraception cases.] . . .

Up to this point in JUSTICE WHITE's analysis, his opinion is fully consistent with the accepted teachings of the Court and with the major premises of *Roe v. Wade*. For reasons that are not entirely clear, however, JUSTICE WHITE abruptly announces that the interest in "liberty" that is implicated by a decision not to bear a child that is made a few days after conception is *less* fundamental than a comparable decision made before conception. There may, of course, be a significant difference in the

strength of the countervailing state interest, but I fail to see how a decision on child-bearing becomes *less* important the day after conception than the day before. Indeed, if one decision is more "fundamental" to the individual's freedom than the other, surely it is the post-conception decision that is the more serious. Thus, it is difficult for me to understand how JUSTICE WHITE reaches the conclusion that restraints upon this aspect of a woman's liberty do not "call into play anything more than the most minimal judicial scrutiny."

If JUSTICE WHITE were correct in regarding the post-conception decision of the question whether to bear a child as a relatively unimportant, second-class sort of interest, I might agree with his view that the individual should be required to conform her decision to the will of the majority. But if that decision commands the respect that is traditionally associated with the "sensitive areas of liberty" protected by the Constitution, as JUSTICE WHITE characterized reproductive decisions in *Griswold*, 381 U.S., at 503, no individual should be compelled to surrender the freedom to make that decision for herself simply because her "value preferences" are not shared by the majority. In a sense, the basic question is whether the "abortion decision" should be made by the individual or by the majority "in the unrestrained imposition of its own, extraconstitutional value preferences." But surely JUSTICE WHITE is quite wrong in suggesting that the Court is imposing value preferences on anyone else.[6]

6. JUSTICE WHITE's characterization of the governmental interest as "protecting those who will be citizens if their lives are not ended in the womb," reveals that his opinion may be influenced as much by his own value preferences as by his view about the proper allocation of decisionmaking responsibilities between the individual and the State. For if federal judges must

JUSTICE WHITE is also surely wrong in suggesting that the governmental interest in protecting fetal life is equally compelling during the entire period from the moment of conception until the moment of birth. Again, I recognize that a powerful theological argument can be made for that position, but I believe our jurisdiction is limited to the evaluation of secular state interests. I should think it obvious that the state's interest in the protection of an embryo—even if that interest is defined as "protecting those who will be citizens,"—increases progressively and dramatically as the organism's capacity to feel pain, to experience pleasure, to survive, and to react to its surroundings increases day by day. The development of a fetus—and pregnancy itself—are not static conditions, and the assertion that the government's interest is static simply ignores this reality.

Nor is it an answer to argue that life itself is not a static condition, and that "there is no nonarbitrary line separating a fetus from a child, or indeed, an adult human being." For, unless the religious view that a fetus is a "person" is adopted—a view JUSTICE WHITE refuses to embrace, *id.*—there is a fundamental and well-recognized difference between a fetus and a human being; indeed, if there is not such a difference, the permissibility of terminating the life of a fetus could scarcely be left to the will of the state legislatures. And if distinctions may be drawn between a fetus and a human

---

allow the State to make the abortion decision, presumably the State is free to decide that a woman may *never* abort, may *sometimes* abort, or, as in the People's Republic of China, must *always* abort if her family is already too large. In contrast, our cases represent a consistent view that the individual is primarily responsible for reproductive decisions, whether the State seeks to prohibit reproduction, *Skinner v. Oklahoma*, 316 U.S. 535 (1942), or to require it, *Roe v. Wade*, 410 U.S. 113 (1973).

being in terms of the state interest in their protection—even though the fetus represents one of "those who will be citizens"—it seems to me quite odd to argue that distinctions may not also be drawn between the state interest in protecting the freshly fertilized egg and the state interest in protecting the 9-month-gestated, fully sentient fetus on the eve of birth. Recognition of this distinction is supported not only by logic, but also by history and by our shared experiences.

Turning to JUSTICE WHITE's comments on *stare decisis*, he is of course correct in pointing out that the Court "has not hesitated to overrule decisions, or even whole lines of cases, where experience, scholarship, and reflection demonstrated that their fundamental premises were not to be found in the Constitution." But JUSTICE WHITE has not disavowed the "fundamental premises" on which the decision in *Roe v. Wade* rests. He has not disavowed the Court's prior approach to the interpretation of the word "liberty" or, more narrowly, the line of cases that culminated in the unequivocal holding, applied to unmarried persons and married persons alike, "that the Constitution protects individual decisions in matters of childbearing from unjustified intrusion by the State." *Carey*, 431 U.S., at 687; *id.* at 702 (WHITE, J., concurring in pertinent part).

Nor does the fact that the doctrine of *stare decisis* is not an absolute bar to the reexamination of past interpretations of the Constitution mean that the values underlying that doctrine may be summarily put to one side. There is a strong public interest in stability, and in the orderly conduct of our affairs, that is served by a consistent course of constitutional adjudication. Acceptance of the fundamental premises that underlie the decision in *Roe v. Wade*, as well as the application of those premises in that case, places the primary responsibility for decision in matters of childbearing squarely in the private sector of our society. The majority remains free to preach the evils of birth control and abortion and to persuade others to make correct decisions while the individual faced with the reality of a difficult choice having serious and personal consequences of major importance to her own future—perhaps to the salvation of her own immortal soul—remains free to seek and to obtain sympathetic guidance from those who share her own value preferences.

In the final analysis, the holding in *Roe v. Wade* presumes that it is far better to permit some individuals to make incorrect decisions than to deny all individuals the right to make decisions that have a profound effect upon their destiny. . . .

CHIEF JUSTICE BURGER, dissenting.

I agree with much of JUSTICE WHITE's and JUSTICE O'CONNOR's dissents. In my concurrence in the companion case to *Roe v. Wade* in 1973, I noted that

> I do not read the Court's holdings today as having the sweeping consequences attributed to them by the dissenting Justices; the dissenting views discount the reality that the vast majority of physicians observe the standards of their profession, and act only on the basis of carefully deliberated medical judgments relating to life and health. Plainly, the Court today rejects any claim that the Constitution requires abortions on demand. (*Doe v. Bolton,* 410 U.S. 179, 208 [1973].)

Later, in *Maher v. Roe,* 432 U.S. 464, 481 (1977), I stated my view that

> [t]he Court's holdings in *Roe* . . . and *Doe v. Bolton* . . . simply require that a State not create an absolute barrier to a woman's decision to have an abortion.

I based my concurring statements in *Roe* and *Maher* on the principle expressed in the Court's opinion in *Roe* that the right to an abortion "is not unqualified and must be considered against important state interests in regulation." 410 U.S., at 154–55. In short, every member of the *Roe* Court rejected the idea of abortion on demand. The Court's opinion today, however, plainly undermines that important principle. . . .

. . . [T]oday the Court astonishingly goes so far as to say that the State may not even require that a woman contemplating an abortion be provided with accurate medical information concerning the risks inherent in the medical procedure which she is about to undergo and the availability of state-funded alternatives if she elects not to run those risks. . . .* We have apparently already passed the point at which abortion is available merely on demand. If the statute at issue here is to be invalidated, the "demand" will not even have to be the result of an informed choice.

The Court in *Roe* further recognized that the State "has . . . an interest in "protecting the potentiality of human life." *Id.* The point at which these interests become "compelling" under *Roe* is at viability of the

---

*The Court's astounding rationale for this holding is that such information might have the effect of "discouraging abortion," as though abortion is something to be advocated and encouraged. This is at odds not only with *Roe* but with our subsequent abortion decisions as well. As I stated in my opinion for the Court in *H.L. v. Matheson,* 450 U.S. 398 (1981), upholding a Utah statute requiring that a doctor notify the parents of a minor seeking an abortion: "The Constitution does not compel a state to fine-tune its statutes so as to encourage or faciliate abortions. To the contrary, state action 'encouraging childbirth except in the most urgent circumstances' is 'rationally related to the legitimate governmental objective of protecting potential life.'" *Id.* at 413 (quoting *Harris v. McRae,* 448 U.S. 297, 325 [1980]).

fetus. *Id.* at 163. Today, however, the Court abandons that standard. . . . The statute at issue in this case requires that a second physician be present during an abortion performed after viability, so that the second physician can "take control of the child and . . . provide immediate medical care . . . taking all reasonable steps necessary, in his judgment, to preserve the child's life and health." 18 Pa. Cons. Stat. § 3210(c).

Essentially this provision simply states that a viable fetus is to be cared for, not destroyed. No governmental power exists to say that a viable fetus should not have every protection required to preserve its life. Undoubtedly the Pennsylvania Legislature added the second physician requirement on the mistaken assumption that this Court meant what it said in *Roe* concerning the "compelling interest" of the states in potential life after viability.

The Court's opinion today is but the most recent indication of the distance traveled since *Roe*. . . .

In discovering constitutional infirmities in state regulations of abortion that are in accord with our history and tradition, we may have lured judges into "roaming at large in the constitutional field." *Griswold v. Connecticut*, 381 U.S. 479, 502 (1965) (Harlan, J., concurring). The soundness of our holdings must be tested by the decisions that purport to follow them. If *Danforth* and today's holding really mean what they seem to say, I agree we should reexamine *Roe*.

JUSTICE WHITE, with whom JUSTICE REHNQUIST joins, dissenting.

Today the Court carries forward the "difficult and continuing venture in substantive due process," *Planned Parenthood of Missouri v. Danforth*, 428 U.S. 52 (1976) (WHITE, J., dissenting), that began with the decision in *Roe v. Wade*, 410 U.S. 113 (1973), and has led the Court further and further afield in the 13 years since that decision

was handed down. I was in dissent in *Roe v. Wade* and am in dissent today. In Part I below, I state why I continue to believe that this venture has been fundamentally misguided since its inception. In part II, I submit that even accepting *Roe v. Wade*, the concerns underlying that decision by no means command or justify the results reached today. Indeed, in my view, our precedents in this area, applied in a manner consistent with sound principles of constitutional adjudication, require reversal of the Court of Appeals on the ground that the provisions before us are facially constitutional.

I

The rule of *stare decisis* is essential if case-by-case judicial decisionmaking is to be reconciled with the principle of the rule of law, for when governing legal standards are open to revision in every case, deciding cases becomes a mere exercise of judicial will, with arbitrary and unpredictable results. But *stare decisis* is not the only constraint upon judicial decisionmaking. Cases—like this one—that involve our assumed power to set aside on grounds of unconstitutionality a State or federal statute representing the democratically expressed will of the people call other considerations into play. Because the Constitution itself is ordained and established by the people of the United States, constitutional adjudication by this Court does not, in theory at any rate, frustrate the authority of the people to govern themselves through institutions of their own devising and in accordance with principles of their own choosing. But decisions that find in the Constitution principles or values that cannot fairly be read into that document usurp the people's authority, for such decisions represent choices that the people have never made and that they cannot disavow through corrective legislation. For this reason, it is essential that this Court maintain the power to restore authority to its proper possessors by correcting constitutional decisions that, on reconsideration, are found to be mistaken.

The Court has therefore adhered to the rule that *stare decisis* is not rigidly applied in cases involving constitutional issues. . . .

In my view, the time has come to recognize that *Roe v. Wade*, no less than the cases overruled by the Court in the past . . ., "departs from a proper understanding" of the Constitution and to overrule it. I do not claim that the arguments in support of this proposition are new ones or that they were not considered by the Court in *Roe* or in the cases that succeeded it.

A

Roe v. Wade posits that a woman has a fundamental right to terminate her pregnancy, and that this right may be restricted only in the service of two compelling state interests: the interest in maternal health (which becomes compelling only at the stage in pregnancy at which an abortion becomes more hazardous than carrying the pregnancy to term) and the interest in protecting the life of the fetus (which becomes compelling only at the point of viability). A reader of the Constitution might be surprised to find that it encompassed these detailed rules, for the text obviously contains no references to abortion, nor, indeed, to pregnancy or reproduction generally; and, of course, it is highly doubtful that the authors of any of the provisions of the Constitution believed that they were giving protection to abortion. As its prior cases clearly show, however, this Court does not subscribe to the simplistic view that constitutional interpretation can possibly be limited to the "plain meaning" of the Constitution's text or to the subjective intention of the Framers. The Constitution is not a deed setting forth the precise metes and bounds of its subject matter; rather, it is a document announcing fundamental principles in value-laden terms that leave ample scope for the exercise of normative judgment by those charged with interpreting and applying it. In particular, the Due Process Clause of the Fourteenth Amendment, which forbids the deprivation of "life, liberty, or property without due process of law," has been read by the majority of the Court to be broad enough to provide substantive protection against State infringement of a broad range of individual interests. *See Moore v. City of East Cleveland*, 431 U.S. 494, 541–52 (WHITE, J., dissenting).

In most instances, the substantive protection afforded the liberty or property of an individual by the Fourteenth Amendment is extremely limited: State action impinging on individual interests need only be rational to survive scrutiny under the Due Process Clause, and the determination of rationality is to be made with a heavy dose of deference to the policy choices of the legislature. Only "fundamental" rights are entitled to the added protection provided by strict judicial scrutiny of legislation that impinges upon them. *See id*. at 499 (opinion of POWELL, J., joined by REHNQUIST, J., dissenting); *id*. at 547–49 (WHITE, J., dissenting). I can certainly agree with the proposition—which I deem indisputable—that a woman's ability to choose an abortion is a species of "liberty" that is subject to the general protections of the Due Process Clause. I cannot agree, however, that this liberty is so "fundamental" that restrictions upon it call into play anything more than the most minimal judicial scrutiny.

Fundamental liberties and interests are most clearly present when the Constitution provides specific textual recognition of their existence and importance. Thus, the Court is on relatively firm ground when it deems certain of the liberties set forth in the Bill of Rights to be fundamental and therefore finds them incorporated in the Fourteenth Amendment's guarantee that no State may deprive any person of liberty without due process of law. When the Court ventures further and defines as "fundamental" liberties that are nowhere mentioned in the Constitution (or that are present only in the so-called "penumbras" of specifically enumerated rights), it must, of necessity, act with more caution, lest it open itself to the accusation that, in the name of identifying constitutional principles to which the people have consented in framing their Constitution, the Court has done nothing more than impose its own controversial choices of value upon the people.

Attempts to articulate the constraints that must operate upon the Court when it employs the Due Process Clause to protect liberties not specifically enumerated in the text of the Constitution have produced varying definitions of "fundamental liberties." One approach has been to limit the class of fundamental liberties to those interests that are "implicit in the concept of ordered liberty" such that "neither liberty nor justice would exist if [they] were sacrificed." *Palko v. Connecticut,*f 302 U.S. 319, 325, 326 (1937); *See Moore v. City of East Cleveland, supra*, at 537 (STEWART, J., joined by REHNQUIST, J., dissenting). Another, broader approach is to define fundamental liberties as those that are "deeply rooted in this Nation's history and tradition." *Id.* at 503 (opinion of POWELL, J.); *see also Griswold v. Connecticut*, 381 U.S., at 501 (Harlan, J., concurring). These distillations of the possible approaches to the identification of unenumerated fundamental rights are not and do not purport to be precise legal tests or "mechanical yardstick[s]," *Poe v. Ullman*, 367 U.S., at 544 (1961) (Harlan, J., dissenting). Their utility lies in their effort to identify some source of constitutional value

that reflects not the philosophical predilections of individual judges, but basic choices made by the people themselves in constituting their system of government—"*the balance struck by this country,*" *id.* at 542 (emphasis added)—and they seek to achieve this end through locating fundamental rights either in the traditions and consensus of our society as a whole or in the logical implications of a system that recognizes both individual liberty and democratic order. Whether either of these approaches can, as Justice Harlan hoped, prevent "judges from roaming at large in the constitutional field," *Griswold*, 381 U.S., at 502, is debatable. What for me is not subject to debate, however, is that either of the basic definitions of fundamental liberties, taken seriously, indicates the illegitimacy of the Court's decision in *Roe v. Wade*.

The Court has justified the recognition of a woman's fundamental right to terminate her pregnancy by invoking decisions upholding claims of personal autonomy in connection with the conduct of family life, the rearing of children, marital privacy and the use of contraceptives, and the preservation of the individual's capacity to procreate. [Citations omitted.] Even if each of these cases was correctly decided and could be properly grounded in rights that are "implicit in the concept of ordered liberty" or "deeply rooted in this Nation's history and tradition," the issues in the cases cited differ from those at stake where abortion is concerned. As the Court appropriately recognized in *Roe v. Wade*, "[t]he pregnant woman cannot be isolated in her privacy," 410 U.S., at 159; the termination of a pregnancy typically involves the destruction of another entity: the fetus. However one answers the metaphysical or theological question whether the fetus is a "human being" or the legal question whether it is a "person" as that term is used in the Constitution, one must at least recognize, first, that the fetus is an entity that bears in its cells all the genetic information that characterizes a member of the species *homo sapiens* and distinguishes an individual member of that species from all others, and second, that there is no nonarbitrary line separating a fetus from a child or, indeed, an adult human being. Given that the continued existence and development—that is to say, the *life*—of such an entity are so directly at stake in the woman's decision whether or not to terminate her pregnancy, that decision must be recognized as *sui generis*, different in kind from the others that the Court has protected under the rubric of personal or family privacy and autonomy.[2]

2. That the abortion decision, like the decisions protected in *Griswold, Einsenstadt,* and *Carey,* concerns childbearing (or, more generally, family life) in no sense necessitates a holding that the liberty to choose abortion is "fundamental." That the decision involves the destruction of the fetus renders it different in kind from the decision not to conceive in the first place. This difference does not go merely to the weight of the state interest in regulating abortion; it affects as well the characterization of the liberty interest itself. For if the liberty to make certain decisions with respect to contraception without governmental constraint is "fundamental," it is not only because those decisions are "serious" and "important" to the individual (STEVENS, J., concurring), but also because some value of privacy or individual autonomy that is somehow implicit in the scheme of ordered liberties established by the Constitution supports a judgment that such decisions are none of government's business. The same cannot be said where, as here, the individual is not "isolated in her privacy."

My point can be illustrated by drawing on a related area in which fundamental liberty interests have been found: childrearing. The Court's decision in *Moore v. East Cleveland, Pierce v. Society of Sisters,* and *Meyer v. Nebraska* can be read for the proposition that parents have a fundamental liberty to make decisions with respect to the upbringing of their children. But no one would suggest that this fundamental liberty extends to

Accordingly, the decisions cited by the Court both in *Roe* and in its opinion today as precedent for the fundamental nature of the liberty to choose abortion do not, even if all are accepted as valid, dictate the Court's classification.

If the woman's liberty to choose an abortion is fundamental, then, it is not because any of our precedents (aside from *Roe* itself) commands or justifies that result; it can only be because protection for this unique choice is itself "implicit in the concept of ordered liberty" or, perhaps, "deeply rooted in this Nation's history and tradition." It seems clear to me that it is neither. The Court's opinion in *Roe* itself convincingly refutes the notion that the abortion liberty is deeply rooted in the history or tradition of our people, as does the continuing and deep division of the people themselves over the question of abortion. As for the notion that choice in the matter of abortion is implicit in the concept of ordered liberty, it seems apparent to me that a free, egalitarian, and democratic society does not presuppose any particular rule or set of rules with respect to abortion. And again, the fact that many men and women of good will and high commitment to constitutional government place themselves on both sides of the abortion controversy strengthens my own conviction that the values animating the Constitution do not compel recognition of the abortion liberty as fundamental. In so denominating that liberty, the Court engages not in constitutional interpretation, but in the un-

---

assaults committed upon children by their parents. It is not the case that parents have a fundamental liberty to engage in such activities and that the State may intrude to prevent them only because it has a compelling interest in the well-being of children; rather, such activities, by their very nature, should be viewed as outside the scope of the fundamental liberty interest.

restrained imposition of its own, extraconstitutional value preferences.[3]

B

A second, equally basic error infects
the Court's decision in *Roe v. Wade*. The detailed set of rules governing state restrictions on abortion that the Court first articulated in *Roe* and has since refined and
elaborated presupposes not only that the
woman's liberty to choose an abortion is
fundamental, but also that the state's countervailing interest in protecting fetal life
(or, as the Court would have it, "potential
human life," 410 U.S., at 159) becomes
"compelling" only at the point at which the
fetus is viable. As JUSTICE O'CONNOR
pointed out three years ago in her dissent
in *Akron v. Akron Center for Reproductive
Health*, 462 U.S. 416, 461 (1983), the Court's
choice of viability as the point at which the
state's interest becomes compelling is entirely arbitrary. The Court's "explanation"
for the line it has drawn is that the state's
interest becomes compelling at viability

"because the fetus then presumably has the
capacity of meaningful life outside the
mother's womb." 410 U.S., at 163. . . .

The governmental interest at issue is in
protecting those who will be citizens if
their lives are not ended in the womb. The
substantiality of this interest is in no way
dependent on the probability that the fetus
may be capable of surviving outside the
womb at any given point in its development, as the possibility of fetal survival is
contingent on the state of medical practice
and technology, factors that are in essence
morally and constitutionally irrelevant.
The State's interest is in the fetus as an entity in itself, and the character of this entity
does not change at the point of viability
under conventional medical wisdom. Accordingly, the State's interest, if compelling
after viability, is equally compelling before
viability.[4]

C

Both the characterization of the abortion liberty as fundamental and the denigration of the State's interest in preserving
the lives of nonviable fetuses are essential
to the detailed set of constitutional rules
devised by the Court to limit the States'
power to regulate abortion. If either or both
of these facets of *Roe v. Wade* were rejected,

---

3. JUSTICE STEVENS asserts that I am "quite
wrong in suggesting that the Court is imposing
value preferences on anyone else" when it de-
nominates the liberty to choose abortion as
"fundamental" (in contra-distinction to such
other, nonfundamental liberties as the liberty to
use dangerous drugs or to operate a business
without governmental interference) and thereby
disempowers state electoral majorities from legislating in this area. I can only respond that I
cannot conceive of a definition of the phrase
"imposing value preferences" that does not encompass the Court's action.

JUSTICE STEVENS also suggests that it is the legislative majority that has engaged in "the unrestrained imposition of its own, extraconstitutional value choices" when a state legislature
restricts the availability of abortion. *Id.* But a legislature, unlike a court, has the inherent power
to do so unless its choices are constitutionally
forbidden, which, in my view, is not the case
here.

4. Contrary to JUSTICE STEVENS' suggestion,
this is no more a "theological" position than is
the Court's own judgment that viability is the
point at which the state interest becomes compelling. (Interestingly, JUSTICE STEVENS omits
any real effort to defend this judgment.) The
point is that the specific interest the Court has
recognized as compelling after the point of
viability—that is, the interest in protecting "potential human life"—is present as well before
viability, and the point of viability seems to bear
no discernible relationship to the strength of that
interest. Thus, there is no basis for concluding
that the essential character of the state interest becomes transformed at the point of viability. . . .

a broad range of limitations on abortion (including outright prohibition) that are now unavailable to the States would again become constitutional possibilities.

In my view, such a state of affairs would be highly desirable from the standpoint of the Constitution. Abortion is a hotly contested moral and political issue. Such issues, in our society, are to be resolved by the will of the people, either as expressed through legislation or through the general principles they have already incorporated into the Constitution they have adopted.[5] *Roe v. Wade* implies that the

---

5. . . . The rejection of what has been characterized as "clause-bound" interpretivism, J. Ely, *Democracy and Distrust* 12 (1980), does not necessarily carry with it a rejection of the notion that constitutional adjudication is a search for values and principles that are implicit (and explicit) in the structure of rights and institutions that the people have themselves created. The implications of those values for the resolution of particular issues will in many if not most cases not have been explicitly considered when the values themselves were chosen—indeed, there will be some cases in which those who framed the provisions incorporating certain principles into the Constitution will be found to have been incorrect in their assessment of the consequences of their decision. *See, e.g., Brown v. Board of Education,* 347 U.S. 483 (1953). Nonetheless, the hallmark of a correct decision of constitutional law is that it rests on principles selected by the people through their Constitution, and not merely on the personal philosophies, be they libertarian or authoritarian, of the judges of the majority. While constitutional adjudication involves judgments of value, it remains the case that some values are indeed "extraconstitutional," in that they have no roots in the Constitution that the people have chosen. The Court's decision in *Lochner v. New York,* 198 U.S. 45 (1905), was wrong because it rested on the Court's belief that the liberty to engage in a trade or occupation without governmental regulation was somehow fundamental—an assessment of value that was unsupported by the Constitution. I believe

people have already resolved the debate by weaving into the Constitution the values and principles that answer the issue. As I have argued, I believe it is clear that the people have never—not in 1787, 1791, 1868, or at any time since—done any such thing. I would return the issue to the people by overruling *Roe v. Wade.*

II

As it has evolved in the decisions of this Court, the freedom recognized by the Court in *Roe v. Wade* and its progeny is essentially a negative one, based not on the notion that abortion is a good in itself, but only on the view that the legitimate goals that may be served by state coercion of private choices regarding abortion are, at least under some circumstances, outweighed by the damage to individual autonomy and privacy that such coercion entails. In other words, the evil of abortion does not justify the evil of forbidding it. . . . But precisely because *Roe v. Wade* is not premised on the notion that abortion is itself desirable (either as a matter of constitutional entitlement or of social policy), the decision does not command the States to fund or encourage abortion, or even to approve of it. Rather, we have recognized that the States may legitimately adopt a policy of encouraging normal childbirth rather than abortion so long as the measures through which that policy is implemented do not amount to direct compulsion of the woman's choice regarding abortion. *Harris v. McRae,* 448 U.S. 297 (1980); *Maher v. Roe,* 432 U.S. 464 (1977); *Beal v. Doe,* 432 U.S. 438 (1977). The provisions before the Court today quite obviously represent the State's effort to implement such a policy.

---

that *Roe v. Wade*—and today's decision as well—rests on similarly extraconstitutional assessments of the value of the liberty to choose an abortion.

The majority's opinion evinces no deference toward the State's legitimate policy. Rather, the majority makes it clear from the outset that it simply disapproves of any attempt by Pennsylvania to legislate in this area. . . . The result is a decision that finds no justification in the Court's previous holdings, departs from sound principles of constitutional and statutory interpretation, and unduly limits the state's power to implement the legitimate (and in some circumstances compelling) policy of encouraging normal childbirth in preference to abortion.

A

The Court begins by striking down statutory provisions designed to ensure that the woman's choice of an abortion is fully informed—that is, that she is aware not only of the reasons for having an abortion, but also of the risks associated with an abortion and the availability of assistance that might make the alternative of normal childbirth more attractive than it might otherwise appear. . . .

. . .

. . . [T]he majority concludes that the informed consent provisions are invalid because they "intrud[e] upon the discretion of the pregnant woman's physician," violate "the privacy of the informed-consent dialogue between the woman and her physician," and "officially structur[e]" that dialogue. The provisions thus constitute "state medicine" that "infringes upon [the physician's] professional responsibilities." This is nonsensical. I can concede that the Constitution extends its protection to certain zones of personal autonomy and privacy, *see Griswold v. Connecticut*, 381 U.S. 479, 502 (1965) (WHITE, J., concurring in judgment), and I can understand, if not share, the notion that that protection may extend to a woman's decision regarding abortion. But I cannot concede the possibility that the Constitution provides more than minimal protection for the manner in which a physician practices his or her profession or for the "dialogues" in which he or she chooses to participate in the course of treating patients. I had thought it clear that regulation of the practice of medicine, like regulation of other professions and of economic affairs generally, was a matter peculiarly within the competence of legislatures, and that such regulation was subject to review only for rationality. *See, e.g., Williamson v. Lee Optical of Oklahoma, Inc.,* 348 U.S. 483 (1955).

. . .

. . . [It is] obvious that the talk of "infringement of professional responsibility" is mere window-dressing for a holding that must stand or fall on other grounds. And because the informed-consent provisions do not infringe the essential right at issue—the right of the woman to choose to have an abortion—the majority's conclusion that the provisions are unconstitutional is without foundation.

B

The majority's decision to strike down the reporting requirements of the statute is equally extraordinary. The requirements obviously serve legitimate purposes.

. . .

Nonetheless, the majority strikes down the reporting requirements because it finds that notwithstanding the explicit statutory command that the reports be made public only in a manner ensuring anonymity, "the amount of information about [the patient] and the circumstances under which she had an abortion are so detailed that identification is likely," and that "[i]dentification is the obvious purpose of these extreme reporting requirements." Where these "findings" come from is mysterious, to say the least. The Court of Appeals did not make any such findings on the record before it, and the District Court expressly found that "the requirements of confidentiality in § 3214(e) regarding the identity of both patient and physician prevent any invasion of privacy which could present a legally significant burden on the abortion decision." 552 F. Supp. 791, 804 (E.D. Pa. 1982). Rather than pointing to anything in the record that demonstrates that the District Court's conclusion is erroneous, the majority resorts to the handy, but mistaken, solution of substituting its own view of the facts and strikes down the statute.

I can accept the proposition that a statute whose purpose and effect are to allow harassment and intimidation of citizens for their constitutionally protected conduct is unconstitutional, but the majority's action in striking down the Pennsylvania statute on this basis is procedurally and substantively indefensible.

. . .

C

The majority resorts to linguistic nitpicking in striking down the provision requiring physicians aborting viable fetuses to use the method of abortion most likely to result in fetal survival unless that method would pose a "significantly greater medical risk to the life or health of the pregnant woman" than would other available methods. The majority concludes that the statute's use of the word "significantly" indicates that the statute represents an unlawful "trade-off" between the woman's health and the chance of fetal survival. Not only is this conclusion based on a wholly unreasonable interpretation of the statute, but the statute would also be constitutional even if it meant what the majority says it means.

. . .

The Court's ruling in this respect is not even *consistent* with its decision in *Roe v. Wade*. In *Roe*, the Court conceded that the State's interest in preserving the life of a viable fetus is a compelling one, and the Court has never disavowed that concession. The Court now holds that this compelling interest cannot justify *any* regulation that imposes a quantifiable medical risk upon the pregnant woman who seeks to abort a viable fetus: if attempting to save the fetus imposes any additional risk of injury to the woman, she must be permitted to kill it. This holding hardly accords with the usual understanding of the term "compelling interest," which we have used to describe those governmental interests that are so weighty as to justify substantial and ordinarily impermissible impositions on the individual—impositions that, I had thought, could include the infliction of some degree of risk of physical harm. . . . [Here he discusses the military draft and smallpox vaccinations.]

. . .

The Court's ruling today that any trade-off between the woman's health and fetal survival is impermissible is not only inconsistent with *Roe's* recognition of a compelling state interest in viable fetal life; it directly contradicts one of the essential holdings of *Roe*—that is, that the State may forbid *all* post-viability abortions except when *necessary* to protect the life or health of the pregnant woman. As is evident, this holding itself involves a trade-off between maternal health and protection of the fetus, for it plainly permits the State to forbid a postviability abortion even when such an abortion may be statistically safer than carrying the pregnancy to term, provided that the abortion is not medically necessary.

. . .

The framework of rights and interest devised by the Court in *Roe v. Wade* indicates that just as a State may prohibit a post-viability abortion unless it is necessary to protect the life or health of the woman, the State may require that postviability abortions be conducted using the method most protective of the fetus unless a less protective method is necessary to protect the life or health of the woman. Under this standard, the Pennsylvania statute—which does not require the woman to accept any significant health risks to protect the fetus—is plainly constitutional.

D

The Court strikes down the statute's second-physician requirement because, in its view, the existence of a medical emergency requiring an immediate abortion to save the life of the pregnant woman would not be a defense to a prosecution under the statute. The Court does not question the proposition, established in the *Ashcroft* case, that a second-physician requirement accompanied by an exception for emergencies is a permissible means of vindicating the compelling state interest in protecting the lives of viable fetuses. Accordingly, the majority's ruling on this issue does not on its face involve a substantial departure from the Court's previous decisions.

What is disturbing about the Court's opinion on this point is not the general principle on which it rests, but the manner in which that principle is applied. The Court brushes aside the fact that the section of the statute in which the second-physician requirement is imposed states that "[i]t shall be a complete defense to *any* charge brought against a physician for violating the requirements *of this section* that he had concluded, in good faith, in his best medical judgment, . . . that the abortion was necessary to preserve maternal life or health." (Emphasis added.) 18 Pa. Cons. Stat. § 3210(a) (1982). This language is obviously susceptible of the construction the State advances: namely, that it is a defense to

a charge of violating the second-physician requirement that the physician performing the abortion believed that performing an abortion in the absence of a second physician was necessary to the life or health of the mother.

. . .

The Court's rejection of a perfectly plausible reading of the statute flies in the face of the principle—which until today I had thought applicable to abortion statutes as well as to other legislative enactments— that "[w]here fairly possible, courts should construe a statute to avoid a danger of unconstitutionality." *Planned Parenthood Assn. v. Ashcroft*, 462 U.S., at 493. The Court's reading is obviously based on an entirely different principle: that in cases involving abortion, a permissible reading of a statute is to be avoided at all costs. . . .

E

[Discussion of injunction procedures omitted.]

III

The decision today appears symptomatic of the Court's own insecurity over its handiwork in *Roe v. Wade* and the cases following that decision. Aware that in *Roe* it essentially created something out of nothing and that there are many in this country who hold that decision to be basically illegitimate, the Court responds defensively. Perceiving, in a statute implementing the State's legitimate policy of preferring childbirth to abortion, a threat to or criticism of the decision in *Roe v. Wade*, the majority indiscriminately strikes down statutory provisions that in no way contravene the right recognized in *Roe*. I do not share the warped point of view of the majority, nor can I follow the tortuous path the majority treads in proceeding to strike down the statute before us. I dissent.

JUSTICE O'CONNOR, with whom JUSTICE REHNQUIST joins, dissenting.

. . . Today's decision . . . makes it painfully clear that no legal rule or doctrine is safe from ad hoc nullification by this Court when an occasion for its application arises in a case involving state regulation of abortion. . . .

[Here followed a very lengthy critique of the majority's failure to follow proper procedures for injunctive remedies. She argued that most of the issues decided were not properly before the Court.]

. . .

I agree with much of what JUSTICE WHITE has written in part II of his dissenting opinion, and the arguments he has framed might well suffice to show that the provisions at issue are facially constitutional. Nonetheless, I believe the proper course is to decide this case as the Court of Appeals should have decided it, lest appellees suffer the very prejudice the Court sees fit to inflict on appellants. For me, then, the question is not one of "success" but of the "likelihood of success." In addition, because Pennsylvania has not asked the Court to reconsider or overrule *Roe v. Wade*, 410 U.S. 113 (1973), I do not address that question.

I do, however, remain of the views expressed in my dissent in *Akron*, 462 U.S., at 459–66. The State has compelling interests in ensuring maternal health and in protecting potential human life, and these interests exist "throughout pregnancy." *Id.* at 461 (O'CONNOR, J., dissenting). Under this Court's fundamental-rights jurisprudence, judicial scrutiny of state regulation of abortion should be limited to whether the state law bears a rational relationship to legitimate purposes such as the advancement of these compelling interests, with heightened scrutiny reserved for instances in which the State has imposed an "undue burden" on the abortion decision. *Id.* at 461–63 (O'CONNOR, J., dissenting). An undue burden will generally be found "in situations involving absolute obstacles or severe limitations on the abortion decision," not wherever a state regulation "may 'inhibit' abortions to some degree." *Id.* at 464 (O'CONNOR, J., dissenting). And if a state law does interfere with the abortion decision to an extent that is unduly burdensome, so that it becomes "necessary to apply an exacting standard of review," *id.* at 467 (O'CONNOR, J., dissenting), the possibility remains that the statute will withstand the stricter scrutiny.

. . .

[Here followed arguments that echoed Justice White's on the specific statute, with the one qualification, as Justice O'Connor had remarked in n.16 of the *Akron* dissent, that First Amendment problems might ensue if anyone is forced to "communicate the state's ideology," but she added that in neither case had this issue been raised.]

CASE QUESTIONS

1. Justice Stevens argues that, if the freedom to choose not to bear a child is so important to the American way of life that it amounts to a basic constitutional right at the time of buying a contraceptive and at the time of using the con-

traceptive, it does not make sense to say that the right disappears on the day after the contraceptive failed to work. Justice White replies that it does make sense because the embryo/fetus is a "separate entity." Is Justice White convincing in his argument that a fertilized egg is more of an entity than is either the egg or the sperm that combine to make it up? Is the previability/postviability line more arbitrary than Justice White's egg/fertilized egg line? Less arbitrary?

2. All the dissenters insist that the majority is now more anti-abortion than the majority was in *Roe v. Wade*. The majority justices insist that they are following *Roe* and that the dissenters' reading would be watering down the principles of *Roe*. Who is correct?

Money for Abortions

In such states as Missouri (from which the *Planned Parenthood v. Danforth* case originated), where popular antagonism toward the Supreme Court's 1973 abortion decision was intense, legislative reaction extended beyond the overt restrictions, such as husband consent requirements, that the Court prohibited in *Danforth*. In addition, these states prohibited the use of state Medicaid funds for "nontherapeutic" abortions, or for abortions not "medically necessary." Statutory definition of these terms varied from state to state. (It is worth noting, however, that the Supreme Court had made clear in the 1971 case of *U.S. v. Vuitch* [described above in the text for n.36] that such phrases as "necessary for the mother's health" in these statutes would be interpreted to mean "appropriate for mental and emotional health as well as for physical health." This judicial gloss had liberally interpreted the category "therapeutic abortion.")

Challenges to these refusals to fund abortions arose from two different directions. One line of attack rested on the Constitution itself, using a combination of the equal protection clause and the right to privacy. This approach maintained that the right of privacy required the state to treat equally the decision to give birth and the decision to abort. To fund one but not the other was to rig the scales in the case of indigent women, making it impossible for them to choose "freely" the more expensive alternative. Although a case presenting this argument, *Singleton v. Wulff*,[42] did reach the Supreme Court in advance of one presenting the other line of attack, the Court chose at first to avoid a head-on clash on this issue. On July 1, 1976, the Court sidestepped a decision on the merits in *Singleton v. Wulff*, sending it, on technical grounds, back to the lower courts for reconsideration.

One year later, almost to the day, the Supreme Court responded both to the second line of attack on denials of Medicaid funds for abortion and to the first. The second approach rested on statutory interpretation, and it was presented in the case of *Beal v. Doe*. Federal law establishes the Medicaid program (Title XIX of the Social Security Act), and this program provides federal funds for medical services to the "medically needy" (persons too poor to pay for medical care including those who are not already on welfare). State participation in the program is optional. But if states do participate, they must abide by any federal regulations that are part of the program. This obligation follows from the basic principle of our legal system that federal law always overrides state law in case of a conflict.[43] This second line of attack maintained that the wording of the federal Medicaid law implied that abortions had to be funded by all states participating in the Medicaid program.

The precise wording at issue was the statute's requirement that

> A state plan for medical assistance must . . . include *reasonable standards . . . for determining eligibility* for and *the extent of medical assistance* under the plan which . . . are consistent with the objectives of this [Title].[44] (Emphasis added.)

The wording by which the statute described its own "objective" included the phrase "to meet the costs of necessary medical services."[45] Thus, this decision hinged on whether the Supreme Court was willing to view certain abortions as "unnecessary" medical services. Six members of the Court were.

The particular Pennsylvania statute against which this attack was launched refused Medicaid funds to any abortions not "medically necessary" as the statute itself defined that term. "Medically necessary," as Pennsylvania viewed it, included abortions only (1) when continued pregnancy threatened the mother's health, (2) when the infant faced a probability of being born with a physical or mental deficiency, of (3) when the pregnancy resulted from rape or incest and constituted a threat to the mother's "mental or physical health." One of these conditions had to be documented by "medical evidence" and certified in writing by three physicians before the state would consider an abortion "medically necessary." The U.S. Supreme Court interpreted Title XIX of the Social Security Act to permit the imposition of these three conditions, but it withheld judgment on the requirement for written certification by two physicians in addition to the woman's own doctor. The Supreme Court expressed concern that this three-physician clause of the state law might conflict with the basic intent of Title XIX. Because the court of appeals had ignored that precise issue, however, the U.S. Supreme Court remanded that particular question back to the court of appeals for the development of a fuller court record on the operation of the clause in question.

In the excerpt that follows, only those portions of the Supreme Court opinion dealing with the parts of the state statute that were upheld are included, because these constituted the definitive sections of the decision. The court of appeals[46] had interpreted Title XIX as forbidding state denials of Medicaid funds for abortions, so this decision was a reversal.[47]

Frank Beal et al. v. Ann Doe et al., 432 U.S. 438 (1977)

MR. JUSTICE POWELL delivered the opinion of the Court.

II

The only question before us is one of statutory construction: whether Title XIX requires Pennsylvania to fund under its medicaid program the cost of *all* abortions that are permissible under state law. "The starting point in every case involving construction of a statute is the language itself." *Blue Chip Stamps v. Manor Drug Stores,* 421 U.S. 723, 756 (1975) (POWELL, J., concurring). Title XIX makes no reference to abortions, or, for that matter, to any other particular medical procedure. . . . But nothing in the statute suggests that participating States are required to fund every medical procedure that falls within the delineated categories of medical care. Indeed, the statute expressly provides that:

A State plan for medical assistance must . . . include reasonable standards . . . of determining eligibility for and the extent of medical assistance under the plan which . . . are consistent with the objectives of this [Title] . . . (42 U.S.C. § 1396[a][17]).

This language confers broad discretion on the States to adopt standards for determining the extent of medical assistance, requiring only that such standards be "reasonable" and "consistent with the objectives" of the Act.

Pennsylvania's regulation comports fully with Title XIX's broadly stated primary objective to "enabl[e] each State, as far as practicable under the conditions in such State, to furnish . . . medical assistance [to] individuals . . . whose income and resources are insufficient to meet the costs of necessary medical services." *Id.* § 1396. Although serious statutory questions might be presented if a state medicaid plan excluded necessary medical treatment from its coverage, it is hardly inconsistent with the objectives of the Act for the State to refuse to fund unnecessary—though perhaps desirable—medical services.

The thrust of respondents' argument is that the exclusion of nontherapeutic abortions from medicaid coverage is unreasonable on both economic and health grounds. The economic argument is grounded on the view that abortion is generally a less expensive medical procedure than childbirth. Since a pregnant woman normally will either have an abortion or carry her child full term, a State that elects not to fund nontherapeutic abortions will eventually be confronted with the greater expenses associated with childbirth. Consequently, respondents argue, the economic and health considerations that ordinarily support the reasonableness of state limitations on financing of unnecessary medical services are not applicable to pregnancy.

Accepting respondents' assumptions as accurate, we do not agree that the exclusion of nontherapeutic abortions from medicaid coverage is unreasonable under Title XIX. As we acknowledged in *Roe v. Wade,* 410 U.S. 113 (1973), the State has a valid and important interest in encouraging childbirth. We recognized . . . the "important and legitimate interest [of the State] in protecting the potentiality of human life." *Id.* at 162. That interest alone does not, at least until approximately the third trimester, become sufficiently compelling to justify unduly burdensome state interference with the woman's constitutionally protected private interest. But it is a significant state interest existing throughout the course of the woman's pregnancy. Respondents point to nothing in either the language or the legislative history of Title XIX that suggests that it is unreasonable for a participating State to further this unquestionably strong and legitimate interest in encouraging normal childbirth.[10] Absent such a showing, we will not presume that Congress intended to condition a State's participation in the Medicaid Program on its willingness to undercut this important interest by subsidizing the cost of nontherapeutic abortions.

Our interpretation of the statute is reinforced by two other relevant considerations. First when Congress passed Title XIX in 1965, nontherapeutic abortions were unlawful in most States. In view of the then prevailing state law, the contention that Congress intended to require—rather than permit—participating States to fund nontherapeutic abortions requires far more convincing proof than respondents have offered. Second, the Department of Health, Education, and Welfare, the agency charged with the administration of this complicated statute, takes the position that Title XIX allows—but does not mandate—funding for such abortions. "[W]e must be

mindful that 'the construction of the statute by those charged with its execution should be followed unless there are compelling indications that it is wrong. . . .'" *New York Department of Social Services v. Dublino*, 413 U.S. 405, 421 (1973), quoting *Red Lion Broadcasting Co. v. FCC*, 395 U.S. 367, 381 (1969). Here, such indications are completely absent.

We therefore hold that Pennsylvania's refusal to extend medicaid coverage to nontherapeutic abortions is not inconsistent with Title XIX. We make clear, however, that the federal statute leaves a State free to provide such coverage if it so desires. . . .

Mr. Justice Brennan, with Mr. Justice Marshall and Mr. Justice Blackmun, dissenting.

The Court holds that the "necessary medical services" which Pennsylvania must fund for individuals eligible for Medicaid do not include services connected with elective abortions.

I dissent.

Though the question presented by this case is one of statutory interpretation, a difficult constitutional question would be raised if the Act were read not to require funding of elective abortions. *Maher v. Roe* (1977), *Doe v. Bolton*, 410 U.S. 179 (1973), *Roe v. Wade*, 410 U.S. 113 (1973). Since the Court should "first ascertain whether a construction of the statute is fairly possible by which the [constitutional] question may be avoided," *Ashwander v. TVA*, 297 U.S. 341, 348 (1936) (Brandeis, J., concurring), *Westby v. Doe*, 420 U.S. 968 (1975), the Act, in my view, read fairly in light of the principle of avoidance of unnecessary constitutional decisions, requires agreement with the Court of Appeals that the legislative history of the Medicaid statute and our abortion cases compel the conclusion that elective abortions constitute medically nec-

---

10. Respondents rely heavily on the fact that in amending Title XIX in 1972 to include "family planning services" within the five broad categories of required medical treatment Congress did not expressly exclude abortions as a covered service. Since Congress had expressly excluded abortions as a method of family planning services in prior legislation, *see* 42 U.S.C. § 300a–6, respondents conclude that the failure of Congress to exclude coverage of abortions in the 1972 amendments to Title XIX "strongly indicates" an intention to require coverage of abortions. This line of reasoning is flawed. The failure to exclude abortions from coverage indicates only that Congress intended to allow such coverage, not that such coverage is mandatory for nontherapeutic abortions.

essary treatment for the condition of pregnancy. I would therefore find that Title XIX of the Social Security Act, 42 U.S.C. § 1396, *et seq.*, requires that Pennsylvania pay the costs of elective abortions for women who are eligible participants in the Medicaid program.

Pregnancy is unquestionably a condition requiring medical services. Treatment for the condition may involve medical procedures to bring the pregnancy to term, resulting in a live birth. . . . The Medicaid statutes leave the decision as to choice among pregnancy procedures exclusively with the doctor and his patient, and make no provision whatever for intervention by the State in that decision. Section 1396 (a)(19) expressly imposes the obligation upon participating States to incorporate safeguards in their programs that assure medical "care and services will be provided in a manner consistent with . . . the best interests of the recipients." And, significantly, the Senate Committee Report on the Medicaid bill expressly stated that the "physician is to be the key figure in determining utilization of health service." *Report of the Committee on Finance to Accompany H.R. 6675*, S.R. 404, 89th Cong., 1st Sess. 46. Thus the very heart of the congressional scheme is that the physician and patient should have complete freedom to choose those medical procedures for a given condition which are best suited to the needs of the patient.

The Court's original abortion decisions dovetail precisely with the congressional purpose under Medicaid to avoid interference with the decision of the woman and her physician. *Roe v. Wade*, 410 U.S. 113, 163 (1973), held that "[t]he attending physician, in consultation with his patient, is free to determine without regulation by the State, that in his medical judgment the patient's pregnancy should be terminated." And *Doe v. Bolton*, 410 U.S. 179, 192, 197

(1973), held that "the medical judgment may be exercised in the light of all factors—physical, emotional, psychological, familial, and the woman's age—relevant to the well-being of the patient. All these factors may relate to health. This allows the attending physician the room he needs to make his best medical judgment. And it is room that operates for the benefit, not the disadvantage of the pregnant woman."* Once

*The Court states that Pennsylvania has left the abortion decision to the patient and her physician in the manner prescribed in *Doe v. Bolton*. Pennsylvania indeed does allow the attending physician to provide a certificate of medical necessity "on the basis of all relevant factors," *id.*, but Pennsylvania's concept of relevance does not extend far enough to permit doctors freely to provide certificates of medical necessity for all elective abortions. At oral argument, counsel for Pennsylvania carefully stated the State's position as follows:

". . . [A] physician, in examining a patient, may take psychological, physical, emotional, familial considerations into mind and in the light of those considerations, may determine if those factors affect the health of the mother to such an extent as he would deem an abortion necessary.

"I think the key in the *Bolton* language and key in the *Vuitch* language is . . . that the physician, using all of these facts—and there are probably more that he should use—must determine if the woman's health—that is, her physical or psychological health [—] is jeopardized by the condition of pregnancy.

"That, is not to say, obviously, as I believe the Plaintiffs are asserting, that the fact that the family is going to increase makes an abortion medically necessary." Tr. of Oral Arg.

Pennsylvania's "concession" only goes so far as to permit an attending physician to consider an abortion as it relates to a woman's health. *Doe* recognized that the factors considered by a physician "may relate to health," but in the very same paragraph made clear that those factors were more broadly directed to the "well-being" of the woman. 410 U.S., at 192. (Emphasis added.) While the right to privacy does implicate

medical treatment of some sort is necessary, the Act does not dictate what the treatment should be. In the face of the Act's emphasis upon the joint autonomy of the physician and his patient in the decision of how to treat the condition of pregnancy, it is beyond comprehension how treatment for therapeutic abortions and live births constitutes "necessary medical services" under the Act, but that for elective abortions does not.

If Pennsylvania is not obligated to fund medical services rendered in performing elective abortions because they are not "necessary" within the meaning of § 1396, it must follow that Pennsylvania also would not violate the statute if it refused to fund medical services for "therapeutic" abortions or live births. . . . This highlights the violence done the congressional mandate by today's decision. If the State must pay the costs of therapeutic abortions and of live birth as constituting medically necessary responses to the condition of pregnancy, it must, under the command of § 1396, also pay the costs of elective abortions; the procedures in each case constitute necessary medical treatment for the condition of pregnancy.

The 1972 family planning amendment to the Act, 42 U.S.C. § 1396(a)(4)(C), buttresses my conclusion that the Court's construction frustrates the objectives of the Medicaid program. Section 1396(a) states that an explicit purpose of Medicaid is to assist eligible indigent recipients to "attain or retain capability for independence or

---

health considerations, the constitutional right recognized and protected by the Court's abortion decisions is the "right of the individual, married or single, to be free of unwarranted governmental intrusion into matters so fundamentally affecting a person as the decision whether to bear or beget a child." *Eisenstadt v. Baird*, 405 U.S. 438, 453 (1972).

self-care." The 1972 amendment furthered this objective by assisting those who "desire to control family size in order to enhance their capacity and ability to seek employment and better meet family needs." *Report of the Committee on Finance to Accompany H.R. 1, S.R. 92–1230, 92nd Cong., 2d Sess. 297.* Though far less than an ideal family planning mechanism, elective abortions are one method for limiting family size and avoiding the financial and emotional problems that are the daily lot of the impoverished. . . .

It is no answer that abortions were illegal in 1965 when Medicaid was enacted, and in 1972 when the family planning amendment was adopted. Medicaid deals with general categories of medical services, not with specific procedures, and nothing in the statute even suggests that Medicaid is designed to assist in payment for only those medical services that were legally permissible in 1965 and 1972. . . . Nor is the administrative interpretation of the Department of Health, Education, and Welfare that funding of elective abortions is permissible but not mandatory dispositive of the construction of "necessary medical services." The principle of according weight to agency interpretation is inapplicable when a departmental interpretation, as here, is patently inconsistent with the controlling statute. *Townsend v. Swank*, 404 U.S. 282, 286 (1971).

Finally, there is certainly no affirmative policy justification of the State that aids the Court's construction of "necessary medical services" as not including medical services rendered in performing elective abortions. The State cannot contend that it protects its fiscal interests. . . . Nor can the State contend that it protects the mother's health by discouraging an abortion, for not only may Pennsylvania's exclusion force the pregnant woman to use of measures dangerous to her life and health but *Roe v. Wade, supra,*

410 U.S., at 149, concluded that elective abortions by competent licensed physicians are now "relatively safe" and the risks to women undergoing abortions by such means "appear to be as low or lower . . . than for normal childbirth."

The Court's construction can only result as a practical manner in forcing penniless pregnant women to have children they would not have borne if the State had not weighted the scales to make their choice to have abortions substantially more oner-

ous. . . . The Court's construction thus makes a mockery of the congressional mandate that States provide "care and services . . . in a manner consistent with . . . the best interests of the recipients." We should respect the congressional plan. . . .

[The separate dissents of JJ. Marshall and Blackmun are included in *Maher v. Roe*, to which they also apply. They address the issue of the constitutionality of the majority's version of the congressional statute.]

CASE QUESTIONS

1. Is it Justice Powell's position that the potential life of an embryo in the first trimester of pregnancy is not a compelling enough interest to forbid the potential mother to abort it, but that it is a compelling enough interest to justify the state's making it impossible for certain potential mothers (the poor) to abort their embryos? Does this comport with the reasoning of *Roe v. Wade*?

2. Powell stresses the statute's reference to "medically necessary" services whereas Brennan stresses the statute's requirement that medical "services be provided in a manner consistent with . . . the best interests of the recipients." Because the statute contained both phrases, is it equally liable to either interpretation? Should the fact that freedom to choose an abortion is supposed to be a fundamental right influence the choice of statutory interpretation?

3. Powell (and the rest of the majority) chose to follow the guidelines of HEW, "the agency charged with the statute," whereas the three dissenters rejected those guidelines. Yet two of the dissenters here (Marshall and Brennan) had argued in *General Electric v. Gilbert* (see below) that the administrative guidelines of another executive agency, the Equal Employment Opportunity Commission (EEOC) were entitled to "great deference," and in that case five of the six justices here in the majority (minus only Stevens) had rejected those guidelines. Does this pattern imply anything about the judicial impact of administrative guidelines?

4. Once Powell has argued that some abortions are not a "necessary medical service," how can he conclude that states may, nevertheless, if they wish, fund these abortions through Medicaid?

On the same day that the Supreme Court handed down *Beal v. Doe,* it handed down two more decisions affecting the availability of abortions. In the first of these, *Maher v. Roe,* the Court faced squarely the constitutional attack on a state's denial of Medicaid funds for abortions not "medically necessary."[48] A sizable hint as to the outcome in *Maher,* had been revealed in the Court's *Beal v. Doe* decision, but Justice Powell had kept his constitutional reasoning substantially under wraps in that decision. Not much more than its basic contours were apparent.

The legal situation in *Maher v. Roe* turned the spotlight directly onto the constitutional question. The district court had reasoned that Susan Roe, who was suing the Connecticut's commissioner of social services (Maher) in behalf of the class of all pregnant indigent women needing Medicaid funds for abortions, had a constitutional right to such funds. This right was not a right to a state-financed abortion, as such, but was a right that originated once the state had decided to fund normal childbirth. Once it covered those expenses, the district court had reasoned, the state would no longer be providing "equal protection of the law" if it refused to cover the expenses incident to a choice to abort. For the freedom to make that choice had been enshrined (in *Roe*) as "fundamental," and it could not now be infringed on by financial pressure from the state. Six other lower federal courts had announced decisions agreeing with this reasoning of the district court in *Maher.*[49]

In sustaining the constitutional attack on state denial of abortion funds, the district court was acting within a complex legal environment. A substantial series of cases had announced that the Constitution forbids the government to condition the exercise of fundamental civil rights on wealth or on the payment of a fee. This rule of law had been used to strike down state laws that forbid entry into the state by indigents,[50] that required even impoverished convicts to pay fees for various trial records needed to appeal their own convictions,[51] that refused to supply free attorneys to impoverished criminal defendants,[52] that imposed poll taxes on the privilege of voting,[53] that imposed a property ownership requirement on people running for public office,[54] and that required even the impoverished to pay filing fees before they could sue for divorce.[55] These cases involved, respectively, the right to travel freely among the states, the right to due process of law, the right to counsel, the right to vote and run for office, and the right of marital freedom. Although the Court announced in the poll-tax case that "lines drawn on the basis of wealth or property, like those of race, are traditionally disfavored,"[56] the Court has nonetheless never invalidated a law *solely* because it drew a line on the basis of poverty. To do that would imply that existing welfare laws and many current tax laws are unconstitutional. And even the conditioning of certain legal procedures on the payment of a fee has not always been held unconstitutional. In 1973 the Court held that the Bankruptcy Act's requirement of a 500 dollar filing fee was not unconstitutional because (among other reasons) "bankruptcy is not a 'fundamental right.'"[57]

Neither the combination of poverty with the fundamental right of privacy, which the *Maher* case presented, nor the equal protection reasoning of the district court, persuaded the U.S. Supreme Court to rule for Susan Roe. Having just rejected in *Beal* the statutory attack on denials of Medicaid for abortion, the Supreme Court in *Maher* now rejected this constitutional attack. Included in the excerpt that follows are the *Beal* dissents of Justices Marshall and Blackmun, which actually apply to *Maher* and *Poelker* as well, because they address specifically the constitutionality question.

Edward Maher v. Susan Roe et al., 432 U.S. 464 (1977)

J. POWELL delivered the opinion of the Court.

II

The Constitution imposes no obligation on the States to pay the pregnancy-related medical expenses of indigent women, or indeed to pay any of the medical expenses of indigents. But when a State decides to alleviate some of the hardships of poverty by providing medical care, the manner in which it dispenses benefits is subject to constitutional limitations. Appellee's claim is that Connecticut must accord equal treatment to both abortion and childbirth, and may not evidence a policy preference by funding only the medical expenses incident to childbirth. This challenge to the classifications established by the Connecticut regulation presents a question arising under the Equal Protection Clause. . . . The basic framework of analysis of such a claim is well-settled:

> We must decide, first, whether [state legislation] operates to the disadvantage of some suspect class or impinges upon a fundamental right explicitly or implicitly protected by the Constitution, thereby requiring strict judicial scrutiny. . . . If not, the [legislative] scheme must still be examined to determine whether it rationally furthers some legitimate, articulated state purpose and therefore does not constitute an invidious discrimination. . . . (*San Antonio School District v. Rodriguez*, 411 U.S. 1, 17 [1973].)

Applying this analysis here, we think the District Court erred in holding that the Connecticut regulation violated the Equal Protection Clause of the Fourteenth Amendment.

A

This case involves no discrimination against a suspect class. An indigent woman desiring an abortion does not come within the limited category of disadvantaged classes so recognized by our cases. Nor does the fact that the impact of the regulation falls upon those who cannot pay lead to a different conclusion. In a sense, every denial of welfare to an indigent creates a wealth classification as compared to nonindigents who are able to pay for the desired goods or services. But this Court has never held that financial need alone identifies a suspect class for purposes of equal protection analysis. *See Rodriguez*, at 29; *Dandridge v. Williams*, 397 U.S. 471 (1970). Accordingly, the central question in this case is whether the regulation "impinges upon a fundamental right explicitly or implicitly protected by the Constitution." The District Court read court decisions in *Roe v. Wade* and the subsequent cases applying it, as establishing a fundamental right to abortion and therefore concluded that nothing less than a compelling state interest would justify Connecticut's different treatment of abortion and childbirth. We think the District Court misconceived the nature and scope of the fundamental right recognized in *Roe.*

B

At issue in *Roe* was the constitutionality of a Texas law making it a crime to procure or attempt to procure an abortion, except on medical advice for the purpose of saving the life of the mother. Drawing on a group of disparate cases restricting governmental intrusion, physical coercion, and criminal prohibition of certain activities, we concluded that the Fourteenth Amendment's concept of personal liberty affords constitutional protection against state interference with certain aspects of an individual's personal "privacy," including a woman's decisions to terminate her pregnancy.[7] 410 U.S., at 153.

The Texas statute imposed severe criminal sanctions on the physicians and other medical personnel who performed abortions, thus drastically limiting the availability and safety of the desired service. As MR. JUSTICE STEWART observed, "It is difficult to imagine a more complete abridgement of a constitutional freedom. . . ." *Id.* at 170 (STEWART, J., concurring). We held

---

7. A woman has at least an equal right to choose to carry her fetus to term as to choose to abort it. Indeed, the right of procreation without state interference has long been recognized as "one of the basic civil rights of man . . . fundamental to the very existence and survival of the race." *Skinner v. Oklahoma,* 316 U.S. 535, 541 (1942).

that only a compelling state interest would justify such a sweeping restriction on a constitutionally protected interest, and we found no such state interest during the first trimester. Even when judged against this demanding standard, however, the State's dual interests in the health of the pregnant woman and the potential life of the fetus were deemed sufficient to justify substantial regulation of abortions in the second and third trimesters. "These interests are separate and distinct. Each grows in substantiality as the woman approaches term and, at a point during pregnancy, each becomes 'compelling,'" *Id.* at 162–63. In the second trimester, the State's interest in the health of the pregnant woman justifies state regulation reasonably related to that concern. *Id.* at 163. At viability, usually in the third trimester, the State's interest in the potential life of the fetus justifies prohibition with criminal penalties, except where the life or health of the mother is threatened. *Id.* at 163–64.

The Texas law in *Roe* was a stark example of impermissible interference with the pregnant woman's decision to terminate her pregnancy. In subsequent cases, we have invalidated other types of restrictions, different in form but similar in effect, on the woman's freedom of choice. Thus, in *Planned Parenthood of Missouri v. Danforth,* 428 U.S. 52, 70–71, n.11 (1976), we held that Missouri's requirement of spousal consent was unconstitutional because it "granted [the husband] the right to prevent unilaterally, and for whatever reason, the effectuation of his wife's and her physician's decision to terminate her pregnancy." Missouri had interposed an *"absolute obstacle* to a woman's decision that *Roe* held to be constitutionally protected from such interference." (Emphasis added.) Although a state-created obstacle need not be absolute to be impermissible, *see Doe v. Bolton; Carey v. Population Services International* (1977), we have held that a requirement for a lawful abortion "is not unconstitutional unless it unduly burdens the right to seek an abortion." *Bellotti v. Baird*, 428 U.S. 132, 147 (1976). We recognized in *Bellotti* that "not all distinction between abortion and other procedures is forbidden" and that "[t]he constitutionality of such distinction will depend upon its degree and the justification for it." *Id.* at 149–50. . . .

These cases recognize a constitutionally protected interest "in making certain kinds of important decisions" free from governmental compulsion. *Whalen v. Roe*, nn.24 and 26 (1977). As *Whalen* makes clear, the right in *Roe v. Wade* can be understood only by considering both the woman's interest and the nature of the State's interference with it. *Roe* did not declare an unqualified "constitutional right to an abortion," as the District Court seemed to think. Rather, the right protects the woman from unduly burdensome interference with her freedom to decide whether to terminate her pregnancy. It implies no limitation on the authority of a State to make a value judgment favoring childbirth over abortion, and to implement that judgment by the allocation of public funds.

The Connecticut regulation before us is different in kind from the laws invalidated in our previous abortion decisions. The Connecticut regulation places no obstacles—absolute or otherwise—in the pregnant woman's path to an abortion. An indigent woman who desires an abortion suffers no disadvantage as a consequence of Connecticut's decision to fund childbirth; she continues as before to be dependent on private sources for the service she desires. The State may have made childbirth a more attractive alternative, thereby influencing the woman's decision, but it has imposed no restriction on access to abortion that was not already there. The indigency that may make it difficult—and in some cases, perhaps, impossible—for some women to have abortions is neither created nor in any way affected by the Connecticut regulation. We conclude that the Connecticut regulation does not impinge upon the fundamental right recognized in *Roe*.[8]

8. Appellees rely on *Shapiro v. Thompson*, 394 U.S. 618 (1969), and *Memorial Hospital v. Maricopa County*, 415 U.S. 250 (1974). In those cases durational residence requirements for the receipt of public benefits were found to be unconstitutional because they "penalized" the exercise of the constitutional right to travel interstate.

Appellees' reliance on the penalty analysis of *Shapiro* and *Maricopa County* is misplaced. In our view there is only a semantic difference between appellees' assertion that the Connecticut law unduly interferes with a woman's right to terminate her pregnancy and their assertion that it penalizes the exercise of that right. Penalties are most familiar to the criminal law, where criminal sanctions are imposed as a consequence of proscribed conduct. *Shapiro* and *Maricopa County* recognized that denial of welfare to one who had recently exercised the right to travel across state lines was sufficiently analogous to a criminal fine to justify strict judicial scrutiny.

If Connecticut denied general welfare benefits to all women who had obtained abortions and who were otherwise entitled to the benefits, we would have a close analogy to the facts in *Shapiro*, and strict scrutiny might be appropriate under either the penalty analysis or the analysis we have applied in our previous abortion decisions. But the claim here is that the State "penalizes" the woman's decision to have an abortion by refusing to pay for it. *Shapiro* and *Maricopa County* did not hold that States would penalize the right to travel interstate by refusing to pay the bus fares of the indigent travelers. We find no support in the right to travel cases for the view that Connecticut must show a compelling interest for its decision not to fund elective abortions.

Sherbert v. Verner, 37 U.S. 398 (1963), similarly is inapplicable here. In addition, that case was decided in the significantly different context of a constitutionally imposed "governmental obligation of neutrality" originating in the Establish-

C

Our conclusion signals no retreat from *Roe* or the cases applying it. There is a basic difference between direct state interference with a protected activity and state encouragement of an alternative activity consonant with legislative policy. Constitutional concerns are greatest when the State attempts to impose its will by force of law; the State's power to encourage actions deemed to be in the public interest is necessarily far broader.

This distinction is implicit in two cases cited in *Roe* in support of the pregnant woman's right under the Fourteenth Amendment. *Meyer v. Nebraska*, 262 U.S. 390 (1923), involved a Nebraska law making it criminal to teach foreign languages to children who had not passed the eighth grade. *Id.* at 396–97. Nebraska's imposition of a criminal sanction on the providers of desired services makes *Meyer* closely analogous to *Roe*. In sustaining the constitutional challenge brought by a teacher convicted under the law, the Court held that the teacher's "right thus to teach and the right of parents to engage him so to instruct their children" were "within the liberty of the Amendment." *Id.* at 400. In *Pierce v. Society of Sisters*, 268 U.S. 510 (1925), the Court relied on *Meyer* to invalidate an Oregon criminal law requiring the parent or guardian of a child to send him to a public school, thus precluding the choice of a private school. Reasoning that the Fourteenth Amendment's concept of liberty "excludes any general power of the State to standardize its children by forcing them to accept instruction from public teachers only," the Court held that the law "unreasonably interfere[d] with the liberty of parents and guardians to direct the up-

bringing and education of children under their control." *Id.* at 534–35.

Both cases invalidated substantial restrictions on constitutionally protected liberty interests: in *Meyer*, the parent's right to have his child taught a particular foreign language; in *Pierce*, the parent's right to choose private rather than public school education. But neither case denied to a State the policy choice of encouraging the preferred course of action. Indeed, in *Meyer* the Court was careful to state that the power of the State "to prescribe a curriculum" that included English and excluded German in its free public schools "is not questioned." 262 U.S., at 402. Similarly, *Pierce* casts no shadow over a State's power to favor public education by funding it—a policy choice pursued in some States for more than a century. *See Brown v. Board of Education*, 347 U.S. 483, 489 n.4 (1954). Indeed, in *Norwood v. Harrison*, 413 U.S. 455, 462 (1973), we explicitly rejected the argument that *Pierce* established a "right of private or parochial schools to share with public schools in state largesse," noting that "[i]t is one thing to say that a State may not prohibit the maintenance of private schools and quite another to say that such schools must, as a matter of equal protection, receive state aid." Yet, were we to accept appellees' argument, an indigent parent could challenge the state policy of favoring public rather than private schools, or of preferring instruction in English rather than German, on grounds identical in principle to those advanced here. We think it abundantly clear that a State is not required to show a compelling interest for its policy choice to favor normal childbirth any more than a State must so justify its election to fund public but not private education.

D

The question remains whether Connecticut's regulation can be sustained un-

---

ment and Freedom of Religion Clauses of the First Amendment. *Id.* at 409.

der the less demanding test of rationality that applies in the absence of a suspect classification or the impingement of a fundamental right. This test requires that the distinction drawn between childbirth and nontherapeutic abortion by the regulation be "rationally related" to a "constitutionally permissible" purpose. *Lindsey v. Normet*, 405 U.S. 56, 74 (1972); *Massachusetts Board v. Murgia*, 427 U.S., at 314. We hold that the Connecticut funding scheme satisfies this standard.

Roe itself explicitly acknowledged the State's strong interest in protecting the potential life of the fetus. That interest exists throughout the pregnancy, "grow[ing] in substantiality as the woman approaches term." *Roe, supra,* at 162–63. Because the pregnant woman carries a potential human being, she "cannot be isolated in her privacy. . . . [Her] privacy is no longer sole and any right of privacy she possesses must be measured accordingly." *Id.* at 159. The State unquestionably has a "strong and legitimate interest in encouraging normal childbirth," *Beal v. Doe, ante,* an interest honored over the centuries.[11] Nor can there be any question that the Connecticut regulation rationally furthers that interest. . . . The subsidizing of cost incident to childbirth is a rational means of encouraging childbirth.

We certainly are not unsympathetic to the plight of an indigent woman who desires an abortion, but "the Constitution does not provide judicial remedies for every social and economic ill," *Lindsey v. Normet,* 405 U.S., at 74. Our cases uniformly have accorded the States a wider latitude in choosing among competing demands for limited public funds. . . .

The decision whether to expend state funds for nontherapeutic abortion is fraught with judgments of policy and value over which opinions are sharply divided. Our conclusion that the Connecticut regulation is constitutional is not based on a weighing of its wisdom or social desirability. . . . Indeed, when an issue involves policy choices as sensitive as those implicated by public funding of nontherapeutic abortions, the appropriate forum for their resolution in a democracy is the legislature. We should not forget that "legislatures are ultimate guardians of liberties and welfare of the people in quite as great a degree as the courts." *Mo., Kan. and Tex. Ry. Co. v. May,* 194 U.S. 267, 270 (1904) (Holmes, J.)[13]

In conclusion, we emphasize that our decision today does not proscribe government funding of nontherapeutic abortions. It is open to Congress to require provision of medicaid benefits for such abortions as a condition of state participation in the medicaid program. Also, under Title XIX as construed in *Beal v. Doe, ante,* Connecticut is free—through normal democratic processes—to decide that such benefits should be provided. We hold only that the Constitution does not require a judicially imposed resolution of these difficult issues. . . .

MR. CHIEF JUSTICE BURGER, concurring.

I join the Court's opinion. Like the Court, I do not read any decision of this Court as requiring a State to finance a non-

11. In addition to the direct interest in protecting the fetus, a State may have legitimate demographic concerns about its rate of population growth. Such concerns are basic to the future of the State and in some circumstances could constitute a substantial reason for departure from a position of neutrality between abortion and childbirth.

13. Much of the rhetoric of the three dissenting opinions would be equally applicable if Connecticut had elected not to fund either abortions or childbirth. Yet none of the dissents goes so far as to argue that the Constitution requires such assistance for all indigent pregnant women.

therapeutic abortion. The Court's holdings in *Roe* and *Doe, supra,* simply require that a State not create an absolute barrier to a woman's decision to have an abortion. These precedents do not suggest that the State is constitutionally required to assist her in procuring it.

From time to time, every state legislature determines that, as a matter of sound public policy, the government ought to provide certain health and social services to its citizens. Encouragement of childbirth and child care is not a novel undertaking in this regard. Various governments, both in this country and in others, have made such a determination for centuries. In recent times, they have similarly provided educational services. The decision to provide any one of these services—or not to provide them—is not required by the Federal Constitution. Nor does the providing of a particular service require, as a matter of federal constitutional law, the provision of another.

Here, the State of Connecticut has determined that it will finance certain childbirth expenses. That legislative determination places no state-created barrier to a woman's choice to procure an abortion, and it does not require the State to provide it. Accordingly, I concur in the judgment.

MR. JUSTICE BRENNAN, with MR. JUSTICE MARSHALL and MR. JUSTICE BLACKMUN, dissenting.

. . .

This court reverses on the ground that "the District Court misconceived the nature and scope of the fundamental right recognized in *Roe [v. Wade],*" and therefore that Connecticut was not required to meet the "compelling interest" test to justify its discrimination against elective abortion by only "the less demanding test of rationality that applies in the absence of . . . the infringement of a fundamental right." This holding, the Court insists, "places no ob-

stacles—absolute or otherwise—in the pregnant woman's path to an abortion"; she is still at liberty to finance the abortion from "private sources." True, "the state may [by funding childbirth] have made childbirth a more attractive alternative, thereby influencing the woman's decision, but it has imposed no restriction on access to abortions that was not already there." True, also, indigency "may make it more difficult—and in some cases, perhaps impossible—for some women to have abortions," but the regrettable consequence "is neither created nor in any way affected by the Connecticut regulation." *Ante.*

But a distressing insensitivity to the plight of impoverished pregnant women is inherent in the Court's analysis. The stark reality for too many, not just "some," indigent pregnant women is that indigency makes access to competent licensed physicians not merely "difficult" but "impossible." As a practical matter, many indigent women will feel they have no choice but to carry their pregnancies to term because the State will pay for other associated medical services, even though they would have chosen to have abortions if the State had also provided funds for that procedure, or indeed if the State had provided funds for neither procedure. This disparity in funding by the State clearly operates to coerce indigent pregnant women to bear children they would not otherwise choose to have, and just as clearly, this coercion can only operate upon the poor, who are uniquely the victims of this form of financial pressure. Mr. Justice Frankfurter's words are apt:

> To sanction such a ruthless consequence, inevitably resulting from a money hurdle erected by the State, would justify a latter-day Anatole France to add one more item to his ironic comments on the "majestic equality" of the law. "The law, in its majestic equality, forbids the rich as well

as the poor to sleep under bridges, to beg in the streets, and to steal bread". . . . (*Griffin v. Illinois*, 351 U.S. 12, 23 [1956], [Frankfurter, J., concurring].)

None can take seriously the Court's assurance that its "conclusion signals no retreat from *Roe [v. Wade]* or the cases applying it." That statement must occasion great surprise among the Courts of Appeals and District Courts that, relying upon *Roe* and *Doe v. Bolton*, have held that States are constitutionally required to fund elective abortions if they fund pregnancies carried to term. [Citations omitted.] Indeed, it cannot be gainsaid that today's decision seriously erodes the principles that *Roe* and *Doe* announced to guide the determination of what constitutes an unconstitutional infringement of the fundamental right of pregnant women to be free to decide whether to have an abortion.

The Court's premise is that only an equal protection claim is presented here. Claims of interference with enjoyment of fundamental rights have, however, occupied a rather protean position in our constitutional jurisprudence. Whether or not the Court's analysis may reasonably proceed under the Equal Protection Clause, the Court plainly errs in ignoring, as it does, the unanswerable argument of appellee, and holding of the District Court, that the regulation unconstitutionally impinges upon her claim of privacy derived from the Due Process Clause.

Roe v. Wade and cases following it hold that an area of privacy invulnerable to the State's intrusion surrounds the decision of a pregnant woman whether or not to carry her pregnancy to term. The Connecticut scheme clearly infringes upon that area of privacy by bringing financial pressures on indigent women that force them to bear children they would not otherwise have. That is an obvious impairment of the fundamental right established by *Roe*. Yet the

Court concludes that "the Connecticut regulation does not impinge upon [that] fundamental right." This conclusion is based on a perceived distinction, on the one hand, between the imposition of criminal penalties for the procurement of an abortion present in *Roe v. Wade* and *Doe v. Bolton* and the absolute prohibition present in *Planned Parenthood v. Danforth*, and, on the other, the assertedly lesser inhibition imposed by the Connecticut scheme. . . .

We . . . rejected this approach in other abortion cases. *Doe v. Bolton*, the companion to *Roe*, in addition to striking down the Georgia criminal prohibition against elective abortions, struck down the procedural requirements of certification of hospitals, of approval by a hospital committee, and of concurrence . . . by two doctors other than the woman's own doctor. None of these requirements operated as an absolute bar to elective abortions in the manner of the criminal prohibitions present in the other aspect of the case or in *Roe*, but this was not sufficient to save them from unconstitutionality. In *Planned Parenthood*, we struck down a requirement for spousal consent to an elective abortion which the Court characterizes today simply as an "absolute obstacle" to a woman obtaining an abortion. But the obstacle was "absolute" only in the limited sense that a woman who was unable to persuade her spouse to agree to an elective abortion was prevented from obtaining one. Any woman whose husband agreed, or could be persuaded to agree, was free to obtain an abortion, and the State never imposed directly any prohibition of its own. This requirement was qualitatively different from the criminal statutes that the Court today says are comparable, but we nevertheless found it unconstitutional.

. . .

Finally, cases involving other fundamental rights also make clear that the

Court's concept of what constitutes an impermissible infringement upon the fundamental right of a pregnant woman to choose to have an abortion makes new law. We have repeatedly found that infringements of fundamental rights are not limited to outright denials of those rights. First Amendment decisions have consistently held in a wide variety of contexts that the compelling state interest test is applicable not only to outright denials but also to restraints that make exercise of those rights more difficult. *See, e.g., Sherbert v. Verner*, 374 U.S. 398 (1963) (free exercise of religion), *NAACP v. Button*, 371 U.S. 415 (1963) (freedom of expression and association), *Linmark Associates v. Township of Willingboro*, 431 U.S. 85 (1977) (freedom of expression). The compelling state interest test has been applied in voting cases, even where only relatively small infringements upon voting power, such as dilution of voting strength caused by malapportionment, have been involved. *See, e.g., Reynolds v. Sims*, 377 U.S. 533, 562, 566 (1964), *Chapman v. Meier*, 420 U.S. 1 (1975), *Connor v. Finch*, 431 U.S. 407 (1977). Similarly, cases involving the right to travel have consistently held that statutes penalizing the fundamental right to travel must pass muster under the compelling state interest test, irrespective of whether the statutes actually deter travel. *Memorial Hospital v. Maricopa County*, 415 U.S. 250, 257–58 (1974), *Dunn v. Blumstein*, 405 U.S. 330, 339–41 (1972), *Shapiro v. Tompson*, 394 U.S. 618 (1969). And indigents asserting a fundamental right of access to the courts have been excused payment of entry costs without being required first to show their indigency was an absolute bar to access. *Griffin v. Illinois*, 351 U.S. 12 (1956). *Douglas v. California*, 372 U.S. 353 (1963), *Boddie v. Connecticut*, 401 U.S. (1971).

Until today, I had not thought the nature of the fundamental right established in *Roe* was open to question, let alone susceptible to the interpretation advanced by the Court. The fact that the Connecticut scheme may not operate as an absolute bar preventing all indigent women from having abortions is not critical. What is critical is that the State has inhibited their fundamental right to make that choice free from state interference.

Nor does the manner in which Connecticut has burdened the right freely to choose to have an abortion save its Medicaid program. The Connecticut scheme cannot be distinguished from other grants and withholdings of financial benefits that we have held unconstitutionally burdened a fundamental right. *Sherbert v. Verner* struck down a South Carolina statute that denied unemployment compensation to a woman who for religious reasons could not work on Saturday, but that would have provided such compensation if her unemployment had stemmed from a number of other nonreligious causes. Even though there was no proof of indigency in that case, *Sherbert* held that "the pressure upon her to forgo [her religious] practice [was] unmistakable," 374 U.S., at 414, and therefore held the effect was the same as a fine imposed for Saturday worship. Here, though the burden is upon the right to privacy derived from the Due Process Clause and not upon freedom of religion under the Free Exercise Clause of the First Amendment, the governing principle is the same, for Connecticut grants and withholds financial benefits in a manner that discourages significantly the exercise of a fundamental constitutional right. Indeed, the case for application of the principle actually is stronger than in *Verner* since appellees are all indigents and therefore even more vulnerable to the financial pressures imposed by the Connecticut regulations.

Bellotti v. Baird, 428 U.S. 132, 147 (1976), held, and the Court today agrees, that a state requirement is unconstitutional if it "unduly" burdens the fundamental right of pregnant women to be free to choose to have an abortion because the State has advanced no compelling state interest to justify its interference in that choice.

Although Connecticut does not argue it as justification, the Court concludes that the State's interest "in protecting the potential life of the fetus" suffices.* Since only the first trimester of pregnancy is involved in this case, that justification is totally foreclosed if the Court is not overruling the holding of *Roe v. Wade* that "[w]ith respect to the State's important and legitimate interest in potential life, the 'compelling point is at viability,'" occurring at about the end of the second trimester. 410 U.S., at 163. The State also argues a further justification not relied upon by the Court, namely, that it needs "to control the amount of its limited public funds which will be allocated to its public welfare budget." Brief. The District Court correctly held, however, that the asserted interest was "wholly chimerical" because the "state's assertion that it saves money when it declines to pay the cost of a welfare mother's abortion is simply contrary to indisputed facts." 408 F. Supp., at 664. . . .

MR. JUSTICE MARSHALL, dissenting, [announced in *Beal v. Doe*].

It is all too obvious that the governmental actions in these cases, ostensibly taken to "encourage" women to carry pregnancies to term, are in reality intended to

*The Court also suggests, *ante* at n.[11], that a "state may have legitimate demographic concerns about the rate of population growth" which might justify a choice to favor live births over abortions. While it is conceivable that under some circumstances this might be an appropriate factor to be considered . . . no one contends that this is the case here. . . .

impose a moral viewpoint that no State may constitutionally enforce. *Roe v. Wade; Doe v. Bolton.* Since efforts to overturn those decisions have been unsuccessful, the opponents of abortion have attempted every imaginable means to circumvent the commands of the Constitution and impose their moral choices upon the rest of society. *See, e.g., Planned Parenthood of Missouri v. Danforth; Singleton v. Wulff,* 428 U.S. 106 (1976); *Bellotti v. Baird,* (1976). The present cases involve the most vicious attacks yet devised. The impact of the regulations here falls tragically upon those among us least able to help or defend themselves. As the Court well knows, these regulations inevitably will have the practical effect of preventing nearly all poor women from obtaining safe and legal abortions.[1]

1. Although an abortion performed during the first trimester of pregnancy is a relatively inexpensive surgical procedure, usually costing under $200, even this modest sum is far beyond the means of most Medicaid recipients. And "if one does not have it and is unable to get it the fee might well be" one hundred times as great. *Smith v. Bennett,* 365 U.S. 708, 712 (1961). . . . The inevitable human tragedy that will result is reflected in a government report: "[F]or some women, non-availability of public funding for legal abortion acted as a deterrent to their obtaining the safe procedures. The following case history of a death which occurred during 1975 exemplifies such a situation:

" . . . A 41-year-old black married female with 6 previous pregnancies, 5 living children, and 1 previous abortion, sought an illegal abortion from a local dietician. . . . Her stated reason for seeking an illegal procedure was financial. . . . [It] cost $30, compared to an estimated $150 for a legal procedure. . . . Allegedly, the operation was performed by inserting a metal rod to dilate the cervix. . . . [The woman died of cardiac arrest after two weeks of intensive hospital care and two operations.]" U.S. Dept. of HEW, Center for Disease Control, *Abortion Surveillance, 1975* (1977) (hereafter "CDC *Surveillance*").

The enactments challenged here brutally coerce poor women to bear children whom society will scorn for every day of their lives. . . . And opposition remains strong against increasing AFDC benefits for impoverished mothers and children, so that there is little chance for the children to grow up in a decent environment. *Cf. Dandridge v. Williams*, 397 U.S. 471 (1970). I am appalled at the ethical bankruptcy of those who preach a "right to life" that means, under present social policies, a bare existence in utter misery for so many poor women and their children.

I

The Court's insensitivity to the human dimension of these decisions is particularly obvious in its cursory discussion of respondent's equal protection claims in *Maher v. Roe*. . . . In the present case, in its evident desire to avoid strict scrutiny—or indeed any meaningful scrutiny—of the challenged legislation, which would almost surely result in its invalidation the Court pulls from thin air a distinction between laws that absolutely prevent exercise of the fundamental right to abortion and those that "merely" make its exercise difficult for some people. *See Maher v. Roe.* MR. JUSTICE BRENNAN demonstrates that the challenged regulations are little different from a total prohibition from the viewpoint of the poor. But the Court's legal legerdemain has produced the desired result: a fundamental right is no longer at stake and mere rationality becomes the appropriate mode of analysis. To no one's surprise, application of that test—combined with misreading of *Roe v. Wade* to generate a "strong" state interest in "potential life" during the first trimester of pregnancy . . ." leaves little doubt about the outcome; the challenged legislation is [as] always upheld." *Massachusetts v. Murgia*, 427 U.S., at 321. And once again, "relevant factors [are] misapplied or ignored." 427 U.S., at 321, while

the Court "forego[es] all judicial protection against discriminatory legislation bearing upon a right "vital to the flourishing of a free society" and a class "unfairly burdened by invidious discrimination unrelated to the individual worth of [its] members." *Id.* at 320.

As I have argued before, an equal protection analysis far more in keeping with the actions rather than the words of the Court, *see id.* at 320–21, carefully weighs three factors—"the importance of the governmental benefits denied, the character of the class, and the asserted state interests," *id.* at 322. Application of this standard would invalidate the challenged regulations.

The governmental benefits at issue here, while perhaps not representing large amounts of money for any individual, are nevertheless of absolutely vital importance in the lives of the recipients. The right of every woman to choose whether to bear a child is, as *Roe v. Wade* held, of fundamental importance. An unwanted child may be disruptive and destructive of the life of any woman, but the impact is felt most by those too poor to ameliorate those efforts. If funds for an abortion are unavailable, a poor woman may feel that she is forced to obtain an illegal abortion that poses a serious threat to her health and even her life. *See* n.1, *supra.* If she refuses to take this risk, and undergoes the pain and danger of state-financed pregnancy and childbirth, she may well give up all chance of escaping the cycle of poverty. Absent day-care facilities, she will be forced into full-time child care for years to come; she will be unable to work so that her family can break out of the welfare system or the lowest income brackets. If she already has children, another infant to feed and clothe may well stretch the budget past the breaking point. All chance to control the direction of her own life will have been lost.

. . . While poverty alone does not entitle a class to claim government benefits, it is surely a relevant factor in the present inquiry. *See San Antonio School District v. Rodriguez*, 411 U.S. 1, 70, 117–24 (MARSHALL, J., dissenting). Indeed, it was in the *San Antonio* case that MR. JUSTICE POWELL for the Court stated a test for analyzing discrimination on the basis of wealth that would, if fairly applied here, strike down the regulations. The Court there held that a wealth discrimination claim is made out by persons who share "two distinguishing characteristics: because of their impecunity they [are] completely unable to pay for some desired benefit, and as a consequence they sustain an absolute deprivation of a meaningful opportunity to enjoy that benefit." *Id.* at 20. Medicaid recipients are, almost by definition, "completely unable to pay for" abortions, and are thereby completely denied "a meaningful opportunity" to obtain them.[2]

It is no less disturbing that the effect of the challenged regulations will fall with great disparity upon women of minority races. Nonwhite women now obtain abortions at nearly twice the rate of whites, and it appears that almost 40 percent of minority women—more than five times the proportion of whites—are dependent upon medicaid for their health care. Even if this strongly disparate racial impact does not alone violate the Equal Protection Clause, *see Washington v. Davis*, 426 U.S. 229 (1976); *Jefferson v. Hackney*, 406 U.S. 535 (1972), "at some point a showing that state action has a devastating impact on the lives of minor-

ity racial groups must be relevant." *Id.* at 558, 575–76 (MARSHALL, J., dissenting).

Against the brutal effect that the challenged laws will have must be weighed the asserted state interest. The Court describes this as a "strong interest in protecting the potential life of the fetus." Yet in *Doe v. Bolton*, the Court expressly held that any state interest during the first trimester of pregnancy, when 88 percent of all abortions occur, CDC *Surveillance*, was wholly insufficient to justify state interference with the right to abortion. *Id.* at 192–200.[5] If a State's interest in potential human life before the point of viability is insufficient to justify requiring several physicians' concurrence for an abortion, *id.*, I cannot comprehend how it magically becomes adequate to allow the present infringement on rights of disfavored classes. If there is any state interest in potential life before the point of viability, it certainly does not outweigh the deprivation or serious discouragement of a vital constitutional right of especial importance to poor and minority women.[6]

Thus, taking account of all relevant factors under the flexible standards of equal protection review, I would hold the Connecticut and Pennsylvania medicaid regulations and the St. Louis public hospital policy violative of the Fourteenth Amendment.

---

5. Requirements that the abortion be performed by a physician exercising his best clinical judgment, and in a facility meeting narrowly tailored health standards, are allowable. *Id.*

6. Application of the flexible equal protection standard would allow the Court to strike down the regulations in these cases without calling into question laws funding public education or English language teaching in public schools. *See Maher v. Roe.* By permitting a court to weigh all relevant factors, the flexible standard does not logically require acceptance of any equal protection claim that is "identical in principle" under the traditional approach to those advanced here. *See id.*

2. If public funds and facilities for abortions are sharply reduced, private charities, hospital, clinics, and doctors willing to perform abortions for far less than the prevailing fee will, I trust, accommodate some of the need. But since abortion services are inadequately available even now, *see* n.1, *supra*, such private generosity is unlikely to give many poor women "a meaningful opportunity" to obtain abortions.

II

. . . The abortion decisions are sound law and undoubtedly good policy. They have never been questioned by the Court and we are told that today's cases "signal no retreat from *Roe* or the cases applying it." *Maher v. Roe.* The logic of those cases inexorably requires invalidation of the present enactments. Yet I fear that the Court's decisions will be an invitation to public officials, already under extraordinary pressure from well financed and carefully orchestrated lobbying campaigns, to approve more such restrictions. The effect will be to relegate millions of people to lives of poverty and despair. When elected leaders cower before public pressure, this Court, more than ever, must not shirk its duty to enforce the Constitution for the benefit of the poor and powerless.

Mr. Justice Blackmun, with whom Mr. Justice Brennan and Mr. Justice Marshall join, dissenting [announced in *Beal v. Doe*].

The Court today, by its decisions in these cases, allows the States, and such municipalities as choose to do so, to accomplish indirectly what the Court in *Roe v. Wade* and *Doe v. Bolton*—by a substantial majority and with some emphasis, I had thought—said they could not do directly. The Court concedes the existence of a constitutional right but denies the realization and enjoyment of that right on the ground that existence and realization are separate and distinct. For the individual woman concerned, indigent and financially helpless, as the Court's opinions in the three cases concede her to be, the result is punitive and tragic. Implicit in the Court's holdings is the condescension that she may go elsewhere for her abortion. I find that disingenuous and alarming, almost reminiscent of "let them eat cake."

The result the Court reaches is particularly distressing in *Poelker v. Doe*, where a presumed majority, in electing as mayor one whom the record shows campaigned on the issue of closing public hospitals to nontherapeutic abortions, punitively impresses upon a needy minority its own concepts of the socially desirable, the publicly acceptable, and the morally sound, with a touch of the devil-take-the-hindmost. This is not the kind of thing for which our Constitution stands.

The Court's financial argument, of course, is specious. To be sure, welfare funds are limited and welfare must be spread perhaps as best meets the community's concept of its needs. But the cost of a nontherapeutic abortion is far less than the cost of maternity care and delivery, and holds no comparison whatsoever with the welfare costs that will burden the State for the new indigents and their support in the long, long years ahead.

Neither is it an acceptable answer, as the Court well knows, to say that the Congress and the States are free to authorize the use of funds for nontherapeutic abortions. Why should any politician incur the demonstrated wrath and noise of the abortion opponents when mere silence and nonactivity accomplish the results the opponents want?

There is another world "out there," the existence of which the Court, I suspect, either chooses to ignore or fears to recognize. And so the cancer of poverty will continue to grow. This is a sad day for those who regard the Constitution as a force that would serve justice to all evenhandedly, and in so doing, would better the lot of the poorest among us.

CASE QUESTIONS

1. Justice Powell asserts that *Roe* "implies no limitation on the authority of the state to make a value judgment favoring childbirth over abortion, and to implement that judgment by the allocation of public funds." Does this assertion mean that he would hold constitutional a state's imposition of a fine or fee of $2000 on all abortions performed within the state? How would such a situation differ from the present one?

2. Suppose that a state, in an effort to alleviate the shortage of babies for adoption, offered a $5000 award to any mother giving up her illegitimate infant for adoption. If this particular state nonetheless paid out Medicaid funds for abortions, would the dissenters still object?

3. The First Amendment says, "Congress shall make no law abridging freedom of speech. . . ." If Congress, through its support of national public television, happens to fund a program in which various scholars extol the virtues of American democracy, would the First Amendment be violated by Congress' failure then to fund a program in which the virtues of communism are extolled? Would such a combination of Congressional decisions deny "equal protection of law" to advocates of communism? What if the Democratic-controlled Congress were to pass a law providing funds for all television campaign expenses of Democratic candidates, and none for Republicans or others? What would be the precise constitutional flaw with the latter? Would it apply to the funding of childbirth but not of abortion?

4. Justice Brennan argues that if the state had chosen to fund neither pregnancy nor abortion, certain women would choose to abort, and yet that under the scheme challenged here those same women would be "coerced" (by the fact that childbirth will be "free") into carrying the fetus to term. Is this really a plausible scenario? Would the women not realize that childbirth, in the long run, would be more expensive? If the women could obtain abortion funds in the first instance (where the state was not funding childbirth), why could the same women not obtain the funds in the second instance (where the state was funding childbirth)? If one rejects the assumption that an indigent woman who finds herself pregnant is less likely to have an abortion when the state funds childbirth than she would be if the state funded neither childbirth nor abortion, does the dissenters' position boil down to a right of "free abortion on demand"?

5. Is there a difference of constitutional dimensions between a state's imposing a burden on a right and a state's failing to alleviate a burden (that exists for social reasons) on the same right?

6. Does this decision signal a retreat from the principles of *Roe v. Wade* and *Doe v. Bolton*, or does it just refuse to extend them further?

7. The Court here and in *Beal* acknowledged the state's "valid and important interest in encouraging childbirth," but in *Akron* and *Thornburgh* the justices blocked efforts by the State to have abortion clinic personnel provide such encouragement. Would it be constitutional under *Beal* and *Akron* for the state to publish anti-abortion pamphlets and require that a woman consenting to an abortion certify that she has read the pamphlet?

Finally, on the same day that the Court announced *Beal* and *Maher*, the majority, in a third case, sustained another variety of a state effort to limit the availability of abortions. St. Louis had issued an outright prohibition on "nontherapeutic" abortions within its two city-owned hospitals. The city defined "nontherapeutic" as covering any abortion not needed to save the mother's life or to save her from "grave physiological injury." Since this definition amounted to an outright governmental prohibition, although one of limited extent because private hospitals did function in St. Louis, it is somewhat surprising that the court majority devoted less effort to settling this case, *Poelker v. Doe*, than to either *Beal* or *Maher*. The Court majority issued only a brief per curiam opinion for this case, treating the city's decision not as a limited prohibition on abortions but rather as a refusal to provide a government subsidy (via its subsidy of the hospital facilities) for abortion services. The same three justices as in *Beal* and *Maher* dissented here, and the dissents of Justices Blackmun and Marshall, included in *Maher v. Roe*, apply as well to this case.

John Poelker et al. v. Jane Doe, etc., 432 U.S. 519 (1977)

Per curiam.

. . . Relying on our decisions in *Roe v. Wade,* and *Doe v. Bolton,* the Court of Appeals held that the city's policy and the hospital's staffing practice denied the "constitutional rights of indigent pregnant women . . . long after those rights had been clearly enunciated" in *Roe* and *Doe*. 515 F.2d, at 547. The court cast the issue in an equal protection mold, finding that the provision of publicly financed hospital services for childbirth but not for elective abortions constituted invidious discrimination. In support of its equal protection analysis, the court also emphasized the contrast between nonindigent women who can afford to obtain abortions in private hospitals and indigent women who cannot. . . .

We agree that the constitutional question presented here is identical in principle with that presented by a State's refusal to provide Medicaid benefits for abortions while providing them for childbirth. This

was the issue before us in *Maher v. Roe*. For the reasons set forth in our opinion in that case, we find no constitutional violation by the city of St. Louis in electing, as a policy choice, to provide publicly financed hospital services for childbirth without providing corresponding services for nontherapeutic abortions.

In the decision of the Court of Appeals and in the briefs supporting that decision, emphasis is placed on Mayor Poelker's personal opposition to abortion, characterized as "a wanton, callous disregard" for the constitutional rights of indigent women. 515 F.2d, at 547. Although the Mayor's personal position on abortion is irrelevant to our decision, we note that he is an elected official responsible to the people of St. Louis. His policy of denying city funds for abortions such as that desired by Doe is subject to public debate and approval or disapproval at the polls. We merely hold, for the reasons stated in *Maher*, that the Constitution does not forbid a State or city, pursuant to democratic processes, from expressing a preference for normal childbirth as St. Louis has done.

The judgment of the Court of Appeals for the Eighth Circuit is reversed, and the case is remanded for further proceedings consistent with this opinion.

MR. JUSTICE BRENNAN, with MR. JUSTICE MARSHALL and MR. JUSTICE BLACKMUN, dissenting.

The Court holds that St. Louis may constitutionally refuse to permit the performance of elective abortions in its city-owned hospitals while providing hospital services to women who carry their pregnancies to term. As stated by the Court of Appeals,

> Stripped of all rhetoric, the city here, through its policy and staffing procedure, is simply telling indigent women, like Doe, that if they choose to carry their pregnancies to term, the city will provide physicians and medical facilities for full maternity care; but if they choose to exercise their constitutionally protected right to determine that they wish to terminate the pregnancy, the city will not provide physicians and facilities for the abortion procedure, even though it is probably safer than going through a full pregnancy and childbirth. (515 F.2d 541, 544 [1975].)

The Court of Appeals held that St. Louis could not in this way "interfer[e] in her decision of whether to bear a child or have an abortion simply because she is indigent and unable to afford private treatment," *id.*, because it was constitutionally impermissible that indigent women be "'subjected to State coercion to bear children which they do not wish to bear [while] no

other women similarly situated are so coerced,'" *id.* at 545.

For the reasons set forth in my dissent in *Maher v. Roe*, I would affirm the Court of Appeals. Here the fundamental right of a woman freely to choose to terminate her pregnancy has been infringed by the city of St. Louis through a deliberate policy based on opposition to elective abortions on moral grounds by city officials. While it may still be possible for some indigent women to obtain abortions in clinics or private hospitals, it is clear that the city policy is a significant, and in some cases insurmountable, obstacle to indigent pregnant women who cannot pay for abortions in those private facilities. Nor is the closing of St. Louis' public hospitals an isolated instance with little practical significance. The importance of today's decision is greatly magnified by the fact that during 1975 and the first quarter of 1976 only about 18 percent of all public hospitals in the country provided abortion services, and in 10 States there were no public hospitals providing such services.[1]

A number of difficulties lie beneath the surface of the Court's holding. Public hospitals that do not permit the performance of elective abortions will frequently have physicians on their staffs who would willingly perform them. This may operate in some communities significantly to reduce the number of physicians who are both willing and able to perform abortions in a hospital setting. It is not a complete answer that many abortions may safely be performed in clinics, for some physicians will not be affiliated with those clinics, and some abortions may pose unacceptable risks if performed outside a hospital. Indeed, such an answer would be ironic, for

1. Sullivan, Tietze, and Dryfoos, "Legal Abortion in the United States, 1975–1976," 9 *Family Planning Perspectives* 116, 121, 128 (1977).

if the result is to force some abortions to be performed in a clinic that should properly be performed in a hospital, the city policy will have operated to increase rather than reduce health risks associated with abortions; and in *Roe* the Court permitted regulation by the State solely to protect maternal health. 410 U.S., at 163.

The Court's holding will also pose difficulties in small communities where the public hospital is the only nearby health care facility. If such a public hospital is closed to abortion, any woman—rich or poor—will be seriously inconvenienced; and for some women—particularly poor women—the unavailability of abortions in the public hospital will be an insuperable obstacle. Indeed, a recent survey suggests that the decision in this case will be felt most strongly in rural areas, where the public hospital will in all likelihood be closed to elective abortions, and where there will not be sufficient demand to support a separate abortion clinic.[2]

Because the city policy constitutes "coercion [of women] to bear children they do not wish to bear," *Roe v. Wade* and the

cases following it require that the city show a compelling state interest that justifies this infringement upon the fundamental right to choose to have an abortion. "[E]xpressing a preference for normal childbirth," does not satisfy that standard. *Roe* explicitly held that during the first trimester no state interest in regulating abortions was compelling, and that during the second trimester the State's interest was compelling only insofar as it protected maternal health. 410 U.S., at 162–64. Under *Roe*, the State's "important and legitimate interest in potential life," *id.* at 163,—which I take to be another way of referring to a State's "preference for normal childbirth"—becomes compelling only at the end of the second trimester. Thus it is clear that St. Louis' policy preference is insufficient to justify its infringement on the right of women to choose to have abortions during the first two trimesters of pregnancy without interference by the State on the ground of moral opposition to abortions. St. Louis' policy therefore "unduly burdens the right to seek an abortion," *Bellotti v. Baird*, 428 U.S. 132, 147 (1976).

I would *Affirm* the Court of Appeals.

2. "The concentration of services among relatively few providers—mostly clinics—in the nation's larger cities is clearly associated with the failure of hospitals—especially the smaller hospitals that are the major health institutions in small cities and nonmetropolitan areas—to offer abortions along with their other health services. Since public hospitals are even less likely than private hospitals to provide abortions, it is the poor, rural and very young women who are most likely to be denied abortions as a result of the need to travel outside their own communities to obtain terminations. It is these women who are least likely to have the funds, the time or the familiarity with the medical system that they need to be able to cope with the problems associated with such travel." *Id.* at 121.

CASE QUESTIONS

1. Does Justice Brennan's dissent slide into the position that communities must provide abortion services, as distinguished from the position that communities may

not rig the scales by providing childbirth services but not abortion services?

2. The Fourteenth Amendment says that no state may deprive a person of life without due process of law. Does this phrase mean that a starving person has a right to have the state provide food? An indigent sick person, a right to free health care? Do the dissenters imply an affirmative answer to these questions?

3. How does a local ordinance forbidding abortions in city-run hospitals differ from the state law (declared void in *Doe*) restricting abortions to JCAH-accredited hospitals?

4. Under the majority's reasoning, could a state deny police and fire protection to abortion-providing clinics on the grounds that such protection was a subsidy of abortion services?

Even before *Beal*, *Maher*, and *Poelker* were handed down (on June 20, 1977), Congress, in an effort orchestrated by Representative Henry Hyde, had added its voice to the chorus opposing public financing of abortions. In a series of amendments to annual appropriations bills, each called a Hyde Amendment, Congress began in September 1976 to forbid the use of federal funds to reimburse the cost of abortions for Medicaid recipients, with a very narrow range of permitted exceptions. The 1977 fiscal year appropriation made an exception for those pregnancies that endangered the life of the mother. The Hyde Amendments for 1978 and 1979 additionally exempted abortions to end pregnancies that were the result of "promptly reported" rape or incest or that would cause "severe and long-lasting health damage" to the mother. The 1980 Hyde Amendment removed the health damage exemption but retained the exemptions for rape or incest or life-threatening pregnancies.

On September 30, 1976, the day the first Hyde Amendment was enacted, Cora McRae, a pregnant Medicaid recipient in New York, brought suit with a number of other plaintiffs to enjoin the enforcement of the funding restriction on the grounds that it was unconstitutional. The Secretary of HEW was joined on the defendant side by Senators James Buckley and Jesse Helms and by Representative Hyde. The district court certified the suit as a class action suit on behalf of all pregnant or potentially pregnant women eligible for Medicaid in New York state who choose to seek an abortion and all abortion service providers, and granted an injunction against enforcing the law, pending a full hearing. Then *Beal* and *Maher* were decided and the Supreme Court vacated the injunction and remanded to the district court for reconsideration in light of the reasoning in those decisions. A number of additional plaintiffs joined the first group for the reconsideration trial.

The plaintiffs argued along both statutory and constitutional lines. First, they claimed that Title XIX of the Social Security Act even with the Hyde Amendments still obliged the states to pay for medically necessary abortions, for they were necessary medical services within the meaning of the Act. The district court rejected this argument, and none of the Supreme Court justices in their disposition quarreled with that statutory interpretation.

The plaintiffs' constitutional arguments, on the other hand, met with more success at the district court. They claimed that the Hyde Amendment violated the First Amendment clauses forbidding laws "respecting an establishment of religion," or prohibiting the free exercise of religion, and also violated the equal protection component of the Fifth Amendment Due Process Clause. They succeeded in convincing the district court of both the free exercise and the Fifth Amendment arguments. The district court then enjoined (again) the Secretary of HEW from enforcing the Hyde Amendment. The Secretary appealed to the Supreme Court for a stay of the injunction pending appeal, but the Supreme Court refused to grant it. After hearing the appeal, however, in the case of *Harris v. McRae* (448 U.S. 297) the Supreme Court did (on June 24, 1980) overturn the district court's order and permit the Hyde Amendment to take effect. The excerpt below omits the Court's statutory reasoning but includes the essence of the constitutional arguments. The decision here is 5–4, because Justice Stevens has joined the *Maher* dissent group of Brennan, Marshall, and Blackmun. The decision was accompanied by that of *Williams v. Zbaraz* (448 U.S. 358), which decided essentially on the same grounds the constitutionality of an Illinois version of the Hyde Amendment.

Patricia R. Harris, Secretary of Health and Human Services,* v. Cora McRae, 448 U.S. 297 (1980)

MR. JUSTICE STEWART delivered the opinion of the Court.

III

. . .

The appellees assert that the funding restrictions of the Hyde Amendment violate several rights secured by the Constitution—(1) the right of a woman, implicit in the Due Process Clause of the Fifth Amendment, to decide whether to terminate a pregnancy, (2) the prohibition under the Establishment Clause of the First Amendment against any "law respecting an estab-

lishment of religion," and (3) the right to freedom of religion protected by the Free Exercise Clause of the First Amendment. The appellees also contend that, quite apart from substantive constitutional rights, the Hyde Amendment violates the equal protection component of the Fifth Amendment.

. . .

A

We address first the appellees' argument that the Hyde Amendment, by restricting the availability of certain medi-

*Formerly Health, Education and Welfare (HEW).—Au.

cally necessary abortions under Medicaid, impinges on the "liberty" protected by the Due Process Clause as recognized in *Roe v. Wade*, 410 U.S. 113, and its progeny.

. . . The constitutional underpinning of *Wade* was a recognition that the "liberty" protected by the Due Process Clause of the Fourteenth Amendment includes not only the freedoms explicitly mentioned in the Bill of Rights, but also a freedom of personal choice in certain matters of marriage and family life. This implicit constitutional liberty, the Court in *Wade* held, includes the freedom of a woman to decide whether to terminate a pregnancy.

But the Court in *Wade* also recognized that a State has legitimate interests during a pregnancy in both ensuring the health of the mother and protecting potential human life. These state interests, which were found to be "separate and distinct" and to "grow[] in substantiality as the woman approaches term," *id.* at 162–63, pose a conflict with a woman's untrammeled freedom of choice. . . .

In *Maher v. Roe*, 432 U.S. 464, the Court was presented with the question whether the scope of personal constitutional freedom recognized in *Roe v. Wade* included an entitlement to Medicaid payments for abortions that are not medically necessary. . . . The doctrine of *Roe v. Wade*, the Court held in *Maher*, "protects the woman from unduly burdensome interference with her freedom to decide whether to terminate her pregnancy," *id.* at 473–74, such as the severe criminal sanctions at issue in *Roe v. Wade*, *supra*, or the absolute requirement of spousal consent for an abortion challenged in *Planned Parenthood of Central Missouri v. Danforth*, 428 U.S. 52.

But the constitutional freedom recognized in *Wade* and its progeny, the *Maher* Court explained, did not prevent Connecticut from making "a value judgment favoring childbirth over abortion, and . . .

implement[ing] that judgment by the allocation of public funds." At 474.

. . .

The Hyde Amendment, like the Connecticut welfare regulation at issue in *Maher*, places no governmental obstacle in the path of a woman who chooses to terminate her pregnancy, but rather, by means of unequal subsidization of abortion and other medical services, encourages alternative activity deemed in the public interest. The present case does differ factually from *Maher* insofar as that case involved a failure to fund nontherapeutic abortions, whereas the Hyde Amendment withholds funding of certain medically necessary abortions. Accordingly, the appellees argue that because the Hyde Amendment affects a significant interest not present or asserted in *Maher*—the interest of a woman in protecting her health during pregnancy—and because that interest lies at the core of the personal constitutional freedom recognized in *Wade*, the present case is constitutionally different from *Maher*. It is the appellees' view that to the extent that the Hyde Amendment withholds funding for certain medically necessary abortions, it clearly impinges on the constitutional principle recognized in *Wade*.

It is evident that a woman's interest in protecting her health was an important theme in *Wade*. . . . In fact, although the Court in *Wade* recognized that the state interest in protecting potential life becomes sufficiently compelling in the period after fetal viability to justify an absolute criminal prohibition of nontherapeutic abortions, the Court held that even after fetal viability a State may not prohibit abortions "necessary to preserve the life or health of the mother." *Id.* at 164. . . .

But, . . . it simply does not follow that a woman's freedom of choice carries with it a constitutional entitlement to the financial resources to avail herself of the full range of protected choices. The reason why was explained in *Maher:* although government may not place obstacles in the path of a woman's exercise of her freedom of choice, it need not remove those not of its own creation. Indigency falls in the latter category. The financial constraints that restrict an indigent woman's ability to enjoy the full range of constitutionally protected freedom of choice are the product not of governmental restrictions on access to abortions, but rather of her indigency. . . . The Hyde Amendment leaves an indigent woman with at least the same range of choice in deciding whether to obtain a medically necessary abortion as she would have had if Congress had chosen to subsidize no health care costs at all. We are thus not persuaded that the Hyde Amendment impinges on the constitutionally protected freedom of choice recognized in *Wade*.[19]

19. The appellees argue that the Hyde Amendment is unconstitutional because it "penalizes" the exercise of a woman's choice to terminate a pregnancy by abortion. *See Memorial Hospital v. Maricopa County*, 415 U.S. 250; *Shapiro v. Thompson*, 394 U.S. 618. This argument falls short of the mark. In *Maher*, the Court found only a "semantic difference" between the argument that Connecticut's refusal to subsidize nontherapeutic abortions "unduly interfere[d]" with the exercise of the constitutional liberty recognized in *Wade* and the argument that it "penalized" the exercise of that liberty. 432 U.S., at 474, n.8. And, regardless of how the claim was characterized, the *Maher* Court rejected the argument that Connecticut's refusal to subsidize protected conduct, without more, impinged on the constitutional freedom of choice. This reasoning is equally applicable in the present case. A substantial constitutional question would arise if Congress had attempted to withhold all Medicaid benefits from an otherwise eligible candidate simply because that candidate had exercised her constitutionally protected freedom to terminate her pregnancy by abortion. This would be analo-

Although the liberty protected by the Due Process Clause affords protection against unwarranted government interference with freedom of choice in the context of certain personal decisions, it does not confer an entitlement to such funds as may be necessary to realize all the advantages of that freedom. To hold otherwise would mark a drastic change in our understanding of the Constitution. It cannot be that because government may not prohibit the use of contraceptives, *Griswold v. Connecticut*, 381 U.S. 479, or prevent parents from sending their child to a private school, *Pierce v. Society of Sisters*, 268 U.S. 510, government, therefore, has an affirmative constitutional obligation to ensure that all persons have the financial resources to obtain contraceptives or send their children to private schools. To translate the limitation on governmental power implicit in the Due Process Clause into an affirmative funding obligation would require Congress to subsidize the medically necessary abortion of an indigent woman even if Congress had not enacted a Medicaid program to subsidize other medically necessary services. Nothing in the Due Process Clause supports such an extraordinary result. Whether freedom of choice that is constitutionally

gous to *Sherbert v. Verner*, 374 U.S. 398, where this Court held that a State may not, consistent with the First and Fourteenth Amendments, withhold *all* unemployment compensation benefits from a claimant who would otherwise be eligible for such benefits but for the fact that she is unwilling to work one day per week on her Sabbath. But the Hyde Amendment, unlike the statute at issue in *Sherbert*, does not provide for such a broad disqualification from receipt of public benefits. Rather, the Hyde Amendment, like the Connecticut welfare provision at issue in *Maher*, represents simply a refusal to subsidize certain protected conduct. A refusal to fund protected activity, without more, cannot be equated with the imposition of a "penalty" on that activity.

protected warrants federal subsidization is a question for Congress to answer, not a matter of constitutional entitlement. Accordingly, we conclude that the Hyde Amendment does not impinge on the due process liberty recognized in *Wade*.

B

The appellees also argue that the Hyde Amendment contravenes rights secured by the Religion Clauses of the First Amendment. It is the appellees' view that the Hyde Amendment violates the Establishment Clause because it incorporates into law the doctrines of the Roman Catholic Church concerning the sinfulness of abortion and the time at which life commences. Moreover, insofar as a woman's decision to seek a medically necessary abortion may be a product of her religious beliefs under certain Protestant and Jewish tenets, the appellees assert that the funding limitations of the Hyde Amendment impinge on the freedom of religion guaranteed by the Free Exercise Clause.

1

It is well settled that "a legislative enactment does not contravene the Establishment Clause if it has a secular legislative purpose, if its principal or primary effect neither advances nor inhibits religion, and if it does not foster an excessive governmental entanglement with religion." *Committee for Pub. Ed. & Rel. Lib. v. Regan*, 444 U.S. 646. Applying this standard, the District Court properly concluded that the Hyde Amendment does not run afoul of the Establishment Clause. . . .

2

We need not address the merits of the appellees' arguments concerning the Free Exercise Clause, because the appellees lack standing to raise a free exercise challenge to the Hyde Amendment. . . . [N]one al-leged, much less proved, that she sought an abortion under compulsion of religious belief. . . .

C

It remains to be determined whether the Hyde Amentment violates the equal protection component of the Fifth Amendment. This challenge is premised on the fact that, although federal reimbursement is available under Medicaid for medically necessary services generally, the Hyde Amendment does not permit federal reimbursement of all medically necessary abortions. The District Court held, and the appellees argue here, that this selective subsidization violates the constitutional guarantee of equal protection.

The guarantee of equal protection under the Fifth Amendment is not a source of substantive rights or liberties, but rather a right to be free from invidious discrimination in statutory classifications and other governmental activity.

I

For the reasons stated above, we have already concluded that the Hyde Amendment violates no constitutionally protected substantive rights. We now conclude as well that it is not predicated on a constitutionally suspect classification. In reaching this conclusion, we again draw guidance from the Court's decision in *Maher v. Roe*. . . .

It is our view that the present case is indistinguishable from *Maher* in this respect. Here, as in *Maher*, the principal impact of the Hyde Amendment falls on the indigent. But that fact does not itself render the funding restriction constitutionally invalid, for this Court has held repeatedly that poverty, standing alone, is not a suspect classification. *See, e.g., James v. Valtierra*, 402 U.S. 137. . . .

2

The remaining question then is whether the Hyde Amendment is rationally related to a legitimate governmental objective. It is the Government's position that the Hyde Amendment bears a rational relationship to its legitimate interest in protecting the potential life of the fetus. We agree.

. . . [T]he Hyde Amendment, by encouraging childbirth except in the most urgent circumstances, is rationally related to the legitimate governmental objective of protecting potential life. By subsidizing the medical expenses of indigent women who carry their pregnancies to term while not subsidizing the comparable expenses of women who undergo abortions (except those whose lives are threatened), Congress has established incentives that make childbirth a more attractive alternative than abortion for persons eligible for Medicaid. These incentives bear a direct relationship to the legitimate congressional interest in protecting potential life. Nor is it irrational that Congress has authorized federal reimbursement for medically necessary services generally, but not for certain medically necessary abortions.[28] Abortion is inherently different from other medical procedures, because no other procedure involves the purposeful termination of a potential life.

. . .

Where, as here, the Congress has neither invaded a substantive constitutional right or freedom, nor enacted legislation

28. In fact, abortion is not the only "medically necessary" service for which federal funds under Medicaid are sometimes unavailable to otherwise eligible claimants. *See* 42 U.S.C. § 1396d(a)(17)(B) (inpatient hospital care of patients between 21 and 65 in institutions for tuberculosis or mental disease not covered by Title XIX).

that purposefully operates to the detriment of a suspect class, the only requirement of equal protection is that congressional action be rationally related to a legitimate governmental interest. The Hyde Amendment satisfies that standard. It is not the mission of this Court or any other to decide whether the balance of competing interests reflected in the Hyde Amendment is wise social policy. If that were our mission, not every Justice who has subscribed to the judgment of the Court today could have done so. . . .

IV

For the reasons stated in this opinion, we hold that a State that participates in the Medicaid program is not obligated under Title XIX to continue to fund those medically necessary abortions for which federal reimbursement is unavailable under the Hyde Amendment. We further hold that the funding restrictions of the Hyde Amendment violate neither the Fifth Amendment nor the Establishment Clause of the First Amendment. It is also our view that the appellees lack standing to raise a challenge to the Hyde Amendment under the Free Exercise Clause of the First Amendment. Accordingly, the judgment of the District Court is reversed, and the case is remanded to that court for further proceedings consistent with this opinion.

It is so ordered.

MR. JUSTICE WHITE, concurring.

I join the Court's opinion and judgment with these additional remarks.

Roe v. Wade, 410 U.S. 113 (1973), held that prior to viability of the fetus, the governmental interest in potential life was insufficient to justify overriding the due process right of a pregnant woman to terminate her pregnancy by abortion. In the last trimester, however, the State's interest in fetal life was deemed sufficiently strong to warrant a ban on abortions, but only if continuing the pregnancy did not threaten the life or health of the mother. In the latter event, the State was required to respect the choice of the mother to terminate the pregnancy and protect her health.

Drawing upon *Roe v. Wade* and the cases that followed it, the dissent extrapolates the general proposition that the governmental interest in potential life may in no event be pursued at the expense of the mother's health. It then notes that under the Hyde Amendment, Medicaid refuses to fund abortions where carrying to term threatens maternal health but finances other medically indicated procedures, including childbirth. The dissent submits that the Hyde Amendment therefore fails the first requirement imposed by the Fifth Amendment and recognized by the Court's opinion today—that the challenged official action must serve a legitimate governmental goal.

The argument has a certain internal logic, but it is not legally sound. The constitutional right recognized in *Roe v. Wade* was the right to choose to undergo an abortion without coercive interference by the government. As the Court points out, *Roe v. Wade* did not purport to adjudicate a right to have abortions funded by the government, but only to be free from unreasonable official interference with private choice. At an appropriate stage in a pregnancy, for example, abortions could be prohibited to implement the governmental interest in potential life, but in no case to the damage of the health of the mother, whose choice to suffer an abortion rather than risk her health the government was forced to respect.

Roe v. Wade thus dealt with the circumstances in which the governmental interest in potential life would justify official inter-

ference with the abortion choices of pregnant women. There is no such calculus involved here. The government does not seek to interfere with or to impose any coercive restraint on the choice of any woman to have an abortion. The woman's choice remains unfettered, the government is not attempting to use its interest in life to justify a coercive restraint, and hence in disbursing its Medicaid funds it is free to implement rationally what *Roe v. Wade* recognized to be its legitimate interest in a potential life by covering the medical costs of childbirth but denying funds for abortions. Neither *Roe v. Wade* nor any of the cases decided in its wake invalidates this legislative preference. We decided as much in *Maher v. Roe*, 432 U.S. 464 (1977), when we rejected the claims that refusing funds for nontherapeutic abortions while defraying the medical costs of childbirth, although not an outright prohibition, nevertheless infringed the fundamental right to choose to terminate a pregnancy by abortion and also violated the equal protection component of the Fifth Amendment. I would not abandon *Maher* and extend *Roe v. Wade* to forbid the legislative policy expressed in the Hyde Amendment.

. . .

Mr. Justice Brennan, with whom Mr. Justice Marshall and Mr. Justice Blackmun join, dissenting.

I agree entirely with my Brother Stevens that the State's interest in protecting the potential life of the fetus cannot justify the exclusion of financially and medically needy women from the benefits to which they would otherwise be entitled solely because the treatment that a doctor has concluded is medically necessary involves an abortion. *See post.* I write separately to express my continuing disagreement with the Court's mischaracterization of the nature of the fundamental right recognized in *Roe v. Wade,* 410 U.S. 113 (1973), and its misconception of the manner in which that right is infringed by federal and state legislation withdrawing all funding for medically necessary abortions.

Roe v. Wade held that the constitutional right to personal privacy encompasses a woman's decision whether or not to terminate her pregnancy. *Roe* and its progeny established that the pregnant woman has a right to be free from state interference with her choice to have an abortion—a right which, at least prior to the end of the first trimester, absolutely prohibits any governmental regulation of that highly personal decision. The proposition for which these cases stand thus is not that the State is under an affirmative obligation to ensure access to abortions for all who may desire them; it is that the State must refrain from wielding its enormous power and influence in a manner that might burden the pregnant woman's freedom to choose whether to have an abortion. The Hyde Amendment's denial of public funds for medically necessary abortions plainly intrudes upon this constitutionally protected decision, for both by design and in effect it serves to coerce indigent pregnant women to bear children that they would otherwise elect not to have.[4]

4. My focus throughout this opinion is upon the coercive impact of the congressional decision to fund one outcome of pregnancy—childbirth—while not funding the other—abortion. Because I believe this alone renders the Hyde Amendment unconstitutional, I do not dwell upon the other disparities that the Amendment produces in the treatment of rich and poor, pregnant and nonpregnant. I concur completely, however, in my Brother STEVENS' discussion of those disparities. Specifically, I agree that the congressional decision to fund all medically necessary procedures except for those that require an abortion is entirely irrational either as a

When viewed in the context of the Medicaid program to which it is appended, it is obvious that the Hyde Amendment is nothing less than an attempt by Congress to circumvent the dictates of the Constitution and achieve indirectly what *Roe v. Wade* said it could not do directly. Under

means of allocating health-care resources or otherwise serving legitimate social welfare goals. And that irrationality in turn exposes the Amendment for what it really is—a deliberate effort to discourage the exercise of a constitutionally protected right.

It is important to put this congressional decision in human terms. Nonpregnant women may be reimbursed for all medically necessary treatments. Pregnant women with analogous ailments, however, will be reimbursed only if the treatment involved does not happen to include an abortion. Since the refusal to fund will in some significant number of cases force the patient to forego medical assistance, the result is to refuse treatment for some genuine maladies not because they need not be treated, cannot be treated, or are too expensive to treat, and not because they relate to a deliberate choice to abort a pregnancy, but merely because treating them would as a practical matter require termination of that pregnancy. Even were one of the view that legislative hostility to abortions could justify a decision to fund obstetrics and child delivery services while refusing to fund nontherapeutic abortions, the present statutory scheme could not be saved. For here, that hostility has gone a good deal farther. Its consequence is to leave indigent sick women without treatment simply because of the medical fortuity that their illness cannot be treated unless their pregnancy is terminated. Antipathy to abortion, in short, has been permitted not only to ride roughshod over a woman's constitutional right to terminate her pregnancy in the fashion she chooses, but also to distort our Nation's health care programs. As a means of delivering health services, then, the Hyde Amendment is completely irrational. As a means of preventing abortions, it is concededly rational—brutally so. But this latter goal is constitutionally forbidden.

Title XIX of the Social Security Act, the Federal Government reimburses participating States for virtually all medically necessary services it provides to the categorically needy. The sole limitation of any significance is the Hyde Amendment's prohibition against the use of any federal funds to pay for the costs of abortions (except where the life of the mother would be endangered if the fetus were carried to term). As my Brother STEVENS persuasively demonstrates, exclusion of medically necessary abortions from Medicaid coverage cannot be justified as a cost-saving device. Rather, the Hyde Amendment is a transparent attempt by the Legislative Branch to impose the political majority's judgment of the morally acceptable and socially desirable preference on a sensitive and intimate decision that the Constitution entrusts to the individual. Worse yet, the Hyde Amendment does not foist that majoritarian viewpoint with equal measure upon everyone in our Nation, rich and poor alike; rather, it imposes that viewpoint only upon that segment of our society which, because of its position of political powerlessness, is least able to defend its privacy rights from the encroachments of state-mandated morality. The instant legislation thus calls for more exacting judicial review than in most other cases. . . .

Moreover, it is clear that the Hyde Amendment not only was designed to inhibit, but does in fact inhibit the woman's freedom to choose abortion over childbirth. "Pregnancy is unquestionably a condition requiring medical services. . . . Treatment for the condition may involve medical procedures for its termination, or medical procedures to bring the pregnancy to term, resulting in a live birth. '[A]bortion and childbirth, when stripped of the sensitive moral arguments surrounding the abortion controversy, are simply two alternative medical methods of dealing with pregnancy. . . .'" *Beal v. Doe, supra,* at 449 (BRENNAN, J., dissenting) (quoting *Roe v. Norton,* 408 F. Supp. 660, 663, n.3 [Conn. 1975]). In every pregnancy, one of these two courses of treatment is medically necessary, and the poverty-stricken woman depends on the Medicaid Act to pay for the expenses associated with that procedure. But under the Hyde Amendment, the Government will fund only those procedures incidental to childbirth. By thus injecting coercive financial incentives favoring childbirth into a decision that is constitutionally guaranteed to be free from governmental intrusion, the Hyde Amendment deprives the indigent woman of her freedom to choose abortion over maternity, thereby impinging on the due process liberty right recognized in *Roe v. Wade.*

The Court's contrary conclusion is premised on its belief that "[t]he financial constraints that restrict an indigent woman's ability to enjoy the full range of constitutionally protected freedom of choice are the product not of governmental restrictions on access to abortions, but rather of her indigency." *Ante.* Accurate as this statement may be, it reveals only half the picture. For what the Court fails to appreciate is that it is not simply the woman's indigency that interferes with her freedom of choice, but the combination of her own poverty and the government's unequal subsidization of abortion and childbirth.

The fundamental flaw in the Court's due process analysis, then, is its failure to acknowledge that the discriminatory distribution of the benefits of governmental largesse can discourage the exercise of fundamental liberties just as effectively as can an outright denial of those rights through criminal and regulatory sanctions. Implicit in the Court's reasoning is the notion that as long as the government is not obligated to provide its citizens with certain benefits or privileges, it may condition the grant of such benefits on the recipient's relinquishment of his constitutional rights.

It would belabor the obvious to expound at any great length on the illegitimacy of a state policy that interferes with the exercise of fundamental rights through the selective bestowal of governmental favors. It suffices to note that we have heretofore never hesitated to invalidate any scheme of granting or withholding financial benefits that incidentally or intentionally burdens one manner of exercising a constitutionally protected choice. To take but one example of many, *Sherbert v. Verner*, 374 U.S. 398 (1963), involved a South Carolina unemployment insurance statute that required recipients to accept suitable employment when offered, even if the grounds for refusal stemmed from religious convictions. Even though the recipients possessed no entitlement to compensation, the Court held that the State could not cancel the benefits of a Seventh Day Adventist who had refused a job requiring her to work on Saturdays. The Court's explanation is particularly instructive for the present case:

Here not only is it apparent that appellant's declared ineligibility for benefits derives solely from the practice of her religion, but the pressure upon her to forego that practice is unmistakable. The ruling forces her to choose between following the precepts of her religion and forfeiting benefits, on the one hand, and abandoning one of the precepts of her religion in order to accept work, on the other hand. Governmental imposition of such a choice puts the same kind of burden upon the free exercise of religion as would a fine imposed against appellant for her Saturday worship.

Nor may the South Carolina court's construction of the statute be saved from constitutional infirmity on the ground that unemployment compensation benefits are not appellant's 'right' but merely a 'privilege.' It is too late in the day to doubt that the liberties of religion and expression may be infringed by the denial of or placing of conditions upon a benefit or privilege. . . . [T]o condition the availability of benefits upon the appellant's willingness to violate a cardinal principle of her religious faith effectively penalizes the free exercise of her constitutional liberties. (*Id.* at 404–6.)

See also *Frost & Frost Trucking Co. v. Railroad Comm'n*, 271 U.S. 583 (1926); *Speiser v. Randall*, 357 U.S. 513 (1958); *Elfbrandt v. Russell*, 384 U.S. 11 (1966); *Goldberg v. Kelly*, 397 U.S. 254 (1970); *United States Dept. of Agric. v. Moreno*, 413 U.S. 528 (1973); *Southeastern Promotions, Ltd. v. Conrad*, 420 U.S. 546 (1975). Cf. *Shapiro v. Thompson*, 394 U.S. 618 (1969); *Memorial Hospital v. Maricopa County*, 415 U.S. 250 (1974).

The Medicaid program cannot be distinguished from these other statutory schemes that unconstitutionally burdened fundamental rights.[6] Here, as in *Sherbert*,

---

6. The Court rather summarily rejects the argument that the Hyde Amendment unconstitutionally penalizes the woman's exercise of her right to choose an abortion with the comment that "[a] refusal to fund protected activity, without more, cannot be equated with the imposition of a 'penalty' on that activity." *Ante*, n.19. To begin with, the Court overlooks the fact that there is "more" than a simple refusal to fund a protected activity in this case; instead, there is a program that selectively funds but one of two choices of a constitutionally protected decision, thereby penalizing the election of the disfavored option.

Moreover, it is no answer to assert that no "penalty" is being imposed because the State is only refusing to pay for the specific costs of the

the government withholds financial benefits in a manner that discourages the exercise of a due process liberty: The indigent woman who chooses to assert her constitutional right to have an abortion can do so only on pain of sacrificing health care benefits to which she would otherwise be entitled. Over 50 years ago, Mr. Justice Sutherland, writing for the Court in *Frost & Frost Trucking Co. v. Railroad Comm'n, supra,* at 593–94, made the following observation, which is as true now as it was then:

> It would be a palpable incongruity to strike down an act of state legislation which, by words of express divestment, seeks to strip the citizen of rights guaranteed by the federal Constitution, but to uphold an act by which the same result is accomplished under the guise of a surrender of a right in exchange for a valuable privilege which the state threatens otherwise to withhold. It is not necessary to challenge the proposition that, as a general rule, the state, having power to deny a privilege altogether, may grant it upon such conditions as it sees fit to impose. But the power of the state in

---

protected activity rather than withholding other Medicaid benefits to which the recipient would be entitled or taking some other action more readily characterized as "punitive." Surely the government could not provide free transportation to the polling booths only for those citizens who vote for Democratic candidates, even though the failure to provide the same benefit to Republicans "represents simply a refusal to subsidize certain protected conduct," *id.*, and does not involve the denial of any other governmental benefits. Whether the State withholds only the special costs of a disfavored option or penalizes the individual more broadly for the manner in which she exercises her choice, it cannot interfere with a constitutionally protected decision through the coercive use of governmental largesse.

that respect is not unlimited; and one of the limitations is that it may not impose conditions which require the relinquishment of constitutional rights. If the state may compel the surrender of one constitutional right as a condition of its favor, it may, in like manner, compel a surrender of all. It is inconceivable that guaranties embedded in the Constitution of the United States may thus be manipulated out of existence.

I respectfully dissent.

MR. JUSTICE MARSHALL, dissenting.

. . . Under the Hyde Amendment, federal funding is denied for abortions that are medically necessary and that are necessary to avert severe and permanent damage to the health of the mother. The Court's opinion studiously avoids recognizing the undeniable fact that for women eligible for Medicaid—poor women—denial of a Medicaid-funded abortion is equivalent to denial of legal abortion altogether. By definition, these women do not have the money to pay for an abortion themselves. If abortion is medically necessary and a funded abortion is unavailable, they must resort to back-alley butchers, attempt to induce an abortion themselves by crude and dangerous methods, or suffer the serious medical consequences of attempting to carry the fetus to term. Because legal abortion is not a realistic option for such women, the predictable result of the Hyde Amendment will be a significant increase in the number of poor women who will die or suffer significant health damage because of an inability to procure necessary medical services.

The denial of Medicaid benefits to individuals who meet all the statutory criteria for eligibility, solely because the treatment that is medically necessary involves the exercise of the fundamental right to choose abortion, is a form of discrimination repugnant to the equal protection of the laws guaranteed by the Constitution. The Court's decision today marks a retreat from *Roe v. Wade* and represents a cruel blow to the most powerless members of our society. I dissent.

I

In its present form, the Hyde Amendment restricts federal funding for abortion to cases in which "the life of the mother would be endangered if the fetus were carried to term" and "for such medical procedures necessary for the victims of rape or incest when such rape or incest has been reported promptly to a law enforcement agency or public health service." Federal funding is thus unavailable even when severe and long-lasting health damage to the mother is a virtual certainty. Nor are federal funds available when severe health damage, or even death, will result to the fetus if it is carried to term.

The record developed below reveals that the standards set forth in the Hyde Amendment exclude the majority of cases in which the medical profession would recommend abortion as medically necessary. . . .

The impact of the Hyde Amendment on indigent women falls into four major categories. First, the Hyde Amendment prohibits federal funding for abortions that are necessary in order to protect the health and sometimes the life of the mother. Numerous conditions—such as cancer, rheumatic fever, diabetes, malnutrition, phlebitis, sickle cell anemia, and heart disease—substantially increase the risks associated with pregnancy or are themselves aggravated by pregnancy. Such conditions may make an abortion medically necessary in the judgment of a physician, but cannot be funded under the Hyde Amendment. Further, the health risks of undergoing an abortion increase dramatically as pregnancy becomes more advanced. By the time a pregnancy has progressed to the point where a physician is able to certify that it endangers the life of the mother, it is in many cases too late to prevent her death because abortion is no longer safe. There are also instances in which a woman's life will not be immediately threatened by carrying the pregnancy to term, but aggravation of another medical condition will significantly shorten her life expectancy. These cases as well are not fundable under the Hyde Amendment.

Second, federal funding is denied in cases in which severe mental disturbances will be created by unwanted pregnancies. The result of such psychological disturbances may be suicide, attempts at self-abortion, or child abuse. . . .

Third, the Hyde Amendment denies funding for the majority of women whose pregnancies have been caused by rape or incest. The prerequisite of a report within 60 days serves to exclude those who are afraid of recounting what has happened or are in fear of unsympathetic treatment by the authorities. . . .

Finally, federal funding is unavailable in cases in which it is known that the fetus itself will be unable to survive. . . . The Hyde Amendment, purportedly designed to safeguard "the legitimate governmental interest of protecting potential life," *ante*, excludes federal funding in such cases.

An optimistic estimate indicates that as many as 100 excess deaths may occur each year as a result of the Hyde Amendment. The record contains no estimate of the health damage that may occur to poor women, but it shows that it will be considerable.

II

The Court resolves the equal protection issue in this case through a relentlessly formalistic catechism. Adhering to its "two-tiered" approach to equal protection, the Court first decides that so-called strict scrutiny is not required because the Hyde Amendment does not violate the Due Process Clause and is not predicated on a constitutionally suspect classification. . . . Observing that previous cases have recognized "the legitimate governmental objective of protecting potential life," *ante,* the Court concludes that the Hyde Amendment "establishe[s] incentives that make childbirth a more attractive alternative than abortion for persons eligible for Medicaid," *id.,* and is therefore rationally related to that governmental interest.

I continue to believe that the rigid "two-tiered" approach is inappropriate and that the Constitution requires a more exacting standard of review than mere rationality in cases such as this one. Further, in my judgment the Hyde Amendment cannot pass constitutional muster even under the rational-basis standard of review.

A

This case is perhaps the most dramatic illustration to date of the deficiencies in the Court's obsolete "two-tiered" approach to the Equal Protection Clause. [Citations omitted.] With all deference, I am unable to understand how the Court can afford the same level of scrutiny to the legislation involved here—whose cruel impact falls exclusively on indigent pregnant women—that it has given to legislation distinguishing opticians from opthalmologists, or to other legislation that makes distinctions between economic interests more than able to protect themselves in the political process. . . .

B

. . .

The class burdened by the Hyde Amendment consists of indigent women, a substantial proportion of whom are members of minority races. As I observed in *Maher,* nonwhite women obtain abortions at nearly double the rate of whites, *id.* at 459. In my view, the fact that the burden of the Hyde Amendment falls exclusively on financially destitute women suggests "a special condition, which tends seriously to curtail the operation of those political processes ordinarily to be relied upon to protect minorities, and which may call for a correspondingly more searching judicial inquiry." *United States v. Carolene Products,* 304 U.S. 144, 152–53, n.4 (1938). For this reason, I continue to believe that "a showing that state action has a devastating impact on the lives of minority racial groups must be relevant" for purposes of equal protection analysis. *Jefferson v. Hackney,* 406 U.S. 535, 575–76 (1972) (MARSHALL, J., dissenting).

As I explained in *Maher,* the asserted state interest in protecting potential life is insufficient to "outweigh the deprivation or serious discouragement of a vital constitutional right of especial importance to poor and minority women." 432 U.S., at 461. In *Maher,* the Court found a permissible state interest in encouraging normal childbirth. *Id.* at 477, 478, 479. The governmental interest in the present case is substantially weaker than in *Maher,* for under the Hyde Amendment funding is refused even in cases in which normal childbirth will not result: one can scarcely speak of "normal childbirth" in cases where the fetus will die shortly after birth, or in which the mother's life will be shortened or her health otherwise gravely impaired by the birth. Nevertheless, the Hyde Amendment denies funding even in such cases. In these circumstances, I am unable to see how even a minimally rational legislature could conclude that the interest in fetal life outweighs the brutal effect of the Hyde Amendment on indigent women. Moreover, both the legislation in *Maher* and the Hyde Amendment were designed to deprive poor and minority women of the constitutional right to choose abortion. That purpose is not constitutionally permitted under *Roe v. Wade.*

C

Although I would abandon the strict-scrutiny/rational-basis dichotomy in equal protection analysis, it is by no means necessary to reject that traditional approach to conclude, as I do, that the Hyde Amendment is a denial of equal protection. . . .

The Court treats this case as though it were controlled by *Maher.* To the contrary, this case is the mirror image of *Maher.* The result in *Maher* turned on the fact that the legislation there under consideration discouraged only nontherapeutic, or medically unnecessary, abortions. In the Court's view, denial of Medicaid funding for nontherapeutic abortions was not a denial of equal protection because Medicaid funds were available only for medically necessary procedures. Thus the plaintiffs were seeking benefits which were not available to others similarly situated. I continue to believe that *Maher* was wrongly decided. But it is apparent that while the plaintiffs in *Maher* were seeking a benefit not available to others similarly situated, respondents are protesting their exclusion from a benefit that is available to all others similarly situated. This, it need hardly be said, is a crucial difference for equal protection purposes.

Under Title XIX and the Hyde Amendment, funding is available for essentially all necessary medical treatment for the poor. Respondents have met the statutory re-

quirements for eligibility, but they are excluded because the treatment that is medically necessary involves the exercise of a fundamental right, the right to choose an abortion. In short, respondents have been deprived of a governmental benefit for which they are otherwise eligible, solely because they have attempted to exercise a constitutional right. The interest asserted by the government, the protection of fetal life, has been declared constitutionally subordinate to respondents' interest in preserving their lives and health by obtaining medically necessary treatment. *Roe v. Wade, supra.* And finally, the purpose of the legislation was to discourage the exercise of the fundamental right. In such circumstances the Hyde Amendment must be invalidated because it does not meet even the rational-basis standard of review.

III

. . .

In this case, the Federal Government has taken upon itself the burden of financing practically all medically necessary expenditures. One category of medically necessary expenditure has been singled out for exclusion, and the sole basis for the exclusion is a premise repudiated for purposes of constitutional law in *Roe v. Wade.* The consequence is a devastating impact on the lives and health of poor women. I do not believe that a Constitution committed to the equal protection of the laws can tolerate this result. I dissent.

Mr. Justice Blackmun, dissenting.

I join the dissent of Mr. Justice Brennan and agree wholeheartedly with his and Mr. Justice Stevens' respective observations and descriptions of what the Court is doing in this latest round of "abortion cases."

Mr. Justice Stevens, dissenting.

"The federal sovereign, like the States, must govern impartially. The concept of equal justice under law is served by the Fifth Amendment's guarantee of due process, as well as by the Equal Protection Clause of the Fourteenth Amendment." *Hampton v. Mow Sun Wong*, 426 U.S. 88, 100. When the sovereign provides a special benefit or a special protection for a class of persons, it must define the membership in the class by neutral criteria; it may not make special exceptions for reasons that are constitutionally insufficient.

This case involves the pool of benefits that Congress created by enacting Title XIX of the Social Security Act in 1965. Individuals who satisfy two neutral statutory criteria—financial need and medical need—are entitled to equal access to that pool. The question is whether certain persons who satisfy those criteria may be denied access to benefits solely because they must exercise the constitutional right to have an abortion in order to obtain the medical care they need. Our prior cases plainly dictate the answer to that question.

A fundamentally different question was decided in *Maher v. Roe*, 432 U.S. 464. Unlike these plaintiffs, the plaintiffs in *Maher* did not satisfy the neutral criterion of medical need; they sought a subsidy for nontherapeutic abortions—medical procedures which by definition they did not need. In rejecting that claim, the Court held that their constitutional right to choose that procedure did not impose a duty on the State to subsidize the exercise of that right. Nor did the fact that the State had undertaken to pay for the necessary medical care associated with childbirth require the State also to pay for abortions that were not necessary; for only necessary medical procedures satisfied the neutral statutory criteria. Nontherapeutic abortions were simply outside the ambit of the medical benefits program. Thus, in *Maher*, the plaintiffs' desire to exercise a constitutional right gave rise to neither special access nor special exclusion from the pool of benefits created by Title XIX.

This case involves a special exclusion of women who, by definition, are confronted with a choice between two serious harms: serious health damage to themselves on the one hand and abortion on the other. The competing interests are the interest in maternal health and the interest in protecting potential human life. It is now part of our law that the pregnant woman's decision as to which of these conflicting interests shall prevail is entitled to constitutional protection.

In *Roe v. Wade*, 410 U.S. 113, and *Doe v. Bolton*, 410 U.S. 179, the Court recognized that the States have a legitimate and protectible interest in potential human life. 410 U.S., at 162. But the Court explicitly held that prior to fetal viability that interest may not justify any governmental burden on the woman's choice to have an abortion nor even any regulation of abortion except in furtherance of the State's interest in the woman's health. In effect, the Court held that a woman's freedom to elect to have an abortion prior to viability has absolute constitutional protection, subject only to valid health regulations. Indeed, in *Roe v. Wade* the Court held that even after fetal viability, a State may "regulate, and even proscribe, abortion *except where it is necessary, in appropriate medical judgment, for the preservation of the life or health of the mother.*" 410 U.S., at 165. (Emphasis added.) We have a duty to respect that holding. The Court simply shirks that duty in this case.

If a woman has a constitutional right to place a higher value on avoiding either serious harm to her own health or perhaps an abnormal childbirth[3] than on protecting

---

3. The Court rests heavily on the premise—recognized in both *Roe* and *Maher*—that the

potential life, the exercise of that right cannot provide the basis for the denial of a benefit to which she would otherwise be entitled. The Court's sterile equal protection analysis evades this critical though simple point. The Court focuses exclusively on the "legitimate interest in protecting the potential life of the fetus." *Ante.* It concludes that since the Hyde amendments further that interest, the exclusion they create is rational and therefore constitutional. But it is misleading to speak of the Government's legitimate interest in the fetus without reference to the context in which that interest was held to be legitimate. For *Roe v. Wade* squarely held that the States may not protect that interest when a conflict with the interest in a pregnant woman's health exists. It is thus perfectly clear that neither the Federal Government nor the States may exclude a woman from medical benefits to which she would otherwise be entitled solely to further an interest in potential life when a physician, "in appropriate medical judgment," certifies that an abortion is necessary "for the preservation of the life or health of the mother." *Roe v. Wade, supra,* 410 U.S., at 165. The Court totally fails to explain why this reasoning is not dispositive here.[4]

_____

State's legitimate interest in preserving potential life provides a sufficient justification for funding medical services that are necessarily associated with normal childbirth without also funding abortions that are not medically necessary. The *Maher* opinion repeatedly referred to the policy of favoring "normal childbirth." *See* 432 U.S., at 477, 478, 479. But this case involves a refusal to fund abortions which are medically necessary to avoid abnormal childbirth.

4. This case thus illustrates the flaw in the method of equal protection analysis by which one chooses among alternative "levels of scrutiny" and then determines whether the extent to which a particular legislative measure furthers a given governmental objective transcends the

It cannot be denied that the harm inflicted upon women in the excluded class is grievous.[5] As the Court's comparison of the

_____

predetermined threshold. *See Craig v. Boren,* 429 U.S. 190, 211–212 (STEVENS, J., concurring). That method may simply bypass the real issue. The relevant question in this case is whether the Court must attach greater weight to the individual's interest in being included in the class than to the governmental interest in keeping the individual out. Since *Roe v. Wade* squarely held that the individual interest in the freedom to elect an abortion and the State interest in protecting maternal health *both* outweigh the State's interest in protecting potential life prior to viability, the Court's "equal protection analysis" is doubly erroneous.

In responding to my analysis of this case, MR. JUSTICE WHITE has described the constitutional right recognized in *Roe v. Wade* as "the right to choose to undergo an abortion without coercive interference by the Government" or a right "only to be free from unreasonable official interference with private choice." *Ante.* No such language is found in the *Roe* opinion itself. Rather, that case squarely held that State interference is unreasonable if it attaches a greater importance to the interest in potential life than to the interest in protecting the mother's health. One could with equal justification describe the right protected by the First Amendment as the right to make speeches without coercive interference by the Government and then sustain a Government subsidy for all medically needy persons except those who publicly advocate a change of administration.

5. The record is replete with examples of serious physical harm. *See, e.g.,* Judge Dooling's opinion in 79–1268, slip op., at 106:

"Women, particularly young women, suffering from diabetes are likely to experience high risks of health damage to themselves and their fetuses; the woman may become blind through the worsening during pregnancy of a diabetic retinopathy; in the case, particularly, of the juvenile diabetic, Dr. Eliot testified there is evidence that a series of pregnancies advances the diabetes faster; given an aggravated diabetic condition,

differing forms of the Hyde Amendment that have been enacted since 1976 demonstrates, the Court expressly approves the exclusion of benefits in "instances where

---

other risks increased through pregnancy are kidney problems, and vascular problems of the extremities."

See also the affidavit of Jane Doe in 79–1268:

"3. I am twenty-five years old. I am married with four living children. Following the birth of my third child in November of 1976, I developed a serious case of phlebitis from which I have not completely recovered. Carrying another pregnancy to term would greatly aggravate this condition and increase the risk of blood clots to the lung.

"4. On July 29, 1977, I went to the Fertility Control Clinic at St. Paul-Ramsey Hospital, St. Paul, Minnesota to request an abortion. They informed me that a new law prohibits any federal reimbursement for abortions except those necessary to save the life of the mother and that they cannot afford to do this operation free for me.

"5. I cannot afford to pay for an abortion myself, and without Medicaid reimbursement, I cannot obtain a safe, legal abortion. According to the doctor, Dr. Jane E. Hodgson, without an abortion I might suffer serious and permanent health problems." App. in No. 79–1268, at 109–10.

And see the case of the Jane Doe in 79–4, 79–5, 79–491, as recounted in Dr. Zbaraz' affidavit:

"Jane Doe is thirty-eight years old and has had nine previous pregnancies. She has a history of varicose veins and thrombophlebitis (blood clots) of the left leg. The varicose veins can be, and in her case were, caused by multiple pregnancies: the weight of the uterus on her pelvic veins increased the blood pressure in the veins of her lower extremities; those veins dilated and her circulation was impaired resulting in thrombophlebitis of her left leg. The varicosities of her lower extremities became so severe that they required partial surgical removal in 1973.

"2. Given this medical history, Jane Doe's varicose veins are almost certain to recur if she continues her pregnancy. Such a recurrence would

severe and long lasting physical health damage to the mother" is the predictable consequence of carrying the pregnancy to term. Indeed, as the Solicitor General acknowledged with commendable candor, the logic of the Court's position would justify a holding that it would be constitutional to deny funding to a medically and financially needy person even if abortion were the only lifesaving medical procedure available. Because a denial of benefits for medically necessary abortions inevitably causes serious harm to the excluded women, it is tantamount to severe punishment. In my judgment, that denial cannot be justified unless Government may, in effect, punish women who want abortions. But as the Court unequivocally held in *Roe v. Wade*, this the Government may not do.

Nor can it be argued that the exclusion of this type of medically necessary treatment of the indigent can be justified on fiscal grounds. There are some especially costly forms of treatment that may reasonably be excluded from the program in order to preserve the assets in the pool and extend its benefits to the maximum number of needy persons. Fiscal considerations may compel certain difficult choices in order to improve the protection afforded to

---

require a second operative procedure for their removal. Given her medical history, there is also about a 30 percent risk that her thrombophlebitis will recur during the pregnancy in the form of 'deep vein' thrombophlebitis (the surface veins of her left leg having previously been partially removed). This condition would impair circulation and might require prolonged hospitalization with bed rest.

"3. Considering Jane Doe's medical history of varicose veins and thrombophlebitis, particularly against the background of her age and multiple pregnancies, it is my view that an abortion is medically necessary for her, though not necessary to preserve her life." App. in 79–4, 79–5, 79–491, at 92.

the entire benefited class. But, ironically, the exclusion of medically necessary abortions harms the entire class as well as its specific victims. For the records in both *McRae* and *Zbaraz* demonstrate that the cost of an abortion is only a small fraction of the costs associated with childbirth. Thus, the decision to tolerate harm to indigent persons who need an abortion in order to avoid "serious and long lasting health damage" is one that is financed by draining money out of the pool that is used to fund all other necessary medical procedures. Unlike most invidious classifications, this discrimination harms not only its direct victims but also the remainder of the class of needy persons that the pool was designed to benefit. . . .

Having decided to alleviate some of the hardships of poverty by providing necessary medical care, the Government must use neutral criteria in distributing benefits. It may not deny benefits to a financially and medically needy person simply be-cause he is a Republican, a Catholic, or an Oriental—or because he has spoken against a program the Government has a legitimate interest in furthering. In sum, it may not create exceptions for the sole purpose of furthering a governmental interest that is constitutionally subordinate to the individual interest that the entire program was designed to protect. The Hyde amendments not only exclude financially and medically needy persons from the pool of benefits for a constitutionally insufficient reason; they also require the expenditure of millions and millions of dollars in order to thwart the exercise of a constitutional right, thereby effectively inflicting serious and long lasting harm on impoverished women who want and need abortions for valid medical reasons. In my judgment, these amendments constitute an unjustifiable, and indeed blatant, violation of the sovereign's duty to govern impartially.

I respectfully dissent.

CASE QUESTIONS

1. All of the *Poelker* and *Maher* questions could fruitfully be reconsidered for *Harris v. McRae.* In addition, one might ask whether anything would remain of the dissenters' constitutional argument, if Congress, in response to the district court injunction and in a desire to avoid an equal protection obligation to finance abortions, had simply abolished Medicaid.

2. In the case of, say, a diabetic pregnant and indigent woman who needs an abortion for medical reasons, is the state refusal to provide an abortion more analogous to imposing a fine on the abortion choice or more analogous to a state refusal to provide private school tuition for the needy?

3. The number of abortions performed annually in the U.S. did not drop in the years after the Hyde Amendment took effect. Does this fact poke any holes in the "coercion" argument of most of the dissenters?

Penalties on Pregnancy

Prohibitions on abortion and contraception, or refusals to fund them, have not been the only methods utilized by states to restrict women's freedom in matters of childbearing. Indirect techniques of governmental control have included (1) firing women from state jobs once they become visibly pregnant, (2) refusing to fund maternity-related medical costs in state-operated medical disability insurance programs, and (3) denying unemployment compensation to unemployed pregnant women.

From the point of view of the women litigants who challenged these ordinances, all these statutes imposed penalties by which the state restricted these women's freedom of choice. From the point of view of the state, however, not all these laws were aimed at penalizing individual childbearing choices. Mandatory pregnancy leaves, at least in the eye of some legislators, aimed at promoting maternal health. The exclusion of maternity benefits from employee health insurance plans and the denial of unemployment compensation to pregnant women were perceived as money-saving measures. (By contrast, state or national government decisions to eliminate abortion funding from Medicaid programs, while providing funding for childbirth expenses, must be characterized as deliberate attempts to indicate a government stamp of disapproval on the choice of abortion.)

The Supreme Court's variegated responses to these differing governmental constraints on the constitutional "right of privacy" were not readily predictable from *Eisenstadt* and *Roe v. Wade*. In fact, the question of the consistency between those responses and the earlier precedents is a matter that has provoked, and no doubt will continue to provoke, controversy in the legal commentary.

The assertion that these statutes infringe on the right to privacy has not been the only basis on which legal challenges to them have been mounted. Governmental and private employee insurance plans that excluded maternity costs from the surgical and hospitalization benefits available to workers have also been challenged as instances of sex discrimination. These challenges have relied on the equal protection clause for the case of state-run programs (*Geduldig v. Aiello*), on Title VII of the Civil Rights Act for the case of private employer's programs (*General Electric v. Gilbert*), and finally on the Pregnancy Discrimination Act amendment to Title VII (*Newport News Shipbuilding v. EEOC*). Challenges to denials of Medicaid funds for abortions have also relied in part on the equal protection clause. Of these antidiscrimination challenges to funding arrangements, only the challenge based on Congress's own Pregnancy Discrimination Act met with success at the Supreme Court.

In settling the earliest challenges to a state-imposed penalty on a childbearing decision, the Supreme Court did not apply this anti-discrimination analysis, even though an equal protection violation had been the basis of holdings of unconstitutionality in the lower courts.[58] Instead, the Court majority focused on the degree of state infringement into the right of privacy and on the quality of the state's justification for that infringement. When the Court agreed to analyze the statute in these terms, the challengers to the law emerged victorious.

Two statutes were at issue in this first challenge: the Cleveland, Ohio, Board of Education had a rule requiring pregnant teachers to take an unpaid leave five months in advance of the expected date of childbirth and to stay away from the job until the semester that began after the baby was three months old; the Chesterfield County, Virginia, School Board had a rule requiring pregnant teachers to leave work at least four months before the expected birth and to stay away from the job until the beginning of a semester following a physician's certification of postchildbirth fitness. Two separate lawsuits challenging these rules had been launched by pregnant schoolteachers early in 1971. Jo Carol LaFleur and Ann Elizabeth Nelson attacked the Cleveland rule, and Susan Cohen attacked the Chesterfield rule. LaFleur and Nelson lost at the district court level[59] but won at the circuit court of appeals.[60] Cohen won at the district court level[61] but lost at the court of appeals.[62] The U.S. Supreme Court consolidated the two suits into *Cleveland Board of Education et al. v. LaFleur et al.*[63] and handed down its decision in January 1974, almost one year after the groundbreaking abortion decisions *Roe* and *Doe*.

Cleveland Board of Education v. LaFleur, 414 U.S. 632 (1974)

MR. JUSTICE STEWART delivered the opinion of the Court.

. . .

These cases call upon us to decide the constitutionality of the school boards' rule. . . .

II

This Court has long recognized that freedom of personal choice in matters of marriage and family life is one of the liberties protected by the Due Process Clause of the Fourteenth Amendment. *Roe v. Wade*, 410 U.S. 113; *Loving v. Virginia*, 388 U.S. 1, 12; *Griswold v. Connecticut*, 381 U.S. 479; *Pierce v. Society of Sisters*, 268 U.S. 510; *Meyer v. Nebraska*, 262 U.S. 390. *See also Prince v. Massachusetts*, 321 U.S. 158; *Skinner*

v. Oklahoma, 316 U.S. 535. As we noted in *Eisenstadt v. Baird*, 405 U.S. 438, 453, there is a right "to be free from unwarranted governmental intrusion into matters so fundamentally affecting a person as the decision whether to bear or beget a child."

By acting to penalize the pregnant teacher for deciding to bear a child, overly restrictive maternity leave regulations can constitute a heavy burden on the exercise of these protected freedoms. Because public school maternity leave rules directly affect "one of the basic civil rights of man," *Skinner v. Oklahoma, supra*, at 541, the Due Process Clause of the Fourteenth Amendment requires that such rules must not needlessly, arbitrarily, or capriciously impinge upon this vital area of a teacher's constitutional liberty. The question before us in these cases is whether the interests advanced in support of the rules of the Cleveland and Chesterfield County School Boards can justify the particular procedures they have adopted.

The school boards in these cases have offered two essentially overlapping explanations for their mandatory maternity leave rules. First, they contend that the firm cutoff dates are necessary to maintain continuity of classroom instruction, since advance knowledge of when a pregnant teacher must leave facilitates the finding and hiring of a qualified substitute. Secondly, the school boards seek to justify their maternity rules by arguing that at least some teachers become physically incapable of adequately performing certain of their duties during the latter part of pregnancy. By keeping the pregnant teacher out of the classroom during these final months, the maternity leave rules are said to protect the health of the teacher and her unborn child, while at the same time assuring that students have a physically capable instructor in the classroom at all times.[9]

9. The records in these cases suggest that the maternity leave regulations may have originally been inspired by other, less weighty, considerations. For example, Dr. Mark C. Schinnerer, who served as Superintendent of Schools in Cleveland at the time the leave rule was adopted, testified in the District Court that the rule had been adopted in part to save pregnant teachers from embarrassment at the hands of giggling schoolchildren; the cutoff date at the end of the fourth month was chosen because this was when the teacher "began to show." Similarly, at least several members of the Chesterfield County School Board thought a mandatory leave rule was justified in order to insulate schoolchildren from the sight of conspicuously pregnant women. One member of the school board thought that it was "not good for the school system" for student to view pregnant teachers, "because some of the kids say, my teacher swallowed a watermelon, things like that."

It cannot be denied that continuity of instruction is a significant and legitimate educational goal. Regulations requiring pregnant teachers to provide early notice of their condition to school authorities undoubtedly facilitate administrative planning toward the important objective of continuity. But, as the Court of Appeals for the Second Circuit noted in *Green v. Waterford Board of Education*, 473 F.2d 629, 635:

> Where a pregnant teacher provides the Board with a date certain for commencement of leave . . . that value [continuity] is preserved; an arbitrary leave date set at the end of the fifth month is no more calculated to facilitate a planned and orderly transition between the teacher and a substitute than is a date fixed closer to confinement. Indeed, the latter . . . would afford the Board more, not less, time to procure a satisfactory long-term substitute. (Footnote omitted.)

Thus, while the advance-notice provisions in the Cleveland and Chesterfield County rules are wholly rational and may well be necessary to serve the objective of continuity of instruction, the absolute requirements of termination at the end of the fourth or fifth month of pregnancy are not. . . .

In fact, since the fifth or sixth month of pregnancy will obviously begin at different

---

The school boards have not contended in this Court that these considerations can serve as a legitimate basis for a rule requiring pregnant women to leave work; we thus note the comments only to illustrate the possible role of outmoded taboos in the adoption of the rules. *Cf. Green v. Waterford Board of Education*, 473 F.2d, at 635 ("Whatever may have been the reaction in Queen Victoria's time, pregnancy is no longer a dirty word").

times in the school year for different teachers, the present Cleveland and Chesterfield County rules may serve to hinder attainments of the very continuity objectives that they are purportedly designed to promote. For example, the beginning of the fifth month of pregnancy for both Mrs. LaFleur and Mrs. Nelson occurred during March of 1971. Both were thus required to leave work with only a few months left in the school year, even though both were fully willing to serve through the end of the term. Similarly, if continuity were the only goal, it seems ironic that the Chesterfield County rule forced Mrs. Cohen to leave work in mid-December 1970 rather than at the end of the semester in January, as she requested.

We thus conclude that the arbitrary cutoff dates embodied in the mandatory leave rules before us have no rational relationship to the valid state interest of preserving continuity of instruction. . . .

The question remains as to whether the cutoff dates at the beginning of the fifth and sixth months can be justified on the other ground advanced by the school boards—the necessity of keeping physically unfit teachers out of the classroom. There can be no doubt that such an objective is perfectly legitimate, both on educational and safety grounds. And, despite the plethora of conflicting medical testimony in these cases, we can assume, *arguendo,* that at least some teachers become physically disabled from effectively performing their duties during the latter stages of pregnancy.

The mandatory termination provisions of the Cleveland and Chesterfield County rules surely operate to insulate the classroom from the presence of potentially incapacitated pregnant teachers. But the question is whether the rules sweep too broadly. *See Shelton v. Tucker,* 364 U.S. 479. That question must be answered in the

affirmative, for the provisions amount to a conclusive presumption that every pregnant teacher who reaches the fifth or sixth month of pregnancy is physically incapable of continuing. There is no individualized determination by the teacher's doctor—or the school board's—as to any particular teacher's ability to continue at her job. The rules contain an irrebuttable presumption of physical incompetency, and that presumption applies even when the medical evidence as to an individual woman's physical status might be wholly to the contrary.

As the Court noted last Term in *Vlandis v. Kline,* 412 U.S. 441, 446, "permanent irrebuttable presumptions have long been disfavored under the Due Process Clauses of the Fifth and Fourteenth Amendments." . . .

Similarly, in *Stanley v. Illinois,* 405 U.S. 645, the Court held that an Illinois statute containing an irrebuttable presumption that unmarried fathers are incompetent to raise their children violated the Due Process Clause. . . . As the Court put the matter:

> It may be, as the State insists, that most unmarried fathers are unsuitable and neglectful parents. . . . But all unmarried fathers are not in this category; some are wholly suited to have custody of their children. (*Id.* at 654, [footnotes omitted].)

These principles control our decision in the cases before us. While the medical experts in these cases differed on many points, they unanimously agreed on one—the ability of any particular pregnant woman to continue at work past any fixed time in her pregnancy is very much an individual matter. Even assuming, *arguendo,* that there are some women who would be physically unable to work past the particular cutoff dates embodied in the challenged rules, it is evident that there are large numbers of teachers who are fully capable of continuing work for longer than the Cleveland and Chesterfield County regulations will allow. . . .

The school boards have argued that the mandatory termination dates serve the interest of administrative convenience, since there are many instances of teacher pregnancy, and the rules obviate the necessity for case-by-case determinations. Certainly, the boards have an interest in devising prompt and efficient procedures to achieve their legitimate objectives in this area. But, as the Court stated in *Stanley v. Illinois, supra,* at 656:

> [T]he Constitution recognizes higher values than speed and efficiency. Indeed, one might fairly say of the Bill of Rights in general, and the Due Process Clause in particular, that they were designed to protect the fragile values of a vulnerable citizenry from the overbearing concern for efficiency and efficacy that may characterize praiseworthy government officials no less, and perhaps more, than mediocre ones. (Footnote omitted.)

While it may be easier for the school boards to conclusively presume that all pregnant women are unfit to teach past the fourth or fifth month[,] or even the first month, of pregnancy, administrative convenience alone is insufficient to make valid what otherwise is a violation of due process of law.[13] The Fourteenth Amendment requires the school boards to employ alternative administrative means, which do not so broadly infringe upon basic constitutional liberty, in support of their legitimate goals.[14]

We conclude, therefore, that neither the necessity for continuity of instruction nor the state interest in keeping physically unfit teachers out of the classroom can justify the sweeping mandatory leave regulations that the Cleveland and Chesterfield County School Boards have adopted. While the regulations no doubt represent a good-faith attempt to achieve a laudable goal, they cannot pass muster under the Due Process Clause of the Fourteenth Amendment, because they employ irrebuttable presumptions that unduly penalize a female teacher for deciding to bear a child.

III

In addition to the mandatory termination provisions, both the Cleveland and

---

13. This is not to say that the only means for providing appropriate protection for the rights of pregnant teachers is an individualized determination in each case and in every circumstances. We are not dealing in these cases with maternity leave regulations requiring a termination of employment at some firm date during the last few weeks of pregnancy. We therefore have no occasion to decide whether such regulations might be justified by considerations not presented in these records—for example, widespread medical consensus about the "disabling" effect of pregnancy on a teacher's job performance during these latter days, or evidence showing that such firm cutoffs were the only reasonable method of avoiding the possibility of labor beginning while some teacher was in the classroom, or proof that adequate substitutes could not be procured without at least some minimal lead time and certainty as to the dates upon which their employment was to begin.

14. The schools boards have available to them reasonable alternative methods of keeping physically unfit teachers out of the classroom. For example, they could require the pregnant teacher to submit to medical examination by a school board physician, or simply require each teacher to submit a current certification from her obstetrician as to her ability to continue work. Indeed, when evaluating the physical ability of a teacher to *return* to work, each school board in this case relies upon precisely such procedures.

Chesterfield County rules contain limitations upon a teacher's eligibility to return to work after giving birth. Again, the school boards offer two justifications for the return rules—continuity of instruction and the desire to be certain that the teacher is physically competent when she returns to work. As is the case with the leave provisions, the question is not whether the school board's goals are legitimate, but rather whether the particular means chosen to achieve those objectives unduly infringe upon the teacher's constitutional liberty. . . . The provisions concerning a medical certificate or supplemental physical examination are narrowly drawn methods of protecting the school board's interest in teacher fitness; these requirements allow an individualized decision as to the teacher's condition, and thus avoid the pitfalls of the presumptions inherent in the leave rules. Similarly, the provision limiting eligibility to return to the semester following delivery is a precisely drawn means of serving the school board's interest in avoiding unnecessary changes in classroom personnel during any one school term.

The Cleveland rule, however, does not simply contain these reasonable medical and next-semester eligibility provisions. In addition, the school board requires the mother to wait until her child reaches the age of three months before the return rules begin to operate. The school board has offered no reasonable justification for this supplemental limitation, and we can perceive none. . . . The presumption, moreover, is patently unnecessary, since the requirement of a physician's certificate or a medical examination fully protects the school's interests in this regard. . . .

Thus, we conclude that the Cleveland return rule, insofar as it embodies the three-month age provision, is wholly arbitrary and irrational, and hence violates the Due Process Clause of the Fourteenth Amendment. The age limitation serves no legitimate state interest, and unnecessarily penalizes the female teacher for asserting her right to bear children.

We perceive no such constitutional infirmities in the Chesterfield County rule. In that school system, the teacher becomes eligible for re-employment upon submission of a medical certificate from her physician; return to work is guaranteed no later than the beginning of the next school year following the eligibility determination. . . . In short, the Chesterfield County rule manages to serve the legitimate state interests here without employing unnecessary presumptions that broadly burden the exercise of protected constitutional liberty. . . .

Mr. Justice Douglas concurs in the result.

Mr. Justice Powell, concurring in the result.

I concur in the Court's result, but I am unable to join its opinion. In my view these cases should not be decided on the ground that the mandatory maternity leave regulations impair any right to bear children or create an "irrebuttable presumption." It seems to me that equal protection analysis is the appropriate frame of reference.

These regulations undoubtedly add to the burdens of childbearing. But certainly not every government policy that burdens childbearing violates the Constitution. Limitations on the welfare benefits a family may receive that do not take into account the size of the family illustrate this point. *See Dandridge v. Williams,* 397 U.S. 471 (1970). Undoubtedly Congress could, as another example, constitutionally seek to discourage excessive population growth by limiting tax deductions for dependents. That would represent an intentional governmental effort to "penalize" childbearing. *See ante,* at 640. The regulations here do not have that purpose. Their deterrent impact is wholly incidental. If some intentional efforts to penalize childbearing are constitutional, and if *Dandridge, supra,* means what I think it does, then certainly these regulations are not invalid as an infringement of any right to procreate.

I am also troubled by the Court's return to the "irrebuttable presumption" line of analysis of *Stanley v. Illinois,* 405 U.S. 645 (1972) (POWELL, J., not participating), and *Vlandis v. Kline,* 412 U.S. 441 (1973). Although I joined the opinion of the Court in *Vlandis* and continue fully to support the result reached there, the present cases have caused me to reexamine the "irrebuttable presumption" rationale. This has led me to the conclusion that the Court should approach that doctrine with extreme care. There is much to what MR. JUSTICE REHNQUIST says in his dissenting opinion, *post* about the implications of the doctrine for the traditional legislative power to operate by classification. As a matter of logic, it is difficult to see the terminus of the road upon which the Court has embarked under the banner of "irrebuttable presumptions." If the Court nevertheless uses "irrebuttable presumption" reasoning selectively, the concept at root often will be something else masquerading as a due process doctrine. That something else, of course, is the Equal Protection Clause.

These cases present precisely the kind of problem susceptible of treatment by classification. Most school teachers are women, a certain percentage of them are pregnant at any given time, and pregnancy is a normal biological function possessing, in the great majority of cases, a fairly well defined term. The constitutional difficulty is not that the boards attempted to deal with this problem by classification. Rather, it is that the boards chose irrational classifications.

A range of possible school board goals emerge from the cases. Several may be put to one side. The records before us abound with proof that a principal purpose behind the adoption of the regulations was to keep visibly pregnant teachers out of the sight of schoolchildren. The boards do not advance this today as a legitimate objective, yet its initial primacy casts a shadow over these cases. Moreover, most of the after-the-fact rationalizations proposed by these boards are unsupported in the records. The boards emphasize teacher absenteeism, classroom discipline, the safety of schoolchildren, and the safety of the expectant mother and her unborn child. No doubt these are legitimate concerns. But the boards have failed to demonstrate that these interests are in fact threatened by the continued employment of pregnant teachers.

To be sure, the boards have a legitimate and important interest in fostering continuity of teaching. And, even a normal pregnancy may at some point jeopardize that interest. But the classifications chosen by these boards, so far as we have been shown, are either counterproductive or irrationally overinclusive even with regard to this significant, nonillusory goal. Accordingly, in my opinion these regulations are invalid under rational-basis standards of equal protection review. . . .

[For reasons similar to those explained in the majority opinion,] I believe the linkage between the boards' legitimate ends and their chosen means is too attenuated to support those portions of the regulations overturned by the Court. Thus, I concur in the Court's result. But I think it important to emphasize the degree of latitude the Court, as I read it, has left the boards for dealing with the real and recurrent problems presented by teacher pregnancies. Boards may demand in every case "substantial advance notice of [pregnancy]. . . ." *Ante.* Subject to certain restrictions, they may require all pregnant teachers to cease teaching "at some firm date during the last few weeks of pregnancy. . . ." *Id.* at n.13. The Court further holds that boards may in all cases restrict re-entry into teaching to the outset of the school term following delivery. *Id.*

In my opinion, such class-wide rules for pregnant teachers are constitutional under traditional equal protection standards. . . . My concern with the Court's opinion is that, if carried to logical extremes, the emphasis on individualized treatment is at war with [the] need for discretion. Indeed, stringent insistence on individualized treatment may be quite impractical in a large school district with thousands of teachers.

But despite my reservations as to the rationale of the majority, I nevertheless conclude that in these cases the gap between the legitimate interest of the boards and the particular means chosen to attain them is too wide. A restructuring generally along the lines indicated in the Court's opinion seems unavoidable. Accordingly, I concur in its result.

MR. JUSTICE REHNQUIST, with whom THE CHIEF JUSTICE joins, dissenting.

The Court rests its invalidation of the school regulations involved in these cases on the Due Process Clause of the Fourteenth Amendment, rather than on any claim of sexual discrimination under the Equal Protection Clause of that Amendment. My Brother STEWART thereby enlists the Court in another quixotic engagement in his apparently unending war on irrebuttable presumptions. In these cases we are told that although a regulation "requiring a termination of employment at some firm date during the last few weeks of pregnancy," *ante*, at n.13, might pass muster, the regulations here challenged requiring

termination at the end of the fourth or fifth month of pregnancy violate due process of law.

As THE CHIEF JUSTICE pointed out in his dissent last year in *Vlandis v. Kline*, 412 U.S. 441, "literally thousands of state statutes create classifications permanent in duration, which are less than perfect, as all legislative classifications are, and might be improved on by individualized determinations. . . ." *Id.* at 462. Hundreds of years ago in England, before Parliament came to be thought of as a body having general lawmaking power, controversies were determined on an individualized basis without benefit of any general law. Most students of government consider the shift from this sort of determination, made on an *ad hoc* basis by the King's representative, to a relatively uniform body of rules enacted by a body exercising legislative authority, to have been a significant step forward in the achievement of a civilized political society. It seems to me a little late in the day for this Court to weigh in against such an established consensus.

Countless state and federal statutes draw lines such as those drawn by the regulations here which, under the Court's analysis, might well prove to be arbitrary in individual cases. The District of Columbia Code, for example, draws lines with respect to age for several purposes. The Code requires that a person to be eligible to vote be eighteen years of age, that a male be eighteen and a female be sixteen before a valid marriage may be contracted, that alcoholic beverages not be sold to a person under the age of twenty-one years, or beer or light wines to any person under the age of eighteen years. A resident of the District of Columbia must be sixteen years of age to obtain a permit to operate a motor vehicle, and the District of Columbia delegate to the United States Congress must be twenty-five years old. Nothing in the Court's opinion clearly demonstrates why its logic would not equally well sustain a challenge to these laws from a seventeen-year-old who insists that he is just as well informed for voting purposes as an eighteen-year-old, from a twenty-year-old who insists that he is just as able to carry his liquor as a twenty-one-year-old, or from the numerous other persons who fall on the outside of lines drawn by these and similar statutes.

More closely in point is the jeopardy in which the Court's opinion places long-standing statutes providing for mandatory retirement of government employees. [T]he Court will have to strain valiantly in order to avoid having today's opinion lead to the invalidation of mandatory retirement statutes for governmental employees. In that event federal, state, and local governmental bodies will be remitted to the task, thankless both for them and for the employees involved, of individual determinations of physical impairment and senility.

It has been said before, *Williamson v. Lee Optical Co.*, 348 U.S. 483 (1955), but it bears repeating here: All legislation involves the drawing of lines, and the drawing of lines necessarily results in particular individuals who are disadvantaged by the line drawn being virtually indistinguishable for many purposes from those individuals who benefit from the legislative classification. The Court's disenchantment with "irrebuttable presumptions," and its preference for "individualized determination," is in the last analysis nothing less than an attack upon the very notion of lawmaking itself.

[The evidence suggests that] in some cases there may be physical impairment at the stage of pregnancy fastened on by the regulations in questions, and that the probability of physical impairment increases as the pregnancy advances. If legislative bodies are to be permitted to draw a general line anywhere short of the delivery room, I can find no judicial standard of measurement which says the ones drawn here was invalid. I therefore dissent.

CASE QUESTIONS

1. Did the constitutional infirmity of these statutes lay in their irrebuttable presumptions or in their infringement on the right of familial privacy? The combination of the two? Is Justice Powell correct in suggesting that the problem with the statutes is their irrationality?

2. Does this majority opinion imply that mandatory retirement ages are unconstitutional?

3. Does Justice Rehnquist's dissent (joined by Justice Burger) suggest that a mandatory leave even for women only one or two months pregnant would be constitutional? Does it imply that school boards could forbid married women under the age of, say, forty to teach in their schools, on the grounds that married women are more likely than single women to become pregnant?

Turner v. Department of Employment (1975), discussion

Late in 1975 the Supreme Court handed down a brief per curiam opinion in a 5–3 summary judgment for the case of *Mary Ann Turner v. Department of Employment Security of Utah* (423 U.S. 44). As in *Cleveland v. LaFleur,* the challenger to the legislative penalty on a childbearing decision prevailed. *Turner v. Department of Employment* was similar to *Cleveland v. LaFleur* in reasoning as well as result. It was the only other challenge to a penalty on a childbearing decision in which the litigants managed to persuade the Court majority to examine the statute from a perspective that acknowledged and focused on the statute's clash with the right of familial privacy.[64]

The Supreme Court in *Turner* noted that "freedom of personal choice in matters of marriage and family life is one of the liberties protected by the due process clause" and that any infringement on such "basic human liberties" must be imposed by carefully "individualized means" instead of by sweeping categorical presumptions. In this instance the presumption at issue was Utah's belief that women in the last three months of pregnancy and the first six weeks after childbirth are unfit for gainful employment and therefore should be denied unemployment compensation. The Court declared such a presumption an unconstitutional infringement on the right of familial privacy.

In three other challenges to penalties on childbearing decisions stretching from 1974 through 1977, however, the Supreme Court applied an equal protection or antidiscrimination, rather than a right of privacy, analysis, and the first two of these equal-protection-approach decisions upheld the statute or practice under attack. These dealt with denials of funds for abortion or for childbirth or both. Conceivably, if the Court had wanted to declare unconstitutional any of these funding denials, it could have done so, at least for government programs, on the basis of the compelling-interesting/right-of-privacy approach of *Roe* and its progeny.

These three cases began with *Geduldig v. Aiello*[65] in June 1974. Geduldig was director of the Department of Human Resources in California, and Carolyn Aiello was one of the four employees within the state who initiated a lawsuit against California's system of disability benefits for its citizens. That system paid medical disability and hospital benefits to its workers out of a fund created by deducting one percent of those workers' wages. Normal pregnancies, unlike other occasions for hospitalization, were specifically excluded from coverage. This exclusion was the target of the legal attack on the statute.

The statute included certain other specific exclusions, and these figured prominently in the Court's rationale for upholding it. It excluded coverage for disabilities that did not require hospitalization and that lasted fewer than eight days, for disabilities extending beyond twenty-six weeks, and for disabilities producing "court commitment as a dipsomaniac, drug addict, or sexual psychopath." The litigants had no quarrel with these exclusions, but, evidently inspired by the *Reed* and *Frontiero* successes, they claimed that the denial of pregnancy benefits amounted to sex discrimination and thereby violated the constitutional command of equal protection. The district court agreed with the women employees,[66] but the women's attorneys were not so successful with the U.S. Supreme Court.

Geduldig v. Aiello, 417 U.S. 484 (1974)

Mr. Justice Stewart delivered the opinion of the Court.

II

It is clear that California intended to establish this benefit system as an insurance program that was to function essentially in accordance with insurance concepts. Since the program was instituted in 1946, it has been totally self-supporting, never drawing on general state revenues to finance disability or hospital benefits. The Disability Fund is wholly supported by the one percent of wages annually contributed by participating employees. . . .

Over the years California has demonstrated a strong commitment not to increase the contribution rate above the 1 percent level. The State has sought to provide the broadest possible disability protection that would be affordable by all employees, including those with very low incomes. . . .

In ordering the State to pay benefits for disability accompanying normal pregnancy and delivery, the District Court acknowledged the State's contention "that coverage of these disabilities is so extraordinarily expensive that it would be impossible to maintain a program supported by employee contributions if these disabilities are included." 359 F. Supp., at 798. There is considerable disagreement between the parties with respect to how great the in-

creased costs would actually be, but they would clearly be substantial. For purposes of analysis the District Court accepted the State's estimate, which was in excess of $100 million annually, and stated: "[I]t is clear that including these disabilities would not destroy the program. The increased costs could be accommodated quite easily by making reasonable changes in the contribution rate, the maximum benefits allowable, and the other variables affecting the solvency of the program." *Id.*

Each of these "variables"—the benefit level deemed appropriate to compensate employee disability, the risks selected to be insured under the program, and the contribution rate chosen to maintain the solvency of the program and at the same time to permit low income employees to participate with minimal personal sacrifice—represents a policy determination by the State. The essential issue in this case is whether the Equal Protection Clause requires such policies to be sacrificed or compromised in order to finance the payment of benefits to those whose disability is attributable to normal pregnancy and delivery.

We cannot agree that the exclusion of this disability from coverage amounts to invidious discrimination under the Equal Protection Clause. California does not discriminate with respect to the persons or groups . . . eligible for disability insurance protection under the program. The classification challenged in this case relates to the asserted underinclusiveness of the set of risks that the State has selected to insure. Although California has created a program to insure most risks of employment disability, it has not chosen to insure all such risks, and this decision is reflected in the level of annual contributions exacted from participating employees. This Court has held that, consistently with the Equal Protection Clause, a State "may take one step at a time, addressing itself to the phase of the problem which seems most acute to the legislative mind. . . . The legislature may select one phase of one field and apply a remedy there neglecting the others. . . ." *Williamson v. Lee Optical Co.*, 348 U.S. 483, 489 (1955); *Jefferson v. Hackney*, 406 U.S. 535 (1972). Particularly with respect to social welfare programs, so long as the line drawn by the State is rationally supportable, the courts will not interpose their judgment as to the appropriate stopping point. "[T]he Equal Protection Clause does not require that a State must choose between attacking every aspect of a problem or not attacking the problem at all." *Dandridge v. Williams*, 397 U.S. 471, 486–87 (1970).

The District Court suggested that moderate alterations in what it regarded as "variables" of the disability insurance program could be made to accommodate the substantial expense required to include normal pregnancy within the program's protection. The same can be said, however, with respect to the other expensive class of disabilities that are excluded from coverage—short-term disabilities. If the Equal Protection Clause were thought to compel disability payments for normal pregnancy, it is hard to perceive why it would not also compel payments for short-term disabilities suffered by participating employees.

It is evident that a totally comprehensive program would be substantially more costly than the present program and would inevitably require state subsidy, a higher rate of employee contribution, a lower scale of benefits for those suffering insured disabilities, or some combination of these measures. There is nothing in the Constitution, however, that requires the State to subordinate or compromise its legitimate interests solely to create a more comprehensive social insurance program than it already has.

The State has a legitimate interest in maintaining the self-supporting nature of its insurance program. Similarly, it has an interest in distributing the available resources in such a way as to keep benefit payments at an adequate level for disabilities that are covered, rather than to cover all disabilities inadequately. Finally, California has a legitimate concern in maintaining the contribution rate at a level that will not unduly burden participating employees, particularly low-income employees who may be most in need of the disability insurance.

These policies provide an objective and wholly non-invidious basis for the State's decision not to create a more comprehensive insurance program than it has. There is no evidence in the record that the selection of the risks insured by the program worked to discriminate against any definable group or class in terms of the aggregate risk protection derived by that group or class from the program.[20] There is

20. The dissenting opinion to the contrary, this case is thus a far cry from cases like *Reed v. Reed* and *Frontiero v. Richardson*, involving discrimination based upon gender as such. The California insurance program does not exclude anyone from benefits eligibility because of gender but merely removes one physical condition—pregnancy—from the list of compensable disabilities. While it is true that only women can become pregnant, it does not follow that every legislative classification concerning pregnancy is a sex-based classification like those considered in *Reed* and *Frontiero*. Normal pregnancy is an

no risk from which men are protected and women are not. Likewise, there is no risk from which women are protected and men are not.

The appellee simply contends that, although she has received insurance protection equivalent to that provided all other participating employees, she has suffered discrimination because she encountered a risk that was outside the program's protection. For the reasons we have stated, we hold that this contention is not a valid one under the Equal Protection Clause of the Fourteenth Amendment.

Reversed.

Mr. Justice Brennan, with Mr. Justice Douglas and Mr. Justice Marshall, dissenting.

Relying upon *Dandridge v. Williams,* 397 U.S. 471 (1970), and *Jefferson v. Hackney,* 406 U.S. 535 (1972), the Court today rejects appellees' equal protection claim and upholds the exclusion of normal-pregnancy-related disabilities from coverage under

California's disability insurance program on the ground that the legislative classification rationally promotes the State's legitimate cost-saving interests. . . . Because I believe that *Reed v. Reed* and *Frontiero v. Richardson* mandate a stricter standard of scrutiny which the State's classification fails to satisfy, I respectfully dissent.

. . . [C]ompensation is paid for virtually all disabling conditions without regard to cost, voluntariness, uniqueness, predictability, or "normalcy" of the disability.[3] Thus, for example, workers are compensated for costly disabilities such as heart attacks, voluntary disabilities such as cosmetic surgery or sterilization, disabilities unique to sex or race such as prostatectomies or sickle-cell anemia, pre-existing conditions inevitably resulting in disability such as degenerative arthritis or cataracts, and "normal" disabilities such as removal of irritating wisdom teeth or other orthodontia.

Despite the Code's broad goals and scope of coverage, compensation is denied for disabilities suffered in connection with a "normal" pregnancy—disabilities suffered only by women. Cal. Unemp. Ins. Code § 2626, 2626.2 (Supp. 1974). Disabilities caused by pregnancy, however, like other physically disabling conditions covered by the Code, require medical care, often include hospitalization, anesthesia and surgical procedures, and may involve genuine risk to life. Moreover, the economic effects caused by pregnancy-related

---

objectively identifiable physical condition with unique characteristics. Absent a showing that distinctions involving pregnancy are mere pretexts designed to effect an invidious discrimination against the members of one sex or the other, lawmakers are constitutionally free to include or exclude pregnancy from the coverage of legislation such as this on any reasonable basis, just as with respect to any other physical condition.

The lack of identity between the excluded disability and gender as such under this insurance program becomes clear upon the most cursory analysis. The program divides potential recipients into two groups—pregnant women and nonpregnant persons. While the first group is exclusively female, the second includes members of both sexes. The fiscal and actuarial benefits of the program thus accrue to members of both sexes.

3. While the Code technically excludes from coverage individuals under court commitment for dipsomania, drug addiction, or sexual psychopathy, Cal. Unemp. Ins. Code § 2678, the Court was informed by the Deputy Attorney General of California at oral argument that court commitment for such disabilities is "a fairly archaic practice" and that "it would be unrealistic to say that they constitute valid exclusions."

disabilities are functionally indistinguish-able from the effects caused by any other disability: wages are lost due to a physical inability to work, and medical expenses are incurred for the delivery of the child and for postpartum care.[5] In my view, by sin-gling out for less favorable treatment a gender-linked disability peculiar to women, the State has created a double standard for disability compensation: a limitation is imposed upon the disabilities for which women workers may recover, while men re-ceive full compensation for all disabilities suffered, including those that affect only . . . their sex, such as prostatectomies and circumcision. . . . In effect, one set of rules is applied to females and another to males. Such dissimilar treatment of men and women, on the basis of physical char-acteristics inextricably linked to one sex, inevitably constitutes sex discrimination.

The same conclusion has been reached by the Equal Employment Opportunity Commission, the federal agency charged with enforcement of Title VII of the Civil Rights Act of 1964, as amended by the Equal Employment Opportunity Act of 1972, 42 U.S.C. § 2000e *et seq.* (Supp. II 1970), which prohibits employment dis-crimination on the basis of sex. . . .

In the past, when a legislative classifi-cation has turned on gender, the Court has justifiably applied a standard of judicial scrutiny more strict than that generally ac-corded economic or social welfare pro-grams. Compare *Reed v. Reed* and *Frontiero v. Richardson* with *Dandridge v. Williams* and *Jefferson v. Hackney.* Yet by its decision

5. Nearly two-thirds of all women who work do so of necessity: either they are unmarried or their husbands earn less than $7,000 per year. *See* United States Department of Labor, Women's Bureau, *Why Women Work* (rev. ed. 1972); United States Department of Labor, Employment Stan-dards Administration, *The Myth and the Reality* (May 1974 rev.). . . .

today, the Court appears willing to aban-don that higher standard of review without satisfactorily explaining what differentiates the gender-based classification employed in this case from those found unconstitu-tional in *Reed* and *Frontiero.* The Court's de-cision threatens to return men and women to a time when "traditional" equal protec-tion analysis sustained legislative classifi-cations that treated differently members of a particular sex solely because of their sex. *See, e.g., Muller v. Oregon,* 208 U.S. 412 (1908); *Goesaert v. Cleary,* 335 U.S. 464 (1948); *Hoyt v. Florida,* 368 U.S. 57 (1961).

I cannot join the Court's apparent re-treat. I continue to adhere to my view that "classifications based upon sex, like classi-fications based upon race, alienage, or na-tional origin, are inherently suspect, and must therefore be subjected to strict judi-cial scrutiny." *Frontiero,* at 688. When, as in this case, the State employs a legislative classification that distinguishes between beneficiaries solely by reference to gender-linked disability risks, "[t]he Court is not . . . free to sustain the statute on the ground that it rationally promotes legiti-mate governmental interests; rather, such suspect classification can be sustained only when the State bears the burden of demon-strating that the challenged legislation serves overriding or compelling interests that cannot be achieved either by a more carefully tailored legislative classification or by the use of feasible, less drastic means." *Kahn v. Shevin,* 416 U.S. 351, 357–58 (1974) (BRENNAN, J., dissenting).

The State has clearly failed to meet that burden in the present case. . . . For while "a State has a valid interest in preserving the fiscal integrity of its programs[,] . . .a State may not accomplish such a purpose by invidious distinctions between classes of its citizens. . . . The saving of welfare costs cannot justify an otherwise invidious classification." *Shapiro v. Thompson,* 394

U.S. 618, 633 (1969). Thus, when a statutory classification is subject to strict judicial scrutiny, the State "must do more than show that denying [benefits to the excluded class] saves money." *Memorial Hospital v. Maricopa County*, 415 U.S. 250, 263 (1974). *See also Graham v. Richardson*, 403 U.S. 365, 374–75 (1971). . . .

CASE QUESTIONS

1. The majority insist (see footnote 20) that this is not a matter of sex discrimination. Would they be so insistent on the matter of discrimination if California were to exclude from its disability coverage the disease of sickle-cell anemia, a disease that strikes black people almost exclusively? Would such an exclusion violate the equal protection clause? If it would, why does the same reasoning not apply to a maternity exclusion?

2. Would the dissenters' objections be answered if California were to exclude *all* voluntary disabilities (cosmetic surgery, suicide attempts, etc., as well as pregnancy)?

3. Does the dissenters' position imply that paid maternity leave (if paternity leave is not provided) for state employees would be unconstitutional? Would it violate Title VII?

4. Justice Brennan's dissent predates the development of *Craig*-level scrutiny, so he is still advocating a compelling interest test. Would the application of the *Craig* test change his conclusion?

Of course, the equal protection clause of the Fourteenth Amendment does not explicitly mention either sex discrimination or discriminatory employment practices. But Title VII of the 1964 Civil Rights Act explicitly forbids sex discrimination in employment practices. Thus, when Martha Gilbert, in December 1976 presented her class-action case against the maternity-exclusion clause of General Electric Company's employee disability plan (identical to the one in *Geduldig v. Aiello*), many Court-watchers expected her to be more successful than the *Aiello* litigants. Indeed, the district court for this particular case[67] and six different courts of appeal that received such cases had reached decisions that such exclusion did violate Title VII.[68] But once again the Supreme Court rejected the argument that a penalty on the process of childbirth constitutes a sex discrimination.

General Electric Company v. Martha Gilbert, 429 U.S. 125 (1976)

MR. JUSTICE REHNQUIST delivered the opinion of the Court.

II

. . . In *Geduldig*, the disability insurance system was funded entirely from contributions deducted from the wages of participating employees, at a rate of 1 percent of the employee's salary up to an annual maximum of $85. In other relevant respects, the operation of the program was similar to General Electric's disability benefits plan, *see* 417 U.S., at 487–89.

We rejected appellee's Equal Protection challenge to this statutory scheme. We first noted that:

> We cannot agree that the exclusion of this disability from coverage amounts to invidious discrimination under the Equal Protection Clause. California does not discriminate with respect to the persons or groups which are eligible for disability insurance protection under the program. The classification challenged in this case relates to the asserted underinclusiveness of the set of risks that the State has selected to insure. (417 U.S., at 494.)

This point was emphasized again, when later in the opinion we noted that

> This case is thus a far cry from cases like *Reed v. Reed* and *Frontiero v. Richardson*, involving discrimination based upon gender as such. The California insurance program does not exclude anyone from benefit eligibility because of gender but merely removes one physical condition—pregnancy—from the list of compensable disabilities. While

it is true that only women can become pregnant, it does not follow that every legislative classification concerning pregnancy is a sex-based classification like those considered in *Reed* and *Frontiero*. Normal pregnancy is an objectively identifiable physical condition with unique characteristics. Absent a showing that distinctions involving pregnancy are mere pretexts designed to effect an invidious discrimination against the members of one sex or the other, lawmakers are constitutionally free to include or exclude pregnancy from the coverage of legislation such as this on any reasonable basis, just as with respect to any other physical condition.

> The lack of identity between the excluded disability and gender as such under this insurance program becomes clear upon the most cursory analysis. The program divides potential recipients into two groups—pregnant women and non-pregnant persons. While the first group is exclusively female, the second includes members of both sexes. (417 U.S., at 496–97, n.20.)

The quoted language from *Geduldig* leaves no doubt that our reason for rejecting appellee's equal protection claim in that case was that the exclusion of pregnancy from coverage under California's disability benefits plan was not in itself discrimination based on sex.

We recognized in *Geduldig*, of course, that the fact that there was not sex-based discrimination as such was not the end of the analysis, should it be shown "that distinctions involving pregnancy are mere pretexts designed to effect an invidious discrimination against the members of one sex or the other," 417 U.S., at 496–97, n.20. But we noted that no semblance of such a showing had been made:

> There is no evidence in the record that the selection of the risks insured by the program worked to discriminate against any definable group or class in terms of the aggregate risk protection derived by that group or class from the program. There is no risk from which men are protected and women are not. Likewise, there is no risk from which women are protected and men are not. (417 U.S., at 496–97.)

Since gender-based discrimination had not been shown to exist either by the terms of the plan or by its effect, there was no need to reach the question of what sort of standard would govern our review had there been such a showing. *See Frontiero; Reed.*

The Court of Appeals was therefore wrong in concluding that the reasoning of *Geduldig* was not applicable to an action under Title VII. Since it is a finding of sex-based discrimination that must trigger, in a case such as this, the finding of an unlawful employment practice under § 703(a)(1), 42 U.S.C. § 2000e–2(a)(1), *Geduldig* is precisely in point in its holding that an exclusion of pregnancy from a disability benefits plan providing general coverage is not a gender-based discrimination at all.

There is no more showing in this case than there was in *Geduldig* that the exclusion of pregnancy benefits is a mere "pretext designed to effect an invidious discrimination against the members of one sex or the other." . . . [A] distinction which on its face is not sex related might nonetheless violate the Equal Protection Clause if it were in fact a subterfuge to accomplish a forbidden discrimination. But we have here

no question of excluding a disease or disability comparable in all other respects to covered diseases or disabilities and yet confined to the members of one race or sex. Pregnancy is of course confined to women, but it is in other ways significantly different from the typical covered disease or disability. The District Court found that it is not a "disease" at all, and is often a voluntarily undertaken and desired condition, 375 F. Supp., at 375, 377. We do not therefore infer that the exclusion of pregnancy disability benefits from petitioner's plan is a simple pretext for discriminating against women. . . .

As in *Geduldig,* respondents have not attempted to meet the burden of demonstrating a gender-based discriminatory effect resulting from the exclusion of pregnancy-related disabilities from coverage.[15] Whatever the ultimate probative value of the evidence introduced before the District Court on this subject in the instant case, at the very least it tended to illustrate that the selection of risks covered by the Plan did not operate, in fact, to discriminate against women. As in *Geduldig,* we start from the indisputable baseline that "[t]he fiscal and actuarial benefits of the program . . . accrue to members of both sexes," 417 U.S., at 497 n.20. We need not disturb the findings of the District Court to note that there is not . . . any evidence which would support a finding that the financial benefits of the Plan "worked to discriminate against any definable group or class in terms of the aggregate risk protection derived by that group or class from the program," *id.* at 496. The Plan, in effect . . . is nothing more than an insurance package, which covers some risks, but

15. Absent a showing of gender-based discrimination, as that term is defined in *Geduldig,* or a showing of gender-based effect, there can be no violation of § 703(a)(1) [Title VII].

excludes others, *see id.* at 494, 496–97. The "package" going to relevant identifiable groups we are presently concerned with— General Electric's male and female employees—covers exactly the same categories of risk, and is facially nondiscriminatory in the sense that "[t]here is no risk from which men are protected and women are not. Likewise, there is no risk from which women are protected and men are not." *Geduldig*, 417 U.S., at 496–97. As there is no proof that the package is in fact worth more to men than to women, it is impossible to find any gender-based discriminatory effect in this scheme simply because an employer's disability benefits plan is less than all inclusive.[17] For all that appears,

pregnancy-related disabilities constitute an *additional* risk, unique to women, and the failure to compensate them for this risk does not destroy the presumed parity of the benefits, accruing to men and women alike, which results from the facially even-handed *inclusion* of risks. To hold otherwise would endanger the common-sense notion that an employer who has no disability program at all does not violate Title VII even though the "underinclusion" of risks impacts, as a result of pregnancy-related disabilities, more heavily upon one gender than upon the other.[18] Just as there is no facial gender-based discrimination in that case, so, too, there is none here. . . .

III

. . .

There are also persuasive indications that the more recent EEOC guideline [forbidding this kind of exclusion of maternity benefits] sharply conflicts with other indicia of the proper interpretation of the sex-discrimination provisions of Title VII. The legislative history of Title VII's prohibition of sex discrimination is notable primarily for its brevity. Even so, however,

---

17. Absent proof of different values, the cost to "insure" against the risks is, in essence, nothing more than extra compensation to the employees, in the form of fringe benefits. If the employer were to remove the insurance fringe benefits and, instead, increase wages by an amount equal to the cost of the "insurance," there would clearly be no gender-based discrimination, even though a female employee who wished to purchase disability insurance that covered all risks would have to pay more than would a male employee who purchased identical disability insurance, due to the fact that her insurance had to cover the "extra" disabilities due to pregnancy. While respondents seem to acknowledge that the failure to provide any benefit plan at all would not constitute sex-based discrimination in violation of Title VII, *see* note 18, they illogically also suggest that the present scheme does violate Title VII because "A female must spend her own money to buy a personal disability policy covering pregnancy disability if she wants to be fully insured against a period of disability without income, whereas a male without extra expenditure is fully insured by GE against every period of disability." Supplemental Brief for Martha Gilbert *et al*, on Reargument, at 11. Yet, in both cases—the instant case and the case where there is no disability coverage at all— the ultimate result is that a woman who wished

to be fully insured would have to pay an incremental amount over her male counterpart due solely to the possibility of pregnancy-related disabilities. Title VII's proscription on discrimination does not require, in either case, the employer to pay that incremental amount. The District Court was wrong in assuming, as it did, 375 F. Supp., at 383, that Title VII's ban on employment discrimination necessarily means that "greater economic benefit[s]" must be required to be paid to one sex or the other because of their differing roles in "the scheme of human existence."

18. Respondents tacitly admit that this situation would not violate Title VII. They acknowledge that "G.E. had no obligation to establish any fringe benefits program," Brief for Martha Gilbert *et al*. . . .

Congress paid especial attention to the provisions of the Equal Pay Act. 29 U.S.C. § 206(d), when it amended § 703(h) of Title VII by adding the following sentence:

> It shall not be an unlawful employment practice under this subchapter for any employer to differentiate upon the basis of sex in determining the amount of the wages or compensation paid or to be paid to employees of such employer if such differentiation is authorized by the provisions of § 206(d) of Title 29. (42 U.S.C. § 2000e–2[h].)

This sentence was proposed as the Bennett Amendment to the Senate Bill, 110 Cong. Rec. 13647 (1964), and Senator Humphrey, the floor manager of the bill, stated that the purpose of the amendment was to make it "unmistakably clear" that "differences of treatment in industrial benefit plans, including earlier retirement options for women, may continue in operation under this bill if it becomes law," 110 Cong. Rec. 13663–4 (1964). Because of this amendment, interpretations of § 6(d) of the Equal Pay Act are applicable to Title VII as well, and an interpretive regulation promulgated by the Wage and Hour Administrator under the Equal Pay Act explicitly states:

> If employer contributions to a plan providing insurance or similar benefits to employees are equal for both men and women, no wage differential prohibited by the equal pay provisions will result from such payments, even though the benefits which accrue to the employees in question are greater for one sex than for the other. The mere fact that the employer may make unequal contributions for employees of opposite sexes in such a situation will not, however, be considered to indicate that the employer's payments are in violation of § 6(d), if the resulting benefits are equal for such employees. (29 CFR § 800.116[d] [1975].)

Thus even if we were to depend for our construction of the critical language of Title VII solely on the basis of "deference" to interpretative regulations by the appropriate administrative agencies, we would find ourselves pointed in diametrically opposite directions by the conflicting regulations of the EEOC, on the one hand, and the Wage and Hour Administrator, on the other. Petitioner's exclusion of benefits for pregnancy disability would be declared an unlawful employment practice under § 703(a)(1), but would be declared not to be an unlawful employment practice under § 703(h).

We are not reduced to such total abdication in construing the statute. The EEOC guideline of 1972, conflicting as it does with earlier pronouncements of that agency, and containing no suggestion that some new source of legislative history had been discovered in the intervening eight years, stands virtually alone. Contrary to it are the consistent interpretation of the Wage and Hour Administrator, and the quoted language of Senator Humphrey, the floor manager of Title VII in the Senate. They support what seems to us to be the "plain meaning" of the language used by Congress when it enacted § 703(a)(1). . . .

MR. JUSTICE STEWART, concurring.

I join the opinion of the Court. . . . Unlike my Brother BLACKMUN, I do not understand the opinion to question . . . the significance generally of proving a discriminatory effect in a Title VII case.

MR. JUSTICE BLACKMUN, concurring in part.

I join the judgment of the Court and concur in its opinion insofar as it holds (a) that General Electric's exclusion of disability due to pregnancy is not *per se* a violation of § 703(a)(1) of Title VII; (b) that the plaintiffs in this case therefore had at least the burden of proving discriminatory effect, and (c) that they failed in that proof. I do not join any inference or suggestion in the Court's opinion—if any such inference or suggestion is there—that effect may never be a controlling factor in a Title VII case. . . .

MR. JUSTICE BRENNAN, with whom MR. JUSTICE MARSHALL concurs, dissenting.

The Court holds today that without violating Title VII of the Civil Rights Act, 42 U.S.C. 2000e, a private employer may adopt a disability plan that compensates employees for all temporary disabilities except one affecting exclusively women, pregnancy. I respectfully dissent. Today's holding not only repudiates the applicable administrative guideline promulgated by the agency charged by Congress with implementation of the Act, but also rejects the unanimous conclusion of all six Courts of Appeals that have addressed this question. [Citations omitted.]

I

This case is unusual in that it presents a question the resolution of which at first glance turns largely upon the conceptual framework chosen to identify and describe the operational features of the challenged disability program. By directing their focus upon the risks excluded from the otherwise comprehensive program, and upon the purported justifications for such exclusions, the Equal Employment Opportunity Commission, the women plaintiffs, and the lower courts that the pregnancy exclusion constitutes a prima facie violation of Title

VII. This violation is triggered, they argue, because the omission of pregnancy from the program has the intent and effect of providing that "only women [are subjected] to a substantial risk of total loss of income because of temporary medical disability." Brief of EEOC.

The Court's framework is diametrically different. It views General Electric's plan as representing a gender-free assignment of risks in accordance with normal actuarial techniques. From this perspective the lone exclusion of pregnancy is not a violation of Title VII insofar as all other disabilities are mutually covered for both sexes. This reasoning relies primarily upon the descriptive statement borrowed from *Geduldig v. Aiello*, 417 U.S. 484, 496–97 (1974): "There is no risk from which men are protected and women are not. Likewise, there is no risk from which women are protected and men are not." According to the Court, this assertedly neutral sorting process precludes the pregnancy omission from constituting a violation of Title VII.

Presumably, it is not self-evident that either conceptual framework is more appropriate than the other, which can only mean that further inquiry is necessary to select the more accurate and realistic analytical approach. At the outset, the soundness of the Court's underlying assumption that the plan is the untainted product of a gender-neutral risk-assignment process can be examined against the historical backdrop of General Electric's employment practices and the existence or nonexistence of gender-free policies governing the inclusion of compensable risks. Secondly, the resulting pattern of risks insured by General Electric can then be evaluated in terms of the broad social objectives promoted by Title VII. I believe that the first inquiry compels the conclusion that the Court's assumption that General Electric engaged in a gender-neutral risk-assignment process is purely fanciful. The second demonstrates that the EEOC's interpretation that the exclusion of pregnancy from a disability insurance plan is incompatible with the overall objectives of Title VII has been unjustifiably rejected.

II

Geduldig v. Aiello, purports to be the starting point for the Court's analysis. There a state-operated disability insurance system containing a pregnancy exclusion was held not to violate the Equal Protection Clause. Although it quotes primarily from one footnote of that opinion at some length, the Court finally does not grapple with *Geduldig* on its own terms.

Considered most favorably to the Court's view, *Geduldig* established the proposition that a pregnancy classification standing alone cannot be said to fall into the category of classifications that rest explicitly on "gender as such," 417 U.S., at 496 n.20. Beyond that, *Geduldig* offers little analysis helpful to decision of this case. Surely it offends common-sense to suggest, that a classification resolving around pregnancy is not, at the minimum, strongly "sex related." *See, e.g., Cleveland Board of Education v. LaFleur*, 414 U.S. 632, 652 (1974) (POWELL, J., concurring). Indeed, even in the insurance context where neutral actuarial principles were found to have provided a legitimate and independent input into the decisionmaking process, *Geduldig's* outcome was qualified by the explicit reservation of a case where it could be demonstrated that a pregnancy-centered differentiation is used as a "mere pretext . . . designed to effect an invidious discrimination against the members of one sex. . . ." 417 U.S., at 496–97, n.20.

Thus, *Geduldig* itself obliges the Court to determine whether the exclusion of a sex-linked disability from the universe of compensable disabilities was actually the

product of neutral, persuasive actuarial considerations, or rather stemmed from a policy that purposefully downgraded women's role in the labor force. In *Geduldig*, that inquiry coupled with the normal presumption favoring legislative action satisfied the Court that the pregnancy exclusion in fact was prompted by California's legitimate fiscal concerns, and therefore that California did not deny equal protection in effectuating reforms "one step at a time." 417 U.S., at 495. But the record in this case makes such deference impossible here. Instead, in reaching its conclusion that a showing of purposeful discrimination has not been made, the Court simply disregards a history of General Electric practices that have served to undercut the employment opportunities of women who become pregnant while employed.[1] More-

1. General Electric's disability program was developed in an earlier era when women openly were presumed to play only a minor and temporary role in the labor force. As originally conceived in 1926, General Electric offered no benefit plan to its female employees because "women did not recognize the responsibilities of life, for they probably were hoping to get married soon and leave the Company." Vol. III. App. 958, excerpted from D. Loth, *Swope of General Electric: Story of Gerald Swope and G.E. in American Business* (1958). It was not until the 1930s and 1940s that the Company made female employees eligible to participate in the disability program. In common with general business practice, however, General Electric continued to pursue a policy of taking pregnancy and other factors into account in order to scale women's wages at ⅔ the level of men's. *Id.* at 1002. More recent company policies reflect common stereotypes concerning the potentialities of pregnant women . . . and have coupled forced maternity leave with the nonpayment of disability payments. Thus, the District Court found, "In certain instances it appears that the pregnant employee was required to take leave of her position three months prior to birth and not permitted to return until six

over, the Court studiously ignores the undisturbed conclusion of the District Court that General Electric's "discriminatory attitude" toward women was "a motivating factor in its policy," 375 F. Supp. 367, 383 (E.D. Va. 1974), and that the pregnancy exclusion was neither "neutral on its face" nor "in its intent." *Id.* at 382.

Plainly then, the Court's appraisal of General Electric's policy as a neutral process of sorting risks and "not a gender-based discrimination at all," cannot easily be squared with the historical record in this case. The Court, therefore, proceeds to a discussion of purported neutral criteria that suffice to explain the lone exclusion of pregnancy from the program. The Court argues that pregnancy is not "comparable" to other disabilities since it is a "voluntary" condition rather than a "disease." The fallacy of this argument is that even if "nonvoluntariness" and "disease" are to be construed as the operational criteria for inclusion of a disability in General Electric's program, application of these criteria is inconsistent with the Court's gender-neutral interpretation of the company's policy.

For example, the characterization of pregnancy as "voluntary"[3] is not a persuasive factor, for as the Court of Appeals correctly noted, "other than for childbirth disability, [General Electric] has never construed its plan as eliminating *all* so-called 'voluntary' disabilities," including sport injuries, attempted suicides, venereal disease, disabilities incurred in the commission of a crime or during a fight, and elective cosmetic surgery," 519 F.2d, at 665. Similarly, the label "disease" rather than "disability" cannot be deemed determinative since General Electric's pregnancy disqualification also excludes the 10 percent of pregnancies that end in debilitating miscarriages, 375 F. Supp., at 377, the 10 percent of cases where pregnancies are complicated by "diseases" in the intuitive sense of the word, *id.*, and cases where women recovering from childbirth are stricken by severe diseases unrelated to pregnancy.[4]

Moreover, even the Court's principal argument for the plan's supposed gender neutrality cannot withstand analysis. The central analytical framework relied upon to demonstrate the absence of discrimination is the principle described in *Geduldig:* "There is no risk from which men are pro-

---

weeks after the birth. In other instances the periods varies. . . . In short, of all the employees it is only pregnant women who have been required to cease work regardless of their desire and physical ability to work and only they have been required to remain off their job for an arbitrary period after the birth of their child." 375 F. Supp., at 385. In February 1973, approximately coinciding with commencement of this suit, the company abandoned its forced maternity-leave policy by formal directive.

3. Of course, even the proposition that pregnancy is a voluntary condition is overbroad, for the District Court found that "a substantial incidence of negligent or accidental conception also occurs." 375 F. Supp., at 377. I may assume, however, for purposes of this argument, that the high incidence of voluntary pregnancies and

the inability to differentiate between voluntary and involuntary conceptions, except perhaps through obnoxious, intrusive means, could justify the decision-maker's treating pregnancies as voluntarily induced.

4. The experience of one of the class plaintiffs is instructive of the reach of the pregnancy exclusion. On April 5, 1972, she took a pregnancy leave, delivering a stillborn baby some 9 days later. Upon her return home, she suffered a blood clot in the lung, a condition unrelated to her pregnancy, and was rehospitalized. The Company declined her claim for disability payments on the ground that pregnancy severed her eligibility under the plan. *See* 375 F. Supp., at 732. Had she been separated from work for any other reason—for example, during a work stoppage—the plan would have fully covered the embolism.

tected and women are not, . . . [and] no risk from which women are protected and men are not." 417 U.S., at 496–97. In fostering the impression that it is faced with a mere underinclusive assignment of risks in a gender-neutral fashion—that is, all other disabilities are insured irrespective of gender—the Court's analysis proves to be simplistic and misleading. For although all mutually contractible risks are covered irrespective of gender, *but see* n.4 *supra*, the plan also insures risks such as prostatectomies, vasectomies, and circumcisions that are specific to the reproductive system of men. . . . Again, pregnancy affords the only disability, sex-specific or otherwise, that is excluded from coverage.[5] Accordingly, the District Court appropriately remarked: "[T]he concern of defendants in reference to pregnancy risks, coupled with the apparent lack of concern regarding the balancing of other statistically sex-linked disabilities, buttresses the Court's conclusion that the discriminatory attitude characterized elsewhere in the Court's finding was in fact a motivating factor in its policy." 375 F. Supp., at 383.

If decision of this case, therefore, turns upon acceptance of the Court's view of

General Electric's disability plan as a sex-neutral assignment of risks, or plaintiffs' perception of the plan as a sex-conscious process expressive of the secondary status of women in the company's labor force, the history of General Electric's employment practices and the absence of definable gender-neutral sorting criteria under the plan warrants rejection of the Court's view in deference to the plaintiffs'.

III

. . .

General Electric's disability program has three divisible sets of effects. First, the plan covers all disabilities that mutually inflict both sexes. *But see* n.4 *supra*. Second, the plan insures against all disabilities that are male-specific or have a predominant impact on males. Finally, all female-specific and -impacted disabilities are covered, except for the most prevalent, pregnancy. The Court focuses on the first factor—the equal inclusion of mutual risks—and therefore understandably can identify no discriminatory effect arising from the plan. In contrast, EEOC and plaintiffs rely upon the unequal exclusion manifested in effects two and three to pinpoint an adverse impact on women. However one defines the profile of risks protected by General Electric, the determinative question must be whether the . . . aims to be furthered by Title VII and filtered through the phrase "to discriminate" contained in § 703(a)(1) fairly forbid an ultimate pattern of coverage that insures all risks except a commonplace one that is applicable to women but not to men.

As a matter of law and policy, this is a paradigm example of the type of complex economic and social inquiry that Congress wisely left to resolution by the EEOC pursuant to its Title VII mandate. *See* H.R. Rep. No. 92–238, 92d Cong., 2d Sess., U.S.

---

5. Indeed, the shallowness of the Court's "underinclusive" analysis is transparent. Had G.E. assembled a catalogue of all ailments that befall humanity, and then systematically proceeded to exclude from coverage every disability that is female-specific or predominantly inflicts women, the Court could still reason as here that the plan operates equally: Women, like men, would be entitled to draw disability payments for their circumcisions and prostatectomies, and neither sex could claim payment for pregnancies, breast cancer, and the other excluded female-dominated disabilities. Along similar lines, any disability that occurs disproportionately in a particular group—sickle-cell anemia, for example—could be freely excluded from the plan without troubling the Court's analytical approach.

[Code] Cong. & Admin. News, at 2144 (1972). And, accordingly, prior Title VII decisions have consistently acknowledged the unique persuasiveness of EEOC interpretations in this area. These prior decisions, rather than providing merely that Commission guidelines are "entitled to consideration," as the Court allows, hold that EEOC's interpretations should receive "great deference." *Albermarle Paper Co. v. Moody,* 422 U.S., at 431; *Griggs v. Duke Power Co.,* 401 U.S., at 433–34; *Phillips v. Martin Marietta Corp.,* at 400 U.S. 542, 545 (1971) (MARSHALL, J., concurring). Nonetheless, the Court today abandons this standard in order squarely to repudiate the 1972 Commission guideline providing that "[d]isabilities caused or contributed to by pregnancy . . . are, for all job-related purposes, temporary disabilities . . . [under] any health or temporary disability insurance or sick leave plan. . . ." 29 C.F.R. § 1604.10(b). This rejection is attributed to two interrelated events: a seven-year delay between Title VII's enactment and the promulgation of the Commission's guideline, and interim letters by EEOC's General Counsel expressing the view that pregnancy is not necessarily includable as a compensable disability. Neither event supports the Court's refusal to accord "great deference" to EEOC's interpretation.

It is true, as noted, that only brief mention of sex discrimination appears in the early legislative history of Title VII. It should not be surprising, therefore, that the EEOC, charged with a fresh and uncharted mandate, candidly acknowledged that further study was required before the contours of sex discrimination as proscribed by Congress could be defined. . . . These investigations on the role of pregnancy in the labor market coupled with the Commission's "review . . . [of] its case decision on maternity preparatory to issuing formal guidelines," *id.*, culminated in the 1972 guideline, the agency's first formalized, systematic statement on "Employment policies relating to pregnancy and childbirth."

Therefore, while some seven years had elapsed prior to the issuance of the 1972 guideline, and earlier opinion letters had refused to impose liability on employers during this period of deliberation, no one can or does deny that the final EEOC determination followed thorough and well-informed consideration. Indeed, realistically viewed, this extended evaluation of an admittedly complex problem and an unwillingness to impose additional, potentially premature costs on employers during the decisionmaking stages ought to be perceived as a practice to be commended. It is bitter irony that the care that preceded promulgation of the 1972 guideline is today condemned by the Court as tardy indecisiveness, its unwillingness irresponsibly to challenge employers' practices during the formative period is labelled as evidence of inconsistency, and this indecisiveness and inconsistency are bootstrapped into reasons for denying the Commission's interpretation its due deference.

For me, the 1972 regulation represents a particularly conscientious and reasonable product of EEOC deliberations and, therefore, merits our "great deference." Certainly, I can find no basis for concluding that the regulation is out of step with congressional intent. . . . On the contrary, prior to 1972, Congress enacted just such a pregnancy-inclusive rule to govern the distribution of benefits for "sickness" under the Railroad Unemployment Insurance Act, 45 U.S.C. § 351(K)(2). Furthermore, shortly following the announcement of the EEOC's rule, Congress approved and the President signed an essentially identical promulgation by the Department of Health, Education, and Welfare under Title IX of the Education Amendments of 1972, 20

U.S.C. (Supp. II) § 1681(a). *See* 45 C.F.R. § 86.57(c). Moreover, federal workers subject to the jurisdiction of the Civil Service Commission now are eligible for maternity and pregnancy coverage under their sick leave program. *See* Federal Personnel Manual, ch. 630, subch. 13, § 13–2 (April 30, 1975).

These policy formulations are reasonable responses to the uniform testimony of governmental investigations which show that pregnancy exclusions built into disability programs both financially burden women workers and act to break down the continuity of the employment relationship, thereby exacerbating women's comparatively transient role in the labor force. *See, e.g.,* U.S. Dept. of Commerce, Consumer Income (Series P–60, No. 93, July 1974); Women's Bureau, U.S. Dept. of Labor, *Underutilization of Women Workers* (rev. ed. 1971). In dictating pregnancy coverage under Title VII, EEOC's guideline merely settled upon a solution now accepted by every other Western industrial country. Dept. of HEW, *Social Security Programs Throughout the World,* 1971, at ix, xviii, xix. I find it difficult to comprehend that such a construction can be anything but a "sufficiently reasonable" one to be "accepted by the reviewing courts." *Train v. Natural Resources Defense Council,* 421 U.S. 60, 75 (1975). . . .

MR. JUSTICE STEVENS, dissenting.

The word "discriminate" does not appear in the Equal Protection Clause. Since the plaintiffs' burden of proving a prima facie violation of that constitutional provision is significantly heavier than the burden of proving a prima facie violation of a statutory prohibition against discrimination, the constitutional holding in *Geduldig v. Aiello,* 417 U.S. 484 (1974), does not control the question of statutory interpretation presented by this case. And, of course,

when it enacted Title VII of the Civil Rights Act of 1964, Congress could not possibly have relied on language which this Court was to use a decade later in the *Geduldig* opinion. We are, therefore, presented with a fresh, and rather simple, question of statutory construction: Does a contract between a company and its employees which treats the risk of absenteeism caused by pregnancy differently from any other kind of absence discriminate against certain individuals because of their sex?

An affirmative answer to that question would not necessarily lead to a conclusion of illegality, because a statutory affirmative defense might justify the disparate treatment of pregnant women in certain situations. In this case, however, the company has not established any such justification. On the other hand, a negative answer to the threshold question would not necessarily defeat plaintiffs' claim because facially neutral criteria may be illegal if they have a discriminatory effect. An analysis of the effect of a company's rules relating to absenteeism would be appropriate if those rules referred only to neutral criteria, such as whether an absence was voluntary or involuntary, or perhaps particularly costly. This case, however, does not involve rules of that kind.

Rather, the rule at issue places the risk of absence caused by pregnancy in a class by itself. By definition, such a rule discriminates on account of sex; for it is the capacity to become pregnant which primarily differentiates the female from the male. The analysis is the same whether the rule relates to hiring, promotion, the acceptability of an excuse for absence, or an exclusion from a disability insurance plan. Accordingly, without reaching the questions of motive, administrative expertise, and policy, which MR. JUSTICE BRENNAN so persuasively exposes, or the question of effect to which MR. JUSTICE STEWART and

MR. JUSTICE BLACKMUN refer, I conclude that the language of the statute plainly requires the result which the courts of appeals have reached unanimously.

CASE QUESTIONS

1. The Equal Rights Amendment states: "Equality of rights under the law shall not be denied or abridged . . . on account of sex." Would this amendment, if ratified, under the Court's reasoning forbid the exclusion of maternity disability benefits from the benefit packages of state employees?

2. Justice Brennan's dissent (in which Justice Marshall concurs) weights heavily the history of sexist employment practices of General Electric Company. Does this rhetorical strategy imply that employers without such histories of "bad faith" would be permitted under Title VII to exclude pregnancy disabilities from benefit plans?

3. What is the most important difference between Justice Stevens' dissent and that of Brennan and Marshall?

4. Consider the hypothetical plan outlined in Brennan's footnote 5. Would the Court majority accept such a plan as nondiscriminatory? If they would not, what is it that makes the singling out of pregnancy different from the singling out of *all* female-specific disabilities?

5. Who is correct in the dispute between Justice Blackmun and Justice Stewart whether the majority opinion implies that group impact can be considered as evidence of discrimination? Does it matter? See Justice Blackmun's opinion in the 1978 *Manhart* case (chapter 5) for an elaboration of his concern.

The denial of disability benefits for maternity leaves was not the only penalty that employers imposed on pregnant workers. Some companies also imposed on returning employees, after they had taken maternity leaves, the sanction of depriving them of all the seniority they had accumulated at that company. Because seniority generally brings with it a variety of privileges, this practice imposed a substantial burden on those female workers who happened to give birth to children.

One such employee, Nora Satty, who had worked for the Nashville Gas Company for three years was required by her employer to take a maternity leave five weeks before her baby was due to be born. When she tried to return to work, seven weeks after giving birth, her original job had been eliminated for economic reasons. Had Nora Satty not been deprived of her seniority benefits, she would have had first priority for new job openings at the company. It was company policy at Nashville Gas, however, to take away seniority benefits from persons on maternity leave, although the company did allow persons on leave for reasons of disease or injury to retain all seniority benefits on their return to work. So Nora Satty was given only a temporary job at the company, at a lower salary than she was earning when she left work. While in that temporary job, she applied for openings for three different permanent positions at higher salaries. Each of those jobs was gven to someone who had been hired while she was on leave and who, therefore, by the company's rule had more seniority than she (even though, she had three years of prior experience at the company and her competitors had only a few months on the job).

Nora Satty brought a lawsuit to a federal district court, claiming that this policy violated the prohibition in Title VII on sex discrimination in employment. Since *G.E. v. Gilbert* had not yet been decided, she also alleged that the company's denial of disability leave benefits to women on maternity leave constituted sex discrimination. The federal district court and a circuit of appeals sustained both of her claims.

The Supreme Court (in a unanimous decision in December 1977), however, sustained only her claim on seniority benefits. As for her claim on maternity leave pay, they remanded that portion of the case back to the lower courts for reconsideration in the light of the *Gilbert* ruling, which had been announced *after* the original court of appeals decision. But, in the "remand" section of his Supreme Court opinion, Justice Rehnquist carried only four other justices with him. Justice Powell, on the question of maternity leave pay, aligned himself with the *Gilbert* dissenters (Brennan, Marshall, and Stevens). Whether this shift was a sign that he was now willing to vote to overrule *Gilbert* is a question better addressed after reading the opinions in the case:

Nashville Gas Company v. Satty, 434 U.S. 136 (1977)

Mr. Justice Rehnquist delivered the opinion of the Court.

. . .

We conclude that petitioner's policy of denying accumulated seniority to female employees returning from pregnancy leave violates § 703(a)(2) of Title VII, 42 U.S.C. § 2000e–2(a)(2). That section declares it to be an unlawful employment practice for an employer to:

limit, segregate, or classify his employees or applicants for employment

in any way which would deprive or tend to deprive any individual of employment opportunities . . . because of such individual's . . . sex . . .

On its face, petitioner's seniority policy appears to be neutral in its treatment of male and female employees.[2] If an em-

2. The appearance of neutrality rests in part on petitioner's contention that its pregnancy leave policy is identical to the formal leave of absence granted to employees, male or female, in order that they may pursue additional education. However, petitioner's policy of denying ac-

ployee is forced to take a leave of absence from his job because of disease or any disability other than pregnancy, the employee, whether male or female, retains accumulated seniority and, indeed, continues to accrue seniority while on leave. If the employee takes a leave of absence for any other reason, including pregnancy, accumulated seniority is divested. Petitioner's decision not to treat pregnancy as a disease or disability for purposes of seniority retention is not on its face a discriminatory policy. "Pregnancy is, of course, confined to women, but it is in other ways significantly different from the typical covered disease or disability." *Gilbert*, at 136.

We have recognized, however, that both intentional discrimination and policies neutral on their face but having a discriminating effect may run afoul of § 703(a)(2). *Griggs v. Duke Power Co.*, 401 U.S. 424 (1971). It is beyond dispute that petitioner's policy of depriving employees returning from pregnancy leave of their accumulated seniority acts . . . to deprive them "of employment opportunities." . . . It is apparent from the previous recitation of the events which occurred following respondent's return from pregnancy leave that petitioner's policy denied her specific employment opportunities that she otherwise would have obtained. Even if she had ultimately been able to regain a permanent position with petitioner, she would have felt the effects of a lower seniority level, with its attendant relegation to less desirable and lower paying jobs, for the remainder of her career with petitioner.

---

cumulated seniority to employees returning from leaves of absence has not to date been applied outside of the pregnancy context. Since 1962, only two employees have requested formal leaves of absence to pursue a college degree; neither employee has returned. . . .

In *Gilbert*, there was no showing that General Electric's policy of compensating for all nonjob-related disabilities except pregnancy favored men over women. No evidence was produced to suggest that men received more benefits from General Electric's disability insurance fund than did women; both men and women were subject generally to the disabilities covered and presumably drew similar amounts. . . . We therefore upheld the plan under Title VII.

As there is no proof that the package is in fact worth more to men than to women, it is impossible to find any gender-based discriminatory effect in this scheme simply because women disabled as a result of pregnancy do not receive benefits; that is to say, gender-based discrimination does not result simply because an employer's disability benefits plan is less than all-inclusive. For all that appears pregnancy-related disabilities constitute an *additional* risk, unique to women, and the failure to compensate them for this risk does not destroy the presumed parity of the benefits, accruing to men and women alike, which results from the facially even-handed *inclusion* of risks. (429 U.S., at 138–40.)

Here, by comparison, petitioner has not merely refused to extend to women a benefit that men cannot and do not receive, but has imposed on women a substantial burden that men need not suffer. The distinction between benefits and burdens is more than one of semantics. We held in *Gilbert* that § 703(a)(1) did not require that greater economic benefits be paid to one sex or the other "because of their different roles in the scheme of existence, *Gilbert*, at 139, n.17. But that holding does not allow us to read § 703(a)(2) to permit an employer to burden female employees in such a way as to deprive them of employment opportunities because of their different role.

Recognition that petitioner's facially neutral seniority system does deprive women of employment opportunities because of their sex does not end the inquiry. . . . If a company's business necessitates the adoption of particular leave policies, Title VII does not prohibit the company from applying these policies to all leaves of absence, including pregnancy leaves; Title VII is not violated even though the policies may burden female employees. *Griggs*, 401 U.S. at 431; *Dothard v. Rawlinson*, 433 U.S. at 321, n.14. But we agree with the District Court in this case that since there was no proof of any business necessity adduced with respect to the policies in question, that court was entitled to "assume no justification exists." 384 F. Supp., at 771.

II

On the basis of the evidence presented to the District Court, petitioner's policy of not awarding sick-leave pay to pregnant employees is legally indistinguishable from the disability insurance program upheld in *Gilbert*. . . . We emphasized in *Gilbert* that exclusions of this kind are not *per se* violations of Title VII: "an exclusion of pregnancy from a disability-benefits plan providing general coverage is not a gender-based discrimination at all." 429 U.S., at 136. Only if a plaintiff through the presentation of other evidence can demonstrate that exclusion of pregnancy from the compensated conditions is a mere "[pretext] deigned to effect an invidious discrimination against the members of one sex or the other" does Title VII apply. *Id.*

In *Gilbert*, evidence had been introduced indicating that women drew substantially greater sums than did men from General Electric's disability insurance program, even though it excluded pregnancy. *Id.* at 130–31, nn.9 and 10. But our holding

did not depend on this evidence. The District Court in *Gilbert* expressly declined to find "that the present actuarial value of the coverage was equal as between men and women." We upheld the disability program on the ground "that neither [was] there a finding, nor was there any evidence which would support a finding, that the financial benefits of the Plan 'worked to discriminate against any definable group or class in terms of the aggregate risk protection derived by that group or class from the program.'" *Id.* at 138. When confronted by a facially neutral plan, whose only fault is underinclusiveness, the burden is on the plaintiff to show that the plan discriminates on the basis of sex in violation of Title VII. *Albemarle Paper Co. v. Moody*, 422 U.S. 405, 425 (1975); *McDonnell Douglas Corp. v. Green*, 411 U.S. 792, 802 (1973).

. . .

The District Court sitting as a trier of fact made no such finding in this case, and we are not advised whether it was requested to or not. The decision of the Court of Appeals was not based on any such finding, but instead embodied generally the same line of reasoning as the Court of Appeals for the Fourth Circuit followed in its opinion in *Gilbert v. General Electric Co.*, 519 F.2d 661 (1975). Since we rejected that line of reasoning in our opinion in *Gilbert*, the judgment of the Court of Appeals with respect to petitioner's sick pay policies must be vacated. That court and the District Court are in a better position than we are to know whether respondent adequately preserved in those courts the right to proceed further in the District Court on the theory which we have just described.[6]

6. Our Brother POWELL in his concurring opinion suggests that we also remand to allow respondent to develop a theory not articulated to

Affirmed in part, vacated in part, and remanded.

Mr. Justice Powell, with whom Mr. Justice Brennan and Mr. Justice Marshall join, concurring in the result and concurring in part.

I join part I of the opinion of the Court affirming the decision of the Court of Appeals that petitioner's policy denying accumulated seniority for job-bidding purposes to female employees returning from pregnancy leave violates Title VII.[1]

I also concur in the result in part II, for the legal status under Title VII of petitioner's policy of denying accumulated sick-pay benefits to female employees while on pregnancy leave requires further factual development in light of *G.E. v. Gilbert.* I write separately, however, because the Court appears to have constricted unnecessarily the scope of inquiry on remand by holding prematurely that respondent has failed to meet her burden of establish-

ing a prima facie case that petitioner's sick-leave policy is discriminatory under Title VII. This case was tried in the District Court and reviewed in the Court of Appeals before our decision in *Gilbert.* The appellate court upheld her claim in accord with the then uniform view of the courts of appeals that any disability plan that treated pregnancy differently from other disabilities was *per se* violative of Title VII. Since respondent had no reason to make the showing of gender-based discrimination required by *Gilbert,* I would follow our usual practice of vacating the judgment below and remanding to permit the lower court to reconsider its sick-leave ruling in light of our intervening decision.

The issue is not simply one of burden of proof, which properly rests with the Title VII plaintiff [citations omitted,] but of a "full opportunity for presentation of the relevant facts," *Harris v. Nelson,* 394 U.S. 286, 298 (1969). Given the meandering course that Title VII adjudication has taken . . . often . . . the parties or the lower courts proceeded on what was ultimately an erroneous theory of the case. Where the mistaken theory is premised on the pre-existing understanding of the law, and where the record as constituted does not foreclose the arguments made necessary by our ruling, I would prefer to remand . . . and permit the lower courts to pass on the new contentions in light of whatever additional evidence is deemed necessary. . . .

Here, respondent has abandoned the theory that enabled her to prevail in the [courts below]. Instead, she urges that her case is distinguishable from *Gilbert:*

> Respondent submits that because the exclusion of sick pay is only one of the many ways in which female employees who experience pregnancy are treated differently by petitioner, the holding in *Gilbert* is not controlling. . . . [and]

---

us, viz., that petitioner's sick-leave plan is monetarily worth more to men than to women.
Our opinion in *Gilbert* on this and other issues, of course, speaks for itself; we do not think it can rightly be characterized as so drastic a change in the law as it was understood to exist in 1974 as to enable respondent to raise or reopen issues on remand that she would not under settled principle be otherwise able to do. We assume that the Court of Appeals and the District Court will apply these latter principles in deciding what claims may be open to respondent on remand.

1. I would add, however, that petitioner's seniority policy, on its face, does not "appear to be neutral in its treatment of male and female employees." *Ante.* As the District Court noted below, "only pregnant women are required to take leave and thereby lose job-bidding seniority and no leave is required in other non-work related disabilities. . . ." 384 F. Supp. 765, 771 (M.D. Tenn. 1974). . . .

that petitioner's policies are much more pervasive than the mere under-inclusiveness of the Sickness and Accident Insurance Plan in *Gilbert*. (Brief for the Respondent.)

. . . First, . . . only pregnant women are required to take a leave of absence and are denied sick-leave benefits while in all other cases of nonoccupational disability sickleave benefits are available. 384 F. Supp., at 767, 771. Second, the sickleave policy is necessarily related to petitioner's discriminatory denial of job-bidding seniority to pregnant woman on mandatory maternity leave, presumably because both policies flow from the premise that a female employee is no longer in active service when she becomes pregnant.

Although respondent's theory is not fully articulated, she presents a plausible contention, one not required to have been raised until *Gilbert* and not foreclosed by the stipulated evidence or record. . . . It is not inconceivable that on remand respondent will be able to show that the combined operation of petitioner's mandatory maternity leave policy and denial of accumulated sick-pay benefits yielded significantly less net compensation for petitioner's female employees than for the class of male employees. A number of the former, but not the latter endured forced absence from work without sick pay or other compensation. The parties stipulated that, between July 2, 1965 and August 27, 1974, petitioner had placed 12 employees on pregnancy leave, and that some of these employees were on leave for periods of two months or more. It is possible that these women had not exhausted their sick-pay benefits at the time they were compelled to take a maternity leave, and that the denial of sick pay for this period of absence resulted in a relative loss of net compensation for petitioner's female workforce. Petitioner's male employees, on the other hand, are not sub-ject to a mandatory leave policy, and are eligible to receive compensation in some form for any period of absence from work due to sickness or disability.

In short, I would not foreclose the possibility that the facts as developed on remand will support a finding that "the package is in fact worth more to men than to women." *Gilbert*, 429 U.S., at 138. If such a finding were made, I would view respondent's case as not barred by *Gilbert*. . . .

I do not view the record in this case as precluding a finding of discrimination in compensation within the principles enunciated in *Gilbert*.[6] I would simply remand the sick-pay issue for further proceedings in light of our decision in that case.

MR. JUSTICE STEVENS, concurring in the judgment.

Petitioner enforces two policies that treat pregnant employees less favorably than other employees who incur a temporary disability. First, they are denied seniority benefits during their absence from work and thereafter; second, they are denied sick pay during their absence. The Court holds that the former policy is unlawful whereas the latter is lawful. I concur in the Court's judgment, but because I believe that its explanation of the legal distinction between the two policies may engender some confusion among those who must make compliance decisions on a day-to-day basis, I advance a separate, and rather pragmatic, basis for reconciling the two parts of the decision with each other and with *G.E. v. Gilbert*.

The general problem is to decide when

6. . . . I do not suggest that mathematical exactitude can or need be shown in every § 703(a)(1) case. But essential equality in compensation for comparable work is at the heart of § 703(a)(1). In my view, proof of discrimination in this respect would establish a prima facie violation.

a company policy which attaches a special burden to the risk of absenteeism caused by pregnancy is a *prima facie* violation of the statutory prohibition against sex discrimination. The answer "always," which I had thought quite plainly correct, is foreclosed by the Court's holding in *Gilbert*. The answer "never" would seem to be dictated by the Court's view that a discrimination against pregnancy is "not a gender-based discrimination at all." The Court has, however, made it clear that the correct answer is "sometimes." Even though a plan which frankly and unambiguously discriminates against pregnancy is "facially neutral," the Court will find it unlawful if it has a "discriminatory effect." The question, then is how to identify this discriminatory effect.

. . . The Court seems to rely on the difference between a benefit and a burden. . . . In my judgment, these differences are illusory.[4] I agree with the Court that the effect of the respondent's seniority plan is significantly different from that of the General Electric disability plan in *Gilbert*, but I suggest that the difference may be described in this way: although the *Gilbert* Court was unwilling to hold that discrimination against pregnancy—as compared with other physical disabilities—is discrimination on account of sex, it may nevertheless be true that discrimination against pregnant or formerly pregnant employees—as compared with other employees—does constitute sex discrimination. This distinction may be pragmatically expressed in terms of whether the employer has a policy which adversely affects

4. Differences between benefits and burdens cannot provide a meaningful test of discrimination since, by hypothesis, the favored class is always benefited and the disfavored class is equally burdened. The grant of seniority is a benefit which is not shared by the burdened class; conversely, the denial of sick pay is a burden which the benefited class need not bear. . . .

a woman beyond the term of her pregnancy leave.

Although the opinion in *Gilbert* characterizes as "facially neutral" a company policy which differentiates between an absence caused by pregnancy and an absence caused by illness, the factual context of *Gilbert* limits the reach of the broad characterization. Under the Court's reasoning, the disability plan in *Gilbert* did not discriminate against pregnant employees or formerly pregnant employees while they were working for the company. If an employee, whether pregnant or nonpregnant, contracted the measles, he or she would receive disability benefits; moreover, an employee returning from maternity leave would also receive those benefits. On the other hand, pregnancy, or an illness occurring while absent on maternity leave, was not covered. During that period of maternity leave, the pregnant woman was temporarily cut off from the benefits extended by the Company's plan. At all other times, the woman was treated the same as other employees in terms of her eligibility for the plan's benefits.

The Company's seniority plan in this case has a markedly different effect. In attempting to return to work, the formerly pregnant woman is deprived of all previously accumulated seniority. The policy affects both her ability to re-enter the work force, and her compensation when she does return. The company argues that these effects are permissible because they flow from its initial decision to treat pregnancy as an unexcused absence. But this argument misconceives the scope of the protection afforded by *Gilbert* to such initial decisions. For the G.E. plan did not attach any consequences to the condition of pregnancy that extended beyond the period of maternity leave. *Gilbert* allowed the employer to treat pregnancy leave as a temporal gap in the full employment status of a woman. During that period, the employer may treat the employee in a manner consistent with the determination that pregnancy is not an illness. In this case, however, the Company's seniority policy has an adverse impact on the employee's status after pregnancy leave is terminated. The formerly pregnant person is permanently disadvantaged as compared to the rest of the work force. And since the persons adversely affected by this policy comprise an exclusively female class, the Company's plan has an obvious discriminatory effect.[8]

Under this analysis, it is clear that petitioner's seniority rule discriminating against formerly pregnant employees is invalid. It is equally clear that the denial of sick pay during maternity leave is consistent with the *Gilbert* rationale, since the Company was free to withhold those benefits during that period.[9]

---

8. This analysis is consistent with the approach taken by lower courts to post-Gilbert claims of pregnancy-based discrimination, which have recognized that *Gilbert* "[has] nothing to do with foreclosing employment opportunity." *Cook v. Arentzen*, 14 EPD Par. 7544, p. 4702 (4th Cir. 1977); *MacLennan v. American Airlines, Inc.*, 46 U.S.L.W. 2215 (Va. Oct. 21, 1977). . . .

9. In his concurring opinion, Mr. Justice Powell seems to suggest that even when the

As is evident from my dissent in *Gilbert*, I would prefer to decide this case on a simpler rationale. Since that preference is foreclosed by *Gilbert*, I concur in the Court's judgment on the understanding that as the law now stands, although some discrimination against pregnancy—as compared with other physical disabilities—is permissible, discrimination against pregnant or formerly pregnant employees is not.

---

employer's disparate treatment of a pregnant employee is limited to the period of the pregnancy leave, it may still violate Title VII if the Company's rule has a greater impact on one sex than another. If this analysis does not require an overruling of *Gilbert* it must be applied with great caution, since the laws of probability would invalidate an inordinate number or rules on such a theory. It is not clear to me what showing, beyond "mathematical exactitude," . . . is necessary before this Court will hold that a classification, which is by definition gender-specific, discriminates on the basis of sex. Usually, statistical disparities aid a court in determining whether an apparently neutral classification is, in effect, gender or race specific. Here, of course, statistics would be unnecessary to prove that point. In all events, I agree with the Court that this issue is not presented to us in this case, and accordingly concur in the Court's determination of the proper scope of the remand.

CASE QUESTIONS

1. Is Justice Rehnquist convincing in his claim that principled differences can be drawn between (a) denying sick-leave pay for maternity leave but not for any other physical disability-related leave and (b) denying seniority benefits to returnees from maternity leave but not to returnees from any other physical disability-related leave? Is Justice Stevens' explanation more convincing? Is there a third explanation that might distinguish the two situations in a principled way?

2. Is Justice Powell having second thoughts about his vote in *Gilbert*? What is the import of Justice Stevens' critique of Jus-

tice Powell's opinion in footnote 9? Does it indicate that Justice Stevens is now willing to give up his opposition to the *Gilbert* rule? That he believes that Justice Powell now opposes the *Gilbert* rule?

3. Consider the fourth paragraph of part I and the second paragraph of part II of Justice Rehnquist's opinion regarding the basis of the *Gilbert* decision. A few months after he handed down the *Satty* decision, the Supreme Court announced, over the dissent of Justice Rehnquist, in *Los Angeles Department of Water and Power v. Manhart* (see chapter 5) that Title VII forbids the predication of employee benefits packages on group characteristics of a sex or a race. Does that announcement undermine the reasoning of *Gilbert* or not?

4. If the Court chose to follow Justice Stevens' suggestion concerning the application of Title VII to pregnant employees, would it be legal for an airline company to require that a stewardess take a leave from work during her ninth month of pregnancy?

Despite Rehnquist's efforts to reconcile *G.E. v. Gilbert* with *Nashville Gas v. Satty*, the two decisions do seem to be in conflict with each other. One holds that under Title VII pregnancy may be singled out for unique treatment by employers and the other holds that (in an only slightly different context) it may not. The explanation for the Court's change of tune may lie outside its chambers, in the political arena. During the interlude between the two decisions, Congress had not been idle. Recall (see text for n.83 in chapter 2) that ERA proponents in Congress in the early 1970s had endorsed the idea that legislation providing special treatment for maternity benefits should not be viewed as sex discrimination, since that would be an instance of taking account of actual physiological differences of reproductive function between the sexes. This view was fully compatible with *Geduldig* and *Gilbert*. But in 1977, in response to fierce reaction against *G.E. v. Gilbert* by feminist groups, the Senate voted overwhelmingly (75–11) for the Pregnancy Discrimination Act (PDA), a bill that specifically amended Title VII by defining pregnancy discrimination as a type of forbidden sex discrimination. Because of conflicts over how to treat employee abortion costs, the bill did not become law until October 1978 (ten months after *Satty*).[69] But anyone who read the Washington newspapers would have had a clear picture, by the time of *Satty*, of a dramatic change in the sense of Congress as to the moral and legal import of pregnancy discrimination. The public and therefore the Congressional consciousness of what constituted unfair sex discrimination had actually evolved in the course of the decade, and the Supreme Court did not lag far behind. The finishing touches on this portrait of an evolving legal concept were penned by the Supreme Court in 1983 in *Newport News Shipbuilding v. EEOC* (462 U.S. 669) when the justices ruled 7–2 that employers who provide medical expenses for spouses of their employees must include equal coverage for the medical expenses of maternity care for employees' wives.

Since the PDA referred specifically only to the treatment of pregnant employees, this conclusion was not obvious from the language of the statute. Indeed, three federal district courts and two out of three federal circuit courts of appeals had concluded otherwise concerning the impact of the PDA on spouse benefits. The circuit court of appeals whose decision was being appealed in *Newport News Shipbuilding*, however, had reasoned that the PDA, in addition to forbidding discrimination in employer-provided benefits for pregnant workers, had also transformed the very concept of sex discrimination so that it now included pregnancy discrimination. Thus, if the spouses of female employees had coverage for all medical expenses but the spouses of male employees did not have coverage for maternity-incurred medical expenses, those male employees suffered "discrimination on the basis of sex" in their job benefits. This reasoning was persuasive to a Supreme Court majority, although not to Justices Rehnquist and Powell.

Most of the Supreme Court debate in *Newport News* is over Congressional intent. In contrast to the reaction to the *Gilbert* decision, Congress has shown no inclination to overturn the *Newport News* reading of its statutory intent. Still, the Court's presentation of the legislative history of the PDA is instructive in that it seems to show a certain evasiveness on the part of the PDA sponsors as to the ultimate reach of the statute. The reader might consider whether the immediate political "payoff" of such evasiveness is worth its longterm costs to representative democracy, in that it seems to delegate considerably more power than necessary to nonelected, life-tenure judges. The Court debate over that legislative history follows.

Newport News Shipbuilding and Drycock v. Equal Employment Opportunity Commission (EEOC), 462 U.S. 669 (1983)

JUSTICE STEVENS delivered the opinion of the Court.

. . .

Ultimately the question we must decide is whether petitioner has discriminated against its male employees with respect to their compensation, terms, conditions, or privileges of employment because of their sex [in violation] . . . of § 703(a)(1) of Title VII. Although the Pregnancy Discrimination Act has clarified the meaning of certain terms in this section, neither that Act nor the underlying statute contains a defi-

nition of the word "discriminate." In order to decide whether petitioner's plan discriminates against male employees because of *their* sex, we must therefore go beyond the bare statutory language. Accordingly, we shall consider whether Congress, by enacting the Pregnancy Discrimination Act, not only overturned the specific holding in *General Electric v. Gilbert*, but also rejected the test of discrimination employed by the Court in that case. We believe it did. Under the proper test petitioner's plan is unlawful, because the protection it affords to married male employees is less comprehensive than the protection it affords to married female employees.

I

. . .

As a matter of statutory interpretation, the dissenters [in *Gilbert*] rejected the Court's holding that the plan's exclusion of disabilities caused by pregnancy did not constitute discrimination based on sex. As JUSTICE BRENNAN explained, it was facially discriminatory for the company to devise "a policy that, but for pregnancy, offers protection for all risks, even those that are 'unique to' men or heavily male dominated." 429 U.S., at 160. It was inaccurate to describe the program as dividing potential recipients into two groups, pregnant women and non-pregnant persons, because insurance programs "deal with future *risks* rather than historic facts." Rather, the appropriate classification was "between persons who face a risk of pregnancy and those who do not." *Id.* at 161–62, n.5 (STEVENS, J., dissenting). The company's plan, which was intended to provide employees with protection against the risk of uncompensated unemployment caused by physical disability, discriminated on the basis of sex by giving men protection for all categories of risk but giving women only partial protection. Thus, the dissenters asserted that the statute had been violated because conditions of employment for females were less favorable than for similarly situated males.

When Congress amended Title VII in 1978, it unambiguously expressed its disapproval of both the holding and the reasoning of the Court in the *Gilbert* decision. It incorporated a new subsection in the "definitions" applicable "[f]or the purposes of this subchapter." 42 U.S.C. § 2000e–2 (1976 ed., Supp. V). The first clause of the Act states, quite simply: "The terms 'because of sex' or 'on the basis of sex' include, but are

not limited to, because of or on the basis of pregnancy, childbirth, or related medical conditions." § 2000e–(k). The House Report stated, "It is the Committee's view that the dissenting Justices correctly interpreted the Act." Similarly, the Senate Report quoted passages from the two dissenting opinions, stating that they "correctly express both the principle and the meaning of title VII." Proponents of the bill repeatedly emphasized that the Supreme Court had erroneously interpreted Congressional intent and that amending legislation was necessary to reestablish the principles of Title VII law as they had been understood prior to the *Gilbert* decision. Many of them expressly agreed with the views of the dissenting Justices.

As petitioner argues, congressional discussion focused on the needs of female members of the work force rather than spouses of male employees. This does not create a "negative inference" limiting the scope of the act to the specific problem that motivated its enactment. . . . When the question of differential coverage for dependents was addressed in the Senate Report, the Committee indicated that it should be resolved "on the basis of existing title VII principles." [20] The legislative context makes it clear that Congress was not thereby referring to the view of Title VII reflected in this

20. "Questions were raised in the committee's deliberations regarding how this bill would affect medical coverage for dependents of employees, as opposed to employees themselves. In this context it must be remembered that the basic purpose of this bill is to protect women employees, it does not alter the basic principles of title VII law as regards sex discrimination. Rather, this legislation clarifies the definition of sex discrimination for title VII purposes. Therefore the question in regard to dependents' benefits would be determined on the basis of existing title VII principles." Leg. Hist. at 42–43; S. Rep. No. 95–331, *supra* n.16, at 6.
This statement does not imply that the new stat-

Court's *Gilbert* opinion. Proponents of the legislation stressed throughout the debates that Congress had always intended to protect *all* individuals from sex discrimination in employment—including but not limited to pregnant women workers.[21] Against this

_____

utory definition has no applicability; it merely acknowledges that the new definition does not itself resolve the question.

The dissent quotes extensive excerpts from an exchange on the Senate floor between Senators Hatch and Williams. Taken in context, this colloquy clearly deals only with the second clause of the bill, and Senator Williams, the principal sponsor of the legislation, addressed only the bill's effect on income maintenance plans. Leg. Hist. at 80. Senator Williams first stated, in response to Senator Hatch, "With regard to more maintenance plans for pregnancy-related disabilities, I do not see how this language could be misunderstood." Upon further inquiry from Senator Hatch, he replied, "If there is any ambiguity, with regard to income maintenance plans, I cannot see it." At the end of the same response, he stated, "It is narrowly drawn and would not give any employee the right to obtain income maintenance as a result of the pregnancy of someone who is not an employee." *Id.* These comments, which clearly limited the scope of Senator Williams' responses, are omitted from the dissent's lengthy quotation.

Other omitted portions of the colloquy make clear that it was logical to discuss the pregnancies of employees' spouses in connection with income maintenance plans. Senator Hatch asked, "what about the status of a woman coworker who is not pregnant but rides with a pregnant woman and cannot get to work once the pregnant female commences her maternity leave or the employed mother who stays home to nurse her pregnant daughter?" The reference to spouses of male employees must be understood in light of these hypothetical questions; it seems to address the situation in which a male employee wishes to take time off from work because his wife is pregnant.

21. *See, e.g.,* 123 Cong. Rec. 7539 (1977) (remarks of Sen. Williams) ("the Court has ignored the congressional intent in enacting title VII of the Civil Rights Act—that intent was to protect

background we review the terms of the amended statute to decide whether petitioner has unlawfully discriminated against its male employees.

II

Section 703(a) makes it an unlawful employment practice for an employer to "discriminate against any individual with respect to his compensation, terms, conditions, or privileges of employment, because of such individual's race, color, religion, sex, or national origin. . . ." 42 U.S.C. § 2002e–2(a) (1976). Health insurance and other fringe benefits are "compensation, terms, conditions, or privileges of employment." Male as well as female employees are protected against discrimination. Thus, if a private employer were to provide complete health insurance coverage for the dependents of its female employees, and no coverage at all for the dependents of its male employees, it would violate Title VII. Such a practice would not pass the simple test of Title VII discrimination that we

_____

all individuals from unjust employment discrimination, including pregnant workers"); *id.* at 29385, 29652. In light of statements such as these, it would be anomalous to hold that Congress provided that an employee's pregnancy is sex-based, while a spouse's pregnancy is gender-neutral.

During the course of the Senate debate on the Pregnancy Discrimination Act, Senator Bayh and Senator Cranston both expressed the belief that the new act would prohibit the exclusion of pregnancy coverage for spouses if spouses were otherwise fully covered by an insurance plan. *See* 123 Cong. Rec. 29642, 29663 (1977). Because our holding relies on the 1978 legislation only to the extent that it unequivocally rejected the *Gilbert* decision, and ultimately we rely on our understanding of general Title VII principles, we attach no more significance to these two statements than to the many other comments by both Senators and Congressmen disapproving the Court's reasoning and conclusion in *Gilbert*.

enunciated in *Los Angeles Department of Water & Power v. Manhart*, 435 U.S. 702, 711 (1978), for it would treat a male employee with dependents "in a manner which but for that person's sex would be different."* The same result would be reached even if the magnitude of the discrimination were smaller. For example, a plan that provided complete hospitalization coverage for the spouses of female employees but did not cover spouses of male employees when they had broken bones would violate Title VII by discriminating against male employees.

Petitioner's practice is just as unlawful. Its plan provides limited pregnancy-related benefits for employees' wives, and affords more extensive coverage for employees' spouses for all other medical conditions requiring hospitalization. Thus the husbands of female employees receive a specified level of hospitalization coverage for all conditions; the wives of male employees receive such coverage except for pregnancy-related conditions. Although *Gilbert* concluded that an otherwise inclusive plan that singled out pregnancy-related benefits for exclusion was nondiscriminatory on its face, because only women can become pregnant, Congress has unequivocally rejected that reasoning. The 1978 Act makes clear that it is discriminatory to treat pregnancy-related conditions less favorably than other medical conditions. Thus petitioner's plan unlawfully gives married male employees a benefit package for their dependents that is less inclusive than the dependency coverage provided to married female employees.

There is no merit to petitioner's argument that the prohibitions of Title VII do not extend to discrimination against pregnant spouses because the statute applies only to discrimination in employ-

ment. A two-step analysis demonstrates the fallacy in this contention. The Pregnancy Discrimination Act has now made clear that, for all Title VII purposes, discrimination based on a woman's pregnancy is, on its face, discrimination because of her sex. And since the sex of the spouse is always the opposite of the sex of the employee, it follows inexorably that discrimination against female spouses in the provision of fringe benefits is also discrimination against male employees. *Cf. Wengler v. Druggists Mutual Ins. Co.*, 446 U.S. 142, 147 (1980).[25] By making clear that an employer could not discriminate on the basis of an employer's pregnancy, Congress did not erase the original prohibition against discrimination on the basis of an employee's sex.

In short, Congress' rejection of the premises of *General Electric v. Gilbert* forecloses any claim that an insurance program excluding pregnancy coverage for female beneficiaries and providing complete coverage to similarly situated male beneficiaries does not discriminate on the basis of sex. Petitioner's plan is the mirror image of the plan at issue in *Gilbert*. The pregnancy limitation in this case violates Title VII by discriminating against male employees.

The judgment of the Court of Appeals is

Affirmed.

25. . . . This reasoning does not require that a medical insurance plan treat the pregnancies of employees' wives the same as the pregnancies of female employees. For example, as the EEOC recognizes . . . an employer might provide full coverage for employees and no coverage at all for dependents. Similarly, a disability plan covering employees' children may exclude or limit maternity benefits. Although the distinction between pregnancy and other conditions is, according to the 1978 Act, discrimination "on the basis of sex," the exclusion affects male and female *employees* equally since both may have pregnant dependent daughters.

*See chapter 5.—Au.

JUSTICE REHNQUIST, with whom JUS-
TICE POWELL joins, dissenting.

. . .

Congress, of course, was free to legislatively overrule *Gilbert* in whole or in part,
and there is no question but what the Pregnancy Discrimination Act manifests congressional dissatisfaction with the result
we reached in *Gilbert*. But I think the court
reads far more into the Pregnancy Discrimination Act than Congress put there,
and that therefore it is the Court, and not
Congress, which is now overruling *Gilbert*.

In a case presenting a relatively simple
question of statutory construction, the
Court pays virtually no attention to the language of the Pregnancy Discrimination Act
or the legislative history pertaining to that
language. The Act provides in relevant part:

> The terms "because of sex" or "on the
> basis of sex" include, but are not lim-
> ited to, because of or on the basis of
> pregnancy, childbirth, or related medi-
> cal conditions; and women affected
> by pregnancy, childbirth, or related
> medical conditions shall be treated the
> same for all employment-related pur-
> poses, including receipt of benefits
> under fringe benefit programs, as
> other persons not so affected but
> similar in their ability or inability to
> work. . . . (Pub. L. 95–555, 92 Stat.
> 2076, 42 U.S.C. § 2000e[k].)

The Court recognizes that this provision is merely definitional and that "[u]l-
timately the question we must decide
is whether petitioner has discriminated
against its male employees . . . because of
their sex within the meaning of § 703(a)(1)"
of Title VII. Section 703(a)(1) provides in
part:

> It shall be an unlawful employment
> practice for an employer . . . to fail or
> refuse to hire or to discharge any indi-
> vidual, or otherwise to discriminate
> against any individual with respect to
> his compensation, terms, conditions,
> or privileges of employment, because
> of such individual's race, color, reli-
> gion, sex, or national origin. . . . (42
> U.S.C. § 2000e–2[a][1].)

It is undisputed that in § 703(a)(1) the word
"individual" refers to an employee or applicant for employment. As modified by the
first clause of the definitional provision
of the Pregnancy Discrimination Act, the
proscription in § 703(a)(1) is for discrimination "against any individual . . . *because of
such individual's . . . pregnancy*, childbirth,
or related medical conditions." This can
only be read as referring to the pregnancy
of an *employee*.

That this result was not inadvertent on
the part of Congress is made very evident
by the second clause of the Act, language
that the Court essentially ignores in its
opinion. When Congress in this clause
further explained the proscription it was
creating by saying that "women affected
by pregnancy . . . shall be treated the
same . . . as other persons not so affected
but *similar in their ability or inability to work*"
it could only have been referring to *female
employees*. The Court of Appeals below
stands alone in thinking otherwise.

. . .

The plain language of the Pregnancy
Discrimination Act leaves little room for
the Court's conclusion that the Act was
intended to extend beyond female employees. The Court concedes that "congressional discussion focused on the needs
of female members of the work force rather
than spouses of male employees." In fact,
the singular focus of discussion on the
problems of the *pregnant worker* is striking.

When introducing the Senate Report
on the bill that later became the Pregnancy

Discrimination Act, its principal sponsor, Senator Williams, explained:

> Because of the Supreme Court's decision in the *Gilbert* case, this legislation is necessary to provide fundamental protection against sex discrimination for our Nation's 42 million *working women*. This protection will go a long way toward insuring that American women are permitted to assume their rightful place in our Nation's economy.
>
> In addition to providing protection to *working women* with regard to fringe benefit programs, such as health and disability insurance programs, this legislation will prohibit other employment policies which adversely affect *pregnant workers*. (124 Cong. Rec. S18,977 [daily ed. Oct. 13, 1978] [emphasis added].)

As indicated by the examples in the margin,[5] the Congressional Record is overflowing with similar statements by individual members of Congress expressing their intention to insure with the Pregnancy Discrimination Act that working women are not treated differently because of pregnancy. Consistent with these views, all three committee reports on the bills that led to the Pregnancy Discrimination Act expressly state that the Act would require employers to treat pregnant employees the same as "other employees."

The Court tries to avoid the impact of this legislative history by saying that it "does not create a 'negative inference' limiting the scope of the act to the specific problem that motivated its enactment." This reasoning might have some force if the legislative history was silent on an arguably

5. [This note cited references to "women workers" or "women employees" by 22 different members of Congress.]

related issue. But the legislative history is not silent. The Senate Report provides:

> Questions were raised in the committee's deliberations regarding how this bill would affect medical coverage for dependents of employees, as opposed to employees themselves. In this context it must be remembered that the basic purpose of this bill is to protect women employees, it does not alter the basic principles of title VII law as regards sex discrimination. . . . [T]he question in regard to dependents' benefits would be determined on the basis of existing title VII principles. . . . *[T]he question of whether an employer who does cover dependents, either with or without additional cost to the employee, may exclude conditions related to pregnancy from that coverage is a different matter.* Presumably because plans which provide comprehensive medical coverage for spouses of women employees but not spouses of male employees are rare, we are not aware of any title VII litigation concerning such plans. It is certainly not this committee's desire to encourage the institution of such plans. If such plans should be instituted in the future, the question would remain whether, under title VII, the affected employees were discriminated against on the basis of their sex as regards the extent of coverage for their dependents. (S. Rep. No. 331. 95th Cong., 1st Sess. 5–6 [1977], Leg. Hist., at 42–43 [emphasis added].)

This plainly disclaims any intention to deal with the issue presented in this case. Where Congress says that it would not want "to encourage" plans such as petitioner's, it cannot plausibly be argued that Congress has intended "to prohibit" such plans. Senator Williams was questioned on this point by Senator Hatch during discussions on the floor and his answers are to the same effect.

MR. HATCH: . . . The phrase "women affected by pregnancy, childbirth or related medical conditions," . . . appears to be overly broad, and is not limited in terms of employment. It does not even require that the person so affected be pregnant.

Indeed under the present language of the bill, it is arguable that spouses of male employees are covered by this civil rights amendment. . . .

Could the sponsors clarify exactly whom that phrase intends to cover?

. . .

MR. WILLIAMS: . . . I do not see how one can read into this any pregnancy other than that pregnancy that relates to the employee, and if there is any ambiguity, *let it be clear here and now that this is very precise. It deals with a woman, a woman who is an employee,* an employee in a work situation where all disabilities are covered under a company plan that provides income maintenance in the event of medical disability; that her particular period of disability, when she cannot work because of childbirth or anything related to childbirth is excluded. . . .

. . .

MR. HATCH: So the Senator is satisfied that, though the committee language I brought up, "woman affected by pregnancy" seems to be ambiguous, what it means is that *this act only applies to the particular woman who is actually pregnant, who is an employee and has become pregnant after her employment?*

. . .

MR. WILLIAMS: *Exactly.* (123 Cong. Rec. S15,038–39 [daily ed. Sept. 16, 1977], Leg. Hist., at 80 [emphasis added].)[7]

It seems to me that analysis of this case should end here. Under our decision in *General Electric Co. v. Gilbert* petitioner's exclusion of pregnancy benefits for male employee's spouses would not offend Title VII. Nothing in the Pregnancy Discrimination Act was intended to reach beyond female employees. Thus, *Gilbert* controls and requires that we reverse the Court of Appeals. But it is here, at what should be the stopping place, that the Court begins. The Court says:

Although the Pregnancy Discrimination Act has clarified the meaning of certain terms in this section, neither that Act nor the underlying statute contains a definition of the word "discriminate." In order to decide whether petitioner's plan discriminates against male employees because of *their* sex, we must therefore go beyond the bare statutory language. Accordingly, we shall consider whether Congress, by enacting the Pregnancy Discrimination Act, not only overturned the specific holding in *General Electric v. Gilbert, supra,* but also rejected the test of discrimination employed by the Court in that case. We believe it did. (*Ante.*)

7. The Court suggests that in this exchange Senator Williams is explaining only that spouses of male employees will not be put on "income maintenance plans" while pregnant. *Ante,* at n.20. This is utterly illogical. Spouses of employees have no income from the relevant employer to be maintained. Senator Williams clearly says that the Act is limited to female employees and as to such employees it will ensure income maintenance where male employees would receive similar disability benefits. Senator

It would seem that the Court has refuted its own argument by recognizing that the Pregnancy Discrimination Act only clarifies the meaning of the phrases "because of sex" and "on the basis of sex," and says nothing concerning the definition of the word "discriminate." Instead the Court proceeds to try and explain that while Congress said one thing, it did another.

The crux of the Court's reasoning is that even though the Pregnancy Discrimination Act redefines the phrases "because of sex" and "on the basis of sex" only to include discrimination against female employees affected by pregnancy, Congress also expressed its view that in *Gilbert* "the Supreme Court . . . erroneously interpreted Congressional intent." *Ante*. Some-

how the Court then concludes that this renders all of *Gilbert* obsolete.

In support of its argument, the Court points to a few passages in congressional reports and several statements by various members of the 95th Congress to the effect that the Court in *Gilbert* had, when it construed Title VII, misperceived the intent of the 88th Congress. *Ante*, at n.17. The Court also points out that "[m]any of [the members of 95th Congress] expressly agreed with the views of the dissenting Justices." *Ante*. Certainly *various members of Congress* said as much. But the fact remains that *Congress as a body* has not expressed these sweeping views in the Pregnancy Discrimination Act.

. . . I dissent.

Hatch's final question and Senator Williams' response could not be clearer. The Act was intended to affect *only* pregnant workers. This is exactly what the Senate Report said and Senator Williams confirmed that this is exactly what Congress intended.

The only indications arguably contrary to the views reflected in the Senate Report and the exchange between Senators Hatch and Williams are found in two isolated remarks by Senators Bayh and Cranston. 123 Cong. Rec. S15,037, S15,058 (daily ed. Sept. 16, 1977), Leg. Hist., at 75, 131. These statements, however, concern these two Senators' view concerning Title VII sex

discrimination as it existed prior to the Pregnancy Discrimination Act. Their conclusions are completely at odds with our decision in *General Electric Co. v. Gilbert*, 429 U.S. 125 (1976), and are not entitled to deference here. We have consistently said that "[t]he views of members of a later Congress, concerning different [unamended] sections of Title VII . . . are entitled to little if any weight. It is the intent of the Congress that enacted [Title VII] in 1964 . . . that controls." *Teamsters v. United States*, 431 U.S. 324, 354 n.39 (1977). *See also Southeastern Community College v. Davis*, 442 U.S. 397, 411 n.11 (1979).

Congress' adoption in 1978 of the Pregnancy Discrimination Act more or less mandated that an antidiscrimination approach supersede the penalty-on-a-fundamental-right analysis, which the Court had employed with regard to government programs in the *LaFleur* and *Turner* cases but had ignored in the 1974–1977 cases on denials of benefits to pregnant employees. Although this legislation clearly prohibited the obvious employer discriminations against pregnancy such as the one the Court had confronted in *G.E. v. Gilbert*, the federal statute's impact on affirmative protections for pregnant workers was less clear. Congress had not been contemplating such protections when it commanded that female employees "affected by pregnancy, childbirth, or related medical conditions . . .

be treated the same for all employment-related purposes . . . as other persons not so affected but similar in their ability or inability to work."

In deciding whether this federal law conflicted with and overrode a California statute that required employers to provide, at employee option, (unpaid) leave of up to four months for medical disability due to pregnancy (see chapter 1, *California Fed. Savings v. Guerra*, 1987), the Supreme Court chose not to return to the *LaFleur* line of analysis. Conceivably, in the *Guerra* case the Court could have taken into account that California was acting to enhance the exercise of a fundamental constitutional right, the right to choose to bear a child. Instead, all members of the Court looked simply at the question of discrimination. The Court majority insisted that the federal law should be read as forbidding only discrimination *against* pregnant employees while the dissenters insisted to the contrary that all discrimination, for or against, pregnant workers was forbidden (and that since the state statute favored pregnant workers, it had to be struck down.) Although the Court has continued to eschew the fundamental rights approach of *LaFleur* and *Turner,* that analysis may crop up again as the Court examines new variations on *Guerra*-type statutes that mandate special benefits for mothers in the workforce.

The latest rounds of Court decisions affecting the treatment of abortion and pregnancy have made two things clear. First, the Supreme Court is not prepared, at least for now, to overrule either the basic *Roe v. Wade* and *Doe v. Bolton* decisions or the basic *Cleveland v. LaFleur* decision. No state may impose criminal penalties on the obtaining of a safe abortion in the pre-viability stages of pregnancy, and no state may fire someone from a job for which she is competent, just because she is pregnant.

Second, if women expect government help in financing the cost of abortion or of pregnancy, that help is not going to come solely from court orders, not now anyway. The women's rights movement, in this area, at least, had to move out of the courtroom and into the political arena. Only effective legislative lobbying and successful electoral activity enabled women to alter the Court's analysis of the treatment of pregnancy in employee benefit plans. And in a good many states, successful legislative politicking has obtained state funding for abortions for the indigent. That such benefits have not been judged constitutional rights does not mean that they are unobtainable, and the dust has not yet settled on this particular front of the women's rights battlefield.

CHAPTER 5

Congressional
Enforcement
of Equal Protection [1]

Employment

The First Decade of Judicial Implementation

Although courses in constitutional law generally focus on Supreme Court interpretations of the Constitution, to the exclusion of Supreme Court interpretations of federal statutes, a substantial portion of the public policy impact of the Supreme Court (and other federal courts) derives from their role as interpreters of federal statute law. Congress, after all, is charged, in the Fourteenth Amendment (section 5), with the "power to enforce, by appropriate legislation, the provisions of this article." Thus, much of what the Supreme Court has to say about the Fourteenth Amendment arises in the context of interpreting such "appropriate legislation."

When litigants bring pleas to court solely on the basis of statutory claims, statutory interpretation of necessity becomes decisive. Still, the question of constitutional rights is never absent from these cases. For, in such situations, the Court's job is to interpret Congress' legislation, if at all possible, in a manner that will comport with the Constitution. Since Congress, too, is governed by the Constitution, in these statutory cases the Court, in effect, is interpreting Congress' interpretation of the Constitution.

I have already noted that 1971 was a watershed year for constitutional interpretation: it produced the turning-point case of *Reed v. Reed*, in which the Court moved sex (at least if one examines outcomes of cases, as distinguished from official doctrine) from the category of ordinary classification to semi-suspect classification. The same year ushered in a second major turning point in women's rights litigation: in the case of *Phillips v. Martin-Marietta Corp.*, the Supreme Court began to implement the sex discrimination provisions of Title VII of the 1964 Civil Rights Act.

The Equal Employment Opportunity Commission (EEOC), the enforcement agency for this act, still had no effective mechanism for enforcing the act. Suit against Martin-Marietta Corporation, therefore, was brought by a private individual, Ida Phillips. Ms. Phillips had tried to apply for a job with Martin-Marietta and had met with the response that the company did not accept job applications from women with pre-school-age children. Ms. Phillips viewed this practice as discrimination based on sex, and she sued in federal court to obtain an order that she be hired.

Title VII makes it unlawful for an employer "to refuse to hire . . . any individual . . . because of such individual's race, color, religion, sex, or national origin" except where "religion, sex, or national origin is a bona fide occupational qualification reasonably necessary to the normal operation of that particular business." Martin-Marietta did hire men with pre-school-age children. However, in the job slot for which Ms. Phillips tried to apply, assembly trainee, 70–75 percent of the applicants, and 75–80 percent of the persons hired for the job, were women.

Because of these figures, the federal district court granted "summary judgment" (judgment without a full-blown, formal hearing) in favor of the corporation, stating that a pattern of "bias against women as such" had not been presented. The circuit court of appeals upheld the district court. The Supreme Court in a per curiam opinion sent the case back to the court of appeals for reconsideration, with the following terse advice:

Phillips v. Martin-Marietta Corporation, 400 U.S. 542 (1971)

Per Curiam.

. . .

Section 703(a) of the Civil Rights Act of 1964 requires that persons of like qualifications be given employment opportunities irrespective of their sex. The Court of Appeals therefore erred in reading this section as permitting one hiring policy for women and another for men—each having pre-school-age children. The existence of such conflicting family obligations, if demonstrably more relevant to job performance for a woman than for a man, could arguably be a basis for distinction under § 703(e) of the Act. But that is a matter of evidence tending to show that the condition in question "is a bona fide occupational qualification reasonably necessary

to the normal operation of that particular business or enterprise." The record before us, however, is not adequate for resolution of these important issues. Summary judgment was therefore improper and we remand for fuller development of the record and for further consideration.

Vacated and remanded.

MR. JUSTICE MARSHALL, concurring.

While I agree that this case must be remanded for a full development of the facts, I cannot agree with the Court's indication that a "bona fide occupational qualification reasonably necessary to the normal operaton of" Martin-Marietta's business could be established by a showing that some women, even the vast majority, with pre-school-age children have family responsibilities that interfere with job performance and that men do not usually have such responsibilities. Certainly, an employer can require that all of his employees, both men and women, meet minimum performance standards, and he can try to insure compliance by requiring parents, both mothers and fathers, to provide for the care of their children so that job performance is not interfered with.

But the Court suggests that it would not require such uniform standards. I fear that in this case, where the issue is not squarely before us, the Court has fallen into the trap of assuming that the Act permits ancient canards about the proper role of women to be a basis for discrimination. Congress, however, sought just the opposite result.

By adding the prohibition against job discrimination based on sex to the 1964 Civil Rights Act Congress intended to prevent employers from refusing "to hire an individual based on stereotyped characterizations of the sexes." EEOC Guidelines on Discrimination Because of Sex, 29 CFR § 1604.1(a)(i)(iii). . . . Even characterizations of the proper domestic roles of the sexes were not to serve as predicates for restricting employment opportunity. The exception of a "bona fide occupational qualification" was not intended to swallow the rule.

That exception has been construed by the EEOC, whose regulations are entitled to "great deference," *Udall v. Tallman*, 380 U.S. 1, 16, to be applicable only to job situations that require specific physical characteristics necessarily possessed by only one sex.[3] Thus the exception would

sex should be interpreted narrowly. Labels—'Men's jobs' and 'Women's jobs'—tend to deny employment opportunities unnecessarily to one sex or the other.

"(1) The Commission will find that the following situations do not warrant the application of the bona fide occupational qualification exception:

"(i) The refusal to hire a woman because of her sex, based on assumption of the comparative employment characteristics of women in general. For example, the assumption that the turnover rate among women is higher than among men.

"(ii) The refusal to hire an individual based on steretyped characterizations of the sexes. Such stereotypes include, for example, that men are less capable of assembling intricate equipment; that women are less capable of aggressive salesmanship. The principle of non-discrimination requires that individuals be considered on the basis of individual capacities and not on the basis of any characteristics generally attributed to the group.

. . .

"(b) (1) Many States have enacted laws or promulgated administrative regulations with respect to the employment of females. Among these laws are those which prohibit or limit the employment of females, e.g., the employment of females in certain occupations, in jobs requiring the lifting or carrying of weights exceeding certain prescribed limits, during certain hours of the night, or for more than a specified number of hours per day or per week.

"(2) The Commission believes that such State laws and regulations, although originally promulgated for the purpose of protecting females, have ceased to be relevant to our technology or to the expanding role of the female worker in our economy. The Commission has found that such laws and regulations do not take into account the capacities, preferences, and abilities of individual females and tend to discriminate rather than protect. Accordingly, the Commission has concluded that such laws and regulations conflict with Title VII of the Civil Rights Act of 1964 and will not be considered a defense to an otherwise established unlawful employment practice or as a basis for the application of the bona fide occupational qualification exception." 29 C.F.R. § 1604.1.

3. The Commission's regulations provide:

"Sex as a bona fide occupational qualification.

"(a) The Commission believes that the bona fide occupational qualification exception as to

apply where necessary "for the purpose of authenticity or genuineness" in the employment of actors or actresses, fashion models and the like. If the exception is to be limited as Congress intended, the Commission has given it the only possible construction.

When performance characteristics of an individual are involved, even when parental roles are concerned, employment opportunity may be limited only by employment criteria that are neutral as to the sex of the applicant.

CASE QUESTIONS

1. Is Justice Marshall sensible in fearing that when the Court says that "conflicting family obligations" must be demonstrated by evidence in court before "a woman" is refused a job on that basis, the Court really means that proof need only be presented regarding "some women" or most women? If he were right, would the Court majority be undermining the spirit of the statute?

2. The EEOC guidelines quoted in Marshall's footnotes suggest that state labor legislation intended to be protective of women, which singles them out for special treatment as a group, is no longer valid, because it conflicts with Title VII. As so interpreted, does Title VII improve American public policy?

Only in March 1972, after the Supreme Court had begun in the *Phillips* case to take a really searching look at sex discrimination, did Congress provide the EEOC with the power to sue discriminating employers in court. That weapon provided the commission with the clout to back up their conciliation efforts; now that the commission could threaten court action, the possibilities for generous out-of-court settlements were considerably broadened. In January 1973 the EEOC obtained its first really substantial out-of-court settlement. The American Telephone and Telegraph Company (AT&T) consented to pay $15 million in back pay to thousands of discriminated-against female employees.[2]

Corning Glass Works v. Brennan (1974), discussion

The EEOC was not the only agency within the federal executive branch that had power to take employers to court for discriminating against women. The Department of Labor had authority under the Equal Pay Act of 1963[3] to seek court injunctions against discriminatory employment practices and to seek back-pay restitution for victims of such discrimination. A case resulting from such an action reached the Supreme Court in 1974.

This case, *Corning Glass Works v. Brennan*, 417 U.S. 188, arose out of an extremely complex situation. Perhaps the complexity, or ambiguity of the factual background partially explains the shift in judicial alignment that the case produced. Instead of the 8–1 division of *Frontiero, Stanton, and Taylor,* the Court here divides 5–3 (with Stewart not participating).

The *Corning Glass* case had its roots in a New York State law dating back to 1927. This law prohibited the employment of women between 10 p.m. and 6 a.m. Before 1925, Corning had operated only a day shift, and all its inspector jobs were filled by women. After that date, technological changes made a night shift feasible; to fill the night inspector jobs, men were hired. Women day inspectors earned twenty to thirty cents an hour; men night inspectors received fifty-three cents an hour. During this same period, persons who worked at night received no special bonus for night work (what is called a "shift differential"); a day-shift worker in other jobs in the plant earned the same wage as his night-shift counterpart.

Beginning in 1944, a labor union agreement forced Corning Glass to pay a shift differential to night workers. This differential (by 1974, sixteen cents an hour extra for night work) did not replace the wage difference between men night inspectors and women day inspectors; rather, it was superimposed on top of the preexisting difference. The male-female wage gap was exacerbated.

In 1953 it became legal throughout New York State for women to work at night, and in 1964 the Congressional Equal Pay Act became effective at Corning Glass (Congress had permitted a one-year grace period before the act took effect). Corning made no effort to comply with the Equal Pay Act until June 1966. Their first effort at compliance took the form of opening up night-shift inspector jobs to females. As vacancies occurred, females could now compete with males, on a company seniority basis, for the higher-paying night inspector jobs.

What the Equal Pay Act requires is that employers pay equal wages to employees of opposite sexes "for equal work on jobs the performance of which requires equal skill, effort, and responsibility, and *which are performed under similar working conditions.*" (Emphasis added.) When a violation of the act is alleged, the burden of proof fails on the secretary of labor—in this case, Peter Brennan—to show that this command has been disobeyed. Then the accused employer has the opportunity of showing that the unequal pay in question is justified by at least one of four specified exceptions to the equal pay requirement: "(i) a seniority system; (ii) a merit system; (iii) a system which measures earnings by quantity or quality of production; or (iv) *a differential based on any other factor other than sex.*" (Emphasis added.) At this point, the burden of proof falls on the accused employer. The italicized passages are the phrases whose meaning was at issue in this decision.

The facts of this case were further complicated in January 1969, at which time Corning Glass made equal the pay of all starting inspector positions—day and night. This new wage meant a substantial raise for the previous day inspectors.

Previous night inspectors, however, received the regular (company-wide) 8 percent raise of their base wage. This made their base pay higher than that of all new inspectors, day or night; and they were allowed to remain (by virtue of what is called a "red circle" provision) at this higher wage. In other words, as of 1969, all persons who had been inspectors before 1969 remained in a two-track wage system. The pre-1969 night inspectors continued to earn a higher base wage than the pre-1969 day inspectors, even though all new inspectors would receive a single base wage (equal to that now received by the pre-1969 day inspectors).

The Supreme Court really had to answer two questions about this complicated situation. First, did working the night shift constitute a difference in "working conditions"? If it did, then Corning was paying unequal pay for unequal work and would not be in violation of the statute. Second, could the extra pay for the job of night inspector be justified on the grounds of a "factor other than sex," such as the additional stress attendant to nighttime employment? Two different federal circuit courts gave opposite answers to the first of these questions.

The Supreme Court's answer to both questions was negative; they held further that the changes implemented by Corning in 1966 and 1969 were inadequate remedies to the illegal situation. Justice Marshall wrote the opinion for the majority of five, and it consisted essentially of a detailed legislative history of the Equal Pay Act, with particular attention to deciphering Congress's meaning in regard to the phrases "working conditions" and "factor other than sex." Their conclusions are summarized in the following excerpts from Marshall's opinion:

> While laymen might well assume that time of day worked reflects one aspect of a job's "working conditions," the term has a different and much more specific meaning in the language of industrial relations. As Corning's own representative testified at the hearings, the element working conditions encompasses two subfactors: "surroundings" and "hazards." "Surroundings" measures the elements, such as toxic chemicals or fumes, regularly encountered by a worker, their intensity, and their frequency. "Hazards" takes into account the physical hazards regularly encountered, their frequency, and the severity of injury they can cause. This definition of "working conditions" is not only manifested in Corning's own job evaluation plans but is also well accepted across a wide range of American industry.

> Nowhere in any of these definitions is time of day worked mentioned as a relevant criterion. The fact of the matter is that the concept of "working conditions," as used in the specialized language of job evaluation systems, simply does not encompass shift differentials.
>
> . . .
>
> This does not mean, of course, that there is no room in the Equal Pay Act for nondiscriminatory shift differentials. Work on a steady night shift no doubt has psychological and physiological impacts making it less attractive than work on a day shift. The Act contemplates that a male night worker may receive a higher

wage than a female day worker, just as it contemplates that a male employee with 20 years' seniority can receive a higher wage than a woman with two years' seniority. Factors such as these play a role under the Act's four exceptions—the seniority differential under the specific seniority exception, the shift differential under the catchall exception for differentials "based on any other factor other than sex."

The question remains, however, whether Corning carried its burden of proving that the higher rate paid for night inspection work, until 1966 performed solely by men, was in fact intended to serve as compensation for night work, or rather constituted an added payment based upon sex. We agree that the record amply supports the District Court's conclusion that Corning had not sustained its burden of proof. As its history revealed, "the higher night rate was in large part the product of the generally higher wage level of male workers and the need to compensate them for performing what were regarded as demeaning tasks." 474 F.2d, at 233. . . . That the company took advantage of such a situation may be understandable as a matter of economics, but its differential nevertheless became illegal once Congress enacted into law the principle of equal pay for equal work.

. . .

. . . [T]he issue before us is not whether the company, in some abstract sense, can be said to have treated men the same as women after 1966. Rather, the question is whether the company remedied the specific violation of the Act which the Secretary proved. We agree with the Second Circuit, as well as with all other circuits that have had occasion to consider this issue, that the company could not cure its violation except by equalizing the base wages of female day inspectors [, which it has not done]. . . .[4]

Another 1970s Title VII sex discrimination complaint handled by the Supreme Court, like the one in *Phillips v. Martin-Marietta*, called for an interpretation of the section of the Civil Rights Act of 1964 (Title VII, or 42 U.S.C. § 2000e–2[a]) that made it unlawful not only to "to fail to hire . . . any individual . . . because of such individual's race . . . or sex" but also to "classify . . . applicants for employment in any way which would deprive *or tend to deprive* any individual of equal employment opportunities . . . because of such individual's race . . . or sex." (Emphasis added.)

In this case, *Dothard v. Rawlinson*, the sex discrimination was not as blatant as that in *Phillips*. In the latter, gender discrimination had been pretty obvious; male parents were eligible for jobs for which female parents were considered automatically ineligible. Dianne Rawlinson was excluded from a "correctional counselor" (prison guard) job by the Alabama Board of Corrections (headed by E. C. Dothard) not explicitly on the basis of gender, but rather on the basis of a height and weight requirement. Diane Rawlinson contended that the 5 feet 2 inches height minimum and the 120-pound weight minimum had a tendency to exclude otherwise qualified women. (Ms. Rawlinson herself was 5 feet 2 inches tall and weighed 115 pounds. She was a 22-year-old college graduate who had majored in Correctional Psychology.)

The Supreme Court by 1977 had already handed down two decisions interpreting the "tend to" discriminate clause of Title VII; both cases had presented allegations of racial rather than sex discrimination,[5] but they did establish procedural precedents that would apply likewise to claims of sex discrimination. If a plaintiff wants to claim that a particular job requirement, which looks neutral (nondiscriminatory) on the surface, in fact has a *tendency* to discriminate against one sex (or one race), the plaintiff can present general statistical evidence on the disproportionate impact that the particular requirement has on one sex (or one race). In other words, if something like 98 percent of males meet a particular job requirement, but only 2 percent of females meet the requirement, clear evidence of a sex-lined disproportionate impact of the requirement would be present.

Once such evidence has been presented, however, the Court's work has only begun. This evidence creates what is called a "prima facie" case of sex discrimination. That means that the job requirement in question is then presumed to be discriminatory, until proven otherwise. The burden of proof then shifts from the plaintiff to the defendant-employer. If the employer can prove that the requirement bears "a manifest relation to the employment in question,"[6] that the requirement is reasonably necessary to avoid undermining "the essence of the business operation,"[7] the employer can succeed in shifting the burden of proof to the plaintiff. At this point the plaintiff must show that other, nondiscriminatory selection devices are available that would achieve the same goal as the discriminatory one. If the plaintiff can do this, the Court is supposed to strike down the discriminatory requirement.

In attacking the height and weight requirements, Dianne Rawlinson had no trouble demonstrating their disproportionate impact on women. More than 99 percent of American men are taller than 5 feet 2 inches and weigh more than 120 pounds. Only 59 percent of American women meet those physical requirements. The disproportion is obvious.

At the district court level, where Ms. Rawlinson first took her case,[8] the Alabama Corrections Board argued that the height and weight requirements achieved a certain level of physical strength in their prison guards. They presented no evidence to support their assumption, and they offered no argument why a direct strength test could not be substituted for the height and weight test. After hearing both sides, the district court concluded that this height and weight requirement for Alabama prison guards violated Title VII of the Civil Rights Act.

While Ms. Rawlinson's case was pending at the district court, the Alabama Board of Corrections adopted a new regulation, Number 204, which established a same-sex rule for all correctional counselors (prison guards) working in "contact positions" within maximum-security institutions. Contact positions are those requiring continual close physical proximity to prisoners. Like most states,

Alabama operated separate prisons for men and for women. Since more prisoners in maximum-security jails are men, this meant that more prison guard jobs would be available to men. More precisely, this new rule closed off access for women to all but 25 percent of the prison guard jobs in the State of Alabama. When Regulation 204 was adopted, Dianne Rawlinson amended her complaint to include a protest against it, too, as a violation of Title VII. The district court decided in her favor on this count, too.

A description of conditions in these maximum-security prisons is useful for assessing the needfulness of the same-sex guard requirement. In these institutions in Alabama, living quarters are arranged by large dormitories, with communal showers and toilets that are open to view from the dormitories and hallways. In two of the male penitentiaries, because of their farming operations, "strip searches" of prisoners, to look for contraband, were frequent. In American prisons "strip searches" not uncommonly include anal inspections and, in the case of women prisoners, vaginal inspections.

In Alabama's nonmaximal-security prisons, women did work in "contact positions" among male prisoners. Women guards performed most of the usual duties including inspections of shower-room and toilet areas, but they did not engage in searches and frisks of nude male prisoners. In the two male maximum-security institutions where strip searches were frequent, only 25–33 percent of the guards actually were involved in the task of conducting strip searches. The possibility that maximum-security prisons, too, could assign male guards to perform this particular task and could nonetheless employ female guards to perform other tasks had figured prominently in the district court's decision that Regulation 204 amounted to arbitrary sex discrimination.[9]

The U.S. Supreme Court split three ways over this decision. A majority of six justices, headed by Justice Stewart, agreed with the district court that the height and weight requirement violated Title VII, but they disagreed as to Regulation 204. They held that Alabama had bona-fide job-related reasons for excluding women guards from contact jobs within male maximum-security penitentiaries. Two justices, Brennan and Marshall, dissented on the Regulation 204 question; they agreed with the district court. Justice White dissented entirely, because he believed that Rawlinson had never made a valid statistical demonstration of prima facie discrimination, and that therefore the case should simply have been thrown out of court. Three of the six justices in the majority—Rehnquist, Burger, and Blackmun—indicated in a separate opinion that they might be more willing to uphold height and weight requirements in future cases. Nonetheless, this left a clear five-judge majority on record against height and weight requirements, at least for the job of prison guard. The reasons proffered by each group of justices follows.

Dothard v. Rawlinson, 433 U.S. 321 (1977)

MR. JUSTICE STEWART delivered the opinion of the Court.

. . . We turn . . . to the appellants' argument that they have rebutted the prima facie case of discrimination by showing that the height and weight requirements are job related. These requirements, they say, have a relationship to strength, a sufficient but unspecified amount of which is essential to effective job performance as a correctional counselor. In the district court, however, the appellants produced no evidence correlating the height and weight requirements with the requisite amount of strength thought essential to good job performance. Indeed, they failed to offer evidence of any kind in specific justification of the statutory standards.

If the job-related quality that the appellants identify is bona fide, their purpose could be achieved by adopting and validating a test for applicants that measures strength directly. Such a test, fairly administered, would fully satisfy the standards of Title VII because it would be one that "measure[s] the person for the job and not the person in the abstract." *Griggs v. Duke Power Co.*, 401 U.S., at 436. But nothing in the present record even approaches such a measurement.

For the reasons we have discussed, the District Court was not in error in holding that Title VII of the Civil Rights Act of 1964, as amended, prohibits application of the statutory height and weight requirements to Rawlinson and the class she represents.

III

Unlike the statutory height and weight requirements, Regulation 204 explicitly discriminates against women on the basis of their sex. In defense of this overt discrimi-nation, the appellants rely on § 703e of Title VII, which permits sex-based discrimination "in those certain instances where . . . sex . . . is a bona fide occupational qualification reasonably necessary to the normal operation of that particular business or enterprise."

The District Court rejected the bona fide occupational qualification (bfoq) defense, relying on the virtually uniform view of the federal courts that § 703e provides only the narrowest of exceptions to the general rule requiring equality of employment opportunities. This view has been variously formulated. In . . . an earlier case, *Weeks v. Southern Bell Telephone and Telegraph Co.*, 408 F.2d 228, 235, the [5th Circuit Court of Appeals] said that an employer could rely on the bfoq exception only by proving "that he had reasonable cause to believe, that is, a factual basis for believing, that all or substantially all women would be unable to perform safely and efficiently the duties of the job involved." *See also Phillips v. Martin-Marietta Corp.*, 400 U.S. 542. But whatever the verbal formulation, the federal courts have agreed that it is impermissible under Title VII to refuse to hire an individual woman or man on the basis of stereotyped characterizations of the sexes, and the District Court in the present case held in effect that Regulation 204 is based on just such stereotypical assumptions.

We are persuaded—by the restrictive language of § 703e, the relevant legislative history, and the consistent interpretation of the EEOC that the bfoq exception was in fact meant to be an extremely narrow exception to the general prohibition of discrimination on the basis of sex. In the particular factual circumstances of this case, however, we conclude that the District

Court erred in rejecting the State's contention that Regulation 204 falls within the narrow gambit of the bfoq exception.

The environment in Alabama's penitentiaries is a peculiarly inhospitable one for human beings of whatever sex. Indeed, a federal district court has held that the conditions of confinement in the prisons of the State, characterized by "rampant violence" and a "jungle atmosphere," are constitutionally intolerable. *James v. Wallace*, 406 F. Supp. 318, 325 (M.D. Ala.). The record in the present case shows that because of inadequate staff and facilities, no attempt is made in the four maximum security male penitentiaries to classify or segregate inmates according to their offense or level of dangerousness—a procedure that, according to expert testimony, is essential to effective penological administration. Consequently, the estimated 20 percent of the male prisoners who are sex offenders are scattered throughout the penitentiaries' dormitory facilities.

In this environment of violence and disorganization, it would be an oversimplification to characterize Regulation 204 as an exercise in "romantic paternalism." In the usual case, the argument that a particular job is too dangerous for women may appropriately be met by the rejoinder that it is the purpose of Title VII to allow the individual woman to make that choice for herself. More is at stake in this case, however, than an individual woman's decision to weigh and accept the risks of employment. . . .

The essence of a correctional counselor's job is to maintain prison security. A woman's relative ability to maintain order in a male, maximum security, unclassified penitentiary of the type Alabama now runs could be directly reduced by her womanhood. There is a basis in fact for expecting that sex offenders who have criminally assaulted women in the past would be moved to do so again if access to women were established within the prison. There would also be a real risk that other inmates, deprived of a normal heterosexual environment, would assault women guards because they were women.[22] In a prison system where violence is the order of the day, where inmate access to guards is facilitated by dormitory living arrangements, where every institution is understaffed, and where a substantial portion of the inmate population is composed of sex offenders mixed at random with other prisoners, there are few visible deterrents to inmate assaults on women custodians.

The plaintiff's own expert testified that dormitory housing for aggressive inmates poses a greater security problem than single-cell lock-ups, and further testified that it would be unwise to use women as guards in a prison where even 10 percent of the inmates had been convicted of sex crimes and were not segregated from the other prisoners.[23] The likelihood that inmates would assault a woman because she was a woman would pose a real threat not only to the victim of the assault but also to the basic control of the penitentiary and protection of its inmates and the other

---

22. The record contains evidence of an attack on a female clerical worker in an Alabama prison, and of an incident involving a woman student who was taken hostage during a visit to one of the maximum security institutions.

23. Alabama's penitentiaries are evidently not typical. The appellees' two experts testified that in a normal, relatively stable maximum security prison—characterized by control over the inmates, reasonable living conditions, and segregation of dangerous offenders—women guards could be used effectively and beneficially. Similarly, an *amicus* brief filed by the State of California attests to that State's success in using women guards in all-male penitentiaries.

security personnel. The employee's very womanhood would thus directly undermine her capacity to provide the security that is the essence of a correctional counselor's responsibility.

There was substantial testimony from experts on both sides of the litigation that the use of women as guards in "contact" positions under the existing conditions in Alabama maximum security male penitentiaries would pose a substantial security problem, directly linked to the sex of the prison guard. On . . . that evidence, we conclude that the District Court was in error in ruling that being male is not a bfoq for the job of correctional counselor in a "contact" position in an Alabama male maximum security penitentiary.[24]

The judgment is accordingly affirmed in part and reversed in part. . . .

Mr. Justice Rehnquist, with whom The Chief Justice and Mr. Justice Blackmun join, concurring in the result and concurring in part.

I agree with, and join, parts I and III of the Court's opinion in this case and with its judgment. While I also agree with the Court's conclusion in part II of its opinion, holding that the District Court was "not in error" in holding the statutory height and weight requirements in this case to be invalidated by Title VII, the issues with which that part deals are bound to arise so frequently that I feel obliged to separately

state the reasons for my agreement with its result. I view affirmance of the District Court in this respect as essentially dictated by the peculiarly limited factual and legal justifications offered below by appellants on behalf of the statutory requirements. For that reason, I do not believe—and do not read the Court's opinion as holding—that all or even many of the height and weight requirements imposed by States on applicants for a multitude of law enforcement agency jobs are pretermitted by today's decision.

I agree that the statistics relied upon in this case are sufficient, absent rebuttal, to sustain a finding of a prima facie violation of § 703(a)(2), in that they reveal a significant discrepancy between the numbers of men, as opposed to women, who are automatically disqualified by reason of the height and weight requirements. . . .

Appellants, in order to rebut the prima facie case under the statute, had the burden placed on them to advance job-related reasons for the qualification. *McDonnell Douglas Corp. v. Green*, 411 U.S. 792, at 802 (1973). . . . The District Court was confronted . . . with only one suggested job-related reason for the qualification—that of strength. Appellants argued only the job-relatedness of actual physical strength; they did not urge that an equally job-related qualification for prison guards is the appearance of strength. As the Court notes, the primary job of correctional counselor in Alabama prisons "is to maintain security and control of the inmates . . ." a function that I at least would imagine is aided by the psychological impact on prisoners of the presence of tall and heavy guards. If the appearance of strength had been urged upon the District Court here as a reason for the height and weight minima, I think that the District Court would surely have been entitled to reach a different re-

---

24. The record shows by contrast, that Alabama's minimum security facilities, such as work-release centers, are recognized by their inmates as privileged confinement situations not to be lightly jeopardized by disobeying applicable rules of conduct. Inmates assigned to these institutions are thought to be the "cream of the crop" of the Alabama prison population.

sult than it did. . . . As appellants did not even present the "appearance of strength" contention to the District Court as an asserted job-related reason for the qualification requirements, I agree that their burden was not met. . . .

Mr. Justice Marshall, with whom Mr. Justice Brennan joins, concurring in part and dissenting in part.

I agree entirely with the Court's analysis of Alabama's height and weight requirements for prison guards, and with its finding that these restrictions discriminate on the basis of sex in violation of Title VII. Accordingly, I join parts I and II of the Court's opinion. I also agree with much of the Court's general discussion in part III of the bfoq exception contained in § 703(e) of Title VII. The Court is unquestionably correct when it holds "that the bfoq exception was in fact meant to be an extremely narrow exception to the general prohibition of discrimination on the basis of sex." I must, however, respectfully disagree with the Court's application of the bfoq exception in this case.

The court properly rejects two proffered justifications for denying women jobs as prison guards. It is simply irrelevant here that a guard's occupation is dangerous and that some women might be unable to protect themselves adequately. Those themes permeate the testimony of the state officials below, but as the Court holds, "the argument that a particular job is too dangerous for women" is refuted by the "purpose of Title VII to allow the individual woman to make that choice for herself." Some women, like some men, undoubtedly are not qualified and do not wish to serve as prison guards, but that does not justify the exclusion of all women from this employment opportunity. . . .

What would otherwise be considered unlawful discrimination against women is justified by the Court, however, on the basis of the "barbaric and inhumane" conditions in Alabama prisons, conditions so bad that state officials have conceded that they violate the Constitution. To me, this analysis sounds distressingly like saying two wrongs make a right. It is refuted by the plain words of § 706(e). The statute requires that a bfoq be "reasonably necessary to the normal operation of that particular business or enterprise." But no governmental "business" may operate "normally" in violation of the constitution. Every action of government is constrained by constitutional limitations. While those limits may be violated more frequently than we would wish, no one disputes that the "normal operation" of all government functions takes place within them. A prison system operating in blatant violation of the Eighth Amendment is an exception that should be remedied with all possible speed as Judge Johnson's comprehensive order in *James v. Wallace, supra,* is designed to do. In the meantime, the existence of such violations should not be legitimatized by calling them "normal." Nor should the Court accept them as justifying conduct that would otherwise violate a statute intended to remedy age-old discrimination.

The Court's error in statutory construction is less objectionable, however, than the attitude it displays toward women. Though the Court recognizes that possible harm to women guards is an unacceptable reason for disqualifying women, it relies instead on an equally speculative threat to prison discipline supposedly generated by the sexuality of female guards. There is simply no evidence in the record to show that women guards would create any danger to security in Alabama prisons significantly greater than already exists. All of the dangers—with one exception discussed below—are inherent in a prison setting whatever the gender of the guards.

The Court first sees women guards as a threat to security because "there are few visible deterrents to inmate assaults on women custodians." In fact, any prison guard is constantly subject to the threat of attack by inmates. . . . No prison guard relies primarily on his or her ability to ward off an inmate attack to maintain order. Guards are typically unarmed and sheer numbers of inmates could overcome the normal complement. Rather, like all other law enforcement officers, prison guards must rely primarily on the moral authority of their office and the threat of future punishment for miscreants. As one expert testified below, common sense, fairness, and mental and emotional stability are the qualities a guard needs to cope with the dangers of the job. Well qualified and properly trained women, no less than men, have these psychological weapons at their disposal.

The particular severity of discipline problems in the Alabama maximum security prisons is also no justification for the discrimination sanctioned by the Court. The District Court found in *James v. Wallace* that guards "must spend all their time attempting to maintain control or to protect themselves." 406 F. Supp., at 325. If male guards face an impossible situation, it is difficult to see how women could make the problem worse, unless one relies on precisely the type of generalized bias against women that the Court agrees Title VII was intended to outlaw. For example much of the testimony of appellants' witnesses ignores individual differences among members of each sex and reads like "ancient canards about the proper role of women." *Phillips v. Martin-Marietta Corp.*, 400 U.S., at 545. The witnesses claimed that women

guards are not strict disciplinarians; that they are physically less capable of protecting themselves and subduing unruly inmates; that inmates take advantage of them as they did their mothers, while male guards are strong father figures who easily maintain discipline, and so on. Yet the record shows that the presence of women guards has not led to a single incident amounting to a serious breach of security in any Alabama institution.[3] . . .

It appears that the real disqualifying factor in the Court's view is "[t]he employee's very womanhood." The Court refers to the large number of sex offenders in Alabama prisons, and to "the likelihood that inmates would assault a woman because she was a woman." In short, the fundamental justification for the decision is that women as guards will generate sexual assaults. With all respect, this rationale regrettably perpetuates one of the most insidious of the old myths about women—that women, wittingly or not, are seductive sexual objects. The effect of the decisions, made I am sure with the best of intentions, is to punish women because their very presence might provoke sexual assault. It is women who are made to pay the price in lost job opportunities for the threat of depraved conduct by prison inmates. Once again, "[t]he pedestal upon which women have been placed has . . . upon closer inspection, been revealed as a cage." *Sail'er Inn, Inc. v. Kirby*, 585 P.2d 329 (1971). It is particularly ironic that the cage is erected here in response to feared misbehavior by imprisoned criminals.

. . . [T]he danger in this emotionally laden context is that common sense will be

---

3. The Court refers to two incidents involving potentially dangerous attacks on women in prisons, at n.22. But these did not involve trained corrections officers. . . .

used to mask the "romantic paternalism" and persisting discriminatory attitudes that the Court properly eschews. To me [it is clear] that the incidence of sexually motivated attacks on guards will be minute compared to the "likelihood that inmates will assault" a guard because he or she is a guard.

The proper response to inevitable attacks on both female and male guards is not to limit the employment opportunities of law-abiding women who wish to contribute to their community, but to take swift and sure punitive action against the inmate offenders. . . . To deprive women of job opportunities because of the threatened behavior of convicted criminals is to turn our social priorities upside down.[5]

Although I do not countenance the sex

---

5. The appellants argue that restrictions on employment of women are also justified by consideration of inmates' privacy. It is strange indeed to hear state officials who have for years been violating the most basic principles of human decency in the operation of their prisons suddenly become concerned about inmate privacy. It is stranger still that these same officials allow women guards in contact positions in a number of nonmaximum security institutions, but strive to protect inmates' privacy in the prisons where personal freedom is most severely restricted. I have no doubt on this record that appellants' professed concern is nothing but a feeble excuse for discrimination.

As the District Court suggested, it may well be possible, once constitutionally adequate staff

discrimination condoned by the majority, it is fortunate that the Court's decision is carefully limited to the facts before it. I trust the lower courts will recognize that the decision was impelled by the shockingly inhuman conditions in Alabama prisons. . . .

MR. JUSTICE WHITE, dissenting.

. . . I am unwilling to believe that the percentage of women applying or interested in applying for jobs as prison guards in Alabama approximates the percentage of women either in the national or state population. . . . I am not now convinced that a large percentage of the actual women applicants, or of those who are seriously interested in applying, for prison guard positions would fail to satisfy the height and weight requirements. Without a more satisfactory record in this issue, I cannot conclude that appellee has made out a prima facie case for the invalidity of the restrictions. . . .

---

is available, to rearrange work assignments so that legitimate inmate privacy concerns are respected without denying jobs to women. Finally, if women guards behave in a professional manner at all times they will engender reciprocal respect from inmates, who will recognize that their privacy is being invaded no more than if a woman doctor examines them. The suggestion implicit in the privacy argument that such behavior is unlikely on either side is an insult to the professionalism of guards and the dignity of inmates.

CASE QUESTIONS

1. Justice Marshall argues that it is unpersuasive to use sexual attacks on a female clerical worker and female student as evidence that the presence of female prison guards would provoke sexual assaults. Suppose there had been two sex-

ual assaults on women guards in the male penitentiary over the past five years; would that change Marshall's position? Ten sexual assaults? Is it correct to say that "the effect of the decision . . . is to punish women because their very presence might provoke sexual assaults"? What would be the best response by prison officials, already hard-pressed for operating funds, to a situation where women guards in a male penitentiary were being victimized by sexual assaults? To a situation where sexual assaults on women guards are increasing the total of already too-frequent disruptions of prison security and order?

2. Suppose that state officials, in a sincere effort to promote the privacy and dignity of prison inmates, ordered that all guards whose jobs placed them in view of shower and toilet areas be of the same sex as inmates. Suppose further that because so many more prisoners are male than female, this order denied women access to 80 percent of prison guard

jobs? Would this be a violation of Title VII? Consider Marshall's suggestion in footnote 5 that prisoners should view the situation of exposure to opposite-sex guards as similar to being examined by a doctor of the opposite sex. Are civilians generally compelled to select a doctor of the opposite sex? Are there other significant differences between the two situations?

3. Justice Rehnquist, joined by Justices Burger and Blackmun, suggests that it would be reasonable for prison administrators to desire the appearance of physical strength in prison guards. Does a man who is 5 feet 3 inches tall and who weighs 130 pounds look very strong? What about a woman who is 5 feet 6 inches and weighs 150 pounds? Might "appearance" of strength be affected by sex-based prejudices of the observer? Is Rehnquist's reasonableness argument undermined by the fact that women guards have been used successfully in California's all-male maximum security prisons?

CASENOTE

Three major Supreme Court decisions interpreting Title VII of the 1964 Civil Rights Act examined questions involving the treatment of pregnant employees. These are included with the Equal Protection Clause case dealing with pregnancy, *Geduldig v. Aiello*, in chapter 4 under the section Penalties on Pregnancy.

Pensions

In 1978 the Supreme Court handed down another decision interpreting Title VII; this time the statutory clause at issue was § 703[a][1], the one forbidding sex discrimination "with respect to . . . compensation, terms, conditions, or privileges of employment." In a 6–2 vote, with Chief Justice Burger and Justice Rehnquist in dissent (and with Justice Brennan not participating), the Supreme Court ruled, in *Los Angeles Department of Water and Power v. Manhart et al.* that requiring female employees to make larger monthly pension fund contributions than male employees constituted illegal sex discrimination.

Because women on the average live longer than men, such distinctions were common practice among American employers. The particular pension plan on which the Court ruled in *Manhart* worked as follows: Men and women employees contributed to the retirement fund a certain portion of their salaries, and the department matched that contribution at a rate of 110 percent. Upon retirement, former employees received a monthly benefit calculated on the basis of age, seniority, and former salary, regardless of sex. The sex-based differential in average life expectancy, however, was taken into account by requiring women to pay larger amounts into the fund during each month that they were employed. One woman involved in the lawsuit, for example, had contributed a total of over $18,000 into her pension fund. A similarly situated male would have contributed less than $3,000. Obviously, this meant that if a woman and a man were hired at the same time to work in an identical job at the Department of Water and Power, the man's take-home monthly income would be substantially higher than the woman's.

A group of the department's female employees, joined by their union, the International Brotherhood of Electrical Workers, launched a class action suit in a federal district court, on behalf of all women employed or formerly employed at the department. They requested not only a court order that the discrimination cease but also that the Department be compelled to return to all members of the "class" of workers involved all the money they had contributed in excess of what male employees in their positions would have contributed.

During the process of this litigation, the California legislature enacted a law forbidding all municipal agencies to discriminate on a gender basis in assessing employee contributions to pension funds. So, when the case reached the Supreme Court, the practice at issue was no longer going on.

However, since the district court and the circuit court of appeals not only had found the sex discrimination in employee contribution assessments to be illegal but had also agreed to the request for the restitution of back pay, the controversy was still very much a "live" one between the original parties. To decide whether to order the backpay restored, the Supreme Court first had to decide whether the extra payroll deduction was illegal in the first place (even though this particular employer was no longer engaged in this sex-differentiating deduction policy).

Six of the justices agreed with the two lower courts that Title VII prohibited this kind of sex-based distinction in assessment of pension contributions. But seven of the eight justices participating (with Marshall in dissent) disagreed with the lower courts about the retroactive impact of this decision. Their reasons were as follows:

Los Angeles Department of Water and Power v. Manhart, 435 U.S. 702 (1978)

MR. JUSTICE STEVENS delivered the opinion of the court.

As a class, women live longer than men. For this reason, the Los Angeles Department of Water and Power required its female employees to make larger contributions to its pension fund than its male employees. . . .

I

There are both real and fictional differences between women and men. It is true that the average man is taller than the average women; it is not true that the average woman driver is more accident-prone than the average man. Before the Civil Rights Act of 1964 was enacted, an employer could fashion his personnel policies on the basis of assumptions about the differences between men and women, whether or not the assumptions were valid.

It is now well recognized that employment decisions cannot be predicated on mere "stereotyped" impressions about the characteristics of males or females. Myths and purely habitual assumptions about a woman's inability to perform certain kinds of work are no longer acceptable reasons for refusing to employ qualified individuals, or for paying them less. This case does not, however, involve a fictional difference between men and women. It involves a generalization that the parties accept as unquestionably true: women, as a class, do live longer than men. . . . It is equally true, however, that all individuals in the respective classes do not share the characteristic which differentiates the average class representatives. Many women do not live as long as the average man and many men

outlive the average woman. The question, therefore, is whether the existence or nonexistence of "discrimination" is to be determined by comparison of class characteristics or individual characteristics. A "stereotyped" answer to that question may not be the same as the answer which the language and purpose of the statute command.

The statute makes it unlawful "to discriminate against any *individual* with respect to his compensation, terms, conditions or privileges of employment, because of such *individual's* race, color, religion, sex, or national origin." 42 U.S.C. § 2000e–2(a)(1). (Emphasis added.) The statute's focus on the individual is unambiguous. It precludes treatment of individuals as simply components of a racial, religious, sexual, or national class. If height is required for a job, a tall woman may not be refused employment merely because, on the average, women are too short. Even a true generalization about the class is an insufficient reason for disqualifying an individual to whom the generalization does not apply.

That proposition is of critical importance in this case because there is no assurance that any individual woman working for the Department will actually fit the generalization on which the Department's policy is based. Many of those individuals will not live as long as the average man. While they were working, those individuals received smaller paychecks because of their sex, but they will receive no compensating advantage when they retire.

It is true, of course, that while contributions are being collected from the employees, the Department cannot know which individuals will predecease the average woman. Therefore, unless women as a class are assessed an extra charge, they will be subsidized, to some extent, by the class of male employees.[14] It follows, according to the Department, that fairness to its class of male employees justifies the extra assessment against all of its female employees.

But the question of fairness to various classes affected by the statute is essentially a matter of policy for the legislature to address. Congress had decided that classifications based on sex, like those based on national origin or race, are unlawful. Actuarial studies could unquestionably identify differences in life expectancy based on race or national origin, as well as sex.[15] But a statute which was designed to make race irrelevant in the employment market, *see Griggs v. Duke Power Co.*, 401 U.S. 424, 436, could not reasonably be construed to permit a take-home pay differential based on a racial classification.[16]

Even if the statutory language were less clear, the basic policy of the statute requires that we focus on fairness to individuals rather than fairness to classes. Practices

which classify employees in terms of religion, race, or sex tend to preserve traditional assumptions about groups rather than thoughtful scrutiny of individuals. The generalization involved in this case illustrates the point. Separate mortality tables are easily interpreted as reflecting innate differences between the sexes; but a significant part of the longevity differential may be explained by the social fact that men are heavier smokers than women.[17]

Finally, there is no reason to believe that Congress intended a special definition of discrimination in the context of employee group insurance coverage. It is true that insurance is concerned with events that are individually unpredicable, but that is characteristic of many employment decisions. Individual risks, like individual performance, may not be predicted by resort to classifications proscribed by Title VII. Indeed, the fact that this case involves a group insurance program highlights a basic flaw in the department's fairness argument. For when insurance risks are grouped, the better risks always subsidize the poorer risks. Healthy persons subsidize medical benefits for the less healthy; unmarried workers subsidize the pensions of married workers;[18] persons who eat, drink, or smoke to excess may subsidize pension benefits for persons whose habits are more temperate. Treating different

---

14. The size of the subsidy involved in this case is open to doubt, because the Department's plan provides for survivors' benefits. Since female spouses of male employees are likely to have greater life expectancies than the male spouses of female employees, whatever benefits men lose in "primary" coverage for themselves, they may regain in "secondary" coverage for their wives.

15. For example, the life expectancy of a white baby in 1973 was 72.2 years; a nonwhite baby could expect to live 65.9 years, a difference of 6.3 years. *See* Public Health Service, IIA *Vital Statistics of the United States 1973*, Table 5–3.

16. Fortifying this conclusion is the fact that some States have banned higher life insurance rates for blacks since the nineteenth century. *See generally* M. James, *The Metropolitan Life—A Study in Business Growth* 338–39.

17. *See* R. Retherford, *The Changing Sex Differential in Mortality* 71–82 (1975). Other social causes, such as drinking or eating habits—perhaps even the lingering effects of past employment discrimination—may also affect the mortality differential.

18. A study of life expectancy in the United States for 1949–1951 showed that 20-year-old men could expect to live to 60.6 years of age if they were divorced. If married, they could expect to reach 70.9 years of age, a difference of more than 10 years. R. Retherford, *The Changing Sex Differential in Mortality* 93 (1975).

classes of risks as though they were the same for purposes of group insurance is a common practice which has never been considered inherently unfair. To insure the flabby and the fit as though they were equivalent risks may be more common than treating men and women alike;[19] but nothing more than habit makes one "subsidy" seem less fair than the other.[20]

An employment practice which requires 2,000 individuals to contribute more money into a fund than 10,000 other employees simply because each of them is woman, rather than a man, is in direct conflict with both the language and the policy of the Act. Such a practice does not pass the simple test of whether the evidence shows "treatment of a person in a manner which but for the person's sex would be dif-

19. The record indicates, however, that the Department has funded its death benefit plan by equal contributions from male and female employees. A death benefit—unlike a pension benefit—has less value for persons with longer life expectancies. Under the Department's concept of fairness, then, this neutral funding of death benefits is unfair to women as a class.

20. A variation on the Department's fairness theme is the suggestion that a gender-neutral pension plan would itself violate Title VII because of its disproportionately heavy impact on male employees. Cf. Griggs v. Duke Power Co., 401 U.S. 424. This suggestion has no force in the sex discrimination context because each retiree's total pension benefits are ultimately determined by his actual life span; any differential in benefits paid to men and women in the aggregate is thus "based on [a] factor other than sex," and consequently immune from challenge under the Equal Pay Act. Even under Title VII itself—assuming disparate impact analysis applies to fringe benefits, cf. Nashville Gas Co. v. Satty—the male employees would not prevail. Even a completely neutral practice will inevitably have some disproportionate impact on one group or another. Griggs does not imply, and this Court has never held, that discrimination must always be inferred from such consequences.

ferent." It constitutes discrimination and is unlawful unless exempted by the Equal Pay Act or some other affirmative justification.

II

Shortly before the enactment of Title VII in 1964, Senator Bennett proposed an amendment providing that a compensation differential based on sex would not be unlawful if it was authorized by [any of the exceptions authorized in] the Equal Pay Act, which had been passed a year earlier. . . . The Department contends that the fourth exception applies here. That exception authorizes a "differential based on any other factor other than sex."

The Department argues that the different contributions exacted from men and women were based on the factor of longevity rather than sex. It is plain, however, that any individual's life expectancy is based on a number of factors, of which sex is only one. The record contains no evidence that any factor other than the employee's sex was taken into account in calculating the 14.84 percent differential between the respective contributions by men and women. We agree with Judge Duniway's observation that one cannot "say that an actuarial distinction based entirely on sex is 'based on any other factor other than sex.' Sex is exactly what it is based on." 553 F.2d, at 588.

We are also unpersuaded by the Department's reliance on a colloquy between Senator Randolph and Senator Humphrey during the debate on the Civil Rights Act of 1964. Commenting on the Bennett Amendment, Senator Humphrey expressed his understanding that it would allow many differences in the treatment of men and women under industrial benefit plans, including earlier retirement options for women.[25] Though he did not address dif-

25. . . . 110 Cong. Rec. 13663–13664 (1964).

ferences in employee contributions based on sex, Senator Humphrey apparently assumed that the 1964 Act would have little, if any, impact on existing pension plans. His statement cannot, however, fairly be made the sole guide. . . . We conclude that Senator Humphrey's isolated comment on the Senate floor cannot change the effect of the plain language of the statute itself.

III

The Department argues that reversal is required by *General Electric Co. v. Gilbert,* 429 U.S. 125. We are satisfied, however, that neither the holding nor the reasoning of *Gilbert* is controlling. . . . On its face, this plan discriminates on the basis of sex whereas the General Electric plan discriminated on the basis of a special physical disability.

In *Gilbert* the Court did note that the plan as actually administered had provided more favorable benefits to women as a class than to men as a class. This evidence supported the conclusion that not only had plaintiffs failed to establish a prima facie case by proving that the plan was discriminatory of its face, but they had also failed to prove any discriminatory effect.[29]

In this case, however, the Department argues that the absence of a discriminatory effect on women as a class justifies an employment practice which, on its face, discriminated against individual employees because of their sex. But even if the Department's actuarial evidence is sufficient to prevent plaintiffs from establishing a prima facie case on the theory that the effect of the practice on women as a class was discriminatory, that evidence does not defeat the claim that the practice, on its face, discriminated against every individual woman employed by the Department.

In essence, the Department is arguing that the prima facie showing of discrimination based on evidence of different contributions for the respective sexes is rebutted by its demonstration that there is a like difference in the cost of providing benefits for the respective classes. . . . But neither Congress nor the courts have recognized such a defense under Title VII.

Although we conclude that the Department's practice violated Title VII, we do not suggest that the statute was intended to revolutionize the insurance and pension industries. All that is at issue today is a requirement that men and women make unequal contributions to an employer-operated pension fund. Nothing in our holding implies that it would be unlawful for an employer to set aside equal retirement contributions for each employee and let each retiree purchase the largest benefit which his or her accumulated contributions could command in the open market.[33] Nor does it call into question the insurance industry practice of considering the composition of an employer's work force in determining the probable cost of a retirement or death benefit plan. Finally, we recognize that in a case of this kind it may be necessary to take special care in fashioning appropriate relief.

IV

The Department challenges the District Court's award of retroactive relief to the entire class of female employees and retirees. Title VII does not require a district court to

29. As the Court recently noted in *Nashville Gas Co. v. Satty* [see chapter 4], the *Gilbert* holding "did not depend on this evidence." Rather, the holding rested on the plaintiff's failure to prove either facial discrimination or discriminatory effect.

33. Title VII and the Equal Pay Act govern relations between employees and their employers, not between employees and third parties. We do not suggest, of course, that an employer can avoid its responsibilities by delegating discriminatory programs to corporate shells. . . .

grant any retroactive relief. A court that finds unlawful discrimination "may enjoin [the discrimination] and order such affirmative action as may be appropriate, which may include, but is not limited to, reinstatement . . . with or without back pay . . . or any other equitable relief as the court deems appropriate." 42 U.S.C. § 2000e – 5(g). To the point of redundancy, the statute stresses that retroactive relief "may" be awarded if is "appropriate."

In *Albemarle Paper Co. v. Moody,* 422 U.S. 405, the Court reviewed the scope of a district court's discretion to fashion appropriate remedies for a Title VII violation and concluded that "back pay should be denied only for reasons which, if applied generally, would not frustrate the central statutory purposes of eradicating discrimination throughout the economy and making persons whole for injuries suffered through past discrimination." *Id.* at 421. Applying that standard, the Court ruled that an award of backpay should not be conditioned on a showing of bad faith. *Id.* at 422–23. But the *Albemarle* Court also held that backpay was not to be awarded automatically in every case.

The *Albemarle* presumption in favor of retroactive liability can seldom be overcome, but it does not make meaningless the district courts' duty to determine that such relief is appropriate. For several reasons, we conclude that the District Court gave insufficient attention to the equitable nature of Title VII remedies. Although we now have no doubt about the application of the statute in this case, we must recognize that conscientious and intelligent administrators of pension funds, who did not have the benefit of the extensive briefs and arguments presented to us, may well have assumed that a program like the Department's was entirely lawful. The agencies had conflicting views. The Department's failure to act more swiftly is a sign, not of its recalcitrance, but of the problem's com-

plexity. As commentators have noted, pension administrators could reasonably have thought it unfair—or even illegal—to make male employees shoulder more than their "actuarial share" of the pension burden. There is no reason to believe that the threat of a backpay award is needed to cause other administrators to amend their practices to conform to this decision.

Nor can we ignore the potential impact which changes in rules affecting insurance and pension plans may have on the economy. Fifty million Americans participate in retirement plans other than Social Security. The assets held in trust for these employees are vast and growing—more than $400 billion were reserved for retirement benefits at the end of 1977 and reserves are increasing by almost $50 billion a year. These plans, like other forms of insurance, depend on the accumulation of large sums to cover contingencies. The amounts set aside are determined by a painstaking assessment of the insurer's likely liability. Risks that the insurer foresees will be included in the calculation of liability, and the rates or contributions charged will reflect that calculation. The occurrence of major unforeseen contingencies, however, jeopardizes the insurer's solvency and, ultimately the insureds' benefits. Drastic changes in the legal rules governing pension and insurance funds, like other unforeseen events, can have this effect. Consequently, the rules that apply to these funds should not be applied retroactively unless the legislature has plainly commanded that result. . . .

. . . Retroactive liability could be devastating for a pension fund. The harm would fall in large part on innocent third parties. . . .

. . . [W]e conclude that it was error to grant [retroactive] relief in this case. Accordingly, . . . we remand the case for further proceedings consistent with this opinion.

Mr. Justice Brennan took no part in the consideration or decision of this case.

Mr. Chief Justice Burger, with whom Mr. Justice Rehnquist joins, concurring in part and dissenting in part.

I join part IV of the Court's opinion; as to parts I, II, and III, I dissent.

Gender-based actuarial tables have been in use since at least 1843, and their statistical validity has been repeatedly verified. The vast life insurance, annuity and pension plan industry is based on these tables. As the Court recognizes, it is a fact that "women, as a class, do live longer than men." It is equally true that employers cannot know in advance when individual members of the classes will die. Yet, if they are to operate economically workable group pension programs, it is only rational to permit them to rely on statistically sound and proven disparities in longevity between men and women. Indeed, it seems to me irrational to assume Congress intended to outlaw use of the fact that, for whatever reasons or combination of reasons, women as a class outlive men.

The Court's conclusion that the language of the civil rights statute is clear, admitting of no advertence to the legislative history, such as there was, is not soundly based. An effect upon pension plans so revolutionary and discriminatory—this time favorable to women at the expense of men—should not be read into the statute without either a clear statement of that intent in the statute, or some reliable indication in the legislative history that this was Congress' purpose. The Court's casual dismissal of Senator Humphrey's apparent assumption that the "Act would have little, if any, impact on existing pension plans," is to dismiss a significant manifestation of what impact on industrial benefit plans was contemplated. It is reasonably clear there was no intention to abrogate an em-

ployer's right, in this narrow and limited context, to treat women differently from men in the fact of historical reliance on mortality experience statistics. *Cf. ante,* at n.25.

The reality of differences in human mortality is what mortality experience tables reflect. The difference is the added longevity of women. All the reasons why women statistically outlive men are not clear. But categorizing people on the basis of sex, the one acknowledged immutable difference between men and women, is to take into account all of the unknown reasons, whether biologically or culturally based, or both, which give women a significantly greater life expectancy than men. It is therefore true as the Court says, "that any individual's life expectancy is based on a number of factors of which sex is only one." But it is not true that by seizing upon the only constant, "measurable" factor, no others were taken into account. All other factors, whether known but variable—or unknown—are the elements which automatically account for the actuarial disparity. And all are accounted for when the constant factor is used as a basis for determining the costs and benefits of a group pension plan.

Here, of course, petitioners are discriminating in take-home pay between men and women. The practice of petitioners, however, falls squarely under the exemption provided by the Equal Pay Act, incorporated into Title VII by the so-called Bennett Amendment. That exemption tells us that an employer may not discriminate between employees on the basis of sex by paying one sex lesser compensation than the other "except where such payment is made pursuant to . . . a differential based on any other factor other than sex. . . ." The "other factor other than sex" is longevity; sex is the umbrella-constant under which all of the elements leading to differences in longevity are grouped and assimilated, and the only objective feature upon which an employer—or anyone else, including insurance companies—may reliably base a cost differential for the "risk" being insured.

This is in no sense a failure to treat women as "individuals" in violation of the statute. . . .

Of course, women cannot be disqualified from, for example, heavy labor just because the generality of women are thought not as strong as men—a proposition which perhaps may sometime be statistically demonstrable, but will remain individually refutable. When, however, it is impossible to tailor a program such as a pension plan to the individual, nothing should prevent application of reliable statistical facts to the individual, for whom the facts cannot be disproved until long after planning, funding, and operating the program has been undertaken.

I find it anomalous, if not contradictory, that the Court's opinion tells us, in effect, that the holding is not really a barrier to responding to the complaints of men employees, as a group. The Court states that employers may give each employee precisely the same dollar amount and require them to secure their own annuities directly from an insurer, who, of course, is under no compulsion to ignore 135 years of accumulated, recorded longevity experiences.[3]

MR. JUSTICE MARSHALL, concurring in part and dissenting in part.

I agree that Title VII of the Civil Rights Act of 1964, as amended, forbids petitioners' practice of requiring female employees to make larger contributions to a pension fund than do male employees. I therefore join all of the Court's opinion except part IV.

I also agree with the Court's statement in part IV that, once a Title VII violation is found, *Albemarle Paper Co. v. Moody*, 422 U.S. 405 (1975), establishes a "presumption in favor of retroactive liability" and that this presumption "can seldom be overcome." But I do not agree that the presumption should be deemed overcome in this case, especially since the relief was granted by the District Court in the exercise of its discretion and was upheld by the Court of Appeals. I would affirm the decision below and therefore cannot join part IV of the Court's opinion or the Court's judgment. . . .

. . . The retroactive relief ordered by the District Court ran from April 5, 1972, through December 31, 1974, after which date petitioners changed to an equal contribution program.

. . . No one has suggested . . . that the relatively modest award at issue—involving a small percentage of the amounts withheld from respondents' paychecks for pension purposes over a 33-month period, *see* 553 F.2d 581, 592 (9th Cir. 1976)—could in any way be considered "devastating," *ante.* And if a "devastating" award were made in some future case, this Court could have ample opportunity to strike it down at that time. . . .

. . . There is every indication, in short, that the factors which the Court thinks might be important in some hypothetical case are of no concern to the petitioners who would have had to pay the award in this case.

. . . I would affirm the judgment of Court of Appeals.

MR. JUSTICE BLACKMUN, concurring in part and concurring in the judgment.

MR. JUSTICE STEWART wrote the opin-

3. This case, of course, has nothing to do with discrimination becuse of race, color, religion, or national origin. The qualification the Bennett Amendment permitted by its incorporation of the Equal Pay Act pertained only to claims of discrimination because of sex.

ions for the Court in *Geduldig v. Aiello,* and joined the Court's opinion in *General Electric Co. v. Gilbert.* MR. JUSTICE WHITE and MR. JUSTICE POWELL joined both *Geduldig* and *General Electric.* MR. JUSTICE STEVENS, who writes the opinion for the Court in the present case, dissented in *General Electric.* MR. JUSTICE MARSHALL, who joins the Court's opinion in large part here, dissented in both *Geduldig and General Electric.* My own discomfort with the latter case was apparent, I believe, for my separate concurrence there.

These "line-ups" surely are not without significance. The participation of my Brothers STEWART, WHITE and POWELL in today's majority opinion should be a sign that the decision in this case is not in tension with *Geduldig* and *General Electric* and, indeed, is wholly consistent with them. I am not at all sure that this is so; the votes of MR. JUSTICE MARSHALL and MR. JUSTICE STEVENS would indicate quite the contrary.

Given the decisions in *Geduldig* and *General Electric*—the one constitutional, the other statutory—the present case just cannot be an easy one for the Court. I might have thought that those decisions would have required the Court to conclude that the critical difference in the Department's pension payments was based on life expectancy, a nonstigmatizing factor that demonstrably differentiates females from males and that is not measurable on an individual basis. I might have thought, too, that there is nothing arbitrary, irrational, or "discriminatory" about recognizing the objective and accepted disparity in female-male life expectancies in computing rates for retirement plans. Moreover, it is unrealistic to attempt to force, as the Court does, an individualized analysis upon what is basically an insurance context. Unlike the possibility, for example, of properly testing job applicants for qualifications before employ-

ment, there is simply no way to determine in advance when a particular employee will die.

The Court's rationale, of course, is that Congress, by Title VII of the Civil Rights Act of 1964, as amended, intended to eliminate, with certain exceptions, "race, color, religion, sex, or national origin," 42 U.S.C. § 2000e–2(a)(1), as factors upon which employers may act. A program such as the one challenged here does exacerbate gender consciousness. But the program under consideration in *General Electric* did exactly the same thing and yet was upheld against challenge.

The Court's distinction between the present case and *General Electric*—that the permitted classes there were "pregnant women and non-pregnant persons," both female and male,—seems to me to be just too easy.* It is probably the only distinction that can be drawn. For me, it does not serve to distinguish the case on any principled basis. I therefore must conclude that today's decision cuts back on *General Electric,* and inferentially on *Geduldig,* the reasoning of which was adopted there, 420 U.S., at 133–36, and, indeed, makes the recognition of those cases as continuing precedent somewhat questionable. I do not say that this is necessarily bad. If that is what Congress has chosen to do by Title VII—as the Court today with such assurance asserts—so be it. I feel, however, that we should meet the posture of the ear-

---

*It is of interest that MR. JUSTICE STEVENS, in his dissent in *General Electric,* strongly protested the very distinction he now must make for the Court. "It is not accurate to describe the program as dividing '"potential recipients into two groups—pregnant women and nonpregnant persons"' . . . The classification is between persons who face a risk of pregnancy and those who do not." 429 U.S., at 161–62, n.5.

lier cases head-on and not by thin rationalization that seeks to distinguish but fails in its quest.

I therefore join only part IV of the Court's opinion, and concur in its judgment.

CASE QUESTIONS

1. Chief Justice Burger's dissent (joined by Justice Rehnquist) seems to assume that Title VII permits differentiating among employees on the basis of sex whenever two conditions hold: (a) The group difference between the sexes on which the discrimination is based has to be a genuine (not mythical) one, and (b) the group difference has to be one not disprovable as applied to particular individuals (by such techniques, for example, as a strength test). How would their approach apply to a hypothetical employer who refused to hire any women on the grounds that their presence would cause undue distraction among his male employees?

2. Is it possible that a statute can mean the opposite of what its main supporters in Congress said it means during the debate over its passage?

3. What precisely is the parallel that Justice Blackmun sees between the views of the *Gilbert* dissenters (see chapter 4) and those of the majority here? How many of the arguments used in the majority opinion of Justice Rehnquist in the *Gilbert* case are repeated by Chief Justice Burger here in dissent, and now rejected by the majority? What is left that still distinguishes the reasoning of the two cases?

4. Justice Marshall's partial dissent seems to maintain that the majority's arguments on the back-pay question make more sense as applied to other cases than to this one. Is it possible that the majority's ruling on the retroactivity issue is aimed at keeping the federal courts from being deluged with future lawsuits, rather than at settling this particular dispute? Would this approach be unfair to Ms. Manhart and her co-workers?

A number of American employers, rather than take bigger deductions for women's pension plans, chose to equalize the sex-longevity-differential by providing smaller monthly benefits for women retirees. A case challenging this practice did not take long to reach the Court after *Manhart*. The case, *Arizona Governing Committee v. Norris*, 463 U.S. 1073 (1983), was complicated by the involvement of a third party, an insurance company.

The state of Arizona, in order to have its employees' pension contributions qualify for income tax deductions for employees, held the contributions and deposited them in a pension fund, which was then managed by one of a group of insurance companies. The group was designated by the employer but the employee chose the company. Upon retirement, the worker could choose one of three options: (a) a lump sum payment, (b) a monthly annuity for a fixed number of years, or (c) a lifetime monthly annuity. Most people chose the third option, and women who chose it received a substantially smaller monthly payment than men.

To some degree, the logic of *Manhart* governed this case, but *Manhart* had left the loophole that employers could give retirees funds with which to purchase insurance "on the open market," with the clear implication that that market itself could continue to discriminate. An important issue in this case was whether the symbiotic relationship between the employer and the selected insurance companies was sufficient to pull this case out of that loophole. The Court majority thought so but apparently Justice Blackmun did not, for he joined the *Manhart* dissenters, Burger and Rehnquist, this time. As with *Manhart*, the Court here chose to make its ruling non-retroactive because of the need for reliable, long-term future planning with pension funds.

This case was initiated by a lawsuit in a federal district court brought by Nathalie Norris, an employee in the Arizona Department of Economic Security. She asked that it be certified as a class action on behalf of all female employees of the state enrolled in the pension plan. The district court in a summary judgment did so, and also ruled for the plaintiff class that the plan violated Title VII, and ordered an immediate change in benefits paid. 486 F. Supp. 645. The Circuit Court of Appeals, with one dissent, affirmed. 671 F.2d 330 (1982). The U.S. Supreme Court affirmed, except as to what they viewed as retroactive elements of the order. Their explanation was as follows:

Arizona Governing Committee v. Norris, 463 U.S. 1073 (1983)

Per Curiam.

Petitioners in this case administer a deferred compensation plan for employees of the State of Arizona. The respondent class consists of all female employees who are enrolled in the plan or will enroll in the plan in the future. Certiorari was granted to decide whether Title VII of the Civil Rights Act of 1964, as amended, 42 U.S.C. § 2000e *et seq.*, prohibits an employer from offering its employees the option of receiving retirement benefits from one of several companies selected by the employer, all of which pay a woman lower monthly retirement benefits than a man who has made the same contributions; and whether, if so, the relief awarded by the District Court was proper. The Court holds that this practice does constitute discrimination on the basis of sex in violation of Title VII, and that all retirement benefits derived from contributions made after the decision today must be calculated without regard to the sex of the beneficiary. This position is expressed in parts I, II, and III of the opinion of JUSTICE MARSHALL, which are joined by JUSTICE BRENNAN, JUSTICE WHITE, JUSTICE STEVENS, and JUSTICE O'CONNOR. The Court further holds that benefits derived from contributions made prior to this decision may be calculated as provided by the existing terms of the Arizona plan. This position is expressed in part III of the opinion of JUSTICE POWELL, *post*, which is joined by THE CHIEF JUSTICE, JUSTICE BLACKMUN, JUSTICE REHNQUIST, and JUSTICE O'CONNOR. Accordingly, the judgment of the Court of Appeals is affirmed in part, reversed in part, and the case is remanded for further proceedings consistent with this opinion. [This judgment is effective August 1, 1983.]

JUSTICE MARSHALL, with whom JUSTICE BRENNAN, JUSTICE WHITE, JUSTICE STEVENS, and JUSTICE O'CONNOR join as to parts I, II, and III, concurring in the judgment in part, and with whom JUSTICE BRENNAN, JUSTICE WHITE, and JUSTICE STEVENS join as to part IV

There is no question that the opportunity to participate in a deferred compensation plan constitutes a "conditio[n] or privileg[e] of employment," and that retirement benefits constitute a form of "compensation." The issue we must decide is whether it is discrimination "because of . . . sex" to pay a retired woman lower monthly benefits than a man who deferred the same amount of compensation.

In *Los Angeles Dept. of Water & Power v. Manhart*, 435 U.S. 702 (1978), we held that an employer had violated Title VII by requiring its female employees to make larger contributions to a pension fund than male employees in order to obtain the same monthly benefits upon retirement. Noting that Title VII's "focus on the individual is

unambiguous," *id.* at 708, we emphasized that the statute prohibits an employer from treating some employees less favorably than others because of their race, religion, sex, or national origin. *Id.*, at 708–9. While women as a class live longer than men, *id.* at 704, we rejected the argument that the exaction of greater contributions from women was based on a "factor other than sex"—i.e., longevity—and was therefore permissible under the Equal Pay Act:

> [A]ny individual's life expectancy is based on a number of factors, of which sex is only one . . . [O]ne cannot "say that an actuarial distinction based entirely on sex is 'based on any other factor than sex.' Sex is exactly what it is based on." (435 U.S. at 712–13.)

We concluded that a plan requiring women to make greater contributions than men discriminates "because of . . . sex" for the simple reason that it treats each woman "'in a manner which but for [her] sex would [have been] different.'" 435 U.S., at 710.

We have no hesitation in holding, as have all but one of the lower courts that have considered the question, that the classification of employees on the basis of sex is no more permissible at the pay-out stage of a retirement plan than at the pay-in stage.[10] We reject petitioners' contention that the Arizona plan does not discriminate on the basis of sex because a woman and a man

---

10. It is irrelevant that female employees in *Manhart* were required to participate in the pension plan, whereas participation in the Arizona deferred compensation plan is voluntary. Title VII forbids all discrimination concerning "compensation, terms, conditions, or privileges of employment," not just discrimination concerning those aspects of the employment relationship as to which the employee has no choice. . . .

who defer the same amount of compensation will obtain upon retirement annuity policies having approximately the same present actuarial value.[11] Arizona has simply offered its employees a choice among different levels of annuity benefits, any one of which, if offered alone, would be equivalent to the plan at issue in *Manhart*, where the employer determined both the monthly contributions employees were required to make and the level of benefits that they were paid. If a woman participating in the Arizona plan wishes to obtain monthly benefits equal to those obtained by a man, she must make greater monthly contributions than he, just as the female employees in *Manhart* had to make greater contributions to obtain equal benefits. For any particular level of benefits that a woman might wish to receive, she will have to make greater monthly contributions to obtain that level of benefits than a man would have to make. The fact that Arizona has offered a range of discriminatory benefit levels, rather than only one such level, obviously provides no basis whatsoever for distinguishing *Manhart*.

[P]etitioners incorrectly assume that Title VII permits an employer to classify employees on the basis of sex in predicting their longevity. Otherwise there would be no basis for postulating that a woman's an-

nuity policy has the same present actuarial value as the policy of a similarly situated man even though her policy provides lower monthly benefits. This underlying assumption—that sex may properly be used to predict longevity—is flatly inconsistent with the basic teaching of *Manhart*: that Title VII requires employers to treat their employees as *individuals*, not "as simply components of a racial, religious, sexual, or national class." 435 U.S., at 708. *Manhart* squarely rejected the notion that, because women as a class live longer than men, an employer may adopt a retirement plan that treats every individual woman less favorably than every individual man. *Id.* at 716–17.

As we observed in *Manhart*, "[a]ctuarial studies could unquestionably identify differences in life expectancy based on race or national origin, as well as sex." *Id.* at 709. If petitioners' interpretation of the statute were correct, such studies could be used as a justification for paying employees of one race lower monthly benefits than employees of another race. We continue to believe that "a statute that was designed to make race irrelevant in the employment market," *id.*, citing *Griggs v. Duke Power Co.*, 401 U.S. 424, 436 (1971), could not reasonably be construed to permit such a racial classification. And if it would be unlawful to use race-based actuarial tables, it must also be unlawful to use sex-based tables, for under Title VII a distinction based on sex stands on the same footing as a distinction based on race unless it falls within one of a few narrow exceptions that are plainly inapplicable here.

What we said in *Manhart* bears repeating: "Congress has decided that classifications based on sex, like those based national origin or race, are unlawful." 435 U.S., at 709. The use of sex-segregated actuarial tables to calculate retirement benefits violates Title VII whether or not the tables reflect an accurate prediction of the

11. The present actuarial value of an annuity policy is determined by multiplying the present value (in this case, the value at the time of the employee's retirement) of each monthly payment promised by the probability, which is supplied by an actuarial table, that the annuitant will live to receive that payment. An annuity policy issued to a retired female employee under a sex-based retirement plan will have roughly the same present actuarial value as a policy issued to a similarly situated man, since the lower value of each monthly payment she is promised is offset by the likelihood that she will live longer and therefore receive more payments.

longevity of women as a class, for under the statute "[e]ven a true generalization about [a] class cannot justify classbased treatment.[14] *Id.* An individual woman may not be paid lower monthly benefits simply because women as a class live longer than men.[15]

14. In his separate opinion in *Manhart*, JUSTICE BLACKMUN expressed doubt that that decision could be reconciled with this Court's previous decision in *General Electric Co. v. Gilbert.* 429 U.S. 125 (1976). . . .
The tension in our cases that JUSTICE BLACKMUN noted in *Manhart* has since been eliminated by the enactment of the Pregnancy Discrimination Act of 1978 (PDA). . . .
The enactment of the PDA buttresses our holding in *Manhart* that the greater cost of providing retirement benefits for women as a class cannot justify differential treatment based on sex. 435 U.S., at 716–17. . . . In enacting the PDA, Congress recognized that requiring employers to cover pregnancy on the same terms as other disabilities would add approximately $200 million to their total costs, but concluded that the PDA was necessary "to clarify [the] original intent" of Title VII. H.R. Rep. No. 948, 95th Cong., 2d Sess. 4, 9 (1978). Since the purpose of the PDA was simply to make the treatment of pregnancy consistent with general Title VII principles, *see Newport News Shipbuilding and Dry Dock Co. v. EEOC*, at n.16, Congress' decision to forbid special treatment of pregnancy despite the special costs associated therewith provides further support for our conclusion in *Manhart* that the greater costs of providing retirement benefits for female employees does not justify the use of a sex-based retirement plan. . . .
15. . . . There is no support in either logic or experience for the view, referred to by JUSTICE POWELL, *post*, that an annuity plan must classify on the basis of sex to be actuarially sound. Neither Title VII nor the Equal Pay Act "makes it unlawful to determine the funding requirements for an establishment's benefit plan by considering the [sexual] composition of the entire force," *Manhart*, 435 U.S., at 718, n.34, and it is simply not necessary either to exact greater contributions from women than from men or to pay

We conclude that it is just as much discrimination "because of . . . sex" to pay a woman lower benefits when she has made the same contributions as a man as it is to make her pay larger contributions to obtain the same benefits.

III

Since petitioners plainly would have violated Title VII if they had run the entire deferred compensation plan themselves, the only remaining question as to liability is whether their conduct is beyond the reach of the statute because it is the companies chosen by petitioners to participate in the plan that calculate and pay the retirement benefits.

Title VII "primarily govern[s] relations between employees and their employer, not between employees and third parties." *Manhart*, 435 U.S., at 718, n.33. Recognizing this limitation on the reach of the statute, we noted in *Manhart* that

> Nothing in our holding implies that it would be unlawful for an employer to set aside equal retirement contributions for each employee and let each retiree purchase the largest benefits which his or her accumulated contributions could command in the open market. (*Id.*, at 717–18.)

Relying on this caveat, petitioners contend that they have not violated Title VII because the life annuities offered by the companies participating in the Arizona plan reflect what is available in the open market. . . .

women lower benefits than men. For example, the Minnesota Mutual Life Insurance Company and the Northwestern National Life Insurance Company have offered an annuity plan that treats men and women equally. *See The Chronicle of Higher Education*, Vol. 25, No. 7, Oct. 13, 1982, at 25–26.

It is no defense that all annuities immediately available in the open market may have been based on sex-segregated actuarial tables. . . . It is irrelevant whether any other insurers offered annuities on a sex-neutral basis, since the State did not simply set aside retirement contributions and let employees purchase annuities on the open market. On the contrary, the State provided the opportunity to obtain an annuity as part of its own deferred compensation plan. It invited insurance companies to submit bids outlining the terms on which they would supply retirement benefits and selected the companies that were permitted to participate in the plan. Once the State selected these companies, it entered into contracts with them governing the terms on which benefits were to be provided to employees. Employees enrolling in the plan could obtain retirement benefits only from one of those companies. . . .

Under these circumstances there can be no serious question that petitioners are legally responsible for the discriminatory terms on which annuities are offered by the companies chosen to participate in the plan. Having created a plan whereby employees can obtain the advantages of using deferred compensation to purchase an annuity only if they invest in one of the companies specifically selected by the State, the State cannot disclaim responsibility for the discriminatory features of the insurers' options. Since employers are ultimately responsible for the "compensation, terms, conditions, [and] privileges of employment" provided to employees, an employer that adopts a fringe-benefit scheme that discriminates among its employees on the basis of race, religion, sex, or national origin violates Title VII regardless of whether third parties are also invited in the discrimination. . . . It would be inconsistent with the broad remedial purposes of Title VII to hold that an employer who adopts a dis-

criminatory fringe benefit plan can avoid liability on the ground that he could not find a third party willing to treat his employees on a nondiscriminatory basis.[24] An employer who confronts such a situation must either supply the fringe benefit himself, without the assistance of any third party, or not provide it at all.

IV

We turn finally to the relief awarded by the District Court. The court enjoined petitioners to assure that future annuity payments to retired female employees shall be equal to the payments received by similarly situated male employees.[25]

. . . Once a violation of the statute has been found, retroactive relief "should be denied only if for reasons which, if applied generally, would not frustrate the central statutory purposes of eradicating discrimination throughout the economy and making persons whole for injuries suffered through past discrimination." *Albemarle Paper v. Moody*, 422 U.S. 405, at 421. Applying this standard, we held that the mere absence of bad faith on the part of the em-

24. Such a result would be particularly anomalous where, as here, the employer made no effort to determine whether third parties would provide the benefit on a neutral basis. Contrast *The Chronicle of Higher Education*, note 15, *supra*, at 25–26 (explaining how the University of Minnesota obtained agreements from two insurance companies to use sex-neutral annuity tables to calculate annuity benefits for its employees). Far from bargaining for sex-neutral treatment of its employees, Arizona asked companies seeking to participate in its plan to list their annuity rates for men and women separately.

25. The court did not explain its reasons for choosing this remedy. Since respondents did not appeal the District Court's refusal to award damages for benefit payments made prior to the court's decision, there is no need to consider the correctness of that ruling.

ployer is not a sufficient reason for denying such relief. *Id.* at 422–23.

Although this Court noted in *Manhart* that "[t]he *Albemarle* presumption in favor of retroactive liability can seldom be overcome." 435 U.S., at 719, the Court concluded that under the circumstances the District Court had abused its discretion in requiring the employer to refund to female employees all contributons they were required to make in excess of the contributions demanded of men. The Court explained that "conscientious and intelligent administrators of pension funds, who did not have the benefit of the extensive briefs and arguments presented to us, may well have assumed that a program like the Department's was entirely lawful," since "[t]he courts had been silent on the question, and the administrative agencies had conflicting views." *Id.* at 720. . . .

While the relief ordered here affects only benefit payments made after the date of the District Court's judgment, it does not follow that the relief is wholly prospective in nature, as an injunction concerning future conduct ordinarily is, and should therefore be routinely awarded once liability is established. When a court directs a change in benefits based on contributions made before the court's order, the court is awarding relief that is fundamentally retroactive in nature. This is true because retirement benefits under a plan such as that at issue here represent a return on contributions which were made during the employee's working years and which were intended to fund the benefits without any additional contributions from any source after retirement.

A recognition that the relief awarded by the District Court is partly retroactive is only the beginning of the inquiry. Absent special circumstances a victim of a Title VII violation is entitled to whatever retroactive relief is necessary to undo any damage re-

sulting from the violation. *See Albemarle Paper Co. v. Moody*, 422 U.S. at 418–19, 421. As to any disparity in benefits that is attributable to contributions made after our decision in *Manhart*, there are no special circumstances justifying the denial of retroactive relief. Our ruling today was clearly foreshadowed by *Manhart*. That decision should have put petitioners on notice that a man and a woman who make the same contributions to a retirement plan must be paid the same monthly benefits.[26] To the extent that any disparity in benefits coming due after the date of the District Court's judgment is attributable to contributions made after *Manhart*, there is therefore no unfairness in requiring petitioners to pay retired female employees whatever sum is necessary each month to bring them up to the benefit level that they would have enjoyed had their post-*Manhart* contributions been treated in the same way as those of similarly situated male employees.

To the extent, however, that the disparity in benefits that the District Court required petitioners to eliminate is attributable to contributions made before *Manhart*, the court gave insufficient attention to this Court's recognition in *Manhart* that until that decision the use of sex-based table might reasonably have been assumed to be lawful. Insofar as this portion of the disparity is concerned, the District Court should have inquired into the circumstances in which petitioners, after *Manhart*, could have applied sex-neutral tables to the pre-*Manhart* contributions of a female employee and a similarly situated male employee without violating any contractual rights that the latter might have had on the basis of his pre-*Manhart* contributions. If, in the case of a particular

26. . . . After *Manhart* an employer could not reasonably have assumed that a sex-based plan would be lawful. . . .

female employee and a similarly situated male employee, petitioners could have applied sex-neutral tables to pre-*Manhart* contributions without violating any contractual right of the male employee, they should have done so in order to prevent further discrimination in the payment of retirement benefits in the wake of this Court's ruling in *Manhart*.[27] Since a female employee in this situation should have had sex-neutral tables applied to her pre-*Manhart* contributions, it is only fair that petitioners be required to supplement any benefits coming due after the District Court's judgment by whatever sum is necessary to compensate her for their failure to adopt sex-neutral tables.

If, on the other hand, sex-neutral tables could not have been applied to the pre-*Manhart* contributions of a particular female employee and any similarly situated male employee without violating the male employee's contractual rights, it would be inequitable to award such relief. . . .

The record does not indicate whether some or all of the male participants in the plan who had not retired at the time *Manhart* was decided had any contractual right to a particular level of benefits that would have been impaired by the appli-

cation of sex-neutral tables to their pre-*Manhart* contributions. The District Court should address this question on remand.

JUSTICE POWELL, with whom THE CHIEF JUSTICE, JUSTICE BLACKMUN, and JUSTICE REHNQUIST join as to parts I and II, dissenting in part and with whom THE CHIEF JUSTICE, JUSTICE BLACKMUN, JUSTICE REHNQUIST, and JUSTICE O'CONNOR join as to part III, concurring in part.

The Court today holds that an employer may not offer its employees life annuities from a private insurance company that uses actuarially sound, sex-based mortality tables. This holding will have a far-reaching effect on the operation of insurance and pension plans. Employers may be forced to discontinue offering life annuities, or potentially disruptive changes may be required in long-established methods of calculating insurance and pensions.[1] Either course will work a major change in the way the cost of insurance is determined—to the probable detriment of *all* employees. This is contrary to our explicit recognition in *Los Angeles Dept. of Water & Power v. Manhart*, 435 U.S. 702, 717 (1978), that Title VII "was [not] intended to revolutionize the insurance and pension industries."

---

27. Since the actual calculation and payment of retirement benefits was in the hands of third parties under the Arizona plan, petitioners would not automatically have been able to apply sex-neutral tables to pre-*Manhart* contributions even if pre-existing contractual rights posed no obstacle. However, petitioners were in a position to exert influence on the companies participating in the plan, which depended upon the State for the business generated by the deferred compensation plan, and we see no reason why petitioners should stand in a better position because they engaged third parties to pay the benefits than they would be in had they run the entire plan themselves.

1. The cost of continuing to provide annuities may become prohibitive. The *minimum* additional cost necessary to equalize benefits prospectively would range from $85 to $93 million each year for at least the next 15 years. . . . If employers are required to "top up" benefits—i.e., calculate women's benefits at the rate applicable to men rather than apply a unisex rate to both men and women—the cost of providing purely prospective benefits would range from $428 to $676 million each year for at least the next 15 years.

I

. . .

[T]o achieve tax benefits under federal law, the life annuity must be purchased from a company designated by the retirement plan. Accordingly, Arizona contracts with private insurance companies to make life annuities available to its employees. The companies that underwrite the life annuities, as do the vast majority of private insurance companies in the United States, use sex-based mortality tables. Thus, the only effect of Arizona's third option is to allow its employees to purchase at a tax saving the same annuities they otherwise would purchase on the open market.

The Court holds that Arizona's voluntary plan violates Title VII. In the majority's view, Title VII requires an employer to follow one of three courses. An employer must provide unisex annuities itself, contract with insurance companies to provide such annuities, or provide no annuities to its employees. The first option is largely illusory. Most employers do not have either the financial resources or administrative ability to underwrite annuities. Or, as in this case, state law may prevent an employer from providing annuities. If unisex annuities are available, an employer may contract with private insurance companies to provide them. It is stipulated, however, that the insurance companies with which Arizona contracts do not provide unisex annuities, nor do insurance companies generally underwrite them. The insurance industry either is prevented by state law from doing so or it views unisex mortality tables as actuarially unsound. An employer, of course, may choose the third option. It simply may decline to offer its employees the right to purchase annuities at a substantial tax saving. It is difficult to see the virtue in such a compelled choice.

II

As indicated above, the consequences of the Court's holding are unlikely to be beneficial. If the cost to employers of offering unisex annuities is prohibitive or if insurance carriers choose not to write such annuities, employees will be denied the opportunity to purchase life annuities—concededly the most advantageous pension plan—at lower cost.[4] If, alternatively, insurance carriers and employers choose to offer these annuities, the heavy cost burden of equalizing benefits probably will be passed on to current employees. There is no evidence that Congress intended Title VII to work such a change. Nor does *Manhart* support such a sweeping reading of this statute. That case expressly recognized the limited reach of its holding—a limitation grounded in the legislative history of Title VII and the inapplicability of Title VII's policies to the insurance industry.

A

We were careful in *Manhart* to make clear that the question before us was narrow. We stated: "All that is at issue today is a requirement that men and women make unequal contributions to an *employer-operated* pension fund." 435 U.S., at 717.

4. This is precisely what has happened in this case. Faced with the liability resulting from the Court of Appeals' judgment, the State of Arizona discontinued making life annuities available to its employees. Tr. of Oral Arg. 8. Any employee who now wishes to have the security provided by a life annuity must withdraw his or her accrued retirement savings from the state pension plan, pay federal income tax on the amount withdrawn, and then use the remainder to purchase an annuity on the open market—which most likely will be sex-based. The adverse effect of today's holding apparently will fall primarily on the State's employees.

(Emphasis added.) And our holding was limited expressly to the precise issue before us. We stated that "[a]lthough we conclude that the Department's practice violated Title VII; we do not suggest that the statute was intended to revolutionize the insurance and pension industries." *Id.*

The Court in *Manhart* had good reason for recognizing the narrow reach of Title VII in the particular area of the insurance industry. Congress has chosen to leave the primary responsibility for regulating the insurance industry to the respective States. *See* McCarran-Ferguson. Act, 59 Stat 33, as amended, 15 U.S.C. §1011 *et seq*. . . . Given the consistent policy of entrusting insurance regulation to the States, the majority is not justified in assuming that Congress intended in 1964 to require the industry to change long-standing actuarial methods, approved over decades by state insurance commissions.

Nothing in the language of Title VII suports this pre-emption of state jurisdiction. Nor has the majority identified any evidence in the legislative history that Congress considered the widespread use of sex-based mortality tables to be discriminatory or that it intended to modify its previous grant by the McCarran-Ferguson Act of exclusive jurisdiction to the States to regulate the terms of protection offered by insurance companies. Rather, the legislative history indicates precisely the opposite.

The only reference to this issue occurs in an explanation of the Act by Senator Humphrey during the debates on the Senate floor. He stated that it was "unmistakably clear" that Title VII did not prohibit different treatment of men and women under industrial benefit plans.[7] *See* 110

Cong. Rec 13663–13664 (1964). As we recognized in *Manhart*, "[alt]hough he did not address differences in employee contributions based on sex, Senator Humphrey apparently assumed that the 1964 Act would have little, if any, impact on existing pension plans." 435 U.S., at 714. This statement was not sufficient, as *Manhart* held, to preclude the application of Title VII to an *employer*-operated plan. *See id.* But Senator Humphrey's explanation provides strong support for Manhart's recognition that Congress intended Title VII to have *only* that indirect effect on the private insurance industry.

B

As neither the language of the statute nor the legislative history supports its holding, the majority is compelled to rely on its perception of the policy expressed in Title

---

7. Senator Humphrey's statement was based on the adoption of the Bennett amendment, which incorporated the affirmative defenses of the Equal Pay Act, 77 Stat. 56, 29 U.S.C. § 206(d),

into Title VII. *See County of Washington, Ore. v. Gunther,* 452 U.S. 161, 175, n.15 (1981). Although not free from ambiguity, the legislative history of the Equal Pay Act provides ample support for Senator Humphrey's interpretation of that Act. In explaining the Equal Pay Act's affirmative defenses, the Senate Report on that statute noted that pension costs were "higher for women than men . . . because of the longer life span of women." S. Rep. No. 176, 88th Cong., 1st Sess. 39 (1963). It then explained that the question of additional costs associated with employing women was one "that can only be answered by an ad hoc investigation." *Id.* Thus, it concluded that where it could be shown that there were in fact higher costs for women than men, an exception to the Equal Pay Act could be permitted "similar to those . . . for a bona fide seniority system or other exception noted above." *Id.*

Even if other meanings might be drawn from the Equal Pay Act's legislative history, the crucial question is how Congress viewed the Equal Pay Act in 1964 when it incorporated it into Title VII. The only relevant legislative history that exists on this point demonstrates unmistakably that Congress perceived—with good reason—that

VII. The policy, of course, is broadly to proscribe discrimination in employment practices. But the statute itself focuses specifically on the individual and "precludes treatment of individuals as simply components of a racial, religious, sexual or national class." *Id.* at 708. This specific focus had little relevance to the business of insurance. *See id.* at 724 (BLACKMUN, J., concurring in part and concurring in the judgment). . . . Insurance companies cannot make individual determinations of life expectancy; they must consider instead the life expectancy of identifiable groups. Given a sufficiently large group of people, an insurance company can predict with considerable realiability the rate and frequency of deaths within the group based on the past mortality experience of similar groups. Title VII's concern for the effect of employment practices on the individual thus is simply inapplicable to the actuarial predictions that must be made in writing insurance and annuities.

C

. . . The most accurate classification system would be to identify all attributes that have some verifiable correlation with mortality and divide people into groups accordingly, but the administrative cost of such an undertaking would be prohibitive. Instead of identifying all relevant attributes, most insurance companies classify individuals according to criteria that provide both an accurate and efficient measure of longevity, including a persons's age and sex. These particular criteria are readily identifiable, stable, and easily verifiable. *See* Benston, *The Economics of Gender Discrimination in Employee Fringe Benefits:* Manhart

Revisited, 49 U. Chi. L. Rev. 489, 499–501 (1982).

It is this practice—the use of a sex-based group classification—that the majority ultimately condemns. The policies underlying Title VII, rather than supporting the majority's decision, strongly suggest—at least for me—the opposite conclusion. This remedial statute was enacted to eradicate the types of discrimination in employment that then were pervasive in our society. The entire thrust of Title VII is directed against *discrimination*—disparate treatment on the basis of race or sex that intentionally or arbitrarily affects an individual. But as JUSTICE BLACKMUN has stated, life expectancy is a "nonstigmatizing factor that demonstrably differentiates females from males and that is not measurable on an individual basis. . . . [T]here is nothing arbitrary, irrational, or 'discriminatory' about recognizing the objective and accepted . . . disparity in female-male life expectancies in computing rates for retirement plans." *Manhart,* 435 U.S., at 724 (opinion concurring in part and concurring in the judgment). Explicit sexual classifications, to be sure, require close examination, but they are not automatically invalid. Sex-based mortality tables reflect objective actuarial experience. Because their use does not entail discrimination in any normal understanding of that term,[9] a court should hesitate to invalidate this long-approved practice on the basis of its own policy judgment.

Congress may choose to forbid the use of any sexual classifications in insurance, but nothing suggests that it intended to do so in Title VII. And certainly the policy underlying Title VII provides no warrant

---

"the 1964 Act [Title VII] would have little, if any, impact on existing pension plans." *Manhart,* 435 U.S., at 714.

9. Indeed, if employers and insurance carriers offer annuities based on unisex mortality tables, men as a class will receive less aggregate benefits than similarly situated women.

for extending the reach of the statute beyond Congress' intent.

III

. . . The Court today affirms the Court of Appeals' judgment insofar as it holds that Arizona's voluntary pension plan violates Title VII. But this finding of a statutory violation provides no basis for approving the retroactive relief awarded by the District Court. To approve this award would be both unprecedented and manifestly unjust.

We recognized in *Manhart* that retroactive relief is normally appropriate in the typical Title VII case, but concluded that the District Court had abused its discretion in awarding such relief. As we noted, the employer in *Manhart* may well have assumed that its pension program was lawful. More importantly, a retroactive remedy would have had a potentially disruptive impact on the operation of the employer's pension plan. The business of underwriting insurance and life annuities requires careful approximation of risk. Reserves normally are sufficient to cover only the cost of funding and administering the plan. Should an unforeseen contingency occur, such as a drastic change in the legal rules governing pension and insurance funds, both the insurer's solvency and the insured's benefits could be jeopardized.

This case presents no different considerations. *Manhart* did put all employer-operated pension funds on notice that they could not "requir[e] that men and women make unequal contributions to [the] fund," at 717, but expressly confirmed that an employer could set aside equal contributions and let each retiree purchase whatever benefits his or her contributions could command on the "open market," *id*. at 718. Given this explicit limitation, an employer reasonably could have assumed that it would be lawful to make available to its employees annuities offered by insurance companies on the open market.

As in *Manhart*, holding employers liable retroactively would have devastating results. The holding applies to all employer-sponsored pension plans, and the cost of complying with the District Court's award of retroactive relief would range from $817 to $1260 million annually for the next 15 to 30 years. *Department of Labor Cost Study* 32. In this case, the cost would fall on the State of Arizona. Presumably other state and local governments also would be affected directly by today's decision. Imposing such unanticipated financial burdens would come at a time when many States and local governments are struggling to meet substantial fiscal deficits. . . . Accordingly, liability should be prospective only.[12]

JUSTICE O'CONNOR, concurring.

This case requires us to determine whether Title VII prohibits an employer from offering an annuity plan in which the participating insurance company uses sex-based tables for calculating monthly benefit payments. It is important to stress that our judicial role is simply to discern the intent of the 88th Congress in enacting Title VII of the Civil Rights Act of 1964,[1] a statute covering only discrimination in employment. What we, if sitting as legislators,

12. In this respect, I agree with JUSTICE O'CONNOR that only benefits derived from contributions collected after the effective date of the judgment need be calculated without regard to the sex of the employee.

1. The 92nd Congress made important amendments to Title VII, including extending its coverage to state employers such as the State of Arizona. The 1972 Amendments did not change the substantive requirements of Title VII, however. Thus, it is the intent of the 88th Congress that is controlling here.

might consider wise legislative policy is irrelevant to our task. . . . Finally, our decision must ignore (and our holding has no necessary effect on) the larger issue of whether considerations of sex should be barred from all insurance plans, including individual purchases of insurance, an issue that Congress is currently debating. *See* S. 372, 98th Cong., 1st Sess. (1983); H.R. 100, 98th Cong., 1st Sess. (1983).

Although the issue presented for our decision is a narrow one, the answer is far from self-evident. As with many other narrow issues of statutory construction, the general language chosen by Congress does not clearly resolve the precise question. Our polestar, however, must be the intent of Congress, and the guiding lights are the language, structure, and legislative history of Title VII. Our inquiry is made somewhat easier by . . . *City of Los Angeles Department of Water and Power v. Manhart.* . . .

. . . I am persuaded that the result in *Manhart* is not distinguishable from the present situation. *Manhart* did note that Title VII would allow an employer to set aside equal retirement contributions for each employee and let the retiree purchase whatever annuity his or her accumulated contributions could command on the open market. *Id.* at 717–18. In that situation, the employer is treating each employee without regard to sex. If an independent insurance company then classifies persons on the basis of sex, the disadvantaged female worker cannot claim she was denied a privilege of employment, any more than she could complain of employment discrimination when the employer pays equal wages in a community where local merchants charge women more than men for identical items. As I stressed above, Title VII covers only discrimination in *employment*, and thus simply does not reach these other situations.

Unlike these examples, however, the employer here has done more than set aside equal lump sums for all employees. Title VII clearly does not allow an employer to offer a plan to employees under which it will collect equal contributions, hold them in a trust account, and upon retirement disburse greater monthly checks to men than women. Nor could an employer escape Title VII's mandate by using a third-party bank to hold and manage the account. In the situation at issue here, the employer has used third-party insurance companies to administer the plan, but the plan remains essentially a "privileg[e] of employment," and thus is covered by Title VII. 42 U.S.C. §2000e–2(a)(1).

For these reasons, I join parts I, II, and III of JUSTICE MARSHALL's opinion. Unlike JUSTICE MARSHALL, however, I would not make our holding retroactive. Rather, for reasons explained below, I agree with JUSTICE POWELL that our decision should be prospective. I therefore join part III of JUSTICE POWELL's opinion.

In *Chevron Oil Co. v. Huson*, 404 U.S. 97, 105–9 (1971), we set forth three criteria for determining when to apply a decision of statutory interpretation prospectively. First, the decision must establish a new principle of law, either by overruling clear past precedent or by deciding an issue of first impression whose resolution was not clearly foreshadowed. *Id.* at 106. Ultimately, I find this case controlled by the same principles of Title VII articulated by the Court in *Manhart*. If this first criterion were the sole consideration for prospectivity, I might find it difficult to make today's decision prospective. As reflected in JUSTICE POWELL's dissent, however, whether *Manhart* foreshadows today's decision is sufficiently debatable that the first criterion of the *Chevron* test does not compel retroactivity here. Therefore, we must examine the remaining criteria of the *Chevron* test as well.

The second criterion is whether retro-activity will further or retard the operation of the statute. *Chevron, supra*, at 106–7. *See also Albemarle Paper Co. v. Moody*, 422 U:S. 405, 421 (backpay should be denied only for reasons that will not frustrate the central statutory purposes). *Manhart* held that a central purpose of Title VII is to prevent employers from treating individual workers on the basis of sexual or racial group characteristics. Although retroactive application will not retard the achievement of this purpose, that goal in no way requires retroactivity. I see no reason to believe that a retroactive holding is necessary to ensure that pension plan administrators, who may have thought until our decision today that Title VII did not extend to plans involving third-party insurers, will not now quickly conform their plans to ensure that individual employees are allowed equal monthly benefits regardless of sex.[3]

In my view, the third criterion—whether retroactive application would impose inequitable results—compels a prospective decision in these circumstances. Many working men and women have based their retirement decisions on expectations of a certain stream of income during retire-

ment. These decisions depend on the existence of adequate reserves to fund these pensions. A retroactive holding by this Court that employers must disburse greater annuity benefits than the collected contributions can support would jeopardize the entire pension fund. If a fund cannot meet its obligations, "[t]he harm would fall in large part on innocent third parties." *Manhart*, at 722–23. This real danger of bankrupting pension funds requires that our decision be made prospective. Such a prospective holding is, of course, consistent with our equitable powers under Title VII to fashion an appropriate remedy.

In my view then, our holding should be made prospective in the following sense. I would require employers to ensure that benefits derived from contributions collected after the effective date of our judgment be calculated without regard to the sex of the employee.[4] For contributions collected before the effective date of our judgment, however, I would allow employers and participating insurers to calculate the resulting benefits as they have in the past.

3. Another goal of Title VII is to make persons whole for injuries suffered from unlawful employment discrimination. *See Albemarle Paper Co. v. Moody*, 422 U.S. 405, 418 (1975). Although this goal would suggest that the present decision should be made retroactive, it does not necessarily control the decision on retroactivity. *See Manhart, supra*, at 719.

4. In other words, I would require employers to use longevity tables that reflect the average longevity of all their workers. The Equal Pay Act proviso, 29 U.S.C. §206(d)(1) which forbids employers from curing violations of the Act by reducing the wage rate of any employee would not require that employers "top up" benefits by using male-longevity tables for all workers. . . . The language of the Equal Pay Act proviso seems to apply only to wages. . . .

CASE QUESTIONS

1. Does this decision in effect force employers to discriminate against male employees? Is it unfair to male employees?

2. If employer-selected insurance companies moved toward computerized, individualized projections of life expec-

tancy, based on annual questionnaires and examinations (that covered weight, smoking, drinking, marital status, drinking habits, etc.) and used this to produce combined assessments of death benefits and pension benefits (so as to neutralize the incentives for lying in either direction), could those projections then take sex into account? Race?

Note on Comparable Worth

While the Equal Pay Act and Title VII of the Civil Rights Act of 1964 certainly forbid overt sex discrimination in wages, hiring and firing, it is not as clear whether those laws cover or should be read as covering, the matter of comparable worth, often called the civil rights issue of the 1980s. "Comparable worth" refers generally to a program of providing equal pay for jobs involving comparable overall effort, skill, responsibility, and working conditions. The issue is a pressing one on the feminist agenda, for women full-time workers continue to earn roughly 60 percent of what males earn, and that gap is largely attributable to the fact that jobs held largely by women tend to have lower wages than jobs held largely by men.

The Equal Pay Act of 1963 seems deliberately to have avoided a "comparable worth" mandate, for it states that employers may not

> discriminate . . . between employees on the basis of sex by paying wages . . . at a rate less than the rate *that he pays to employees of the opposite sex [in the same establishment]* . . . *for equal work* on jobs the performance of which requires equal skill, effort, and responsibility, and which are performed under similar working conditions, except where such payment is made pursuant to (i) a seniority system; (ii) a merit system; (iii) a system which measures earnings by quantity or quality of production; or (iv) a differential based on any other factor other than sex. (29 U.S.C. §206[d][1] [emphasis added].)

When sex discrimination was added to the list of discriminations forbidden by Title VII, Senator Bennett successfully offered an amendment to limit the reach of Title VII. The Bennett Amendment, 42 U.S.C. §2000e–2(h), provides that

> It shall not be an unlawful employment practice . . . for an employer to differentiate upon the basis of sex in determining . . . wages or compensation . . . if such differentiation is authorized by . . . §206(d) of title 29 [the Equal Pay Act].

County of Washington v. Gunther (1981), discussion

In 1981 the U.S. Supreme Court decided *County of Washington v. Gunther*, 452 U.S. 161, a case that required interpretation specifically of the question whether the Bennett Amendment had incorporated the Equal Pay Act rule that the equal pay mandate applied only to workers of the opposite sex in the same establishment performing equal work, or whether, on the other hand, it had incorporated only the four Equal Pay Act affirmative defenses to sex differentials in pay (seniority, merit system, etc.). The issue of comparable worth lurked prominently in the background of *Gunther*. The majority went out of its way to deny that it was endorsing "the controversial theory of 'comparable worth'" (at 166), and the dissenters reiterated the point. What the majority did decide was that the "equal work" limitation of the Equal Pay Act had not been incorporated into Title VII.

Consequently the women in Washington County, hired for the job of guard in the women's jail, even though the job had been ruled not "substantially equal" to men's jail guard (because there were so many fewer prisoners in the former), and even though no males were ever hired for the job of guard in the women's jail, still could bring a Title VII lawsuit, the Supreme Court ruled. The women claimed that the county administrators had evaluated the women's job as worth 95 percent of the men's and had then downgraded the women's salary to 70 percent of the men's because they knew that women will work for less than men. In other words, the allegation was that the women's wages had been lowered well below the degree appropriate for non-comparability of the work on the basis of sheer sex discrimination. The Court reasoned that this case presented a valid Title VII claim and sent it back to the lower courts for hearings as to proof of the allegation.

Some comparable worth advocates have taken encouragement from this decision. Their hope is that they will be able to convince courts of the weakness of employers' claim that paying lower wages for women-dominated jobs is simply a response to market forces, which fit into the "factor other than sex" defense for differentials in pay. The counter-argument to this claim is that sex discrimination pervades the market and thus shapes the market forces; therefore, market forces cannot be a "factor other than sex." To date, three different federal circuit courts of appeal have rejected this counter-argument—i.e., have rejected the theory that Title VII requires equal pay for work of comparable worth,[10] and the U.S. Supreme Court has refused a request to review one of those decisions.[11]

Meanwhile, a substantial number of states have moved on their own to implement comparable worth pay programs for state employees, sometimes dubbing these "pay equity" programs in order to avoid the connotation of "controversy" surrounding "comparable worth."[12] Some of these programs have come through legislative mandate calling for gradual adjustment over a period of years, as in Minnesota, Washington, Iowa, and Wisconsin. In other states, such as Ohio, Connecticut, Massachusetts, and New York, movement toward pay equity has come through executive initiatives, supplementing budgets, and collective bargaining agreements.[13] In short, while the right to receive equal pay for work of comparable value appears to be increasing in prevalence as a legal right of state employees, at the national level it has not attained the status of either constitutional right or legal right.

First Amendment Rights vs. Anti-Discrimination Law

The Fourteenth Amendment (in its Due Process Clause) protects values of liberty as well as (in its Equal Protection Clause) those of equality. Sooner or later, in many areas of American politics these values bump into each other and limit each other at the edges. Anti-discrimination law is no exception. At least four cases that posed conficts between prohibitions on sex discrimination and First Amendment freedoms have already been resolved by the Supreme Court, and a number of others are winding their way through the lower courts.[14]

Pittsburgh Press v. Human Relations Commission (1973), discussion

The first of these occurred relatively early in the Court's history of enforcing anti-discrimination law. In 1973, in *Pittsburgh Press v. Human Relations Commission*, 413 U.S. 376, the Supreme Court sustained an administrative order forbidding *Pittsburgh Press* to run sex-designated help wanted ads (such as "Help Wanted—Female" or "Help Wanted—Male," which used to be common advertisements in American newspapers.) The Court's logic was that since sex discrimination in hiring was a federal crime, there was no constitutional problem with forbidding the press to be an "accessory before the fact." Four justices dissented, however, on the grounds that federal law did permit a narrow category of jobs for which gender was a "bona fide occupational qualification." They argued that it should be left to the editorial judgment of the press to decide which ads might lawfully qualify rather than let the government ban them all in advance. This group of dissenters drew support from the traditional interpretation of the freedom of press clause, which places particularly strong condemnation on any government censorship *prior* to publication. Despite that tradition, however, the Court majority found the Congressional ban on sex discrimination to be the more weighty concern here, and upheld the Human Relations Commission order.

Hishon v. King & Spaulding (1984), discussion

A more recent First Amendment clash with equal protection concerns, *Elizabeth Hishon v. King & Spaulding*, 467 U.S. 69, was settled in May, 1984. Elizabeth Hishon had been hired by the King & Spaulding law firm as an associate in 1972, and she alleged that part of the firm's recruitment policy had been the assurance that satisfactory job performance would yield promotion to partner status within five or six years. She further alleged that the firm then refused to consider women for partnership promotion on a "fair and equal basis," but instead discriminated against them on the basis of sex. The law firm countered with the argument that Title VII did not apply to selections of partners, and both the federal district court and appeals court accepted that argument. The U.S. Supreme Court was unanimous in its reversal.

The Supreme Court insisted that opportunity for promotion in a law firm to partner status was indisputably a "term, condition, or privilege of employment," within the meaning of Title VII. It tersely disposed of King & Spaulding's First Amendment argument as follows:

> [R]espondent argues that application of Title VII in this case would infringe constitutional rights of expression or association. Although we have recognized that the activities of lawyers may make a "distinctive contribution . . . to the ideas and beliefs of our society," *NAACP v. Button*, 371 U.S. 415, 431 (1963), respondent has not shown how its ability to fulfill such a function would be inhibited by a requirement that it consider petitioner for partnership on her merits. Moreover, as we have held in another context, "[i]nvidious private discrimination may be characterized as a form of exercising freedom of association protected by the First Amendment, but it has never been accorded affirmative constitutional protections." *Norwood v. Harrison*, 413 U.S. 455, 470 (1973). There is no constitutional right, for example, to discriminate in the selection of who may attend a private school or join a labor union. (*Runyon, v. McCrary*, 427 U.S. 160 [1976]; *Railway Mail Association v. Corsi*, 326 U.S. 88, 93–94 [1945].)

Justice Powell authored a lone separate concurrence in which he made three points: (1) First Amendment rights of association are very much implicated by decisions to admit someone to partnership in a law firm, since the partnership is the managing body of the firm. (2) In this case, King & Spaulding have no First Amendment defense because they voluntarily contracted (orally at the time of hiring) to consider Hishon on a "fair and equal basis" for partnership. (They cannot have a First Amendment right to renege on their contracts with only female employees, and an attempt to do so would put them in violation of Title VII.) (3) it is beneficial to society and the law if law firms refrain from discrimination on the basis of sex. Justice Powell left unclear whether in his view the combination of Title VII and the First Amendment would permit a law firm to hire associates with an explicit understanding that women could never be promoted to partnership, but the combination of his arguments seems to suggest that he would find such an arrangement lawful. (On the other hand, the import of his third argument may be that anti-discrimination laws serve an interest compelling enough to override the First Amendment claim.)

Roberts v. U.S. Jaycees (1984), discussion

Two months after *Hishon*, the Supreme Court handed down a decision rejecting a challenge by the national Jaycees organization to a civil rights law of the state of Minnesota, *Roberts v. U.S. Jaycees*, 468 U.S. 609. Because membership in the Jaycees was eagerly sold to any male aged eighteen to thirty-five, authorities in Minnesota had ruled that the Jaycees constituted a "place of public accommodation" within the meaning of their civil rights law, and they had ruled that the organization had to stop discriminating on the basis of sex. Minnesota argued that since the Jaycees were not selective (in any way other than age and sex) in their membership the organization's claims of First Amendment rights of association rang hollow. The U.S. Supreme Court (in a unanimous judgment in which Burger and Blackmun did not participate, and with which O'Connor concurred in a separate opinion and Rehnquist concurred with no opinion) found this argument persuasive.

The Jaycees presented a freedom of expression argument that gave the Court a bit more trouble. The claim was that admitting women would alter the message the Jaycees could express. The Court opinion resolved this claim with the compelling interest test, reasoning that even if the Jaycees' expressive freedom suffered "some incidental abridgement," that abridgement was no greater than the amount necessary for attaining the state's compelling interest in assuring women equal opportunity to participate fully in the public life of society. Justice O'Connor wrote separately to argue that this freedom of expression analysis was inappropriate since the Jaycees were essentially a commercial operation rather than "an expressive association" and consequently should be accorded only the most minimal of First Amendment rights.

Hudnut v. American Booksellers' Association (1986), discussion

Third in this recent series, in February 1986, the Supreme Court, without hearing oral argument, rejected an innovative anti-pronography ordinance of Indianapolis. *Hudnut v. American Booksellers' Association*, 54 U.S. L.W. 3560. The ordinance, typical of those promoted in various parts of the U.S. by feminist author Andre Dworkin and law professor Catherine MacKinnon, asserted that the sale or production of pornography constituted "sex discrimination" (in that it promoted a climate of opinion which restricted women's opportunities to participate freely and equally in community life) and would be an actionable offense—i.e., women could bring lawsuits for damages to halt such activity. In contrast to judicial doctrine that removes "obscenity" from First Amendment protection on the grounds that it is not part of the exchange of ideas and lacks serious artistic, literary, political, scientific or other redeeming value (by court-created legal definition),[15] these ordinances define pornography with reference to its graphicness in the depiction of sex combined with its degrading portrayal of women as either desirous of sexual subjugation or suited to be sexually subjugated and dominated. These ordinances do not exempt from their coverage works of artistic, literary, or other merit. That flaw (among others) proved fatal at the circuit court of appeals level (771 F.2d 323), as well as at the district court (598 F. Supp. 1316), where the judge happened to be a woman. The Supreme Court simply upheld the circuit court decision without comment (although three justices did indicate that they believed oral argument should have been set for the case). It is probable that an anti-pornography ordinance that more carefully tracked the Court's definition of obscenity, with regard especially to protection for genuine exchange of ideas, though still couched in anti-discrimination terms, would pass muster at the Supreme Court, because the Court repeatedly and without exception has ruled that "obscenity" (the Court's usual term for pornography), as the Court defines it, is NOT protected by the First Amendment.

Education

Having voted overwhelmingly for the ERA, Congress in 1972 expanded the coverage of federal civil rights law in a number of ways. For instance, the Title VII ban on employment discrimination was extended to cover employees of state and local governments. Another critical expansion of anti-discrimination law was Title IX of the 1972 Education Amendments, which is commonly known simply as Title IX (20 U.S.C. § 1681[a] and § 1682). This set of provisions mandated, "No person in the United States shall, on the basis of sex, be excluded from participation in, be denied the benefits of, or be subjected to discrimination under any education program or activity receiving Federal financial assistance . . ." (§901[a] of Title IX). If a recipient of federal funds were found in violation of this mandate, that recipient was to lose the financial assistance, with the proviso that such loss of funds "shall be limited in its effect to the particular program, or part thereof, in which such noncompliance has been found . . ." (§902).

In terms of media attention, the spotlight on Title IX has focused on its impact upon high school and college athletics programs (which impact was indeed substantial: The number of females participating in intercollegiate sports in the U.S. went from 16,000 in 1972 to over 150,000 by 1984).[16] Expansions in athletic programs, however, are only small pieces of the changes wrought by Title IX. High school vocational training programs, once totally sex segregated, had to become non-discriminatory; college admission programs (e.g., at Cornell University) that had openly discriminated against females, both by admitting fewer women than men and by imposing stiffer admission standards on females, had to stop discriminating.

The legal force of Title IX was dramatically altered by a Supreme Court decision in February of 1984, *Grove City College v. T. H. Bell, Secretary of Education*, 465 U.S. 555. Prior to that decision, the reference in §902 to termination of funds for any discriminating recipient in respect to "the particular program, or part thereof, in which noncompliance has been so found" was thought to refer an entire university. That is, it was generally believed that if any part of a university discriminated, the university would lose all of its federal funds. The executive branch had interpreted the law in this way from its passage in 1972, through the district court and court of appeals levels of the *Grove City* case, but by the time the case was argued at the Supreme Court, the Carter administration had become the Reagan Administration, and the Department of Education (formerly HEW) had altered its "own" position in court. At the Supreme Court, the Department of Education argued that the program-specific language of Title IX should be understood as applying to parts of universities, rather than as treating each whole university as an indivisible "program." Thus, a university could take federal aid, say, to construct science buildings but still discriminate in admissions or in sports programs. Six members of the Supreme Court bought this argument. Two (Brennan and Marshall) dissented, and one (Stevens) argued that the *Grove City* case did not even properly present the question of what the program-specific language meant for financial aid to colleges in general. Thus, in his view the court did not have jurisdiction to issue the specific ruling against which Brennan and Marshall were dissenting.

This case began when the Department of Education moved in 1977 to declare Grove City College ineligible to receive federal funds in the form of Basic Educational Opportunity Grants (BEOGs) because the college refused to fulfill the legal requirement of completing certain government forms asserting that it refrained from discriminating on the basis of sex (Assurance of Compliance). Grove City was a coed liberal arts college of about 2200 students, of whom about 140 received BEOGs. The record was clear and undisputed on Grove City's innocence of any racial or sex-based discrimination. But Grove City College as a matter of principle—insisting on its independence from government control—took no money from the government. (The BEOGs went directly to individual students who then used them to pay tuition.) Likewise, on principle, Grove City refused to fill out these bureaucratic forms. The college went to Court to block the federal cutoff of funds from its students, arguing that the college was not a recipient of federal funds under the statute and thus should not have to fill out the forms. The Supreme Court was unanimous in rejecting this claim. But six justices stated that Grove City, in order to keep receiving the funds, would have to fill out Assurance of Compliance forms *only* as to its financial aid program, for it took federal money only for that program. This part of the decision has evoked considerable controversy.

A bill aimed at overturning this decision (H.R. 5490) passed in the House by a vote of 375–32 on June 26, 1984, and its Senate counterpart (S. 2568) had 63 co-sponsors as of August 1984. The bill, dubbed the Civil Rights Act of 1984, whose coverage would also have extended to laws prohibiting discrimination against the handicapped and the elderly, became entangled in anti-abortion politics and in a number of side issues (e.g., Would ranchers whose animals drank water from federal water projects have to hire the handicapped?). Conservatives, such as Orrin Hatch and Jeremiah Denton, led the campaign against it and succeeded in preventing its enactment. Excerpts from the court decision follow.

Grove City College v. T.H. Bell, Secretary of Education, 465 U.S. 555 (1984)

JUSTICE WHITE delivered the opinion of the Court.

I

. . . [W]e now affirm the Court of Appeals' judgment that the Department could terminate BEOGs received by Grove City's students to force the College to execute an Assurance of Compliance.

II

In defending its refusal to execute the Assurance of Compliance required by the Department's regulations, Grove City first contends that neither it nor any "education program or activity" of the College receives any federal financial assistance within the meaning of Title IX by virtue of the fact that some of its students receive BEOGs and use them to pay for their education. We disagree.

. . . The linchpin of Grove City's argument that none of its programs receives any federal assistance is a perceived distinction between direct and indirect aid, a distinction that finds no support in the text of § 901(a). . . . The economic effect of direct and indirect assistance often is indistinguishable. . . .

Congress undoubtedly comprehended this reality in enacting the Education Amendments of 1972. The legislative history of the amendments is replete with statements evincing Congress' awareness that the student assistance programs established by the amendments would significantly aid colleges and universities. In fact, one of the stated purposes of the student aid provisions was to "provid[e] assistance to institutions of higher education." Pub.

L. 92–318, § 1001(c)(1), 86 Stat. 381, 20 U.S.C. § 1070(a)(5).

. . .

Persuasive evidence of Congress' intent concerning student financial aid may also be gleaned from its subsequent treatment of Title IX. . . . Under the statutory "laying before" procedure of the General Education Provisions Act, Pub. L. 93–380, 88 Stat. 567, as amended, 20 U.S.C. § 1232(d)(1), Congress was afforded an opportunity to invalidate aspects of the regulations it deemed inconsistent with Title IX. The regulations were clear, and Secretary Weinberger left no doubt concerning [HEW]'s position that "the furnishing of student assistance to a student who uses it at a particular institution . . . [is] Federal aid which is covered by the statute." Yet, neither House passed a disapproval resolution. Congress' failure to disapprove the regulations is not dispositive, but . . . it strongly implies that the regulations accurately reflect congressional intent. Congress has never disavowed this implication and in fact has acted consistently with it on a number of occasions.

With the benefit of clear statutory language, powerful evidence of Congress' intent, and a longstanding and coherent administrative construction of the phrase "receiving Federal financial assistance," we have little trouble concluding that Title IX coverage is not foreclosed because federal funds are granted to Grove City's students rather than directly to one of the College's educational programs. There remains the question, however, of identifying the "education program or activity" of the College that can properly be characterized as "receiving" federal assistance through grants to some of the students attending the College.

III

An analysis of Title IX's language and legislative history led us to conclude in *North Haven Board of Education v. Bell*, 456 U.S., at 538, that "an agency's authority under Title IX both to promulgate regulations and to terminate funds is subject to the program-specific limitations of §§ 901 and 902." Although the legislative history contains isolated suggestions that entire institutions are subject to the nondiscrimination provison whenever one of their programs receives federal assistance, *see* 1975 Hearings 178 (Sen. Bayh), we cannot accept the Court of Appeals' conclusion that in the circumstances present here Grove City itself is a "program or activity" that may be regulated in its entirety. Nevertheless, we find no merit in Grove City's contention that a decision treating BEOGs as "Federal financial assistance" cannot be reconciled with Title IX's program-specific language since BEOGs are not tied to any specific "education program or activity."

. . . [H]owever, the fact that federal funds eventually reach the College's general operating budget cannot subject Grove City to institution-wide coverage. . . .

To the extent that the Court of Appeals' holding that BEOGs received by Grove City's students constitute aid to the entire institution rests on the possibility that federal funds received by one program or activity free up the College's own resources for use elsewhere, the Court of Appeals' reasoning is doubly flawed. First, there is no evidence that the federal aid received by Grove City's students results in the diversion of funds from the College's own financial aid program to other areas

within the institution. Second, and more important, the Court of Appeals' assumption . . . is inconsistent with the program-specific nature of the statute. Most federal educational assistance has economic ripple effects throughout the aided institution, and it would be difficult, if not impossible, to determine which programs or activities derive such indirect benefits. Under the Court of Appeals' theory, an entire school would be subject to Title IX merely because one of its students received a small BEOG or because one of its departments received an earmarked federal grant. This result cannot be squared with Congress' intent.

. . .

We conclude that the receipt of BEOGs by some of Grove City's students does not trigger institution-wide coverage under Title IX. In purpose and effect, BEOGs represent federal financial assistance to the College's own financial aid program, and it is that program that may properly be regulated under Title IX.

IV

Since Grove City operates an "education program or activity receiving Federal financial assistance," the Department may properly demand that the College execute an Assurance of Compliance with Title IX. 34 C.F.R. § 106.4 (1982). . . .

. . . [T]he Assurance of Compliance currently in use, like the one Grove City refused to execute, does not on its face purport to reach the entire College; it certifies compliance with respect to those "education programs and activities receiving Federal financial assistance." . . .

A refusal to execute a proper program-specific Assurance of Compliance warrants termination of federal assistance to the student financial aid program. The College's contention that termination must be preceded by a finding of actual discrimination finds no support in the language of § 902, which plainly authorizes that sanction to effect "[c]ompliance with any requirement adopted pursuant to this section." . . .

. . . We conclude, therefore, that the Department may properly condition federal financial assistance on the recipient's assurance that it will conduct the aided program or activity in accordance with Title IX and the applicable regulations.

V

Grove City's final challenge to the Court of Appeals' decision—that conditioning federal assistance on compliance with Title IX infringes First Amendment rights of the College and its students—warrants only brief consideration. Congress is free to attach reasonable and unambiguous conditions to federal financial assistance that educational institutions are not obligated to accept. E.g., *Pennhurst State School & Hospital v. Halderman*, 451 U.S. 1, 17 (1981). Grove City may terminate its participation in the BEOG program and thus avoid the requirements of § 901(a). Students affected by the Department's action may either take their BEOGs elsewhere or attend Grove City without federal financial assistance. Requiring Grove City to comply with Title IX's prohibition of discrimination as a condition for its continued eligibility to participate in BEOG program infringes no First Amendment rights of the College or its students.

Accordingly, the judgment of the Court of Appeals is

Affirmed.

Justice Powell, with whom Chief Justice Burger and Justice O'Connor join, concurring.

As I agree that the holding in this case is dictated by the language and legislative history of Title IX, and the Regulations of the Department of Education, I join the Court's decision. I do so reluctantly and write briefly to record my view that the case is an unedifying example of overzealousness on the part of the Federal Government.

. . .

. . . The undisputed fact is that Grove City does not discriminate—and so far as the record in this case shows—never has discriminated against anyone on account of sex, race, or national origin. This case has nothing whatever to do with discrimination past or present. . . .

. . . The College, in view of its policies and principles of independence and its record of non-discrimination, objected to executing this Assurance. One would have thought that the Department, confronted as it is with cases of national importance that involve actual discrimination, would have respected the independence and admirable record of this college. But common sense and good judgment failed to prevail. The Department chose to litigate, and instituted an administrative proceeding to compel Grove City to execute an agreement to operate all of its programs and activities in full compliance with all of the regulations promulgated under Title IX—despite the College's record as an institution that had operated to date in full accordance with the letter and spirit of Title IX. . . .

. . .

The College prevailed in the District Court but lost in the Court of Appeals. Only after Grove City had brought its case before this Court, did the Department retreat to its present position that Title IX applies only to Grove City's financial aid office. On this narrow theory, the Department has prevailed, having taken this small independent college, which it acknowledges has engaged in no discrimination whatever, through six years of litigation with the full weight of the federal government opposing it. I cannot believe that the Department will rejoice in its "victory."

JUSTICE STEVENS, concurring in part and concurring in the result.

For two reasons, I am unable to join part III of the Court's opinion. First, it is an advisory opinion unnecessary to today's decision, and second, the advice is predicated on speculation rather than evidence.

The controverted issue in this litigation is whether Grove City College may be required to execute the "Assurance of Compliance with Title IX" tendered to it by the Secretary in order to continue receiving the benefits of the federal financial assistance provided by the BEOG program. . . . The Court today holds (in part II of its opinion) that Grove City is a recipient of federal financial assistance within the meaning of Title IX, and (in part IV) that Grove City must execute the Assurance of Compliance in order to continue receiving that assistance. These holdings are fully sufficient to sustain the judgment the Court reviews, as the Court acknowledges by affirming that judgment.

In part III of its opinion, the Court holds that Grove City is not required to refrain from discrimination on the basis of sex except in its financial aid program. In so stating, the Court decides an issue that is not in dispute. The Assurance of Compliance merely requires that it comply with Title IX "to the extent applicable to it." The Secretary, who is responsible for administering Title IX, construes the statute as applicable only to Grove City's financial aid

program. All the Secretary seeks is a judgment that Title IX requires Grove to promise not to discriminate in its financial aid program. The Court correctly holds that this program is subject to the requirements of Title IX, and that Grove City must promise not to discriminate in its operation of the program. But, there is no reason for the Court to hold that Grove City need not make a promise that the Secretary does not ask it to make, and that it in fact would not be making by signing the Assurance, in order to continue to receive federal financial assistance. . . .

Moreover, the record in this case is far from adequate to decide the question raised in part III. Assuming for the moment that participation in the BEOG program could not in itself make Title IX applicable to the entire institution, a factual inquiry is nevertheless necessary as to which of Grove City's programs and activities can be said to receive or benefit from federal financial assistance. This is the import of the applicable regulation, upheld by the Court today which states that Title IX applies "to every recipient and to each education program or activity operated by such recipient which receives or benefits from Federal financial assistance." 34 C.F.R. § 106.11 (1982). The Court decides that a small scholarship for just one student should not subject the entire school to coverage. But why should this case be judged on the basis of that hypothetical example instead of a different one? What if the record showed— and I do not suggest that it does—that all of the BEOG money was reserved for, or merely happened to be used by, talented athletes and that their tuition payments were sufficient to support an entire athletic program that would otherwise be abandoned? Would such a hypothetical program be covered by Title IX? And if this athletic program discriminated on the basis of sex, could it plausibly be contended that Congress intended that BEOG money could be used to enable such a program to survive? Until we know something about the character of the particular program, it is inappropriate to give advice about an issue that is not before us.

Accordingly, while I subscribe to the reasoning in parts I, II, and IV of the Court's opinion, I am unable to join part III.

JUSTICE BRENNAN, with whom JUSTICE MARSHALL joins, concurring in part and dissenting in part.

The Court today concludes that Grove City College is "receiving Federal financial assistance" within the meaning of Title IX of the Education Amendments of 1972, 20 U.S.C. § 1681(a), because a number of its students receive federal education grants. . . . [H]owever, I cannot join part III of the Court's opinion, in which the Court interprets the language in Title IX that limits application of the statute to "any education program or activity" receiving federal monies. By conveniently ignoring [the] controlling indicia of congressional intent, the Court also ignores the primary purposes for which Congress enacted Title IX. The result—allowing Title IX coverage for the College's financial aid program, but rejecting institution-wide coverage even though federal monies benefit the entire College—may be superficially pleasing to those who are uncomfortable with federal intrusion into private educational institutions, but it has no relationship to the statutory scheme enacted by Congress.

I

. . .

When reaching that question today,[1] the Court completely disregards the broad

remedial purposes of Title IX that consistently have controlled our prior interpretations of this civil rights statute. Moreover, a careful examination of the statute's legislative hisory, the accepted meaning of similar statutory language in Title VI, and the postenactment history of Title IX will demonstrate that the Court's narrow definition of "program or activity" is directly contrary to congressional intent.

A

. . .

In sum, although the contemporaneous legislative history does not definitively explain the intended meaning of the program-specific language included in Title IX, it lends no support to the interpretation adopted by the Court. What is clear, moreover, is that Congress intended enforcement of Title IX to mirror the policies and procedures utilized for enforcement under Title VI.

B

"Title IX was patterned after Title VI of the Civil Rights Act of 1964." *Cannon v. University of Chicago*, 441 U.S. 677, at 694. Except for the substitution of the word "sex" in Title IX to replace the words "race, color, or national origin" in Title VI, and for the limitation of Title IX to "education" programs or activities, the two statutes use identical language to describe their scope. The interpretation of this critical language as it already existed under Title VI is therefore crucial to an understanding of con-

1. There is much to commend the suggestion, made by JUSTICE STEVENS, that part III of the

Court's opinion is no more than an advisory opinion, unnecessary to the resolution of this case and unsupported by any factual findings made below. *See ante* (concurring in part and concurring in the result). Because the Court has not heeded that suggestion, however, I feel compelled to express my view on the merits of the issue decided by the Court.

gressional intent in 1972 when Title IX was enacted using the same language.

The voluminous legislative history of Title VI is not easy to comprehend, especially when one considers the emotionally and politically charged atmosphere operating at the time of its enactment. And there are no authoritative committee reports explaining the many compromises that were eventually enacted, including the program-specific limitations that found their way into Title VI. . . .

Without completely canvassing several volumes of the *Congressional Record*, I believe it is safe to say that, by including the programmatic language in Title VI, Congress sought to allay fears on the part of many legislators that one isolated violation of the statute's antidiscrimination provisions would result in the wholesale termination of federal funds. In particular, "Congress was primarily concerned with two facets of the termination power: the possibility that noncompliance in a single school district might lead to termination of funds to the entire state; and the possibility that discrimination in the education program might result in the termination of federal assistance to unrelated federally financed programs, such as highways." Comment, 118 U. Pa. L. Rev. 1113, 1119–20 (1970) (footnotes omitted). *See id.* at 1116–24.

. . . [W]hat is crucial in ascertaining the meaning of the program-specific language included in Title IX is the understanding that the 92d Congress had at the time it enacted the identical language. *Cf. Cannon, supra,* at 696–98. And there were two principal indicators of the accepted interpretation of the program-specific language in Title VI that were available to Members of Congress in 1972 when Title IX was enacted—the existing administrative regulations promulgated under Title VI, and the available judicial decisions that had already interpreted those provisions.

The Title VI regulations first issued by the Department of Health, Education, and Welfare during the 1960's, and remaining in effect during 1972, could not have been clearer in the way they applied to educational institutions. For example, [45 C.F.R.] § 80.4(d) explained the assurances required from, among others, institutions of higher education that received Federal financial assistance:

(d) *Assurances from institutions.* (1) In the case of any application for Federal financial assistance to an institution of higher education (including assistance for construction, for research, for a special training project, for a student loan program, or for any other purpose), the assurance required by this section shall extend to admission practices *and to all other practices relating to the treatment of students.*

(2) The assurance required with respect to an institution of higher education, . . . insofar as the assurance relates to the institution's practices with respect to admission or other treatment of individuals as students, . . . or to the opportunity to participate in the provision of services or other benefits to such individuals, *shall be applicable to the entire institution unless the applicant establishes, to the satisfaction of the responsible Department official, that the institution's practices in designated parts or programs of the institution will in no way affect its practices in the program of the institution for which Federal financial assistance is sought, or the beneficiaries of or participants in such program.* . . .

It must have been clear to the Congress enacting Title IX, therefore, that the administrative interpretation of that statute would follow a similarly expansive approach.

C

If any doubt remains about the congressional intent underlying the program-specific language included in Title IX, it is removed by the unique postenactment history of the statute.

Regulations promulgated by the Department to implement Title IX, both as proposed, 39 Fed. Reg. 22228 (1974), and as finally adopted, 40 Fed. Reg. 24128 (1975), included an interpretation of program specificity consistent with the view of Title VI and with the congressional intent behind Title IX outlined above. In particular, the regulations prohibited sex discrimination "under any academic, extracurricular, research, occupational training, or other education program or activity operated by a recipient which receives or benefits from Federal financial assistance." *Id.* at 24140 (now codified at 34 C.F.R. § 106.31 [1983]). . . .

Moreover . . ., these regulations were submitted to Congress for review. . . . [T]his "laying before" procedure afforded Congress an opportunity to disapprove any regulation that it found to be "inconsistent with the Act from which it derives its authority." And although the regulations interpreting the program-specific limitations of Title IX were explicitly considered by both Houses of Congress, no resolutions of disapproval were passed by the Legislature.

In particular, two resolutions to invalidate the Department's regulations were proposed in the Senate, each specifically challenging the regulations because of the program-specificity requirements of Title IX. One resolution would have provided a blanket disapproval of the regulations, S. Con. Res. 46, 94th Cong., 1st Sess. (1975), premised in part on the view that "[t]he regulations are inconsistent with the enactment in that they apply to programs or activities not receiving Federal funds such as

athletics and extracurricular activities," 121 Cong. Rec. 17300 (remarks of Sen. Helms). The other resolution was aimed more particularly at the regulation of athletic programs and activities not receiving direct federal monies, but also was premised on the program-specific limitations in the statute. See S. Con. Res. 52, 94th Cong., 1st Sess. (1975). Neither resolution, however, was acted upon after referral to the appropriate committee.

. . .

Despite the attention focused upon, and the strong defense offered in support of, the programmatic reach of the Department's regulations at these hearings, the House offered no formal resistance to the regulations. Indeed, among the several resolutions of disapproval introduced in the House, only one directly mentioned this aspect of the regulations, and this resolution was not acted upon either by committee or by the full House. H.R. Con. Res. 311, 94th Cong., 1st Sess. (1975) (disapproving regulations that "would apply to athletic programs and grants which neither receive nor benefit from Federal financial assistance"); *see* 121 Cong. Rec. 19209 (1975).

Although the failure of Congress to disapprove the Department's regulations is not itself determinative, it does "len[d] weight to the argument" that the regulations were consistent with congressional intent. *North Haven, supra,* at 534. Moreover, "the relatively insubstantial interest given the resolutions of disapproval that were introduced seems particularly significant since Congress has proceeded to amend [Title IX] when it has disagreed with [the Department's] interpretation of the statute." *North Haven, supra,* at 534. Indeed, those amendments, by exempting from the reach of Title IX various facilities or services at educational institutions that themselves do not receive direct federal aid, strongly suggest that Congress understands the statute otherwise to encompass such programs or activities.

In conclusion, each of the factors relevant to the interpretation of the program-specificity requirements of Title IX, taken individually or collectively, demonstrates that the Court today limits the reach of Title IX in a way that was wholly unintended by Congress. The contemporaneous legislative history of Title IX, the relevant interpretation of similar language in Title VI, and the administrative and legislative interpretations of Title IX since the statute's original enactment all lead to the same conclusion: that Title IX coverage for an institution of higher education is appropriate if federal monies are received by or benefit the entire institution.

II

A proper application of Title IX to the circumstances of this case demonstrates beyond peradventure that the Court has unjustifiably limited the statute's reach. Grove City College enrolls approximately 140 students who utilize Basic Educational Opportunity Grants (BEOGs) to pay for their education at the College. Although the grant monies are paid directly to the students, . . . a principal purpose underlying congressional enactment of the BEOG program is to provide funds that will benefit colleges and universities as a whole. It necessarily follows, in my view, that the entire undergraduate institution operated by Grove City College is subject to the antidiscrimination provisions included in Title IX.

A

In determining the scope of Title IX coverage, the primary focus should be on the purposes meant to be served by the particular federal funds received by the institution.[13] In this case, Congress has clearly

13. Because I believe that BEOG monies are in-

indicated that BEOG monies are intended to benefit any college or university that enrolls students receiving such grants. . . .

In many respects, therefore, Congress views financial aid to students, and in particular BEOGs, as the functional equivalent of general aid to institutions. Given this undeniable and clearly stated congressional purpose, it would seem to be self-evident that Congress intended colleges or universities enrolling students who receive BEOGs to be covered, in their entirety, by the antidiscrimination provisions of Title IX. . . .

Under the Court's holding, in contrast, Grove City College is prohibited from discriminating on the basis of sex in its own "financial aid program," but is free to discriminate in other "programs or activities" operated by the institution. Underlying this result is the unstated and unsupportable assumption that monies received through BEOGs are meant only to be utilized by the College's financial aid program. But it is undisputed that BEOG monies, paid to the institution as tuition and fees and used in the general operating budget, are utilized to support most, and perhaps all, of the facilities and services that together comprise Grove City College.

. . .

B

. . .

[T]he Court rejects the notion that the federal funds disbursed under the BEOG program are received by the entire institution because they effectively "free up" the

tended by Congress to benefit institutions of higher education in their entirety, I find it unnecessary in this case to decide whether Title IX's reach would be the same when more targeted federal aid is being received by an institution. For such cases, it may be appropriate to examine carefully not only the purposes but also the actual effects of the federal monies received.

College's own resources for use by all programs or activities that are operated by Grove City College. But coverage of an entire institution that receives BEOGs through its students is not dependent upon such a theory. Instead, Title IX coverage for the whole undergraduate institution at Grove City College is premised on the congressional intent that BEOG monies would provide aid for the college or university as a whole. Therefore, whatever merit the Court's argument may have for federal monies that are intended solely to benefit a particular aspect of an educational institution, such as a research grant designed to assist a specific laboratory or professor, *see* n.13, *supra,* the freeing-up theory is simply irrelevant when the federal financial assistance is meant to benefit the entire institution.

Finally, although not explicitly offered as a rationale, the Court's holding might be explained by its willingness to defer to the Government's position as it has been represented to this Court. But until the Government filed its briefs in this case, it had consistently argued that Title IX coverage for the entire undergraduate institution operated by Grove City College was authorized by the statute. The latest position adopted by the Government, irrespective of the motivations that might underlie this recent change, is therefore entitled to little, if any, deference. *Cf. North Haven, supra,* at nn.12, 29 (deference not appropriate when "there is no consistent administrative interpretation of the Title IX regulations"). The interpretation of statutes as important as Title IX should not be subjected so easily to shifts in policy by the executive branch.

. . .

CASE QUESTIONS

1. The majority uses the fact that Grove City College ultimately receives the BEOGs to argue that the college must assure compliance with anti-discrimination rules. Does that very argument undermine the majority's later conclusion that only the financial aid office must assure compliance? (Does that BEOG money stay within the financial aid office?)

2. If a more clear-cut Title IX case reaches the Court, one where a university takes money for one program but frankly discriminates in another program, might the Supreme Court utilize the strange history of the Civil Right Act of 1984 (no passage, but voting support from 90 percent of voting Representatives and sponsorship by 63 percent of the Senate) to overturn the *Grove City* reading of the program-specific language of Title IX? Should the Court be guided by such events?

Sexual Harassment

The same Catherine MacKinnon who was mentioned above in the context of anti-pornography legislation published a book in 1979 entitled *Sexual Harassment of Working Women.* She stated in the preface that up until that time, "Sexual harassment . . . has been legally unthinkable." [17] By that she meant that the laws as written and as enforced at that time did not conceptualize the sexual harassment of women on the job or in educational institutions as "discrimination on the basis of sex." It is a mark of the profundity and rapidity of the current and still on-going revolution in women's legal rights (as well as a tribute to the efforts of people like Catherine MacKinnon) that within seven years of this remark the U.S. Supreme Court unanimously acknowledged not only that sexual harassment is a violation of federal anti-discrimination law but also that employers can be held legally culpable if they fail to take action to ensure that their supervisory personnel refrain from sexual harassment of other employees, *Meritor Savings Bank v. Mechelle Vinson*, 54 U.S.L.W. 4703 (June 19, 1986). The facts of the case that elicited these pronouncements, as well as the reasoning, are included in the following excerpt.

Meritor Savings Bank v. Mechelle Vinson, 54 U.S.L.W. 4703 (1986).

JUSTICE REHNQUIST delivered the opinion of the Court.

This case presents important questions concerning claims of workplace "sexual harassment" brought under Title VII of the Civil Rights Act of 1964, 78 Stat. 253, as amended, 42 U.S.C. § 2000e *et seq.*

I

In 1974, respondent Mechelle Vinson met Sidney Taylor, a vice president of what is now petitioner Meritor Savings Bank (the bank) and manager of one of its branch offices. . . . With Taylor as her supervisor, respondent started as a teller-trainee, and thereafter was promoted to teller, head teller, and assistant branch manager. She worked at the same branch for four years, and it is undisputed that her advancement there was based on merit alone. In September 1978, respondent notified Taylor that she was taking sick leave for an indefinite period. On November 1, 1978, the bank discharged her for excessive use of that leave.

Respondent brought this action against Taylor and the bank, claiming that during her four years at the bank she had "constantly been subjected to sexual harassment" by Taylor in violation of Title VII. She sought injunctive relief, compensatory and punitive damages against Taylor and the bank, and attorney's fees.

At the 11-day bench trial, the parties presented conflicting testimony about Taylor's behavior during respondent's employment. Respondent testified that during her probationary period as a teller-trainee, Taylor treated her in a fatherly way and made no sexual advances. Shortly thereafter, however, he invited her out to dinner and, during the course of the meal, suggested that they go to a motel to have sexual relations. At first she refused, but out of what she described as fear of losing her job she eventually agreed. According to respondent, Taylor thereafter made repeated demands upon her for sexual favors, usually at the branch, both during and after business hours; she estimated that over the next several years she had intercourse with him some 40 or 50 times. In addition, respondent testified that Taylor fondled her in front of other employees, followed her into the women's restroom when she went there alone, exposed himself to her, and even forcibly raped her on several occasions. These activities ceased after 1977, respondent stated, when she started going with a steady boyfriend.

Respondent also testified that Taylor touched and fondled other women employees of the bank, and she attempted to call witnesses to support this charge. But while some supporting testimony apparently was admitted without objection, the District Court did not allow her "to present wholesale evidence of a pattern and practice relating to sexual advances to other female employees in her case in chief, but advised her that she might well be able to present such evidence in rebuttal to the defendants' cases." *Vinson v. Taylor*, 23 F.E.P. Cases 37, 38–39, n.1 (D. D.C. 1980). Respondent did not offer such evidence in rebuttal. Finally, respondent testified that because she was afraid of Taylor she never reported his harassment to any of his supervisors and never attempted to use the bank's complaint procedure.

Taylor denied respondent's allegations of sexual activity, testifying that he never fondled her, never made suggestive remarks to her, never engaged in sexual intercourse with her and never asked her to do so. He contended instead that respondent made her accusations in response to a business-related dispute. The bank also denied respondent's allegations and asserted that any sexual harassment by Taylor was unknown to the bank and engaged in without its consent or approval.

The District Court denied relief, but did not resolve the conflicting testimony about the existence of a sexual relationship between respondent and Taylor. It found instead that

If [respondent] and Taylor did engage in an intimate or sexual relationship

during the time of [respondent's] employment with [the bank], that relationship was a voluntary one having nothing to do with her continued employment at [the bank] or her advancement or promotions at that institution. (*Id.* at 42 [footnote omitted].)

The court ultimately found that respondent "was not the victim of sexual harassment and was not the victim of sexual discrimination" while employed at the bank. *Id.* 43.

. . .

The Court of Appeals for the District of Columbia Circuit reversed. 753 F.2d 141 (1985). . . . [T]he court stated that a violation of Title VII may be predicated on either of two types of sexual harassment: harassment that involves the conditioning of concrete employment benefits on sexual favors, and harassment that, while not affecting economic benefits, creates a hostile or offensive working environment. The court drew additional support for this position from the Equal Employment Opportunity Commission's Guidelines on Discrimination Because of Sex, 29 C.F.R. § 1604.11(a) (1985), which set out these two types of sexual harassment claims. Believing that "Vinson's grievance was clearly of the [hostile environment] type," 753 F.2d, at 145, and that the District Court had not considered whether a violation of this type had occurred, the court concluded that a remand was necessary.

The court further concluded that the District Court's finding that any sexual relationship between respondent and Taylor "was a voluntary one" did not obviate the need for a remand. "[U]ncertain as to precisely what the [district] court meant" by this finding, the Court of Appeals held that if the evidence otherwise showed that "Taylor made Vinson's toleration of sexual harassment a condition of her employment," her voluntariness "had no materiality whatsoever." 753 F.2d, at 146. The court then surmised that the District Court's finding of voluntariness might have been based on "the voluminous testimony regarding respondent's dress and personal fantasies," testimony that the Court of Appeals believed "had no place in this litigation." 753 F.2d, at 146, n.36.

As to the bank's liability, the Court of Appeals held that an employer is absolutely liable for sexual harassment practiced by supervisory personnel, whether or not the employer knew or should have known about the misconduct. The court relied chiefly on Title VII's definition of "employer" to include "any agent of such a person." 42 U.S.C. § 2000e(b), as well as on the EEOC guidelines. The court held that a supervisor is an "agent" of his employer for Title VII purposes, even if he lacks authority to hire, fire, or promote, since "the mere existence—or even the appearance—of a significant degree of influence in vital job decisions gives any supervisor the opportunity to impose on employees." 753 F.2d, at 150.

In accordance with the foregoing, the Court of Appeals reversed the judgment of the District Court and remanded the case for further proceedings. . . . We . . . now affirm but for different reasons.

II

Title VII of the Civil Rights Act of 1964 makes it "an unlawful employment practice for an employer . . . to discriminate against any individual with respect to his compensation, terms, conditions, or privileges of employment, because of such individual's race, color, religion, sex, or national origin." 42 U.S.C. § 2000e-2 (a)(1). . . .

Respondent argues, and the Court of Appeals held, that unwelcome sexual advances that create an offensive or hostile working environment violate Title VII. Without question, when a supervisor sexually harasses a subordinate because of the

subordinate's sex, that supervisor "discriminate[s]" on the basis of sex. Petitioner apparently does not challenge this proposition. It contends instead that in prohibiting discrimination with respect to "compensation, terms, conditions, or privileges" of employment, Congress was concerned with what petitioner describes as "tangible loss" of "an economic character," not "purely psychological aspects of the workplace environment." . . .

We reject petitioner's view. First, the language of Title VII is not limited to "economic" or "tangible" discrimination. The phrase "terms, conditions, or privileges of employment" evinces a congressional intent "to strike at the entire spectrum of disparate treatment of men and women" in employment. *Los Angeles Department of Water and Power v. Manhart*, 435 U.S. 702, 707, n.13 (1978). . . .

Second, in 1980 the EEOC issued guidelines specifying that "sexual harassment," as there defined, is a form of sex discrimination prohibited by Title VII. As an "administrative interpretation of the Act by the enforcing agency," *Griggs v. Duke Power Co.*, 401 U.S. 424, 433–34 (1971), these guidelines, "'while not controlling upon the courts by reason of their authority, do constitute a body of experience and informed judgment to which courts and litigants may properly resort for guidance,'" *General Electric Co. v. Gilbert*, 429 U.S. 125, 141–42 (1976). . . .

In defining "sexual harassment," the guidelines first describe the kinds of workplace conduct that may be actionable under Title VII. These include "[u]nwelcome sexual advances, requests for sexual favors, and other verbal or physical conduct of a sexual nature." 29 C.F.R. § 1604.11(a) (1985). Relevant to the charges at issue in this case, the guidelines provide that such sexual misconduct constitutes prohibited "sexual harassment," whether or not it is directly linked to the grant or denial of an economic *quid pro quo*, where "such conduct has the purpose or effect of unreasonably interfering with an individual's work performance or creating an intimidating, hostile, or offensive working environment." § 1604.11(a)(3).

In concluding that so-called "hostile environment" (*i.e.*, non *quid pro quo*) harassment violates Title VII, the EEOC drew upon a substantial body of judicial decisions and EEOC precedent holding that Title VII affords employees the right to work in an environment free from discriminatory intimidation, ridicule, and insult. *See generally* 45 Fed. Reg. 74676 (1980). *Rogers v. EEOC*, 454 F.2d 234 (5th Cir. 1971), *cert. denied*, 406 U.S. 957 (1972), was apparently the first case to recognize a cause of action based upon a discriminatory work environment. In *Rogers*, the . . . court explained that an employee's protections under Title VII extend beyond the economic aspects of employment:

> . . . One can readily envision working environments so heavily polluted with discrimination as to destroy completely the emotional and psychological stability of minority group workers. . . . (454 F.2d, at 238.)

Courts applied this principle to harassment based on race, *e.g.*, *Firefighters Institute for Racial Equality v. St. Louis*, 549 F.2d 506, 514–15 (8th Cir.) (1977); *Gray v. Greyhound Lines, East*, 545 F.2d 169, 176 (1976), religion, *e.g.*, *Compston v. Borden, Inc.*, 424 F. Supp. 157 (S.D. Ohio 1976), and national origin, *e.g.*, *Cariddi v. Kansas City Chiefs Football Club*, 568 F.2d 87, 88 (8th Cir. 1977). Nothing in Title VII suggests that a hostile environment based on discriminatory *sexual* harassment should not be likewise prohibited. The guidelines thus appropriately drew from, and were fully consistent with, the existing caselaw.

Since the guidelines were issued, courts have uniformly held, and we agree, that a plaintiff may establish a violation of Title VII by proving that discrimination based on sex has created a hostile or abusive work environment. As the Court of Appeals for the Eleventh Circuit wrote in *Henson v. Dundee*, 682 F.2d 897, 902 (1982):

> Sexual harassment which creates a hostile or offensive environment for members of one sex is every bit the arbitrary barrier to sexual equality at the workplace that racial harassment is to racial equality. Surely, a requirement that a man or woman run a guantlet of sexual abuse in return for the privilege of being allowed to work and make a living can be as demeaning and disconcerting as the harshest of racial epithets.

Of course, as the courts in both *Rogers* and *Henson* recognized, not all workplace conduct that may be described as "harassment" affects a "term, condition, or privilege" of employment within the meaning of Title VII. . . . For sexual harassment to be actionable, it must be sufficiently severe or pervasive "to alter the conditions of [the victim's] employment and create an abusive working environment." *Henson, supra*, at 904. Respondent's allegations in this case—which include not only pervasive harassment but also criminal conduct of the most serious nature—are plainly suffficient to state a claim for "hostile environment" sexual harassment. Since it appears that the District Court made its findings without ever considering the "hostile environment" theory of sexual harassment, the Court of Appeals' decision to remand was correct.

Second, the District Court's conclusion that no actionable harassment occurred might have rested on its earlier "finding" that "[i]f [respondent] and Taylor did engage in an intimate or sexual relationship . . . , that relationship was a voluntary one." 23 F.E.P. cases, at 42. But the fact that sex-related conduct was "voluntary," in the sense that the complainant was not forced to participate against her will, is not a defense to a sexual harassment suit brought under Title VII. The gravamen of any sexual harassment claim is that the alleged sexual advances were "unwelcome." 29 C.F.R. § 1604.11(a) (1985). While the question whether particular conduct was indeed unwelcome presents difficult problems of proof and turns largely on credibility determinations committed to the trier of fact, the District Court in this case erroneously focused on the "voluntariness" of respondent's participation in the claimed sexual episodes. The correct inquiry is whether respondent by her conduct indicated that the alleged sexual advances were unwelcome, not whether her actual participation in sexual intercourse was voluntary.

Petitioner contends that even if this case must be remanded to the District Court, the Court of Appeals erred in one of the terms of its remand. Specifically, the Court of Appeals stated that testimony about respondent's "dress and personal fantasies," 753 F.2d, at 146, n.36, which the District Court apparently admitted into evidence, "had no place in this litigation." *Id.* The apparent ground for this conclusion was that respondent's voluntariness *vel non* in submitting to Taylor's advances was immaterial to her sexual harassment claim. While "voluntariness" in the sense of consent is not a defense to such a claim, it does not follow that a complainant's sexually provocative speech or dress is irrelevant as a matter of law in determining whether he or she found particular sexual advances unwelcome. To the contrary, such evidence is obviously relevant. The EEOC guidelines emphasize that the trier of fact must determine the existence of sexual harassment in light of "the record as a whole" and "the totality of circumstances, such as

the nature of the sexual advances and the context in which the alleged incidents occurred." 29 C.F.R. § 1604.11(b) (1985). Respondent's claim that any marginal relevance of the evidence in question was outweighed by the potential for unfair prejudice is the sort of argument properly addressed to the District Court. In this case the District Court concluded that the evidence should be admitted, and the Court of Appeals' contrary conclusion was based upon the erroneous, categorical view that testimony about provocative dress and publicly expressed sexual fantasies "had no place in this litigation." 753 F.2d, at 146, n.36. While the District Court must carefully weigh the applicable considerations in deciding whether to admit evidence of this kind, there is no *per se* rule against its admissibility.

III

Although the District Court concluded that respondent had not proved a violation of Title VII, it nevertheless went on to consider the question of the bank's liability. Finding that "the bank was without notice" of Taylor's alleged conduct, and that notice to Taylor was not the equivalent of notice to the bank, the court concluded that the bank therefore could not be held liable for Taylor's alleged actions. The Court of Appeals took the opposite view, holding that an employer is strictly liable for a hostile environment created by a supervisor's sexual advances, even though the employer neither knew nor reasonably could have known of the alleged misconduct. The court held that a supervisor, whether or not he possesses the authority to hire, fire, or promote, is necessarily an "agent" of his employer for all Title VII purposes, since "even the appearance" of such authority may enable him to impose himself on his subordinates.

. . .

Petitioner argues that respondent's failure to use its established grievance procedure, or to otherwise put it on notice of the alleged misconduct, insulates petitioner from liability for Taylor's wrongdoing. A contrary rule would be unfair, petitioner argues, since in a hostile environment harassment case the employer often will have no reason to know about, or opportunity to cure, the alleged wrongdoing.

The EEOC, in its brief as *amicus curiae,* contends . . . that where a supervisor exercises the authority actually delegated to him by his employer, by making or threatening to make decisions affecting the employment status of his subordinates, such actions are properly imputed to the employer whose delegation of authority empowered the supervisor to undertake them. Brief for United States and Equal Employment Opportunity Commission as *Amicus Curiae* 22. Thus, the courts have consistently held employers liable for the discriminatory discharges of employees by supervisory personnel, whether or not the employer knew, should have known, or approved of the supervisor's actions.

The EEOC suggests that when a sexual harassment claim rests exclusively on a "hostile environment" theory, however, the usual basis for a finding of agency will often disappear. In that case, the EEOC believes, agency principles lead to

a rule that asks whether a victim of sexual harassment had reasonably available an avenue of complaint regarding such harassment, and, if available and utilized, whether that procedure was reasonably responsive to the employee's complaint. If the employer has an expressed policy against sexual harassment and has implemented a procedure specifically designed to resolve sexual harassment claims, and if the victim does not take advantage of

that procedure, the employer should be shielded from liability absent actual knowledge of the sexually hostile environment (obtained, *e.g.,* by the filing of a charge with the EEOC or a comparable state agency). In all other cases, the employer will be liable if it has actual knowledge of the harassment or if, considering all the facts of the case, the victim in question had no reasonably available avenue for making his or her complaint known to appropriate management officials. (Brief for United States and Equal Opportunity Employment Commission as *Amici Curiae,* 26.)

As respondent points out, this suggested rule is in some tension with the EEOC guidelines, which hold an employer liable for the acts of its agents without regard to notice. 29 C.F.R. § 1604.11(c) (1985). The guidelines do require, however, an "examin[ation of] the circumstances of the particular employment relationship and the job [f]unctions performed by the individual in determining whether an individual acts in either a supervisory or agency capacity." *Id.*

This debate over the appropriate standard for employer liability has a rather abstract quality about it given the state of the record in this case. We do not know at this stage whether Taylor made any sexual advances toward respondent at all, let alone whether those advances were unwelcome, whether they were sufficiently pervasive to constitute a condition of employment, or whether they were "so pervasive and so long continuing . . . that the employer must have become conscious of [them]," *Taylor v. Jones,* 653 F.2d 1193, 1197–99 (8th Cir. 1981)

We therefore decline the parties' invitation to issue a definitive rule on employer liability, but we do agree with the EEOC that Congress wanted courts to look to agency principles for guidance in this area.

While such common-law principles may not be transferable in all their particulars to Title VII, Congress' decision to define "employer" to include any "agent" of an employer, 42 U.S.C. § 2000e(b), surely evinces an intent to place some limits on the acts of employees for which employers under Title VII are to be held responsible. For this reason, we hold that the Court of Appeals erred in concluding that employers are always automatically liable for sexual harassment by their supervisors. For the same reason, absence of notice to an employer does not necessarily insulate that employer from liability.

Finally, we reject petitioner's view that the mere existence of a grievance procedure and a policy against discrimination, coupled with respondent's failure to invoke that procedure, must insulate petitioner from liability. While those facts are plainly relevant, the situation before us demonstrates why they are not necessarily dispositive. Petitioner's general nondiscrimination policy did not address sexual harassment in particular, and thus did not alert employees to their employer's interest in correcting that form of discrimination. Moreover, the bank's grievance procedure apparently required an employee to complain first to her supervisor, in this case Taylor. Since Taylor was the alleged perpetrator, it is not altogether surprising that respondent failed to invoke the procedure and report her grievance to him.

. . .

IV

In sum, we hold that a claim of "hostile environment" sex discrimination is actionable under Title VII, that the District Court's findings were insufficient to dispose of respondent's hostile environment claim, and that the District Court did not err in admitting testimony about respondent's sexually provocative speech and dress. As to employer liability, we conclude

that the Court of Appeals was wrong to entirely disregard agency principles and impose absolute liability on employers for the acts of their supervisors, regardless of the circumstances of a particular case.

Accordingly, the judgment of the Court of Appeals reversing the judgment of the District Court is affirmed, and the case is remanded for further proceedings consistent with this opinion.

It is so ordered.

Justice STEVENS, concurring.

Because I do not see any inconsistency between the two opinions, and because I believe the question of statutory construction that Justice MARSHALL has answered is fairly presented by the record, I join both the Court's opinion and Justice MARSHALL's opinion.

Justice MARSHALL, with whom Justice BRENNAN, Justice BLACKMUN, and Justice STEVENS join, concurring in the judgment.

I fully agree with the Court's conclusion that workplace sexual harassment is illegal, and violates Title VII. Part III of the Court's opinion, however, leaves open the circumstances in which an employer is responsible under Title VII for such conduct. Because I believe that question to be properly before us, I write separately.

The issue the Court declines to resolve is addressed in the EEOC Guidelines on Discrimination Because of Sex, which are entitled to great deference. *See Griggs v. Duke Power Co.*, 401 U.S. 424, 433–34 (1971) The Guidelines explain:

> Applying general Title VII principles, an employer . . . is responsible for its acts and those of its agents and supervisory employees with respect to sex-

ual harassment regardless of whether the specific acts complained of were authorized or even forbidden by the employer and regardless of whether the employer knew or should have known of their occurrence. The Commission will examine the circumstances of the particular employment relationship and the job functions performed by the individual in determining whether an individual acts in either a supervisory or agency capacity.

With respect to conduct between fellow employees, an employer is responsible for acts of sexual harassment in the workplace where the employer (or its agents or supervisory employees) knows or should have known of the conduct, unless it can show that it took immediate and appropriate corrective action. (29 C.F.R. §§ 1604.11[c], [d] [1985].)

. . . I would adopt the standard set out by the Commission.

An employer can act only through individual supervisors and employees; discrimination is rarely carried out pursuant to a formal vote of a corporation's board of directors. Although an employer may sometimes adopt company-wide discriminatory policies violative of Title VII, acts that may constitute Title VII violations are generally effected through the actions of individuals, and often an individual may take such a step even in defiance of company policy. Nonetheless, Title VII remedies, such as reinstatement and backpay, generally run against the employer as an entity. The question thus arises as to the circumstances under which an employer will be held liable under Title VII for the acts of its employees.

The answer supplied by general Title VII law, like that supplied by federal labor law, is that the act of a supervisory employee or agent is imputed to the employer. Thus, for example, when a supervisor discriminatorily fires or refuses to promote a black employee, that act is, without more, considered the act of the employer. The courts do not stop to consider whether the employer otherwise had "notice" of the action. . . . Following that approach, every Court of Appeals that has considered the issue has held that sexual harassment by supervisory personnel is automatically imputed to the employer when the harassment results in tangible job detriment to the subordinate employee. [Citations omitted.]

The brief filed by the Solicitor General on behalf of the EEOC in this case suggests that a different rule should apply when a supervisor's harassment "merely" results in a discriminatory work environment. The Solicitor General . . . , departing from the EEOC Guidelines, . . . argues that the case of a supervisor merely creating a discriminatory work environment is different because the supervisor "is not exercising, or threatening to exercise, actual or apparent authority to make personnel decisions affecting the victim." In the latter situation, he concludes, some further notice requirement should therefore be necessary.

The Solicitor General's position is untenable. A supervisor's responsibilities do not begin and end with the power to hire, fire, and discipline employees, or with the power to recommend such actions. Rather, a supervisor is charged with the day-to-day supervision of the work environment and with ensuring a safe, productive, workplace. There is no reason why abuse of the latter authority should have different consequences than abuse of the former. In both cases it is the authority vested in the supervisor by the employer that enables him to commit the wrong: it is precisely because the supervisor is understood to be clothed with the employer's authority that he is able to impose unwelcome sexual conduct on subordinates. There is therefore no justification for a special rule, to be applied *only* in "hostile environment" cases, that sexual harassment does not create employer liability until the employee suffering the discrimination notifies other supervisors. . . .

Agency principles and the goals of Title VII law make appropriate some limitation on the liability of employers for the acts of supervisors. Where, for example, a supervisor has no authority over an employee, because the two work in wholly different parts of the employer's business, it may be improper to find strict employer liability. *See* 29 C.F.R. § 1604.11(c) (1985). Those considerations, however, do not justify the creation of a special "notice" rule in hostile environment cases.

Further, nothing would be gained by crafting such a rule. In the "pure" hostile environment case, where an employee files an EEOC complaint alleging sexual harassment in the workplace, the employee seeks not money damages but injunctive relief. *See Bundy v. Jackson*, 641 F.2d 934, 936, n.12 (1981). Under Title VII, the EEOC must notify an employer of charges made against it within 10 days after receipt of the complaint. 42 U.S.C. § 2000e – 5(b). If the charges appear to be based on "reasonable cause,"

the EEOC must attempt to eliminate the offending practice through "informal methods of conference, conciliation, and persuasion." An employer whose internal procedures assertedly would have redressed the discrimination can avoid injunctive relief by employing these procedures after receiving notice of the complaint or during the conciliation period. Where a complaint, on the other hand, seeks backpay on the theory that a hostile work environment effected a constructive termination, the existence of an internal complaint procedure may be a factor in determing not the employer's liability but the remedies available against it. Where a complainant without good reason bypassed an internal complaint procedure she knew to be effective, a court may be reluctant to find constructive termination and thus to award reinstatement or backpay.

I therefore reject the Solicitor General's position. I would apply in this case the same rules we apply in all other Title VII cases, and hold that sexual harassment by a supervisor of an employee under his supervision, leading to a discriminatory work environment, should be imputed to the employer for Title VII purposes regardless of whether the employee gave "notice" of the offense.

CASE QUESTIONS

1. How pervasive do sexist remarks have to be before a workplace becomes an environment hostile to women?

2. Is the ban on sexual harassment only a ban on unwelcome sexual advances, or does the phrase "other verbal conduct of a sexual nature" also proscribe re-

marks, joking or otherwise, that describe women in vulgar ways, as merely brainless body parts? Is the telling of certain dirty jokes forbidden? Does an assumption that workers must avoid telling dirty jokes in the presence of female workers imply another sort of discriminatory attitude toward women (i.e., the view that women need extra protection from the harsh side of life)? Does that regulation forbid repeated remarks to the effect that women's place is in the home, that women are not fit to be fire-fighters, etc.? Is there a danger to legitimate First Amendment values lurking here?

3. Is it unfair to allow a sexual harassment defendant to introduce testimony about a plaintiff's allegedly provocative clothing and remarks? Unfair not to?

Affirmative Action

At least since the early 1970s it has been clear that the federal courts were willing to employ race-conscious remedies to counteract the lingering effects of prior illegal or unconstitutional racial discrimination. In the context of public schools, such remedies often included court-ordered busing. In the context of employment discrimination, such remedies have included group awards of backpay or temporary affirmative hiring quotas to bring a workforce into line with where it would have been "but for" the illegal discrimination. For sex-based discrimination, courts have employed similar affirmative remedies.

In addition to remedies for specific wrongdoing, the U.S. Supreme Court in 1980 (*Fullilove v. Klutznick,* 448 U.S. 448) upheld a mandate by Congress that federal public works contracts had to be awarded in such a way that at least 10 percent of the contracts went to businesses owned by members of designated racial minorities. The Court interpreted this law as a remedy imposed by Congress to a long history of racial discrimination in the contracting industries and upheld it within that remedial framework.

Where race-conscious affirmative action efforts have been taken by employers or university admissions personnel outside of a specific remedial context—i.e., without proof or confession of previous wrongdoing by the party implementing affirmative action—the Supreme Court has issued decidedly mixed messages about the legality of such voluntary affirmative action. And before 1987 the Supreme Court had been utterly silent about the legality of voluntary affirmative efforts to increase percentages of women in jobs or educational programs from which they had previously been excluded or discouraged by society at-large, albeit not by the particular party offering the affirmative action program.

In the matter of voluntary race-conscious affirmative action programs, the two leading Supreme Court precedents are *Regents of California v. Bakke,* 438 U.S. 265 (1978) and *United Steelworkers v. Weber,* 443 U.S. 193 (1979). In the former, the majority (of five) ruled that the prohibition on race discrimination by educational institutions receiving federal funds, which comprises Title VI of the 1964 Civil Rights Act, forbade fixed racial quotas in university admissions, however benevolently motivated. On the other hand, the majority said that Title VI did permit taking minority racial status into account as a "plus" factor in the admission decision.

In the *Weber* case just a year later, a majority of five ruled that Title VII, which bans discrimination on the basis of race in hiring and promotion, *did* permit rigid racial quotas of an affirmative nature. (It was Justice Stewart who switched sides from the *Bakke* majority.) If an employer wished to implement such quotas voluntarily, in order "to eliminate conspicuous racial imbalance in traditionally segregated job categories," Title VII, despite its language to the contrary, would permit it. Justice Brennan writing for the majority, explained that sometimes what appears to contradict the letter of the law fulfills its spirit, and that the goal of the Civil Rights Act was to enhance economic opportunity for those races that had previously suffered discrimination. Justice Blackmun wrote a concurring opinion in which he took pains to explain that a "traditionally segregated job category" meant one where there had been "a societal history of purposeful exclusion of blacks from the job category, resulting in a persistent disparity between the proportion of blacks in the labor force and the proportion . . . who hold jobs within the category." Thus, the *Weber* majority appeared to view permissible voluntary affirmative action programs as remedial measures, even if not as remedies specifically for discrimination perpetrated by the particular employer and union adopting the program.

These two cases, *Bakke* and *Weber*, framed the legal background for the decision on March 25, 1987 of *Paul Johnson v. Transportation Agency of Santa Clara*, 55 U.S.L.W. 4379, the Supreme Court's first statement on the legality of voluntary gender-based affirmative action. And since *Johnson v. Agency* arose in an employment context, *Weber* was accorded great prominence in the debate between the majority, led by Justice Brennan, and the dissenters, led by Justice Scalia. Justice Scalia, (Burger's replacement on the Court) argued forcefully that *Weber* should be overruled.

The Johnson case began when Paul Johnson was passed over in a competition for the job of road dispatcher for Santa Clara County, California. The County chose instead to promote into the position another of their employees, Diane Joyce.

The County acknowledged that this selection occurred pursuant to their Affirmative Action Plan, adopted in December, 1978, with the goal of remedying "the effects of past practices and . . . [attaining] an equitable representation of minorities, women and handicapped persons." The Plan indicated that in making appointments for "a traditionally segregated job classification in which women have been significantly underrepresented, the Agency is authorized to consider as one factor the sex of a qualified applicant." The Plan described traditionally segregated jobs as ones for which women "had not been strongly motivated to seek training or employment 'because of the limited opportunities that have existed in the past for them to work in such classifications.'" (Justice Brennan quoting the Plan, 55 U.S.L.W. 4380–4381.) The Plan set no fixed quotas; it aimed ultimately at attaining proportions of women in each job that would match those in the local labor force, but acknowledged that more realistic annual goals should be geared to proportions of women in the labor force who possess relevant job qualifications. (The Plan said similar things about racial minorities and the handicapped, but those were not specifically at issue in the Johnson case.)

When the vacancy for road dispatcher was announced, twelve county employees applied for it, including Diane Joyce and Paul Johnson. Nine of those, again including Joyce and Johnson were deemed qualified for the job (on the basis of such criteria as work experience) and were then interviewed by a two-person committee. Applicants were scored on the basis of the interview; a 70 was passing, and seven people earned passing scores. The highest score given was an 80, Johnson ranked next with 75 and Joyce ranked next with 73. All seven thereby judged qualified were then scheduled for a second interview by a board of three Agency supervisors.

Because Diane Joyce had previously clashed with two of the three scheduled interviewers, in incidents some of which apparently reflected gender prejudice, she at this point contacted the County's Affirmative Action Office to express fear that she would receive biased treatment in her second interview. The Supreme Court's description of her previous difficulties with these men is set forth below.

> Joyce testified that she had had disagreements with two of the three members of the second interview panel. One had been her first supervisor when she began work as a road maintenance worker. In performing arduous work in this job, she had not been issued coveralls, although her male co-workers had received them. After ruining her pants, she complained to her supervisor, to no avail. After three other similar incidents, ruining clothes on each occasion, she filed a grievance, and was issued four pair of coveralls the next day. Tr. 89–90. Joyce had dealt with a second member of the panel for a year and a half in her capacity as chair of the Roads Operations Safety Committee, where she and he "had several differences of opinion on how safety should be implemented." Id. at 90–91. In addition, Joyce testified that she had informed the person responsible for arranging her second interview that she had a disaster preparedness class on a certain day the following week. By this time about ten days had passed since she had notified this person of her availability, and no date had yet been set for the interview. Within a day or two after this conversation, however, she received a notice setting her interview at a time directly in the middle of her disaster preparedness class. Id. at 94–95. The same panel member had earlier described Joyce as a "rebel-rousing, skirt-wearing person." (Tr. 153.)

The Coordinator of the Affirmative Action Office, whose job includes apprising the Director of the Agency of qualified women (and minorities and handicapped) for particular openings, then recommended that Joyce receive the promotion to road dispatcher. At the time no women held that job.

The Director of the Agency, James Graebner, then received a recommendation from the second interview panel to hire Paul Johnson. Technically authorized to select any of the seven, Graebner chose Diane Joyce. He later explained that he had taken into account "the whole picture"—both persons' experience, background, expertise, test scores, and "affirmative action matters." he indicated further that he viewed both Johnson and Joyce as "well-qualified" and that the difference between test scores of 75 and 73 on an interview was insignificant.

After Joyce's appointment Paul Johnson went to federal court with a complaint that sex had been "the determining factor" in Diane Joyce's selection over him, and the District Court was persuaded by his argument that this selection procedure violated Title VII. The Circuit Court of Appeals reversed, and Johnson appealed to the U.S. Supreme Court.

At the Supreme Court, the Reagan-staffed Justice Department submitted an *amicus* brief. In 1986 the Justice Department had argued in three different cases that all voluntary affirmative action violates the law (and for government agencies, the Constitution), and that even affirmative action remedies to illegal discrimination should be limited to proven individual victims of the discrimination. Rebuffed by the Supreme Court in all three cases, the Justice Department in *Johnson* v. *Agency* had modified its position, but still insisted that the Santa Clara plan swept too broadly and had invaded Paul Johnson's legal rights. The Supreme Court again rejected that Department's arguments.

Paul E. Johnson v. Transportation Agency, Santa Clara County, 55 U.S.L.W. 4379 (1987)

JUSTICE BRENNAN delivered the opinion of the Court.

. . .

In reviewing the employment decision at issue in this case, we must first examine whether that decision was made pursuant to a plan prompted by concerns similar to those of the employer in *Weber*. Next, we must determine whether the effect of the plan on males and non-minorities is comparable to the effect of the plan in that case.

The first issue is therefore whether consideration of the sex of applicants for skilled craft jobs was justified by the existence of a "manifest imbalance" that reflected underrepresentation of women in

"traditionally segregated job categories." *Id*. at 197. In determining whether an imbalance exists that would justify taking sex or race into account, a comparison of the percentage of minorities or women in the employer's work force with the percentage in the area labor market or general population is appropriate in analyzing jobs that require no special expertise, see *Teamsters v. United States*, 431 U.S. 324 (1977) (comparison between percentage of blacks in employer's work force and in general population proper in determining extent of imbalance in truck driving positions), or training programs designed to provide expertise, see *Weber, supra* (comparison between proportion of blacks working at plant and proportion of blacks in area labor force appropriate in calculating imbalance for purpose of establishing preferential admission to craft training program). Where a job requires special training, however, the comparison should be with those in the labor force who posess the relevant qualifications. *See Hazelwood School District v. United States*, 433 U.S. 299 (1977) (must compare percentage of blacks in employer's work ranks with percentage of qualified black teachers in area labor force in determining underrepresentation in teaching positions). The requirement that the "manifest imbalance" relate to a "traditionally segregated job category" provides assurance both that sex or race will be taken into account in a manner consistent with Title VII's purpose of eliminating the effects of employment discrimination, and that the interests of those employees not benefitting from the plan will not be unduly infringed.

A manifest imbalance need not be such that it would support a prima facie case against the employer, as suggested in Justice O'Connor's concurrence, *post*, since we do not regard as identical the constraints of Title VII and the federal constitution on voluntarily adopted affirmative action plans. Application of the "prima facie" standard in Title VII cases would be inconsistent with *Weber's* focus on statistical imbalance, and could inappropriately create a significant disincentive for employers to adopt an affirmative action plan. *See Weber, supra*, at 204 (Title VII intended as a "catalyst" for employer efforts to eliminate vestiges of discrimination). A corporation concerned with maximizing return on investment, for instance, is hardly likely to adopt a plan if in order to do so it must compile evidence that could be used to subject it to a colorable Title VII suit.

It is clear that the decision to hire Joyce was made pursuant to an Agency plan that directed that sex or race be taken into account for the purpose of remedying underrepresentation. The Agency Plan acknowledged the "limited opportunities that have existed in the past," App. 57, for women to find employment in certain job classifications "where women have not been traditionally employed in significant numbers." *Id.* at 51.[12] As a result, observed the Plan, women were concentrated in traditionally female jobs in the Agency, and represented a lower percentage in other job classifications than would be expected if such traditional segregation had not occurred. . . . The Plan sought to remedy these imbalances through "hiring, training and promotion of . . . women throughout the Agency in all major job classifications where they are underrepresented." *Id.* at 43.

. . .

As the Agency Plan recognized, women were most egregiously underrepresented in the Skilled Craft job category, since *none* of the 238 positions was occupied by a woman. In mid-1980, when

12. For instance, the description of the Skilled Craft Worker category, in which the road dispatcher position is located, is as follows:

"Occupations in which workers perform jobs which require special manual skill and a thorough and comprehensive knowledge of the process involved in the work which is acquired through on-the-job training and experience or through apprenticeship or other formal training programs. Includes: mechanics and repairmen; electricians, heavy equipment operators, stationary engineers, skilled machining occupations, carpenters, compositors and typesetters and kindred workers." App. 108.

As the Court of Appeals said in its decision below, "A plethora of proof is hardly necessary to show that women are generally underrepresented in such positions and that strong social pressures weigh against their participation." 748 F.2d, at 1313.

Joyce was selected for the road dispatcher position, the Agency was still in the process of refining its short-term goals for Skilled Craft Workers in accordance with the directive of the Plan. This process did not reach fruition until 1982, when the Agency established a short-term goal for that year of three women for the 55 expected openings in that job category—a modest goal of about 6 percent for that category.

. . . The Agency's Plan emphasized that the long-term goals were not to be taken as guides for actual hiring decisions, but that supervisors were to consider a host of practical factors in seeking to meet affirmative action objectives, including the fact that in some job categories women were not qualified in numbers comparable to their representation in the labor force.

By contrast, had the Plan simply calculated imbalances in all categories according to the proportion of women in the area labor pool, and then directed that hiring be governed solely by those figures, its validity fairly could be called into question. This is because analysis of a more specialized labor pool normally is necessary in determining underrepresentation in some positions. If a plan failed to take distinctions in qualifications into account in providing guidance for actual employment decisons, it would dictate mere blind hiring by the numbers, for it would hold supervisors to "achievement of a particular percentage of minority employment or membership . . . regardless of circumstances such as economic conditions or the number of qualified minority applicants . . ." *Sheet Metal Workers' v. EEOC*, 478 U.S. — (1986) (O'CONNOR, J., concurring in part and dissenting in part).

The Agency's Plan emphatically did *not* authorize such blind hiring. It expressly directed that numerous factors be taken into account in making hiring decisions, including specifically the qualifications of female applicants for particular jobs. . . .

. . . Given the obvious imbalance in the Skilled Craft category, and given the Agency's commitment to eliminating such imbalances, it was plainly not unreasonable for the Agency to determine that it was appropriate to consider as one factor the sex of Ms. Joyce in making its decision. The promotion of Joyce thus satisfies the first requirement enunciated in *Weber*, since it was undertaken to further an affirmative action plan designed to eliminate Agency work force imbalances in traditionally segregated job categories.

We next consider whether the Agency Plan unnecessarily trammeled the rights of male employees or created an absolute bar to their advancement. In contrast to the plan in *Weber*, which provided that 50 percent of the positions in the craft training program were exclusively for blacks, and to the consent decree upheld last term in *Firefighters v. Cleveland*, 478 U.S. — (1986), which required the promotion of specific numbers of minorities, the Plan sets aside no positions for women. The Plan expressly states that "[t]he 'goals' established for each Division should not be construed as 'quotas' that must be met." App. 64. Rather, the Plan merely authorizes that consideration be given to affirmative action concerns when evaluating qualified applicants. As the Agency Director testified, the sex of Joyce was but one of numerous factors he took into account in arriving at his decision. Tr. 68. The Plan thus resembles the "Harvard Plan" approvingly noted by JUSTICE POWELL in *University of California Regents v. Bakke*, 438 US. 265, 316–19 (1978), which considers race along with other criteria in determining admission to the college. . . . Similarly, the Agency Plan requires women to compete with all other qualified applicants. *No* persons are automatically excluded from consideration; *all* are able to have their qualifications weighed against those of other applicants.

In addition, petitioner had no absolute entitlement to the road dispatcher position. Seven of the applicants were classified as qualified and eligible, and the Agency Director was authorized to promote any of the seven. Thus, denial of the promotion unsettled no legitimate firmly rooted expectation on the part of the petitioner. Furthermore, while the petitioner in this case was denied a promotion, he retained his employment with the Agency, at the same salary and with the same seniority, and remained eligible for other promotions.

Finally, the Agency's Plan was intended to *attain* a balanced work force, not to maintain one. The Plan contains ten references to the Agency's desire to "attain" such a balance, but no reference whatsoever to a goal of maintaining it.

. . . Express assurance that a program is only temporary may be necessary if the program actually sets aside positions according to specific numbers. *See, e.g., Firefighters, supra*, (four-year duration for consent decree providing for promotion of particular number of minorities); *Weber*, 443 U.S., at 199 (plan requiring that blacks constitute 50 percent of new trainees in effect until percentage of employer work force equal to percentage in local labor force). This is necessary both to minimize the effect of the program on other employees, and to ensure that the plan's goals "[are] not being used simply to achieve and maintain . . . balance, but rather as a benchmark against which" the employer may measure its progress in eliminating the underrepresentation of minorities and women. *Sheet Metal Workers supra*. In this case, however, substantial evidence shows that the Agency has sought to take a moderate, gradual approach to eliminating the imbalance in its work force, one which es-

tablishes realistic guidance for employment decisions, and which visits minimal intrusion on the legitimate expectations of other employees. Given this fact, as well as the Agency's express commitment to "attain" a balanced work force, there is ample assurance that the Agency does not seek to use its Plan to maintain a permanent racial and sexual balance.

III

In evaluating the compliance of an affirmative action plan with Title VII's prohibition on discrimination, we must be mindful of "this Court's and Congress' consistent emphasis on 'the value of voluntary efforts to further the objectives of the law.'" *Wygant*, 476 U.S., at —— (O'CONNOR, J., concurring in part and concurring in judgment) (quoting *Bakke, supra*, at 364). The Agency in the case before us has undertaken such a voluntary effort, and has done so in full recognition of both the difficulties and the potential for intrusion on males and non-minorities. The Agency has identified a conspicuous imbalance in job categories traditionally segregated by race and sex. It has made clear from the outset, however, that employment decisions may not be justified solely by reference to this imbalance, but must rest on a multitude of practical, realistic factors. It has therefore committed itself to annual adjustment of goals so as to provide a reasonable guide for actual hiring and promotion decisions. The Agency earmarks no positions for anyone; sex is but one of several factors that may be taken into account in evaluating qualified applicants for a position.[17] As

---

17. The dissent predicts that today's decision will loose a flood of "less qualified" minorities and women upon the workforce, as employers seek to forestall possible Title VII liability. *Post.* The first problem with this projection is that it is by no means certain that employers could

both the Plan's language and its manner of operation attest, the Agency has no intention of establishing a work force whose permanent composition is dictated by rigid numerical standards.

We therefore hold that the Agency appropriately took into account as one factor the sex of Diane Joyce in determining that she should be promoted to the road dispatcher position. The decision to do so was made pursuant to an affirmative action plan that represents a moderate, flexible case-by-case approach to effecting a gradual improvement in the representation of minorities and women in the Agency's work force. Such a plan is fully consistent with Title VII, for it embodies the contribution that voluntary employer action can make in eliminating the vestiges of discrimination in the workplace. Accordingly, the judgment of the Court of Appeals is

Affirmed.

---

in every case necessarily avoid liability for discrimination merely by adopting an affirmative action plan. . . .

A second, and more fundamental, problem with the dissent's speculation is that it ignores the fact that "[i]t is a standard tenet of personnel administration that there is rarely a single, 'best qualified' person for a job. An effective personnel system will bring before the selecting official several fully-qualified candidates who each may possess different attributes which recommend them for selection. Especially where the job is an unexceptional, middle-level craft position, without the need for unique work experience or educational attainment and for which several well-qualified candidates are available, final determinations as to which candidate is 'best qualified' are at best subjective." Brief for American Society for Personnel Administration as *Amicus Curiae* 9.

This case provides an example of precisely this point. Any differences in qualifications between Johnson and Joyce were minimal, to say the least. . . .

JUSTICE STEVENS, concurring.

While I join the Court's opinion, I write separately to explain my view of this case's position in our evolving antidiscrimination law and to emphasize that the opinion does not establish the permissible outer limits of voluntary programs undertaken by employers to benefit disadvantaged groups.

I

. . . As a shield, an antidiscrimination statute can . . . help a member of a protected class by assuring decisionmakers in some instances that, when they elect for good reasons of their own to grant a preference of some sort to a minority citizen, they will not violate the law. The Court properly holds that the statutory shield allowed respondent to take Diane Joyce's sex into account in promoting her to the road dispatcher position.

Prior to 1978 the Court considered the Civil Rights Act of 1964 as an absolute blanket prohibition against discrimination which neither required nor permitted discriminatory preferences for any group, minority or majority. The Court unambiguously endorsed the neutral approach, first in the context of gender discrimination[1] and then in the context of racial discrimination against a white person.[2] As I ex-

---

1. "Discriminatory preference for any group, minority or majority, is precisely and only what Congress has proscribed. What is required by Congress is the removal of artificial, arbitrary, and unnecessary barriers to employment when the barriers operate invidiously to discriminate on the basis of racial or other impermissible classification." *Griggs v. Duke Power Co.*, 401 U.S. 424, 431 (1971).

2. "Similarly the EEOC, whose interpretations are entitled to great deference, [401 U.S.,] at 433–34, has consistently interpreted Title VII to proscribe racial discrimination in private em-

plained in my separate opinion in *University of California Regents v. Bakke,* 438 U.S. 265, 412–18 (1978), and as the Court forcefully stated in *McDonald v. Santa Fe Trail Transportation Co.,* 427 U.S. 273, 280 (1976), Congress intended "'to eliminate all practices which operate to disadvantage the employment opportunities of any group protected by Title VII including Caucasians.'" (Citations omitted.) If the Court had adhered to that construction of the Act, petitioner would unquestionably prevail in this case. But it has not done so.

In the *Bakke* case in 1978 and again in *Steelworkers v. Weber,* 443 U.S. 193 (1979), a majority of the Court interpreted the antidiscriminatory strategy of the statute in a fundamentally different way. The Court held in the *Weber* case that an employer's program designed to increase the number of black craftworkers in an aluminum plant did not violate Title VII.[3] It remains clear

that the Act does not *require* any employer to grant preferential treatment on the basis of race or gender, but since 1978 the Court has unambiguously interpreted the statute to *permit* the voluntary adoption of special programs to benefit members of the minority groups for whose protection the statute was enacted. Neither the "same standards" language used in *McDonald,* nor the "color blind" rhetoric used by the Senators and Congressmen who enacted the bill, is now controlling. Thus, as was true in *Runyon v. McCrary,* 427 U.S. 160, 189 (1976) (STEVENS, J., concurring), the only problem for me is whether to adhere to an authoritative construction of the Act that is at odds with my understanding of the actual intent of the authors of the legislation. I conclude without hesitation that I must answer that question in the affirmative, just as I did in *Runyon. Id.* at 191–92.

Bakke and *Weber* have been decided and are now an important part of the fabric of our law. This consideration is sufficiently compelling for me to adhere to the basic construction of this legislation that the Court adopted in *Bakke* and in *Weber.* There is an undoubted public interest in "stability and orderly development of the law." 427 U.S., at 190.

The logic of antidiscrimination legislation requires that judicial constructions of Title VII leave "breathing room" for employer initiatives to benefit members of minority groups. If Title VII had never been enacted, a private employer would be free to hire members of minority groups for any reason that might seem sensible from a business or a social point of view. The

ployment against whites on the same terms as racial discrimination against nonwhites, holding that to proceed otherwise would

'constitute a derogation of the Commission's Congressional mandate to eliminate all practices which operate to disadvantage the employment opportunities of any group protected by Title VII, including Caucasians.' EEOC Decision No. 74–31, 7 FEP Cases 1326, 1328, CCh EEOC Decisions § 6404, at 4084 (1973)."

"This conclusion is in accord with uncontradicted legislative history to the effect that Title VII was intended to 'cover white men and white women and all Americans,' 110 Cong. Rec. 2578 (1964) (remarks of Rep. Celler), and create an 'obligation not to discriminate against whites,' *id.* at 7218 (memorandum of Sen. Clark). *See also id.* at 7213 (memorandum of Sens. Clark and Case); *id.* at 8912 (remarks of Sen. Williams). We therefore hold today that Title VII prohibits racial discrimination against the white petitioners in this case upon the same standards as would be applicable were they Negroes and Jackson white." *McDonald v. Santa Fe Trail Transportation Co.,* 427 U.S. 273, 279–80 (footnotes omitted).

3. Toward the end of its opinion, the Court

mentioned certain reasons why the plan did not impose a special hardship on white employees or white applicants for employment. *Steelworkers v. Weber,* 443 U.S. 193, 208 (1979). I have never understood those comments to constitute a set of conditions that every race-conscious plan must satisfy in order to comply with Title VII.

Court's opinion in *Weber* reflects the same approach; the opinion relied heavily on legislative history indicating that Congress intended that traditional management prerogatives be left undisturbed to the greatest extent possible. *See* 443 U.S., at 206–7. As we observed Last Term, "'[i]t would be ironic indeed if a law triggered by a Nation's concern over centuries of racial injustice and intended to improve the lot of those who had "been excluded from the American dream for so long" constituted the first legislative prohibition of all voluntary, private, race-conscious efforts to abolish traditional patterns of racial segregation and hierarchy.'" *Firefighters, v. Cleveland,* 478 U.S. ——, —— (1986) (citing *Weber,* 443 U.S., at 204). In *Firefighters,* we again acknowledged Congress' concern in Title VII to avoid "undue federal interference with managerial discretion." 478 U.S., at ——.[5]

As construed in *Weber* and in *Firefighters,* the statute does not absolutely prohibit preferential hiring in favor of minorities; it was merely intended to protect historically disadvantaged groups *against* discrimination and not to hamper managerial efforts to benefit members of disadvantaged groups that are consistent with that paramount purpose. The preference granted by respondent in this case does not violate the statute as so construed; the

record amply supports the conclusion that the challenged employment decision served the legitimate purpose of creating diversity in a category of employment that had been almost an exclusive province of males in the past. Respondent's voluntary decision is surely not prohibited by Title VII as construed in *Weber.*

II

Whether a voluntary decision of the kind made by respondent would ever be prohibited by Title VII is a question we need not answer until it is squarely presented. Given the interpretation of the statute the Court adopted in *Weber,* I see no reason why the employer has any duty, prior to granting a preference to a qualified minority employee, to determine whether his past conduct might constitute an arguable violation of Title VII. Indeed, in some instances the employer may find it more helpful to focus on the future. Instead of retroactively scrutinizing his own or society's possible exclusions of minorities in the past to determine the outer limits of a valid affirmative-action program— or indeed, any particular affirmative-action decision—in many cases the employer will find it more appropriate to consider other legitimate reasons to give preferences to members of under-represented groups. Statutes enacted for the benefit of minority groups should not block these forward-looking considerations.

Public and private employers might choose to implement affirmative action for many reasons other than to purge their own past sins of discrimination. The Jackson school board, for example, said it had done so in part to improve the quality of education in Jackson— whether by improving black students' performance or by dispelling for black and white students alike any idea that white supremacy governs our social

5. As Justice Blackmun observed in *Weber,* 443 U.S., at 209, 214–15 (Blackmun, J., concurring): "Strong considerations of equity support an interpretation of Title VII that would permit private affirmative action to reach where Title VII itself does not. The bargain struck in 1964 with the passage of Title VII guaranteed equal opportunity for white and black alike, but where Title VII provides no remedy for blacks, it should not be construed to foreclose private affirmative action from supplying relief. . . . Absent compelling evidence of legislative intent, I would not interpret Title VII itself as a means of 'locking in' the effects of discrimination for which Title VII provides no remedy."

institutions. Other employers might advance different forward-looking reasons for affirmative action: improving their services to black constituencies, averting racial tension over the allocation of jobs in a community; or increasing the diversity of a work force, to name but a few examples. Or they might adopt affirmative action simply to eliminate from their operations all de facto embodiment of a system of racial caste. All of these reasons aspire to a racially integrated future, but none reduces to "racial balancing for its own sake." (Sullivan, *The Supreme Court— Comment, Sins of Discrimination: Last Term's Affirmative Action Cases,* 100 Harv. L. Rev. 78, 96 [1986].)

The Court today does not foreclose other voluntary decisions based in part on a qualified employee's membership in a disadvantaged group. Accordingly, I concur.

Justice O'Connor, concurring in the judgment.

In *Steelworkers v. Weber,* 443 U.S. 193 (1979), this Court held that § 703(d) of Title VII does not prohibit voluntary affirmative action efforts if the employer sought to remedy a "manifest . . . imbalanc[e] in traditionally segregated job categories." *Id.* at 197. As Justice Scalia illuminates with excruciating clarity, § 703 has been interpreted by *Weber* and succeeding cases to permit what its language read literally would prohibit. Section 703(d) prohibits employment discrimination "against *any individual* because of his race, color, religion, sex, or national origin." 42 U.S.C. § 2000e– 2(d). (Emphasis added.) The *Weber* Court, however, concluded that voluntary affirmative action was permissible in some circumstances because a prohibition of every type of affirmative action would "'bring

about an end completely at variance with the purpose of the statute.'" 443 U.S., at 202 (quoting *United States v. Public Utilities Comm'n,* 345 U.S. 295, 315 (1953). This purpose, according to the Court, was to open employment opportunities for blacks in occupations that had been traditionally closed to them.

None of the parties in this case have suggested that we overrule *Weber* and that question was not raised, briefed, or argued in this Court or in the courts below. If the Court is faithful to its normal prudential restraints and to the principle of *stare decisis* we must address once again the propriety of an affirmative action plan under Title VII in light of our precedents, precedents that have upheld affirmative action in a variety of circumstances. This time the question posed is whether a public employer violates Title VII by promoting a qualified woman rather than a marginally better qualified man when there is a statistical imbalance sufficient to support a claim of a pattern or practice of discrimination against women under Title VII.

I concur in the judgment of the Court in light of our precedents. I write separately, however, because the Court has chosen to follow an expansive and ill-defined approach to voluntary affirmative action by public employers despite the limitations imposed by the Constitution and by the provisions of Title VII, and because the dissent rejects the Court's precedents and addresses the question of how Title VII should be interpreted as if the Court were writing on a clean slate. The former course of action gives insufficient guidance to courts and litigants; the latter course of action serves as a useful point of academic discussion, but fails to reckon with the reality of the course that the majority of the Court has determined to follow.

In my view, the proper initial inquiry in evaluating the legality of an affirmative action plan by a public employer under Title VII is no different from that required by the Equal Protection Clause. In either case, consistent with the congressional intent to provide some measure of protection to the interests of the employer's nonminority employees, the employer must have had a firm basis for believing that remedial action was required. An employer would have such a firm basis if it can point to a statistical disparity sufficient to support a prima facie claim under Title VII by the employee beneficiaries of the affirmative action plan of a pattern or practice claim of discrimination.

In *Weber*, this Court balanced two conflicting concerns in construing § 703(d): Congress' intent to root out invidious discrimination against *any* person on the basis of race or gender, *McDonald v. Santa Fe Transp. Co.*, 427 U.S. 273 (1976), and its goal of eliminating the lasting effects of discrimination against minorities. Given these conflicting concerns, the Court concluded that it would be inconsistent with the background and purpose of Title VII to prohibit affirmative action in all cases. As I read *Weber*, however, the Court also determined that Congress had balanced these two competing concerns by permitting affirmative action only as a remedial device to eliminate actual or apparent discrimination or the lingering effects of this discrimination.

Contrary to the intimations in JUSTICE STEVENS' concurrence, this Court did not approve preferences for minorities "for any reason that might seem sensible from a business or a social point of view." *Ante.* Indeed, such an approach would have been wholly at odds with this Court's holding in *McDonald* that Congress intended to prohibit practices that operate to discriminate against the employment opportunities of nonminorities as well as minorities. Moreover, in *Weber* the Court was careful to consider the effects of the affirmative action

plan for black employees on the employment opportunities of white employees. 443 U.S., at 208. Instead of a wholly standardless approach to affirmative action, the Court determined in *Weber* that Congress intended to permit affirmative action only if the employer could point to a "manifest . . . imbalanc[e] in traditionally segregated job categories." *Id.* at 197. This requirement both "provides assurance that sex or race will be taken into account in a manner consistent with Title VII's purpose of eliminating the effects of employment discrimination," *ante,* and is consistent with this Court's and Congress' consistent emphasis on the value of voluntary efforts to further the antidiscrimination purposes of Title VII. *Wygant v. Jackson Board of Education,* 476 U.S. ——, —— (1986) (O'CONNOR, J., concurring in part and concurring in judgment).

The *Weber* view of Congress' resolution of the conflicting concerns of minority and nonminority workers in Title VII appears substantially similar to this Court's resolution of these same concerns in *Wygant v. Jackson Board of Education, supra,* which involved the claim that an affirmative action plan by a public employer violated the Equal Protection Clause. In *Wygant,* the Court was in agreement that remedying past or present racial discrimination by a state actor is a sufficiently weighty interest to warrant the remedial use of a carefully constructed affirmative action plan. The Court also concluded, however, that "[s]ocietal discrimination, without more, is too amorphous a basis for imposing a racially classified remedy." *Id.* at ——. Instead, we determined that affirmative action was valid if it was crafted to remedy past or present discrimination by the employer. Although the employer need not point to any contemporaneous findings of actual discrimination, I concluded in *Wygant* that the employer must point to evidence sufficient to establish a firm basis for believing that remedial action is required, and that a statistical imbalance sufficient for Title VII prima facie case against the employer would satisfy this firm basis requirement. . . .

The *Wygant* analysis is entirely consistent with *Weber.* . . . Here, however, the evidence of past discrimination is more complex. The number of women with the qualifications for entry into the relevant job classification was quite small. A statistical imbalance between the percentage of women in the work force generally and the percentage of women in the particular specialized job classification, therefore, does not suggest past discrimination for purposes of proving a Title VII prima facie case. *See Hazelwood School District v. United States,* 433 U.S. 299, 308, and n.13 (1977).

Unfortunately, the Court today gives little guidance for what statistical imbalance is sufficient to support an affirmative action plan. Although the Court denies that the statistical imbalance need be sufficient to make out a prima facie case of discrimination against women, the Court fails to suggest an alternative standard. Because both *Wygant* and *Weber* attempt to reconcile the same competing concerns, I see little justification for the adoption of different standards for affirmative action under Title VII and the Equal Protection Clause.

While employers must have a firm basis for concluding that remedial action is necessary, neither *Wygant* nor *Weber* places a burden on employers to prove that they actually discriminated against women or minorities. Employers are "trapped between the competing hazards of liability to minorities if affirmative action is *not* taken to remedy apparent employment discrimination and liability to nonminorities if affirmative action is taken." *Wygant v. Jackson Board of Education,* 476 U.S., at —— (O'Connor, J., concurring in part and concurring in judgment). Moreover, this Court

has long emphasized the importance of voluntary efforts to eliminate discrimination. *Id.* at ——. Thus, I concluded in *Wygant* that a contemporaneous finding of discrimination should not be required because it would discourage voluntary efforts to remedy apparent discrimination. . . . Evidence sufficient for a prima facie Title VII pattern or practice claim against the employer itself suggests that the absence of women or minorities in a workforce cannot be explained by general societal discrimination alone and that remedial action is appropriate.

In applying these principles to this case, it is important to pay close attention to both the affirmative action plan, and the manner in which that plan was applied to the specific promotion decision at issue in this case. . . .

The long-term goal of the plan was "to attain a work force whose composition in all job levels and major job classifications approximates the distribution of women . . . in the Santa Clara County work force." App., at 54. If this long-term goal had been applied to the hiring decisions made by the Agency, in my view, the affirmative action plan would violate Title VII. "[I]t is completely unrealistic to assume that individuals of each [sex] will gravitate with mathematical exactitude to each employer . . . absent unlawful discrimination." *Sheet Metal Workers, supra,* (O'Connor, J., concurring in part and dissenting in part.) Thus, a goal that makes such an assumption, and simplistically focuses on the proportion of women and minorities in the workforce without more, is not remedial. Only a goal that takes into account the number of women and minorities qualified for the relevant position could satisfy the requirement that an affirmative action plan be remedial. This long-range goal, however, was never used as a guide for actual hiring decisions. Instead, the goal was merely a statement of aspiration wholly without operational significance. . . . Instead, the plan provided for the development of short-term goals, which alone were to guide the respondents . . . [;] these short-term goals were to be focused on remedying past apparent discrimination, and would "[p]rovide an objective standard for use in determining if the representation of minorities, women and handicapped persons in particular job classifications is at a reasonable level in comparison with estimates of the numbers of persons from these groups in the area work force who can meet the educational and experience requirements for employment." App., at 61.

. . .

As JUSTICE SCALIA views the record in this case, the Agency Director made the decision to promote Joyce rather than petitioner solely on the basis of sex and with indifference to the relative merits of the two applicants. In my view, however, the record simply fails to substantiate the picture painted by JUSTICE SCALIA. The Agency Director testified that he "tried to look at the whole picture, the combination of [Joyce's] qualifications and Mr. Johnson's qualifications, their test scores, their experience, their background, affirmative action matters, things like that." Tr. 68. Contrary to JUSTICE SCALIA's suggestion, the Agency Director knew far more than merely the sex of the candidates and that they appeared on a list of candidates eligible for the job. The Director had spoken to individuals familiar with the qualifications of both applicants for the promotion, and was aware that their scores were rather close. Moreover, he testified that over a period of weeks he had spent several hours making the promotion decision, suggesting that Joyce was not selected solely on the basis of her sex. Tr. 63. Additionally, the Director stated that had Joyce's experience been less than that of petitioner by a larger margin, petitioner

might have received the promotion. *Id.* at 69–70. As the Director summarized his decision to promote Joyce, the underrepresentation of women in skilled craft positions was only one element of a number of considerations that led to the promotion of Ms. Joyce. *Id.* While I agree with the dissent that an affirmative action program that automatically and blindly promotes those marginally qualified candidates falling within a preferred race or gender category, or that can be equated with a permanent plan of "proportionate representation by race and sex" would violate Title VII, I cannot agree that this is such a case. Rather, as the Court demonstrates, Joyce's sex was simply used as a "plus" factor.

In this case, I am also satisfied that the respondent had a firm basis for adopting an affirmative action program. Although the District Court found no discrimination against women in fact, at the time the affirmative action plan was adopted, there were *no* women in its skilled craft positions. The petitioner concedes that women constituted approximately 5 percent of the local labor pool of skilled craft workers in 1970. Reply Brief for Petitioner 9. Thus, when compared to the percentage of women in the qualified work force, the statistical disparity would have been sufficient for a prima facie Title VII case brought by unsuccessful women job applicants. *See Teamsters,* 431 U.S., at 342, n.23 ("[F]ine tuning of the statistics could not have obscured the glaring absence of minority line drivers. . . . [T]he company's inability to rebut the inference of discrimination came not from a misuse of statistics but from 'the inexorable zero'").

. . . Accordingly, I concur in the judgment of the Court.

JUSTICE WHITE, dissenting.

I agree with parts I and II of JUSTICE

SCALIA's dissenting opinion. Although I do not join part III, I also would overrule *Weber*. My understanding of *Weber* was, and is, that the employer's plan did not violate Title VII because it was designed to remedy intentional and systematic exclusion of blacks by the employer and the unions from certain job categories. That is how I understood the phrase "traditionally segregated jobs" we used in that case. The Court now interprets it to mean nothing more than a manifest imbalance between one identifiable group and another in an employer's labor force. As so interpreted, that case, as well as today's decision, as JUSTICE SCALIA so well demonstrates, is a perversion of Title VII. I would overrule *Weber* and reverse the judgment below.

JUSTICE SCALIA, with whom THE CHIEF JUSTICE joins, and with whom JUSTICE WHITE joins in parts I and II, dissenting.

With a clarity which, had it not proven so unavailing, one might well recommend as a model of statutory draftsmanship, Title VII of the Civil Rights Act of 1964 declares:

> It shall be an unlawful employment practice for an employer—
> (1) to fail or refuse to hire or to discharge any individual, or otherwise to discriminate against any individual with respect to his compensation, terms, conditions, or privileges of employment, because of such individual's race, color, religion, sex, or national origin; or
> (2) to limit, segregate, or classify his employees or applicants for employment in any way which would deprive or tend to deprive any individual of employment opportunities or otherwise adversely affect his status as an employee, because of such individual's race, color, religion, sex, or national origin. (42 U.S.C. § 2000e–2[a].)

The Court today completes the process of converting this from a guarantee that race or sex will *not* be the basis for employment determinations, to a guarantee that it often *will*. . . .

I

. . .

Several salient features of the plan should be noted. Most importantly, the plan's purpose was assuredly not to remedy prior sex discrimination by the Agency. It could not have been, because there was no prior sex discrimination to remedy. The majority, in cataloguing the Agency's alleged misdeeds, neglects to mention the District Court's finding that the Agency "has not discriminated in the past, and does not discriminate in the present against women in regard to employment opportunities in general and promotions in particular." App. to Pet. for Cert. 13a. This finding was not disturbed by the Ninth Circuit.

Not only was the plan not directed at the results of past sex discrimination by the Agency, but its objective was not to achieve the state of affairs that this Court has dubiously assumed would result from an absence of discrimination—an overall work force "more or less representative of the racial and ethnic composition of the population in the community." *Teamsters v. United States*, 431 U.S. 324, 340, n.20 (1977). Rather, the oft-stated goal was to mirror the racial and sexual composition of the entire county labor force, not merely in the Agency work force as a whole, but in each and every individual job category at the Agency. In a discrimination-free world, it would obviously be a statistical oddity for every job category to match the racial and sexual composition of even that portion of the county work force *qualified* for that job; it would be utterly miraculous for each of them to match, as the plan expected, the composition of the *entire* work force. Quite obviously, the plan did not seek to replicate what a lack of discrimination would produce, but rather imposed racial and sexual tailoring that would, in defiance of normal expectations and laws of probability, give each protected racial and sexual group a governmentally determined "proper" proportion of each job category.

That the plan was not directed at remedying or eliminating the effects of past discrimination is most clearly illustrated by its description of what it regarded as the *"Factors Hindering Goal Attainment"*—*i.e.*, the existing impediments to the racially and sexually representative work force that it pursued. The plan noted that it would be "difficult," App. 55, to attain its objective of across-the-board statistical parity in at least some job categories, because:

a. Most of the positions require specialized training and experience. Until recently, relatively few minorities, women and handicapped persons sought entry into these positions. Consequently, the number of persons from these groups in the area labor force who possess the qualifications required for entry into such job classifications is limited.

. . .

c. many of the Agency positions where women are underrepresented involve heavy labor, *e.g.*, Road Maintenance Worker. Consequently, few women seek entry into these positions.

. . .

f. Many women are not strongly motivated to seek employment in job classifications where they have not been traditionally employed because of the limited opportunities that have existed in the past for them to work in such classifications. (*Id.* at 56–57.)

That is, the qualifications and desires of women may fail to match the Agency's Platonic ideal of a work force. The plan concluded from this, of course, not that the ideal should be reconsidered, but that its attainment could not be immediate. *Id.* at 58–60. . . .

Finally, the one message that the plan unmistakably communicated was that concrte results were expected, and supervisory personnel would be evaluated on the basis of the affirmative-action numbers they produced. . . . As noted earlier, supervisors were reminded of the need to give attention to affirmative action in every employment decision, and to explain their reasons for *failing* to hire women and minorities whenever there was an opportunity to do so.

The petitioner in the present case, Paul E. Johnson, had been an employee of the Agency since 1967, coming there from a private company where he had been a road dispatcher for seventeen years. . . . When the Road Dispatcher job next became vacant, in 1979, he was the leading candidate—and indeed was assigned to work out of class full-time in the vacancy, from September of 1979 until June of 1980: There is no question why he did not get the job.

The fact of discrimination against Johnson is much clearer, and its degree more shocking, than the majority and Justice O'Connor's concurring opinion would suggest—largely because neither of them recites a single one of the District Court findings that govern this appeal, relying instead upon portions of the transcript which those findings implicitly rejected, and even upon a document (favorably comparing Joyce to Johnson), that was prepared *after* Joyce was selected. *See* App. 27–28; Tr.

223–27. It is worth mentioning, for example, the trier of fact's determination that, if the Affirmative Action Coordinator had not intervened, "the decision as to whom to promote . . . would have been made by [the Road Operations Division Director]," App. to Pet. for Cert. 12a, who had recommended that Johnson be appointed to the position. *Id.* Likewise, the even more extraordinary findings that James Graebner, the Agency Director who made the appointment, "did not inspect the applications and related examination records of either [Paul Johnson] or Diane Joyce before making his decision," *id.*, and indeed "did little or nothing to inquire into the results of the interview process and conclusions which [were] described as of critical importance to the selection process." *Id.* at 3a. In light of these determinations, it is impossible to believe (or to think that the District Court believed) Graebner's self-serving statements relied upon by the majority and concurrence, such as the assertion that he "tried to look at the whole picture. . . ." It was evidently enough for Graebner to know that both candidates (in the words of Johnson's counsel, to which Graebner assented) "met the M. Q.'s, the minimum. Both were minimally qualified." Tr. 25. When asked whether he had "any basis," *id.*, for determining whether one of the candidates was more qualified than the other, Graebner candidly answered, "No. . . . As I've said, they both appeared, and my conversations with people tended to corroborate, that they were both capable of performing the work." *Id.*

After a two-day trial, the District Court concluded that Diane Joyce's gender was *"the determining factor,"* *id.* at 4a, in her selection for the position. . . . The Ninth Circuit did not reject these factual findings as clearly erroneous, nor could it have done so on the record before us. We are bound by those findings under Federal Rule of Civil Procedure 52(a).

II

The most significant proposition of law established by today's decision is that racial or sexual discrimination is permitted under Title VII when it is intended to overcome the effect, not of the employer's own discrimination, but of societal attitudes that have limited the entry of certain races, or of a particular sex, into certain jobs. Even if the societal attitudes in question consisted exclusively of conscious discrimination by other employers, this holding would contradict a decision of this Court rendered only last Term. *Wygant v. Jackson Board of Education*, 476 U.S. —— (1986), held that the objective of remedying societal discrimination cannot prevent remedial affirmative action from violating the Equal Protection Clause. *See id.* (O'CONNOR, J., concurring in part and concurring in judgment) (White, J., concurring in judgment). While Mr. Johnson does not advance a constitutional claim here, it is most unlikely that Title VII was intended to place a *lesser* restraint on discrimination by public actors than is established by the Constitution. . . . Because, therefore, those justifications (*e.g.*, the remedying of past societal wrongs) that are inadequate to insulate discriminatory action from the racial discrimination prohibitions of the Constitution are also inadequate to insulate it from the racial discrimination prohibitions of Title VII; and because the portions of Title VII at issue here treat race and sex equivalently; *Wygant*, which dealt with race discrimination, is fully applicable precedent, and is squarely inconsistent with today's decision.[4]

4. JUSTICE O'CONNOR's concurrence at least makes an attempt to bring this term into accord with last. Under her reading of Title VII, an employer may discriminate affirmatively, so to speak, if he has a "firm basis" for believing that he might be guilty of (nonaffirmative) discrimination under the Act, and if his action is de-

[T]oday's decision goes well beyond merely allowing racial or sexual discrimination in order to eliminate the effects of prior societal *discrimination*. The majority opinion often uses the phrase "traditionally segregated job category" to describe the evil against which the plan is legitimately (according to the majority) directed. As originally used in *Steelworkers v. Weber*, 443 U.S. 193 (1979), that phrase described skilled jobs from which employers and unions had systematically and intentionally excluded black workers—traditionally segregated jobs, that is, in the sense of conscious, exclusionary discrimination. *See id.* at 197–98. But that is assuredly not the sense in which

signed to remedy that suspected prior discrimination. *Ante*. This is something of a half-way house between leaving employers scot-free to discriminate against disfavored groups, as the majority opinion does, and prohibiting discrimination, as do the words of Title VII. In the present case, although the District Court found that in fact no sex discrimination existed, JUSTICE O'CONNOR would find a "firm basis" for the agency's *belief* that sex discrimination existed in the "inexorable zero"; the complete absence, prior to Diane Joyce, of any women in the Agency's skilled positions. There are two problems with this: First, even positing a "firm basis" for the Agency's belief in prior discrimination, as I have discussed above the plan was patently not *designed to remedy* that prior discrimination, but rather to establish a sexually representative work force. Second, even an absolute zero is not "inexorable." While it may inexorably provide "firm basis" for belief in the mind of an outside observer, it cannot conclusively establish such a belief *on the employer's part*, since he may be aware of the particular reasons that account for the zero. That is quite likely to be the case here, given the nature of the jobs we are talking about, and the list of "*Factors Hindering Goal Attainment*" recited by the Agency plan. *See supra*. The question is in any event one of fact, which, if it were indeed relevant to the outcome, would require a remand to the District Court rather than an affirmance.

the phrase is used here. It is absurd to think that the nationwide failure of road maintenance crews, for example, to achieve the Agency's ambition of 36.4 percent female representation is attributable primarily, if even substantially, to systematic exclusion of women eager to shoulder pick and shovel. It is a "traditionally segregated job category" *not* in the *Weber* sense, but in the sense that, because of longstanding social attitudes, it has not been regarded *by women themselves* as desirable work. Or as the majority opinion puts the point, quoting approvingly the Court of Appeals: "'A plethora of proof is hardly necessary to show that women are generally underrepresented in such positions and that strong social pressures weigh against their participation.'" *Ante*, at n.12 (quoting 748 F.2d 1308, 1313 (9th Cir. 1984). Given this meaning of the phrase, it is patently false to say that "[t]he requirement that the 'manifest imbalance' relate to a 'traditionally segregated job category' provides assurance that sex or race will be taken into account in a manner consistent with Title VII's purpose of eliminating the effects of employment discrimination." *Ante*. There are, of course, those who believe that the social attitudes which cause women themselves to avoid certain jobs and to favor others are as nefarious as conscious, exclusionary discrimination. Whether or not that is so (and there is assuredly no consensus on the point equivalent to our national consensus against intentional discrimination), the two phenomena are certainly distinct. And it is the alteration of social attitudes, rather than the elimination of discrimination, which today's decision approves as justification for state-enforced discrimination. This is an enormous expansion, undertaken without the slightest justification or analysis.

III

. . . [U]ntil today the applicability of *Weber* to public employers remained an open question. . . . *Weber* rested in part on the assertion that the 88th Congress did not wish to intrude too deeply into private employment decisions. *See* 443 U.S., at 206–7. *See also Firefighters v. Cleveland, supra,* at ——. Whatever validity that assertion may have with respect to private employers (and I think it negligible), it has none with respect to public employers or to the 92d Congress that brought them within Title VII. *See* Equal Employment Opportunity Act of 1972, Pub. L. 92–261, § 2, 86 Stat. 103, 42 U.S.C. § 2000e(a). Another reason for limiting *Weber* to private employers is that state agencies, unlike private actors, are subject to the Fourteenth Amendment. As noted earlier, it would be strange to construe Title VII to permit discrimination by public actors that the Constitution forbids.

In truth, however, the language of 42 U.S.C. § 2000e–2 draws no distinction between private and public employers, and the only good reason for creating such a distinction would be to limit the damage of *Weber.* It would be better, in my view, to acknowledge that case as fully applicable precedent, and to use the Fourteenth Amendment ramifications—which *Weber* did not address and which are implicated for the first time here—as the occasion for reconsidering and overruling it. It is well to keep in mind just how thoroughly *Weber* rewrote the statute it purported to construe. The language of that statute, as quoted at the outset of this dissent, is unambiguous: it is an unlawful employment practice "to fail or refuse to hire or to discharge any individual, or otherwise to discriminate against any individual with respect to his compensation, terms, conditions, or privileges of employment, because of such individual's race, color, reli-

gion, sex, or national origin." 42 U.S.C. § 2000e–2(a). *Weber* disregarded the text of the statute, invoking instead its "'spirit,'" 443 U.S., at 201 (quoting *Holy Trinity Church v. United States,* 143 U.S. 457, 459 [1892]), and "practical and equitable [considerations] only partially perceived, if perceived at all, by the 88th Congress," 443 U.S., at 209 (BLACKMUN, J., concurring). It concluded, on the basis of these intangible guides, that Title VII's prohibition of intentional discrimination on the basis of race and sex does not prohibit intentional discrimination on the basis of race and sex, so long as it is "designed to break down old patterns of racial [or sexual] segregation and hierarchy," "does not unnecessarily trammel the interests of the white [or male] employees," "does not require the discharge of white [or male] workers and their replacement with new black [or female] hirees," "does [not] create an absolute bar to the advancement of white [or male] employees," and "is a temporary measure . . . not intended to maintain racial [or sexual] balance, but simply to eliminate a manifest racial [or sexual] imbalance." *Id.* at 208. In effect, *Weber* held that the legality of intentional discrimination by private employers against certain disfavored groups or individuals is to be judged not by Title VII but by a judicially crafted code of conduct, the contours of which are determined by no discernible standard, aside from (as the dissent convincingly demonstrated) the divination of congressional "purposes" belied by the face of the statute and by its legislative history. We have been recasting that self-promulgated code of conduct ever since—and what it has led us to today adds to the reasons for abandoning it.

The majority's response to this criticism of *Weber,* at n.7, asserts that, since "Congress has not amended the statute to reject our construction, . . . we . . . may assume that our interpretation was correct." This assumption, which frequently haunts our opinions, should be put to rest. It is based, to begin with, on the patently false premise that the correctness of statutory construction is to be measured by what the current Congress desires, rather than by what the law as enacted meant. To make matters worse, it assays the current Congress' desires *with respect to the particular provision in isolation,* rather than (the way the provision was originally enacted) as part of a total legislative package containing many *quids pro quo. . . .* But even accepting the flawed premise that the intent of the current Congress, with respect to the provision in isolation, is determinative, one must ignore rudimentary principles of political science to draw any conclusions regarding that intent from the *failure* to enact legislation. The "complicated check on legislation," *The Federalist* No. 62, at 378 (C. Rossiter ed. 1961), erected by our Constitution creates an inertia that makes it impossible to assert with any degree of assurance that congressional failure to act represents (1) approval of the status quo, as opposed to (2) inability to agree upon how to alter the status quo, (3) unawareness of the status quo, (4) indifference to the status quo, or even (5) political cowardice. It is interesting to speculate on how the principle that congressional inaction proves judicial correctness would apply to another issue in the civil rights field, the liability of municipal corporations under § 1983. In 1961, we held that that statute did not reach municipalities. *See Monroe v. Pape,* 365 U.S. 167, 187 (1961). Congress took no action to overturn our decision, but we ourselves did, in *Monell v. New York City Dept. of Social Services,* 436 U.S. 658, 663 (1978). On the majority's logic, *Monell* was wrongly decided, since Congress' seventeen years of silence established that *Monroe* had not "misperceived the political will," and one could therefore, "assume that [*Monroe's*] inter-

pretation was correct." On the other hand, nine years have now gone by since *Monell,* and Congress *again* has not amended § 1983. Should we now "assume that [*Monell's*] interpretation was correct"? Rather, I think we should admit that vindication by congressional inaction is a canard.

JUSTICE STEVENS' concurring opinion emphasizes "the underlying public interest in 'stability and orderly development of the law,'" *ante,* (citation omitted), that often requires adherence to an erroneous decision. As I have described above, however, today's decision is a demonstration not of stability and order but of the instability and unpredictable expansion which the substitution of judicial improvisation for statutory text has produced. For a number of reasons, *stare decisis* ought not to save *Weber.* First, this Court has applied the doctrine of *stare decisis* to civil rights statutes less rigorously than to other laws. . . . Second, as JUSTICE STEVENS acknowledges in his concurrence, *Weber* was itself a dramatic departure from the Court's prior Title VII precedents, and can scarcely be said to be "so consistent with the warp and woof of civil rights law as to be beyond question." *Monell v. New York City Dept. of Social Services, supra,* at 696. Third, *Weber* was decided a mere seven years ago, and has provided little guidance to persons seeking to conform their conduct to the law, beyond the proposition that Title VII does not mean what it says. Finally, "even under the most stringent test for the propriety of overruling a statutory decision . . . —'that it appear beyond doubt . . . that [the decision] misapprehended the meaning of the controlling provision,'" 436 U.S., at 700 (quoting *Monroe v. Pape,* 365 U.S., at 192 [Harlan, J., concurring]), *Weber* should be overruled.

. . .

The majority emphasizes, as though it is meaningful, that "*No* persons are automatically excluded from consideration; *all* are able to have their qualifications weighed against those of other applicants." *Id.* One is reminded of the exchange from Shakespeare's King Henry the Fourth, part I: "GLENDOWER: I can call Spirits from the vasty Deep. HOTSPUR: Why, so can I, or so can any man. But will they come when you do call for them?" Act III, Scene I, lines 53–55. Johnson was indeed entitled to have his qualifications weighed against those of other applicants—but more to the point, he was virtually assured that, after the weighing, if there was any minimally qualified applicant from one of the favored groups, he would be rejected.

Similarly hollow is the Court's assurance that we would strike this plan down if it "failed to take distinctions in qualifications into account," because that "would dictate mere blind hiring by the numbers." *Ante.* For what the Court means by "taking distinctions in qualifications into account" consists of no more than eliminating from the applicant pool those who are not even *minimally qualified* for the job. Once that has been done, once the promoting officer assures himself that all the candidates before him are "M. Q.s" (minimally qualifieds), he can then ignore, as the Agency Director did here, how much better than minimally qualified some of the candidates may be, and can proceed to appoint from the pool solely on the basis of race or sex, until the affirmative action "goals" have been reached. . . .

Today's decision does more, however, than merely reaffirm *Weber,* and more than merely extend it to public actors. It is impossible not to be aware that the practical effect of our holding is to accomplish *de facto* what the law—in language even plainer than that ignored in *Weber,* see 42 U.S.C. § 2000e–2(j)—forbids anyone from accomplishing *de jure:* in many contexts it effectively *requires* employers, public as well as private, to engage in intentional discrimination on the basis of race or sex. This Court's prior interpretations of Title VII, especially the decision in *Griggs v. Duke Power Co.,* 401 U.S. 424 (1971), subject employers to a potential Title VII suit whenever there is a noticeable imbalance in the representation of minorities or women in the employer's work force. Even the employer who is confident of ultimately prevailing in such a suit must contemplate the expense and adverse publicity of a trial, because the extent of the imbalance, and the "job relatedness" of his selection criteria, are questions of fact to be explored through rebuttal and counter-rebuttal of a "prima facie case. . . ." . . . If, however, employers are free to discriminate through affirmative action, without fear of "reverse discrimination" suits by their nonminority or male victims, they are offered a threshold defense against Title VII liability premised on numerical disparities. Thus, after today's decision the *failure* to engage in reverse discrimination is economic folly, and arguably a breach of duty to shareholders or taxpayers, wherever the cost of anticipated Title VII litigation exceeds the cost of hiring less capable (though still minimally capable) workers. (This situation is more likely to obtain, of course, with respect to the least skilled jobs—perversely creating an incentive to discriminate against precisely those members of the nonfavored groups *least* likely to have profited from societal discrimination in the past.) It is predictable, moreover, that this incentive will be greatly magnified by economic pressures brought to bear by government contracting agencies upon employers who refuse to discriminate in the fashion we have now approved. A statute designed to establish a color-blind and gender-blind workplace has thus been converted into a powerful engine of racism and sexism, not merely *permitting* intentional race- and sex-based discrimination, but often making it, through operation of the legal system, practically compelled.

. . . [The] losers in the process are the Johnsons of the country, for whom Title VII has been not merely repealed but actually inverted. The irony is that these individuals—predominantly unknown, unaffluent, unorganized—suffer this injustice at the hands of a Court fond of thinking itself the champion of the politically impotent. I dissent.

CASE QUESTIONS

1. In the majority's depiction of the facts, Diane Joyce and Paul Johnson were about equally qualified for the job. In Justice Scalia's version Johnson was clearly more qualified and lost the job only because he was a male. Which version of the facts was more convincing? Does it matter which version was accurate?

2. The majority argues that Congress's acceptance of the Court's *Weber* reading of Title VII (as permitting voluntary affirmative action) is convincing evidence of Congressional intent. Justice Scalia replies that what Congress intends now is irrelevant; what counts is what the people in Congress wanted when they enacted Title VII 23 years ago. Has Justice Scalia turned the theory of representative democracy on its head? Should Congress be allowed to let the meaning of statutes evolve in order to reflect current (rather than past) moral sentiments?

3. Does the Court's description of Diane Joyce's on-the-job clashes with her supervisors make it appear that she has suffered actual sex discrimination, as distinguished from mere "social pressure"? Should federal law penalize gender-based hiring by private employers who *would* like to engage in affirmative efforts to counteract those social pressures that have limited women's opportunities? What about similar hiring by government employers?

Epilogue

The first edition of this book contained a set of conclusions describing the pattern of Supreme Court alterations in the body of law comprising women's constitutional rights. Some of the patterns there identified still hold; some amendments and refinements would be necessary, were I redescribing the pattern for this edition. But I have decided to abjure that kind of conclusory summary, for the reader by this point can identify the patterns discernible to her or him, and the pattern is likely to continue shifting over the next several years.

Instead, I simply add that I was struck, during my rethinking of the material for this volume, by the profound degree to which the Supreme Court has been influenced by the activities of other national level governmental actors. (It may be that this amenability to influence from the other branches is an especially distinctive trait of the Burger Court, which court brought about the twentieth-century revolution in women's constitutional rights.) This is observable not only in the very obvious cases, as when the Supreme Court follows EEOC guidelines on sexual harassment or Department of Education interpretations of Title IX, or goes along with Congress's desire to refrain from funding abortions, or obeys Congress's mandate in the Pregnancy Discrimination Act. It is also observable in the more subtle interplay between constitutional politics at the legislative level and Court readings of the Constitution in its case decisions.

The Court's profound and seemingly abrupt shift in treatment of the equal protection clause in *Reed v. Reed* is rendered much more understandable if one pays attention to the twenty to one margin of victory for the ERA in the House of Representatives preceding the *Reed* decision and to the Congressional discussions of the ERA that castigated the Court for not making that shift earlier. Similarly, the Court's peculiar view that pregnancy discrimination did not amount to sex discrimination is rendered less peculiar when one reads the remarks of prominent ERA proponents who espoused rather similar views long before *Geduldig* and *Gilbert* were handed down.

None of these observations is intended to denigrate the important and independent contribution that the Supreme Court has made to the constitutional law of women's rights. These remarks do suggest, however, that a fuller understanding of these rights would require attention also to the other functioning parts of the American political system.

Notes

**Timetable of
Women's Rights Cases**

Appendices

Case Index

Notes

Chapter 1. Ancient History

1. A very few limits were placed on state governments. In regard to citizen rights, states are forbidden from passing "bills of attainder" (laws that label named individuals as criminals, regardless of whether they have committed any illegal acts), "ex post facto" laws (statutes that declare punishments for past actions which, at the time they were committed, were legal), and laws "impairing the obligation of contracts" (e.g., a law saying that particular debts would not have to be paid, thereby depriving the lender of his property right). (*See* U.S. Const. art. I, § 10.) The states had to provide a "republican form of government" (art. IV, § 4) and to refrain from granting titles of nobility (art. I, § 10). States were ordered to give cognizance to property rights recognized by other states (art. IV, § 1), including the property right in runaway "persons held to service or labor" (art. IV, § 2). Finally, states had to grant "all privileges and immunities of citizens in the several states" to the citizens of each state. This confusingly worded clause (art. IV, § 2) simply meant that states were not allowed to discriminate against out-of-staters in basic legal rights, such as access to the courts, the rights to buy and sell, the right to be hired for a job.

2. 4 Washington's Circuit Court 380, cited in *Slaughter-House Cases*, 16 Wall. 36, 117.

3. 16 Wall., at 78.

4. *See Swayne* dissent, 16 Wall., at 127.

5. 16 Wall., at 81.

6. A classic analysis of the Fourteenth Amendment suggests that this is due to the "primacy of the American concern with liberty over equality." Joseph Tussman and Jacobus ten Broek, "The Equal Protection of the Laws," 37 *California Law Review* 341 (1949). The tremendous upsurge in equal protection litigation in the post-World War II era (desegregation, state legislative reapportionment, welfare rights, illegitimate children's rights, prisoners' rights, in addition to the subject of this book) probably indicates that equality, as against liberty, has taken on increased importance in American political ideology.

7. *Yick Wo v. Hopkins*, 118 U.S. 365 (1886).

8. *Truax v. Raich*, 235 U.S. 33. A later case supporting the same principle was *Takahashi v. Fish and Game Commission*, 334 U.S. 410. The present Justice Rehnquist still disagrees with this development, despite its firmly implanted roots. He would limit the condemned classification doctrine to racial classifications. See his dissent in *Sugarman v. Dougall*, 413 U.S. 634 (1973).

9. *Heath and Milligan v. Worst*, 207 U.S. 338, 354 (1907). (Emphasis added.) The interior quote is from *Mobile County v. Kimball*, 102 U.S. 691. Significantly, that case was upholding a law passed before the Fourteenth Amendment had been adopted.

10. *See Chicago, Milwaukee and St. Paul Railway v. Minnesota*, 134 U.S. 418 (1980);

Allgeyer v. Louisiana, 165 U.S. 578 (1897); *Smyth v. Ames,* 169 U.S. 466 (1898).

11. The Supreme Court did hear arguments on Oregon's minimum-wage law for women in 1916 (*Settler v. O'Hara,* 243 U.S. 629) but the vote on that case was a 4–4 tie, creating no precedent.

12. *Morehead v. New York ex rel Tipaldo,* 298 U.S. 587. An attorney for the National Consumers League, Dorothy Kenyon, submitted an *amicus curiae* brief endorsing the constitutionality of New York's women-only minimum wage law. The same attorney

in 1961 presented the Supreme Court case against Florida's women-only automatic jury exemption (*see Hoyt v. Florida,* chapter 2). Ms. Kenyon also presented an *amicus curiae* brief in the 1971 *Phillips v. Martin-Marietta* employment discrimination case (see chapter 2). For the latter two cases, Ms. Kenyon was in the employ of the American Civil Liberties Union.

13. Kai Bird and Max Holland, "The Garland Case," *The Nation* July 5–12, 1986, at 8.

14. *New York Times,* Feb. 3, 1987, at A18, col. 4.

Chapter 2. The Equal Protection Clause and Gender Discrimination

1. 16 Wall. 130.

2. Edward James, *Notable American Women, 1607–1950* 3 vols. 1:223–25, 2:492–93 (Cambridge, Mass.: Belknap Press, 1971).

3. See discussion of *Slaughter-House Cases* in chapter 1.

4. As explained in the chapter 1 discussion of *Slaughter-House Cases,* Miller's interpretation of the Privileges or Immunities Clause turned it into mere repetition of principles already embodied in the Constitution. Even before the adoption of the Fourteenth Amendment, no state would have been permitted to interfere with rules of the federal courts. This is because of the Supremacy Clause, Article VI, § 2.

5. 16 Wall. 36, 109–10.

6. 16 Wall. 36, 122.

7. David Morgan, *Suffragists and Democrats: The Politics of Women's Suffrage in America* 18, (East Lansing: Michigan State University Press, 1972).

8. Until 1869 it was known as the Equal Rights Society. In 1869 it split into the National Women's Suffrage Association and the American Woman's Suffrage Association. These groups reunited in 1890 as the National American Woman's Suffrage Association. *Id.* 16–17, 21.

9. Albert McKinley, *The Suffrage Franchise in the Thirteen English Colonies in America* 53–54, and notes therein (Philadelphia: University of Pennsylvania, 1905).

10. *Id.* at 434 and n.1.

11. *Id.* at 192–93. Generally, the town meeting would nominate and the colony director would make the final choice of magistrates. Often, however, the nomination process became the election—in Lady Moody's town, that was said to be the case.

12. Abigail Adams on March 31, 1776, wrote to her husband, John: "and by the way in the new code of laws which I suppose it will be necessary for you to make, I desire you to remember the ladies, and be more generous and favorable to them than your ancestors. Do not put such unlimited power into the hands of the husbands. Remember all men would be tyrants if they could. If particular care and attention is not paid to the ladies, we are determined to foment a rebellion, and will not hold ourselves bound by any laws in which we have no voice or representation." Reprinted in several books; *See, e.g.,* Miriam Schneir, ed., *Feminism: The Essential Historical Writings* 3 (New York: Vintage, 1972).

13. Historical material in this paragraph

and the two following paragraphs comes from Elizabeth Cady Stanton, Susan B. Anthony, and Matilda Joslyn Gage, *History of Woman Suffrage*. 6 vols. 1:447–55 (New York: Fowler & Wells, 1881–1922) (hereinafter Stanton).

14. Susan B. Anthony and Ida Husted Harper, *History of Woman Suffrage* 5 vols. 4:674 (Rochester: Susan B. Anthony, 1902).

15. Stanton, *Woman Suffrage* 1:189–94.

16. Anthony and Harper, *Woman Suffrage* 4:465–1011. By 1890 women had school suffrage in fourteen states and territories.

17. Morgan, *Suffragists and Democrats* 17; *see also* Alan P. Grimes, *The Puritan Ethic and Women Suffrage* (New York: Oxford University Press, 1967). But compare Eleanor Flexner, *Century of Struggle* 159–62, 178 (New York: Atheneum, 1970) for the argument that in Wyoming, at least, women's rights ideology was a major factor in the suffrage victory.

18. Flexner, *Century of Struggle* 165.

19. Anne R. Scott and Andrew M. Scott, *One Half the People: The Fight for Woman Suffrage* 19–20 (Philadelphia: J. B. Lippincott, 1975).

20. The year 1875 did see the eventual attainment of women's school suffrage in Minnesota. Anthony and Harper, *Woman Suffrage* 4:777–79.

21. Scott and Scott, *One Half the People* 20. A women's suffrage amendment with different wording had been introduced unsuccessfully as early as 1868. Flexner, *Century of Struggle* 173.

22. Flexner, *Century of Struggle* 173–75, 220–22.

23. Carrie Chapman Catt and Nettie Rogers Shirler, *Women Suffrage and Politics* 107 (New York: Charles Scribner's Sons, 1923). The description is Ms. Catt's.

24. Flexner, *Century of Struggle* 291. The Flexner book contains the fullest account of the suffragist effort that can be found in a single volume. The five-volume *History of Women Suffrage* by Anthony and Harper is more complete but not as well organized.

25. Flexner, *Century of Struggle* 248–57.

26. *Id.* at 254–68.

27. *Id.* at 264.

28. *Id.* at 265.

29. *Id.* at 272–73.

30. *Id.* at 269.

31. *Id.* at 279.

32. Doris Stevens, *Jailed for Freedom* 102 (New York: Boni & Liveright, 1920).

33. Flexner, *Century of Struggle* 285.

34. *Id.* at 286.

35. *Id.* at 290.

36. *Id.* at 291–92.

37. V. O. Key, *Politics, Parties, and Pressure Groups* 616 (5th ed., New York: Thomas Y. Crowell, 1964).

38. Flexner, *Century of Struggle,* 312–14.

39. The southern states were pressured into ratifying the Fourteenth Amendment by a set of congressional requirements that, for the decision-making process, enfranchised blacks and disfranchised participants in the rebellion, and that also made ratification a precondition for regaining representation in Congress. For further details, see A. Kelly and W. Harbison, *The American Constitution* 465–73 (4th ed., New York: W. W. Norton, 1970).

40. *Strauder v. Virginia,* 100 U.S. 303.

41. *Yick Wo v. Hopkins,* 118 U.S. 356 (1886).

42. *Truax v. Raich,* 239 U.S. 33 (1915). Although the law involved here (as well as various later ones that discriminated against aliens) was declared unconstitutional, the equal protection clause does allow some "discrimination" against aliens, e.g., the limitation of suffrage rights to American citizens. For the explanation of what is considered good enough "reason" to deprive aliens of certain privileges, see the following text.

43. See the two preceding notes. The former involved Chinese persons trying to get

licenses in San Francisco to operate laundries. The latter involved a law that applied to all nonnaturalizable aliens in a community where the only such people were Chinese.

44. *See, e.g., Edwards v. California,* 314 U.S. 160 (1941). This case, while not based explicitly on equal protection, clearly expanded the constitutional rights of "paupers."

45. *See Griffin v. Illinois,* 351 U.S. 12 (1956); *Douglas v. California,* 372 U.S. 353 (1963); *Roberts v. LaVallee,* 389 U.S. 40 (1967); *Harper v. Board of Elections,* 383 U.S. 663 (1966); *Williams v. Illinois,* 399 U.S. 235 (1970); *Boddie v. Connecticut,* 401 U.S. 371 (1971); *James v. Strange,* 407 U.S. 128 (1972). *But contrast James v. Valtierra,* 402 U.S. 137 (1971); and *San Antonio Independent School District v. Rodriguez,* 411 U.S. 1 (1973).

46. *McDonald v. Board of Election Commissioners,* 349 U.S. 802, 807.

47. For a discussion of this problem, see Michelman, "Foreword: On Protecting the Poor through the Fourteenth Amendment," 83 *Harvard Law Review* 7 (1969).

48. Illegitimates as a group have met with mixed success in asserting claims that illegitimacy should be a suspect classification. *See Levy v. Louisiana,* 391 U.S. 68 (1968); *Labine v. Vincent,* 401 U.S. 532 (1971); and *Weber v. Aetna,* 406 U.S. 164 (1972).

49. 411 U.S. 677.

50. 379 US. 184 (1964).

51. *Loving v. Virginia,* 388 U.S. 1 (1967).

52. *Korematsu v. United States,* 323 U.S. 214 (1944). Three unusually bitter dissents were recorded for that case and the majority opinion upholding the incarceration remains controversial to this day.

53. *North Carolina Board of Education v. Swann,* 402 U.S. 43.

54. *Id.* The Court also noted in passing in *Swann v. Charlotte-Mecklenburg,* 402 U.S. 1 (1971), the decision that unanimously upheld court-ordered busing, that if a school board, on its own, wished to use race-conscious busing to promote integration in a non-remedial context (i.e., where there had been no previous constitutional violation) the school board was permitted to do so. The Court did not detail there the nature of the "overriding interest" being served.

55. The ERA was "proposed" by two-thirds of both houses of Congress on March 22, 1972. It had seven years from that date to gain ratification before needing to be re-proposed. On October 6, 1978, Congress, by majority vote, extended the ratification deadline to June 30, 1982. By that deadline the proposed amendment had attained ratification in only 35 of the needed 38 states (70 percent instead of 75 percent). Since that time ERA politics have become entangled in anti-abortion politics, and the amendment remains stalled in Congress.

56. *Yick Wo v. Hopkins,* 118 U.S. 356, 369 (1886).

57. *Barbier v. Connolly,* 113 U.S. 27, 31.

58. *Lindsley v. Natural Carbonic Gas,* 220 U.S. 61, 78.

59. *Royster Guano v. Virginia,* 253 U.S. 412, 415.

60. *Heath and Milligan v. Worst,* 207 U.S. 338, 354 (1907). See chapter 1, note 9.

61. The terms strict scrutiny or rigid scrutiny, and ordinary or minimum scrutiny are also used in discussions of the due process clause. For explanation see chapter 4.

62. *See,* for example, Judith Baer, *The Chains of Protection* (Westport, Conn: Greenwood Press, 1977).

63. Chinese-American, that is, in the sense that he was a permanent resident of America and was of Chinese descent. No person born in China was permitted to become a naturalized American citizen until 1943, when China was our wartime ally. Persons born in India, the Philippines, and Japan were barred from citizenship until

even later. See *Takahashi v. Fish and Game Committee*, 334 U.S. 410 (1948), for a discussion of these developments.

64. *Harper v. Board of Elections*, 383 U.S. 663.

65. 335 U.S. 464. *Radice v. New York* (1924) in chapter 1 presented an additional example of the Court's kidglove treatment of the equal protection clause in this period. While the Court took the due process argument seriously there, its response to the equal protection argument was relatively cavalier: The legislature may proceed "step by step"; "it is not necessary that the prohibition . . . be all-embracing [i.e., cover everyone equally]." This is standard logic under ordinary equal protection scrutiny.

66. 74 F. Supp. 735, 739.

67. *McDonald v. Board of Elections*, 394 U.S. 802, 809.

68. *Id.; see also Edwards v. California*, 314 U.S. 160 (1941); *Griffin v. Illinois*, 351 U.S. 12 (1956); *Douglas v. California*, 372 U.S. 353 (1963); *Lane v. Brown*, 372 U.S. 477 (1963); *Long v. District Court*, 385 U.S. 192 (1966); *Robert v. La Vallee*, 389 U.S. 40 (1967); *Harper v. Board of Elections*, 383 U.S. 663 (1966). But for a clarification, or narrowing, of this principle, see *San Antonio Independent School District v. Rodriguez*, 411 U.S. 1 (1973).

69. *Skinner v. Oklahoma*, 316 U.S. 535.

70. For post-Skinner developments concerning procreation, see chapter 4.

71. *Reynolds v. Sims*, 377 U.S. 533 (1964); *Carrington v. Rash*, 380 U.S. 89 (1965); *Harper v. Board of Elections*, 383 U.S. 663 (1966); *Kramer v. Union Free School District*, 395 U.S. 621 (1969).

72. *Shapiro v. Thompson*, 394 U.S. 618 (1969). This case too, had roots in *Edwards v. California*; see chapter 2, note 68.

73. *Levy v. Louisiana*, 391 U.S. 68 (1968); *Glona v. American Guarantee and Liability Insurance*, 391 U.S. 73 (1968).

74. The term "rationality with bite" comes from Gerald Gunther, *American Constitu-*

tional Law 758 (9th ed., Mineola, N.Y.: Foundation Press, 1975).

75. 429 U.S. 190.

76. This organization submitted an *amicus curiae* brief, arguing the women's rights position, in the 1971 case of *Reed v. Reed*. Presenting this brief at the Supreme Court was Senator Birch Bayh.

77. Jo Freeman, *The Politics of Women's Liberation* (New York: David McKay, 1975), gives an account of these two developments.

78. *Rutgers Law Review* (1970), *Harvard Civil Rights-Civil Liberties Law Review* (1971), *Women's Law Journal* (1971), *Valparaiso Law Review* (1971), *New York Law Forum* (1971), and *Journal of Family Law* (1971).

79. *Sail'er Inn v. Kirby*, 485 P.2d. 529.

80. For a detailed look at Congressional ERA politics, see Gilbert Steiner, *Constitutional Inequality* (Washington, D.C.: The Brookings Institution, 1985).

81. *Bolling v. Sharpe*, 347 U.S. 497 (1954).

82. 37 U.S.C. § 401(1); 10 U.S.C. § 1072(A).

83. *Equal Rights for Men and Women, 1972,* Senate Report No. 689, 92d Cong., 2d Sess. 12, 16, 20 (1972); *Equal Rights for Men and Women, 1971,* House of Representatives Report No. 359, 92d Cong., 1st Sess. 7 (1971); *Equal Rights, 1970: Hearings Before the Senate Committee on the Judiciary*, 91st Cong., 2d Sess. 183, 299, 303 (1970); Barbara Brown, Thomas Emerson, Gail Falk, and Ann Freedman, "The Equal Rights Amendment: A Constitutional Basis for Equal Rights for Women," 80 *Yale Law Journal*, 871, at 893–94 (hereinafter Brown).

84. Brown, 904–5.

85. In the latter case, they had filed briefs only as *amicus curiae* representing the American Civil Liberties Union.

86. The Louisiana legislature actually ended this practice two weeks before the Supreme Court handed down its decision. The Supreme Court went ahead because the legislative change did not affect people already in prison, like Taylor. And, of course,

the Court decision affects any state that might in the future consider re-instituting the practice.

87. *Alexander v. Louisiana*, 405 U.S. 625, 633 (1972). Only Justice Douglas reached the issue, 405 U.S., at 639–41.

88. In February 1975 and in January 1977 the pro-ERA forces obtained ratification in the thirty-fourth and thirty-fifth states, respectively.

89. 407 U.S. 493.

90. Justice White wrote the opinion, and Justices Powell and Brennan concurred.

91. The justice to decide who writes the Court opinion is the most senior member of the majority. In this case that justice was Douglas and he assigned the opinion to Marshall. After Marshall wrote it, evidently, Powell, White, and Brennan decided that they could not go along with its reasoning, and so White then wrote the second three-judge opinion.

92. 407 U.S., at 500.

93. 407 U.S., at 501–2.

94. 407 U.S., at 503.

95. 391 U.S. 145.

96. 329 U.S. 187 (1946).

97. The development of the fundamental rights/strict scrutiny doctrine is explained under "Sex as a Semi-Suspect Classification."

98. The quote is from Justice Bradley's concurring opinion in *Bradwell v. Illinois* (1873).

99. Justice Brennan had used this kind of argument in his *Frontiero* opinion, but at that time he spoke for only four justices. See his note 23 in that case.

100. The reader will recall, however, that they did not achieve victory in *Kahn v. Shevin*.

101. Justice Rehnquist concurred only in the result.

102. He does, however, employ the overriding or compelling interest test in terms of the father's constitutional right to the companionship and care of his children. In other words, he uses it on the grounds of a fundamental right rather than suspect classification.

103. This is a very time-honored equal protection rule, but in the traditional formulation, the phrase is "persons similarly situated" rather than "men and women similarly situated."

104. Between June and September 1972, the amount was somewhat less: about $200.

Chapter 3. Gender and "More Rigid Scrutiny"

1. Janet Boles, *The Politics of the Equal Rights Amendment* 63–64 (New York: Longman, 1979).

2. Also on the Ginzburg-Wulf team were attorneys Kathleen Willert Peratis and Nadine Taub. *Califano v. Goldfarb* constituted this team's fourth major Supreme Court victory against sex discrimination and their second victory specifically against sex discrimination in the Social Security code. Their only "loss" by the end of the 1976–1977 term was *Kahn v. Shevin*.

3. Ruth Bader Ginzburg, "Women, Equality, and the *Bakke* Case," The Civil Liberties Review, Nov.–Dec. 1977, 8–16, at 13.

4. 446 U.S. 142.

5. *Califano v. Westcott*, 443 U.S. 76. The court was divided, however, on whether to eliminate the benefits, or to extend them to both groups. The latter course prevailed on a 5–4 vote.

6. The third (and eldest) had been taken from the Stanleys at an earlier date on grounds of neglect. At that time the family

court had believed erroneously that the Stanleys were married.

7. *Pierce v. Society of Sister,* 268 U.S. 510 (1925), and *Meyer v. Nebraska,* 262 U.S. 390 (1923). The "fundamental rights" phrase is from Meyer.

8. *Pierce v. Society of Sisters.*

9. *Meyer v. Nebraska.*

10. *Skinner v. Oklahoma,* 316 U.S. 535 (1942). See chapter 4.

11. 316 U.S., at 541.

12. *Griswold v. Connecticut,* 381 U.S. 479. See chapter 4.

13. *Eisenstadt v. Baird,* 405 U.S. 438. See chapter 4.

14. 405 U.S., at 453.

15. Although the *Eisenstadt* decision was handed down almost two weeks before the *Stanley* decision, oral arguments in *Stanley* predated the oral arguments in *Eisenstadt.* Thus, Stanley's lawyers could not possibly have made reference to the *Eisenstadt* precedent, but they did have *Griswold* and its predecessors on the record. The early drafts of the Supreme Court opinion in *Stanley* evidently predated the *Eisenstadt* decision, for *Griswold* is cited in *Stanley* but *Eisenstadt* is not.

16. The Supreme Court relegates *Reed v. Reed* to a footnote in the *Stanley* decision, but the two cases seem to be pieces of a single pattern of increasing Supreme Court hostility to gender-based discrimination.

17. *Planned Parenthood v. Danforth,* 428 U.S. 52 (1976). See chapter 4.

18. *See,* for example, *United States v. Curtiss-Wright Export,* 299 U.S. 304 (1936).

19. The most extreme example of this tendency was probably *Korematsu v. United States,* 323 U.S. 214 (1944), in which the mass incarceration of more than 100,000 Japanese-Americans during wartime was held to be not unconstitutional.

20. In a classic interpretation of the freedom of speech guarantee, for example, Justice Oliver Wendell Holmes said: "When a

nation is at war many things that might be said in time of peace are such a hindrance to its effort that their utterance will not be endured so long as men fight, and that no court could regard them as protected by any constitutional right." (*Schenck v. United States,* 249 U.S. 47 [1919].)

21. 430 U.S. 787 (1977).

22. These precedents began in 1968 with the case of *Levy v. Louisiana,* 391 U.S. 68; they are listed in Justice Marshall's dissent.

23. The quote is from *Marshall v. Diaz,* 426 U.S. 67, at 80 (1976).

24. 434 U.S. 246 (1978).

25. 441 U.S. 380 (1979).

26. 463 U.S. 248 (1983).

27. 441 U.S. 347.

28. 463 U.S. 248 (1983).

29. An excellent survey of these is provided in Leo Kanowitz, *Women and the Law* (Albuquerque: University of New Mexico Press, 1969).

30. *Forbush v. Wallace,* 405 U.S. 970.

31. 440 U.S. 268.

32. 450 U.S. 455.

33. For a review of these cases, see Gayle Binion, "'Intent' and Equal Protection: A Reconsideration," *Supreme Court Review* 397–457 (1983).

34. 326 U.S. 229.

35. 442 U.S. 256.

36. For a discussion of its divisiveness, see Jane Mansbridge, "Who's in Charge Here? Decision by Accretion and Gate-Keeping in the Struggle for the ERA," 13 *Politics and Society* 343–82 (1984).

37. For a review of the evidence, see Leslie F. Goldstein, "The ERA and the U.S. Supreme Court," 1 *Research in Law and Policy Studies* 145 (1987).

38. See discussion under "Father's Rights".

39. 453 U.S. 57.

40. *Coker v. Georgia,* 433 U.S. 584 (1977).

41. 347 U.S. 483.

42. Although the official legality of racial

segregation ended in 1954, it took more than ten years before schools designated officially as "white" or "colored" were eliminated in southern states. Most of this elimination took place in the late 1960s after the federal government, under President Johnson, threatened to withdraw funds from any school district refusing to desegregate.

43. *Sweatt v. Painter*, 339 U.S. 629 (1950).
44. *McLaurin v. Oklahoma*, 339 U.S. 637 (1950).
45. 409 U.S. 951.
46. The case reviewed was *Vorchheimer v. School District of Philadelphia*, 532 F.2d 880 (1975), affirmed by an equally divided court, 430 U.S. 703 (1977).

Chapter 4. Women, Procreation, and the Right of Privacy

1. This earliest "strict scrutiny" test was formulated by the Court majority as follows: "The mere asserton that the [law's] subject relates though but in a remote degree to the public health does not necessarily render the enactment valid. The act must have a *more direct relation, as a means to an end,* and the end itself must be appropriate and legitimate, before an act can be held to be valid which interferes with the general right of an individual to be free . . . in his power to contract in relation to his own labor. (*Lochner v. New York*, 198 U.S. 45 [1905]. (Emphasis added.) (See chapter 1.)

2. *Lochner*; see chapter 1.

3. See note 1 for the *Lochner* majority's statement of the level of scrutiny to be applied to infringements on the "right of contract." By contrast, three of the *Lochner* dissenters explained the rule of ordinary due process scrutiny as follows: "[If] the question [of the public welfare value of a statute] is one about which there is room for debate and for an honest difference of opinion . . . that ought to be the end of the case, for the State is not amenable to the judiciary, in respect of its legislative enactments, unless such enactments are plainly, palpably, beyond all question, inconsistent with the Constitution. . . ."

4. 262 U.S. 390.

5. 268 U.S. 510.

6. Not even Holmes dissented, even though he had dissented in the 1923 *Meyer* case, and even though only twenty years earlier, in *Lochner*, he had asserted: "I think the Fourteenth Amendment is perverted when it is held to prevent the natural outcome of a dominant opinion, unless it can be said that a rational and fair man necessarily would admit that the statute proposed would infringe fundamental principles as they have been understood by the traditions of our people and our law." This suggests that in 1925 Holmes was willing to imply that the majority of the Oregon legislature consisted of irrational and/or unfair people.

7. *Gitlow v. New York*, 268 U.S. 652 (1925).

8. *Near v. Minnesota*, 283 U.S. 697 (1931).

9. *DeJonge v. Oregon*, 299 U.S. 353 (1937).

10. *Meyer v. Nebraska*; see chapter 4, note 4 and accompanying text.

11. *Cantwell v. Connecticut*, 310 U.S. 296 (1940). Interestingly, in adding freedom from the establishment of religion to the other First Amendment freedoms protected by the Fourteenth Amendment, the Supreme Court cites only one precedent (*Schneider v. State*, 308 U.S. 147), one which nowhere mentions that particular freedom.

12. *West Coast Hotel v. Parrish*, 300 U.S. 379 (1937).

13. This is a summary of note 4 of *United*

States v. Carolene Products, 304 U.S. 144 (1938), known as the "Carolene Products footnote."

14. Even when it did become clear in 1965 that they were live precedents, Justice Black dissented vehemently, insisting that the substantive due process reasoning which undergirded the *Meyer* and *Pierce* cases had been "repudiated" by "many later opinions."

15. *Reynolds v. Sims*, 377 U.S. 533 (1964), asserted for the first time that the right to vote is "constitutionally protected," that it is "one of the basic civil rights of man," and that it "is . . . fundamental . . . in a free and democratic society." The right in question involved general suffrage in state legislative elections, a matter which the Constitution implicitly (art. I, § 2) left to state discretion. Of course, the Fifteenth, Nineteenth, and (later) the Twenty-sixth Amendments do protect the right to vote for certain groups (blacks, women, and eighteen-to-twenty-year olds), but no part of the Constitution explicitly addresses general suffrage rights in state elections. The Supreme Court in 1964 asserted that the equal protection clause implicitly does protect such a right.

16. *NAACP v. Alabama*, 357 U.S. 449 (1959). The right of political association is all but spelled out in the Constitution's protection of the "right of the people peaceably to assemble and petition the government for redress of grievance" (First Amendment).

17. *Crandall v. Nevada*, 6 Wall. 35.

18. Article I, § 8, cl. 3. Its explicit message is that "Congress shall have the power . . . to regulate commerce with foreign nations and among the states."

19. The first of these rules dates back at least to 1824. *Gibbons v. Ogden*, 9 Wheat 1. This reasoning formed the basis of the concurring opinions of Justice Clifford and Chief Justice Chase in *Crandall*. The latter

rationale was the basis of the Court opinion in *Crandall*, authored by Justice Miller.

20. *Edwards v. California*, 314 U.S. 160 (1941).

21. *Kent v. Dulles*, 357 U.S. 116.

22. *Aptheker v. Secretary of State*, 378 U.S. 500.

23. *Id.* at 517. Justice Douglas in a lone concurring opinion wrote at some length on why the freedom to travel was important in a free society. But he also had only a brief comment on the constitutional basis of the right: "Freedom of movement is kin to the rights of assembly and the right of free association. These rights may not be abridged." *Id.* at 520.

24. Stephen Gould, "Carrie Buck's Daughter," 2 *Constitutional Commentary* 331, at 336–37 (1985).

25. In fact, legislative requirements mandating just this sort of equality of penalty in first degree murder cases were declared unconstitutional by the Supreme Court in 1976. *Woodson v. North Carolina*, 428 U.S. 280 and *Roberts v. Louisiana*, 428 U.S. 325.

26. Justice Holmes, author of the *Buck v. Bell* Court opinion, had written the dissenting opinion (for a group of four justices) in *Meyer v. Nebraska*.

27. But see chapter 4, note 14.

28. *Poe v. Ullman*, 367 U.S. 497 (1961); *Tileston v. Ullman*, 318 U.S. 44 (1943).

29. In *Poe* the Court claimed that there was not yet a "controversy" (as required in art. III) because no one had been arrested under the statute; and to expect that this outdated law would ever be enforced taxed the judicial credibility. Griswold later provoked enforcement by opening up a public birth-control clinic.

In *Tileston* the Supreme Court said that Dr. Tileston (a physician) did not have standing (see discussion of *Taylor v. Louisiana* in chapter 2) to claim that his patients' lives were being threatened by the statute in violation of "due process of law." Only his patients, said the Court, could raise that claim.

30. The Bill of Rights applies only to the federal government. But in the post-World War II period, the Supreme Court has held that most of those commands are implied in the Fourteenth Amendment's requirement that states observe "due process of law." For example, "due process of law" at the state level now includes the right to a lawyer, the right to trial by jury, the right against unreasonable searches, and the right against compulsory self-incrimination. It did not include any of these before the 1940s.

31. Justice Douglas, like Justice Black, was an FDR appointee. The term "incorporation" refers to the idea that the phrase "due process" in the Fourteenth Amendment "incorporates" the restraints of the Bill of Rights and applies them to state governments.

32. See his explanation in *Roe v. Wade.*

33. On the day after the abortion decision, January 23, 1973, the *New York Times* reported that the number of women intending to terminate their pregnancies at the time was estimated at 1.6 million.

34. Michaels was from a small town in a rural section of the state. He explained in interviews that conversations with his teen-aged children had caused him to change his mind on the issue. As he had predicted, he was defeated in the next election.

This information comes from the *New York Times*, Apr. 10, 20, 23, 27; May 4; June 5, 24, 1972.

35. *New York Times*, Apr. 16, 1972.

36. *United States v. Vuitch*, 402 U.S. 62.

37. Thus, it is not sheer accident that in March 1972, in handing down the *Eisenstadt* decision, the Court spoke in terms not of contraception but of the choice "whether to bear or beget a child." The Court had just been listening to arguments to the effect that the right of privacy extended to such a choice.

38. 428 U.S. 132. Because this case returned to the Court with the same title later, this version of it is referred to as *Bellotti I.*

39. 450 U.S. 398.

40. 439 U.S. 379.

41. 462 U.S. 416.

42. 428 U.S. 106.

43. This principle stems from the supremacy clause found in Article VI of the Constitution.

44. 52 U.S.C. § 1396(a)(17).

45. 42 U.S.C. § 1396.

46. 532 F.2d 611.

47. Two other circuit courts of appeals had interpreted Title XIX as permitting the denial of abortion funds. *Roe v. Norton*, 522 F.2d 988, and *Roe v. Ferguson*, 515 F.2d 297. And one other circuit court of appeals had interpreted Title XIX as forbidding that denial. The Supreme Court is obligated, other conditions being equal, to settle those cases where disagreements have arisen between two different federal courts of appeal.

48. All that this Connecticut statute noted about the phrase "medically necessary" is that it included psychiatric necessity and that it should be determined by the attending physician.

49. *Doe v. Rose*, 499 F.2d 1112; *Wulff v. Singleton*, 508 F.2d 211; *Doe v. Westby*, 383 F. Supp. 1143 and 402 F. Supp. 140; *Doe v. Wohlgemuth*, 376 F. Supp. 173 (this case became *Beal v. Doe*); *Doe v. Rampton*, 366 F. Supp. 189; and *Klein v. Nassau County Medical Center*, 347 F. Supp. 496 and 409 F. Supp. 731.

50. *Edwards v. California*, 314 U.S. 160 (1941).

51. *Griffin v. Illinois*, 351 U.S. 12 (1956); *Burns v. Ohio*, 360 U.S. 252 (1959); *Smith v. Bennett*, 365 U.S. 708 (1961); *Long v. District*

Court, 385 U.S. 192 (1966); *Roberts v. La-Vallee*, 389 U.S. 40 (1967); *Mayer v. Chicago*, 404 U.S. 189 (1971).

52. *Gideon v. Wainwright*, 372 U.S. 335 (1963); *Douglas v. California*, 372 U.S. 353 (1963); *Argersinger v. Hamlin*, 407 U.S. 25 (1972).

53. *Harper v. Board of Elections*, 383 U.S. 663 (1966).

54. *Turner v. Fouche*, 396 U.S. 246 (1969).

55. *Boddie v. Connecticut*, 401 U.S. 371 (1971).

56. *Harper v. Board of Elections*, 383 U.S. 663 (1966).

57. *United States v. Kras*, 409 U.S. 434 (1973).

58. *LaFleur v. Cleveland Board of Education*, 466 F.2d 1184; and *Cohen v. Chesterfield County Bd. of Education*, 326 F. Supp. 1159.

59. 326 F. Supp. 128.

60. 465 F.2d 1184.

61. 326 F. Supp. 1159.

62. 474 F.2d 395.

63. 414 U.S. 633.

64. In the 1977 abortion funding decisions, the Court did acknowledge the centrality of the fundamental right of privacy. But it then concluded that a state's decision to refuse to fund abortions through Medicaid does not "impinge on the fundamental right recognized in *Roe*," and it bluntly denied that such a law "penalizes the exercise of that right." *Maher*.

65. 417 U.S. 484.

66. 359 F. Supp. 792.

67. 375 F. Supp. 367.

68. *Communications Workers of America v. AT&T*, 513 F.2d 1024; *Wetzel v. Liberty Mutual Ins.*, 511 F.2d 199; *Gilbert v. G.E.*, 519 F.2d 661; *Tyler v. Vickery*, 517 F.2d 1089; *Satty v. Nashville Gas*, 522 F.2d 850; *Hutchison v. Lake Oswego School District*, 519 F.2d 961.

69. Joyce Gelb and Marian Palley, *Women and Public Policies*, Ch. 7 (2d ed., Princeton: Princeton University Press, 1986).

Chapter 5. Congressional Enforcement of Equal Protection

1. The statutes discussed in this section may appear, at first impression, to have been passed as part of Congress' job of regulating "commerce among the states" (art. I, § 8, cl. 3) rather than as part of its job of enforcing "equal protection of the laws." One reason for this impression is that "equal protection" is an obligation laid upon state governments, whereas the laws dealt with in this section apply to private employers, private universities, etc. Despite that impression, however, regulations imposed upon private individuals are not entirely unrelated to the equal protection clause. The Supreme Court recognized this in the case of *United States v. Guest*, 383 U.S. 745 (1966). Laws regulating private individuals can indirectly promote equal protection of the laws.

For example, intelligent use of the ballot is one way individuals can help to ensure that they will receive equal protection of the laws. A good education facilitates intelligent use of the ballot, and good employment opportunities facilitate a good education in many ways. (It costs money to be able to afford housing in neighborhoods that have good schools; it costs money to go to college; etc.) Thus, when Congress commanded in 1963 that women receive equal pay for equal work, and in 1964 that women not be barred from jobs on the basis of sex, Congress may have had a dual purpose. They were certainly barring particular unfair economic practices, but at the same time, they were arguably facilitating women's quest for "equal protection of the laws," and thereby enforcing the Fourteenth Amendment.

2. A detailed account of this settlement can be found in Lisa Cronin Wohl, "Liberating Ma Bell," *Ms.*, Nov. 1973, at 52.

3. In the successful AT&T case the Department of Labor had joined forces with the EEOC in a coordinated attack. *Id.*

4. The three dissenters, Burger, Rehnquist, and Blackmun, simply stated that they endorsed the contrary opinion of Judge Adams of the Circuit Court of Appeals. He had argued that extra pay for nighttime work was properly interpreted as compensation for a more stressful working condition, and he, too, had based his argument on his reading of the legislative history.

5. *Griggs v. Duke Power*, 401 U.S. 424 (1971); and *Albemarle Paper v. Moody*, 422 U.S. 405 (1975).

6. *Griggs*, 401 U.S., at 432.

7. *Diaz v. Pan-American World Airways*, 422 F.2d 385, 388.

8. Ms. Rawlinson brought suit as a class action on behalf of herself and other women similarly situated.

9. *Meth v. Dothard*, 418 F. Supp. 1169, 1184–85.

10. *Washington v. AFSCME*, 770 F.2d 1401 (9th Cir. Sept. 5, 1985); *Spaulding v. University of Washington*, 740 F.2d 686 (9th Cir. 1984); *Lemons v. Denver*, 620 F.2d 228 (10th Cir. 1980); *Christenson v. Iowa*, 563 F.2d 353 (8th Cir. 1977).

11. *Spaulding v. University of Washington*, 740 F.2d 686, *cert. denied* 469 U.S. 1036 (Nov. 26, 1984).

12. Keon S. Chi, "Comparable Worth in State Government: Trends and Issues," 5 *Policy Studies Review* 800–14, at 813. (May 1986)

13. *Id.* at 811. Gasaway, "Comparable Worth: A Post-*Gunther* Overview," 69 *Georgia Law Journal* 1123, at 1159 (1981) includes Idaho in the list of states that have moved toward comparable worth for government employees.

14. On June 27, 1986, the Supreme Court sent a case back to Ohio for further proceedings. It involved a fundamentalist Christian school in a dispute over Ohio anti-discrimination law. The school asserted that its religious teachings required it to fire any women who became mothers, because a mother's proper place was home with her children. 54 U.S.L.W. 4860.

In New York State, as this book went to press, a case was pending in federal district court because Chasidic Jewish groups do not want their children riding on (publicly funded) schoolbuses driven by women; their religious teachings proscribe physical contact between males and non-family females. The Chasids assert that the state is obligated to provide them with male drivers. "Who Should Drive Hasidic Schoolboys?," *New York Times*, Sept. 15, 1986, A14, col. 1.

15. *Miller v. California*, 413 U.S. 15 (1973) and *Paris Adult Theater v. Slaton*, 413 U.S. 49 (1973).

16. Kenneth H. Bastian, Jr., "Thank Title IX for Some of That Gold," *Washington Post*, Aug. 5, 1984, C7, col. 1.

17. *Sexual Harassment* xi (New Haven, Conn.: Yale University Press).

Timetable of Women's Rights Cases

Date	Case	Result
1873	*Bradwell v. Illinois* 83 U.S. (16 Wall) 130	Law prohibiting women from being lawyers held CONSTITUTIONAL.
1875	*Minor v. Happersett* 88 U.S. (21 Wall) 162	State law denying women the vote held CONSTITUTIONAL.
1908	*Muller v. Oregon* 208 U.S. 412	Law limiting workday to ten hours for women only held CONSTITUTIONAL.
1912	*Quong Wing v. Kirkendall* 223 U.S. 62	Law providing tax exemption to women (only) running small laundries held CONSTITUTIONAL.
1920	(CONSTITUTIONAL AMENDMENT)	Women guaranteed the vote.
1923	*Adkins v. Children's Hospital* and *Adkins v. Lyons* 216 U.S. 525	Minimum-wage law for women held UNCONSTITUTIONAL.
1924	*Radice v. New York* 264 U.S. 292	Law prohibiting women from working certain jobs between 10 P.M. and 6 A.M. held CONSTITUTIONAL.
1927	*Buck v. Bell* 274 U.S. 200	Forced sterilization of "feeble-minded" women (and men) held CONSTITUTIONAL.
1936	*Morehead v. New York ex. rel. Tipaldo* 298 U.S. 587	Reaffirmed result of *Adkins v. Children's Hospital*.
1937	*West Coast Hotel v. Parrish* 300 U.S. 379	Overruled *Adkins v. Children's Hospital*; minimum wage law for women held CONSTITUTIONAL.

Date	Case	Result
1937	*Breedlove v. Suttles* 302 U.S. 277	Poll tax required of all nonblind males ages 21–60 but only of those females in the age group who registered to vote held CONSTITUTIONAL.
1942	*Skinner v. Oklahoma* 316 U.S. 535	Law requiring sterilization of male (and female) repeat offenders of certain crimes held UNCONSTITUTIONAL.
1946	*Ballard v. United States* 329 U.S. 187	California practice of not summoning women for federal jury service when they are legally eligible (though rarely called) for state jury service held VIOLATION OF (implications in) FEDERAL LAW. Ruling applied only to the 60 percent of states in which women were eligible for state jury duty, but wording of opinion implied that women's eligibility was necessary for jury impartiality.
1948	*Goesaert v. Cleary* 335 U.S. 464	Law prohibiting women from working as bartender in most situations held CONSTITUTIONAL.
1961	*Hoyt v. Florida* 368 U.S. 57	State practice of systematically excluding women from (state) jury held CONSTITUTIONAL.
1963	(Legislation)	Congress requires equal wages paid for equal work regardless of sex.
1964	(Legislation)	Congress forbids sex discrimination in employment.
1965	*Griswold v. Connecticut* 381 U.S. 479	State law prohibiting the use of contraceptive devices by anyone held UNCONSTITUTIONAL (with explicit reference to married persons).
1967	(Executive order)	President forbids sex discrimination by employers under federal contract or subcontract.
1968	*State v. Hall* 385 U.S. 98	Supreme Court refuses to review issue settled in *Hoyt v. Fla.*
August 1970	[CONSTITUTIONAL AMENDMENT?]	House of Representatives votes for ERA, 350–15.
January 1971	*Phillips v. Martin-Marietta* 400 U.S. 542	Practice by private employer of refusing to hire women with preschool-age children held VIOLATION OF FEDERAL LAW that prohibits employment discrimination on the basis of sex.

Date	Case	Result
March 1971	*Williams v. McNair* 401 U.S. 951	State law excluding men from certain state colleges and women from others held CONSTITUTIONAL.
October 1971	[CONSTITUTIONAL AMENDMENT?]	House of Representatives again votes for ERA, 354–24.
November 1971	*Reed v. Reed* 404 U.S. 71	State law establishing automatic preferences for males over otherwise equally situated females as administrators of wills held UNCONSTITUTIONAL. First case in which Supreme Court held unconstitutional a law imposing sex discrimination. Court claimed to use a "reasonableness" test to reach this result.
6 March 1972	*Forbush v. Wallace* 405 U.S. 970	Court without written opinion held CONSTITUTIONAL state law requiring a married woman to use husband's name on driver's license.
8 March 1972	(Legislation)	Congress empowers Equal Employment Opportunity Commission to enforce via lawsuits the 1964 prohibition on sex and race discrimination in employment.
22 March 1972	(CONSTITUTIONAL AMENDMENT?)	Senate votes 84–8 for the Equal Rights Amendment to the Constitution, sending it to the states for ratification.
22 March 1972	*Eisenstadt v. Baird* 405 U.S. 438	Law prohibiting the dispensing of contraceptives to any unmarried person, or by anyone other than a physician or pharmacist, held UNCONSTITUTIONAL.
3 April 1972	*Alexander v. Louisiana* 405 U.S. 625	Court noted, in passing, that systematic exclusion of women from state grand juries was CONSTITUTIONAL.
3 April 1972	*Stanley v. Illinois* 405 U.S. 645	Law automatically denying child custody to the only surviving male parent of an illegitimate child while automatically granting such custody to the only surviving female parent held UNCONSTITUTIONAL.
June 1972	(Legislation)	Congress forbids sex discrimination in educational institutions that receive federal funds (except for admission to single-sex schools).

Date	Case	Result
January 1973	*Roe v. Wade* and *Doe v. Bolton* 410 U.S. 113 and 410 U.S. 179	Laws prohibiting abortion held UNCONSTITUTIONAL, except where such laws are restricted to last three months of pregnancy, or to stage of fetal "viability."
May 1973	*Frontiero v. Richardson* 411 U.S. 677	Law requiring married women army officers to prove "actual dependency" of spouse to qualify for spouse benefits, although married male officers automatically received such benefits, held UNCONSTITUTIONAL.
June 1973	*Pittsburgh Press v. Human Relations Commission* 413 U.S. 376	Administrative order forbidding sex-specific "Help Wanted" ads held CONSTITUTIONAL (under First Amendment).
January 1974	*Cleveland Board of Education v. LaFleur* 414 U.S. 632	Law requiring schoolteachers to leave job when they became five months pregnant held UNCONSTITUTIONAL.
April 1974	*Kahn v. Shevin* 416 U.S. 351	Law granting automatic property tax exemption to sole surviving female spouse while denying it to all males (and other females) held CONSTITUTIONAL.
3 June 1974	*Corning Glass v. Brennan* 417 U.S. 188	Company policy of paying night inspectors (whose jobs until 1966 were denied to women) more than day inspectors (whose jobs were historically held by women), in a situation where the pay difference was substantially in excess of the company shift differential, held VIOLATION OF FEDERAL LAW that prohibits giving unequal pay, on the basis of sex, for equal work performed.
17 June 1974	*Geduldig v. Aiello* 417 U.S. 484	State denial of pregnancy disability benefits to workers held CONSTITUTIONAL.
15 January 1975	*Schlesinger v. Ballard* 419 U.S. 498	Law permitting women members of the armed forces more time to attain promotion as officers than is permitted to men held CONSTITUTIONAL.
21 January 1975	*Taylor v. Louisiana* 419 U.S. 522	State practice of systematically excluding women from state jury duty held UNCONSTITUTIONAL.

Date	Case	Result
March 1975	*Weinberger v. Wiesenfeld* 420 U.S. 636	Law providing Social Security benefits to sole surviving female parents of dependent children, when such parents have low or no earnings and when the deceased spouse has contributed Social Security taxes, but denying such benefits to sole surviving male parents in parallel situation held UNCONSTITUTIONAL.
April 1975	*Stanton v. Stanton* 421 U.S. 7	Law establishing age of female adulthood at 18 but age of male adulthood at 21, for purpose of determining how to continue financial support payments from divorced parent, held UNCONSTITUTIONAL.
October 1975	(Legislation and Executive Action)	Congress, with Federal Reserve Board regulations, forbids sex discrimination in credit transactions.
November 1975	*Turner v. Department of Employment Security* 423 U.S. 44	Law denying unemployment compensation any woman in last three months of pregnancy held UNCONSTITUTIONAL.
1 July 1976	*Planned Parenthood v. Danforth* 428 U.S. 52	State law prohibiting abortion by saline amniocentesis held UNCONSTITUTIONAL. State law prohibiting abortion without written consent of husband or, for unmarried minors, without written consent of parent held UNCONSTITUTIONAL. State law requiring physician to attempt to preserve life of aborted fetus held UNCONSTITUTIONAL. State laws establishing special record-keeping rules for abortions, requiring written consent of the pregnant women for an abortion, and forbidding abortions of "viable" fetuses held CONSTITUTIONAL.
7 December 1976	*General Electric v. Gilbert* 429 U.S. 125	Denial by private employers of medical disability benefits to workers absent for maternity-related reasons held NOT A VIOLATION OF FEDERAL LAW.
20 December 1976	*Craig v. Boren* 429 U.S. 190	State law permitting 18–20-year-old females the right to drink "3.2" beer while denying the right to 18–20-year-old males held UNCONSTITUTIONAL. For the first time, the U.S. Supreme Court majority acknowledged that something stricter than the reasonableness test applies to sex discriminations.

Date	Case	Result
2 March 1977	*Califano v. Goldfarb* 430 U.S. 199	Federal law providing Social Security benefits to surviving female spouses of persons who paid Social Security taxes but denying such benefits to surviving male spouses unless the males could prove "actual dependency" on their wives held UNCONSTITUTIONAL.
21 March 1977	*Califano v. Webster* 430 U.S. 313	Federal law providing women a more generous technique than that provided to men for calculating their Social Security benefits in relation to their earnings held CONSTITUTIONAL.
19 April 1977	*Vorchheimer v. School Board of Philadelphia* 430 U.S. 703	Local law establishing one girls-only and one boys-only high school, at which attendance was voluntary (i.e., coed alternatives were available), held CONSTITUTIONAL by virtue of a Supreme Court nondecision (a 4–4 tie) that left the lower court opinion in effect.
26 April 1977	*Fiallo v. Bell* 430 U.S. 787	Federal law providing preferred immigrant status to illegitimate children of American mothers and to mothers of illegitimate American children, but denying preferred immigrant status to illegitimate children of American fathers and to fathers of illegitimate American children held CONSTITUTIONAL.
9 June 1977	*Carey v. Population Services* 431 U.S. 678	State law prohibiting distribution of contraceptives to persons under age 16 held UNCONSTITUTIONAL.
20 June 1977	*Beal v. Doe* 432 U.S. 438	State law denying Medicaid benefits for "unnecessary" abortions held NOT A VIOLATION OF FEDERAL LAW.
20 June 1977	*Maher v. Roe* 432 U.S. 464	State law denying Medicaid benefits for "unnecessary" abortions held CONSTITUTIONAL.
20 June 1977	*Poelker v. Doe* 432 U.S. 519	Local law forbidding the performance of "unnecessary" abortions in publicly funded hospitals held CONSTITUTIONAL.
27 June 1977	*Dothard v. Rawlinson* 433 U.S. 321	Minimum height and weight requirements for the job of prison guard held VIOLATION OF FEDERAL LAW. "Males-only" requirement for "contact positions" within maximum-security male penitentiaries characterized by "violence and disorganization" and in which sex offenders are mixed with other prisoners held NOT A VIOLATION OF FEDERAL LAW.

Date	Case	Result
6 December 1977	*Nashville Gas v. Satty* 434 U.S. 136	Deprivation of previously accumulated seniority benefits of women returning from maternity leave (where employees returning from other kinds of disability leave do not lose benefits) held VIOLATION OF FEDERAL LAW.
10 January 1978	*Quilloin v. Walcott* 434 U.S. 246	State law not permitting unwed father to block the adoption of natural son by the child's step-father but permitting divorced fathers to block such proceedings held CONSTITUTIONAL as applied to an unwed father who had never sought nor held custody of child. Court REFUSED TO REACH MERITS on whether statute's discrimination between unwed fathers and unwed mothers (who also could block adoption) was unconstitutional.
24 April 1978	*Los Angeles Department of Water and Power v. Manhart* 435 U.S. 702	Deductions by employer of larger amounts from wages of female employees than from male employees for pension fund held VIOLATION OF FEDERAL LAW.
6 October 1978	(CONSTITUTIONAL AMENDMENT?)	Congress by majority vote (233–189) extends ratification deadline for ERA from 22 March 1977 to 30 June 1982.
October 1978	(Legislation)	Congress forbids employment discrimination on grounds of pregnancy.
9 January 1979	*Colautti v. Franklin* 439 U.S. 379	State law requiring life-saving efforts by physician performing abortion on fetus who "may be viable" held UNCONSTITUTIONAL on vagueness grounds.
5 March 1979	*Orr v. Orr* 440 U.S. 268	State law permitting alimony awards only to women held UNCONSTITUTIONAL.
24 April 1979	*Parham v. Hughes* 441 U.S. 347	State law permitting mothers but not fathers of illegitimate children to sue for wrongful death of child held CONSTITUTIONAL.
24 April 1979	*Caban v. Mohammed* 441 U.S. 380	State law requiring mother's but not father's permission to release illegitimate child for adoption held UNCONSTITUTIONAL.

Date	Case	Result
5 June 1979	*Personnel Administrator v. Feeney* 442 U.S. 256	State law providing sweeping military veterans' preference for non-clerical civil service jobs in setting where 98 percent of veterans were male held CONSTITUTIONAL on grounds that statute was not a product of intentional sex discrimination.
25 June 1979	*Califano v. Westcott*	Federal law providing welfare benefits to families with unemployed father, but not to families with unemployed mother, held UNCONSTITUTIONAL
2 July 1979	*Bellotti v. Baird (II)* 443 U.S. 622	State law requiring that unmarried minor obtain written consent from both parents or, after they refuse, permission from a judge "on good cause" before obtaining an abortion held UNCONSTITUTIONAL.
22 April 1980	*Wengler v. Druggists Mutual Insurance* 446 U.S. 142	State workmen's compensation program providing death benefits to widows, but not widowers, of workers held UNCONSTITUTIONAL.
30 June 1980	*Harris v. McRae* 448 U.S. 297	Federal law subsidizing maternity costs for the poor but not their abortion costs, even if medically "necessary," held CONSTITUTIONAL.
23 March 1981	*H. L. v. Matheson* 450 U.S. 398	State law requiring parental notification "if possible" prior to performing abortion on a minor held CONSTITUTIONAL as applied to immature minor living with parents.
23 March 1981	*Kirchberg v. Feenstra* 450 U.S. 455	State law giving husbands unilateral control over marital property unanimously held UNCONSTITUTIONAL.
23 March 1981	*Michael M. v. Sonoma County* 450 U.S. 464	State law making criminal sexual intercourse by 14–17-year-old male with 14–17-year-old consenting female but treating the female as innocent of crime held CONSTITUTIONAL.
8 June 1981	*Washington County v. Gunther* 452 U.S. 161	State practice of paying women jail guards substantially less than officials believed would have to be paid if men were hired for the same job held VIOLATION OF FEDERAL LAW.
25 June 1981	*Rostker v. Goldberg* 453 U.S. 57	Federal law requiring that only males register for the Selective Service (draft) held CONSTITUTIONAL.

Date	Case	Result
1 July 1982	*Mississippi University for Women v. Hogan* 458 U.S. 718	State law reserving state nurses' college admission to females only UNCONSTITUTIONAL.
15 June 1983	*Akron v. Akron Center for Reproductive Health* 462 U.S. 416	Local statute requiring that all post-first-trimester abortions be in a hospital held UNCONSTITUTIONAL; that doctors say that life begins at conception and detail all possible negative consequences of abortions and inform woman of adoption services, all prior to obtaining her abortion consent held UNCONSTITUTIONAL; that abortions not be performed sooner than 24 hours after women give consent to the procedure held UNCONSTITUTIONAL; and that post-abortion remains of embryo or fetus be disposed of in "humane and sanitary manner" held UNCONSTITUTIONAL (on grounds of vagueness).
15 June 1983	*Planned Parenthood v. Ashcroft* 462 U.S. 476	State law requiring presence of a second physician for preservation of fetus whenever "abortion" is performed after fetus is viable held CONSTITUTIONAL; law requiring pathologist's report on all abortions also held CONSTITUTIONAL.
15 June 1983	*Simopoulos v. Virginia* 462 U.S. 506	State law requiring that all post-first-trimester abortions be either in a full-service hospital or in a licensed out-patient clinic held CONSTITUTIONAL.
20 June 1983	*Newport News Shipbuilding v. EEOC* 462 U.S. 669	Refusal to provide employee benefits paying maternity costs for spouses of male workers when spouses of female workers were receiving benefits covering all medical costs held VIOLATION OF FEDERAL LAW.
27 June 1983	*Lehr v. Robertson* 463 U.S. 248	State law that, as applied, denied to unmarried father opportunity for legitimation hearing for purpose of blocking adoption of his child by the mother's husband held NOT A VIOLATION OF THE CONSTITUTION, despite fact that mother had refused to allow father to develop a relationship with his child.

Date	Case	Result
6 July 1983	*Arizona Governing Committee v. Norris* 463 U.S. 1073	Practice of having employees select from one of several pension companies, each of which provided lower monthly retirement benefits to females than to males, held VIOLATION OF FEDERAL LAW.
15 November 1983	(CONSTITUTIONAL AMENDMENT?)	Attempt in Congress to re-adopt ERA, which had attained state ratification by only 35 rather than the needed 38 states prior to ratification deadline, fell short of needed two-thirds (278–147).
28 February 1984	*Grove City College v. Bell* 465 U.S. 555	Title IX of Education Amendments, forbidding gender discrimination in universities receiving federal funds held applicable only to specific programs that receive the funds.
22 May 1984	*Hishon v. King Spaulding* 467 U.S. 69	Sex discrimination in promotion to "partner" of law firm held VIOLATION OF FEDERAL LAW.
3 July 1984	*Roberts v. Jaycees* 468 U.S. 609	Application of state law forbidding gender discrimination to association open on non-selective basis to all 18–35-year-old males held CONSTITUTIONAL (under First Amendment).
24 February 1986	*Hudnut v. American Booksellers Assoc.*	Local anti-pornography ordinance defining trafficking in pornography as discrimination against women held UNCONSTITUTIONAL on First Amendment grounds (by summary affirmance of lower court opinion).

Date	Case	Result
11 June 1986	*Thornburgh v. ACOG*	State law requiring each of the following held UNCONSTITUTIONAL: (1) that physician or other abortion facility personnel, prior to obtaining consent for abortion, recite a litany of specified information on several specified topics, including fetal development, the risks of abortion, and the availability of adoption services; (2) that public records be kept of physician and facility performing each abortion, the woman's political subdivision of residence, the woman's age, race, marital status, and number of prior pregnancies, the method of payment, the probable gestational age of the fetus, and any evidence as to whether a medical emergency necessitated the abortion; (3) for any abortion performed on a viable fetus that a second physician be present to try to save the fetus (unlike the similar requirement upheld in *Ashcroft* this provision contained no implication of exceptions for medical emergencies for the mother); (4) for a viable fetus the abortion technique must be selected that offers the best opportunity for live birth unless that technique "would present a significantly greater risk to the life or health of the mother."
19 June 1986	*Meritor Savings Bank v. Vinson*	Sexual harassment by employers of employees, or by supervisory employees of supervised employees, held VIOLATION OF FEDERAL LAW. Court also ruled that it is LAWFUL in sexual harassment trials to introduce evidence aiming to show provocative or seductive behavior by harassed employee.
13 January 1987	*California Federal Savings and Loan v. Guerra*	State law mandating up to four months leave for employees disabled by pregnancy held NOT A VIOLATION OF FEDERAL LAW (which forbade employer discrimination on the basis of pregnancy).

20 January 1987	*Wimberly v. Labor and Industrial Relation Commission*	State law refusing unemployment benefits to women who leave work voluntarily to have a baby and later cannot be rehired when they try, in context where benefits are refused to all others who leave work voluntarily, is NOT A VIOLATION OF FEDERAL LAW that forbids denying such benefits "solely on the basis of pregnancy."
25 March 1987	*Johnson v. Transportation Agency*	Affirmative action hiring program for jobs from which women had traditionally been excluded, even when operated by an employer who neither acknowledged, nor had been proven to have engaged in, previous discrimination against women, held NOT A VIOLATION OF FEDERAL LAW.

Appendix A

How the Supreme Court Operates

Jurisdiction

The Constitution mandates the establishment of a Supreme Court and grants that court jurisdiction over all "cases and controversies" involving diplomatic personnel, legal clashes on the seas, clashes between citizens or governments of two different states, legal disputes betwen Americans and foreigners, and all cases "arising under" any of the three forms of national law: federal statutes, treaties, or clauses of the Constitution. This grant of power in a variety of ways imposes limits on the Court's powers.

First, no legal dispute that is wholly an in-state matter may go to the federal courts. If the clash involves only the *state* law (and the bulk of laws affecting our daily lives *are* state laws), and the parties to the dispute all live within that state, no federal court may intervene. The federal courts may be brought in *only* if some element of federal law is at issue, such as, for example, the prohibition within the federal Constitution against unreasonable searches and seizures. (If a party in a local trial wishes to appeal the case later to a federal court, that party must raise the issue of federal law at the initial trial. People are not permitted to wait until they lose at the local level and then try to dream up new "federal" issues so that they can keep appealing to the federal courts.)

Second, the federal courts will hear only genuine, live "controversies"; that is, cases in which the court's ruling will settle someone's pending claim. The federal courts will not hand out "advisory opinions," that is, general opinions as to a law's merits or its constitutionality which do not settle actual live disputes between concrete individuals or groups. The Supreme Court, for this reason, avoids "moot" cases; these are cases in which the resolution of the initial legal claim has (usually by the passage of time) somehow been taken out of the power of the court. A mother who objects to prayers in public school but whose children have graduated from school by the time her case gets to the highest court would be one example of someone whose case had been "mooted" by the passage of time.

By inference from the "cases and controversies" phrase, the Supreme Court requires that the parties who present cases have an actual, tangible stake in the outcome. This requirement that the parties involved must somehow stand to gain or lose directly from the outcome of the case, is called the "standing" requirement. The federal courts apply it with a certain flexibility; it is one way for them to bow out tactfully from politically "hot" cases. For cases that the justices want to decide, they occasionally bend the rules of standing.

In all cases involving diplomatic personnel and in those where one state government is opposing another government or an out-of-state citizen, the Constitution gave the Supreme Court original jurisdiction. That means that the Supreme Court hears the case on the initial round, before any other judicial body hears it. (Only about 150 cases in the entire history of the Supreme Court have been handled in this way.) All the rest of the Supreme Court's jurisdiction is appellate (cases come to it on appeal from the decision of lower courts, both state and federal). The Constitution gives Congress the power to make exceptions to these rules of jurisdiction and to create lower federal courts to supplement the work of the Supreme Court.

Congress also has the power to alter the number of justices on the Supreme Court, and it has done this on a number of occasions over the past 190 years. The official size of the Supreme Court has remained steadily at nine for more than a century.

In the Judiciary Act of 1921, Congress made the bulk of the Supreme Court's appellate jurisdiction discretionary. (In practice, the Supreme Court makes that portion of its jurisdiction not covered by this part of the Judiciary Act also discretionary.) The Supreme Court exercises this discretion to select for decision only those cases of importance to the legal system of the country as a whole. In other words, the Supreme Court is more likely to accept a case for decision if that case presents a legal issue of national importance than if one of the parties in the case simply happened to receive unfair treatment.

Structure and Workload of the Federal Courts

The vast majority of legal cases in the United States are handled in the state court system. (This system includes county and municipal courts.) In additon, about 150,000 cases each year are initiated in the federal court system at the level of the district courts.

The United States is divided into eighty-eight judicial districts, and the District of Columbia and Puerto Rico each constitute an additional district. Each of these has its own federal district court. There are 517 federal district judges. The district courts have original jurisdiction for cases arising under federal laws. They also have appellate jurisdiction to hear cases from the state courts in which a convicted criminal claims that his conviction process was in some way unconstitutional. Generally, district judges hear cases as individuals, but if a case presents a major constitutional issue, a panel of three district judges will hear it.

Anyone who loses at the district court level has a right to appeal to the one of the eleven U.S. circuit courts of appeals whose circuit includes the district of the original case. The courts of appeals must hear cases appealed to them. Roughly 10 percent of cases heard in district courts are taken to the circuit courts of appeals. There are 132 circuit court judges and at the circuit level the use of three-judge panels to decide cases is much more typical than in the district courts. The number of court of appeals judges per circuit varies according to the size of the circuit. Whenever possible, the three-judge panels are designed so as to include at least two judges from states other than the one where the case arose. Very rarely (for the purpose of avoiding differing decisions by three-judge panels) all the judges of a circuit will hear a case together, or *en banc.*

Federal Court opinions are reprinted in *Federal Supplement* (F. Supp.). State Supreme Court decisions are reprinted by region in collections such as *Northwest Reporter* (N.W.) or *Northeast Reporter Second Series* (N.E. 2d) or published in state collections such as *Idaho Reports* (Idaho).

Supreme Court Proceedings

About 5,000 cases each year are appealed to the Supreme Court. Some of these (about 30 percent) come from state supreme courts and a few directly from federal district courts, but most come from the circuit courts of appeals. Ninety percent of these appeals for Supreme Court review are rejected outright. A few hundred of them are disposed of in "summary" proceedings, in which no further argument is presented to the Supreme Court. Sometimes a summary disposition will have no explanatory opinion at all; the Supreme Court can just announce a summary affirmance or reversal. Often summary proceedings include very brief (three or four sentence) per curiam opinions authored anonymously for the Court as a group. Each year only about 150 cases are accepted for full argument at the United States Supreme Court.

To be accepted for review by the Supreme Court, a case must garner the votes of four of the nine justices in favor of its petition for review. About one hundred petitions arrive every week. These petitions are read by the justices (or their clerks), and any single justice can request that a particular petition be discussed at the next available conference. Seventy percent of the petitions never arouse such a request and are, therefore, rejected without any discussion.

The Supreme Court session begins on the first Monday in October and lasts until early July. The Court's sessions consists of alternating two-week periods in which the justices first hear oral arguments and then spend time drafting and re-drafting opinions to explain their decisions for the cases they have heard argued. Fridays are set aside for conferences.

These conferences begin at 9:30 A.M. with a series of handshakes between every justice and each of the other eight justices. The proceedings are kept completely secret. No one else is present. Only the chief justice takes notes (and these are not made public). If any books or papers are needed, the most "junior" justice (based on the date of appointment to the Court) goes to the door and hands a message to the bailiff, who is always waiting there.

The chief justice starts the discussion of each case, and the other justices then comment in order of descending seniority. When each justice speaks he or she indicates a tentative vote on the case, or on the petition for review. Once all nine have spoken, an official vote is taken, but this time in reverse order of seniority. In other words, the chief justice can see how everyone else has voted before he casts his vote. Any petition for review that obtains four votes in this process is then scheduled for full briefing and oral argument, usually several months hence.

The attorneys on both sides of cases accepted by the Court then submit written "briefs" (often hundreds of pages long), detailing their legal arguments. In addition, other parties (individuals, groups or government agencies) who feel they have a stake in the outcome of the case, often request the opportunity to submit *amicus curiae* ("friend of the court") briefs, supplementing the original brief with arguments presenting their own perspective on the case. These briefs may be submitted either by permission of both parties or by permission of the Supreme Court.

Once the Supreme Court justices have read the briefs and have had time, with the help of their (three or four per justice) law clerks (generally people who recently graduated at the top of their law school class) to research the cases further, they then hear oral argument. Oral argument is usually limited to thirty minutes for each side. The process of oral argument is a rather awesome spectacle. All nine justices sit in a row of high-backed chairs on an elevated platform behind a long table. They all wear black robes and the solicitor general, who argues cases for the federal government, dons a formal morning coat. The attorney stands facing the justices (with back to the small audience) and begins his or her argument. He or she generally manages no more than a few sentences before the justices begin to pepper him or her with questions. The rest of the "argument" then consists of a lively interchange between justices and attorney.

On the Friday following oral argument, the case is again discussed in conference. The justices follow the same procedures of speaking and voting, and, of course, a majority (rather than a vote of four) is now decisive. If the chief justice votes with the majority, he assigns the job of writing the "Court" opinion. If the chief justice is in the minority, the most senior of the associate justices assigns the Court opinion. Some effort is made to distribute the opinion-writing responsibility evenly around the Court; each justice authors about thirteen to eighteen majority opinions a year. Once the selected justice has drafted the intended majority opinion, he or she circulates this rough version to every other justice. At this point the other justices jot down various suggestions for changing the draft; a justice in the original minority, for example, may offer to change sides if a particular point is added or deleted, strengthened or weakened. Likewise, an original member of the majority may threaten to break ranks if the opinion is not modified to his or her specifications. Meanwhile, if the vote on the case was nonunanimous (as 75 percent of them are), a dissenting opinion will also be circulating. Occasionally, a dissent is so persuasive, or a majority opinion so unpersuasive, that the initial dissent becomes a majority opinion before the consulting process has ended. These opinion drafts are frequently revised several times, and any justice is free to change sides until

the official decision is announced in open court. Any justice who wants to may also write his or her own concurring or dissenting opinion.

Opinions are "read aloud" in Court, often on Mondays and Tuesdays. These days, justices generally summarize their main arguments and read only selected portions of the opinion. When the opinion is being announced, complete copies of it are distributed to journalists from the news media and are also mailed to the litigants and the lower courts involved.

Supreme Court opinions are reprinted every week in a journal called *U.S. Law Week: Supreme Court Section* (abbreviated U.S.L.W. or L.W.), which is available in every law library. All law schools have law libraries, as do all county seats. Eventually the opinions are also reprinted in each of three edited series: *United States Reports* (abbreviated U.S.), the official version of the Government Printing Office; *The Supreme Court Reporter* (abbreviated S. Ct.), and *United States Supreme Court, Lawyers' Edition* (abbreviated L. Ed.), both published by West Publishing, a private company. At least one of these editions is always available in law libraries.

Court cases use a legal notation form for citing cases. For example, in the citation 198 U.S. 45, 47, the letters U.S. are the abbreviation of the title of the collection in which the case can be found (in this instance, United States Supreme Court Reports); the first number, 198, refers to the volume number in that collection; the second number, 45, refers to the page on which the case begins; the third number, 47, refers to the page on which the particular quotation is found. For other forms of citation and further help, see a legal handbook or *A Uniform System of Citation* (currently in the fourteenth edition).

Appendix B

The Constitution of the United States

Preamble

We the People of the United States, in Order to form a more perfect Union, establish Justice, ensure domestic Tranquility, provide for the common defence, promote the general Welfare, and secure the Blessings of Liberty to ourselves and our Posterity, do ordain and establish this Constitution for the United States of America.

Article 1

Section 1. All legislative Powers herein granted shall be vested in a Congress of the United States, which shall consist of a Senate and House of Representatives.

Section 2. [1] The House of Representatives shall be composed of Members chosen every second Year by the People of the several States, and the Electors in each State shall have the Qualifications requisite for Electors of the most numerous Branch of the State Legislature.

[2] No Person shall be a Representative who shall not have attained to the Age of twenty five Years, and been seven Years a Citizen of the United States, and who shall not, when elected, be an Inhabitant of that State in which he shall be chosen.

[3] Representatives and direct Taxes shall be apportioned among the several States which may be included within this Union, according to their respective Numbers, which shall be determined by adding to the whole Number of free Persons, including those bound to Service for a Term of Years, and excluding Indians not taxed, three fifths of all other Persons. The actual Enumeration shall be made within three Years after the first Meeting of the Congress of the United States, and within every subsequent Term of ten Years, in such Manner as they shall by Law direct. The Number of Representatives shall not exceed one for every thirty Thousand, but each State shall have at Least one Representative; and until such enumeration shall be made, the State of New Hampshire shall be entitled to chuse three, Massachusetts eight. Rhode Island and Providence Plantations one, Connecticut five, New York six, New Jersey four, Pennsylvania eight, Delaware one, Maryland six, Virginia ten, North Carolina five, South Carolina five, and Georgia three.

[4] When vacancies happen in the Representation from any State, the Executive Authority thereof shall issue Writs of Election to fill such Vacancies.

[5] The House of Representatives shall chuse their Speaker and other Officers; and shall have the sole Power of Impeachment.

Section 3. [1] The Senate of the United States shall be composed of two Senators from each State, chosen by the Legislature thereof, for six Years; and each Senator shall have one Vote.

[2] Immediately after they shall be assembled in Consequence of the first Election, they shall be divided as equally as may be into three Classes. The Seats of the Senators of the first Class shall be vacated at the Expiration of the Second Year, of the second Class at the Expiration of the fourth Year, and of the third Class at the Expiration of the sixth Year, so that one third may be chosen every second Year; and if Vacancies happen by Resignation, or otherwise, during the Recess of the Legislature of any State, the Executive thereof may make temporary Appointments until the next Meeting of the Legislature, which shall then fill such Vacancies.

[3] No Person shall be a Senator who shall not have attained to the Age of thirty Years, and been nine Years a Citizen of the United States, and who shall not, when elected, be an Inhabitant of that State for which he shall be chosen.

[4] The Vice President of the United States shall be President of the Senate, but shall have no Vote, unless they be equally divided.

[5] The Senate shall chuse their other Officers, and also a President pro tempore, in the Absence of the Vice President, or when he shall exercise the Office of President of the United States.

[6] The Senate shall have the sole Power to try all Impeachments. When sitting for that Purpose, they shall be on Oath or Affirmation. When the President of the United States is tried, the Chief Justice shall preside: And no Person shall be convicted without the Concurrence of two thirds of the Members present.

[7] Judgment in Cases of Impeachment shall not extend further than to removal from Office, and disqualification to hold and employ any Office of honor, Trust, or Profit under the United States: but the Party convicted shall nevertheless be liable and subject to Indictment, Trial, Judgment, and Punishment, according to Law.

Section 4. [1] The Times, Places and Manner of holding Elections for Senators and Representatives, shall be prescribed in each State by the Legislature thereof; but the Congress may at any time by Law make or alter such Regulations, except as to the Places of chusing Senators.

[2] The Congress shall assemble at least once in every Year, and such Meeting shall be on the first Monday in December, unless they shall by Law appoint a different Day.

Section 5. [1] Each House shall be the Judge of the Elections, Returns, and Qualifications of its own Members, and a Majority of each shall constitute a Quorum to do Business; but a smaller Number may adjourn from day to day, and may be authorized to compel the Attendance of absent Members, in such Manner, and under such Penalties as each House may provide.

[2] Each House may determine the Rules of its Proceedings, punish its Members for disorderly Behavior, and, with the Concurrence of two thirds, expel a Member.

[3] Each House shall keep a Journal of its Proceedings, and from time to time publish the same, excepting such Parts as may in their Judgment require Secrecy; and the Yeas and Nays of the Members of either House on any question shall, at the Desire of one fifth of those Present, be entered on the Journal.

[4] Neither House, during the Session of Congress, shall, without the Consent of the other, adjourn for more than three days, nor to any other Place than that in which the two Houses shall be sitting.

Section 6. [1] The Senators and Representatives shall receive a Compensation for their Services, to be ascertained by Law, and paid out of the Treasury of the United States. They shall in all Cases, except Treason, Felony and Breach of the Peace, be privileged from Arrest during their Attendance at the Session of their respective Houses, and in going to and returning from the same; and for any Speech and Debate in either House, they shall not be questioned in any other Place.

[2] No Senator or Representative shall, during the Time for which he was elected, be appointed to any civil Office under the Authority of the United States, which shall have been created, or the Emoluments whereof shall have been increased during such time; and no Person holding any Office under the United States, shall be a Member of either House during his Continuance in Office.

Section 7. [1] All Bills for raising Revenue shall originate in the House of Representatives; but the Senate may propose or concur with Amendments as on other Bills.

[2] Every Bill which shall have passed the House of Representatives and the Senate, shall, before it become a Law, be presented to the President of the United States; If he approve he shall sign it, but if not he shall return it, with his Objections to the House in which it shall have originated, who shall enter the Objections at large on their Journal, and proceed to reconsider it. If after such Reconsideration two thirds of that House shall agree to pass the Bill, it shall be sent together with the Objections, to the other House, by which it shall likewise be reconsidered, and if approved by two thirds of that House, it shall become a Law. But in all such Cases the Votes of both Houses shall be determined by Yeas and Nays, and the Names of the Persons voting for and against the Bill shall be entered on the Journal of each House respectively. If any Bill shall not be returned by the President within ten Days (Sundays excepted) after it shall have been presented to him, the Same shall be a Law, in like Manner as if he had signed it, unless the Congress by

their Adjournment prevent its Return in which Case it shall not be a Law.

[3] Every Order, Resolution, or Vote, to Which the Concurrence of the Senate and House of Representatives may be necessary (except on a question of Adjournment) shall be presented to the President of the United States; and before the Same shall take Effect, shall be approved by him, or being disaproved by him, shall be repassed by two thirds of the Senate and House of Representatives, according to the Rules and Limitations prescribed in the Case of a Bill.

Section 8. [1] The Congress shall have Power To lay and collect Taxes, Duties, Imposts and Excises, to pay the Debts and provide for the common Defence and general Welfare of the United States; but all Duties, Imposts and Excises shall be uniform throughout the United States;

[2] To borrow money on the credit of the United States;

[3] To regulate Commerce with foreign Nations, and among the several States, and with the Indian Tribes;

[4] To establish an uniform Rule of Naturalization, and uniform Laws on the subject of Bankruptcies throughout the United States;

[5] To coin Money, regulate the Value thereof, and of foreign Coin, and fix the Standard of Weights and Measures;

[6] To provide for the Punishment of counterfeiting the Securities and current Coin of the United States;

[7] To Establish Post Offices and Post Roads;

[8] To promote the Progress of Science and useful Arts, by securing for limited Times to Authors and Inventors the exclusive Right to their respective Writings and Discoveries;

[9] To constitute Tribunals inferior to the supreme Court;

[10] To define and punish Piracies and

Felonies committed on the high Seas, and Offenses against the Law of Nations;

[11] To declare War, grant Letters of Marque and Reprisal, and make Rules concerning Captures on Land and Water;

[12] To raise and support Armies, but no Appropriation of Money to that Use shall be for a longer Term than two Years;

[13] To provide and maintain a Navy;

[14] To make Rules for the Government and Regulation of the land and naval Forces;

[15] To provide for calling forth the Militia to execute the Laws of the Union, suppress Insurrections and repel Invasions;

[16] To provide for organizing, arming, and disciplining, the Militia, and for governing such Part of them as may be employed in the Service of the United States, reserving to the States respectively, the Appointment of the Officers, and the Authority of training the Militia according to the discipline prescribed by Congress;

[17] To exercise exclusive Legislation in all Cases whatsoever, over such District (not exceeding ten Miles square) as may, by Cession of particular States, and the Acceptance of Congress, become the Seat of the Government of the United States, and to exercise like Authority over all Places purchased by the Consent of the Legislature of the State in which the Same shall be, for the Erection of Forts, Magazines, Arsenals, dock-Yards, and other needful Buildings;—And

[18] To make all Laws which shall be necessary and proper for carrying into Execution the foregoing Powers, and all other Powers vested by this Constitution in the Government of the United States, or in any Department or Officer thereof.

Section 9. [1] The Migration or Importation of Such Persons as any of the States now existing shall think proper to admit, shall not be prohibited by the Congress prior to the Year one thousand eight hundred and eight, but a Tax or duty may be imposed on such importation, not exceeding ten dollars for each Person.

[2] The privilege of the Writ of Habeas Corpus shall not be suspended, unless when in Cases of Rebellion or Invasion the public Safety may require it.

[3] No Bill of Attainder or ex post facto Law shall be passed.

[4] No Capitation, or other direct, Tax shall be laid, unless in Proportion to the Census or Enumeration herein before directed to be taken.

[5] No Tax or Duty shall be laid on Articles exported from any State.

[6] No Preference shall be given by any Regulation of Commerce or Revenue to the Ports of one State over those of another: nor shall Vessels bound to, or from, one State be obliged to enter, clear, or pay Duties in another.

[7] No money shall be drawn from the Treasury, but in Consequence of Appropriations made by Law; and a regular Statement and Account of the Receipts and Expenditures of all public Money shall be published from time to time.

[8] No Title of Nobility shall be granted by the United States; And no Person holding any Office of Profit or Trust under them, shall, without the Consent of the Congress, accept of any present, Emolument, Office, or Title, of any kind whatever, from any King, Prince, or foreign State.

Section 10. [1] No State shall enter into any Treaty, Alliance, or Confederation; grant Letters of Marque and Reprisal; coin Money; emit Bills of Credit; make any Things but gold and silver Coin a Tender in Payment of Debts; pass any Bill of Attainder, ex post facto Law, or Law impairing the Obligation of Contracts, or grant any Title of Nobility.

[2] No State shall, without the Consent of the Congress, lay any Imposts or Duties on Imports or Exports, except what may be

absolutely necessary for executing its inspection Laws: and the net Produce of all Duties and Imposts, laid by any State on Imports or Exports, shall be for the Use of the Treasury of the United States; and all such Laws shall be subject to the Revision and Controul of the Congress.

[3] No State shall, without the Consent of Congress, lay any Duty of Tonnage, keep Troops, or Ships of War in time of Peace, enter into any Agreement or Compact with another State or with a foreign Power, or engage in War, unless actually invaded, or in such imminent Danger as will not admit of delay.

Article 2

Section 1. [1] The executive Power shall be vested in a President of the United States of America. He shall hold his Office during the Term of four Years, and, together with the Vice President, chosen for the same Term, be elected, as follows:

[2] Each State shall appoint, in such Manner as the Legislature thereof may direct, a Number of Electors, equal to the whole Number of Senators and Representatives to which the State may be entitled in the Congress; but no Senator or Representative, or Person holding an Office of Trust or Profit under the United States, shall be appointed an Elector.

[3] The Electors shall meet in their respective States, and vote by Ballot for two Persons, of whom one at least shall not be an Inhabitant of the same State with themselves. And they shall make a List of all the Persons voted for, and of the number of Votes for each; which List they shall sign and certify, and transmit sealed to the Seat of the Government of the United States, directed to the President of the Senate. The President of the Senate shall, in the Presence of the Senate and House of Represen-

tatives, open all the Certificates, and the Votes shall then be counted. The Person having the greatest Number of Votes shall be the President, if such Number be a Majority of the whole Number of Electors appointed; and if there be more than one who have such Majority, and have an equal Number of Votes, then the House of Representatives shall immediately chuse by Ballot one of them for President; and if no Person have a Majority, then from the five highest on the List the said House shall in like Manner chuse the President. But in chusing the President, the Votes shall be taken by States the Representation from each State having one Vote; A quorum for this Purpose shall consist of a Member or Members from two thirds of the States, and a Majority of all the States shall be necessary to a Choice. In every Case, after the Choice of the President, the Person having the greater Number of Votes of the Electors shall be the Vice President. But if there should remain two or more who have equal Votes, the Senate shall chuse from them by Ballot the Vice President.

[4] The Congress may determine the Time of chusing the Electors, and the Day on which they shall give their Votes; which Day shall be the same throughout the United States.

[5] No person except a natural born Citizen, or a Citizen of the United States, at the time of the Adoption of this Constitution, shall be eligible to the Office of President; neither shall any Person be eligible to that Office who shall not have attained to the Age of thirty five Years, and been fourteen Years a Resident within the United States.

[6] In case of the removal of the President from Office, or of his Death, Resignation or Inability to discharge the Powers and Duties of the said Office, the Same shall devolve on the Vice President, and the Congress may by Law provide for the Case of Removal, Death, Resignation or Inability,

both of the President and Vice President, declaring what Officer shall then act as President, and such Officer shall act accordingly, until the Disability be removed, or a President shall be elected.

[7] The President shall, at stated Times, receive for his Services, a Compensation, which shall neither be increased nor diminished during the Period for which he shall have been elected, and he shall not receive within that Period any other Emolument from the United States, or any of them.

[8] Before he enter on the Execution of his Office, he shall take the following Oath or Affirmation: "I do solemnly swear (or affirm) that I will faithfully execute the Office of President of the United States, and will to the best of my Ability, preserve, protect and defend the Constitution of the United States."

Section 2. [1] The President shall be Commander in Chief of the Army and Navy of the United States, and of the militia of the several States, when called into the actual Service of the United States; he may require the Opinion, in writing, of the principal Officer in each of the Executive Departments, upon any Subject relating to the Duties of their respective Offices, and he shall have Power to grant Reprieves and Pardons for Offenses against the United States, except in Cases of Impeachment.

[2] He shall have Power, by and with the Advice and Consent of the Senate to make Treaties, provided two thirds of the Senators present concur; and he shall nominate, and by and with the Advice and Consent of the Senate, shall appoint Ambassadors, other public Ministers and Consuls, Judges of the supreme Court, and all other Officers of the United States, whose Appointments are not herein otherwise provided for, and which shall be established by Law; but the Congress may by Law vest the Appointment of such inferior Officers, as they think proper, in the President alone, in the Courts of Law, or in the Heads of Departments.

[3] The President shall have Power to fill up all Vacancies that may happen during the Recess of the Senate, by granting Commissions which shall expire at the End of their next Session.

Section 3. He shall from time to time give to the Congress Information of the State of the Union, and recommend to their Consideration such Measures as he shall judge necessary and expedient; he may, on extraordinary Ocasions, convene both Houses, or either of them, and in Case of Disagreement between them, with Respect to the Time of Adjournment, he may, on extraordinary Occasions, convene both Houses, or either of them, and in and other public Ministers; he shall take Care that the Laws be faithfully executed, and shall Commission all the Officers of the United States.

Section 4. The President, Vice President and all civil Officers of the United States, shall be removed from Office on Impeachment for, and Conviction of, Treason, Bribery, or other high Crimes and Misdemeanors.

Article 3

Section 1. The judicial Power of the United States, shall be vested in one supreme Court, and in such inferior Courts as the Congress may from time to time ordain and establish. The Judges, both of the supreme and inferior Courts, shall hold their Offices during good Behaviour, and shall, at stated Times, receive for their Services a Compensation, which shall not be diminished during their Continuance in Office.

Section 2. [1] The judicial Power shall extend to all Cases, in Law and Equity, arising under this Constitution, the Laws of the United States, and Treaties made, or which shall be made, under their Authority;—to all Cases affecting Ambassadors, other public Ministers and Consuls;—to all Cases of admiralty and maritime Jurisdiction;—to Controversies to which the United States shall be a Party;—to Controversies between two or more States;—between Citizens of the same State claiming Lands under the Grants of different States, and between a State, or the Citizens thereof, and foreign States, Citizens or Subjects.

[2] In all Cases affecting Ambassadors, other public Ministers and Consuls, and those in which a State shall be a Party, the Supreme Court shall have original Jurisdiction. In all the other Cases before mentioned, the supreme Court shall have appellate Jurisdiction, both as to Law and Fact, with such Exceptions, and under such Regulations as the Congress shall make.

[3] The trial of all Crime, except in Cases of Impeachment, shall be by Jury; and such Trial shall be held in the State where the said Crimes shall have been committed; but when not committed within any State, the Trial shall be at such Place or Places as the Congress may by Law have directed.

Section 3. [1] Treason against the United States, shall consist only in levying War against them, or, in adhering to their Enemies, giving them Aid and Comfort. No Person shall be convicted of Treason unless on the Testimony of two Witnesses to the same overt Act, or on Confession in open Court.

[2] The Congress shall have Power to declare the Punishment of Treason, but no Attainder of Treason shall work Corruption of Blood, or Forfeiture except during the Life of the Person attainted.

Article 4

Section 1. Full Faith and Credit shall be given in each State to the public Acts, Rec-

ords, and judicial Proceedings of every other State. And the Congress may by general Laws prescribe the Manner in which such Acts, Records and Proceedings shall be proved, and the Effect thereof.

Section 2. [1] The Citizens of each State shall be entitled to all Privileges and Immunities of Citizens in the several States.

[2] A Person charged in any State with Treason, Felony, or other Crime, who shall flee from Justice, and be found in another State, shall on demand of the executive Authority of the State from which he fled, be delivered up, to be removed to the State having Jurisdiction of the Crime.

[3] No Person held to Service or Labour in one State, under the Laws thereof, escaping into another, shall, in Consequence of any Law or Regulation therein, be discharged from such Service or Labour, but shall be delivered up on Claim of the Party to whom such Service or Labour may be due.

Section 3. [1] New States may be admitted by the Congress into this Union; but no new State shall be formed or erected within the Jurisdiction of any other State; nor any State be formed by the Junction of two or more States, or Parts of States, without the Consent of the Legislatures of the States concerned as well as of the Congress.

[2] The Congress shall have Power to dispose of and make all needful Rules and Regulations respecting the Territory or other Property belonging to the United States; and nothing in this Constitution shall be so construed as to Prejudice any Claims of the United States, or of any particular State.

Section 4. The United States shall guarantee to every State in this Union a Republican Form of Government, and shall protect each of them against Invasion; and on Application of the Legislature, or of the Executive (when the Legislature cannot be convened) against domestic Violence.

Article 5

The Congress, whenever two thirds of both Houses shall deem it necessary, shall propose Amendments to this Constitution, or, on the Application of the Legislatures of two thirds of the several States, shall call a Convention for proposing Amendments, which, in either Case, shall be valid to all Intents and Purposes, as part of this Constitution, when ratified by the Legislatures of three fourths of the several States, or by Conventions in three fourths thereof, as the one or the other Mode of Ratification may be proposed by the Congress; Provided that no Amendment which may be made prior to the Year One thousand eight hundred and eight shall in any Manner affect the first and fourth Clauses in the Ninth Section of the first Article; and that no State, without its Consent, shall be deprived of its equal Suffrage in the Senate.

Article 6

[1] All Debts contracted and Engagements entered into, before the Adoption of this Constitution shall be as valid against the United States under this Constitution, as under the Confederation.

[2] This Constitution, and the Laws of the United States which shall be made in Pursuance thereof; and all Treaties made, or which shall be made under the Authority of the United States, shall be the supreme Law of the Land; and the Judges in every State shall be bound thereby, any Things in the Constitution or Laws of any State to the Contrary notwithstanding.

[3] The Senators and Representatives before mentioned, and the Members of the several State Legislatures, and all executive and judicial Officers, both of the United States and of the several States, shall be bound by Oath or Affirmation, to support this Constitution; but no religious Test shall ever be required as a Qualification to any Office or public Trust under the United States.

Article 7

The Ratification of the Conventions of nine States shall be sufficient for the Establishment of this Constitution between the States so ratifying the Same.

ARTICLES IN ADDITION TO, AND AMENDMENT OF, THE CONSTITUTION OF THE UNITED STATES OF AMERICA, PROPOSED BY CONGRESS, AND RATIFIED BY THE LEGISLATURES OF THE SEVERAL STATES PURSUANT TO THE FIFTH ARTICLE OF THE ORIGINAL CONSTITUTION.

Amendment I [1791]

Congress shall make no law respecting an establishment of religion, or prohibiting the free exercise thereof; or abridging the freedom of speech, or of the press; or the right of the people peaceably to assemble, and to petition the Government for a redress of grievances.

Amendment II [1791]

A well regulated Militia, being necessary to the security of a free State, the right of the people to keep and bear Arms, shall not be infringed.

Amendment III [1791]

No Soldier shall, in time of peace be quartered in any house, without the consent of the Owner, nor in time of war, but in a manner to be prescribed by law.

Amendment IV [1791]

The right of the people to be secure in their persons, houses, papers, and effects, against unreasonable searches and seizures, shall not be violated, and no Warrants shall issue, but upon probable cause, supported by Oath or affirmation, and particularly describing the place to be searched, and the persons or things to be seized.

Amendment V [1791]

No person shall be held to answer for a capital, or otherwise infamous crime, unless on a presentment or indictment of a Grand Jury, except in cases arising in the land or naval forces, or in the Militia, when in actual service in time of War or public danger; nor shall any person be subject for the same offence to be twice put in jeopardy of life or limb; nor shall be compelled in any criminal case to be a witness against himself, nor be deprived of life, liberty, or property, without due process of law; nor shall private property be taken for public use, without just compensation.

Amendment VI [1791]

In all criminal prosecutions, the accused shall enjoy the right to a speedy and public trial, by an impartial jury of the State and district wherein the crime shall have been committed, which district shall have been previously ascertained by law, and to be informed of the nature and cause of the accusation; to be confronted with the witnesses against him; to have compulsory process for obtaining witnesses in his favor, and to have the Assistance of Counsel for his defence.

Amendment VII [1791]

In Suits at common law, where the value in controversy shall exceed twenty dollars, the right of trial by jury shall be preserved, and no fact tried by jury, shall be otherwise reexamined in any Court of the United States, than according to the rules of the common law.

Amendment VIII [1791]

Excessive bail shall not be required, nor excessive fines imposed, nor cruel and unusual punishments inflicted.

Amendment IX [1791]

The enumeration in the Constitution, of certain rights, shall not be construed to deny or disparage others retained by the people.

Amendment X [1791]

The powers not delegated to the United States by the Constitution, nor prohibited by it to the States, are reserved to the States respectively, or to the people.

Amendment XI [1798]

The Judicial power of the United States shall not be construed to extend to any suit in law or equity, commenced or prosecuted against one of the United States by Citizens of another State, or by Citizens or Subjects of any Foreign State.

Amendment XII [1804]

The Electors shall meet in their respective states and vote by ballot for President and

Vice-President, one of whom, at least, shall not be an inhabitant of the same state with themselves; they shall name in their ballots the person voted for as President, and in distinct ballots the person voted for as Vice-President, and they shall make distinct lists of all persons voted for as President, and of all persons voted for as Vice-President, and of the number of votes for each, which lists they shall sign and certify, and transmit sealed to the seat of the government of the United States, directed to the President of the Senate;—The President of the Senate shall, in the presence of the Senate and House of Representatives, open all the certificates and the votes shall then be counted;—The person having the greatest number of votes for President, shall be the President, if such number be a majority of the whole number of Electors appointed; and if no person have such majority, then from the persons having the highest numbers not exceeding three on the list of those voted for as President, the House of Representatives shall choose immediately, by ballot, the President. But in choosing the President, the votes shall be taken by states, the representation from each state having one vote; a quorum for this purpose shall consist of a member or members from two-thirds of the States, and a majority of all the states shall be necessary to a choice. And if the House of Representatives shall not choose a President whenever the right of choice shall devolve upon them before the fourth day of March next following, then the Vice-President shall act as President, as in the case of the death or other constitutional disability of the President.—The person having the greatest number of votes as Vice-President, shall be the Vice-President, if such number be a majority of the whole number of Electors appointed, and if no person have a majority, then from the two highest numbers on the list, the Senate shall choose the Vice-

President; a quorum for the purpose shall consist of two-thirds of the whole number of Senators, and a majority of the whole number shall be necessary to a choice. But no person constitutionally ineligible to the office of President shall be eligible to that of Vice-President of the United States.

Amendment XIII [1865]

Section 1. Neither slavery nor involuntary servitude, except as a punishment for crime whereof the party shall have been duly convicted, shall exist within the United States, or any place subject to their jurisdiction.

Section 2. Congress shall have power to enforce this article by appropriate legislation.

Amendment XIV [1868]

Section 1. All persons born or naturalized in the United States, and subject to the jurisdiction thereof, are citizens of the United States and of the State wherein they reside. No State shall make or enforce any law which shall abridge the privileges or immunities of citizens of the United States; nor shall any State deprive any person of life, liberty, or property, without due process of law; nor deny to any person within its jurisdiction the equal protection of the laws.

Section 2. Representatives shall be apportioned among the several States according to their respective numbers, counting the whole number of persons in each State, excluding Indians not taxed. But when the right to vote at any election for the choice of electors for President and Vice President of the United States, Representatives in Congress, the Executive and Judicial officers of a State, or the members of the Legislature thereof, is denied to any of the male inhabitants of such State, being twenty-one years of age, and citizens of the United

States, or in any way abridged, except for participation in rebellion, or other crime, the basis of representation therein shall be reduced in the proportion which the number of such male citizens shall bear to the whole number of male citizens twenty-one years of age in such State.

Section 3. No person shall be a Senator or Representative in Congress, or elector of President and Vice President, or hold any office, civil or military, under the United States, or under any State, who having previously taken an oath, as a member of Congress, or as an officer of the United States, or as a member of any State legislature, or as an executive or judicial officer of any State, to support the Constitution of the United States, shall have engaged in insurrection or rebellion against the same, or given aid or comfort to the enemies thereof. But Congress may by a vote of two-thirds of each House, remove such disability.

Section 4. The validity of the public debt of the United States, authorized by law, including debts incurred for payment of pensions and bounties for services in suppressing insurrection or rebellion, shall not be questioned. But neither the United States nor any State shall assume or pay any debt or obligation incurred in aid of insurrection or rebellion against the United States, or any claim for the loss or emancipation of any slave; but all such debts, obligations and claims shall be held illegal and void.

Section 5. The Congress shall have power to enforce, by appropriate legislation, the provisions of this article.

Amendment XV [1870]

Section 1. The right of citizens of the United States to vote shall not be denied or abridged by the United States or by any State on account of race, color, or previous condition of servitude.

Section 2. The Congress shall have power to enforce this article by appropriate legislation.

Amendment XVI [1913]

The Congress shall have power to lay and collect taxes on incomes, from whatever source derived, without apportionment among the several States, and without regard to any census or enumeration.

Amendment XVII [1914]

[1] The Senate of the United States shall be composed of two Senators from each State, elected by the people thereof, for six years; and each Senator shall have one vote. The electors in each State shall have the qualifications requisite for electors of the most numerous branch of the State legislatures.

[2] When vacancies happen in the representation of any State in the Senate, the executive authority of such State shall issue writs of election to fill such vacancies: *Provided,* That the legislature of any State may empower the executive thereof to make temporary appointments until the people fill the vacancies by election as the legislature may direct.

[3] This amendment shall not be so construed as to affect the election or term of any Senator chosen before it becomes valid as part of the Constitution.

Amendment XVIII [1919]

Section 1. After one year from the ratification of this article the manufacture, sale, or transportation of intoxicating liquors within, the importation thereof into, or the exportation thereof from the United States and all territory subject to the jurisdiction thereof for beverage purposes is hereby prohibited.

Section 2. The Congress and the several States shall have concurrent power to enforce this article by appropriate legislation.

Section 3. This article shall be inoperative unless it shall have been ratified as an amendment to the Constitution by the legislatures of the several States, as provided in the Constitution, within seven years from the date of the submission hereof to the States by the Congress.

Amendment XIX [1920]

[1] The right of citizens of the United States to vote shall not be denied or abridged by the United States or by any State on account of sex.

[2] Congress shall have power to enforce this article by appropriate legislation.

Amendment XX [1933]

Section 1. The terms of the President and Vice President shall end at noon on the 20th day of January, and the terms of Senators and Representatives at noon on the 3d day of January, of the years in which such terms would have ended if this article had not been ratified; and the terms of their successors shall then begin.

Section 2. The Congress shall assemble at least once in every year, and such meeting shall begin at noon on the 3d day of January, unless they shall by law appoint a different day.

Section 3. If, at the time fixed for the beginning of the term of the President, the President elect shall have died, the Vice President elect shall become President. If the President shall not have been chosen before the time fixed for the beginning of his term, or if the President elect shall have failed to qualify, then the Vice President

elect shall act as President until a President shall have qualified; and the Congress may by law provide for the case wherein neither a President elect nor a Vice President elect shall have qualified, declaring who shall then act as President, or the manner in which one who is to act shall be selected, and such person shall act accordingly until a President or Vice President shall have qualified.

Section 4. The Congress may by law provide for the case of the death of any of the persons from whom the House of Representatives may choose a President whenever the right of choice shall have devolved upon them, and for the case of the death of any of the persons from whom the Senate may choose a Vice President whenever the right of choice shall have devolved upon them.

Section 5. Sections 1 and 2 shall take effect on the 15th day of October following the ratification of this article.

Section 6. This article shall be inoperative unless it shall have been ratified as an amendment to the Constitution by the legislatures of three-fourths of the several States within seven years from the date of its submission.

Amendment XXI [1933]

Section 1. The eighteenth article of amendment to the Constitution of the United States is hereby repealed.

Section 2. The transportation or importation into any State, Territory, or possession of the United States for delivery or use therein of intoxicating liquors, in violation of the laws thereof, is hereby prohibited.

Section 3. This article shall be inoperative unless it shall have been ratified as an amendment to the Constitution by conventions in the several States, as provided in the Constitution, within seven years from the date of the submission hereof to the States by the Congress.

Amendment XXII [1951]

Section 1. No person shall be elected to the office of the President more than twice, and no person who has held the office of President, or acted as President, for more than two years of a term to which some other person was elected President shall be elected to the office of President more than once. But this Article shall not apply to any person holding the office of President when this Article was proposed by the Congress, and shall not prevent any person who may be holding the office of President, or acting as President, during the term within which this Article becomes operative from holding the office of President or acting as President during the remainder of such term.

Section 2. This article shall be inoperative unless it shall have been ratified as an amendment to the Constitution by the legislatures of three-fourths of the several States within seven years from the date of its submission to the States by the Congress.

Amendment XXIII [1961]

Section 1. The District constituting the seat of Government of the United States shall appoint in such manner as the Congress may direct:

A number of electors of President and Vice President equal to the whole number of Senators and Representatives in Congress to which the District would be entitled if it were a State, but in no event more than the least populous state; they shall be in addition to those appointed by the states, but they shall be considered, for the purposes of the election of President and Vice President, to be electors appointed by

a state; and they shall meet in the District and perform such duties as provided by the twelfth article of amendment.

Section 2. The Congress shall have power to enforce this article by appropriate legislation.

Amendment XXIV [1964]

Section 1. The right of citizens of the United States to vote in any primary or other election for President or Vice President, for electors for President or Vice President, or for Senator or Representative in Congress, shall not be denied or abridged by the United States or any State by reason of failure to pay any poll tax or other tax.

Section 2. The Congress shall have power to enforce this article by appropriate legislation.

Amendment XXV [1967]

Section 1. In case of the removal of the President from office or of his death or resignation, the Vice President shall become President.

Section 2. Whenever there is a vacancy in the office of the Vice President, the President shall nominate a Vice President who shall take office upon confirmation by a majority vote of both Houses of Congress.

Section 3. Whenever the President transmits to the President pro tempore of the Senate and the Speaker of the House of Representatives his written declaration that he is unable to discharge the powers and duties of his office, and until he transmits to them a written declaration to the contrary, such powers and duties shall be discharged by the Vice President as Acting President.

Section 4. Whenever the Vice President and a majority of either the principal officers of the executive departments or of such other body as Congress may by law provide, transmit to the President pro tempore of the Senate and the Speaker of the House of Representatives their written declaration that the President is unable to discharge the powers and duties of his office, the Vice President shall immediately assume the powers and duties of the office as Acting President.

Thereafter, when the President transmits to the President pro tempore of the Senate and the Speaker of the House of Representatives his written declaration that no inability exists, he shall resume the powers and duties of his office unless the Vice President and a majority of either the principal officers of the executive department or of such other body as Congress may by law provide, transmit within four days to the President pro tempore of the Senate and the Speaker of the House of Representatives their written declaration that the President is unable to discharge the powers and duties of his office. Thereupon Congress shall decide the issue, assembling within forty-eight hours for that purpose if not in session. If the Congress, within twenty-one days after receipt of the latter written declaration, or, if Congress is not in session, within twenty-one days after Congress is required to assemble, determines by two-thirds vote of both Houses that the President is unable to discharge the powers and duties of his office, the Vice President shall continue to discharge the same as Acting President; otherwise, the President shall resume the powers and duties of his office.

Amendment XXVI [1971]

Section 1. The right of citizens of the United States, who are eighteen years of age or older, to vote shall not be denied or abridged by the United States or by any State on account of age.

Section 2. The Congress shall have power to enforce this article by appropriate legislation.

Equal Rights Amendment (ERA)

Amendment XXVII [Proposed but not ratified][†]

Section 1. Equality of rights under the law shall not be denied or abridged by the United States or by any State on account of sex.

Section 2. The Congress shall have the power to enforce, by appropriate legislation, the provisions of this article.

Section 3. This amendment shall take effect two years after the date of ratification.

†The proposed 27th Amendment was submitted to the states on March 22, 1972. Although about half of the necessary number of states approved the Amendment in the first three months after submission, the drive for adoption of the Equal Rights Amendment slowed thereafter. By the ratification deadline, support for the Amendment still fell three short of the required 38 ratifying state legislatures. A three-year extension of the seven-year ratification period produced no additional state ratifications.

Case Index

The following is a case index. Those cases indicated in boldface type are excerpted in this book. The number in boldface type is the page where the excerpt begins.

Abele v. Markle, 351
Adair v. United States, 26
Adams v. City of Milwaukee, 124
Adams v. Tanner, 320
Adkins v. Children's Hospital, xii, 9, 24, 25, **26**, 37, 39, 41, 42, 44, 45, 46, 48, 101, 320, 321, 601
Adkins v. Lyons, 24, 29 n, 601
Aetna Insurance Co. v. Hyde, 100
Akron v. Akron Center for Reproductive Health, **375**, 387, 396, 397, 407, 412, 433, 609
Albermarle Paper Co. v. Moody, 246, 247, 478, 483, 519, 521, 528, 529, 536
Alexander v. Davis, 246
Alexander v. Louisiana, 603
Allgeyer v. Louisiana, 10, 15, 21, 26
Allied Stores v. Bowers, 129
American Sugar Refining Co. v. Louisiana, 39, 97
Anderson v. Martin, 91
Apodaca v. Oregon, 144, 148
Aptheker v. Secretary of State, 344, 350
Arizona Governing Committee v. Norris, 523, **524**, 610
Arkansas Natural Gas Co. v. Railroad Commission, 40
Arlington Heights v. Metropolitan Housing Development Corp., 238, 243, 244, 245 n, 246
Armour Packing Co. v. Lacy, 97
Armstrong v. Manzo, 229
Ashwander v. Tennessee Valley Authority, 330, 356, 416
Atkin v. Kansas, 16, 18, 27

Baggett v. Bullitt, 312
Baker v. Carr, 167, 234, 237

Ballard v. United States, 105, 106, 143, 145, 602
Baltimore & Ohio R. Co. v. Interstate Commerce Commission, 49
Barbier v. Connolly, 15, 113
Barenblatt v. United States, 312
Barrows v. Jackson, 167, 168, 173
Bates v. Little Rock, 317
Beal v. Doe, 273, 376 n, 378, 408, 413, **415**, 420, 421, 425, 429, 432, 433, 434, 437, 606
Bell v. Burson, 200
Bellotti v. Baird I (1976), 373, 375 n, 386, 391, 395, 423, 428, 429, 436
Bellotti v. Baird II (1979), 376 n, 378 n, 382, 391, 392, 395, 608
Black v. Cutter Laboratories, 287 n
Blake v. McClung, 349
Blodgett v. Holden, 250
Board of Education v. Barnette, 313
Board of Regents v. Roth, 229
Boddie v. Connecticut, 428
Bolling v. Sharpe, 91, 117 n, 350
Bosley v. McLaughlin, 34, 35, 39, 40, 44, 46, 100
Bowers v. Hardwick, 333
Boyd v. United States, 313, 343, 352 n
Bradwell v. Illinois, xii, 4, 63, 66, 67, 68, **70**, 101, 118, 152, 601
Breard v. Alexandria, 313
Breed v. Jones, 364
Breedlove v. Suttles, 99, **100**, 602
Brimmer v. Rebman, 14
Brown v. Allen, 143, 149
Brown v. Board of Education, 91, 243, 272, 283, 284, 408 n, 424
Brown v. Louisiana, 328
Buck v. Bell, 303, **304**, 305, 307, 308, 309, 310, 344, 354, 359, 601

Bundy v. Jackson, 561
Bunting v. Oregon, 23, 25, 28, 33, 34, 35, 36, 43, 48, 49, 101
Butchers' Union Co. v. Crescent City Co., 26

Caban v. Mohammed, 58, 63, 208, **209,** 221, 222, 224, 226, 229, 230n, 232, 243, 248, 260, 277, 287, 607
Cafeteria Workers v. McElroy, 198, 225
Califano v. Goldfarb, 179, **180,** 192, 193, 194, 195, 212, 236, 243, 247, 253, 269n, 277, 279, 605
Califano v. Webster, 192, **193,** 194, 234, 235, 236, 248, 253, 269, 272, 289, 606
Califano v. Wescott, 58, 254, 260, 277, 608
California Federal Savings & Loan v. Guerra, 50, **52,** 496, 497, 611
California v. LaRue, 103, 173
Cannon v. University of Chicago, 548, 549
Cantwell v. Connecticut, 344
Carey v. Population Services International, 274, 333, 378n, 399, 401, 406n, 422, 606
Cargill Co. v. Minnesota, 97
Cariddi v. Kansas City Chiefs Football Club, 556
Carrington v. Rash, 121, 130, 350, 353
Carroll v. Greenwich Insurance Co., 40, 46
Carter v. Jury Comm'n., 143, 149
Carter v. Virginia, 102
Castaneda v. Partida, 247
CBS, Inc. v. Democratic National Committee, 250, 251
Chapman v. Meier, 428
Chevron Oil Co. v. Huson, 220, 535, 536
Chicago B. & Q. R. Co. v. McGuire, 43
Church of the Holy Trinity v. United States, 54
City of. See under name
Cleveland Board of Education v. LaFleur, 169, **456,** 464, 475, 496, 497, 604
Colautti v. Franklin, 374, 375, 377, 385, 388, 393, 607
Committee for Pub. Ed. & Rel. Lib. v. Regan, 441
Commonwealth v. Baird, 324, 329
Compston v. Borden, Inc., 556
Connecticut v. Menillo, 375n, 379n
Connolly v. Union Sewer Pipe Co., 39, 97, 98
Connor v. Finch, 428
Cook v. Arentzen, 487n
Cooper v. Aaron, 399
Coppage v. Kansas, 26, 39, 320, 321

Corfield v. Coryell, 5, 6
Corning Glass v. Brennan, 501, 604
Craig v. Boren, 63, 111, 165, **166,** 178, 179, 182n, 183, 184, 193, 194, 195, 209, 221, 222, 228, 234, 235, 236, 240, 241, 243, 248, 249, 252, 256, 260, 261, 262, 268, 274, 276, 279n, 286, 288, 294, 452n, 469, 605
Cramer v. United States, 245n
Crowley v. Christensen, 10

Dandridge v. Williams, 117, 123, 174, 176, 421, 430, 460, 461, 466, 467, 468
Davidson v. New Orleans, 15
DeFunis v. Odegaard, 167
De Jonge v. Oregon, 313
Doe v. Bolton, xi, 334, 336, 337, 339, **347,** 352, 357, 359, 360, 362, 377, 380, 384, 391n, 402, 416, 417, 422, 426, 427, 429, 431, 432, 433, 434, 437, 451, 497, 604
Dothard v. Rawlinson, 483, 504, **507,** 606
Douglas v. California, 428
Duke Power Company v. Carolina Environmental Study Group, Inc., 238
Duncan v. Louisiana, 143, 144, 149, 150, 151
Dunn v. Blumstein, 428

Eisenstadt v. Baird, 168, 173, 179, 323, **324,** 333, 334, 336, 338, 343, 344, 345, 351, 359, 363, 377, 399, 406n, 418n, 455, 456, 603
Elfbrandt v. Russell, 446
Ellis v. United States, 27
Entick v. Carrington, 313
Eubanks v. Louisiana, 108

Falbo v. United States, 254
Fay v. New York, 107, 147n, 148
Ferguson v. Skrupa, 129, 350, 353n
Fiallo v. Bell, 205, 206, 207, 606
Finley v. California, 306
Firefighters Institute for Racial Equality v. St. Louis, 556
Firefighters v. Cleveland, 567, 568, 571, 580
Flemming v. Nestor, 117, 157
Florida Lime & Avocado Growers, Inc. v. Paul, 53, 58
Forbush v. Wallace, 603
Frank v. Maryland, 313–314
Frontiero v. Laird, 122
Frontiero v. Richardson, 90, 92, 115, **116,** 127, 129n, 130, 131, 132, 133, 135, 136, 139, 140, 151, 152, 153, 154, 155, 157, 158, 160, 168,

169n, 172n, 174, 175, 180, 183, 188, 190, 191, 194, 213, 243, 262, 288, 289, 334, 465, 466n, 468, 470, 471, 604
Frost & Frost Trucking Co. v. Railroad Comm'n., 446, 447
Fullilove v. Klutznick, 272, 562
Funk v. U.S., 232

Gaines v. Canada, 307
Gault, In re, 364
Geduldig v. Aiello, 160, 455, 464, **465**, 469, 470, 471, 472, 474, 475, 479, 488, 513, 522, 585, 604
General Electric v. Gilbert, 52, 55, 57, 279n, 419, 455, 469, **470**, 481, 482, 483, 484, 485, 486, 487, 488, 489, 490, 491, 492, 493, 494, 495, 496, 518, 522, 523, 527n, 555, 585, 605
German Alliance Insurance Co. v. Lewis, 35
Gideon v. Wainwright, 149
Gilligan v. Morgan, 251
Ginsberg v. New York, 364
Glasser v. United States, 143, 147n, 149
Glidden Company v. Zdanok, 388
Glona v. American Guarantee Co., 199
Goesaert v. Cleary, 101, **102**, 152, 170n, 178, 233, 468, 602
Goldberg v. Kelly, 199, 446
Gomez v. Perez, 216n
Gomillion v. Lightfoot, 243, 246
Goss v. Board of Education, 246
Goss v. Lopez, 229, 364
Graham v. Richardson, 469
Gray v. Greyhound Lines, East, 556
Green v. Waterford Board of Education, 457
Griffin v. Illinois, 246, 427, 428
Griggs v. Duke Power Co., 57, 60, 478, 482, 483, 507, 516, 517n, 526, 555, 559, 569n, 582
Griswold v. Connecticut, xi, 168, 173, 199, 274, 310, 311, **312**, 322, 323, 324, 325, 326, 327, 329, 331, 332, 333, 335, 338, 343, 344, 345, 350, 351, 352, 353, 355, 359, 363, 377, 399, 400, 405, 406n, 409, 440, 456, 602
Grove City College v. Bell, 297, 542, 543, **544**, 552, 610
Guinn v. United States, 243

Hamilton v. Kentucky Distilleries & Warehouse Co., 251
Hampton v. Mow Sun Wong, 184, 186, 451
Harlow v. Fitzgerald, 296n
Harris v. McRae, 274, 376n, 383n, 386, 390, 391, 392, 394, 402n, 408, 437, **438**, 454, 608

Harris v. Nelson, 484
Harrison v. NAACP, 393
Hawker v. New York, 306
Hawley v. Walker, 35
Hayes v. Missouri, 39
Hazelwood School District v. United States, 566, 574
Heaton v. Bristol, 295n
Heim v. McCall, 27
Henson v. Dundee, 556
Hernandez v. Texas, 107, 108
Hill v. Texas, 108
Hines v. Davidowitz, 53
Hirabayashi v. United States, 91
Hishon v. King & Spaulding, 539, 540, 610
H. L. v. Matheson, 274, 374, 376n, 378n, 390, 391, 394, 402n, 608
Holden v. Hardy, 11, 15, 21, 27, 33, 39, 43, 49, 299
Holy Trinity Church v. United States, 580
Hostetter v. Idlewild Bon Voyage Liquor Corp., 173
Hoyt v. Florida, xi, xii, 105, **106**, 109, 111, 115, 140, 142, 146, 147, 148, 149, 150, 151, 152, 468, 602
Hudnut v. American Booksellers' Association, 541, 610

Ingraham v. Wright, 229
In re. *See* name of individual party

Jacobson v. Massachusetts, 16, 304, 327, 344, 354
James v. Valtierra, 441
James v. Wallace, 508, 511
Jay Burns Baking Co. v. Bryan, 320, 321
Jefferson v. Hackney, 117, 174, 190, 431, 449, 446, 467, 468
Johnson v. Transportation Agency, 563, 564, **565**, 612
Jones v. Rath Packing Co., 53

Kahn v. Shevin, xii, 127, **128**, 132, 133, 135, 136, 138, 153, 154, 155, 159, 160, 168n, 175n, 180n, 182n, 183, 184, 185, 186, 187, 188, 190, 191, 192, 193, 194, 236, 237, 252n, 269, 270, 274, 468, 604
Katz v. United States, 343, 350n
Katzenbach v. Morgan, 291
Kemmler, In re, 10
Kent v. Dulles, 350, 353

Keokee Coke Co. v. Taylor, 40, 46, 307
Kilbourn v. Thompson, 352 n
Kirchberg v. Feenstra, 240, 260, 277, 287, 608
Kohr v. Weinberger, 194
Korematsu v. United States, 91
Kovacs v. Cooper, 199, 317
Kramer v. Union Free School District, 344, 353

Lane v. Wilson, 243
Lanza v. New York, 313
Lassiter v. Department of Social Services, 230
Lau v. Nichols, 57
Lawton v. Steele, 15
Lehnhausen v. Lake Shore Auto Parts Co., 129
Lehr v. Robertson, 224, 232, 609
Levy v. Louisiana, 199
Lichter v. United States, 251
Linda R. S. v. Richard D., 234
Lindsey v. Normet, 425
Lindsley v. Natural Carbonic Gas Co., 113
Linmark Associates v. Township of
   Willingboro, 428
Little v. Streater, 230
Liverpool N. Y. & Phil. S. S. Co. v. Commis-
   sioners of Emigration, 162, 356
Lochner v. New York, xi, 8, 9, **10**, 20, 21, 22,
   25, 26, 27, 28, 33, 36, 298, 311, 320, 356, 408
**Los Angeles Dept. of Water and Power v. Man-
   hart,** 57, 460, 488, 492, 513, 514, **515**, 524, 525,
   526, 527, 529, 530, 531, 532, 533, 534, 535,
   536, 555, 607
Loving v. Virginia, 325 n, 343, 345, 351, 353,
   377, 456

McCulloch v. Maryland, 16
McDonald v. Board of Election Commissioners,
   113
McDonald v. Santa Fe Trail Transportation Co.,
   570, 573
McDonnell Douglas Corp. v. Green, 483, 509
McGowan v. Maryland, 117, 174
McLaughlin v. Florida, 88, 90, **91**, 95, 243, 272,
   317
McLean v. Arkansas, 97, 306
MacLennan v. American Airlines, 487
Maher v. Roe, 273, 376 n, 383 n, 386, 398, 391,
   402, 408, 416, 419, 420, **421**, 430, 431 n, 432,
   434, 435, 437, 439, 440, 441, 443, 449, 450,
   451, 452, 454, 606
Mahoney v. Joseph Triner Corp., 173
Malloy v. Hogan, 149

Malone v. White Motor Corp., 53, 54
Malpica-Orsini, In re, 210, 211, 215 n, 218 n,
   219 n
Mapp v. Ohio, 313
Martin v. Struthers, 312
Maryland v. Louisiana, 53
Massachusetts v. Murgia, 243, 425, 430
Mathews v. Eldridge, 229
Mathews v. Lucas, 173 n, 183, 184, 248
Matthews v. Rodgers, 393
May v. Anderson, 199
Maynard v. Hill, 363
Meachum v. Fano, 229
Memorial Hospital v. Maricopa County, 423 n,
   428, 446, 469
Meritor Savings Bank v. Vinson, 553, 610
Meyer v. Nebraska, 199, 225, 300, 310, 311, 312,
   313, 314, 315, 316, 317, 320, 343, 345, 350,
   351, 353 n, 377, 399, 406 n, 424, 440 n, 456
Michael M. v. Sonoma County, 252, 253, 256,
   268, 278 n, 608
Miller v. Wilson, 34, 35, 39, 40, 44, 46, 100, 306
Milligan, Ex parte, 251
Minnesota v. Barber, 14, 16
Minor v. Happersett, 73, **76**, 601
Mississippi University for Women v. Hogan,
   284, 285, **286**, 609
Missouri K. & T. R. Co. v. May, 391, 425
Monell v. New York City Dept. of Social Ser-
   vices, 581
Monroe v. Board of Commissioners, 246
Monroe v. Pape, 313, 581
Moore v. East Cleveland, 225, 226, 399, 405, 406 n
Moore v. Missouri, 306
Moose Lodge v. Irvis, 355
Morehead v. New York ex. rel. Tipaldo, 46, 601
Morey v. Doud, 203, 348
Morrison v. California, 308
Morrissey v. Brewer, 225, 229
Mountain Timber Co. v. Washington, 43
Mugler v. Kansas, 10, 16
Mullane v. Central Hanover Trust, 231
Muller v. Oregon, 19, **20**, 26, 28, 33, 34, 35, 39,
   43, 48, 49, 63, 96, 97, 100, 101, 129, 132, 468,
   601
Munn v. Illinois, 27

NAACP v. Alabama, 313, 314, 353
NAACP v. Button, 428, 540
Nashville Gas Co. v. Satty, 55, 455, 480, **481**,
   488, 517 n, 518 n, 607

National Mutual Ins. Co. v. Tidewater Transfer Co., 351
Newport News Shipbuilding v. EEOC, 52n, 55, 61, 455, 488, **489**, 527n, 609
New York Central R. Co. v. White, 43
New York Department of Social Services v. Dublino, 416
New York Life Insurance Co. v. Dodge, 26
New York Transit Authority v. Beazer, 228, 243
Norris v. Alabama, 108
North Haven Board of Education v. Bell, 545, 550, 552
Norwood v. Harrison, 424, 540

Oliver, In re, 149
Olmstead v. United States, 343, 353
Orr v. Orr, 213, **233**, 238, 243, 247, 248, 260, 270n, 271, 277, 287, 294, 607
Orsini v. Blasi, 210

Pacific Gas & Electric Co. v. State Energy Resources Conservation and Development Commission, 56–57
Packard v. Banton, 39, 46
Palko v. Connecticut, 316, 343, 405
Papachristou v. City of Jacksonville, 353
Parham v. Hughes, 222, 268, 269, 272, 607
Parham v. J. R., 389
Patsone v. Pennsylvania, 40, 306, 307
Pennhurst State School & Hospital v. Halderman, 546
People v. Hernandez, 278n
Personnel Administrator v. Feeney, 241, 249, 250, 261, 287, 607
Peters v. Kiff, 141, 143, 144, 145n
Phillips v. Martin Marietta, 57, 260, 334, 478, 498, **499**, 504, 507, 511, 602
Pierce v. Society of Sisters, 225, 300, 310, 311, 312, 313, 315, 316, 317, 320, 343, 345, 350, 351, 353, 377, 399, 406n, 424, 440, 456
Pittsburgh Press v. Human Relations Commission, 539, 604
Planned Parenthood v. Ashcroft, 375, 395, 399, 411, 609
Planned Parenthood v. Danforth, 204, 207, 216n, 298, 360, **361**, 365n, 374, 375, 378, 379, 382, 383, 384, 387, 388, 389, 390, 391, 394, 397, 403, 413, 422, 427, 429, 439, 605
Plessy v. Ferguson, 272
Plyler v. Doe, 386
Poe v. Ullman, 316, 351, 377, 405

Poelker v. Doe, 274, 432, **434**, 437, 454, 606
Pointer v. Texas, 149
Powell v. Alabama, 149, 315
Prince v. Massachusetts, 199, 225, 316, 317, 343, 351, 364, 456
Public Utilities Comm'n. v. Pollak, 313, 328

Quilloin v. Walcott, 207, 208, 226, 227n, 228, 230n, 232, 607
Quong Wing v. Kirkendall, 36, 44, 96, **97**, 100, 601

Radice v. New York, 37, **38**, 46, 101, 601
Railway Express Agency v. New York, 113, 327
Railway Mail Association v. Corsi, 540
Rawlins v. Georgia, 146
Red Lion Broadcasting Co. v. FCC, 416
Reed v. Reed, 112, **113**, 115, 117, 118, 120, 121, 123n, 124, 125, 127, 129, 130, 131, 133, 135, 136, 140, 151, 152, 153, 157, 160, 165, 166, 168, 169, 170, 173, 175, 180, 181, 183, 190, 196, 200n, 209, 210, 213, 228, 232, 234, 235, 243, 248, 252, 256, 274, 284, 285, 287, 289, 325, 334, 465, 466n, 468, 470, 471, 498, 585, 603
Reitman v. Mulkey, 269, 271n
Rescue Army v. Municipal Court, 162, 163
Reynolds v. Sims, 428
Rice v. Santa Fe Elevator Corp., 53
Richardson v. Belcher, 117, 174, 175, 182
Riley v. Massachusetts, 34, 35, 39, 44, 100
Rinaldi v. Yeager, 124, 268
Roberts v. Jaycees, 540, 610
Roe v. Norton, 445
Roe v. Wade, xi, 334, 336, 337, 347, 349, 350, 352, 353n, 355, 357, 359, 360, 361, 362, 363, 367, 368, 370, 372, 373, 374, 375, 376n, 377, 378, 379, 380, 381, 383, 385, 386, 387, 388, 389, 390, 391, 392n, 396, 400, 401, 402, 403, 404, 405, 406, 407, 408, 409, 410, 411, 412, 413, 415, 416, 417, 418, 419, 422, 423, 424, 425, 426, 427, 428, 429, 430, 432, 433, 434, 436, 439, 440, 441, 442, 443, 444, 445, 450, 451, 452, 453, 455, 456, 497, 604
Rogers v. EEOC, 556
Rosenthal v. New York, 100, 307
Rostker v. Goldberg, 250, 608
Royster Guano Co. v. Virginia, 114, 161, 170, 211, 325
Rundlett v. Oliver, 271
Runyon v. McCrary, 540, 570

Sail'er Inn, Inc. v. Kirby, 511
San Antonio School District v. Rodriguez, 390, 421, 431
Santosky v. Kramer, 226
Schlesinger v. Ballard, 113, **134,** 140, 160, 168, 175n, 181, 182n, 183, 191, 193, 194, 213, 214, 235, 249, 250, 253, 255, 256, 269, 272, 274, 289, 294, 604
Schneider v. Rusk, 117n
Schroeder v. City of New York, 231
Schware v. Board of Bar Examiners, 317, 350
Seagram & Sons v. Hostetter, 173
Semler v. Oregon Board, 46
Shapiro v. Thompson, 117n, 121, 123n, 130, 325n, 344, 349, 350, 353, 423n, 428, 440n, 446, 468
Shaw v. Delta Air Lines, Inc., 53, 54n
Sheet Metal Workers v. EEOC, 567, 568, 574
Shelton v. Tucker, 317, 458
Sherbert v. Verner, 344, 353, 423n, 428, 440n, 446
Sierra Club v. Morris, 355
Simon v. Eastern Kentucky Welfare Rights Org., 238
Simopoulos v. Virginia, 375, 387n, 392, 395, 609
Singleton v. Wulff, 167, 413, 429
Skinner v. Oklahoma, 199, 305, **306,** 309, 314, 317, 327, 343, 345, 351, 353, 368, 401n, 422n, 456, 602
Slaughter-House Cases, 4, 6, 7, 8, 66, 67, 68, 69, 88, 93
Smith v. Allwright, 388
Smith v. Bennett, 429n
Smith v. Organization of Foster Families, 215n, 226, 229, 230
Smith v. Texas, 143, 144, 148, 149
Smith v. Wayne Probate Judges, 307
Snyder v. Massachusetts, 314, 315, 357
Socialist Labor Party v. Gilligan, 163
Southeastern Community College v., Davis, 496n
Southeastern Promotions, Ltd. v. Conrad, 446
Speiser v. Randall, 446
Springer v. Bliss, 170
Sproles v. Binford, 46
Stanley v. Georgia, 327
Stanley v. Illinois, 121, 156, 168, 169, 175n, 180, 183, 196, **197,** 204, 206, 207, 213, 215n, 223, 224, 226, 232, 334, 345, 368, 370, 458, 459, 461, 603

Stanton v. Stanton, 159, 168, 169, 170n, 174, 179, 181, 183, 193, 212, 213, 235, 247, 268, 285, 290, 605
State Board of Equalization v. Young's Market Co., 173
State ex rel. Springer v. Bliss, 170
State Farm Mutual Automobile Ins. Co. v. Duel, 201
State v. Hall, 109, 602
Stern v. Stern, 235
Strauder v. West Virginia, 107, 147n
Street v. New York, 357
Stromberg v. California, 328
Sturgis v. Attorney General, 325
Sullivan v. Little Hunting Park, 168, 173
Swann v. Board of Education, 244
Sweezy v. New Hampshire, 312

Taylor v. Georgia, 308
Taylor v. Jones, 558
Taylor v. Louisiana, xi, xii, 140, 141, **142,** 151, 152, 154n, 159, 161, 164, 168, 179, 183, 196, 604
Teamsters v. United States, 496n, 565, 576
Terry v. Ohio, 343
Thiel v. Southern Pacific, 105, 144
Thornburgh v. ACOG, 395, **396,** 433, 611
Tigner v. Texas, 102, 268
Tinker v. Des Moines School District, 364
Toomer v. Witsell, 349
Tot v. United States, 124
Toth v. Quarles, 253
Townsend v. Swank, 418
Train v. Colorado Public Interest Research Group, Inc., 54
Train v. Natural Resources Defense Council, 479
Trammel v. U. S., 232
Trimble v. Gordon, 216n, 225n, 248
Truax v. Raich, 39, 350
Turner v. Department of Employment Security, 464, 496, 605

Udall v. Tallman, 500
Union Pacific R. Co. v. Botsford, 342, 354
United Jewish Organizations v. Carey, 236, 245
United States Dept. of Agric. v. Moreno, 446
United States v. American Trucking Assns., 54–55
United States v. Butler, 239

United States v. Carolene Products Co., 308, 449

United States v. Darby, xi, 48, **49**

United States v. Dege, 232, 233

United States v. Gaston County, 120 *n*

United States v. Guest, 350

United States v. Harriss, 385

United States v. Maryland Savings-Share Insurance Co., 123

United States v. O'Brien, 251, 270 *n*

United States v. Public Utilities Comm'n., 572

United States v. Raines, 173, 325, 330

United States v. Robel, 266

United States v. Vuitch, 345, 348, 352, 354, 358, 417 *n*

United States v. Yazell, 225

United Steel Workers v. Weber, 51, 59, 562, 563, 565, 566, 567, 570, 571, 572, 573, 574, 476, 579, 580, 581, 582, 583

University of California Regents v. Bakke, 562, 563, 567, 568, 570

Village of. *See under* name

Virginia, Ex parte, 291

Virginia Board of Elections v. Hamm, 91

Vlandis v. Kline, 458, 461, 462

Vorchheimer v. Philadelphia, 285, 287 *n*, 606

Ward v. Maryland, 349

Warth v. Seldin, 168, 237

Washington County v. Gunther, 532 *n*, 537, 538, 608

Washington v. Davis, 240, 241, 243, 244, 245, 247, 431

Watson v. City of Memphis, 91

Weber v. Aetna Casualty & Surety Co., 119, 172 *n*, 215 *n*

Weeks v. Southern Bell Telephone and Telegraph Co., 507

Weinberger v. Wiesenfeld, xii, 152, 153, **154**, 159, 160, 168, 169 *n*, 175 *n*, 180, 181, 182, 183, 184, 187, 188, 191, 192, 193, 194, 213, 236, 243, 247, 248, 269, 274, 289, 290 *n*, 605

Wengler v. Druggists Mutual Insurance Co., 58, 63, 195, 260, 277, 287, 295, 492, 608

West Coast Hotel v. Parrish, xi, xii, 41, **42**, 48, 49, 601

Westby v. Doe, 416

Whalen v. Roe, 377, 378 *n*, 384, 399, 423

Wieman v. Updegraff, 312

Williams v. Fears, 97

Williams v. Florida, 144

Williams v. McNair, 284, 285, 295 *n*, 603

Williams v. Zbaraz, 274, 451

Williamson v. Lee Optical Co., 174, 190, 326, 356, 392, 409, 463, 466

Wimberly v. Labor and Industrial Relations Commission, 65, 611

Wisconsin v. Yoder, 227

Wolf v. Schroering, 365

Wygant v. Jackson Board of Education, 568, 573, 574, 578

Yick Wo v. Hopkins, 15, 97–98, 243, 307, 317, 357

Yot Sang, In re, 97

Zemel v. Rusk, 318

DESIGNED BY MIKE BURTON
COMPOSED BY G&S TYPESETTERS, INC., AUSTIN, TEXAS
MANUFACTURED BY CUSHING MALLOY, INC., ANN ARBOR, MICHIGAN
TEXT AND DISPLAY LINES ARE SET IN PALATINO

Library of Congress Cataloging-in-Publication Data
Goldstein, Leslie Friedman, 1945–
The constitutional rights of women.
Includes index.
1. Sex discrimination against women—Law and
legislation—United States—Cases.   2. Women—Legal
status, laws, etc.—United States—Cases.
3. Sociological jurisprudence—Cases.   4. United
States. Supreme Court.   I. Title.
KF4758.A7G66   1988   342.73′0878   87-40361
ISBN 0-299-11240-3   347.302878
ISBN 0-299-11244-6 (pbk.)

Technical Communication Today

FIFTH EDITION

Richard Johnson-Sheehan
Purdue University

PEARSON

Boston   Columbus   Indianapolis   New York   San Francisco   Upper Saddle River
Amsterdam   Cape Town   Dubai   London   Madrid   Milan   Munich   Paris   Montreal   Toronto
Delhi   Mexico City   São Paulo   Sydney   Hong Kong   Seoul   Singapore   Taipei   Tokyo

To Tracey, Emily, and Collin

Senior Acquisitions Editor: Brad Potthoff
Senior Development Editor: Anne Brunell
　Ehrenworth
Executive Field Marketing Manager:
　Joyce Nilsen
Product Marketing Manager:
　Jennifer Edwards
Executive Digital Producer: Stefanie Snajder
Digital Editor: Sara Gordus
Senior Supplements Editor: Donna Campion
Project Manager: Denise Phillip Grant
Project Coordination, Text Design, and
　Electronic Page Makeup: Cenveo®
　Publisher Services
Cover Design Manager: Heather Scott
Senior Manufacturing Buyer: Roy Pickering
Printer/Binder: R.R. Donnelley/Harrisonburg
Cover Printer: R.R. Donnelley/Harrisonburg

Cover Photos: Bottom, first row right,
ocean scene within pad: Lev Kropotov/
Shutterstock; bottom second row, second
from left cloud with colored arrows: Alex
Millos/Shutterstock; bottom first row,
right pad with hands: Tcey/Shutterstock;
bottom second row first from left, hand
with phone: Syda Productions/Fotolia;
bottom second row, fifth from left,
conference phone: Area 381/Fotolia;
bottom first row left laptop: Tsiumpa/
Fotolia; bottom second row, fourth from
left, RSS feed icon: Alex White/Fotolia;
top middle group of 4 people at table:
Jupiter Images/Getty Images; top left and
top right: Robert Churchhill/Getty Images;
bottom second row third from left, safety
glasses: 4X Image/Getty Images.

Credits and acknowledgments borrowed from other sources and reproduced, with permission, in this textbook appear on the appropriate page within text or on pages C-1 to C-2.

Library of Congress Cataloging-in-Publication Data
Johnson-Sheehan, Richard, author.
　Technical communication today / Richard Johnson-Sheehan, Purdue University. -- Fifth edition.
　　pages cm
　Includes bibliographical references and index.
　ISBN 978-0-321-90798-1 -- ISBN 0-321-90798-1
1. Communication of technical information. I. Title.
　T10.5.J64 2015
　601'.4--dc23

　　　　　　　　　　　　　2014022467

Copyright © 2015, 2012, 2010 by Pearson Education, Inc.

10 9 8 7 6 5 4 — DOC —17 16 15

www.pearsonhighered.com
Student Edition ISBN 10: 0-321-90798-1
Student Edition ISBN 13: 978-0-321-90798-1

A la Carte ISBN 10: 0-321-99665-8
A la Carte ISBN 13: 978-0-321-99665-7

PEARSON

Contents

Preface *xviii*

Part 1: Elements of Technical Communication

CHAPTER 1 | **Communicating in the Technical Workplace** *1*

Developing a Workplace Writing Process *2*

Genres and the Technical Writing Process *3*

Stage 1: Planning Out Your Project and Doing Start-up Research *4*

Stage 2: Organizing and Drafting *6*

Stage 3: Improving the Style *8*

Stage 4: Designing *8*

Stage 5: Revising and Editing *8*

What Is Technical Communication? *9*

Technical Communication Is Interactive and Adaptable *10*

Technical Communication Is Reader Centered *10*

Technical Communication Relies on Teamwork *11*

Technical Communication Is Visual *12*

Technical Communication Has Ethical, Legal, and Political Dimensions *12*

Technical Communication Is International and Transcultural *14*

How Important Is Technical Communication? *14*

What You Need to Know *15*

Exercises and Projects *16*

CHAPTER 2 | **Communicating in a Reader-Focused Way** *18*

Creating a Reader Profile *19*

Step 1: Identify Your Readers *20*

Step 2: Identify Your Readers' Needs, Values, and Attitudes *21*

Step 3: Identify the Contexts in Which Readers Will Experience Your Document *22*

Using Profiles to Your Advantage *24*

Global and Transcultural Communication *24*

Differences in Content *24*

Differences in Organization *29*

Differences in Style   30

Differences in Design   31

Listen and Learn: The Key to Global and Transcultural
    Communication   32

What You Need to Know   33

Exercises and Projects   33

Case Study: Installing a Medical Waste Incinerator   35

CHAPTER

3

Working in Teams   *39*

The Stages of Teaming   *40*

Forming: Strategic Planning   *40*

Step 1: Define the Project Mission and Objectives   *41*

Step 2: Identify Project Outcomes   *41*

Step 3: Define Team Member Responsibilities   *42*

Step 4: Create a Project Calendar   *42*

Step 5: Write Out a Work Plan   *42*

Step 6: Agree on How Conflicts Will Be Resolved   *43*

Storming: Managing Conflict   *44*

Running Effective Meetings   *48*

Mediating Conflicts   *50*

Firing a Team Member   *51*

Norming: Determining Team Roles   *51*

Revising Objectives and Outcomes   *52*

Help: Virtual Teaming   *52*

Redefining Team Roles and Redistributing Workload   *54*

Using Groupware to Facilitate Work   *54*

Performing: Improving Quality   *54*

The Keys to Teaming   *57*

What You Need to Know   *57*

Exercises and Projects   *58*

Case Study: Not a Sunny Day   *59*

CHAPTER

4

Managing Ethical Challenges   *60*

What Are Ethics?   *61*

Where Do Ethics Come From?   *64*

Personal Ethics   *64*

Social Ethics   *65*

Conservation Ethics   *67*

Resolving Ethical Dilemmas   69
   Step 1: Analyze the Ethical Dilemma   69
   Step 2: Make a Decision   70
   Step 3: React Appropriately When You Disagree with Your Employer   72
   Help: Stopping Cyberbullying and Computer Harassment   74

Ethics in the Technical Workplace   76
   Copyright Law   76
   Trademarks   76
   Patents   77
   Privacy   77
   Information Sharing   77
   Proprietary Information   77
   Libel and Slander   78
   Fraud   78

Copyright Law in Technical Communication   78
   Asking Permission   79
   Copyrighting Your Work   80
   Plagiarism   80

What You Need to Know   80

Exercises and Projects   81
   Case Study: This Company Is Bugging Me   82

Part 2: Genres of Technical Communication

CHAPTER 5

Letters, Memos, and E-Mail   83

Features of Letters, Memos, and E-Mails   84
   Quick Start: Letters, Memos, and E-Mails   85

Step 1: Make a Plan and Do Research   88
   Determining the Rhetorical Situation   89

Step 2: Decide What Kind of Letter, Memo, or E-Mail Is Needed   90
   Inquiries   90
   Responses   90
   Transmittals   90
   Claims or Complaints   93
   Adjustments   93
   Refusals   96

Step 3: Organize and Draft Your Message   96
    Introduction with a Purpose and a Main Point   96
    Body That Provides Need-to-Know Information   101
    Conclusion That Restates the Main Point   102
    Microgenre: Workplace Texting and Tweeting   103

Step 4: Choose the Style, Design, and Medium   104
    Strategies for Developing an Appropriate Style   105
    Formatting Letters   106
    Formatting Envelopes   109
    Formatting Memos   109

Using E-Mail for Transcultural Communication   111

What You Need to Know   113

Exercises and Projects   113
    Case Study: The Nastygram   117

CHAPTER

6

Technical Descriptions and Specifications   *119*

Step 1: Make a Plan and Do Research   120
    Planning   120
    Quick Start: Technical Descriptions and Specifications   121
    Addressing ISO 9000/ISO 14000 Issues   125
    Researching   125

Step 2: Partition Your Subject   127

Step 3: Organize and Draft Your Technical
    Description   128
    Specific and Precise Title   131
    Introduction with an Overall Description   131
    Description by Features, Functions, or Stages   135
    Description by Senses, Similes, Analogies,
        and Metaphors   136
    Conclusion   137
    Help: Using Digital Photography in Descriptions   138

Step 4: Choose the Style, Design, and Medium   139
    Plain, Simple Style   139
    Page Layout That Fits the Context of Use   139
    Graphics That Illustrate   140
    Medium That Allows Easy Access   140
    Microgenre: Technical Definitions   144

What You Need to Know   146

Exercises and Projects   146
    Case Study: In the Vapor   150

CHAPTER 7

Instructions and Documentation   *152*

Types of Technical Documentation   *153*

Step 1: Make a Plan and Do Research   *153*

    Quick Start: Instructions and Documentation   *154*

    Planning   *155*

    Researching   *165*

Step 2: Organize and Draft Your Documentation   *167*

    Specific and Precise Title   *167*

    List of Parts, Tools, and Conditions Required   *168*

    Sequentially Ordered Steps   *170*

    Safety Information   *176*

    Conclusion That Signals Completion of Task   *177*

    User-Testing Your Documentation   *179*

    Help: On-Screen Documentation   *183*

Step 3: Choose the Style, Design, and Medium   *184*

    Plain Style with a Touch of Emotion   *184*

    Functional, Attractive Page Layout   *185*

    Graphics That Reinforce Written Text   *186*

    Medium That Improves Access   *188*

Working with Transcultural Documentation   *188*

    Verbal Considerations   *188*

    Design Considerations   *189*

    Microgenre: Emergency Instructions   *189*

What You Need to Know   *191*

Exercises and Projects   *192*

    Case Study: Purified Junk   *194*

CHAPTER 8

Proposals   *195*

Types of Proposals   *196*

Step 1: Make a Plan and Do Research   *196*

    Planning   *196*

    Quick Start: Proposals   *197*

    Researching   *202*

Step 2: Organize and Draft Your Proposal   *203*

    Writing the Introduction   *206*

    Describing the Current Situation   *206*

    Describing the Project Plan   *208*

    Describing Qualifications   *211*

    Concluding with Costs and Benefits   *218*

Step 3: Choose the Style, Design, and Medium   *218*
     A Balance of Plain and Persuasive Styles   *220*
     An Attractive, Functional Design   *220*
     A Dynamic Use of Medium   *222*
     Microgenre: The Elevator Pitch   *223*

What You Need to Know   *225*

Exercises and Projects   *225*
     Case Study: The Mole   *229*

CHAPTER 9   Activity Reports   *230*

Types of Activity Reports   *231*
     Progress Reports   *231*
     White Papers and Briefings   *231*
     Quick Start: Activity Reports   *232*
     Incident Reports   *232*
     Laboratory Reports   *236*

Step 1: Make a Plan and Do Research   *236*
     Analyzing the Rhetorical Situation   *236*

Step 2: Organize and Draft Your Activity Report   *239*
     Writing the Introduction   *240*
     Writing the Body   *241*
     Writing the Conclusion   *241*

Step 3: Choose the Style, Design, and Medium   *241*
     Keeping the Style Plain and Straightforward   *243*
     Designing for Simplicity and Illustrating with Graphics   *243*
     Writing for Electronic Media   *243*
     Microgenre: The Status Report   *248*

What You Need to Know   *250*

Exercises and Projects   *250*
     Case Study: Bad Chemistry   *252*

CHAPTER 10   Analytical Reports   *253*

Types of Analytical Reports   *254*
     Quick Start: Analytical Report   *255*

Step 1: Make a Plan and Do Research   *259*
     Planning   *259*
     Researching   *260*

Step 2: Organize and Draft Your Report   *265*

Writing the Introduction   *265*

Describing Your Methodology   *266*

Summarizing the Results of the Study   *266*

Discussing Your Results   *266*

Concluding with Recommendations   *267*

**Help: Using Google Drive to Collaborate
on Global Projects**   *277*

Step 3: Draft the Front Matter and Back Matter   *278*

Developing Front Matter   *278*

Developing Back Matter   *284*

Step 4: Choose the Style, Design, and Medium   *285*

Using Plain Style in a Persuasive Way   *285*

A Straightforward Design   *286*

Microgenre: The Poster Presentation   *287*

What You Need to Know   *289*

Exercises and Projects   *289*

Case Study: The X-File   *292*

CHAPTER

11 | Starting Your Career   293

Setting Goals, Making a Plan   *294*

Setting Goals   *294*

Making Your Plan   *294*

Quick Start: Career Materials   *295*

Preparing a Résumé   *298*

Types of Résumés   *298*

Chronological Résumé   *299*

Functional Résumé   *307*

Designing the Résumé   *308*

Help: Designing a Searchable Résumé   *310*

Writing Effective Application Letters   *312*

Content and Organization   *312*

Style   *316*

Revising and Proofreading the Résumé
and Letter   *317*

Creating a Professional Portfolio   *317*

Collecting Materials   *317*

Organizing Your Portfolio   *318*

Assembling the Portfolio in a Binder   *319*

Creating an Electronic Portfolio   *319*

Interviewing Strategies   *320*

       Preparing for the Interview   *320*
       At the Interview   *321*
       Writing Thank You Letters and/or E-Mails   *322*
       Microgenre: The Bio   *324*

  What You Need to Know   *326*

  Exercises and Projects   *326*
       Case Study: The Lie   *328*

Part 3: Planning and Doing Research

CHAPTER
12 | Strategic Planning, Being Creative   *329*

  Using Strategic Planning   *330*
       Step 1: Set Your Objectives   *330*
       Step 2: Create a List of Tasks
          (or Task List)   *331*
       Step 3: Set a Timeline   *332*
       Help: Planning with Online Calendars   *333*

  Generating New Ideas   *334*
       Tips for Being More Creative   *334*
       Inventing Ideas   *335*

  What You Need to Know   *339*

  Exercises and Projects   *340*
       Case Study: Getting Back to Crazy   *342*

CHAPTER
13 | Persuading Others   *343*

  Persuading with Reasoning   *344*
       Reasoning with Logic   *349*
       Reasoning with Examples and Evidence   *350*

  Persuading with Values   *351*
       Help: Persuading Readers Online   *352*
       Appealing to Common Goals and Ideals   *353*
       Framing Issues from the Readers'
          Perspective   *356*

  Persuasion in High-Context Cultures   *357*

  What You Need to Know   *361*

  Exercises and Projects   *361*
       Case Study: Trying to Stay Neutral   *363*

CHAPTER 14 **Researching in Technical Workplaces** **364**

Beginning Your Research *365*

Step 1: Define Your Research Subject *366*
    Mapping Out Your Ideas *367*
    Narrowing Your Research Subject *367*

Step 2: Formulate a Research Question or Hypothesis *368*

Step 3: Develop a Research Methodology *368*
    Mapping Out a Methodology *369*
    Describing Your Methodology *370*
    Using and Revising Your Methodology *370*

Step 4: Collect Evidence Through Sources *371*
    Using Electronic Sources *371*
    Using Print Sources *372*
    Using Empirical Sources *374*

Step 5: Triangulate Your Sources *375*

Step 6: Take Careful Notes *378*
    Taking Notes *379*
    Documenting Your Sources *383*
    Help: Using a Citation Manager *385*

Step 7: Appraise Your Evidence *387*
    Is the Source Reliable? *387*
    How Biased Is the Source? *387*
    Am I Biased? *388*
    Is the Source Up to Date? *388*
    Can the Evidence Be Verified? *388*
    Have I Plagiarized Any of My Sources? *388*

Step 8: Revise, Accept, or Abandon Your Hypothesis *390*

What You Need to Know *390*

Exercises and Projects *391*
    Case Study: The Life of a Dilemma *393*

Part 4: Drafting, Designing, and Revising

CHAPTER 15 **Organizing and Drafting** **394**

Basic Organization for Any Document *395*
Using Genres for Outlining *395*
Organizing and Drafting the Introduction *399*

Six Opening Moves in an Introduction   *399*
Drafting with the Six Moves   *400*

Organizing and Drafting the Body   402

Carving the Body into Sections   *402*
Patterns of Arrangement   *403*

Organizing and Drafting the Conclusion   411

Five Closing Moves in a Conclusion   *411*

Organizing Transcultural Documents   414

Indirect Approach Introductions   *415*
Indirect Approach Conclusions   *416*

What You Need to Know   418

Exercises and Projects   418

Case Study: The Bad News   *420*

CHAPTER

16 | Using Plain and Persuasive Style   421

What Is Style?   422

Writing Plain Sentences   422

Basic Parts of a Sentence   *423*
Eight Guidelines for Plain Sentences   *423*
Creating Plain Sentences with
a Computer   *427*
Help: Translating and Translation Programs   *429*

Writing Plain Paragraphs   430

The Elements of a Paragraph   *430*
Using the Four Types of Sentences
in a Paragraph   *432*
Aligning Sentence Subjects in a Paragraph   *433*
The Given/New Method   *434*

When Is It Appropriate to Use Passive Voice?   435

Persuasive Style   437

Elevate the Tone   *437*
Use Similes and Analogies   *438*
Use Metaphors   *439*
Change the Pace   *440*

Balancing Plain and Persuasive Style   442

What You Need to Know   443

Exercises and Projects   443

Case Study: Going Over the Top   *445*

CHAPTER 17 — Designing Documents and Interfaces   446

Five Principles of Design   *447*

Design Principle 1: Balance   *447*
  Weighting a Page or Screen   *448*
  Using Grids to Balance a Page Layout   *451*

Design Principle 2: Alignment   *455*

Design Principle 3: Grouping   *456*
  Using Headings   *457*
  Using Borders and Rules   *460*

Design Principle 4: Consistency   *461*
  Choosing Typefaces   *461*
  Labeling Graphics   *464*
  Creating Sequential and Nonsequential Lists   *464*
  Inserting Headers and Footers   *466*

Design Principle 5: Contrast   *466*

Transcultural Design   *468*

What You Need to Know   *470*

Exercises and Projects   *471*
  Case Study: Bugs on the Bus   *473*

CHAPTER 18 — Creating and Using Graphics   476

Guidelines for Using Graphics   *477*
  Guideline One: A Graphic Should Tell
    a Simple Story   *477*
  Guideline Two: A Graphic Should Reinforce
    the Written Text, Not Replace It   *477*
  Guideline Three: A Graphic Should Be Ethical   *479*
  Guideline Four: A Graphic Should Be Labeled
    and Placed Properly   *479*

Displaying Data with Graphs, Tables, and Charts   *481*
  Line Graphs   *481*
  Bar Charts   *483*
  Tables   *484*
  Pie Charts   *485*
  Flowcharts   *486*

Using Pictures and Drawings   *487*
  Photographs   *488*
  Inserting Photographs and Other Images   *490*
  Illustrations   *491*

Using Transcultural Symbols   *492*

What You Need to Know   *495*

Exercises and Projects   *495*

    Case Study: Looking Guilty   *497*

CHAPTER 19

Revising and Editing for Usability   *498*

Levels of Edit   *499*

Level 1 Editing: Revising   *499*

Level 2 Editing: Substantive Editing   *501*

Level 3 Editing: Copyediting   *503*

Level 4 Editing: Proofreading   *505*

    Grammar   *505*

    Punctuation   *505*

    Spelling and Typos   *506*

    Word Usage   *508*

Using Copyediting Symbols   *509*

Lost in Translation: Transcultural Editing   *509*

Document Cycling and Usability Testing   *512*

    Document Cycling   *512*

    Usability Testing   *512*

What You Need to Know   *516*

Exercises and Projects   *516*

    Case Study: A Machine by Any Other Name   *518*

Part 5: Connecting with Clients

CHAPTER 20

Preparing and Giving Presentations   *520*

Planning and Researching Your Presentation   *521*

    Defining the Rhetorical Situation   *523*

    Allotting Your Time   *525*

Choosing the Right Presentation Technology   *526*

Organizing the Content of Your Presentation   *529*

    Building the Presentation   *530*

    The Introduction: Tell Them What You're Going to Tell Them   *530*

    Help: Giving Presentations with Your Mobile Phone or Tablet   *534*

The Body: Tell Them *535*

The Conclusion: Tell Them What You Told Them *537*

Preparing to Answer Questions *539*

Choosing Your Presentation Style *540*

Creating Visuals *542*

Designing Visual Aids *542*

Using Graphics *544*

Slides to Avoid *544*

Delivering the Presentation *545*

Body Language *545*

Voice, Rhythm, and Tone *547*

Using Your Notes *547*

Rehearsing *548*

Evaluating Your Performance *548*

Working Across Cultures with Translators *548*

What You Need to Know *554*

Exercises and Projects *554*

Case Study: The Coward *556*

CHAPTER

21 | **Writing for the Web** *557*

Writing for Websites *558*

Basic Features of a Website *558*

Step 1: Develop the Content *560*

Step 2: Organize and Draft Your Webpage
or Website *560*

Step 3: Choose the Style and Design of Your Webpage
or Website *561*

Step 4: Add Images *563*

Step 5: Anticipate the Needs of Transcultural Readers *563*

Step 6: Upload Your Website *565*

Using Social Networking in the Workplace *565*

Step 1: Create Your Social Networking Account *566*

Step 2: Choose Your Friends (Wisely) *566*

Step 3: Maintain Your Site *567*

Step 4: Collaborate with Others, But Carefully *567*

Step 5: Communicate with Your Company's "Fans" *567*

Creating Blogs and Microblogs *568*

Step 1: Choose Your Blog's Host Site *568*

Step 2: Write and Maintain Your Blog *569*

Step 3: Let Others Join the Conversation *569*

Making Internet Videos and Podcasts   569
    Step 1: Write the Script   569
    Step 2: Shoot the Video or Record the Podcast   570
    Step 3: Edit Your Video or Podcast   570
    Step 4: Upload Your Video or Podcast   570

Writing Articles for Wikis   571
    Step 1: Write the Text   571
    Step 2: Post Your Article   571
    Step 3: Return to Edit Your Articles   572

What You Need to Know   572

Exercises and Projects   572
    Case Study: My Boss Might Not "Like" This   574

Appendix A: Grammar and Punctuation Guide   *A-1*

The Top Ten Grammar Mistakes   *A-1*
    Comma Splice   *A-1*
    Run-On Sentence *A-2*
    Fragment   *A-3*
    Dangling Modifier   *A-3*
    Subject-Verb Disagreement   *A-4*
    Pronoun-Antecedent Disagreement   *A-5*
    Faulty Parallelism   *A-5*
    Pronoun Case Error (*I* and *Me*, *We* and *Us*)   *A-6*
    Shifted Tense   *A-7*
    Vague Pronoun   *A-7*

Punctuation Refresher   *A-8*
    Period, Exclamation Point, Question Mark   *A-9*
    Commas   *A-9*
    Semicolon and Colon   *A-11*
    Apostrophe   *A-13*
    Quotation Marks   *A-14*
    Dashes and Hyphens   *A-16*
    Parentheses and Brackets   *A-17*
    Ellipses   *A-18*

Appendix B: English as a Second Language Guide   *A-19*

Using Articles Properly   *A-19*
Putting Adjectives and Adverbs in the Correct Order   *A-20*
Using Verb Tenses Appropriately   *A-21*

Appendix C: Documentation Guide   *A-24*

APA Documentation Style   *A-25*
   APA In-Text Citations   *A-25*
   The References List for APA Style   *A-27*
   Creating the APA References List   *A-30*

CSE Documentation Style (Citation-Sequence)   *A-30*
   The References List for CSE Citation-Sequence Style   *A-31*
   Creating the CSE References List (Citation-Sequence Style)   *A-34*

MLA Documentation Style   *A-34*
   MLA In-Text Citations   *A-35*
   The Works Cited List for MLA Style   *A-36*
   Creating the MLA Works Cited List   *A-39*

References   *R-1*
Credits   *C-1*
Index   *I-1*
Sample Documents   *Inside Back Cover*

Preface

In the technical workplace, people use their computers to help them research, compose, design, revise, and deliver technical documents and presentations. Networked computers and mobile devices are the central nervous system of the technical workplace, and *Technical Communication Today* helps students and professionals take full advantage of these important workplace tools.

New media and communication technologies are dramatically altering technical fields at an astounding rate. People are working more efficiently, more globally, and more visually. These changes are exciting, and they will continue to accelerate in the technical workplace. This new edition of *Technical Communication Today* continues to help writers master these changing communication tools that are critical to success in technical fields.

Today, as the centrality of technology in our lives has expanded, almost all professionals find themselves needing to communicate technical information. To meet this need, this book addresses a broad range of people, including those who need to communicate in business, computer science, the natural sciences, the social sciences, public relations, medicine, law, and engineering.

What's New in the Fifth Edition?

This edition has been streamlined so that students can quickly find the key information they are looking for in every chapter. Many chapters have also been reframed to present the writing process for any document as a series of steps. In addition:

- **A new Chapter 21, "Writing for the Web,"** provides an overarching look at how to write for the Web, with coverage on creating and designing websites, social media pages, blogs, videos, podcasts, and wikis.
- **An updated Chapter 11, "Starting Your Career,"** reflects the electronic shift in the job search process. In addition, it provides more guidance on creating chronological résumés and designing a searchable résumé.
- **A revised Chapter 14, "Researching in the Technical Workplace,"** now provides step-by-step guidance on the research process, with more help on beginning research with primary and secondary sources; collecting evidence through print, electronic, and empirical sources; and new coverage of revisiting a hypothesis to determine its validity.
- **New sample documents** provide even more examples of the types of communications students will encounter in the workplace, including technical descriptions (Chapter 6), instructions (Chapter 7), reports (Chapter 10), and a résumé from an international student (Chapter 11).
- **New Microgenre examples** in Part 2, including tweeting at work (Chapter 5), demonstrate how elements of broad genres can be applied to narrower rhetorical situations.

- **Four new case studies** prepare students for real workplace situations by presenting ethical challenges for reflection and rich class discussion.

  - Responding to a memo from a senior management official who has expressed dissatisfaction with the way one of his offices is being "run" (Chapter 5).
  - Determining whether or not it is ethical for a fiberoptic telecommunications company to block certain content from reaching its users (Chapter 13).
  - Creating a brochure designed specifically for parents of school-aged children, raising awareness about bed bugs (Chapter 17).
  - Addressing a cross-cultural issue involving the unfortunate translation of the name of an x-ray machine in another country (Chapter 19).

- **Newly titled chapter reviews, "What You Need to Know,"** reinforce key points for students.
- **New exercises and projects** throughout.
- **Updated APA and MLA** documentation coverage.

Guiding Themes

In this book, I have incorporated the newest technology in workplace communication, but the basics have not been forgotten. *Technical Communication Today* is grounded in a solid core of rhetorical principles that have been around since the beginning. These core principles have held up well and, in fact, are even more relevant as we return to a more visual and oral culture.

Computers as Thinking Tools

This book's foremost theme is that networked computers and mobile devices are integral and indispensable in technical communication. *Technical Communication Today* shows students how to fully use computers and succeed in a complex and fast-moving technical workplace.

Visual-Spatial Reading, Thinking, and Composing

Documents are "spaces" where information is stored and flows. Visual-spatial reading, thinking, and composing involve interacting with text in real time. *Technical Communication Today* shows students how to engage, compose, and interact with texts in four important ways:

- It shows writers how to use visual-spatial techniques to research, invent, draft, design, and edit their work.
- It teaches students how to write and speak visually, while designing highly navigable documents and presentations.
- It provides guidance on composing visual-spatial multimodal documents and presentations.
- It practices what it preaches by providing information in an accessible, visual-spatial format.

The International, Transcultural Workplace

As with each edition, international and transcultural issues have been expanded as the world becomes more globalized. This topic has been woven into the main chapter discussion, rather than placed on its own, because issues of globalization are not separable from technical communication.

The Activity of Technical Communication

Technical Communication Today continues to stress the activity of technical communication—producing effective documents and presentations. Each chapter follows a step-by-step process approach that mirrors how professionals in the technical workplace communicate. As someone who has consulted and taught technical communication for over two decades, I know that students today rarely read their textbooks, but instead raid them for specific information. For this reason, like any good technical communicator, I have tried to make this book as "raidable" as possible. That way, students can get in the book, get what they need, and get things done.

Resources for Students and Instructors

MyWritingLab Now Available for Technical Communication

Integrated solutions for writing. *MyWritingLab* is an online homework, tutorial, and assessment program that provides engaging experiences for today's instructors and students. New features, built on *MyWritingLab's* hallmark foundation, offer instructors:

- A new Composing Space for students
- Customizable Rubrics for assessing and grading student writing
- Multimedia instruction on all aspects of technical communication
- Advanced reporting to analyze class performance

Adaptive learning powered by multimedia instruction. For students who enter the course under-prepared, *MyWritingLab* offers pre-assessments and personalized remediation so students see improved results and instructors spend less time in class reviewing the basics. Rich multimedia resources are built in to engage students and support faculty throughout the course. Visit *www.mywritinglab.com* for more information.

Instructor's Manual

The *Instructor's Manual,* available online at pearsonhighered.com, offers chapter-specific teaching strategies, prompts for class discussion, strategies for improving students' writing and presentations, in-and-out-of-class activities, and quizzes (with suggested answers). Additional instructor resources include a Test Bank and PowerPoint slides.

CourseSmart

Students can subscribe to this book as a *CourseSmart eText* at coursesmart.com. The subscription includes all of the book's content in a format that enables students to search, bookmark, take notes, and print reading assignments that incorporate lecture notes.

Acknowledgments

Every edition of *Technical Communication Today* has given me the opportunity to work with many people at Pearson and at colleges around the country. I wish to thank the following individuals for their insight and support: Teresa Aggen, Pikes Peak Community College; Sherrie L. Amido, California Polytechnic State University—San Luis Obispo; James Baker, Texas A&M University; Lauri M. Baker, University of Florida; Russell Barrett, Blinn College; Eric Bateman, San Juan College; Norman Douglas Bradley, University of California—Santa Barbara; Lee Brasseur, Illinois State University; Jonathon Briggs, Central New Mexico Community College; Stuart Brown, New Mexico State University; Ellie Bunting, Edison College; Maria J. Cahill, Edison State College; Tracy L. Dalton, Missouri State University; Roger Friedman, Kansas State University; Timothy D. Giles, Georgia Southern University; Mark Gula, Northern Arizona University; Jeffrey Jablonski, University of Nevada—Las Vegas; Rebecca Jackson, Texas State University; Leslie Janac, Blinn College—Bryan Campus; Miles A. Kimball, Texas Tech University; Christy L. Kinnion, Wake Technical Community College; Barry Lawler, Oregon State University; Barbara L'Eplattenier, University of Arkansas—Little Rock; Anna Maheshwari, Schoolcraft College; Barry Maid, Arizona State University; Jodie Marion, Mt. Hood Community College; Steve Marsden, Stephen F. Austin State University; Mary S. McCauley, Wake Technical Community College; Kenneth Mitchell, Southeastern Louisiana University; Jacqueline S. Palmer, Texas A&M University; Andrea M. Penner, San Juan College; Cindy Raisor, Texas A&M University; Sherry Rankins-Robertson, Arizona State University; Mark T. Rooze, Florence-Darlington Technical College; Carlos Salinas, The University of Texas at El Paso; Teryl Sands, Arizona State University; Paul Sawyer, Southeastern Louisiana University; Jennifer Sheppard, New Mexico State University; Rick Simmons, Louisiana Technical University; Nancy Small, Texas A&M University; Kara Smith, Brunswick Community College; Krista Soria, University of Alaska Anchorage; Karina Stokes, University of Houston—Downtown; Christine Strebeck, Louisiana Tech University; Valerie Thomas, University of New Mexico; Christopher Toth, Iowa State University; Jack Trotter, Trident Technical College; Greg Wilson, Iowa State University; Alan Zemel, Drexel University.

Editors Brad Potthoff and Anne Brunell Ehrenworth were essential in the revision of this book and I thank them for their ideas. Thanks also to my colleagues, Professors Scott Sanders, Charles Paine, and David Blakesley. Finally, thanks to Gracemarie Mike and Mary McCall for their assistance.

Most important, I would like to thank my wife, Tracey, and my children, Emily and Collin, for their patience, because sometimes working on books like this one takes time away from them.

RICHARD JOHNSON-SHEEHAN
PURDUE UNIVERSITY

CHAPTER

1

Communicating
in the Technical
Workplace

Developing a Workplace Writing
   Process 2

Genres and the Technical Writing
   Process 3

What Is Technical
   Communication? 9

How Important Is Technical
   Communication? 14

What You Need to Know 15

Exercises and Projects 16

In this chapter, you will learn:

- How to develop a writing process that is suitable for the technical workplace.

- How genres are used in technical workplaces to develop documents.

- How to use your computer to overcome writer's block.

- To define technical communication as a process of managing information in ways that allow people to take action.

- The importance of communication in today's technical workplace.

- The importance of effective written and spoken communication to your career.

When new college graduates begin their technical and scientific careers, they are often surprised by the amount of writing and speaking required in their new jobs. They knew technical communication would be important, but they never realized it would be so crucial to their success.

Communication is the central nervous system of the technical workplace. People who can write and speak effectively using a variety of media tend to be successful. Meanwhile, people with weak communication skills are often passed over for jobs and promotions. Technical communication will be vitally important to your career, whether you are an engineer, scientist, doctor, nurse, psychologist, social worker, anthropologist, architect, technical writer, or any other professional in a technical field.

Developing a Workplace Writing Process

One of the major differences between workplace writing and college writing is the pace at which you need to work. Computer networks and smartphones have greatly increased the speed of the technical workplace, and they allow people to work around the clock. So, you need to work smarter, not harder.

To help you work smarter, this book will teach you a *genre-based approach* to technical communication. Genres are patterns that reflect how communities, including people in technical workplaces, get things done. A genre shapes a project's content, organization, style, and design, as well as the medium in which it is delivered.

For example, an analytical report follows a different genre than technical specifications (Figure 1.1). Reports and specifications are written for completely different purposes and for different kinds of readers. Their content, organization, style, and design are also very different. Yet, in most technical workplaces, you would need to know how to use both of these genres.

Communication Is the Central Nervous System of the Workplace

Your ability to communicate with others through computer networks will be critical to your career.

Two Different Genres

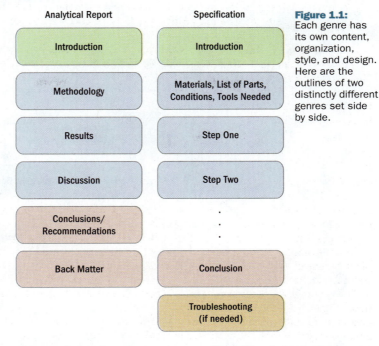

Analytical Report

- Introduction
- Methodology
- Results
- Discussion
- Conclusions/ Recommendations
- Back Matter

Specification

- Introduction
- Materials, List of Parts, Conditions, Tools Needed
- Step One
- Step Two
- .
- .
- .
- Conclusion
- Troubleshooting (if needed)

Figure 1.1: Each genre has its own content, organization, style, and design. Here are the outlines of two distinctly different genres set side by side.

Genres do much more than help you organize your ideas. They help you interpret workplace situations and make sense of what is happening around you. Genres are not formulas or recipes to be followed mechanically. Instead, genres reflect the activities and practices of technical workplaces. Genres are flexible, allowing them to be adapted to many different kinds of projects.

In this book, you will learn a *genre set* that will be helpful to you throughout your career. Learning these technical communication genres will allow you produce clear documents and give authoritative presentations so you can achieve your goals.

Genres and the Technical Writing Process

In your previous courses on writing and public speaking, you probably learned a *writing process*. This process included a few stages such as prewriting, drafting, revising, and proofreading.

The technical writing process modifies these stages and adds in a few new ones, as shown in Figure 1.2. In this book, this process is divided into five stages: (1) Planning and Researching, (2) Organizing and Drafting, (3) Improving Style, (4) Designing, and (5) Revising and Editing.

While writing a document or presentation, you will need to move back and forth among these stages. For example, while organizing and drafting your document, you may realize that you need to do a little more research on your topic. While editing, you may realize that the style of the document needs to be changed to fit the needs of the readers. Generally, though, this technical writing process will guide you from the beginning to the end of the project.

The Technical Writing Process

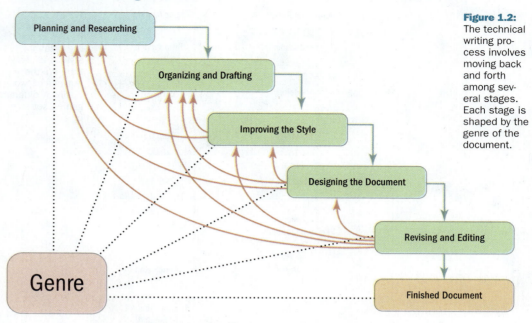

Meanwhile, as shown in Figure 1.2, the genre of your document guides each stage in your writing process. The genre helps you make decisions about the content, organization, style, and design of your document, as well as the most appropriate medium for your ideas.

Stage 1: Planning Out Your Project and Doing Start-Up Research

During the planning and researching stage, you should accomplish three tasks: analyze the rhetorical situation, do start-up research, and refine your purpose.

ANALYZING THE RHETORICAL SITUATION   Understanding the rhetorical situation means gaining a firm grasp of your document's subject, purpose, readers, and context of use (Figure 1.3).

To define the rhetorical situation, start out by asking the *Five-W and How Questions:* who, what, why, where, when, and how.

- *Who* are my readers, and who else is involved with the project?
- *What* do the readers want and need, and what do I want and need?
- *Why* do the readers need the information in this document?
- *Where* do they need the information, and *where* will they use it?
- *When* will the information be used, and *when* is it needed?
- *How* should I achieve my purpose and goals?

Defining the Rhetorical Situation

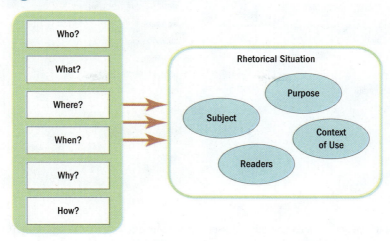

Figure 1.3: The Five-W and How Questions can help you determine the rhetorical situation for your technical document or presentation.

The Five-W and How Questions will give you an overall sense of your document's rhetorical situation.

Now, spend some time taking notes on the following four elements of the rhetorical situation:

> **Subject**—What is the document about? What is it *not* about? What kinds of information will my readers need to make a decision or complete a task? What is the scope of the project?
>
> **Purpose**—What does this document need to achieve or prove? Why do my readers need this document and what do they need to know?
>
> **Readers**—Who are the readers of this document? What are their specific needs and interests? What are they looking for in this document?
>
> **Context of use**—Where and when will this document be used? What physical, economic, political, and ethical constraints will shape this text?

Defining the rhetorical situation may seem like an added step that will keep you from writing. Actually, knowing your document's rhetorical situation will save you time and effort, because you will avoid dead ends, unnecessary revision, and writer's block.

DEFINING YOUR PURPOSE   Among the four elements of the rhetorical situation, your document's purpose is the most important. Your purpose is what you want to do—and what you want the document to achieve.

The purpose statement of your document is like a compass. You can use that purpose statement to guide your decisions about the content, organization, style, and design of your document.

When defining your purpose, try to express exactly what you want your document to achieve. Sometimes it helps to find an appropriate action verb and then build your purpose statement around it. Here are some useful action verbs that you might use:

Link

To learn about adapting texts to readers and contexts, go to Chapter 2, page 19.

INFORMATIVE DOCUMENTS	PERSUASIVE DOCUMENTS
inform	persuade
describe	convince
define	influence
review	support
demonstrate	change
instruct	advocate
advise	recommend
announce	defend
explain	justify
notify	urge

Using the action verb you have chosen, state your purpose in one sentence. It might help to finish the phrase "The purpose of my document is to . . ."

> The purpose of my report is to review the successes and failures of wolf reintroduction programs in the western United States.

> The purpose of my proposal is to recommend significant changes to flood control strategies in the Ohio River Valley.

Hammering your purpose statement down into one sentence is hard work, but worth the effort. Your one-sentence purpose statement will focus your writing, saving you time. Chapter 12 on strategic planning provides some helpful ideas for figuring out your purpose statement, especially with larger, more complex projects.

RESEARCHING YOUR SUBJECT   Solid research is your next step. Computers have significantly changed the way we do research in technical workplaces. Before computers and Internet search engines, finding enough information was usually a writer's main challenge. Today, there is almost too much information available on any given subject. So, it is important that you learn how to *manage* the information you collect, sorting through all the texts, scraps, junk, and distortions to uncover what you need. Your documents should give your readers only the information they require to make a decision or take action. Leave out anything else.

While researching your subject, gather information from a variety of sources, including the electronic sources, print documents, and empirical methods (e.g., experiments, surveys, observations, interviews). Chapters 14 and 15 will help you do effective research and evaluate your sources.

Stage 2: Organizing and Drafting

While organizing and drafting, you are essentially doing two things at the same time:

> **Organizing the content**—Using common genres to shape your ideas into patterns that will be familiar to readers.

> **Drafting the content**—Generating the written text of your document by weaving together facts, data, reasoning, and examples.

The genre you are using will help you understand how to organize the information you've collected in a way that achieves your purpose. For example, the document in Figure 1.4 is easily recognizable as a *set of instructions* because it is following the genre.

Chapters 5 through 11 will teach you how to use the most common genres in technical workplaces. In most situations, you will already know which genre you need because your supervisor or instructor will ask you to write a "specification," "report," or "proposal." But if you are uncertain which genre suits your needs, pay attention to your document's purpose. Then, find the genre that best suits the purpose you are trying to achieve.

Sample of Genre: Instructions

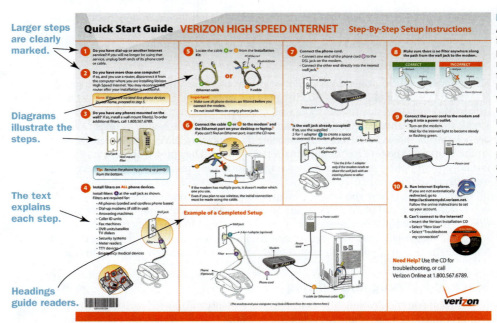

Figure 1.4: A genre follows a pattern that readers will find familiar. Readers would immediately recognize this document as a set of instructions and be able to use it.

Source: "Quick Start Guide," Verizon Wireless, used by permission.

Stage 3: Improving the Style

All documents have a style, whether it is effective or not. Good style is a choice you can and should make. In Chapter 16, you will learn about two kinds of style that are widely used in technical documents: plain style and persuasive style.

> **Plain style**—Plain style stresses clarity and accuracy. By paying attention to your sentences and paragraphs, you can make your ideas clearer and easier to understand.

> **Persuasive style**—Persuasive style motivates readers by appealing to their values and emotions. You can use similes and analogies to add a visual quality to your work. You can use metaphors to change your readers' perspective on issues. Meanwhile, you can use tone and pace to add energy and color to your work.

Most workplace texts are written in the plain style, but technical documents sometimes need the extra energy and vision provided by the persuasive style.

Stage 4: Designing

Designing a document only takes minutes with a computer, and you can create graphics with a few clicks of a button. So, design is not only possible, but your readers will *expect* your technical documents to be well designed.

As you think about the design of your document, keep this saying in mind: *Readers are "raiders" for information.* Your readers want the important parts highlighted for them so they can raid the text for the information they need. They prefer documents that use effective graphics and layout to make the information more accessible, interesting, and attractive (Figure 1.5).

Chapter 17 will show you how to design workplace documents. Chapter 18 will show you how to create and place graphics in your documents. As you draft and revise your document, look for places where you can use visual design to help readers locate the information they need. Look for places where graphics might support or reinforce the written text. The design of your document should make it both attractive and easy to read.

Stage 5: Revising and Editing

In technical communication, it is crucial to leave plenty of time for revising, editing, and proofreading. Clarity and accuracy are essential if your readers are going to understand what you are trying to tell them.

In Chapter 19, you will learn about four levels of revising and editing:

> **Level 1: Revising**—Re-examine your subject and purpose while thinking again about the information your readers need to know.

> **Level 2: Substantive editing**—Look closely at the content, organization, and design of the document to make sure your readers can find the information they need.

> **Level 3: Copyediting**—Pay close attention to the document's sentences, paragraphs, and graphics to make sure they are clear, accurate, and efficient.

> **Level 4: Proofreading**—Carefully proofread your document to eliminate grammar problems, typos, spelling errors, and usage mistakes. In workplace documents, errors are a signal of low-quality work.

Document Design Is Very Important

The organization's name is easy to locate.

Topics are listed clearly.

Text is highly scannable because it is in groups.

Figure 1.5: Because readers are raiders of information, you want the design of your document to be visually accessible.

Color adds energy.

Pictures add a human quality.

Source: American Red Cross, http://www.redcross.org

Your supervisors will expect you to do much more revising and editing than your college professors do because documents with even the smallest errors will be rejected by readers. Small errors can even cause customers and clients to doubt whether you or your company cares about quality, which can damage your or your company's relationships with them.

What Is Technical Communication?

Let's step back for a moment to look at the big picture. Here is the definition of technical communication that will be used throughout this book:

Technical communication is a process of managing technical information in ways that allow people to take action.

The key words in this definition are *process, manage,* and *action.* In this book, you will learn the *process* of technical communication so you can *manage* large amounts of information in ways that allow you to take *action.* Technical communication involves learning how to manage the flow of information so you can get things done (Figure 1.6). Let's look closer at some of the special qualities of technical communication.

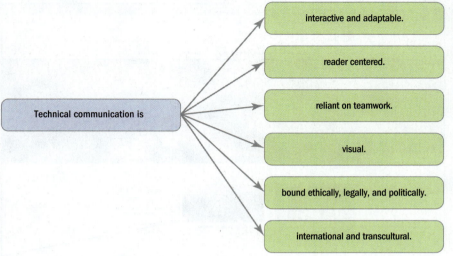

Technical communication is
- interactive and adaptable.
- reader centered.
- reliant on teamwork.
- visual.
- bound ethically, legally, and politically.
- international and transcultural.

Figure 1.6:
Technical communication puts much more emphasis on managing information and taking action than most other forms of writing.

Technical Communication Is Interactive and Adaptable

One of the most significant changes brought about by computers is the amount of *interactivity* and *collaboration* among people in the technical workplace. In the computer-networked workplace, people are constantly communicating with each other and sharing their ideas.

As a result of this interactivity, it is possible for you to quickly adapt documents and presentations to fit the specific needs of various readers and situations. Websites are an especially interactive form of technical communication (Figure 1.7). Using a website, people can find the information that is most helpful to them. And if they cannot find the information they are looking for on the website, they can send an e-mail to get the answers they need.

Similarly, paper-based documents can also be adapted to the changing needs of readers. Before computers, it was difficult to adjust and revise paper-based documents. Once they were printed, documents were hard to change. Today, with computers, you can easily update documents to reflect changes in your company's products and services. Or, you can quickly revise documents to address unexpected changes in the workplace.

Technical Communication Is Reader Centered

In technical communication, readers play a much more significant role than they do in other kinds of writing. When writing a typical college essay, you are trying to express *your* ideas and opinions. Technical communication turns this situation around. It concentrates on what the readers "need to know" to take action, not on what you, as the writer, want to tell them.

Sample Webpage

The webpage is highly visual, including color.

Links make the text interactive.

Document is highly scannable and adaptive to reader's needs by using small columns.

Ethics and politics are an important concern in all technical documents.

Links take readers to more information about a subject.

Source: National Human Genome Research Institute, http://www.genome.gov

Figure 1.7: Websites are highly interactive, allowing readers to follow a variety of paths to find information.

Because it is reader centered, effective technical communication tends to be highly pragmatic. Technical communication needs to be efficient, easy to understand, accessible, action oriented, and adaptable.

Technical Communication Relies on Teamwork

Technical workplaces are highly collaborative, meaning you will likely work with a team of specialists on almost every project. Writing and presenting with a team are crucial skills in any technical workplace.

Computers have only heightened the team orientation of the technical workplace. Today, it is common for many people to be working on a document at the same time because documents can be shared through e-mail and virtual storage sites like Google Drive or Dropbox. In some cases, your team might be adjusting and updating technical documents on an ongoing basis.

Link

For more information on working in teams, see Chapter 3, page 40.

Link

For more information on visual design, see Chapter 17, page 447.

Technical Communication Is Visual

By making texts highly visual, you can help readers quickly locate the information they need. Visual cues, like headings, lists, diagrams, and margin comments, are common in technical documents (Figure 1.8). Graphics also play an important role in technical communication. By using charts, graphs, drawings, and pictures, you can clarify and strengthen your arguments in any technical document. Today's readers quickly grow impatient with large blocks of text. They prefer graphics that reinforce the text and help them quickly gain access to important information.

Link

To learn about using graphics in documents, turn to Chapter 18, page 477.

Technical Communication Has Ethical, Legal, and Political Dimensions

In the increasingly complex technical workplace, issues involving ethics, laws, and politics are always present. Ethical and legal standards can be violated if you aren't careful. Moreover, computers have created new micro- and macropolitical challenges that need to be negotiated in the workplace. To communicate effectively in the technical workplace, you need to be aware of the ethical, legal, and political issues that shape your writing and speaking.

As management structures become flatter—meaning there are fewer layers of management—employees are being asked to take on more decision-making responsibilities than ever. In most corporations, fewer checks and balances exist, meaning that all employees need to be able to sort out the ethical, legal, and political aspects of a decision for themselves.

Link

Ethical, legal, and political issues are discussed in Chapter 4, starting on page 61.

Working with a team can be fun and rewarding. Teams take advantage of the strengths and knowledge of different people to succeed.

Figure 1.8: Visual design is an essential part of technical communication.

Visuals add color and emotion.

An easy-to-read title identifies the document's subject.

Headings make the text highly scannable.

The two-column format makes the text easy to scan.

Ecosystems

NOS Releases Two National Progress Reports on Reef Conservation

This year, NOS released two major progress reports on coral reef research, monitoring and management. *The State of Coral Reef Ecosystems of the United States and Pacific Freely Associated States: 2005* established the first quantitative baseline of the conditions of shallow water coral reef ecosystems in the U.S., the Republic of Palau, the Republic of the Marshall Islands, and the Federated States of Micronesia. More than 160 scientists and resource managers contributed to the report, which documents the geographic extent of reef ecosystems and the status of water quality, benthic habitats, associated biological communities and key threats to coral ecosystem health. The second report, *Implementation of the National Coral Reef Action Strategy: Report on U.S. Coral Reef Agency Activities from 2002 to 2003,* highlights the activities of NOAA and the U.S. Coral Reef Task Force under each of the 13 national conservation goals defined by the 2002 U.S. National Coral Reef Action Strategy. The report indicates that collective research and management actions are moving in the right direction, citing examples like the creation of 14 new coral reef protected areas and the creation of Local Action Strategies for conservation.

Tortugas Ecological Reserve Show Signs of Species Abundance

Four years after the establishment of the Tortugas Ecological Reserve, NOS scientists are studying how the ecosystem is changing as a result of reserve status. This year, scientists conducted 253 dives to collect data and fish samples, and found that certain fish species are increasingly abundant.

New Tide and Water Quality Monitoring Station Includes Multiple Features

In August, NOS installed a tide and water quality monitoring station at the Wells National Estuarine Research Reserve (NERR), in Wells, Maine. The station combines the capabilities of the National Water Level Observation Network (NWLON) and the System-wide Monitoring Network. The station, which is the first of its kind installed at a NERR, includes primary and backup water level sensors, a suite of meteorological sensors, and a water quality sensor that measures several parameters. The NWLON technology allows Wells NERR staff to access water level, weather, and water quality data all from the same platform at the same time. Products generated from these data will benefit both short-term (such as habitat restoration) and long-term (such as sea level trends) applications, as well as research and education objectives.

Restoration Efforts at Blackwater National Wildlife Refuge

NOS and NOAA Fisheries are working with the U.S. Geological Survey (USGS), U.S. Army Corps of Engineers, U.S. Fish and Wildlife Service, National Aquarium in Baltimore, and others to restore 8,000 acres of wetlands at the Blackwater National Wildlife Refuge in eastern Maryland. Under common observing and data management principles of the Integrated Ocean Observing System, the partners are collecting water level data so that NOAA can process and conduct analyses of the data to apply to the restoration project. The Refuge also hosted a workshop on the importance of geodetic control for tidal analysis and applications. After the workshop, a global positioning system survey was conducted to connect NOAA's and USGS's water level stations, and USGS's surface elevation tables to the same geodetic network.

NOAA'S NATIONAL OCEAN SERVICE: ACCOMPLISHMENTS 2005

Source: National Ocean Service, 2005

Link

To learn about communicating internationally and cross-culturally, go to Chapter 2, page 24.

Technical Communication Is International and Transcultural

Computers have also increased the international nature of the technical workplace. Today, professionals regularly communicate with people around the world. Almost all companies and institutions compete in a global marketplace. Many have offices, communication hubs, and manufacturing sites in Europe, Asia, Africa, Australia, and South America. The growth of international and transcultural trade means you will find yourself working with people who speak other languages and have other customs. They will also hold different expectations about how technical documents should look and the way presentations should be made.

How Important Is Technical Communication?

At this point, you're probably still wondering how important technical communication will be to your career. Surveys regularly show that oral and written communication skills are among the most important in the technical workplace. According to a 2013 survey by the Workforce Solutions Group, over 60 percent of employers report that new applicants lack the "communication and interpersonal skills" needed for the technical workplace. Proficiency in math and science are important, according to the survey, but "communications ranked as the top basic skill in demand" (p. 30).

These findings are in line with conclusions from other surveys. When members of the American Institute of Aeronautics and Astronautics (AIAA) were asked to evaluate their educational preparation for their jobs, they ranked the following areas as the ones needing improvement in engineering education.

Areas of Needed Improvement in Education for Engineers

1. Oral communication
2. Visualization in three dimensions
3. Technical writing
4. Understanding the processes of fabrication and assembly
5. Using CAD, CAM, and solid modeling
6. Estimating solutions to complex problems without using computer models
7. Sketching and drawing

The membership of the AIAA is made up mostly of engineers, so it is interesting that two out of three of the top skills they listed stress the importance of technical communication.

Corporations spend billions each year to improve the writing skills of their employees, according to the report "A Ticket to Work . . . or a Ticket Out," from the National Commission on Writing. Poor writing skills are the "kiss of death," according to the report, because 51 percent of companies say they "frequently or almost always take writing into consideration when hiring salaried employees" (p. 9).

Fortunately, you can learn how to write and speak effectively in the technical workplace. The ability to communicate effectively is not something people are born with. With guidance and practice, anyone can learn to write and speak well. Right now, you

In the global market, the ability to communicate is the key to success.

have a golden opportunity to develop these important technical communication skills. They will help you land the job you want, and they will help you succeed.

If you are reading this book, you are probably in a class on technical communication or are looking to improve your skills in the technical workplace. This book will give you the tools you need for success.

- By consciously developing a writing process, you will learn how to write more efficiently. In other words, you will "work smarter, not harder."

- A useful workplace writing process includes the following stages: planning and researching, organizing and drafting, improving the style, designing, and revising and editing.

- Technical writing genres are helpful for organizing information into patterns that your readers will expect.

- Computers, the Internet, and instant forms of communication have had an enormous impact on communication in the technical workplace.

- Technical communication is defined as a process of managing technical information in ways that allow people to take action.

- Technical communication is a blend of actions, words, and images. Readers expect technical documents to use writing, visuals, and design to communicate effectively.

- Technical communication is interactive, adaptable, reader centered, and often produced in teams.

- Technical communication has ethical, political, international, and transcultural dimensions that must be considered.

- Effective written and spoken communication will be vital to your career.

Individual or Team Projects

1. Locate a document that is used in a technical workplace through a search engine like Google, Bing, or Yahoo. To find documents, type in keywords like "report," "proposal," "instructions," and "presentation."

   What characteristics make the document you found a form of technical communication? Develop a two-minute presentation for your class in which you highlight these characteristics of the document. Compare and contrast the document with academic essays you have written for your other classes.

2. Using a search engine on the Internet, locate a professional who works in your chosen field. Write an e-mail asking that person what kinds of documents or presentations he or she needs to produce. Ask how much time he or she devotes to communication on the job. Ask whether he or she has some advice about how to gain and improve the communication skills that you will need in your career. Write a memo to your instructor in which you summarize your findings.

3. Using the information in this chapter, write a memo to your instructor in which you compare and contrast the kinds of writing you have done for classes in the past (e.g., essays, short answer, short stories) with the kinds of writing you expect to do in your career. Then, tell your instructor how this class would best help you prepare for your career in a technical workplace.

Collaborative Project: Writing a Course Mission Statement

As you begin this semester, it is a good idea for your class to develop a common understanding of the course objectives and outcomes. Companies develop mission statements to help focus their efforts and keep their employees striving toward common ends. Corporate mission statements are typically general and nonspecific, but they set an agenda or tone for how the company will do business internally and with its clients.

Your task in this assignment is to work with a group to develop a "Course Mission Statement" in which you lay out your expectations for the course, your instructor, and yourselves. To write the mission statement, follow these steps:

1. Use an Internet search engine to find examples of mission statements. Just type "mission statement" into Google, Bing, or Yahoo.

2. In class, with your group, identify the common characteristics of these mission statements. Pay special attention to their content, organization, and style. Make note of their common features.

3. With your group, write your own course mission statement. Be sure to include goals you would like the course to meet. You might also want to develop an "ethics statement" that talks about your approach to ethical issues associated with assignments, course readings, and attendance.

4. Compare your group's course mission statement with other groups' mission statements. Note places where your statement is similar to and different from their statements.

When your course mission statement is complete, it should provide a one-paragraph description of what you are trying to achieve in your class.

Visit MyWritingLab for a Post-test and more technical writing resources.

CHAPTER

2

Communicating in a Reader-Focused Way

Creating a Reader Profile *19*

Using Reader Profiles to Your Advantage *24*

Global and Transcultural Communication *24*

What You Need to Know *33*

Exercises and Projects *33*

Case Study: Installing a Medical Waste Incinerator *35*

In this chapter, you will learn:

- How to develop a comprehensive profile of a document's readers.

- How to use the computer as a reader analysis tool.

- How to sort your readers into primary, secondary, tertiary, or gatekeeper audiences.

- Techniques for identifying readers' needs, values, and attitudes about you and your document.

- How to analyze the physical, economic, political, and ethical contexts of use that influence the way readers will interpret your text.

- How to anticipate the needs of global and transcultural readers.

When communicating in the workplace, you should focus on your readers' needs, values, and attitudes. Today, more than ever, readers don't have time to slog through information they don't need. So, you should find out exactly what your readers need to know and how they want that information presented. Then, as you are writing, speaking, or designing your message, focus on giving them the information they need in ways that are most useful to them.

Another concern is the ever-increasing importance of global communication through electronic networks. In technical fields, you *will* find yourself regularly communicating with people who speak other languages, have different customs, and hold different expectations. Computers have broken down many of the geographical barriers that once separated people and cultures.

This chapter will show you the steps needed to better understand your readers and the contexts in which they will be reading your technical document.

Creating a Reader Profile

A *reader profile* is an analysis of your readers' distinct needs, backgrounds, abilities, and experiences. In technical communication, documents are designed to target the needs of specific types of readers. Your reader profile will give you detailed information about how your readers will use your document and the contexts in which they will use it.

Keep in mind the following guidelines about your readers and how they prefer to read.

Guideline One: Readers are "raiders" for information—People don't usually read technical documents for fun. Instead, most readers are *raiding* your document for the information they need to make decisions or take action.

Guideline Two: Readers are wholly responsible for interpreting your text—You won't be available to explain what your document means, so your readers need to be able to easily figure out on their own what you are telling them.

Your readers only want the information they need to make a decision or take action. As the writer, it is your job to find out what they need and how they want the information presented.

Guideline Three: Readers want only "need-to-know" information—Readers want you to give them only the information they need, nothing more. Any additional material only makes the information they want harder to find.

Guideline Four: Readers prefer concise texts—The shorter, the better. Usually, the longer the document is, the less likely it is that people are going to read it. Your readers prefer documents that get to the point and highlight the important information.

Guideline Five: Readers prefer documents with graphics and effective page design—We live in a visual culture. Large blocks of text intimidate most readers, so include graphics and use page design to make your document more readable.

About Your Readers

- Readers are "raiders" for information.
- Readers are wholly responsible for interpreting your text.
- Readers want only "need-to-know" information.
- Readers prefer concise texts.
- Readers prefer documents with graphics and effective page design.

AT A GLANCE

Step 1: Identify Your Readers

You should always begin by identifying exactly who are the target readers of your document. Figure 2.1 shows a Writer-Centered Analysis Chart that will help you identify the various kinds of people who might read your text (Mathes & Stevenson, 1976). Put yourself, as the writer, in the center ring. Then, in each ring farther from yourself, identify your readers from most important (primary readers) to least important (tertiary readers).

In your Writer-Centered Chart, fill in the names and titles of the primary, secondary, tertiary, and gatekeeper readers who will or might look over your work.

PRIMARY READERS (ACTION TAKERS) The primary readers are the people to whom your document is addressed. They are usually *action*

Writer-Centered Analysis Chart

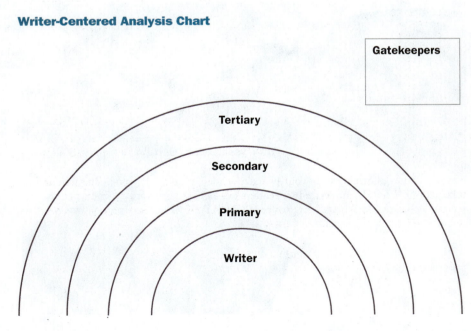

Gatekeepers

Tertiary

Secondary

Primary

Writer

Figure 2.1: A Writer-Centered Analysis Chart starts with you in the center and identifies the various people who may be interested in your document.

takers because the information you are providing will allow them to do something or make a decision. Usually, your document will have only one or two primary readers or types of primary readers.

SECONDARY READERS (ADVISORS)   The secondary readers are people who *advise* the primary readers. Usually, they are experts in the field, or they have special knowledge that the primary readers require to make a decision.

TERTIARY READERS (EVALUATORS)   The tertiary readers include others who may have an interest in your document's information. They are often *evaluators* of you, your team, or your company. These readers might be local news reporters, lawyers, auditors, historians, politicians, community activists, environmentalists, or perhaps your company's competitors.

GATEKEEPERS (SUPERVISORS)   The gatekeepers are people who will need to look over your document before it is sent to the primary readers. Your most common gatekeeper is your immediate supervisor. In some cases, though, your company's lawyers, accountants, and others may need to sign off on the document before it is sent out.

Each of these four types of readers will look for different kinds of information. The primary readers are the most important, so their needs come first. Nevertheless, a well-written document also anticipates the needs of the secondary, tertiary, and gatekeeper readers.

Step 2: Identify Your Readers' Needs, Values, and Attitudes

Don't assume that your readers have the same needs, values, and attitudes as you do. Readers often have very different needs and expectations than the writers of a technical document.

As you begin considering your readers, think about some of the following issues:

- Readers' familiarity with the subject
- Readers' professional experience
- Readers' educational level
- Readers' reading and comprehension level
- Readers' skill level

A Reader Analysis Chart, like the one shown in Figure 2.2, can help you identify your readers' needs, values, and attitudes toward your text. To use the Reader Analysis Chart, fill in the boxes with your understanding of your readers' needs, values, and attitudes.

NEEDS   What information do your primary readers require to make a decision or take action? What do the secondary readers need if they are going to make positive recommendations to the primary readers? What might the tertiary and gatekeeper readers be looking for in your document?

VALUES   What do your readers value most? Do they value efficiency and consistency? Do they value accuracy? Is profit a key concern? How much do they value environmental or social concerns?

Reader Analysis Chart

Readers	Needs	Values	Attitudes
Primary			
Secondary			
Tertiary			
Gatekeepers			

Figure 2.2: To better understand your readers, fill in this Reader Analysis Chart with notes about their characteristics.

AT A GLANCE

Determining How Readers Make Decisions

- *Needs*—information the readers need to take action or make a decision
- *Values*—issues, goals, or beliefs that the readers feel are important
- *Attitudes*—the readers' emotional response to you, your project, or your company

ATTITUDES What are your readers' attitudes toward you, your company, and the subject of your document? Will your readers be excited, upset, wary, positive, hopeful, careful, concerned, skeptical, or heartened by what you are telling them?

As you fill in the Reader Analysis Chart, make strategic guesses about your readers. Put a question mark (?) in spaces where you aren't sure about your readers' needs, values, or attitudes. These question marks signal places where you need to do more research on your readers. You can look them up on the Internet with search engines, or you might interview people who are Subject Matter Experts (SMEs) at your company or who hire themselves out as consultants. These experts may be able to give you insights into your readers' likely characteristics.

The overall goal of your reader profile is to help you see your subject through your readers' perspective. When you know who they are, as well as their needs, values, and attitudes, you can make better decisions about the content, organization, style, and design of your document or presentation.

Step 3: Identify the Contexts in Which Readers Will Experience Your Document

Perhaps the most obvious concern is the *physical context* in which your readers will use your document. Will they be in their office or at a meeting? Will they be on the factory floor, trying to repair a robotic arm? Or are they in the emergency room, trying to save someone's life? Each of these physical contexts will alter the way your readers interpret your document.

Context Analysis Chart

	Physical Context	Economic Context	Political Context	Ethical Context
Primary Readers				
Readers' Company				
Readers' Industry				

Figure 2.3: Each reader is influenced by physical, economic, political, and ethical concerns. A Context Analysis Chart anticipates these concerns for the primary readers, their company, and their industry.

AT A GLANCE

Context of Use

- *Physical context*—the places where the readers will use your document
- *Economic context*—the money-related issues that will restrict the kinds of actions possible
- *Political context*—the micropolitical and macropolitical trends that will guide your readers
- *Ethical context*—the personal, social, and environmental issues that shape the readers' responses

But context of use goes beyond your readers' physical context. Your readers may also be influenced by the economic, ethical, and political issues that shape how they see the world. To help you sort out these various contexts, you can use a Context Analysis Chart like the one shown in Figure 2.3.

To use the Context Analysis Chart, fill in what you know about the physical, economic, political, and ethical issues that might influence the primary readers, their company, and their industry.

PHYSICAL CONTEXT   Where will your readers use your document? How do these various places affect how they will read your document? How should you write and design the document to fit these places?

ECONOMIC CONTEXT   What are the economic issues that will influence your readers' decisions? What are the costs and benefits of your ideas? How would accepting your ideas change the financial situation of your readers, their company, or their industry?

POLITICAL CONTEXT   What are the political forces influencing you and your readers? On a micropolitical level, how will your ideas affect your readers' relationships with you, their supervisors, or their colleagues? On a macropolitical level, how will political trends at the local, state, federal, and global levels shape how your readers interpret your ideas?

Link

For more help with identifying ethical issues, see Chapter 4, page 61.

ETHICAL CONTEXT How will your ideas affect the rights, values, and well-being of others? Does your document involve any social or environmental issues that might be of concern to your readers? Will any laws or rules be bent or broken if your readers do what you want?

Put a question mark (?) in spaces where you don't have specific information about your readers' physical, economic, political, and ethical contexts. You can then do research on the Internet or you can interview SMEs who may have the answers you need.

Using Reader Profiles to Your Advantage

You are now ready to use your reader profile to strengthen your writing and make your technical document more informed and persuasive. In your Reader Analysis and Context Analysis charts, circle or highlight the most important terms, concepts, and phrases. The items you circle will help you make better decisions about the content, organization, style, and design of your document.

For example, Figures 2.4 and 2.5 show two documents from the same website about the same topic, West Nile virus. The documents, though, are written for two different types of readers. The first document, Figure 2.4, is written for the general public. Notice how its content, organization, style, and design are shaped to appeal to this general audience. The second document, Figure 2.5, is written for medical personnel. Notice how the content is far more complex and the style is less personal.

Different reader profiles for each of these documents allowed the author (probably the same person) to effectively present the same information to two very different kinds of readers.

Global and Transcultural Communication

Computers and mobile devices have greatly blurred geographical and political boundaries. Whether you are developing software documentation or describing a heart transplant procedure, your documents will be read and used by people around the world. In any technical or scientific field, you will be working with people from different cultures (Hoft, 1995; Reynolds & Valentine, 2004). It's all very exciting—and very challenging.

Global and transcultural issues will affect the content, organization, style, and design of your document.

Differences in Content

Cultures have different expectations about content in technical documentation:

- In business, the Chinese tend to trust relationships above all, so in documents they tend to look for facts, and they do not like overt attempts to persuade. An effective document will usually present the facts, with the underlying relationship between writer and reader being the basis for doing business.
- In Mexico, South America, and many African countries, family and personal backgrounds are of great importance. It is common for family-related issues to be mentioned in public relations, advertising, and documentation. Business relationships and meetings often start with exchanges about families and personal interests.

Document Written for the General Public

West Nile Virus (WNV) Fact Sheet

What Is West Nile Virus?

West Nile virus infection can cause serious disease. WNV is established as a seasonal epidemic in North America that flares up in the summer and continues into the fall. This fact sheet contains important information that can help you recognize and prevent West Nile virus.

What Can I Do to Prevent WNV?

The easiest and best way to avoid WNV is to prevent mosquito bites.

- When outdoors, use repellents containing DEET, picaridin, IR3535, some oil of lemon eucalyptus or para-menthane-diol. Follow the directions on the package.
- Many mosquitoes are most active from dusk to dawn. Be sure to use insect repellent and wear long sleeves and pants at these times or consider staying indoors during these hours.
- Make sure you have good screens on your windows and doors to keep mosquitoes out.
- Get rid of mosquito breeding sites by emptying standing water from flower pots, buckets and barrels. Change the water in pet dishes and replace the water in bird baths weekly. Drill holes in tire swings so water drains out. Keep children's wading pools empty and on their sides when they aren't being used.

What Are the Symptoms of WNV?

- **Serious Symptoms in a Few People.** About 1 in 150 people infected with WNV will develop severe illness. The severe symptoms can include high fever, headache, neck stiffness, stupor, disorientation, coma, tremors, convulsions, muscle weakness, vision loss, numbness and paralysis. These symptoms may last several weeks, and neurological effects may be permanent.
- **Milder Symptoms in Some People.** Up to 20 percent of the people who become infected will have symptoms which can include fever, headache, body aches, nausea, vomiting, and sometimes swollen lymph glands or a skin rash on the chest, stomach and back. Symptoms can last for as short as a few days to as long as several weeks.
- **No Symptoms in Most People.** Approximately 80 percent of people who are infected with WNV will not show any symptoms at all, but there is no way to know in advance if you will develop an illness or not.

How Does West Nile Virus Spread?

- **Infected Mosquitoes.**
  WNV is spread by the bite of an infected mosquito. Mosquitoes become infected when they feed on infected birds. Infected mosquitoes can then spread WNV to humans and other animals when they bite.
- **Transfusions, Transplants, and Mother-to-Child.**
  In a very small number of cases, WNV also has been spread directly from an infected person through blood transfusions, organ transplants, breastfeeding and during pregnancy from mother to baby.
- **Not through touching.**
  WNV is not spread through casual contact such as touching or kissing a person with the virus.

How Soon Do Infected People Get Sick?

People typically develop symptoms between 3 and 14 days after they are bitten by the infected mosquito.

How Is WNV Infection Treated?

There is no specific treatment for WNV infection. In cases with milder symptoms, people experience symptoms such as fever and aches that pass on their own, although illness may last weeks to months. In more severe cases, people usually need to go to the hospital where they can receive supportive treatment including intravenous fluids, help with breathing, and nursing care.

What Should I Do if I Think I Have WNV?

Milder WNV illness improves on its own, and people do not need to seek medical attention for this infection though they may choose to do so. If you develop symptoms of severe WNV illness, such as unusually severe headaches or confusion, seek medical attention immediately. Severe WNV illness usually requires hospitalization. Pregnant women and nursing mothers are encouraged to talk to their doctor if they develop symptoms that could be WNV.

National Center for Emerging and Zoonotic Infectious Diseases
Division of Vector-Borne Diseases

CDC

CS242240-A

Headings help readers raid document for information.

Examples are used to illustrate points.

Questions are used to anticipate readers' concerns.

Figure 2.4: This document on West Nile virus was written for the general public. It is action oriented and not very technical. The images also help reinforce the message, and the layout makes it highly raidable for information.

Source: Centers for Disease Control and Prevention (CDC), http://www.cdc.gov/westnile/index.html

(continued)

Figure 2.4:
(continued)

Bulleted lists help readers locate specific information.

Images reinforce written text.

What Is the Risk of Getting Sick from WNV?

- **People over 50 at higher risk to get severe illness.** People over the age of 50 are more likely to develop serious symptoms of WNV if they do get sick and should take special care to avoid mosquito bites.

- **Being outside means you're at risk.** The more time you're outdoors, the more time you could be bitten by an infected mosquito. Pay attention to avoiding mosquito bites if you spend time outside, either working or playing.

- **Risk through medical procedures is very low.** All donated blood is checked for WNV before being used. The risk of getting WNV through blood transfusions and organ transplants is very small, and should not prevent people who need surgery from having it. If you have concerns, talk to your doctor.

What Is CDC Doing About WNV?

CDC is working with state and local health departments, the Food and Drug Administration and other government agencies, as well as private industry, to prepare for and prevent new cases of WNV.

Some things CDC is doing include:

- Coordinating a nation-wide electronic database where states share information about WNV
- Helping states develop and carry out improved mosquito prevention and control programs
- Developing better, faster tests to detect and diagnose WNV
- Creating new education tools and programs for the media, the public, and health professionals
- Working with partners to develop vaccines.

What Else Should I Know?

West Nile virus infects birds. In nature, West Nile virus cycles between mosquitoes and birds. Some infected birds can develop high levels of the virus in their bloodstream and mosquitoes can become infected by biting these infected birds. Some, but not all infected birds get sick and die of disease. One way health officials conduct surveillance for West Nile virus is by testing local birds. Finding dead birds may be a sign that West Nile virus is circulating between birds and the mosquitoes in an area. By reporting dead birds to state and local health departments, you can play an important role in monitoring West Nile virus. State and local agencies have different policies for collecting and testing birds, so check with your county or state health department to find information about reporting dead birds in your area.

If you find a dead bird: Don't handle the body with your bare hands. Contact your local health department for instructions on reporting and disposing of the body. They may tell you to dispose of the bird after they log your report.

For more information, visit www.cdc.gov/westnile, or call CDC at 800-CDC-INFO (English and Spanish) or 888-232-6348 (TTY).

Document Written for Experts

Clinical Evaluation & Disease

Diagnosis & Reporting

West Nile virus (WNV) disease should be considered in any person with a febrile or acute neurologic illness who has had recent exposure to mosquitoes, blood transfusion, or organ transplantation, especially during the summer months in areas where virus activity has been reported. The diagnosis should also be considered in any infant born to a mother infected with WNV during pregnancy or while breastfeeding. More information on WNV in pregnancy and breastfeeding is available here. (/westnile/faq/pregnancy.html)

In addition to other more common causes of encephalitis and aseptic meningitis (e.g. herpes simplex virus and enteroviruses), other arboviruses (e.g., La Crosse, St. Louis encephalitis, Eastern equine encephalitis, and Powassan viruses) should also be considered in the differential etiology of suspected WNV illness.

WNV disease is a nationally notifiable condition. All cases should be reported to local public health authorities in a timely manner. Reporting can assist local, state, and national authorities to recognize outbreaks and to implement control measures to reduce future infections.

Clinical Signs & Symptoms

The incubation period for WNV disease is typically 2 to 6 days but ranges from 2 to 14 days and can be several weeks in immunocompromised people.

An estimated 70-80% of human WNV infections are subclinical or asymptomatic. Most symptomatic persons experience an acute systemic febrile illness that often includes headache, weakness, myalgia, or arthralgia; gastrointestinal symptoms and a transient maculopapular rash also are commonly reported. Less than 1% of infected persons develop neuroinvasive disease, which typically manifests as meningitis, encephalitis, or acute flaccid paralysis.

- WNV meningitis is clinically indistinguishable from viral meningitis due to other etiologies and typically presents with fever, headache, and nuchal rigidity.
- WNV encephalitis is a more severe clinical syndrome that usually manifests with fever and altered mental status, seizures, focal neurologic deficits, or movement disorders such as tremor or parkinsonism.
- WNV acute flaccid paralysis is usually clinically and pathologically identical to poliovirus-associated poliomyelitis, with damage of anterior horn cells, and may progress to respiratory paralysis requiring mechanical ventilation. WNV poliomyelitis often presents as isolated limb paresis or paralysis and can occur without fever or apparent viral prodrome. WNV-associated Guillain-Barré syndrome and radiculopathy have also been reported and can be distinguished from WNV poliomyelitis by clinical manifestations and electrophysiologic testing.

Rarely, cardiac dysrhythmias, myocarditis, rhabdomyolysis, optic neuritis, uveitis, chorioretinitis, orchitis, pancreatitis, and hepatitis have been described in patients with WNV disease.

Source: Centers for Disease Control and Prevention (CDC), http://www.cdc.gov/westnile/index.html

(continued)

The language is much more technical.

Document is more focused on providing information than encouraging action.

Figure 2.5: This document was written for clinicians and other medical personnel. It is far more technical in style and design than the document written for the general public. Nevertheless, it contains much of the same information.

Figure 2.5:
(continued)

Most women known to have been infected with WNV during pregnancy have delivered infants without evidence of infection or clinical abnormalities. In the best-documented, confirmed congenital WNV infection, the mother developed neuroinvasive WNV disease during the twenty-seventh week of gestation, and her neonate was born with cystic lesions in brain tissue and chorioretinitis. One infant who apparently acquired WNV infection through breastfeeding remained asymptomatic. Guidelines for the evaluation of fetal and neonatal WNV infections are available at www.cdc.gov/mmwr/preview/mmwrhtml/mm5307a4.htm (http://www.cdc.gov/mmwr/preview/mmwrhtml/mm5307a4.htm) .

Clinical Evaluation

Routine clinical laboratory studies are generally nonspecific. In patients with neuroinvasive disease, CSF examination generally shows lymphocytic pleocytosis, but neutrophils may predominate early in the course of illness. Brain magnetic resonance imaging is frequently normal, but signal abnormalities in the basal ganglia, thalamus, and brainstem may be seen in patients with encephalitis, and in the anterior spinal cord in patients with poliomyelitis.

Outcomes

Most patients with non-neuroinvasive WNV disease or WNV meningitis recover completely, but fatigue, malaise, and weakness can linger for weeks or months. Patients who recover from WNV encephalitis or poliomyelitis often have residual neurologic deficits. Among patients with neuroinvasive disease, the overall case-fatality ratio is approximately 10%, but it is significantly higher for patients with WNV encephalitis and poliomyelitis than WNV meningitis.

Recent studies have raised questions about the possible persistence of WNV infection and subsequent renal disease. More information is available here. (/westnile/healthCareProviders/healthCareProviders-PersistentInfections.html)

Page last reviewed: June 7, 2013
Page last updated: June 7, 2013
Content source: Centers for Disease Control and Prevention
National Center for Emerging and Zoonotic Infectious Diseases (NCEZID)
Division of Vector-Borne Diseases (DVBD)

Centers for Disease Control and Prevention 1600 Clifton Rd. Atlanta, GA 30333, USA
800-CDC-INFO (800-232-4636) TTY: (888) 232-6348 - Contact CDC–INFO

Design is more text-heavy and less easy to raid for information.

- In the Middle East, Arabs tend to enjoy negotiating and bargaining. As a result, it is crucial that all the details in documents be spelled out exactly before the two sides try to work out a deal. In most cases, though, the first offer you make will rarely be considered the final offer.
- In Asian countries, the reputation of the writer or company is essential for establishing the credibility of the information (Haneda & Shima, 1983). Interpersonal relationships and prior experiences can sometimes even trump empirical evidence in Asia.
- Also in Asia, contextual cues can be more important than content. In other words, *how* someone says something may be more important than *what* he or she is saying. For example, when Japanese people speak or write in their own language, they rarely refuse a request with the word *no*. Instead, they rely on contextual cues to signal the refusal. As a result, when Japanese is translated into English, these "high-context" linguistic strategies are often misunderstood (Chaney & Martin, 2004). Similarly, in Indonesia, the phrase "Yes, but" actually means "no" when someone is speaking.

Link

To learn more about working in high-context cultures, go to Chapter 13, page 357.

- In India, business is often conducted in English because the nation has over a dozen major languages and hundreds of minor languages. So, don't be surprised when your Indian partners are very fluent in English and expect you to show a high level of fluency, especially if you are a native English speaker.
- In several African countries, including Tunisia and Morocco, business tends to be conducted in French, even though the official language of the country is Arabic.

Differences in Organization

The organization of a document often needs to be altered to suit a global audience. Organizational structures that Americans perceive to be "logical" or "common sense" can seem confusing and even rude in some cultures.

- In Arab cultures, documents and meetings often start out with statements of appreciation and attempts to build common bonds among people. The American tendency to "get to the point" can be seen as rude. Both documents and meetings should demonstrate patience.
- Also in Arabic cultures, documents rely on repetition to make their points. To North Americans, this repetition might seem like the document is moving one step back for every two steps forward. To Arabs, American documents often seem incomplete because they lack this repetition.
- Asians often prefer to start out with contextual information about nonbusiness issues. For example, it is common for Japanese writers to start out letters by saying something about the weather. To some Asians, American documents seem abrupt, because Americans tend to bluntly highlight goals and objectives up front.

- In India, the term *thank you* is considered a form of payment and is used more formally than in American culture. So, if an associate or colleague has done something for you, including a favor, you should accept with appreciation but without saying "thank you." Even when doing business with others, "thank you" is not common.

Differences in Style

Beyond difficulties with translation, style is usually an important difference among cultures:

- In China, overt attempts at persuasion are often seen as rude and aggressive. Instead, documents and meetings should be used to build relationships and present factual information. Strong relationships lead to good business, not the other way around.
- Arabic style may seem ornamental to North Americans, making Arabic documents and presentations seem colorful to non-Arabs. On the other hand, the American reliance on "plain language" can offend the sensibilities of Arabs, who prefer a more ornate style in formal documents.
- In Mexico and much of South America, an informal style often suggests a lack of respect for the project, the product, or the readers. Mexicans especially value formality in business settings, so the use of first names and contractions in business prose can be offensive.
- In sub-Saharan Africa, readers prefer a document's tone to stress a win–win situation. Your tone, therefore, should imply that both sides will benefit from the arrangement.

Computers, especially networked computers, have increased opportunities to work across cultures.

- Some Native Americans prefer the sense that everyone had input on the document. Therefore, a direct writing or presentation style will meet resistance because it will seem to represent the opinion of only one person.
- In North America, women are more direct than women in other parts of the world, including Europe. This directness often works to their advantage in other countries, because they are viewed as confident and forward thinking. However, as writers and speakers, women should not be too surprised when people from other cultures react in ways that seem to show resistance.

Differences in Design

Even the design of documents is important when you are working with global and cross-cultural readers:

- Arabic and some Chinese scripts are read from right to left, unlike English, which is read from left to right (Figure 2.6). As a result, Arabic and some Chinese readers tend to scan pages and images differently than Americans or Europeans do.
- Some icons that show hand gestures—like the OK sign, a pointing finger, or a peace sign with the back of the hand facing outward—can be highly offensive in some cultures. Imagine a document in which a hand with the middle finger extended is used to point at things. You get the picture.
- In China, presentations are often black and white because many colors have unexpected meanings that are negative. Yellow, for example, is typically associated with pornography. A man shown wearing a green hat is being cheated upon.
- In many South American and Asian cultures, the use of the right hand is preferred when handing items (e.g., business cards, documents, products) to people. Therefore, pictures or drawings in documents should show people using their right hands to interact.
- In some Asian cultures, a white flower or white dress can symbolize death. As a result, a photograph of white flowers or white dresses can signal a funeral or mourning.

Different Ways of Scanning a Page

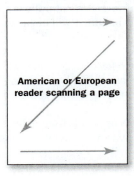

American or European
reader scanning a page

Arabic or Chinese
reader scanning a page

Figure 2.6:
Readers from other cultures may scan the page differently. The design needs to take their preferences into account.

- Europeans find that American texts include too many graphics and use too much white space. Americans, meanwhile, often find that the small margins in European texts make the documents look crowded and cramped.
- Graphs and charts that seem to have obvious meanings to Americans can be baffling and confusing to readers from other cultures. If your global document includes graphs and charts, you should seek out someone from the readers' culture to help you determine whether your visuals will be understood.
- When giving presentations in some Native American cultures, hand gestures should be limited and eye contact should be minimized. Ironically, this advice is exactly the opposite of what most public speaking coaches suggest for non-Native audiences.

Listen and Learn: The Key to Global and Transcultural Communication

With all these differences in content, organization, style, and design, how can you possibly write for global or transcultural readers? Here are four helpful strategies:

LISTEN CAREFULLY   Careful listening is a valued skill in all cultures, and you will learn a great amount by simply paying attention to what your readers expect the document to include and how it should look.

BE POLITE   Politeness in one culture tends to translate well into other cultures. For example, words like *please* and *thank you* are viewed as polite in workplace settings. Even in places where words like "thank you" have different nuances, such as India, the receiver will understand that you are trying to be polite. Smiles and a friendly tone are almost always welcome. There are subtle differences in how these words and gestures are used in other cultures, but your readers will understand that you are trying to be polite.

RESEARCH THE TARGET CULTURE   Use the Internet to do some research into your readers' cultural expectations for technical documents. On the Internet or at your workplace, you might also find some model texts from the readers' culture. Use them to help guide your decisions about content, organization, style, and design.

AVOID HUMOR   Jokes, funny stories, and wordplay rarely translate well across cultures, and they can often be interpreted as offensive. Even if you are a naturally funny person in your own culture, chances are good your attempts at humor will offend or confuse people from other cultures.

TALK TO YOUR COLLEAGUES   You may also seek out co-workers or colleagues who are from the target culture or who have lived there. You can ask them about conventions that might make your document or presentation more effective. They can also help you avoid doing anything awkward or offensive.

Overall, when you are communicating with global readers or people from different cultures, be observant and listen to what they tell you. Do some research into their expectations, and be ready to learn from your mistakes.

- When communicating in the workplace, you should make your readers' needs the focal point of your writing, speaking, and design.

- Early in the writing process, you should begin developing a profile of the types of people who may be interested in your document.

- You can use your computer as a reader analysis tool to better tailor your document's content, organization, style, and design to the needs of your readers.

- Your readers will include *primary readers* (action takers), *secondary readers* (advisors), *tertiary readers* (evaluators), and *gatekeepers* (supervisors).

- In your documents and presentations, you should anticipate various readers' needs, values, and attitudes.

- You should anticipate the document's contexts of use, which include the physical, economic, political, and ethical factors that may influence a reader's ideas.

- The emergence of the Internet has heightened the importance of global and transcultural communication. You need to adjust the content, organization, style, and design of your text to be sensitive to transcultural needs.

Individual or Team Projects

1. Choose two websites that are designed for very different types of readers. Write a memo to your instructor in which you compare and contrast the websites, showing how they approach their readers differently. How do they use content, organization, style, and design to meet the needs, values, and attitudes of their readers?

   Some pairs of websites you might consider include (chevrolet.com versus www.miniusa.com) for cars, (time.com versus outsidemag.com) for magazines, or (samsung.com versus apple.com) for mobile phones. Look for websites for similar products that pursue different kinds of customers.

2. Consider the advertisement in Figure 2.7 and "reverse-engineer" its reader analysis. Using a Writer-Centered Analysis Chart and a Reader Analysis Chart, identify the primary, secondary, and tertiary readers of the text. Then make guesses about the needs, values, and attitudes of these readers.

   Write a memo to your instructor in which you use your charts to discuss the readers of this document. Then show how the advertisement anticipates these readers' needs.

3. Choose a country or culture that interests you. Then, find two texts written by people from that country or culture. Write a memo to your instructor in which you discuss any similarities or differences between the texts and your own expectations for texts. Pay close attention to differences in content, organization, style, and design of these texts.

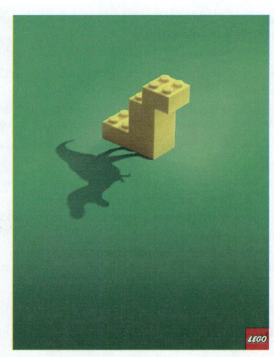

Figure 2.7: Who are the intended readers of this advertisement? What are their needs, values, and attitudes?

Source: LEGO and the LEGO Logo are trademarks of the LEGO Group of Companies, used here by permission. © 2014 The LEGO Group.

Collaborative Project

With a group of people from your class, create a website that explores the needs, values, and attitudes of people from a different country or culture. The website does not need to be complex. On the Internet, identify various websites that offer information on that country or culture. Then, organize those websites by content and create links to them. Specifically, pay attention to the ways in which this country's physical, economic, political, and ethical contexts shape the way its people conduct their lives.

When you are finished with the website, give a presentation to your class in which your group discusses how this country or culture differs from your own. Answer the following question: If you were going to offer a product or service to the people of this country or culture, what considerations would you need to keep in mind? If you needed to write a proposal or a set of instructions to people from this country or culture, how might you need to adjust it to fit their unique qualities?

Visit MyWritingLab for a Post-test and more technical writing resources.

Installing a Medical Waste Incinerator

Duane Jackson knew this decision was going to be difficult. As the assistant city engineer for Dover City, he was frequently asked to study construction proposals sent to the city council. He would then write a report with a recommendation. So, when the proposal for constructing a medical waste incinerator crossed his desk, he knew there was going to be trouble.

Overall, the proposal from Valley Medical, Inc., looked solid. The incinerator would be within 3 miles of the two major hospitals and a biotech research facility. And it would bring about 30 good jobs to the Blue Park neighborhood, an economically depressed part of town.

The problem was that people in Blue Park were going to be skeptical. Duane grew up in a neighborhood like Blue Park, primarily African American and lower middle class. He knew that hazardous industries often put their operations in these kinds of neighborhoods because the locals did not have the financial resources or political clout to fight them. In the past, companies had taken advantage of these neighborhoods' political weaknesses, leaving the areas polluted and unhealthy.

Powerful interests were weighing in on this issue. Dover City's mayor wanted the incinerator badly because she wanted the economic boost the new business would provide. Certainly, the executives at the hospitals and research laboratory were enthusiastic, because a nearby incinerator would help them cut costs. The city councilor who represented Blue Park wanted the jobs, but not at the expense of his constituents' health. Environmental groups, health advocates, and neighborhood associations were cautious about the incinerator.

Analyzing the Readers

After a few weeks of intense study, Duane's research convinced him that the incinerator was not a health hazard to the people of Blue Park. Similar incinerators built by Valley Medical had spotless records. Emissions would be minimal because advanced "scrubbers" would remove almost all the particles left over after incineration. The scrubbers were very advanced, almost completely removing any harmful pollutants such as dioxin and mercury.

Also, the company had a good plan for ensuring that medical waste would not sit around in trucks or containers, waiting to be burned. The waste would be immediately incinerated on arrival.

Duane decided to write a report to the city council that recommended the incinerator be built. That decision was the easy part. Now he needed to write a report that would convince the skeptics.

After identifying the subject and purpose of the report, Duane decided to do a thorough analysis of his readers and the report's contexts of use. He began with a Writer-Centered Analysis Chart (Figure 2.8). He then used a Reader Analysis Chart to identify the various readers' needs, values, and attitudes (Figure 2.9). Finally, Duane filled out a Context Analysis Chart to identify the physical, economic, political, and ethical issues involved (Figure 2.10).

Duane's Writer-Centered Analysis Chart

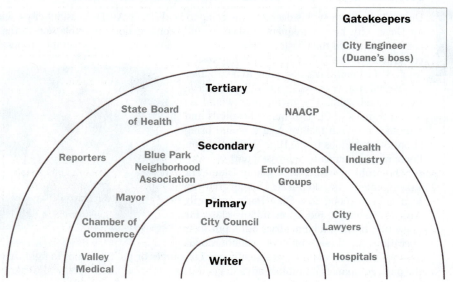

Gatekeepers

City Engineer
(Duane's boss)

Figure 2.8: Duane's Writer-Centered Analysis Chart showed how many readers his report would have.

What Should Duane Do Now?

On the facts alone, Duane was convinced that the incinerator would be well placed in the Blue Park neighborhood. But his reader analysis charts showed that facts alone were not going to win over his primary audience, the members of the city council. They would have numerous other economic, political, and ethical issues to consider besides the facts. In many ways, these factors were more important than the empirical evidence for the incinerator.

One important thing Duane noticed was that although the city council members were the "action takers," they were heavily influenced by the secondary readers. These secondary readers, the "advisors," would play a large role in the council's decision.

How can Duane adjust the content, organization, style, and design to better write his report? If you were Duane's readers, what kinds of information would you expect in this kind of report?

Duane's Reader Analysis Chart

	Needs	Values	Attitudes
Primary • City Council	Reliable information Environmental impact data Clear recommendation Impartial commentary	Citizen safety Economic development Fairness	Optimistic Cautious
Secondary • Valley Medical • Chamber of Commerce • Mayor • Neighborhood Association • Environmental Groups • City Lawyers • Hospitals	Impartial commentary Specific facts about emissions Cultural and social considerations Valley Medical wants profits.	Maintaining character of Blue Park Economic development Environmental safety Safe disposal of waste	Mayor and hospitals are positive and hopeful. Neighborhood association and environmental groups are skeptical, perhaps resistant. Valley Medical hopeful
Tertiary • Reporters • State Board of Health • NAACP • Health Industry	Impartial decision Reassurance that race or poverty are not factors Basic facts about incinerator	Fairness and honesty Lack of bias Protection of people with little political power	Skeptical Open-minded
Gatekeepers • City Engineer	Reliable information Clear decision based on reliable data	Minimal trouble with mayor and council Low profile; stay out of politics Honesty	Impartial to project Concerned that report may cause tensions

Figure 2.9: Duane filled in a Reader Analysis Chart, noting everything he knew about the various readers of his report. He noticed that most readers wanted impartial and reliable information. Some readers were positive; others were skeptical.

Duane's Context Analysis Chart

	Physical Context	Economic Context	Political Context	Ethical Context
Primary Readers • City Council	Initially at their office Later, in city council meeting	Looking to improve city economics	Re-election is always an issue. Mayor wants it. BP city councilor would like it.	Exploiting poor neighborhood? Racial issues? Environmental issues
Readers' Company • Dover City	City Hall Engineers' office City website	The jobs are a financial plus. Home values in neighborhood decline? Good for hospitals	Voters are wary. Neighborhood and environmental groups draw attention. Racial politics?	City liable if mistake? Environmental impact Infringement of people's rights? Legal issues
Readers' Industry • City government	Reports on Internet about project	Job creation Economic growth	Pressure on mayor Shows Dover City is positive about this kind of business	Public relations Don't want to seem exploitative

Figure 2.10: Duane's Context Analysis Chart revealed some interesting tensions between the economics and politics of the decision on the incinerator.

CHAPTER

3

Working in Teams

The Stages of Teaming *40*

Forming: Strategic Planning *40*

Storming: Managing Conflict *44*

Norming: Determining Team Roles *51*

Help: Virtual Teaming *52*

Performing: Improving Quality *54*

The Keys to Teaming *57*

What You Need to Know *57*

Exercises and Projects *58*

Case Study: Not a Sunny Day *59*

In this chapter, you will learn:

- Why working in teams is essential in technical workplaces.

- The four stages of teaming in the workplace: forming, storming, norming, and performing.

- How to use strategic planning to form a team and begin a project.

- Strategies for managing team conflict in the storming stage.

- How to define team roles in the norming stage to improve productivity.

- How to improve performance with Total Quality Management (TQM) strategies.

- How to work as part of a "virtual" team.

Working in teams happens every day in the technical workplace. In fact, when managers are surveyed about the abilities they look for in new employees, they often put "works well with a team" near the top of their list. The ability to collaborate with others is an essential skill if you are going to succeed in today's networked workplace.

Computers have only increased the ability and necessity to work in teams. Communication tools like smartphones, social networking, e-mail, texting, file and image sharing sites, and websites allow people to work together electronically. Telecommuting, teleworking, and virtual offices are becoming more common, and people are increasingly finding themselves working outside the traditional office setting. Now, more than ever, you need to learn how to work with teams of others.

The Stages of Teaming

It would be nice if people worked well together from the start. But in reality, team members often need time to set goals and adjust to each other's working styles and abilities. In 1965, Bruce Tuckman introduced a four-stage model of how most teams learn to work together: Forming, Storming, Norming, and Performing (Figure 3.1).

Tuckman's stages are not rigid. Instead, a team tends to move back and forth among the stages as the project evolves and moves forward.

Forming: Strategic Planning

Forming is an important part of the team-building process. When a team is first created, the members are usually excited and optimistic about the new project. They are often a little anxious, because each person is uncertain about the others' expectations.

So, in the forming stage, members should spend time getting to know each other and assessing each other's strengths and abilities.

When forming a new team, strategic planning is the key to effective teamwork. By working through the following steps at the beginning of a project, you will give your team time to form properly, often saving yourselves time and frustration as the project moves forward.

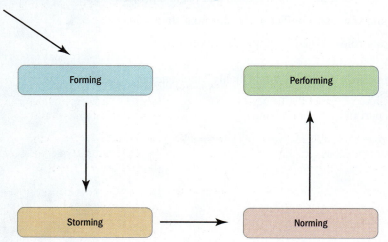

Tuckman's Four Stages of Teaming

Figure 3.1: A team will typically go through four stages: forming, storming, norming, and performing. Give your team time to properly evolve as a unit.

Step 1: Define the Project Mission and Objectives

Don't just rush in. Take some time to first determine what your team is being asked to accomplish. A good way to start forming is to define the rhetorical situation in which your team is working:

Link

For more help defining the rhetorical situation, turn to Chapter 1, page 4.

> **Subject**—What are we being asked to develop? What are the boundaries of our project? What are we *not* being asked to do?
>
> **Purpose (mission statement)**—What is the mission of the project? Why are we being asked to do this? What are the end results (deliverables) that we are being asked to produce?
>
> **Readers**—Who are our clients? What are their needs, values, and attitudes? Who will be evaluating our work?
>
> **Context**—What are the physical, economic, political, and ethical factors that will influence this project? How should we adjust to them?

You and your team should write down your mission statement in one sentence. For example:

Our Mission:

The purpose of this Staph Infection Task Force is to determine the level of staph infection vulnerability at St. Thomas Medical Center and to develop strategies for limiting our patients' exposure to staph, especially MRSA.

Step 2: Identify Project Outcomes

Your *project outcomes* are the visible and measurable results of the team's efforts. To identify the outcomes of your project, make a list of the two to five measurable goals that you can use to show the progress of your team.

Organizations often like to talk about outcomes in terms of "deliverables." *Deliverables* are the real products or services that you will deliver to the client during the project and after it is completed. Sometimes it is helpful to convert each project outcome into a deliverable. For example:

Outcome 1: Collection of current data and research literature on staph infections. Interviews with other hospitals about successful control methods. → **Deliverable:** A report on the findings, due May 25

Outcome 2: More awareness of the problem here at the hospital → **Deliverable:** Pamphlets and posters raising awareness and describing staph control procedures

Outcome 3: Results of experiments that quantify the staph risk at the hospital → **Deliverable:** Report to the administration about the extent of the problem, due June 2

Outcome 4: Development of strategies for preventing and containing staph infections → **Deliverable:** A contingency plan that offers concrete steps for controlling staph. Training modules to educate staff about the problem.

Step 3: Define Team Member Responsibilities

Ask team members to identify ways they could best contribute to the project. That way, each person can take advantage of his or her strengths. Discuss any time limitations or potential conflicts that might arise during the project.

If your team's project involves writing a document, you should identify each team member's responsibilities while dividing up the writing task. For example, here are four jobs you might consider:

> **Coordinator**—The coordinator is responsible for maintaining the project schedule and running the meetings. The coordinator is not the "boss." Rather, he or she is a facilitator who helps keep the project on track.
>
> **Researchers**—One or two people in the group should be assigned to collect information. They are responsible for doing Internet searches, digging up materials in the library, and coordinating the team's empirical research.
>
> **Editor**—The editor is responsible for the organization and style of the document. He or she identifies places where content is missing or where information needs to be reorganized to achieve the project's purpose.
>
> **Designer**—The designer is responsible for laying out the document, collecting images, and making tables, graphs, and charts.

Notice that there is no designated "writer" among these roles. Each person in the group should be responsible for writing at least one major part of the document.

Step 4: Create a Project Calendar

Project calendars are essential for meeting deadlines. Numerous project management software packages like Microsoft Project, Clarizen, AtTask, and Genius Project help teams lay out calendars for completing projects. These programs are helpful for setting deadlines and specifying when interrelated parts of the project need to be completed (Figure 3.2).

You don't need project management software for smaller projects. A reliable time management technique is to use *backward planning* to determine when you need to accomplish specific tasks and meet smaller and final deadlines.

To do backward planning, start out by putting the project's deadline on a calendar. Then, work backward from that deadline, writing down the dates when specific project tasks need to be completed (Figure 3.3).

The advantage of a project calendar is that it keeps the team on task. The calendar shows the milestones for the project, so everyone knows how the rest of the team is progressing. That way, everyone on the team knows when his or her part of the project needs to be completed.

Step 5: Write Out a Work Plan

Link

For help writing work plans as proposals, turn to Chapter 8, page 210.

A work plan is a description of how the project will be completed (Figure 3.4). Some work plans are rather simple, perhaps using an outline to describe how the project will go from start to finish. Other work plans, like the one in Figure 3.4, are very detailed and thorough.

A work plan will do the following:

- Identify the mission and objectives of the project.
- Lay out a step-by-step plan for achieving the mission and objectives.

Project Planning Software

Colors show parts of project.

Windows give more information on tasks.

Figure 3.2: Project planning software can be helpful when setting a calendar for the team. In this screen, the calendar is represented visually to show how tasks relate to each other over time.

Tasks are identified each day.

Source: AtTask, www.attask.com

- Establish a project calendar.
- Estimate a project budget if needed.
- Summarize the results/deliverables of the project.

A work plan is helpful for both small and large projects because team members need to see the project overview in writing. Otherwise, they will walk away from meetings with very different ideas about what needs to be accomplished.

By writing up a work plan, your team specifies how the project will be completed and who is responsible for which parts of the project. That way, team members can review the work plan if they are uncertain about (1) what tasks are being completed, (2) when the tasks will be finished, and (3) who is responsible for completing them.

Step 6: Agree on How Conflicts Will Be Resolved

Finally, your team should talk about how it will handle conflicts. Conflict is a natural, even healthy, part of a team project. Constructive conflict often leads to more creativity and closer bonds among team members. But destructive conflict can lead to dysfunctional working relationships, frustration, and lower morale.

AT A GLANCE

Six Steps for Strategic Planning

- Define the project mission and objectives.
- Identify project outcomes.
- Define team member responsibilities.
- Create a project calendar.
- Write out a work plan.
- Agree on how conflicts will be resolved.

Backward Planning Calendar

Project Calendar: Staph Infection Training Modules				
Monday	**Tuesday**	**Wednesday**	**Thursday**	**Friday**
4 Staff Meeting	**5** ←	**6**	**7**	**8** Complete Collection of Data
11 ←	**12**	**13** Report on Findings Due	**14** ←	**15**
18 ←	**19** Brochures, Pamphlets Printed	**20** ←	**21**	**22** Proofread Training Materials
25 ←	**26**	**27** Training Modules Completed	**28** ←	**29** ← Deadline: Training Day

Figure 3.3: Backward planning is a process of working backward from the deadline. Starting with the deadline, chart out when each task needs to be completed.

Here is the deadline. Work backward from this date.

To avoid destructive conflict, your team should discuss up front how conflicts will be handled during the project. Here are some questions you can answer:

How will important decisions be decided—by majority rule or full consensus?

If a deadlock arises among group members, who should be asked to referee the discussion?

How can team members call a team meeting to discuss conflicts?

How should alterations in the project plan be recorded so everyone knows exactly what has changed?

Storming: Managing Conflict

Soon after the forming stage, a team will typically go through a storming phase. At this point, it's normal for tension to surface among team members. When the storming phase happens, team members will need to negotiate, adapt, and compromise to achieve the team's mission.

Figure 3.4:
A work plan
specifies the
*who, what,
where, when,
why,* and *how*
of the project.

St. Thomas Medical Center

Date: April 28, 2014
To: Staff Infection Task Force (M. Franks, C. Little, J. Archuleta,
          L. Drew, V. Yi, J. Matthews, J. McManus)
From: Alice Falsworthy, Infections Specialist
Re: Work Plan for Combating Staph Infection

Last week, we met to discuss how we should handle the increase in staph
infections here at the St. Thomas Medical Center. We defined our mission,
defined major tasks, and developed a project calendar. The purpose of this
memo is to summarize those decisions and lay out a work plan that we
will follow.

**Purpose of
the work plan**

I cannot overstate the importance of this project. Staph infections are
becoming an increasing problem at hospitals around the country. Of
particular concern are antibiotic-resistant bacteria called methicillin-
resistant *Staphylococcus aureus* (MRSA), which can kill patients with
otherwise routine injuries. It is essential that we do everything in our
power to control MRSA and other forms of staph.

Please post this work plan in your office to keep you on task and on
schedule.

**Mission
statement**

Project Mission
Our Mission: The purpose of this Staph Infection Task Force is to
determine the level of staph infection vulnerability at St. Thomas Medical
Center and to develop strategies for limiting our patients' exposure to
staph, especially MRSA.

**Team
objectives**

Secondary Objectives:
• Gain a better understanding of current research on staph and its
  treatments.
• Raise awareness of staph infections among our medical staff and
  patients.
• Assess the level of staph risk, especially MRSA, here at the hospital.
• Develop methods for controlling staph on hospital surfaces.

(continued)

Project Plan

To achieve our mission and meet the above objectives, we developed the following five-action plan:

Action One: Collect Current Research on Staph Infections and Their Treatments

Mary Franks and Charles Little will collect and synthesize current research on staph infections, the available treatments, and control methods. They will run Internet searches, study the journals, attend workshops, and interview experts. They will also contact other hospitals to collect information on successful control methods. They will write a report on their findings and present it to the group on May 25 at our monthly meeting.

Action Two: Create Pamphlets and Other Literature That Help Medical Personnel Limit Staph Infections

Juliet Archuleta will begin developing a series of pamphlets and white papers that stress the importance of staph infections and offer strategies for combating them. These documents will be aimed at doctors and nurses to help them understand the importance of using antibiotics responsibly. Juliet will begin working on these documents immediately, but she will need the information collected by Mary and Charles to complete her part of the project. The documents will be completed by July 13, so we can have them printed to hand out at training modules.

Action Three: Conduct Experiments to Determine Level of Staph Risk at St. Thomas Medical Center

Lisa Drew and Valerie Yi will collect samples around the medical center to determine the risk of staph infection here at St. Thomas. The Center's Administration has asked us to develop a measurable knowledge of the problem at the Center. Lisa and Valerie will write a report to the Administration in which they discuss their findings. The report will be completed and delivered to the task force by June 2.

Action Four: Develop Contingency Plans for Handling Staph Instances

John Matthews and Joe McManus will develop contingency plans for handling instances of staph infections at the Center. These plans will offer

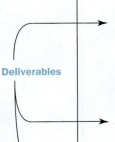

Step-by-step actions

Deliverables

concrete steps that the staph task force can take to limit exposure to staph bacteria. These plans will be based on the research collected by Mary and Charles. They will be completed by July 13.

Action Five: Develop Training Modules
When our research is complete, all of the members of this task force will develop training modules to raise awareness of staph infections, offer prevention strategies, and provide information on proper use of antibiotics. Different modules will be developed for doctors, nurses, and custodial staff. Alice Falsworthy and Charles Little will coordinate the development of these training modules. The training modules will be ready by August 29.

Deliverables

Project Calendar
Here is a chart that illustrates the project calendar and its deadlines:

Timeline for achieving goals

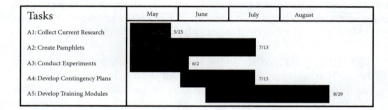

Tasks	May	June	July	August
A1: Collect Current Research		5/25		
A2: Create Pamphlets			7/13	
A3: Conduct Experiments		6/2		
A4: Develop Contingency Plans			7/13	
A5: Develop Training Modules				8/29

Conclusion
If anyone on the task force would like to change the plan, we will call a meeting to discuss the proposed changes. If you wish to call a meeting, please contact me at ext. 8712, or e-mail me at Alice_Falsworthy@stthomasmc.com.

During the storming stage, team members may:

- resist suggestions for improvement from other members.
- have doubts about the work plan's ability to succeed.
- compete for resources or recognition.
- resent that others are not listening to their ideas.
- want to change the team's objectives.
- raise issues of ethics or politics that need to be addressed.
- believe they are doing more than their share of the work.

Storming is rarely pleasant, but it is a natural part of the teaming process. When storming, teams realize that even the best work plans are never perfect and that people don't always work the same way or have the same expectations. The important thing is to not let small conflicts or disagreements sidetrack the project.

Running Effective Meetings

One way to constructively work through the storming phase is to conduct effective meetings. Typically, storming becomes most evident during meetings. People grow frustrated and even angry as the team struggles to accomplish its objectives. That's why running effective meetings is so important. Creating a predictable structure for meetings can lower the level of frustration, allowing you to get work done.

CHOOSE A MEETING FACILITATOR   In the workplace, usually a manager or supervisor runs the meeting, so he or she is responsible for setting the time and agenda. An interesting workplace trend, though, is to rotate the facilitator role among team members. That way, each team member has the opportunity to take on leadership roles. In classroom situations, your team should rotate the facilitator role to maintain a more democratic approach.

SET AN AGENDA   An agenda is a list of topics to be discussed at the meeting (Figure 3.5). The meeting coordinator should send out the meeting agenda at least a couple of days before the meeting. That way, everyone will know what issues will be discussed and decided on. Begin each meeting by first making sure everyone agrees to the agenda. Then, during the meeting, use the agenda to avoid going off track into nonagenda topics.

START AND END MEETINGS PROMPTLY   If team members are not present, start the meeting anyway. Waiting for latecomers can be frustrating, so you should insist that people arrive on time. If people know the meeting will start on time, they will be punctual. Likewise, end meetings on time.

ADDRESS EACH AGENDA ITEM SEPARATELY   Discuss each agenda item separately before moving on to the next one. If someone wants to move ahead to a future agenda item, first make sure the current item of discussion has been fully addressed before moving on.

ENCOURAGE PARTICIPATION   Everyone on the team should say something about each item. If one of the team members has not spoken, the facilitator should give that person an opportunity to speak.

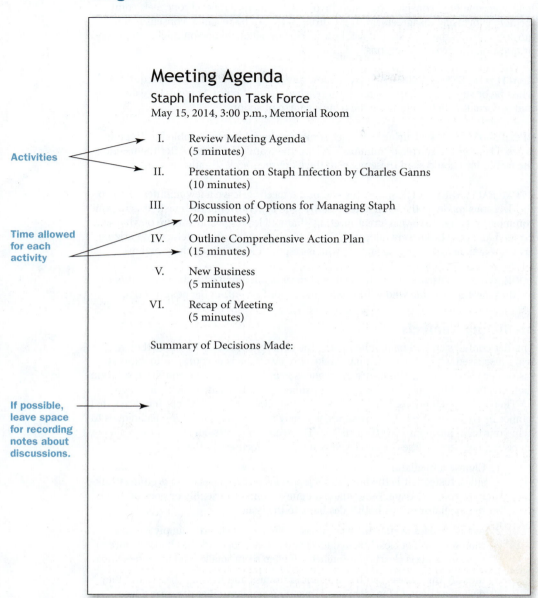

Figure 3.5:
A simple agenda is a helpful tool for keeping the meeting on track.

Meeting Agenda

Staph Infection Task Force
May 15, 2014, 3:00 p.m., Memorial Room

Activities

I.   Review Meeting Agenda
     (5 minutes)

II. Presentation on Staph Infection by Charles Ganns
     (10 minutes)

III. Discussion of Options for Managing Staph
     (20 minutes)

Time allowed for each activity

IV. Outline Comprehensive Action Plan
     (15 minutes)

V.   New Business
     (5 minutes)

VI. Recap of Meeting
     (5 minutes)

Summary of Decisions Made:

If possible, leave space for recording notes about discussions.

ALLOW DISSENT At meetings, it is fine to disagree. Active debate about issues will help everyone fully consider the issues involved. So, make sure everyone feels comfortable expressing disagreement. If the group seems to be reaching consensus too quickly, a group member should ask how a critic or skeptical person might challenge or question the group's decisions.

REACH CONSENSUS AND MOVE ON Allow any group member to "call the question" when he or she feels consensus has been reached. At that point, you can take an informal or formal vote to determine the team's course of action.

RECORD DECISIONS During meetings, someone should be responsible for keeping notes. The notes (also called "minutes") record the team's decisions. After the meeting, the facilitator should send these notes to the team members, usually via e-mail.

RECAP EACH AGENDA ITEM At the end of the meeting, leave a few minutes to recap the decisions made by the team and to clarify who is performing each task. It is not uncommon for teams to have a "great meeting" that still leaves people unsure of what was decided and how tasks were allocated. So, go through each agenda item, summarizing (1) what actions will be taken and (2) who is responsible for taking those actions.

LOOK AHEAD Discuss when the team will meet again along with the expectations for that meeting. Decide who will be responsible for facilitating the next meeting.

Mediating Conflicts

Smaller conflicts should be handled using the conflict resolution methods that your team discussed when it was forming. Make sure everyone is encouraged to express his or her views openly. Make sure everyone is heard. Then, use the conflict resolution methods (vote, full consensus, or appeal to supervisor) to decide which way to go.

There will be situations, however, when personalities or ideas will clash in ways that cannot be easily resolved. At these times, you may want to use mediation techniques to help your team move forward (Figure 3.6). The secret to successful mediation is a focus on issues, not personalities or perceived wrongs. Stay focused on the task.

1. **Choose a mediator**—A mediator is like a referee. He or she does not take sides. Instead, it is the mediator's job to keep both sides of an argument talking about the issue. When the dialogue becomes unfriendly or goes off track, the mediator brings both sides back to the issues.

2. **Ask both sides to state their positions**—Often, conflicts arise simply because each side has not clearly stated its position. Once each side has had a chance to explain its ideas clearly, the conflict will often seem smaller and more resolvable.

3. **Identify the issues**—Both sides should discuss and identify the "issues" they disagree about. Often, disputes hinge on a small number of issues. Once these issues are identified, it becomes easier to talk about them.

4. **Prioritize the issues from most to least important**—Some issues are more important than others. By prioritizing the issues, both sides can usually find places where they already agree. Or, in some cases, a top priority to one side is not a foremost concern to the other side. By prioritizing the issues, both sides often begin to see room for negotiation.

Link

Ethical issues are often a source of conflict. To learn more about ethics, go to Chapter 4, page 61.

The Steps of Mediation

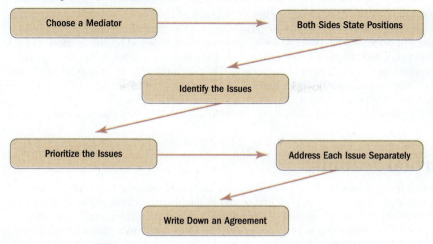

Choose a Mediator → Both Sides State Positions

Identify the Issues

Prioritize the Issues → Address Each Issue Separately

Write Down an Agreement

Figure 3.6: When more formal mediation is needed, you can follow these steps toward a resolution of the problem.

5. **Address each issue separately, trying to find a middle ground that is acceptable to both sides of the dispute**—Focus on each issue separately and keep looking for middle ground between both sides. When both sides realize that they have many common interests, they will usually come up with solutions to the conflict.

6. **Write down an agreement that both sides can accept**—As the mediation continues, both sides usually find themselves agreeing on ways to resolve some or all of the issues. At this point, it helps to write down any compromises that both sides can accept.

Firing a Team Member

Sometimes a team member is not doing his or her share of the work. When this happens, the team might consider removing that person from the project. The best way to handle these situations is to first mediate the problem. The members of the team should meet to talk about their expectations, giving the person a chance to explain why he or she is not doing a fair share of the work.

After hearing this person's side of the story, the team might decide to give him or her a second chance. At that point, an agreement should be written that specifies exactly what this person needs to do for the project.

If the person still isn't doing his or her share, the supervisor (perhaps your instructor) should be asked about removing the person from the team. The supervisor should be present when the team tells the problematic team member that he or she is being removed.

Norming: Determining Team Roles

The storming period can be frustrating, but soon afterward, your team should enter the *norming* stage. In this stage, members of your team will begin to accept their responsibilities and their roles in the project. A sense of team unity will develop as people begin to trust each other. Criticism will become increasingly constructive as team members strive to achieve the project's mission and objectives.

Revising Objectives and Outcomes

The storming stage often reveals the flaws in the work plan. So, when norming, you might find it helpful to revisit and refine the team's original decisions about objectives and outcomes. The team may also want to revise the project schedule and reallocate the workload.

You don't need to completely rewrite the work plan from scratch. You should stay with your original work plan in most cases. The plan probably just needs to be revised and refined, not completely rewritten.

HELP

Virtual Teaming

Increasingly, technical workplaces are turning to virtual teaming to put the right people on any given project. Virtual teaming allows people to work on projects collaboratively through electronic networks, using e-mail, instant messaging, conference calls, and Internet conferencing to stay in contact. Electronic networks, called *intranets*, are often used to share information and documents among team members.

Virtual teams, just like teams working together in an office, schedule regular meetings, share ideas and documents, and work toward achieving specific goals. The main differences between on-site teams and virtual teams are how people communicate and where they are located. Software, such as Virtual Office, Good Collaboration Suite, PlanetIntra's Noodle, MS Outlook, and Google Drive, help people stay in touch and collaborate on projects.

Trends in the technical workplace support virtual teaming. Today, more people are "telecommuting" or "teleworking" from home or remote sites. Also, the global economy sometimes results in people on the same project working thousands of miles away from each other. Meanwhile, wireless technologies allow people to work just about anywhere. Chances are, you will find yourself working with a virtual team in the near future—if you aren't already.

Interestingly, virtual teaming does not change traditional teaming strategies—it only makes them more necessary. A virtual team will go through the forming, storming, norming, and performing stages, just like an on-site team. Good planning, communication, and conflict resolution are even more important in virtual teams. After all, communicating with your virtual team is a little more difficult, because you cannot physically visit each other.

Here are some strategies for managing a successful virtual team:

Develop a work plan and stick to it—Members of virtual teams do not bump into each other in the hallway or the break room. So, they need a clear work plan to keep everyone moving together toward the final goal. Your team's work plan should (1) define the mission, (2) state objectives and measurable outcomes, (3) spell out each stage and task in the project, (4) specify who is responsible for each task, and (5) lay out a project calendar.

Communicate regularly—In virtual teams, the old saying "out of sight, out of mind" now becomes "out of communication, out of mind." Each member of the virtual team should agree to communicate with the others regularly (e.g., two times a day). Your team can use e-mail, social networking, phones, texting, or chat rooms to contact each other. You and your team members should constantly keep each other up to date on your progress. And if someone does not

Teleconferencing

A hidden webcam sends video to the other participants in the virtual meeting.

The screen can be used to show people, documents, or presentations.

Figure A: Teleconferencing allows team members to hold meetings virtually.

communicate for a day or two, the team leader should track him or her down and urge the team member to resume communications.

Hold teleconferences and videoconferences—There are many ways to hold real-time virtual meetings with team members. Your team members can tele-conference over the phone, or you can use a chat room or instant messaging to exchange ideas. Increasingly, broadband technology is allowing people to hold videoconferences in which people meet and see each other with Internet cameras (webcams) through computer screens (Figure A). Like on-site meetings, virtual meetings should be preplanned and follow an agenda. The only significant difference between on-site meetings and virtual meetings is that people are not in the same room.

Build trust and respect—One of the shortcomings of virtual teaming is the lack of nonverbal cues (smiles, shrugs, scowls) that help people to avoid misunderstandings. As a result, people in virtual teams can feel insulted or disrespected much more easily than people in on-site teams. So it is doubly important that team members learn how to build trust with others and show respect. Trust is built by communicating effectively, meeting deadlines, and doing high-quality work. Respect is fostered by giving compliments and using "please" and "thank you" in messages. When conflicts do arise (and they will), focus on issues and problem solving, not personalities or perceived slights.

Keep regular hours—Time management is always important, even if you are working in a virtual team. During regular office hours, team members should be confident that they can contact each other. You and your team members should be ready to answer the phone, text each other, or answer e-mail as though you were all working together in a typical office.

Redefining Team Roles and Redistributing Workload

As the project moves forward, your team will notice that certain group members are better suited to some aspects of the project than others.

Now that the project is in the norming phase, your team should reconsider each of your roles in the project. Perhaps one of your group members is not as strong at editing as she thought. Maybe she feels more comfortable doing research for the project. Perhaps another group member has a big exam coming up, so he doesn't have the time to create graphs and charts this week. However, he does have time to design the document this weekend when the exam is over.

As your team settles into the project, you may need to redefine your roles in the project and redistribute the workload to achieve a better balance and take advantage of team members' strengths and time availability.

Using Groupware to Facilitate Work

When working in a team, you might need to use *groupware*, a kind of software that helps move information and documents around. Groupware allows team members to communicate and work collaboratively through the Internet, a local area network (LAN), or an intranet.

Perhaps the most common use of groupware is sharing documents and sending messages. The two most popular workplace groupware packages are MS Exchange and Smartsheet (Figure 3.7). Meanwhile, Google Drive and Microsoft Outlook® can be used to manage group projects. These software packages and others like them support the following kinds of activities:

Scheduling and calendaring—One of the more powerful features of groupware is the ability to schedule meetings and keep a common calendar for the team. With this feature, team members can regularly check the calendar to stay on task.

Discussion lists and instant messaging—Groupware offers easy access to discussion lists (usually via e-mail) and instant messaging. With these tools, team members can post notes to each other on a discussion list or have real-time discussions through instant messaging.

Document posting and commenting—Files can be posted to a common site, allowing team members to view documents, comment on them electronically, or download them.

Using groupware effectively takes some practice. Eventually, the team will begin using the groupware as a meeting place and a posting board. It will become an integral part of the project.

Link

For more ideas about improving quality through document cycling, see Chapter 19, page 512.

Performing: Improving Quality

Your team is *performing* when members are comfortable with the project and their roles in it. Team members will recognize the other members' talents and weaknesses. They also begin to anticipate each other's needs and capabilities.

Using Groupware

Major tasks of project are outlined.

Timelines are shown here.

Toolbox for enhancing task lists and timelines.

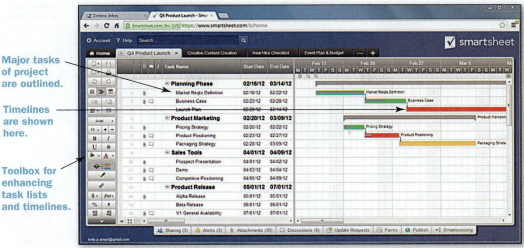

Figure 3.7: With groupware like Smartsheet, shown here, members of a group can keep a common calendar, post notes, and send e-mails to each other. In this screen, the calendar shows how parts of the project overlap and deadlines for each part.

Source: Copyright © 2014 SmartSoft Ltd. Used with permission.

When your team is performing, you can start looking for ways to improve the quality of your work. W. Edwards Deming developed many of the principles behind Total Quality Management (TQM) and Continuous Quality Improvement (CQI), which are widely used in technical workplaces. Deming argued that teams should put an emphasis on improving the *process* rather than simply exhorting people to improve the product (Deming, 2000).

How can you improve quality in your team? While performing, a helpful technique is to develop *quality feedback loops* in which your team regularly compares the team's outcomes to the mission statement of the project.

You will also hear managers talking about measuring outcomes against "metrics." Metrics are used by corporations and organizations to measure the performance of teams in key areas like client satisfaction, return on investment (ROI), quality improvement, and production and innovation. Metrics are gauges that help companies and organizations measure whether they are reaching their objectives.

Teams also need to regularly review the performance of their own members. Figure 3.8 shows a "Team Performance Review" form that is similar to ones found in the workplace. Your team and instructor can use this form to assess the performance of your team and look for places to improve.

A performing team will have its ups and downs. There may even be times when the team regresses into the norming or even the storming stages. Eventually, though, the performing team usually regroups and puts the focus back on quality.

Team Performance Review

Date: _____

Name: _____

Name of Project: _____

The purpose of this performance review is to evaluate the participation of you and your team members on the project we just completed. Your feedback on this form will be taken into account when determining each member's "participation" part of the grade for this assignment.

Describe your role on the team and list your top four contributions to the project.

My role:

My contributions to the project:

1.

2.

3.

4.

Describe the role and list the contributions of your team members.

Team Member	a.	b.	c.
Role on team			
Contributions			

Rate the participation (1–10 with 10 being the highest) of your team members.

Team Member	a.	b.	c.
Attended team meetings			
Did her/his share of the project			
Contributed good ideas			
Respected the ideas of others			
Handled conflict and stress			
Communicated with team			
Overall Participation Rating (1–10)			

On the back of this sheet, write detailed comments about how well your team worked together. What were its strengths? What could have been improved? Which team members were essential to the project and why were they so important? Which team members should have done more?

The Keys to Teaming

The keys to good teaming are good planning and effective communication. The planning strategies discussed in this chapter might seem like extra work, especially when time is limited and your team is eager to start working on the project. But good planning will save your team time in the long run. Each person needs a clear understanding of the mission and the steps in the project. Then, you need to keep the communication lines open. Plan to communicate regularly by phone, e-mail, and instant messaging.

Telecommuting, or teleworking, is becoming much more common in today's technical workplace. Sometimes your team members will be working a few days per week at home. Or, they may be working while they are on the road. Some telecommuters work almost exclusively from home, going to the office only when absolutely necessary. Good planning and effective communication are the keys to success in these virtual workplace environments.

- Teams have several advantages. They can concentrate strengths, foster creativity, share the workload, and improve morale. Disadvantages include conflict with other members and disproportionate workloads.

- Tuckman's four stages of teaming are forming, storming, norming, and performing.

- In the forming stage, use strategic planning to define the mission, set objectives, define roles, and establish a project schedule.

- In the storming stage, use conflict management techniques to handle emerging disagreements, tension and anxiety, leadership challenges, and frustration.

- In the norming stage, revise the work plan to form consensus, refine the team's objectives and outcomes, and solidify team roles.

- In the performing stage, pay attention to improving the process in ways that improve the quality of the work.

- Virtual teaming, or working together from a distance, requires good planning and effective communication.

- W. Edwards Deming developed many of the principles behind Total Quality Management (TQM) and Continuous Quality Improvement (CQI), which are common in technical workplaces today.

Individual or Team Projects

1. If you have a job now, write a report to your instructor in which you talk about how your co-workers fluctuate among Tuckman's four stages. What are some of the indications that the team is forming, storming, norming, and performing? How does the team tend to react during each of these stages? Does your team aid in forming strategic planning? How do you mediate conflicts during storming? How is norming achieved at your workplace? What does performing look like?

2. Imagine that your class is a workplace. What are the objectives and outcomes of this course? How are conflicts resolved in the classroom? Do members of your class take on various team roles in the classroom? How could you and your instructor create quality feedback loops to improve your learning experience? In a class, discuss how teaming strategies might be helpful in improving the way the class is managed.

3. On the Internet, research the theories and writings of Tuckman and Deming. Write a report to your instructor in which you summarize the principles of one of their theories. Then, discuss the ways in which you might apply this theory to your own life and work.

Collaborative Project

With a team, try to write a report in one hour on a topic of interest to all of you. For example, you might write about a problem on campus or at your workplace. While you are writing the report, pay attention to how your group forms, norms, storms, and performs. Pay attention to how the group plans and divides up the responsibilities. Then, as the project moves forward, pay attention to the ways conflict is resolved. Finally, identify the different roles that group members tend to play as the group develops norms for the project.

When your one-hour report is finished, talk among yourselves about how the group project went. Did the group form and plan properly? Did you handle conflict well? Did the group members take on identifiable roles? Do you think you ever reached the performing stage? If you were going to do the project over, how might your group do things differently?

Visit MyWritingLab for a Post-test and more technical writing resources.

Not a Sunny Day

Veronica Norton liked working on teams. She liked interacting with others, and she liked how working with others allowed her to accomplish projects that were too big for one person. Veronica also had a strong interest in building solar-powered motors, like the ones that went into solar-powered cars. She hoped to find a job in the automotive industry building solar vehicles.

As a result, Veronica decided to join her university's team in the American Solar Challenge race competition. She and a group of ten other students were going to build a solar car to race across the country against cars from other universities.

The first meeting of the team went great. Everyone was excited. Several engineering departments were contributing money and resources, and a local aerospace engineering firm was matching university funds dollar for dollar. The firm was also letting the team use its wind tunnel to help streamline the car. There were other local sponsors who wanted to participate.

The team rushed right into the project. They sketched out a design for the car, ordered supplies, and began welding together a frame for the car. Veronica began designing a solar motor that would be long lasting and have plenty of power. She thought that the overall plan for the car was not well thought out, but she went along with it anyway. At least they were making progress.

One of the team members, George Franks, began emerging as the leader. He was finishing up his engineering degree, so he had only a couple of classes left to take. He had plenty of time to work on the solar car.

Unfortunately, he didn't like to follow plans. Instead, he just liked to tinker, putting things together as he saw fit. It wasn't long before the team started running into problems. George's tinkering approach was creating a car that would be rather heavy. Also, each time Veronica visited the shop, the dimensions of the car had changed, so the motor she was building needed to be completely redesigned.

Perhaps the worst problem was that they were running out of money. George's tinkering meant lots of wasted materials. As a result, they had almost used up their entire budget. Sally, who was in charge of the finances for the project, told everyone they were going to be out of money in a month. Everyone was getting anxious.

Finally, at one of the monthly meetings, things fell apart. People were yelling at each other. After being blamed for messing up the project, George stormed out of the meeting. Things looked pretty hopeless. Everyone left the meeting unsure of what to do.

Veronica still wanted to complete the project, though. If you were Veronica, how might you handle this situation? What should she do to get the project going again?

CHAPTER

4

Managing Ethical Challenges

What Are Ethics? *61*

Where Do Ethics Come From? *64*

Resolving Ethical Dilemmas *69*

Help: Stopping Cyberbullying and Computer Harassment *74*

Ethics in the Technical Workplace *76*

Copyright Law in Technical Communication *78*

What You Need to Know *80*

Exercises and Projects *81*

Case Study: This Company Is Bugging Me *82*

In this chapter, you will learn:

- A working definition of ethics.

- About three ethical systems: personal, social, and conservation.

- To consider social ethics in terms of rights, justice, utility, and care.

- Strategies for resolving ethical conflicts in technical workplaces.

- How to balance the many issues involved in an ethical dilemma.

- How copyright law affects technical communication.

- About the new ethical challenges that face the computer-centered workplace.

In the technical workplace, you will regularly encounter ethical challenges that you and your team will need to resolve. In these situations, you need to know how to identify what is at stake and then make an informed decision. Ethical behavior is more than a matter of personal virtue—it is good business.

What Are Ethics?

For some people, ethics are about issues of morality. For others, ethics are a matter of law. Actually, ethics bring together many different ideas about appropriate behavior in a society.

Ethics are systems of moral, social, or cultural values that govern the conduct of an individual or community. For many people, acting ethically simply means "doing the right thing," a phrase that actually sums up ethics quite well. The hard part, of course, is figuring out the right thing to do. Ethical choices, after all, are not always straightforward.

Every decision you make has an ethical dimension, whether it is apparent or not. In most workplace situations, the ethical choice is apparent, so you do not pause to consider whether you are acting ethically. Occasionally, though, you will be presented with an *ethical dilemma* that needs more consideration. An ethical dilemma offers a choice among two or more unsatisfactory courses of action. At these decision points, it is helpful to ponder the ethics of each path so you can make the best choice.

In technical workplaces, resolving ethical dilemmas will be a part of your job. Resources, time, and reputations are at stake, so you will feel pressure to overpromise, underdeliver, bend the rules, cook the numbers, or exaggerate results. Technical fields are also highly competitive, so people sometimes stretch a little further than they should. Ethical dilemmas can force us into situations where all choices seem unsatisfactory.

Why do some people behave unethically? People rarely set out to do something unethical. Rather, they find themselves facing a tough decision in which moving forward means taking risks or treating others unfairly. In these situations, they may be tempted to act unethically due to a fear of failure, a desire to survive, pressure from others, or just a series of bad decisions. Small lies lead to bigger lies until the whole house of cards collapses on them.

Keep in mind, though, that ethics are not always about deception or fraud. A famous decision involving Albert Einstein offers an interesting example. Figure 4.1 shows a letter that Einstein wrote to President Franklin Roosevelt encouraging research into the development of the atom bomb. Throughout the rest of his life, Einstein, who was an ardent pacifist, was troubled by this letter. Five months before his death, he stated:

> I made one great mistake in my life . . . when I signed the letter to President Roosevelt recommending that atom bombs be made; but there was some justification—the danger that the Germans would make them. (Clark, 1971, p. 752)

In this quote, you see the ethical dilemma weighing on Einstein. He deeply regretted the atom bomb's development and use on Japan. However, he also recognized that his letter may have alerted Roosevelt to a very real danger. Historians have pointed

AT A GLANCE

Definitions of *Ethics* and *Ethical Dilemma*

- Ethics—systems of moral, social, or cultural values that govern the conduct of an individual or community
- Ethical dilemma—a choice among two or more unsatisfactory courses of action

Einstein's Letter to Roosevelt About the Atom Bomb

Albert Einstein
Old Grove Rd.
Nassau Point
Peconic, Long Island

August 2nd 1939

F.D. Roosevelt
President of the United States
White House
Washington, D.C.

Sir:

Some recent work by E.Fermi and L. Szilard, which has been communicated to me in manuscript, leads me to expect that the element uranium may be turned into a new and important source of energy in the immediate future. Certain aspects of the situation which has arisen seem
to call for watchfulness and, if necessary, quick action on the part
of the Administration. I believe therefore that it is my duty to bring
to your attention the following facts and recommendations:

In the course of the last four months it has been made probable -
through the work of Joliot in France as well as Fermi and Szilard in
America - that it may become possible to set up a nuclear chain reaction
in a large mass of uranium, by which vast amounts of power and large quantities of new radium-like elements would be generated. Now it appears
almost certain that this could be achieved in the immediate future.

This new phenomenon would also lead to the construction of bombs,
and it is conceivable - though much less certain - that extremely powerful bombs of a new type may thus be constructed. A single bomb of this
type, carried by boat and exploded in a port, might very well destroy
the whole port together with some of the surrounding territory. However,
such bombs might very well prove to be too heavy for transportation by
air.

Here is Einstein's main point.

Einstein expresses the imminent problem.

He points out the possible threat of these new kinds of weapons.

Source: Argonne National Laboratory, http://www.anl.gov/OPA/frontiers96arch/aetofdr.html

Figure 4.1: In 1939, Einstein wrote this letter to President Franklin Roosevelt. The atom bomb would have been built without Einstein's letter, but his prodding jump-started the U.S. nuclear program.

-2-

The United States has only very poor ores of uranium in moderate quantities. There is some good ore in Canada and the former Czechoslovakia, while the most important source of uranium is Belgian Congo.

In view of the situation you may think it desirable to have more permanent contact maintained between the Administration and the group of physicists working on chain reactions in America. One possible way of achieving this might be for you to entrust with this task a person who has your confidence and who could perhaps serve in an inofficial capacity. His task might comprise the following:

a) to approach Government Departments, keep them informed of the further development, and put forward recommendations for Government action, giving particular attention to the problem of securing a supply of uranium ore for the United States;

b) to speed up the experimental work, which is at present being carried on within the limits of the budgets of University laboratories, by providing funds, if such funds be required, through his contacts with y private persons who are willing to make contributions for this cause, and perhaps also by obtaining the co-operation of industrial laboratories which have the necessary equipment.

I understand that Germany has actually stopped the sale of uranium from the Czechoslovakian mines which she has taken over. That she should have taken such early action might perhaps be understood on the ground that the son of the German Under-Secretary of State, von Weizsäcker, is attached to the Kaiser-Wilhelm-Institut in Berlin where some of the American work on uranium is now being repeated.

Yours very truly,

A. Einstein

(Albert Einstein)

Einstein offers a potential solution.

He points out that the Nazis may already be working on nuclear technology, potentially a bomb.

Einstein with Robert Oppenheimer

Einstein meets with Robert Oppenheimer, the leader of the U.S. efforts to develop an atom bomb. Later, Einstein regretted his involvement, though minimal, with its development.

out that Einstein's letter may have helped prevent the Nazis from creating an atom bomb. Ethical dilemmas put people in these kinds of quandaries.

Where Do Ethics Come From?

How can you identify ethical issues and make appropriate choices? To begin, consider where values come from:

> **Personal ethics**—Values derived from family, culture, and faith
>
> **Social ethics**—Values derived from constitutional, legal, utilitarian, and caring sources
>
> **Conservation ethics**—Values that protect and preserve the ecosystem in which we live

These ethical systems intertwine, and sometimes they even conflict with each other (Figure 4.2).

Personal Ethics

By this point in your life, you have developed a good sense of right and wrong. More than likely, your personal ethics derive from your family, your culture, and your faith. Your family, especially your parents, taught you some principles to live by. Meanwhile, your culture, including the people in your neighborhood or even the people you watch on television, has shaped how you make decisions. And for many people, faith gives them specific principles about how they should live their lives.

Intertwined Ethical Systems

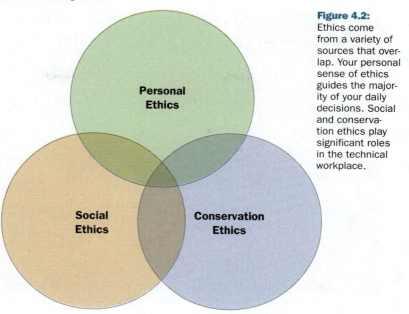

Figure 4.2: Ethics come from a variety of sources that overlap. Your personal sense of ethics guides the majority of your daily decisions. Social and conservation ethics play significant roles in the technical workplace.

In the technical workplace, a strong sense of personal values is essential, because these values offer a reliable touchstone for ethical behavior. A good exercise is making a list of values that you hold dear. Perhaps some of these values are honesty, integrity, respect, candor, loyalty, politeness, thoughtfulness, cautiousness, thriftiness, and caring. By articulating these values and following them, you will likely find yourself acting ethically in almost all situations.

Social Ethics

In technical workplaces, the most difficult ethical dilemmas are usually found in the social realm. Social ethics require you to think more globally about the consequences of your or your company's actions.

Ethics scholar Manuel Velasquez (2002) offers a helpful four-part categorization of social ethical situations:

> **Rights**—Rights are fundamental freedoms that are innate to humans or granted by a nation to its citizens. *Human rights,* like those mentioned in the *U.S. Declaration of Independence* (life, liberty, and the pursuit of happiness), are innate to humans and cannot be taken away. *Constitutional rights* (freedom of speech, right to bear arms, protection against double jeopardy) are the rights held in common by citizens of a nation.

> **Justice**—Justice involves fairness among equals. Justice takes its most obvious form in the laws that govern a society. Our laws are a formalized ethical system that is designed to ensure that people are treated equally and fairly. Similarly, *corporate policies* are the rules that ensure fairness within a company.

Four Categories of Social Ethics

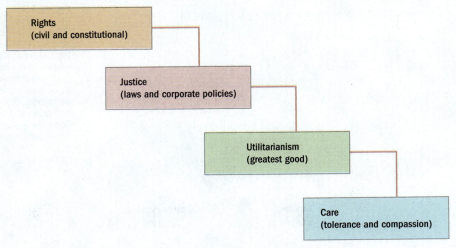

Figure 4.3: Social ethics can be ranked. Concerns about rights usually have more gravity than justice issues, and so on.

Utility—Utility suggests that the interests of the majority should outweigh the interests of the few. Of paramount importance to utilitarianism is *the greatest good for the greatest number of people.*

Care—Care suggests that tolerance and compassion take precedence over rigid, absolute rules. Ethics of care suggest that each situation should be judged on its own, putting heightened attention on concern for the welfare of people and preserving relationships. It also recognizes that some relationships, like those involving friends and family, will often lead to ethical choices that transcend rights, justice, and utility.

Link

For more information on working with transcultural readers, see Chapter 2, page 24.

Legal issues, usually involving rights and justice, are especially important in technical communication, because the temptation to break the law to gain a competitive edge can be great. Legal issues of copyright law, patent law, liability, privacy, and fraud (all of which are discussed later in this chapter) are crucial concerns that affect how individuals and companies conduct themselves. You should be aware of the laws that apply to your discipline.

When facing an ethical dilemma or a controversy involving ethics, you should first identify which of these four ethical categories applies to your situation. Ethical issues that involve human or constitutional rights usually have the most gravity (Figure 4.3). Issues involving care are still important, but they have the least gravity. In other words, if an ethical decision involves human or constitutional rights, it will take on much more importance than a decision that involves issues of justice, utility, or care.

By sorting ethical dilemmas into these four categories, you can often decide which course of action is best. For example, consider the following case study:

Case Study: Your company makes a popular action figure toy with many tiny accessories. Countless children enjoy the toy, especially all those tiny boots, hats, backpacks, weapons, and so on. However, a few children have choked on some of the small pieces that go with the toy. How would the four levels of ethics govern how to handle this situation?

Answer: In this case, a human right (life) has more weight than utility (thousands of children versus a few). So, the ethical choice would be to alter the toy or stop selling it.

Social ethical issues are rarely this clear cut, though. After all, rights, justice, utility, and care are open to interpretation and debate. A union organizer, for example, may see a company's resistance to unionizing as a violation of the "right to free assembly" provided by the U.S. Constitution. The company, on the other hand, may point to federal laws that allow it to curb union activities. This kind of debate over rights and justice happens all the time.

Another problem is that people miscategorize their ethical issue.

Case Study: Your town's city council has decided to implement a no-smoking policy that includes all public property and restaurants. Many smokers now find it impossible to have their smoke break around public buildings and in restaurants. They argue that their "right to smoke" is being violated. How might you resolve this ethical issue?

Answer: Actually, there is no such thing as a right to smoke. Smoking is a legal issue (a matter of justice) and a utility issue (the health interests of the nonsmoking majority versus the interests of a smoking minority). So, if the city chooses to ban smoking on public property or in restaurants, it can do so legally as long as it applies the law fairly to all. It is not violating anyone's human or constitutional rights.

Of course, defenders of smoking may point out that restricting smoking may hurt businesses like bars and restaurants (a utility argument). Advocates of nonsmoking places might counter that secondhand smoke may cause cancer in patrons and employees of these establishments (also a utility argument). The city council may take these arguments into consideration before passing a new law.

Ethics
• Rights—Civil rights and constitutional rights
• Justice—Laws and corporate policies
• Utility—Greatest good (majority rules)
• Care—Tolerance and compassion for others

When making decisions about social ethical issues, it is important to first decide which ethical categories fit the ethical dilemma you are pondering. Then, decide which set of ethics has more significance, or gravity. In most cases:

- issues involving *rights* will have more gravity than issues involving *laws*.
- issues involving *laws* will have more gravity than issues involving *utility*.
- issues involving *utility* will have more gravity than issues involving *care*.

There are, of course, exceptions. In some cases, utility may be used to argue against laws that are antiquated or unfair. For example, it was once legal to smoke just about anywhere, including the workplace (and the college classroom). By using utility arguments, opponents of smoking have successfully changed those laws. Today, smoking is ever more restricted in public.

Conservation Ethics

Increasingly, issues involving our ecosystems are becoming sources of ethical dilemmas. With issues such as global warming, nuclear waste storage, toxic waste disposal, and overpopulation, we must move beyond the idea that conservation is a personal virtue. We are now forced to realize that human health and survival are closely tied to the health and survival of the entire ecosystem in which we live. Conservation ethics involve issues of water conservation, chemical and nuclear production and waste, management of insects and weeds in agriculture, mining, energy production and use, land use, pollution, and other environmental issues.

One of America's prominent naturalists, Aldo Leopold, suggested that humans need to develop a *land ethic.* He argued:

> All ethics so far evolved rest upon a single premise: that the individual
> is a member of a community of interdependent parts. . . . The land ethic
> simply enlarges the boundaries of the community to include soils, waters,
> plants, and animals, or collectively: the land. (1986, p. 239)

In other words, your considerations of ethics should go beyond the impact on humans and their communities. The health and welfare of the ecosystem around you should also be carefully considered.

People who work in technical fields need to be especially aware of conservation ethics, because we handle so many tools and products that can damage the ecosystem. Without careful concern for use and disposal of materials and wastes, we can do great harm to the environment.

Aldo Leopold and the Land Ethic

Aldo Leopold, a naturalist and conservationist, developed the concept of a "land ethic," which defines a sustainable relationship between humans and nature.

Ultimately, conservation ethics are about *sustainability*. Can humans interact with their ecosystem in ways that are sustainable in the long term? Conservation ethics recognize that resources must be used. They simply ask that people use resources in sustainable ways. They ask us to pay attention to the effects of our decisions on the air, water, soil, plants, and animals on this planet.

Conservation ethics are becoming increasingly important. The twenty-first century has been characterized as the "Green Century," because humans have reached a point where we can no longer ignore the ecological damage caused by our decisions. For example, within this century, estimates suggest that human-caused climate change will raise global temperatures between 2 and 10 degrees. Such a rise would radically alter our ecosystem.

Moreover, as emerging markets such as China and India continue to grow, the world economy will need to learn how to use its limited resources in ways that are fair and conscientious.

Resolving Ethical Dilemmas

No doubt, you will be faced with numerous ethical dilemmas during your career. There is no formula or mechanism you can use to come up with the right answer. Rather, ethical dilemmas usually force us to choose among uncomfortable alternatives.

Doing the right thing can mean putting your reputation and your career on the line. It might mean putting the interests of people above profits. It also might mean putting the long-term interests of the environment above short-term solutions to waste disposal and use of resources.

Step 1: Analyze the Ethical Dilemma

When faced with an ethical dilemma, your first step is to analyze it from all three ethical perspectives: personal, social, and conservation (Figure 4.4).

Personal ethics—How does my upbringing in a family, culture, and faith guide my decision? How can I do unto others as I would have them do unto me?

Social ethics—What rights or laws are involved in my decision? What is best for the majority? How can I demonstrate caring by being tolerant and compassionate?

Conservation ethics—How will my decision affect the ecosystem? Will my choice be ecologically sustainable in the long term?

With most ethical dilemmas, you will find that ethical stances conflict. To resolve the dilemma, it helps to first locate the "ethical tension"—the point where two or more ethical stances are incompatible. For example:

- An emergency room doctor who treats gunshot victims believes gun ownership should be highly restricted. Constitutional law, however, makes gun ownership a right. *Here, rights are in tension with utility.*
- Someone offers you a draft of your competitor's proposal for an important project. With that information, your company would almost certainly win the contract. However, your industry's code of ethics regarding proprietary information forbids you from looking at it. *Here, justice is in tension with utility.*
- Your company owns the rights to the timber in a forest, but an endangered species of eagle lives there and its habitat, by law, should be protected. *Here, justice, rights, and conservation are in tension.*

Balancing the Different Issues in an Ethical Dilemma

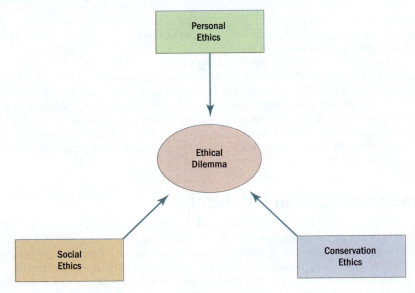

Figure 4.4: Resolving an ethical dilemma requires you to consider it from various ethical perspectives.

- A legal loophole allows your company to pump tons of pollution into the air even though this pollution harms the health of the residents in a small town a few miles downwind. *Here, personal and conservation ethics are in tension with justice.*

You will better be able to resolve the ethical dilemma if you can identify the tension that is causing it.

Step 2: Make a Decision

Making a decision will likely be difficult because ethical dilemmas almost always force people to choose one set of values over another. When faced with an ethical dilemma, you can use the following five questions to help you make a good decision. These questions are a variation of the ones developed by Professor Sam Dragga in an article on ethics in technical communication (1996).

Do any laws or rules govern my decision?—In many cases, laws at the federal, state, and local levels will specify the appropriate action in an ethical case. You can look to your company's legal counsel for guidance in these matters. Otherwise, companies often have written rules or procedures that address ethical situations.

Do any corporate or professional codes of ethics offer guidance?— Most companies and professional organizations have published codes of ethics. They are usually rather abstract, but they can help frame ethical situations so you can make clearer decisions. Figure 4.5 shows the code of ethics for the Institute of Electrical and Electronics Engineers (IEEE).

AT A GLANCE

Resolving Ethical Dilemmas

- Do any laws or rules govern my decision?
- Do any corporate or professional codes of ethics offer guidance?
- Are there any historical records to learn from?
- What do my colleagues think?
- What would moral leaders do?

Sample Code of Ethics

IEEE CODE OF ETHICS

WE, THE MEMBERS OF THE IEEE, in recognition of the importance of our technologies in affecting the quality of life throughout the world and in accepting a personal obligation to our profession, its members and the communities we serve, do hereby commit ourselves to the highest ethical and professional conduct and agree:

1. to accept responsibility in making decisions consistent with the safety, health and welfare of the public, and to disclose promptly factors that might endanger the public or the environment;

2. to avoid real or perceived conflicts of interest whenever possible, and to disclose them to affected parties when they do exist;

3. to be honest and realistic in stating claims or estimates based on available data;

4. to reject bribery in all its forms;

5. to improve the understanding of technology, its appropriate application, and potential consequences;

6. to maintain and improve our technical competence and to undertake technological tasks for others only if qualified by training or experience, or after full disclosure of pertinent limitations;

7. to seek, accept, and offer honest criticism of technical work, to acknowledge and correct errors, and to credit properly the contributions of others;

8. to treat fairly all persons regardless of such factors as race, religion, gender, disability, age, or national origin;

9. to avoid injuring others, their property, reputation, or employment by false or malicious action;

10. to assist colleagues and co-workers in their professional development and to support them in following this code of ethics.

Approved by the IEEE Board of Directors | February 2006

Source: Institute of Electrical and Electronics Engineers. © 2006 IEEE. Reprinted with permission of the IEEE.

Figure 4.5:
Like the IEEE, just about every established field has a code of ethics you can turn to for guidance.

Are there any historical records to learn from?—Look for similar situations in the past. Your company may keep records of past decisions, or you can often find ethical cases discussed on the Internet. By noting successes or failures in the past, you can make a more informed decision.

What do my colleagues think?—Your co-workers, especially people who have been around for a while, may have some insight into handling difficult ethical situations. First, they can help you assess the seriousness of the situation. Second, they may be able to help you determine the impact on others. At a minimum, talking through the ethical dilemma may help you sort out the facts.

What would moral leaders do?—You can look for guidance from moral leaders that you respect. These might include spiritual leaders, civil rights advocates, business pioneers, or even your friends and relatives. In your situation, what would they do? Sometimes their convictions will help guide your own. Their stories may give you the confidence to do what is right.

Facing an ethical dilemma, you will probably need to make a judgment call. In the end, you want to make an informed decision. If you fully consider the personal, social, and conservation perspectives, you will likely make a good decision.

Step 3: React Appropriately When You Disagree with Your Employer

Ethical conflicts between you and your employer need to be handled carefully. If you suspect your company or your supervisors are acting unethically, there are a few paths you can take:

Link

For more on persuasion strategies, see Chapter 13, page 344.

Persuasion through costs and benefits—After you have collected the facts, take some time to discuss the issue with your supervisor in terms of costs and benefits. Usually, unethical practices are costly in the long term. Show the supervisor that the ethical choice will be beneficial over time.

Seek legal advice—Your company or organization likely has an attorney who can offer legal counsel on some issues. You may visit legal counsel to sort out the laws involved in the situation. If your company does not have legal counsel or you don't feel comfortable using it, you may need to look outside the company for legal help.

Link

For more information on resolving conflicts, see Chapter 3, page 40.

Mediation—The human resources office at your company can sometimes offer access to mediators who can facilitate meetings between you and your employer. Mediators will not offer judgments on your ethical case, but they can help you and others identify the issues at stake and work toward solutions.

Memos to file—In some cases, you will be overruled by your supervisors. If you believe an ethical mistake is being made, you may decide to write a *memo to file* in which you express your concerns. In the memo, write down all the facts and your concerns as objectively as possible. Then, present the memo to your supervisors and keep a copy for yourself. These memos are usually filed to document your concerns if the ethical dilemma turns into a major problem.

Whistle-blowing—In serious cases, especially where people's lives are at stake, you may even choose to be a whistle-blower. Whistle-blowing usually involves going to legal authorities, regulatory agencies, or the news media. Being a whistle-blower is a serious decision. It will affect your career and your company. Federal laws exist that protect whistle-blowers but there is always a personal price to be paid.

Resign—In the news, you will sometimes hear about people resigning because they cannot work for a company or organization that is behaving in an unethical way. If you truly think your organization is behaving unethically, resignation may be your only option. Before resigning, though, you should first sit down with your supervisor to tell him or her that you are considering resignation and why you have come to this decision. Perhaps the threat of losing you (and perhaps other employees and clients) will urge your employer to change the unethical practices.

Ethical situations should be carefully considered, but they should not be ignored. When faced with an ethical dilemma, it is tempting to walk away from it or pretend it isn't there. In any ethical situation, you should take some kind of action. Inaction on your part is ethically wrong, and it might leave you or your company vulnerable to liability lawsuits. At a minimum, taking action will allow you to live with your conscience.

Websites exist that can help you make your decision by considering ethical case studies. For example, the Online Ethics Center at the National Academy of Engineering offers many case studies that are discussed by ethics experts (Figure 4.6). Perhaps one of these cases is similar to the one you face, and you can use the wisdom of these experts to make the ethical decision.

Online Ethics

Figure 4.6: The Online Ethics Center at the National Academy of Engineering is a great place to learn about ethics in scientific and technical disciplines.

Source: The Online Ethics Center at the National Academy of Engineering, http://www.onlineethics.org

Stopping Cyberbullying and Computer Harassment

Have you ever been cyberbullied or harassed via computer? Cyberbullying is the use of a computer to harm or threaten others psychologically, economically, or in a way that damages their careers or personal lives. Computer harassment involves using a computer to disturb or threaten others because of their race, gender, sexual orientation, disability, ancestry, religious affiliation, or other inherent characteristics. People also use computers to sexually harass others by making unwanted sexual advances and making demeaning or humiliating sexual comments.

To combat cyberbullying and computer harassment, anti-harassment policies are being developed by schools, workplaces, video game manufacturers, Internet service providers, and social networking sites. Figure A, for example, shows Facebook's policies for addressing issues like cyberbullying and harassment.

In some cases, people don't even realize they are bullying or harassing others. When e-mailing or texting others, they use aggressive language such as "I'll have you fired for this," or "I'm going to kill myself," or "Tomorrow, I think I'll bring my assault rifle to the meeting." Or, they might think it's funny to e-mail dirty jokes or pornographic cartoons or images to their co-workers.

Unfortunately, these kinds of behaviors are not uncommon on campuses and in today's workplace. So what should you do if someone is bullying or harassing you electronically? Here are some tips for preventing and stopping cyberbullying and harassment:

Figure A: Facebook's Policies on Bullying and Harassment

Bullying and harassment are not new in school or in the workplace, but computers add some important new elements that make these activities especially harmful. Bullies and harassers can mask their identities or pretend to be someone else. Social networking and video game sites often allow people to do things they would not do in real life. Meanwhile, people can spread rumors and harmful information quickly through electronic means.
Source: Facebook. See https://www.facebook.com/communitystandards for full listing.

Preventing It

NEVER GIVE OUT PERSONAL INFORMATION ONLINE—This includes social networking sites. You might think only your friends can access your Facebook or MySpace page, but it is not that difficult for someone else to gain access to that information through one of your "friends." Your e-mails and text messages can also be easily forwarded, so any personal information may fall into the wrong hands.

DON'T PUT COMPROMISING CONTENT ONLINE—Compromising pictures, video, or statements have a way of being copied, leaked, and forwarded. If you have done or written something that would look bad to your classmates, parents, instructors, or a future employer, you should not put it online or send it through your phone. Once it's out there, it can be saved and used against you.

REFUSE TO PASS ALONG MESSAGES FROM CYBERBULLIES AND HARASSERS—Instead, tell the cyberbully or harasser to stop sending the messages and report the incident to your instructors, the Dean of Students, or your supervisor at work. Even if you are just making a victim aware that harmful things are being said about him or her, your forwarding of the message to the victim or others is really doing work for the bully or harasser.

KNOW WHO YOU ARE TALKING TO—Cyberbullies, harassers, and predators often try to build relationships with their victims over time. Then, once a "friendship" is established, they try to exploit their victim's trust. As soon as your "friend" does or says something strange or offensive or makes an inappropriate request, you should end the relationship.

Stopping It

STEP 1: TELL THE PERSON TO STOP—The person who is bullying or harassing you may not realize he or she is being intimidating or offensive. Firmly tell that person that his or her messages are not welcome and that they should cease.

STEP 2: BLOCK THEIR MESSAGES—Social networking and video game sites, Internet service providers, and mobile phones almost always give you the ability to block messages or disconnect from people you don't want to hear from.

STEP 3: SAVE AND PRINT HARASSING MESSAGES—By saving and printing these messages, you are collecting evidence that can be used against the cyberbully or harasser. Even if you don't want to take action now or you don't know who is doing it, you should keep any messages in case the problem escalates and the person is identified.

STEP 4: FILE A COMPLAINT—Most social networking and game sites have a procedure for filing a complaint that will warn, suspend, or ban the person who is bullying or harassing you. If you are being bullied or harassed in college, you should file a complaint with your university's Dean of Students office or the Equal Opportunity Office at your campus. At a workplace, you should contact the Human Resources office of your company.

   If you are being threatened or you believe someone is stalking you, you should get law enforcement involved. Call your campus or local police.

Ethics in the Technical Workplace

Some legal and ethics scholars have speculated that the Information Age requires a new sense of ethics, or at least an updating of commonly held ethics. These scholars may be right. After all, our ethical systems, especially those involving forms of communication, are based on the printing press as the prominent technology. Laws and guidelines about copyright, plagiarism, privacy, information sharing, and proprietary information are all based on the idea that information is "owned" and shared on paper.

The fluid, shareable, changeable nature of electronic files and text brings many of these laws and guidelines into discussion. For example, consider the following case study:

> **Case Study:** You and your co-workers are pulling together a training package by collecting information from the Internet. You find numerous sources of information on the websites of consultants and college professors. Most of it is well written, so you cut and paste some of the text directly into your materials. You also find some great pictures and drawings on the Internet to add to your presentation. At what point does your cutting and pasting of text become a violation of copyright law? How can you avoid any copyright problems?

In the past, these kinds of questions were easier to resolve, because text was almost exclusively paper based. Printed text is rather static, so determining who "owns" something is a bit easier. Today, the flexibility and speed of electronic media make these questions much more complicated.

At this time, many of our laws governing the use of information and text are evolving to suit new situations.

Copyright Law

Today, copyright law is being strained by the electronic sharing of information, images, and music. In legal and illegal forms, copies of books, songs, and software are all available on the Internet. According to the law, these materials are owned by the people who wrote or produced them; however, how can these materials be protected when they can be shared with a few clicks of a mouse? You can find out more about copyright law at the website of the U.S. Copyright Office (www.copyright.gov). Later in this chapter, U.S. copyright law is discussed in depth.

Trademarks

People or companies can claim a symbol, word, or phrase as their property by trademarking it. Usually, a trademark is signaled with a ™ symbol. For example, the Internet search engine Google™ is a trademarked name. The trademark signals that the company is claiming this word for its use in the area of Internet search engines.

To gain further protection, a company might register its trademark with the U.S. Patent and Trademark Office, which allows the company to use the symbol ® after the logo, word, or phrase. Once the item is registered, the trademark owner has exclusive rights to use that symbol, word, or phrase. For example, IBM's familiar blue symbol is its registered trademark, and it has the exclusive right to use it. There are exceptions, though. The First Amendment of the U.S. Constitution, which protects free speech, has allowed trademarked items to be parodied or critiqued without permission of the trademark's owner.

Patents

Inventors of machines, processes, products, and other items can protect their inventions by patenting them. Obtaining a patent is very difficult because the mechanism being patented must be demonstrably unique. But once something is patented, the inventor is protected against others' use of his or her ideas to create new products.

Privacy

Whether you realize it or not, your movements are regularly monitored through electronic networks. Surveillance cameras are increasingly prevalent in our society, and your online movements are tracked. Websites will send or ask for *cookies* that identify your computer. These cookies can be used to build a profile of you. Meanwhile, at a workplace, your e-mail and phone conversations can be monitored by your supervisors. Privacy laws are only now being established to cover these issues.

Information Sharing

Through electronic networks, companies can build databases with information about their customers and employees that can be shared with other companies. Information sharing, especially involving medical information, is an important issue that will probably be resolved in the courts.

Proprietary Information

As an employee of a company, you have access to proprietary information that you are expected not to share with others outside the company. In government-related work,

Privacy in an Electronic World

Electronic networks offer many more opportunities for surveillance.

you may even have a *security clearance* that determines what kinds of information you have access to. When you leave that company, you cannot take copies of documents, databases, or software with you. In some cases, you may even be asked to sign papers that prevent you from sharing your previous employer's secrets with your new employer.

Libel and Slander

You or your company can be sued for printing falsehoods (libel) or speaking untruths (slander) that damage the reputation or livelihood of another person or company. With the broadcasting capabilities of the Internet, libel and slander have much greater reach. For example, a website that libels another person or company may be a target for legal retaliation. If you use e-mail to libel others, these messages could be used against you.

Fraud

The Internet is also opening whole new avenues for fraud. Con artists are finding new victims with classic fraud schemes. Websites, especially, can sometimes give the appearance of legitimacy to a fraudulent operation. Meanwhile, con artists use e-mail to find victims. (Have you received any e-mails from the widows of wealthy Nigerian dictators recently?)

Copyright Law in Technical Communication

An interesting flash point today is copyright law. A copyright gives someone an exclusive legal right to reproduce, publish, or sell his or her literary, musical, or artistic works. Copyright law in the United States was established by Article I of the U.S. Constitution. The U.S. law that governs copyright protection is called "Title 17" of the U.S. Code. You can find this code explained on the U.S. Copyright Office website at www.copyright.gov (Figure 4.7).

Essentially, a copyright means that a creative work is someone's property. If others would like to duplicate that work, they need to ask permission and possibly pay the owner. Authors, musicians, and artists often sign over their copyrights to publishers, who pay them royalties for the right to duplicate their work.

New electronic media, however, have complicated copyright law. For example,

- When you purchase something, like a music CD, you have the right to duplicate it for your own personal use. What happens if you decide to copy a song off a CD and put it on your website for downloading? You might claim that you put the song on your website for your personal use, but now anyone else can download the song for free. Are you violating copyright law?
- According to Title 17, section 107, you can reproduce the work of others "for purposes such as criticism, comment, news reporting, teaching (including multiple copies for classroom use), scholarship, or research." This is referred to as "fair use." So, is it illegal to scan whole chapters of books for "teaching purposes" and put them on Google Drive or Dropbox for fellow students or co-workers?
- Technology like webcasting (using digital cameras to broadcast over the Internet) allows people to produce creative works. If you decided to webcast your and your roommates' dorm room antics each evening, would you be protected by copyright law?
- Blogs and microblogs, like Twitter, have become popular ways to broadcast news and opinions. Are these materials copyrighted?

The U.S. Copyright Office Website

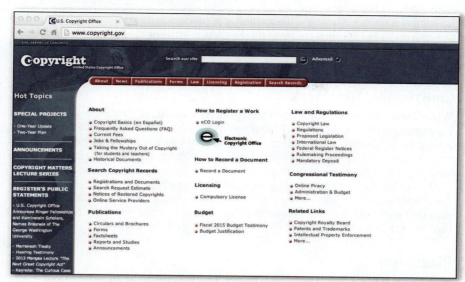

Figure 4.7:
You can visit the U.S. Copyright Office website to learn more about copyright law or to protect your own work.

Source: United States Copyright Office, http://www.copyright.gov

The answer to these questions is "yes," but the laws are still being worked out. It is illegal to allow others to download songs from your website. It would be illegal to scan large parts of a book, even if you claimed they were being used for educational purposes. Meanwhile, you can protect webcasting and blogs through the copyright laws.

The problem is the ease of duplication. Before computers, copyrights were easier to protect because expensive equipment like printing presses, sound studios, and heavy cameras were required to copy someone else's work. Today, anyone can easily duplicate the works of others with a scanner, computer or digital video recorder.

Ultimately, violating copyright is like stealing someone else's property. The fact that it is easier to steal today does not make it acceptable. Nevertheless, a few scholars have argued that copyright law is antiquated and that this kind of electronic sharing is how people will use text and music in the future.

Asking Permission

To avoid legal problems, it is best to follow copyright law as it is currently written. You need to ask permission if you would like to duplicate or take something from someone else's work. You can ask permission by writing a letter or e-mail to the publisher of the materials. Publishers can almost always be found on the Internet. On their websites, they will often include a procedure for obtaining permissions. Tell them exactly what you want to use and how it will be used.

In some cases, especially when you are a student, your use may fall under the "fair use clause" of the Copyright Act. Fair use allows people to copy works for purposes of "criticism, comment, news reporting, teaching (including multiple copies for classroom use), scholarship, or research" (17 U.S. Code, sec. 107). If your use of the materials falls under these guidelines, you may have a *limited* right to use the materials without asking permission.

For example, fair use would likely allow you to use a song legally downloaded from the Internet as background music in a presentation for your class. However, it does not allow you to distribute that song freely to your friends, even if you claim you are doing so for educational purposes.

Copyrighting Your Work

What if you write a novel, take a picture, produce a movie, or create a song? How do you copyright it? The good news is that you already have. In the United States, a work is copyrighted as soon as it exists in written form. If you want, you can add the copyright symbol "©" to your work to signal that it is copyrighted. The copyright symbol, however, is no longer necessary to protect a work.

If you want to formally protect your work from copyright infringement (i.e., so you can sue someone who uses your work without your permission), you should register your copyright with the U.S. Copyright Office. This step is not necessary to protect your work, but it makes settling who owns the material much easier.

Plagiarism

One type of copyright infringement is plagiarism. In Chapter 14, plagiarism is discussed in depth, but the subject is worth briefly mentioning here. Plagiarism is the use of someone else's text or ideas as your own without giving credit. Plagiarism is a violation of copyright law, but it is also a form of academic dishonesty that can have consequences for your education and your career.

For example, cutting and pasting words and images from the Internet and "patchwriting" them into your documents is a form of plagiarism, unless those materials are properly cited. To avoid questions of plagiarism, make sure you cite your sources properly and, when needed, ask permission to use someone else's work.

WHAT YOU NEED TO KNOW

- Ethics are systems of moral, social, or cultural values that govern the conduct of an individual or community.

- Ethical dilemmas force us to choose among uncomfortable alternatives.

- When you are faced with an ethical dilemma, consider it from all three ethical perspectives: personal, social, and conservation.

- You can turn to sources like laws, professional codes of ethics, historical records, your colleagues, or moral leaders to help you make ethical choices.

- When you disagree with the company, use persuasion first to discuss costs and benefits. You may turn to legal avenues if persuasion doesn't work.

- Ethical guidelines are evolving to suit the new abilities of computers.

- Privacy and information sharing are also becoming hot topics, because computer networks facilitate the collection of so much information.

- Copyright law and plagiarism are two rapidly evolving areas of ethics in this computer-centered world.

Individual or Team Projects

1. Describe a real or fictional situation that involves a communication-related ethical dilemma. As you describe the situation, try to bring personal, social, and conservation ethics into conflict. At the end of the situation, leave the readers with a difficult question to answer.

   In a memo to your instructor, identify the ethical issues at stake in the situation you described and offer a solution to the ethical dilemma. Then give your description to someone else in your class. He or she should write a memo to you and your instructor discussing the ethical issue at stake and offering a solution to the problem. Compare your original solution to your classmate's solution.

2. Find examples of advertising that seem to stretch ethics by making unreasonable claims. Choose one of these examples and write a short report to your instructor in which you discuss why you find the advertisement unethical. Use the terminology from this chapter to show how the advertisement challenges your sense of personal ethics, social ethics, or conservation ethics.

3. Find the Code of Conduct for your college, university, or workplace. Your college or university may actually have two codes of conduct, one for the organization as a whole and another, the student code of conduct. In a memo to your instructor, use the concepts from this chapter to critique the various aspects of this code of conduct. How are personal, social, and environmental ethics represented in the code of conduct? Are there any parts of the code of conduct that you believe should be updated? Are there any items (e.g., a section on cyberbullying) that need to be added?

Collaborative Project

The case study at the end of this chapter discusses a difficult case in which a company might be doing something unethical. Read and discuss this case with a group of others. Sort out the ethical issues involved by paying attention to the personal, social, and conservation factors that shape the ethical dilemma.

If you were Hanna, how would you react to this ethical dilemma? How would you use writing to turn your reaction into action? Would you write a memo to your supervisor? Would you contact a government agency? Would a memo to file be appropriate? Would you blow the whistle?

Whichever path you choose, write a letter or memo to a specific reader (e.g., your supervisor, corporate management, the human resources office, a newspaper journalist) that urges the reader to take action. Summarize the situation for the reader of your document, and then suggest an appropriate course of action. Support your recommendation by highlighting the ethical issues involved and discussing the ramifications of inaction.

Visit **My**WritingLab for a Post-test and more technical writing resources.

This Company Is Bugging Me

Last week, Hanna Simpson's employer, Ventron United, sent out an identical memo and e-mail to all 50 employees. The memo/e-mail announced that all employees would be required to have a Radio Frequency Identification (RFID) chip inserted into their left or right hand. The RFID would allow employees to open secure doors, use equipment, and log on to computers throughout the company's campus in Portland, Oregon.

The announcement explained that the company would be working on some projects that required high security. So, management wanted to ensure that only employees who were supposed to enter secure areas or use secure computers would have access. Also, the company experienced a break-in a couple of months ago. The thieves took a few laptop computers, but the rumor was that the thieves were really looking for information on Ventron United's new security-related products. The thieves had used an employee's access card, which was reported missing the next day.

Hanna's two closest co-workers, Jim Peters and Georgia Miller, had very different reactions to the memo. Jim thought it was a great idea. He already had a personal RFID implanted in one of his hands. "It's about the size of a grain of rice. I don't notice it at all. But now I don't need to carry keys anymore. The RFID opens the doors to my house, and I can turn on my car with just a button. I'm looking forward to the day when I can pay for my groceries with the wave of my hand."

Georgia was less enthusiastic, even paranoid. She confided to Hanna, "I think they're just trying to track our movements around here. Besides, my body is my personal space. These RFIDs are an invasion of my privacy."

"But would you quit your job over this?" Hanna asked Georgia.

"I hope it doesn't come to that, but yes I would," Georgia replied. "I'm not some dog that needs a chip implanted in me to keep track of me."

Other employees were worried about the health implications of the chips. Some just felt uncomfortable about the idea of a chip being injected into their hands. Some were considering a lawsuit if the company didn't back down on the issue.

Do some research on the Internet about RFIDs. What ethical issues are in conflict here?

CHAPTER

5

Letters, Memos, and E-Mail

Features of Letters, Memos, and E-mails *84*

Step 1: Make a Plan and Do Research *88*

Step 2: Decide What Kind of Letter, Memo, or E-mail Is Needed *90*

Step 3: Organize and Draft Your Message *96*

Microgenre: Workplace Texting and Tweeting *103*

Step 4: Choose the Style, Design, and Medium *104*

Using E-Mail for Transcultural Communication *111*

What You Need to Know *113*

Exercises and Projects *113*

Case Study: The Nastygram *117*

In this chapter, you will learn:

- The role of correspondence in the technical workplace.
- The basic features of letters, memos, and e-mails.
- How to plan, organize, and draft letters, memos, and e-mails.
- Common patterns for letters, memos, and e-mails.
- How to choose an appropriate style for correspondence.
- How to design and format letters and memos.

etters, memos, and e-mails are forms of *correspondence*, meaning they are used to correspond with clients, supervisors, colleagues, and others. They are used to share information, make requests, and convey decisions. Writing these documents will be a regular part of your job, but it can also be a drain on your time. The key is to learn how to write these documents quickly and efficiently, within the natural flow of your workday.

Letters and Memos Usually Convey Formal Messages

Letters and memos are generally used to convey formal messages, while e-mail is used for less formal messages.

Features of Letters, Memos, and E-Mails

These three types of correspondence are used for similar purposes, so their content, organization, and style are also similar. Here is how they differ:

Letters are written to people *outside* the company or organization. Primarily, letters are used in formal situations in which an employee is acting as a representative of the company. Letters can be used to make requests or inquiries, accept or refuse claims, communicate important information, record agreements, and apply for jobs.

Memos are written to people *inside* the company or organization. They are used to convey decisions, meeting agendas, policies, internal reports, and short proposals. When a message is too important or proprietary for e-mail, most people will send a memo instead. Memos are still more reliable than e-mails for information that should not be broadly released.

E-mails can be written to people *inside* or *outside* the company or organization. E-mail is used in situations that previously called for less formal memos, letters, or phone calls. Increasingly, e-mail is being used for formal communication, too.

Until recently, an obvious difference was that letters and memos appeared on paper, while e-mails appeared on screen. Today, though, it is not unusual for letters and memos to be written as electronic documents that are sent and received as PDF files (PDF stands for "Portable Document Format").

Letters, Memos, and E-Mails

This model shows a typical pattern for organizing a letter, memo, or e-mail. These kinds of documents are used for many different purposes, so the pattern shown here is designed to be flexible.

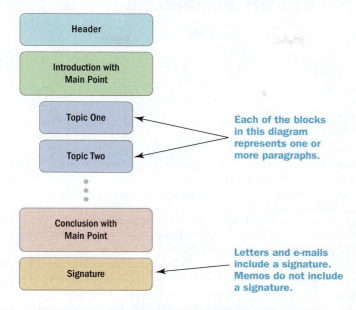

Header

Introduction with Main Point

Topic One

Topic Two

Each of the blocks in this diagram represents one or more paragraphs.

Conclusion with Main Point

Signature

Letters and e-mails include a signature. Memos do not include a signature.

Basic Features of Letters, Memos, and E-mails

A letter, memo, or e-mail will generally have the following features:

- **Header** with the company name and address of the sender, as well as recipient's name and address
- **Greeting** or **salutation** for the recipient (not included in memos)
- **Introduction** that states a clear main point
- **Body paragraphs** that provide need-to-know information
- **Conclusion** that restates the letter's main point
- **Signature** of the sender (not included in memos)

Letters, memos, and e-mails primarily differ in the way they are *formatted* (how they appear on the page or screen). Figure 5.1 shows how the same information would look in letter format, memo format, and as an e-mail.

- A letter includes a letterhead, the date, an inside address, a greeting, and a closing with the writer's signature.
- A memo includes a memohead, the date, and lines for the reader ("To:"), the sender ("From:"), and the subject ("Subject:").
- An e-mail includes a header with an addressee line for the readers' e-mail addresses ("To:"), carbon copy lines ("Cc:" and "Bcc:"), a subject line ("Subject:") and an attachments line ("Attach:").

(a)

Letterhead

Date

Inside
Address

Greeting

Closing with
Signature

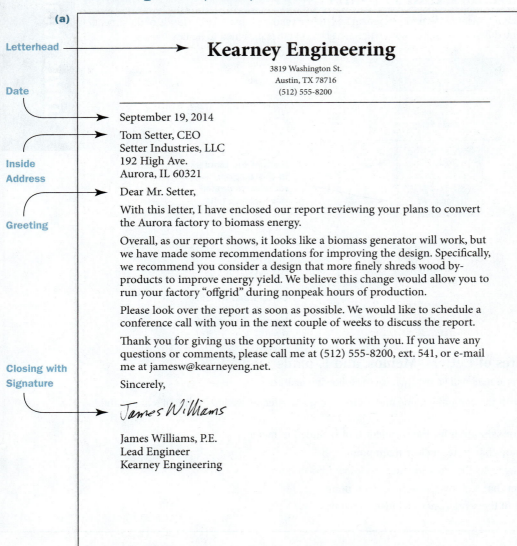

Kearney Engineering

3819 Washington St.
Austin, TX 78716
(512) 555-8200

September 19, 2014

Tom Setter, CEO
Setter Industries, LLC
192 High Ave.
Aurora, IL 60321

Dear Mr. Setter,

With this letter, I have enclosed our report reviewing your plans to convert
the Aurora factory to biomass energy.

Overall, as our report shows, it looks like a biomass generator will work, but
we have made some recommendations for improving the design. Specifically,
we recommend you consider a design that more finely shreds wood by-
products to improve energy yield. We believe this change would allow you to
run your factory "offgrid" during nonpeak hours of production.

Please look over the report as soon as possible. We would like to schedule a
conference call with you in the next couple of weeks to discuss the report.

Thank you for giving us the opportunity to work with you. If you have any
questions or comments, please call me at (512) 555-8200, ext. 541, or e-mail
me at jamesw@kearneyeng.net.

Sincerely,

James Williams

James Williams, P.E.
Lead Engineer
Kearney Engineering

Figure 5.1:
Letters (a),
memos (b),
and e-mails
(c) are basi-
cally the
same, ex-
cept in their
formatting.
The main dif-
ferences are
that letters
are written to
readers out-
side the com-
pany, whereas
memos
are written
to readers
inside the
company.
E-mail can
be written to
readers both
inside and
outside the
company.

(b)

Header ————————→ **Kearney Engineering**

Memorandum

Date ————————→ Date: September 19, 2014

To and From ——→ To: Louis Kearney, CEO
Lines   From: James Williams, Lead Engineer

Subject Line ——→ Subject: Report on biomass options for Setter Industries

I have enclosed our report on Setter Industries' plans to convert its Aurora factory to biomass energy.

Overall, as our report shows, it looks like a biomass generator will work, but we have made some recommendations for improving the design. Specifically, we recommend they consider a design that more finely shreds wood byproducts to improve energy yield. We believe this change would allow them to run the factory "offgrid" during nonpeak hours of production.

Please look over the enclosed report as soon as possible. We would like to schedule a conference call with their CEO, Tom Setter, in the next couple of weeks to discuss the report.

If you have any questions or comments, please call me at ext. 541 or e-mail me at jamesw@kearneyeng.net.

No Signature ——→

(continued)

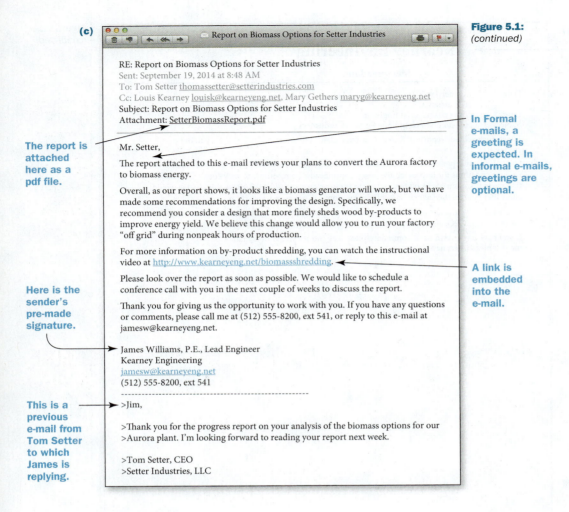

(c)

Figure 5.1:
(continued)

The report is attached here as a pdf file.

In Formal e-mails, a greeting is expected. In informal e-mails, greetings are optional.

RE: Report on Biomass Options for Setter Industries
Sent: September 19, 2014 at 8:48 AM
To: Tom Setter thomassetter@setterindustries.com
Cc: Louis Kearney louisk@kearneyeng.net, Mary Gethers maryg@kearneyeng.net
Subject: Report on Biomass Options for Setter Industries
Attachment: SetterBiomassReport.pdf

Mr. Setter,

The report attached to this e-mail reviews your plans to convert the Aurora factory to biomass energy.

Overall, as our report shows, it looks like a biomass generator will work, but we have made some recommendations for improving the design. Specifically, we recommend you consider a design that more finely sheds wood by-products to improve energy yield. We believe this change would allow you to run your factory "off grid" during nonpeak hours of production.

For more information on by-product shredding, you can watch the instructional video at http://www.kearneyeng.net/biomassshredding.

A link is embedded into the e-mail.

Please look over the report as soon as possible. We would like to schedule a conference call with you in the next couple of weeks to discuss the report.

Thank you for giving us the opportunity to work with you. If you have any questions or comments, please call me at (512) 555-8200, ext 541, or reply to this e-mail at jamesw@kearneyeng.net.

Here is the sender's pre-made signature.

James Williams, P.E., Lead Engineer
Kearney Engineering
jamesw@kearneyeng.net
(512) 555-8200, ext 541

>Jim,

This is a previous e-mail from Tom Setter to which James is replying.

>Thank you for the progress report on your analysis of the biomass options for our
>Aurora plant. I'm looking forward to reading your report next week.

>Tom Setter, CEO
>Setter Industries, LLC

Step 1: Make a Plan and Do Research

When you begin writing a letter, memo, or e-mail, first consider how your readers will use the information you are providing. You might start by answering the Five-W and How Questions:

Who is the reader of my letter, memo, or e-mail?

Why am I writing to this person?

What is my point? What do I want my reader to do?

Where will the letter, memo, or e-mail be read?

When will the letter, memo, or e-mail be used?

How will the reader use this document now and in the future?

Determining the Rhetorical Situation

If the message is informal or routine, you should be ready to start typing right now. However, if your message is formal or especially important, you should explore the rhetorical situation in more depth.

SUBJECT Pay attention to what your readers need to know to take action. Letters, memos, and e-mails should be as concise as possible, so include only need-to-know information.

PURPOSE The purpose of your letter, memo, or e-mail should be immediately obvious to your readers. Some action words for your purpose statement might include the following:

to inform	*to apologize*
to explain	*to discuss*
to complain	*to clarify*
to congratulate	*to notify*
to answer	*to advise*
to confirm	*to announce*
to respond	*to invite*

Your purpose statement might sound like one of the following:

> We are writing to inform you that we have accepted your proposal to build the Washington Street overpass.

> I would like to congratulate the Materials Team for successfully patenting the fusion polymer blending process.

> This memo explains and clarifies the revised manufacturing schedule for the remainder of this year.

READERS Letters, memos, and e-mails can be written to individuals or to whole groups of people. Since these documents are often shared or filed, you need to anticipate all possible readers who might want a copy of your document.

Primary readers (action takers) are the people who will take action after they read your message. Your letter, memo, or e-mail needs to be absolutely clear about what you want these readers to do.

Secondary readers (advisors) are the people to whom your primary readers will turn if they need advice. They may be experts in the area, support staff, supervisors, or colleagues.

Tertiary readers (evaluators) are any other people who may have an interest in what you are saying. Keep in mind that letters, memos, and e-mails have a strange way of turning up in unexpected places, including the hands of lawyers, reporters, auditors, and even competitors. Before sending any correspondence, think carefully about how the document would look if it were made public.

Gatekeeper readers (supervisors), such as your supervisor or your company's lawyer, may need to look over an especially important correspondence before it is sent out. These gatekeepers may want to ensure that you are communicating appropriately and correctly with clients.

Link
For more information about distinguishing between need-to-know and want-to-tell information, go to Chapter 14, page 378.

Link
For more guidance on defining a document's purpose, see Chapter 1, page 4.

Link
For more information on analyzing readers, turn to Chapter 2, page 19.

Link

For strategies to help identify contextual issues, go to Chapter 2, page 20.

CONTEXT OF USE   Consider the physical, economic, political, and ethical factors that will influence the way your readers will interpret and respond to your message. Put yourself in their place, imagining how the readers' location, finances, relationships, and values will influence the way they interpret your message.

Step 2: Decide What Kind of Letter, Memo, or E-Mail Is Needed

In the technical workplace, letters, memos, and e-mails are used for a variety of purposes. Now that you know your purpose, you can figure out what kind of correspondence you are writing.

Inquiries

The purpose of an *inquiry* is to gather information, especially answers to questions about important or sensitive subjects. In these situations, you could use e-mail, but a printed document is sometimes preferable because the recipients will view it as a formal request.

Here are some guidelines to follow when writing a letter, memo, or e-mail of inquiry:

- Clearly identify your subject and purpose.
- State your questions clearly and concisely.
- Limit your questions to five or fewer.
- If possible, offer something in return.
- Thank readers in advance for their response.
- Provide contact information (address, e-mail address, or phone number).

Figure 5.2 shows a typical letter of inquiry. Notice how the author of the letter is specific about the kinds of information she wants.

Responses

A response is written to answer an inquiry. The response should answer each of the inquirer's questions in specific detail. The amount of detail you provide will depend on the kinds of questions asked. In some situations, you may need to offer a lengthy explanation. In other situations, a simple answer or referral to the corporate website or enclosed product literature will be sufficient.

Here are some guidelines to follow when writing a response:

- Thank the writer for the inquiry.
- Clearly state the subject and purpose of the letter, memo, or e-mail.
- Answer any questions point by point.
- Offer more information, if available.
- Provide contact information (address, e-mail address, or phone number).

Figure 5.3 shows an example of a response letter. Pay attention to the author's point-by-point response to the questions in the original letter of inquiry (Figure 5.2).

Transmittals

When sending documents or materials through the mail or e-mail, you should include a letter, memo, or e-mail of transmittal. Also called "cover letters" or "cover memos," the purpose of these documents is to explain the reason the enclosed or attached

Figure 5.2: A letter of inquiry needs to be clear about the information it is seeking. In this letter, notice how the writer has listed her questions in an unmistakable way.

Arctic Information Associates
2315 BROADWAY, FARGO, ND 58102

February 23, 2014

Customer Service
Durable Computers
1923 Hanson Street
Orono, Maine 04467

Dear Customer Service:

State the subject and purpose of the letter.

My research team is planning a scientific expedition to the northern Alaskan tundra to study the migration habits of caribou. We are looking for a Rugged Laptop that will stand up to the unavoidable abuse that will occur during our trip. Please send us detailed information on your Yeti Rugged Laptop. We need answers to the following questions:

State questions clearly and concisely.

- How waterproof is the laptop?
- How far can the laptop fall before serious damage will occur?
- How well does the laptop hold up to vibration?
- Does the laptop interface easily with GPS systems?
- Can we receive a discount on a purchase of 20 computers?

Offer something in return.

Upon return from our expedition, we would be willing to share stories about how your laptops held up in the Alaskan tundra.

Thank the readers.

Thank you for addressing our questions. Please respond to these inquiries and send us any other information you might have on the Yeti Rugged Laptop. Information can be sent to me at Arctic Information Associates, 2315 Broadway, Fargo, ND 58102. I can also be contacted at 701-555-2312 or salvorman@arcticia.com.

Provide contact information.

Sincerely,

S Vorman

Sally Vorman, Ph.D.
Arctic Specialist

Response Letter

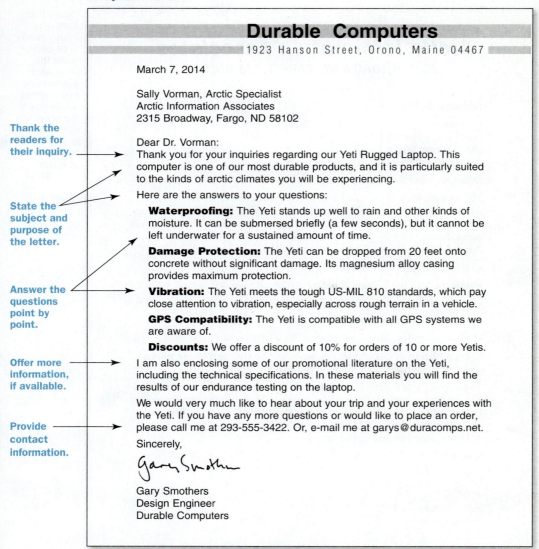

Thank the readers for their inquiry.

State the subject and purpose of the letter.

Answer the questions point by point.

Offer more information, if available.

Provide contact information.

Durable Computers

1923 Hanson Street, Orono, Maine 04467

March 7, 2014

Sally Vorman, Arctic Specialist
Arctic Information Associates
2315 Broadway, Fargo, ND 58102

Dear Dr. Vorman:

Thank you for your inquiries regarding our Yeti Rugged Laptop. This computer is one of our most durable products, and it is particularly suited to the kinds of arctic climates you will be experiencing.

Here are the answers to your questions:

Waterproofing: The Yeti stands up well to rain and other kinds of moisture. It can be submersed briefly (a few seconds), but it cannot be left underwater for a sustained amount of time.

Damage Protection: The Yeti can be dropped from 20 feet onto concrete without significant damage. Its magnesium alloy casing provides maximum protection.

Vibration: The Yeti meets the tough US-MIL 810 standards, which pay close attention to vibration, especially across rough terrain in a vehicle.

GPS Compatibility: The Yeti is compatible with all GPS systems we are aware of.

Discounts: We offer a discount of 10% for orders of 10 or more Yetis.

I am also enclosing some of our promotional literature on the Yeti, including the technical specifications. In these materials you will find the results of our endurance testing on the laptop.

We would very much like to hear about your trip and your experiences with the Yeti. If you have any more questions or would like to place an order, please call me at 293-555-3422. Or, e-mail me at garys@duracomps.net.

Sincerely,

Gary Smothers
Design Engineer
Durable Computers

materials are being sent. For example, if you were sending a proposal to the vice president of your company, you would likely add a memo of transmittal like the one shown in Figure 5.4. Earlier in this chapter, the documents in Figure 5.1 also showed a letter, memo, and e-mail of transmittal.

A transmittal letter or memo should do the following:

• Identify the materials enclosed.
• State the reason the materials are being sent.
• Summarize the information being sent.
• Clearly state any action requested or required of readers.
• Provide contact information.

You should keep your comments brief in transmittal letters, memos, and e-mails. After all, readers are mostly interested in the enclosed materials, not your transmittal.

Why should you include a letter, memo, or e-mail of transmittal in the first place? There are a few good reasons:

• If a document, such as a report, shows up in your readers' mailbox or inbox without a transmittal letter, memo, or e-mail, they may not understand why it is being sent to them and what they should do with it.
• Transmittals give you an opportunity to make a personal connection with the readers.
• Transmittals also give you an opportunity to set a specific tone for readers, motivating them to respond positively to the document or materials you have enclosed or attached.

Claims or Complaints

In the technical workplace, products break and errors happen. In these situations, you may need to write a claim, also called a complaint. The purpose of a claim is to explain a problem and ask for amends. Here are some guidelines to follow when writing a claim:

• State the subject and purpose clearly and concisely.
• Explain the problem in detail.
• Describe how the problem inconvenienced you.
• State what you would like the receiver to do to address the problem.
• Thank your reader for his or her response to your request.
• Provide contact information.

Figure 5.5 shows a claim letter with these features.

A claim should always be professional in tone. Angry letters, memos, and e-mails might give you a temporary sense of satisfaction, but they are less likely to achieve your purpose—to have the problem fixed. If possible, you want to avoid putting readers on the defensive, because they may choose to ignore you or halfheartedly try to remedy the situation.

Adjustments

If you receive a claim or complaint, you may need to respond with an *adjustment* letter, memo, or e-mail. The purpose of an adjustment is to respond to the issue described by the client, customer, or co-worker. These documents need to do more than simply respond to the problem, though. They should also try to rebuild a potentially damaged relationship with the reader.

Figure 5.4:
A transmittal memo should be concise. Make sure any action items are clearly stated.

Rockford Services

MEMORANDUM

Date: May 8, 2014
To: Brenda Young, VP of Services
From: Valerie Ansel, Outreach Coordinator
cc: Hank Billups, Pat Roberts
Re: Outreach to Homeless Youth

Enclosed is the Proposal for the Rockford Homeless Youth Initiative, which you requested at the Board Meeting on February 17. We need you to look it over before we write the final version.

The proposal describes a broad-based program in which Rockford Services will proactively reach out to the homeless youth in our city. In the past, we have generally waited for these youths to find their way to our shelter on the west side of town. We always knew, though, that many youths are reluctant or unable to come to the shelter, especially the ones who are mentally ill or addicted to drugs. The program described in this proposal offers a way to reach out to these youths in a nonthreatening way, providing them a gateway to services or treatment.

Please look over this proposal. We welcome any suggestions for improvement you might have. We plan to submit the final version of this proposal to the Board on May 26th at the monthly meeting.

Thank you for your help. You can contact me by phone at 555-1242, or you can e-mail me at valansel@rockfordservices.org.

Enclosed: Proposal for the Rockford Homeless Youth Initiative

Identify the enclosed materials.

State the reason materials are being sent.

Summarize the enclosed materials.

State the action item clearly.

Provide contact information.

Claim Letter

Figure 5.5:
A claim letter should explain the problem in a professional tone and describe the remedy being sought.

State the subject and purpose of the letter.

Explain the problem in detail.

Describe how the problem inconvenienced you.

State what the reader should do.

Thank the reader for the anticipated response.

Provide contact information.

Outwest Engineering

2931 Mission Drive, Provo, UT 84601 (801) 555-6650

June 15, 2014

Customer Service
Optima Camera Manufacturers, Inc.
Chicago, IL 60018

Dear Customer Service:

We are requesting the repair or replacement of a damaged ClearCam Digital Camcorder (#289PTDi), which we bought directly from Optima Camera Manufacturers in May 2011.

Here is what happened. On June 12, we were making a promotional film about one of our new products for our website. As we were making adjustments to the lighting on the set, the camcorder was bumped and it fell ten feet to the floor. Afterward, it would not work, forcing us to cancel the filming, causing us a few days' delay.

We paid a significant amount of money for this camcorder because your advertising claims it is "highly durable." So, we were surprised and disappointed when the camcorder could not survive a routine fall.

Please repair or replace the enclosed camcorder as soon as possible. I have provided a copy of the receipt for your records.

Thank you for your prompt response to this situation. If you have any questions, please call me at 801-555-6650, ext. 139.

Sincerely,

Paul Williams

Paul Williams
Senior Product Engineer

Here are some guidelines to follow when writing an adjustment:

- Express regret for the problem *without directly taking blame.*
- State clearly what you are going to do about the problem.
- Tell your reader when he or she should expect results.
- Show appreciation for his or her continued business with your company.
- Provide contact information.

Figure 5.6 shows an adjustment letter with these features.

Why shouldn't you take direct blame? Several factors might be involved when something goes wrong. So, it is fine to acknowledge that something unfortunate happened. For example, you can say, "We are sorry to hear about your injury when using the Zip-2000 soldering tool." But it is something quite different to say, "We accept full responsibility for the injuries caused by our Zip-2000 soldering tool." This kind of statement could make your company unnecessarily liable for damages.

Ethically, your company may need to accept full responsibility for an accident. In these situations, legal counsel should be involved with the writing of the letter.

Refusals

Refusals, also called "bad news" letters, memos, or e-mails, always need to be carefully written. In these documents, you are telling the readers something they don't want to hear (i.e., "no"). Yet, if possible, you want to maintain a professional or business relationship with these customers or clients.

When writing a refusal, show your readers how you logically came to your decision. In most cases, you will not want to start out immediately with the bad news (e.g., "We have finished interviewing candidates and have decided not to hire you"). However, you also do not want to make readers wait too long for the bad news.

Here are some guidelines for writing a refusal:

- State your subject.
- Summarize your understanding of the facts.
- Deliver the bad news, explaining your reasoning.
- Offer any alternatives, if they are available.
- Express a desire to retain the relationship.
- Provide contact information.

Keep any apologizing to a minimum, if you feel you must apologize at all. Some readers will see your apology as an opening to negotiate or complain further. An effective refusal logically explains the reasons for the turndown, leaving your reader satisfied with your response—if a bit disappointed. Figure 5.7 shows a sample refusal letter with these features.

Step 3: Organize and Draft Your Message

Like any technical document, your letter, memo, or e-mail should have an introduction, a body, and a conclusion. To help you organize and draft quickly, keep in mind that the introductions and conclusions of these texts tend to make some predictable moves.

Introduction with a Purpose and a Main Point

In the introduction, you should make at least three moves: (a) identify your *subject,* (b) state your *purpose,* and (c) state your *main point* (Figure 5.8). Depending on your

Adjustment Letter

O C M

Optima Camera Manufacturers, Inc.
Chicago, IL 60018 312-555-9120

July 1, 2014

Paul Williams, Senior Product Engineer
Outwest Engineering Services
2931 Mission Drive
Provo, UT 84601

Dear Mr. Williams,

Express regret for the problem.

We are sorry that the ClearCam Digital Camcorder did not meet your expectations for durability. At Optima, we take great pride in offering high-quality, durable cameras that our customers can rely on. We will make the repairs you requested.

State what will be done.

After inspecting your camera, our service department estimates the repair will take two weeks. When the camera is repaired, we will return it to you by overnight freight. The repair will be made at no cost to you.

Tell when results should be expected.

We appreciate your purchase of a ClearCam Digital Camcorder, and we are eager to restore your trust in our products.

Show appreciation to the customer.

Thank you for your letter. If you have any questions, please contact me at 312-555-9128.

Provide contact information.

Sincerely,

Ginger Faust

Ginger Faust
Customer Service Technician

Figure 5.6:
An adjustment letter should express regret for the problem and offer a remedy.

Refusal Letter

Figure 5.7:
A refusal letter should deliver the bad news politely and offer alternatives if available. You should strive to maintain the relationship with the person whose request is being refused.

O C M

Optima Camera Manufacturers, Inc.
Chicago, IL 60018   312-555-9120

July 1, 2014

Paul Williams, Senior Product Engineer
Outwest Engineering Services
2931 Mission Drive
Provo, UT 84601

Dear Mr. Williams,

State the subject. → We are sorry that the ClearCam Digital Camcorder did not meet your expectations for durability. At Optima, we take great pride in offering high-quality, durable cameras that our customers can rely on.

Summarize what happened. → According to the letter you sent us, the camcorder experienced a fall and stopped working. After inspecting your camcorder, we have determined that we will need to charge for the repair. According to the warranty, repairs can only be made at no cost when problems are due to manufacturer error. A camcorder that experienced a fall like the one you described is not covered under the warranty.

Deliver the bad news, explaining your reasoning.

Offer alternatives. → We sent your camcorder to the service department for a repair estimate. After inspecting your camera, they estimate the repair will take two weeks at a cost of $156.00. When it is repaired, we will return it to you by overnight freight.

Provide contact information. → If you would like us to repair the camcorder, please send a check or money order for $156.00. If you do not want us to repair the camcorder, please call me at 312-555-9128. Upon hearing from you, we will send the camcorder back to you immediately.

Express a desire to retain the relationship. → Again, we are sorry for the damage to your camcorder. We appreciate your purchase of a ClearCam Digital Camcorder, and we are eager to retain your business.

Sincerely,

Ginger Faust

Ginger Faust
Customer Service Technician

Enclosed: Warranty Information

message, you might also make two additional moves: (d) offer some *background information* and (e) stress the *importance of the subject.*

SUBJECT   Your *subject* should be identified in the first or second sentence of the introduction. Simply tell your readers what you are writing about. *Do not assume* that they already know what you are writing about.

> Recently, the Watson Project has been a source of much concern for our company.

> This memo discusses the equipment thefts that have occurred in our office over the last few months.

PURPOSE   Your *purpose* should also be stated almost immediately in the first paragraph, preferably in the first or second sentence.

> Now that we have reached Stage Two of the Oakbrook Project, I would like to re-evaluate and re-distribute project tasks among our team members.

> The purpose of this letter is to inform you about our new transportation policies for low-level nuclear waste sent to the WIPP Storage Facility in New Mexico.

MAIN POINT   All letters, memos, and e-mails should have a *main point* that you want your readers to grasp or remember. In many cases, "the point" is something you want your readers to do (an "action item") when they are finished reading. In other words, state the big idea you want your readers to remember or the action you want them to take.

> We request the hiring of three new physician's assistants to help us with the recent increases in emergency room patients.

> My main point in this letter is the following: Our subcontractors must meet ISO-9001 quality standards on this project, and we will work with you to ensure compliance.

It may seem odd to state your main point up front in the introduction. Wouldn't it be better to lead up to the point, perhaps putting it in the conclusion? No. Most of your readers will only skim your letter, memo, or e-mail. So, by putting your main point (the big idea or action item) up front, you will ensure that they do not miss it.

BACKGROUND INFORMATION   Writers often like to start their letters, memos, and e-mails with a statement that gives some background information or makes a personal connection to readers.

> Our staff meeting on June 28 was very productive, and I hope we all came away with a better understanding of the project. In this memo. . . .

> When you and I met at the NEPSCORE Convention last October, our company was not ready to provide specifics about our new ceramic circuit boards. Now we are ready. . . .

IMPORTANCE OF THE SUBJECT   In some cases, you might also want your introduction to stress the importance of the subject.

> This seems like a great opportunity to expand our network into the Indianapolis market. We may not see this opportunity again.

Link

For more information on writing introductions, see Chapter 15, page 399.

Figure 5.8:
This memo shows the basic parts of a correspondence. The introduction sets a context, the body provides information, and the conclusion restates the main point.

Morris Blue Industries

Date: November 18, 2014
To: Hanna Marietta, Chief Executive Officer
From: Jason Santos, Corporate Health Officer
Subject: Bird Flu Contingency Plan

The subject is identified in the first sentence.

Last week, the Executive Board inquired about our company's contingency plans if a bird flu pandemic occurs. As the Board mentioned, the exposure of our overseas manufacturing operations, especially in the Asian Pacific region, puts our company at special risk. At this point, we have no approved contingency plan, but my team strongly believes we need to create one as soon as possible. In this memo, I will highlight important issues to consider, and my team requests a meeting with you to discuss developing a plan for Board approval.

Background information is offered to remind the reader about the subject.

The main point and purpose are clearly stated up front.

The body provides need-to-know information.

Despite the media hype, a bird flu pandemic is not imminent. A remote possibility exists that the H5N1 avian influenza virus could mutate into a form that can be transmitted among humans. To this point, though, only a small number of bird flu infections have occurred in humans. In these cases, birds have infected humans through close contact. The World Health Organization (WHO) reported in January 2014 that only about 600 confirmed deaths had occurred worldwide since 2003, almost all in Asia. Human-to-human transmissions of bird flu are extremely rare.

This paragraph uses facts to inform the readers.

Nevertheless, the risk of a pandemic is real and the WHO recommends the immediate development of contingency plans. We recommend the following actions right now:

A. Develop a decision tree that outlines how our company will respond to a pandemic.
B. Design an alert system that notifies managers how to identify bird flu symptoms, when to be watchful, when to send employees home, and how to evacuate them.

This list makes important details easy to find.

C. Strengthen ties with local health authorities and law enforcement near our factories to speed the flow of information to local managers.

D. Create a training package for managers to educate them about bird flu and our company's response to a pandemic.

The Executive Board should also consider (a) whether we want to procure stocks of antiviral drugs like Tamiflu and Relenza, (b) whether our sick leave policies need to be adjusted to handle a pandemic, and (c) how our medical insurance would cover prevention and recovery for employees. These issues will require legal counsel from each country in which we have employees.

Thank you for contacting me about this matter. We believe a contingency plan should be developed as soon as possible. To get things rolling, we would like to schedule an appointment with you to go over these issues in more depth. You or your assistant can reach me at ext. 2205 or e-mail me at jsantos@morrisblue.com.

A "thank you" signals the conclusion of the memo.

The conclusion restates the main point and action item, while looking to the future.

Contact information is provided.

If we don't start planning a next-generation facility now, we may find ourselves struggling to keep up with the demand for our products.

Introductions should be as concise as possible. Any information that goes beyond these five moves should be put in the body of the correspondence.

Body That Provides Need-to-Know Information

The body is where you will provide your readers with the information they need to make a decision or take action. As shown in Figure 5.8, the body is the largest part of the memo or letter, and it will take up one or more paragraphs.

As you begin drafting the body of your text, divide your subject into the two to five major topics you need to discuss with your readers. Each of these major topics will likely receive one or more paragraphs of coverage.

If you are struggling to develop the content, you can use mapping to put your ideas on the screen or a piece of paper (Figure 5.9). Start out by putting the purpose statement in the center of the screen or at the top of a piece of paper. Then, branch out into two to five major topics. You can use mapping to identify any supporting information that will be needed for those topics.

While drafting, keep looking back at your purpose statement in the introduction. Ask yourself, "What information do I need to provide to achieve this purpose?" Then, include any facts, examples, data, and reasoning that will help support your argument.

Link

For more information on using logical mapping, go to Chapter 13, page 356.

AT A GLANCE

Elements of a Letter, Memo, or E-mail

- Header
- Introduction—subject, purpose, main point, background information, importance of the subject
- Body—discussion topics, usually with one paragraph per topic
- Conclusion—thank you, main point (restated), and a look to the future

Using Mapping to Generate Content

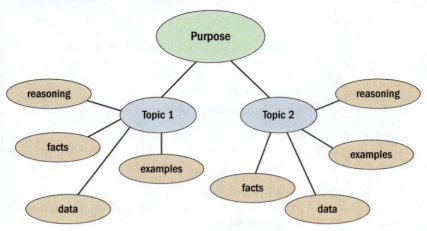

Figure 5.9: Using your purpose as a guide, identify the topics you will need to cover in your correspondence.

Conclusion That Restates the Main Point

The conclusion of your letter, memo, or e-mail should be short and to the point. Nothing essential should appear in the conclusion that has not already been stated in the introduction or body.

Conclusions in these documents tend to make three moves: *thank the readers, restate your main point,* and *look to the future.*

THANK THE READERS   By thanking your readers at the end, you leave them with a positive impression as you conclude.

> Thank you for your time and attention to this important matter.

> We appreciate your company's efforts on this project, and we look forward to working with you over the next year.

RESTATE YOUR MAIN POINT   Remind your readers of the action you would like them to take.

> Time is short, so we will need your final report in our office by Friday, September 12, at 5:00.

> Please discuss this proposal right away with your team so that we can make any final adjustments before the submission deadline.

LOOK TO THE FUTURE   Try to end your correspondence by looking forward in some way.

> When this project is completed, we will have taken the first revolutionary step toward changing our approach to manufacturing.

> If you have questions or comments, please call me at 555–1291 or e-mail me at sue.franklin@justintimecorp.com.

Link

To learn more about writing conclusions, go to Chapter 15, page 411.

Your conclusion should run about one to three sentences. If you find yourself writing a conclusion that is more than a small paragraph, you probably need to trim the added information or move some of it into the body of the letter, memo, or e-mail.

Workplace Texting and Tweeting

In the technical workplace, texting and social media are used regularly to keep in touch with co-workers and connect with the public. Texting is a quick way to share information and update your team on your status. Similarly, Twitter and other micro-blogging platforms are used to interact with colleagues, customers, and clients. These microblogging platforms are becoming increasingly common ways of keeping colleagues informed about the status of a project and any new developments.

Here are some tips for effective texting and tweeting at work:

Write longer text messages. Your messages should offer useful information and/or make a specific request. A typical workplace text or tweet will run one or two full sentences. When texting or tweeting with your friends, a ping is fine (e.g., "wazup"), but these kinds of brief messages shouldn't be sent to co-workers or the public because they can be disruptive or misunderstood.

Spell out most words and punctuate. Text messages are usually limited to 160 characters and tweets are limited to 140 characters, so abbreviating is common. However, in a workplace text message or tweet, you should spell out most words and punctuate properly, so your readers can understand what you are saying. It's better to send longer texts that are spelled out than a garble of abbreviations that people won't understand.

E-mail or call when it's important. Don't rely on people to read your texts and tweets. These messages are often overlooked, especially when people are busy.

Make sure you're doing work. It's easy to get caught up texting or tweeting with others, but remember, you're on company time. If you're texting or tweeting about something other than work, it's probably time to end the conversation.

Don't text or tweet during meetings. In many workplaces, supervisors will react negatively if people are looking down at their phones during a meeting or presentation, even if the texting and tweeting are work-related. You can usually keep your phone on the table in front of you, but wait until the meeting or presentation is over to respond to any texts or tweets.

Don't use texting to flirt at work. There is a fine line between playful text messages and sexual harassment in the workplace. Messages can be saved and used against you.

Remember: Texts and tweets sent with company phones are not private. If your company issues you a mobile phone, do not use it for private texting or tweeting. Your company can access those messages, and this has led to people being fired for misuse of company property.

(continued)

Write

Try using texting to communicate on your next team project. In class, try following the above texting guidelines instead of talking. When you are finished for the day, print out your conversation. What are the pros and cons of texting while working on a project?

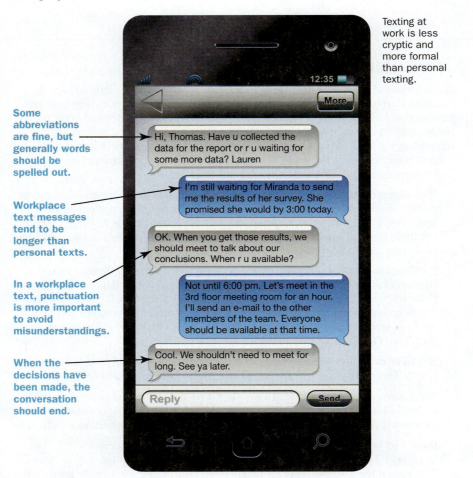

Texting at work is less cryptic and more formal than personal texting.

Some abbreviations are fine, but generally words should be spelled out.

Hi, Thomas. Have u collected the data for the report or r u waiting for some more data? Lauren

I'm still waiting for Miranda to send me the results of her survey. She promised she would by 3:00 today.

Workplace text messages tend to be longer than personal texts.

OK. When you get those results, we should meet to talk about our conclusions. When r u available?

In a workplace text, punctuation is more important to avoid misunderstandings.

Not until 6:00 pm. Let's meet in the 3rd floor meeting room for an hour. I'll send an e-mail to the other members of the team. Everyone should be available at that time.

When the decisions have been made, the conversation should end.

Cool. We shouldn't need to meet for long. See ya later.

Step 4: Choose the Style, Design, and Medium

The style and design of a letter, memo, or e-mail can make a big difference. One thing to keep in mind is this: *All letters, memos, and e-mails are personal.* They make a one-to-one connection with readers. Even if you are writing a memo to the whole company or sending out a form letter to your company's customers, you are still making a personal, one-to-one connection with each of those readers.

Strategies for Developing an Appropriate Style

Since letters, memos, and e-mails are personal documents, their style needs to be suited to their readers and contexts of use. Here are some strategies for projecting the appropriate style:

- Use the "you" style.
- Create an appropriate tone.
- Avoid bureaucratic phrasing.

USE THE "YOU" STYLE   When you are conveying neutral or positive information, you should use the word *you* to address your readers. The "you" style puts the emphasis on the readers rather than on you, the author.

> Well done. Your part of the project went very smoothly, saving us time and money.

> We would like to update your team on the status of the Howards Pharmaceutical case.

> You are to be congratulated for winning the Baldrige Award for high-quality manufacturing.

In most cases, negative information should not use the "you" style, because readers will tend to react with more hostility than you expect.

> **Offensive:** Your lack of oversight and supervision on the assembly line led to the recent work stoppage.

> **Improved:** Increased oversight and supervision will help us avoid work stoppages in the future.

> **Offensive:** At our last meeting, your ideas for new products were not fully thought through. In the future, you should come more prepared.

> **Improved:** Any ideas for new products should be thoroughly considered before they are presented. In the future, we would like to see presenters more prepared.

Don't worry about whether your readers will notice that you are criticizing them. Even without the "you" style, they will figure out that you are conveying negative information or criticisms. By avoiding "you" in these negative situations, you will create a constructive tone and avoid an overly defensive reaction from your readers.

Link

For more advice about choosing an appropriate style, see Chapter 16, page 422.

CREATE A TONE   Think about the image you want to project. Put yourself into character as you compose your message. Are you satisfied, hopeful, professional, pleased, enthusiastic, or annoyed? Write your message with that tone in mind.

Brainstorming is an especially good way to project a specific tone in your correspondence. For example, perhaps you want to argue that you are an "expert." Put the word *expert* on the top of your screen or a piece of paper. Then, brainstorm a list of words associated with this word. For example, brainstorming about the word *expert* would give you a list of words like *authority, professional, specialist, master, knowledgeable, trained, certified, experienced, thorough understanding,* and *solid background.*

You can then weave these expert-related words into your letter, memo, or e-mail. If the words are used strategically, your readers will subconsciously sense the tone you are trying to create.

AVOID BUREAUCRATIC PHRASING   When writing correspondence, especially a formal letter, some people feel a strange urge to use phrasing that sounds bureaucratic:

> **Bureaucratic:** Pursuant to your request, please find the enclosed materials.

> **Nonbureaucratic:** We have included the materials you requested.

Bureaucratic phrasing depersonalizes the letter, undermining the one-to-one relationship between writer and reader. Here are a few other bureaucratic phrases and ways they can be avoided:

Bureaucratic Phrase	Nonbureaucratic Phrase
Per your request	As you requested
In lieu of	Instead of
Attached, please find	I have attached
Enclosed, please find	I have enclosed
Contingent upon receipt	When we receive
In accordance with your wishes	As you requested
In observance with	According to
Please be aware that	We believe
It has come to our attention	We know
Pursuant to	In response to
Prior to receipt of	Before receiving

A simple guideline is not to use words and phrases that you would not use in everyday speech. If you would not use words like *lieu, contingent,* or *pursuant* in a conversation, you should not use them in a letter, memo, or e-mail.

Formatting Letters

Letters and memos usually have a rather plain design because they typically follow standardized formats and templates that prescribe how they will look. Most companies have premade word-processing templates for letters and memos that you can download on your computer. These templates allow you to type your letter or memo directly into a word-processing file. When you print out the document, the letterhead or memo header appears at the top.

Letter formats typically include some predictable features: a header (letterhead), an inside address, a greeting, the message, and a closing with a signature (Figure 5.10).

LETTERHEAD   Companies typically have letterhead available as a premade word-processor template or as stationery. Letterhead includes the company name and

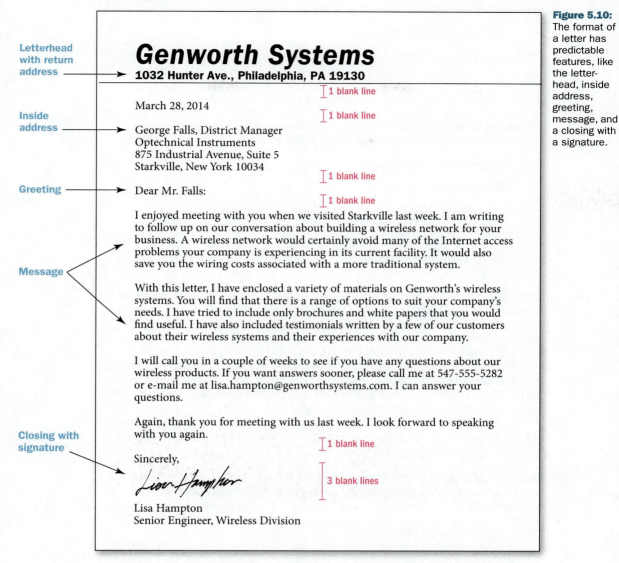

Letterhead with return address

Genworth Systems
1032 Hunter Ave., Philadelphia, PA 19130

[1 blank line

March 28, 2014

[1 blank line

Inside address

George Falls, District Manager
Optechnical Instruments
875 Industrial Avenue, Suite 5
Starkville, New York 10034

[1 blank line

Greeting

Dear Mr. Falls:

[1 blank line

Message

I enjoyed meeting with you when we visited Starkville last week. I am writing to follow up on our conversation about building a wireless network for your business. A wireless network would certainly avoid many of the Internet access problems your company is experiencing in its current facility. It would also save you the wiring costs associated with a more traditional system.

With this letter, I have enclosed a variety of materials on Genworth's wireless systems. You will find that there is a range of options to suit your company's needs. I have tried to include only brochures and white papers that you would find useful. I have also included testimonials written by a few of our customers about their wireless systems and their experiences with our company.

I will call you in a couple of weeks to see if you have any questions about our wireless products. If you want answers sooner, please call me at 547-555-5282 or e-mail me at lisa.hampton@genworthsystems.com. I can answer your questions.

Again, thank you for meeting with us last week. I look forward to speaking with you again.

[1 blank line

Closing with signature

Sincerely,

[3 blank lines

Lisa Hampton
Senior Engineer, Wireless Division

address. If letterhead is not available, you should enter your return address followed by the date. Do not include your name in the return address.

> 1054 Kellogg Avenue, Apt. 12
>
> Hinsdale, Illinois 60521
>
> January 23, 2014

The return address is best set along the left margin of the letter.

INSIDE ADDRESS   The address of the person to whom you are sending the letter (called the *inside address*) should appear two lines below the date or return address.

> George Falls, District Manager
>
> Optechnical Instruments
>
> 875 Industrial Avenue, Suite 5
>
> Starkville, New York 10034

The inside address should be the same as the address that will appear on the letter's envelope.

GREETING   Include a greeting two lines below the inside address. It is common to use the word "Dear," followed by the name of the person to whom you are sending the letter. A comma or colon can follow the name, although in business correspondence a colon is preferred.

If you do not know the name of the person to whom you are sending the letter, choose a gender-neutral title like "Human Resources Director," "Production Manager," or "Head Engineer." A generic greeting like "To Whom It May Concern" is inappropriate because it is too impersonal. With a little thought, you can usually come up with a neutral title that better targets the reader of your letter.

Also, remember that it is no longer appropriate to use gender-biased terms like "Dear Sirs" or "Dear Gentlemen." You will offend at least half the receivers of your letters with these kinds of gendered titles.

MESSAGE   The message should begin two lines below the greeting. Today, most letters are set in *block format,* meaning the message is set against the left margin with no indentation. In block format, a space appears between each paragraph.

CLOSING WITH SIGNATURE   Two lines below the message, you should include a closing with a signature underneath. In most cases, the word "Sincerely," followed by a comma, is preferred. Your signature should appear next, with your name and title typed beneath it. To save room for your signature, you should leave three blank lines between the closing and your typed name.

> Sincerely,
>
> *Lisa Hampton*
>
> Lisa Hampton
>
> Senior Engineer, Wireless Division

Formatting for an Envelope

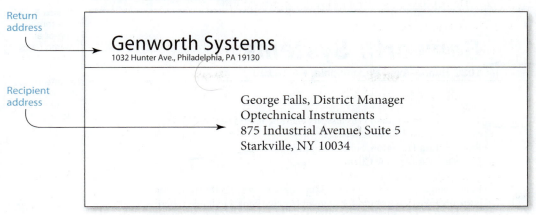

If you are sending the letter electronically, you can create an image of your signature with a scanner. Then, insert the image in your letter.

Formatting Envelopes

Once you have finished writing your letter, you will need to put it in an envelope. Fortunately, with computers, putting addresses on envelopes is not difficult. Your word-processing program can capture the addresses from your letter (Figure 5.11). Then, with the Envelopes and Labels function (or equivalent), you can have the word processor put the address on an envelope or label. Most printers can print envelopes.

An envelope should have two addresses, the *return address and the recipient address*. The return address is printed in the upper left-hand corner of the envelope, a couple of lines from the top edge of the envelope. The recipient address is printed in the center of the envelope, about halfway down from the top edge of the envelope.

If your company has premade envelopes with the return address already printed on them, printing an envelope will be easier. You will only need to add the recipient address.

Formatting Memos

Memos are easier to format than letters because they include only a header and a message.

HEADER   Most companies have stationery available that follows a standard memo format (Figure 5.12). If memo stationery is not available, you can make your own by typing the following list:

Date:

To:

cc:

From:

Subject:

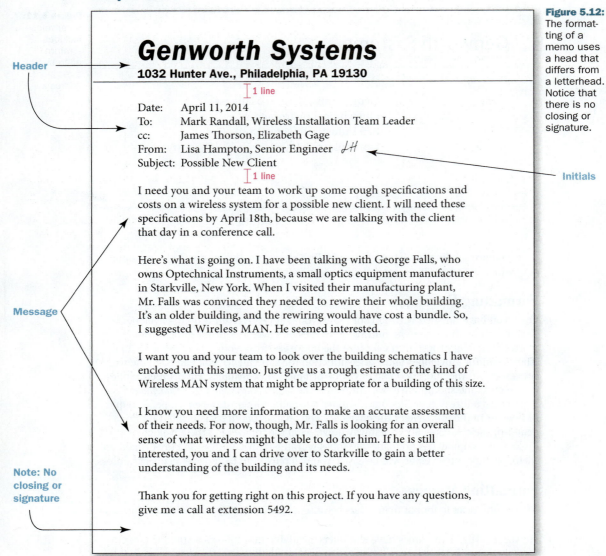

Header

Genworth Systems

1032 Hunter Ave., Philadelphia, PA 19130

↕ 1 line

Date: April 11, 2014
To: Mark Randall, Wireless Installation Team Leader
cc: James Thorson, Elizabeth Gage
From: Lisa Hampton, Senior Engineer *LH*
Subject: Possible New Client

↕ 1 line

Initials

Message

I need you and your team to work up some rough specifications and costs on a wireless system for a possible new client. I will need these specifications by April 18th, because we are talking with the client that day in a conference call.

Here's what is going on. I have been talking with George Falls, who owns Optechnical Instruments, a small optics equipment manufacturer in Starkville, New York. When I visited their manufacturing plant, Mr. Falls was convinced they needed to rewire their whole building. It's an older building, and the rewiring would have cost a bundle. So, I suggested Wireless MAN. He seemed interested.

I want you and your team to look over the building schematics I have enclosed with this memo. Just give us a rough estimate of the kind of Wireless MAN system that might be appropriate for a building of this size.

I know you need more information to make an accurate assessment of their needs. For now, though, Mr. Falls is looking for an overall sense of what wireless might be able to do for him. If he is still interested, you and I can drive over to Starkville to gain a better understanding of the building and its needs.

Thank you for getting right on this project. If you have any questions, give me a call at extension 5492.

Note: No closing or signature

Figure 5.12: The formatting of a memo uses a head that differs from a letterhead. Notice that there is no closing or signature.

The "Subject" line should offer a descriptive and specific phrase that describes the content of the memo. Most readers will look at the subject line first to determine if they want to read the memo. If it is too generic (e.g., "Project" or "FYI"), they may not read the memo. Instead, give them a more specific phrase like "Update on the TruFit Project" or "Accidental Spill on 2/2/14."

The "cc" line (optional) includes the names of any people who will receive copies of the memo. Often, copies of memos are automatically sent to supervisors to keep them informed.

If possible, sign your initials next to your name on the "From" line. Since memos are not signed, these initials serve as your signature on the document.

MESSAGE   Memos do not include a "Dear" line or any other kind of greeting. They just start out with the message. The block style (all lines set against the left margin and spaces between paragraphs) is preferred, though some writers indent the first line of each paragraph.

Longer memos should include headings to help readers identify the structure of the text. In some cases, you might choose to include graphics to support the written text.

It is important to remember that memos do *not* include a closing or signature. When your conclusion is complete, the memo is complete. No closing or signature is needed.

Link

For more ideas about designing documents, go to Chapter 17, page 447.

Using E-Mail for Transcultural Communication

The speed of e-mail makes it an ideal way to communicate and build relationships with clients and co-workers in other cultures. In many cases, e-mail has replaced both phone calls and letters, because it has the immediacy of the phone while giving readers the time to translate and consider the message being sent. When working across cultures, you will discover that many clients and co-workers prefer to conduct business via e-mail.

North Americans tend to view e-mail as an "informal" or even "intimate" medium for communication. As a result, they regularly stumble over the social norms and conventions of people from other cultures who use e-mail more formally. Too quickly, Americans try to become too friendly and too informal. Also, Americans can be sloppy with grammar, spelling, and word usage in their e-mails, causing significant problems for non-English speakers who are trying to translate.

Here are some tips for using e-mail across cultures:

Allow time to form a relationship—Introduce yourself by name and title, and provide some background information about your company and yourself. Tell the readers where you are writing from and where you are in relation to a major city. Don't rush into making a request, because doing so will often come across as pushy or rude.

Use titles and last names—Titles are often much more important in other cultures than in the United States. Minimally, you should use titles like Mr., Ms., or Dr. (Mrs. can be risky). If you know the proper titles from the readers' culture, such as Madame, Herr, Signora, then you should use them. Eventually, your clients or co-workers may want to move to a first-name relationship, but it's often a good idea to let them make that first move.

Focus on the facts—In your message, concentrate on factual issues regarding the who, what, where, when, how, and why. Cut out other nonessential information because it will cloud your overall message.

Talk about the weather—If you want to personalize your message, talking about the weather is a safe topic. People are often curious about the weather in other parts of the world. It's a safe, universal topic that will allow you to get beyond just factual information. (*Hint:* Convert all temperatures to Celsius and measurements into metric.)

Use attachments only when needed—In some parts of the world, e-mail systems cannot handle large attachments. Inbox quotas may be too small or download speeds may be too slow. A good approach is to send an initial e-mail that asks if an attachment would be welcome. Then, if the reader tells you it will work, you can send it in a follow-up e-mail.

Use plain text—You should assume that your readers can only receive plain text. So, turn off any special characters (smart quotes, dashes, emoticons, etc.) because they will often come out as gibberish at the other end. Also, assume that any embedded hyperlinks and e-mail addresses won't be shown as links. You should spell these addresses out in full, so readers can cut and paste them for their own use.

Limit or avoid photographs and graphics—Photographs, background images, and other graphics don't always transfer properly when they are sent globally, and they can require a great amount of memory. Plus, photographs can mean something unexpected to readers from other cultures.

Avoid clichés at the closing—Commonly used closings like "Do not hesitate to contact me," "If there's a problem, just holler," or "Don't be afraid to call," do not translate well into other languages and may be confusing to the readers.

Avoid humor—Attempts to be funny or tell jokes can backfire. Humor usually relies on cultural knowledge, so a joke or a clever play on words can be misinterpreted by readers. In some cases, the humor might be seen as insulting.

Create a simple signature file with your contact information—In other cultures, e-mails are sometimes printed out, which can cause the sender's e-mail address and other contact information to be separated from the message. A concise signature file that appears at the bottom of each e-mail should include your name, title, e-mail address, postal address, phone number, and corporate website.

Use simple grammar and proofread carefully—Simple sentences are easier for human and machine translators to interpret. Complex grammar or grammatical errors greatly increase problems with translation.

WHAT YOU NEED TO KNOW

- Writing letters, memos, and e-mails can be a drain on your time. You should learn how to write them quickly and efficiently.

- Letters, memos, and e-mails are essentially the same kind of document, called a *correspondence.* They use different formats, but they tend to achieve the same purposes. Letters are used for messages that go outside the company. Memos are for internal messages. E-mails can be used for messages both inside and outside the company.

- Letters, memos, and e-mails are always personal. They are intended to be a one-to-one communication to a reader, even if they are sent to more than one person.

- Letters, memos, and e-mails share the same basic features: header, introduction, informative body, and conclusion. They differ mostly in *format,* not content or purpose.

- The introduction should identify the subject, purpose, and point of the correspondence. If you want readers to take action, put that action up front.

- The body of the correspondence should give readers the information they need to take action or make a decision.

- The conclusion should thank the readers, restate your main point, and look to the future.

- To develop an appropriate style, use the "you" style, create a deliberate tone, and avoid bureaucratic phrasing.

- Use standard formats for letters, memos, and e-mails. These formats will make the nature of your message easier to recognize.

- When corresponding with people from other cultures, avoid being too familiar too quickly. Stick to the facts and avoid trying to be funny.

EXERCISES AND PROJECTS

Individual or Team Projects

1. Find a sample letter or memo on the Internet. In a memo to your instructor, discuss why you believe the letter is effective or ineffective. Discuss how the content, organization, style, and design (format) are effective/ineffective. Then, make suggestions for improvement.

2. Think of something that bothers you about your college campus. To a named authority, write a letter in which you complain about this problem and discuss how it has inconvenienced you in some way. Offer some suggestions about how the problem might be remedied. Be sure to be tactful.

3. Imagine that you are the college administrator who received the complaint letter in Exercise 2. Write a response letter to the complainant in which you offer a reasonable response to the writer's concerns. If the writer is asking for a change that requires a great amount of money, you may need to write a letter that refuses the request.

Collaborative Project

With a group, choose three significantly different cultures that interest you. Then, research these cultures' different conventions, traditions, and expectations concerning letters, memos, and e-mails. You will find that correspondence conventions in countries such as Japan or Saudi Arabia are very different from those in the United States. The Japanese often find American correspondence to be blunt and rude. Arabs often find American correspondence to be bland (and rude, too).

Write a brief report, in memo form, to your class in which you compare and contrast these three different cultures' expectations for correspondence. In your memo, discuss some of the problems that occur when a person is not aware of correspondence conventions in other countries. Then offer some solutions that might help the others in your class become better intercultural communicators.

Present your findings to the class.

> Visit MyWritingLab for a Post-test and more technical writing resources.

Revision Challenge

The memo shown in Figure A needs to be revised before it is sent to its primary readers. Using the concepts and strategies discussed in this chapter, analyze the weaknesses of this document. Then, identify some ways it could be improved through revision.

- What information in the memo goes beyond what readers need to know?

- How can the memo be reorganized to highlight its purpose and main point?

- What is the "action item" in the memo, and where should it appear?

- How can the style of the memo be improved to make the text easier to understand?

- How might design be used to improve the readers' understanding?

Write an e-mail to your instructor in which you explain how you improved this memo to make it more effective.

ChemConcepts, LLC

Memorandum

Date: November 5, 2013
To: Laboratory Supervisors
cc: George Castillo, VP of Research and Development
From: Vicki Hampton, Safety Task Force
Re: FYI

It is the policy of ChemConcepts to ensure the safety of its employees at all times. We are obligated to adhere to the policies of the State of Illinois Fire and Life Safety Codes as adopted by the Illinois State Fire Marshal's Office (ISFMO). The intent of these policies is to foster safe practices and work habits throughout companies in Illinois, thus reducing the risk of fire and the severity of fire if one should occur. The importance of chemical safety at our company does not need to be stated. Last year, we had four incidents of accidental chemical combustion in our laboratories. We needed to send three employees to the hospital due to the accidental combustion of chemicals stored or used in our laboratories. The injuries were minor and these employees have recovered; but without clear policies it is only a matter of time before a major accident occurs. If such an accident happens, we want to feel assured that all precautions were taken to avoid it, and that its effects were minimized through proper procedures to handle the situation.

In the laboratories of ChemConcepts, our employees work with various chemical compounds that cause fire or explosions if mishandled. For example, when stored near reducing materials, oxidizing agents such as peroxides, hydroperoxides and peroxyesters can react at ambient temperatures. These unstable oxidizing agents may initiate or promote combustion in materials around them. Of special concern are organic peroxides, the most hazardous chemicals handled in our laboratories. These

(continued)

compounds form extremely dangerous peroxides that can be highly combustible. We need to have clear policies that describe how these kinds of chemicals should be stored and handled. We need policies regarding other chemicals, too. The problem in the past is that we have not had a consistent, comprehensive safety policy for storing and handling chemicals in our laboratories. The reasons for the lack of such a comprehensive policy are not clear. In the past, laboratories have been asked to develop their own policies, but our review of laboratory safety procedures shows that only four of our nine laboratories have written safety policies that specifically address chemicals. It is clear that we need a consistent safety policy that governs storage and handling of chemicals at all of our laboratories.

So, at a meeting on November 3, it was decided that ChemConcepts needs a consistent policy regarding the handling of chemical compounds, especially ones that are flammable or prone to combustion. Such a policy would describe in depth how chemicals should be stored and handled in the company's laboratories. It should also describe procedures for handling any hazardous spills, fires, or other emergencies due to chemicals. We are calling a mandatory meeting for November 11 from 1:00–5:00 in which issues of chemical safety will be discussed. The meeting will be attended by the various safety officers in the company, as well as George Castillo, VP of Research and Development. Before the meeting, please develop a draft policy for chemical safety for your laboratory. Make fifteen copies of your draft policy for distribution to others in the meeting. We will go over the policies from each laboratory, looking for consistencies. Then, merging these policies, we will draft a comprehensive policy that will be applicable throughout the corporation.

The Nastygram

Jim Brand is a biomedical engineer who works for BioNextGen, a medical supplies manufacturer that is headquartered in Boston. He works in the Chicago satellite office, which specializes in CAT scan equipment. In the past few years, he has picked up more managerial responsibilities and is now second-in-charge of the satellite office.

Last week, a vice president from the Boston office, Charles Franklin, was visiting for a two-hour sales meeting that was scheduled for 2:00 pm. Due to snow, his flight was delayed and he arrived at 6:00 pm.

It wasn't a good time to visit. Jim's boss, Sharon Vonn, had fallen on some ice that day and hurt her shoulder. The office's administrative assistant was on vacation, and two of the other staffers had called in sick with the flu. A co-op engineering student was answering the phone, trying to handle technical questions. Two technicians were out on service calls. Jim had allowed one technician to go home at 5:00 pm to take care of a sick child.

Besides Jim, only the co-op and a sales representative were in the office when Charles arrived, so there were many empty desks. Phones were ringing.

The vice president, Charles, seemed irritated by what he saw. He and Jim met in the conference room to talk about the new products that BioNextGen was going to introduce next year. During the meeting, the co-op and sales rep needed to interrupt them so Jim could help handle emergencies.

Charles and Jim talked until 7:30 pm about strategies for managing the new products in the Chicago area. Then, the next day Charles caught an early-morning flight back to Boston.

Later that week, all managers at BioNextGen received the memo in Figure B as an attachment to an e-mail. If you were Jim, how would you respond to this situation? He knew his own boss, Sharon, would be upset by the memo, possibly with him.

BioNextGen

Date:	February 20, 2014
To:	Managers at BioNextGen
From:	Harmon Young, CEO
Re:	Get Your Damn Employees Working

It has come to my attention that the productivity at BioNextGen has fallen to a low. Employees, including here in Boston, are strolling in somewhere around 8:00 am and leaving at 5:00 sharp, if not earlier. We have technicians out "on call" who are apparently parked somewhere doing who knows what.

The only explanation for this is EMPLOYEE LAZINESS and a LACK OF OVERSIGHT from their managers. We are paying full-time wages for these so-called employees but we are not getting anything near 40 hours of full-time work. We're a company trying to grow, so we should be getting more than 40 hours, not less!

A recent site visit by one of our executives to Chicago was only the most recent incident. He witnessed a NEARLY VACANT OFFICE with phones going unanswered. The parking lot was almost completely empty at 5:15 pm! Clearly, the managers were not doing their jobs.

As managers, it is your job to ensure that your employees are working and that they are being productive. If you don't know where your people are, YOU NEED TO FIND OUT. If they are wasting time and not giving you a full day's work, then you need to either light a fire under them or get rid of them. DO YOUR DAMN JOB AND THEY WILL DO THEIRS!

Consider this your only warning. You have two weeks to motivate your employees or you will be fired!

Figure B: Sometimes it is difficult to respond professionally to a nasty memo or letter like this one.

CHAPTER

6

**Technical
Descriptions and
Specifications**

Step 1: Make a Plan and Do
  Research *120*

Step 2: Partition Your Subject *127*

Step 3: Organize and Draft Your
  Technical Description *128*

Help: Using Digital Photography
  in Descriptions *138*

Step 4: Choose the Style, Design,
  and Medium *139*

Microgenre: Technical Definitions
  144

What You Need to Know *146*

Exercises and Projects *146*

Case Study: In the Vapor *150*

In this chapter, you will learn:

- How descriptions and specifications are used in technical workplaces.

- Common features of descriptions and specifications.

- How to determine the rhetorical situation for a description.

- Strategies for partitioning objects, places, or processes into major and minor parts.

- Techniques for organizing and drafting descriptions and specifications.

- How to use plain style to make descriptions and specifications understandable.

- How to use page layout and graphics to highlight and illustrate important concepts.

Technical descriptions are detailed explanations of objects, places, or processes. There are several types of technical descriptions, written for various purposes in the technical workplace:

Technical description—Manufacturers use technical descriptions to describe their products for patents, quality control, and sales.

Patents—An application for a patent requires a detailed technical description of an invention.

Specifications (often referred to as "specs")—Engineers write specifications to describe a product in great detail, providing exact information about features, dimensions, power requirements, and other qualities.

Field notes—Naturalists, anthropologists, sociologists, and others use field notes to help them accurately describe people, animals, and places.

Observations—Scientists and medical personnel need to accurately describe what they observe, so they can measure changes in their patients' conditions.

Descriptions appear in almost every technical document, including experimental reports, user's manuals, reference materials, proposals, marketing literature, magazine articles, and conference presentations. Specifications, meanwhile, are used to establish a standard and an exact set of requirements for a product or service. Often, when a product or service does not meet these standards, it is referred to as "out of spec."

Figure 6.1 shows a technical description of the Hubble Space Telescope, which has been orbiting the Earth for over two decades. The exactness of the description allows a variety of readers to better understand the function and abilities of this important device.

Step 1: Make a Plan and Do Research

During the planning and researching phase, you should identify what kinds of information your readers need to know, how they will use that information, and the contexts in which they will use it.

Planning

As you begin planning your technical description, it is important that you first have a good understanding of the situation in which your description will be used. Start by considering the Five-W and How Questions:

Who might need this description?

Why is this description needed?

What details and facts should the description include?

Where will the description be used?

When will the description be used?

How will this description be used?

Technical Descriptions and Specifications

This model shows a typical organizational pattern for a technical description. You should alter this pattern to fit the unique features of the object, place, or process that you are describing.

Basic Features of Technical Descriptions

A technical description can be part of a larger document, or it can stand alone as a separate document. A stand-alone technical description will generally have the following features:

- **Title** that is specific to the subject being described
- **Introduction** with a definition and overall description of the subject
- **Body paragraphs** that partition the subject into its features, functions, or stages
- **Graphics** that illustrate the subject and its parts
- **Conclusion**, if needed, that describes the subject in operation

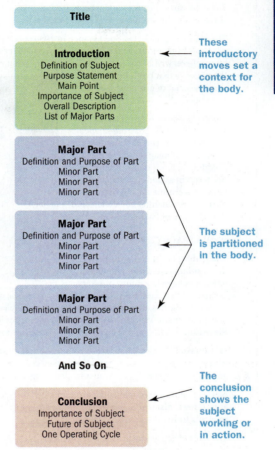

Title

Introduction
Definition of Subject
Purpose Statement
Main Point
Importance of Subject
Overall Description
List of Major Parts

These introductory moves set a context for the body.

Major Part
Definition and Purpose of Part
Minor Part
Minor Part
Minor Part

Major Part
Definition and Purpose of Part
Minor Part
Minor Part
Minor Part

The subject is partitioned in the body.

Major Part
Definition and Purpose of Part
Minor Part
Minor Part
Minor Part

And So On

Conclusion
Importance of Subject
Future of Subject
One Operating Cycle

The conclusion shows the subject working or in action.

Figure 6.1: Here is a technical description of the Hubble Space Telescope.

The Telescope: Hubble Essentials

Since the earliest days of astronomy, since the time of Galileo, astronomers have shared a single goal — to see more, see farther, see deeper.

The Hubble Space Telescope's launch in 1990 sped humanity to one of its greatest advances in that journey. Hubble is a telescope that orbits Earth. Its position above the atmosphere, which distorts and blocks the light that reaches our planet, gives it a view of the universe that typically far surpasses that of ground-based telescopes.

The introduction states the topic and stresses its importance.

Hubble is one of NASA's most successful and long-lasting science missions. It has beamed hundreds of thousands of images back to Earth, shedding light on many of the great mysteries of astronomy. Its gaze has helped determine the age of the universe, the identity of quasars, and the existence of dark energy.

WHY A SPACE TELESCOPE

The Hubble Space Telescope is the direct solution to a problem that telescopes have faced since the very earliest days of their invention: the atmosphere. The quandary is twofold: Shifting air pockets in Earth's atmosphere distort the view of telescopes on the ground, no matter how large or scientifically advanced those telescopes are. This "atmospheric distortion" is the reason that the stars seem to twinkle when you look up at the sky.

The atmosphere also partially blocks or absorbs certain wavelengths of radiation, like ultraviolet, gamma- and X-rays, before they can reach Earth. Scientists can best examine an object like a star by studying it in all the types of wavelengths that it emits.

Newer ground-based telescopes are using technological advances to try to correct atmospheric distortion, but there's no way to see the wavelengths the atmosphere prevents from even reaching the planet.

The most effective way to avoid the problems of the atmosphere is to place your telescope beyond it. Or, in Hubble's case, 353 miles (569 km) above the surface of Earth.

Source: NASA, hubblesite.org/the_telescope/hubble_essentials

HOW IT WORKS

Every 97 minutes, Hubble completes a spin around Earth, moving at the speed of about five miles per second (8 km per second) — fast enough to travel across the United States in about 10 minutes. As it travels, Hubble's mirror captures light and directs it into its several science instruments.

Hubble is a type of telescope known as a Cassegrain reflector. Light hits the telescope's main mirror, or primary mirror. It bounces off the primary mirror and encounters a secondary mirror. The secondary mirror focuses the light through a hole in the center of the primary mirror that leads to the telescope's science instruments.

When light strikes the concave primary mirror of the Hubble Space Telescope, it is reflected to the convex secondary mirror, then back through a hole in the center of the primary mirror. There, the light comes to the focal point and passes to one of Hubble's instruments. Telescopes of this design are called Cassegrain telescopes, after the person who designed the first one.

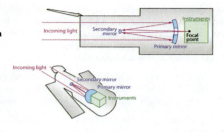

People often mistakenly believe that a telescope's power lies in its ability to magnify objects. Telescopes actually work by collecting more light than the human eye can capture on its own. The larger a telescope's mirror, the more light it can collect, and the better its vision. Hubble's primary mirror is 94.5 inches (2.4 m) in diameter. This mirror is small compared with those of current ground-based telescopes, which can be 400 inches (1,000 cm) and up, but Hubble's location beyond the atmosphere gives it remarkable clarity.

Once the mirror captures the light, Hubble's science instruments work together or individually to provide the observation. Each instrument is designed to examine the universe in a different way.

The Wide Field Camera 3 (WFC3) sees three different kinds of light: near-ultraviolet, visible and near-infrared, though not simultaneously. Its resolution and field of view are much greater than that of Hubble's other instruments. WFC3 is one of Hubble's two newest instruments, and will be used to study dark energy and dark matter, the formation of individual stars and the discovery of extremely remote galaxies previously beyond Hubble's vision.

Major features are described.

(continued)

The Cosmic Origins Spectrograph (COS), Hubble's other new instrument, is a spectrograph that sees exclusively in ultraviolet light. Spectrographs act something like prisms, separating light from the cosmos into its component colors. This provides a wavelength "fingerprint" of the object being observed, which tells us about its temperature, chemical composition, density, and motion. COS will improve Hubble's ultraviolet sensitivity at least 10 times, and up to 70 times when observing extremely faint objects.

← **Minor features are used to add detail.**

The Advanced Camera for Surveys (ACS) sees visible light, and is designed to study some of the earliest activity in the universe. ACS helps map the distribution of dark matter, detects the most distant objects in the universe, searches for massive planets, and studies the evolution of clusters of galaxies. ACS partially stopped working in 2007 due to an electrical short, but was repaired during Servicing Mission 4 in May 2009.

← **Details are used to fill out the text.**

The Space Telescope Imaging Spectrograph (STIS) is a spectrograph that sees ultraviolet, visible and near-infrared light, and is known for its ability to hunt black holes. While COS works best with small sources of light, such as stars or quasars, STIS can map out larger objects like galaxies. STIS stopped working due to a technical failure on August 3, 2004, but was also repaired during Servicing Mission 4.

The Near Infrared Camera and Multi-Object Spectrometer (NICMOS) is Hubble's heat sensor. Its sensitivity to infrared light — perceived by humans as heat — lets it observe objects hidden by interstellar dust, like stellar birth sites, and gaze into deepest space.

Finally, the Fine Guidance Sensors (FGS) are devices that lock onto "guide stars" and keep Hubble pointed in the right direction. They can be used to precisely measure the distance between stars, and their relative motions.

All of Hubble's functions are powered by sunlight. Hubble sports solar arrays that convert sunlight directly into electricity. Some of that electricity is stored in batteries that keep the telescope running when it's in Earth's shadow, blocked from the Sun's rays.

Now, define your description's rhetorical situation: subject, purpose, readers, and context of your description.

Link

For more help defining your subject, see Chapter 1, page 4.

SUBJECT   What exactly is your subject? What are its major features? What are its boundaries?

PURPOSE   What should your technical description achieve? Do the readers want exact detail, or do they want an overall familiarity with the subject?

In one sentence, write down the purpose of your description. Here are some verbs that might help you write that sentence:

to describe	*to show*	*to portray*
to clarify	*to explain*	*to characterize*
to illustrate	*to depict*	*to represent*
to reveal		

Link

For more information on defining a document's purpose, see Chapter 1, page 5.

Your purpose statement might say something like the following:

The purpose of this description is to show how a fuel cell generates power.

In this description, I will explain the basic features of the International Space Station.

If your purpose statement goes beyond one sentence, you probably need to be more specific about what you are trying to achieve.

READERS   Technical descriptions tend to be written for readers who are unfamiliar with the subject. So, you will also need to adjust the detail and complexity of your description to suit their specific interests and needs.

> **Primary readers** (action takers) are individuals who most need to understand your description. What exactly do they need to know?
>
> **Secondary readers** (advisors) will likely be experts who understand your subject, such as engineers, technicians, or scientists. How much technical detail and accuracy will these readers need to advise the primary readers?
>
> **Tertiary readers** (evaluators) could include just about anyone who has an interest in the product, place, or process you are describing, including reporters, lawyers, auditors, or concerned citizens. What kinds of information should be given to them and what should be held back?
>
> **Gatekeeper readers** (supervisors) within your company will want to review your materials for exactness and correctness.

Link

For more information on analyzing readers, see Chapter 2, page 19.

CONTEXT OF USE   Use your imagination to visualize your primary readers using your technical description. Where are they likely to read and use the document? What economic, ethical, and political factors will influence how they interpret the text?

Link

For more ideas about analyzing the context of use, see Chapter 2, page 22.

Addressing ISO 9000/ISO 14000 Issues

One important issue involving context of use is whether your technical description needs to conform to ISO 9000 or ISO 14000 standards. These voluntary standards are accepted internationally and managed by the International Organization for Standardization (ISO). ISO 9000 standards involve quality management systems, while ISO 14000 standards involve environmental management systems. Many high-tech companies, especially ones working for the U.S. government, follow these quality management and environmental management standards. Figure 6.2 shows an introduction to the ISO 9000 standards drawn from the ISO website (www.iso.org).

The ISO standards cannot be discussed in sufficient depth here, but you should be aware that they exist. If your company follows ISO standards, any descriptions and specifications you write will need to reflect and conform to these standards.

Researching

In most cases, doing research for a technical description is primarily experiential. In other words, you will likely need to personally observe the object, thing, or process you are describing. Here are some strategies that are especially applicable to writing descriptions and specifications.

Link

For more information on doing research, go to Chapter 14, page 365.

DO BACKGROUND RESEARCH   You should know as much as possible about your subject. On the Internet, use search engines to find as much information as you can. Then, collect print sources like books, documents, and other literature.

ISO 9000

Figure 6.2: The ISO standards are crucial to maintaining quality and consistency in national and international manufacturing.

Source: International Organization for Standardization, http://www.iso.org/iso/home/standards/management-standards/iso_9000.htm

USE YOUR SENSES   Use all of your available senses to study your subject. As much as possible, take notes about how something looks, sounds, smells, feels, and tastes. Pay special attention to colors and textures, because they will add depth and vividness to your description.

TAKE MEASUREMENTS   When possible, measure qualities like height, width, depth, and weight. Exact measurements are especially important if you are writing a specification that will set standards for a product or device.

DESCRIBE MOTION AND CHANGE   Pay attention to how your subject moves or changes. Look for movement patterns. Note situations where your subject changes or transforms in some way.

DESCRIBE THE CONTEXT   Take notes about the surroundings of the subject. Pay attention to how your subject acts or interacts with the objects and people around it.

CREATE OR LOCATE GRAPHICS   If available, collect graphics that illustrate your subject, or create them yourself. You can make drawings or take pictures of your subject.

ASK SUBJECT MATTER EXPERTS (SMEs)   If possible, find SMEs who can answer your questions and fill in any gaps in your understanding.

When you are finished researching, you should figure out how much your readers already know about the subject and how much they need to know. You can then prioritize the content of your description to suit their needs.

Step 2: Partition Your Subject

Now you are ready to *partition* your subject. Partitioning means dividing your subject into its features, functions, or its stages of a process.

> **By features**—You might separately describe the subject's parts or features. For example, a description of a computer might describe it part by part, partitioning it into a monitor, keyboard, external hard drives, and a central processing unit (CPU).
>
> **By functions**—You might note how the subject's different parts function. A description of the International Space Station, for example, might partition it function by function into research, power generation, infrastructure, habitation, and docking sections.
>
> **By stages of its process**—You might break down the subject chronologically by showing how it works. A description of Hodgkin's disease, for example, might walk readers step by step through detection, diagnosis, staging, and remission stages. A description of a machine might show how it moves step by step through its operations.

Logical mapping can help you break down (partition) your subject into major and minor parts (Figure 6.3).

To use logical mapping to help describe something, follow these steps:

1. Put the name of your subject in the middle of your screen or a sheet of paper.

2. Write down the two to five major parts in the space around it.

3. Circle each major part.

4. Partition each major part into two to five minor parts.

For example, in Figure 6.4, NASA's description of the Mars Curiosity Rover partitions the subject into

Body

Brains

Eyes and Other Senses

Arm and Hand

Wheels and Legs

Energy

Communications

Link

For more help using logical mapping, see Chapter 14, page 367.

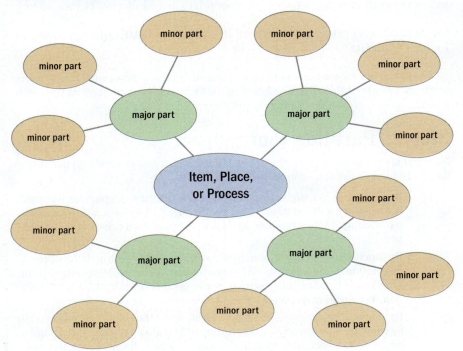

In this example, notice how the description carves the subject into its major parts. Then, each of these major parts is described in detail by paying attention to its minor parts.

Step 3: Organize and Draft Your Technical Description

With your subject partitioned into major and minor features, you are ready to start organizing and drafting your description. You can describe your subject in many ways, but it is best to choose an organizational pattern that demonstrates an obvious logic that readers will immediately recognize. The Quick Start at the beginning of this chapter shows a basic model to help you get started.

Figure 6.4:
This description of the Mars Curiosity Rover shows how a subject can be partitioned into major and minor parts.

Definition of the subject →

Mars Curiosity Rover

Curiosity is a car-sized, six-wheeled robot destined for Gale Crater on Mars. Its mission: to see if Mars ever could have supported small life forms called microbes… and if humans could survive there someday! In addition to super-human senses that help us understand Mars as a habitat for life, Curiosity's parts are similar to what a human would need to explore Mars (body, brains, eyes, arms, legs, etc.). Check it out though—sometimes they are located in odd places!

The Rover's "Body"

The rover body is called the warm electronics box, or "WEB" for short. Like a car body, the rover body is a strong, outer layer that protects the rover's computer and electronics (which are basically the equivalent of the rover's brains and heart). The rover body thus keeps the rover's vital organs protected and temperature-controlled.

Major parts →

The warm electronics box is closed on the top by a piece called the Rover Equipment Deck (RED). The Rover Equipment Deck makes the rover like a convertible car, allowing a place for the rover mast and cameras to sit out in the martian air, taking pictures and clearly observing the martian terrain as it travels.

The Rover's "Brains"

Unlike people and animals, the rover brains are in its body. The rover computer (its "brains") is inside a module called "The Rover Compute Element" (RCE) inside the rover body. The communication interface that enables the main computer to exchange data with the rover's instruments and sensors is called a "bus." This bus is an industry standard interface bus to communicate with and control all of the rover motors, science instruments, and communication functions.

The Rover's "Eyes" And Other "Senses"

The rover has seventeen "eyes." Six engineering cameras aid in rover navigation and four cameras perform science investigations. Each camera has an application-specific set of optics:

- **Four Pairs of Engineering Hazard Avoidance Cameras (Hazcams):** Mounted on the lower portion of the front and rear of the rover, these black-and-white cameras use visible light to capture three-dimensional (3-D) imagery.   ← **Minor parts are used to fill in the details.**
- **Two Pairs of Engineering Navigation Cameras (Navcams):** Mounted on the mast (the rover "neck and head"), these black-and-white cameras use visible light to gather panoramic, three-dimensional (3D) imagery.
- **Four Science Cameras: MastCam (one pair), ChemCam, MAHLI:** Mast Camera will take color images, three-dimensional stereo images, and color video footage of the martian terrain and have a powerful zoom lens.
- **One Descent Imager–MARDI:** MARDI (Mars Descent Imager) provided four frame-per-second video at a high resolution during Curiosity's landing. The images are "true color," or as the human eye would see.

Curiosity's "Arm" and "Hand"

The Robot Arm holds and maneuvers the instruments that help scientists get up-close and personal with martian rocks and soil. Much like a human arm, the robotic arm has flexibility through three joints: the rover's shoulder, elbow, and wrist. The arm enables a tool belt of scientists' instruments to extend, bend, and angle precisely against a rock to work as a human geologist would: grinding away layers, taking microscopic images, and analyzing the elemental composition of the rocks and soil.

At the end of the arm is a turret, shaped like a cross. This turret, a hand-like structure, holds various tools that can spin through a 350-degree turning range. At the tip of the arm is the turret structure on which 5 devices are mounted. Two of these devices are in-situ or contact instruments known as the Alpha Particle X-ray Spectrometer (APXS) and the Mars Hand Lens Imager (MAHLI). The remaining three devices are associated with sample acquisition and sample preparation functions.

Source: NASA, http://mars.jpl.nasa.gov/msl/mission/rover/

(continued)

The Rover's Wheels and "Legs"

The Mars Science Laboratory has six wheels, each with its own individual motor. The two front and two rear wheels also have individual steering motors (1 each). This steering capability allows the vehicle to turn in place, a full 360 degrees. The 4-wheel steering also allows the rover to swerve and curve, making arching turns.

The design of the suspension system for the wheels is based on heritage from the "rocker-bogie" system on the Pathfinder and Mars Exploration Rover missions. The suspension system is how the wheels are connected to and interact with the rover body. The term "bogie" comes from old railroad systems. A bogie is a train undercarriage with six wheels that can swivel to curve along a track. The term "rocker" comes from the design of the differential, which keeps the rover body balanced, enabling it to "rock" up or down depending on the various positions of the multiple wheels. Of most importance when creating a suspension system is how to prevent the rover from suddenly and dramatically changing positions while cruising over rocky terrain. If one side of the rover were to travel over a rock, the rover body would go out of balance without a "differential" or "rocker," which helps balance the angle the rover is in at any given time. When one side of the rover goes up, the differential or rocker in the rover suspension system automatically makes the other side go down to even out the weight load on the six wheels. This system causes the rover body to go through only half of the range of motion that the "legs" and wheels could potentially experience without a "rocker-bogie" suspension system.

The rover is designed to withstand a tilt of 45 degrees in any direction without overturning. However, the rover is programmed through its "fault protection limits" in its hazard avoidance software to avoid exceeding tilts of 30 degrees during its traverses.

The rover rocker-bogie design allows the rover to go over obstacles (such as rocks) or through holes that are more than a wheel diameter (50 centimeters or about 20 inches) in size. Each wheel also has cleats, providing grip for climbing in soft sand and scrambling over rocks.

The Rover's Energy

The rover requires power to operate. Without power, it cannot move, use its science instruments, or communicate with Earth. The Mars Science Laboratory rover carries a radioisotope power system that generates electricity from the heat of plutonium's radioactive decay. This power source gives the mission an operating lifespan on Mars' surface of at least a full Martian year (687 Earth days) or more while also providing significantly greater mobility and operational flexibility, enhanced science payload capability, and exploration of a much larger range of latitudes and altitudes than was possible on previous missions to Mars.

The Rover's Communications

Curiosity has three antennas that serve as both its "voice" and its "ears." They are located on the rover equipment deck (its "back"). Having multiple antennas provides back-up options just in case they are needed.

Most often, Curiosity will likely send radio waves through its ultra-high frequency (UHF) antenna (about 400 Megahertz) to communicate with Earth through NASA's Mars Odyssey and Mars Reconnaissance Orbiters. Because the rover's and orbiters' antennas are close-range, they act a little like walky-talkies compared to the long range of the low-gain and high-gain antennas. Using orbiters to relay messages is beneficial because they are closer to the rover than the Deep Space Network (DSN) antennas on Earth and they have Earth in their field of view for much longer time periods than the rover does on the ground. That allows them to send more data back to Earth at faster rates. Mars Reconnaissance Orbiter will likely relay most of the data between the rover and Earth.

Curiosity will likely use its high-gain antenna to receive commands for the mission team back on Earth. The high-gain antenna can send a "beam" of information in a specific direction, and it is steerable, so the antenna can move to point itself directly to any antenna on Earth. The benefit of having a steerable antenna is that the entire rover doesn't necessarily have to change positions to talk to Earth. Like turning your neck to talk to someone beside you rather than turning your entire body, the rover can save energy by moving only the antenna.

Curiosity will likely use its low-gain antenna primarily for receiving signals. This antenna can send and receive information in every direction; that is, it is "omni-directional." The antenna transmits radio waves at a low rate to the Deep Space Network antennas on Earth.

Major parts

Minor parts are used to go into more details.

Specific and Precise Title

The title of your technical description should clearly identify the purpose of the document. For example,

> Description of the Mars Curiosity Rover
>
> Specifications for the Intel® Xeon Phi™ Coprocessor
>
> How Does a Fuel Cell Work?
>
> Lung Cancer: Profile of a Killer

Your title should clearly distinguish your document as a technical description.

Introduction with an Overall Description

Typically, the introduction will set a framework or context by including some or all of the following features:

DEFINITION OF SUBJECT   A sentence definition of your subject includes three parts: the *term*, the *class* in which the subject belongs, and the *characteristics* that distinguish the subject from the other members in its class.

> The International Space Station is a multinational research facility that houses six state-of-the-art laboratories in orbit.
>
> Hodgkin's disease is a type of cancer that starts in the lymph nodes and other organs that are the body's system for making blood and protecting against germs.

The definition of the subject should appear early in the introduction, preferably in the first sentence. The description of "Solar and Lunar Eclipses" in Figure 6.5 shows how definitions are used to lead off descriptions of both kinds of major eclipses: solar eclipse and lunar eclipse.

PURPOSE STATEMENT   Directly or indirectly state that you are describing something.

> This description of the International Space Station will explain its major features, highlighting its research capabilities.
>
> In this article, we will try to demystify Hodgkin's disease, so you can better understand its diagnosis and treatment.

MAIN POINT   Give your readers an overall claim that your description will support or prove.

> Building the International Space Station is an incredible engineering feat that has challenged the best scientists and engineers from many nations.
>
> To fight Hodgkin's disease, you first need to understand it.

Link

For more information on writing definitions, see the Microgenre on page 144.

Figure 6.5: These technical descriptions of solar and lunar eclipses allow readers to use comparison to learn about both types.

SOLAR AND LUNAR ECLIPSES

A sentence definition is used to define the subject.

A **solar eclipse** occurs when the Moon passes between the Sun and Earth, casting the Moon's shadow on Earth. A solar eclipse can only happen during a New Moon. The Moon's orbit is tilted 5 degrees to Earth's orbit around the Sun. Therefore a solar eclipse is a relatively rare phenomena and a **Total** or **Annular eclipse** even more rare.

Data is used to add specific detail to the description.

To understand the difference between a **total** and **annular eclipse** of the Sun, we must state that the Moon has an elliptical orbit around Earth. In fact, the Moon's distance from Earth varies from a minimum of 221,000 to a maximum of 252,000 miles. *Therefore the Moon's apparent size in our sky will vary by 13%.* When the Moon's orbit is toward its minimum distance from Earth, the Moon will appear *visually as a larger disk* than the Sun. If an eclipse occurs during this time, it will be a **total solar eclipse** because the Moon has totally obscured the Sun's disk, producing the beautiful solar corona ejecting outward from the Sun. One important element to remember though is that the Moon's shadow will obviously become narrower as it is cast from the Moon to Earth (in a shape of a cone with the wide end being at the Moon and the narrow end on Earth). Therefore the path of totality on Earth is narrow. It is also very short-lived as the Moon is moving quickly away from its perfect location of being situated between the Sun and Earth.

Variations of eclipses are described here.

An **annular solar eclipse** is different than Totality in that it occurs when the Moon is closer to its maximum distance from Earth in its orbit. If an eclipse happens during this situation, the Moon will appear *visually smaller* than the Sun and its shadow cast will not be long enough to reach Earth. What reaches Earth is the antumbral or "negative" shadow. If you are within the antumbral shadow, you will see a solar eclipse where a thin ring or annulus of bright sunlight surrounds the Moon. Therefore **annular solar eclipses** are still spectacular in that they are almost total, but the solar corona is not seen due to the brightness of the annulus. Like a **total** eclipse, the **annular solar eclipse** will have a narrow path on Earth with short duration, most often less than 10 minutes.

Source: National Weather Service Weather Forecast Office, NOAA , http://www.crh.noaa.gov/fsd/?n=suneclipse

DO NOT observe a solar eclipse with the naked eye. Serious eye damage can result. Use approved solar filters (camera film negatives do not count) or cut a pin hole in a shoe box and watch the Sun's light cast through the pin hole onto a smooth surface such as cardboard.

A sentence definition is used to define the subject.

A lunar eclipse occurs when the Sun casts Earth's shadow onto the Moon. For this to happen, the Earth must be physically between the Sun and Moon with all three bodies lying on the same plane of orbit. A lunar eclipse can only occur during a Full Moon and when the Moon passes through all or a portion of Earth's shadow.

The outer portion of the shadow cast from Earth is known as the *penumbral* shadow, which is an area where Earth obstructs only a part of the Sun's light from reaching the Moon. The *umbral* shadow is the "inner" shadow, which is the area where Earth blocks all direct sunlight from reaching the Moon. A **penumbral lunar eclipse** is subtle and very difficult to observe. A **partial lunar eclipse** is when a portion of the Moon passes through the Earth's umbral shadow. Finally, a **total lunar eclipse** is when the entire Moon passes into the Earth's umbral shadow. During a total lunar eclipse, the sequence of eclipses are penumbral, partial, total, partial and back to penumbral.

Technical jargon is defined when it is first used.

Variations of eclipses are described here.

Unlike solar eclipses, a **total lunar eclipse** lasts a few hours, with totality itself usually averaging anywhere from about 30 minutes to over an hour. This is due to the large relative size of Earth over the Moon (the Moon's diameter is only about 2150 miles), therefore casting a large umbral shadow on the Moon. In addition, lunar eclipses are more frequent than their solar counterparts. There are zero to three lunar eclipses per year (although possibly not all at the same location on Earth) where the Moon passes through at least a portion of the Earth's umbral shadow (producing a partial to total eclipse). As stated above in the solar eclipse explanation, the Moon's orbit is tilted 5 degrees from Earth's orbit. For an eclipse to occur, the Moon and Earth have to be on the same orbital plane with the Sun, so the Earth's shadow can be cast onto the Moon from the Sun. This is why lunar eclipses only occur on average one or two times a year instead of every month.

(continued)

Even though the Moon is immersed in the Earth's umbral shadow, indirect sunlight will still reach the Moon thus illuminating it slightly. This is because indirect sunlight reaches the Moon and also the Earth's atmosphere will bend a very small portion of sunlight onto the Moon's surface. Many times during lunar totality, the color of the Moon will take on a dark red hue or brown/orange color. As sunlight passes through Earth's atmosphere, the blue-light is scattered out. The amount of illumination of the Moon will vary depending on how much dust is in the Earth's atmosphere. The more dust present in the atmosphere, the less illuminated the Moon will be.

Lunar eclipses are totally safe to be viewed by the naked eye, through binoculars or a telescope.

Source: National Weather Service Weather Forecast Office, NOAA , http://www.crh.noaa.gov/fsd/?n=suneclipse

IMPORTANCE OF THE SUBJECT For readers who are unfamiliar with your subject, you might want to include a sentence or paragraph that stresses its importance.

> The ISS provides scientists and other researchers an excellent platform from which to study space.

> Hodgkin's disease is one of the most acute forms of cancer, and it needs to be aggressively treated.

OVERALL DESCRIPTION OF THE SUBJECT Descriptions sometimes offer an overall look at the item being described.

> From a distance, the International Space Station looks like a large collection of white tubes with two rectangular solar panels jutting out like ears from its side.

> Hodgkin's disease spreads through the lymphatic vessels to other lymph nodes. It enlarges the lymphatic tissue, often putting pressure on vital organs and other important parts of the body.

This overall description will help your readers visualize how the parts fit together as they read further.

LIST OF THE MAJOR FEATURES, FUNCTIONS, OR STAGES In many descriptions, especially longer descriptions, the introduction will list the major features, functions, or stages of the subject.

> The International Space Station includes five main features: modules, nodes, trusses, solar power arrays, and thermal radiators.

> Once Hodgkin's has been detected, doctors will usually (1) determine the stage of the cancer, (2) offer treatment options, and (3) make a plan for remission.

You can then use this list of features, functions, or stages to organize the body of your description.

Link

For more information on writing introductions, see Chapter 15, page 399.

Description by Features, Functions, or Stages

The body of your description will concentrate on describing your subject's features, functions, or stages. Address each major part separately, defining it and describing it in detail. Within your description of each major part, identify and describe the minor parts.

Definition of major part ⟶ **Modules** are pressurized cylinders of habitable space on board the Station. They may contain research facilities, living quarters, and any

Minor parts ⟶ vehicle operational systems and equipment the astronauts may need to access.

If necessary, each of these minor parts could then be described separately. In fact, you could extend your description endlessly, teasing out the smaller and smaller features of the subject.

Figure 6.6 shows a description of a subject by "stages in a process." In this description of a fuel cell, the author walks readers through the energy generation process, showing them step by step how the fuel cell works.

A Technical Description: Stages in a Process

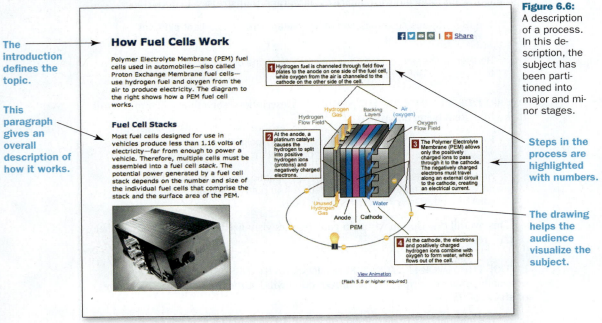

The introduction defines the topic.

This paragraph gives an overall description of how it works.

Steps in the process are highlighted with numbers.

The drawing helps the audience visualize the subject.

How Fuel Cells Work

Polymer Electrolyte Membrane (PEM) fuel cells used in automobiles—also called Proton Exchange Membrane fuel cells—use hydrogen fuel and oxygen from the air to produce electricity. The diagram to the right shows how a PEM fuel cell works.

Fuel Cell Stacks

Most fuel cells designed for use in vehicles produce less than 1.16 volts of electricity—far from enough to power a vehicle. Therefore, multiple cells must be assembled into a fuel cell *stack*. The potential power generated by a fuel cell stack depends on the number and size of the individual fuel cells that comprise the stack and the surface area of the PEM.

1. Hydrogen fuel is channeled through field flow plates to the anode on one side of the fuel cell, while oxygen from the air is channeled to the cathode on the other side of the cell.

2. At the anode, a platinum catalyst causes the hydrogen to split into positive hydrogen ions (protons) and negatively charged electrons.

3. The Polymer Electrolyte Membrane (PEM) allows only the positively charged ions to pass through it to the cathode. The negatively charged electrons must travel along an external circuit to the cathode, creating an electrical current.

4. At the cathode, the electrons and positively charged hydrogen ions combine with oxygen to form water, which flows out of the cell.

View Animation
(Flash 5.0 or higher required)

Source: U.S. Office of Transportation & Air Quality, http://www.fueleconomy.gov/feg/fcv_PEM.shtml

Description by Senses, Similes, Analogies, and Metaphors

The key to a successful technical description is the use of vivid details to bring your subject to life—to make it seem real. To add this level of detail, you might consider using some of the following techniques:

DESCRIPTION THROUGH SENSES   Consider each of your five senses separately, asking yourself, "How does it look?" "How does it sound?" "How does it smell?" "How does it feel?" and "How does it taste?"

> A visit to a Japanese car manufacturing plant can be an overwhelming experience. Workers in blue jumpsuits seem to be in constant motion. Cars of every color—green, yellow, red—are moving down the assembly line with workers hopping in and out. The smell of welding is in the air, and you can hear the whining hum of robots at work somewhere else in the plant.

SIMILES   A simile describes something by comparing it to something familiar to the readers ("A is like B").

> The mixed-waste landfill at Sandia Labs is like a football field with tons of toxic chemical and nuclear waste buried underneath it.

Similes are especially helpful for nonexpert readers, because they make the unfamiliar seem familiar.

Link

For more information on using similes, analogies, and metaphors, see Chapter 16, page 438.

ANALOGIES   Analogies are like similes, but they work on two parallel levels ("A is to B as C is to D").

> Circuits on a semiconductor wafer are like tiny interconnected roads crisscrossing a city's downtown.

METAPHORS   Metaphors are used to present an image of the subject by equating two different things ("A is B"). For example, consider these two common metaphors:

> The heart is a pump: it has valves and chambers, and it pushes fluids through a circulation system of pipes called arteries and veins.

> Ants live in colonies: a colony will have a queen, soldiers, workers, and slaves.

The use of senses, similes, analogies, and metaphors will make your description richer and more vivid. Readers who are unfamiliar with your subject will especially benefit from these techniques, because concepts they understand are being used to describe things that are new to them.

Conclusion

The conclusion of a technical description should be short and concise. Conclusions often describe one working cycle of the object, place, or process.

> The International Space Station is a center of activity. Researchers are conducting experiments. Astronomers study the stars. Astronauts are constantly working, sleeping, exercising, and relaxing. The solar power arrays pump energy into the station, keeping it powered up and running.

> Fighting Hodgkin's disease is difficult but not impossible. After detection and diagnosis, you and your doctors will work out treatment options and staging objectives. If treatment is successful, remission can continue indefinitely.

Some technical descriptions won't include a conclusion. They stop when the last item has been described.

Using Digital Photography in Descriptions

Digital cameras and scanners offer an easy way to insert visuals into your descriptions. These digitized pictures are inexpensive, alterable, and easily added to a text. Moreover, they work well in print and on-screen texts. Here are some photography basics to help you use a camera more effectively.

Resolution—Digital cameras will usually allow you to set the resolution at which you shoot pictures. If you are using your camera to put pictures on the web, you should use the 640 × 480 pixel setting. This setting will allow the picture to be downloaded quickly, because the file is smaller. If you want your picture to be a printed photograph, a minimum 1280 × 1024 pixel setting is probably needed. Online pictures are usually best saved in jpeg or png format, while print photos should be saved as tiff files.

ISO sensitivity—ISO is the amount of light the camera picks up. A high ISO number like 400 is good for shooting in dark locations or snapping something that is moving quickly. A low ISO number like 100 produces a higher-quality shot. You might leave your camera's ISO setting on "auto" unless you need to make adjustments.

Shutter speed—Some digital cameras will allow you to adjust your shutter speed. The shutter speed determines how much light is allowed into the camera when you push the button. Shutter speeds are usually listed from 1/1000 of a second to 1 second. Slower speeds (like 1 second) capture more detail but risk blurring the image, especially if your subject is moving. Faster speeds (like 1/1000 second) will not capture as much detail, but they are good for moving subjects.

Cropping—Once you have downloaded your picture to your computer, you can "crop" the picture to remove things you don't want. Do you want to remove an

Cropping a Digital Photograph

The toolbar offers a variety of options for altering the picture.

Figure A: Using the cropping tool, you can focus the photograph on the subject. Or, you can eliminate things or people you don't want in the picture.

The cropping tool lets you frame the part of the picture you want.

old roommate from your college pictures? You can use the cropping tool to cut him or her out of the picture. Most word processors have a cropping tool that you can use to carve away unwanted parts of your pictures (Figure A).

Retouching—One of the main advantages of digital photographs is the ease with which they can be touched up. Professional photographers make ample use of programs like Adobe Photoshop to manipulate their photographs. If the picture is too dark, you can lighten it up. If the people in the photo have "red-eye," you can remove that unwanted demonic stare.

One of the nice things about digital photography, including pictures taken with your phone, is that you can make any photograph look professional. With a digital camera, since the "bullets are free," as photographers say, you can experiment freely.

Step 4: Choose the Style, Design, and Medium

The style, design, and medium of your technical description or specification should reflect your readers' needs and context, as well as the places in which they will be using the document. Your style should be simple and straightforward, and the design should clarify and support the written text. The medium you choose should make your text easy to find and use.

Plain, Simple Style

Most technical descriptions are written in the plain style. Here are some suggestions for improving the style of your technical description:

Use simple words and limit the amount of jargon.

Focus on the details your readers need to know, and cut the extras.

Keep sentences short, within breathing length.

Remove any subjective qualifier words like "very," "easy," "hard," "amazing."

Use the senses to add color, texture, taste, sound, and smell.

In most cases, the best style for a technical description is an unobtrusive one. However, the style of your technical description will depend on the context in which it will be used. A technical description that will be part of your company's sales literature, for example, will usually be more persuasive than a technical specification kept in your company's files.

Page Layout That Fits the Context of Use

The page layout of your description or specification likely depends on your company's existing documentation or an established corporate design. If you are given a free hand to design the text, you might consider these design features:

Use a two-column or three-column format to leave room for images.

List any minor parts in bulleted lists.

Add a sidebar that draws attention to an important part or feature.

Use headings to clarify the organization.

Put measurements in a table.

Link

For more information on designing documents, see Chapter 17, page 447.

Use your imagination when you design the document. Figure 6.7, for example, shows how columns and tables can be used to pack in a solid amount of information while still presenting the information in an attractive way.

Graphics That Illustrate

Graphics are especially effective in technical descriptions. Pictures, illustrations, and diagrams help readers visualize your subject and its parts.

Using your computer, you can collect or create a wide range of graphics. Many free-use graphics are widely available on the Internet. (Reminder: Unless the site specifies that the graphics are free to reproduce, you must ask permission to use them.) If you cannot find graphics on the Internet, you can use a digital camera to take photographs that can be downloaded into your text. You can also use a scanner to digitize pictures, illustrations, and diagrams.

Here are some guidelines for using graphics in a technical description or specification:

Link

For more information on using graphics, see Chapter 18, page 477.

Use a title and figure number with each graphic, if possible.

Refer to the graphic by number in the written text.

Include captions that explain what the graphic shows.

Label specific features in the graphic.

Place the graphic on the page where it is referenced or soon afterward.

It is not always possible to include titles, numbers, and captions with your graphics. In these situations, graphics should appear immediately next to or immediately after the places in the text where they are discussed.

As we become more entrenched in this visual and global age, readers will expect technical descriptions to be more and more visual. For example, Scott McCloud, a well-known graphic artist, was brought in to illustrate the technical description of Google's Internet browser, Chrome (Figure 6.8). Technical descriptions will almost certainly become more visual and interactive in the future.

Medium That Allows Easy Access

You can choose from a variety of media to present and distribute your technical description or specification. Increasingly, these kinds of documents are being made available through websites, so readers can view them on the screen or download them as PDF files.

Consider the following as you are choosing the appropriate medium:

Paper or printable is often best for situations in which the text needs to be portable.

Websites are more accessible to a broader public because they are searchable.

PDF is a useful format for creating downloadable specifications.

PowerPoint, Keynote, and Prezi are good ways to demonstrate steps in a process.

Graphics are welcome in all media.

Today, you should assume that any technical descriptions or specifications will eventually need to be available electronically. So, make sure your document will work in a variety of media or can be easily converted from paper to electronic form.

A Specification

The title is clearly stated at the top of the text.

Photo shows product

The narrower column makes the text easier to scan.

Source: Solarworld

(continued)

Figure 6.7: The design of this specification allows readers to quickly gain access to the information they need. Notice how information is presented in easy-to-access blocks.

Company name and logo are framed with white space

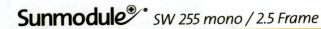

Sunmodule⊕ SW 255 mono / 2.5 Frame

PERFORMANCE UNDER STANDARD TEST CONDITIONS (STC)*

Maximum power	P_{max}	255 Wp
Open circuit voltage	V_{oc}	37.8 V
Maximum power point voltage	V_{mpp}	31.4 V
Short circuit current	I_{sc}	8.66 A
Maximum power point current	I_{mpp}	8.15 A

*STC: 1000 W/m², 25°C, AM 1.5

THERMAL CHARACTERISTICS

NOCT	48 °C
TC I_{sc}	0.004 %/K
TC V_{oc}	-0.30 %/K
TC P_{mpp}	-0.45 %/K
Operating temperature	-40°C to 85°C

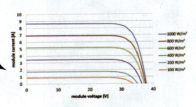

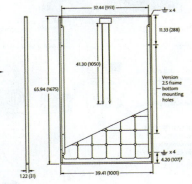

PERFORMANCE AT 800 W/m², NOCT, AM 1.5

Maximum power	P_{max}	184.1 Wp
Open circuit voltage	V_{oc}	34.0 V
Maximum power point voltage	V_{mpp}	28.3 V
Short circuit current	I_{sc}	6.99 A
Maximum power point current	I_{mpp}	6.52 A

Minor reduction in efficiency under partial load conditions at 25°C: at 200 W/m², 95% (+/-3%) of the STC efficiency (1000 W/m²) is achieved.

COMPONENT MATERIALS

Cells per module	60
Cell type	Mono crystalline
Cell dimensions	6.14 in x 6.14 in (156 mm x 156 mm)
Front	Tempered glass (EN 12150)
Frame	Clear anodized aluminum
Weight	46.7 lbs (21.2 kg)

SYSTEM INTEGRATION PARAMETERS

Maximum system voltage SC II		1000 V
Max. system voltage USA NEC		600 V
Maximum reverse current		16 A
Number of bypass diodes		3
UL Design Loads*	Two rail system	113 psf downward 64 psf upward
UL Design Loads*	Three rail system	170 psf downward 64 psf upward
IEC Design Loads*	Two rail system	113 psf downward 50 psf upward

* Please refer to the Sunmodule installation instructions for the details associated with these load cases.

ADDITIONAL DATA

Power sorting†	-0 Wp / +5 Wp
J-Box	IP65
Connector	MC4
Module efficiency	15.21 %
Fire rating (UL 790)	Class C

VERSION 2.5 FRAME
- Compatible with both "Top-Down" and "Bottom" mounting methods
- ↓Grounding Locations:
  - 4 corners of the frame
  - 4 locations along the length of the module in the extended flange†

1) Measuring tolerance traceable to TUV Rheinland: +/- 2% (TUV Power Controlled). All units provided are imperial. SI units provided in parentheses.

SolarWorld AG reserves the right to make specification changes without notice.

SW-01-6001US 03-2013

The layout balances the design features of the page.

This table lists the specifications of the product.

These annotations help readers understand the parts of the product.

Technical Descriptions Are Becoming More Visual

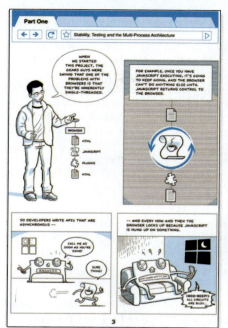

Figure 6.8: As our culture becomes more visual, even technical descriptions need to be as visual as possible. Scott McCloud drew these images for Google's Chrome browser.

Technical Definitions

In workplace documents, you need to provide clear and precise definitions of technical terms, especially in detailed documents like technical descriptions, patents, specifications, experiments, and field observations.

Technical definitions are used a variety of ways. In most cases, they are embedded in other, larger documents. They are usually written into the main text, and they sometimes appear in the margins. In larger technical documents, definitions of technical terms will often appear before the introduction, or a *glossary of technical terms* will be added as an appendix.

A basic definition, often called a *sentence definition*, has three parts: (1) the term being defined, (2) the category in which the term belongs, and (3) the distinguishing features that differentiate it from its category.

Category

An ion is an atom that has a negative or positive charge because it has more electrons or fewer electrons than usual.

Distinguishing characteristics

An *extended definition* starts with a sentence definition like this one and then expands on it in the following ways:

Word history and etymology. Use a dictionary to figure out where a technical term originated and how its meaning has evolved (e.g., "The word *ion,* which means 'going' in Greek, was coined by physicist Michael Faraday in 1834.")

Examples. Include examples of how the term is used in a specific field (e.g., "For example, when hydrogen chloride (HCl) is dissolved in water, it forms two ions, H^+ and Cl^-.")

Negation. Define your subject by explaining what it is *not* (e.g., "An ion is not a subatomic particle.")

Division into parts. Divide the subject into its major parts and define each of those parts separately (e.g., "An ion has protons, electrons, and neutrons. Protons are subatomic particles with a positive charge found in the nucleus, while electrons . . .").

Similarities and differences. Compare your subject to objects or places that are similar, highlighting their common characteristics and their differences (e.g., "An ion is an atom with a nucleus and electrons, except an ion does not have an equal number of protons and electrons like a stable atom.")

Analogy. Compare your subject to something completely different but with some similar qualities (e.g., "An ion is like an unattached, single person at a dance, searching for oppositely-charged ions to dance with.")

Graphics. Use a drawing, picture, diagram, or other kind of graphic to provide an image of your subject.

Write

Write your own technical definition. List five technical terms that are important to your field of study. Write a sentence definition for each of them. Then, choose one of these sentence definitions and write a 300-word extended definition of that term.

An extended
definition
starts with
a sentence
definition.
Then it uses a
variety of rhe-
torical tools
to expand
and sharpen
the meaning
of the term.

The Definition of Ionic Compounds

The technical
definition
starts out
with a
sentence
definition.

The word *ionic* refers to any compound between one or more cations and one or more anions. A cation is an ion that has fewer electrons than protons, which makes it positive. An anion is an ion that has more electrons than protons, which makes it negative. This makes an ionic compound neutral. When a metal with the tendency to lose electrons combines with a nonmetal with the tendency to gain electrons, one or more electrons transfer from the metal to the nonmetal. This creates positive and negative ions that are then attracted to each other. Such a bond between elements is an ionic bond.

The drawing
illustrates
the subject.

The sodium (Na) atom has an extra electron and the chlorine atom (Cl) is missing one. Together, they make an ionic compound.

How Many Types of Ionic Compounds Are There?

Comparison

Use of
examples

There are two types of ionic compounds. First, there are the ionic compounds that contain a metal with an invariant charge. In other words, it does not vary from compound to compound. A good example is sodium. Sodium has a 1+ charge in all of its compounds. Secondly are the ionic compounds that contain a metal with a charge that differs in various compounds. These metals can form more than one kind of cation. An example is iron. Iron has a charge 2+ in some compounds and a charge of 3+ in others.

What Is An Example of an Ionic Compound?

Division
into parts

Word
etymology

The classical example of an ionic compound is sodium chlorine (NaCl), popularly known as table salt. Salt results from a synthesis reaction between sodium and chlorine. In a synthesis reaction, two simpler substances combine to make a more complex substance. About 60 percent of salt is made of chlorine and 40 percent of sodium. The chemical formula of salt, NaCl indicates that the sodium and chlorine atoms are in a 1:1 ratio. The name for table salt, sodium chloride (NaCl), consists of the name of the cation, in this case the sodium, followed by the base name of the anion, in this case chlor, with the ending *-ide*. The two form an ionic compound. This is the standard format name of a salt.

Source: ChemAnswers, http://chem.answers.com/definitions/the-definition-of-ionic-compounds

- Technical descriptions and specifications are written to describe objects, places, phenomena, and processes. They are important documents in all technical workplaces.

- Basic features of a technical description or specification include a title, introduction, body, graphics, and conclusion.

- An object, place, or process can be partitioned according to its features, functions, or stages.

- Technical descriptions and specifications tend to be written in the "plain style," meaning that words and sentences are simple, direct, and concise.

- To add a visual element to the description, use the senses, similes, analogies, and metaphors to describe the subject.

- Graphics are crucial in technical descriptions, because the purpose of the description is to allow the readers to "see" the object, place, or process. You can use pictures, illustrations, and diagrams to add graphics to your text.

- The design of the description will depend on how it is being used. In sales literature, the design will probably be colorful or ornate. A specification for the company's files, on the other hand, might be rather plainly designed.

Individual or Team Projects

1. Find a technical description on the Internet or in your workplace or home. First, determine the rhetorical situation (subject, purpose, readers, context) for which the description was written. Then, study its content, organization, style, and design. Write a two-page memo to your instructor in which you offer a critique of the description. What do you find effective about the description? What could be improved?

2. Your company sells a variety of products, listed below. Choose one of these items and write a one-page technical description. Your description should be aimed at a potential customer who might purchase one of these products:

plasma-screen television	washing machine
DVD player	baby stroller
MP3 player	toaster
bicycle	coffeemaker
clock radio	video camera
telescope	

3. Find a common process that you can describe. Then, describe that process, walking your readers through its stages. In your description, you should define any jargon or technical terms that may be unfamiliar to your readers.

Collaborative Project

Your group has been assigned to describe a variety of renewable energy sources that might be used in your state. These energy sources could include solar, wind, geothermal, biomass generators, and fuel cells. While keeping the energy needs and limitations of your region in mind, offer a brief description of each of these renewable energy sources, showing how it works, its advantages, and its disadvantages.

In a report to your state's energy commissioner, describe these energy sources and discuss whether you think they offer possible alternatives to nonrenewable energy sources.

Revision Challenge

Figure B shows a fact sheet from the Occupational Safety and Health Administration (OSHA). The description of flooding and flooding cleanup in this document is fine for an office environment. However, the size of the document makes it not particularly portable into areas that have been flooded.

Revise and redesign this document so that it fits on a 3 × 5 inch card that will be given out to first responders. This "Quickcard" will be easier to carry, and it can be stored in pockets and small storage areas. It could also be laminated, so it would hold up in severe conditions, like those found in flood zones.

Using the principles discussed in this chapter, analyze the content, organization, style, and design of this document. Then, revise this fact sheet so that it would be suitable for the kinds of emergency situations in which it would be used.

Visit MyWritingLab for a Post-test and more technical writing resources.

OSHA **Fact**Sheet

Flood Cleanup

Flooding can cause the disruption of water purification and sewage disposal systems, overflowing of toxic waste sites, and dislodgement of chemicals previously stored above ground. Although most floods do not cause serious outbreaks of infectious disease or chemical poisonings, they can cause sickness in workers and others who come in contact with contaminated floodwater. In addition, flooded areas may contain electrical or fire hazards connected with downed power lines.

Floodwater

Floodwater often contains infectious organisms, including intestinal bacteria such as E. coli, Salmonella, and Shigella; Hepatitis A Virus; and agents of typhoid, paratyphoid and tetanus. The signs and symptoms experienced by the victims of waterborne microorganisms are similar, even though they are caused by different pathogens. These symptoms include nausea, vomiting, diarrhea, abdominal cramps, muscle aches, and fever. Most cases of sickness associated with flood conditions are brought about by ingesting contaminated food or water. Tetanus, however, can be acquired from contaminated soil or water entering broken areas of the skin, such as cuts, abrasions, or puncture wounds. Tetanus is an infectious disease that affects the nervous system and causes severe muscle spasms, known as lockjaw. The symptoms may appear weeks after exposure and may begin as a headache, but later develop into difficulty swallowing or opening the jaw.

Floodwaters also may be contaminated by agricultural or industrial chemicals or by hazardous agents present at flooded hazardous waste sites. Flood cleanup crew members who must work near flooded industrial sites also may be exposed to chemically contaminated floodwater. Although different chemicals cause different health effects, the signs and symptoms most frequently associated with chemical poisoning are headaches, skin rashes, dizziness, nausea, excitability, weakness, and fatigue.

Pools of standing or stagnant water become breeding grounds for mosquitoes, increasing the risk of encephalitis, West Nile virus or other mosquito-borne diseases. The presence of wild animals in populated areas increases the risk of diseases caused by animal bites (e.g., rabies) as well as diseases carried by fleas and ticks.

Protect Yourself

After a major flood, it is often difficult to maintain good hygiene during cleanup operations. To avoid waterborne disease, it is important to wash your hands with soap and clean, running water, especially before work breaks, meal breaks, and at the end of the work shift. Workers should assume that any water in flooded or surrounding areas is not safe unless the local or state authorities have specifically declared it to be safe. If no safe water supply is available for washing, use bottled water, water that has been boiled for at least 10 minutes or chemically disinfected water. (To disinfect water, use 5 drops of liquid household bleach to each gallon of water and let it sit for at least 30 minutes for disinfection to be completed.) Water storage containers should be rinsed periodically with a household bleach solution.

If water is suspected of being contaminated with hazardous chemicals, cleanup workers may need to wear special chemical resistant outer clothing and protective goggles. Before entering a contaminated area that has been flooded, you should don plastic or rubber gloves, boots, and other protective clothing needed to avoid contact with floodwater.

Source: Occupational Safety and Health Administration www.osha.gov/OshDoc/data_Hurricane_Facts/floodcleanup.pdf.

Figure B: This fact sheet is somewhat long-winded and not easy to access in an emergency situation. Try turning it into a "Quickcard" that fits on a 3 × 5 inch card. You can use both sides of the card.

Decrease the risk of mosquito and other insect bites by wearing long-sleeved shirts, long pants, and by using insect repellants. Wash your hands with soap and water that has been boiled or disinfected before preparing or eating foods, after using the bathroom, after participating in flood cleanup activities, and after handling articles contaminated by floodwater. In addition, children should not be allowed to play in floodwater or with toys that have been in contact with floodwater. Toys should be disinfected.

What to Do If Symptoms Develop

If a cleanup worker experiences any of the signs or symptoms listed above, appropriate first aid treatment and medical advice should be sought. If the skin is broken, particularly with a puncture wound or a wound that comes into contact with potentially contaminated material, a tetanus vaccination may be needed if it has been five years or more since the individual's last tetanus shot.

Tips to Remember

- Before working in flooded areas, be sure that your tetanus shot is current (given within the last 10 years). Wounds that are associated with a flood should be evaluated for risk; a physician may recommend a tetanus immunization.

- Consider all water unsafe until local authorities announce that the public water supply is safe.

- Do not use contaminated water to wash and prepare food, brush your teeth, wash dishes, or make ice.

- Keep an adequate supply of safe water available for washing and potable water for drinking.

- Be alert for chemically contaminated floodwater at industrial sites.

- Use extreme caution with potential chemical and electric hazards, which have great potential for fires and explosions. Floods have the strength to move and/or bury hazardous waste and chemical containers far from their normal storage places, creating a risk for those who come into contact with them. Any chemical hazards, such as a propane tank, should be handled by the fire department or police.

- If the safety of a food or beverage is questionable, throw it out.

- Seek immediate medical care for all animal bites.

This is one in a series of informational fact sheets highlighting OSHA programs, policies or standards. It does not impose any new compliance requirements. For a comprehensive list of compliance requirements of OSHA standards or regulations, refer to Title 29 of the Code of Federal Regulations. This information will be made available to sensory impaired individuals upon request. The voice phone is (202) 693-1999; teletypewriter (TTY) number: (877) 889-5627.

For more complete information:

OSHA Occupational Safety and Health Administration

U.S. Department of Labor
www.osha.gov
(800) 321-OSHA

DSTM 9/2005

In the Vapor

Linda Galhardy, a computer engineer at Gink, rushed to finish her technical description of FlashTime, a new handheld video game console her team had developed. She and her team had suffered through two long months of 18-hour days with no weekends off in order to get to this point. They were exhausted.

But, they succeeded in developing a prototype of the console, and they had created a couple of innovative games. The purpose of Linda's technical description was to update Gink's management on the project and persuade them to begin planning for production. If everything worked out, the game console could be released in October.

This mad rush all started when Gink's management read on gaming blogs that CrisMark, Gink's main competitor, was only six months away from developing a new handheld gaming device that would revolutionize the market. According to the bloggers, CrisMark's console had a small screen, much like a PlayStation Vita, but it also allowed the gamer to project video onto any blank wall. According to reports, CrisMark had figured out a way to keep that video from shaking or turning with the controller. If true, this handheld game would revolutionize the market and take away a significant chunk of Gink's marketshare.

Fortunately, Gink had some smart engineers like Linda, and it had a reputation for more reliable and innovative consoles and games. Consumers tempted to buy CrisMark's console would probably be willing to wait a couple of extra months for a similar console from Gink. Gink's engineers and designers would have time to catch up.

Gink's management was impressed with Linda's presentation, including her technical description and the prototype. The marketing division was brought in immediately to begin working up the advertising and public relations campaign. Linda was congratulated and told to wait for management's answer.

A week later, Linda's supervisor, Thomas Hale, sent her a text message with a link to a popular consumer electronics blog. On the front page of the blog was a picture of Linda's prototype and a story taken from "leaked" sources. The story was surprisingly accurate.

She was furious, but she didn't know whom to blame. Did the marketing department leak the information? A week later, several consumer electronics blogs reported that CrisMark was abandoning its attempt to develop their revolutionary new handheld console. Anonymous sources said CrisMark abandoned the project when they heard Gink was ahead of them in developing the new product.

Soon afterward, Linda's boss, Thomas, called her into his office and told her the FlashTime project was being "slow-tracked."

"You mean we're being killed slowly," Linda said angrily.

"Well," replied Thomas, "we need to make it look like we weren't just floating vaporware. So, you and a couple designers are going to stay on the project part-time. A year from now, we'll quietly pull the plug."

"That's garbage. We can do this, Thomas!" Linda said loudly. "We can make this console!"

Thomas said in a reassuring voice, "This thing was never going to get made anyway, Linda. Management just wanted to get something into the blogs to head off CrisMark. It worked. As soon as our 'leaked' story hit the blogs, CrisMark's stock dropped like a rock. They had to cancel the project to concentrate on their current products. Management just wanted to scare them off."

Linda couldn't believe what she was hearing. "So we were just making up some vaporware to scare off CrisMark?"

Thomas nodded. "Yeah, and it worked. Congratulations."

If you were Linda, what would you do at this point? Would you play along? Would you try to convince management to continue the project? Would you leak the truth to the blogs? Would you strike out on your own?

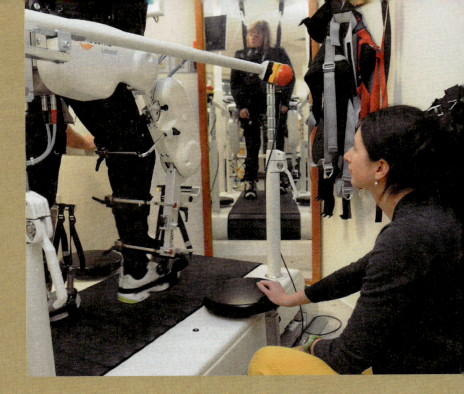

CHAPTER 7

Instructions and Documentation

Types of Technical Documentation
153

Step 1: Make a Plan and Do
Research 153

Step 2: Organize and Draft Your
Documentation 167

Help: On-Screen Documentation
183

Step 3: Choose the Style, Design,
and Medium 184

Working with Transcultural
Documentation 188

Microgenre: Emergency
Instructions 189

What You Need to Know 191

Exercises and Projects 192

Case Study: Purified Junk 194

In this chapter, you will learn:

- The importance of instructions, specifications, and procedures in the technical workplace.

- The basic features of instructions, specifications, and procedures.

- How to plan and research instructions, specifications, and procedures.

- How to organize and draft instructions, specifications, and procedures.

- How style and design can be used to highlight and reinforce written text.

- About the needs of transcultural readers.

More than likely, you have read and used countless sets of instructions in your lifetime. Instructions are packaged with the products we buy, such as smartphones, cameras, and televisions. In the technical workplace, documentation helps people complete simple and complex tasks, such as downloading software, building an airplane engine, drawing blood from a patient, and assembling a computer motherboard.

Types of Technical Documentation

Instructions and other kinds of documentation are among the least noticed but most important documents in the technical workplace. Documentation tends to fall into three categories:

> **Instructions**—Instructions describe how to perform a specific task. They typically describe how to assemble a product or do something step by step.
>
> **Specifications**—Engineers and technicians write specifications (often called "specs") to describe in exact detail how a product is assembled or how a routine process is completed.
>
> **Procedures/Protocols**—Procedures and protocols are written to ensure consistency and quality in a workplace. In hospitals, for example, doctors and nurses are often asked to write procedures that describe how to handle emergency situations or treat a specific injury or illness. Similarly, scientists will use protocols to ensure consistent methods in the laboratory.

To avoid confusion in this chapter, the word *documentation* will be used as a general term to mean instructions, procedures, and specifications. When the chapter discusses issues that are specific to instructions, procedures, or specifications, those terms will be used.

Documentation can take on many different forms, depending on when and where it will be used. For example, Figure 7.1 shows a humorous set of instructions that was created for the Centers for Disease Control and Prevention.

Figure 7.2 shows an example of a protocol used at a hospital. This protocol works like most sets of instructions. A numbered list of steps explains what to do if someone is experiencing chest pain. The protocol includes helpful visuals, like the gray boxes and pictures of a doctor, to signal situations where a doctor should be called.

Figure 7.3, on pages 161–164, is a testing specification used by civil engineers. The numbers and indentation help engineers follow the procedure consistently.

Link

For more information on writing descriptions, go to Chapter 6, page 120.

Step 1: Make a Plan and Do Research

When you are asked to write documentation for a product or procedure, you should first consider the situations in which it might be used. You also need to research the process you are describing so that you fully understand it and can describe it in detail.

Instructions and Documentation

These models illustrate a couple of common organizational patterns for instructions, procedures, and specifications. You should adjust these patterns to fit the process you are describing.

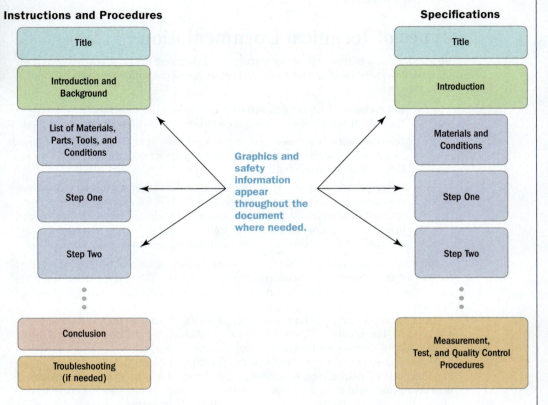

Instructions and Procedures

- Title
- Introduction and Background
- List of Materials, Parts, Tools, and Conditions
- Step One
- Step Two
- Conclusion
- Troubleshooting (if needed)

Graphics and safety information appear throughout the document where needed.

Specifications

- Title
- Introduction
- Materials and Conditions
- Step One
- Step Two
- Measurement, Test, and Quality Control Procedures

Basic Features

Documentation tends to follow a consistent step-by-step pattern, whether you are describing how to make coffee or how to assemble an automobile engine. The pattern shown here should be changed to fit the needs of your subject, purpose, readers, and context of use.

Here are the basic features in most forms of documentation:

- **Title** that is specific to the subject being described
- **Introduction** with background information on the subject
- **Parts list** that identifies materials, tools, and conditions needed
- **Safety information** that helps users avoid injury or product damage
- **Steps** that are sequentially ordered
- **Graphics** that illustrate the steps
- **Conclusion** that signals the completion of the task

Instructions, procedures, and specifications are important, though often unnoticed, documents.

Planning

When planning, first gain a thorough grasp of your subject, your readers, and their needs. A good way to start is to answer the Five-W and How Questions:

Who might use this documentation?

Why is this documentation needed?

What should the documentation include?

Where will the documentation be used?

When will the documentation be used?

How will this documentation be used?

Once you have answered these questions, you are ready to define the rhetorical situation that will shape how you write the text.

SUBJECT   Give yourself time to use the product or follow the process. What is it, and what does it do? Are there any unexpected dangers or difficulties?

PURPOSE   Take a moment to consider and compose your purpose statement, limiting yourself to one sentence. Some key verbs for the purpose statement might include the following:

to instruct	*to show*	*to illustrate*	*to explain*	*to teach*
to guide	*to lead*	*to direct*	*to train*	*to tutor*

Here are a few purpose statements that might be used in a set of instructions:

The purpose of these instructions is to show you how to use your new QuickTake i700 digital video camera.

These procedures will demonstrate the suturing required to complete and close up a knee operation.

These specifications illustrate the proper use of the Series 3000 Router to trim printed circuit boards.

Link

For more information on defining a document's purpose, see Chapter 1, page 5.

Figure 7.1: In this humorous set of instructions, the author includes an introduction, body, and conclusion. Pay attention to how he uses these humorous instructions to introduce the readers to the more serious topic of emergency preparedness.

Preparedness 101: Zombie Apocalypse

Ali S. Kahn, Centers for Disease Control and Prevention

The introduction explains the purpose and stresses the importance of the subject.

There are all kinds of emergencies out there that we can prepare for. Take a zombie apocalypse for example. That's right, I said z-o-m-b-i-e a-p-o-c-a-l-y-p-s-e. You may laugh now, but when it happens you'll be happy you read this, and hey, maybe you'll even learn a thing or two about how to prepare for a *real* emergency.

Better Safe than Sorry

So what do you need to do before zombies . . . or hurricanes or pandemics for example, actually happen? First of all, you should have an emergency kit in your house. This includes things like water, food, and other supplies to get you through the first couple of days before you can locate a zombie-free refugee camp (or in the event of a natural disaster, it will buy you some time until you are able to make your way to an evacuation shelter or utility lines are restored). Below are a few items you should include in your kit; for a full list visit the CDC Emergency page.

A list of needed supplies is put up front.

- **Water** (1 gallon per person per day)
- **Food** (stock up on non-perishable items that you eat regularly)
- **Medications** (this includes prescription and non-prescription meds)
- **Tools and Supplies** (utility knife, duct tape, battery powered radio, etc.)
- **Sanitation and Hygiene** (household bleach, soap, towels, etc.)
- **Clothing and Bedding** (a change of clothes for each family member and blankets)
- **Important documents** (copies of your driver's license, passport, and birth certificate to name a few)
- **First Aid supplies** (although you're a goner if a zombie bites you, you can use these supplies to treat basic cuts and lacerations that you might get during a tornado or hurricane)

Once you've made your emergency kit, you should sit down with your family and come up with an **emergency plan**. This includes where you would go and who you would call if zombies started appearing outside your door step. You can also implement this plan if there is a flood, earthquake, or other emergency.

Source: Centers for Disease Control and Prevention

1. **Identify the types of emergencies that are possible in your area.** Besides a zombie apocalypse, this may include floods, tornadoes, or earthquakes. If you are unsure contact your local Red Cross chapter for more information.

2. **Pick a meeting place for your family to regroup in case zombies invade your home … or your town evacuates because of a hurricane.** Pick one place right outside your home for sudden emergencies and one place outside of your neighborhood in case you are unable to return home right away.

3. **Identify your emergency contacts.** Make a list of local contacts like the police, fire department, and your local zombie response team. Also identify an out-of-state contact that you can call during an emergency to let the rest of your family know you are ok.

4. **Plan your evacuation route.** When zombies are hungry they won't stop until they get food (i.e., brains), which means you need to get out of town fast! Plan where you would go and multiple routes you would take ahead of time so that the flesh eaters don't have a chance! This is also helpful when natural disasters strike and you have to take shelter fast.

Never Fear – CDC is Ready

If zombies did start roaming the streets, CDC would conduct an investigation much like any other disease outbreak. CDC would provide technical assistance to cities, states, or international partners dealing with a zombie infestation. This assistance might include consultation, lab testing and analysis, patient management and care, tracking of contacts, and infection control (including isolation and quarantine). It's likely that an investigation of this scenario would seek to accomplish several goals: determine the cause of the illness, the source of the infection/virus/toxin, learn how it is transmitted and how readily it is spread, how to break the cycle of transmission and thus prevent further cases, and how patients can best be treated. Not only would scientists be working to identify the cause and cure of the zombie outbreak, but CDC and other federal agencies would send medical teams and first responders to help those in affected areas (I will be volunteering the young nameless disease detectives for the field work).

To learn more about what CDC does to prepare for and respond to emergencies of all kinds, visit: http://emergency.cdc.gov/cdc/orgs_progs.asp

To learn more about how you can prepare for and stay safe during an emergency visit: http://emergency.cdc.gov/

Numbered list highlights steps in procedure.

This part explains how the process works when it is in action.

The conclusion offers additional information if needed.

A Procedure

Header shows identification number of procedure.

Title of emergency procedure

Brief introduction defines medical condition.

Steps of the procedure

Gray areas signal situations in which a doctor needs to be involved.

Figure 7.2: Procedures like this one are used for training. They also standardize care.

EMT-Paramedic Treatment Protocol
4202

Chest Pain/Discomfort Acute Coronary Syndrome (ACS)	Page 1 of 3

WEST VIRGINIA EMS SYSTEM

A. Indications for this protocol include one or more of the following:

  1. Male over 25 years of age or female over 35 years of age, complaining of substernal chest pain, pressure or discomfort unrelated to an injury.

  2. History of previous ACS/AMI with recurrence of "similar" symptoms.

  3. Any patient with a history of cardiac problems who experiences lightheadedness or syncope.

  4. Patients of any age with suspected cocaine abuse and chest pain.

B. Perform **MAMP (4201).**

C. Obtain 12 lead ECG, if available and causes no delay in treatment or transport.

D. If patient has no history of allergy to aspirin **and** has no signs of active bleeding (i.e., bleeding gums, bloody or tarry stools, etc.), then administer 4 (four) 81 mg chewable aspirin orally (324 mg total). Note: May be administered prior to establishment of IV access.

E. If blood pressure > 90 systolic and patient has **not** taken *Viagra* or *Levitra* within last 24 hours (or *Cialis* within the last 48 hours):

  1. Administer nitroglycerine 0.4 mg (1/150 gr) SL. Note: May be administered prior to establishment of IV access.

  2. Repeat every 3-5 minutes until pain is relieved.

  3. If blood pressure falls below 90 systolic or decreases more than 30 mm Hg below patient's normal baseline blood pressure, then discontinue dosing and **contact MCP** to discuss further treatment.

West Virginia Office of Emergency Medical Services - State ALS Protocols
4602 Stroke.doc   Finalized 12/1/01, Revised 9/11/07

Source: West Virginia EMS System, 2007.

Header is retained from first page.

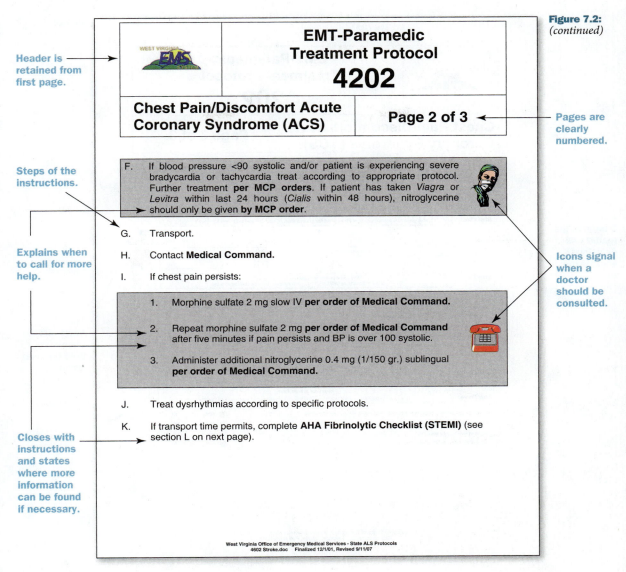

EMT-Paramedic
Treatment Protocol
4202

Chest Pain/Discomfort Acute
Coronary Syndrome (ACS)

Page 2 of 3

Pages are clearly numbered.

Steps of the instructions.

F.   If blood pressure <90 systolic and/or patient is experiencing severe bradycardia or tachycardia treat according to appropriate protocol. Further treatment **per MCP orders**. If patient has taken *Viagra* or *Levitra* within last 24 hours (*Cialis* within 48 hours), nitroglycerine should only be given **by MCP order**.

G.   Transport.

Explains when to call for more help.

H.   Contact **Medical Command.**

I.   If chest pain persists:

1.   Morphine sulfate 2 mg slow IV **per order of Medical Command.**

2.   Repeat morphine sulfate 2 mg **per order of Medical Command** after five minutes if pain persists and BP is over 100 systolic.

3.   Administer additional nitroglycerine 0.4 mg (1/150 gr.) sublingual **per order of Medical Command.**

Icons signal when a doctor should be consulted.

J.   Treat dysrhythmias according to specific protocols.

K.   If transport time permits, complete **AHA Fibrinolytic Checklist (STEMI)** (see section L on next page).

Closes with instructions and states where more information can be found if necessary.

West Virginia Office of Emergency Medical Services - State ALS Protocols
4602 Stroke.doc   Finalized 12/1/01, Revised 9/11/07

(continued)

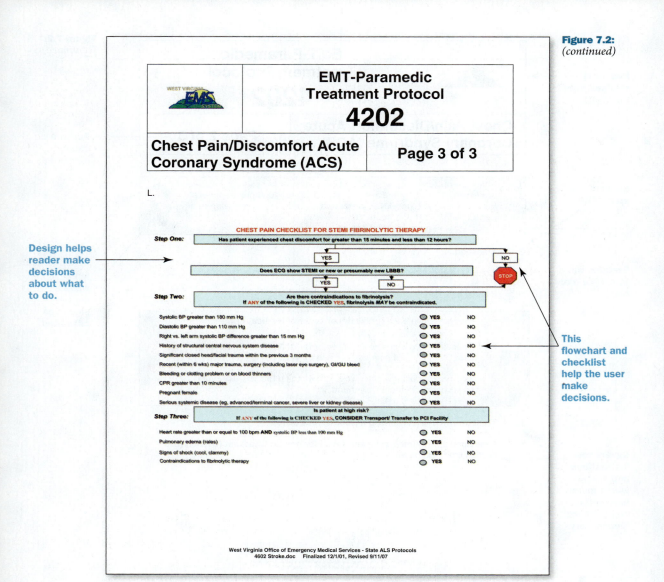

EMT-Paramedic
Treatment Protocol
4202

Chest Pain/Discomfort Acute
Coronary Syndrome (ACS)

Page 3 of 3

L.

Design helps reader make decisions about what to do.

This flowchart and checklist help the user make decisions.

CHEST PAIN CHECKLIST FOR STEMI FIBRINOLYTIC THERAPY

Step One: Has patient experienced chest discomfort for greater than 15 minutes and less than 12 hours?

YES — Does ECG show STEMI or new or presumably new LBBB?

NO — STOP

YES / NO

Step Two: Are there contraindications to fibrinolysis?
If ANY of the following is CHECKED YES, fibrinolysis MAY be contraindicated.

	YES	NO
Systolic BP greater than 180 mm Hg	YES	NO
Diastolic BP greater than 110 mm Hg	YES	NO
Right vs. left arm systolic BP difference greater than 15 mm Hg	YES	NO
History of structural central nervous system disease	YES	NO
Significant closed head/facial trauma within the previous 3 months	YES	NO
Recent (within 6 wks) major trauma, surgery (including laser eye surgery), GI/GU bleed	YES	NO
Bleeding or clotting problem or on blood thinners	YES	NO
CPR greater than 10 minutes	YES	NO
Pregnant female	YES	NO
Serious systemic disease (eg, advanced/terminal cancer, severe liver or kidney disease)	YES	NO

Step Three: Is patient at high risk?
If ANY of the following is CHECKED YES, CONSIDER Transport/ Transfer to PCI Facility

	YES	NO
Heart rate greater than or equal to 100 bpm AND systolic BP less than 100 mm Hg	YES	NO
Pulmonary edema (rales)	YES	NO
Signs of shock (cool, clammy)	YES	NO
Contraindications to fibrinolytic therapy	YES	NO

West Virginia Office of Emergency Medical Services - State ALS Protocols
4602 Stroke.doc   Finalized 12/1/01, Revised 9/11/07

A Specification

Figure 7.3:
This speci-
fication ex-
plains how a
civil engineer
would con-
duct a mate-
rials test.

INDIANA DEPARTMENT OF TRANSPORTATION
OFFICE OF MATERIALS MANAGEMENT

DRY FLOW TESTING
OF
FLOWABLE BACKFILL MATERIALS
ITM No. 217-07T

1.0   SCOPE.

Introduction
explains the
purpose of the
specifications.

1.1   This test method covers the procedure for the determination of the flow time of dry flowable backfill materials for the purpose of verifying changes in sand sources for an approved Flowable Backfill Mix Design (FBMD).

1.2   The values stated in either acceptable English or SI metric units are to be regarded separately as standard, as appropriate for a specification with which this ITM is used. Within the text, SI metric units are shown in parentheses. The values stated in each system may not be exact equivalents; therefore, each system shall be used independently of the other, without combining values in any way.

1.3   This ITM may involve hazardous materials, operations, and equipment. This ITM may not address all of the safety problems associated with the use of the test method. The user of the ITM is responsible for establishing appropriate safety and health practices and determining the applicability of regulatory limitations prior to use.

2.0   REFERENCES.

2.1   AASHTO Standards.

M 231   Weighing Devices Used in the Testing of Materials

T 304   Uncompacted Void Content of Fine Aggregate

T 248   Reducing Samples of Aggregate to Testing Size

3.0   TERMINOLOGY.   Definitions for terms and abbreviations shall be in accordance with the Department's Standard Specifications, Section 101, except as follows.

3.1   Dry flow time. The time to for a specified sample size of dry flowable materials to flow through a specified funnel

Source: Indiana Department of Transportation, http://www.in.gov/indot/div/M&T/itm/pubs/ 217_testing.pdf.

(continued)

4.0   SIGNIFICANCE AND USE.

4.1   This ITM is used to determine the time of dry flow of loose uncompacted flowable backfill material through a flow cone. The flowable backfill material includes sand or sand and fly ash mixture. The test result is done to ensure that an alternate sand shall have the same flow characteristic as the sand in the approved FBMD.

4.2   The dry flow cone test characterizes the state of flow of dry materials on any sand of known grading that may provide information about the sand or sand and fly ash mixture angularity, spherical shape, and surface texture.

4.3   Other test procedures or test methods exist for various flow cones with different dimensions and cone tip forms and sizes that may or may not have a correlation with the AASHTO T 304 flow cone.

5.0   APPARATUS.

5.1   Cylindrical measure, in accordance with AASHTO T 304, except the nominal 100-mL cylindrical measure is replaced by a one quart glass jar

The testing apparatus is clearly described. →

5.2   Metal spatula, with a blade approximately 4 in. (100 mm) long, and at least ¾ in. (20 mm) wide, with straight edges. The end shall be cut at a right angle to the edges. (The straight edge of the spatula blade is used to strike off the fine aggregate.)

This "nested" numbering system is commonly used with specifications for easy reference.

5.3   Timing device, such as a stop watch, with an accuracy to within ± 0.1 seconds

5.4   Balance, Class G2, conforming to the requirements of AASHTO M 231

5.5   Sample splitter, in accordance with AASHTO T 248 for fine aggregate

6.0   SAMPLE PREPARATION.

6.1   The sample may consist of sand or a sand and fly ash mixture proportioned according to the FBMD. The sample shall be oven dried at 230 ± 9° F (110 ± 5° C) for 24 h. Upon completion of the drying, the sample shall be split to a sample size of approximately 1,500 g using a small sample splitter for fine aggregate in accordance with AASHTO T 248.

6.2   The dry sample of sand or sand and fly ash mixture shall be thoroughly mixed with the spatula until the sample appears to be homogenous.

7.0 PROCEDURE.

7.1 Place the dry sample into the one quart glass jar and put the lid on. Agitate the glass jar to mix the dry sample for 30 seconds.

7.2 Place a finger at the end of the funnel to block the opening of the funnel.

7.3 Pour and empty the dry sample of sand or sand and fly ash mixture from the glass jar into the Mason jar.

The testing procedure is explained step by step. →

7.4 Level the dry sample in the Mason jar with a spatula.

7.5 Place the empty glass jar directly centered under the funnel.

7.6 Remove the finger and allow the dry sample to fall freely into the glass jar, and start timing the dry flow.

7.7 Record the time T_1 of the dry flow to an accuracy of ±0.1 second.

7.8 Repeat 7.1 through 7.6 for times T_2 and T_3.

8.0 CALCULATIONS.

8.1 Calculate the average dry flow time of the dry flowable backfill materials as follows:

$$T_{average} = \frac{T_1 + T_2 + T_3}{3}$$

where:

$T_{average}$ = Average dry flow time, s
T_1 = Dry flow time on first trial, s
T_2 = Dry flow time on second trial, s
T_3 = Dry flow time on third trial, s

9.0 REPORT.

9.1 Report the average dry flow time to within ± 0.1 seconds.

(continued)

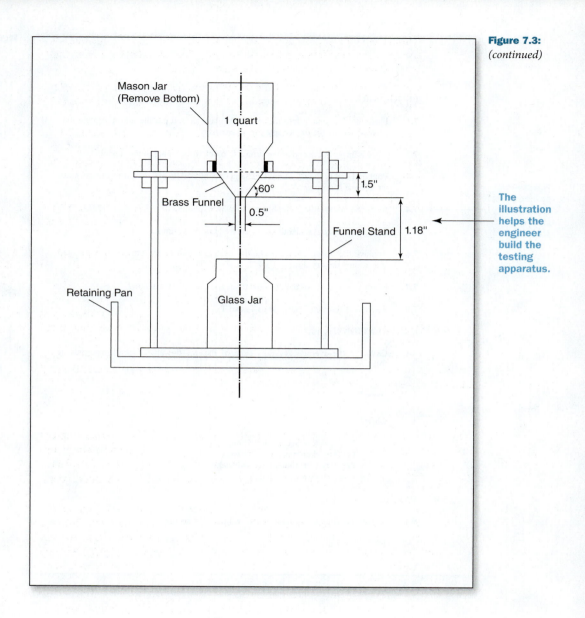

Mason Jar
(Remove Bottom)

1 quart

Brass Funnel

60°

0.5"

1.5"

Funnel Stand   1.18"

Retaining Pan

Glass Jar

The
illustration
helps the
engineer
build the
testing
apparatus.

READERS   Of course, it is difficult to anticipate all the types of people who might use your documentation. But people who decide to use a specific set of instructions, a set of specifications, or a procedure usually have common characteristics, backgrounds, and motivations that you can use to make your documentation more effective.

Primary readers (action takers) are people who will use your documentation to complete a task. What is their skill level? How well do they understand the product or process? What is their age and ability?

Secondary readers (advisors) are people who might supervise or help the primary readers complete the task. What is the skill level of these secondary readers? Are they training/teaching the primary readers?

Tertiary readers (evaluators) often use documentation to ensure quality. Auditors and quality experts review procedures and specifications closely when evaluating products or processes in a technical workplace. Also, sets of instructions can be used as evidence in lawsuits.

Gatekeeper readers (supervisors) who may or may not be experts in your field will need to look over your documentation before it is sent out with a product or approved for use in the workplace. They will be checking the accuracy, safety, and quality of your documentation.

Take care not to overestimate your readers' skills and understanding. In most cases, you are better off giving your readers more information than they need.

CONTEXT OF USE   Put yourself in your readers' place for a moment. When and where will your readers use the documentation? In their living rooms? At a workbench? At a construction site? In an office cubicle? At night? Each of these different places and times will require you to adjust your documentation to your readers' needs.

Context of use also involves safety and liability issues. If users of the documentation are at risk for injury or an accident, you are ethically obligated to warn them about the danger and tell them how to avoid it.

Link

For more information on analyzing readers, see Chapter 2, page 19.

Researching

Once you have defined the rhetorical situation, you should spend some time doing research on the task you are describing. Research consists of gaining a thorough understanding of your subject by considering it from several angles (Figure 7.4). Here are a few research strategies that are especially useful when writing documentation.

DO BACKGROUND RESEARCH   You should research the history and purpose of the product or process you are describing. If the product or process is new, find out why it was developed and study the documents that shaped its development. If the product or process is not new, determine whether it has evolved or changed. Also, collect any prior instructions, procedures, or specifications that might help you write your own documentation.

MAKE OBSERVATIONS   Observe people using the product. If, for example, you are writing instructions for using a coffeemaker, observe someone making coffee with the machine. Pay attention to his or her experiences, especially any mistakes. Your notes from these experiments will help you anticipate some of the situations and problems your readers will experience.

Researching for Documentation

Figure 7.4: When doing research to write documentation, you should study your subject from a few different perspectives.

ASK SUBJECT MATTER EXPERTS (SMEs)   Interview experts who are familiar with the product or have used the procedure. They may be able to give you some insight or pointers into how the product is actually used or how the procedure is completed. They might also be able to point out trouble spots where nonexperts might have problems.

USE YOUR SENSES   Where appropriate, take notes about appearance, sounds, smells, textures, and tastes. These details will add depth to your documentation. They will also help your readers determine if they are following the directions properly.

DESCRIBE MOTION AND CHANGE   Pay special attention to the movements of your subject and the way it changes as you complete the steps. Each step will lead to some kind of motion or change. By noting these motions and changes, you will be better able to describe them.

COLLECT VISUALS   If available, collect graphics that can help you illustrate the steps you are describing in your documentation. If necessary, you can take photographs with a digital camera or mobile phone, or you can use drawings to illustrate your subject.

Link

For more information on doing research, go to Chapter 14, page 365.

Step 2: Organize and Draft Your Documentation

Like other technical documents, instructions and documentation should include an introduction, body, and conclusion. The introduction typically offers background information on the task being described. The body describes the steps required to complete the task. The conclusion usually offers readers a process for checking their work.

Specific and Precise Title

The title of your documentation should clearly describe the specific task the reader will complete.

> **Not descriptive:** RGS-90x Telescope

> **Descriptive:** Setting Up Your RGS-90x Telescope

> **Not descriptive:** Head Wound

> **Descriptive:** Procedure for Treating a Head Wound

INTRODUCTION   The length of the introduction depends on the complexity of the task and your readers' familiarity with it. If the task is simple, your introduction might be only a sentence long. If the task is complex or your readers are unfamiliar with the product or process, your introduction may need to be a few paragraphs long.

Introductions should include some or all of the following moves.

STATE THE PURPOSE   Simple or complex, all documentation should include some kind of statement of purpose.

> These instructions will help you set up your RGS-90x telescope.

> The Remington Medical Center uses these procedures to treat head wounds in the emergency room.

STATE THE IMPORTANCE OF THE TASK   You may want to stress the importance of the product or perhaps the gravity of doing the task correctly.

> Your RGS-90x telescope is one of the most revolutionary telescope systems ever developed. You should read these instructions thoroughly so that you can take full advantage of the telescope's numerous advanced features.

> Head wounds of any kind should be taken seriously. The following procedures should be followed in all head wound cases, even the cases that do not seem serious.

DESCRIBE THE NECESSARY TECHNICAL ABILITY   You may want to describe the necessary technical background that readers will need to use the product or to complete the task. Issues like age, qualifications, education level, and prior training are often important considerations that should be mentioned in the introduction.

With advanced features similar to those found in larger and more specialized telescopes, the RGS-90x can be used by casual observers and serious astronomers alike. Some familiarity with telescopes is helpful but not needed.

Because head wounds are usually serious, a trained nurse should be asked to bandage them. Head wounds should never be bandaged by trainees without close supervision.

IDENTIFY THE TIME REQUIRED FOR COMPLETION If the task is complex, you may want to estimate the time readers will need to complete all the steps.

Initially, setting up your telescope should take about 15 to 20 minutes. As you grow more familiar with it, though, setup should take only 5 to 10 minutes.

Speed is important when treating head wounds. You may have only a few minutes before the patient goes into shock.

MOTIVATE THE READER An introduction is a good place to set a positive tone. Add a sentence or two to motivate readers and make them feel positive about the task they are undertaking.

With push-button control, automatic tracking of celestial objects, and diffraction-limited imaging, an RGS-90x telescope may be the only telescope you will ever need. With this powerful telescope, you can study the rings of the planet Saturn or observe the feather structure of a bird from 50 yards away. This telescope will meet your growing interests in astronomical or terrestrial viewing.

Head wounds of any kind are serious injuries. Learn and follow these procedures so you can effectively treat these injuries without hesitation.

Procedures and specifications often also include motivational statements about the importance of doing the job right, as companies urge their employees to strive for the highest quality.

List of Parts, Tools, and Conditions Required

After the introduction, you should list the parts, tools, and conditions required for completing the task.

LIST THE PARTS REQUIRED This list should identify all the necessary items required to complete the task. Your parts list will allow readers to check whether all the parts were included in the package (Figure 7.5). Other items not included with the package, like adhesive, batteries, and paint, should be mentioned at this point so readers can collect these items before beginning the task.

IDENTIFY TOOLS REQUIRED Nothing is more frustrating to readers than discovering midway through a set of instructions that they need a tool that was not previously mentioned. The required tools should be listed up front so readers can gather them before starting.

A Parts List

The opening encourages readers to check the kit's parts.

The parts are listed and given letters so that they can be checked against the graphic.

PARALLAX 599 Menlo Drive
Rocklin, California 95765, USA
Office: (916) 624-8333
Fax: (916) 624-8003

Technical: support@parallax.com
Web Site: www.parallax.com
Educational: www.parallax.com/education

Crawler Kit for the Boe-Bot® Robot (#30055)

The Crawler Kit Rev B V2.1

This kit allows your Parallax Boe-Bot® Robot to walk on six legs. Assembly takes approximately 60 minutes to complete. Before getting started, take an inventory of the parts in your kit. Use **Fig 1** to identify each part to the parts list. Once you have inventoried your kit, proceed to **Step #1**. Parallax Boe-Bot® Robot (#28132 or #28832) is sold separately

Recommended Tools

- Small needle nosed pliers
- Phillips #2 point screwdriver
- A sharp-tipped hobby knife, such as an X-Acto® knife -OR- A hand drill with 7/64"(2.8 mm) bit

WARNING!

DO NOT use electric screwdrivers with this kit. Please assemble using hand tools only to avoid damaging your Crawler.

Parts List

Item	Qty	Description
A	(2)	Crawler Side
B	(2)	Servo Horn
C	(4)	End Leg
D	(6)	Rubber Feet, Black
E	(4)	#4 1/16" Nylon Spacer
F	(2)	#4 1/8" Nylon Spacer
G	(4)	Extension Arm
H	(2)	3/4" Hex Nylon Standoff
I	(4)	4-40 1" Hex Nylon Standoff
J	(2)	4-40 5/8" Phillips Pan Head Screw
K	(6)	4-40 ½" Phillips Self Taping Screw
L	(10)	4-40 3/8" Phillips Pan Head Screw
M	(6)	4-40 Hex Nut
N	(6)	4-40 Nylon Insert Locknut
O	(2)	Center Leg
P	(6)	4-40 ¼" Phillips Pan Head Screw
Q	(12)	Plastic Screw Cover, Black
R	(8)	#4 .031" Nylon Washer, Large

Fig 1

© Parallax, Inc. 2004 - Crawler Kit for Boe-Bot® Robot   1

The graphic illustrates the parts in the kit.

Figure 7.5: A parts list for a set of instructions. Many instructions begin by asking readers to check whether all the parts were included in the kit.

Source: Parallax, Inc.

SPECIFY SPECIAL CONDITIONS   If any special conditions involving temperature, humidity, or light are required, mention them up front.

> Paint is best applied when temperatures are between 50°F and 90°F.

> If the humidity is above 75 percent, do not solder the microchips onto the printed circuit board. High humidity may lead to a defective joint.

Sequentially Ordered Steps

The steps are the centerpiece of any form of documentation, and they will usually make up the bulk of the text. These steps need to be presented logically and concisely, allowing readers to easily understand them and complete the task.

As you divide the task you are describing into steps, you might use logical mapping to sort out the major and minor steps (Figure 7.6). First, put the overall task you

Using Logical Mapping to Identify Steps in a Task

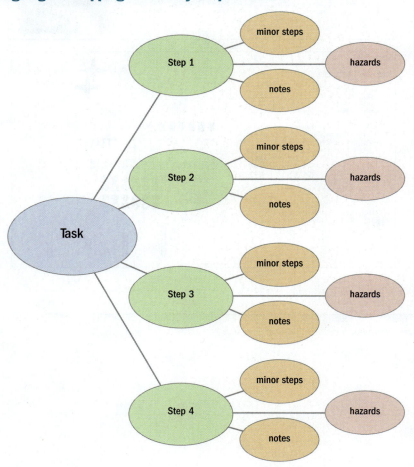

Figure 7.6: With logical mapping, the task is broken down into major and minor steps. Places where notes and hazard statements might appear are also noted.

are describing on the left-hand side of the screen or a sheet of paper. Then, break the task down into its major and minor steps. Also, take note of any steps that might require hazard statements.

Once you have organized the task into major and minor steps, you are ready to draft your instructions.

USE COMMAND VOICE   Steps should be written in *command voice,* or imperative mood. To use command voice, start each step with an action verb.

1. Place the telescope in an upright position on a flat surface.

2. Plug the coil cord for the Electronic Controller into the HBX port (see Figure 5).

In most steps, the verb should come first in the sentence. This puts the action up front, while keeping the pattern of the steps consistent.

STATE ONE ACTION PER STEP   Each step should express only one action (Figure 7.7). You might be tempted to state two smaller actions in one step, but your readers will appreciate following each step separately.

Ineffective

2. Place the telescope securely on its side as shown in Figure 4 and open the battery compartment by simultaneously depressing the two release latches.

Revised

2. Place the telescope securely on its side as shown in Figure 4.

3. Open the battery compartment by simultaneously depressing the two release latches.

However, when two actions must be completed at the same time, you should put them in the same sentence.

6. Insert a low-power eyepiece (e.g., 26mm) into the eyepiece holder and tighten the eyepiece thumbscrew.

If two actions need to be stated in one step, completion of the first action should require the other action to be handled at the same time.

KEEP THE STEPS CONCISE   Use concise phrasing to describe each step. Short sentences allow readers to remember each step while they work.

7. Adjust the focus of the telescope with the focusing knob.

8. Center the observed object in the lens.

If your sentences seem too long, consider moving some information into a follow-up "Note" or "Comment" that elaborates on the step.

Instructions with Sequentially Ordered Steps

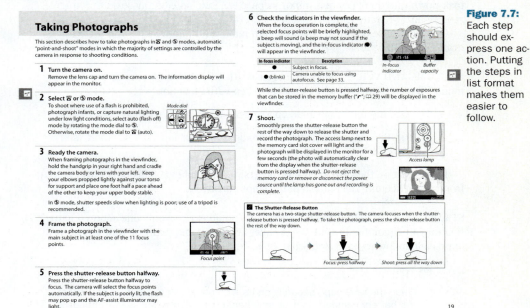

Figure 7.7: Each step should express one action. Putting the steps in list format makes them easier to follow.

Source: Nikon D5100 User Manual, pages 10 and 11. © 2014 Nikon Corporation Used by permission.

NUMBER THE STEPS In most kinds of documentation, steps are presented in a numbered list. Start with the number 1 and mark each step sequentially with its own number. Notes or warnings should not be numbered, because they do not state steps to be followed.

Incorrect

9. Aim the telescope with the electronic controller.

10. Your controller is capable of moving the telescope in several directions. It will take practice to properly aim the telescope.

There is no action in step 10 above, so a number should not be used.

Correct

9. Aim the telescope with the electronic controller.

Your controller is capable of moving the telescope in several directions. It will take practice to properly aim the telescope.

An important exception to this "number only steps" guideline involves the numbering of procedures and specifications. Procedures and specifications often use an itemized numbering system in which lists of cautions or notes are "nested" within lists of steps.

10.2.1 Putting on Clean Room Gloves, Hood, and Coveralls

10.2.1.1 Put on coveralls.

10.2.1.2 Put on a pair of clean room gloves so they are fully extended over the arm and the coverall sleeves. Glove liners are optional.

10.2.1.3 Put a face/beard mask on, completely covering the mouth and nose.

Cautions and notes receive numbers in some specifications and procedures.

10.2.1.3.1 *Caution: No exposed hair is allowed in the fab.*

10.2.1.3.2 *Caution: Keep your nose covered at all times while in the fab.*

10.2.1.3.3 *Note: Do not wear the beard cover as a facemask. A beard cover should be used with a facemask to cover facial hair.*

In specifications, comments and hazard statements are numbered because the numbers help people refer to specific lines in the document.

In some cases, you may also want to use *paragraph style* to describe the steps (Figure 7.8). In these situations, you can use headings or sequential transitions to highlight the steps. Numerical transitions ("first," "second," "third," "finally") are best in most cases. In shorter sets of steps, you might use transitions like "then," "next," "5 minutes later," and "finally" to mark the actions. In Figure 7.9, headings are used to mark transitions among the major steps.

Readers often find paragraph style harder to follow because they cannot easily find their place again in the list of instructions. In some cases, though, paragraph style takes up less space and sounds more friendly and conversational.

ADD COMMENTS, NOTES, OR EXAMPLES   After each step, you can include additional comments or examples that will help readers complete the action. Comments after steps might include additional advice or definitions for less experienced readers. Or, comments might provide troubleshooting advice in case the step did not work out.

3.   Locate a place to set your telescope.

Finding a suitable place to set up your telescope can be tricky. A paved area is optimal to keep the telescope steady. If a paved area is not available, find a level place where you can firmly set your telescope's tripod in the soil.

Comments and examples are often written in the "you" style to maintain a positive tone.

Chain Saws — Safety, Operation, Tree Felling Techniques

KANSAS FOREST SERVICE
KANSAS STATE UNIVERSITY

A chain saw is a valuable, labor-saving tool for homeowners, forest landowners, and professional loggers. When used improperly, however, it can cause serious injuries. Read and follow operating manual instructions provided with the chain saw.

Good judgment and common sense are essential to operating a chain saw safely. Equipment varies, but if a chain saw manual is not available, the following guidelines provide important information about chain saw safety, operation, and tree felling techniques.

Safety

Many safety advancements in chain saw design have been made, but accidents still happen. Chain saw users must observe safety practices. Working safely requires a personal commitment to being constantly aware of your actions and the possible

reactions they may cause, as well as your surroundings.

Select a chain saw with good safety features, including features to reduce kickback and an anti-vibration system to reduce saw vibration to the user's hands. This reduces user fatigue and ensures greater safety. Chain saw operators should know their physical limitations, work slowly, rest often, and remain alert to potential problems and hazards. Saws also should be equipped with a continuous pressure throttle control system that shuts off the power to the saw's chain when pressure is reduced.

Wear comfortable, close-fitting clothing when using a chain saw. Also, include the following protective equipment (see Figure 1):

- safety boots with steel toes and nonskid soles.

- face shields or plastic goggles to prevent injuries from wood chips and sawdust.
- ear plugs or muffs to prevent hearing loss. Chain saw noise is greater than the human ear can tolerate. Sustained exposure can cause hearing loss that cannot be restored.
- heavy-duty, leather gloves to protect hands from cuts and scrapes.
- leg protective pants or chaps that cover the upper thigh to boot tops. Chaps protect against cuts and can stop the chain before it causes harm if it accidentally contacts the user's leg.
- first-aid kit available at the work site.

Before starting the chain saw, check the operating manual for the recommended fuel mixture, choke setting, and throttle control. Always start the saw with the chain brake on. Properly adjust the saw so the chain stops when the throttle is released. Start the chain saw at least 10 feet away from the fueling area. Always fill the oil reservoir when refueling the saw.

When starting the saw, hold the saw firmly on the ground with your right foot in the rear handle. Grip the front handle with the left hand. Be sure the area under the bar and chain is clear. Check to see that the starter mechanism is engaged, then pull the starter rope sharply with the right hand while keeping a firm hold on the

Figure 1. *Chain saw operator's safety equipment.*

- Hard Hat
- Ear Muffs
- Face Shield
- Safety Boots
- Leg Protection
- Leather Gloves

Kansas Forest Service

K·STATE
Kansas State University

Source: "Chain Saws—Safety, Operation, Tree Felling Techniques," by Eric Ward, Kansas Forest Service. Published by Kansas State University, Manhattan, KS, April 2011, MF2013Rev.

Figure 7.8: Paragraph style often takes up less space. It is a little harder to read at a glance, but this style can often be more personal. In these instructions the pictures show helpful details to clarify the steps.

Paragraphs slow the readers down.

Figures are numbered and referenced in the written text.

Drawings are used to illustrate complex steps.

Safety equipment is used in drawings.

Lists are used where needed to highlight specific details.

starter handle as the rope retracts. Rev the engine briefly to release the throttle control latch and let the saw idle.

Another method of starting a chain saw that should only be used by experienced operators is known as the "crotch clamp" method. This involves the operator clamping the rear handle of the saw between his or her legs to stabilize the saw during the starting procedure. **Never start a saw on your knee or by drop starting!**

Operation

When handling the saw, the following techniques allow the user to keep control:

- maintain a firm footing with legs well apart to support the body. Keep the body away from the saw's cutting path. Keep the weight of the saw close to the body, arms slightly flexed, allowing the trunk and legs to carry the weight, relieving the load on the back and arms. The hands and arms mainly serve to guide the saw, bearing as little weight as possible.
- when working in a crouched position, avoid back strain by supporting the elbows on the knees.
- keep wrists straight to prevent muscle strain in the arms.
- keep the thumb around the front handle to prevent the saw from being wrenched from the hands in the event of a kickback. Let the left hand slide along the handle to keep the saw stable and to change positions.
- do not operate the saw with the power head higher than your shoulders.

The safest and least tiring way of sawing is to cut with the backward-running or lower part of the saw bar close to the bumper. Sawing with the forward-running or upper part makes it difficult to control the saw and increases the risk of kickback.

Do not overreach while using a chain saw. Overreaching causes loss of grip and chain saw instability. Avoid forcing the saw when cutting. Be alert for wire, nails, and other foreign objects in the wood.

Never carry a saw with a moving chain. The saw should be shut off or the chain brake engaged when carrying for distances of greater than 50 feet, or when terrain and other physical factors make carrying a running saw hazardous.

Chain saw kickback can cause serious injuries without giving the operator time to react. When cutting, the chain is traveling about 65 feet per second. If kickback occurs, it will be over within $2/10$ of a second. The most common cause of kickback is when the teeth come in contact with an object as they rotate around the tip of the bar. This causes the saw to kickback rapidly, backward and upward, toward the operator (see Figure 2):

Prevent kickback injuries by:

- holding the saw firmly with both hands.
- keeping the thumb around the top handle.
- using a saw equipped with a chain brake or kickback guard.
- watching for twigs that can snag.
- not pinching the bar.
- sawing with the lower part of the bar, not on the top near the nose.
- maintaining adequate saw speed when beginning or completing a cut.
- selecting chains designed to reduce kickback.
- avoiding situations where the nose of the bar is likely to encounter a fixed object.

Figure 2. *Chain saw kickback*

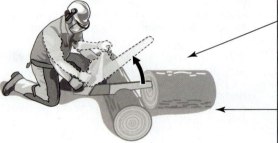

Breaking chains can cause serious accidents and are nearly always the result of a poorly maintained saw. Because of the saw's high speed, the flying cutters can embed themselves in the body. There is little risk of breakage in a chain that is properly sharpened, well lubricated, and correctly adjusted for tension.

Tree Felling Techniques

Accurate tree felling takes practice to master. Because of the hazards involved, never work alone.

The first step in felling a tree is to identify all the hazards around the tree, such as structures, power lines, roads, vehicles, and other trees. Also look for hazardous, dead branches or rot on the tree being felled. Make sure the area is clear of people and animals before beginning. Check to be sure the chain saw has enough gas and chain oil to finish felling the tree. Work behind and slightly to the side of the direction of the fall.

The second step is to determine the height of the tree and the direction it should fall. The tree's high center of gravity causes instability and makes its movement difficult to predict and control. Other factors to consider in felling a tree include wind direction and velocity. Never attempt to fell a tree into the wind. Trees that have a definite lean should be felled in the direction of the lean, if possible.

Figures are numbered and referenced in the written text.

Drawings depict action.

This drawing shows how a dangerous mistake might happen.

2

PROVIDE FEEDBACK   After a difficult step or group of steps, you might offer a paragraph of feedback to help readers assess their progress.

> When you finish these steps, the barrel of your telescope should be pointed straight up. The tripod should be stable so that it does not teeter when touched. The legs of the tripod should be planted firmly on the ground.

REFER TO THE GRAPHICS   In the steps, refer readers to any accompanying graphics. A simple statement like, "See Figure 4" or "(Figure 4)" will notify readers that a graphic is available that illustrates the step. After reading the step, they can look at the graphic for help in completing the step properly.

If graphics are not labeled, they should appear immediately next to the step or below it so readers know which visual goes with each step.

Safety Information

Safety information should be placed early in the documentation and in places where the reader will be completing difficult or dangerous steps. A common convention in technical writing is to use a three-level rating for safety information and warnings: *Danger, Warning,* and *Caution.*

DANGER   "Danger" signals that readers may be at risk for serious injury or even death. This level of warning is the highest, and it should be used only when the situation involves real danger to the readers.

> *Danger:* Do not remove grass from beneath your riding lawn mower while the engine is running (even if the blade is stopped). The blade can cause severe injury. To clear out grass, turn off the lawn mower and disconnect the spark plug before working near the blade.

WARNING   "Warning" signals that the reader may be injured if the step is done improperly. To help readers avoid injury, warnings are used frequently.

> *Warning:* When heated, your soldering iron will cause burns if it touches your skin. To avoid injury, always return the soldering iron to its holder between uses.

CAUTION   "Caution" alerts readers that mistakes may cause damage to the product or equipment. Cautions should be used to raise readers' awareness of difficult steps.

> *Caution:* The new oil filter should be tightened by hand only. Do not use an oil filter wrench for tightening, because it will cause the filter to seal improperly.

Safety information should tell your readers the following three things: (1) the hazard, (2) the seriousness of the hazard, and (3) how to avoid injury or damage. As shown in Figure 7.9, safety information should appear in two places:

- If a hazard is present throughout the procedure, readers should be warned before they begin following the steps. In these cases, danger and warning statements should appear between the introduction and the steps.
- If a hazard relates to a specific step, a statement should appear prominently before that step. It is important for readers to see the hazard statement *before* the step so that they can avoid damage or injury.

You can use symbols to highlight safety information. Icons are available to reinforce and highlight special hazards such as radioactive materials, electricity, or chemicals. Figure 7.9 shows a few examples of icons commonly used in safety information.

In our litigious culture, the importance of safety information should not be underestimated. Danger, warning, and caution notices will not completely protect your company from lawsuits, but they will give your company some defense against legal action.

Conclusion That Signals Completion of Task

When you have listed all the steps, you should offer a closing that tells readers they are finished with the task. Closings can be handled a few different ways.

SIGNAL COMPLETION OF THE TASK   Tell readers that they are finished with the steps. Perhaps you might offer a few comments about the future.

> Congratulations! You have finished setting up your RGS-90x telescope. You will now be able to spend many nights exploring the night skies.

> When completed, the bandaging of the head wound should be firm but not too tight. Bleeding should stop within a minute. If bleeding does not stop, call an emergency room doctor immediately.

Safety Symbols

Source: Peckham, Geoffrey. "Safety Symbols," originally appearing in Compliance Engineering Magazine. Used with permission, Clarion Safety Systems, LLC.

Figure 7.9: Here are a few examples of ISO and IEC symbols used on safety signs (hot surface, laser, radiation).

Placement of Hazard Statements

Warning statements are prominently displayed.

Symbols draw attention to warnings.

Boxes are used to capture the readers' attention.

Figure demonstrates proper use of the machine, including use of appropriate safety devices like glasses, earmuffs, and gloves.

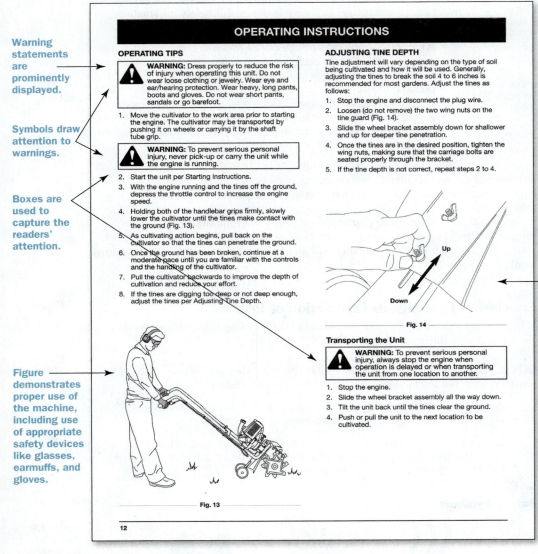

OPERATING INSTRUCTIONS

OPERATING TIPS

⚠ **WARNING:** Dress properly to reduce the risk of injury when operating this unit. Do not wear loose clothing or jewelry. Wear eye and ear/hearing protection. Wear heavy, long pants, boots and gloves. Do not wear short pants, sandals or go barefoot.

1. Move the cultivator to the work area prior to starting the engine. The cultivator may be transported by pushing it on wheels or carrying it by the shaft tube grip.

⚠ **WARNING:** To prevent serious personal injury, never pick-up or carry the unit while the engine is running.

2. Start the unit per Starting Instructions.
3. With the engine running and the tines off the ground, depress the throttle control to increase the engine speed.
4. Holding both of the handlebar grips firmly, slowly lower the cultivator until the tines make contact with the ground (Fig. 13).
5. As cultivating action begins, pull back on the cultivator so that the tines can penetrate the ground.
6. Once the ground has been broken, continue at a moderate pace until you are familiar with the controls and the handling of the cultivator.
7. Pull the cultivator backwards to improve the depth of cultivation and reduce your effort.
8. If the tines are digging too deep or not deep enough, adjust the tines per Adjusting Tine Depth.

ADJUSTING TINE DEPTH

Tine adjustment will vary depending on the type of soil being cultivated and how it will be used. Generally, adjusting the tines to break the soil 4 to 6 inches is recommended for most gardens. Adjust the tines as follows:

1. Stop the engine and disconnect the plug wire.
2. Loosen (do not remove) the two wing nuts on the tine guard (Fig. 14).
3. Slide the wheel bracket assembly down for shallower and up for deeper tine penetration.
4. Once the tines are in the desired position, tighten the wing nuts, making sure that the carriage bolts are seated properly through the bracket.
5. If the tine depth is not correct, repeat steps 2 to 4.

Up

Down

— Fig. 14 —

Transporting the Unit

⚠ **WARNING:** To prevent serious personal injury, always stop the engine when operation is delayed or when transporting the unit from one location to another.

1. Stop the engine.
2. Slide the wheel bracket assembly all the way down.
3. Tilt the unit back until the tines clear the ground.
4. Push or pull the unit to the next location to be cultivated.

— Fig. 13 —

12

Figure 7.10: Hazard statements need to be prominent in the page design. In this user's manual, the warnings stand out because boxes and symbols draw attention to them.

A close-up graphic shows how to accomplish important tasks.

Source: Ryobi, 2000.

DESCRIBE THE FINISHED PRODUCT   You might describe the finished product as a conclusion. Or, you might offer information about how the product works and how it can be modified.

> When you have completed setting up your telescope, it should be firmly set on the ground and the eyepiece should be just below the level of your eyes. With the Electronic Controller, you should be able to move the telescope horizontally and vertically with the push of a button. Figure 5 shows how a properly set up telescope should look.
>
> Your bandaging of the patient's head should look like Figure B. The bandaging should be neatly wound around the patient's head with a slight overlap in the bandage strips.

The "Discussion" in Figure 7.11 shows how a set of instructions can serve as a learning tool. In this set of instructions, the author explains the physics of a match stick rocket.

OFFER TROUBLESHOOTING ADVICE   Depending on the complexity of the task, you might end your documentation by anticipating some of the common problems that could occur. Simple tasks may require only a sentence or two of troubleshooting advice. More complex tasks may require a table that lists potential problems and their remedies (Figure 7.12 on page 182.). Depending on your company's ability to provide customer service, you may also include a web address or a phone number where readers can obtain additional help.

User-Testing Your Documentation

When you have finished drafting your documentation, you should do some user-testing to see how real readers will react to it. Chapter 19, "Revising and Editing for Usability," discusses four kinds of tests that would be helpful while user-testing your documentation: (1) read-and-locate tests, (2) understandability tests, (3) performance tests, and (4) safety tests. These tests would strengthen the usability of your documentation, while helping you identify places where you may have overlooked small or significant aspects of the documentation.

A Set of Instructions as a Learning Tool

Figure 7.11: Some sets of instructions will conclude by explaining the finished product and offering possible variations.

Descriptive title →

Introduction →

Steps in procedure →

Helpful graphic →

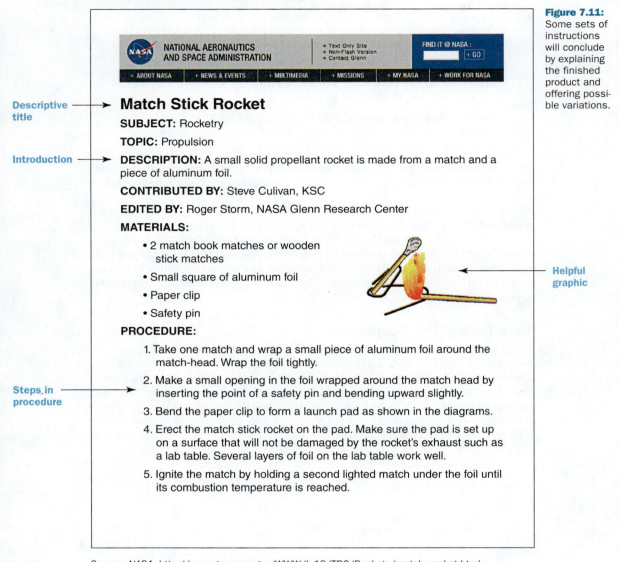

NATIONAL AERONAUTICS AND SPACE ADMINISTRATION

+ Text Only Site
+ Non-Flash Version
+ Contact Glenn

FIND IT @ NASA :

+ GO

+ ABOUT NASA   + NEWS & EVENTS   + MULTIMEDIA   + MISSIONS   + MY NASA   + WORK FOR NASA

Match Stick Rocket

SUBJECT: Rocketry

TOPIC: Propulsion

DESCRIPTION: A small solid propellant rocket is made from a match and a piece of aluminum foil.

CONTRIBUTED BY: Steve Culivan, KSC

EDITED BY: Roger Storm, NASA Glenn Research Center

MATERIALS:

- 2 match book matches or wooden stick matches
- Small square of aluminum foil
- Paper clip
- Safety pin

PROCEDURE:

1. Take one match and wrap a small piece of aluminum foil around the match-head. Wrap the foil tightly.
2. Make a small opening in the foil wrapped around the match head by inserting the point of a safety pin and bending upward slightly.
3. Bend the paper clip to form a launch pad as shown in the diagrams.
4. Erect the match stick rocket on the pad. Make sure the pad is set up on a surface that will not be damaged by the rocket's exhaust such as a lab table. Several layers of foil on the lab table work well.
5. Ignite the match by holding a second lighted match under the foil until its combustion temperature is reached.

Source: NASA, http://www.grc.nasa.gov/WWW/k-12/TRC/Rockets/match_rocket.html

Clear caution statement

Caution: Be sure the match rocket is pointed away from people or burnable materials. It is recommended to have water or some other fire extinguishant available. The foil head of the rocket will be very hot!

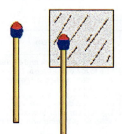
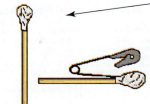

This graphic illustrates the steps for preparing the rocket.

The discussion offers an explanation of physics involved.

DISCUSSION: The match stick rocket demonstrates Isaac Newton's Laws of Motion as they relate to rocketry. Newton's third law states that for every action, there is an opposite and equal reaction. The exhaust of the fire products from the burning match (smoke and gas) is the "action" and the movement of the rocket in the other direction is the "reaction." The action thrust is produced when the match burns in an enclosed environment. The aluminum foil acts as a rocket combustion chamber. Because the opening in the foil is small, pressure builds up in the chamber that eventually escapes as a rapid stream of smoke and gas.

In an interesting variation of the experiment, try making holes of different diameters to let the combustion products out at different rates. A larger opening permits the smoke and gas to escape before it has time to build up much pressure. The escape of the products will be slower than produced by a match stick rocket with a smaller opening. Isaac Newton's second law states that the force or thrust of a rocket is equal to the mass of the smoke and gas escaping the rocket times how fast it escapes. In this experiment, the mass of the smoke and gas is the same for both cases. The difference is in how fast it escapes. Compare the distance traveled with the two match stick rockets.

Variations on the procedure are provided.

Source: NASA, http://www.grc.nasa.gov/WWW/k-12/TRC/Rockets/match_rocket.html

Troubleshooting Guide

Troubleshooting

Problem	Possible Cause	Solution
Aircraft will not respond to the throttle but responds to other controls.	ESC is not armed. Throttle channel is reversed.	Lower throttle stick and throttle trim to lowest settings. Reverse throttle channel on transmitter.
Extra propeller noise or extra Vibration.	Damaged spinner, propeller. motor or motor mount. Loose propeller and spinner parts. Propellor installed backwards.	Replaced damaged parts. Tighten parts for propeller adapter, propeller and spinner.
Reduced flight time or aircraft underpowered.	Flight battery charge is low. Propeller installed backward. Flight battery damaged.	Remove and install propeller correctly.Completely recharge Flight battery. Remove and install propeller correctly. Replace flight battery and obey flight battery instructions.
Control surface does not move, or is slow to respond to control inputs.	Control surface, control horn, linkage or servo damage, Wire damaged or connections loose.	Replace or repair damaged parts and adjust controls. Do a check of connections for loose wiring.
Control reversed.	Channels need to be reversed in the transmitter.	Do the Control Direction Test and adjust controls for aircraft and transmitter.
Motor loses power. Motor power pulses then motor loses power.	Damage to motor, or battery. Lose of power to aircraft. ESC uses default soft Low Voltage Cutoff(LVC).	Do a check of batteries, transmitter, receiver, ESC, motor and wiring for damage (replace as needed). Land aircraft immediately and Recharge flight battery.
LED on receiver flashes slowly.	Power loss to receiver.	Check connection from ESC to receiver. Check servos for damage. Check linkages for binding.

Battery Selection and Installation.

1. We recommend the 11.1V 1100mAh 15C Li-Po battery.
2. If using another battery, the battery must be at least a 11.1V 1100mAh 15C battery.
3. Your battery should be approximately the same capacity ,dimension and weight as the 11.1V 1100mAh 15C Li-Po battery to fit in the fuselage without changing the center of gravity

 For More Info Vist: www.motionrc.com

page 15

Source: Motion RC

Figure 7.12: Troubleshooting guides are often provided in a table format with problems on the left and solutions on the right. Note the positive, constructive tone in this table.

On-Screen Documentation

One of the major changes brought about by computers is the availability of on-screen documentation. Today, user's manuals and instructions for products are often available through a website, provided on a CD or DVD, or included with the Help feature in a software package.

The advantages of online documentation are numerous, and the disadvantages are few. The greatest advantage is reduced cost. After all, with some products like software, the accompanying user's manual costs more to print than the software itself. By putting the manual on a website, CD or DVD, or online Help, a company can save thousands of dollars almost immediately. Also, online documentation can be updated regularly to reflect changes in the product or revisions to the documentation.

Companies are also putting specifications and procedures online, usually on the company's intranet. That way, all employees can easily call up the documents they need on their desktop.

Several options are available for on-screen documentation:

Online Help—Increasingly, the online Help features that come with software packages are being used to present instructions (Figure A). Online Help features allow readers to access the instructions more quickly, because they do not need to hunt around for the user's manual. As more documents move online, it is likely that instructions will increasingly be offered as online Help. To write instructions as online Help, you will need Help-authoring software, such as RoboHelp, Helpinator, and Help & Manual, which simplifies the writing of Help features.

Online Help

Users can use the search function to find help on specific topics.

The instructions are listed here.

A screen shot shows users how the screen will look.

Figure A: Online Help features are another place where instructions are commonly found, especially for software programs. These instructions are from the online Help feature for Mozilla Firefox.

Source: Mozilla Firefox.

CD or DVD—Increasingly, computers have a CD burner as a standard feature. To make a CD or DVD, you can use web development software such as Adobe Dreamweaver or Microsoft Expression Web to create the files. Then, burn the files to a CD or DVD the same way you would save to a disk. Browser programs like Firefox, Safari, or Explorer will be able to read these multimedia documents.

Website—You can put your documentation on a website for use through the Internet or a company intranet. These files can be created with web development software such as Dreamweaver or Expression Web.

Portable document format (PDF)—Software programs such as Adobe Acrobat can turn your word-processing files into PDFs, which retain the formatting and color of the original document. PDFs can be read by almost any computer, and they store information efficiently. They can also be password protected so that readers cannot tamper with the text. PDFs can be placed on a website for easy downloading.

Step 3: Choose the Style, Design, and Medium

People often assume that technical documentation should sound dry and look boring. But documentation can be—and sometimes should be—written in a more interesting style and can use an eye-catching design. A variety of media could also be used to make technical documentation more accessible to the readers.

Plain Style with a Touch of Emotion

Documentation tends to be written in the plain style. Here are some suggestions for improving the style of your technical description:

> **Use simple words and limit the amount of jargon.**
>
> **Define any words that might not be familiar to your readers.**
>
> **Keep sentences short, within breathing length.**
>
> **Use the command or imperative style (verb first) for any instructional steps.**
>
> **Keep it simple and don't over-explain basic steps or concepts.**

Link

For more ideas about improving style, go to Chapter 16, page 422.

How can you further improve the style of your documentation? First, look at your original analysis of your readers and the contexts in which your document will be used. Pay attention to your readers' needs, values, and attitudes. Then, try to identify the emotions and attitudes that shape how they will be reading and using the instructions. Will they be enthusiastic, frustrated, happy, apprehensive, or excited?

Identify a word that best reflects readers' feelings as they are using your documentation. Then, use logical mapping to come up with some words that are associated with that word (Figure 7.13).

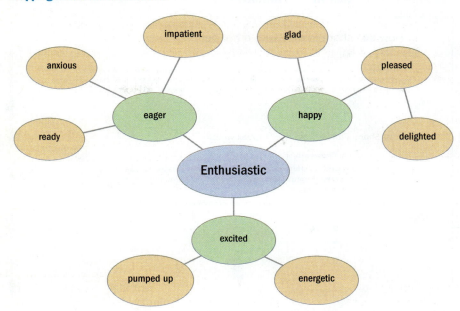

Figure 7.13: You can create an enthusiastic tone by finding synonyms associated with the word "enthusiastic."

After you have found words that are associated with the appropriate tone, use them in the introduction, notes, and conclusion. These words, when used strategically, will reflect your readers' attitudes or emotions.

If your readers have a negative attitude (perhaps they are annoyed that they need to read instructions), you can use antonyms to counteract their feelings. For example, to soothe annoyed readers, use words like *satisfy, pleasure, please, delight,* and *fulfill* to counteract their negativity. Don't overuse them, though, because angry readers may detect your attempt to soothe them and feel like you are being patronizing.

Functional, Attractive Page Layout

The page layout of your documentation should be both functional and attractive, like the example in Figure 7.14. Here are some techniques that you might try:

> **Incorporate graphics that illustrate and reinforce the written text.**
>
> **Try using a two- or three-column format that leaves room for graphics.**
>
> **Use boxes, borders, and lines to highlight important information, especially safety information.**
>
> **Use headings that clearly show the levels of information in the text.**

If you are not sure how to design your instructions, study sample texts from your home or workplace. You can use these examples as models for designing your own documentation.

Link
For more help on document design, see Chapter 17, page 447.

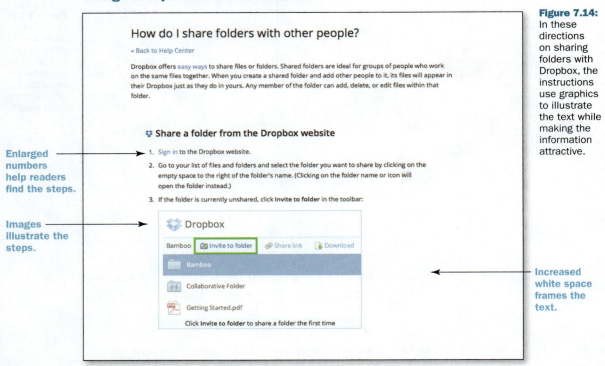

Figure 7.14: In these directions on sharing folders with Dropbox, the instructions use graphics to illustrate the text while making the information attractive.

Source: Used with permission from Dropbox.

Graphics That Reinforce Written Text

With computers, a variety of methods are available for you to add graphics to your documentation. You can add illustrations and diagrams (as in Figure 7.14). Or, you can use a digital camera or scanner to add graphics to your text. Here are some tips:

Link

For more information on using graphics, see Chapter 18, page 477.

Number and title your graphics, so readers can locate them.

Refer to the graphics by number in the written steps.

Put each graphic next to or below the step that refers to it.

Place graphics on the same page as the step that refers to them.

Check whether the graphics you have chosen could be misunderstood by or offensive to cross-cultural readers.

Keep in mind that the graphics should reinforce, not replace, the written text.

If the folder is already being shared, click **Shared folder options**:

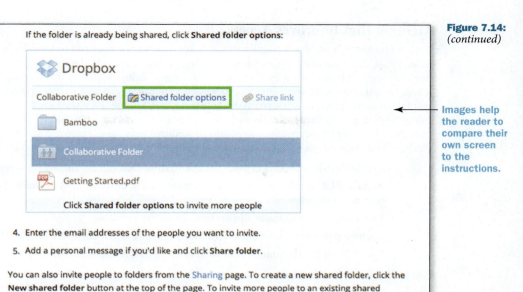

Images help the reader to compare their own screen to the instructions.

4. Enter the email addresses of the people you want to invite.

5. Add a personal message if you'd like and click **Share folder**.

You can also invite people to folders from the Sharing page. To create a new shared folder, click the **New shared folder** button at the top of the page. To invite more people to an existing shared folder, find it in the list and click its **Options** link.

Share a folder on Mac OS X

You can share a folder right from your computer if you've installed the Dropbox desktop application.

1. Open your Dropbox folder.

2. Right-click or Control-click on the folder you want to share to bring up a menu.

3. Select **Dropbox > Share This Folder...**. This will open the **Sharing** page on the Dropbox website.

Instructions are easy to find in this numbered list.

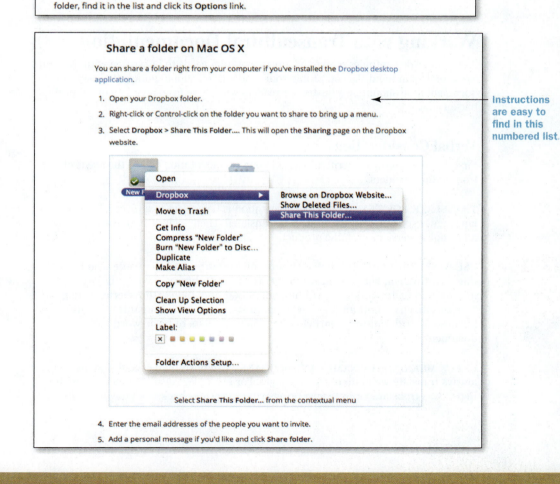

4. Enter the email addresses of the people you want to invite.

5. Add a personal message if you'd like and click **Share folder**.

Figure 7.14: *(continued)*

Medium that Improves Access

Let's be honest. People don't usually save the instructions for the products they buy—or they lose them. Increasingly, consumers expect to have access to documentation on-line. The same is true of specifications and procedures. Today, people in the technical workplace, such as engineers, doctors, nurses, and technicians, prefer to call up documentation on their computer screens or mobile devices. Online documentation is better because it is searchable, and they don't need to look through a file cabinet of papers for the instructions, specifications, and procedures they need. Here are some strategies for making documentation more accessible:

> **Create website versions of your documentation that can be viewed on-screen.**
>
> **Make a PDF version of any paper documentation that can be downloaded or sent as an attachment.**
>
> **Use more photographs as illustrations in online versions.**
>
> **Archive past versions of documentation, marking when each was updated.**
>
> **Use links in the documentation to help users find additional information.**

You might also create a video version of your documentation that can be placed on a site like YouTube.

Working with Transcultural Documentation

As world trade continues to expand, documentation needs to be written with transcultural readers in mind. As you profile your readers, you should anticipate how your documentation should be adjusted for readers who come from a variety of cultural backgrounds.

Verbal Considerations

First, figure out how the written parts of your documentation will fit the needs of transcultural readers.

TRANSLATE THE TEXT   If the documentation is being sent to a place where another language is spoken, you should have it translated. Then, include both the translated and English versions with the product.

USE BASIC ENGLISH   If the documentation might be sent to people who are not fluent in English, you should use basic words and phrases. Avoid any jargon, idioms, and metaphors that will be understood only by North Americans (e.g., "senior citizens," "bottom line," or "back to square one"). Companies that do business in transcultural markets often maintain lists of basic words to use in documentation.

CHECK MEANINGS OF NAMES AND SLOGANS   Famously, names and slogans don't always translate well into other languages. For example, Pepsi's "Come alive with Pepsi" was translated into, "Pepsi brings your ancestors back from the grave" in

Taiwan. In Spanish, the name of Chevrolet's popular car the "Nova" means "It doesn't go." Coors's slogan "Turn it loose" translated into "Suffer from diarrhea" in some Spanish-speaking countries. So, check with people who are familiar with the target culture and its language to see if your names and slogans have meanings other than those intended.

Design Considerations

Next, do some research to figure out the best way to present your documentation visually to your target readers.

USE ICONS CAREFULLY   Some symbols commonly used in North America can be offensive to other cultures. A pointing finger, for example, is offensive in some Central and South American countries. An "OK" sign is offensive in Arab nations. Dogs are "unclean" animals in many parts of the world, so cartoon dogs often do not work well in documentation for transcultural readers. To avoid these problems, minimize your use of animals, human characters, or body parts whenever possible. Make sure that any icons you use will not confuse or offend your readers in some unintended way.

USE IMAGES CAREFULLY   Images can convey unintended messages to readers, especially in high-context cultures like those of Asia, parts of Africa, and the Middle East. For instance, the way people are dressed in photographs can signal respect or disrespect. Obvious displays of emotion in professional settings can be seen as rude. In some conservative Middle Eastern countries, meanwhile, photographs of people are used for identification only. So, before moving forward with your documentation, you might ask someone from the target culture to look over the images for any unintended meanings.

Link

For more information on working with cross-cultural readers, go to Chapter 2, page 24.

Emergency Instructions

Most of the time, emergency instructions go almost unnoticed. They are posted on a wall or put in the pocket of an airplane seat. But when an emergency happens, these instructions may make the difference between life and death. People need to take action, and they have little time to do so.

Emergency instructions need to be highly visual and brief. Here are some strategies for writing them:

Put the title in large lettering. Big lettering (at least 26-point font size) will help people locate your emergency instructions in a crisis.

MICROGENRE

ON-BOARD TRAIN EMERGENCY INSTRUCTIONS

This set of emergency instructions is designed to help train passengers handle a variety of potential crises.

ALWAYS — Use the Passenger Emergency Intercom to contact a Train Crew Member

Listen for Announcements

FIRE — Move to an unaffected car

Remain inside — tracks are electrified

Follow instructions of emergency workers

Train crews can access fire extinguishers

Do not activate emergency cord

MEDICAL — If a passenger is in distress, notify a crew member immediately

If you are medically qualified and able to assist,

identify yourself to the crew

POLICE — Notify the crew of any unlawful or suspicious activity on board your train

Train crews can contact the police en route

EVACUATION — Open panel above side door

Pull red handle down

Slide door open

Exit the train only when directed

Source: New York Metropolitan Transportation Authority, http://www.mta.info/lirr/safety/bilevel3.htm.

Use only one side of a page or placard. Your emergency instructions should fit on one side of a page, poster, sign, or placard, because people must be able to read them at a glance.

Use familiar icons. Highlight specialized information with icons that represent fire, water, electricity, hazardous materials, police, first aid, fire extinguishers, and so on.

Group information into visual blocks. Use lines, boxes, and white space to create frames around information that belongs together.

Put the safety of people first. Keeping people safe should always be your first concern. Instructions for saving property, machines, or information should be secondary.

Use command voice and keep sentences brief. Each of your commands should fit on one line and should have as few words as possible.

Minimize unnecessary explanations. In a crisis, people need to know what to do, not why to do it that way. So don't clutter up the sign with explanations.

Tell readers to call for help. Remind readers that they should call 911 or contact emergency responders as soon as possible.

Write

Write your own emergency instructions. Pick a potential emergency situation on campus or in your home. Create emergency instructions that fit on one side of a standard piece of paper. Make sure you include icons that highlight important points.

- Documentation describes step by step how to complete a task.

- Basic features of documentation include a specific and precise title; an introduction; a list of parts, tools, and conditions required; sequentially ordered steps; graphics; safety information; a conclusion; and troubleshooting information.

- Determine the rhetorical situation by asking the Five-W and How Questions and analyzing the document's subject, purpose, readers, and context of use.

- Organize and draft your documentation step by step, breaking tasks down into their major and minor actions.

- Safety information should (1) identify the hazard, (2) state the level of risk (Danger, Warning, or Caution), and (3) offer suggestions for avoiding injury or damage.

- User-testing your documentation with sample readers is an effective way to work out any bugs and locate places for improvement. Your observations of these sample readers should help you revise the document.

- Try to use a style that reflects or counters readers' attitudes as they follow the steps.

- Graphics offer important support for the written text. They should be properly labeled by number and inserted on the page where they are referenced.

- Documentation designed for transcultural readers should be mindful about the meanings of symbols and colors in other cultures.

Individual or Team Projects

1. Find an example of documentation in your home or workplace. Using concepts discussed in this chapter, develop a set of criteria to evaluate its content, organization, style, and design. Then, write a two-page memo to your instructor in which you analyze the documentation. Highlight any strengths and make suggestions for improvements.

2. On the Internet or in your home, find information on first aid (handling choking, treating injuries, using CPR, handling drowning, treating shock, dealing with alcohol or drug overdoses). Then, turn this information into a text that is specifically aimed at college students living on campus. You should keep in mind that these individuals will be reluctant to read this text—until it is actually needed. So, write and design it in a way that will be both appealing before injuries occur and highly usable when an injury has occurred.

3. The Case Study at the end of this chapter presents a difficult ethical decision. Pretend you are Jim Helena who is the main character in the case. As Jim, write a memo to your company's CEO in which you express your concerns about the product. Tell the CEO what you think the company should do about the problem. Keep in mind, though, that you are going over the head of Vonn, your supervisor.

4. Choose a culture that is quite different from your own. Through the Internet and your library, research how documentation is written and designed in that culture. Look for examples of documentation designed for people of that culture. Then, write a memo to your instructor in which you explain how documentation is different in that target culture.

Collaborative Projects

Have someone in your group bring to class an everyday household appliance (toaster, blender, hot air popcorn popper, clock radio, MP3 player, etc.). With your group, write and design documentation for this appliance that would be appropriate for 8-year-old children. Your documentation should keep the special needs of these readers in mind. The documentation should also be readable and interesting to these readers, so they will actually use it.

> Visit **My**Writing**Lab** for a Post-test and more technical writing resources.

Revision Challenge

These instructions for playing Klondike are technically correct; however, they are hard to follow. Can you use visual design to revise these instructions to make them more readable?

Playing Klondike (Solitaire)

Many people know Klondike simply as solitaire, because it is such a widely played solitaire game. Klondike is not the most challenging form of solitaire, but it is very enjoyable and known worldwide.

To play Klondike, use one regular pack of cards. Dealing left to right, make seven piles from 28 cards. Place one card on each pile, dealing one fewer pile each round. When you are finished dealing, the pile on the left will have one card, the next pile on the left will have two cards, and so on. The pile farthest to the right will have seven cards. When you are finished dealing the cards, flip the top card in each pile face up.

You are now ready to play. You may move cards among the piles by stacking cards in decreasing numerical order (king to ace). Black cards are placed on red cards and red cards are placed on black cards. For example, a red four can be placed on a black five. If you would like to move an entire stack of face up cards, the bottom card being moved must be placed on a successive card of the opposite color. For example, a face up stack with the jack of hearts as the bottom card can be moved only to a pile with a black queen showing on top. You can also move partial stacks from one pile to another as long as the bottom card you are moving can be placed on the top face up card on the pile to which you are moving it. If a facedown card is ever revealed on top of a pile, it should be turned face up. You can now use this card. If the cards in a pile are ever completely removed, you can replace the pile by putting a king (or a stack with a king as the bottom face up card) in its place.

The rest of the deck is called the "stock." Turn up cards in the stock one by one. If you can play a turned-up card on your piles, place it. If you cannot play the card, put it in the discard pile. As you turn up cards from the stock, you can also play the top card off the discard pile. For example, let us say you have an eight of hearts on top of the discard pile. You turn up a nine of spades from the stock, which you find can be played on a ten of diamonds on top of one of your piles. You can then play the eight of hearts on your discard pile on the newly placed nine of spades.

When an ace is uncovered, you may move it to a scoring pile separate from the seven piles. From then on, cards of the same suit may be placed on the ace in successive order. For example, if the two of hearts is the top face up card in one of your piles, you can place it on the ace of hearts. As successive cards in the suit are the top cards in piles or revealed in the stock, you can place them on your scoring piles.

When playing Klondike properly, you may go through the stock only once (variations of Klondike allow you to go through the stock as many times as you like, three cards at a time). When you are finished going through the stock, count up the cards placed in your scoring piles. The total cards in these piles make up your score for the game.

Purified Junk

Jim Helena is a design engineer at AquaSafe Water Purifiers. It's a great job, and he feels really good about designing whole-house water purifiers that remove trace bacteria, chemicals, and other elements from the public water supply.

Recently, Jim was asked to complete a special project because the lead engineer resigned. The prior engineer was designing and building prototypes of solar-powered water purifiers for use in developing countries in South America and Africa. These specialized purifiers would allow small villages to filter contaminated water for drinking. The marketing arm of AquaSafe had already been featuring the project in "feel good" advertisements that presented a positive image of the company. AquaSafe's stock was rising in value because of the positive press and the additional sales it was receiving due to the high-profile project.

Initially, Jim was impressed when he saw the prototypes and read through the specs. A lack of clean drinking water is a major problem in parts of South America and Africa, so these water purifiers could make a big difference in people's lives. Meanwhile, their solar-power energy source would allow villages who have no electricity to purify significant amounts of drinking water.

But then, Jim noticed a problem in the documentation. It warned that the purifiers were designed for use with treated tap water only, which is standard in North America but not in the villages where these purifiers would be used. The filters were not designed to remove the kinds of contaminants that are common in untreated water in developing countries. The documentation was very clear about the limitations of the filters.

He ran some tests and estimated that the filters would only last a few weeks if used with contaminated water supplies. That meant villages in Africa and South America would need to obtain at least 15–20 replacement filters per purifier per year. That would be expensive.

Jim asked his supervisor, Vonn Huston, whether there was a plan for supplying replacement filters with each purifier. Vonn said, "We're not a charity. We'll get each village started with a couple filters, but they are going to need to import more filters if they want to keep the program going. Maybe an aid organization can supply them more filters, but we can't." Jim mentioned that there was no way people who are struggling to find enough food would be able to buy replacement water filters. Vonn shrugged his shoulders and said, "It is what it is. We're supposed to start delivering those purifiers in three months, so you better get something into production."

Jim realized that the purifiers, no matter how well designed, were going to be nothing more than junk within a couple months because the filters would get clogged and stop working. Then villagers would need to return back to drinking contaminated water.

How do you think Jim should address this problem?

CHAPTER

8

Proposals

Types of Proposals *196*

Step 1: Make a Plan and Do
Research *196*

Step 2: Organize and Draft Your
Proposal *203*

Step 3: Choose the Style, Design,
and Medium *218*

Microgenre: The Elevator
Pitch *223*

What You Need to Know *225*

Exercises and Projects *225*

Case Study: The Mole *229*

In this chapter, you will learn:

- The purpose of proposals and their uses in the workplace.

- The basic features and types of proposals.

- How to plan and do research for a proposal.

- How to organize and draft the major sections in a proposal.

- Strategies for using plain and persuasive style to make a proposal influential.

- How document design and graphics can enhance a proposal.

Proposals are the lifeblood of the technical workplace. Whatever your field, you will be asked to write proposals that describe new projects, present ideas, offer new strategies, and promote services. The purpose of a proposal is to present your ideas and plans for your readers to consider. Almost all projects begin with proposals, so you need to master this important genre to be successful.

Types of Proposals

Proposals are categorized in a couple of different ways. *Internal* proposals are used within a company to plan or propose new projects or products. *External* proposals are used to offer services or products to clients outside the company.

Proposals are also classified as *solicited* or *unsolicited,* depending on whether they were requested by the readers.

Solicited proposals are proposals requested by the readers. For example, your company's management might request proposals for new projects. Or, your team might be "solicited" to write a proposal that answers a request for proposals (RFP) sent out by a client.

Unsolicited proposals are proposals not requested by the readers. For example, your team might prepare an unsolicited internal proposal to pitch an innovative idea to your company's management. Or, your team might use an unsolicited external proposal as a sales tool to offer your company's clients a product or service.

Figure 8.1 shows an internal, solicited proposal. In this example, a team within the company is pitching a plan to overhaul the company's website. This proposal is being used to persuade management to agree to the team's ideas.

Another kind of proposal is the grant proposal. Researchers and nonprofit organizations prepare grant proposals to obtain funding for their projects. For example, one of the major funding sources for grants in science and technology is the National Science Foundation (NSF). Through its website, the NSF offers funding opportunities for scientific research (Figure 8.2).

Step 1: Make a Plan and Do Research

Because proposals are difficult to write, it is important to follow a reliable writing process that will help you develop your proposal's content, organization, style, and design. An important first step in this process is to start with a planning and researching phase. During this phase, you will define the rhetorical situation and start collecting content for the proposal.

Planning

A good way to start planning your proposal is to analyze the situations in which it will be used. Begin by answering the Five-W and How Questions:

Who will be able to say yes to my ideas, and what are their characteristics?

Why is this proposal being written?

What information do the readers need to make a decision?

Where will the proposal be used?

When will the proposal be used?

How will the proposal be used?

Proposals

Here is a basic model for organizing a proposal. This organizational pattern, though, is flexible, allowing the contents of a proposal to be arranged in a variety of ways. The proposal genre is not a formula to be followed mechanically. You should alter this pattern to suit the needs of your proposal's subject, purpose, readers, and context of use.

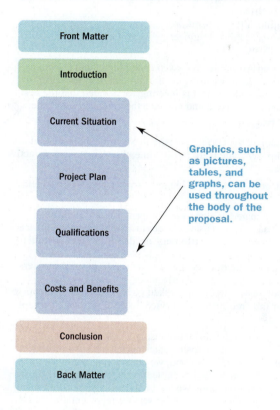

Front Matter

Introduction

Current Situation

Project Plan

Qualifications

Costs and Benefits

Conclusion

Back Matter

Graphics, such as pictures, tables, and graphs, can be used throughout the body of the proposal.

Basic Features of Proposals

In technical workplaces, proposals tend to have the following features:

- **Introduction** that identifies the problem and your solution
- **Description** of the current situation that explains the problem, including its causes and effects
- **Description** of the project plan that shows step by step how the problem can be solved
- **Graphics and graphs** that illustrate the problem and the project plan
- **Qualifications** that describe who will participate in the project
- **Summary** of costs and benefits
- **Budget** that itemizes the costs of the project

An Internal Solicited Proposal

Figure 8.1:
This small proposal is an internal proposal that is pitching a new idea to a manager. After a brief introduction, it describes the current situation and offers a plan for solving a problem. It concludes by highlighting the benefits of the plan.

JumperCom

Date: April 11, 2014
To: Jim Trujillo, VP of Operations
From: Sarah Voss, Lambda Engineering Team Leader
Re: Cutting Costs

Internal proposals are often written in memo format.

At our meeting on April 4th, you asked each project team to come up with one good idea for cutting costs. Our team met on April 7th to kick around some ideas. At this meeting we decided that the best way to cut costs is to expand and enhance the company's website.

The main point of the proposal is stated up front.

Our Current Website

Background information signals that the proposal was solicited.

When we developed the current website in Spring 2008, it served our company's purposes quite well. For its time, the website was attractive and interactive.

This section describes the current situation.

Six years later, our website is no longer cutting edge—it's obsolete. The website

- looks antiquated, making our company seem out of touch
- does not address our customers' questions about current products
- does not address our customers' needs for product documentation
- is not a tool that our salespeople can use to provide answers and documentation to the customers
- does not answer frequently asked questions, forcing clients to call our toll-free customer service lines for answers to simple questions.

As a result, our outdated website is causing a few important problems. First, we are likely losing sales because our customers don't see us as cutting edge. Second, we are wasting hundreds of thousands of dollars on printed documents that the customers throw away after a glance. And, third, we are unnecessarily spending many more thousands of dollars on customer service representatives and tollfree phone lines. *A conservative estimate suggests that our outdated website could be costing us around $400,000 each year.*

Renovating the Website

We believe a good way to cut costs and improve customer relations is to renovate the website. We envision a fully interactive site that customers can use to find answers to their questions, check on prices, and communicate with our service personnel. Meanwhile, our sales staff can use the website to discuss our products with clients. Instead of lugging around printed documents, our salespeople would use their tablet computers to show products or make presentations.

This section offers a plan for the readers' consideration.

Renovating the site will require four major steps:

Step One: Study the Potential Uses of Our Website

With a consultant, we should study how our website might be better used by customers and salespeople. The consultant would survey our clients and salespeople to determine what kind of website would be most useful to them. The consultant would then develop a design for the website.

Step Two: Hire a Professional Web Designer to Renovate the Site

The plan is described step by step.

We should hire a professional web designer to implement our design, because modern websites are rather complex. A professional would provide us with an efficient, well-organized website that would include all the functions we are seeking.

Step Three: Train One of Our Employees to Be a Webmaster

We should hire or retrain one of our employees to be the webmaster of the site. We need someone who is working on the site daily and making regular updates. Being the webmaster for the site should be this employee's job description.

Step Four: User-Test the New Website with Our Customers and Salespeople

Once we have created a new version of the website, we should user-test it with our customers and salespeople. Perhaps we could pay some of our customers to try out the site and show us where it could be improved. Our salespeople will certainly give us plenty of feedback.

2

(continued)

At the end of this process, we would have a fully functioning website that would save us money almost immediately.

Costs and Benefits of Our Idea

Proposal concludes by discussing costs and benefits of the plan.

Renovating the website would have many advantages:

- The new website will save us printing costs. We estimate that the printing costs at our company could be sliced in half—perhaps more—because our customers would be able to download our documents directly from the website, rather than ask us to send these documents to them. That's a potential savings of $300,000.
- The new website will provide better service to our customers. Currently, our customers go to the website first when they have questions. By providing more information in an interactive format, we can cut down dramatically on calls to our customer service center. We could save up to $120,000 in personnel costs and long-distance charges.
- Our sales staff will find the new website a useful tool when they have questions. When products change, salespeople will immediately see those changes reflected on the website. As a result, more sales might be generated because product information will be immediately available online.

A quick estimate shows that a website renovation would cost us about $40,000. We would also need to shift the current webmaster's responsibilities from part time to full time, costing us about $20,000 per year more. The savings, though, are obvious. For an initial investment of $60,000 and a yearly investment of $20,000 thereafter, we will minimally save about $400,000 a year.

Thank you for giving us this opportunity to present our ideas. If you would like to talk with us about this proposal, please call me at 555-1204, or e-mail me at sarahv@jumpercom.net.

3

The National Science Foundation Home Page

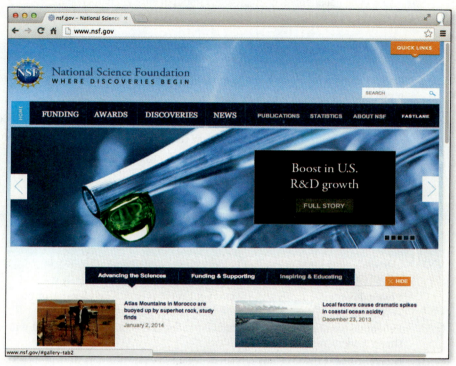

Figure 8.2:
The National Science Foundation (NSF) website offers information on grant opportunities. The home page, shown here, discusses some of the recent research projects that have received grants.

Source: National Science Foundation, http://www.nsf.gov

Once you have answered these questions, you are ready to start thinking in-depth about your proposal's subject, purpose, readers, and context of use.

SUBJECT Define exactly what your proposal is about. Where are the boundaries of the subject? What need-to-know information must readers have if they are going to say yes to your ideas?

PURPOSE Clearly state the purpose of your proposal in one sentence. What should the proposal achieve?

Some key action verbs for your purpose statement might include the following:

to persuade	*to argue for*	*to offer*
to convince	*to advocate*	*to suggest*
to provide	*to present*	*to recommend*
to describe	*to propose*	*to support*

A purpose statement might look something like this:

> The purpose of this proposal is to recommend that our company change its manufacturing process to include more automation.

Link

For more help on defining need-to-know information, go to Chapter 2, page 20.

Link

To read more about defining your purpose, go to Chapter 1, page 5.

In this proposal, our aim is to persuade the state of North Carolina to develop a multimodal approach to protect itself from stronger hurricanes, which may be caused by climate change.

READERS   More than any other kind of document, proposals require you to fully understand your readers and anticipate their needs, values, and attitudes.

Primary readers (action takers) are the people who can approve your ideas. They need good reasons and solid evidence to understand and agree to your ideas.

Secondary readers (advisors) are usually technical experts in your field. They won't be the people who say yes to your proposal, but their opinions will be highly valued by your proposal's primary readers.

Tertiary readers (evaluators) can be just about anyone else who might have an interest in the project and could potentially undermine it. These readers might include lawyers, journalists, and community activists, among others.

Gatekeepers (supervisors) are the people at your own company who will need to look over your proposal before it is sent out. Your immediate supervisor is a gatekeeper, as are your company's accountants, lawyers, and technical advisors.

Link
For more strategies for analyzing your readers, see Chapter 2, page 19.

CONTEXT OF USE   The document's context of use will also greatly influence how your readers interpret the ideas in your proposal.

Physical context concerns the places your readers may read, discuss, or use your proposal.

Economic context involves the financial issues and economic trends that will shape readers' responses to your ideas.

Ethical context involves any ethical or legal issues involved in your proposed project.

Political context concerns the people inside and outside your company who will be affected by your proposal.

Link
For more help defining the context of use, turn to Chapter 2, page 22.

Proposals are legal documents that can be brought into court if a dispute occurs, so you need to make sure that everything you say in the proposal is accurate and truthful.

Researching

After defining your proposal's rhetorical situation, you should start collecting information and creating the content of your document (Figure 8.3). Chapter 14 describes how to do research, so research strategies won't be fully described here. As a brief review, here are some research strategies that are especially applicable for writing proposals:

DO BACKGROUND RESEARCH   The key to writing a persuasive proposal is to fully understand the problem you are trying to solve. Use the Internet, print sources, and empirical methods to find as much information about your subject as you can.

ASK SUBJECT MATTER EXPERTS (SMEs)   Spend time interviewing experts who know a great amount about your subject. They can give you insight into the problem you are trying to solve and suggest some potential solutions.

Doing Research on Your Subject

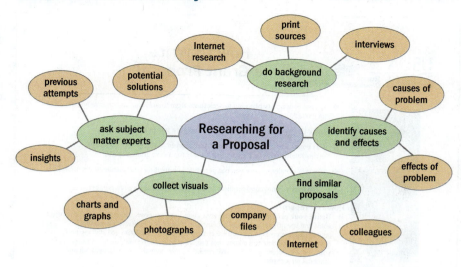

Figure 8.3:
A logical map, like this one, might help you research your subject from a variety of directions. When researching the background of a proposal, collect as much information as possible.

PAY ATTENTION TO CAUSES AND EFFECTS All problems have causes, and all causes create effects. In your analysis of the problem your proposal is trying to solve, identify any causes and effects.

FIND SIMILAR PROPOSALS On the Internet or at your workplace, you can probably locate proposals that have dealt with similar problems in the past. They might give you some insight into how those problems were solved.

COLLECT VISUALS Proposals are persuasive documents, so they often include plenty of graphics, such as photographs, charts, illustrations, and graphs. Collect any materials, data, and information that will help you add a visual dimension to your proposal. If appropriate, you might use a digital camera or your mobile phone to take pictures to include in the document.

Link

To learn more about doing research, turn to Chapter 14, page 365.

Step 2: Organize and Draft Your Proposal

Writing the first draft of a proposal is always difficult because proposals describe the future—a future that you are trying to envision for your readers and yourself.

A good way to draft your proposal is to write it one section at a time. Think of the proposal as four or five separate mini-documents that can stand alone. When you finish drafting one section, move on to the next.

Also, before drafting, check if your readers require a specific format or arrangement for the proposal. The information sheet in Figure 8.4, for example, includes helpful advice on writing community-planning proposals from the Rural Development Offices of the US Department of Agriculture. As demonstrated in this information sheet, each scientific and technical discipline alters the proposal genre to fit its specific needs.

Figure 8.4:
These guidelines explain how this government agency prefers proposals to be written.

How to Write a Grant Proposal

USDA Rural Development
--
Cooperative Programs
--
TN-13
Updated:
January 2008

By:
Justin Goetz
&
Llana Varallyay
--
www.ocdweb.sc.egov.usda.gov

CD Technotes

❖ Is your community planning to seek funds from foundations or corporations as part of an overall fundraising plan?

❖ Have you already applied for funding and been turned down?

❖ Has your community already created a nonprofit, 501(c)(3) development organization and is that organization ready to receive grant monies?

❖ Are you wondering how you can get started on funding your community's needs?

If so, you may want to consider these tips for writing effective grant proposals.

How To Prepare

1) **Define your project** by clarifying your underlying purpose. Determine general project goals and specific objectives to accomplish. You should consider a timetable, anticipated outcomes, a method for evaluating results, and estimated staffing needs. You also should determine how your project adheres to the philosophy or mission of your agency. Potential funders will consider more favorably well thought out and practical project plans.

2) **Estimate costs and identify the right funding sources** by looking for consistency between the purpose/goals of your project and those of the funder. Direct contact with the funder is imperative. Be sure to inquire into the maximum amount of money available, the average size of awards, and whether the funder has a geographic preference for applicant projects. You also should find out how they make decisions and what types of projects it funds (project funding, capital funding, seed funding, etc.). If possible, identify a project officer to be your liaison to address your questions.

3) **Acquire proposal guidelines and submission requirements** by requesting this information from the funder. You should find a potential funder who will support your proposal so you are not caught trying to change your goals to fit those of the funder. To fully gauge this support, send the funder a "letter of intent" with basic information on your project idea to see if they would be interested in viewing your proposal. Follow up this letter with telephone calls or face-to-face meetings to develop a relationship with the funder, a key to the success of the proposal. The more the funder knows you, the more likely they will fund your project.

How To Write an Effective Proposal

1) The *Executive Summary* conveys all key information and serves to convince the reader of the importance of your project and its potential in successfully addressing your goals. It should include a brief statement of the problem/need recognized by your organization and a concise description of the proposed solution. You also should explain the amount of grant money required for your project and any plans for future funding. You may wish to briefly state the name, history, and activities of your organization, emphasizing its capacity to carry out the proposal. Also, list any experts or partnerships associated with your organization (particularly those that are associated with the project proposal).

Cooperative Programs • 1400 Independence Ave SW. • Stop 3254 • Washington, DC 20250-3254
Committed to the future of rural communities.
Rural Development is an Equal Opportunity Lender, Provider, and Employer. Complaints of discrimination should be sent to USDA, Director, Office of Civil Rights, Washington, DC 20250-9410

Source: Rural Development, USDA, http://www.rurdev.usda.gov/SupportDocuments/tn13GrantProposal.pdf

2) The *Statement of Need* presents the facts and evidence that support your project. It should demonstrate that your program addresses a need in an inventive manner that is particularly effective in meeting the need. Remember to include goals and measurable objectives, provide a compelling narrative of the need, and ensure that the focus of the document is placed on the particular, unique need(s) of the community (and not the needs of your organization).

3) The *Project Description* presents your plan by aligning your project with the purpose/goals of the funding source. It should include specific details of the method and process by which the goals and objectives will be accomplished. Be sure to note the distinction between methods, objectives, and goals. You should also outline the proposed activities and their expected outcomes. A description of personnel functions with names and credentials of key staff/consultants often proves beneficial in this portion of the proposal.

4) The *Evaluation Plan* indicates that you take your objectives seriously and want to know how well you have achieved them. There are three types of evaluations—formative (showing the small changes brought by the project over time), summative (a pre-test of needs before the project and a post-test of needs at the end of the project to show progress), and outcome (a description of how the community was improved overall by the project). You should describe the manner in which evaluation information will be collected and how it will be analyzed and the results reported. Ask funders for their evaluation preference.

5) The *Budget* lists all the personnel and non-personnel items included in your project, specifying estimated costs. Costs should be grouped into subcategories, reflecting the critical areas of expense. A narrative portion might help explain unusual items in the budget, though it is not always needed. Be sure to budget *for all expenses*, no matter how trivial. More often than not, organizations do not consider the full costs of project operation, leaving out smaller costs like supplies (pens, paper, etc., an average cost, in 2007, of $150 per project employee per year) and transportation. Also, be sure to highlight the contributions of your own organization to this project—whether money or in-kind support. The more in-house resources you can chalk up to the effort, the more likely the funder will fund your project. Even volunteer hours can be counted as in-house contributions, complete with a dollar value (depending upon the fair-market value of the jobs they are given or the generally accepted "volunteer rate," which was $18.77 per hour for 2006).

6) Find out if *Supporting Materials* are allowed or desired by the funder. If so, you may wish to attach a résumé of your nonprofit organization, describing its structure, programs, and special expertise. Attach a list of the board of directors. Examples of supporting materials include letters of recommendation, certifications, or information about project personnel.

7) The *Sustainability Component and Conclusion* calls attention to the future, perhaps outlining possible follow-up activities. It should state how the project might carry-on without further grant support to assure the funders that they are making an investment in something that will last. A good way of assuring the funders of a proposal's sustainability is to show that the project has a large amount of public support, and that fundraising or fund generating will be a part of and help accomplish the project's mission. A good way of assuring funders of this quality is to show that the project arose from your community's strategic planning process and that the project is a part of or is in keeping with its strategic plan (carrying with it a great amount of influence). As this is the last chance to make an appeal for your project, you may want to briefly restate what your organization wants to do, its importance, and why you need funding to accomplish it.

Additional Resources

- Idealist.org Nonprofit Resources/FAQs – **http://www.idealist.org/if/i/en/npofaq**
- Foundation Center, "Learn About Proposal Writing" – **http://foundationcenter.org/getstarted/learnabout/proposalwriting.html**
- Rural Information Center's Guide to Funding Resources – **http://www.nal.usda.gov/ric/ricpubs/funding/fundguide.html**
- Independent Sector "Value of Volunteer Time" – http://www.independentsector.org/programs/**research/volunteer_time.html**

Writing the Introduction

As with all documents, the proposal's introduction sets a context, or framework, for the body of the document. A proposal's introduction will usually include up to six moves:

Link

For additional help on writing introductions, see Chapter 15, page 399.

Move 1: Define the *subject,* stating clearly what the proposal is about.

Move 2: State the *purpose* of the proposal, preferably in one sentence.

Move 3: State the proposal's *main point.*

Move 4: Stress the *importance of the subject.*

Move 5: Offer *background information* on the subject.

Move 6: Forecast the *organization* of the proposal.

These moves can be made in just about any order, depending on your proposal, and they are not all required. Minimally, your proposal's introduction should clearly identify your *subject, purpose,* and *main point.* The other three moves are helpful, but they are optional. Figure 8.5 shows a sample introduction that uses all six moves.

Describing the Current Situation

The aim of the *current situation* section—sometimes called the *background* section—is to define the problem your plan will solve. You should accomplish three things in this section of the proposal:

- Define and describe the problem.
- Discuss the causes of the problem.
- Discuss the effects of the problem if nothing is done.

For example, let us say you are writing a proposal to improve safety at your college or workplace. Your current situation section would first define the problem by proving there is a lack of safety and showing its seriousness. Then, it would discuss the causes and effects of that problem.

MAPPING OUT THE SITUATION Logical mapping is a helpful technique for developing your argument in the current situation section. Here are some steps you can follow to map out the content:

The Current Situation

- Define and describe the problem.
- Discuss the causes of the problem.
- Discuss the effects if nothing is done about the problem.

AT A GLANCE

1. Write the problem in the middle of your screen or piece of paper. Put a circle around the problem.

2. Write down the two to five major causes of that problem. Circle them, and connect them to the problem.

3. Write down some minor causes around each major cause, treating each major cause as a separate problem of its own. Circle the minor causes and connect them to the major causes.

Figure 8.6 illustrates how your logical map for the current situation section might look.

Growth and Flexibility with Telecommuting

A Proposal to Northside Design from Insight Systems

Offers background information.

Founded in 2002, Northside Design is one of the classic entrepreneurial success stories in architecture. Today, this company is one of the leading architectural firms in the Chicago market with over 50 million dollars in annual revenue. With growth, however, comes growing pains, and Northside now faces an important decision about how it will manage its growth in the near future. The right decision could lead to more market share, increased sales, and even more prominence in the architectural field. However, Northside also needs to safeguard itself against over-extension in case the Chicago construction market unexpectedly begins to recede.

Defines the subject.

Stresses the importance of the subject.

"Northside needs to safeguard itself against over-extension in case the Chicago construction market unexpectedly begins to recede."

To help you make the right decision, this proposal offers an innovative strategy that will support your firm's growth while maintaining its flexibility. Specifically, we propose Northside implement a telecommuting network that allows selected employees to work a few days each week at home. Telecommuting will provide your company with the office space it needs to continue growing. Meanwhile, this approach will avoid a large investment in new facilities and disruption to the company's current operations.

States the purpose of the proposal.

States the main point.

Forecasts the body of the proposal.

In this proposal, we will first discuss the results of our research into Northside's office space needs. Second, we will offer a plan for using a telecommuting network to free up more space at Northside's current office. Third, we will review Insight Systems' qualifications to assist Northside with its move into the world of telecommuting. And finally, we will go over some of the costs and advantages of our plan.

1

Figure 8.5: This introduction makes all six "moves." As a result, it is somewhat lengthy. Nevertheless, this introduction prepares readers to understand the information in the body of the proposal.

Mapping Out the Current Situation

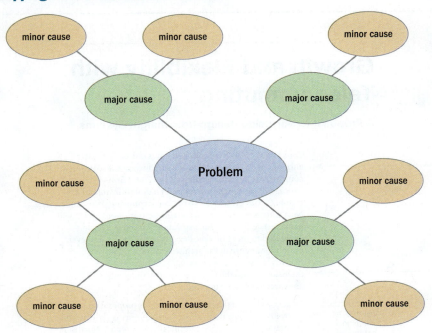

DRAFTING THE CURRENT SITUATION SECTION   Your proposal's current situation section should include an opening, a body, and a closing:

> **Opening**—Identify and define the problem you will describe.
>
> **Body**—Discuss the *causes* of the problem, showing how these causes brought about the problem.
>
> **Closing**—Discuss the *effects* of not doing anything about the problem.

The length of the current situation section depends on your readers' familiarity with the problem. If readers are new to the subject, then several paragraphs or even pages might be required. However, if they fully understand the problem already, maybe only a few paragraphs are needed. Figure 8.7 shows an example of the current situation section from a proposal.

Describing the Project Plan

A proposal's *project plan* section offers a step-by-step method for solving the problem. Your goal is to tell your readers *how* you would like to handle the problem and *why* you would handle it that way. In this section, you should do the following:

- Identify the solution.
- State the objectives of the plan.
- Describe the plan's major and minor steps.
- Identify the deliverables or outcomes.

Example Current Situation Section

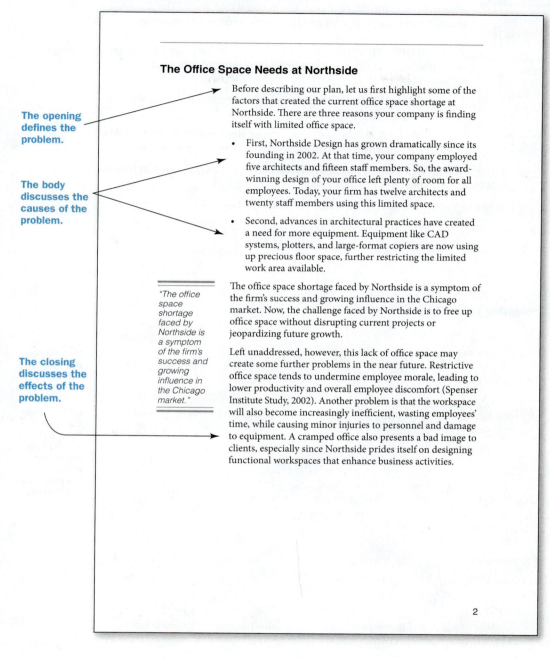

The opening defines the problem.

The body discusses the causes of the problem.

The closing discusses the effects of the problem.

The Office Space Needs at Northside

Before describing our plan, let us first highlight some of the factors that created the current office space shortage at Northside. There are three reasons your company is finding itself with limited office space.

- First, Northside Design has grown dramatically since its founding in 2002. At that time, your company employed five architects and fifteen staff members. So, the award-winning design of your office left plenty of room for all employees. Today, your firm has twelve architects and twenty staff members using this limited space.

- Second, advances in architectural practices have created a need for more equipment. Equipment like CAD systems, plotters, and large-format copiers are now using up precious floor space, further restricting the limited work area available.

"The office space shortage faced by Northside is a symptom of the firm's success and growing influence in the Chicago market."

The office space shortage faced by Northside is a symptom of the firm's success and growing influence in the Chicago market. Now, the challenge faced by Northside is to free up office space without disrupting current projects or jeopardizing future growth.

Left unaddressed, however, this lack of office space may create some further problems in the near future. Restrictive office space tends to undermine employee morale, leading to lower productivity and overall employee discomfort (Spenser Institute Study, 2002). Another problem is that the workspace will also become increasingly inefficient, wasting employees' time, while causing minor injuries to personnel and damage to equipment. A cramped office also presents a bad image to clients, especially since Northside prides itself on designing functional workspaces that enhance business activities.

2

Figure 8.7:
The current situation section includes an opening, a body, and a closing. The causes of the problem are discussed mainly in the body paragraphs, while the effects are usually discussed at the end of the section.

The Project Plan

• Identify the solution.
• State the objectives of the plan.
• Describe the plan's major and minor steps.
• Identify the deliverables or outcomes.

As you begin drafting this section, look back at your original purpose statement for the proposal, which you wrote during the planning phase. Now, imagine a solution that might achieve that purpose.

MAPPING OUT THE PROJECT PLAN   When you have identified a possible solution, you can again use logical mapping to turn your idea into a plan:

1. Write your solution in the middle of your screen or a sheet of paper. Circle this solution.

2. Write down the two to five major steps needed to achieve that solution. Circle them and connect them to the solution.

3. Write down the minor steps required to achieve each major step. Circle them and connect them to the major steps.

As shown in Figure 8.8, your map should illustrate the basic steps of your plan.

Mapping Out a Project Plan

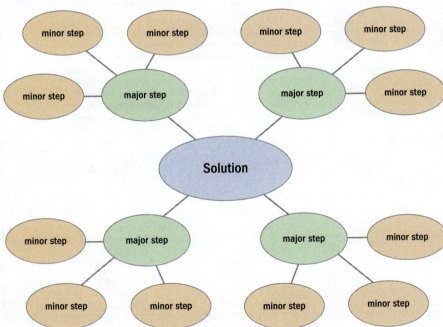

Figure 8.8: Logical mapping will help you figure out how to solve the problem. In a map like the one shown here, you can visualize your entire plan by writing out the major and minor steps.

DRAFTING THE PROJECT PLAN SECTION   Your project plan section should have an opening, a body, and a closing. This section will describe step by step how you will achieve your project's purpose.

> **Opening**—Identify your overall solution to the problem. You can even give your plan a name to make it sound more real (e.g., the "Restore Central Campus Project"). Your opening might also include a list of project objectives so readers can see what goals your plan is striving to achieve.
>
> **Body**—Walk the readers through your plan step by step. Address each major step separately, discussing the minor steps needed to achieve that major step. It is also helpful to tell readers *why* each major and minor step is needed.
>
> **Closing**—Summarize the final *deliverables,* or outcomes, of your plan. The deliverables are the goods and services that you will provide when the project is finished.

As shown in the example proposal in Figure 8.9, the project plan section explains *why* each step is needed and identifies *what* will be delivered when the project is finished.

Describing Qualifications

The qualifications section presents the credentials of your team or company, showing why your team is qualified to carry out the project plan. Minimally, the aim of this section is to demonstrate that your team or company is able to do the work. Ideally, you also want to prove that your team or company is *best qualified* to handle the project.

As you begin drafting this section, keep the following saying in mind: *What makes us different makes us attractive.* In other words, pay attention to the qualities that make your team or company different from your competitors. What are your company's strengths? What makes you better than the others?

A typical qualifications section offers information on three aspects of your team or company:

> **Description of personnel**—Short biographies of managers who will be involved in the project; demographic information on the company's workforce; description of support staff.
>
> **Description of organization**—Corporate mission, philosophy, and history of the company; corporate facilities and equipment; organizational structure of the company.
>
> **Previous experience**—Past and current clients; a list of similar projects that have been completed; case studies that describe past projects.

Figure 8.10 shows a sample qualifications section that includes these three kinds of information. Pay attention to how this section does more than *describe* the company—it makes an argument that the bidders are uniquely qualified to handle the project.

You should never underestimate the importance of the qualifications section in a proposal. In the end, your readers will not accept the proposal if they do not believe that your team or company has the personnel, facilities, or experience to do the work.

Figure 8.9:
An effective project plan section includes an opening, a body, and a closing. The opening states the solution and offers some objectives. The body walks the readers through the plan's steps. The closing identifies the major deliverables of the plan.

Our Plan: Flexibility and Telecommuting

Managing Northside's limited office space requires a solution that allows the company to grow but does not sacrifice financial flexibility. Therefore, we believe a successful solution must meet the following objectives:

Objectives →

- minimize disruption to Northside's current operations
- minimize costs, preserving Northside's financial flexibility
- retain Northside's current office on Michigan Avenue
- foster a dynamic workplace that will be appealing to Northside's architects and staff.

Our Objectives:
- *minimize disruption*
- *minimize costs*
- *retain Northside's current office*
- *foster a dynamic workplace*

To meet these objectives, Insight Systems proposes to collaborate with Northside to develop a telecommunication network that allows selected employees to work at home. ←

Solution to problem

The primary advantage of telecommuting is that it frees up office space for the remaining employees who need to work in the main office. Telecommuting will also avoid overextending Northside's financial resources, so the firm can quickly react to the crests and valleys of the market.

Our plan will be implemented in four major phases. First, we will study Northside's telecommuting options. Second, we will design a local area network (LAN) that will allow selected employees to telecommute from a home office. Third, we will train Northside's employees in telecommuting basics. And finally, we will assess the success of the telecommuting program after it has been implemented.

Phase One: Analyzing Northside's Telecommuting Needs

We will start out by analyzing the specific workplace requirements of Northside's employees and management. The results of this analysis will allow us to work closely with Northside's management to develop a telecommuting program that fits the unique demands of a dynamic architecture firm.

3

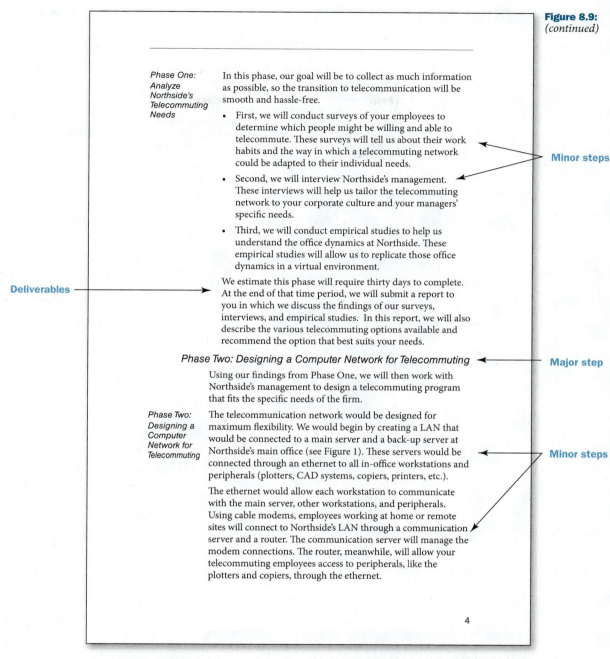

Phase One: Analyze Northside's Telecommuting Needs

In this phase, our goal will be to collect as much information as possible, so the transition to telecommunication will be smooth and hassle-free.

- First, we will conduct surveys of your employees to determine which people might be willing and able to telecommute. These surveys will tell us about their work habits and the way in which a telecommuting network could be adapted to their individual needs.

- Second, we will interview Northside's management. These interviews will help us tailor the telecommuting network to your corporate culture and your managers' specific needs.

- Third, we will conduct empirical studies to help us understand the office dynamics at Northside. These empirical studies will allow us to replicate those office dynamics in a virtual environment.

Minor steps

We estimate this phase will require thirty days to complete. At the end of that time period, we will submit a report to you in which we discuss the findings of our surveys, interviews, and empirical studies. In this report, we will also describe the various telecommuting options available and recommend the option that best suits your needs.

Deliverables

Phase Two: Designing a Computer Network for Telecommuting

Major step

Using our findings from Phase One, we will then work with Northside's management to design a telecommuting program that fits the specific needs of the firm.

Phase Two: Designing a Computer Network for Telecommuting

The telecommunication network would be designed for maximum flexibility. We would begin by creating a LAN that would be connected to a main server and a back-up server at Northside's main office (see Figure 1). These servers would be connected through an ethernet to all in-office workstations and peripherals (plotters, CAD systems, copiers, printers, etc.).

Minor steps

The ethernet would allow each workstation to communicate with the main server, other workstations, and peripherals. Using cable modems, employees working at home or remote sites will connect to Northside's LAN through a communication server and a router. The communication server will manage the modem connections. The router, meanwhile, will allow your telecommuting employees access to peripherals, like the plotters and copiers, through the ethernet.

4

(continued)

The router will also allow Northside's main office to connect easily with future branch offices and remote clients.

To ensure the security of the LAN, we will equip the network with the most advanced security hardware and software available. The router (hardware) will be programmed to serve as a "firewall" against intruders. We will also install the most advanced encryption and virus software available to protect your employees' transmissions.

Figure 1: The Local Area Network

The graphic illustrates a complex concept.

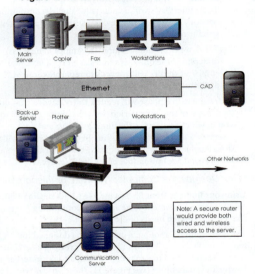

Figure 1: An ethernet allows you to interconnect the office internally and externally.

5

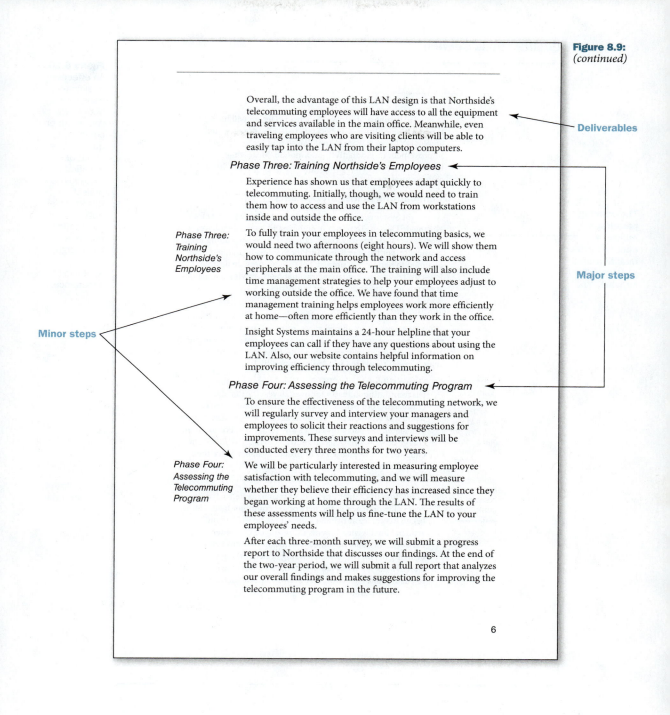

Overall, the advantage of this LAN design is that Northside's telecommuting employees will have access to all the equipment and services available in the main office. Meanwhile, even traveling employees who are visiting clients will be able to easily tap into the LAN from their laptop computers.

Deliverables

Phase Three: Training Northside's Employees

Experience has shown us that employees adapt quickly to telecommuting. Initially, though, we would need to train them how to access and use the LAN from workstations inside and outside the office.

Phase Three: Training Northside's Employees

To fully train your employees in telecommuting basics, we would need two afternoons (eight hours). We will show them how to communicate through the network and access peripherals at the main office. The training will also include time management strategies to help your employees adjust to working outside the office. We have found that time management training helps employees work more efficiently at home—often more efficiently than they work in the office.

Major steps

Minor steps

Insight Systems maintains a 24-hour helpline that your employees can call if they have any questions about using the LAN. Also, our website contains helpful information on improving efficiency through telecommuting.

Phase Four: Assessing the Telecommuting Program

To ensure the effectiveness of the telecommuting network, we will regularly survey and interview your managers and employees to solicit their reactions and suggestions for improvements. These surveys and interviews will be conducted every three months for two years.

Phase Four: Assessing the Telecommuting Program

We will be particularly interested in measuring employee satisfaction with telecommuting, and we will measure whether they believe their efficiency has increased since they began working at home through the LAN. The results of these assessments will help us fine-tune the LAN to your employees' needs.

After each three-month survey, we will submit a progress report to Northside that discusses our findings. At the end of the two-year period, we will submit a full report that analyzes our overall findings and makes suggestions for improving the telecommuting program in the future.

6

Qualifications Section

Figure 8.10: An effective qualifications section shows why your team or company is qualified, or is the best qualified, to handle a project. In this sample, notice how the section makes a clean argument by appealing to experience.

When we complete this plan, Northside Design will have a fully functional telecommuting network that will allow selected employees to work from home. You should see an immediate improvement in productivity and morale. Meanwhile, you will be able to stay financially flexible to compete in the Chicago architectural market.

Qualifications at Insight Systems

The opening paragraph makes a claim that the qualifications section will support.

At Insight Systems, we know this moment is a pivotal one for Northside Design. To preserve and expand its market share, Northside needs to grow, but it cannot risk overextending itself financially. For these reasons, Insight Systems is uniquely qualified to handle this project, because we provide flexible, low-cost telecommuting networks that help growing companies stay responsive to shifts in their industries.

Management and Labor

With over seventy combined years in the industry, our management team offers the insight and responsiveness required to handle your complex growth needs. (The résumés of our management team are included in Appendix B).

> "With over seventy combined years in the industry, our management team offers the insight and responsiveness required to handle your complex growth needs."

Hanna Gibbons, our CEO, has been working in the telecommuting industry for over 20 years. After she graduated from MIT with a Ph.D in computer science, she worked at Krayson International as a systems designer. Then years later, she had worked her way up to Vice President in charge of Krayson's Telecommuting Division. In 2005, Dr. Gibbons took over as CEO of Insight Systems. Since then, Dr. Gibbons has built this company into a major industry leader with gross sales of $15 million per year.

Description of personnel

Frank Roberts, Chief Engineer at Insight Systems, has 30 years of experience in the networked computer field. He began his career at Brindle Labs, where he worked on artificial intelligence systems using analog computer networks. In 2000, he joined the Insight Systems team, bringing his unique understanding of networking to our team. Frank is very detail oriented, often working long hours to ensure that each computer network meets each client's exact specifications and needs.

7

Lisa Miller, Insight System's Senior Computer Engineer, has successfully led the implementation of thirty-three telecommuting systems in companies throughout the United States. Earning her computer science degree at Iowa State, Lisa has won numerous awards for her innovative approach to computer networking. She believes that clear communication is the best way to meet her clients' needs.

Our management is supported by one of the most advanced teams of high technology employees. Insight Systems employs twenty of the brightest engineers and technicians in the telecommunications industry. We have aggressively recruited our employees from the most advanced universities in the United States, including Stanford, MIT, Illinois, Iowa State, New Mexico, and Syracuse. Several of our engineers have been with Insight Systems since it was founded.

Corporate History and Facilities

Insight Systems has been a leader in the telecommuting industry from the beginning. In 2002, the company was founded by John Temple, a pioneer in the networking field. Since then, Insight Systems has followed Dr. Temple's simple belief that computer-age workplaces should give people the freedom to be creative.

Description of organization

"Insight Systems earned the coveted '100 Companies to Watch' designation from Business Outlook Magazine."

Recently, Insight Systems earned the coveted "100 Companies to Watch" designation from *Business Outlook Magazine* (May 2013). The company has worked with large and small companies, from Vedder Aerospace to the Cedar Rapids Museum of Fine Arts, to create telecommuting options for companies that want to keep costs down and productivity high.

Insight Systems' Naperville office has been called "a prototype workspace for the information age" (*Gibson's Computer Weekly*, May 2006). With advanced LAN systems in place, only ten of Insight System's fifty employees actually work in the office. Most of Insight Systems' employees telecommute from home or on the road.

Experience You Can Trust

Our background and experience give us the ability to help Northside manage its needs for a more efficient, dynamic office space. Our key to success is innovation, flexibility, and efficiency.

8

Concluding with Costs and Benefits

Most proposals end by summarizing the benefits of the project and identifying the costs of the project. The conclusion of a proposal usually makes most of these five moves:

Move 1: Make an obvious *transition* that signals the conclusion.

Move 2: State the *costs* of the project.

Move 3: Summarize the *benefits* of the project.

Move 4: Briefly *describe the future* if the readers say yes.

Move 5: *Thank* the readers and offer contact information.

Start out this section by making an obvious transition that will wake up your readers. Say something like, "Let us conclude by summarizing the costs and benefits of our plan." Then, tell them the costs in a straightforward way without an apology or sales pitch.

As shown in our budget, this renovation will cost $287,000.

We anticipate that the price for retooling your manufacturing plant will be $5,683,000.

After the costs, summarize or list the two to five major benefits of saying yes to your project. Usually, these benefits are the deliverables you mentioned in the project plan section earlier in your proposal. By putting these benefits right after the costs, you can show readers exactly what they will receive for their investment.

Link

For more information on writing conclusions, go to Chapter 15, page 411.

Then, add a paragraph in which you describe the future benefits for the readers if they agree to your ideas. Describe how their investment in your plan will improve their company or organization.

Finally, thank the readers for their consideration of the proposal and offer contact information (e.g., phone number and e-mail address) where they can reach you if they have more questions or need more information.

In most cases, your discussion of the benefits should not add new ideas to the proposal. In Figure 8.11, for example, notice that this proposal's costs and benefits section really doesn't add anything new to the proposal, except the cost of the project.

Step 3: Choose the Style, Design, and Medium

Good choices about the style, design, and medium are crucial to your proposal's success. A clear, persuasive proposal that is attractive and easy to navigate will be much more competitive than one that sounds boring and looks plain. Plus, good style and design help inspire trust in your readers. The appropriate media, meanwhile, will make your proposal easier to access, while enhancing your readers' experience.

Costs and Benefits Section

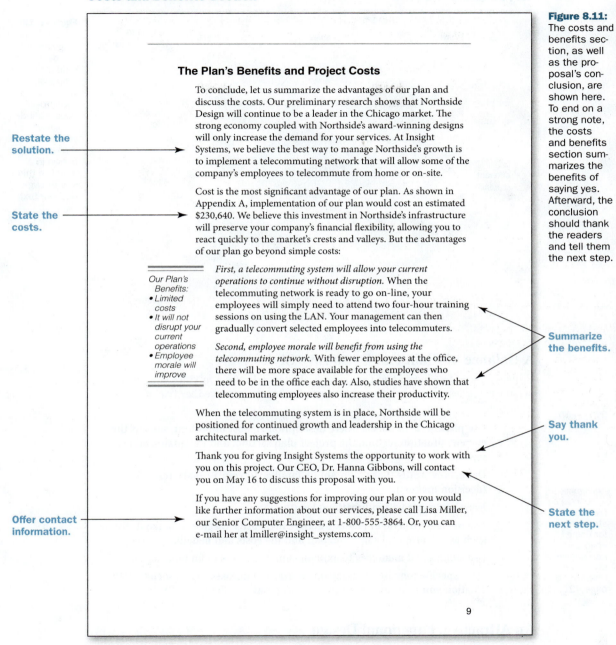

Restate the solution.

State the costs.

Offer contact information.

The Plan's Benefits and Project Costs

To conclude, let us summarize the advantages of our plan and discuss the costs. Our preliminary research shows that Northside Design will continue to be a leader in the Chicago market. The strong economy coupled with Northside's award-winning designs will only increase the demand for your services. At Insight Systems, we believe the best way to manage Northside's growth is to implement a telecommuting network that will allow some of the company's employees to telecommute from home or on-site.

Cost is the most significant advantage of our plan. As shown in Appendix A, implementation of our plan would cost an estimated $230,640. We believe this investment in Northside's infrastructure will preserve your company's financial flexibility, allowing you to react quickly to the market's crests and valleys. But the advantages of our plan go beyond simple costs:

Our Plan's Benefits:
- Limited costs
- It will not disrupt your current operations
- Employee morale will improve

First, a telecommuting system will allow your current operations to continue without disruption. When the telecommuting network is ready to go on-line, your employees will simply need to attend two four-hour training sessions on using the LAN. Your management can then gradually convert selected employees into telecommuters.

Second, employee morale will benefit from using the telecommuting network. With fewer employees at the office, there will be more space available for the employees who need to be in the office each day. Also, studies have shown that telecommuting employees also increase their productivity.

When the telecommuting system is in place, Northside will be positioned for continued growth and leadership in the Chicago architectural market.

Thank you for giving Insight Systems the opportunity to work with you on this project. Our CEO, Dr. Hanna Gibbons, will contact you on May 16 to discuss this proposal with you.

If you have any suggestions for improving our plan or you would like further information about our services, please call Lisa Miller, our Senior Computer Engineer, at 1-800-555-3864. Or, you can e-mail her at lmiller@insight_systems.com.

9

Summarize the benefits.

Say thank you.

State the next step.

Figure 8.11: The costs and benefits section, as well as the proposal's conclusion, are shown here. To end on a strong note, the costs and benefits section summarizes the benefits of saying yes. Afterward, the conclusion should thank the readers and tell them the next step.

Mapping to Set a Tone

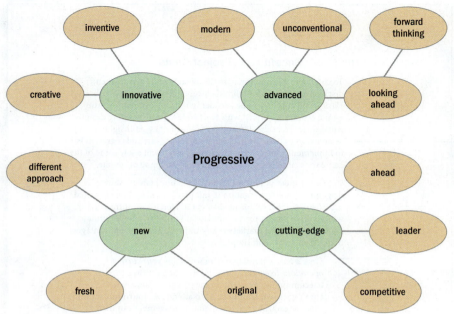

Figure 8.12: Logical mapping can help you develop a tone for your proposal. To make your proposal sound "progressive," you can use the words shown in a map like this one throughout your text.

A Balance of Plain and Persuasive Styles

Proposals need to educate and persuade, so they tend to use a mixture of plain and persuasive styles. Here are a few suggestions for how to improve the style of your proposal:

> Use plain style in places where description is most important, such as the current situation section, the project plan section, and the qualifications section.
>
> Define any words that might not be familiar to your primary readers (decision makers).
>
> Keep sentences within breathing length.
>
> Use persuasive style in places where readers are expected to make decisions, such as the proposal's introduction and the costs and benefits section.
>
> Use similes and analogies to explain complex issues in familiar terms.
>
> Set a specific tone by mapping out words and phrases that associate with an emotion you want to project in your proposal (see Figure 8.12).

Link

For more strategies for using plain and persuasive style, see Chapter 16, page 422.

An Attractive, Functional Design

The design of your proposal needs to be visually appealing, while helping readers find the information they need. Figure 8.13, for example, shows the first page of a

Sample Proposal Design

Figure 8.13: The page design of this proposal sets a professional tone while helping readers scan for important information. The tone is set with positive words and phrasings, while the graphics and headings make the information easy to access.

Header adds color and anchors the top of the page.

Title of proposal is bold and easy to read.

Headings provide access points into text.

Two-column format makes text more scannable.

Graphic supports text while adding color.

A Proposal for Upgrading the National-Scale Soil Geochemical Database for the United States

The most requested data from the U.S. Geological Survey's (USGS) National Geochemical Database is a set of 1,323 soil samples. Why? Consider the following examples:

Example 1—Imagine for a moment that you are employed by an environmental regulatory agency of either the Federal or a State Government. Your assignment is to establish a "remediation value" for arsenic in soil at a contaminated site where a wood preservative facility once operated. Current arsenic values in soils at the facility range from 15 to 95 ppm and you must decide the concentration of arsenic that is acceptable after remediation efforts are completed. Scientists refer to the natural or native concentration of an element in soils as the "background concentration." Given the fact that arsenic occurs naturally in all soils, how would you determine the background concentration of arsenic in soils for this particular area?

Example 2—Your environmental consulting firm has been assigned to work with a team of specialists conducting a risk-based assessment of land contaminated with lead, zinc, and cadmium from a metal foundry. The assessment would determine the likelihood of adverse health or ecological effects caused by the contaminants. Again, an important part of this determination is, "What is the background concentration of these elements in the soil?"

What data are available for persons responsible for making the determinations of background concentrations for soils contaminated with potentially toxic metals? The most-often-quoted data set for background concentrations of metals and other trace elements in soil of the conterminous United States consists of only 1,323 samples collected during the 1960s and 1970s by the U.S. Geological Survey (Boerngen and Shacklette, 1981; Shacklette and Boerngen, 1984). (There is a similar data set for Alaska (Gough and others, 1984, 1988)). Samples for the "Shacklette data" were collected from a depth of about 1 ft, primarily from noncultivated fields having native vegetation, and samples were analyzed for more than 40 elements. Data in this study represent about one sample per 2,300 mi², indicating that very few samples were collected in each State. For example, the State of Arizona is covered by only 47 samples, and Pennsylvania has only 16. Despite the low number of samples, this data set is still being used on a regular basis to determine background concentrations of metals in soil to aid in remediation or risk-based assessments of contaminated land.

The only other national-scale soil geochemical data set for the United States was generated by the Natural Resources Conservation Service (NRCS), formerly the Soil Conservation Service (Holmgren and others, 1993). This data set consists of 3,045 samples of agricultural soil collected from major crop-producing areas of the conterminous United States. The primary purpose of this study was to assess background levels of lead and cadmium in major food crops and in soils on which these crops grow. Thus, the samples were only analyzed for five metals—lead, cadmium, copper, zinc, and nickel.

The Shacklette data set allows us to produce geochemical maps for specific elements, such as that shown on figure 1 for arsenic (Gustavsson and others, 2001). A map produced from such sparse data points obviously carries a large degree of uncertainty with it and does not have the resolution needed to answer many of the questions raised by land-management and regulatory agencies, earth scientists, and soil scientists. An example of the poor data set resolution is illustrated for Pennsylvania (fig. 2). The State is divided into major soil taxonomic units referred to as Suborders (Soil Survey Staff, 1999). Suborders group similar soil types in any region. The dots represent the sample points from the Shacklette data set. The few sample points shown on figure 2 illustrate that this data set would be inadequate for someone who must define the arsenic content of a given soil. At this time, no data set exists that will allow us to make these kinds of determinations.

The USGS and NRCS are currently studying the feasibility of a national-scale soil geochemical survey that will increase the sample density of the Shacklette data set by at least a factor of 10. This project, called Geochemical Landscapes, began in October 2002. The first 3 years will be devoted to determining how such a survey should be conducted. Therefore, we are actively soliciting input from potential customers of the new data. Interested members of the private sector, government, or academic communities

Figure 1. Map of arsenic distribution in soils and other surficial materials of the conterminous United States based on 1,323 sample localities as represented by the black dots.

ARSENIC

U.S. Department of the Interior
U.S. Geological Survey

Printed on recycled paper

USGS Fact Sheet FS-015-03
March 2003

Source: U.S. Geological Survey, 2003

well-designed proposal. Notice how the design of the proposal sets a professional, progressive tone for the whole document—even before you start reading.

Here are some design tips for proposals:

Where possible, put data into tables or charts that the readers can review.

Use graphs to illustrate any trends in the data or facts.

Clarify and reinforce important points with images, illustrations, and maps.

Expand the outside margin to provide room for pull quotes or reader notes.

Use page numbers to allow easy references in meetings.

Add color to give energy, especially to headings, headers, and footers.

Use headings and lists to help readers locate the information they need.

Professional design is crucial for catching and holding your readers' attention. Don't expect your proposal's content alone to persuade them to say yes.

A Dynamic Use of Medium

The appropriate medium is also an important choice. Paper is still the norm for most proposals, but increasingly, companies are using multimedia, websites, and presentation software to deliver their ideas. Here are a few suggestions for using media to enhance your proposal:

Use presentation software, such as PowerPoint or Keynote, to summarize your proposal into slides.

Add in videos that are embedded in the text or that can be linked to sites on the Internet.

Create a companion website that allows readers to learn more about the problem you are trying to solve and the products or services you are promoting.

Include appropriate background music in a multimedia version of the proposal.

Create a model or display that can demonstrate how the finished product or project will look.

Increasingly, proposals use a variety of communication media, such as video, audio, and oral presentations to provide a multimedia package to the readers. You should look for ways to use media to do something extra that will make your proposal stand out.

Link

For more information on using graphics, see Chapter 18, page 477.

Link

For more information on page and screen layout, see Chapter 17, page 451.

Link

For more information on developing oral presentations with presentation software, see Chapter 20, page 526.

The Elevator Pitch

An elevator pitch is a one- or two-minute proposal that pitches a new idea, project, or service to potential investors or clients. If you type "Elevator Pitch Competition" into an Internet search engine, you will find videos of competitions in which entrepreneurs or college students compete to give the best elevator pitches. The best elevator pitches sell a good idea quickly.

Here is how to create your own elevator pitch:

Introduce yourself and establish your credibility. Remember that people invest in other *people,* not in projects. So tell them *who* you are and *what* you do.

Grab them with a good story. You need to grab your listeners' attention right away, so ask them, "What if _____?" or explain, "Recently, _____ happened and we knew there must be a better way."

Present your big idea in one sentence. Don't make them wait. Hit them with your best idea up front in one sentence.

Give them your best two or three reasons for doing it. The secret is to sell your idea, not explain it. List your best two or three reasons with minimal explanation.

Mention something that distinguishes you and your idea from the others. What is unique about your idea? How does your idea uniquely fit your listener's prior investments?

Offer a brief cost-benefits analysis. Show them very briefly that your idea is worth their investment of time, energy, or money.

Make sure they remember you. End your pitch by telling them something memorable about you or your organization. Make sure you put your contact information in their hand (e.g., a business card or résumé). If they allow it, leave them a written version of your pitch.

Write

Make your own elevator pitch. Think of a new product or service that might be useful to students at your university. Then, with a team of other students, write a persuasive one-minute elevator pitch. If time allows, present your pitch to your class.

Elevator Pitch: Pocket Drone

The Pocket Drone is the personal flying robot that enables anyone to capture amazing video and photos from the sky. The year 2014 is going to be the "Year of the Drone." Personal and professional photography is literally beginning to take off. Everybody can already take great looking photos and videos with their camera phones and share them online, but they have been limited to what could seen from the ground. Now with the Pocket Drone, it's never been easier to capture spectacular aerial images that open up a whole new perspective and insight that had previously been unseen.

We aim to change the status quo through our little project with a BIG impact. We love flying robots, and we're building them to share with the world.

Until now, most people could not participate in this awesome new technology revolution—the cost was too great, the drones too bulky, and the software too difficult to operate. And to top it off, it always seemed like either mom or dad (the photographer) was missing from family pictures. We're proud to announce the launch of *The Pocket Drone* to address these challenges. Many of our supporters are calling it the "GoPro of drones."

The Pocket Drone Key Features

1. Unique cutting-edge collapsible compact design

2. Easy to fly and simple to maintain

3. Lightweight with maximum payload

4. Ready to fly (RTF) with everything you need out of the box and quick to deploy

5. Advanced software and systems with autopilot and "follow me" mode

6. Longest flight time of any multicopter under $500

7. High quality materials and components

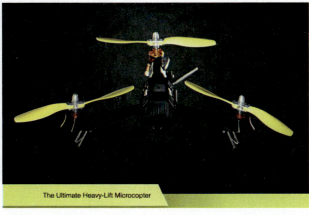

The Pocket Drone is a flying robot created by AirDroids. With this pitch, it was successfully funded on the crowdfunding platform, Kickstarter.

The Ultimate Heavy-Lift Microcopter

Source: Team AirDroids

8. Upgradeable, expandable and hackable

9. Designed with multiple safety features

We are also proud that our project has been selected from numerous other hardware innovations as a finalist at the **TechCrunch Hardware Battlefield 2014** at the Consumer Electronics Show (CES) in Las Vegas.

WHAT YOU NEED TO KNOW

- Proposals are documents that present ideas or plans for consideration.

- Proposals can be internal or external and solicited or unsolicited.

- Proposals usually include five sections: (1) introduction, (2) current situation, (3) project plan, (4) qualifications, and (5) costs and benefits.

- When planning the proposal, start out by defining the Five-W and How Questions. Then, define the rhetorical situation (subject, purpose, readers, context of use).

- When organizing and drafting the proposal, each major section should be written separately with an opening, a body, and a closing.

- Proposals should use a combination of plain and persuasive styles to motivate readers.

- Design is absolutely essential in professional proposals. You should look for places where page layout, graphics, and multimedia will improve the readability of your proposal.

EXERCISES AND PROJECTS

Individual or Team Projects

1. Analyze the "Concept Proposal for Drone-Based Security at Salisbury College" at the end of this chapter. A concept proposal is brief start-up proposal that describes a new idea or product. Study the content, organization, style, and design of the proposal. Does it cover the four areas (current situation, project plan, qualifications, costs and benefits) that were discussed in this chapter? Where does it include more or less information than you would expect in a proposal?

    Write a two-page memo to your instructor in which you discuss whether you believe the proposal was effectively written and designed. Discuss the content, organization, style, and design in specific detail. Highlight the proposal's strengths and suggest ways in which it could be improved.

2. Find a Request for Proposals (RFP) at www.fedbizopps.gov or by searching the Internet. Analyze the RFP according to the Who, What, Where, When, Why, and How Questions. Then, prepare a presentation for your class in which you (a) summarize the contents of the RFP, (b) discuss why you believe the RFP was sent out, and (c) explain what kinds of projects would be suitable for this RFP.

3. Find a proposal on the Internet that demonstrates weak style and/or design. Using the style and design techniques discussed in this chapter and in Chapters 17–19, revise the document so that it is more persuasive and more visual. Locate places where blocks of text could be turned into lists, and identify places where graphics would reinforce the text.

Collaborative Project: Improving Campus

As students, you are aware—perhaps more so than the administrators—of some of the problems on campus. Write a proposal that analyzes the causes of a particular problem on campus and then offers a solution that the administration might consider implementing. The proposal should be written to a *named* authority on campus who has the power to approve your proposal and put it into action.

Some campus-based proposals you might consider include the following:

- improving lighting on campus to enhance safety at night.
- improving living conditions in your dorm or fraternity/sorority.
- creating a day-care center on campus.
- creating an adult commuter room in the student union.
- improving campus facilities for individuals with special needs.
- improving security in buildings on campus.
- creating a university public relations office run by students.
- increasing access to computers on campus.
- improving the parking situation.
- reducing graffiti and/or litter on campus.
- improving food service in the student union.
- helping new students make the transition to college.
- changing the grading system at the university.
- encouraging more recycling on campus.
- reducing the dependence on cars among faculty and students.

Use your imagination to come up with a problem to which you can offer a solution. You don't need to be the person who implements the program. Just offer some guidance for the administrators. In the qualifications section of your proposal, you will likely need to recommend that someone else should do the work.

Revision Challenge

This proposal in Figure A is written well, but it could be strengthened in organization, style, and design. Read through the proposal and identify five ways in which you could make it stronger.

Visit MyWritingLab for a Post-test and more technical writing resources.

Concept Proposal for Drone-Based Security at Salisbury College

April 12, 2014

The STEM Radicals:
Stacy Phillips, James Johnson, Jose Hernandez, and Helen Peterson

The purpose of this proposal is to offer an innovative way to improve night-time security on campus at Salisbury College. Admittedly, we are pushing the ethical boundaries on this issue by proposing that we use drones for surveillance on our campus. But, we believe that drones offer possibilities that other kinds of security, like video cameras and human security officers do not. Plus, in times when the budget is tight, drones are about as expensive as a video camera system, and they are easier to upgrade. Certainly, they are less expensive than human officers. One human officer can monitor up to five drones at a time, which would greatly expand his or her ability to increase security on campus.

Current State of Security on Campus

Recently, it feels like crime has been going up on campus. A look at last week's *Campus Journal* confirms that crime on campus is on the rise. On Wednesday night, a student was robbed near Engineering Hall. This weekend, some cars were broken into by the Sigma Nu fraternity. An iPhone and textbooks were stolen.

The college administration, meanwhile, has been encouraging students to take more classes at night, so the college can increase revenue and expand course offerings. As the college seeks to attract more "non-traditional" students to take professional classes, more people will be on campus at night.

So, the problem is that we don't have drones for surveillance of these night-time activities. Without drones, students walking on campus cannot feel safe because no one is keeping track of what is happening. Instead, people are often forced to walk across campus alone in the dark. If they knew drones were hovering above campus, keeping an eye on things, then they would feel much more secure about being on campus at night.

Using Drones for Campus Security

As a surveillance technology, drones are relatively new but they show great promise. A typical video-equipped surveillance drone costs anywhere from $200 to $1000. For example, the DJI Phantom FC40 Quadcopter ($459) has an FPV

Source: *Association for the Advancement of Sustainability in Higher Education*

(continued)

Figure A: A concept proposal is a brief proposal that presents a new idea or product for further consideration. If the concept proposal is accepted, then a full proposal would be written. This proposal is well written, but not perfect. How might you revise this to make its content, organization, style, and design even stronger?

Camera and transmitter that can send video. It works by having four helicopter-type propellers that allow it to hover and capture video from a suspended camera. A drone like this one could be used to follow people as they are walking across campus. Then, if something bad was about to happen, like a robbery, the person monitoring drones at the Campus Police could send help. Here is our plan:

Step 1: Buy the Drones—Drones can be purchased from a variety of places. The people buying the drones could compare prices on the Internet and find the best value, as well as the best kind of drones for surveillance. We suggest buying electric-motor drones because they are quiet. Gas-powered drones often make buzzing noises that would be distracting.

Step 2: Train Police Officers to Use Drones—Police officers can get a Unmanned Aerial Vehicle (UAV) Certificate from a variety of places. Places like the Unmanned Vehicle University offer videos and simulators to train people how to fly drones at home. Then, the police officers would go to Florida to attend a three-day flight school to complete their training.

Step 3: Develop a Strategy for Using Drones—The drones would need to be positioned around the edges of campus. When a person walks onto the campus, a drone would follow him or her and send video back to the campus police station.

Step 4: Ethical Problems—Some people have mentioned ethical problems with tracking people walking on campus. Their concerns, though, seem a bit paranoid. The drones would be there for their own safety, and they wouldn't even notice them. If they aren't doing anything wrong, they have nothing to fear from drones.

Costs and Benefits: Let's Do This

We estimate that a drone surveillance program for campus would cost about $10,450. That would include buying 10 drones and paying for the training of three police officers to fly and monitor them. Obviously, security would be greatly enhanced on campus. People who want to do crimes would know that they are being watched. Meanwhile students and faculty would be comforted by the idea that someone at the Campus Police is looking out for their safety. More people, especially professionals, would be willing to take classes at night, which would increase revenue for our college.

If you like this concept, contact us. We will expand this concept proposal into a full proposal with all the necessary details.

The Mole

Henry Espinoza knew this proposal was important to his company, Valen Industries. If the proposal was successful, it could be worth millions of dollars in short-term and long-term projects for his employer. For Henry, winning the project meant a likely promotion to vice president and a huge raise in salary. The company's CEO was calling him daily to check up and see if it was going well. That meant she was getting stressed out about the project.

Through the grapevine, Henry knew his company really had only one major competitor for the project. So the odds were good that Valen Industries would win the contract. Of course, Henry and his team needed to put together an innovative and flawless proposal to win, because their major competitor was going all out to get this project.

Then, one day, something interesting happened. One of Henry's team members, Vera Houser, came to him with an e-mail from one of her friends, who worked for their main competitor. In the e-mail, this person offered to give Valen Industries a draft of its competitor's proposal. Moreover, this friend would pass along any future drafts as the proposal evolved. In the e-mail, Vera's friend said he was very frustrated working at his "slimy" company, and he was looking for a way out. He also revealed that his company was getting "inside help" on the proposal, but Henry wasn't sure what that meant.

Essentially, this person was hinting that he would give Henry's team a copy of the competitor's proposal and work as a mole if they considered hiring him at Valen Industries. Henry knew he would gain a considerable advantage over his only competitor if he had a draft of its proposal to look over. The ability to look at future drafts would almost ensure that he could beat his competitor. Certainly, he thought, with this kind of money on the line, a few rules could be bent. And it seemed that his competitor was already cheating by receiving inside help.

Henry went home to think it over. What would be the ethical choice in this situation? How do you think Henry should handle this interesting opportunity?

CHAPTER

9

Activity Reports

Types of Activity Reports 231

Step 1: Make a Plan and Do
   Research 236

Step 2: Organize and Draft Your
   Activity Report 239

Step 3: Choose the Style, Design,
   and Medium 241

Microgenre: The Status Report 248

What You Need to Know 250

Exercises and Projects 250

Case Study: Bad Chemistry 252

In this chapter, you will learn:

- The basic features of activity reports.

- About the different kinds of activity reports and how they are used in the workplace.

- How to determine the rhetorical situation for an activity report.

- How to organize and draft an activity report.

- Strategies for using an appropriate style.

- How to design and format activity reports.

Today, companies are using computer networks to create management structures that are less hierarchical. As a result, companies require fewer levels of managers than before, because computer networks help top executives better communicate with employees throughout the company.

These "flatter" management structures require more communication, quicker feedback, and better accountability among employees in the company. As a result, activity reports are more common than ever in the technical workplace.

Activity reports are used to objectively present ideas or information within a company. This genre has many variations, making it adaptable to many situations that you will encounter in the technical workplace.

Types of Activity Reports

Activity reports are called a variety of names that reflect their different purposes. These small reports share one goal—to objectively inform readers about (1) what happened, (2) what is happening, and (3) what will happen in the near future.

Progress Reports

A progress report is written to inform management about the progress or status of a project. These reports are usually written at regular intervals—weekly, biweekly, or monthly—to update management on what has happened since the last progress report was submitted. Your company's management may also periodically request a progress report to stay informed about your or your team's activities.

A typical progress report will provide the following information:

- a summary of completed activities
- a discussion of ongoing activities
- a forecast of future activities

Figure 9.1, for example, shows a progress report that is designed to update management on a project.

White Papers and Briefings

White papers and briefings are used to inform management or clients about an important issue. Typically, white papers are print documents, while briefings are presented verbally. Occasionally, briefings will also appear as "briefs" in written form.

White papers and briefings typically present gathered facts in a straightforward and impartial way. They include the following kinds of information:

- a summary of the facts
- a discussion of the importance of these facts
- a forecast about the importance of these facts in the future

An effective briefing presents the facts as concisely as possible, leaving time for questions and answers. When you brief an audience on your subject, try to do so as objectively as possible. Then, after presenting the facts, interpret their importance based on evidence, not on speculation. It is up to the readers to decide what actions are appropriate.

Figure 9.2 on page 234 shows the first page of a white paper written by RSA, a computer and network security company.

Activity Reports

This is a basic model for organizing an activity report. There are many different types of activity reports, so this pattern can and should be altered to fit the content and purpose of your document.

Basic Features of Activity Reports

An activity report usually includes the following features, which can be modified to suit the needs of the situations in which the report will be used:

- **Introduction** that clearly states the report's purpose and main point
- **Summary** of activities that occurred within the reporting period
- **Results** of activities or research within the reporting period
- **Graphics and charts** that illustrate activities or present data
- **Description** of future activities or research
- **Record of Expenses** incurred within the reporting period
- **Conclusion** that restates the main point and looks to the future

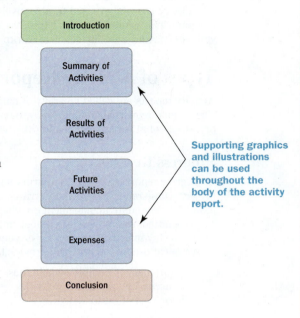

Introduction

Summary of Activities

Results of Activities

Future Activities

Expenses

Conclusion

Supporting graphics and illustrations can be used throughout the body of the activity report.

Incident Reports

Incident reports describe an event, usually an accident or irregular occurrence, and they identify what corrective actions have been taken. As with other kinds of activity reports, incident reports present the facts as objectively as possible. They provide the following information:

- a summary of what happened (the facts)
- a discussion of why it happened
- a description of how the situation was handled
- a discussion of how the problem will be avoided in the future

It is tempting, especially when an accident was your fault, to make excuses or offer apologies, but an incident report is not the place to do so. As with other activity reports, you should concentrate on the facts. Describe what happened as honestly and clearly as possible. You can make excuses or apologize later.

Figure 9.3 on page 235 shows a typical incident report in which management is notified of an accident in a laboratory.

Hanson Engineering

March 14, 2014
To: Charlie Peterson, Director
From: Sue Griego, Iota Team Manager
Subject: Progress Report, March 14

Subject, purpose, and main point are identified up front.

This month, we made good progress toward developing a new desalinization method that requires less energy than traditional methods.

Ongoing activities are described objectively.

Our activities have centered around testing the solar desalinization method that we discussed with you earlier this year. With solar panels, we are trying to replicate the sun's natural desalinization of water (Figure A). In our system, electricity from the photovoltaic solar panels evaporates the water to create "clouds" in a chamber, similar to the way the sun makes clouds from ocean water. The salt deposits are then removed with reverse osmosis, and freshwater is removed as steam.

The graphic supports the text.

Figure A: The Desalinator

Results are presented.

We are succeeding on a small scale. Right now, our solar desalinator can produce an average of 2.3 gallons of freshwater an hour. Currently, we are working with the system to improve its efficiency, and we soon hope to be producing 5 gallons of freshwater an hour.

Report ends with a look to the future and a brief conclusion.

We are beginning to sketch out plans for a large-scale solar desalinization plant that would be able to produce thousands of gallons of freshwater per hour. We will discuss our ideas with you at the April 18 meeting.

Our supplies and equipment expenses for this month were $8,921. Looks like things are going well. E-mail me if you have questions. (Suegriego@hansoneng.net)

Figure 9.2:
A white paper presents technical information objectively, allowing readers to make decisions based on the facts.

Bioenergy Science White Paper
U.S. Department of Agriculture
Research, Education and Economics
Office of the Chief Scientist
July 24, 2012

The Nation is aggressively developing the capacity to meet some of our energy needs through biofuels and biopower. The Energy Independence and Security Act of 2007 (EISA) calls for 36 billion gallons per year (BGY) of renewable fuels by 2022 and establishes new categories of renewable fuels, each with specific volume requirements and life cycle greenhouse gas (GHG) performance thresholds.[1,2] As mandated by EISA, the Renewable Fuel Standard was implemented in 2009. Additionally, the Food, Conservation, and Energy Act of 2008 authorized many bioenergy research, demonstration, and deployment efforts currently being implemented by the U.S. Department of Agriculture (USDA) and the Department of Energy (DOE). State and national initiatives such as the National Bioeconomy Blueprint are also exploring the use of biomass to produce high value chemicals, biobased products, and heat and power. All these applications increase demand for biomass production.

Emerging bioenergy systems hold the promise of helping to reduce our dependence on foreign oil, increase rural prosperity, and reduce greenhouse gas emissions. Meeting the energy demands of the future requires the development of transformative, ecologically based agricultural systems that ensure sustainable environmental, economic, and social outcomes. Successful bioenergy systems require strategic approaches that pose many scientific research, economic, data management, and communication challenges. The bioenergy supply chain (Figure 1) that drives these systems depends on the cooperation of researchers, landowners, industrial sectors, and market suppliers.

Figure 1.

THE BIOENERGY SUPPLY CHAIN

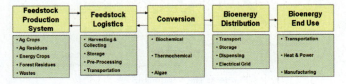

Strategic Approaches Needed

A multidisciplinary, integrated systems approach. The significant expansion and modification of existing and new interrelated components of the bioenergy supply chain is creating effective systems. These systems incorporate new partnerships and investments, innovative grower

---

[1] 15 BGY of corn ethanol; 21 BGY of "advanced biofuels" with a 50 percent reduction in life cycle GHG emissions, compared with fossil fuels; 16 BGY of that coming from cellulosic sources with a required 60 percent reduction in life cycle GHG emissions. An additional 1 BGY of biomass-based diesel is also required.

[2] This national standard is expected to reduce GHG emissions more than 138 million metric tons per year when fully phased in by 2022.

Source: U.S. Department of Agriculture

An Incident Report

Red Hills Health Sciences Center (RH)

Testing and Research Division
201 Hospital Drive, Suite A92
Red Hills, CA 92698

March 11, 2014

To: Brian Jenkins, Safety Assurance Officer
From: Hal Chavez, Testing Laboratory Supervisor
Subject: Incident Report: Fire in Laboratory

Subject and purpose are stated up front.

I am reporting a fire in Testing Laboratory 5, which occurred yesterday, March 10, 2014, at 3:34 p.m.

What happened is described objectively.

The fire began when a sample was being warmed with a bunsen burner. A laboratory notebook was left too close to the burner, and it caught fire. One of our laboratory assistants, Vera Cather, grabbed the notebook and threw it into a medical waste container. The contents of the waste container then lit on fire, filling the room with black smoke. At that point, another laboratory assistant, Robert Jackson, grabbed the fire extinguisher and emptied its contents into the waste container, putting out the fire. The overhead sprinklers went off, dousing the entire room.

What was done about it is noted.

Even though everyone seemed fine, we decided to send all lab personnel down to the emergency room for an examination. While we were in the waiting room, Vera Cather developed a cough and her eyes became red. She was held for observation and released that evening when her condition was stable. The rest of us were looked over by the emergency room doctors, and they suggested that we stay out of the laboratory until it was thoroughly cleaned.

I asked the hospital's HazMat team to clean up the mess that resulted from the fire. We had been working with samples of *Borrelia burgdorferi* bacteria, which causes Lyme disease. I was not sure if the waste container held any of our discarded samples. So, I thought it appropriate to clean up the laboratory with the utmost care. Even if the samples were in the waste container, it would be unlikely that the bacteria survived the fire, but I asked the HazMat team to do a Type 3 cleaning anyway.

The costs are specified.

The HazMat team will be charging us $2,405 for the cleaning. The water damage to the laboratory was about $3,529. We will pay these costs out of our operating budget for now. We will file a claim with the Center's insurance company.

What will happen in the future is described.

In the future, we will be more careful about fire hazards in the laboratory. We are currently developing policies to avoid these kinds of situations in the future. We will also develop an action and evacuation plan to handle these sorts of situations if they occur again.

Contact information concludes the memo.

Thank you for your attention. If you have any questions or would like to talk further about this incident, please call me at 5-9124.

Figure 9.3: An incident report is not the place to make apologies or place blame. You should state the facts as objectively as possible.

Laboratory Reports

Laboratory reports are written to describe experiments, tests, or inspections. If you have taken a laboratory class, you are no doubt familiar with lab reports. These reports describe the experiment, present the results, and discuss the results. Lab reports typically include the following kinds of information:

* a summary of the experiment (methods)
* a presentation of the results
* a discussion of the results

Lab reports, like other activity reports, emphasize the facts and data. A lab report is not the place to speculate or to develop a new theory. Instead, your lab report should present the results as objectively as possible and use those results to support the reasoned discussion that follows.

Figure 9.4 shows an example of a laboratory report. In this report, the writer describes the results of the testing as objectively as possible.

Step 1: Make a Plan and Do Research

One of the nice things about writing activity reports is that you have already developed most of the content. In almost all situations, you are familiar with your readers. So, minimal planning is required, and the research has been mostly completed. These internal reports, after all, are supposed to describe your activities.

A good workplace practice you might adopt is keeping an *activity journal* or *work log* on your computer or in a notebook. In your journal, start out each day by jotting down the things you need to accomplish. As you complete each of these activities, note the dates and times they were completed and the results.

At first, keeping an activity journal will seem like extra work. But you will soon realize that your journal keeps you on task and saves you time in the long run. Moreover, when you need to report on your activities for the week or month, you will have a record of all the things you accomplished.

Analyzing the Rhetorical Situation

With your notes in front of you, you are ready to plan your activity report. You should begin by briefly answering the Five-W and How Questions:

> *Who might read or use this activity report?*
>
> *Why do they want the report?*
>
> *What information do they need to know?*
>
> *Where will the report be used?*
>
> *When will the report be used?*
>
> *How might the report be used?*

After considering these questions, you can begin thinking about the rhetorical situation that will shape how you write the activity report or present your briefing.

SUBJECT   The subject of your report includes your recent activities. Include only information your readers need to know.

A Lab Report

FEND-LAB, INC.

www.fendlabcal.com

2314 Universal St., Suite 192
San Francisco, CA 94106
(325) 555-1327

Test Address
NewGen Information Technology, LLC
3910 S. Randolph
Slater, CA 93492

Client
Brian Wilson
Phone: 650-555-1182
Fax: 650-555-2319
e-mail: brian_wilson@cssf.edu

Mold Analysis Report
Report Number: 818237-28
Date of Sampling: 091313
Arrival Date: 091613
Analysis Date: 092013
Technician: Alice Valles

Lab Report: Mold Test

The introduction states the subject, purpose, and main point.

In this report, we present the results of our testing for mold at the offices of NewGen Information Technology, at 3910 S. Randolph in Slater, California. Our results show above-normal amounts of allergenic mold, which may lead to allergic reactions among the residents.

Testing Methods

Methods are described, explaining how the study was done.

On 13 September 2013, we took samples from the test site with two common methods: Lift Tape Sampling and Bulk Physical Sampling.

Lift Tape Sampling. We located 10 areas around the building where we suspected mold or spores might exist (e.g., water stains, dusty areas, damp areas). Using 8-cm-wide strips of transparent tape, we lifted samples and pressed them into the nutrient agar in petri dishes. Each sample was sealed and sent to our laboratory, where it was allowed to grow for one week.

Bulk Physical Sampling. We located 5 additional areas where we observed significant mold growth in ducts or on walls. Using a sterilized scraper, we removed samples from these areas and preserved them in plastic bags. In one place, we cut a 1-inch-square sample from carpet padding because it was damp and contained mold. This sample was saved in a plastic bag. All the samples were sent to our laboratory.

At the laboratory, the samples were examined through a microscope. We also collected spores in a vacuum chamber. Mold species and spores were identified.

Results of Microscopic Examination

The following chart lists the results of the microscope examination:

Mold Found	Location	Amount
Trichoderma	Break room counter	Normal growth
Geotrichum	Corner, second floor	Normal growth
Cladosporium	Air ducts	Heavy growth
Penicillium spores	Corkboard in bathroom	Normal growth

1

Figure 9.4:
A lab report walks readers through the methods, results, and discussion. Then, it offers any conclusions, based on the facts.

(continued)

Descriptions of molds found:

Trichoderma: Trichoderma is typically found in moistened paper and unglazed ceramics. This mold is mildly allergenic in some humans, and it can create antibiotics that are harmful to plants.

Geotrichum: Geotrichum is a natural part of our environment, but it can be mildly allergenic. It is usually found in soil in potted plants and on wet textiles.

Cladosporium: Cladosporium can cause serious asthma and it can lead to edema and bronchiospasms. In chronic cases, this mold can lead to pulmonary emphysema.

Penicillium: Penicillium is not toxic to most humans in normal amounts. It is regularly found in buildings and likely poses no threat.

Results are presented objectively, without interpretation.

Discussion of Results

It does not surprise us that the client and her employees are experiencing mild asthma attacks in their office, as well as allergic reactions. The amount of Cladosporium, a common culprit behind mold-caused asthma, is well above average. More than likely, this mold has spread throughout the duct system of the building, meaning there are probably no places where employees can avoid coming into contact with this mold and its spores.

The other molds found in the building could be causing some of the employees' allergic reactions, but it is less likely. Even at normal amounts, Geotrichum can cause irritation to people prone to mold allergies. Likewise, Trichoderma could cause problems, but it would not cause the kinds of allergic reactions the client reports. Penicillium in the amounts found would not be a problem.

The results of our analysis lead us to believe that the Cladosporium is the main problem in the building.

Results are interpreted and discussed.

Conclusions

The mold problem in this building will not go away over time. Cladosporium has obviously found a comfortable place in the air ducts of the building. It will continue to live there and send out spores until it is removed.

We suggest further testing to confirm our findings and measure the extent of the mold problem in the building. If our findings are confirmed, the building will not be safely habitable until a professional mold remover is hired to eradicate the mold.

Ignoring the problem would not be wise. At this point, the residents are experiencing mild asthma attacks and occasional allergic reactions. These symptoms will only grow worse over time, leading to potentially life-threatening situations.

Contact us at (325) 555-1327 if you would like us to further explain our methods and/or results.

The conclusion restates the main point and recommends action.

2

PURPOSE The purpose of your report is to describe what happened and what will happen in the future. In your introduction, state your purpose directly:

> In this memo, I will summarize our progress on the Hollings project during the month of August 2014.

> The purpose of this briefing is to update you on our research into railroad safety in northwestern Ohio.

You might use some of the following action verbs to describe your purpose:

to explain	to show	to demonstrate
to illustrate	to present	to exhibit
to justify	to account for	to display
to outline	to summarize	to inform

READERS Think about the people who will need to use your report. The readers of activity reports tend to be your supervisors. Occasionally, though, these kinds of reports are read by clients (lab reports or briefings) or are used to support testimony (white papers). An incident report, especially when it concerns an accident, may have a range of readers, such as lawyers and insurance adjusters, who plan to use the document in a variety of ways.

CONTEXT OF USE The context of use for your activity report will vary. In most cases, your readers will simply scan and file your report. Similarly, oral briefings are not all that exciting. Your listeners will perk up for the information that interests them, but they will mostly be checking to see if you are making progress.

Nevertheless, take a moment to decide whether your activity report discusses any topics that involve troublesome ethical or political issues. When mistakes happen, auditors and lawyers will go through your activity reports, looking for careless statements or admissions of fault. So, your statements need to reflect your actual actions and the results of your work.

Moreover, if you are reporting expenses in your activity report, the entries need to be accurate. Auditors and accountants will look at these numbers closely. If your numbers don't add up, you may have some explaining to do.

Step 2: Organize and Draft Your Activity Report

Remember, organizing and drafting activity reports should not take too much time. If you find yourself taking more than an hour to write an activity report, you are probably spending too much time on this routine task.

To streamline your efforts, remember that all technical documents have an introduction, a body, and a conclusion. Each of these parts of the document makes predictable moves that you can use to guide your drafting of the report.

Link

To learn more about defining a purpose, go to Chapter 1, page 5.

Link

For more ideas about reader analysis, turn to Chapter 2, page 19.

Link

For more help defining the context, go to Chapter 2, page 22.

Writing the Introduction

Readers of your activity report are mostly interested in the facts. So, your introduction should give them only a brief framework for understanding those facts. To provide this framework, you should concisely

Link

For more advice on writing introductions, turn to Chapter 15, page 399.

- define your subject.
- state your purpose.
- state your main point.

Figures 9.1, 9.3, and 9.4 show example reports with concise introductions that include these three common introductory moves.

If your readers are not familiar with your project (e.g., you are giving a demonstration to clients), you might want to expand the introduction by also offering background information, stressing the importance of the subject, and forecasting the body of the report. For example, Figure 9.5 shows the introduction of a document that would accompany a demonstration for people who would not be familiar with micromachines.

Full Introduction for an Activity Report

Figure 9.5: When readers are less familiar with the subject, you might add background information, stress the importance of the subject, and forecast the rest of the document.

Wilson National Laboratory
Always Moving Forward

Nanotech Micromachines Demonstration for Senators Laura Geertz and Brian Hanson
Presented by Gina Gould, Head Engineer

Background information is offered for readers unfamiliar with the topic. →

Nanotechnology is the creation and utilization of functional materials, devices, and systems with novel properties and functions that are achieved through the control of matter, atom by atom, molecule by molecule, or at the macromolecular level. A revolution has begun in science, engineering, and technology, based on the ability to organize, characterize, and manipulate matter systematically at the nanoscale.

Purpose and main point are mentioned here. →

In this demonstration, we will show you how the 5492 Group at Wilson National Laboratory is applying breakthroughs in nanotechnology science toward the development of revolutionary new micromachines. Our work since 2010 has yielded some amazing results that might dramatically expand the capacity of these tiny devices.

Forecasting shows the structure of the briefing. →

Today, we will exhibit a few of the prototype micromachines we have developed with nanotechnology principles. Then, we will present data gathered from testing these prototypes. And finally, we will discuss future uses of nanotechnology in micromachine engineering.

Writing the Body

In the body of the activity report, you should include some or all of the following:

Summary of activities—In chronological order, summarize the project's two to five major events since your previous activity report. Highlight any advances or setbacks in the project.

Results of activities or research—In order of importance, list the two to five most significant results or outcomes of your project. To help a reader scan, you might even use bullets to highlight these results.

Future activities or research—Tell readers what you will be doing during the next work period.

Expenses—If asked, you should state the costs incurred over the previous week or month. Highlight any places where costs are deviating from the project's budget.

The body of the activity report shown in Figure 9.6 includes these four items.

Writing the Conclusion

The conclusion should be as brief as possible. You should

- restate your main point.
- restate your purpose.
- make any recommendations, if appropriate.
- look to the future.

These concluding moves should be made in a maximum of two to four sentences.

> To conclude, in this demonstration, our goal was to update you on our progress toward developing nanotechnology micromachines. Overall, it looks like we are making solid progress toward our objectives, and we seem to be on schedule. Over the next couple of months, we will be facing some tough technical challenges. At that point, we will know if micromachines are feasible with current technology.

The conclusion shown in Figure 9.6 is probably more typical than the example above. Most conclusions in analytical reports are limited to one or two sentences.

Link

For more ideas about writing conclusions, go to Chapter 15, page 411.

Step 3: Choose the Style, Design, and Medium

Generally, activity reports follow a plain style and use a simple design. These documents are mostly informative, not overly persuasive, so you should try to keep them rather straightforward.

Progress Report

Memo header identifies primary readers and subject of report.

TIGER INDUSTRIES
Automation Development Division

Date: 28 February 2014
To: Hal Roberts, Division Head
From: Sally Fenker, Green Robot Project Manager
Subject: Progress Report on Green Robot Project

The introduction is concise.

We are pleased to report that we have made significant progress in coding for the X53 Manufacturing Robot.

In September, we coded for the lateral movement of the robot's arm. We developed several usable subroutines that should improve its placement accuracy.

The month's activities are summarized without interpretation.

The results are clearly stated.

So far, the results of our work are looking good:

- placement accuracies of .009 mm
- speed of 20 placements per minute
- frozen arm only 3 times in 100 trials.

In March, we hope to complete development of the software. One member of our team is currently debugging. Right now, it looks like we're on schedule for the May rollout of the robot. Of course, that depends on the folks over in manufacturing.

Future activities are discussed.

At this point, we're running a bit over budget, due to higher-than-expected contractor costs. We're perhaps $2,000 over.

Update on costs is given.

Otherwise, we're on schedule and looking forward to finishing. Call me (505.555.0180) or e-mail me (sallyf@tigeradd.com) if you have any questions.

The conclusion is brief and looks ahead.

Keeping the Style Plain and Straightforward

As you choose the style of your document, pay attention to the following elements:

> Using plain style techniques, make sure that (1) the subject is the "doer" of most sentences and (2) the verb expresses the action in most sentences.
>
> Begin each paragraph with a topic sentence that makes a direct statement or claim that the rest of the paragraph will support.
>
> Use an objective, professional tone and avoid any attempts at humor or irony.
>
> State negative information candidly and with no apologies, which might leave you or your organization liable.

Link

For more information on using plain style, see Chapter 16, page 422.

Designing for Simplicity and Illustrating with Graphics

The design of your activity report should also be straightforward:

> Follow the format prescribed by your organization, such as a memo template or a standardized form for lab reports.
>
> Use photos or illustrations to illustrate important concepts, objects, or processes.
>
> Use tables to present data and graphs to illustrate trends.
>
> Center graphics in the text and place them after the point where you refer to them.
>
> Graphs are always helpful for showing trends in the data.

Link

For more information on using an appropriate tone, go to Chapter 16, page 437.

Link

For help using templates, go to Chapter 17, page 452.

If your company or organization regularly produces activity reports, you will probably be asked to use a template to design your document. Figure 9.7, for example, shows the first three pages of a government white paper. This template is used for all white papers produced by the Congressional Research Service.

Writing for Electronic Media

Increasingly, activity reports are being circulated and archived in a variety of media. A progress report or white paper might be originally written as a paper document, but it will then be circulated via blog or social networking. Later, it could be archived in a searchable database or consolidated into a larger report. Here are some ways to write for multiple media:

> Include embedded links that allow readers to learn more about the subject from the Internet.
>
> Embed videos that demonstrate the product, service, process, or phenomenon.
>
> Use presentation software like PowerPoint, Keynote, or Prezi to summarize the contents of the report.
>
> Use file sharing sites like Google Drive or Dropbox to share and archive activity reports so they are widely available.
>
> Convert documents into PDFs so they can be more easily sent and shared across media.

It's safe to say that activity reports will appear increasingly in electronic form and less on paper. So, you should write these reports in ways that can be easily converted from one electronic medium to another.

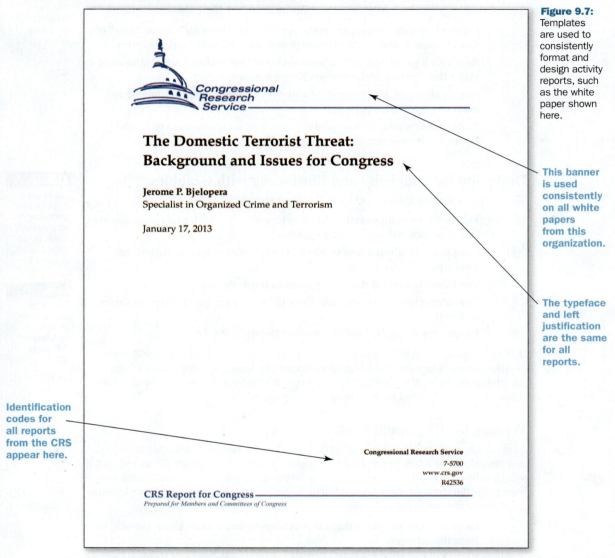

Figure 9.7: Templates are used to consistently format and design activity reports, such as the white paper shown here.

This banner is used consistently on all white papers from this organization.

The typeface and left justification are the same for all reports.

Identification codes for all reports from the CRS appear here.

The Domestic Terrorist Threat:
Background and Issues for Congress

Jerome P. Bjelopera
Specialist in Organized Crime and Terrorism

January 17, 2013

Congressional Research Service
7-5700
www.crs.gov
R42536

CRS Report for Congress
Prepared for Members and Committees of Congress

Source: Congressional Research Service, http://fpc.state.gov/documents/organization/203741.pdf

The template automatically inserts this header at the top of each page.

Headings are formatted consistently in the report.

Summary

The emphasis of counterterrorism policy in the United States since Al Qaeda's attacks of September 11, 2001 (9/11) has been on jihadist terrorism. However, in the last decade, domestic terrorists—*people who commit crimes within the homeland and draw inspiration from U.S.-based extremist ideologies and movements*—have killed American citizens and damaged property across the country. Not all of these criminals have been prosecuted under terrorism statutes. This latter point is not meant to imply that domestic terrorists should be taken any less seriously than other terrorists.

The Department of Justice (DOJ) and the Federal Bureau of Investigation (FBI) do not officially list domestic terrorist organizations, but they have openly delineated domestic terrorist "threats." These include individuals who commit crimes in the name of ideologies supporting animal rights, environmental rights, anarchism, white supremacy, anti-government ideals, black separatism, and anti-abortion beliefs.

The boundary between constitutionally protected legitimate protest and domestic terrorist activity has received public attention. This boundary is especially highlighted by a number of criminal cases involving supporters of animal rights—one area in which specific legislation related to domestic terrorism has been crafted. The Animal Enterprise Terrorism Act (P.L. 109-374) expands the federal government's legal authority to combat animal rights extremists who engage in criminal activity. Signed into law in November 2006, it amended the 1992 Animal Enterprise Protection Act (P.L. 102-346).

Five discussion topics in this report may help explain domestic terrorism's significance for policymakers:

- **Level of Activity.** Domestic terrorists have been responsible for orchestrating more than two-dozen incidents since 9/11, and there appears to be growth in anti-government extremist activity as measured by watchdog groups in the last several years.

- **Use of Nontraditional Tactics.** A large number of domestic terrorists do not necessarily use tactics such as suicide bombings or airplane hijackings. They have been known to engage in activities such as vandalism, trespassing, and tax fraud, for example.

- **Exploitation of the Internet.** Domestic terrorists—much like their jihadist analogues—are often Internet savvy and use the medium as a resource for their operations.

- **Decentralized Nature of the Threat.** Many domestic terrorists rely on the concept of *leaderless resistance*. This involves two levels of activity. On an operational level, militant, underground, ideologically motivated cells or individuals engage in illegal activity without any participation in or direction from an organization that maintains traditional leadership positions and membership rosters. On another level, the above-ground public face (the "political wing") of a domestic terrorist movement may focus on propaganda and the dissemination of ideology—engaging in protected speech.

The template also inserts this footer at the bottom of each page.

(continued)

The Domestic Terrorist Threat: Background and Issues for Congress

- **Prison Radicalization.** Prison has been highlighted as an arena in which terrorist radicalization can occur. Some prison gangs delve into radical or extremist ideologies that motivate domestic terrorists, and in a number of instances, these ideologies are integral to fashioning cohesive group identities within prison walls. It must be reiterated, however, that even for gangs that exhibit these ideological dimensions, criminal enterprises such as drug trafficking—not radical beliefs—largely drive their activities.

Congress may choose to consider issues in three areas regarding the federal role in combating domestic terrorism. First is the issue of definitions. It is difficult to assess the scope of domestic terrorism because federal agencies use varying terms to describe it. Even more basically, there is no clear sense of how many domestic terrorist attacks have occurred or how many plots the government has foiled in recent years. Second, Congress may review the adequacy of domestic terrorism intelligence collection efforts. For intelligence gathering and program prioritization purposes, there is no standard set of intelligence collection priorities across federal agencies that can be applied to domestic terrorism cases. Also, there likely is no established standard for the collection of intelligence from state and local investigators—aside from suspicious activity reporting. Finally, it may be of value to explore how domestic terrorism fits into the Obama Administration's community outreach-driven strategy to quell terrorism-related radicalization in the United States. Congress may query the Administration on which brand of domestic terrorists it plans to focus on under the strategy and which local community groups it intends to engage regarding domestic terrorism issues.

Congressional Research Service

The Domestic Terrorist Threat: Background and Issues for Congress

Contents

The template automatically constructs a table of contents to make this large white paper more accessible to the readers.

Introduction... 1

Domestic Terrorism Defined... 2

What Is Domestic Terrorism?... 3

Toward a Narrower Definition.. 4

Ambiguity Regarding "U.S.-Based Extremist Ideologies".. 5

Factors Complicating the Descriptions of the Domestic Terrorism Threat 5

Counting Terrorism Cases... 5

Sifting Domestic Terrorism from Other Illegal Activity 6

Extremism vs. Terrorism... 7

The Lack of an Official Public List.. 9

Toward a Practical Definition: Threats Not Groups 10

Animal Rights Extremists and Environmental Extremists... 11

Anarchist Extremists.. 13

White Supremacist Extremists 16

Anti-Government Extremists 22

Black Separatist Extremists 31

Anti-Abortion Extremists 32

Protected Activities vs. Terrorism—Divergent Perceptions of the ALF.......................... 34

A Serious Domestic Concern or "Green Scare?" 34

Assessing Domestic Terrorism's Significance... 38

Counting Incidents... 39

Growth in Hate Groups and Anti-Government Extremism 40

"Non-Violent" Strategies 42

Direct Action 42

The ALF: "Live Liberations" and "Economic Sabotage" 43

The ELF: "Monkeywrenching".. 43

"Paper Terrorism": Liens, Frivolous Lawsuits, and Tax Schemes 47

The Internet and Domestic Terrorists 49

A Decentralized Threat... 51

Leaderless Resistance... 52

Lone Wolves 54

Prison Radicalization.. 58

Policy Considerations for Congress.. 60

Scoping the Threat... 60

Terminology 61

Designating Domestic Terrorist Groups... 61

A Public Accounting of Plots and Incidents 62

Intelligence 63

How Does Domestic Terrorism Fit into the U.S. Countering Violent Extremism
Strategy?.. 64

"Leader" tabs are used by the template to line up the numbers in the table of contents.

Figures

Figure 1. Hate Groups and Militia Groups, 2000-2010... 41

Congressional Research Service

The Status Report

A status report is a short, barebones e-mail or text that highlights your or your team's recent activities. In some ways, they are similar to the "status updates" on Facebook and other social networking sites, because they are intended to keep people up to date on what you are doing. Status reports in the workplace, though, are longer and they are submitted weekly, sometimes daily. Here is how to write one:

Identify the purpose and date in the subject line. You can type something like "Status Report for T. Jennings: 9/22/14" in the subject line.

Put your name, project name, and date at the top of the e-mail message. These items will help readers identify the report if the text of the e-mail is separated from the subject line.

Describe the project's status. Use brief phrases to list your activities. Sometimes, you will be asked to estimate the amount of time devoted to each task.

Record any tasks you have completed. If you have finished something, tell the readers it's done.

Identify tasks for the next reporting period. List the things you plan to accomplish before the next status report is due.

Highlight any problems or concerns. List any short-term or long-term issues that might sidetrack the project.

Identify any costs. If you spent any money on the project, identify those costs. Normal operating costs usually don't need to be reported.

Increasingly, microblogs like Twitter are being used as status update tools, so all this information may need to be crammed into 140-word posts.

Write

Write your own status report. While working on your current project, e-mail two status reports each week to your instructor and your other team members.

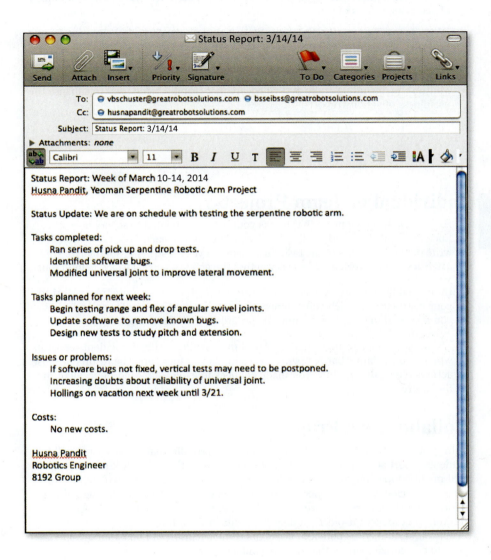

- Activity reports include progress reports, white papers, briefings, incident reports, and lab reports.

- An activity report typically includes the following sections: introduction, summary of activities, results of activities, future activities, expenses, and conclusion.

- While preparing to write an activity report, analyze the rhetorical situation by anticipating the readers and the context in which the report will be used.

- The style and design of activity reports should be plain and straightforward.

- Multimedia, including audio and video, are increasingly being used to enhance the usefulness of activity reports.

Individual or Team Projects

1. For a week, keep a journal that tracks your activities related to school or work. Each day, make up a "to do" list. Then, as you complete each task, cross it off and write down the results of the task. In a memo to your instructor, summarize your activities for the week and discuss whether the activity journal was a helpful tool.

2. In the middle of a large project in this class or another, write a progress report to your instructor in which you summarize what you have accomplished and what you still need to complete. Submit the progress report in memo format.

3. Think back to an accident that occurred in your life. Write an incident report in which you explain what happened, the actions you took, and the results of those actions. Then, discuss how you made changes to avoid that kind of accident in the future.

Collaborative Project

Your group has been asked to develop a standardized information sheet that will help students report accidents on your campus. Think of all the different kinds of accidents that might happen on your campus. Your information sheet should explain how to report an accident to the proper authorities on campus. Encourage the users of the information sheet to summarize the incident in detail, discuss the results, and make recommendations for avoiding similar accidents in the future.

Of course, numerous potential accidents could occur on campus. Your group may need to categorize them so that readers contact the right authorities.

> Visit MyWritingLab for a Post-test and more technical writing resources.

Revision Challenge

The incident report below is intended to describe an accident in which hazardous chemicals were spilled. Imagine you are Mary Valesquez, the recipient of this report, and you are rightfully concerned about what happened. Using the facts from this incident report, rewrite it for the CEO of Bridgeford Chemicals to explain what happened.

Bridgeford Industries

Making Your World Better

Date: May 9, 2014
To: Mary Valesquez, Assistant Director of Public Relations
From: Vincent Helms, Transportation Supervisor
Subject: Incident Report: Leaking TDI Waste Tank Truck

While you were on vacation, we had a problem that you may or may not have heard about. I think this is something we need to take seriously because if the federal government or the media finds out about it, things could get ugly. Our best path is to keep things quiet and finish cleaning up this problem. We will, of course, need to submit the appropriate forms to the state's Department of Environmental Issues and maybe the Department of Transportation. However, we can phrase things in such a way to keep publicity to a minimum and avoid any damages. It's helpful that the current governor seems to be looking the other way on environmental issues because she wants to encourage industry to relocate to our state.

Right now, we're hosing off the road that it happened on. That's not really the way we're supposed to do this, but I can't figure out any way to deal with a problem this big. We're hoping the hazardous waste will just make its way to Salt Creek (slowly) and get diluted along the way.

This is what happened. Between 2:00 and 3:00 pm on May 6th, the trailer of one of our tank trucks began leaking liquid waste left over from our usage of touluene diisocyanate (TDI) as it was driving down Highway 43 away from our Bridgeford plant. We use TDI to produce urethane foam, and then we burn the waste byproduct to generate energy in the Ulane plant, which is ten miles away. That's where the truck was going. It was transporting the TDI waste to the other plant. The stuff is pretty nasty. I wouldn't want to be around it, and I'm glad I don't need to breathe around the stuff.

Anyway, one of the valves was left partially open, and TDI waste basically leaked out on the highway. The driver only noticed when he arrived at the Ulane plant. So, it's possible the truck was spilling liquid the whole ten miles. These tank trucks hold about 6000 gallons, and there were about 4000 gallons left when it arrived at the plant. So, we could have lost anywhere from 1000-2000 gallons along the way.

Fortunately, it's not like our trucks drive through urban areas. It's mostly farmland between the Bridgeford Plant and the Ulane Plant. So, there aren't as many people. They don't ask questions, and I doubt they would care even if they knew what happened. Heck, they all think environmentalists are troublemakers who use these kinds of incidents to get publicity.

Listen, I'm really sorry this happened but it's not my fault. The driver is responsible for checking that valve before he drives off. He didn't, and now we have a mess on our hands. I chewed him out really good.

Don't worry. I'll get this cleaned up and submit the report to the state DOEI and the DOT. I just thought you should know.

Bad Chemistry

Amanda Jones works as a chemical engineer at BrimChem, one of the top plastics companies in the country. Recently, a bright new chemical engineer named Paul Gibson was hired in her division. Paul was tall and good-looking, and he was always polite. At lunch during Paul's first week, Amanda and a co-worker teased him about being a "Chippendales guy." Paul laughed a little, but it was apparent that the comment offended him. So, Amanda was careful from then on about her comments regarding his appearance.

A few months after starting at BrimChem, Paul went to a convention and came back somewhat agitated. Amanda asked him what was wrong. After a pause, Paul told her that one of the managers, Linda Juno, had made a pass at him one evening at the convention, suggesting he come up to her room "for a drink." When he declined, she became angry and said, "Paul, you need to decide whether you want to make it in this company." She didn't speak to him for the rest of the convention.

Paul told Amanda he was a bit worried about keeping his job with the company, since he was still on "probationary" status for his first year. Being on probation meant Linda or anyone else could have him fired for the slightest reason.

Later that day, though, Linda came down to Paul's office and seemed to be patching things up. After Linda left his office, Paul flashed Amanda a thumbs-up signal to show that things were all right.

The next week, Amanda was working late and passed by Paul's office. Linda was in his office giving him a backrub. He was obviously not enjoying it. He seemed to be making the best of it, though, and he said, "OK, thank you. I better finish up this report."

Linda was clearly annoyed and said, "Paul, I let you off once. You better not disappoint me again." A minute later, Linda stormed out of Paul's office.

The next day, Paul stopped Amanda in the parking lot. "Amanda, I know you saw what happened last night. I'm going to file a harassment complaint against Linda. If I'm fired, I'll sue the company. I'm tired of being harassed by her and other women in this company."

Amanda nodded. Then Paul asked, "Would you write an incident report about what you saw last night? I want to put some materials on file." Amanda said she would.

A week later, Paul was fired for a minor mistake. Amanda hadn't finished writing up the incident report.

If you were Amanda, what would you do at this point? If you would finish writing the incident report, what would you say and how would you say it?

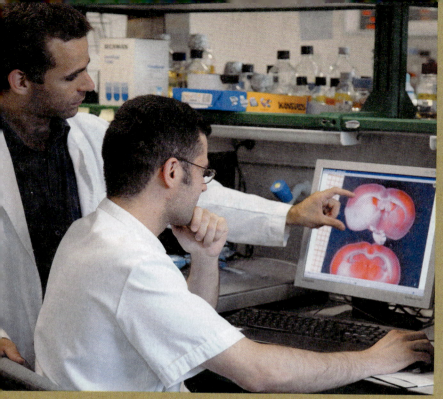

CHAPTER

10
Analytical
Reports

Types of Analytical Reports 254

Step 1: Make a Plan and Do
Research 259

Step 2: Organize and Draft Your
Report 265

Help: Using Google Drive to
Collaborate on Global
Projects 277

Step 3: Draft the Front Matter and
Back Matter 278

Step 4: Choose the Style, Design,
and Medium 285

Microgenre: The Poster
Presentation 287

What You Need to Know 289

Exercises and Projects 289

Case Study: The X-File 292

In this chapter, you will learn:

- About the various kinds of analytical reports used in technical workplaces.

- How to use the IMRaD pattern for organizing reports.

- How to determine the rhetorical situation for your reports.

- How to develop a methodology for collecting and analyzing information.

- Strategies for organizing and drafting an analytical report.

- How to use style and design to highlight important information and make it understandable.

Analytical reports are some of the most common large documents produced in the technical workplace. An analytical report is usually a formal response to a research question. It typically describes a research methodology, presents results, discusses those results, and makes recommendations.

The diagram in the Quick Start shows a general pattern for organizing an analytical report. To help you remember this generic report pattern, you might do what many researchers do—memorize the acronym IMRaD (Introduction, Methods, Results, and Discussion).

The IMRaD pattern for reports is flexible and should be adapted to the specific situation in which you are writing. For example, in some reports, the methodology section can be moved into an appendix at the end of the report, especially if your readers do not need a step-by-step description of your research approach. In other reports, you may find it helpful to combine the results and discussion sections into one larger section.

As with other genres, the IMRaD pattern is not a formula to be followed strictly. Rather, it is a guide to help you organize the information you have collected.

Types of Analytical Reports

Analytical reports are formal documents that present findings and make recommendations. Here are a few types:

Research reports—The purpose of a research report is to present the findings of a study. Research reports often stress the causes and effects of problems or trends, showing how events in the past have developed into the current situation.

Empirical research reports—Empirical research reports are written when a scientific project is completed. They first define a research question and hypothesis. Then, they describe the methods of study and the results of the research project. And finally, they discuss these results and draw conclusions about what was discovered as a result of the project.

Completion reports—Most projects in technical workplaces conclude with a completion report. These documents are used to report back to management or to the client, assessing the outcomes of a project or initiative.

Recommendation reports—Recommendation reports are often used to make suggestions about the best course of action. These reports are used to study a problem, present possible solutions, and then recommend what actions should be taken.

Feasibility reports—Feasibility reports are written to determine whether developing a product or following a course of action is possible or sensible. Usually, these reports are produced when management or the clients are not sure whether something can be done. The feasibility report helps determine whether the company should move forward with a project.

Link

For more strategies on organizing information in large documents, see Chapter 15, page 395.

Link

For more information on the scientific method, turn to Chapter 14, page 367.

Analytical Reports

Analytical reports tend to follow the IMRaD pattern as shown here. However, reports can be organized in a variety of ways. You should adjust this pattern to suit your subject and purpose.

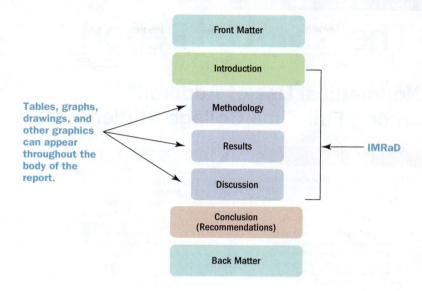

Tables, graphs, drawings, and other graphics can appear throughout the body of the report.

Basic Features of Analytical Reports

Analytical reports typically include the following basic features:

- **Introduction** that identifies the research question or hypothesis
- **Methodology** that explains step by step how the research was conducted
- **Results** that present the facts, data, and evidence collected while doing research
- **Graphics, graphs, and tables** that illustrate the results of the research
- **Discussion** of the results, relating them to the research question or hypothesis
- **Conclusions** that state the report's main point and make recommendations

Figure 10.1 shows a research report on Adderall abuse among college students. Like any research report, it defines a research question and offers a methodology for studying that research question. Then, it presents the results of the study and discusses those results. The report does not advocate a particular course of action. If this report were a recommendation report, it would make recommendations for ways to address Adderall abuse in young adults.

A Research Report

A clear title for the report is placed up front.

National Survey on Drug Use and Health
The NSDUH Report

April 7, 2009

Nonmedical Use of Adderall® among Full-Time College Students

In Brief

- Full-time college students aged 18 to 22 were twice as likely as their counterparts who were not full-time college students to have used Adderall® nonmedically in the past year (6.4 vs. 3.0 percent)

- Full-time college students who were nonmedical users of Adderall® were almost 3 times as likely as those who had not used Adderall® nonmedically to have used marijuana in the past year (79.9 vs. 27.2 percent), 8 times more likely to have used cocaine in that period (28.9 vs. 3.6 percent), 8 times more likely to have been nonmedical users of prescription tranquilizers (24.5 vs. 3.0 percent), and 5 times more likely to have been nonmedical users of prescription pain relievers (44.9 vs. 8.7 percent)

- Nearly 90 percent of full-time college students who used Adderall® nonmedically in the past year were past month binge alcohol users, and more than half were heavy alcohol users

Main points are placed up front in an easy-to-access box.

Nonmedical use of Adderall® is of special interest to policymakers because, as an amphetamine, Adderall® is among the group of legally approved drugs classified as having the highest potential for dependence or abuse.[1] A prior study of nonmedical use of stimulants such as Adderall® by college students reported considerably higher rates of frequent binge alcohol use, marijuana use, and cocaine use among students who used stimulants nonmedically in the past year compared with their counterparts who had not.[2] Use of both cocaine and stimulants is problematic because each increases the risk for heart attack or stroke.[3,4]

This issue of *The NSDUH Report* examines the rates of nonmedical use of Adderall® in the past year among full-time college students aged 18 to 22 and comparably aged persons who were not full-time college students.[5,6] All findings presented in this report are annual averages based on combined 2006 and 2007 data.

Background information stresses the importance of the subject.

The purpose of the report is stated.

Nonmedical Use of Adderall®, by College Enrollment Status

Full-time college students aged 18 to 22 were twice as likely as their counterparts who were

The NSDUH Report is published periodically by the Office of Applied Studies, Substance Abuse and Mental Health Services Administration (SAMHSA). All material appearing in this report is in the public domain and may be reproduced or copied without permission from SAMHSA. Additional copies of this report or other reports from the Office of Applied Studies are available online: http://oas.samhsa.gov. Citation of the source is appreciated. For questions about this report, please e-mail: shortreports@samhsa.hhs.gov.

NSDUH_117

Source: Office of Applied Studies Substance Abuse and Mental Health Services Administration [SAMHSA], 2009

Graphs show trends in data while supporting written text.

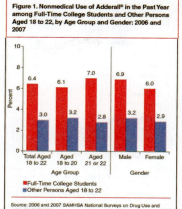

Figure 1. Nonmedical Use of Adderall® in the Past Year among Full-Time College Students and Other Persons Aged 18 to 22, by Age Group and Gender: 2006 and 2007

Source: 2006 and 2007 SAMHSA National Surveys on Drug Use and Health (NSDUHs).

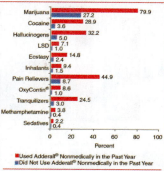

Figure 2. Other Drug Use in the Past Year among Full-Time College Students Aged 18 to 22, by Past Year Nonmedical Use of Adderall®: 2006 and 2007

Source: 2006 and 2007 SAMHSA National Surveys on Drug Use and Health (NSDUHs).

not full-time college students to have used Adderall® nonmedically in the past year (6.4 vs. 3.0 percent) (Figure 1). This pattern was found for both males and females and for persons aged 18 to 20 as well as for those 21 or 22 years old.

Other Drug Use

Among full-time college students, those who had used Adderall® nonmedically in the past year were more likely than those who had not used Adderall® nonmedically to have used illicit drugs or to have used other prescription drugs nonmedically in the past year. Full-time college students who were nonmedical users of Adderall® were almost 3 times as likely as those who had not used Adderall® nonmedically to have used marijuana in the past year (79.9 vs. 27.2 percent), 8 times more likely to have used cocaine in that period (28.9 vs. 3.6 percent), 8 times more likely to have been nonmedical users of prescription tranquilizers (24.5 vs. 3.0 percent), and 5 times more likely to have been nonmedical users of prescription pain relievers (44.9 vs. 8.7 percent) (Figure 2).

Results are described.

Alcohol Use

Among full-time college students aged 18 to 22, those who used Adderall® nonmedically in the past year were more than 1.5 times as likely as their counterparts to have used alcohol in the past month (95.4 vs. 63.0 percent), more than twice as

likely to have been binge alcohol users (89.5 vs. 41.4 percent), and more than 3 times as likely to have been heavy alcohol users (55.2 vs. 15.6 percent) (Figure 3). Similar patterns were observed for underage full-time college students (i.e., those aged 18 to 20) who used Adderall® nonmedically in the past year and for nonmedical Adderall® users of legal drinking age compared with their counterparts who had not used it nonmedically (data not shown).

Demographic Differences

Among full-time college students aged 18 to 22, nonmedical use of Adderall® in the past year was more likely among whites (8.6 percent) than blacks (1.0 percent), Asians (2.1 percent), Hispanics (2.2 percent), or persons of two or more races (2.7 percent) (Table 1). Nonmedical use of Adderall® among full-time college students was highest among students whose annual family incomes were less than $20,000 (8.9 percent), followed by those with annual family incomes of $75,000 or more (6.0 percent). Rates were lower for students with annual family incomes of $20,000 to $49,999 (3.0 percent) or $50,000 to $74,999 (4.0 percent).

Headings make the text easy to scan.

Discussion

The higher rate of nonmedical use of Adderall® among full-time college students than among others in the same

(continued)

April 7, 2009   NSDUH REPORT: NONMEDICAL USE OF ADDERALL® AMONG FULL-TIME COLLEGE STUDENTS

Charts are used to present results visually in ways that are easy to scan.

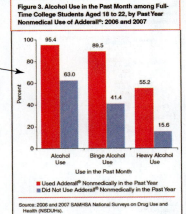

Figure 3. Alcohol Use in the Past Month among Full-Time College Students Aged 18 to 22, by Past Year Nonmedical Use of Adderall®: 2006 and 2007

Percent (y-axis, 0 to 100)

- Alcohol Use: 95.4, 63.0
- Binge Alcohol Use: 89.5, 41.4
- Heavy Alcohol Use: 55.2, 15.6

Use in the Past Month

■ Used Adderall® Nonmedically in the Past Year
■ Did Not Use Adderall® Nonmedically in the Past Year

Source: 2006 and 2007 SAMHSA National Surveys on Drug Use and Health (NSDUHs).

Table 1. Nonmedical Use of Adderall® in the Past Year among Full-Time College Students Aged 18 to 22, by Selected Demographic Characteristics: 2006 and 2007

Demographic Characteristic	%
*Race/Ethnicity**	
White	8.6
Black or African American	1.0
Asian	2.1
Two or More Races	2.7
Hispanic or Latino	2.2
Annual Family Income	
Less than $20,000	8.9
$20,000 to $49,999	3.0
$50,000 to $74,999	4.0
$75,000 or More	6.0

Source: 2006 and 2007 SAMHSA National Surveys on Drug Use and Health (NSDUHs).

age range is a public health concern because of this drug's potential for dependence or abuse. Educators, counselors, and others who work with students also need to be aware that polydrug use was prevalent among full-time college students who used Adderall® nonmedically in the past year. As noted previously, both cocaine and stimulants such as Adderall® increase a person's risk for heart attack or stroke. Students who use Adderall® nonmedically also may need to take central nervous system depressants such as pain relievers or tranquilizers—which carry their own risks of dependence or abuse—to counteract the stimulant effects of Adderall®. Finally, high rates of binge and heavy alcohol use among full-time college students who used Adderall® nonmedically in the past year are a cause for concern because of the well-documented associations between excessive drinking among college students and the adverse consequences for students' physical and mental health, safety, and environment.[7]

The authors choose not to include a conclusion because the report is brief and does not make recommendations.

End Notes

1 Prescription drug classifications (or schedules) based on the Controlled Substances Act (CSA) can be found online at http://www.usdoj.gov/dea/pubs/scheduling.html. For definitions of drug schedules under the CSA, see http://www.usdoj.gov/dea/pubs/csa/812.htm#a

2 McCabe, S. E., Knight, J. R., Teter, C. J., & Wechsler, H. (2005). Non-medical use of prescription stimulants among US college students: Prevalence and correlates from a national survey. *Addiction, 100*, 96-106.

3 National Institute on Drug Abuse. (2008, August). *NIDA InfoFacts: Cocaine*. Retrieved March 4, 2009, from http://www.drugabuse.gov/Infofacts/cocaine.html

4 National Institute on Drug Abuse. (2008, June). *NIDA InfoFacts: Stimulant ADHD medications – Methylphenidate and amphetamines*. Retrieved March 4, 2009, from http://www.drugabuse.gov/Infofacts/ADHD.html

5 Nonmedical use is defined as the use of prescription-type drugs not prescribed for the respondent by a physician or used only for the experience or feeling they caused. For this analysis, respondents with missing data for their lifetime or past year nonmedical use of Adderall® were treated as though they were nonusers.

6 Respondents were classified as full-time college students if they reported that they were in their first through fourth year (or higher) at a college or university and that they were enrolled full time. Respondents who were on break were considered enrolled if they intended to return to college or university when the break ended. Respondents aged 18 to 22 who were not full-time college students included those who were enrolled part time in college, enrolled in secondary school, or not enrolled. Respondents with unknown enrollment status were excluded from this analysis.

7 College Drinking – Changing the Culture, National Institute on Alcohol Abuse and Alcoholism. (2007, July 11 [last reviewed]). *A snapshot of annual high-risk college drinking consequences*. Retrieved March 4, 2009, from http://www.collegedrinkingprevention.gov/facts/snapshot.aspx

Table and Figure Notes

* Data are not shown for American Indians or Alaska Natives and for Native Hawaiians or Other Pacific Islanders because these estimates were of low precision.

Suggested Citation

Substance Abuse and Mental Health Services Administration, Office of Applied Studies. (April 7, 2009). *The NSDUH Report: Nonmedical Use of Adderall® among Full-Time College Students*. Rockville, MD.

Sources are listed.

Step 1: Make a Plan and Do Research

An analytical report can be a large, complex document, so it is important that you plan properly with a full understanding of the report's rhetorical situation.

Planning

You should start planning the document by first identifying the elements of the rhetorical situation. Begin by answering the Five-W and How Questions:

Who might read this report?

Why was this report requested?

What kinds of information or content do readers need?

Where will this report be read?

When will this report be used?

How will this report be used?

With the answers to these questions fresh in your mind, you can begin defining the rhetorical situation in which your report will be used.

SUBJECT   What exactly will the report cover, and what are the boundaries of its subject? What information and facts do readers need to know to make a decision?

PURPOSE   What should the report accomplish, and what do the readers expect it to accomplish? What is its main goal or objective?

You should be able to express the purpose of your report in one sentence. A good way to begin forming your purpose statement is to complete the phrase "The purpose of my report is to . . . ." You can then use some of the following action verbs to express what the report will do:

to analyze	to develop	to determine
to examine	to formulate	to recommend
to investigate	to devise	to decide
to study	to create	to conclude
to inspect	to generate	to offer
to assess	to originate	to resolve
to explore	to produce	to select

READERS   Who are the intended readers of your report, and who else might be interested in your findings and analysis?

Primary readers (action takers) are the people who need the report's information to make some kind of decision. What information do they need to make this decision?

Secondary readers (advisors) are usually experts or other specialists who will advise the primary readers.

Tertiary readers (evaluators) might be people you didn't expect to read the report, like reporters, lawyers, auditors, and perhaps even historians.

Gatekeeper readers (supervisors) will probably include your immediate supervisor, as well as your company's legal counsel, accountants, or technical experts.

Link

For more help defining your readers and their characteristics, go to Chapter 2, page 19.

CONTEXT OF USE   Where, when, and how will the report be used? What are the economic, political, and ethical factors that will influence the writing of the report and how readers will interpret it?

Physical context—Consider the various places where your report might be used, such as in a meeting or at a convention.

Economic context—Anticipate the financial issues that may influence how your readers will interpret the results and recommendations in your report.

Political context—Think about how local, national, and international politics will shape the reception of your report.

Ethical context—Consider any legal, environmental, or ethical issues that might affect your report and the methods you will use to collect information.

Link

For more information on defining the context of use, go to Chapter 2, page 22.

If you are writing a report with a team, collaborate on your answers to these questions about the rhetorical situation. If your team begins the project with a clear understanding of the subject, purpose, readers, and context of use, you will likely avoid unnecessary conflict and wasted time.

Researching

With the rhetorical situation fresh in your mind, you can start collecting information for your report. It is important that you define a research question and develop a plan (a methodology) for conducting research on your subject.

Research in technical fields typically follows a predictable process:

1. Define a research question.

2. State a hypothesis.

3. Develop a research methodology.

4. Collect information by following the research methodology.

5. Analyze gathered information and use it to modify the hypothesis.

The most effective methodologies collect information from a variety of sources (Figure 10.2).

Researching a Subject

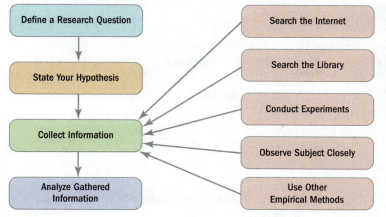

Figure 10.2: A research methodology is a plan for gathering information, preferably from a variety of sources.

DEFINE A RESEARCH QUESTION AND HYPOTHESIS   Reports are usually written to answer a specific *research question* or test a *hypothesis*. So, you should begin by defining the question you are trying to answer. Write down the question in one sentence.

> Could we convert one of our campus buildings to a renewable heating source, like solar?

> Why are the liver cancer rates in Horn, Nevada, higher than the national average?

> How much would it cost to automate our factory in Racine, Wisconsin?

> Is it feasible to reintroduce wolves into the Gila Wilderness Area?

At this point, you should also write down a one-sentence hypothesis. A hypothesis is essentially an educated guess or tentative explanation that answers your research question.

> We believe we could convert a building like Engineering Hall to a solar heating source.

> Our hypothesis is that liver cancer rates in Horn, Nevada, are high because of excessive levels of arsenic in the town's drinking water.

> Automating our Racine plant could cost $2 million, but the savings will offset that figure in the long run.

> Reintroducing wolves to the Gila Wilderness Area is feasible, but there are numerous political obstacles and community fears to be overcome.

Link

To learn more about forming a hypothesis, turn to Chapter 14, page 366.

As you move forward with your research, you usually need to modify this hypothesis to fit your findings. In some cases, you might even need to abandon your original hypothesis completely and come up with a new one.

DEVELOP A METHODOLOGY   A *methodology* is the series of steps you will take to answer your research question or test your hypothesis. A good way to invent your methodology is to use logical mapping (Figure 10.3).

1. Write your research question in the middle of a sheet of paper or a document on your computer.

2. Around your research question, insert two to five major steps you would need to take to answer that question.

3. Around each major step, insert two to five minor steps needed to achieve that major step.

4. Keep filling out and revising your map until you have fully described the major and minor steps in your methodology.

Using Logical Mapping to Develop a Methodology

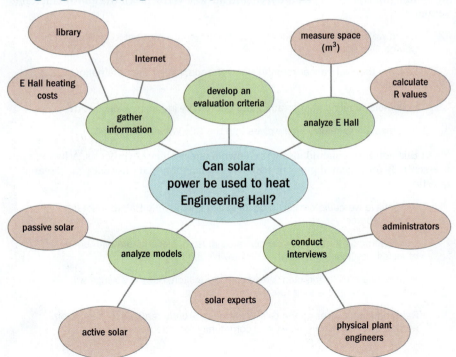

Figure 10.3: When mapping a methodology, ask yourself how you might answer the research question. Then, decide on the major and minor steps in your methodology.

Allow yourself to be creative at this point. As you keep mapping out farther, your methodology will likely evolve in front of you. You can cross out some steps and combine others. In the end, a reasonable methodology is one that is "replicable," meaning that readers can obtain the same results if they redo your research.

COLLECT INFORMATION   Once you have described your methodology, you can use it to guide your research. The information you collect will become the results section of your report.

There are many places to find information:

> **Internet searches**—With some well-chosen keywords, you can use search engines to collect information on the subject. Websites like the ones from the U.S. Census Bureau and the National Science Foundation offer a wealth of information (Figures 10.4 and 10.5).

Link

For more strategies for using search engines, see Chapter 14, page 371.

U.S. Census Bureau Website

Source: www.census.gov

Figure 10.4: The U.S. Census Bureau website is an excellent resource for statistics. The website offers statistics on income, race, trade, and lifestyle issues.

An Archive on the Internet

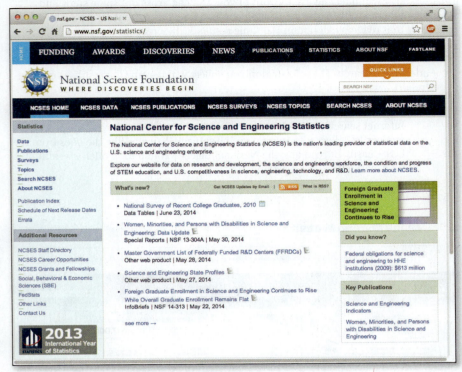

Figure 10.5
The web-site for the National Science Foundation archives many informative reports and data sets that can be used in projects related to science, technology, and engineering.

Source: The National Science Foundation, www.nsf.gov

Link

Chapter 14 offers a full discussion of research. For more research strategies, see page 365.

Library research—Using your library's catalogs, databases, and indexes, start searching for articles, reports, books, and other print documents that discuss your subject.

Experiments and observations—Your report might require experiments and measurable observations to test your hypothesis. Learn about the research methodologies used in your field and use them to generate empirical data.

Other empirical methods—You might conduct interviews, pass out surveys, or do case studies to generate empirical information that you can use to confirm or challenge the information you find in print or electronic forms.

To avoid any problems with plagiarism or copyright issues, you need to carefully cite your sources in your notes. Chapter 15 offers note-taking strategies that will help you avoid any issues of plagiarism or copyright. Chapter 4 discusses ethical issues involving copyright.

While collecting information, you will likely find that your methodology will evolve. These kinds of changes in the research plan are not unusual. Keep track of any changes, because you will need to note them in the methodology section of your report.

ANALYZE INFORMATION AND USE IT TO MODIFY YOUR HYPOTHESIS Using the material you collected, try to locate two to five major findings about your subject. Then, look back at your original research question and hypothesis. You can now modify your hypothesis, if needed, to fit your findings.

Don't worry if your original hypothesis ends up needing modifications. It was just a guess anyway. In the end, the facts in your final report are more important than your original guess about what you would discover.

Link

For more information on plagiarism and copyright, go to Chapter 14, page 388.

Link

For more information on developing and modifying research questions and hypotheses, turn to Chapter 14, page 367.

Step 2: Organize and Draft Your Report

Organizing your information and drafting analytical reports will not be difficult if you stay focused on your purpose. Your purpose statement will help you include only need-to-know information in the report. Although you might be tempted to include everything you collected, don't do this. Anything beyond need-to-know information will only muddle your document, making the most important ideas harder for your readers to find.

AT A GLANCE

Moves in an Introduction

- Define the subject.
- State the purpose.
- State the main point.
- Stress the importance of the subject.
- Offer background information.
- Forecast the remainder of the report.

Writing the Introduction

Your report should begin with an introduction that grabs your readers' attention and sets a framework for the rest of the document (Figure 10.6 on pp. 268–276). Typically, the introduction will include some or all of the following six moves, though not necessarily in this order:

Move 1: Define the *subject* of the report.

Move 2: State the *purpose* of the report, preferably in one sentence.

Move 3: State the report's *main point,* which is likely your main conclusion or recommendation.

Move 4: Stress the *importance of the subject,* especially to the readers.

Move 5: Offer *background information* on the subject.

Move 6: Forecast the *organization* of the report.

It is fine to be straightforward, even blunt, in the introduction of your report because these documents need to be as clear as possible. You can make statements like, "The purpose of this report is to . . ." and "In this report, we demonstrate that . . . ." Your readers will appreciate your clear and forthright approach.

Link

For more information on writing introductions, see Chapter 15, page 399.

Link

For more information on writing a purpose statement, see Chapter 1, page 5.

Describing Your Methodology

Following the introduction, reports typically include a methodology section that describes step by step how the study was conducted. This section should include an opening, body, and closing.

Link

For help organizing sections in larger documents, see Chapter 15, page 395.

- In the opening paragraph, describe your overall approach to collecting information in one or two sentences (Figure 10.6). If you are following an established methodology, you might mention where it has been used before and who used it.
- In the body of this section, walk your readers step by step through the major parts of your study. After you describe each major step, you should also discuss the minor steps that were part of it.
- In the closing paragraph, you should discuss some of the limitations of the study. For example, your study may have been conducted with a limited sample (e.g., college students at a small Midwestern university). By identifying your study's limitations, you will show your readers that you are aware that other conditions may yield different results.

Summarizing the Results of the Study

In the results section, you should summarize the major *findings* of your study. A helpful guideline is to discuss only your two to five most important findings. That way, these important findings won't be lost in a list of not-so-important findings. This section should include an opening, a body, and perhaps a closing.

Link

For help making tables, charts, and graphs, see Chapter 18, starting on page 477.

- In your opening paragraph for the results section, briefly summarize your major results (Figure 10.6).
- In the body of this section, devote at least one paragraph to each of these major results, using data to support each finding.
- In the closing (if needed), you can again summarize your major results. Often, results sections do not include a closing paragraph.

Your aim in this section is to present your findings as objectively and clearly as possible. To achieve this aim, state your results with minimal interpretation. You should wait until the discussion section to offer your interpretation of the results.

If your study generated numerical data, you should use tables, graphs, and charts to present your data in this section. As discussed in Chapter 19, these graphics should support the written text, not replace it.

Discussing Your Results

The results of your research are analyzed in the discussion section. As you review your findings, identify the two to five major conclusions you have drawn from your information or data. Like other sections in the report, the discussion section should include an opening, a body, and perhaps a closing.

- The discussion section should start out with an opening paragraph that briefly states your overall conclusions about the results of your study (Figure 10.6).
- In the body of this section, you should devote a paragraph or more to each of your major conclusions. Discuss the results of your study, detailing what you think your results show about your subject.
- A closing paragraph, usually only found in large reports, can be used to summarize your major conclusions.

Concluding with Recommendations

The conclusion of a report should be concise. You should make some or all of the following six moves, which are typical in a larger document:

AT A GLANCE

Moves in the Conclusion
- Make an obvious transition.
- Restate the main points.
- State your recommendations.
- Re-emphasize the importance of the study.
- Look to the future.
- Say thank you and offer contact information.

MAKE AN OBVIOUS TRANSITION A heading like "Our Recommendations" or "Summary" will cue readers that you are concluding. Or, you can use phrases like "In conclusion" or "To sum up" to signal that the report is coming to an end.

RESTATE YOUR MAIN POINT State clearly what you think your research discovered about your subject. Boil the information down to its essence.

STATE YOUR RECOMMENDATIONS If you have been asked to make recommendations, your conclusion should identify two to five actions that your readers should consider. A good way to handle recommendations is to present them in a bulleted list (Figure 10.6).

RE-EMPHASIZE THE IMPORTANCE OF THE STUDY Tell your readers why your study is important, especially to them.

LOOK TO THE FUTURE You might discuss future research paths that could be pursued. Or, you could describe the future you envision if readers follow your recommendations.

Link

For more ideas on writing conclusions, see Chapter 15, page 411.

SAY "THANK YOU" AND OFFER CONTACT INFORMATION After thanking your readers for their interest, you might also provide contact information, such as a phone number and e-mail address.

Your conclusion doesn't need to make these moves in this order, nor are all the moves necessary. Minimally, you should restate your main point and present any recommendations.

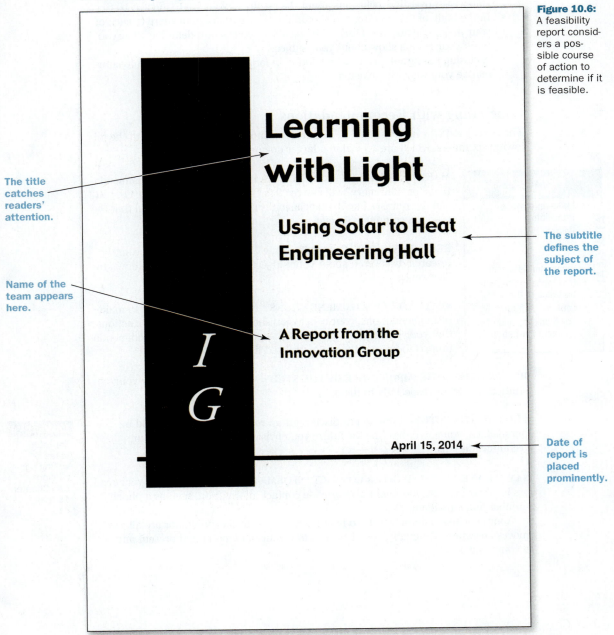

Figure 10.6: A feasibility report considers a possible course of action to determine if it is feasible.

The title catches readers' attention.

Learning with Light

Using Solar to Heat Engineering Hall

The subtitle defines the subject of the report.

Name of the team appears here.

A Report from the Innovation Group

I G

April 15, 2014

Date of report is placed prominently.

The table of contents is clearly signaled by a heading.

The headings of the report are listed here as they appear in the report.

The abstract is clearly identified by a header.

The main point is stated up front.

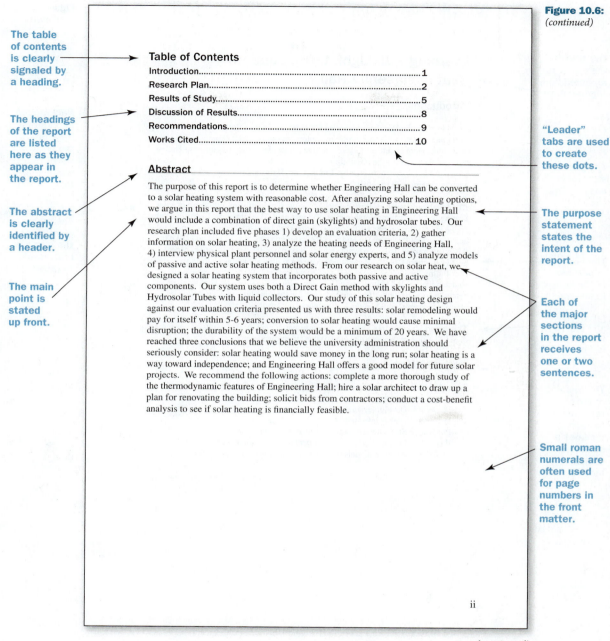

Table of Contents

Introduction...1

Research Plan..2

Results of Study...5

Discussion of Results...8

Recommendations..9

Works Cited... 10

"Leader" tabs are used to create these dots.

Abstract

The purpose of this report is to determine whether Engineering Hall can be converted to a solar heating system with reasonable cost. After analyzing solar heating options, we argue in this report that the best way to use solar heating in Engineering Hall would include a combination of direct gain (skylights) and hydrosolar tubes. Our research plan included five phases 1) develop an evaluation criteria, 2) gather information on solar heating, 3) analyze the heating needs of Engineering Hall, 4) interview physical plant personnel and solar energy experts, and 5) analyze models of passive and active solar heating methods. From our research on solar heat, we designed a solar heating system that incorporates both passive and active components. Our system uses both a Direct Gain method with skylights and Hydrosolar Tubes with liquid collectors. Our study of this solar heating design against our evaluation criteria presented us with three results: solar remodeling would pay for itself within 5-6 years; conversion to solar heating would cause minimal disruption; the durability of the system would be a minimum of 20 years. We have reached three conclusions that we believe the university administration should seriously consider: solar heating would save money in the long run; solar heating is a way toward independence; and Engineering Hall offers a good model for future solar projects. We recommend the following actions: complete a more thorough study of the thermodynamic features of Engineering Hall; hire a solar architect to draw up a plan for renovating the building; solicit bids from contractors; conduct a cost-benefit analysis to see if solar heating is financially feasible.

The purpose statement states the intent of the report.

Each of the major sections in the report receives one or two sentences.

Small roman numerals are often used for page numbers in the front matter.

ii

(continued)

The title of
the report is
repeated here
(optional).

Learning with Light: Using Solar to Heat Engineering Hall

Introduction

Background
information
familiarizes
the readers
with the
report's
topic.

On March 14, the President of Kellen College, Dr. Sharon Holton, asked our Energy Dynamics class (Engineering 387) to explore ways to convert campus buildings to renewable energy sources. Our research team decided to use Engineering Hall as a test case for studying the possibility of conversion to solar heating. The purpose of this report is to determine whether Engineering Hall can be converted to a solar heating system with reasonable cost.

The purpose
statement is
easy to find.

After analyzing solar heating options, we argue that in this report the use of solar heating would require a combination of direct gain (skylights) and hydrosolar tubes. At the end of this report, we recommend that the university begin designing a solar heating system this summer, and we offer specific steps toward that goal. We believe this effort toward using renewable energy is a step in the right direction, especially here in southern Colorado where we receive a significant amount of sunlight. In the near future, the United States will need to wean itself off non-renewable energy sources, like oil and natural gas. The conversion of Engineering Hall from an oil heater to solar heating offers us a test case for studying how the conversion to renewable energy could be made throughout our campus.

The main
point gives
the report a
statement
to prove.

The
importance
of the subject
is stressed.

This report includes four sections: a) our research plan, b) the results of our research, c) a discussion of these results, and d) our recommendations.

The structure
of the report
is forecasted.

Research Plan

To study whether heating Engineering Hall with solar is feasible, we followed a five-part research plan:

The opening
of the
research
section
includes a
summary
of the
methodology.

Phase 1:	Develop evaluation criteria
Phase 2:	Gather information
Phase 3:	Study the heating needs of Engineering Hall
Phase 4:	Interview physical plant personnel and solar energy experts
Phase 5:	Analyze models of passive and active solar heating models

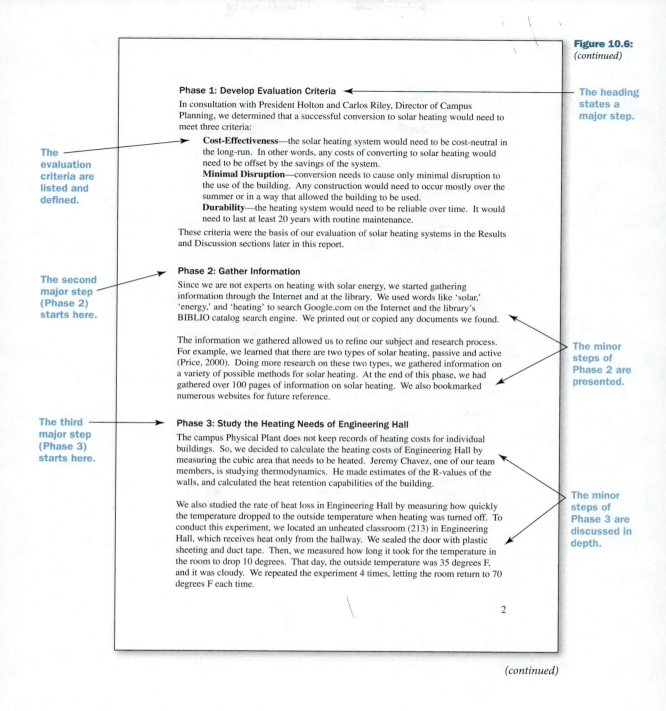

Phase 1: Develop Evaluation Criteria ◄─── *The heading states a major step.*

In consultation with President Holton and Carlos Riley, Director of Campus Planning, we determined that a successful conversion to solar heating would need to meet three criteria:

The evaluation criteria are listed and defined.

Cost-Effectiveness—the solar heating system would need to be cost-neutral in the long-run. In other words, any costs of converting to solar heating would need to be offset by the savings of the system.
Minimal Disruption—conversion needs to cause only minimal disruption to the use of the building. Any construction would need to occur mostly over the summer or in a way that allowed the building to be used.
Durability—the heating system would need to be reliable over time. It would need to last at least 20 years with routine maintenance.

These criteria were the basis of our evaluation of solar heating systems in the Results and Discussion sections later in this report.

Phase 2: Gather Information

The second major step (Phase 2) starts here.

Since we are not experts on heating with solar energy, we started gathering information through the Internet and at the library. We used words like 'solar,' 'energy,' and 'heating' to search Google.com on the Internet and the library's BIBLIO catalog search engine. We printed out or copied any documents we found.

The information we gathered allowed us to refine our subject and research process. For example, we learned that there are two types of solar heating, passive and active (Price, 2000). Doing more research on these two types, we gathered information on a variety of possible methods for solar heating. At the end of this phase, we had gathered over 100 pages of information on solar heating. We also bookmarked numerous websites for future reference.

The minor steps of Phase 2 are presented.

Phase 3: Study the Heating Needs of Engineering Hall

The third major step (Phase 3) starts here.

The campus Physical Plant does not keep records of heating costs for individual buildings. So, we decided to calculate the heating costs of Engineering Hall by measuring the cubic area that needs to be heated. Jeremy Chavez, one of our team members, is studying thermodynamics. He made estimates of the R-values of the walls, and calculated the heat retention capabilities of the building.

We also studied the rate of heat loss in Engineering Hall by measuring how quickly the temperature dropped to the outside temperature when heating was turned off. To conduct this experiment, we located an unheated classroom (213) in Engineering Hall, which receives heat only from the hallway. We sealed the door with plastic sheeting and duct tape. Then, we measured how long it took for the temperature in the room to drop 10 degrees. That day, the outside temperature was 35 degrees F, and it was cloudy. We repeated the experiment 4 times, letting the room return to 70 degrees F each time.

The minor steps of Phase 3 are discussed in depth.

2

(continued)

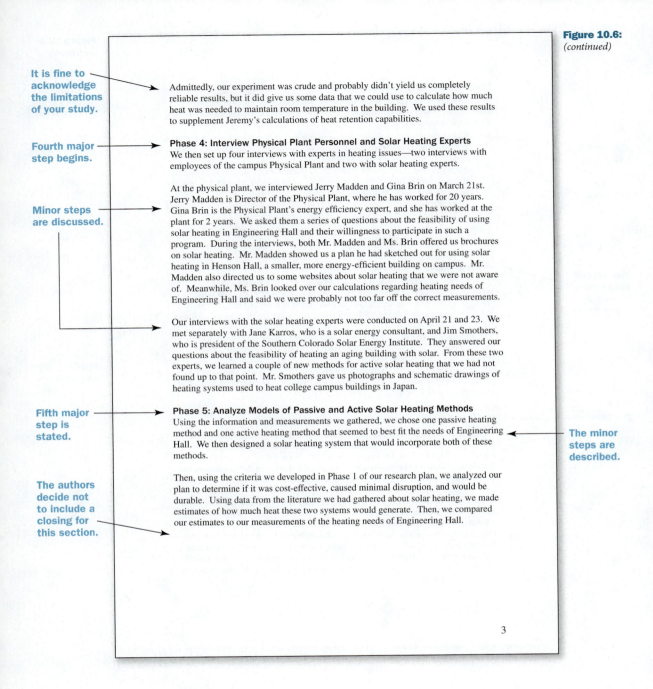

It is fine to acknowledge the limitations of your study.

Admittedly, our experiment was crude and probably didn't yield us completely reliable results, but it did give us some data that we could use to calculate how much heat was needed to maintain room temperature in the building. We used these results to supplement Jeremy's calculations of heat retention capabilities.

Fourth major step begins.

Phase 4: Interview Physical Plant Personnel and Solar Heating Experts
We then set up four interviews with experts in heating issues—two interviews with employees of the campus Physical Plant and two with solar heating experts.

Minor steps are discussed.

At the physical plant, we interviewed Jerry Madden and Gina Brin on March 21st. Jerry Madden is Director of the Physical Plant, where he has worked for 20 years. Gina Brin is the Physical Plant's energy efficiency expert, and she has worked at the plant for 2 years. We asked them a series of questions about the feasibility of using solar heating in Engineering Hall and their willingness to participate in such a program. During the interviews, both Mr. Madden and Ms. Brin offered us brochures on solar heating. Mr. Madden showed us a plan he had sketched out for using solar heating in Henson Hall, a smaller, more energy-efficient building on campus. Mr. Madden also directed us to some websites about solar heating that we were not aware of. Meanwhile, Ms. Brin looked over our calculations regarding heating needs of Engineering Hall and said we were probably not too far off the correct measurements.

Our interviews with the solar heating experts were conducted on April 21 and 23. We met separately with Jane Karros, who is a solar energy consultant, and Jim Smothers, who is president of the Southern Colorado Solar Energy Institute. They answered our questions about the feasibility of heating an aging building with solar. From these two experts, we learned a couple of new methods for active solar heating that we had not found up to that point. Mr. Smothers gave us photographs and schematic drawings of heating systems used to heat college campus buildings in Japan.

Fifth major step is stated.

Phase 5: Analyze Models of Passive and Active Solar Heating Methods
Using the information and measurements we gathered, we chose one passive heating method and one active heating method that seemed to best fit the needs of Engineering Hall. We then designed a solar heating system that would incorporate both of these methods.

The minor steps are described.

The authors decide not to include a closing for this section.

Then, using the criteria we developed in Phase 1 of our research plan, we analyzed our plan to determine if it was cost-effective, caused minimal disruption, and would be durable. Using data from the literature we had gathered about solar heating, we made estimates of how much heat these two systems would generate. Then, we compared our estimates to our measurements of the heating needs of Engineering Hall.

3

The heading
clearly signals
a new section.

Results of Study

In this section, we will first describe the solar heating system we devised. Then, we will show the results of our evaluation of this solar heating system measured against the criteria we developed.

The opening
paragraph
states the
subject and
purpose of
the section.

One result
of the
research was
the design
chosen.

Our Solar Heating Design

On the advice of Mr. Madden, the Director of the Physical Plant, we designed a solar heating system that incorporated both passive and active components. Our system uses both a Direct Gain method with skylights and Hydrosolar Tubes with liquid collectors.

Direct Gain (passive system)—this method would use a south-facing skylight that is mounted on the roof of the building to heat the second floor of Engineering Hall. In the winter, when the sun is low in the southern sky, the skylight lets in full sunlight (see Figure 1). On the opposite wall from the skylight, a thermal storage wall made of brick would collect the heat so it could be released gradually throughout the day. According to one of our sources, each square foot of glass in the skylight can heat 10 square feet of floor space (Solar Thermal Energy Group, 2003). If so, we would need 200 square feet of glass to heat the 2000 sq. ft. on the second floor of Engineering Hall. In other words, we would need the equivalent of a 5 ft. by 40 ft. skylight across the roof of the building.

Solar design
is described.

Graphics help
illustrate
complex
concepts.

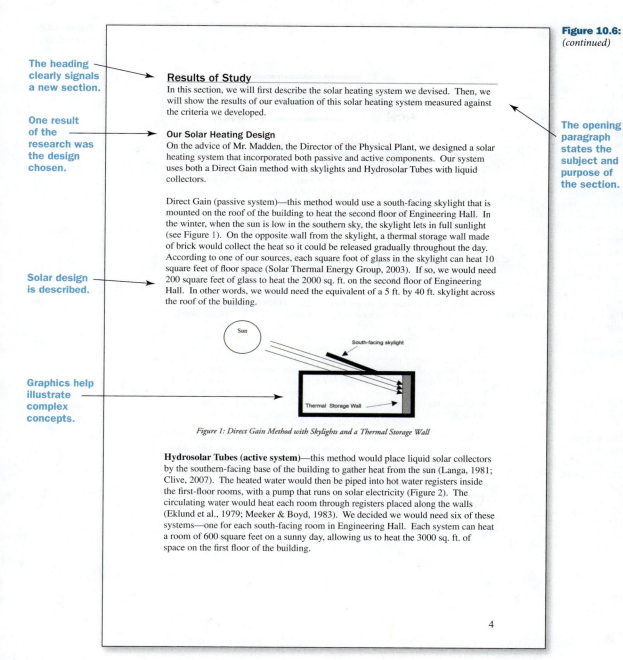

Figure 1: Direct Gain Method with Skylights and a Thermal Storage Wall

Hydrosolar Tubes (active system)—this method would place liquid solar collectors by the southern-facing base of the building to gather heat from the sun (Langa, 1981; Clive, 2007). The heated water would then be piped into hot water registers inside the first-floor rooms, with a pump that runs on solar electricity (Figure 2). The circulating water would heat each room through registers placed along the walls (Eklund et al., 1979; Meeker & Boyd, 1983). We decided we would need six of these systems—one for each south-facing room in Engineering Hall. Each system can heat a room of 600 square feet on a sunny day, allowing us to heat the 3000 sq. ft. of space on the first floor of the building.

4

(continued)

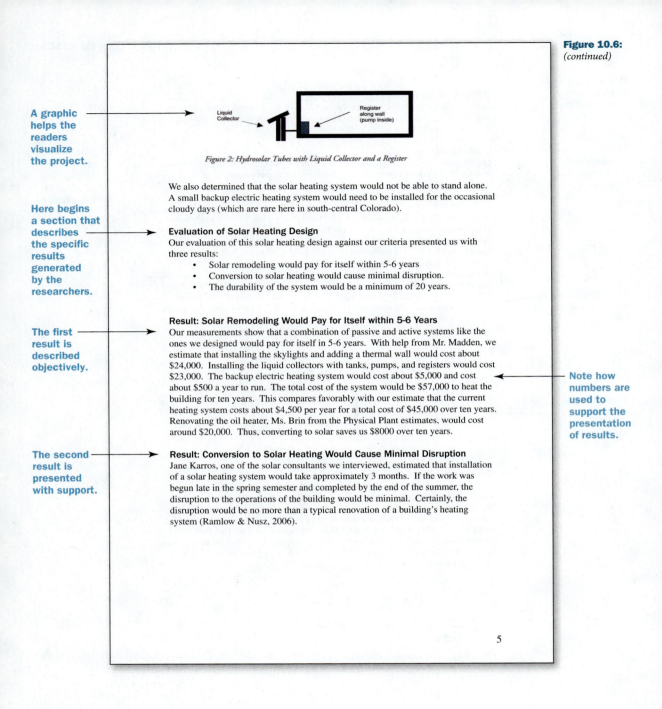

Figure 2: Hydrosolar Tubes with Liquid Collector and a Register

A graphic helps the readers visualize the project.

We also determined that the solar heating system would not be able to stand alone. A small backup electric heating system would need to be installed for the occasional cloudy days (which are rare here in south-central Colorado).

Here begins a section that describes the specific results generated by the researchers.

Evaluation of Solar Heating Design

Our evaluation of this solar heating design against our criteria presented us with three results:

- Solar remodeling would pay for itself within 5-6 years
- Conversion to solar heating would cause minimal disruption.
- The durability of the system would be a minimum of 20 years.

The first result is described objectively.

Result: Solar Remodeling Would Pay for Itself within 5-6 Years

Our measurements show that a combination of passive and active systems like the ones we designed would pay for itself in 5-6 years. With help from Mr. Madden, we estimate that installing the skylights and adding a thermal wall would cost about $24,000. Installing the liquid collectors with tanks, pumps, and registers would cost $23,000. The backup electric heating system would cost about $5,000 and cost about $500 a year to run. The total cost of the system would be $57,000 to heat the building for ten years. This compares favorably with our estimate that the current heating system costs about $4,500 per year for a total cost of $45,000 over ten years. Renovating the oil heater, Ms. Brin from the Physical Plant estimates, would cost around $20,000. Thus, converting to solar saves us $8000 over ten years.

Note how numbers are used to support the presentation of results.

The second result is presented with support.

Result: Conversion to Solar Heating Would Cause Minimal Disruption

Jane Karros, one of the solar consultants we interviewed, estimated that installation of a solar heating system would take approximately 3 months. If the work was begun late in the spring semester and completed by the end of the summer, the disruption to the operations of the building would be minimal. Certainly, the disruption would be no more than a typical renovation of a building's heating system (Ramlow & Nusz, 2006).

5

The third result is presented.

Result: The Durability of the System Would Be a Minimum of 10 Years

The literature we gathered estimates that the durability of this solar heating system would be a minimum of 20 years (Price, 2000). The direct gain system, using the skylight and thermal storage wall, could be used indefinitely with minor upkeep. The hydrosolar tube system, using liquid solar collectors and a solar pump, would likely need to be renovated in 20 years. These systems have been known to go 25 years without major renovation.

Discussion of Results

Based on our research and calculations, we have reached three conclusions, which suggest that a solar heating system would be a viable option for Engineering Hall.

The discussion section starts out with an opening paragraph to redirect the discussion.

The results of the research are discussed.

Solar Heating Would Save Money in the Long Run

Engineering Hall is one of the oldest, least efficient buildings on campus. Yet, our calculations show that putting in skylights and liquid collectors would be sufficient to heat the building on most days. According to our estimates, the solar remodeling would more than pay for itself in 10 years. Moreover, we would eliminate the need for the current oil heating system in the building, which will likely need to be replaced in that time period.

Solar Heating Is a Way Toward Independence

Our dependence on imported oil and natural gas puts our society at risk a few different ways (US DOE, 2004). Engineering Hall's use of oil for heating pollutes our air, and it contributes to our nation's dependence on other countries for fuel. By switching over to solar heating now, we start the process of making ourselves energy independent. Engineering Hall's heating system will need to be replaced soon anyway. Right now would be a good time to think seriously about remodeling to use solar.

Note how the authors are offering their opinions in this section.

Engineering Hall Offers a Good Model for Future Projects

Engineering Hall is one of the older buildings on campus. Consequently, it presents some additional renovation challenges that we would not face with the newer buildings. We believe that Engineering Hall provides an excellent model for conversion to solar energy because it is probably one of the more difficult buildings to convert. If we can make the conversion with this building, we can almost certainly make the conversion with other buildings.

It might also be noteworthy that our discussions with Mr. Madden and Ms. Brin at the Physical Plant showed us that there is great enthusiasm for making this kind of renovation to buildings like Engineering Hall.

6

(continued)

The recommendations section is clearly signaled here.

Recommendations

In conclusion, we think the benefits of remodeling Engineering Hall to use solar heating clearly outweigh the costs. We recommend the following actions:

- Complete a more thorough study of the heating needs of Engineering Hall.
- Hire a solar architect to draw up a plan for renovating the building.
- Solicit bids from contractors.
- Conduct a formal cost-benefit analysis to see if solar heating is financially feasible for Engineering Hall.

The recommendations are put in bullet form to make them easy to read.

Here is the main point and a look to the future.

If all goes well, remodeling of Engineering Hall could be completed in the summer of 2015. When the remodeling is complete, the college should begin saving money within ten years. Moreover, our campus would house a model building that could be studied to determine whether solar heating is a possibility for other buildings on campus.

Thank you for your time and consideration. After you have looked over this report, we would like to meet with you to discuss our findings and recommendations. Please call Dan Garnish at 555-9294.

Offering contact information is a good way to end the report.

References

Clive, K. (2007). *Build your own solar heating system.* Minneapolis, MN: Lucerno.

Eklund, K. (1979). *The solar water heater workshop manual* (2nd ed.). Seattle, WA: Ecotape Group.

Langa, F. (1981). *Integral passive solar water heating book.* Davis, CA: Passive Solar Institute.

Meeker, J., & Boyd, L. (1983). Domestic hot water installations: The great, the good, and the unacceptable. *Solar Age* 6, 28-36.

Price, G. (2000). *Solar remodeling in southern New Mexico.* Las Cruces, NM: NMSU Energy Institute.

Ramlow, B., & Nusz, B. (2006). *Solar water heating.* Gabriola Island, BC: New Society Publishers.

Solar Thermal Energy Group. (2003). *Solar home and solar collector plans.* Retrieved from http://www.jc-solarhomes.com

U.S. Department of Energy. (2004). Residential solar heating retrofits. Retrieved from http://www.eere.energy.gov/consumerinfo/factsheets/ac6.html

The materials cited in the report are listed here in APA format.

7

Using Google Drive to Collaborate on Global Projects

In the universe of Google products, there is a helpful collaboration tool called Google Drive (**http://drive.google.com**). Google Drive is useful in two ways. First, it includes a free, web-based suite of online software that can be used for writing documents, creating spreadsheets, and making presentations. It's similar to the Microsoft Office software package.

Second, and more importantly, Google Drive allows you to collaborate with others by storing and "sharing" documents (Figure A). When a file is placed in Google Drive, the creator can share it with other members of the team. They can then work on the document, too.

Figure A shows the Google Drive interface. In the center of the screen, you can see a list of files that are being shared among different collaborative groups. On the left-hand side of the screen, the user names of regular team members are listed, allowing the creator of a document to designate quickly who can read or edit each file.

People working on collaborative projects, especially with global teams, find Google Drive to be an amazingly helpful workspace. With Google Drive, everyone can access and edit the most recent versions of any document. This allows teams to avoid the usual questions about whether everyone has the latest version of the file.

Another advantage is that this free software is available to everyone. One of the problems with working transculturally is that team members in different parts of the world are often using a variety of software for word processing, spreadsheets, and presentations on different operating systems. So document sharing among members of a global team can get bogged down with tricky conversions between software packages and operating systems. But if the whole team is using Google Drive, everyone has access to the same software.

Even if your team agrees to use a common software package (e.g., MS Word), members may be using different versions or running old versions of Windows, Linux,

HELP

Link
For more advice about working in teams, see Chapter 3, page 52.

The Google Drive Interface

Source: GOOGLE is a trademark of Google Inc.

Figure A: Google Drive provides a common space for sharing documents with international teams.

or Mac OS. Google Drive solves that problem because everyone will be using the up-to-date versions of its software. Since the software is free, you won't hear the common complaints from your team members about how their management won't pay for software or operating system upgrades.

The main drawback to Google Drive is that the software suite is not as advanced as Microsoft or Adobe products (despite Google's claims to the contrary). Also, when documents from other software applications, like MS Word, are placed on Google Drive, they can lose some of their formatting and design. Plus, you should always remember that with Google Drive, your files are being stored on a server outside your company. So, any high-security files should not be stored or shared on Google Drive.

Google Drive isn't perfect, but for transcultural teams, its benefits can outweigh its shortcomings. The ability to share documents with Google Drive and use common software makes collaborating with others much easier.

Step 3: Draft the Front Matter and Back Matter

Most reports also include front matter and back matter. Front matter includes the letter of transmittal, title page, table of contents, and other items that are placed before the first page of the main report. Back matter includes appendixes, glossaries, and indexes that are placed after the main report.

Developing Front Matter

Link

For more information on writing letters and memos of transmittal, see Chapter 5, page 84.

Front matter may include some or all of the following items:

LETTER OR MEMO OF TRANSMITTAL   Typically, reports are accompanied by a letter or memo of transmittal. A well-written letter or memo gives you an opportunity to make positive personal contact with your readers before they read your report.

TITLE PAGE   Title pages are an increasingly common feature in analytical reports. A well-designed title page sets a professional tone while introducing readers to the subject of the report. The title page should include all or some of the following features:

- a specific title for the report
- the names of the primary readers, their titles, and the name of their company or organization
- the names of the writers, their titles, and the name of their company or organization
- the date on which the report was submitted
- company logos, graphics, or rules (lines) to enhance the design

Link

For graphic design strategies, see Chapter 17, page 447.

The title of your report should give readers a clear idea of what the report is about (Figure 10.7). A title like "Solar Heating" probably is not specific enough. A more descriptive title like "Learning with Light: Using Solar to Heat Engineering Hall" gives readers a solid idea about what the report will discuss.

ABSTRACT OR EXECUTIVE SUMMARY   If your report is longer than ten pages, you should consider including an abstract or executive summary.

Designing the Title Page

Learning with Light:

Using Solar to Heat
Engineering Hall

A Report from the
Innovation Group

April 15, 2014

Learning with Light

Using Solar to Heat Engineering Hall

A Report from the
Innovation Group

April 15, 2014

I
G

Figure 10.7: Designing an effective title page takes only a few moments. Those few moments of work, though, can make a solid first impression on the readers. Most readers would be attracted to the report on the right.

An abstract is a summary of the report that uses the phrasing in the report and follows its organizational structure. When writing an abstract, you should draw key sentences directly from the report itself. Start out with the purpose statement of the report, and then state the main point. From there, draw one or two key sentences from each major section. In an abstract for a report, for example, you would probably include these items in the following order:

- Purpose statement (one sentence)
- Main point (one sentence)
- Methodology (one or two sentences)
- Results (one or two sentences)
- Discussion (one or two sentences)
- Recommendations (one or two sentences)

You should modify the sentences in places to make the abstract readable, but try to retain the phrasing of the original report as much as possible.

Abstract

Purpose of report leads the abstract.

The main point comes second.

The purpose of this report is to determine whether the Engineering Hall's heating system can be converted to solar with reasonable cost. After analyzing solar heating options, we argue in this report that the best way to add solar heating to Engineering Hall would include a combination of direct gain (skylights) and hydrosolar tubes. Our research plan included five phases: (1) develop evaluation criteria, (2) gather information on solar heating, (3) analyze the heating needs of Engineering Hall, (4) interview physical plant personnel and solar energy experts, and (5) analyze models of passive and active solar heating methods. From our research, we designed a solar heating system that incorporates both passive and active components. Our system uses both a direct gain method with skylights and hydrosolar tubes with liquid collectors. Our evaluation of this solar heating design using our evaluation criteria yielded three results: Solar remodeling would pay for itself within 5–6 years; conversion to solar heating would cause minimal disruption; the durability of the system would be a minimum of 10 years. We have reached three conclusions that we believe the university administration should seriously consider: Solar heating would save money in the long run; solar heating is a way toward independence; and Engineering Hall offers a good model for future solar projects. We recommend the following actions: Complete a more thorough study of the thermodynamic features of Engineering Hall; hire a solar architect to draw up a plan for renovating the building; solicit bids from contractors; and conduct a cost-benefit analysis to see if solar heating is financially feasible.

An executive summary is a concise, *paraphrased* version of your report (usually one page) that highlights the key points in the text. The two main differences between an abstract and an executive summary are that (1) the summary does not follow the organization of the report, and (2) the summary does not use the exact phrasing of the report. In other words, a summary paraphrases the report and organizes the information to highlight the key points.

Report Summary

This report was written in response to a challenge to our Energy Dynamics class (Engineering 387) from Dr. Sharon Holton, President of Kellen College. She asked us to develop options for converting campus buildings to renewable energy sources. In this report, we discuss the possibility of converting Engineering Hall's heating system to solar. We conclude that heating Engineering Hall with solar sources would require a combination of direct gain (skylights) and hydrosolar tubes. The combination of these two solar technologies would ensure adequate heating for almost all the building's heating needs. A backup heater could be retained for sustained cold spells.

To develop the information for this report, we followed a five-step research plan: (1) develop an evaluation criteria, (2) gather information on solar heating, (3) analyze the heating needs of Engineering Hall, (4) interview physical plant personnel and solar energy experts, and (5) analyze models of passive and active solar heating that would be appropriate for this building.

The results of our research are mostly anecdotal, but they show that solar heating is possible, even for an older building on campus. We believe that our results show that Engineering Hall can be a model for developing solar heating systems around campus, because it is truly one of the more difficult buildings at Kellen to convert to solar heating. Newer buildings on campus would almost certainly be easier to convert. We conclude by pointing out that solar heating would save money in the long run. In the case of Engineering Hall, solar remodeling would pay for itself in 5–6 years.

We appreciate your taking time to read this report. If you have any questions or would like to meet with us, please call Dan Garnish at 555–9294.

The executive summary will often duplicate the contents of the introduction, but it should not replace the introduction. Instead, it should be written so that it can stand alone, apart from the rest of the report.

Figure 10.8 shows the cover page and executive summary that appeared in a 155-page report. In this summary, after a brief overview, the authors use bullet points to draw out the most important items discussed in the report.

Executive Summary Example

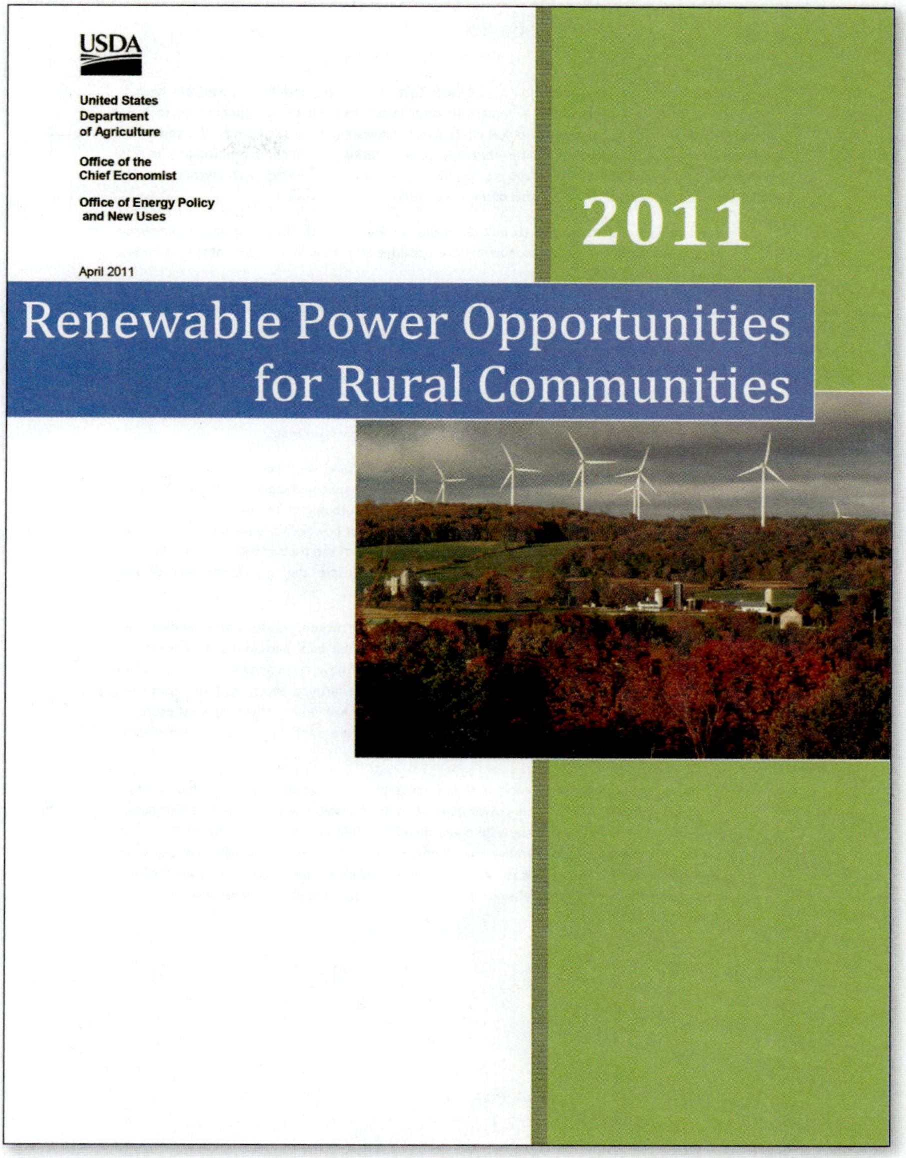

USDA

United States Department of Agriculture

Office of the Chief Economist

Office of Energy Policy and New Uses

April 2011

2011

Renewable Power Opportunities for Rural Communities

Figure 10.8: This executive summary shows how a very large report can be boiled down to its most important points.

Source: USDA, http://www.usda.gov/oce/reports/energy/RenewablePowerOpportunities-Final.pdf

(continued)

Executive Summary

Renewable resources for the generation of electricity (e.g., wind, solar, geothermal, etc.) are typically most abundant and practical for development in rural areas. This creates an opportunity for rural electric utilities, which are at a geographical advantage for investing in these projects. This report is a summary and guide to assist rural utilities that may be considering investing in a renewable electricity generation project and policymakers who may be considering how to encourage such investments. The following points summarize the highlights of the issues addressed in this report.

Brief overview of report's topic and purpose

- Rural utilities are motivated to provide power at least cost to their customers; renewable generation projects must be economically competitive after including all government incentives and tax impacts.

- Ample, unexploited renewable generation resources are available, with some resource types more available in some regions than in others. The Great Plains states are particularly well endowed with both wind and biomass resources, and the Southwestern and Western states are generally well endowed with solar and geothermal resources. With the exception of biomass potential in Maine, the Northeastern and Southeastern states have relatively less renewable generation resources. All coastal states have potential for off-shore wind; however, significant technical and acceptance barriers to developing these resources remain.

Bullet points help readers find essential information.

- One of the challenges to expanding renewable generation in rural areas is that many of the areas with rich resources do not have the transmission capacity needed to get the additional power to demand centers. This capacity limitation is exacerbated by the intermittent nature of some renewable generation sources such as wind and solar power. While a number of plans are currently under consideration for expanding the capacity of the transmission system, there are several issues. Foremost among these is how to allocate the substantial cost of new transmission capacity.

- Due to their typical incorporation as member-customer owned, not-for-profit entities, rural electric utilities are focused on supplying electricity to their local customers. While there are localized exceptions, the prospects for demand growth in these areas appear to be limited. The reasons for this include increasing consolidation in the farming sector and the continuing erosion of the manufacturing sector. Although there are exceptions driven by local economic activities, areas that appear likely to see demand growth are either adjacent to urban areas or offer recreational or retirement amenities.

- Other aspects of the business models of alternative types of rural utilities impact their ability to successfully invest in renewable power generation enterprises. These are due to differences in how they are treated by the tax system and by policies that are targeted to the electric power sector. For example, a cooperative that primarily serves its member-owners may enjoy tax-exempt status. This makes policies with incentives based on tax benefits relatively ineffective in influencing the investment behavior of cooperatives. The benefits of these policies in some

1

cases can be recaptured through the creation of partnerships or wholly owned subsidiary companies that have different business models.

- An important aspect of policy is related to the ability of rural utilities to finance the development of renewable electricity generation projects. Various loan and grant programs at the federal, state, and local levels are targeted specifically to different types of rural utilities and, in some cases, specifically targeted to investments in renewable generation capacity. The nature of these programs may restrict the types of investments that can benefit, and in designing new policies, careful consideration must be given to the provisions of existing policies that may offset the benefits of the new policy.

- The answers to a number of questions regarding a rural utility's opportunities for investing in renewable electricity generation capacity can serve as a basis for prescreening these investments. Beyond the prescreening phase, a full-blown engineering and economic analysis of any investment that passes the prescreening tests will of course be required. While it may be tempting to perform regional analyses to identify promising opportunities for investments, a survey of successful projects indicates that unique local factors often provide an added advantage to the selected technology.

Concluding paragraph sums up the report's overall main point.

In sum, there is clearly substantial latitude for expansion of renewable electricity generation in the United States. The location and the extent of that expansion will depend on many factors, including shifting economic conditions, technological improvements, and government policies. As policymakers consider the alternatives, they will need to take into account the broad impacts of investments in renewable electricity generation, including impacts on the transmission system, the economy (local, national, and international), and national security.

2

TABLE OF CONTENTS If your report runs over ten pages, you should consider adding a table of contents. A table of contents is helpful to readers in two ways. First, it helps them quickly access the information they need in the report. Second, it offers an overall outline of the contents of the report. Since reports tend to be larger documents, your readers will appreciate a quick summary of the report's contents.

In the table of contents, the headings should be the same as the ones used in your report. Then, use tabs or leader tabs to line up the page numbers on the right side. Leader tabs are used to insert a line of dots or dashes from the heading to the page number.

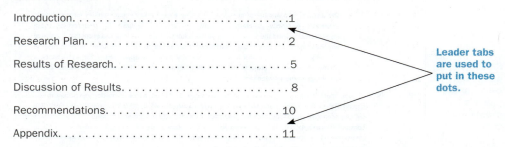

Table of Contents

Introduction 1

Research Plan 2

Results of Research 5

Discussion of Results 8

Recommendations 10

Appendix 11

Leader tabs are used to put in these dots.

Developing Back Matter

Back matter in a report might include appendixes, a glossary of terms, and calculations. Keep in mind, though, that most readers will never look at the back matter. So, if you have something important to say, do not say it here.

APPENDIXES Appendixes are storage areas for information that may or may not be useful to certain readers. For example, additional data tables or charts not needed in the body of the report might be displayed in an appendix. You might include articles or screenshots from newspapers or magazines.

GLOSSARY OF TERMS Depending on the complexity of your report and your readers' familiarity with the subject, you may want to include a short glossary of terms. When creating a glossary, look back over your report and highlight words that may not be familiar to your nonexpert readers. Then, in a glossary at the back of the report, list these terms and write sentence definitions for each.

CALCULATIONS In highly technical reports, you may want to include your calculations in the back matter. Here is where you can demonstrate how you arrived at the figures in the report.

AT A GLANCE

Front Matter and Back Matter

Front matter—items that appear before the main report:
- Letter or memo of transmittal
- Title page
- Abstract or executive summary
- Table of contents

Back matter—items that appear after the main report:
- Appendixes
- Glossary of terms
- Calculations

Link

For more information on writing sentence definitions, see Chapter 6, page 144.

Step 4: Choose the Style, Design, and Medium

Link

For more help with using plain style, see Chapter 16, page 422.

The style and design of an analytical report is typically straightforward and plain. However, your report should not be boring. You can use good style and effective page design to keep your readers' interest, help them locate important information, and make your report attractive.

Using Plain Style in a Persuasive Way

Reports are persuasive in an unstated way, putting the emphasis on the soundness of the methodology, the integrity of the results, and the reasonableness of the discussion. Plain style will make your reports sound straightforward and clear to readers.

While revising your report, you might pay close attention to the following plain style techniques:

Make "doers" the subjects of sentences—Reports tend to overuse the passive voice, which makes them harder to read than necessary. If the passive voice is required in your field, use it. But if you want your writing to be more effective, make your sentences active by making the "doers" the subjects of the sentences.

> **Passive:** Saplings had been eaten during the winter by the deer we monitored, because they were desperate for food.

> **Active:** The deer we monitored ate saplings to survive the winter because they were desperate for food.

Link

For more information on eliminating nominalizations, see Chapter 16, page 425.

Use breathing-length sentences—Reports are notorious for using sentences that are far too long to be understood. As you write and revise your report, look for places where your sentences are too long to be stated in one breath. These sentences should be shortened to breathing length or divided into two breathing-length sentences.

Eliminate nominalizations—Reports often include nominalizations that cloud the meaning of sentences. You should revise these sentences for clarity:

> **Nominalization:** This report offers *a presentation* of our findings.

> **Revised:** This report *presents* our findings.

> **Nominalization:** We made *a decision* to initiate *a replacement* of the Collings CAD software.

> **Revised:** We *decided to replace* the Collings CAD software.

> **Revised further:** We *replaced* the Collings CAD software.

AT A GLANCE

Improving Style in Analytical Reports

- Make "doers" the subjects of sentences.
- Use breathing-length sentences.
- Eliminate nominalizations.
- Define jargon and specialized terms.

Nominalizations may make your report sound more formal, but eliminating them will increase clarity, which readers will appreciate.

Define jargon and specialized terms—Jargon should not be completely eliminated from reports. Instead, these words should be defined for nonexperts.

When you need to use a specialized term, use a sentence definition or parenthetical definition to clarify what the word means.

> **Sentence definition:** A gyrocompass is a directional finding device that uses a gyroscope to compensate for the earth's rotation and thus points to true north.

> **Parenthetical definition:** Spotting a blue grouse, *a plump, medium-sized bird with feathered legs and bluish gray plumage,* is especially difficult because they are well camouflaged and live in higher mountain areas.

Link

For more information on writing sentence and parenthetical definitions, see Chapter 6, page 120.

A Straightforward Design

Link

For more help with document design, see Chapter 17, page 447.

People rarely read reports word for word. Instead, they scan these documents. Therefore, you should use document design and graphics to highlight your main points and offer readers access points to start reading.

Link

For more information on making and using graphs, see Chapter 18, page 477.

Choose a functional document design—Your report's design should reflect the subject of the report and the preferences of your readers. So, you might experiment with page layout, the design of headings, and uses of graphics. You might look for ways to use multicolumn formats, which allow you to add pull quotes, sidebars, and other page layout enhancements (Figure 10.9).

Use graphics to clarify and enhance meaning—Tables and graphs are especially helpful tools for displaying data. As you write the report, you should actively look for places where tables might be used to better display your data or information. Also, look for places where a graph could show trends in the data.

Page Layouts for Reports

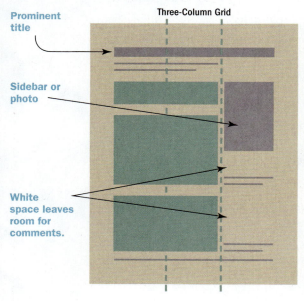
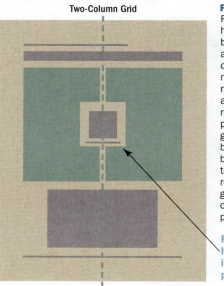

Prominent title

Sidebar or photo

White space leaves room for comments.

Three-Column Grid

Two-Column Grid

Figure 10.9: Reports don't have to look boring. A little attention to design will make your report inviting and easier to read. In these page layouts, grids have been used to balance the text, leaving room for margin text and other access points.

Pull quote to highlight an important point.

The Poster Presentation

Poster presentations have become one of the principal ways to display technical and scientific research. Poster presentations are typically 1 × 1.5 meters (3.5 × 5 feet), and they are often exhibited at conventions and conferences. Readers can study the researcher's methodology and the results of an experiment or research study. Poster presentations are designed to stand alone, but the researcher is often nearby to answer questions. Here is how to make one:

Choose the appropriate software. PowerPoint or Presentation will work fine if you are creating a poster with slides. InDesign or QuarkXPress are better for large, single-page posters, because they allow more flexibility with text and graphics.

Use a prominent title that attracts the reader. Your title should be large and prominent, 70 points or higher, so it catches the reader's attention. The best titles ask a question or hint at an interesting discovery.

Divide your presentation into major sections. Poster presentations usually follow the organization of an analytical report (e.g., IMRaD). Each major section of your report should be represented by a space on the poster. Label each section with a prominent heading.

Keep each section brief and to the point. Each section of the poster will usually have 500 words or less. So, keep the text simple and straightforward. Focus on the facts and need-to-know information.

Use text that is readable from 4 to 5 feet away. Most readers will be standing this distance from the poster, so the font size of the body text should be about 16 points. Headings should be 36 points or higher.

Design an interesting layout. Generally, the flow of information should be left to right and top to bottom. Poster presentations frequently use a three-column or four-column layout.

Include images, graphs, and tables. Readers may not have time to read all your written text, but they will look at the visuals. So, where possible, put your data into visual forms that can be scanned quickly.

Write

Make your own poster presentation. You can use your poster presentation as a way to organize your ideas and data before you write your analytical report. Or, you can turn an existing report into a poster presentation.

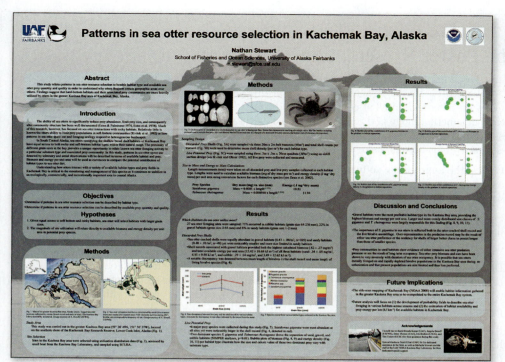

Source: *Used with permission of Nathan Stewart.*

This poster presentation has all the major parts of an analytical report. It also uses graphics well to reinforce the written text.

- Various types of analytical reports are used in the workplace, including research reports, completion reports, recommendation reports, feasibility reports, and empirical research reports.

- Determine the rhetorical situation for your report by considering the subject, purpose, readers, and context of use of your report.

- Define your research question, and formulate a hypothesis to be tested. Then, develop a methodology and identify the two to five major steps you will need to take to establish or refute your hypothesis.

- Collect information using library, Internet, and empirical sources.

- Use the IMRaD acronym to remember the generic report pattern: Introduction, Methods, Results, and Discussion.

- Typically, large sections in reports have their own opening, body, and closing.

- The style and design of analytical reports tends to be plain and straightforward. However, strategic use of phrasing, good design, and graphics can make a report more readable and attractive.

- Organize and draft your report following the separate "moves" for an introduction, body, and conclusion.

- Both the style and the design of analytical reports should serve to clarify the contents of the report.

Individual or Team Projects

1. Write a small report (two or three pages) in which you conduct a preliminary study of a scientific or technical topic that interests you. In your report, create a short methodology that will allow you to collect some overall information about the subject. Then, present the results of your study. In the conclusion, talk about how you might conduct a larger study on the subject and the limitations you might face as you enlarge the project.

2. Devise a research question of interest to you. Then, using logical mapping, sketch out a methodology that would allow you to study that research question in depth. When you have finished outlining the methodology, write a one-page memo to your instructor in which you describe the methodology and discuss the kinds of results your research would produce.

3. Write an executive summary of an article from a scientific or technical journal in your field. You should be able to find journals in your campus library. Your summary should paraphrase the article, highlighting its main points, methodology, results, discussion, and conclusions.

Collaborative Project: Problems in the Community

With a team of classmates, choose a local problem in your community about which you would like to write an analytical report. The readers of your report should be people who can take action on your findings, like the mayor or the city council.

After defining the rhetorical situation in which your report will be used, develop a step-by-step methodology for studying the problem. Then, collect information on the topic. Here are some ideas for topics that might interest you:

• Driving under the influence of alcohol or drugs
• Violence
• Underage drinking
• Illegal drug use
• Homelessness
• Teen pregnancy
• Water usage
• Pollution
• Graffiti
• Environmental health

In your report, present the results of your study and discuss those results. In the conclusion of your report, make recommendations about what local authorities can do to correct the problem or improve the situation.

Revision Challenge

The introduction to the report shown here is somewhat slow and clumsy. How could you revise this introduction to make it sharper and more interesting?

Introduction

Let us introduce ourselves. We are the Putnam Consulting Firm, LLC, based out of Kansas City, KS. We specialize in the detection and mitigation of lead-related problems. We have been in business since 1995, and we have done many studies much like the one we did for you.

Our CEO is Lisa Vasquez. She has been working with lead-related issues for nearly two decades. In her opinion, lead poisoning is one of the greatest epidemics facing the United States today. The effects of lead on children, especially poor children, is acute. Dr. Vasquez has devoted her life to addressing the lead problem so today and tomorrow's children won't be damaged by continued neglect of the issue.

One of today's silent villains is lead poisoning. It is one of the most prevalent sources of childhood health problems. Each year, several hundred children in Yount County are treated for serious cases of lead poisoning. There are countless others who are suffering silently because their symptoms are either too minor or they go unnoticed by parents, teachers, and other authorities. For example, consider the case of Janice Brown in northwestern Yount County. She showed the effects of lead poisoning in her cognitive development, leading to a lower IQ rating. When her house was tested for lead poisoning, it was found that her parents had sandblasted the sides of the home to remove the old paint. Lead had saturated the ground around Janice's home and there was residual lead dust everywhere in the home. The levels of lead in Janice's blood were nearly 10 times the amount that causes problems.

You will find other troubling stories like this one in this report. We were hired by the Yount County Board of Directors to complete this study on the amounts of lead in the county. Unfortunately, we have found that Yount County is in particular trouble. Much of the county's infrastructure and housing was built when lead use was at its peak. Housing in the county relies heavily on lead pipes. Most of the houses were painted inside and out with lead-based paint.

Ironically, lead poisoning is also one of the most preventable problems that face children today. The continual persistence of the problem is a stain on our nation, and it is a particular problem that Yount County must face. In this report, we offer some recommendations.

Visit **My**Writing**Lab** for a Post-test and more technical writing resources.

The X-File

George Franklin works as an environmental engineer for Outdoor Compliance Associates. He and his team are responsible for writing analytical reports called environmental impact statements (EISs) on sites that might be developed for housing or businesses. An EIS is required by the government before any work can begin.

George's responsibility on the team is to track down any historical uses of the site. For example, if he learns that a gas station had once been on the site, his job is to make sure the old underground holding tanks were removed. If the site once held a factory, his job is to make sure that chemicals had not been dumped in the area. George loves being an environmental detective.

A year ago, George's team had written an EIS for a site where a new apartment complex was planned. The site was about a mile from a major research university. While researching the site, George discovered that it had housed part of the city's waste treatment center until the early 1950s. George's discovery wasn't a problem, though, because any contaminants would have disappeared long ago. So, George's team wrote a favorable EIS, clearing the site for development. The building plan was approved by the city, and construction started soon after.

Then, yesterday, an old, yellowed file mysteriously appeared in George's office mailbox. The file was marked "Confidential" and had no return address. George looked inside.

In the file was a report that nuclear weapons research had once been done at the university during the 1940s. Not recognizing the potential harm of the nuclear waste, the scientists had sent tons of radioactive waste down the drain. The nuclear waste ended up at the city's old waste treatment center. The waste, including the nuclear waste, was then spread around the grounds of the waste treatment plant.

George grabbed his Geiger counter and went out to the building site. The apartment development was now half built. When he pulled out his Geiger counter, it immediately began detecting significant levels of radiation.

The radiation wasn't high enough to violate government standards, but it was close. George knew that the building permit still would have been granted even if knowledge of this site's nuclear past had been known. However, he also knew that as soon as people heard about the radiation, no one would want to live in the apartments. That would be a disaster for the developer building them.

If he reported the radiation, there was a good chance George's company would be sued by the builder for missing this important problem with the property. Moreover, other builders would likely never again hire his company to write an EIS. George would almost certainly lose his job, and the company he worked for might be forced out of business. But then, he could keep it quiet. The radiation, after all, was not above government standards.

If you were George, how would you handle this situation?

CHAPTER

11

Starting Your Career

Setting Goals, Making a Plan *294*

Preparing a Résumé *298*

Help: Designing a Searchable
Résumé *310*

Writing Effective Application
Letters *312*

Creating a Professional
Portfolio *317*

Interviewing Strategies *320*

Microgenre: The Bio *324*

What You Need to Know *326*

Exercises and Projects *326*

Case Study: The Lie *328*

In this chapter, you will learn:

- How to set goals and make a plan for finding a career position.

- Methods for using both web-based and traditional networking.

- How to design and prepare a résumé in both electronic (searchable) and traditional formats.

- Techniques for writing a persuasive application letter.

- How to create a targeted, professional portfolio that highlights your background and experience.

- Strategies for effective interviewing.

Finding a good job requires energy, dedication, and optimism—and readiness to hear the word "no." You will probably look for a job at least a few times during your lifetime. U.S. Department of Labor statistics show that people tend to change careers four to six times in their lives, including twelve to fifteen job changes. In other words, being able to find a job is now becoming a necessary skill in a successful career.

Setting Goals, Making a Plan

Like most people, you are probably uncertain about how to get started with the job search. Setting some goals and making a plan will streamline your efforts and shorten the time it takes to land a job.

Setting Goals

Setting goals means asking some big questions about your future and who you want to be:

> *What are my needs and wants in a job/career?*
>
> *Who would I like to work for?*
>
> *Where would I like to live?*
>
> *When do I need to be employed?*
>
> *Why did I choose this career path in the first place?*
>
> *How much salary, vacation, and benefits do I need?*

Write down your answers to these questions. You should be specific about issues like location, salary, vacation, and the amount of time you have to find a job. If you don't know the answers to some of these questions, like salary, then use Internet search engines to help you find the answers.

Be honest with yourself about what you need and want. More than likely, your first job will require you to make some trade-offs. For example, perhaps you might find a job at a great company, but the salary is less than you hoped for. Or, perhaps you might be willing to work at a lower profile company that will give you better opportunities to advance.

Making Your Plan

With your goals in mind, you can begin developing a plan. Your plan should pursue a variety a paths to finding a job.

EMPLOYMENT WEBSITES   The numerous employment websites available on the Internet are good places to start looking for jobs (Figure 11.1). By entering a few keywords, you should be able to locate a variety of job advertisements in your area. You can also post your résumé so potential employers can find you.

Career Materials

These models show typical organizational patterns for a résumé and application letter. These patterns should be altered to fit your background and the kinds of jobs you are applying for.

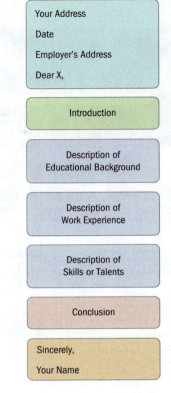

Application Letter

Your Address

Date

Employer's Address

Dear X,

Introduction

Description of Educational Background

Description of Work Experience

Description of Skills or Talents

Conclusion

Sincerely,

Your Name

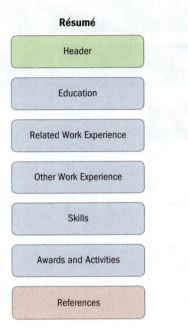

Résumé

Header

Education

Related Work Experience

Other Work Experience

Skills

Awards and Activities

References

Basic Features

Minimally, your career materials will include a résumé and an application letter. These documents will usually have the following features:

Résumé

- Header with your name and contact information
- Career objective/career summary
- Educational background that lists your degrees and training
- Work experience in your field of study
- Other work experience not in your field of study
- Skills related to the career you are pursuing
- Awards you have earned and activities in which you have participated
- References listing employers, professors, and other professionals

Application Letter

- Header with addresses
- Introduction that identifies position being applied for
- Description of your educational background
- Description of your work experience
- Description of your specialized skills or talents
- Conclusion that thanks readers

An Internet Job Search Engine

Figure 11.1: Monster.com is one of the more popular job search engines. It offers a variety of tools to aid your search.

Source: Monster.com. Reprinted by permission.

Here are some of the more popular job search engines:

Indeed.com	*Idealist.com*
SimplyHired.com	*Hotjobs.yahoo.com*
Careerbuilder.com	*Dice.com*
Glassdoor.com	*Monster.com*
CollegegradInternships.com	*UsaJobs.com*

In scientific and technical fields, employment websites are the primary way to find a job, especially after you graduate. You should check these sites regularly and post your résumé on at least a few of them.

SOCIAL NETWORKING More than ever, people are finding jobs through their connections on social networking sites like Facebook and Twitter. There are also business-centered social networking sites like LinkedIn and Plaxo that you should join because they are designed to help people do career networking. You should turn your social networking sites into job-finding tools by including your résumé and any other information you would like potential employers to see.

Before you go on the job market, however, you should spend some time cleaning up your current social networking sites. Interviewers regularly do background checks on their candidates through these sites and search engines. Just about anything on your social networking sites can be found by someone doing a thorough background check.

PERSONAL NETWORKING   Someone you know is probably aware of a job available in your field. Or, they know someone who knows about a job. Make a list of your friends, relatives, and instructors who might be able to help you find a job. Then send each of these people an e-mail that tells them you are "on the market," looking for a job. You might even attach a résumé to your e-mail so they can look it over and perhaps forward it to a potential employer.

PROFESSIONAL NETWORKING   Most career tracks have professional groups associated with them. Engineers, for example, have the Institute of Electrical and Electronics Engineers (IEEE), while medical practitioners have the American Medical Association (AMA). Technical writers have the Society for Technical Communication (STC). These professional groups are especially helpful for networking with people who are already employed in your field. You should become involved with these groups as soon as possible, even if you have not graduated from college. Once people get to know you, they can be very helpful with finding job opportunities.

COLLEGE PLACEMENT OFFICE   Most colleges have a placement office that is available to students. The placement office may have jobs posted on its website, or you can visit the office itself. There, you can sign up for interviews and speak with a counselor about improving your job-searching skills.

TARGETING   Make up a list of ten to twenty "target" companies for which you might want to work. Then, look at their websites, paying special attention to each company's human resources office. From each website, write down notes about the company's mission, products, history, and market. If a target company has a job available, usually you can apply for it through their website. If a job is not available, most companies will allow you to upload your résumé and an application letter in case a position becomes available.

CLASSIFIED ADVERTISEMENTS   In the classifieds section of a newspaper, especially the Sunday edition, you will find job advertisements. Most newspapers have their classified ads online, and you can also search on classified ad websites like Craigslist or Oodle. Keep in mind, though, that newspapers carry advertisements for only a few jobs in any given area. *Most jobs are not advertised in the paper.*

You should plan to use all these pathways in your job search (Figure 11.2). That way, you will get interviews from a variety of sources and eventually land that new job.

The Job-Searching Cycle

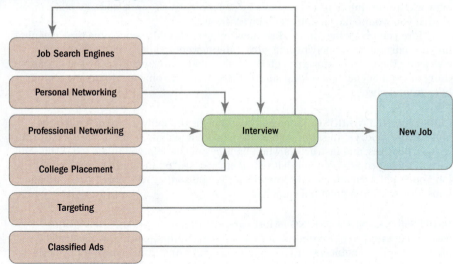

Figure 11.2: There are many tools available for finding a job and building a career. You should take advantage of all of them.

Preparing a Résumé

A résumé is a summary of your background, experience, and qualifications. Usually, résumés for entry-level jobs fit on one page. Résumés for advanced positions will often take up two pages. Your résumé has to make a good first impression because it is usually the first item that employers will look at. If your résumé is badly written or looks unprofessional, employers won't bother to look at your application letter and other employment materials.

Types of Résumés

Résumés tend to follow one of two organizational approaches: the *chronological* approach and the *functional* approach.

> **Chronological approach**—Organizes the résumé according to education and work experience, highlighting a job seeker's qualifications in a few areas. A chronological résumé might be organized into sections such as Education, Work Experience, Skills, and Awards/Activities.

> **Functional approach**—Organizes the résumé according to your talents, abilities, skills, and accomplishments. A functional résumé would be organized into sections such as Leadership, Design Experience, Communication Skills, and Training Abilities.

By far, the chronological approach is the most common in scientific and technical fields, especially for new graduates, because it allows you to highlight the details of your education and qualifications. The functional approach is advantageous for more experienced job seekers who want to highlight their accomplishments and experience.

Chronological Résumé

Chronological résumés can be divided into the following sections, which can be organized in a variety of ways:

- Name and contact information
- Career objective/career summary
- Educational background
- Related work experience
- Other work experience
- Skills
- Awards and activities
- References

The headings in this list are common in chronological résumés but other headings are available. Figures 11.3, 11.4, 11.5, and 11.6 show some variations of these headings.

NAME AND CONTACT INFORMATION At the top of the page, your résumé should include a heading that states your name, address, phone number, and e-mail address. To catch the reader's eye, your name should appear in a larger font size. The heading can be left justified, centered, or right justified, depending on the design of your résumé.

International students often receive conflicting information about how to put their names on résumés, especially if they are applying for jobs in North America, Europe, and South America. Generally, it is best to use the name as it appears on your passport. If you have adopted an English name, you can include it in parentheses as a nickname, but doing so is not necessary. If speakers of other languages have difficulty pronouncing your name, you can include a phonetic spelling, but again doing so is not necessary. Keep in mind that there are many other transnational employees at almost all scientific and technical companies, so your name will not be an issue.

CAREER OBJECTIVE OR CAREER SUMMARY (OPTIONAL) A *career objective* is a phrase or sentence that describes the career you are seeking. Your career objective should specify the type of position you are applying for and the industry in which you want to work.

> Seeking a position as a Physician's Assistant in a research hospital.
>
> A computer programming career working with mainframes in the defense industry.
>
> Looking for a career as a school psychologist working with children who have behavioral problems.
>
> Mechanical Engineer developing nanotechnological solutions for biotech applications.

Avoid writing a career objective that is too narrow or too broad. A career objective that is too narrow might eliminate you from some potential jobs. For example, if you specify that you are looking for a job at a "large engineering firm," the human resources officer at a small engineering firm might assume you are not interested in her company's job. On the other hand, an objective that is too broad, like "a job as an electrical engineer," might give the impression that you are not sure about what kind of career would suit your talents.

Link

For more information on using fonts effectively, go to Chapter 17, page 461.

A *career summary* is a brief sentence or paragraph that describes your career to this point. Career summaries are typically used by people with years of experience.

> I have been employed as a physician's assistant for 10 years, working my way up from the position of licensed practical nurse to head physician's assistant at a major metropolitan hospital.

> My experience as a webmaster includes designing and managing a variety of interactive sites that have been used by large companies to promote their products and solicit new business.

A career objective or career summary is not required in a résumé. Some résumé experts recommend not using space for these statements because they basically describe the job being applied for or they repeat information that can be found elsewhere on the résumé.

EDUCATIONAL BACKGROUND   Your educational background should list your most recent college degree and other degrees in reverse chronological order—most recent to least recent. You can list the degree you are working on now as "expected" with the month and year when you should graduate.

Name each college and list your major, minor, and any distinctions you earned (e.g., scholarships or summa cum laude or distinguished-scholar honors) (Figure 11.3). You might also choose to mention any coursework you have completed that is related to your career (Figures 11.4, 11.5, and 11.6).

Generally, a high school diploma should not be listed on your college résumé, even if you were an honors student or valedictorian. Sometimes, however, international students who are applying for positions in both North America and a home country will list the high school diploma to signal their country of origin.

Any specialized training, such as welding certification, experience with machinery, or military training, might also be listed here with dates of completion.

If you are new to the technical workplace, you should place your educational background early in your résumé. Your degree is probably your most prominent achievement, so you want to highlight it. If you have years of professional work experience, you may choose to put your educational background later in your résumé, allowing you to highlight your work experience.

RELATED WORK EXPERIENCE   Any career-related jobs, internships, or co-ops that you have held should be listed, starting with the most recent and working backward chronologically. For each job, include the title of the position, the company, and dates of employment (month and year).

Below each position, list your workplace responsibilities. As demonstrated in Figures 11.3, 11.4, 11.5, and 11.6, you can describe these responsibilities in a bulleted list or in a brief paragraph. Use action verbs and brief phrases to add a sense of energy to your work experience. Also, where possible, add any numbers or details that reflect the importance of your responsibilities.

> Coordinated a team of 15 student archaeologists in the field.

> Participated in the development of UNIX software for a Cray supercomputer.

> Worked with over 100 clients each year on defining, updating, and restoring their water rights in the Wilkins Valley.

Chronological Résumé

Figure 11.3:
Anne
Franklin's
résumé uses
a list style.
She achieves
a classic
look by using
a serif font
(Garamond)
and left
justification.

Name and contact information are prominently displayed.

Anne Franklin
834 County Line Rd.
Hollings Point, Illinois 62905

Home: 618-555-2993
Mobile: 618-555-9167
e-mail: afranklin@unsb5.net

Career Objective

Career objective describes position sought.

A position as a naturalist, specializing in agronomy, working for a distribution company that specializes in organic foods.

Educational Background

Bachelor of Science, Southern Illinois University, expected May 2014.

Education is highlighted by placement early in the résumé.

Major: Plant and Soil Science
Minor: Entomology
GPA: 3.2/4.0

Work Experience

Intern Agronomist, December 2012–August 2013
Brighter Days Organic Cooperative, Simmerton, Illinois

Work experience lists duties with bullets.

- Consulted with growers on organic pest control methods. Primary duty was sale of organic crop protection products, crop nutrients, seed, and consulting services.
- Prepared organic agronomic farm plans for growers.
- Provided crop-scouting services to identify weed and insect problems.

Field Technician, August 2010–December 2012
Entomology Department, Southern Illinois University
- Collected and identified insects.
- Developed insect management plans.
- Tested organic and nonorganic pesticides for effectiveness and residuals.

Skills

Skills are listed separately for emphasis.

Computer Experience: Access, Excel, Outlook, PowerPoint, and Word. Global Positioning Systems (GPS). Database Management.
Machinery: Field Tractors, Combines, Straight Trucks, and Bobcats.
Communication Skills: Proposal Writing and Review, Public Presentations, Negotiating, Training, Writing Agronomic and Financial Farm Plans.

Awards and Memberships

Awards and memberships are placed later in the résumé.

Awarded "Best Young Innovator" by the Organic Food Society of America, 2012
Member of Entomological Society of America.

References Available Upon Request

Chronological Résumé

James L. Mondragon

576 First Avenue, Rolla, Missouri 65408
Phone: 573-555-4391, e-mail: bigmondy12@umr.edu

Career Summary

My interests in chemical engineering started with a childhood fascination with plastic products. I enrolled at the University of Missouri–Rolla because of their strong chemical engineering program, especially in the area of applied rheology and polymeric materials. I have also completed a co-op with Vertigo Plastics in St. Louis. My background includes strong computer modeling skills, especially involving polymeric materials.

Work Experience

Vertigo Plastics, Inc., St. Louis, Missouri, 5/12–1/13, 5/13–1/14
Co-op Chemical Engineer
   Performed inspections of chemical equipment and plant equipment affected by chemical systems (such as boilers and condensers). Monitored the performance of chemical systems at various sites throughout the Vertigo Plastics system. Performed calculations and wrote reports summarizing the performance of those systems. Helped troubleshoot problems.

Other Work Experience

To Go Pizza, *Server,* Springfield, Missouri, 2/06–7/08

Educational Background

University of Missouri–Rolla, BSE, Expected May 2014
Major: Chemical Engineering
   Advanced Coursework included Chemical Engineering Fluid Flow, Chemical Engineering Heat Transfer, Chemical Engineering Thermodynamics I & II, Process Dynamics and Control, Chemical Engineering Reactor Design, Chemical Engineering Economics, Chemical Process Safety, Chemical Process Design, Chemical Process Materials.

Activities and Awards

Awarded Stevenson Scholarship in Engineering, 2012
Treasurer, UMR Student Chapter, American Institute of Chemical Engineers (AIChE), 2012–Present
Member, Tau Beta Pi, 2012

**Dossier with References Available at UMR Placement Services
(573-555-2941)**

Chronological Résumé of an International Student

Liu Ning

623 W. College Avenue, Apt. #12, State College PA, 16801
Phone: (814) 555-9120, E-mail: liuning5434@psu.edu

Education

Penn State University, B.S. in Computer Engineering, GPA 3.8/4.0, expected May 2014

CMPSC 121: Intro to Programming
CMPSC 122: Intermediate Programming
CMPSC 221: Object Oriented Programming with Web-Based Applications
CMPSC 360: Discrete Mathematics for Computer Science
CMPSC 270: Introduction to Digital Systems
CMPSC 311: Systems Programming
CMPSC 331: Computer Organization and Design
CMPSC 473: Operating Systems
CMPEN 431: Introduction to Computer Architecture

CMPSC 465: Data Structures and Algorithms
CMPEN 362: Communication Networks
CMPEN 455: Digital Image Processing
CMPEN 471: Logical Design of Digital
CMPEN 482W: Computer Engineering Project Design
EE 210: Circuits and Devices
EE 310: Introduction to Electron Devices and Circuits
EE 353: Signals and Systems: Continuous and Discrete-Time
ENGL 202C: Technical Writing

Guangdong Country Garden School, Foshan City, Guangdong Province, PRC, High School Diploma, 2009

Work Experience

NextGenIT, Engineering Co-Op, Bedford MA, Spring and Summer 2012, 2013

- Designed XenDesktop images for aiding self-service access
- Developed scripts to enhance mobile browsing
- Tested use cases to determine if users could achieve specific goals

Languages

Programming Languages: Java, C, C#, C++, Linux, Lisp, Haskell, SysML

Natural Languages: Mandarin Chinese (first-language), English (fluent speaking and writing), German (reading only)

Awards and Associations

Silver Leaf, Philadelphia Entrepreneurs Club Elevator Pitch Contest, 2013
Recipient, Wu Jian Bridge To America Scholarship, 2010
Vice President, Engineers for a Sustainable World, Penn State University
Member, Institute of Electric and Electronics Engineers (IEEE)
Student Member, National Society of Professional Engineers (NSPE)

References Available Upon Request

Chronological Résumé of Student Who Returned to College

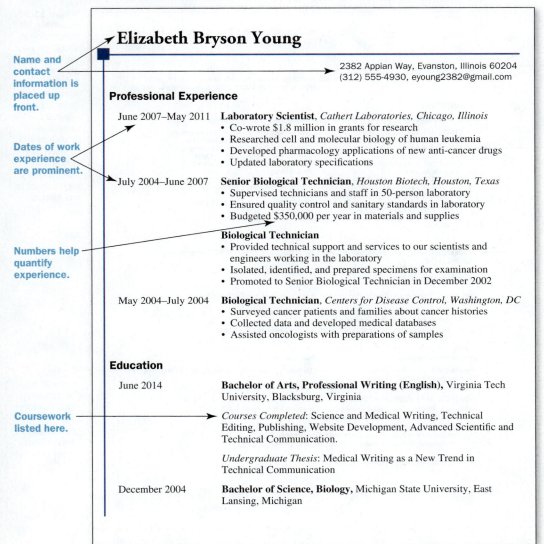

Elizabeth Bryson Young

2382 Appian Way, Evanston, Illinois 60204
(312) 555-4930, eyoung2382@gmail.com

Professional Experience

June 2007–May 2011   **Laboratory Scientist**, *Cathert Laboratories, Chicago, Illinois*
• Co-wrote $1.8 million in grants for research
• Researched cell and molecular biology of human leukemia
• Developed pharmacology applications of new anti-cancer drugs
• Updated laboratory specifications

July 2004–June 2007   **Senior Biological Technician**, *Houston Biotech, Houston, Texas*
• Supervised technicians and staff in 50-person laboratory
• Ensured quality control and sanitary standards in laboratory
• Budgeted $350,000 per year in materials and supplies

Biological Technician
• Provided technical support and services to our scientists and engineers working in the laboratory
• Isolated, identified, and prepared specimens for examination
• Promoted to Senior Biological Technician in December 2002

May 2004–July 2004   **Biological Technician**, *Centers for Disease Control, Washington, DC*
• Surveyed cancer patients and families about cancer histories
• Collected data and developed medical databases
• Assisted oncologists with preparations of samples

Education

June 2014   **Bachelor of Arts, Professional Writing (English),** Virginia Tech University, Blacksburg, Virginia

Courses Completed: Science and Medical Writing, Technical Editing, Publishing, Website Development, Advanced Scientific and Technical Communication.

Undergraduate Thesis: Medical Writing as a New Trend in Technical Communication

December 2004   **Bachelor of Science, Biology,** Michigan State University, East Lansing, Michigan

Name and contact information is placed up front.

Dates of work experience are prominent.

Numbers help quantify experience.

Coursework listed here.

Figure 11.6: This résumé from a student who returned to college features work experience ahead of educational experience.

Figure 11.6:
(continued)

Computer Skills

Word, InDesign, Photoshop, Illustrator, Excel, Dreamweaver, PowerPoint

Awards

AMWA Best Biotech Article in 2009 for "Turning a Corner on Leukemia," *Biotech News*, March 2009

Researcher of the Year, Cathert Laboratories, 2008

Professional Organizations

American Medical Writers Association (AMWA)

Society of Technical Communication (STC)

American Association for the Advancement of Science (AAAS)

Volunteer Work

Volunteer work adds depth to experience and shows maturity.

Health Volunteers Overseas, 2006–2010

Habitat for Humanity, 2001–present

Northern Chicago Urban Ministries, 2013–present

References

References listed on second page.

Thomas VanArsdale, Chief Scientist
Cathert Laboratories
1208 Discovery Lane
Chicago, IL 60626
(312) 654-3864
tvanarsdale@cathertlabs.com

Franklin Charleston, Assistant Professor
Department of English
North Carolina State University
Tompkins Hall, Box 8105
Raleigh, NC 27695-8105
(919) 515-3866
franklcharleston@ncsu.edu

Christina Smith, Associate Professor
Department of English
Virginia Tech University
323 Shanks Hall (0112)
Blacksburg, VA 24061
(540) 231-6501
chrsmith34@vt.edu

Verb-first phrases are preferable to full sentences because they are easier to read and require less space. Some action verbs you might consider using on your résumé include the following:

adapted	devised	organized
analyzed	directed	oversaw
assisted	equipped	planned
collaborated	examined	performed
collected	exhibited	presented
compiled	implemented	proposed
completed	increased	recorded
conducted	improved	researched
constructed	instructed	studied
coordinated	introduced	supervised
corresponded	investigated	taught
designed	managed	trained
developed	observed	wrote

You might be tempted to exaggerate your responsibilities at a job. For example, a cashier at a fast food restaurant might say he "conducted financial transactions." In reality, nobody is fooled by these kinds of puffed-up statements. They simply draw attention to a lack of experience and, frankly, a mild lack of honesty. There is nothing wrong with simply and honestly describing your experiences.

OTHER WORK EXPERIENCE   Almost everyone has worked at jobs that were not related to his or her desired career. If you have worked at a pizza place, waited tables, or painted houses in the summer, those jobs can be listed in your résumé. But they should not be placed more prominently than your related work experience, nor should they receive a large amount of space. Instead, simply list these jobs in reverse chronological order, with names, places, and dates.

Pizza Chef. Giovanni's. Lincoln, Nebraska. September 2013–August 2014.

Painter. Campus Painters. Omaha, Nebraska. May 2014–September 2014.

Server. Crane River Brewpub and Cafe. Omaha, Nebraska. March 2011–May 2014.

Do not offer any additional description. After all, most people are well aware of the responsibilities of a pizza chef, painter, and server. Any more description will only take up valuable space on your résumé.

Don't underestimate the importance of non-career-related jobs on your résumé. If you do not have much professional work experience, any kind of job shows your ability to work and hold a job. As your career progresses, these items should be removed from your résumé.

SKILLS AND LANGUAGES   Résumés will often include a section that lists career-related skills. In this area, you may choose to mention your abilities with computers, including any software or programming languages you know how to use. If you have been trained on any specialized machines or know how to do bookkeeping, these skills might be worth mentioning. If you have proven leadership abilities or communication skills (technical writing or public speaking) you might also list those.

> *Computer Skills:* Word processing (Word, WordPerfect), desktop publishing (InDesign, Quark), web design (Dreamweaver, FrontPage), and data processing (Excel, Access).

> *Leadership Abilities:* President of Wilkins Honor Society, 2013–2014. Treasurer of Lambda Kappa Kappa Sorority, 2011–2014. Volunteer Coordinator at the Storehouse Food Shelter, 2011 to present.

> *Natural Languages:* Spanish (professional fluency), Italian (reading only)

The skills section is a good place to list any training you have completed that does not fit under the "Educational Background" part of your résumé.

Increasingly, due to the globalization of the workplace, proficiency with languages is important. When you list a language other than English, you should indicate your fluency level in speaking, writing, and reading. Some words that you can use include "bilingual," "professional," "reading and writing," and "reading only."

AWARDS AND ACTIVITIES   List any awards you have won and any organized activities in which you have participated. For example, if you won a scholarship for your academic performance, list it here. If you are an active member of a club or fraternity, show those activities in this part of your résumé. Meanwhile, volunteer work is certainly worth mentioning, because it shows your commitment to the community and your initiative.

REFERENCES   Your references are the three to five people whom employers can call to gather more information about you. Your references could include current or former supervisors, instructors, colleagues, and professionals who know you and your work.

They should be people you trust to offer a positive account of your abilities. Each reference listing should include a name, title, address, phone number, and e-mail address. Before putting someone in your list of references, though, make sure you ask permission. Otherwise, he or she may be surprised when a recruiter or human resources officer calls to ask questions about you.

References can take up a large amount of space on a résumé, so they are typically not listed on the résumé itself. Instead, a line at the bottom of the résumé states, "References available upon request." Then the references—listed on a separate sheet of paper under the heading "References"—can be sent to any employer who requests them.

If the employer asks for references to appear on the résumé, you can add them at the bottom of your résumé, usually on a second page (Figure 11.6). To avoid causing your résumé to go over two pages, you may need to list your references in two or three columns on the second page.

AT A GLANCE

Sections in a Chronological Résumé

- Name and contact information
- Career objective/career summary
- Educational background
- Related work experience
- Other work experience
- Skills
- Awards and activities
- References

Functional Résumé

The functional résumé is less common than the chronological résumé, especially for new college graduates. This type of résumé is designed to highlight the job applicant's abilities and skills by placing them up front in the résumé. The advantage of this type of résumé is its ability to boil years of experience down to a few strengths that the job applicant would like to highlight.

Link

For more information on page design, turn to Chapter 18, page 477.

Figure 11.7 shows an example of a functional résumé. In this example, note how the résumé places the applicant's strengths, including awards, early in the document. Then, the remainder of the résumé concisely lists details about the applicant's employment background, educational background, and professional memberships.

Designing the Résumé

The design of your résumé should reflect your personality and the industry in which you want to work. A résumé for an engineering firm, for example, will probably be somewhat plain and straightforward. A résumé for a graphic artist position at a magazine, on the other hand, should demonstrate some of your skills as a designer. There are, of course, exceptions. Some progressive engineering firms, for example, might prefer a layout that reflects your innovative qualities.

Most word-processing programs include résumé templates that you can use to lay out your information. If you use one of these templates, alter the design in some way, because unfortunately, many thousands of people have access to the same templates. So, employers often receive several résumés that look identical. You want yours to stand out.

If you decide to design your own résumé, Chapter 18 offers design principles that are helpful toward creating a design for your résumé. These principles are balance, alignment, grouping, consistency, and contrast. All of these principles should be used to design your résumé.

Balance—Pay attention to the vertical and horizontal balance of the page. Your résumé should not be weighted too heavily toward the left or right, top or bottom.

Alignment—Different levels of information should be consistently indented to make the résumé easy to scan. Don't just align everything at the left margin; instead, use vertical alignment to create two or three levels in the text.

Grouping—Use white space to frame groups of information. For example, a job listed on your résumé with its responsibilities should be identifiable as a chunk of text. Sometimes using rules, especially horizontal lines, is a good way to carve a résumé into quickly identifiable sections (Figure 11.3).

Consistency—The design of your résumé should be internally consistent. Use boldface, italics, and font sizes consistently. Bullets or other symbols should also be used consistently throughout the résumé.

Contrast—Titles and headings should be noticeably different from the body text. To contrast with the body text, you might choose a different serif or sans serif font for your titles and headings. You can increase the font sizes and/or use boldface to make the résumé easy to read.

A helpful strategy for designing your résumé is to collect résumés from other people. There are also numerous books and websites available that offer ideas about designing résumés. You can use these sample résumés as models for designing your own.

A Functional Résumé

Figure 11.7:
A functional résumé puts the applicant's abilities and skills up front where an employer will see them. Other features, such as employment history and education, are minimized.

Name and contact information are placed up front.

Walter David Trimbal

818 Franklin Drive
Atlanta, Georgia 30361
404-555-2915

The objective describes the position sought.

Objective: Senior architect position in a firm that specializes in urban revitalization projects.

Qualities are summarized here, including awards.

Leadership Experience
- Managed design team for additions/alterations for small-scale commercial buildings in downtown Atlanta.
- Led planning charette for Bell Hill Neighborhood renovation.
- Awarded a 2011 "Archi" for design of Delarma Commerce Center.

Technical Expertise
- Experienced with the latest developments in computer-aided drafting hardware and software.
- Able to resolve conflicting building and zoning codes, while preparing site plans.

Community Involvement
- Founding Member of the Better Atlanta Commission in 2004 and served as board member until 2012.
- Served on the Architecture Public Involvement Committee for Atlanta Metropolitan Council of Governments from 2011–2012.

Employment and education histories are very concise, listing only the details.

Employment Background
Vance & Lipton—Architects, Senior Architect, Atlanta, GA, 2008 to present.
Fulton County Planning Department, Planning Architect, Atlanta, GA, 2004–2008.
Ronald Alterman—Architect, Intern, Boston, MA, 2000–2001.

Education Background
B.A. in Architecture, Boston College, Boston, MA, 2004.
A.A. in Computer-Aided Drafting, Augusta Technical College, Augusta, GA, 2001.

Professional Memberships
National Council of Architectural Registration Boards
Greater Atlanta Architects Guild

References Available Upon Request

Designing a Searchable Résumé

Companies will sometimes ask for a *searchable* or *scannable* résumé (Figure A). These kinds of résumés are designed to be processed by computers, which sort and rank candidates. Also, résumés posted on job search engines need to be searchable through keywords. Fortunately, computers and scanning machines do not care about the length or design of your résumé. So, your searchable résumé can be longer than your regular résumé, if needed.

How are searchable résumés used by employers? Usually, after all the résumés are put into a database, a human resources officer or recruiter will enter ten keywords that describe the position. Then the computer returns a ranked list of the applicants who matched the most keywords. To survive the cut, you need to find a way to anticipate the keywords that will be entered. Here's a hint: The job advertisement probably contains many of the keywords the employer will be looking for.

- Use well-known keywords to describe your skills and experience.
- Use terms in predictable ways. For example, you should write "Managed a team of technicians" rather than "Responsible for guiding a contingent of technical specialists."
- Include acronyms specific to your field (e.g., CAD, TQM, APA, IEEE).
- Use common headings found in résumés: Career Objective, Work Experience, Skills, Qualifications, Education, Honors, Publications, Certifications.
- At the end of your résumé, make a list of any additional traits or skills you possess: time management, dependability, efficiency, leadership, responsibility. These may be used as keywords.

Scannable paper résumés are rarely requested anymore, but if you are asked for one here are some suggestions:

- Use white 8½-by-11-inch paper, printed on one side only.
- Do not fold or staple the paper.
- Place your name on its own line at the top of the page.
- Use a standard address format below your name.
- List each phone number on its own line.
- Use standard typefaces like Arial, Helvetica, Times, New York, or Garamond. The computer may have trouble reading other fonts.
- Don't use a font size smaller than 10 points for any of the text.
- Don't use italics, underlining, shadows, or reverse type (white type on a black background) because scanners have trouble reading them.
- Don't use vertical and horizontal lines, graphics, boxes, or shading.
- Don't use two- or three-column formats. One column is easier for the computer to scan.

If you suspect your paper résumé will be scanned by a scanning machine, your best strategy is to make two résumés. One should be your regular résumé and the other should be a scannable version. Your scannable résumé should be clearly identified for the employer with a cover note. That way, the employer won't be confused by the submission of two résumés.

A Searchable Résumé

Figure A: A searchable résumé removes much of the formatting and design, allowing a computer to more easily locate keywords. Compare this résumé with the regular résumé in Figure 11.3.

Name and contact information is plainly presented.

Anne Franklin
834 County Line Rd.
Hollings Point, IL 62905
Home: 618-555-2993
Mobile: 618-555-9167
e-mail: afranklin@unsb5.net

Career Objective: A position as a naturalist, specializing in agronomy, working for a distribution company that specializes in organic foods.

Headings are predictable and easy to locate.

Educational Background
Bachelor of Science, Southern Illinois University, expected May 2014.
> Major: Plant and Soil Science
> Minor: Entomology
> GPA: 3.2/4.0

Work Experience
Intern Agronomist, December 2012–August 2013
Brighter Days Organic Cooperative, Simmerton, IL

Italics have been removed for easier scanning.

> Consulted with growers on organic pest control methods. Primary duty was sale of organic crop protection products, crop nutrients, seed, and consulting services.
> Prepared organic agronomic farm plans for growers.
> Provided crop-scouting services to identify weed and insect problems.

Field Technician, August 2010–December 2012
Entomology Department, Southern Illinois University

Bullets have been removed to simplify text.

> Collected and identified insects.
> Developed insect management plans.
> Tested organic and nonorganic pesticides for effectiveness and residuals.

Skills
Computer Experience: Access, Excel, Outlook, PowerPoint, and Word. Global Positioning Systems (GPS). Database Management.
Machinery: Field Tractors, Combines, Straight Trucks, and Bobcats.
Communication Skills: Proposal Writing and Review, Public Presentations, Negotiating, Training, Writing Agronomic and Financial Farm Plans.

Awards and Memberships
Awarded "Best Young Innovator" by the Organic Food Society of America (OFSA), 2012.
Member of Entomological Society of America (ESA).

Writing Effective Application Letters

Your résumé will provide the employer with facts and details about your education, work experience, and skills. An effective application letter strives to prove that you are uniquely qualified for the available position. Your letter should fit on one page for an entry-level position. Two pages would be a maximum for any job.

Two mistakes are frequently made in application letters. First, applicants sometimes only restate the information available on the résumé, failing to demonstrate why they are the right person for the job. Second, they discuss why the position would be good *for them* (e.g., "A job at Gurson Industries would help me reach my goal to become an electrical engineer working with sensors"). To put it bluntly, employers don't really care whether their job is good for you.

Instead, your letter should prove to potential employers that your education, experience, and skills will allow you to make a valuable contribution to *their* company. Put the emphasis on *their* needs, not yours.

Content and Organization

Like any letter, an application letter will have an introduction, body, and conclusion (Figure 11.8). It will also include common features of a letter such as the header (your address and the employer's address), a greeting ("Dear"), and a closing salutation ("Sincerely") with your signature.

The Basic Pattern of an Application Letter

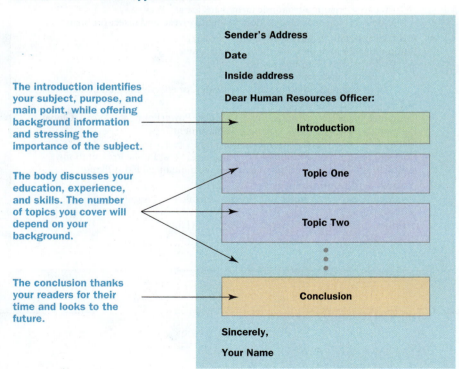

The introduction identifies your subject, purpose, and main point, while offering background information and stressing the importance of the subject.

The body discusses your education, experience, and skills. The number of topics you cover will depend on your background.

The conclusion thanks your readers for their time and looks to the future.

Sender's Address

Date

Inside address

Dear Human Resources Officer:

Introduction

Topic One

Topic Two

Conclusion

Sincerely,

Your Name

Figure 11.8: An application letter includes the common features of a letter, like the sender's address, date, inside address, introduction, body, and closing salutation.

Link

For more information on writing letters, go to Chapter 5, page 84.

INTRODUCTION You should begin your letter by making up to five moves commonly found in the introduction of any document: Identify your subject, state your purpose, state your main point, stress the importance, and offer background information on your subject.

DEAR MS. SIMS:

Subject and purpose → I would like to apply for the Organic Agronomist position you advertised
Background information → through HotJobs.com on March 17. My experience with organic innovations in plant and soil science as well as my minor in entomology would allow me
Main point and importance → to make an immediate contribution to your company.

This introduction makes all five introductory moves, but you don't need to use all five moves for a successful introduction. Minimally, an introduction should identify the subject (the position being applied for), state your purpose ("I would like to apply for your job"), and state your main point ("I am uniquely qualified for your position").

BODY In the body of the letter, you should include two to three paragraphs that show how your educational background, work experience, and skills fit the employer's needs. You should organize the body of your letter to highlight your strengths. If your educational background is your best asset, put that paragraph right after the letter's introduction (Figure 11.9). If your work experience is stronger than your education, then put that information up front (Figure 11.10).

Remember that you are making an argument, so each paragraph should start out with a claim, and the rest of the paragraph should support that claim with examples, facts, and reasoning. Here is a sample paragraph that supports a claim about an agronomist's educational background.

A clear claim → My education and research as an organic agronomist would benefit your company significantly. As a Plant and Soil Science major at Southern Illinois University, I have been studying and researching environmentally safe alternatives to pesticides. Specifically, my mentor, Professor George Roberts,
Support for that claim → and I have been working on using benevolent insects, like ladybird beetles (*Coleomegilla maculata*), to control common pests on various vegetable plants. We have also developed several varieties of organic insecticidal soaps that handle the occasional insect infestation.

In the body, you need to back up your claims with facts, examples, details, and reasoning—you need proof. You should breathe life into your letter by telling stories about yourself.

CONCLUSION Your conclusion should make three moves: thank the reader, offer contact information, and look to the future. Your goal is to leave a positive impression.

Thank you statement → Thank you for this opportunity to apply for your opening. I look forward to
Look to the future → hearing from you about this exciting position. I can be contacted at home
Contact information → (618–555–2993) or through e-mail (afranklin@unsb5.net).

Keep the conclusion concise, and avoid any pleading for the position. Employers will not look favorably on someone who is begging for the job.

Letter of Application Emphasizing Education

Figure 11.9: A letter of application should make an argument, not simply restate items that can be found on the résumé.

834 County Line Rd.
Hollings Point, Illinois 62905

April 1, 2014

Valerie Sims, Human Resources Manager
Sunny View Organic Products
1523 Cesar Chavez Lane
Sunny View, California 95982

Dear Ms. Sims:

Opening paragraph states the subject, purpose, and main point.

I would like to apply for the Organic Agronomist position you advertised through HotJobs.com on March 17. My experience with organic innovations in plant and soil science as well as my minor in entomology would allow me to make an immediate contribution to your company.

Education is discussed up front with examples.

My education and research as an organic agronomist would benefit your company significantly. As a Plant and Soil Science major at Southern Illinois University, I have been studying and researching environmentally safe alternatives to pesticides. Specifically, my mentor, Professor George Roberts, and I have been working on using benevolent insects, like ladybird beetles (*Coleomegilla maculata*), to control common pests on various vegetable plants. We have also developed several varieties of organic insecticidal soaps that handle the occasional insect infestation.

Work experience is used to show potential contributions to employer.

I also worked as an intern for Brighter Days Organic Cooperative, a group of organic farmers, who have an operation similar to Sunny View. From your website, I see that you are currently working toward certification as an organic farm. At Brighter Days, I wrote eleven agronomic plans for farmers who wanted to change to organic methods. My work experience in the organic certification process would be helpful toward earning certification for Sunny View in the shortest amount of time.

Other skills are highlighted to show unique abilities.

Finally, I would bring two other important skills to your company: a background in farming and experience with public speaking. I grew up on a farm near Hollings Point, Illinois. When my father died, my mother and I kept the farm going by learning how to operate machinery, plant the crops, and harvest. We decided to go organic in 2002, because we always suspected that my father's death was due to chemical exposure. Based on our experiences with going organic, I have given numerous public speeches and workshops to the Farm Bureau and Future Farmers of America on organic farming. My farming background and speaking skills would be an asset to your operation.

Conclusion ends on a positive note and offers contact information.

Thank you for this opportunity to apply for your opening. I look forward to hearing from you about this exciting position. I can be contacted at home (618-555-2993) or through e-mail (afranklin@unsb5.net).

Sincerely,

Anne Franklin

Anne Franklin

Letter of Application Emphasizing Work Experience

576 First Avenue
Rolla, Missouri 65408

March 10, 2014

Mr. Harold Brown, Human Resources Director
Farnot Plastic Solutions
4819 Renaissance Lane
Rochester, New York 14608

Dear Mr. Brown:

Opening paragraph uses background information to make personal connection. → Last week, you and I met at the University of Missouri–Rolla engineering job fair. You mentioned that Farnot Plastics might be interviewing entry-level chemical engineers this spring to work on applications of polymeric materials. If a position becomes available, I would like to apply for it. With my experience in applied rheology and polymeric materials, I would be a valuable addition to your company.

Work experience with co-op is highlighted. → My work experience includes two summers as a co-op at Vertigo Plastics, a company similar in size, products, and services to Farnot. My responsibilities included inspecting and troubleshooting the plant's machinery. I analyzed the production process and reported on the performance of the plant's operations. While at Vertigo, I learned to work with other chemical engineers in a team-focused environment.

Paragraph on education makes connections to employer's needs. → My education in chemical engineering at University of Missouri–Rolla would allow me to contribute a thorough understanding of plastics engineering to Farnot. In one of the best programs in the country, I have excelled at courses in thermodynamics, chemical process design, and chemical process materials. In addition, my work in the university's state-of-the-art chemical laboratories has prepared me to do the prototype building and vacuum forming that is a specialty of your company. I also have experience working with the CAD/CAM systems that your company uses.

Conclusion indirectly requests the interview. → The enclosed résumé highlights my other qualifications. I enjoyed speaking with you at the job fair, and I would appreciate an opportunity to talk to you again about opportunities at Farnot. If you would like more information or you would like to schedule an interview, please call me at 573-555-4391 or e-mail me at bigmondy12@umr.edu.

Sincerely,

J. Mondragon

James L. Mondragon
Enclosure: Résumé

Style

Another way an application letter differs from a résumé is in its style. You want to adopt a style that conveys a sense of your own personality and your interest in the position available.

Link

For more information on using the "you" style in letters, go to Chapter 5, page 105.

"YOU" ATTITUDE   Put the emphasis of the letter on your readers by using the *"you" attitude*. By strategically using the words "you" and "your" in the letter, you can discuss your qualifications from your readers' point of view.

To put emphasis on the readers rather than on yourself, you might also change "I" sentences to "my" sentences.

ACTIVE VOICE   In uncomfortable situations, like writing application letters, you might be tempted to switch to passive voice. Passive voice in application letters will make you sound detached and even apathetic.

Link

For more help on using active voice, see Chapter 16, page 422.

> **Passive:** The proposal describing the need for a new bridge over the Raccoon River was completed and presented to the Franklin City Council.

> **Active:** My team completed the proposal for a new bridge over the Raccoon River and presented it to the Franklin City Council.

Why active voice? The active voice shows that you did something. You took action.

NONBUREAUCRATIC TONE   Avoid using business clichés to adopt an artificially formal tone. Phrases such as "per your advertisement" or "in accordance with your needs" only make you sound stuffy and pretentious.

> **Bureaucratic:** Pursuant to your advertisement in the *Chicago Sun-Times,* I am tendering my application toward your available position in pharmaceutical research.

> **Nonbureaucratic:** I am applying for the pharmaceutical researcher position you advertised in the *Chicago Sun-Times.*

Employers are not interested in hiring people who write in such a pretentious way—unless they are looking for a butler.

THEMES   Think of one quality that sets you apart from others. Do you work well in teams? Are you a self-starter? Are you able to handle pressure? Are you quality minded? Some themes you might weave into your letter include the ability to

- make public presentations.
- be a leader.
- manage time effectively.
- motivate yourself and others.
- follow instructions.
- meet deadlines.
- work well in a team.

AT A GLANCE

Style in an Application Letter

- "You" attitude—Put the emphasis on the employer.
- Active voice—Put yourself, not events, in charge.
- Nonbureaucratic tone—No one wants to hire bureaucrats, so don't sound like one.
- Themes—Point out what makes you different or attractive.

- write clearly and persuasively.
- handle stressful situations.

One theme should be enough, because using more than one theme will sound like you are boasting.

Revising and Proofreading the Résumé and Letter

When you are finished writing your résumé and application letter, you should spend a significant amount of time revising and proofreading your materials. Have as many people as possible look over your letter of application and your résumé. For most jobs, even the smallest typos can become good excuses to pitch an application into the recycle bin. Your materials need to be nearly flawless in grammar and spelling.

Creating a Professional Portfolio

Increasingly, it is becoming common for employers to ask applicants to bring a *professional portfolio* to their interview. Sometimes, interviewers will ask that a portfolio be sent ahead of the interview so they can familiarize themselves with the applicant and his or her abilities.

A portfolio is a collection of materials that you can use to demonstrate your qualifications and abilities. Portfolios include some or all of the following items:

- Résumé
- Samples of written work
- Examples of presentations
- Descriptions and evidence of projects
- Diplomas and certificates
- Awards
- Letters of reference

These materials can be placed in a three-ring binder with dividers and/or put on a website, flash drive, or CD.

Your personal portfolio should not be left with the interviewer, because it may be lost or not returned. Instead, you should create a "giveaway" portfolio with copies of your work that you can leave with the employer.

Even if interviewers do not ask you to bring a portfolio, putting one together is still well worth your time. You will have a collection of materials to show your interviewers, allowing you to make the strongest case possible that you have the qualifications and experience they need.

Collecting Materials

If you have not made a portfolio before, you are probably wondering if you have enough materials to put one together.

Much of your written work in college is suitable for your portfolio. Your class-related materials do not need to be directly applicable to the job you are applying for. Instead, potential employers are interested in seeing evidence of your success and your everyday abilities. Documents written for class will show evidence of success.

A Print Portfolio

A portfolio is a useful tool to bring to an interview. It holds all your work in an accessible package so that you can support your claims during your interview.

Even nontechnical materials—like your critical analysis of Beethoven's Ninth Symphony that you wrote for a course in classical music—show your ability to do research, adopt a critical perspective, and write at length. These items are appropriate if you are looking for materials to fill a portfolio.

Organizing Your Portfolio

A particularly good way to organize a portfolio is to follow the categories in a typical résumé:

Cover sheet—A sheet that includes your name, address, phone number, and e-mail address.

Educational background—Diplomas you have received, workshops you have attended, a list of relevant courses, and college transcripts.

Related work experience—Printed materials from your previous jobs, internships, co-ops, and volunteer work. You might include performance reviews, news articles that mention you, or brochures about specific projects. You might even include photographs of places you have worked, projects you have worked on, and people you have worked with.

Specialized skills—Certificates of completion for training, including any coursework you have completed outside of your normal college curriculum.

Writing samples and publications—Examples of your written work, presentations, or websites.

Awards—Any award certificates or letters of congratulation. You might include letters that mention any scholarships you have received.

Other interests—Materials that reflect your other activities, such as volunteer work, sports, or hobbies. Preferably, these materials would be relevant to the kinds of jobs you are seeking.

AT A GLANCE

Organizing Your Portfolio
- Cover sheet
- Educational background
- Related work experience
- Specialized skills
- Writing samples and publications
- Awards
- Other interests
- References

References—Letters of reference from instructors, colleagues, co-workers, or employers. Also, it is helpful to keep a list of references with phone numbers and addresses where they can be contacted.

Assembling the Portfolio in a Binder

Your portfolio needs to be easy to use at an interview. If your portfolio is nothing more than a hodgepodge of paper stuffed in a three-ring binder, you will find it difficult to locate important information.

So, go to an office supply store and purchase the following items:

Three-ring binder—The binder should be at least 2 inches wide to hold your materials, but it should not be too large to be comfortably carried to an interview. Find one that is suitable for a formal situation like an interview.

Dividers with tabs—Tabbed dividers are helpful for separating your materials into larger categories. The tabs are helpful for finding materials quickly, especially in a stressful situation like an interview.

Pocketed folders or clear plastic sleeves—Put your materials in pockets or clear plastic sleeves. That way, you can easily insert and remove your materials when you want.

As you assemble the portfolio, keep professionalism and ease of use in mind:

- Copies of your résumé can usually be placed in a pocket on the inside cover of the three-ring binder. You may need them if interviewers do not have a copy of your résumé in front of them.
- Labels can be used to provide background information on each item in the portfolio. These labels are helpful in jogging your memory during a stressful interview.

Creating an Electronic Portfolio

If you know how to create a basic website, you can create an electronic portfolio for yourself (Figure 11.11). An electronic portfolio has several advantages. It can

- be accessed from anywhere there is a networked computer, including an interviewer's office.
- include multimedia texts such as movies, presentations, and links to websites you have created.
- include materials and links to information that would not typically be found in a nonelectronic portfolio. For example, you might put links to your university and academic department to help interviewers learn about your educational background.

You should keep your electronic portfolio separate from any personal websites you create. The materials you include in your electronic portfolio should be appropriate for discussion in a professional interview. (Your vacation photos from that Aspen skiing trip with your friends probably aren't appropriate.)

Electronic Portfolio

Interviewing Strategies

When you are called for an interview, an employer is already telling you that you are qualified for the position. Now you just need to compete with the other qualified candidates who are also interviewing for the position.

Preparing for the Interview

In many ways, interviewing is a game. It's not an interrogation. The interviewers are going to ask you some questions or put you in situations that will test your problem-solving abilities.

RESEARCH THE COMPANY   Before the interview, find out as much as possible about the company and the people who will be interviewing you. The Internet, especially the company's website, is a great place to start. But you should also look for magazine and newspaper articles on the company in your university or local library. While researching the company, locate facts about the size of the company, its products, and its competitors. You should also be aware of major trends in the company's market.

DRESS APPROPRIATELY   The interview game begins with your appearance. There is an old saying: "Dress for the job you want, not for the job you have." When you are interviewing, you should be dressed in a suitably formal manner, avoiding flashy jewelry or too much cologne or perfume.

The Interview

Interviewing is more like a game than an interrogation. Once you know how the game is played, you can win it.

At the Interview

When you are at the interview, try to relax and present yourself as someone the interviewer would like to hire. Remember that each question from an interviewer is a move in the game, and there are always appropriate countermoves available.

GREET PEOPLE WITH CONFIDENCE When you meet people at the interview, you should greet them with confidence. Most North Americans will expect you to shake their hand firmly and make eye contact. Let the interviewer indicate where you are going to sit. Then, set your briefcase and/or portfolio at your side on the floor. Don't put things on the interviewer's desk, unless he or she asks you to.

ANSWER QUESTIONS Interviewers will usually work from a script of questions. However, most interviews go off the script as interesting topics come up. You should be prepared with answers to some of the following questions:

> **"Tell me about yourself"**—Spend about two minutes talking about your work experience, education, and skills, relating them to the position. Don't start with, "I was born in New York in 1995 . . . ."

> **"What about this position attracted you?"**—Talk about the strengths of the company and what qualities of the position you find interesting.

> **"Why should we hire you?"**—Stress qualifications and skills appropriate to the job that set you apart from the other candidates.

Link

For more information on making a professional presentation, see Chapter 20, page 521.

Link

For more strategies on answering questions, see Chapter 20, page 539.

"Where do you want to be in three to five years?"—Without being too ambitious, talk about doing your job well and moving up in the company.

"What are your salary requirements?"—This question is uncommon, but you should have a salary figure in your head in case it is asked. You don't want to fumble this question or ask for too little or too much.

"What is your greatest strength?"—Discuss a strong qualification, skill, or knowledge area relevant to the job.

"What is your greatest weakness?"—Discuss something you would like to learn that would enhance your ability to do your job (e.g., a new language, more advanced computer skills, greater communication skills). The "weakness" question is not the time to admit your shortcomings. Also, answers like, "I just work too hard" or "I am too committed to doing an excellent job" don't really fool anyone.

USE YOUR PORTFOLIO   No doubt you have been told numerous times, "Show, don't just tell." In your interview, use your professional portfolio to back up your answers to interview questions.

ASK QUESTIONS   As the interview comes to an end, the interviewer will usually ask if you have any questions. You should be ready to ask two or three insightful questions. Here are a few examples of questions that will demonstrate your interest in the company and the job:

Where do you see the company going in the next five years?

What can you tell me about your customers/clients?

What kinds of additional learning opportunities are available?

What happens in a normal day at this position?

Avoid asking questions at this point about salary, vacation, and benefits. Usually these items are discussed after a job offer has been made.

Interviewing Strategies

AT A GLANCE

- Research the company.
- Dress appropriately.
- Greet people with confidence.
- Answer questions.
- Use your portfolio.
- Ask questions.
- Leave with confidence.

LEAVE WITH CONFIDENCE   When the interview is finished, thank the interviewers for their time and say that you are looking forward to hearing from them. Also, ask if they would like you to send them any other information. Then, shake each interviewer's hand firmly and go.

As soon as possible after the interview, find a place where you can write down names and everything you can remember about what you and the interviewers talked about. These notes may be helpful later, especially if a week or two lapses before you hear about the job. Your notes should mention any important discussion points that developed during the interview.

Writing Thank You Letters and/or E-Mails

After an interview, it is polite to write a thank you letter to the people who interviewed you. A basic thank you letter shows your appreciation for the interviewers' time while expressing continued interest in the job. A more sophisticated letter could reinforce one or more of your strengths, in addition to saying thank you and expressing continued interest in the job (Figure 11.12).

A Thank You Letter

Figure 11.12:
A thank you
letter can be
used to rein-
force an im-
portant point
that came
out during the
interview.

Inside address

A thank you
statement
leads off the
letter.

An important
point is rein-
forced with
details from
the interview.

The signature
includes the
full name.

834 County Line Rd.
Hollings Point, Illinois 62905

May 13, 2014

Valerie Sims, Human Resources Manager
Sunny View Organic Products
1523 Cesar Chavez Lane
Sunny View, California 95982

Dear Ms. Sims:

Thank you for interviewing me for the Organic Agronomist position at Sunny
View Organic Products. I enjoyed meeting you and the others at the company.
Now, after speaking with you, I am more interested than ever in the position. ◄— The main
point is
clearly
stated in the
introduction.

I noticed during the interview that my experience with benevolent insects
was a recurring topic of discussion. This area of pest control is indeed very
exciting, and my work with Professor George Roberts is certainly cutting edge.
By paying attention to release times and hatching patterns, we have been able
to maximize the effectiveness of predator insects. I would bring the latest
research in this area to Sunny View's crops.

Again, thank you for the opportunity to interview with you for this position. ◄
I can be contacted at home (618-555-2993) or through e-mail
(afranklin@unsb5.net). Please call or e-mail me if you need more information
or would like to speak with me further about this position.

The
conclusion
thanks the
reader
and offers
contact
information.

Sincerely,

Ann. Franklin

Anne Franklin

If you send a thank you message via e-mail, follow it with a letter through the mail. An e-mail is nice for giving the interviewers immediate feedback, but the letter shows more professionalism.

If all goes well, you will be offered the position. At that point, you can decide if the responsibilities, salary, and benefits fit your needs.

The Bio

In the workplace, you will need to write your professional biography or "bio." A bio is a brief description of your career that highlights your background and accomplishments. Bios are typically included in job-finding materials, social networking sites, "About Us" pages on websites, qualifications sections, and marketing materials. Also, career consultants often ask people to write their own "retirement bio" that describes the careers they hope to have. Writing your own retirement bio might seem a bit odd when you're still in college, but it's a great way to lay out your long-term goals and think about what you want to do with your life.

Here are some strategies for writing your bio:

Be concise. You may be asked to keep your bio to a specific length: one sentence, 100 words, 250 words, or 500 words. Try to say as much as you can in the space available.

Hook the readers. Tell the readers what you do in the first sentence, and highlight what makes you different. For example, "Lisa Geertz is a biomedical engineer who specializes in developing mobility devices for children."

Write in the third-person. You should refer to yourself by name, even though you are writing about yourself. A formal bio will use your last name throughout, while an informal bio will use your first name.

Identify your three to five major achievements. Describe each of your major accomplishments in one sentence or a maximum of two sentences.

Be specific about your accomplishments. Where possible, use numbers, facts, dates, and other figures to quantify the *impact* of your achievements.

Offer personal information. If space allows, you can talk about your family, where you live, or your favorite activities. Personal information adds a human touch.

Contact information. If appropriate, include contact information, such as your e-mail address and phone number.

Write

Write your own retirement bio. Imagine yourself at the end of your career, getting ready to retire. Write a 250-word bio that reviews your career and accomplishments. Go ahead and dream. Set your goals high.

welch architecture

Portfolio Bio Client Access Contact Blog

CLIFF WELCH ARCHITECT

BIOGRAPHY

Cliff is a Dallas Architect whose work has been honored at the local and national levels. His background includes working with the late Dallas modernist Bud Oglesby, was a principal with Design International, and now has his own practice. His firm's focus is modern architecture, concentrating on residential, interiors, and small scale commercial work. He has been a leading resource and proponent for the restoration and preservation of post-war modernism in Dallas.

In addition to his practice, he is past President of the Dallas Architectural Foundation, and has taught graduate level design at the University of Texas, Arlington. Cliff is a past Executive Board member for the Dallas Chapter AIA, served two years as Commissioner of Design, and has Chaired several chapter events such as the Ken Roberts Memorial Delineation Competition, Retrospect, and Home Tours. He has also served as a design awards juror for other chapters around the state.

Cliff was featured in Texas Architect as one of five young design professionals leading the way into the coming century and has been honored as Dallas American Institute of Architects' Young Architect of the Year.

Source: Welch Architecture, http://www.welcharchitecture.com.

- From the beginning, you should adopt a professional approach to job seeking: Set goals and make a plan.

- Your job-searching plan should include employment websites, social networking, personal networking, professional networking, college placement office, targeting, and classified advertisements.

- Two types of résumés are commonly used, the chronological résumé and the functional résumé. Either should summarize your background, experience, and qualifications.

- A well-designed résumé should use the basic principles of design; a searchable résumé incorporates keywords so that it can be sorted electronically.

- An effective application letter can be more individual and specifically targeted than the résumé. It shares the common features of a letter, including the appropriate "moves" for the introduction, body, and conclusion.

- An appropriate style for an application letter uses the "you" attitude, active voice, and nonbureaucratic language; you can also work in a theme that will make your résumé stand out.

- A professional portfolio is a helpful tool for an interview because it can demonstrate your qualifications and abilities; material for your "master" portfolio can be assembled from classroom work, volunteer projects, related work experience, awards, certificates, or letters of reference.

- E-portfolios are becoming common tools for presenting materials to potential employers. You should create one before you begin looking for jobs.

- When you go to your interview, be prepared with information about the company and appropriate questions to ask; dress appropriately for the position; greet people with confidence; and answer questions thoughtfully.

Individual or Team Projects

1. Imagine that you are looking for an internship in your field. Write a one-page résumé that summarizes your education, work experience, skills, awards, and activities. Then, pay attention to issues of design, making sure the text uses principles of balance, alignment, grouping, consistency, and contrast.

2. Using an Internet job search engine, use keywords to find a job for which you might apply after college. Underline the qualifications required and the responsibilities of the position. Then write a résumé and application letter suitable for the job. In a cover memo addressed to your instructor, discuss some of the reasons you would be a strong candidate for the position. Then discuss some areas where you might need to take more courses or gain more experience before applying for the position.

3. Contact a human resources manager at a local company. Request an "informational interview" with this manager (preferably in person, but an e-mail interview is sufficient). If the interview is granted, ask him or her the best way to approach the company about a job. Ask what kinds of qualifications the company is usually looking for in a college graduate. Ask what you can do now to enhance your chances of obtaining a position at the company. After your interview, present your findings to your class.

4. Make an electronic portfolio of your materials. Besides the materials available in your regular portfolio, what are some other links and documents you might include in your electronic portfolio?

Collaborative Project

With a group of people pursuing similar careers, develop a job search plan. Then, send each member of the group out to collect information. One group member should try out job search engines, while another should explore personal and professional networking opportunities. One member should create a list of potential employers in your area. Another should explore newspapers' online classified advertisements.

After your group has collected the information, write a small report for your class and instructor in which you discuss the results of your research. What did your group discover about the job market in your field? Where are the hottest places to find jobs? How can professional groups and personal networking help you make contacts with potential employers?

Individuals in your group should then choose one job that seems interesting. Each member of the group should write an application letter for that job and create a résumé that highlights qualifications and strengths.

Then the group should come up with five questions that might be asked at an interview, four questions that are usually asked at an interview, and one question that is meant to trip up an interviewee.

Finally, take turns interviewing each other. Ask your questions and jot down good answers and bad answers to the questions. Discuss how each member of the group might improve his or her interviewing skills based on your experiences with this project.

Visit MyWritingLab for a Post-test and more technical writing resources.

CASE
STUDY

The Lie

Henry Romero had wanted to be an architect his whole life. Even as a child, he was fascinated by the buildings in nearby Chicago. So, he spent years preparing to be an architect, winning top honors at his university in design.

He was thrilled when one of the top architectural firms, Goming and Cooper, announced it would be visiting his campus looking to interview promising new talent. This firm was certainly one of the top firms in the country. It had designed some of the most innovative buildings in recent years. Henry was especially interested in the firm's international projects, which would allow him to work and live abroad. Recently, in *Architecture Times,* he had read about the firm's successful relationships with companies in France.

So, Henry gave his résumé and a letter of application to the university's placement office personnel and told them to send it to Goming and Cooper. A month later, his placement counselor called him and said he had an interview with the firm. Henry was very pleased.

There was only one problem. On his résumé, Henry had put down that he "read and spoke French fluently." But, in all honesty, he had taken French for only a few years in high school and one year in college. He hadn't really mastered the language. If necessary, he could muddle his way through a conversation in French, but he was hardly fluent.

To make things worse, last week Henry's roommate, Paul, had had a nightmarish interview. He too had reported on his résumé that he spoke a language fluently—in this case, German. When he arrived at the interview, the interviewer decided to break the ice by talking in German. Paul was stunned. He stammered in German for a few minutes. Then the interviewer, clearly angry, showed him the door.

Henry was worried. What if the same thing happened to him? He knew the ability to speak French was probably one of the reasons he had received the interview in the first place. If the interviewer found out he was not fluent in French, there was a good chance the interview would go badly.

If you were Henry, how would you handle this touchy situation?

CHAPTER

12

Strategic Planning, Being Creative

Using Strategic Planning *330*

Help: Planning with Online
  Calendars *333*

Generating New Ideas *334*

What You Need to Know *339*

Exercises and Projects *340*

Case Study: Getting
  Back to Crazy *342*

In this chapter, you will learn:

- To plan a project in an organized way.

- Strategies for identifying your objectives and "top-rank objective."

- To develop a list of tasks and a timeline for your project.

- How to use the technical writing process as a planning tool.

- How to generate new ideas in the technical workplace.

- Strategies for being creative and trusting your instincts.

- Five techniques for generating new ideas.

The writing process for any technical document should begin with a "planning phase" in which you think about how you are going to best inform and persuade your readers. Good planning will save you time while helping you write more efficiently and effectively.

Using Strategic Planning

Effective strategic planning will save you time, while helping you produce higher-quality documents and presentations that are informative and persuasive to your readers. A time-tested method for strategic planning includes three steps: (1) setting objectives, (2) creating a list of tasks or "task list," and (3) setting a timeline (Figure 12.1).

Step 1: Set Your Objectives

To begin the planning process, you first need to figure out what you want your project to achieve.

LIST PROJECT OBJECTIVES   On your computer or a sheet of paper, make a brainstorming list of the objectives of your project. For a smaller project, you may list only a few objectives. For a larger project, your list of objectives will probably include many items that vary in importance. At this point, as you brainstorm, you should list any objectives that come to mind. You can prioritize and condense the list later.

IDENTIFY THE TOP-RANK OBJECTIVE   When your list is complete, rank your objectives from the most important to the least important. Identify your "top-rank objective" (or what a marketing guru would call your "TRO"). That's the main goal that your project will strive to reach. More than likely, your top-rank objective is going to be almost identical to the *purpose* of your project.

Steps of Strategic Planning

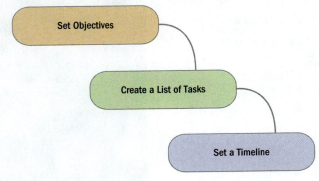

Figure 12.1:
Good project planning involves identifying your objective and then breaking the project down into tasks that are set on a timeline.

Then express your project's top-rank objective in one sentence:

> Our main objective is to persuade the university's vice president of information technology to upgrade the wireless network on campus.

> The primary goal of this project is to develop a solar car that will be competitive in the American Solar Challenge race.

If you are having trouble expressing your top-rank objective or purpose in one sentence, you probably need to narrow the scope of your project. A top-rank objective that requires more than one sentence is probably too complicated to guide your strategic planning.

Step 2: Create a List of Tasks (or Task List)

Once you have identified your top-rank objective, you should then convert the remainder of your objectives into tasks that you will need to perform. Logical mapping and developing a "task list" are helpful ways to make this conversion from objectives to tasks.

MAP OUT THE PROJECT TASKS Put your top-rank objective (purpose) in the middle of your screen or a piece of paper, and ask yourself, "What are the two to five major steps necessary to achieve this goal?" Once you have identified your major steps, then identify the two to five minor steps that will help you achieve each major step.

You shouldn't reinvent the wheel with every new project. For example, if your project involves writing a document, you can use the "technical writing process" described in Chapter 1 to help you figure out the major steps of your project (Figure 12.2). Here are the stages of the writing process again:

Planning and researching

Organizing and drafting

Improving style

Designing

Revising and editing

Once you have identified the major and minor steps of your project, put each of these steps on your calendar along with the other tasks that you need to accomplish to finish the project.

CREATE A TASK LIST When your logical map is finished, you can transform it into a list of tasks, or a *task list* (Figure 12.2). The major steps in your map will become the larger stages of the project. Meanwhile, the minor steps will become individual tasks that you need to complete at each stage.

Link

For more help with identifying your purpose go to Chapter 1, page 5.

Link

For more tips on using logical maps, go to Chapter 14, page 367.

Link

For more information about the technical writing process, go to Chapter 1, page 2.

Mapping Out a Plan

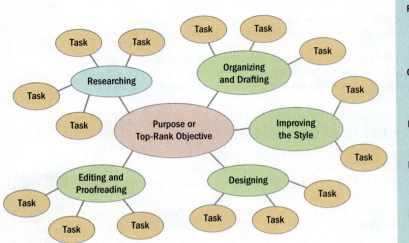

Project Task List

Researching
 Task
 Task
 Task
 Task

Organizing and Drafting
 Task
 Task
 Task

Improving the Style
 Task
 Task

Designing
 Task
 Task
 Task

Editing and Proofreading
 Task
 Task
 Task

Figure 12.2:
To create a project plan, map out the two to five major steps. Then add two to five minor tasks for each major step. Your plan can then be converted into a task list.

Step 3: Set a Timeline

In technical workplaces, setting timelines is essential. A timeline allows you to keep track of your progress toward completing the project. If you are working alone, the timeline will help you avoid procrastination (and a mad rush to the finish). If you are working with a team, the timeline will help everyone work together to reach the same milestones and deadlines.

ASSIGN A DATE TO EACH TASK   Working backward from your project's deadline, identify how much time each part of the project will require. Then, on your task list, write down specific dates when each part of the project should be completed. Online calendars and project planning software are available to help you fill out your timeline (see the Help box). These calendaring programs are widely used in technical workplaces, because they allow team members to check each other's calendars and the project calendar.

Link
For more information on creating a project calendar, go to Chapter 3, page 42.

SCHEDULE MEETINGS OR CHECKPOINTS   At regular intervals on your timeline (each week, every two weeks, or each month), schedule meetings with your team. Meetings can be boring, but people tend to use them as deadlines to get their tasks completed. If you are working alone, you can use the major steps in your project as "checkpoints" to ensure that you are making steady progress toward finishing the project.

Planning with Online Calendars

An online calendar is a helpful tool for planning your project and coordinating with team members. Until recently, the best online calendars have been tied to large software suites like Microsoft Outlook, Corel Office, and IBM Lotus. These calendar programs are closely linked to the e-mail services included with these software suites.

When search engines like Google and Yahoo! jumped into the e-mail game, online calendars took an interesting leap forward. Now, your calendar (like your e-mail) can be accessed through any computer, mobile phone, or tablet that gives you access to Google or Yahoo! portals (Figure A). So, your calendar is no longer tied to your personal computer. You can access it anywhere. That's a significant advantage.

Online calendars are helpful because you can easily schedule events, including any deadlines and meetings (and social activities). Then, you can set up your preferences, and the calendar will send you reminder messages through your e-mail. That way, you won't miss an important meeting, and you will be fully aware when you blow past the deadline for a project—even if there's nothing you can do about it.

You can set up your calendar to let others check your schedule to find times when they can meet with you. If you scheduled a meeting or an after-work gathering, your calendar program can remind people with e-mail messages ("Hey, don't forget we're meeting at Cy's Roost on Thursday at 5:30").

Scheduling with an Online Calendar

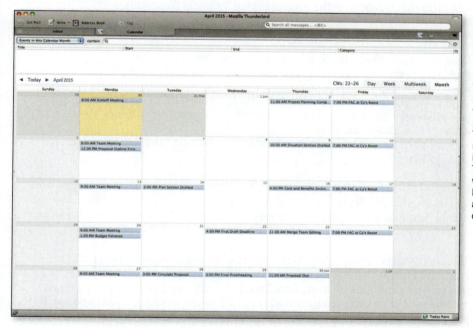

Figure A: Online calendars are widely used in technical workplaces. They are usually linked to e-mail programs. The screen shown here is Mozilla Thunderbird with the Lightning add-on for calendaring.

Source: Mozilla.

Online calendars are especially useful for project planning. Once you have created your list of project tasks, you should enter the items into your calendar. Work backward from the project deadline, as shown in Figure A. Put something like "Proposal Due" on the day of the deadline. From last to first, start entering the other tasks into the calendar. Once all the tasks are entered, you can move them around to create a project timeline.

Finally, set up your preferences so your online calendar sends you reminders about when parts of the project need to be completed. The reminders should keep you on schedule.

Online calendaring is easy, and it's a great way to stay organized. Give it a try.

Generating New Ideas

In today's technical workplace, it is difficult to overestimate the importance of innovation and creative thinking. The ability to "think outside the box" has become a tiresome cliché, but this overused phrase highlights the importance of being creative in the high-tech community. Your company's new products and services will only have a short lead time before competitors have answered with their own versions. So, the ability to generate new ideas and solutions is highly valued.

When you finish strategic planning, it's time to start being creative and "inventing" new ideas that will become the content of your technical documents.

Tips for Being More Creative

Being creative is the ability to come up with new ideas or alternatives for solving problems. Everyone values creativity, but creativity can also be threatening. After all, when you develop something completely new or you do something differently, you're shifting the power balance (MacLoed, 2009). More often than not, the people around you will react with skepticism to new ideas or new ways of doing things. People rarely embrace new ideas right away.

Here are a few guidelines to keep in mind as you begin inventing the content of your document.

CREATIVITY IS HARD WORK   Breakthrough ideas are usually the result of hard work and tough thinking. So, get to work and stop waiting for inspiration to arrive. You will usually figure out what you are doing *while you are working,* not while you are waiting to get to work.

PAY ATTENTION TO CHANGE   When you start a project, focus on the people, processes, and trends that are changing and evolving. Change is usually where you will find new opportunities. Be ready for failure, but don't worry about being wrong. Any entrepreneur or business leader will tell you that failure is common and expected. If you are afraid of being wrong, you won't create anything new.

BE PASSIONATE ABOUT WHAT YOU ARE DOING   Whether the task is interesting or boring, find a way to be passionate about doing it. A positive outlook will help you stay focused and find new ways to succeed. Above all, do it for yourself, not just for someone else.

HEAR NAYSAYERS, BUT DON'T ALWAYS LISTEN TO THEM   People are going to tell you "it won't work" or "it's been tried before." But if you think something will work, follow your instincts and try it out. You might be seeing the problem in a new way, or maybe your good idea's time has arrived. Let your intuitions guide you.

Inventing Ideas

All right, let's put that creativity to work. Sometimes the hardest part about starting a new project is just putting ideas and words on the screen. Fortunately, several *invention techniques* can help you get your ideas out there. Five of the best techniques for technical communication are logical mapping, brainstorming, freewriting, outlining/boxing, and using the journalist's questions. Try them all to see which one works best for you.

LOGICAL MAPPING   Logical mapping is a visual way to invent your ideas, helping you to discover their logical relationships.

To map the content of your document, start by putting your subject in the middle of the screen or a piece of blank paper. Put a circle or box around it. Then, start typing or writing your other ideas around the subject, and put circles or boxes around them (Figure 12.3).

Logical Mapping Software

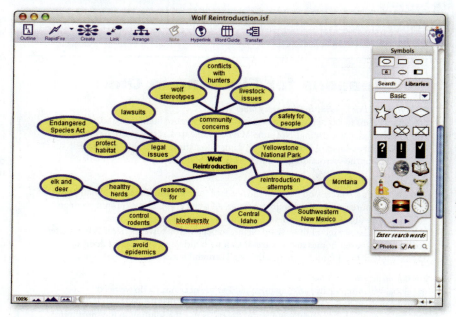

Figure 12.3: A variety of software packages, some of them free, are available for doing logical mapping. The program shown here, Inspiration, will help you map out your ideas. Then, it will turn them into an outline.

Source: Diagram created in Inspiration® by Inspiration Software®, Inc.

Now, fill the screen or page with words and phrases related to the subject. Start connecting related ideas by drawing lines among them. As you draw lines, you will begin to identify the major topics, concepts, or themes that will be important parts of the document you are writing. These major issues can be found in the clusters of your map.

Software programs such as Inspiration (shown in Figure 12.3), Visio, MindManager, and IHMC Concept Mapping Software can help you do logical mapping on screen. Otherwise, you can use the Draw function of your word processor to create "text boxes" and draw lines among them. With a little practice, you will find that you can create logical maps on the screen with little effort.

BRAINSTORMING OR LISTING   Some people like to make lists of their ideas rather than drawing concept maps. Make a quick list of everything you know or believe about your topic. One page or one screen is probably enough. Just write down any words or phrases that come to mind. You're brainstorming.

Then, pick out the best two or three ideas from your list. Make a second list in which you concentrate on these key ideas. Again, write down all the words and phrases that you can think up. Making two lists will force you to think more deeply about your subject while narrowing the scope of your project.

You can continue this brainstorming process indefinitely with a third or fourth list, but eventually you will find it difficult to come up with new ideas. At that point, you should be able to sort your lists into clusters of ideas. These clusters can then be mined for the major topics that will become the content of your text.

Freewriting

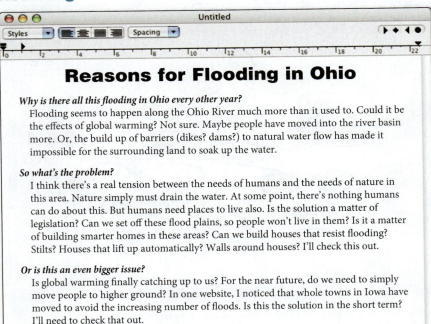

Figure 12.4: While free-writing, just get your ideas on the screen. Simply writing ideas down will help you locate important ideas and directions for research.

FREEWRITING   Freewriting is easy. Simply put your fingers on the keyboard and start typing into a document file in your word processor. Type for 5 to 10 minutes before you stop to look over your work. Don't worry about the usual constraints of writing such as sentences, paragraphs, grammatical correctness, or citations. Just keep typing. Eventually, you will find that you have filled one or more screens with words, sentences, and fragments of sentences (Figure 12.4).

You may or may not end up using many of the words and sentences in your freewriting draft, but the purpose of freewriting is to put your ideas on the screen. It helps you fight through writer's block.

When you're done freewriting, identify the two to five major items in your text that seem most important. Then, spend 5 to 10 minutes freewriting about each of these items separately. Like magic, within half an hour to an hour, your freewriting will probably give you the material you need to write your text.

OUTLINE OR BOXING   Outlines can be used throughout the drafting process. Most word-processing programs will allow you to draft in *Outline* mode or *Document Map* mode (Figure 12.5). Sometimes it helps to sketch an outline before you start drafting. That way, you can see how the document will be structured.

Boxing is less formal. As you plan your document, draw boxes on the screen or a piece of paper that show the major ideas or topics in your document (Figure 12.6). Then, type or write your ideas into the boxes. If you want to make multiple levels in your text, simply create boxes within boxes. You can use the Table function in your word-processing software to make boxes. When using the Table function, start out with a few boxes. Then, add cells to the table as you need more boxes.

Outlining or Document Mapping

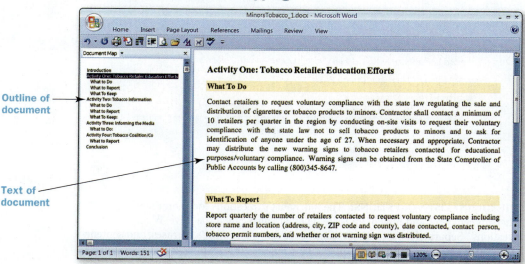

Figure 12.5: In Document Map mode, the computer automatically outlines your document on the left. This feature allows you to keep the whole structure of the document in mind as you work on individual parts.

Boxing

Figure 12.6: Boxing is like outlining. Each of the cells can be filled with your ideas. Then, you organize these ideas into a more structured document.

Introduction: Report on Flooding in Ohio

Purpose Statement: This report will provide strategies for managing flooding in the Ohio River Valley.

Main Point: Solving flooding means restoring wetlands and slowing development.

Importance of Subject: If we don't do something now, it will only become worse as the effects of global warming are felt.

Section One: The Problem

Development in Ohio River Valley

Increased water due to global warming

Additional dams and retaining walls

Section Two: The Plan

Restore wetlands

Limit development along rivers

Create holding reservoirs for water

Remove some retaining walls

Conclusions: We're Running Out of Time

We need to restore wetlands and lessen development on rivers

Advantages of these recommendations

The future

THE JOURNALIST'S QUESTIONS   The journalist's questions focus on the who, what, where, when, why, and how of an issue. They are also called the "Five-W and How questions." Separately, for each question, write down any words, phrases, and sentences that come to mind about your topic. These six questions will help you view your subject from a variety of viewpoints and perspectives.

Who was involved?

What happened?

Where did it happen?

When did it happen?

Why did it happen?

How did it happen?

When using the journalist's questions, pay special attention to anything about your subject that is changing or has changed. If you ask what has changed recently about your subject, you will likely focus in on what is most important about it.

In the workplace, people use a variety of strategies to be creative. The five described here are especially useful for writing technical documents, but you may have your own ways of generating new ideas. Whatever you do, don't be discouraged if your good ideas aren't always accepted. Creativity usually means change, and change can be intimidating to others. Every once in a while, though, an idea catches fire. Those moments make the effort of being creative worth it.

WHAT YOU NEED TO KNOW

- Developing a project plan is a process of identifying tasks and setting a timeline for completing them.

- Start out your project planning by listing your objectives and identifying your "top-rank objective."

- Create a task list and then put those tasks on a timeline.

- Strategic planning will lead to the need to generate new ideas and be creative.

- Being creative is hard work, but you should pay attention to change and trust your instincts.

- Logical mapping, brainstorming, freewriting, outlining/boxing, and the journalist's questions are good ways to generate new ideas.

- Creativity means change, so don't be discouraged if your good ideas are not accepted immediately.

Individual or Team Projects

1. For a project you are working on right now, go through the strategic planning process described in this chapter. First, list your objectives and identify a top-rank objective. Second, express that top-rank objective as a one-sentence purpose statement for the project. Third, create a task list of items that will need to be completed for the project. Fourth, put those tasks on a timeline or calendar and schedule any deadlines or meetings that will be part of the project. If you are working with a group, make sure everyone is following the same objectives, task list, and calendar.

2. In this chapter, you learned five different invention techniques to be creative and generate new ideas. Pick a technical subject. Then, use two different invention techniques to generate ideas about that subject. Compare and contrast the results. Which of the techniques worked better for this subject? Why? Which technique felt more comfortable to you? Is there something about the way you think that might make particular invention techniques more effective than others?

3. Use an Internet search engine to find advice about being creative. Find five ways to be creative that aren't mentioned in this chapter. Do you think these websites are offering good advice? What criticisms or skepticisms might you have about the advice they offer for being more creative? What are your criticisms and skepticisms about the advice offered in this chapter?

Collaborative Project

Imagine that you and your group have been hired to write a travel website about Quebec, Canada, and you need to go there for four days this spring to do your research. More than likely, most of you have never been to Quebec. It's a historic city in eastern Canada that reminds many people of an older European city. Quebec has great food, a fun nightlife, music, and arts and culture. It is also not far from great hiking, whale watching, and other outdoor experiences.

With your group, use listing or brainstorming to come up with a list of "objectives" that you would like to achieve during your trip. Check out Quebec on the Internet to decide on some of the things you would like to explore while you are there. Then, narrow your list to one top-rank objective and a few other major objectives that you would like to reach while you are on the trip.

Now, create a task list of major activities that you will do when you arrive in Quebec. Remember, you only have four days, so you will need to prioritize what you can experience while you are there. Also, the members of your group don't need to do everything together. You can go your separate ways, giving you a chance to explore more of Quebec.

Finally, use an online calendaring program to schedule your visit. On a four-day timeline, assign a time to each activity (task). Identify who will be going where and doing what each hour of the day. Also, schedule daily meetings or checkpoints in which your group will meet to catch up and make adjustments to the plan.

When you are finished, give your plan to your boss (your instructor) for approval.

Extra Challenge: Try to do this collaborative exercise virtually, without meeting face to face.

Visit My WritingLab for a Post-test and more technical writing resources.

Getting Back to Crazy

Lisa Stewart had been working for Fluke!, an Internet search company based in Silicon Valley, California. Her boss, Jack Hansen, would tell her stories about the exciting days when Fluke! began. He said new ideas were always welcome, no matter how crazy or far-fetched. He said there were only a dozen employees working long hours, so they could create just about anything they could imagine. Those were the good days.

One of those crazy ideas became an Internet search engine that made Fluke! a successful company. The search engine used social networking to rank information, products, and services. Advertisers loved it. Fluke! grew into a multi-million dollar company in one year.

Over the years, though, Fluke! had lost its edge. While other search engine companies, like Google, were always coming up with new products and services, the software engineers at Fluke! kept trying to improve its existing search engine. Fluke! was still well regarded, but revenues had dropped off sharply over the last few years.

So, the company's Board of Directors hired a new CEO, Amanda Jackson, who had a reputation for bringing established Silicon Valley companies back to life. The new CEO immediately put everyone in the company through a three-day workshop with "Creativity Engineers," who showed them how to be innovative and inventive. Most employees, including Lisa, were skeptical at first, but they learned a great deal. They were excited about creating some new products and getting back some of that Silicon Valley magic that Lisa's boss, Jack, was always talking about.

On a darker note, though, the new CEO also began circulating a rumor that the company would be going through a dramatic shake-up if creative new products weren't put in the pipeline. Whole teams of software engineers would be fired if they kept doing business as usual.

The Monday after the creativity workshop, Lisa came to work with some new ideas. She was ready to throw out some crazy thoughts to see if her team could come up with something new. Some of her other team members came in with new ideas, too.

Unfortunately, the creativity workshop didn't seem to have any effect on her boss, Jack. Their Monday morning team meeting was the same old boring discussion about how to adjust the Fluke! search engine to improve its speed. There was no talk of new products or crazy ideas.

After the meeting, Lisa was frustrated, and so were some of her fellow team members. Not only did they not have an opportunity to share new ideas, but Lisa was worried about the lack of innovation. If the new CEO was looking for people to fire for lack of creativity, Lisa's team was putting itself on the chopping block. Her boss, Jack, obviously didn't see the threat.

If you were Lisa, what would you do?

CHAPTER

13

Persuading Others

Persuading with Reasoning *344*

Persuading with Values *351*

Help: Persuading Readers Online *352*

Persuasion in High-Context Cultures *357*

What You Need to Know *361*

Exercises and Projects *361*

Case Study: Trying to Stay Neutral *363*

In this chapter, you will learn:

- How people are persuaded by reasoning and values.

- How to reason with logic, examples, and evidence to support your views.

- How to use values to appeal to common goals and ideals while using language familiar to your readers.

- About persuasion in high-context cultures.

When you have finished planning your project and generating ideas, you should spend some time developing your "persuasion strategy." Persuasion is not only about changing other people's minds. It is also about giving people good reasons to do things they might already want to do. In some cases, persuasion is about building someone else's confidence in you, your company, or your company's products and services.

Effective technical documents typically include a blend of reasoning-based and values-based persuasion strategies (Figure 13.1).

Persuading with Reasoning

Let's look at reasoning first. Reasoning is the use of logic and examples to show others the strengths and merits of your ideas. Reasoning has two basic forms:

Reasoning with logic—Using logically constructed statements such as *if . . . then, either . . . or, cause and effect, effect . . . because, costs and benefits,* and *better and worse*

Reasoning with examples and evidence—Using real or realistic statements, such as examples, prior experiences, facts, data, observations, and quotes from experts

Figure 13.2 shows a briefing that uses an assortment of logical statements, examples, and evidence to support its points.

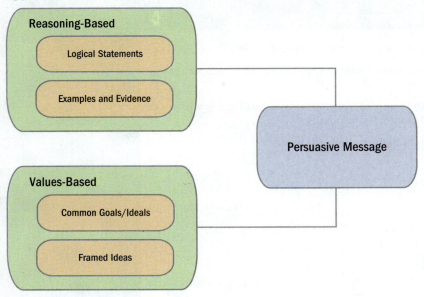

Types of Persuasion

Reasoning-Based
- Logical Statements
- Examples and Evidence

Values-Based
- Common Goals/Ideals
- Framed Ideas

Persuasive Message

Figure 13.1: Technical documents and presentations typically include a blend of reasoning-based and values-based statements.

A Document That Uses Reasoning

Influence of Competitive Food and Beverage Policies on Children's Diets and Childhood Obesity

Healthy Eating Research

Bridging the Gap

Issue Brief, July 2012

Introduction

Statistics are used to support claims.

More than 23 million children and adolescents in the United States—nearly one in three young people—are obese or overweight, putting them at risk for serious health problems. The foods and beverages available in schools have an influence on children's diets and their weight. In fact, children and adolescents consume more than 35 percent of their daily calories at school.

Outside of meal programs, schools sell many foods and beverages to students through à la carte lines in the cafeteria, vending machines, school stores, snack bars, canteens, fundraisers and other venues. Such snack foods often are high in fat, calories, sugar and/or salt, and offer minimal nutritional value. Many schools also sell a variety of unhealthy drinks to students, including high-fat milks and sugar-sweetened beverages (SSBs) such as soda, sports drinks and high-calorie fruit drinks.

A cause and effect statement defines a key term.

Collectively, the snacks and beverages sold or served outside of school meal programs are known as competitive foods because they compete with school meals for students' spending. Despite voluntary agreements by several snack and beverage manufacturers to remove unhealthy

competitive foods from schools, the majority of public school students, particularly middle and high school students, still have ready access to them (Figure 1).

This brief examines the emerging evidence about the influence of competitive food and beverage policies on children's diets and childhood obesity. The research clearly shows a need for comprehensive policies that govern the sale and consumption of these foods and beverages in the school environment.

This issue brief is based on a research review prepared by Jamie Chriqui, PhD, MHS, Health Policy Center in the Institute for Health Research and Policy at the University of Illinois at Chicago. The full research review, which includes citations, is available at www.healthyeatingresearch.org and www.bridgingthegapresearch.org.

Robert Wood Johnson Foundation

Healthy Eating Research and **Bridging the Gap** are programs of the Robert Wood Johnson Foundation.

Source: Robert Wood Johnson Foundation

(continued)

Figure 13.2: In this brief, scientist Jamie Chriqui, Ph.D., MHS, discusses the effects of competitive advertising on children's diets.

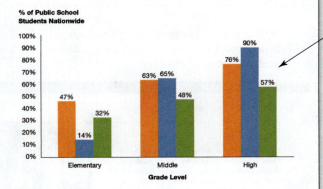

FIGURE 1

Percentage of U.S. Public School Students Nationwide with Access to Unhealthy Foods and Beverages in Competitive Venues by Grade Level, School Year 2009–10

% of Public School Students Nationwide

- ■ Sweet/Salty/High Fat Snacks
- ■ SSBs
- ■ 2% or Whole Milk

Elementary: 47%, 14%, 32%
Middle: 63%, 65%, 48%
High: 76%, 90%, 57%

Grade Level

A graph is used to illustrate data.

The Evidence

Competitive Food and Beverage Policies Influence the School Environment and Student Purchases

- Students purchase and consume fewer unhealthy snack foods and beverages, such as soda and other sugary drinks, high-fat milks, candy and chips, when policies prohibit or restrict schools from offering them. Such policies also increase the availability of healthier options, such as fruits and vegetables.

- Policies that prohibit or restrict unhealthy snack foods and beverages at school quickly and effectively reduce the availability and/or consumption of such products. In some cases, these reductions occurred only a few months after policies were implemented.

- The limited published, peer-reviewed evidence shows that food service revenues increase when schools restrict students' access to unhealthy snack foods and beverages. This is primarily because revenue from increased participation in school meal programs offsets initial declines in sales of competitive products.

Such Policies Influence Students' Diets and Possibly Even Their Weight

- Policies that restrict snack food and beverage offerings and limit portion sizes and the fat, sugar and calorie content of such products also are effective at reducing children's caloric intake.

- When policies allow schools to offer snack foods and beverages that are high in fat, sugar and calories, such items are more available and students consume more of them. Students also consume fewer healthier foods and beverages when schools offer unhealthy options.

- Limited evidence suggests that policies that allow unhealthy snack foods in schools are associated with increased body mass index (BMI) among students. Policies that restrict unhealthy snack foods are associated with lower proportions of overweight or obese students, or lower rates of increase in student BMI.

Cause and effect statements are used to explain trends.

2 **Issue Brief** | Influence of Competitive Food and Beverage Policies on Children's Diets and Childhood Obesity • July 2012

To Be Effective, Policies Must Be Comprehensive

- Policies that only apply to some venues but not all (e.g., to à la carte lines or vending machines, but not school stores) are not as effective as comprehensive policies that apply to all venues.

- Comprehensive policies are key to reducing students' access to and consumption of SSBs in schools. Policies that restrict only soda, but allow sports drinks and other SSBs, do not reduce the overall availability or consumption of SSBs.

- While one study found that school-based policies can affect children's total consumption of SSBs, both in and out of school, most studies show that school-based policies are not associated with students' dietary changes outside of school.

Conclusions and Policy Implications

Causes and effects of policies are explained.

The best evidence available indicates that policies on snack foods and beverages sold in school impact children's diets and their risk for obesity. Strong policies that prohibit or restrict the sale of unhealthy competitive foods and drinks in schools are associated with lower proportions of overweight or obese students, or lower rates of increase in student BMI. Such policies also may boost participation in school meal programs and increase food service revenues.

Better and worse arguments explain the pros and cons.

Research also suggests that when schools provide easy access to unhealthy snack foods and beverages, students consume more of them. Overall, student BMI tends to be higher in schools that sell unhealthy items in competitive venues. Because the school food environment affects the dietary behaviors and weight outcomes of millions of students across the country, implementing strong policies that support healthy eating could lead to sustained changes that would help reverse the childhood obesity epidemic, particularly if those changes were reinforced in environments outside of the school setting.

The federal government and many states, school districts and schools across the country have begun changing policies to create a healthier school environment. The following is a short summary of those efforts, including policy implications based on the findings reported in this brief.

At the Federal Level

As required by the Healthy, Hunger-Free Kids Act of 2010, the U.S. Department of Agriculture (USDA) is working to update national nutrition standards for competitive foods and beverages for the first time since 1979. The findings documented in this brief can help inform USDA in its efforts to develop strong, comprehensive competitive food and beverage standards for all schools across the country.

At the State Level

Costs and benefits are explained.

In the mid- to late-2000s, a number of states enacted or strengthened their competitive food and beverage laws to provide guidance and promote uniformity across districts working to implement their wellness policies. Findings from this brief can help inform policy-makers about effective strategies for restricting or removing unhealthy foods from schools. These results also show that such policies have an almost immediate effect on improving students' diets. Increasing awareness of the link between strong policies and healthier behaviors is one strategy for motivating key decision-makers to support policy changes.

(continued)

At the District and School Level

The federal government required all school districts participating in federal child nutrition programs to implement a wellness policy by the 2006–07 school year. Because it was required to be a part of the wellness policies, most districts do have a policy that addresses foods sold outside of school meals. However, many wellness policies do not set guidelines for all competitive venues, nor do they align with current nutritional recommendations. Further, many districts that have established a wellness policy have not yet implemented its provisions, especially those related to competitive foods and beverages. The findings presented in this brief suggest that districts and schools should continue to strengthen their own nutritional guidelines for competitive products, in order to help students consume a healthier diet. Implementing strong policies for competitive foods also may help districts and schools build revenue, through increased participation in school meal programs.

This issue brief is based on a research review prepared by Jamie Chriqui, PhD, MHS, Health Policy Center in the Institute for Health Research and Policy at the University of Illinois at Chicago. The full research review, which includes citations, is available at www.healthyeatingresearch.org and www.bridgingthegapresearch.org.

 Scan to view the full research review.

About Healthy Eating Research

Healthy Eating Research is a national program of the Robert Wood Johnson Foundation. Technical assistance and direction are provided by the University of Minnesota School of Public Health under the direction of Mary Story, PhD, RD, program director, and Karen M. Kaphingst, MPH, deputy director. The Healthy Eating Research program supports research to identify, analyze, and evaluate environmental and policy strategies that can promote healthy eating among children and prevent childhood obesity. Special emphasis is given to research projects that benefit children and adolescents ages 3 to 18 and their families, especially in lower-income and racial and ethnic populations at highest risk for obesity.

University of Minnesota
School of Public Health
1300 South 2nd St., Suite 300
Minneapolis, MN 55454
www.healthyeatingresearch.org

About Bridging the Gap

Bridging the Gap is a nationally recognized research program of the Robert Wood Johnson Foundation dedicated to improving the understanding of how policies and environmental factors influence diet, physical activity and obesity among youth, as well as youth tobacco use. The program identifies and tracks information at the state, community and school levels; measures change over time; and shares findings that will help advance effective solutions for reversing the childhood obesity epidemic and preventing young people from smoking. Bridging the Gap is a joint project of the University of Illinois at Chicago's Institute for Health Research and Policy and the University of Michigan's Institute for Social Research.

For more information, visit
www.bridgingthegapresearch.org.

About the Robert Wood Johnson Foundation

The *Robert Wood Johnson Foundation* focuses on the pressing health and health care issues facing our country. As the nation's largest philanthropy devoted exclusively to health and health care, the Foundation works with a diverse group of organizations and individuals to identify solutions and achieve comprehensive, measurable, and timely change.

For 40 years the Foundation has brought experience, commitment, and a rigorous, balanced approach to the problems that affect the health and health care of those it serves. When it comes to helping Americans lead healthier lives and get the care they need, the Foundation expects to make a difference in your lifetime. For more information, visit www.rwjf.org. Follow the Foundation on Twitter www.rwjf.org/twitter or Facebook www.rwjf.org/facebook.

Route 1 and College Road East
P.O. Box 2316
Princeton, NJ 08543–2316
www.rwjf.org

4 **Issue Brief** | Influence of Competitive Food and Beverage Policies on Children's Diets and Childhood Obesity • July 2012

Reasoning with Logic

Logic offers you a variety of ways to persuade your readers. When using logic, you are trying to appeal to your readers' common sense or beliefs. Logic allows you to build more complex ideas from simpler facts. When using logical reasoning, you are essentially saying things like, "If you believe X, then you should also believe Y," or "Either you believe X, or you believe Y," or "X is happening because Y happened."

IF . . . THEN   Perhaps the most common logical pattern is the *if . . . then* statement. When using *if . . . then* statements, you persuade your readers by demonstrating that something they already believe leads logically to something else they should also accept. You are basically saying, "If you believe X, then you should also believe Y."

> If we are going to be ready for next summer's hurricane season, then we cannot wait until next spring to begin planning.

> Internet thieves will be able to steal your identity if you don't take steps to protect yourself.

Link

For more on using *if . . . then* and *either . . . or* statements, go to Chapter 15, page 408.

EITHER . . . OR   When using *either . . . or* statements, you are offering your readers a choice between two paths. You are telling them, "Either you believe X or you believe Y."

> Either we take steps to control crime in our area or we risk handing over our streets to criminals.

> We need to either start redesigning the car to use a hybrid engine or take the risky path of hoping oil prices drop dramatically over the next few years.

Either . . . or statements can be risky because readers may choose the path you didn't want them to take, or they may reject both choices. So, you need to make the "correct" path obvious to them if you want them to go in a particular direction.

CAUSE AND EFFECT   When using *cause and effect* statements, you are demonstrating to your readers how specific causes lead to specific effects. You are showing them that "X is caused by Y."

> Gradually, desertification causes a dryland, such as the Sonoran Desert, to lose its ability to support plants and animals.

> The effects of this problem can be sobering. Last year, intoxicated drivers caused 83 accidents in Holt County, killing four people and costing taxpayers $1.1 million.

Link

For more help with using cause and effect and costs and benefits statements, go to Chapter 15, page 403.

Similarly, the word *because* can also signal a cause and effect relationship:

> The Stonyridge Windfarm project should be approved because it will generate electricity and revenue without further polluting our area.

> The Internet went down repeatedly over the summer because the server kept crashing.

COSTS AND BENEFITS   When trying to persuade people, you might find it helpful to show them the *costs and benefits* of your ideas. In most cases, you will want to show them that the benefits outweigh the costs by saying something like "The benefits of doing X will be worth the cost, Y." In some cases, though, you might point out that the costs would be too high for the few benefits gained.

> Building a wireless network in the fraternity house will require an up-front investment, but we would save money because each member would no longer have to pay the phone company for a separate DSL line.

> Since St. Elizabeth Hospital's main building has become obsolete in almost every way, the benefits of remodeling it would not justify the costs.

BETTER AND WORSE   Another persuasive strategy is to show that your ideas are better than the alternatives. You are arguing that "X is better/worse than Y."

> In 2013, we decided to go with AMD's FX-9590 microprocessor for our gaming-dedicated computers. The other chips on the market just couldn't match its balance of speed and reliability.

> In the long run, we would be better off implementing our automation plan right now, while we are retooling the manufacturing plant. If we wait, automating the lines will be almost impossible as we return to full capacity.

Reasoning with Examples and Evidence

Examples and evidence allow you to reason with your readers by showing them real or realistic support for your claims.

FOR EXAMPLE   Using an example is a good way to clarify and support a complex idea while making it seem more realistic to readers. You should say something like, "For example, X happened, which is similar to what we are experiencing now."

> For example, some parasitoid wasps inject polydnaviruses into the egg or larva of the moth host. The wasp eggs survive in the host's body because the virus suppresses the immunity of the host.

> If, for instance, a high-speed railway were to be built between Albuquerque and Santa Fe, commuters would cut their commuting times in half while avoiding the dangerous 50-mile drive.

Phrases like *for example, for instance, in a specific case, to illustrate* and *such as* signal that you are using an example.

EXPERIENCES AND OBSERVATIONS   Personal experiences and observations can often be persuasive as long as readers trust the credibility of the source. You are telling your readers, "I have seen/experienced X before, so I know Y is likely true."

> While we were in the Arctic Circle, we observed a large male polar bear kill and devour a cub, turning to cannibalism to survive.

Link

For more help with using empirical observations, go to Chapter 14, page 374.

When our team began closely monitoring the medications of schizophrenic prisoners at the Oakwood Correctional Facility, we observed a dramatic decline in the number of hallucinations and delusional episodes among the prisoners.

FACTS AND DATA   Empirically proven facts and data generated from experiments and measurements can offer some of the strongest forms of evidence. People generally trust observed facts and numbers.

The facts about influenza epidemics on college campuses are amazing. A 2012 study on college campuses showed that 5 out of 10 students will become infected when the virus finds its way into a dormitory. (Venn, p. 15)

Recently published data shows that for every child who may experience a prolonged benefit from the hemophilus vaccine, two to three children may develop vaccine-induced diabetes. (Akers & Wilson, p. 126)

Always remember to cite any sources when referring to facts and data.

AT A GLANCE	Reasoning-Based Persuasion
	• *If . . . then*
	• *Either . . . or*
	• Cause and effect
	• Costs and benefits
	• Better and worse
	• *For example,*
	• Experiences and observations
	• Facts and data
	• Quotes from experts

QUOTES FROM EXPERTS   A recognized authority on a subject can also be used to support your points. You can use quotes as evidence to back up your claims.

Dr. Jennifer Xu, a scientist at Los Alamos National Laboratory, recently stated, "Our breakthroughs in research on edge localized modes (ELMs) demonstrate that we are overcoming the hurdles to fusion nuclear power" (Xu, 2006).

The lead biologist for the study, Jim Filks, told us that mercury levels in fish from the Wildcat Creek had dropped 18 percent over the last ten years, but levels were still too high for the fish to be safely consumed.

Link

For more ideas about using interviews and observations to collect information, go to Chapter 14, page 374.

Persuading with Values

Values-based persuasion can be more subtle than reasoning-based persuasion. Values-based persuasion is effective because people prefer to say yes to someone who holds the same values and beliefs as they do (Lakoff, 2004). Moreover, confidence and trust go a long way toward convincing people what to believe and what to do.

Values-based persuasion uses two forms:

Goals and ideals—The use of goals, needs, values, and attitudes that you share with your readers

Frames—The use of words, phrases, and themes that reflect your readers' point of view and values

Persuading Readers Online

The Internet offers some interesting persuasion challenges because influencing people is usually best done in person. So, if you need to persuade someone through e-mail, websites, or text messages, you might need to be a little more creative. Noah Goldstein and Steve Martin are researchers who have compiled persuasive strategies into a book called *Yes! 50 Scientifically Proven Ways to Be Persuasive*. Here are ten of their strategies that work well in online situations.

DECREASE THE NUMBER OF OPTIONS   Give clients only a few options, because having too many choices could actually cause them to hesitate and seek a simpler solution.

LABEL THE READER INTO A SPECIFIC GROUP   If you accurately label the person you are trying to persuade (e.g., "engineering major," "doctor," or "instructor") they are more likely to respond favorably.

TELL PEOPLE THEIR PRIOR BELIEFS WERE CORRECT   People don't like to be inconsistent, so they will often cling to prior beliefs for the sake of consistency. So, assure them that their prior beliefs were correct under the old conditions, but new conditions call for them to think and act differently than before.

ASK THEM TO HELP   Readers respond more positively if they think you are asking them to help in some way. Instead of explaining what you need or what you want them to do, ask them for their help in figuring out how to solve the problem.

ADMIT YOU WERE WRONG (IF YOU WERE)   If a product or service didn't work as expected, taking responsibility will actually build trust in readers. In other words, an admission that the team or company came up short is persuasive because it shows you're working toward improvement.

USE "YOU" TO REFER TO READERS   People from Western cultures respond favorably to the word "you" in persuasive situations (e.g., "You will receive the following services"). Interestingly, though, people from Eastern cultures tend to respond more favorably to statements that signal a service or product will be best for all.

USE THE WORD "BECAUSE" TO MAKE YOUR ARGUMENTS SOUND RATIONAL   Simply adding the word "because" to your explanations will signal that you have thought things through and are being reasonable.

RHYME PHRASES TO MAKE THEM MORE CONVINCING   You probably remember rhymes like "An apple a day keeps the doctor away," or "If it doesn't fit, you must acquit." Rhymed phrases are easier to agree with, even if they sound hokey.

CREATE AN IMPRESSION OF SCARCITY   Suggest that the product or service will be available in limited amounts or for a short time.

FACE TIME BEATS E-MAIL TIME   Studies show that people reach agreement and resolve problems better face to face than through e-mail. So, ask yourself whether a meeting or a phone call would be more effective.

When using values-based persuasion, you are trying to convince readers to *identify* with you, your company, or your company's products and services. Advertisers spend billions each year appealing to consumers' sense of values to develop product identification (Figure 13.3). When a company succeeds in associating itself with a particular set of positive values, its written materials will be much more effective.

Appealing to Common Goals and Ideals

To appeal to common goals and ideals, you should begin by looking closely at the profile you developed of your readers, which was discussed in Chapter 2. This profile will contain clues about your readers' goals, needs, values, and attitudes.

Link

For more information about profiling readers, turn to Chapter 2, page 19.

GOALS   Almost all people have personal and professional goals they are striving to reach, and so do most companies. If possible, discuss your readers' goals with them. Then, in your document, you can show them how your product or services will help them reach those goals.

> Solar power will maintain the appearance of your home while adding value. From the street, photovoltaic shingles look just like normal roofing materials, but they will give you energy independence, save you money, and increase the value of your home.

> By renovating Centennial Park, Mason City will go a long way toward reaching its goal of becoming a town that promotes a lifestyle of learning and leisure.

NEEDS   A fundamental difference exists between needs and goals. *Needs* are the basic requirements for survival.

> Your just-in-time manufacturing process requires suppliers to have parts ready to ship within hours. We can guarantee that parts will be shipped within one hour of your order.

> Equipment in the operating room must be sterilized with alcohol to ensure our patients' safety.

If you aren't sure what your readers need, ask them. They will usually be very specific about what they require.

SHARED VALUES   Spend some time identifying any values that your readers, you, and your company have in common. For example, if your readers stress high-quality service, more than likely, they will want to work with suppliers who also value high quality.

> If you have any questions or problems with your custom CAD software, we have engineers available 24/7 through our website and over the phone. When you call, a person, not a machine, will answer the phone.

> Like your organization, our company has a "People First" policy, which we believe is essential in keeping our employees satisfied and productive.

You can usually find shared values by looking on your readers' websites.

Appealing to Values

Figure 13.3:
The purpose of this booklet is to help new diabetes patients adjust to a different lifestyle. The authors appeal to the readers' values to help them make the transition.

Start Here: Living With Type 2 Diabetes

First, take a deep breath.

You have type 2 diabetes. And yes, it's a big deal. But you know what? It's also something you can deal with. And the American Diabetes Association is here to help.

When people first find out that they have diabetes, they sometimes find it really scary, or sad, or even hard to believe. After all, you probably don't feel sick, or any different than you felt before you were told you have diabetes. And yet it is very important to take this disease seriously.

Some people who learn they have diabetes worry that it means their life is over, or that they won't be able to do everything they used to do. Neither of those things is true. What is true is that you may need to change some things about your daily routine. It's not your fault that you got diabetes, but it is your job to take care of yourself.

Luckily, there's a lot that you can do to keep yourself healthy. This booklet will give you the first steps for taking control of your diabetes.

4   www.diabetes.org    American Diabetes Association.   1-800-DIABETES

Words like "sick" or "worry" appeal to the readers' values of health and confidence

The use of "you" appeals to the readers.

Readers identify with people who are happy.

Source: American Diabetes Association

Medicines

Your doctor may prescribe medicine to help get and keep your blood glucose in your target range. There are different types of diabetes medicines that work in different ways to lower blood glucose. Your doctor may prescribe more than one to help you get to your target range. Some people with type 2 diabetes take both pills and insulin or insulin by itself.

If you are starting new medicines, ask your doctor, pharmacist or diabetes educator the following questions:

- How many pills do I take?
- How often should I take them, and when?
- Should I take my medicine on an empty stomach or with food?
- What if I forget to take my medicine and remember later?
- What side effects could I have?
- What should I do if I have side effects?
- Will my diabetes medicine cause a problem with any of my other medicines?

If you think you are having side effects from your medicine, or have questions, call your doctor or pharmacist. Don't stop taking it unless the doctor tells you to. Remember, your medicine will work best if you also make healthy changes to how you eat and if you are active.

Questions are provided that reflect typical concerns that patients might have.

Images of medical personnel are used to build confidence.

Where Do I Begin?   ▲ American Diabetes Association.   Enroll Today!   13

Link

For more strategies on identifying shared values through the Internet, go to Chapter 2, page 21.

ATTITUDES   A reader's attitude toward your subject, you, or your company can greatly determine whether your message is persuasive. So, you might use your reader's positive attitude to your advantage or show understanding when the reader has a negative attitude.

> Purchasing your first new car can be exciting and just a little bit stressful. This guide was created to help you survive your first purchase.

> Like you, we're always a bit nervous when our company upgrades operating systems on all its computers. The process, though, is mostly painless, and the improved speed and new features are worth the effort.

Words alone will rarely change someone's attitude, but you can show that you empathize with your readers' point of view. Perhaps your readers will give you a chance if they think you understand how they feel about the subject.

Framing Issues from the Readers' Perspective

Being persuasive often means seeing and describing an issue from your readers' perspective. Linguists and psychologists call this *framing* an issue (Lakoff, 2004, p. 24). By properly framing or reframing an issue, you can appeal to your readers' sense of values.

Link

For more help on using style persuasively, go to Chapter 17, page 437.

FRAMING   To frame an issue, you should look closely at the profile you developed of the readers. Locate the one or two words or phrases that best characterize your readers' perspective on the issue. For example, let's say your readers are interested in *progress*. Your profile shows that they see the world in terms of *growth* and *advancement*. You can use logical mapping to develop a frame around that concept.

In Figure 13.4, for example, the word "progress" was put in the middle of the screen to create a logical map of ideas. Then, words and phrases that cluster around "progress" were added. As you fill in the logical map, it should show you the frame from which your readers understand the issue you are discussing. Knowing their frame will help you choose content and phrasing that support or reinforce their point of view.

Values-Based Persuasion
• Goals
• Needs
• Shared values
• Attitudes
• Framing
• Reframing

AT A GLANCE

REFRAMING   In some cases, your readers might not see an issue in a way that is compatible with your or your company's views. In these situations, you may need to "reframe" the issue for them. To reframe an issue, look a little deeper into your reader profile to find a value that you and your readers share. Once you locate a common value, you can use logical mapping to reframe the issue in a way that appeals to your readers. For example, the poster in Figure 13.5 shows how NASA is trying to reframe the debate over humans traveling to the moon. They recognize that some people may be skeptical about the need to go to the moon. So, they reframe the argument around common values that most readers will share.

Using Logical Mapping to Create a Frame

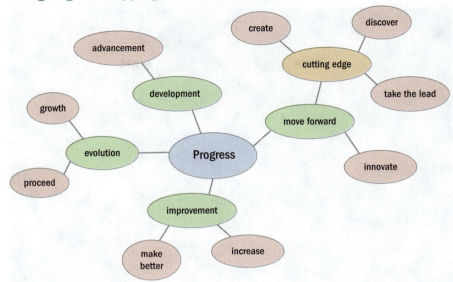

Figure 13.4: Framing is a useful way to describe an idea through the readers' point of view. Here, a logical map shows how the word "progress" would be framed.

Persuasion in High-Context Cultures

Transcultural communication can be difficult, but persuasion is especially challenging when the audience or readers are from a "high-context" culture. High-context cultures, which include many in Asia, the Middle East, and sub-Saharan Africa, usually put more emphasis on community than on individuals. These cultures also often put a high value on consensus, interpersonal harmony, hierarchy, and rituals. They tend to stress long-term goals over short-term gains.

What is not said in a conversation is often very significant, because people from high-context cultures rely on *contextual cues* to interpret what a speaker means. As a result, negotiators from low-context cultures, such as Europe, the Americas, and Australia, tend to mistakenly believe that high-context negotiators are inefficient, indirect, vague, and ambiguous. Meanwhile, negotiators from high-context cultures, such as Japan, China, Korea, Indonesia, and parts of Africa, often find their low-context counterparts, especially Americans, to be abrupt, aggressive, and far too emotional.

Persuasion and negotiation are still important in high-context cultures, but the interactions are more subtle and indirect. Here are some guidelines to help you navigate such interactions:

Guideline 1: Develop long-term relationships—High-context cultures put a high value on existing relationships and reputations. Spend time familiarizing your readers with your company and explaining its reputation in the

Reframing by Using Common Values

Argues that "real benefits" are to be gained from the mission.

Identifies six benefits (values) that are held by most people.

Uses an image with a child to encourage readers to think about the future.

National Aeronautics and Space Administration

WHY THE MOON?

THE DAWN OF THE TRUE SPACE AGE LIES AHEAD OF US.

In the not-too-distant future, people around the world will be able to look through a telescope and see evidence of human and robotic exploration on the moon. In 2004, President Bush directed NASA to send humans back to the lunar surface – this time to stay – and to get ready for a journey to Mars. Since then, we've determined what transportation we'll need, set goals for our activities, identified real benefits of exploring the moon, and even started building the spacecraft to get us there. We'll spend 2007 maturing our ideas on the equipment that future lunar-explorers will need to accomplish these exciting plans.

WHATEVER WE DO, IT WILL BE FOR THE BENEFIT OF ALL MANKIND.

Human Civilization
Extend human presence to the moon to enable eventual settlement.

Global Partnerships
Provide a challenging, shared and peaceful activity that unites nations in pursuit of common objectives.

Scientific Knowledge
Pursue scientific activities that address our fundamental questions about the history of Earth, the solar system and the universe -- and about our place in them.

Economic Expansion
Expand Earth's economic sphere and conduct lunar activities with benefits to life on the home planet.

Exploration Preparation
Test technologies, systems, flight operations and exploration techniques to reduce the risks and increase the productivity of future missions to Mars and beyond.

Public Engagement
Use a vibrant space exploration program to engage the public, encourage students and help develop the high-tech workforce that will be required to address the challenges of tomorrow.

BECAUSE HUMANS EXPLORE

"The earth is the cradle of mind, but one cannot forever live in a cradle."
– Konstantin Tsiolkovsky, 1896

www.nasa.gov

Source: NASA

Figure 13.5: In this poster, NASA uses several common values to argue that travel to the moon is important. NASA's goal is to overcome public skepticism about the cost and necessity of the program.

The answer to the question "Why the Moon?" appeals to an assumed trait of humanity—a desire to explore.

Working in High-Context Cultures

Readers from high-context cultures often use different forms of persuasion.

field. This will take time, because companies and governments from high-context cultures tend to think long term. Your company may need to invest years of effort to build a strong relationship with a company from a high-context culture.

Guideline 2: Use intermediaries to build relationships—In high-context cultures, strangers tend to be handled with caution. So, you might look for a trusted intermediary who knows both parties to help you make connections.

Guideline 3: Rely on facts and reasoning—In high-context cultures, attempts to persuade directly are often viewed negatively. So, a fact-based presentation with solid reasoning tends to be much more effective.

Guideline 4: Avoid arguing strongly for or against—Outward argumentativeness can be viewed as threatening and disrespectful and is often counterproductive. Moreover, arguing directly against someone else's position might be perceived as an attack on that person. Instead, if you disagree with someone, restate the facts of your ideas and use reasoning to explain them.

Guideline 5: Strive to reach consensus—Social harmony is greatly valued in high-context cultures. So, you should strive for consensus with your high-context counterparts. They will tend to react skeptically to plans in which one side seems to benefit more than another. Instead, your ideas will be most persuasive if you present them as a win–win for both sides.

Guideline 6: Speak collectively, not individually—To maintain social harmony, you should tend toward speaking collectively ("we" or "us") rather than individually ("I" or "me"). Avoid saying something like, "Here's my opinion." Instead, strive to characterize what is best for all.

Guideline 7: Be patient and wait for the "point"—People from high-context cultures often approach complex issues holistically, discussing all issues at the same time. To a low-context person, it can seem as though nothing is being decided. People from low-context cultures tend to be eager to "get to the point," while people from high-context cultures usually assume the point is obvious and need not be stated. The point of a discussion or document will tend to arrive near the end, so you should be patient and wait for it.

Guideline 8: Remember that "no" is rarely used—Direct refusal, rejection, and the answer "no" tend to be avoided in high-context cultures, especially in professional settings. A direct refusal can be considered an insult. So, refusals are handled with some care. If you are being refused, you might hear a deferral like, "We will consider your ideas." In some cases, as in Indonesia, you may receive an initial "yes" with a later "but" that signals the refusal. When a "no" needs to be conveyed, often an intermediary will be asked to deliver the bad news.

Guideline 9: Don't be informal—In high-context cultures, hierarchy and rituals are important, and respect for social status is expected. In professional settings, people from high-context cultures tend to address each other formally. The American tendency to quickly become informal and familiar (e.g., "You can just call me Jim") can be viewed as disrespectful or aggressive. Even when you know someone well, you should address that person by title and demonstrate respect for his or her position.

Guideline 10: Defer to hierarchy—High-context cultures tend to put great emphasis on hierarchy and social standing. A person of lower standing is expected to defer to someone of higher standing. Meanwhile, causing someone of higher standing to become embarrassed or agitated, even accidentally, will usually undermine or scuttle any negotiations.

Link

For more strategies on communicating with transcultural readers, go to Chapter 2, page 24.

Guideline 11: Minimize emotions—Smiles are welcome in high-context cultures, but obvious signs of emotion, like anger, hilarity, annoyance, or bemusement, will usually be taken far more seriously than they would in low-context cultures. Losing your composure is almost a sure way to end a professional relationship.

Research is always helpful if you need to communicate with people from another culture. A surprising amount of helpful information can be found on the web.

As technical fields globalize, North Americans are finding it helpful to learn how other cultures operate. To be persuasive, you should learn how people from the target culture tend to think and negotiate. Listen carefully and don't become too frustrated when you make mistakes.

- All technical documents are persuasive in some way, even those that are intended to be strictly "informational."

- Persuasion is about giving people good reasons to do things, while building their confidence in you and your company.

- Technical workplaces tend to rely on reasoning-based persuasion and values-based persuasion.

- Reasoning-based persuasion relies on logic, examples, and evidence to support claims.

- Values-based persuasion uses shared ideals, mutual values, common goals, and credibility to build and strengthen relationships.

- Transcultural communication can be difficult, but persuasion is especially challenging when the audience or readers are from a high-context culture.

Individual or Team Projects

1. Compare and contrast two technical documents that are being used to persuade their audiences. In a PowerPoint presentation, show why one document is more persuasive than the other. How does the more persuasive document use reasoning and values to persuade readers? What would make the other document more persuasive?

2. Find websites that use images and graphics to set a particular tone. How persuasive are the images? Why do you think they persuade or don't persuade the readers? If you were the intended reader of the website, what would make the website more persuasive to you? What would make you do what the authors of the website want you to do?

3. Write a white paper to your class that studies the persuasion strategies of a culture other than your own. For example, you might explore persuasion strategies in China or France. What would typical people from these cultures find persuasive? And what would be the most effective way to persuade them, without offending them? You can learn more about white papers in Chapter 9.

Collaborative Project

Ask one of your team members to bring in a common household product (e.g., toaster, popcorn popper, video game, mobile phone, etc.). Using reasoning-based and values-based persuasion strategies, develop a strategy to promote this item to college students—in other words, people much like your classmates. What would be some of your best arguments in favor of the product? How would you downplay any weaknesses? How might you use the buyers' values to urge them to identify with the product?

Now, let's change the target readers. Imagine that you need to promote this same product to people who are 60 years old or older. How might your persuasion strategies change? What kinds of reasoning would be more appropriate for this audience? How might you encourage them to value the product by identifying with it?

In a 5-minute presentation to your class, compare and contrast your team's strategies for marketing the product to college students and older people. How would your strategies be similar? How would they differ? How might these differences affect the organization, style, and design of the documentation that goes with the product?

Visit MyWritingLab for a Post-test and more technical writing resources.

Trying to Stay Neutral

Tom Young is a computer engineer for VinTel, a growing fiberoptic telecommunications company in the northeastern United States. Recently, the CEO of VinTel, Ben Hammonds, stumbled into a messy public relations mess when he told a reporter that VinTel is against net neutrality. Net neutrality would mean that telecommunications companies, like VinTel, would be required to offer equal access to all Internet content and applications. A non-neutral net would allow VinTel to slow or even block some kinds of content from reaching users.

VinTel's CEO didn't seem to have a full grasp of the issue when the reporter asked about it during an interview. He said, "We should be able

to block whatever we want. We don't plan to, but we should keep the right to do so. They are our fiberoptic cables. We invested in them, not some guy downloading porn."

The media went a bit over the top with the story. The defenders of net neutrality argued vigorously that VinTel would be in the business of censoring free speech and even restricting access to the press. On the other side, opponents of net neutrality argued that companies should have the right and even the responsibility to block the flow of illegal or unsavory activities. As an example, they pointed out that full net neutrality would aid money laundering, cyberterrorism, child pornography, cyberstalking, and perhaps even terrorist acts.

In reality, Tom, as an engineer, knew VinTel's position against net neutrality had little to do with people's rights or security. The company simply wanted to create a laddered payment model that would allow it to charge more money for faster and wider access to the Internet. Customers would need to pay more if they wanted to stream movies or use their broadband connection as a phone. These activities required more bandwidth, and therefore VinTel felt it should be able to charge more for these kinds of usage.

Personally, Tom was a supporter of net neutrality, even though his company was not. He thought it was unethical to decide for customers what kinds of content they should access over the Internet. He also knew his company was only restricting access to movies and peer-to-peer (P2P) services as a way to get customers to pay more. There was no technological reasons for slowing down or blocking these kinds of services. Fiberoptic cables and VinTel's advanced servers could easily handle even the heaviest broadband usage.

Plus, he was worried that some day in the future, the absence of net neutrality could allow companies to snoop on their users. In order to figure out what kinds of services users were consuming, companies might need to look in on people's viewing and usage habits. Tom thought that was an invasion of their privacy that could be exploited.

Yesterday, though, Tom's supervisor came in to give him a "rush" assignment. Tom was supposed to come up with some talking points about net neutrality that VinTel's CEO could use with interviewers in the future. The CEO didn't want to get burned on this issue again. In other words, Tom would be coming up with arguments for a position that he thought was unethical.

If you were Tom, how would you handle this situation? You don't want to quit your job, but you also don't want to support an argument that you find unethical. Do some research on the issue of net neutrality to figure out what you would do. If you were Tom, how would you persuade people to see things your way? Or, would you just write the talking points?

CHAPTER

14

Researching in Technical Workplaces

Beginning Your Research 365

Step 1: Define Your Research
 Subject 366

Step 2: Formulate a Research
 Question or Hypothesis 368

Step 3: Develop a Research
 Methodology 368

Step 4: Collect Evidence Through
 Sources 371

Step 5: Triangulate Your Sources
 375

Step 6: Take Careful Notes 378

Help: Using a Citation Manager
 385

Step 7: Appraise Your Evidence
 387

Step 8: Revise, Accept, or Abandon
 Your Hypothesis 390

What You Need to Know 390

Exercises and Projects 391

Case Study: The Life of a Dilemma
 393

In this chapter, you will learn:

- How to define your research subject using concept mapping to describe its boundaries.

- How to formulate a research question or hypothesis that will guide your research.

- How to develop a research methodology and revise it as needed.

- Methods for triangulating evidence to ensure reliability.

- Strategies for careful note taking.

- How to appraise evidence to ensure its reliability.

Research is a process of inquiring, describing, and explaining the world around us. In the technical workplace, research is usually done for practical reasons. It is used to gather information, test concepts, measure safety, and ensure the reliability of products, procedures, and models. Like all research, the goal of workplace research is to find truth. However, workplace researchers are usually collecting evidence that helps them solve a problem, gain insight, improve results, or prevent wrong turns.

When doing research in the workplace, you will typically blend your own empirical observations with existing evidence that is available through computer networks, archives, and libraries. You need to be an information manager who evaluates, prioritizes, interprets, stores, and shares the information you collect.

Beginning Your Research

In technical fields, researchers typically use a combination of primary and secondary sources to gain a full understanding of a particular subject.

Primary sources—Evidence collected from observations, experiments, surveys, interviews, ethnographies, and testing

Secondary sources—Evidence drawn from academic journals, magazine articles, books, websites, research databases, DVDs, CDs, and reference materials

Most researchers begin their research by first locating the secondary sources available on their subject. Once they have a thorough understanding of their subject, they use primary research to expand on these existing materials.

Empirical research is a critical part of working in technical disciplines.

A Research Process

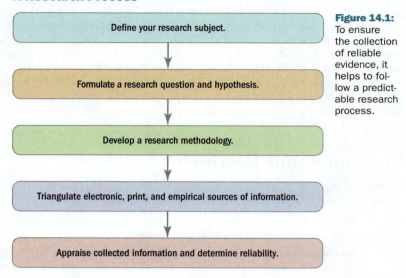

Figure 14.1: To ensure the collection of reliable evidence, it helps to follow a predictable research process.

Your research with primary and secondary sources should follow a process similar to this:

1. Define your research subject.
2. Formulate a research question or hypothesis.
3. Develop a research methodology.
4. Collect evidence through sources.
5. Triangulate your sources.
6. Take careful notes.
7. Appraise your evidence.
8. Revise, accept, or abandon your hypothesis.

A good research process begins by clearly defining the research subject. Then, it follows a research methodology in which a variety of sources are located and appraised for reliability (Figure 14.1).

Step 1: Define Your Research Subject

Your first task is to define your research subject as clearly as possible. You should begin by identifying what you already know about the subject and highlighting areas where you need to do more research.

Mapping Out Your Ideas

A reliable way to start is to develop a *concept map* of your research subject (Figure 14.2). To create a concept map, write your subject in the middle of your screen or on a piece of paper. Then, around that subject, begin jotting down everything you already know or believe about it. As you find relationships among these ideas, you can draw lines connecting them into clusters. In places where you are not sure of yourself, simply put down your thoughts and write question marks (?) after them.

Mapping is widely used in technical disciplines, and it is gaining popularity in highly scientific and technical research where visual thinking is being used to enhance creativity. You might find it strange to begin your research by drawing circles and lines, but mapping will reveal relationships that you would not otherwise discover.

Narrowing Your Research Subject

After defining your subject, you also need to look for ways to narrow and focus your research. Often, when people start the research process, they begin with a very broad subject (e.g., nuclear waste, raptors, lung cancer). Your concept map and a brief search on the Internet will soon show you that these kinds of subjects are too large for you to handle in the time available.

General Subject (too broad)	Angled Research Area (narrowed)
Nuclear waste	Transportation of nuclear waste in western states
Eagles	Bald eagles on the Mississippi
Lung cancer	Effects of secondhand smoke
Water usage	Water usage on the TTU Campus
Violence	Domestic abuse in rural areas

Using Mapping to Find the Boundaries of a Subject

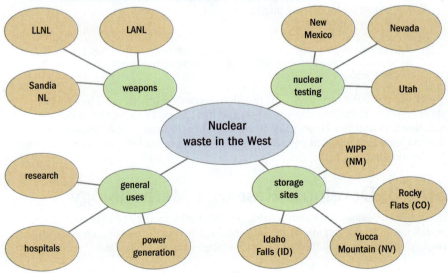

Figure 14.2: A concept map can help you generate ideas about your subject. It can also show you where you need to do research.

To help narrow your subject, you need to choose an *angle* on the subject. An angle is a specific direction that your research will follow. For example, "nuclear waste" is too large a subject, but "the hazards of transporting nuclear waste in the western United States" might be a good angle for your research. Likewise, research on raptors is too large a subject, but "the restoration of bald eagles along the Mississippi River" might be a manageable project.

By choosing an angle, you will be able to narrow your research subject to a manageable size.

Step 2: Formulate a Research Question or Hypothesis

Once you have narrowed your subject, you should then formulate a *research question* and *hypothesis*. The purpose of a research question is to guide your empirical or analytical research.

Try to devise a research question that is as specific as possible:

> Why do crows like to gather on our campus during the winter?

> What are the effects of violent television on boys between the ages of 10 and 16?

> Is solar power a viable energy source for South Dakota?

Your hypothesis is your best guess about an answer to your research question:

> **Hypothesis:** The campus is the best source of available food in the wintertime, because students leave food around. Crows naturally congregate because of the food.

> **Hypothesis:** Boys between the ages of 10 and 16 model what they see on violent television, causing them to be more violent than boys who do not watch violent television.

> **Hypothesis:** Solar power is a viable energy source in the summer, but cloudiness in the winter makes it less economical than other forms of renewable energy.

As you move forward with your research, you will probably need to refine or sharpen your original research question and hypothesis. For now, though, ask the question that you would most like to answer. Then, to form your hypothesis, answer this question to the best of your knowledge. Your hypothesis should be your best guess for the moment.

Step 3: Develop a Research Methodology

A *research methodology* is a step-by-step procedure that you will use to answer your research question. As you and your team consider how to do research on your subject, begin thinking about all the different ways you can collect evidence.

Mapping Out a Methodology

Concept mapping can help. Put the purpose of your research in the middle of your screen or a piece of paper. Ask, "*How* are we going to achieve this purpose?" Then, answer this question by formulating the two to five major steps you will need to take in your research. Each of these major steps can then be broken down into minor steps (Figure 14.3).

Using the map in Figure 14.3, for example, a team of researchers might devise the following methodology for studying their research question:

Methodology for Researching Nuclear Waste Transportation:

- Collect evidence from the Internet for and against nuclear waste storage and transportation.

- Track down news stories in the print media and collect any journal articles available on nuclear waste transportation.

- Interview experts and survey members of the general public.

- Study the Waste Isolation Pilot Plant (WIPP) in New Mexico to see if transportation to the site has been a problem.

Mapping Out a Methodology

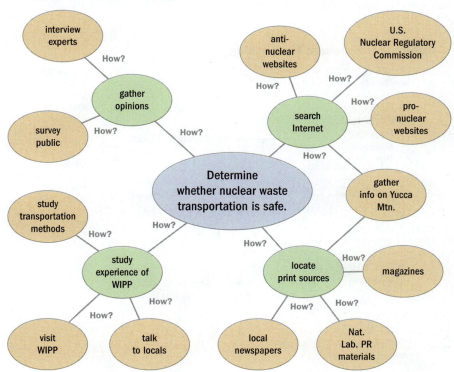

Figure 14.3: Concept mapping can help you sketch out a methodology. Keep asking the *How?* question as you consider the steps needed to complete your project.

Note that these researchers are planning to collect evidence from a range of electronic, print, and empirical sources. A good methodology will collect evidence from all three of these kinds of sources, not just one.

Describing Your Methodology

After mapping out your research methodology, begin describing it in outline form (Figure 14.4).

Sometimes, as shown in Figure 14.4, it is also helpful to identify the kinds of evidence you expect to find in each step. By clearly stating your *expected findings* before you start collecting evidence, you will know if your research methodology is working the way you expected.

At the end of your methodology, add a step called "Analysis of Findings." If you collected data, you will need to do some statistical analysis. If you conducted interviews or tracked down information on the Internet, you will need to spend some time checking and verifying your sources.

Using and Revising Your Methodology

A good methodology is like a treasure map. You and your research team can use it as a guide to uncover answers to questions that intrigue you.

Almost certainly, you will deviate from your methodology while doing your research. Sometimes you will find evidence that takes you down an unexpected path. Sometimes evidence you expected to find is not available. In other cases, experiments and surveys return unexpected findings.

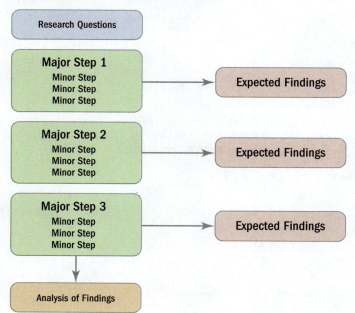

Outlining a Research Methodology

Figure 14.4: The major and minor steps in the research methodology should result in specific kinds of findings. At the end of the methodology, leave time for analyzing your findings.

When you deviate from your methodology, note these changes in direction. A change in methodology is not a sign of failure. It is simply a recognition that research is not formulaic and can be unpredictable. Research is a process of discovery. Sometimes the most important discoveries are made when we deviate from the original plan.

Step 4: Collect Evidence Through Sources

All right, it's time to collect the evidence you need to answer your research question. Solid research draws from three kinds of evidence:

- **Electronic sources:** Websites, DVDs, CDs, listservs, research databases, television and radio, videos, podcasts, blogs
- **Print sources:** Books, journals, magazines and newspapers, government publications, reference materials, microform/microfiche
- **Empirical sources:** Experiments, surveys, interviews, field observations, ethnographies, case studies

Using Electronic Sources

Because electronic sources are so convenient, a good place to start collecting evidence is through your computer.

Websites—Websites are accessible through browsers like Chrome, Firefox, Explorer, or Safari. You can run keyword searches to find evidence on your subject with search engines like Bing, Google, Yahoo, and Ask.com, among many others.

Listservs—Listservs are ongoing e-mail discussions, usually among specialists in a field. Once you find a listserv on your subject, you can usually subscribe to the discussion. A politely phrased question may return some helpful answers from other subscribers to the listserv.

Television and radio—You can find television and radio documentaries or news programs that address your subject. Increasingly, these shows are available through sites like Netflix, Amazon Prime, or Hulu Plus. In some cases, versions of these materials will be available at your library on a DVD.

Research databases—If you are looking for scientific and technical articles on your subject, you might first locate a research database that collects materials about your subject (Figure 14.5). Your campus library likely subscribes to a variety of databases that can be searched electronically.

Podcasts—Podcasts can be played on your computer or any MP3 player (not only on an iPod). They often sound like radio broadcasts. Video podcasts are also becoming more popular.

Videos—Increasingly, documentaries and training videos are available on websites like YouTube or on DVDs. Your library may have these kinds of materials available.

Blogs—Commentators or researchers will sometimes use blogs to "publish" raw or cutting-edge information, opinions, and hearsay.

Figure 14.5: A research database can help you target evidence in specialized fields.

You can browse journals on the subject here.

Here you can enter the terms you want searched.

Source: American Society of Civil Engineers, http://www.ascelibrary.org.

Using Print Sources

Printed documents are often still reliable sources of evidence. In the rush to use electronic sources, many people have forgotten that their nearby library is loaded with books and periodicals on almost any subject. These print sources can usually be located by using your computer to access the library's website (Figure 14.6).

A Library's Search Engine

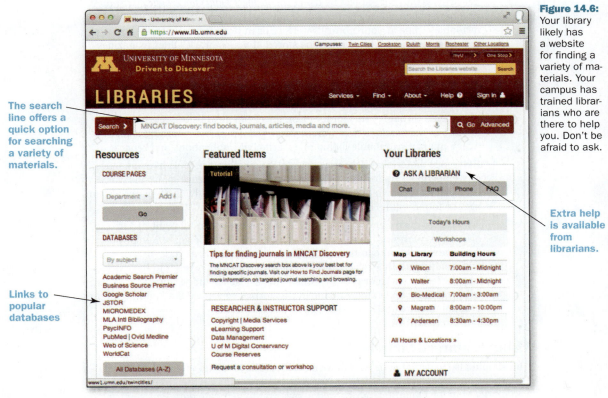

The search line offers a quick option for searching a variety of materials.

Links to popular databases

Source: © 2014 Regents of the University of Minnesota. All rights reserved.

Figure 14.6: Your library likely has a website for finding a variety of materials. Your campus has trained librarians who are there to help you. Don't be afraid to ask.

Extra help is available from librarians.

Here are a few of the many kinds of print materials that you can use:

Books—Almost all libraries have electronic cataloging systems that allow you to use author name, subject, title, and keywords to search for books on your subject. Once you have located a book on your subject, look at the books shelved around it to find other useful materials.

Journals—Using a *periodical index* at your library, you can search for journal articles on your subject. Journal articles are usually written by professors and scientists in a research field, so the articles can be rather detailed and hard to understand. Nevertheless, these articles offer some of the most exact research on any subject. Periodical indexes for journals are usually available online at your library's website, or they will be available as printed books in your library's reference area.

Magazines and newspapers—You can also search for magazine and newspaper articles on your subject by using the *Readers' Guide to Periodical Literature* or a newspaper index. The *Readers' Guide* and newspaper indexes are likely available online at your library's website or in print form. Recent editions of magazines or newspapers might be stored at your library. Older magazines and newspapers have usually been stored on microform or microfiche, also available at your library.

Government publications—The U.S. government produces a surprising number of useful books, reports, maps, and other documents. You can find these documents through your library or on government websites. A good place to start is *The Catalog of U.S. Government Publications* (www.catalog.gpo.gov), which offers a searchable listing of government publications and reports.

Reference materials—Libraries contain many reference tools like almanacs, encyclopedias, handbooks, and directories. These reference materials can help you track down facts, data, and people. Increasingly, these materials can also be found online in searchable formats.

Microform/microfiche—Libraries will often store copies of print materials on microform or microfiche. Microform and microfiche are miniature transparencies that can be read on projectors available at your library. You will usually find that magazines and newspapers over a year old have been transferred to microform or microfiche to save space in the library. Also, delicate and older texts are available in this format to reduce the handling of the original documents.

Using Empirical Sources

You should also generate your own data and observations to support your research. Empirical studies can be *quantitative* or *qualitative,* depending on the kinds of evidence you are looking for. Quantitative research allows you to generate data that you can analyze statistically to find trends. Qualitative research allows you to observe patterns of behavior that cannot be readily boiled down into numbers.

Experiments—Each research field has its own experimental procedures. A controlled experiment allows you to test a hypothesis by generating data. From that data, you can confirm or dispute the hypothesis. Experiments should be *repeatable,* meaning the results can be replicated by another experimenter.

Field observations—Researchers often carry field notebooks to record their observations of their research subjects. For example, an ornithologist might regularly note the birds she observes in her hikes around a lake. Her notebook would include her descriptions of birds and their activities.

Interviews—You can ask experts to answer questions about your subject. On almost any given college campus, experts are available on just about any subject. Your well-crafted questions can draw out very useful information and quotes.

Surveys and questionnaires—You can ask a group of people to answer questions about your subject. Their answers can then be scored and analyzed for trends. Survey questions can be *closed-ended* or *open-ended*. Closed-ended questions ask respondents to choose among preselected answers. Open-ended questions allow respondents to write down their views in their own words. Figure 14.7 shows pages from a survey with both closed-ended and open-ended questions.

Ethnographies—An ethnography is a systematic recording of your observations of a defined group or culture. Anthropologists use ethnographies to identify social or cultural trends and norms.

Case studies—Case studies typically offer in-depth observations of specific people or situations. For example, a case study might describe how a patient reacted to a new treatment regimen that manages diabetes.

Step 5: Triangulate Your Sources

Triangulation is a helpful way to determine whether you are collecting evidence from a variety of sources. Triangulating your sources allows you to compare sources, thereby helping you determine which evidence is reliable and which is not.

Doing Empirical Research

Empirical research requires you to observe your subject directly.

Pages from a Questionnaire on Campus Safety

Introduction explains how to complete the survey.

Campus Survey 75

Campus Perception Survey

The following questions are about how safe you feel or don't feel on campus. For each situation please tell us if you feel: very safe, reasonably safe, neither safe nor unsafe, somewhat unsafe, very unsafe, or if this situation does not apply to you. (Please circle the number that best represents your answer or **NA** if the situation does not apply to you.)

How safe do you feel...

	Very Unsafe	Somewhat Unsafe	Neither Safe Nor Unsafe	Reasonable Safe	Very Safe	
walking alone on campus during daylight hours?	1	2	3	4	5	NA
waiting alone on campus for public transportation during daylight hours?	1	2	3	4	5	NA
walking in parking lots or garages on campus during daylight hours?	1	2	3	4	5	NA
walking alone on campus after dark?	1	2	3	4	5	NA
waiting alone on campus for public transportation after dark?	1	2	3	4	5	NA
walking in parking lots or garages on campus after dark?	1	2	3	4	5	NA
working in the library stacks late at night?	1	2	3	4	5	NA
while alone in classrooms?	1	2	3	4	5	NA
Student Activity Center during the day?	1	2	3	4	5	NA
Student Activity Center at night?	1	2	3	4	5	NA

Are there any specific areas on campus where you do not feel safe? Please specify which areas, which campus, and when; for example, evenings only or any time. _____

_____

Do you have any special needs related to safety on campus? _____

Have you ever used services related to safety issues, sexual harassment, or sexual assault that are provided on campus by the following?

How satisfied were you with help from this source?

			Very Dissatisfied	Somewhat Dissatisfied	Neither Satisfied Nor Dissatisfied	Somewhat Satisfied	Very Satisfied
Campus Police	YES	NO	1	2	3	4	5
Women's Center	YES	NO	1	2	3	4	5
Campus ministry	YES	NO	1	2	3	4	5
Campus counseling (Belknap)	YES	NO	1	2	3	4	5
Student Health Services (Belknap)	YES	NO	1	2	3	4	5
Campus counseling (Health Science)	YES	NO	1	2	3	4	5
Student Health Services (Health Science)	YES	NO	1	2	3	4	5
Psychological Services Ctr (Psychology Clinic)	YES	NO	1	2	3	4	5
Affirmative Action Office	YES	NO	1	2	3	4	5
Security escort services after dark	YES	NO	1	2	3	4	5
Residence Hall staff	YES	NO	1	2	3	4	5
Office of Student Life	YES	NO	1	2	3	4	5
Disability Resource Center	YES	NO	1	2	3	4	5
Access Center	YES	NO	1	2	3	4	5
Faculty member	YES	NO	1	2	3	4	5
Other _____	YES	NO	1	2	3	4	5
(Please specify.)							

Source: Bledsoe & Sar, 2001.

Figure 14.7: A survey is a good way to generate data for your research. In this example, both closed-ended and open-ended questions are being used to solicit evidence.

These closed-ended questions yield numerical data.

Open-ended questions allow participants to elaborate on their answers.

Campus Survey 78

The following are some beliefs that may be held about the role of women and men in today's society. There are no right or wrong answers. (Please circle the response that best describes your opinion.)

	Strongly Disagree		Somewhat Agree		Strongly Agree
A man's got to show the woman who's boss right from the start.	1	2	3	4	5
Women are usually sweet until they've caught a man, but then they let their true self show.	1	2	3	4	5
In a dating relationship a woman is largely out to take advantage of a man.	1	2	3	4	5
Men are out for only one thing.	1	2	3	4	5
A lot of women seem to get pleasure from putting a man down.	1	2	3	4	5
A woman who goes to the home or apartment of a man on their first date implies that she is willing to have sex.	1	2	3	4	5
Any female can get raped.	1	2	3	4	5
Any healthy woman can successfully resist a rapist if she really wants to.	1	2	3	4	5
Many women have an unconscious wish to be raped, and may then unconsciously set up a situation in which they are likely to be attacked.	1	2	3	4	5
If a woman gets drunk at a party and has intercourse with a man she's just met there, she should be considered "fair game" to other males at the party who also want to have sex with her whether she wants to or not.	1	2	3	4	5

The survey uses statements to measure participants' reactions to specific situations or opinions.

What **percentage of women** who report a rape would you say are lying because they are angry and want to get back at the man they accuse? _____ %

What **percentage of reported rapes** would you guess were merely invented by women who discovered they were pregnant and wanted to protect their own reputation? _____ %

Did you attend any type of student orientation conducted by University of Louisville during Summer 2000 or at the beginning of this term? (Please circle your answer). **YES NO**

If your answer was "No, I did not attend orientation", please continue on next page.

At the orientation you attended, how much information about violence against women issues did you receive? (Please circle your answer).	None		Some		A Lot
	1	2	3	4	5

The Research Triangle

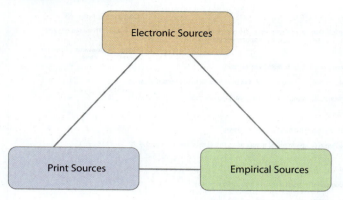

Electronic Sources

Print Sources

Empirical Sources

Figure 14.8: In any research project, try to draw evidence from electronic, print, and empirical sources.

AT A GLANCE

Triangulating Research

Solid research draws from three kinds of evidence:

- Electronic sources—Internet, DVDs, list-servs, television and radio, videos, blogs
- Print sources—books, journals, magazines and newspapers, government publications, reference materials, microform/microfiche
- Empirical sources—experiments, surveys, interviews, field observations, ethnographies, case studies

To triangulate your sources, collect evidence from all three sides of the "research triangle" (Figure 14.8):

- If you find similar facts from all three sides of the research triangle, you can be reasonably confident that the evidence is reliable.
- If you find the evidence from only two sides, the evidence is probably still reliable, though you should be less confident.
- If, however, you find the evidence in only one side of the triangle, it might not be reliable and needs further confirmation.

Make sure you look for sources from a variety of perspectives and opinions. In other words, do not only search for sources that confirm what you already believe because you won't gain a deeper understanding of the subject. After all, even when you absolutely disagree with someone else, his or her argument may give you additional insight into the issue you are researching. Keep an open mind.

Step 6: Take Careful Notes

On almost any subject, you are going to find a wealth of information. At this point, you need to start thinking like an information manager. After all, only some of the information you collect will be important to your project and your readers.

You can sort the evidence you collect into two categories: *need-to-know* information and *want-to-tell* information.

- *Need-to-know information* includes material that your readers will need if they want to take action or make a decision.
- *Want-to-tell information* includes material that you would like to tell your readers but that is not necessary for them to take action or make a decision.

After you have gone through all the effort to collect evidence on your subject, you will want to tell the readers about everything you found. But your readers don't need (or want) all of that information. So, make some difficult decisions about what they need to know.

Taking Notes

Reliable note taking is essential when you do research. If you are organized when you take notes, you will find the evidence you collect easy to use in the document you are writing.

RECORD EACH SOURCE SEPARATELY   Make sure you clearly identify the author, title of the work, and the place where you found the information (Figure 14.9). For information from the Internet, write down the webpage address (URL) and the date and time you found the information. For a print document, write down where the information was published and who published it. Also, record the library call number of the document.

For large research projects, you might consider making a separate word-processing file for each of your authors or sources, like the one shown in Figure 14.9. That way, you can more easily keep your notes organized.

TAKE DOWN QUOTATIONS   When quoting a source, be sure to copy the exact wording of the author. If you are taking a quote from a website, you might avoid errors by using the Copy and Paste functions of your computer to copy the statement directly from your source into your notes.

In your notes, you should put quotation marks around any material you copied word for word from a source.

> According to Louis Pakiser and Kaye Shedlock, scientists for the Earthquake Hazards Program at the U.S. Geological Survey, "the assumption of random occurrence with time may not be true." (1997, para. 3)

Keeping Notes on Your Computer

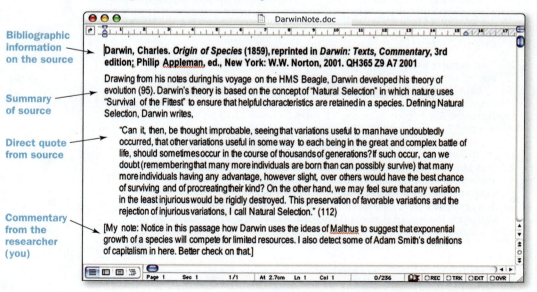

Bibliographic information on the source

Summary of source

Direct quote from source

Commentary from the researcher (you)

Figure 14.9: Most notes include a combination of summaries, paraphrases, direct quotes, and personal comments.

If the quoted material runs more than three lines in your text, you should set off the material by indenting it in the text.

> Louis Pakiser and Kaye Shedlock, scientists for the Earthquake Hazards Program at the U.S. Geological Survey, make the following point:
>
>> When plate movements build the strain in rocks to a critical level, like pulling a rubber band too tight, the rocks will suddenly break and slip to a new position. Scientists measure how much strain accumulates along a fault segment each year, how much time has passed since the last earthquake along the segment, and how much strain was released in the last earthquake. (1997, para. 4)
>
> If we apply this rubber band analogy to the earthquake risk here in California . . .

Link

For more information on citing sources, go to Appendix C, which begins on page A-24.

When you are quoting a source, you also need to include an in-text citation at the end of the quote. In the two examples above, the in-text citation is the information in the parentheses.

Overall, you should use direct quotes sparingly in your technical writing. You might be tempted to use several quotes from a source, because the authors "said it right." If you use too many quotes, though, your writing will sound fragmented and patchy, because the quotes disrupt the flow of your text.

PARAPHRASE IDEAS   When paraphrasing, you are presenting another person's ideas in your own words. You still need to give the original author credit for the ideas, but you do not need to use quotation marks around the text. To paraphrase something, you should:

* reorganize the information to highlight important points.
* use plain language, replacing jargon and technical terms with simpler words.
* include an in-text citation.

In the following example, a quote from an original document is paraphrased:

Original Quote

"But in many places, the assumption of random occurrence with time may not be true, because when strain is released along one part of the fault system, it may actually increase on another part. Four magnitude 6.8 or larger earthquakes and many magnitude 6–6.5 shocks occurred in the San Francisco Bay region during the 75 years between 1836 and 1911. For the next 68 years (until 1979), no earthquakes of magnitude 6 or larger occurred in the region. Beginning with a magnitude 6.0 shock in 1979, the earthquake activity in the region increased dramatically; between 1979 and 1989, there were four magnitude 6 or greater earthquakes, including the magnitude 14.1 Loma Prieta earthquake. This clustering of earthquakes leads scientists to estimate that the probability of a magnitude 6.8 or larger earthquake occurring during the next 30 years in the San Francisco Bay region is about 67 percent (twice as likely as not)."

Effective Paraphrase

In-text citation

Simple language is used.

Pakiser and Shedlock (1997) report that large earthquakes are mostly predictable, because an earthquake in one place usually increases the likelihood of an earthquake somewhere nearby. They point out that the San Francisco area—known for earthquakes—has experienced long periods of minor earthquake activity (most notably from 1911 to 1978, when no earthquakes over magnitude 6 occurred). At other times in San Francisco, major earthquakes have happened with more frequency, because large earthquakes tend to trigger other large earthquakes in the area.

Some of the more technical details have been removed to enhance understanding.

Improper Paraphrase

Much of the original wording is retained.

Pakiser and Shedlock (1997) report the assumption of random occurrence of earthquakes may not be accurate. Earthquakes along one part of a fault system may increase the frequency of earthquakes in another part. For example, the San Francisco Bay region experienced many large earthquakes between 1836 and 1911. For the next six decades until 1979, only smaller earthquakes (below magnitude 6) occurred in the area. Then, there was a large rise in earthquakes between 1979 and 1989. Scientists estimate that the probability of an earthquake of magnitude 6.8 or larger is 67 percent in the next 30 years in the Bay area.

Language is still overly technical for the readers.

The "effective" paraphrase shown here uses the ideas of the original quote, while reordering information to highlight important points and simplifying the language. The "improper" paraphrase duplicates too much of the wording from the original source and does not effectively reorder information to highlight important points. In fact, this improper paraphrase is so close to the original, it could be considered plagiarism.

In many ways, paraphrasing is superior to using direct quotes. A paraphrase allows you to simplify the language of a technical document, making the information easier for readers to understand. Also, you can better blend the paraphrased information into your writing because you are using your writing style, not the style of the source.

Warning: Make sure you are paraphrasing sources properly. Do not use the author's original words and phrases in your notes without quotation marks. Otherwise, when you draft your document, you may forget that you copied some of the wording from the original text. These duplications may leave you vulnerable to charges of plagiarism or copyright violation.

SUMMARIZE SOURCES When summarizing, your goal is to condense the ideas from your source into a brief passage. Summaries usually strip out the examples, details, data, and reasoning from the original text, leaving only the essential information that readers need to know. Like a paraphrase, summaries should be written in your own words. When you are summarizing a source for your notes:

- Read the source carefully to gain an overall understanding.
- Highlight or underline the main point and other key points.
- Condense key points into lists, where appropriate.
- Organize information from most important to least important.
- Use plain language to replace any technical terms or jargon in the original.
- Use in-text citations to identify important ideas from the source.

For example, the original text in Figure 14.10 has been summarized in Figure 14.11. The details in the original text were stripped away, leaving only a condensed version that highlights the main point and a few other key issues. The summary uses the researcher's own words, not the words from the original source.

Link

For more information on plagiarism, see Chapter 14, page 388.

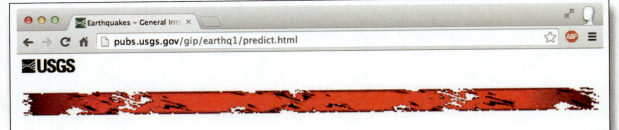

≋USGS

Predicting Earthquakes

The goal of earthquake prediction is to give warning of potentially damaging earthquakes early enough to allow appropriate response to the disaster, enabling people to minimize loss of life and property. The U.S. Geological Survey conducts and supports research on the likelihood of future earthquakes. This research includes field, laboratory, and theoretical investigations of earthquake mechanisms and fault zones. A primary goal of earthquake research is to increase the reliability of earthquake probability estimates. Ultimately, scientists would like to be able to specify a high probability for a specific earthquake on a particular fault within a particular year. Scientists estimate earthquake probabilities in two ways: by studying the history of large earthquakes in a specific area and the rate at which strain accumulates in the rock.

This time-exposure photograph of the electronic-laser, ground-motion movement system in operation at Parkfield, California, to track movement along the San Andreas fault. <u>Full size image - 40 k</u>

Scientists study the past frequency of large earthquakes in order to determine the future likelihood of similar large shocks. For example, if a region has experienced four magnitude 7 or larger earthquakes during 200 years of recorded history, and if these shocks occurred randomly in time, then scientists would assign a 50 percent probability (that is, just as likely to happen as not to happen) to the occurrence of another magnitude 7 or larger quake in the region during the next 50 years.

But in many places, the assumption of random occurrence with time may not be true, because when strain is released along one part of the fault system, it may actually increase on another part. Four magnitude 6.8 or larger earthquakes and many magnitude 6 - 6.5 shocks occurred in the San Francisco Bay region during the 75 years between 1836 and 1911. For the next 68 years (until 1979), no earthquakes of magnitude 6 or larger occurred in the region. Beginning with a magnitude 6.0 shock in 1979, the earthquake activity in the region increased dramatically; between 1979 and 1989, there were four magnitude 6 or greater earthquakes, including the magnitude 7.1 Loma Prieta earthquake. This clustering of earthquakes leads scientists to estimate that the probability of a magnitude 6.8 or larger earthquake occurring during the next 30 years in the San Francisco Bay region is about 67 percent (twice as likely as not).

Another way to estimate the likelihood of future earthquakes is to study how fast strain accumulates. When plate movements build the strain in rocks to a critical level, like pulling a rubber band too tight, the rocks will suddenly break and slip to a new position. Scientists measure how much strain accumulates along a fault segment each year, how much time has passed since the last earthquake along the segment, and how much strain was released in the last earthquake. This information is then used to calculate the time required for the accumulating strain to build to the level that results in an earthquake. This simple model is complicated by the fact that such detailed information about faults is rare. In the United States, only the San Andreas fault system has adequate records for using this prediction method.

Both of these methods, and a wide array of monitoring techniques, are being tested along part of the San Andres fault. For the past 150 years, earthquakes of about magnitude 6 have occurred an average of every 22 years on the San Andreas fault near Parkfield, California. The last shock was in 1966. Because of the consistency and similarity of these earthquakes, scientists have started an experiment to "capture" the next Parkfield earthquake. A dense web of monitoring instruments was deployed in the region during the late 1980s. The main goals of the ongoing Parkfield Earthquake Prediction Experiment are to record the geophysical signals before and after the expected earthquake; to issue a short-term prediction; and to develop effective methods of communication between earthquake scientists and community officials responsible for disaster response and mitigation. This project has already made important contributions to both earth science and public policy.

Scientific understanding of earthquakes is of vital importance to the Nation. As the population increases, expanding urban development and construction works encroach upon areas susceptible to earthquakes. With a greater understanding of the causes and effects of earthquakes, we may be able to reduce damage and loss of life from this destructive phenomenon.

Figure 14.10:
The original text contains many details that can be condensed into a summary.
Source: U.S. Geological Survey, http://pubs.usgs.gov/gip/earthg1/predict.html.

Summary of Original Text

The main point is expressed up front.

The important points are put into list form.

The summary uses plain language.

Figure 14.11: A summary highlights important points and puts the text in plain language.

Summary of "Predicting Earthquakes" by Louis Pakiser and Kaye Shedlock (1997). http://pubs.usgs.gov/gip/earthq1/predict.html. Retrieved March 10, 2014.

The goal of earthquake prediction is to anticipate earthquakes that may cause major damage in a region. According to geologists Louis Pakiser and Kaye Shedlock from the U.S. Geological Survey, scientists are increasingly able to predict the likelihood of an earthquake in a region in the near future (1997). Scientists use two important methods to predict large earthquakes:

- They study the frequency of earthquakes in the past, especially the recent past, because large earthquakes tend to trigger other large earthquakes.

- They measure the strain on the earth to determine the buildup of pressure along fault lines. These measurements can be used to predict when the strain will be released as an earthquake.

As Pakiser and Shedlock point out, earthquakes are not random events. They tend to occur in "clusters" over periods of several years. By paying attention to these clusters of earthquakes, scientists can make rather reliable predictions about the probability of a future large quake.

WRITE COMMENTARY In your notes, you should offer your own commentary to help interpret your sources. Your commentary might help you remember why you collected the evidence and how you thought it could be used. To avoid plagiarism, it is important to visually distinguish your commentary from summaries, paraphrases, and quotations drawn from other sources. You might put brackets around your comments or use color, italics, or bold type to set them off from your other notes.

Documenting Your Sources

As you draft your text, you will need to *document* your sources. Documentation involves (1) naming each source with an *in-text citation* and (2) recording your sources in the *References* list at the end of the document. Documenting your sources offers the advantages of:

- supporting your claims by referring to the research of others.
- helping build your credibility with readers by showing them the support for your ideas.
- reinforcing the thoroughness of your research methodology.
- allowing your readers to explore your sources for more information.

When should you document your sources? Any ideas, text, or images that you draw from a source need to be properly acknowledged. If you are in doubt about whether you need to cite someone else's work, you should go ahead and cite it. Citing sources will help you avoid any questions about the integrity and soundness of your work.

In Appendix C at the end of this book, you will find a full discussion of three documentation systems (APA, CSE, and MLA) that are used in technical fields. Each of these systems works differently.

The most common documentation style for technical fields is offered by the American Psychological Association (APA). The APA style, published in the *Publication Manual of the American Psychological Association,* is preferred in technical fields because it puts emphasis on the year of publication. As an example, let's briefly look at the APA style for in-text citations and full references.

APA IN-TEXT CITATIONS   In APA style, in-text citations can include the author's name, the publication year, and the page number where the information was found.

Link

For a full discussion of documentation, including models for documenting references, turn to Appendix C, page A-24.

One important study showed that physicians were regularly misusing antibiotics to treat viruses (Reynolds, 2003, p. 743).

According to Reynolds (2003), physicians are regularly misusing antibiotics to treat viruses.

According to Reynolds, "Doctors are creating larger problems by mistakenly treating viruses with antibiotics" (2003, p. 743).

These in-text citations are intended to refer the readers back to the list of full references at the end of the document.

Elements of an APA Full Reference

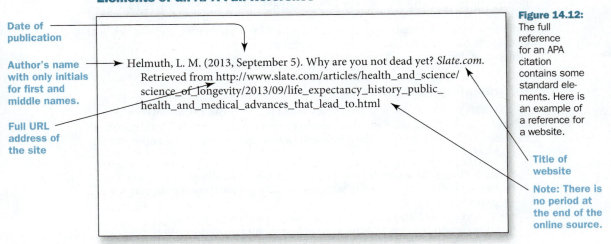

Date of publication

Author's name with only initials for first and middle names.

Helmuth, L. M. (2013, September 5). Why are you not dead yet? *Slate.com.* Retrieved from http://www.slate.com/articles/health_and_science/ science_of_longevity/2013/09/life_expectancy_history_public_ health_and_medical_advances_that_lead_to.html

Full URL address of the site

Figure 14.12: The full reference for an APA citation contains some standard elements. Here is an example of a reference for a website.

Title of website

Note: There is no period at the end of the online source.

APA FULL REFERENCES   The full references at the end of the document provide readers with the complete citation for each source (Figure 14.12).

Helmuth, L. M. (2013, September 5). Why are you not dead yet? *Slate. com*. Retrieved from http://www.slate.com/articles/health_and_science/science_of_longevity/2013/09/life_expectancy_history_public_health_and_medical_advances_that_lead_to.html

Pauling, L., & Wilson, E. B. (1935). *Introduction to quantum mechanics*. New York, NY: Dover Publications.

As you take notes, you should keep track of the information needed to properly cite your sources. That way, when you draft the document and create a references list, you will have this important information available. It can be very difficult to locate the sources of your information again after you finish drafting the document.

Using a Citation Manager

In today's technical workplace, finding information on a subject is rarely a problem. The real problem is managing all the information that is available through the Internet and print sources. You can often find yourself struggling to keep track of the sources you have located.

A good way to organize your sources is to use a *citation manager,* a software program that will help you format and store your references. Some of the more popular citation managers include EndNote, Zotero, RefWorks, and Mendeley. Figure A shows Zotero, a citation management tool that is a free plug-in with Firefox.

Using a citation manager isn't difficult, but it takes some practice. Here's how it works. When you find a source that looks useful, you should enter its details into the citation manager as soon as you can. The software will cue you for information about the author, title, journal title, publisher, pages, date, and so on. Then, the citation manager will automatically format all your sources into APA, MLA, IEEE, CSE, and a variety of other citation styles. You just need to tell it which citation style you are using.

Some citation managers will allow you to click on an icon in the address bar of your Internet browser, which will automatically put the citation in your database of sources (Figure A).

Then, when you need to cite a specific source in your document, select "Add Citation" from your word processor's menu. The citation manager will create an in-text citation for that source. It will also add the source to your document's References list in the appropriate bibliographic format.

Another helpful feature in many citation managers is the ability to include keywords or comments about each source. You can then electronically search your citations to locate the ones that are best for your research project.

When you are working on a team project, citation managers can be especially helpful. You and your team can quickly collect all your sources into a common database. Then, the database can be searched to find the most useful sources for the project. This ability to organize a collection of sources will help your team find the information it needs while identifying any trends or gaps in the research.

Using a Citation Manager

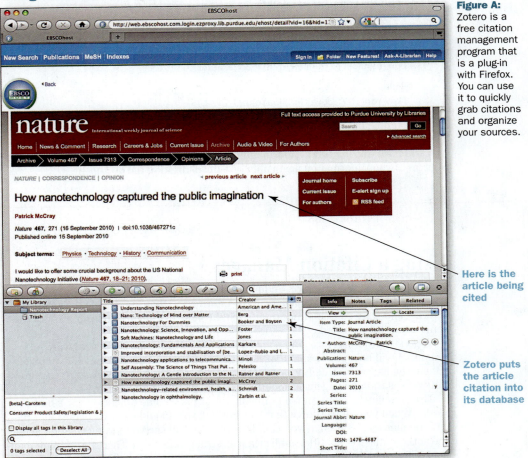

Figure A:
Zotero is a free citation management program that is a plug-in with Firefox. You can use it to quickly grab citations and organize your sources.

Here is the article being cited

Zotero puts the article citation into its database

Something to keep in mind, though, is that citation managers do make formatting mistakes. They are not perfect. So, you should proofread the items in your References list before sending your document to your instructor or a client.

Step 7: Appraise Your Evidence

All evidence is not created equal. In fact, some information you find will be downright wrong or misleading. Keep in mind that even the most respected authorities usually have agendas that they are pursuing with their research. Even the most objective experiment will include some tinge of bias.

To avoid misleading information and researcher biases, you need to appraise the evidence you have collected to develop an overall sense of what the truth might be (Figure 14.13).

Is the Source Reliable?

Usually, the most reliable sources of evidence are those that have limited personal, political, or financial stakes in the subject. For example, claims about the safety of pesticides from a company that sells pesticides need to be carefully verified. On the other hand, a study on pesticides by a university professor should be less biased because the professor is not selling the product.

To ensure that your sources are reliable, you should always do some checking on their authors. Use an Internet search engine like Google or Yahoo to check out the authors, company, or organization that produced the materials. If the researchers have a good reputation, the evidence is probably reliable. If you can find little or no information about the researchers, company, or organization, you should be skeptical about their research.

How Biased Is the Source?

It is safe to say that all sources of information have some bias. There is no such thing as a completely objective source. So, you need to assess the amount of bias in your sources.

Questions for Appraising Your Evidence

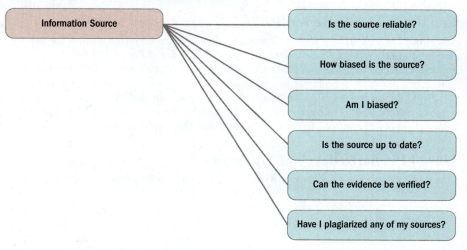

Figure 14.13: Challenge your sources by asking questions about their biases and validity.

Even the most reliable sources have some bias. Researchers, after all, very much want their hypotheses to be true, so irregularities in their results might be overlooked. Bias is a natural part of research. So, when you are assessing bias, consider how much the researchers want their results to be true. If the researchers indicate that they were open to a range of answers, then the bias of the material is probably minimal. If it seems like only one answer was acceptable to the researchers (e.g., climate change does not exist or smoking does not cause lung cancer), then the material should be considered heavily biased.

Am I Biased?

As a researcher, you need to carefully examine your own biases. We all go into a research project with our own beliefs and expectations of what we will find. Our own biases can cause us to overlook evidence that contradicts our beliefs or expectations. For example, our beliefs about gender, race, sexuality, poverty, or religion, among other social issues, can strongly influence the way we conduct research and interpret our findings. These influences cannot be completely avoided, but they can be identified and taken into consideration.

To keep your own biases in check, consider your research subject from an alternative or opposing perspective. At a minimum, considering alternative views will only strengthen your confidence in your research. But, in some cases, you may actually gain a new perspective that can help you further your research.

Is the Source Up to Date?

Depending on the field of study, results from prior research can become obsolete rather quickly. For instance, three-year-old research on skin cancer might already be considered outdated. On the other hand, climate measurements that are over 100 years old are still usable today.

Try to find the most recent sources on your subject. Scientific sources will often offer a *literature review* that traces research on the subject back at least a few years. These literature reviews will show you how quickly the field is changing, while allowing you to judge whether the evidence you have located is current.

Can the Evidence Be Verified?

You should be able to locate more than one independent source that verifies the evidence you find. If you locate the same evidence from a few different independent sources, chances are good that the evidence is reliable. If you find the evidence in only one or two places, it is probably less reliable.

Triangulation is the key to verifying evidence. If you can find the evidence in diverse electronic and print sources, it is probably evidence you can trust. You might also use empirical methods to confirm or challenge the results of others.

Have I Plagiarized Any of My Sources?

One thing to watch out for in your work is plagiarism, whether it is intentional or unintentional.

Plagiarism is the use of others' words, images, or ideas without acknowledgment or permission. In most cases, plagiarism is unintentional. While collecting evidence, a researcher might cut and paste information from websites or duplicate passages from a book. Later, he or she might use the exact text, forgetting that the information was copied directly from a source.

In rare cases, plagiarism is intentional and therefore a form of academic dishonesty. In these cases, instructors and universities will often punish plagiarizers by having them fail the course, putting them on academic probation, or even expelling them. Intentional plagiarism is a serious form of dishonesty.

To avoid plagiarizing, keep careful track of your sources and acknowledge where you found your evidence.

Keep track of sources—Whenever you are gathering evidence from a source, carefully note where that information came from. If you are cutting and pasting information from an online source, make sure you put quotation marks around that material and clearly identify where you found it.

Acknowledge your sources—Any words, sentences, images, data, or unique ideas that you take from another source should be properly cited. If you are taking a direct quote from a source, use quotation marks to set it off from your writing. If you are paraphrasing the work of others, make sure you cite them with an in-text citation and put a full-text citation in a references list.

Ask permission—If you want to include others' images or large blocks of text in your work, write them an e-mail to ask permission. Downloading pictures and graphics from the Internet is really easy. But those images are usually someone's property. If you are using them for educational purposes, you can probably include them without asking permission. But, if you are using them for any other reason, you likely need to obtain permission from their owners.

You do not need to cite sources that offer information that is "common knowledge." If you find the same information in a few different sources, you probably do not need to document that information. But, if you have any doubts, you might want to cite the sources anyway to avoid any plagiarism problems.

Link

For more information on obtaining permission, go to Chapter 4, page 79.

AT A GLANCE

Assessing Your Information

- Is the source reliable?
- How biased is the source?
- Am I biased?
- Is the source up to date?
- Can the evidence be verified?
- Have I plagiarized my sources?

Unfortunately, cases of plagiarism are on the rise. One of the downsides of online texts, such as websites, is the ease of plagiarism. Some students have learned techniques of "patchwriting," in which they cut and paste text from the Internet and then revise it into a document. This kind of writing is highly vulnerable to charges of plagiarism, so it should be avoided.

In the end, plagiarism harms mostly the person doing it. Plagiarism is kind of like running stoplights. People get away with it for only so long. Then, when they are caught, the penalties can be severe. Moreover, whether intentional or unintentional, plagiarizing reinforces some lazy habits. Before long, people who plagiarize find it difficult to do their own work, because they did not learn proper research skills. Your best approach is to avoid plagiarism in the first place.

Step 8: Revise, Accept, or Abandon Your Hypothesis

When you have finished collecting evidence and verifying your sources, you should revisit your hypothesis. As you collected information about your subject, your sources probably revealed some new perspectives or evidence that you didn't expect. Now it's time to determine whether your hypothesis holds up and whether you have truly answered your original research question.

You have a few choices:

> **Accept your hypothesis**—Maybe you were right all along, and your research confirms what you believed. If so, you're ready to start organizing your evidence and writing your document.

> **Modify your hypothesis**—Perhaps your hypothesis was a good guess but the evidence you collected suggests something a little different. If so, you can modify your hypothesis to fit your evidence.

> **Abandon your hypothesis**—In rare cases, you will find that your hypothesis was not correct. In these situations, you should just abandon it and come up with a new hypothesis that fits your evidence.

Eventually, your evidence should lead you to an overall conclusion (your main point) that you can support or prove in your document. The decision to modify or abandon a hypothesis can be difficult, but it happens regularly in the sciences. If you are really open to finding the truth about your subject, you will let the evidence determine what you believe.

WHAT YOU NEED TO KNOW

- Research today involves collecting evidence from diverse sources that are available in many media, including the Internet.

- Concept mapping can be used to define a subject and highlight places where evidence needs to be found.

- A research methodology is a planned, step-by-step procedure that you will use to study the subject. Your research methodology can be revised as needed as your research moves forward.

- Effectively managing existing evidence is often as important as creating new evidence.

- Triangulation is a process of using electronic, print, and empirical sources to obtain and evaluate your findings and conclusions.

- Careful note taking involves summarizing your sources and taking good quotations.

- To appraise your sources, determine how bias influenced the researchers who wrote them, as well as your own bias.

- When your research is finished, you will need to accept, modify, or abandon your original hypothesis.

Individual or Team Projects

1. Think of a technical subject that interests you. Then, collect evidence from electronic and print sources. Write a progress report to your instructor in which you highlight themes in the materials you've found. Discuss any gaps in the evidence that you might be able to fill with more searching or empirical study. Some possible topics might include the following:

   Wildlife on campus
   Surveillance in America
   Hybrid motor cars
   The problems with running red lights on or near campus
   Safety on campus at night
   The effects of acid rain in Canada
   Migration of humpback whales

2. On the Internet, find evidence on a subject that you think is "junk science" or is influenced by junk science. Junk science is faulty or unproven scientific-like evidence that is used to support the agendas of special interests. For example, the tobacco industry used junk science for many years to cast doubt on whether smoking causes cancer. Pay close attention to the reputations of the researchers and their results. Can you find any evidence to back up their claims? Pay special attention to where they receive their funding for the research. When you are finished searching the web, make a report to your class on your findings. Show your audience how junk science influences the debate on your subject.
   Here are a few possible topics:

   Evolution versus creation science
   Genetically engineered foods
   Managing forests to prevent fires
   Mobile phones and cancer
   Experimentation on animals
   Herbicides and insecticides
   Diets and dietary supplements
   Global warming
   Smoking and secondhand smoke
   Air and water pollution
   Resisting vaccinations for children
   Welfare abuse

3. Survey your class on a campus issue that interests you. Write five questions and let your classmates select among answers like "strongly agree," "agree," "disagree," and "strongly disagree." Then, tabulate the results of the survey. Write a memo to your instructor in which you discuss the trends revealed by your findings. In your memo, also point out places where your methodology might be challenged by someone who doubts your findings. Discuss how you might strengthen your survey if you wanted to do a larger study on this subject.

Collaborative Project

With a group, develop a methodology for studying substance abuse (alcohol abuse or abuse of prescription drugs or illegal drugs) on your campus. First, use concept mapping to identify what you already know or believe about substance abuse on your campus. Second, formulate a research question that your research will answer. Third, use concept mapping to sketch out a methodology that would help you generate results to answer your research question.

Your methodology should use triangulation to gather evidence from a broad range of sources. In other words, you should plan to gather evidence from electronic, print, and empirical sources.

Finally, write up your methodology, showing the step-by-step procedures you will use to study substance abuse on campus. Your methodology should be written in such a way that others can duplicate it. It should also clearly identify the kinds of results you expect your research to generate.

Give your methodology to your instructor. At this point, your instructor may ask you to continue your research, following your methodology. As you do your research, note places where you changed your methodology or found evidence you did not expect.

Visit **My**Writing**Lab** for a Post-test and more technical writing resources.

The Life of a Dilemma

Jen Krannert was a third-year student in the biomedical engineering program at North Carolina State University. She was looking forward to doing a co-op semester in the spring, so she could gain some valuable experience (and earn a little money).

She applied to several co-op programs, including programs at Baxter, Biogen, and Boston Scientific. The one that caught her interest most, though, was at GenBenefits, a small biotech laboratory in California. At the interview, GenBenefits' recruiters talked with her about their work on embryonic stem cell research and how they were on the cusp of some major breakthroughs. She was very excited about the possibility of being part of that kind of research.

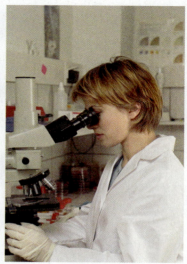

Two weeks after the interview, Allen Marshall, GenBenefits' Vice President of Research, called Jen personally to offer her the co-op position. She accepted right away and spent the next hour e-mailing her other co-op opportunities to tell them she had accepted a position. She also called her parents, who were thrilled for her. They were very excited about her being part of this cutting-edge research.

The next day, she called her best friend Alice Cravitz, who was a student at Duke University. At first, Alice was enthusiastic, but when Jen told her that she would be working with embryonic stem cells, Alice grew quiet.

"What's wrong?" Jen asked.

Alice said, "I just think doing research on embryonic stem cells is unethical. Those are human lives you will be messing around with and ultimately destroying."

Jen became a little defensive. "First, they are embryos, not people. Second, these embryos are the leftover products of fertilization clinics. They will never be implanted and will probably be destroyed anyway. Third, we could save many, many lives with this research."

Sensing Jen's defensiveness, Alice changed the subject. After Jen hung up the phone, she wasn't sure how she felt about her co-op now. She realized she wasn't sure how she felt about embryonic stem cell research, so she didn't know if she believed it was ethical or not. The co-op was a great opportunity. If she turned it down, she would likely not find another for the spring. Plus, she really believed that this research could lead to some incredible medical breakthroughs.

If you were Jen, how might you use the research methods described in this chapter to sort out this ethical dilemma?

CHAPTER
15

Organizing and Drafting

Basic Organization for Any
   Document 395

Using Genres for Outlining 395

Organizing and Drafting the
   Introduction 399

Organizing and Drafting the
   Body 402

Organizing and Drafting the
   Conclusion 411

Organizing Transcultural
   Documents 414

What You Need to Know 418

Exercises and Projects 418

Case Study: The Bad News 420

In this chapter, you will learn:

- A basic organizational pattern that any document can follow.
- How genres offer patterns for organizing documents.
- How to outline the organization of a document.
- How to use presentation software to organize your information.
- How to organize and draft a document's introduction.
- Patterns of arrangement for organizing and drafting sections of a document's body.
- Basic moves used in a document's conclusion.
- Strategies for organizing documents for transcultural readers.

omputers are great tools for helping you manage large amounts of information. Today, "information management" is one of the most significant challenges to communicating in the technical workplace. After all, computer networks put amazing amounts of information at your fingertips. But, you still need to organize that information in ways that make it accessible and understandable to your readers.

When writing a technical document or presentation, you will need to organize the information you've collected into patterns that are familiar to your readers. Your readers, after all, are interested in the information you have gathered. But they need you to present that information in a predictable and usable way. Otherwise, they won't be able to take full advantage of your thoughts and research on the subject.

Basic Organization for Any Document

Despite their differences, technical documents usually have something important in common. They typically include an *introduction, body,* and *conclusion.*

Introduction—The introduction of your document needs to tell readers *what* you are writing about and *why* you are writing about it.

Body—The body of your document presents the content that your readers need to know to take action or make a decision.

Conclusion—The conclusion of your document wraps up your argument by restating your main point(s).

Sometimes it helps to remember the familiar speechwriters' saying, "Tell them what you are going to tell them. Tell them. Then, tell them what you told them."

Introductions and conclusions are especially important in technical documents, because they provide a *context,* or framework, for understanding the *content* in the body of the text (Figure 15.1). To see an example of a good introduction, body, and conclusion, consider the classic memo in Figure 15.2. This memo is referred to as the "smoking gun" memo that demonstrated that NASA and the management at Morton Thiokol were ignoring erosion problems with the *Challenger* shuttle's O-rings.

The problem described in this memo is clear, and its author, Roger Boisjoly, does his best to stress the importance of the problem in the introduction and conclusion. Unfortunately, his and other engineers' warnings were not heeded by higher-ups.

Using Genres for Outlining

As you start organizing and drafting your document, you should first identify the genre you are using. A technical description, for example, follows a different organizational pattern than a proposal. Both genres have an introduction and conclusion, but the bodies of these documents are not alike. Chapters 5–11 in this book describe the major technical communication genres. When you know what genre you are using, you should turn to that chapter for advice about how it is typically organized.

Genres are not formulas to be followed mechanically; but they do offer helpful patterns for figuring out how you are going to organize and draft your document. The Quick Start diagrams at the beginnings of Chapters 5–11 illustrate common organizational patterns for each genre. These chapters also include further advice on how to organize each genre.

For all genres, outlining is often a good way to start sketching out the shape of your document. Outlining may seem a bit old-fashioned, but it is very helpful when you are trying to sort out your ideas, especially as you prepare to write a large

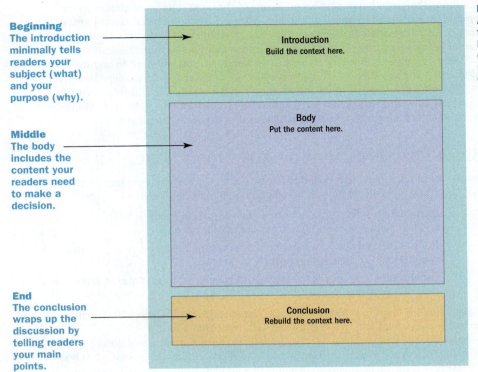

Standard Organization of a Document

Beginning
The introduction minimally tells readers your subject (what) and your purpose (why).

Introduction
Build the context here.

Middle
The body includes the content your readers need to make a decision.

Body
Put the content here.

End
The conclusion wraps up the discussion by telling readers your main points.

Conclusion
Rebuild the context here.

Figure 15.1:
An effective technical text will have a beginning (introduction), middle (body), and end (conclusion).

technical document. In the workplace, most people sketch out a rough outline to help them organize their ideas. In their outline, they type the document's main headings on the screen (Figure 15.3). Then, they list the contents of each section separately. The outline will usually change as new ideas, evidence, or issues emerge.

You might also consider using presentation software like PowerPoint or Keynote to help you outline your document (Figure 15.4). Start out by creating a title slide, an introduction slide, and a conclusion slide. Then, add a slide for each major section in the body of your document. On each slide, list the two to five items you want to include in that section of the document.

Outlining with presentation software has some advantages over traditional paper outlines. The presentation software will automatically put bullets and even roman numerals next to each of your ideas. You can then rearrange the items on each slide to try out different ways to present information.

Another advantage is that you can use the *slide sorter* to move the slides around. That way, you can try out different organizations for the body of your document. You can also make decisions about whether you should:

- combine two smaller sections to make one larger section.
- merge a smaller section into one of the larger sections.
- divide an excessively large section into two smaller sections.
- remove any want-to-tell information that is making some sections too long.
- add any need-to-know information to fill out sections that seem light on content.

The "Smoking Gun" *Challenger* Memo

MORTON THIOKOL, INC

Wasatch Division Interoffice Memo

July 31, 1985

2870:FY86:073

TO:	R. K. Lund
	Vice President, Engineering
CC:	B. C. Brinton, A. J. McDonald, L. H. Sayer, J. R. Kapp
FROM:	R. M. Boisjoly
	Applied Mechanics - Ext. 3525
SUBJECT:	SRM O-Ring Erosion/Potential Failure Criticality

The introduction contains the purpose and main point.

This letter is written to insure that management is fully aware of the seriousness of the current O-ring erosion problem in the SRM joints from an engineering standpoint.

The mistakenly accepted position on the joint problem was to fly without fear of failure and to run a series of design evaluations which would ultimately lead to a solution or at least a significant reduction of the erosion problem. This position is now drastically changed as a result of the SRM 16A nozzle joint erosion which eroded a secondary O-ring with the primary O-ring never sealing.

The body supports the argument.

If the same scenario should occur in a field joint (and it could), then it is a jump ball as to the success or failure of the joint because the secondary O-ring cannot respond to the clevis opening rate and may not be capable of pressurization. The result would be a catastrophe of the highest order— loss of human life.

The conclusion restates the main point.

An unofficial team (a memo defining the team and its purpose was never published) with leader was formed on July 19, 1985 and was tasked with solving the problem for both the short and long term. This unofficial team is essentially nonexistent at this time. In my opinion, the team must be officially given the responsibility and the authority to execute the work that needs to be done on a non-interference basis (full time assignment until completed.)

It is my honest and very real fear that if we do not take immediate action to dedicate a team to solve the problem with the field joint having the number one priority, then we stand in jeopardy of losing a flight along with all the launch pad facilities.

R. M. Boisjoly

Concurred by: J. R. Kapp, Manager

Applied Mechanics

Source: Roger Boisjoly. *Report of the Presidential Commission on the Space Shuttle Challenger Accident, 1986.*

A Rough Outline

This outline follows the proposal genre for organizing the text.

Major headings sketch out the basic structure of the document.

Subheadings begin filling in the content.

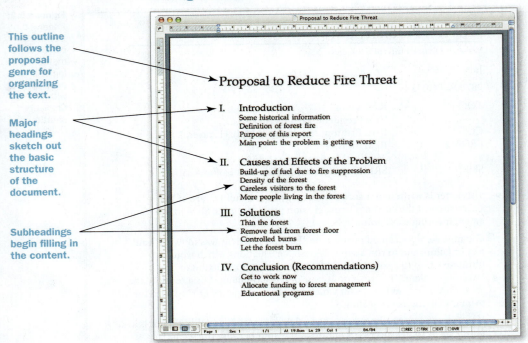

Figure 15.3: An outline doesn't need to be formal, and it should always be open to change. Here is a rough outline with some guesses about what kinds of topics will be discussed in the proposal.

Presentation Software as an Outlining Tool

The slide thumbnails give an overall view of the project.

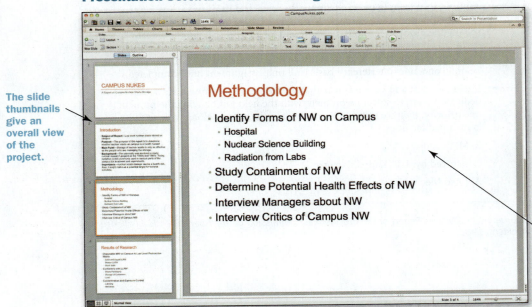

Figure 15.4: Presentation software is especially helpful for creating an outline of your document. It is also helpful when you are brainstorming with a team of co-workers on a large project.

Each major slide outlines what will happen in that section of the document.

Using presentation software as an outlining tool is especially helpful when you are working with a team. When you and your co-workers are brainstorming about a project or document, just toss your ideas into some slides. Then, when you're finished brainstorming, you can start organizing all of the information into a more structured outline. Put a team member's name on each slide to show who is responsible for writing each part of the document.

At the end of the meeting, you can print out the slides or e-mail them to the whole group. That way, everyone will have a guide to drafting of the document.

Overall, an outline should be as flexible as the document itself. A computer-generated outline can be a helpful tool for planning, drafting, and revising your work.

Link

For more information on working with a team, see Chapter 3, page 40.

Organizing and Drafting the Introduction

When organizing and drafting your document, you should put yourself in your readers' place. If you were the reader, what information would you want to know up front?

What is this document about?

Why did someone write this for me?

What is the main point?

Is this information important?

How is this document organized?

When an introduction answers these questions, readers are better able to understand the rest of the document.

Six Opening Moves in an Introduction

These kinds of questions translate into six opening "moves" made in an introduction:

MOVE 1: DEFINE YOUR SUBJECT   Tell readers what your document is about by defining the subject.

> Flooding has become a recurring problem in Darbey, our small town nestled in the Curlew Valley south of St. Louis.

In some cases, to help define the boundaries of your subject, you might also tell readers what your document is *not* going to cover.

MOVE 2: STATE YOUR PURPOSE   Tell readers what you are trying to achieve. Your purpose statement should be clear and easy to find in the introduction. It should plainly tell your readers what the document will do.

> This proposal offers some strategies for managing flooding in the Darbey area.

You should be able to articulate your purpose in one sentence. Otherwise, your purpose may not be clear to your readers—and perhaps not even to you.

Link

For more information on crafting a purpose statement, go to Chapter 1, page 5.

AT A GLANCE

Six Moves in an Introduction

- Move 1: Define your subject.
- Move 2: State your purpose.
- Move 3: State your main point.
- Move 4: Stress the importance of the subject.
- Move 5: Provide background information.
- Move 6: Forecast the content.

MOVE 3: STATE YOUR MAIN POINT   Tell your readers the key idea or main point that you would like them to take away from the document.

> The only long-term way to control flooding around Darbey is to purchase and restore the wetlands around the Curlew River, while enhancing some of the existing flood control mechanisms like levees and diversion ditches.

Are you giving away the ending by telling the readers your main point up front? Yes. Just tell readers your main point in the introduction. That way, as they read the document, they can see how you came to your decision.

MOVE 4: STRESS THE IMPORTANCE OF THE SUBJECT   Make sure you give your readers a reason to care about your subject. You need to answer their "So what?" questions if you want them to pay attention and continue reading.

> If development continues to expand between the town and the river, the flooding around Darbey will only continue to worsen, potentially causing millions of dollars in damage.

MOVE 5: PROVIDE BACKGROUND INFORMATION   Typically, background information includes material that readers already know or won't find controversial. This material could be historical, or it could stress a connection with the readers.

> As we mentioned in our presentation to the city council last month, Darbey has been dealing with flooding since it was founded. Previously, the downtown was flooded three times (1901, 1922, and 1954). In recent years, Darbey has experienced flooding with much more frequency. The downtown was flooded in 1995, 1998, 2010, and 2013.

MOVE 6: FORECAST THE CONTENT   Forecasting describes the structure of the document for your readers by identifying the major topics it will cover.

> In this proposal, we will first identify the causes of Darbey's flooding problems. Then we will offer some solutions for managing future flooding. And finally, we will discuss the costs and benefits of implementing our solutions.

Forecasting helps readers visualize the organization of the rest of the document by listing each major section of the document. Normally, forecasting is only used in longer documents like proposals and analytical reports.

Drafting with the Six Moves

In an introduction, these moves can be made in just about any order. Figure 15.5, for example, shows how the introductory moves can be used in different arrangements.

Any information that goes beyond these six moves should be removed from the introduction. After all, this extra information will only make it more difficult for readers to locate the subject, purpose, and main point of your document.

Two Versions of an Introduction

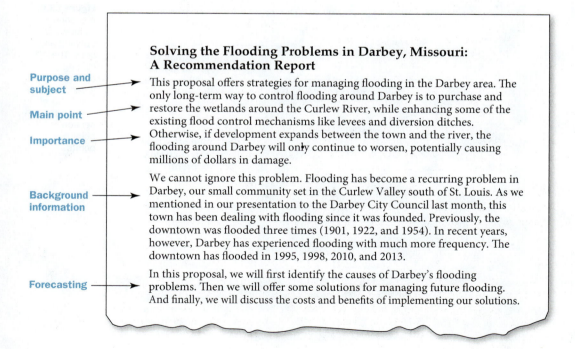

Solving the Flooding Problems in Darbey, Missouri: A Recommendation Report

Subject → Flooding has become a recurring problem in Darbey, our small community
Background information → set in the Curlew Valley south of St. Louis. As we mentioned in our presentation to the Darbey City Council last month, the town has been dealing with flooding since it was founded. Unfortunately, the problem seems to be growing worse. Previously, the downtown was flooded three times (1901, 1922, and 1954). In recent years, though, Darbey has experienced flooding with much more frequency. The downtown has flooded in 1995, 1998, 2010, and 2013.

Purpose → This proposal offers some strategies for managing flooding in the Darbey
Main point → area. We argue that the only long-term way to control flooding around Darbey is to purchase and restore the wetlands around the Curlew River, while enhancing some of the existing flood control mechanisms like levees and
Importance → diversion ditches. Otherwise, if development continues to expand between the town and the river, the flooding around Darbey will only continue to worsen, potentially causing millions of dollars in damage.

Forecasting → In this proposal, we will first identify the causes of Darbey's flooding problems. Then we will offer some solutions for managing future flooding. And finally, we will discuss the costs and benefits of implementing our solutions.

Figure 15.5:
As shown in these two sample introductions, the six introductory moves can be arranged in just about any order. Some arrangements, however, are more effective than others, depending on the subject and purpose of the document.

Solving the Flooding Problems in Darbey, Missouri: A Recommendation Report

Purpose and subject → This proposal offers strategies for managing flooding in the Darbey area. The only long-term way to control flooding around Darbey is to purchase and
Main point → restore the wetlands around the Curlew River, while enhancing some of the existing flood control mechanisms like levees and diversion ditches.
Importance → Otherwise, if development expands between the town and the river, the flooding around Darbey will only continue to worsen, potentially causing millions of dollars in damage.

Background information → We cannot ignore this problem. Flooding has become a recurring problem in Darbey, our small community set in the Curlew Valley south of St. Louis. As we mentioned in our presentation to the Darbey City Council last month, this town has been dealing with flooding since it was founded. Previously, the downtown was flooded three times (1901, 1922, and 1954). In recent years, however, Darbey has experienced flooding with much more frequency. The downtown has flooded in 1995, 1998, 2010, and 2013.

Forecasting → In this proposal, we will first identify the causes of Darbey's flooding problems. Then we will offer some solutions for managing future flooding. And finally, we will discuss the costs and benefits of implementing our solutions.

Organizing and Drafting the Body

The body of the document is where you are going to provide the *content* that readers need to know. Here is where you will give them the information they need (facts, details, examples, and reasoning) to understand your subject and/or take action.

Carving the Body into Sections

The bodies of larger technical documents are typically carved into *sections*. In many ways, sections are like miniature documents, needing their own beginning, middle, and end. They typically include an *opening, body,* and *closing* (Figure 15.6).

OPENING   An opening is usually a sentence or small paragraph that identifies the subject and purpose of the section. The opening usually includes a claim or set of claims that the rest of the section will support.

Results of Our Study

The results of our study allow us to draw two conclusions about the causes of flooding in Darbey. First, Darbey's flooding is mostly due to the recent construction of new levees by towns farther upriver. Second, development around the river is taking away some of the wetlands that have protected Darbey from flooding in the past. In this section, we will discuss each of these causes in depth.

A Section with an Opening, Body, and Closing

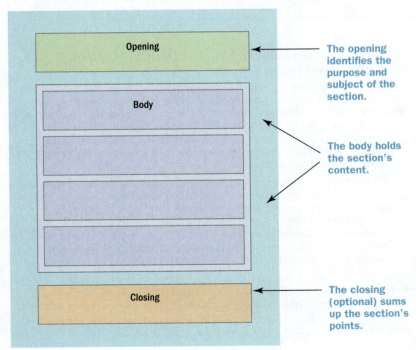

Figure 15.6: A section includes an opening and body. The closing is optional, but it can be helpful to sum up the section's point or points.

BODY   The body of a section is where you will offer support for the claim you made in the opening. The body of a section can run anywhere from one paragraph to many paragraphs, depending on the purpose of the section. For example, if you are discussing the results of a research study, your Results section may require three or more paragraphs in the body—one paragraph per major result.

CLOSING (OPTIONAL)   A large or complex section might need a brief closing paragraph to wrap up the discussion. A closing usually restates the claim you made in the opening of the section. It might also look forward to the next section.

> In sum, these two causes will likely become only more significant over time. As upriver towns grow in population, there will be more pressure than ever to build more levees to protect them. Meanwhile, if development continues in the available wetlands around the Curlew River, Darbey will find that some of its last defenses against flooding have disappeared.

Overall, a section should be able to work as a stand-alone unit in the document. By having its own beginning, middle, and end, a well-written section feels like a miniature document that makes a specific point.

Patterns of Arrangement

When writing each section, you can usually follow a *pattern of arrangement* to organize your ideas. These patterns are based on logical principles, and they can help you organize your information so that your views will be presented in a reasoned way. Major patterns of arrangement are:

- Cause and effect
- Comparison and contrast
- Better and worse
- Costs and benefits
- If … then
- Either … or
- Chronological order
- Problem/needs/solution
- Example

You will find that each section in your document likely follows one of these patterns of arrangement. One section, for example, may discuss the causes and effects of a problem. A later section might use a discussion of the costs and benefits of doing something about the problem. So, as you are organizing and drafting each section, decide which pattern of arrangement best fits your needs.

CAUSE AND EFFECT   In a sense, all events are subject to *causes* and *effects*. For example, if a bridge suddenly collapses, investigators would immediately try to determine the causes for the collapse.

> In 2002, the I-40 bridge over the Arkansas River collapsed for a few different reasons. The actual collapse occurred when a runaway barge on the river rammed into one of the bridge's supports. But other causes were evident. The bridge was already weakened by erosion around the pilings, deteriorated concrete, and attrition due to recent seismic activity.

A cause can also have various effects.

> Leaving a wound untreated can be dangerous. The wound may become contaminated with dirt and germs, thus requiring more healing time. In some cases, the wound may grow infected or even gangrenous, requiring much more treatment at a hospital. Infections can be life threatening.

As you discuss causes and effects, show how effects are the results of specific causes. For example, the white paper shown in Figure 15.7 explains how flooding occurs when specific events (causes) occur.

COMPARISON AND CONTRAST   You can *compare and contrast* just about anything. When comparing and contrasting two things, first identify all the features that make them similar. Then, contrast them by noting the features that make them different (Figure 15.8). By comparing and contrasting two similar things, you can give your readers a deeper understanding of both.

BETTER AND WORSE   In technical workplaces, you are often faced with moments in which you need to choose among different paths. In these cases, you may need to play the advantages off the disadvantages.

The "better" is discussed in terms of advantages. ⟶ Automating our assembly line with robotic workstations has clear advantages. With proper maintenance, robots can work around the clock, every day of the week. They don't take vacations, and they don't require benefits. Moreover, after an initial up-front investment, they are less expensive per unit than human labor.

The "worse" is shown in a less favorable light. ⟶ Our alternative to automation is to stay with human labor. Increasingly, we will become less profitable, because our competitors are moving their operations to offshore facilities, where labor is much cheaper and environmental laws are routinely ignored. Meanwhile, if we do not automate, the increasing costs of health care and an aging workforce will eventually force us to close some of our manufacturing plants in North America.

COSTS AND BENEFITS   By directly weighing the *costs and benefits,* you can show readers that the price is ultimately worth the benefits of moving forward with a project.

Five Reasons a College Education Is Still Worth It

The cost of college has become astronomical and because of the skyrocketing costs, many people have begun to question whether a college education is really worth it. The average private school tuition these days is between $50,000 and $60,000 per year. State universities range anywhere from $20,000 to $50,000. The average yearly tuition at some colleges is more than many Americans earn in an entire year. The four-year tuition at a private college is more than an average house. Yet the value of a college education remains high:

- College graduates make 84 percent more in income during their lifetimes than do high school graduates. That's not quite double, but it's getting closer to double every year.

A Section Using Cause and Effect

Flooding: Causes and Effects

Flooding is primarily caused by natural weather events like rainfall and thunderstorms. Whenever there is heavy rainfall combined with thunderstorms over a short period of time, you can be sure that flooding will occur. Extensive rainfall over a long period of time will also lead to flooding. A flood will also occur when a river overflows its bank and the excess water spills onto the flood plain, which is usually also as a result of heavy rainfall.

The introduction highlights some of the major causes of flooding.

Scientists also say that greenhouse gas emissions have increased the occurrence of extreme weather events, making flooding more likely. In the United Kingdom, research carried out on flood events that occurred in 2000 was attributed to more green house emissions in the atmosphere which led to greenhouse warming and made the floods more likely. Scientists in Oxford University performed a model of the atmosphere as it actually was, and carried out another model of what the atmosphere would have been without the carbon dioxide and other greenhouse gases. Interpolating the two models on a third model, they found that the likelihood of the flood occurring was doubled as a result of humanity's emissions of carbon dioxide and other greenhouse gases. That year, the Hampshire village of Hambledon in the UK was underwater for six weeks and the loss to the country was estimated to be about £1bn.

The causes and effects are explored in greater depth.

Some of the factors that may encourage flooding include:

- A lack of vegetation and woodland. This is because trees and other forms of vegetation obstruct surface runoffs, while roots of trees take up water from the soil. A lack of vegetation will mean that surface runoffs will be high, and this can lead to flooding.
- Rivers surrounded by steep channel may also lead to flooding when the river overflows its bank as a result of excessive rainfall which lead to a high surface run off.
- Drainage basin in urban areas are made of concrete which is impermeable and encourages surface flows. The drainage system takes the water quickly and directly to sewage treatment plants or as in some countries directly to rivers. Heavy rainfall in short periods in instances like this will lead to flooding. Faulty or ill maintained sewer networks and insufficient drainage networks will also encourage flooding.
- Buildings and other developments like car parks in inappropriate places such that they prevent rainfall from draining away naturally can also lead to flood events.

- Canals, reservoirs and other man made structures can fail causing flooding to areas downstream. Industrial activities, water mains and pumping stations can also give rise to flooding due to failure.

The overall effects are explained in the concluding paragraph

The effects of flooding include damage to homes and properties, potential loss of lives, disruption in livelihood and communications and usually an economic loss to the Government. This is because businesses may lose stock, patronage and productivity. Flooding can also affect vital infrastructure. Tourism, agriculture and transportation can also be affected. Road links, canals, rail links may become damaged. The repair cost of the damaged infrastructure can be very high and the period before reinstatement long. Potable water supply may be lost or contaminated and these can have significant health effects as well. One good thing about flooding though is the deposition of silt on the flood plain making it fertile for agriculture and thereby supporting the livelihood of inhabitants of such areas by the provision of food. People living on or near floodplains may rely upon regular flooding to help support their farming and therefore provide food.

Source: Sunmoni, Mobolaji. "Flooding: Causes and Effects" from "The Environmentalist." http://ecoremediation.blogspot.com/2012/07/flooding-causes-and-effects.html. Used by permission of the author.

- As a college graduate you are much more likely to find a job, even in this tough economy. Typically, the unemployment rate for college graduates is about half of that for high school graduates, and that holds true today.

- With a college education, you are much more likely to find a job that is satisfying and enjoyable for your entire life.

- If your family has grown up with financial hardship, getting a college education is the best way to increase your earning power, to provide an example of financial independence for your children, and to improve your family's financial future.

- A recent Georgetown University study showed that as our economy has become less industrial and more knowledge-based, the demand for workers with a college education has increased. In 1973, 72 percent of jobs required a high-school education or less. In 2010, that figure was 41 percent, and by 2020, it is projected to be at 36 percent.

The important thing to remember is that few people pay the actual "sticker price" for college. There are a variety of ways that colleges and universities, as well as the federal government, make it possible to attend college. A college education is still the most sure-fire way to increase your earning power and improve your family's financial situation, now and in the future.

Source, Lili Chamberlain, College Talk, SouthCoastToday.com

Stressing the benefits to your readers is always a good way to reason with them. By putting the costs in contrast to these benefits, you can show how the advantages ultimately outweigh the costs.

A Section Using Comparison and Contrast

Figure 15.8: Comparison and contrast puts two things side by side to show their similarities and differences.

Terrestrial and Jovian Planets

The two types of planets are highlighted for comparison.

With the exception of Pluto, planets in our solar system are classified as either terrestrial (Earth-like) or Jovian (Jupiter-like) planets.

Terrestrial planets include Mercury, Venus, Earth, and Mars. These planets are relatively small in size and in mass. A terrestrial planet has a solid rocky surface, with metals deep in its interior. In the solar system, these planets are closer to the sun and are therefore warmer than the planets located farther out in the solar system. Future space missions are being designed to search remotely for terrestrial planets around other stars.

Describes one of the subjects

The layers of gases surrounding the surface of a planet make up what is known as an atmosphere. The atmospheres of the terrestrial planets range from thin to thick. Mercury has almost no atmosphere. A thick atmosphere made mostly of carbon dioxide covers Venus, trapping heat and raising surface temperatures. Clouds on Venus form from sulfuric acid. Earth's atmosphere is 77 percent nitrogen, 21 percent oxygen, and 1 percent argon, with variable amounts of water vapor, and trace amounts of other gases. White clouds of water vapor hide much of Earth's surface in views of Earth from space. Mars has a very thin atmosphere containing mostly carbon dioxide, with nitrogen, argon, and trace amounts of oxygen and water vapor. The atmosphere also contains thin water and carbon dioxide clouds, and is frequently affected by dust storms.

Jovian planets include Jupiter, Saturn, Uranus, and Neptune. These planets have larger sizes and masses. Jovian planets do not have solid surfaces. They are sometimes called gas giants because they are large and made mostly of gases. Small amounts of rocky materials are only found deep in the cores of Jovian planets. In the solar system, Jovian planets are located farther from the sun than terrestrial planets, and are therefore cooler. Scientists have found more than 100 Jovian planets around other stars. The majority of the extrasolar Jovian planets that have been discovered so far are closer to their stars than the Jovian planets in the solar system are to the sun.

Describes the other subject, while contrasting it to the first subject

The atmospheres of the Jovian planets in our solar system are made mostly of hydrogen and helium. Compounds containing hydrogen, such as water, ammonia, and methane, are also present. Differences in the amounts of these trace gases and variations in the temperatures of these planets contribute to the different colors seen in images taken in visible light. While scientists expect the atmospheres of Jovian planets in other solar systems to be composed mainly of hydrogen and helium, they have not yet measured the properties of their atmospheres.

Source: PBS Nova, http://www.pbs.org/wgbh/nova/education/activities/3113_origins_07.html

IF ... THEN   Perhaps the most common way to reason is using *if ... then* arguments. Essentially, you are saying, "If you believe in X, then you should do Y" or perhaps "If X happens, then Y is likely to happen also" (Figure 15.9). When using *if ... then* arguments, you are leveraging something readers already believe or consider possible to convince them that they should believe or do something further.

EITHER ... OR   When using *either ... or* statements, you are offering readers a choice or showing them two sides of the issue. You are saying, "Either you believe X, or you believe Y" or perhaps "Either X will happen, or Y will happen" (Figure 15.10). Statements using *either ... or* patterns suggest that there is no middle ground, so you should use this strategy only when appropriate. When used appropriately, an *either ... or* argument can prompt your readers to make a decision. When used inappropriately, these arguments can invite readers to make a choice you didn't expect—or perhaps to make no choice at all.

CHRONOLOGICAL ORDER   Time offers its own logic because events happen in chronological order. You can arrange information logically according to the sequence of events.

> Three things happen inside the bronchial tubes and airways in the lungs of people with asthma. The first change is inflammation: The tubes become red, irritated, and swollen. This inflamed tissue "weeps," producing thick mucus. If the inflammation persists, it can lead to permanent thickening in the airways.
>
> Next comes constriction: The muscles around the bronchial tubes tighten, causing the airways to narrow. This is called *bronchospasm* or *bronchoconstriction*.
>
> Finally, there's hyperreactivity. The chronically inflamed and constricted airways become highly reactive to so-called triggers: things like allergens (animal dander, dust mites, molds, pollens), irritants (tobacco smoke, strong odors, car and factory emissions), and infections (flu, the common cold). These triggers result in progressively more inflammation and constriction.
>
> *Source: G. Shapiro, 1998.*

PROBLEM/NEEDS/SOLUTION   The *problem/needs/solution* pattern is a common organizational scheme in technical documents, because technical work often involves solving problems. When using this pattern, you should start by identifying the problem that needs to be solved. Then, state what is needed to solve the problem. Finally, end the section by stating the solution (Figure 15.11). The three-part structure leads readers logically from the problem to the solution.

EXAMPLE   Using an *example* is a good way to support your claims. Your readers might struggle with facts and data, but an example can help make all those technical details more realistic and familiar.

> To fool predators, most butterflies have evolved colors and patterns that allow them to survive. For example, the delicious Red-spotted Purple is often not eaten by birds, because it looks like a Pipevine Swallowtail, a far less appetizing insect. Other butterflies, like angel wings, look like tree bark or leaves when seen from below. If a predator comes near, though, angel wings can surprise it with a sudden burst of color from the topside of their wings. (Pyle, 1981, p. 23)

Figure 15.9:
If ... then
patterns are
used to build
arguments on
uncertainties.

Effects of Climate Change on Forests

The opening sets a premise with two *if . . . then* statements.

The projected 2°C (3.6°F) warming could shift the ideal range for many North American forest species by about 300 km (200 mi.) to the north. If the climate changes slowly enough, warmer temperatures may enable the trees to colonize north into areas that are currently too cold, at about the same rate as southern areas became too hot and dry for the species to survive. If the earth warms 2°C (3.6°F) in 100 years, however, the species would have to migrate about 2 miles every year.

The body of the section explores the implications of those *if . . . then* statements.

Trees whose seeds are spread by birds may be able to spread at that rate. But neither trees whose seeds are carried by the wind, nor nut-bearing trees such as oaks, are likely to spread by more than a few hundred feet per year. Poor soils may also limit the rate at which tree species can spread north. Thus, the range over which a particular species is found may tend to be squeezed as southern areas become inhospitably hot. The net result is that some forests may tend to have a less diverse mix of tree species.

Several other impacts associated with changing climate further complicate the picture. On the positive side, CO_2 has a beneficial fertilization effect on plants, and also enables plants to use water more efficiently. These effects might enable some species to resist the adverse effects of warmer temperatures or drier soils. On the negative side, forest fires are likely to become more frequent and severe if soils become drier. Changes in pest populations could further increase the stress on forests. Managed forests may tend to be less vulnerable than unmanaged forests, because the managers will be able to shift to tree species appropriate for the warmer climate.

The closing poses *if . . . then* statements that are more speculative.

Perhaps the most important complicating factor is uncertainty (see U.S. Climate in the Future Climate section) whether particular regions will become wetter or drier. If climate becomes wetter, then forests are likely to expand toward rangelands and other areas that are dry today; if climate becomes drier, then forests will retreat away from those areas. Because of these fundamental uncertainties, existing studies of the impact of climate change have ambiguous results.

Source: U.S. Environmental Protection Agency, http://yosemite.epa.gov/oar/globalwarming.nsf/content/ImpactsForests.html

The opening sets up two sides with *either . . . or* **statements.**

The remainder of the section discusses the two sides.

Here, the section ends by saying which side won the debate.

Shapley-Curtis Debate

During the 1920s, Harlow Shapley and Heber Curtis debated whether observed fuzzy "spiral nebulae," which are today known as galaxies, exist either in our Milky Way Galaxy or beyond it. Shapley took the stance that these "spiral nebulae" observed in visible light do indeed exist in our galaxy, while the more conservative Curtis believed in the converse. While both sides of this debate seemed to either make too many suppositions or supported their claims with flawed data, the main points of both stances made the debate fairly close at the time.

Shapley's Argument

Shapley argued that these "spiral nebulae" are actually within our galaxy's halo. He presented faulty data which seemed to confirm that M101, a large angular-diameter galaxy, changed angular size noticeably. We know now that for M101 to change angular size appreciably (0.02 arcsecond/year), it would have to recede from us at warp speeds based upon our current knowledge of its diameter and distance. To account for all the galaxies' observed recession from earth, not knowing of the universe's expansion, Shapley invented a special repulsion force to explain this strange phenomenon. He was not cogently able to explain why galaxies observed from earth are less densely distributed along the galactic equator, though.

Curtis's Argument

Curtis remained more conservative in his argument by not introducing outlandish suppositions like the special repulsion forces of Shapley. Curtis, although not able to explain galaxies' redshifts well either, made a convincing claim for the distribution of galaxies in the sky. Because observed galaxies seen edge-on often contain opaque gas lanes, and if our galaxy is similar to those observed galaxies, then we should not see extragalactic objects near our equator because of our own opaque dust lane. Hubble's observation of Cepheid variables in the Andromeda Galaxy confirmed the distance to a galaxy: millions of light-years, not thousands! Curtis was obviously correct.

Source: A. Aversa, 2003

Figure 15.10: The *either . . . or* pattern is helpful when only one belief or action is the right one.

Organizing and Drafting the Conclusion

An effective conclusion rounds out the discussion by bringing readers back to the subject, purpose, and main point of your document.

Five Closing Moves in a Conclusion

Like the introduction of your document, your document's conclusion will make a few predictable moves expected by your audience:

MOVE 1: MAKE AN OBVIOUS TRANSITION By using a heading such as "Final Points" or a transitional phrase such as "To sum up," you will signal to the readers that you are going to tell them your main points. Here are some transitions that will get their attention:

In conclusion,	*Put briefly,*	*Overall,*
To sum up,	*In brief,*	*As a whole,*
Let us sum up,	*Finally,*	*In the end,*
In summary,	*To finish up,*	*On the whole,*
In closing,	*Ultimately,*	

MOVE 2: RESTATE YOUR MAIN POINT In the conclusion, you need to restate your main point one more time to drive it home. After all, your readers now have all the facts, so they should be ready to make a final decision.

> If Darbey is to survive and thrive, we need to take action now to address its increasing flooding problem. By restoring wetlands, developing greenways, and building levees, we can begin preparing for the flooding problems that are almost certainly a risk in the future.

Link

For more information on using transitions, see Chapter 16, page 430.

MOVE 3: RE-EMPHASIZE THE IMPORTANCE OF THE SUBJECT Sometimes readers need to be reminded of why the subject of your document is important to them.

> If we can reduce or eliminate flooding in Darbey, we will save our citizens millions of dollars in lost revenues and reconstruction. Moreover, Darbey will be viewed as a place with a future, because flooding will not continually undo all our hard work.

MOVE 4: LOOK TO THE FUTURE Looking to the future is a good way to end any document (Figure 15.12). A sentence or paragraph that looks to the future will leave your readers with a positive image.

> When we have effectively managed the Curlew River, the city of Darbey and surrounding area will likely see steady growth in population and industry. Once its reputation for flooding has been removed, people and businesses will likely move to this area for its riverside charm and outdoor activities. The town will experience a true revival.

Figure 15.11:
The problem/
needs/solu-
tion pattern
is a good way
to lead peo-
ple logically
toward taking
action.

North Creek Water Cleanup Plan (TMDL)

North Creek does not meet state standards for swimming and wading because there is too much bacteria in the water. Also, the federal government has determined that Chinook salmon are threatened, and other salmon species face continuing pressure from urban development.

Opening paragraph identifies the problem.

In the 1960s, much of the watershed was home to small ranches and hobby farms. Over the past 40 years, much of the land has been redeveloped with a trend towards more urban, commercial, and suburban residential develop-ment. The basin's hydrology, how water is stored and managed throughout the basin, has also changed.

Why Are These Waters Polluted?

Pollution in the North Creek watershed comes from thousands of sources that may not have clearly identifiable emission points; this category of pollution is called "nonpoint" pollution. These nonpoint sources can contribute a variety of pollutants that may come from failing septic systems, livestock and pet wastes, at-home car washing, lawn and garden care, leaky machinery, and other daily activities. Some of these nonpoint sources create fecal coliform bacterial pollution that indicate the presence of fecal wastes from warm-blooded animals. Ecology has confirmed that high levels of fecal coliform bacteria exist in North Creek. For this reason, Total Maximum Daily Loads for fecal coliform bacteria were subsequently established at multiple locations through each watershed.

The section's body elaborates on the problem.

Although wildlife can also contribute bacteria, such sources are not defined as pollution; however, when such natural sources combine with nonpoint pollution, the result can cause the kind of problems found in North Creek.

North Creek became polluted because of the way we do things, not the activities themselves. For example, having dogs, cats, horses, and other animals as part of our life is not a problem; rather, it is the way that we care for these animals. Similarly, roads and parking lots are a necessity of our modern society, but the way we build centers is causing our local streams and creeks to be polluted. There are solutions that can be undertaken by local governments, businesses, organizations, and citizens to solve the problem.

What Can You Do to Improve North Creek?

If cleaning up local waters is important to you, think about what you can do on your own first. Do you always pick up after your pet? Can you use organic

These questions are designed to highlight what is needed.

fertilizer? Do you wash your car on your lawn or take it to a car wash? Can you reduce the amount of stormwater runoff from your property? Can you develop a farm plan to ensure your horse's manure is not reaching local streams? Do you practice good on-site septic system maintenance? The draft Action Plan includes information about current and future activities to clean up local waters.

There are many things residents can do now to reduce pollution reaching water bodies and to improve water quality. Here are some ways that you can help:

- Be responsible for proper septic tank maintenance or repair. If you have questions about your on-site septic system (exactly where it is located, how to maintain it), you can call the Snohomish Health District for technical assistance.

- Can you reduce stormwater leaving your property? To have a free survey of your property for ways to reduce potential water quality problems and improve stormwater management, contact Craig Young, your North Creek Basin steward.

- Keep pet and other animal wastes out of your local streams. Pick up after your pet and work with your community, association, or local government to get a pet waste collection station installed where it is needed most.

Here are the recommended solutions to the problem.

- Use landscaping methods that eliminate or reduce fertilizers and pesticides. If fertilizers are needed, organic products break down more slowly and help prevent big flushes of pollution when we have heavy rains; they also improve soil structure.

- Join local volunteers in planting trees and performing other activities that help local streams. Snohomish County, the Stilly/Snohomish Task Force and North Creek Streamkeepers, and the City of Bothell water quality volunteer program improve water quality by helping with stream restoration activities. They provide help or other opportunities to plant trees on your property or at other needed locations to help water quality (you can also volunteer to plant trees in other areas that need help too).

- Get involved in your local government's programs. Folks interested in sampling their local waters can contact Snohomish County, North Creek Streamkeepers, or your local city to explore the availability of volunteer monitoring opportunities. If you live outside of a city, be a Salmon Watcher or Watershed Keeper, or get involved in other individual or group activities to improve local waters; these are coordinated by Snohomish County staff.

(continued)

The section closes by restating the main point and looking to the future. → How else can you be involved? The solution to polluting our local waters is to do some things a little differently. In this way, we can still live a normal 21st-century lifestyle, have animals as a close part of our lives, and have clean water. Citizen involvement in deciding what needs to be done is essential to making our water bodies safe places for people and fish, and you may be part of helping to design future watershed activities that haven't even been thought of yet! Check out the Related Links page for more ideas.

Source: Washington State Department of Ecology, http://www.ecy.wa.gov/programs/wq/tmdl/watershed/north_creek/solution.html

AT A GLANCE

Five Moves in a Conclusion

- Move 1: Make an obvious transition.
- Move 2: Restate your main point.
- Move 3: Re-emphasize the importance of the subject.
- Move 4: Look to the future.
- Move 5: Say thank you and offer contact information.

MOVE 5: SAY THANK YOU AND OFFER CONTACT INFORMATION You might end your document by saying thank you and offering contact information.

> We appreciate your time and consideration. If you have any questions or would like to meet with us about this report, please contact the task force leader, Mary Subbock, at 555–0912 or e-mail her at msubbock@cdarbey.gov.

This kind of thank you statement leaves readers with a positive feeling and invites them to contact you if they need more information.

Organizing Transcultural Documents

When communicating with transcultural readers, you may need to alter the organization of a document to suit their different expectations. Most readers from other cultures know that North American documents tend to be direct and to the point. Even with this awareness, though, the bluntness might still distract or even irritate them. So, your message may be more effective if you consider your readers' cultural preferences.

When organizing a transcultural document or presentation, perhaps the greatest concern is whether you are communicating with people from a high-context culture like many in Asia, the Middle East, and Africa, or a low-context culture like those in North America or Europe. In a high-context culture, people expect a writer or speaker to provide a significant amount of contextual information before expressing the point or stating the purpose of the document. To most North Americans and Europeans, this up-front contextual information may make the document seem unfocused and its message sound distracted or vague.

Link

For more information on writing cross-cultural texts, see Chapter 2, page 24.

To someone from a high-context culture, however, putting most or all of the contextual information up front signals that the writer is being careful, polite, and deliberate (Figure 15.13). This "indirect approach" signals sensitivity to the importance of the message and the refinement of the writer. In some cultures, this indirectness is intended to allow the reader to save face when problems are mentioned or criticisms are made later in the document.

Sample Conclusion

Figure 15.12:
This conclusion demonstrates all five closing moves that might be found in a document.

An obvious transition →

The main point →

Stresses the importance of the subject →

A look to the future →

A thank you with contact information →

Conclusion

In conclusion, if Darbey is to survive and thrive, we need to take action now to address its increasing flooding problem. By restoring wetlands, developing greenways, and building levees, we can begin preparing for the flooding problems that are almost certainly a risk in the future.

The benefits clearly outweigh the costs. If we can reduce or eliminate flooding in Darbey, we will save our citizens millions of dollars in lost revenues and reconstruction. Moreover, Darbey will be viewed as a place with a future, because flooding will not continually undo all our hard work. When we have effectively managed the Curlew River, Darbey will likely see steady growth in population and industry. Once its reputation for flooding has been removed, people and businesses will likely move to this area for its riverside charm and outdoor activities. The town will experience a true revival.

We appreciate your time and consideration. If you have any questions or would like to meet with us about this report, please contact the task force leader, Mary Subbock, at 555-0912 or e-mail her at msubbock@cdarbey.gov.

Indirect Approach Introductions

The *indirect approach* primarily affects the introductions and conclusions of documents. In Asian cultures, including China, Japan, Korea, and India, writers and speakers often work from the most general information (placed in the introduction) toward the main point (found in the conclusion).

Usually, the first aim in an indirect approach document is to establish a relationship or call attention to the existing relationship. A Japanese introduction may discuss the weather or the changing of the seasons. A Chinese or Korean introduction may refer to any prior relationships between the writer's and the reader's companies.

The example letter in Figure 15.13 plays it safe by mentioning the weather, health, and safety. Notice how the letter starts with general information and works toward more specific information. A letter like this one would be appropriate when the reader has met the writer but the relationship is still new. If the relationship were more established, the second paragraph describing the company would be removed.

For many Asian readers, the preservation of harmony is important, so introductions will likely be subtle, striving to draw attention to common values and experiences. The individual is de-emphasized, while the community and situation are emphasized.

In Arab nations and many Islamic cultures, introductions may include calls for Allah's favor on the reader, family, or business. It is common to find highly ornate statements of appreciation, almost to the point of exaggeration. Arab writers may mention their own accomplishments and the high standing of their acquaintances, while complimenting the reader's achievements and high status. This exaltation of self and acquaintances may seem unnecessary to the North American reader, but the intention is to build a relationship between writer and reader.

Link

For more information on writing introductions in letters, see Chapter 5, page 96.

Letters in Mexico and some South American countries might start with polite inquiries about family members, especially spouses. They then usually move to the main point, much like North American or European documents.

Indirect Approach Conclusions

Link

For more information on writing conclusions in letters, see Chapter 5, page 102.

An indirect approach conclusion usually states the main point of the document but not in an overt way. The most effective conclusion is one in which writer and reader reach a common understanding, often without the main point being stated directly.

For example, in the letter in Figure 15.13, the writer is trying to persuade the reader to buy her company's products. But she does not write, "We would like to sell you our products." Instead, she only makes the catalog and brochures available and explains where orders can be made. The reader in China will recognize that she is trying to sell something.

Hammond Industries

1201 5th Ave., Springfield MO, 65802
417.555.9812

10 February, 2014

Mr. Wu Choa
Northern Construction Company, Ltd.
2550 Hongqiao Road
Shanghai, 200335, China

Dear Mr. Wu Choa,

Weather, health, and safety are common opening topics. →

We hope you are in good health and that you returned home safely from our meeting in Shanghai. Our representatives in Shanghai tell us the weather has been mild and rainy. In our state of Missouri, the weather continues to be cold with more snow than usual, so we are expecting a late spring. We hope spring will bring less moisture.

Hammond Industries greatly appreciates your visit with our company's representatives in Shanghai. Our company was started 25 years ago by Charles Hammond in Missouri. ← **Reinforces relationships with historical information**
Hammond Industries has been supplying solar panels to Asia for 15 years. We have relationships with 8 construction companies in China. Our products are recognized for their reliability and affordability. Our sales and service team in Shanghai is dependable and happy to respond to customers' needs.

China is a growing market for our products. Our goal is to strengthen and expand our connections in the Shanghai province. We hope our products will continue to meet the needs of large construction companies in your province. ← **Becomes more specific by explaining corporate goals**

Main point: Products are available for purchase. →

We have included a catalog and brochures that describe our products. Our representatives in Shanghai are also available to provide more information. Calls can be made to Mr. Sun, our sales representative. Any orders can be made through our website.

Sincerely,

Sally Gualandi

Sally Gualandi
Special Representative for Asia
Hammond Industries

Figure 15.13:
This example letter demonstrates the indirect approach common in many Asian cultures. This kind of letter would be written to a reader who had met the writer, but the relationship is still new.

- The beginning of a document (introduction) builds a context. The middle (body) provides the content. And the end (conclusion) rebuilds the context.

- A genre is a predictable pattern for organizing information to achieve specific purposes.

- Outlining may seem old-fashioned, but it is a very effective way to sketch out the organization of a document.

- Presentation software can help you organize complicated information.

- Introductions usually include up to six opening moves: (1) define your subject, (2) state your purpose, (3) state your main point, (4) stress the importance of the subject, (5) provide background information, and (6) forecast the content.

- The body of larger documents is usually carved into sections. Each section has an opening, a body, and perhaps a closing.

- Sections usually follow patterns of arrangement to organize information.

- Conclusions usually include up to five closing moves: (1) make an obvious transition, (2) restate your main point, (3) re-emphasize the importance of the subject, (4) look to the future, and (5) say thank you and offer contact information.

- Some transcultural readers, especially those from Asia, Africa, and the Middle East, will feel more comfortable with an "indirect approach" document that moves from the general to the specific.

Individual and Team Projects

1. Find a technical document on the Internet that interests you. Write a memo to your instructor in which you critique the organization of the document. Does it have a clear beginning, middle, and end? Does the introduction make some or all of the six opening moves? Is the body divided into sections? Does the conclusion make some or all of the five closing moves? Explain to your instructor how the document's organization might be improved.

2. Find a technical document on the Internet that has an introduction that you think is ineffective. Then, rewrite the introduction so that it includes a clear subject, purpose, and main point. Also, stress the importance of the document's subject, provide some background information, and forecast the structure of the document's body.

3. On the Internet or in a print document, find a section that uses one of the following organizational patterns:

   - Cause and effect
   - Comparison and contrast
   - Better and worse

- Costs and benefits
- *If … then*
- *Either … or*
- Problem/needs/solution
- Example

Prepare a brief presentation to your class in which you show how the text you found follows the pattern.

Collaborative Project

Around campus or on the Internet, find a large document, perhaps a report or proposal. With presentation software, outline the document by creating a slide for each section or subsection. Use the headings of the sections as titles on your slides. Then, on each slide, use bulleted lists to highlight the important points in each section.

When you have finished outlining, look over the presentation. Are there any places where too much information is offered? Are there places where more information is needed? Where could you rearrange information to make it more effective?

Present your findings to your class. Using the presentation software, show the class how the document you studied is organized. Then, discuss some improvements you might make to the organization to highlight important information.

Visit MyWritingLab for a Post-test and more technical writing resources.

The Bad News

In most ways, the project had been a failure. Lisa Franklin was on a chemical engineering team developing a polymer that would protect lightweight tents against desert elements like extreme sun, sandstorms, and chewing insects. Hikers and campers were interested in tents with this kind of protection. But the company Lisa worked for, Outdoor Solutions, wanted to begin selling tents to the military. Bulk sales to the U.S. Army and Marines would improve the company's bottom line, as well as open new opportunities to sell other products.

Despite a promising start, Lisa and the other researchers had not yet developed a stable polymer that would provide the desired protection. The best polymers they had developed were highly flammable. Tent materials covered with these polymers went up like an inferno when exposed to flame. The nonflammable polymers, meanwhile, seemed to break down within three months of use in desert conditions. Lisa's boss, Jim Franklin, was convinced they were close to a breakthrough, but they just couldn't find the right combination to create a nonflammable polymer that would last.

Unfortunately, Lisa's boss had been giving the company president the impression that the polymer was already a success. So, the president had secured a million-dollar loan to retool a factory to produce new lightweight tents coated with the polymer. Renovation was due to begin in a month.

Before starting the factory retooling, the president of the company asked for a final update on the polymer, so Jim wrote a progress report. Then he gave the report to Lisa for final revisions, because he was going out of town on a business trip. He said, "Do whatever you want to revise the report. I'm so frustrated with this project, I don't want to look at this report anymore. When you're done, send the report to the company president. I don't need to see it again."

In the report, Lisa noticed, Jim's facts were all true, but the organization of the report hid the fact that they had not developed a workable polymer. For example, when Jim mentioned that their best polymers were highly flammable, he did so at the end of a long paragraph in the middle of the report. It was highly unlikely that the president would be reading closely enough to see that important fact.

Lisa knew Jim was trying to hide the research team's failure to develop a workable polymer. She didn't want to admit that they had failed either. But she also thought it was important that the company president understand that they had not developed a successful polymer. After all, there was a lot of money on the line.

If you were in Lisa's place, how would you handle this situation?

CHAPTER

16

Using Plain and Persuasive Style

What Is Style? *422*

Writing Plain Sentences *422*

Help: Translating and Translation
  Programs *429*

Writing Plain Paragraphs *430*

When Is It Appropriate to Use
  Passive Voice? *435*

Persuasive Style *437*

Balancing Plain and Persuasive
  Style *442*

What You Need to Know *443*

Exercises and Projects *443*

Case Study: Going Over the
  Top *445*

In this chapter, you will learn:

- The importance of style in technical communication.

- The differences between plain and persuasive style.

- Strategies for writing plain sentences and paragraphs.

- How to tell when it's appropriate to use persuasive style.

- How to use techniques of persuasive style, including tone, similes, analogies, metaphors, and pace.

*S*ometimes, *what you say isn't as important as how you say it.* Your document's style expresses your attitude toward the subject. It reflects your character by embodying the values, beliefs, and relationships you want to share with the readers. In a word, style is about *quality.* Style is about your and your company's commitment to excellence.

One of the great advantages of writing with computers is the ability to move text around. By learning some rather simple techniques, you can make your writing clearer and more persuasive.

What Is Style?

In technical communication, style is not embellishment or ornamentation. Style is not artificial flavoring added to a document to make the content more "interesting." A few added adjectives or exclamation marks won't do much to improve your style.

Good style goes beyond these kinds of superficial cosmetic changes. It involves

- choosing the right words and phrases.
- structuring sentences and paragraphs for clarity.
- using an appropriate tone.
- adding a visual sense to the text.

Historically, rhetoricians have classified style into three levels: plain style, persuasive style, and grand style.

Plain style—Plain style stresses clear wording and simple prose. It is most often used to instruct, teach, or present information. Plain style works best in documents like technical descriptions, instructions, and activity reports.

Persuasive style—There are times when you will need to influence people to accept your ideas and take action. In these situations, persuasive style allows you to add energy and vision to your writing and speaking. This style works best with proposals, letters, articles, public presentations, and some reports.

Grand style—Grand style stresses eloquence. For example, Martin Luther King, Jr., and President John F. Kennedy often used the grand style to move their listeners to do what was right, even if people were reluctant to do it.

In this chapter, we will concentrate solely on plain and persuasive style, because they are most common in technical documents. Grand style is rarely used in technical communication because it often sounds too ornate or formal for the workplace.

Writing Plain Sentences

You have probably been told to "write clearly" or "write in concrete language" as though making up your mind to do so was all it took. In reality, writing plainly is a skill that requires practice and concentration. Fortunately, once you have mastered a few basic guidelines, plain style will become a natural strength in your writing.

Basic Parts of a Sentence

To start, let's consider the parts of a basic sentence. A sentence in English typically has three main parts: a subject, a verb, and a comment.

Subject—What the sentence is about

Verb—What the subject is doing

Comment—What is being said about the subject

English is a flexible language, allowing sentences to be organized in a variety of ways. For example, consider these three variations of the same sentence:

Subject	Verb	Comment
The Institute	provided	the government with accurate crime statistics.
The government	was provided	with accurate crime statistics by the Institute.
Crime statistics	were provided	to the government by the Institute.

Notice that the *content* in these sentences has not changed; only the order of the words has changed. However, the focus of each sentence changes when the subject is changed. The first sentence is *about* the "Institute." The second sentence is *about* the "government." The last sentence is *about* "crime statistics." By changing the subject of the sentence, you essentially shift its focus, drawing your readers' attention to different issues.

Eight Guidelines for Plain Sentences

This understanding of the different parts of a sentence is the basis for eight guidelines that can be used to write plainer sentences in technical documents.

GUIDELINE 1: MAKE THE SUBJECT OF THE SENTENCE WHAT THE SENTENCE IS ABOUT   Confusion often creeps into texts when readers cannot easily identify the subjects of the sentences. For example, what is the subject of the following sentence?

1. Ten months after the Hartford Project began in which a team of our experts conducted close observations of management actions, our final conclusion is that the scarcity of monetary funds is at the basis of the inability of Hartford Industries to appropriate resources to essential projects that have the greatest necessity.

This sentence is difficult to read for a variety of reasons, but the most significant problem is the lack of a clear subject. What is this sentence about? The word "conclusion" is currently in the subject position, but the sentence might also be about "our experts," "the Hartford Project," or "the scarcity of monetary funds."

When you run into a sentence like this one, first decide what the sentence is about. Then, cut and paste to move that subject into the subject slot of the sentence. For example, when this sentence is restructured around "our experts," readers will find it easier to understand:

The subject (underlined) is what this sentence is "about." →

1a. Ten months after the Hartford Project began, <u>our experts</u> have concluded through close observations of management actions that the scarcity of monetary funds is at the basis of the inability of Hartford Industries to appropriate resources to essential projects that have the greatest necessity.

This sentence is still rather difficult to read. Nevertheless, it is easier to understand because the noun in the subject slot ("our experts") is what the sentence is about. We will return to this sentence later in this chapter.

GUIDELINE 2: USE THE "DOER" AS THE SUBJECT OF THE SENTENCE   Readers tend to focus on who or what is doing something in a sentence. For example, which of the following sentences is easier to read?

2a. On Saturday morning, <u>the paperwork</u> was completed in a timely fashion by Jim.

2b. On Saturday morning, <u>Jim</u> completed the paperwork in a timely fashion.

Most readers would say that sentence 2b is easier to read because Jim, the subject of the sentence, is actually doing something. In the first sentence, the paperwork is merely sitting there. People make especially good subjects of sentences, because they are usually active.

GUIDELINE 3: USE A VERB TO EXPRESS THE ACTION, OR WHAT THE DOER IS DOING   Once you have determined who or what is doing something, ask yourself what that person or thing is actually doing. Find the *action* and turn it into the verb of the sentence. For example, consider these sentences:

In these sentences, the action becomes harder and harder to find.

3a. The detective investigated the loss of the payroll.

3b. The detective conducted an investigation into the loss of the payroll.

3c. The detective is the person who is conducting an investigation of the loss of the payroll.

Sentence 3a is easy to understand because the action of the sentence is expressed in the verb. Sentences 3b and 3c are increasingly more difficult to understand, because the action, "investigate," is further removed from the verb of the sentence.

GUIDELINE 4: PUT THE SUBJECT OF THE SENTENCE EARLY IN THE SENTENCE   Subconsciously, your readers start every sentence looking for the subject. The subject anchors the sentence, because it tells readers what the sentence is about.

Consider these two sentences:

It's easier to locate the subject of this sentence because it is up front.

4a. If deciduous and evergreen trees experience yet another year of drought like the one observed in 1997, the entire <u>Sandia Mountain ecosystem</u> will be heavily damaged.

4b. <u>The entire Sandia Mountain ecosystem</u> will be heavily damaged if deciduous and evergreen trees experience yet another year of drought like the one observed in 1997.

The problem with sentence 4a is that it forces readers to hold all those details about trees, drought, and 1997 in short-term memory before it identifies the subject of the sentence. Readers almost feel a sense of relief when they come to the subject, because until that point they cannot figure out what the sentence is about.

Quite differently, sentence 4b tells readers what the sentence is about up front. With the subject early in the sentence, readers immediately know how to connect the comment with the subject.

The first sentence is harder to read because the action is in a nominalization.

GUIDELINE 5: ELIMINATE NOMINALIZATIONS   Nominalizations are perfectly good verbs and adjectives that have been turned into awkward nouns. For example, look at these sentences:

5a. Management has <u>an expectation</u> that the project will meet the deadline.

5b. Management <u>expects</u> the project to meet the deadline.

Here are a whole bunch of nominalizations.

In sentence 5a, "expectation" is a nominalization. Here, a perfectly good verb is being used as a noun. Sentence 5b is not only shorter than sentence 5a, but it also has more energy because the verb "expects" is now an action verb.

Consider these two sentences:

See how reducing them improves the readability?

6a. <u>Our discussion</u> about the matter allowed us to make <u>a decision</u> on <u>the acquisition</u> of the new x-ray machine.

6b. We <u>discussed</u> the matter and <u>decided</u> to <u>acquire</u> the new x-ray machine.

Sentence 6a includes three nominalizations—"discussion," "decision," and "acquisition"—making the sentence hard to understand. Sentence 6b is clearer, because the nominalizations "discussion" and "decision" have been turned into action verbs.

Why do writers use nominalizations in the first place? Two main reasons are:

- First, humans generally think in terms of people, places, and things (nouns), so our first drafts are often filled with nominalizations, which are nouns. While revising, an effective writer will turn those first-draft nominalizations into action verbs.
- Second, some people mistakenly believe that using nominalizations makes their writing sound more formal or important. In reality, though, nominalizations only make sentences harder to read. The best way to sound important is to write sentences that readers can understand.

GUIDELINE 6: ELIMINATE EXCESSIVE PREPOSITIONAL PHRASES Prepositional phrases are necessary in writing, but they are often overused in ways that make text too long and too tedious. Prepositional phrases follow prepositions like *in, of, by, about, over,* and *under.* These phrases are used to modify nouns.

Prepositional phrases become problematic when used in excess. For example, sentence 7a is difficult to read because it links too many prepositional phrases together (the prepositional phrases are underlined and the prepositions are italicized). Sentence 7b shows the same sentence with fewer prepositional phrases:

The prepositional phrases have been reduced, clarifying the sentence's meaning.

> 7a. The decline *in* the number *of* businesses owned *by* locals *in* the town *of* Artesia is a demonstration *of* the increasing hardship faced *in* rural communities *in* the southwest.

> 7b. Artesia's declining number of locally owned businesses demonstrates the increased hardship faced by southwestern rural communities.

You should never feel obligated to eliminate all the prepositional phrases in a sentence. Rather, look for long chains of prepositional phrases. Then, try to condense the sentence by turning some of the prepositional phrases into adjectives.

For example, the phrase "in the town of Artesia" from sentence 7a was reduced in sentence 7b to the adjective "Artesia's." The phrase "in rural communities in the southwest" was reduced to "southwestern rural communities." As a result, sentence 7b is much shorter and easier to read.

Figure 16.1 shows a website in which the authors write plainly. Notice how they have used minimal prepositional phrases.

GUIDELINE 7: ELIMINATE REDUNDANCY IN SENTENCES In your effort to get your point across, you may use redundant phrasing. For example, you might write "unruly mob" as though some kinds of mobs might be orderly. Or, you might talk about "active participants" as though someone can participate without doing anything.

Sometimes buzzwords and jargon lead to redundancies like, "We should collaborate together as a team" or "Empirical observations will provide a new understanding of the subject." In some cases, you might use a synonym to modify a synonym by saying something like, "We are demanding important, significant changes."

You should try to eliminate redundancies because they use two or more words to do the work of one word. As a result, readers need to work twice as hard to understand one basic idea.

GUIDELINE 8: WRITE SENTENCES THAT ARE "BREATHING LENGTH" You should be able to read a sentence out loud in one breath. At the end of the sentence, the period (.) signals, "Take a breath." Of course, when reading silently, readers do not actually breathe when they see a period, but they do take a mental pause at the end of each sentence. If a sentence runs on and on, it forces readers to mentally hold their breath. By the end of an especially long sentence, they are more concerned about when the sentence is going to end than what the sentence is saying.

AT A GLANCE

Eight Guidelines for Plain Sentences

- Guideline 1: The subject of the sentence should be what the sentence is about.
- Guideline 2: The subject should be the "doer" in the sentence.
- Guideline 3: The verb should state the action, or what the doer is doing.
- Guideline 4: The subject of the sentence should come early in the sentence.
- Guideline 5: Eliminate nominalizations.
- Guideline 6: Avoid excessive prepositional phrases.
- Guideline 7: Eliminate redundancy in sentences.
- Guideline 8: Write sentences that are "breathing length."

Writing Plainly

Figure 16.1:
On this web-
page, informa-
tion about
counterterror-
ism is provided
in plain prose.

Nominalizations and prepositional phrases have been kept to a minimum.

Actions are expressed in action verbs.

Subjects are placed up front in sentences.

Source: Lawrence Livermore National Laboratory

The best way to think about sentence length is to imagine how long it takes to comfortably say a sentence out loud.

- If a written sentence is too long to say comfortably, it probably needs to be shortened or cut into two sentences. Avoid asphyxiating the readers with sentences that go on forever.
- If the sentence is very short, perhaps it needs to be combined with one of its neighbors to give it a more comfortable breathing length. You want to avoid making readers hyperventilate over a string of short sentences.

Link

For examples of different breathing-length sentences, see the discussion of pace on page 440.

Creating Plain Sentences with a Computer

Computers give us an amazing ability to manipulate sentences. So, take full advantage of your machine's capabilities. First, write out your draft as you normally would, not paying too much attention to the style. Then, as you revise, identify difficult sentences and follow these seven steps:

1. Identify who or what is doing something in the sentence.
2. Turn that who or what into the subject of the sentence.
3. Move the subject to an early place in the sentence.
4. Identify what the subject is doing, and move that action into the verb slot.
5. Eliminate unnecessary nominalizations and redundancies.
6. Eliminate prepositional phrases, where appropriate, by turning them into adjectives.
7. Shorten, lengthen, combine, or divide sentences to make them breathing length.

With these seven steps in mind, let's revisit sentence 1, the example of weak style earlier in this chapter:

Original

1. Ten months after the Hartford Project began in which a team of our experts conducted close observations of management actions, our final conclusion is that the scarcity of monetary funds is at the basis of the inability of Hartford Industries to appropriate resources to essential projects that have the greatest necessity.

Now, let's apply the seven-step method for revising sentences into the plain style. First, identify who or what is doing something in the sentence, make it the subject, and move it to an early place in the sentence.

The experts are doing something.

The action is now in the verb.

1a. After a ten-month study, our experts have concluded that the scarcity of monetary funds is at the basis of the inability of Hartford Industries to appropriate resources to essential projects that have the greatest necessity.

Now eliminate the prepositional phrases, nominalizations, and redundancies.

1b. After a ten-month study, our experts concluded that Hartford Industries' budget shortfalls are limiting its support for priority projects.

In the revision, the "doers" ("our experts") were moved into the subject position and then moved to an early place in the sentence. Then, the action of the sentence ("concluded") was moved into the verb slot. Prepositional phrases like "after the Hartford Project" and "to appropriate resources to essential projects" were turned into adjectives. Nominalizations ("conclusion," "necessity") were turned into verbs or adjectives. And finally, the sentence was shortened to breathing length.

The resulting sentence still sends the same message—just more plainly.

Translating and Translation Programs

In the *Hitchhiker's Guide to the Galaxy* by Douglas Adams, different creatures are able to communicate with each other by using a Babel fish, which is described as a "yellow and leech-like" creature that can be slipped into the ear.

Unfortunately, these Babel fish are fiction, so we need to translate our own materials or have them translated for us. Professional translators can be expensive, especially if you are just trying to translate an e-mail from one of your overseas clients or figure out a website written in another language.

Several translation software programs are available for purchase, such as Babylon, Power Translator, and Promt. The accuracy of these programs has improved greatly over the last decade. Most Internet search engines, like Bing, have a free online translation service available (Figure A).

Translation software is far from perfect. Certainly, you should not rely exclusively on these tools to translate an important proposal or report into another language. To handle these kinds of projects, you will likely need to hire a translation service. However, for smaller texts, some helpful tips can minimize problems when using translation software:

Use basic sentences—Translation software typically tries to translate whole sentences rather than translate word by word. Cut longer, more complex sentences into smaller, simpler sentences.

Use standard punctuation—Periods, commas, and question marks are fine. Less common punctuation marks like ellipses, dashes, colons, and semicolons often create difficulties for translation software.

Use consistent words—In texts that will be translated, use the same word to mean the same thing.

Avoid metaphors, sayings, and clichés—These kinds of phrases require knowledge of the culture of the source language.

Remove any cultural, historical, or sports-related references—The translation software will not know what you mean if you say something like "That project was our Gettysburg" or "He hit a home run with his presentation."

Back translate all text—After you translate something, have the software translate it back into English. The back translation can signal places where the translation software completely missed the mark.

Use the spellchecker on the original and translated texts—After the text is translated, run it through the spellchecker again, using the target language. Your word processor likely has dictionaries from other languages preloaded, which will allow you to locate misspellings or other errors in the translation.

Avoid words that have double meanings—Try to use words that only have one meaning, not multiple possible meanings.

Minimize jargon and acronyms—Minimize jargon words, and check how any acronyms were translated.

Free Online Translation Tool

Languages are selected here.

Original text is inserted here.

Figure A: Bing Translator is a helpful tool for quick, mostly accurate translations of text and websites.

Translated text appears here.

Source: Free Online Translation Tool: Bing screenshot, Bing screenshot, Bing Translator 291.eda896321. Microsoft Corporation. Copyright 2014.

Avoid puns or other plays on words—The translation software won't understand the double meanings, and they will seem very odd in the translation.

Your translation software is not going to get everything right. So, you might warn the receiver of your text that you are using translation software. That way, he or she will understand that errors and inconsistencies might be in the file. For any critical documents, you should hire a human translator.

Writing Plain Paragraphs

Some rather simple methods are available to help you write plainer paragraphs. As with writing plain sentences, a computer really helps, because you can quickly move sentences around in paragraphs to clarify your meaning.

The Elements of a Paragraph

Paragraphs tend to include four kinds of sentences: a *transition* sentence, a *topic* sentence, *support* sentences, and a *point* sentence (Figure 16.2). Each of these sentences plays a different role in the paragraph.

TRANSITION SENTENCE   The purpose of a transition sentence is to make a smooth bridge from the previous paragraph to the present paragraph. For example, a transition sentence might state the following:

> Keeping these facts about West Nile virus in mind, let us consider the actions we should take.

> How can we help children with learning disabilities succeed in today's "active learning" classrooms?

Types of Sentences in a Typical Paragraph

Figure 16.2: Paragraphs usually contain up to four types of sentences: transition, topic, support, and point sentences.

> Transition Sentence (optional)
>
> Topic Sentence (needed)
>
> Support Sentences (needed)
>
> > examples
> >
> > reasoning
> >
> > facts
> >
> > data
> >
> > definitions
> >
> > descriptions
>
> Point Sentence (optional)

Transition sentences are typically used when the new paragraph handles a significantly different topic than the previous paragraph. They help close the gap between the two paragraphs or redirect the discussion.

TOPIC SENTENCE　The topic sentence is the claim or statement that the rest of the paragraph is going to prove or support:

> To combat the spread of the West Nile virus in Pennsylvania, we recommend three immediate steps: vaccinate all horses, create a public relations campaign to raise public awareness, and spray strategically.

> Children with learning disabilities struggle to cope in the normal classroom, so teachers working in active learning classrooms need to be trained to recognize their special needs.

In technical documents, topic sentences typically appear in the first or second sentence of each paragraph. They are placed up front in each paragraph for two reasons.

- The topic sentence sets a goal for the paragraph. It tells readers the claim the writer is trying to prove. Then, the remainder of the paragraph proves that claim.
- The topic sentence is the most important sentence in any given paragraph. Since readers, especially scanning readers, tend to pay the most attention to the beginning of a paragraph, placing the topic sentence up front ensures that they will read it.

SUPPORT SENTENCES　The bulk of any paragraph is typically made up of support sentences. These sentences contain examples, reasoning, facts, data, anecdotes, definitions, and descriptions.

First, we recommend that all horses be vaccinated against West Nile virus, because they are often the most significant victims of the virus. Last year, nearly 2000 horses died from the virus. Second, we believe a public relations campaign . . .

Children with learning disabilities often struggle to understand their teacher, especially if the teacher lectures for periods longer than ten minutes.

Support sentences are used to prove the claim made in the paragraph's topic sentence.

POINT SENTENCES Point sentences restate the paragraph's main point toward the end of the paragraph. They are used to reinforce the topic sentence by restating the paragraph's original claim in new words. Point sentences are especially useful in longer paragraphs where readers may not fully remember the claim stated at the beginning of the paragraph. They often start with transitional devices like "Therefore," "Consequently," or "In sum," to signal that the point of the paragraph is being restated.

These three recommendations represent only the first steps we need to take. Combating West Nile virus in the long term will require a more comprehensive plan.

Again, learning-disabled children often struggle undetected in the classroom, so teachers need to be trained to recognize the symptoms.

Point sentences are optional in paragraphs, and they should be used only occasionally when a particular claim needs to be reinforced. Too many point sentences will cause your text to sound repetitious and even condescending.

Using the Four Types of Sentences in a Paragraph

Of these four kinds of sentences, only the topic and support sentences are needed to construct a good paragraph. Transition sentences and point sentences are useful in situations where bridges need to be made between paragraphs or specific points need to be reinforced.

Here are the four kinds of sentences used in a paragraph:

8a. How can we accomplish these five goals (transition sentence)? Universities need to study their core mission to determine whether distance education is a viable alternative to the traditional classroom (topic sentence). If universities can maintain their current standards when moving their courses online, then distance education may provide a new medium through which nontraditional students can take classes and perhaps earn a degree (support sentence). Utah State, for example, is reporting that students enrolled in its online courses have met or exceeded the expectations of their professors (support sentence). If, however, standards cannot be maintained, we may find ourselves returning to the traditional on-campus model of education (support sentence). In sum, the ability to meet a university's core mission is the litmus test to measure whether distance education will work (point sentence).

Here is the same paragraph with the transition sentence and point sentence removed:

8b. Universities need to study their core mission to determine whether distance education is a viable alternative to the traditional classroom (topic sentence). If universities can maintain their current standards when moving their courses online, then distance education may provide a new medium through which nontraditional students can take classes and perhaps earn a degree (support sentence). Utah State, for example, is reporting that students enrolled in its online courses have met or exceeded the expectations of their professors (support sentence). If, however, standards cannot be maintained, we may find ourselves returning to the traditional on-campus model of education (support sentence).

As you can see in paragraph 8b, some paragraphs are fine without transition and point sentences. Nevertheless, transition and point sentences can make texts easier to read while amplifying important points.

Aligning Sentence Subjects in a Paragraph

Now let's discuss how you can make paragraphs flow by weaving sentences together effectively. Have you ever read a paragraph in which each sentence seemed to go off in a new direction? Have you ever run into a paragraph that actually felt "bumpy" as you read it? More than likely, the problem was a lack of alignment of the paragraph's sentence subjects. For example, consider this paragraph:

Notice how the subjects of these sentences (underlined) are not in alignment, making the paragraph seem rough to readers.

9. The lack of technical knowledge about the electronic components in automobiles often leads car owners to be suspicious about the honesty of car mechanics. Although they might be fairly knowledgeable about the mechanical workings of their automobiles, car owners rarely understand the nature and scope of the electronic repairs needed in modern automobiles. For instance, the function and importance of a transmission in a car are generally well known to all car owners, but the wire harnesses and printed circuit boards that regulate the fuel consumption and performance of their car are rarely familiar. Repairs for these electronic components can often run over $400—a large amount to a customer who cannot even visualize what a wire harness or printed circuit board looks like. In contrast, a $400 charge for the transmission on the family car, though distressing, is more readily understood and accepted.

There is nothing really wrong with this paragraph—it's just hard to read. Why? Look at the underlined subjects of the sentences in this paragraph. They are all different, causing each sentence to strike off in a new direction. As a result, each sentence forces readers to shift focus to concentrate on a new subject.

With your word processor, you can easily revise paragraphs to avoid this bumpy, unfocused feeling. The secret is lining up the subjects in the paragraph.

To line up subjects, first ask yourself what the paragraph is about. Then, cut and paste words to restructure the sentences to line up on that subject. Here is a revision of paragraph 9 that focuses on the "car owners" as subjects:

Here, the
paragraph
has been
revised to
focus on
people.

9a. Due to their lack of knowledge about electronics, some <u>car owners</u> are skeptical about the honesty of car mechanics when repairs involve electronic components. Most of our <u>customers</u> are fairly knowledgeable about the mechanical features of their automobiles, but <u>they</u> rarely understand the nature and scope of the electronic repairs needed in modern automobiles. For example, most <u>people</u> recognize the function and importance of a transmission in an automobile, but the average <u>person</u> knows very little about the wire harnesses and printed circuit boards that regulate the fuel consumption and performance of his or her car. So, for most of our customers, a <u>$400 repair</u> for these electronic components seems like a large amount, especially when <u>these folks</u> cannot even visualize what a wire harness or printed circuit board looks like. In contrast, <u>most car owners</u> think a $400 charge to fix the transmission on the family car, though distressing, is more acceptable.

In this revised paragraph, you should notice two things:

• First, the words "car owners" are not always the exact two words used in the subject slot. Synonyms and pronouns are used to add variety to the sentences.
• Second, not all the subjects need to be "car owners." In the middle of the paragraph, for example, "$400 repair" is the subject of a sentence. This deviation from "car owners" is fine as long as the majority of the subjects in the paragraph are similar to each other. In other words, the paragraph will still sound focused, even though an occasional subject is not in alignment with the others.

Of course, the subjects of the paragraph could be aligned differently to stress something else in the paragraph. Here is another revision of paragraph 9 in which the focus of the paragraph is "repairs."

9b. <u>Repairs</u> to electronic components often lead car owners, who lack knowledge about electronics, to doubt the honesty of car mechanics. The <u>nature and scope of these repairs</u> are usually beyond the understanding of most nonmechanics, unlike the typical <u>mechanical repairs</u> with which customers are more familiar. For instance, the <u>importance of fixing the transmission</u> in a car is readily apparent to most car owners, but <u>adjustments</u> to electronic components like wire harnesses and printed circuit boards are foreign to most customers— even though these electronic parts are crucial in regulating their car's fuel consumption and performance. So, <u>a repair</u> to these electronic components that costs $400 seems excessive, especially when the <u>repair</u> can't even be visualized by the customer. In contrast, a <u>$400 replacement</u> of the family car's transmission, though distressing, is more readily accepted.

You should notice that paragraph 9a is easier for most people to read than paragraph 9b because sentences that have "doers" in the subject slots are easier for people to read. In paragraph 9a, the car owners are active subjects, while in paragraph 9b, the car repairs are inactive subjects.

The Given/New Method

Another way to write plain paragraphs is to use the "given/new" method to weave sentences together. Every sentence in a paragraph should contain something the readers already know (the given) and something that the readers do not know (the new).

Consider these two paragraphs:

10a. Santa Fe has many beautiful places. Some artists choose to strike off into the mountains to work, while others enjoy working in local studios. The landscapes are wonderful in the area.

10b. Santa Fe offers many beautiful places for artists to work. Some artists choose to strike off into the mountains to work, while others enjoy working in local studios. Both the mountains and the studios offer places to savor the wonderful landscapes in the area.

Both of these paragraphs are readable, but paragraph 10b is easier to read because words are being repeated in a given/new pattern. Paragraph 10a is a little harder to read, because there is nothing "given" that carries over from each sentence to its following sentence.

Using the given/new method is not difficult. In most cases, the given information should appear early in the sentence and the new information should appear later in the sentence. The given information will provide a familiar anchor or context, while the new information will build on that familiar ground. Consider this larger paragraph:

Notice how the chaining of words in this paragraph makes it smoother to read.

11. Recently, an art gallery exhibited the mysterious paintings of Irwin Fleminger, a modernist artist whose vast Mars-like landscapes contain cryptic human artifacts. One of Fleminger's paintings attracted the attention of some young schoolchildren who happened to be walking by. At first, the children laughed, pointing out some of the strange artifacts in the painting. Soon, though, the strange artifacts in the painting drew the students into a critical awareness of the painting, and they began to ask their bewildered teacher what the artifacts meant. Mysterious and beautiful, Fleminger's paintings have this effect on many people, not just schoolchildren.

By chaining together given and new information, the paragraph builds readers' understanding gradually, adding a little more information with each sentence.

In some cases, however, the previous sentence in a paragraph does not offer a suitable subject for the sentence that follows it. In these cases, transitional phrases can be used to provide readers given information in the beginning of the sentence. To illustrate,

12. This public relations effort will strengthen Gentec's relationship with leaders of the community. With this new relationship in place, the details of the project can be negotiated in terms that are fair to both parties.

In this sentence, the given information in the second sentence appears in the transitional phrase, not in the subject slot. A transitional phrase is a good place to include given information when the subject cannot be drawn from the previous sentence.

When Is It Appropriate to Use Passive Voice?

Before discussing the elements of persuasive style, we should expose a writing boogeyman as a fraud. Since childhood, you have probably been warned against using *passive voice*. You have been told to write in *active voice*.

One problem with this prohibition on passive voice is that passive voice is very common in technical communication. In some scientific fields, passive voice is the standard way of writing. So, when is it appropriate to use passive voice?

Passive voice occurs when the subject of the sentence is *being acted upon,* so the verb is in passive voice. Active voice occurs when the subject of the sentence is *doing the acting,* so the verb is an action verb. Here is an example of a sentence written in passive voice and a sentence written in active voice:

13a. The alloy was heated to a temperature of 300°C. (passive)

13b. Andy James heated the alloy to a temperature of 300°C. (active)

The passive voice sentence (sentence 13a) lacks a doer because the subject of the sentence, the alloy, is being acted upon. As a result, sentence 13b might be a bit easier to understand because a doer is the subject of the sentence. But, as you can see, sentence 13a is easy to read and understand, too.

Passive voice does have a place in technical documents. A passive sentence is fine if:

- the readers do not need to know who or what is doing something in the sentence.
- the subject of the sentence is what the sentence is about.

For example, in sentence 13a, the person who heated the alloy might be unknown or irrelevant to the readers. Is it really important that we know that Andy James heated the alloy? Or do we simply need to know that the alloy was heated? If the alloy is what the sentence is about and who heated the alloy is unimportant, then the passive voice is fine.

If you are wondering whether to use the passive voice, consider your readers. Do they expect you to use the passive voice? Do they need to know who did something in a sentence? Go ahead and use the passive voice if your readers expect you to use it or they don't need to know who did what.

Consider these other examples of passive and active sentences:

14a. The shuttle bus will be driven to local care facilities to provide seniors with shopping opportunities. (passive)

14b. Jane Chavez will drive the shuttle bus to local care facilities to provide seniors with shopping opportunities. (active)

15a. The telescope was moved to the Orion system to observe the newly discovered nebula. (passive)

15b. Our graduate assistant, Mary Stewart, moved the telescope to the Orion system to observe the newly discovered nebula. (active)

In both sets of sentences, the passive voice may be more appropriate, unless there is a reason Jane Chavez or Mary Stewart needs to be singled out for special consideration.

When developing a focused paragraph, passive sentences can often help you align the subjects and use given/new strategies (i.e., make the paragraph more cohesive). For example, compare the following paragraphs, one written in passive voice and the other in active voice:

Paragraph
written in
passive
voice

16a. We were shocked by the tornado damage. The downtown of Wheaton had been completely flattened. Brick houses were torn apart. A school bus was tossed into a farm field, as though some fairy-tale giant had crumpled it like a soda can. The town's fallen water tower had been dragged a hundred yards to the east. Amazingly enough, no one was killed by the storm. Clearly, lives were saved by the early warning that the weather bureau had sent out.

Same para-
graph writ-
ten in active
voice

16b. The tornado damage shocked us. The tornado completely flattened the downtown of Wheaton. It had torn apart brick houses. It had tossed a school bus into a farm field, as though some fairy-tale giant had crumpled the bus like a soda can. The tornado had knocked over the town's water tower and dragged it a hundred yards to the east. Amazingly enough, the tornado did not kill anyone. Clearly, the early warning that the weather bureau sent out saved lives.

Most people would find paragraph 16a more interesting and readable because it uses passive voice to put the emphasis on the *damage* caused by the tornado. Paragraph 16b is not as interesting, because the emphasis is repeatedly placed on the *tornado*.

Used properly, passive voice can be a helpful tool in your efforts to write plain sentences and paragraphs. Passive voice is misused only when the readers are left wondering who or what is doing the action in the sentence. In these cases, the sentences should be restructured to put the doers in the subject slots.

Persuasive Style

Link

For more information on reader analysis, go to Chapter 2, page 20.

There are times when you will need to do more than simply present information clearly. You will need to influence your readers to take action or make a decision. In these situations, you should shift to *persuasive style*. When used properly, persuasive style can add emphasis, energy, color, and emotion to your writing.

The following four persuasion techniques will help give your writing more impact. A combination of these, properly used, will make your writing more influential and vivid.

Elevate the Tone

Tone is the resonance or pitch that the readers will "hear" as they read your document. Of course, most people read silently to themselves, but all readers have an inner voice that sounds out the words and sentences. By paying attention to tone, you can influence the readers' inner voice in ways that persuade them to read the document with a specific emotion or attitude.

One easy way to elevate tone in written texts is to first decide what emotion or attitude you want the readers to adopt. Then, use logical mapping to find words and phrases that evoke that emotion or attitude (Figure 16.3).

For example, let's say you want your readers to feel excited as they are looking over your document. You would first put the word "excitement" in the middle of your screen or a sheet of paper. Then, as shown in Figure 16.3, you can map out descriptions and feelings associated with that emotion.

You can use these words at strategic moments in your document. Subconsciously, the readers will detect this tone in your work. Their inner voice will begin reinforcing the sense of excitement you are trying to convey.

Mapping an Emotional Tone

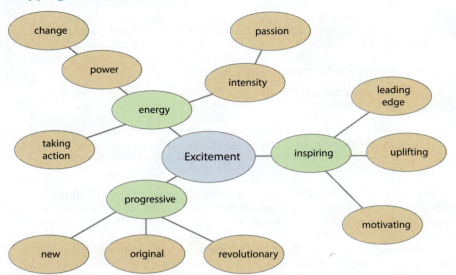

Figure 16.3: You can set an emotional tone by mapping it out and "seeding" the text with words associated with that tone.

Similarly, if you want to create a specific attitude in your text, map out the words associated with it. For instance, let us say you want your document to convey a feeling of "security." A map around "security" might look like the diagram in Figure 16.4.

If you use these words associated with "security" at strategic points in your text, readers will sense the feeling you are trying to convey.

One warning: Use these words sparingly throughout the text. If you overuse them, the emotion or attitude you are setting will be too obvious. You need to use only a few words at strategic moments to set the tone you are seeking.

Use Similes and Analogies

Similes and analogies are rhetorical devices that help writers define difficult concepts by comparing them to familiar things. For example, let's say you are writing a brochure that describes an integrated circuit to people who know almost nothing about these devices. Using a simile, you might describe it this way:

> An integrated circuit is like a miniature Manhattan Island crammed into a space less than 1 centimeter long.

In this case, the simile ("X is like Y") creates an image that helps readers visualize the complexity of the integrated circuit.

Here are a couple of other examples of similes:

> A cell is like a tiny cluttered room with a nucleus inside and walls at the edges. The nucleus is like the cell's brain. It's an enclosed compartment that contains all the information that cells need to form an organism. This information comes in the form of DNA. It's the differences in our DNA that make each of us unique.
>
> (Source: Genetic Science Learning Center, http://gslc.genetics.utah.edu/units/cloning/whatiscloning.)

Mapping an Authoritative Tone

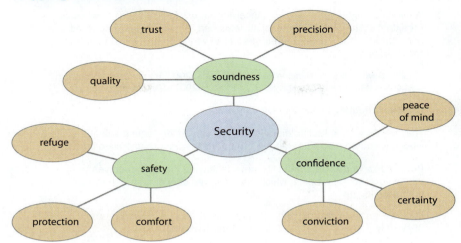

Figure 16.4: If you use these words associated with "security" in your text at strategic points, readers will perceive the sense of security that you are trying to convey.

> Everything that you see is made of things called atoms. An atom is like a very, very small solar system. As you know, the sun is at the center of the solar system. Just like the solar system, there is something at the center of an atom. It is called the nucleus. So the nucleus of an atom is like the sun in our solar system. Around the sun there are planets. They orbit the sun. In an atom, there are things called electrons that orbit the nucleus.
>
> (Source: Chickscope, http://chickscope.beckman.uiuc.edu/about/overview/mrims .html.)

Analogies are also a good way to help readers visualize difficult concepts. An analogy follows the structure "A is to B as X is to Y." For example, a medical analogy might be

> Like police keeping order in a city, white blood cells seek to control viruses and bacteria in the body.

In this case, both parts of the analogy are working in parallel. "Police" is equivalent to "white blood cells," and "keeping order in a city" is equivalent to "control viruses and bacteria in the body."

Use Metaphors

Though comparable to similes and analogies, metaphors work at a deeper level in a document. Specifically, metaphors are used to create or reinforce a particular perspective that you want readers to adopt toward your subject or ideas. For example, a popular metaphor in Western medicine is the "war on cancer."

Off Target In The War On Cancer

We've been fighting the war on cancer for almost four decades now, since President Richard M. Nixon officially launched it in 1971. It's time to admit that our efforts have often targeted the wrong enemies and used the wrong weapons.

(Source: Devra Davis, Washington Post, November 4, 2007, http://www.washington-post.com/wp-dyn/content/article/2007/11/02/AR2007110201648.html.)

Are We Retreating In The War On Cancer?

They are America's foot-soldiers in the war on cancer—young scientists whose research may someday lead to better treatments and even cures.

But experts worry this small elite army is leaving the field in droves because government funding, which once allowed cancer research to flourish, is now drying up.

(Source: CBS News, May 20, 2008, http://www.cbsnews.com/stories/2008/05/20/eveningnews/main4111776.shtml?source=related_story.)

As shown in these examples, by employing this metaphor, the writer can reinforce a particular perspective about cancer research. A metaphor like "war on cancer" would add a sense of urgency, because it suggests that cancer is an enemy that must be defeated, at any cost. Metaphors are powerful tools in technical writing because they tend to work at a subconscious level.

But what if a commonly used metaphor like "war on cancer" is not appropriate for your document? Perhaps you are writing about cancer in a hospice situation, where the patient is no longer trying to "defeat" cancer. In these cases, you might develop a new metaphor and use it to invent a new perspective. For example, perhaps you want your readers to view cancer as something to be managed, not fought.

To manage their cancer, patients become supervisors who set performance goals and lead planning meetings for teams of doctors and nurses. Our doctors become consultants who help patients become better managers of their own care.

In a hospice situation, a "management" metaphor would be much more appropriate than the usual "war" metaphor. It would invite readers to see their cancer from a less confrontational perspective.

If you look for them, you will find that metaphors are commonly used in technical documents. Once you are aware of these metaphors, you can use the ones that already exist in your field, or you might create new metaphors to shift your readers' perspective about your subject. In Figure 16.5, for example, the writer uses metaphors to recast the debate over the use of nuclear energy.

Change the Pace

You can also control the reader's pace as they move through your document. Longer sentences tend to slow down the reading pace, while shorter sentences tend to speed it up. By paying attention to the lengths of sentences, you can increase or decrease the intensity of your text.

A Persuasive Argument

Figure 16.5: In this article, the author uses numerous persuasive style techniques to add energy to his writing. Is the author persuasive?

Patrick Moore: Going nuclear over global warming

By Patrick Moore

For years the Intergovernment Panel on Climate Change (IPCC) of the United Nations has warned us that greenhouse gas emissions from our fossil fuel consumption threaten the world's climate in ways we will regret. This year IPCC won the Nobel Peace Prize for its efforts.

It is the IPCC that former colleagues in Greenpeace, and most of the mainstream environmental movement, look to for expert advice on climate change. Environmental activists take the rather grim but measured language of the IPCC reports and add words like "catastrophe" and "chaos," along with much speculation concerning famine, pestilence, mass extinction and the end of civilization as we know it.

Until the past couple of years, the activists, with their zero-tolerance policy on nuclear energy, have succeeded in squelching any mention by the IPCC of using nuclear power to replace fossil fuels for electricity production. Burning fossil fuels for electricity accounts for 9.5 billion tons of global carbon dioxide emissions while nuclear emits next to nothing. It has been apparent to many scientists and policymakers for years that this would be a logical path to follow. The IPCC has now joined these growing ranks advocating for nuclear energy as a solution.

In its recently issued final report for 2007, the IPCC makes a number of unambiguous references to the fact that nuclear energy is an important tool to help bring about a reduction in fossil fuel consumption. Greenpeace has already made it clear that it disagrees. How credible is it for activists to use the IPCC scientists' recommendations to fuel apocalyptic fundraising campaigns on climate change and then to dismiss the recommendations from the same scientists on what we should do to solve it?

Greenpeace is deliberately misleading the public into thinking that wind and solar, both of which are inherently intermittent and unreliable, can replace baseload power that is continuous and reliable. Only three technologies can produce large amounts of baseload power: fossil fuels, hydroelectric, and nuclear. Given that we want to reduce fossil fuels and that potential hydroelectric sites are becoming scarce, nuclear is the main option. But Greenpeace and its allies remain in denial despite the fact that many independent environmentalists and now the IPCC see the situation clearly.

I have long realized that in retrospect we made a big mistake in the early years of Greenpeace when we lumped nuclear energy together with nuclear weapons as if they were all part of the same holocaust. We were totally fixated, and rightly so, on the threat of all-out nuclear war between the Soviet Union and the United States, and we thought everything nuclear was evil. We failed to distinguish the beneficial and peaceful uses of nuclear technology from its destructive and even evil uses.

The approach would be akin to including nuclear medicine with nuclear weapons just because nuclear medicine uses radioactive materials, most of which are produced in nuclear reactors. Nuclear medicine successfully diagnoses and treats millions of people every year, and it would be ludicrous to ban its use.

Greenpeace and company are basically stuck in the 1970s when it comes to their energy policy as it relates to climate change. They should accept the wisdom of the scientists at the IPCC and recognize that nuclear energy is a big part of the climate change solution. And they should stop misleading the public into thinking that wind and solar can do the job on their own. I will be the first to commend them for their courage.

The author uses metaphors to add energy and imagery.

The "argument is war" metaphor is used throughout the article.

An even pace is created with consistent sentence length.

The author uses an analogy to make an important comparison.

Source: Sacramento Bee, December 12, 2007, http://www.sacbee.com/110/story/560569.html. This article is protected by copyright and should not be printed or distributed for anything except personal use. The Sacramento Bee, 2100 Q St., P. O. Box 15779, Sacramento, CA 95852 Phone: (916) 321-1000.

Long Sentences (Low Intensity)

These long sentences slow the reading down.

According to behavior problem indices, children who experience food insecurity suffer more psychological and emotional difficulties than other children. They exhibit more aggressive and destructive behaviors, as well as more withdrawn and distressed behaviors. Children who are experiencing a great deal of psychological and emotional distress in response to issues of food insecurity will often react to this distress with a range of negative behavioral responses, including acting out and violence toward others. Moreover, a child's psychological and emotional well-being is also negatively affected by food insecurity, which may also have implications for other child development outcomes. Their higher levels of psychological and emotional distress may cause problems in other areas such as school achievement, and these difficulties may interfere with a number of out-of-school activities in which they are involved.

Short Sentences (High Intensity)

Shorter sentences raise the "heartbeat" of the text.

The effect of children's food insecurity can be crucial. According to behavior problem indices, food-insecure children have more psychological and emotional difficulties. They exhibit more aggressive and destructive behaviors. They are more withdrawn and distressed. They react to this distress with a range of behavioral responses, including acting out and violence toward others. The child's overall well-being is negatively affected. This insecurity may have implications for other child development outcomes. These children may have more trouble at school. They also tend to struggle at a number of out-of-school activities.

If a situation is urgent, using short sentences is the best way to show that something needs to be done right away. Your readers will naturally feel compelled to take action. On the other hand, if you want your readers to be cautious and deliberate, longer sentences will decrease the intensity of the text, giving readers the sense that there is no need to rush.

Balancing Plain and Persuasive Style

AT A GLANCE

Persuasive Style Techniques

- Elevate the tone.
- Use similes and analogies.
- Use metaphors.
- Change the pace.

When you are drafting and revising a document for style, look for appropriate places to use plain and persuasive style. Minimally, a document should use plain style. Sentences should be clear and easy to read. Your readers should not have to struggle to figure out what a sentence or paragraph is about.

Persuasive style should be used to add energy and color. It should also be used in places in the document where readers are expected to make a decision or take action. The use of tone, similes, analogies, and metaphors in strategic places should encourage readers to do what you want. You can use short or long sentences to adjust the intensity of your prose.

In the end, developing good style takes practice. At first, revising a document to make it plain and persuasive might seem difficult. Before long, though, you will start writing better sentences while drafting. You will have internalized the style guidelines presented in this chapter.

- The style of your document can convey your message as strongly as the content; *sometimes, what you say isn't as important as how you say it.*

- Style can be classified as plain, persuasive, or grand. Technical communication most often uses plain or persuasive style.

- To write plain sentences, follow these eight guidelines: (1) identify your subject, (2) make the "doer" the subject of the sentence, (3) put the doer's action in the verb, (4) move the subject of the sentence close to the beginning of the sentence, (5) eliminate nominalizations, (6) avoid excess prepositional phrases, (7) eliminate redundancy, and (8) make sure that sentences are "breathing length."

- Writing plain paragraphs involves the use of four types of sentences: transitional and point sentences, which are optional, and topic and support sentences, which are necessary.

- Check sentences in paragraphs for subject alignment, and use the given/new method to weave sentences together.

- Techniques for writing persuasively include elevating the tone; using similes, analogies, and metaphors; and changing the pace.

Individual or Team Projects

1. In your workplace or on campus, find three sentences that seem particularly difficult to read. Use the eight "plain style" guidelines discussed in this chapter to revise them to improve their readability. Make a presentation to your class in which you show how using the guidelines helped make the sentences easier to read.

2. Find a document and analyze its style. Underline key words and phrases in the document. Based on the words you underlined, what is the tone used in the document? Does the document use any similes or analogies to explain difficult concepts? Can you locate any metaphors woven into the text? How might you use techniques of persuasive style to improve this document? Write a memo to your instructor in which you analyze the style of the document. Do you believe the style is effective? If so, why? If not, what stylistic strategies might improve the readability and persuasiveness of the document?

3. While revising some of your own writing, try to create a specific tone by mapping out an emotion or attitude that you would like the text to reflect. Weave a few concepts from your map into your text. At what point is the tone too strong? At what point is the tone just right?

4. Read the Case Study at the end of this chapter. Imagine that you are Henry and write a memo to the managers of NewGenSport expressing your concerns about the safety of the product and its advertising campaign. Make sure you do some research on ephedra so you can add some technical support to your arguments.

Collaborative Project

Metaphors involving "war" are common in American society. We have had wars on poverty, cancer, drugs, and even inflation. More recently, "war on terrorism" has been a commonly used metaphor. With a group of classmates, choose one of these war metaphors and find examples of how it is used. Identify places where the metaphor seems to fit the situation. Locate examples where the metaphor seems to be misused.

With your group, discuss the ramifications of the war metaphor. For example, if we accept the metaphor "war on drugs," who is the enemy? What weapons can we use? What level of force is necessary to win this war? Where might we violate civil rights if we follow this metaphor to its logical end?

Then, try to create a new metaphor that invites people to see the situation from a different perspective. For example, what happens when we use "managing drug abuse" or "healing drug abuse" as new metaphors? How do these new metaphors, for better or worse, change how we think about illegal drugs and react to them?

In a presentation to your class, use examples to show how the war metaphor is used. Then, show how the metaphor could be changed to consider the situation from a different perspective.

Visit MyWritingLab for a Post-test and more technical writing resources.

Going Over the Top

Henry Wilkins is a nutritionist who works for NewGenSport, a company that makes sports drinks. His company's best seller, Overthetop Sports Drink, is basically a fruit-flavored drink with added carbohydrates and salts. As a nutritionist, Henry knows that sports drinks like Overthetop do not really do much for people, but they don't harm them either. Overwhelmingly, the primary benefit of Overthetop is the water, which people need when they exercise. The added carbohydrates and salts are somewhat beneficial, because people deplete them as they exercise.

The advertisements for Overthetop paint a different picture, however. They show overly muscular athletes drinking Overthetop and then dominating opposing players. Henry thinks the advertisements are a bit misleading, but harmless. The product won't lead to the high performance promised by the advertising. But, Henry reasons, that's advertising.

One day, Henry was asked to evaluate a new version of Overthetop, called Overthetop Extreme. The new sports drink would include a small amount of an ephedra-like herbal stimulant formulated to enhance performance and cause slight weight loss. Henry also knew that ephedra had been linked to a few deaths, especially when people took too much. Ephedra was banned by the FDA in 2003, but this new "ephedra-like" herbal stimulant was different enough to be legal. Henry suspected this stimulant would have many of the same problems as its sister drug, ephedra.

Henry's preliminary research indicated that 36 ounces (three bottles) a day of Overthetop Extreme would have no negative effect. But, more than a few bottles a day might lead to complications, perhaps even death in rare cases.

But before Henry could report his findings, the company's marketing team pitched its new advertising campaign for the debut of the new product. In the campaign, as usual, overly muscular athletes were shown guzzling large amounts of Overthetop Extreme and then going on to victory. It was clear that the advertisements were overpromising—as usual. But, they were also suggesting the product be used in a way that would put people at risk. The advertisements were technically accurate, but their style gave an inflated sense of the product's capabilities. In some cases, Henry realized, the style of the advertisements might lead to overconsumption, which could lead to problems.

The company's top executives were very excited about the new product. The advertisements only made them more enthusiastic. They began pressuring Henry to finish his evaluation of Overthetop right away so that they could start advertising and putting the product on store shelves.

Henry, unfortunately, was already concerned about the product's safety. But he was especially concerned that the advertisements were clearly misleading consumers in a dangerous way.

If you were Henry, how would you handle this situation? In your report to the company's management, how would you express your concerns? What else might you do?

CHAPTER

17

Designing Documents and Interfaces

Five Principles of Design 447

Design Principle 1: Balance 447

Design Principle 2: Alignment 455

Design Principle 3: Grouping 456

Design Principle 4: Consistency 461

Design Principle 5: Contrast 466

Transcultural Design 468

What You Need to Know 470

Exercises and Projects 471

Case Study: Bugs on the Bus 473

In this chapter, you will learn:

- How to design technical documents for electronic and paper-based media.

- To use the five principles of design: balance, alignment, grouping, consistency, and contrast.

- To use balancing techniques that enhance readability in a document.

- To use alignment and grouping strategies to add visual structure to text.

- To use consistency and contrast to balance uniformity and difference in the design of a document or interface.

- To anticipate the design expectations of international readers.

Document design has become ever more important with the use and availability of computers. Today, readers expect paper-based documents to be attractive and easy to read, and to include images and color. Meanwhile, readers expect the interfaces of on-screen texts, such as websites and multimedia documents, to be well designed and easy to navigate. Readers don't just *prefer* well-designed documents—they *expect* the design of technical documents to highlight important ideas and concepts.

Five Principles of Design

The readers of your technical documents will almost never read them word for word, sentence by sentence. Instead, they will tend to look over your technical documents at various levels, skimming some parts and paying closer attention to others. Always remind yourself that workplace readers are "raiders" for information, looking specifically for the information they need.

Good design gives your readers obvious "access points" to begin reading and locating the information they need. Here are five basic design principles that will help you make better decisions about how your document should look and function:

Balance—The document looks balanced from left to right and top to bottom.

Alignment—Images and words on the page are aligned to show the document's structure, or hierarchy.

Grouping—Related images and words are placed near each other on the page.

Consistency—Design features in the document are used consistently, so the document looks uniform.

Contrast—Items in the document that are different look significantly different.

These principles are based on theories of Gestalt psychology, a study of how the mind recognizes patterns (Arnheim, 1969; Koffka, 1935). Designers of all kinds, including architects, fashion designers, and artists, have used Gestalt principles in a variety of ways (Bernhardt, 1986). You will find these five principles helpful as you learn about designing documents.

Design Principle 1: Balance

Balance is perhaps the most prominent feature of design in technical documents. On a balanced page or screen, the design features should offset each other to create a feeling of stability.

To balance a text, imagine your page or screen is balanced on a point. Each time you add something to the left side, you need to add something to the right side to maintain balance. Similarly, when you add something to the top, you need to add something to the bottom. Figure 17.1 shows an example of a balanced page and an unbalanced page.

Balanced and Unbalanced Page Layouts

Figure 17.1: The balanced page on the left feels more stable and comfortable. The unbalanced page on the right creates more tension.

In Figure 17.1, the page on the left is balanced because the design features offset each other. The page on the right is unbalanced because the items on the right side of the page are not offset by items on the left. Also, the right page is top-heavy because the design features are bunched at the top of the page.

Balanced page layouts can take on many forms. Figures 17.2 and 17.3 show examples of balanced layouts. The idea is not to create symmetrical pages (i.e., where left and right, top and bottom mirror each other exactly). Instead, you want to balance pages by putting text and images on all sides.

Balance is also important in screen-based documents. In Figure 17.4, the screen interface is balanced because the items on the left offset the items on the right.

Weighting a Page or Screen

When balancing a page or screen, graphic designers will talk about the "weight" of the items on the page. What they mean is that some items on a page or screen attract readers' eyes more than others—these features have more weight. A picture, for example, has more weight than printed words because readers' eyes tend to be drawn toward pictures. Similarly, an animated figure moving on the screen will capture more attention than static items.

Here are some basic weighting guidelines for a page or screen:

• Items on the right side of the page weigh more than items on the left.

The significantly larger title brings your eyes to the beginning of the text.

The elements on the page offset each other to create balance.

Notice how your eyes are drawn to the hawk. Animals or people in a picture usually attract the most attention from readers.

Manitoba's Species At Risk

Threatened

Ferruginous hawk
Buteo regalis

Any native Manitoba species likely to become endangered or at risk due to low or declining numbers in Manitoba if the factors affecting it don't improve. Threatened species are declared as such by regulation under the *Endangered Species Act*.

Ferruginous hawk (*Buteo regalis*) is the largest of North American soaring hawks, with a wingspan of up to 135 cm (53 inches). In flight, the Ferruginous hawk has a light underside with reddish-brown markings on the underside of the wings and on the legs, forming a characteristic dark V against the bird's white underparts. Reddish-brown shoulders and a white window patch on the upper surface of the dark primaries are also distinctive.

The Ferruginous hawk occurs in two colour phases. Dark birds are chocolate brown throughout with a whitish tail and primaries. Although dark birds comprise up to 15 per cent of the population in some areas, in Manitoba they probably make up less than 1 per cent of the population.

Habitat

These birds prefer open areas dominated by native grasses and scattered trees or shrubs, with abundant ground squirrels for food. Isolated trees or some other elevated structure are usually required for the nest site, but the species occasionally uses a highly built-up nest on the ground. Ferruginous hawks typically avoid areas with greater than 30 per cent cultivation, sites that are prone to disturbance, or parkland areas where trees are abundant. However, a few pairs in Manitoba have been found nesting near busy roads, in areas with no surrounding grasslands, or in fairly large clumps of trees.

Life History

Ferruginous hawks arrive in summer nesting grounds by late March. Males usually return first, often coming back to the general area where they were raised. Pairs often maintain the same mate. Successful pairs traditionally use the same nest year after year, but unsuccessful pairs may select an alternative nest within their territory. The nest is built by both adults using large quantities of sticks and roots and lined with dead grass, sod and cow dung. These birds are also comfortable using artificial nesting structures, consisting of a wire basket filled with sticks and

placed in large trees. In Manitoba, nearly three-quarters of the nesting pairs observed since 1990 have occupied artificial nests.

Three to five eggs are laid in late April or early May and are incubated by the female for about 30 days. The male spells off the female on the nest during incubation. Young remain in the nest for six to eight weeks, and are dependent on adults for food for several weeks after they learn to fly. Birds leave their summer grounds in September or October. Young first breed when they are two or three years old. Adults can live for 20 years in the wild.

Ferruginous hawks hunt during the day, eating mostly ground squirrels and prairie dogs. Pocket gophers, voles, mice, rabbits and even birds will also be eaten. Adults frequently perch and hunt from the ground, using the sit-and-wait technique, crouching at the mouth of a burrow and snatching up a ground squirrel as it emerges. They also use trees, hydro poles and power lines as hunting perches.

Distribution

Ferruginous hawks nest in western North America, from the Canadian prairies south to New Mexico and Texas. In Canada, Ferruginous hawks are common in southern Alberta and Saskatchewan. They are rarely found in southern British Columbia, and have recently re-established in southern Manitoba. In Manitoba, the species is concentrated in southwestern Manitoba, as far north and east as Lenore, Brandon and Glenboro. Non-breeding adults have been observed north to St. Lazare and east to Oak Hammock Marsh. Ferruginous hawks winter in the southwestern United States and in Mexico.

Status

The Manitoba Conservation Data Centre lists the Ferruginous hawk as provincially rare (S2). Although it has declined in many provinces and states, it is considered apparently secure (G4) rangewide by NatureServe. Since the early 1900s, populations in North America have

Protecting & Managing *our Future*

Manitoba Conservation

Source: Manitoba Conservation Wildlife and Ecosystem Protection Branch

Figure 17.2: Graphic designers are especially careful about balance. This page layout uses the image of the hawk to balance two columns of written text. Meanwhile, the bold header and footer anchor the text at the top and bottom.

The green header and footer at the top and bottom of the page make it feel balanced and stable.

A Simpler Design That Is Attractive

The two-column format balances the text.

Your eyes naturally flow down and across the page.

Source: Nuclear Weapons Journal, p. 13

This image draws your eyes to it.

Figure 17.3: This page from a magazine is simpler in design than the document shown in Figure 17.2. Notice how the elements on the page offset each other to create a balanced, stable look.

A Balanced Interface

The banner at the top of the screen offsets text and images lower on the page.

Figure 17.4: This screen is balanced, even though it is not symmetrical. The items on the left offset the items on the right.

Left and right images and text are used to balance the screen.

Source: Fermilab

- Items on the top of the page weigh more than items on the bottom.
- Big items weigh more than small items.
- Pictures weigh more than written text.
- Graphics weigh more than written text.
- Colored items weigh more than black-and-white items.
- Items with borders around them weigh more than items without borders.
- Irregular shapes weigh more than regular shapes.
- Items in motion weigh more than static items.

As you are balancing a page, use these weight guidelines to help you offset items. For example, if an image appears on the right side of the page, make sure that there is something on the left side to create balance.

Using Grids to Balance a Page Layout

When designing a page or screen, your challenge is to create a layout that is balanced but not boring. A time-tested way to devise a balanced page design is to use a *page grid* to evenly place the written text and graphics on the page. Grids divide the page vertically into two or more columns. Figure 17.5 shows some standard grids and how they might be used.

Figure 17.6 (on page 454) shows the use of a four-column grid in a report. Notice how the graphics and text offset each other in the page layout.

Grids for Designing Page Layouts

One-column grid

Figure 17.5: Grids can help you place items on a page in a way that makes it look balanced.

One-column grids offer simplicity, but not much flexibility.

Two-column grid

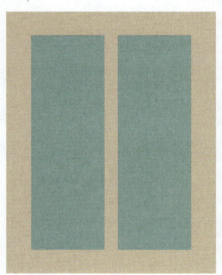

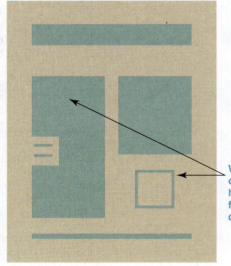

With more columns, you have more flexibility for design.

Three-column grid

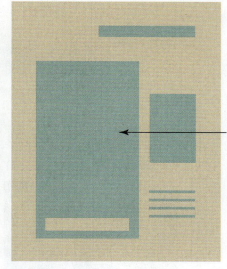

Notice how the text can go over two columns, leaving a large margin on one side.

Four-column grid

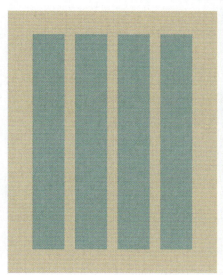

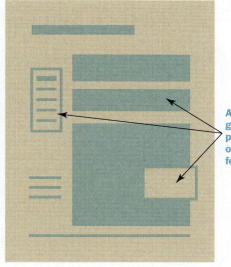

A four-column grid offers plenty of opportunities for creativity.

Figure 17.6: A four-column grid was used to lay out this text in a balanced manner.

The image on the left is offset by the text on the right.

An image can cross two columns, as this one does.

The banner crosses all four columns.

A four-column layout structures the whole page.

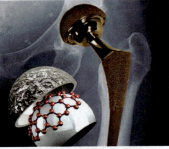

McCormick

Northwestern Engineering

Materials Science and Engineering

Robert R. McCormick School of Engineering and Applied Science
Northwestern University

WINTER 2012

Researchers Create Hips that Function Better and Last Longer

Northwestern researchers have found that graphitic carbon is the key element in metal-on-metal hip implant lubrication.

A team of engineers and physicians have made a surprising discovery that offers a target for designing new materials for hip implants that are less susceptible to the joint's normal wear and tear.

Researchers from Northwestern University, Rush University Medical Center, Chicago, and the University of Duisburg-Essen Germany found that graphitic carbon is a key element in a lubricating layer that forms on metal-on-metal

hip implants. The lubricant is more similar to the lubrication of a combustion engine than that of a natural joint. The study, "Graphitic Tribological Layers in Metal-on-Metal Hip Replacements," was published in December by the journal *Science*.

Prosthetic materials for hips, which include metals, polymers and

"Metal-on-metal implants can vastly improve people's lives, but it's an imperfect technology. Now that we are starting to understand how lubrication of these implants works in the body, we have a target for how to make the devices better." – Professor Laurence D. Marks

ceramics, have a lifetime typically exceeding 10 years. However, beyond 10 years the failure rate generally increases, particularly in young, active individuals. Physicians would love to see that lifespan increased to 30 to 50 years. Ideally, artificial hips should last the patient's lifetime.

"Metal-on-metal implants can vastly improve people's lives, but it's an imperfect technology," said Professor Laurence D. Marks, a co-author on the paper who led the experimental effort at North-

western. "Now that we are starting to understand how lubrication of these implants works in the body, we have a target for how to make the devices better."

The ability to extend the life of implants would have enormous benefits, in terms of both cost and quality of life. More than 450,000

Americans, most with severe arthritis, undergo hip replacement each year, and the numbers are growing. Many more thousands delay the life-changing surgery until they are older, because of the limitations of current implants.

"Hip replacement surgery is the greatest advancement in the treatment of end-stage arthritis in the last century," said co-author and principal investigator Dr. Joshua J. Jacobs, the William A. Hark, M.D./Susanne G. Swift Professor of

Continued on page 7

Please Join us for the 25th Annual Hilliard Symposium and First Annual Alumni Celebration
Thursday, May 17, 2012, Evanston

The Department of Materials Science and Engineering is pleased to host its 25th Annual Hilliard Symposium and First Annual Alumni Celebration on Thursday, May 17.

We are especially excited to announce the morning keynote speaker for the symposium:

NU alum **John Cahn** (Hon. '90), one of the founders of our field, renowned for his many contributions to the thermodynamics and kinetics of phase transformations, and most recently as a winner of the 2011 Kyoto Prize. His presentation will be followed by graduate student talks, providing an opportunity to reflect on

our shared history and learn about the most current research in the department.

Following the day-long Hilliard Symposium, the Alumni Celebration will celebrate accomplishments by faculty, students and alumni, and several milestones: 25 years of the Hilliard Symposium, 30 years since

Cahn-Hilliard Day, and 55 years since the development of the Cahn-Hilliard equation. Program and registration details will be sent via e-mail and are available on the departmental website: www.matsci.northwestern.edu.

Source: Northwestern University

Grids are also used to lay out screen-based texts. Even though screen-based texts tend to be wider than they are long, readers still expect the material to be balanced on the interface. Figure 17.7 shows possible designs using three- and four-grid templates.

In many cases, the columns on a grid do not translate directly into columns of written text. Columns of text and pictures can often overlap one or more columns in the grid.

Grids for Interfaces

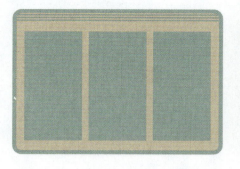

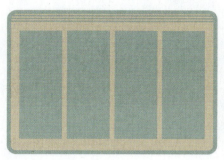

Figure 17.7: Items on screen-based pages should also be evenly placed. This approach creates a sense of stability.

Design Principle 2: Alignment

Items on a page or screen can be aligned vertically and horizontally. By aligning items *vertically* on the page, you can help readers identify different levels of information in a document. By aligning items *horizontally,* you can connect them visually so readers view them as a unit.

In Figure 17.8, for example, the page on the left gives no hint about the hierarchy of information, making it difficult for a reader to scan the text. The page on the right, meanwhile, uses alignment to clearly signal the hierarchy of the text.

Alignment takes advantage of readers' natural tendency to search out visual relationships among items on a page. If a picture, for example, is aligned with a block of text on a page, readers will naturally assume that they go together.

In paper-based documents, look for ways you can use margins, indentation, lists, headings, and graphics to create two or three levels in the text. If you use a consistent alignment strategy throughout the text, you will design a highly readable and accessible document.

Using Vertical Alignment

 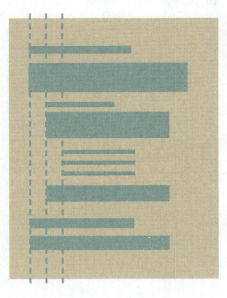

Figure 17.8: Alignment allows readers to see the hierarchy of information in a text.

In technical documents, items are usually aligned on the left side. In rare cases, you might try aligning titles and headings on the right side. But you should use centering only for titles, because it causes alignment problems in the text. Figure 17.9 shows how centering can create unpredictable vertical lines in the text.

Alignment is also very important in on-screen documents. To create a sense of stability, pay attention to the horizontal and vertical alignments of features on the interface. For example, the screen in Figure 17.10 shows how you can align text and graphics to make an interface look stable.

Design Principle 3: Grouping

The principle of grouping means that items on a page that are near each other will be seen as one unit. Grouping allows you to break up the information on a page by dividing the text into scannable blocks.

Humans naturally see items that are placed near each other as a whole unit. So, if two items are placed near each other, like a picture and a caption, readers will assume that they belong together. In Figure 17.10, notice how pictures are put near paragraphs so that they are seen as units. The banner at the top of the page is supposed to be seen as a block unto itself.

Alignment Problems with Centered Text

**Proposal for an
Improved
Wireless Network on Campus**

Written to Sally Johnson, Vice President for Electronic Advancement

Abstract: In this proposal, we argue that Western State Community College needs to improve its wireless network on campus. Currently, the network only covers specific "hot spots" like the Student Union, the Biotechnology Center, and the Computer Science Center. As a result, a majority of students cannot take advantage of it. We recommend creating a wireless cloud over the campus by establishing a grid of Cisco 350 Series Wireless Access Points (WAPs) with a maximum transmission rate of 11 Mbps. The network could be made secure with IPSec and a Cisco 3030 VPN Concentrator. The cost for this network would likely be about $120,000. The benefits, however, would greatly outstrip the costs, because the university could minimize its hardwired computer classrooms.

The Innovation Team

Introduction to Technical Communication, Humanities 381

Figure 17.9: Centering is fine for headings, but too much centered material can make the text look chaotic.

Grouping is also referred to as "using white space" to frame items on the page. White spaces are places where no text or images appear on the page and include:

- the margins of the document
- the space around a list
- the area between an image and the body text
- the space between two paragraphs

These spaces create frames around the items on the page so readers can view them as groups. For example, the white space around a vertical list (like the one in Figure 17.10) helps readers see that list as one unit.

Using Headings

One way to group information is to use headings. When used properly, headings will help your readers quickly understand the structure of your document and how to use it.

An Interface That Uses Alignment and Grouping Well

Figure 17.10: White space and placing items near each other create groups of information that are easy to scan.

Alignment is used well to signal connections and hierarchies in the text.

White space is used to frame parts of the text, making them groups.

Groups of information create blocks of text that are seen as units on the screen.

Source: The Field Museum, Chicago, Illinois, http://www.fieldmuseum.org

Different types of headings should signal the various levels of information in the text.

- **First-level headings** should be sized significantly larger than second-level headings. In some cases, first-level headings might use all capital letters ("all caps") or small capital letters ("small caps") to distinguish them from the body text.

- **Second-level headings** should be significantly smaller and different from the first-level headings. Whereas the first-level headings might be in all caps, the second-level headings might use bold lettering.

- **Third-level headings** might be italicized and a little larger than the body text.

- **Fourth-level headings** are about as small as you should go. They are usually boldfaced or italicized and placed on the same line as the body text.

Figure 17.11 shows various levels of headings and how they might be used.

In most technical documents, the headings should use the same typeface throughout (e.g., Avant Garde, Times Roman, Helvetica). In other words, the first-level heading should use the same typeface as the second-level and third-level headings. Only the font size and style (bold, italics, small caps) should be changed.

Headings should also follow consistent wording patterns. A consistent wording pattern might use gerunds (-*ing* words) to lead off headings. Or, to be consistent, questions might be used as headings.

Headings serve as *access points* for readers, breaking a large text into smaller groups. If headings are used consistently, readers will be able to quickly access your document to find the information they need. If headings are used inconsistently, readers may have difficulty understanding the structure of the document.

Levels of Headings

DOCUMENT TITLE

FIRST-LEVEL HEADING

This first-level heading is 18-point Avant Garde, boldface with small caps. Notice that it is significantly different from the second-level heading, even though both levels are in the same typeface.

Second-Level Heading

This second-level heading is 14-point Avant Garde with boldface.

Third-Level Heading

This third-level heading is 12-point Avant Garde italics. Often, no extra space appears between a third-level heading and the body text, as shown here.

Fourth-Level Heading. This heading appears on the same line as the body text. It is designed to signal a new layer of information without standing out too much.

Figure 17.11: The headings you choose for a document should be clearly distinguishable from the body text and from each other so that readers can see the levels in the text.

Using Borders and Rules

In document design, *borders* and straight lines, called *rules*, can be used to carve a page into smaller groups of information. They can also help break the text into more manageable sections for the readers.

Borders completely frame parts of the document (Figure 17.12). Whatever appears within a border should be able to stand alone. For example, a bordered warning statement should include all the information readers need to avoid a dangerous situation. Similarly, a border around several paragraphs (like a sidebar) suggests that they should be read separately from the main text.

Rules are often used to highlight a banner or carve a document into sections. They are helpful for signaling places to pause in the document. But when they are overused, they can make the text look and feel too fragmented.

Borders and rules are usually easy to create with your word processor. To put a border around something, highlight that item and find the Borders command in your word processor (Figure 17.13). In the window that appears, you can specify what kind of border you want to add to the text.

Rules can be a bit more difficult to use, so you might want to use a desktop layout program, like Adobe InDesign or QuarkXPress. However, if your document is small or simple, you can use the Draw function of your word processor to draw horizontal or vertical rules in your text.

Using Rules and Borders to Group Information

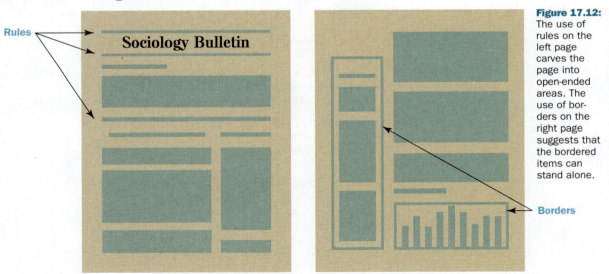

Rules

Sociology Bulletin

Figure 17.12: The use of rules on the left page carves the page into open-ended areas. The use of borders on the right page suggests that the bordered items can stand alone.

Borders

Making Borders

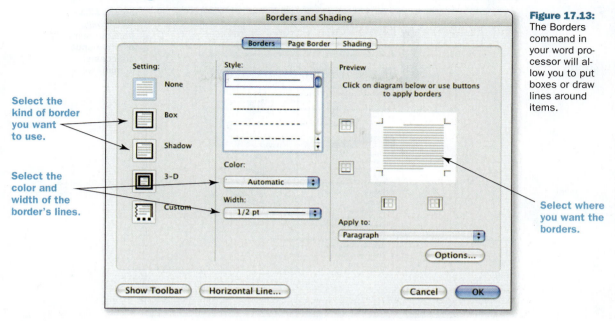

Select the kind of border you want to use.

Select the color and width of the border's lines.

Figure 17.13: The Borders command in your word processor will allow you to put boxes or draw lines around items.

Select where you want the borders.

Design Principle 4: Consistency

The principle of consistency suggests that design features should be used consistently throughout a document or website:

- Headings should be predictable.
- Pages should follow the same grid.
- Lists should use consistent bulleting or numbering schemes.
- Page numbers should appear in the same place on each page.

Consistency is important because it creates a sense of order in a document while limiting the amount of clutter. A consistent page design will help your readers access information quickly, because each page is similar and predictable (Figure 17.14). When design features are used inconsistently, readers will find the document erratic and hard to interpret.

Choosing Typefaces

Consistency should be an important consideration when you choose typefaces for your document. As a rule of thumb, a document should not use more than two typefaces. Most page designers will choose two typefaces that are very different from each other, usually a *serif* typeface and a *sans serif* typeface.

Consistent Layout

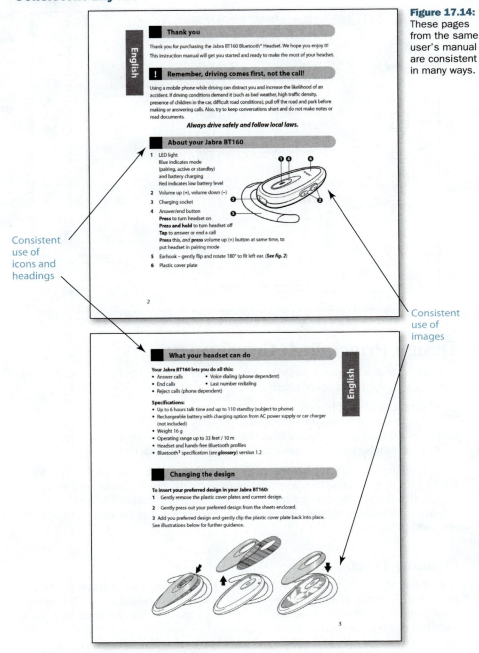

Figure 17.14: These pages from the same user's manual are consistent in many ways.

Consistent use of icons and headings

Consistent use of images

Source: *Jabra BT160 Bluetooth User Manual, pp. 2–5. GN Netcom, Inc.*

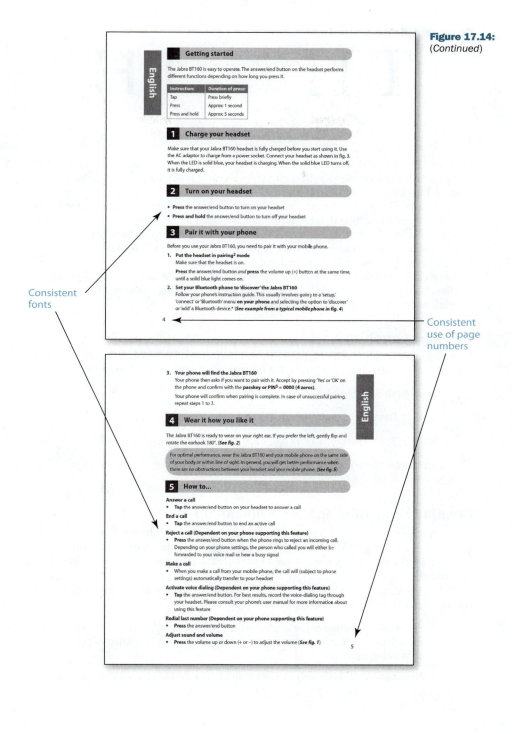

Consistent fonts

Consistent use of page numbers

Getting started

The Jabra BT160 is easy to operate. The answer/end button on the headset performs different functions depending on how long you press it.

Instruction:	Duration of press:
Tap	Press briefly
Press	Approx 1 second
Press and hold	Approx 5 seconds

1 Charge your headset

Make sure that your Jabra BT160 headset is fully charged before you start using it. Use the AC adaptor to charge from a power socket. Connect your headset as shown in fig. 3. When the LED is solid blue, your headset is charging. When the solid blue LED turns off, it is fully charged.

2 Turn on your headset

• **Press** the answer/end button to turn on your headset
• **Press and hold** the answer/end button to turn off your headset

3 Pair it with your phone

Before you use your Jabra BT160, you need to pair it with your mobile phone.

1. **Put the headset in pairing[2] mode**
   Make sure that the headset is on.
   Press the answer/end button *and* **press** the volume up (+) button at the same time, until a solid blue light comes on.

2. **Set your Bluetooth phone to 'discover' the Jabra BT160**
   Follow your phone's instruction guide. This usually involves going to a 'setup,' 'connect' or 'Bluetooth' menu **on your phone** and selecting the option to 'discover' or 'add' a Bluetooth device.* (*See example from a typical mobile phone in fig. 4*)

4

3. **Your phone will find the Jabra BT160**
   Your phone then asks if you want to pair with it. Accept by pressing 'Yes' or 'OK' on the phone and confirm with the **passkey or PIN[3] = 0000 (4 zeros)**.
   Your phone will confirm when pairing is complete. In case of unsuccessful pairing, repeat steps 1 to 3.

4 Wear it how you like it

The Jabra BT160 is ready to wear on your right ear. If you prefer the left, gently flip and rotate the earhook 180°. (*See fig. 2*)

For optimal performance, wear the Jabra BT160 and your mobile phone on the same side of your body or within line of sight. In general, you will get better performance when there are no obstructions between your headset and your mobile phone. (*See fig. 5*)

5 How to...

Answer a call
• **Tap** the answer/end button on your headset to answer a call

End a call
• **Tap** the answer/end button to end an active call

Reject a call (Dependent on your phone supporting this feature)
• **Press** the answer/end button when the phone rings to reject an incoming call. Depending on your phone settings, the person who called you will either be forwarded to your voice mail or hear a busy signal

Make a call
• When you make a call from your mobile phone, the call will (subject to phone settings) automatically transfer to your headset

Activate voice dialing (Dependent on your phone supporting this feature)
• **Tap** the answer/end button. For best results, record the voice-dialing tag through your headset. Please consult your phone's user manual for more information about using this feature

Redial last number (Dependent on your phone supporting this feature)
• **Press** the answer/end button

Adjust sound and volume
• **Press** the volume up or down (+ or –) to adjust the volume (*See fig. 1*)

5

English

English

Serif and Sans Serif Typefaces

Serifs

No Serifs

Figure 17.15: A serif typeface like Bookman (left) includes the small tips at the ends of letters. A sans serif typeface like Helvetica (right) does not include these tips.

A serif typeface like Times Roman, New York, or Bookman has small tips (serifs) at the ends of the main strokes in each letter (Figure 17.15). Sans serif typefaces like Arial or Helvetica do not have these small tips.

Serif fonts, like Times Roman, New York, or Bookman, are usually perceived to be more formal and traditional. Sans serif typefaces like Helvetica seem more informal and progressive. So, designers often use serif fonts for the body of their text and sans serif in the headings, footers, captions, and titles. Using both kinds of typefaces gives a design a progressive and traditional feel at the same time.

Your choice of typefaces, of course, depends on the needs and expectations of your readers. Use typefaces that fit their needs and values, striking the appropriate balance between progressive and traditional design.

Labeling Graphics

Link

For more information on labeling graphics, see Chapter 18, page 481.

Graphics such as tables, charts, pictures, and graphs should be labeled consistently in your document. In most cases, the label for a graphic will include a number.

Graph 5: Growth of Sales in the Third Quarter of 2013

Table C: Data Set Gathered from Beta Radiation Tests

Figure 1.2: Diagram of Wastewater Flow in Hinsdale's Treatment Plant

The label can be placed above the graphic or below it. Use the same style to label every graphic in the document.

Creating Sequential and Nonsequential Lists

Early in the design process, you should decide how lists will be used and how they will look. Lists are very useful for showing a sequence of tasks or setting off a group of items. But if they are not used consistently, they can create confusion for the readers.

When deciding how lists will look, first make decisions about the design of sequential and nonsequential lists (Figure 17.16).

Sequential (numbered) lists are used to present items in a specific order. In these lists, you can use numbers or letters to show a sequence, chronology, or ranking of items.

Nonsequential (bulleted) lists include items that are essentially equal in value or have no sequence. You can use bullets, dashes, or check boxes to identify each item in the list.

Using Sequential and Nonsequential Lists

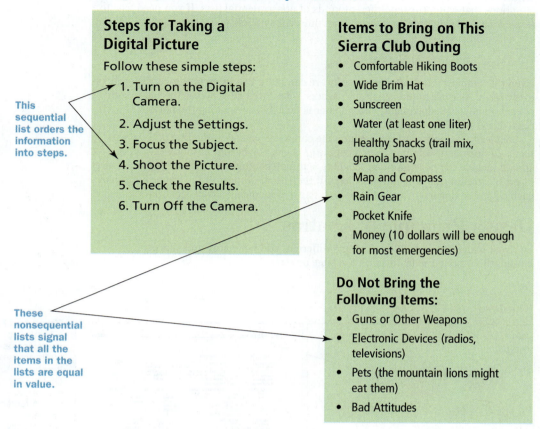

Steps for Taking a Digital Picture

Follow these simple steps:

1. Turn on the Digital Camera.
2. Adjust the Settings.
3. Focus the Subject.
4. Shoot the Picture.
5. Check the Results.
6. Turn Off the Camera.

This sequential list orders the information into steps.

Items to Bring on This Sierra Club Outing

- Comfortable Hiking Boots
- Wide Brim Hat
- Sunscreen
- Water (at least one liter)
- Healthy Snacks (trail mix, granola bars)
- Map and Compass
- Rain Gear
- Pocket Knife
- Money (10 dollars will be enough for most emergencies)

Do Not Bring the Following Items:

- Guns or Other Weapons
- Electronic Devices (radios, televisions)
- Pets (the mountain lions might eat them)
- Bad Attitudes

These nonsequential lists signal that all the items in the lists are equal in value.

Figure 17.16: The sequential list on the left shows an ordering of the information, so it requires numbers. The nonsequential list on the right uses bullets because there is no particular ordering of these items.

Checking for Consistency

AT A GLANCE

The following items should be used consistently in your document:

- typefaces (serif and sans serif)
- labeling of graphics
- lists (sequential and nonsequential)
- headers and footers

Lists make information more readable and accessible. So, you should look for opportunities to use them in your documents. If, for example, you are listing steps to describe how to do something, you have an opportunity to use a sequential list. Or, if you are creating a list of four items or more, ask yourself whether a nonsequential list would present the information in a more accessible way.

Just make sure you use lists consistently. Sequential lists should follow the same numbering scheme throughout the document. For example, you might choose a numbering scheme like (1), (2), (3). If so, do not number the next list 1., 2., 3. and others A., B., C., unless you have a good reason for changing the numbering scheme. Similarly, in nonsequential lists, use the same symbols when setting off lists. Do not use bullets (•) with one list, check marks (✓) with another, and boxes

(■) with a third. These inconsistencies only confuse readers. Of course, there are situations that call for using different kinds of nonsequential lists. If you need lists to serve completely different purposes, then different symbols will work—as long as they are used consistently.

Inserting Headers and Footers

Even the simplest word-processing software can put a header or footer consistently on every page. As their names suggest, a header is text that runs across the top margin of each page in the document, and a footer is text that runs along the bottom of each page (Figure 17.17).

Headers and footers usually include the company's name or the title of the document. In documents of more than a couple of pages, the header or footer (not both) should include the page number. Headers and footers often also include design features like a horizontal rule or a company logo. If these items appear at the top or bottom of each page, the document will tend to look like it is following a consistent design.

Design Principle 5: Contrast

Contrast makes items look distinct and different, adding energy and sharpening boundaries among the features on the page or screen.

Headers and Footers

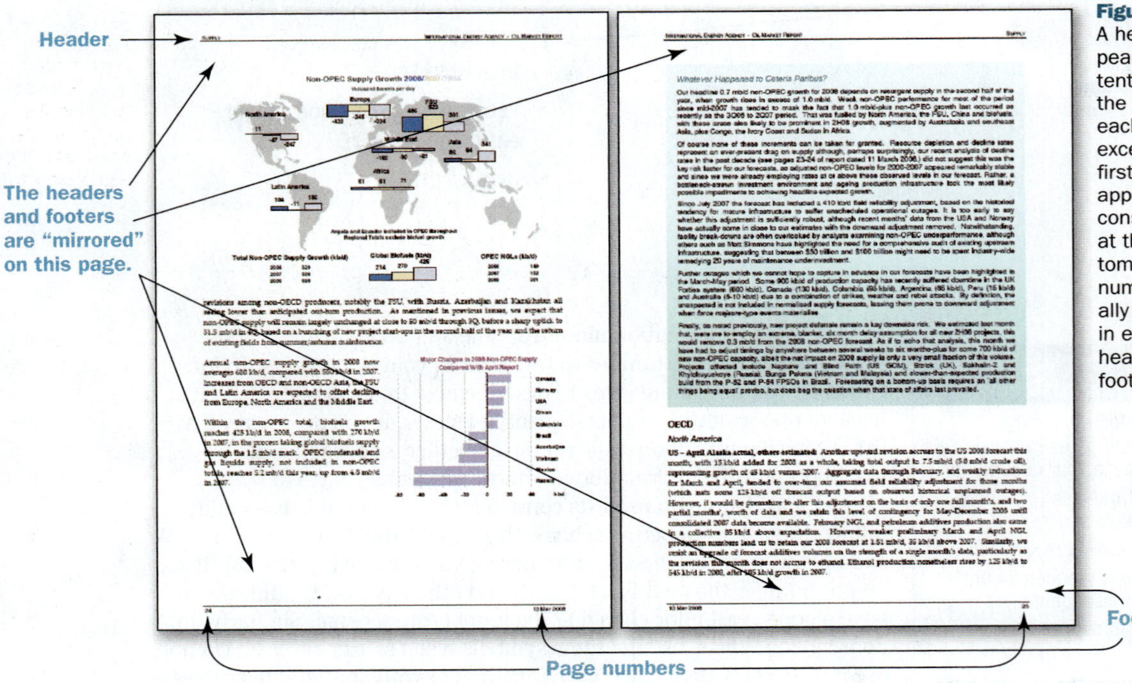

Header

The headers and footers are "mirrored" on this page.

Page numbers

Footer

Figure 17.17: A header appears consistently across the top of each page, except the first. A footer appears consistently at the bottom. A page number usually appears in either the header or the footer.

Source: Oil Market Report, May 13, 2008

AT A GLANCE

Five Principles of Document Design

- balance
- alignment
- grouping
- consistency
- contrast

A good guideline is to "make different things on the page look very different." Contrast, as shown in Figure 17.18, makes design elements lively.

When designing a page, consider your use of contrast carefully. Word processors offer many tools for adding contrast in ways that capture readers' attention. Sometimes, though, you can accidentally create contrast problems with different colors or shading in the background—or by putting too much clutter on the page.

There are a variety of ways to add contrast to a page, including color, shading, highlighting, and changes in font sizes. With the availability of color printers, adding color is an especially good way to add energy to a print document.

Also, when used properly, shading and background color can help highlight important text in a document. However, in some cases these design features can also make texts hard to read on a printed page because the words are sometimes hard to distinguish from the shaded background. Likewise, background color or images can also make text on computer screens difficult to read. So use them carefully and be sure to check how backgrounds work (or don't work) with the text on the screen.

It is fine to use shading, background color, and background images. However, make sure the words on the page contrast significantly with the background behind those words.

Contrast in a Webpage

Images contrast with the text.

Large headings grab the reader.

Color adds contrast to the text.

Reverse type (white on dark green) draws the eye.

Figure 17.18: In this webpage, contrast is used to catch the reader's eye and make the text easier to read.

Source: Medline Plus, http://www.medlineplus.gov

Transcultural Design

As the global economy grows, designing documents for transcultural readers may be one of the greatest challenges facing technical communicators. Today, most international readers are adjusting to Western design practices. But, with the global reach of the Internet and the growth of economies around the world, readers are beginning to expect documents and interfaces to reflect their own cultural design conventions.

When designing transcultural documents, your first consideration is whether your text or interface needs a "culturally deep" or a "culturally shallow" design.

- **Culturally deep** documents and interfaces use the language, symbols, and conventions of the target culture to reflect readers' design preferences and expectations. To develop a culturally deep design, you probably need help from designers or consultants who are familiar with the target culture and understand its design expectations.
- **Culturally shallow** documents and interfaces usually follow Western design conventions, but they adjust to reflect some of the design preferences of the cultures in which they will be used. They also avoid any cultural taboos of the people who are likely to use the text. Culturally shallow designs tend to be used in documents or interfaces that need to accommodate a variety of cultures.

Unless your company is targeting its products or services to a specific nation or culture (e.g., a nation like Korea or Zimbabwe), most of your documents or interfaces will need to be culturally shallow so that they can work across a variety of cultures.

Culturally shallow designs usually consider four design issues: use of color, use of people, use of symbols, and direction of reading.

Use of color—Choice of colors in a document can influence how transcultural readers interpret the message, because colors can have different meanings across cultures. For instance, the use of red in Japan signals anger, while in China red signals happiness. The use of red in Egypt symbolizes death. Meanwhile, the color green in France symbolizes criminality, while in the United States green symbolizes moving forward or environmental consciousness. Figure 17.19 shows how some common colors are perceived across cultures. When designing your document or interface, you should use colors that reflect the expectations of the likely readers (or at least avoid colors that have negative associations).

Use of people—Transcultural texts should use images of people carefully. Avoid big smiles, highly emotional expressions, suggestive behavior, and flashy clothing. In pictures, interactions between women and men should avoid sending mixed signals. In some cultures, especially Islamic cultures, images of people are used only when "needed." The definition of "need" varies among Islamic subcultures, but images tend to be used only for purposes of identification.

Colors in Other Cultures

Color	Japan	France	China	Egypt	United States
Red	Anger, danger	Aristocracy	Happiness	Death	Danger, stop
Blue	Villainy	Freedom, peace	Heavens, clouds	Virtue, faith, truth	Masculine, conservative
Green	Future, youth, energy	Criminality	Ming Dynasty, heavens	Fertility, strength	Safe, go, natural
Yellow	Grace, nobility	Temporary	Birth, wealth, power	Happiness, prosperity	Cowardice, temporary
White	Death	Neutrality	Death, purity	Joy	Purity, peace, marriage

Figure 17.19: Colors can have very different meanings in different cultures. In some cases, the meanings of colors may even be contradictory among cultures.

Source: Patricia Russo and Stephen Boor. 1993. How fluent is your interface?: designing for international users. In Proceedings of the INTERACT '93 and CHI '93 Conference on Human Factors in Computing Systems (CHI '93). ACM, New York, NY, USA, 342–347, Table 1. © 1993 Association for Computing Machinery, Inc. Reprinted by permission. DOI=10.1145/169059.169274 http://doi.acm.org/10.1145/169059.169274.

Use of symbols—Common symbols can have very different meanings in different cultures. For example, in many cultures, the "OK" hand signal is highly offensive. Uses of crescent symbols (i.e., moons) or crosses can have a variety of religious meanings. White flowers or a white dress can signify death in many Asian cultures. To avoid offending readers with symbols, a good approach is to use only simple shapes (e.g., circles, squares, triangles) in transcultural documents.

Direction of reading—Many cultures in the Middle East and Asia read right to left instead of left to right. As a result, some of the guidelines for balancing a page design discussed earlier in this chapter should be reversed. For example, a document or interface that reads right to left tends to be anchored on the right side. Otherwise, the text will look unbalanced to a right-to-left reader. Figure 17.20, for example, shows a website that is designed right to left for Middle Eastern readers.

Transcultural design can be very challenging. The secret is to consult with people from the target culture and/or use consultants to help you design your documents and interfaces. Then, be ready to learn from your mistakes.

Link

For more information on international and transcultural symbols, go to Chapter 18, page 492.

Link

For more help on working with transcultural readers, go to Chapter 2, page 24.

A Right-to-Left Interface Design

Source: Microsoft Corporation.

Figure 17.20: This webpage interface shows how design shifts to fit the target culture. This interface is designed to read from right to left. Notice, however, that some English words, especially brands, have been kept.

- Good design allows readers to (1) easily scan a document, (2) access the document to find the information they need, (3) understand the content more readily, and (4) appreciate the appearance of the document.

- The five principles of document design are balance, alignment, grouping, consistency, and contrast.

- On a balanced page, elements offset each other to create a stable feeling in the text. Unbalanced pages add tension to the reading process.

- Alignment creates relationships among items in a text and helps readers determine the hierarchical levels in the text.

- Grouping divides the text into "scannable" blocks by using headings, rules, and borders to make words and images easier to comprehend.

- Consistency makes documents more accessible by making features predictable; inconsistent documents are harder to read and interpret.

- Contrast can cause text features or elements to stand out, but contrast should be used with restraint so that text elements work together rather than compete against each other.

- Documents and interfaces that need to work transculturally can use a culturally shallow design or a culturally deep design.

- Culturally deep documents use the language, symbols, and conventions of the target culture.

- Culturally shallow documents usually follow Western design conventions, but they adjust to reflect some of the design preferences of the cultures in which they will be used.

Individual or Team Projects

1. On campus or at your workplace, find a poorly or minimally designed document. If you look on any bulletin board, you will find several documents that you can use. In a memo to your instructor, critique this document using the five design principles discussed in this chapter. Explain how the document fails to follow the principles.

2. Read the Case Study at the end of this chapter. Using the design principles discussed in this chapter, sketch out some thumbnails of a better design for this document. Then, using your word processor, develop an improved design. In a memo to your instructor, compare and contrast the old design with the new one, explaining why your new design is superior.

3. Find a document that illustrates good design. Then, change some aspect of its rhetorical situation (purpose, readers, context). Redesign the document to fit that altered rhetorical situation. For example, you might redesign a user's manual to accommodate the needs of eight-year-old children. You might turn a normal-sized document into a poster that can be read from a distance. In a memo to your instructor, discuss the changes you made to the document. Show how the changes in the rhetorical situation led to alterations in the design of the document. Explain why you think the changes you made were effective.

4. On the Internet, find an international company's website that is intended to work in a few different cultures. In a presentation to your class, explain why you believe the site is culturally shallow or culturally deep. How have the designers of the website made adjustments to suit the expectations of people from a different culture? How might they improve the design to make it more effective for the target readers?

Collaborative Project

With other members of your class, choose a provider of a common product or service (for example, a car manufacturer, mobile phone or clothing store, museum, or theater). Then find the websites of three or four competitors for this product or service.

Using the design principles you learned in this chapter, critique these websites by comparing and contrasting their designs. Considering its target audience, which website design seems the most effective? Which is the least effective? Explain your positive and negative criticisms in some depth.

Then, using thumbnails, redesign the weakest site so that it better appeals to its target audience. How can you use balance, alignment, grouping, consistency, and contrast to improve the design of the site?

In a presentation to your class, discuss why the design of one site is stronger and others are weaker from a design perspective. Then, using an overhead projector or smartboard, use your thumbnails to show how you might improve the design of the weakest site you found.

Visit MyWritingLab for a Post-test and more technical writing resources.

Bugs on the Bus

Vera Hernandez is a recent graduate from Rutgers with a degree in Entomology, and she now works as a Pest Management Specialist at the New Jersey Department of Public Health. Her undergraduate research project on bed bugs was a key reason she was hired for the job.

Recently, Jersey City has been experiencing a sudden rise in bed bug infestations. Many children are coming to school with visible bites. Right away, Vera knew what was causing the problem. Bed bugs climb into the kids' backpacks for the trip to school, spread out at the school, and then ride to new homes in other kids' backpacks. That's why the epidemic had been spreading so fast, and why children have been the most obvious victims.

A task force at the Department of Public Health was put together to come up with solutions to the problem. Unfortunately, a city spokesperson revealed that the task force was looking into schools as the main source of the bed bug outbreak. The media was now calling this story the "Bugs on the Bus" crisis and the coverage was causing quite a scare in the public. Yesterday, under intense pressure from parents, the Jersey City mayor declared war on bed bugs and targeted schools as a key "battleground."

The task force needed to move fast. Vera was tasked with designing a two-page pamphlet about bed bugs that could be sent home with children. Each school would also do a one-hour training to show children how to spot bed bugs and how to avoid letting them hitch a ride in their backpacks.

The children would be an important audience for the pamphlet but the real audience would be their parents. Vera wanted to raise their awareness about the bed bug problem and provide some practical advice about how to rid their homes of these persistent pests.

Vera's supervisor gave her the document in Figure A to turn into the pamphlet. It had good information, but the design was not appropriate for children or their parents. It also didn't have any pictures to help identify bed bugs. If you were Vera, how would you redesign this document to make it more useful to both children and adults? You need to keep the length to one sheet of paper, front and back. You cannot go over than amount.

A Document Design That Could Be Improved

New Jersey Department of Health and Senior Services Consumer and Environmental Health Services Public Health, Sanitation and Safety Program

Bed Bug Control for Homes

Bed bugs feed frequently such that the majority of insects would be closest to the host or in the mattress. They do not stay on the host after feeding. They multiply and spread to other parts of the room and eventually other rooms. They are not host specific such that any warm blood will provide nourishment. Forget about trying to starve bed bugs. The bugs may survive 2 months to a year without food depending on various conditions.

CONTROLS

Clothing can be treated by washing in the clothing washer at the high or white clothing temperature of 140°F (thermal death 130°F to 140°F depending on length of time). Remember that due to energy and burn safety, the house water may be tempered. In many cases the clothing washer does not have direct hot water supply before a mixing valve. In other cases the water heater thermostat can be raised for this purpose.

The mattress is a challenge. There are many approaches.

- Throw mattress away and replace with new.

- Encase in plastic or dust mite bag (allergy supplies) to prevent reinfestation until certain the bed bugs are eradicated.

- If you decide to keep the mattress, do not treat mattress with residual insecticides. One product that is used to renovate used mattresses is "Steri-Fab" sanitizer which has the ability to kill dust mites and bed bugs on inanimate surfaces such as mattresses, upholstered chairs, couches, and carpets." You can spray with non-residual insecticide such as a pyrethrum or DDVP (as per label).You can also dust with boric acid powder.

- Make sure any wet treatment dries. Then bag as above.

- There is also a cold method of treating the mattress. Exact time and temperatures are hard to find. Examples—one University says that 5 days in a –10°F walk in refrigerator will work. Another citation says 32°F for 2 to 4 weeks…you would still need a mattress in the meantime.

Source: U.S. Environmental Protection Agency, http://www.epa.gov/pesticides/ipm/schoolipm.

Figure A: This document contains a good amount of useful information, but its design makes it harder to read than necessary. How would you redesign it to be appropriate for children and their parents?

Extermination services are used to control insects in the environment. A good procedure is to spray with a residual spray (labeled for bed bugs) in concentric circles starting with the outside perimeter of the infestation. They would spray any penetration in all surrounding rooms that are on the outside of the target room. Then thoroughly spray all cracks/crevices of the target room perimeter, in the room. Then treat crevices of articles in the room [to be saved and not otherwise treated with hot or cold treatments alluded to above]. Note—Unless sprayed directly, the bed bug eggs will not be destroyed. When they hatch, they should be affected by the residual left in their vicinity. At room temperature the nymphs may take 2 weeks to hatch—at cooler temperatures 4 weeks. In conjunction with insecticide, insect growth regulators (IGR) are considered safe to get rid of tenacious problems (produce sterile bed bugs).

Additionally the exterminator could help with eliminating alternate blood hosts such as rodents, bats, and bird nests. Don't forget pets will provide blood meals for bed bugs.

CLEANING

Frequent vacuuming removes numbers of bugs. Cleaning objects removes eggs which are glued in crevices. Borax cleaner may have some effect because many insects cannot tolerate Boron. Low humidity increases insect death rates. Dehydration is the natural cause of death for most insects.

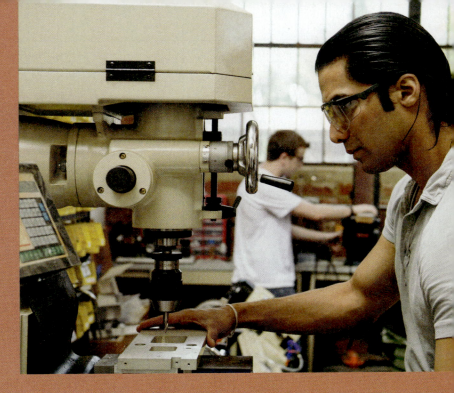

CHAPTER

18

Creating and Using Graphics

Guidelines for Using Graphics 477

Displaying Data with Graphs,
  Tables, and Charts 481

Using Pictures and Drawings 487

Using Transcultural Symbols 492

What You Need to Know 495

Exercises and Projects 495

Case Study: Looking Guilty 497

In this chapter, you will learn:

- The importance of visuals in documents and presentations.

- Four guidelines for using visuals effectively.

- How to use tables, charts, and graphs.

- Strategies for taking photographs and using them in documents and presentations.

- How drawings, icons, and clip art can be effectively used to enhance understanding.

Graphics are an essential part of any technical document or presentation. Your readers will often pay more attention to the visuals in your document than to the written text. For example, think about how you began reading this chapter. More than likely, you did not begin reading at the top of this page. Instead, you probably took a quick glance at the graphics in the chapter to figure out what it is about. Then, you started reading the written text. Your readers will approach your documents the same way.

Guidelines for Using Graphics

As you draft your document, you should look for places where graphics could be used to support the text. Graphics are especially helpful in places where you want to reinforce important ideas or help your readers understand complex concepts or trends.

To help you create and use graphics effectively and properly, there are four guidelines you should commit to memory.

Guideline One: A Graphic Should Tell a Simple Story

A graphic should tell the "story" about your data in a concise way. In other words, your readers should be able to figure out at a quick glance what the graphic says. If they need to pause longer than a moment, there is a good chance readers will not understand what the graphic means.

Figure 18.1, for example, shows how a graph can tell a simple story. Almost immediately, a reader will recognize that obesity rates around the world are going up dramatically. It's also obvious that the United States is the most obese nation and the problem is growing worse.

This first guideline—tell a simple story—also applies to photographs in a document (Plotnik, 1982). At a glance, your readers should be able to figure out what story a photograph is telling. The photograph in Figure 18.2, for example, is not complex, but it tells a clear story about the markings on a fritillary butterfly.

Guideline Two: A Graphic Should Reinforce the Written Text, Not Replace It

Graphics should be used to support the written text, but they cannot replace it altogether. Since technical documents often discuss complex ideas or relationships, it is tempting to simply refer the readers to a graphic (e.g., "See Chart 9 for an explanation of the data"). Chances are, though, that if you cannot explain something in writing, you won't be able to explain it in a graphic, either.

Instead, your written text and visuals should work with each other. The written text should refer readers to the graphics, and the graphics should support the written information. For example, the written text might say, "As shown in Graph 2, the number of high school students who report being in fights has been declining." A graph, like the one in Figure 18.3, would then support this written statement by illustrating this trend.

A Graph That Tells a Simple Story

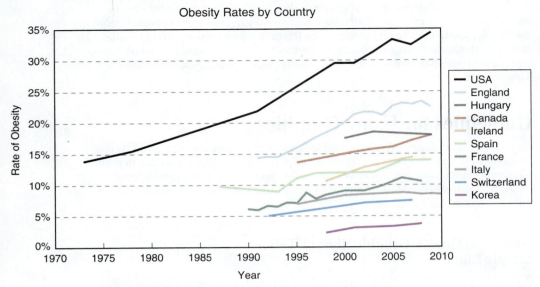

Obesity Rates by Country

*Source: Organisation for Economic Cooperation and Development, "Obesity Update, 2012," p. 2
http://www.oecd.org/health/49716427.pdf*

Figure 18.1: This graph tells a simple story about obesity that readers can grasp at a glance.

A Photograph Should Tell a Simple Story, Too

Figure 18.2: This photograph tells a simple story that reinforces the written text.

Figure B: Fritillaries, a subgroup of the Nymphalidae family, are common in the Rocky Mountains.

A Graph That Reinforces the Written Text

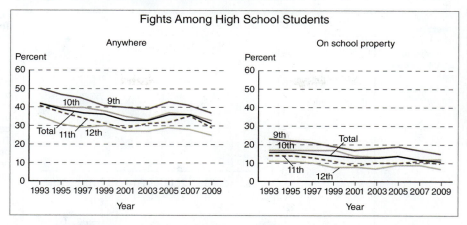

Figure 18.3:
A line graph typically shows a trend over time. This graph shows how fights among high school students have been declining.

Source: National Center for Education Statistics, "Indicators of School Crime and Safety, 2010," http://nces.ed.gov/programs/crimeindicators/crimeindicators2010/figures/figure_13_1.asp

The written text should tell readers the story that the graphic is trying to illustrate. That way, readers are almost certain to understand what the graphic is showing them.

Guideline Three: A Graphic Should Be Ethical

Graphs, charts, tables, illustrations, and photographs should not be used to hide information, distort facts, or exaggerate trends. In a bar chart, for example, the scales can be altered to suggest that more growth has occurred than is actually the case (Figure 18.4). In a line graph, it is tempting to leave out data points that won't allow a smooth line to be drawn. Likewise, photographs can be digitally distorted or doctored.

A good rule of thumb with graphics—and a safe principle to follow in technical communication altogether—is to always be absolutely honest. Your readers are not fools, so attempts to use graphics to distort or stretch the truth will eventually be detected. Once detected, unethical graphics can erode the credibility of an entire document or presentation (Kostelnick & Roberts, 1998). Even if your readers only *suspect* deception in your graphics, they will begin to doubt the honesty of the entire text.

Link

For more information on the ethical use of data, see Chapter 4, page 77.

Guideline Four: A Graphic Should Be Labeled and Placed Properly

Proper labeling and placement of graphics help readers move back and forth between the main text and images. Each graphic should be labeled with an informative title (Figure 18.5). Other parts of the graphic should also be carefully labeled:

- The x- and y-axes of graphs and charts should display standard units of measurement.
- Columns and rows in tables should be labeled so readers can easily locate specific data points.

Link

For more information on designing page layouts, see Chapter 17, page 447.

Unethical and Ethical Bar Charts

This bar chart is unethical. The altered scale makes sales seem to be going up quickly.

This chart is ethical. Notice how the growth in sales seems less dramatic.

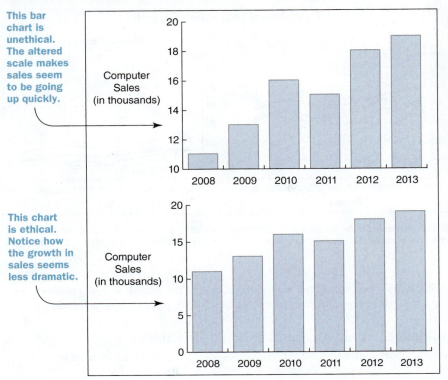

Figure 18.4: The top bar chart is unethical because the y-axis has been altered to exaggerate the growth in sales of computers. The second bar chart presents the data ethically.

- Important features of drawings or illustrations should be identified with arrows or lines and some explanatory text.
- The source of the data used to make the graphic should be clearly identified underneath.

If you include a title with the graph, an explanatory caption is not needed. Nevertheless, a sentence or two of explanation in a caption can often help reinforce or clarify the story the graphic is trying to tell.

When placing a graphic, put it on the page where it is referenced or, at the farthest, put it on the following page. Readers will rarely flip more than one page to look for a graphic.

Even if they *do* make the effort to hunt down a graphic that is pages away, doing so will take them out of the flow of the document, inviting them to start skimming.

Readers should be able to locate a graphic with a quick glance. Then, they should be able to quickly return to the written text to continue reading. When labeled and placed properly, graphics flow seamlessly with the text.

Labeling of a Graphic

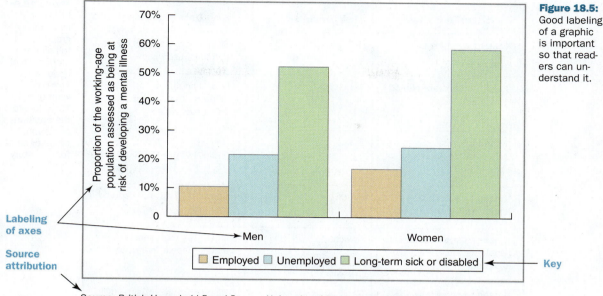

Labeling of axes

Source attribution

Key

Figure 18.5: Good labeling of a graphic is important so that readers can understand it.

Source: British Household Panel Survey, University of Essex, Institute for Social and Economic Research; the data is the average for the five years to 2005/06; updated June 2007. Guy Palmer, The Poverty Site, www.poverty.org.uk http://www.poverty.org.uk

Displaying Data with Graphs, Tables, and Charts

To decide which graphic is best for the data you want to display, first decide what story you want to tell. Then, choose the type of graphic that best fits that story. The chart in Figure 18.6 will help you decide which one works best.

Line Graphs

Line graphs are perhaps the most familiar way to display data. They are best used to show measurements over time. Some of their more common applications include the following:

Showing trends—Line graphs are especially good at showing how quantities rise and fall over time (Figure 18.7). Whether you are illustrating trends in the stock market or charting the changes in temperature during a chemical reaction, a line graph can show how the quantity gradually increases or decreases. When two or more lines are charted on a line graph, you can show how quantities rise and fall in tandem (or don't).

Showing relationships between variables—Line graphs are also helpful when charting the interaction of two different variables. Figure 18.8, for example, shows a line graph that illustrates how a rise in the temperature of a gas is accompanied by a rise in the volume of gas.

Choosing the Appropriate Graphic

The Story to Be Told	Best Graphic	How Data Are Displayed
"I want to show a trend."	Line graph	Shows how a quantity rises and falls, usually over time
"I want to compare two or more quantities."	Bar chart	Shows comparisons among different items or the same items over time
"I need to present data or facts for analysis and comparison."	Table	Displays data in an organized, easy-to-access way
"I need to show how a whole is divided into parts."	Pie chart	Shows data as a pie carved into slices
"I need to show how things, people, or steps are linked together."	Flowchart	Illustrates the connections among people, parts, or steps
"I need to show how a project will meet its goals over time."	Gantt chart	Displays a project schedule, highlighting the phases of the work

Figure 18.6: Different kinds of graphics tell different stories. Think about what story you want to tell. Then, locate the appropriate graph, table, or chart for that story.

A Line Graph Showing a Trend

Figure 18.7: A line graph shows trends. These graphs illustrate the interdependence of wolves and moose on Isle Royale in Lake Superior.

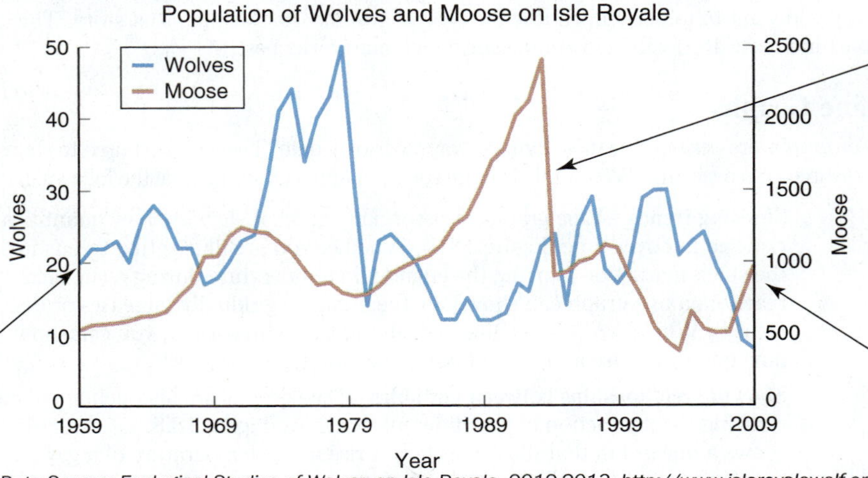

This graph shows the number of wolves over time.

Notice how these graphs show an interesting relationship between these populations of wolves and moose.

This graph shows the number of moose over time.

Population of Wolves and Moose on Isle Royale

Data Source: Ecological Studies of Wolves on Isle Royale, 2012-2013. http://www.isleroyalewolf.org.

A Line Graph Showing a Relationship Between Variables

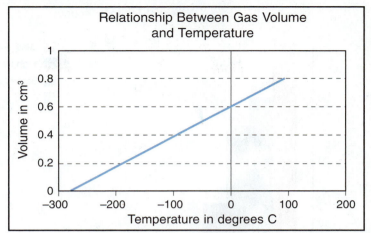

Relationship Between Gas Volume and Temperature

Figure 18.8: Here, the volume of a gas is plotted against the temperature. In this case, an extrapolation of the line allows us to estimate "absolute zero," the temperature at which all molecular activity stops.

Source: Worksafe Department of Commerce, Used with Permission. http://Institute.safetyline. wa.gov.au/mod/lti/view.php?id=2455.

In a line graph, the vertical axis (y-axis) displays a measured quantity such as sales, temperature, production, growth, and so on. The horizontal axis (x-axis) is usually divided into time increments such as years, months, days, or hours. In a line graph, the x- and y-axes do not need to start at zero. Often, by starting one or both axes at a nonzero number, you can better illustrate the trends you are trying to show.

The x-axis in a line graph usually represents the "independent variable," which has a consistently measurable value. For example, in most cases, time marches forward steadily, independent of other variables. So, time is often measured on the x-axis. The y-axis often represents the "dependent variable." The value of this variable fluctuates over time.

You can use more than one line to illustrate trends in a line graph. Depending on your printer, computers also give you the ability to use colors to distinguish the lines. Or, you can use dashes, dots, and solid lines to help your readers distinguish one line from the others.

The drawback of line graphs is their inability to present data in exact numbers. For example, in Figure 18.7, can you tell exactly how many wolves were counted in 2001? No. You can only take a good guess at a number. Line graphs are most effective when the trend you are showing is more significant than the exact figures.

Bar Charts

Bar charts are used to show quantities, allowing readers to make visual comparisons among measurements (Figure 18.9). The width of the bars is kept the same, while the length of the bars varies to represent the quantity measured.

A Bar Chart

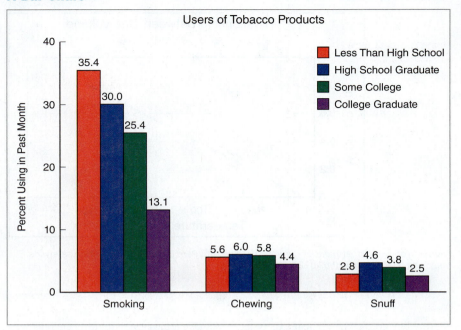

Figure 18.9: A bar chart is especially effective for making comparisons.

Source: Substance Abuse and Mental Health Services Administration, 2009 National Survey on Drug Use and Health.

Computers can be used to enhance bar charts even further. Coloring and shading the bars will help your readers interpret the data and identify trends.

Tables

Tables provide the most efficient way to display data or facts in a small amount of space. In a table, information is placed in horizontal rows and vertical columns, allowing readers to quickly find specific numbers or words that address their needs.

Creating a table takes careful planning, but computers can do much of the hard work for you. For simpler tables, you can use the Table function on your word-processing software. It will allow you to specify how many rows and columns you need (make sure you include enough columns and rows for headings in the table). Then, you can start typing your data or information into the cells.

If the Table function in your word processor is not sufficient for your needs, spreadsheet programs like Microsoft Excel and Corel Quattro Pro also allow you to make quick tables.

After creating the basic table, you should properly label it. In most cases, the table's number and title should appear above it (Figure 18.10). Down the left column,

Parts of a Table

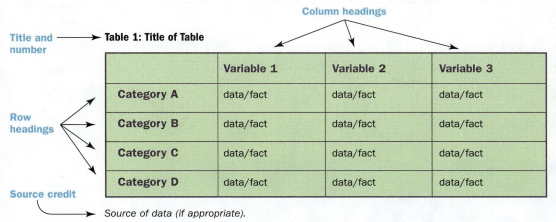

Column headings

Title and number → **Table 1: Title of Table**

	Variable 1	Variable 2	Variable 3
Category A	data/fact	data/fact	data/fact
Category B	data/fact	data/fact	data/fact
Category C	data/fact	data/fact	data/fact
Category D	data/fact	data/fact	data/fact

Row headings

Source credit → *Source of data (if appropriate).*

Figure 18.10: The parts of a table are rather standard. Rows and columns align in ways that allow readers to locate specific pieces of information.

the *row headings* should list the items being measured. Along the top row, the *column headings* should list the qualities of the items being measured. Beneath the table, if needed, a citation should identify the source of the information.

In some cases, tables can be used to present verbal information rather than numerical data. In Figure 18.11, for example, the table is being used to verbally provide health information. With this table, readers can quickly locate their natural skin color and find out their skin cancer risk.

When adding a table to your document, think about what your readers need to know. It is often tempting to include large tables that hold all your data. However, these large tables might clog up your document, making it difficult for readers to locate specific information. You are better off creating small tables that focus on the specific information you want to present. Move larger tables to an appendix, especially if they present data not directly referenced in the document.

Pie Charts

Pie charts are useful for showing how a whole divides into parts (Figure 18.12). Pie charts are popular, but they should be used sparingly. They take up a great amount of space in a document while usually presenting only a small amount of data. The pie chart in Figure 18.12, for instance, uses a third of a page to plot a mere eleven data points.

Pie charts are difficult to construct by hand, but your computer's spreadsheet program (Excel or Quattro Pro) can help you create a basic pie chart of your data. When labeling a pie chart, you should try to place titles and specific numbers in or near the graphic. For instance, in Figure 18.12, each slice of the pie

A Table That Presents Verbal and Visual Information

Figure 18.11: Tables can also present verbal information concisely.

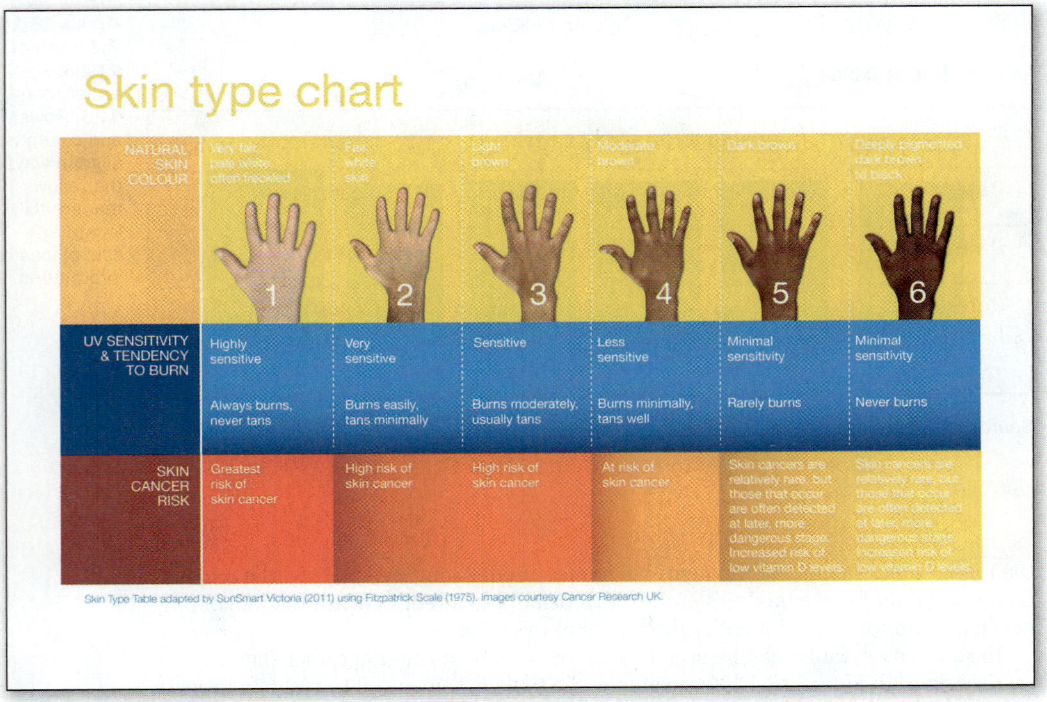

Skin type chart

	1	2	3	4	5	6
NATURAL SKIN COLOUR	Very fair, pale white, often freckled	Fair, white skin	Light brown	Moderate brown	Dark brown	Deeply pigmented dark brown to black
UV SENSITIVITY & TENDENCY TO BURN	Highly sensitive Always burns, never tans	Very sensitive Burns easily, tans minimally	Sensitive Burns moderately, usually tans	Less sensitive Burns minimally, tans well	Minimal sensitivity Rarely burns	Minimal sensitivity Never burns
SKIN CANCER RISK	Greatest risk of skin cancer	High risk of skin cancer	High risk of skin cancer	At risk of skin cancer	Skin cancers are relatively rare, but those that occur are often detected at later, more dangerous stage. Increased risk of low vitamin D levels.	Skin cancers are relatively rare, but those that occur are often detected at later, more dangerous stage. Increased risk of low vitamin D levels.

Skin Type Table adapted by SunSmart Victoria (2011) using Fitzpatrick Scale (1975). Images courtesy Cancer Research UK.

Source: Skin Type table adapted by SunSmart Victoria (2011) using Fitzpatrick scale (1975). Images courtesy Cancer Research UK. http://www.sunsmart.com.au/skin-cancer/risk-factors

chart is labeled and includes measurements to show how the pie was divided. These labels and measurements help readers compare the data points plotted in the chart.

The key to a good pie chart is a clear story. For example, what story is the pie chart in Figure 18.12 trying to tell? Heart disease and cancer are the most significant causes of death among women.

Flowcharts

Link

For more information on writing instructions, go to Chapter 7, page 154.

Flowcharts are used to visually guide readers through a series of decisions, actions, or steps. They typically illustrate a process described in the written text. Arrows are used to connect parts of the flowchart, showing the direction of the process.

As shown in Figure 18.13, flowcharts are helpful for illustrating instructions, especially when judgment calls need to be made by the user of the instructions. A flowchart typically cannot replace written instructions, especially if the steps are complex. But it can illustrate the steps in the process to help readers understand the written text.

A Pie Chart

Ten Leading Causes of Death Among Women

Figure 18.12: A pie chart is best for showing how a whole can be divided into parts.

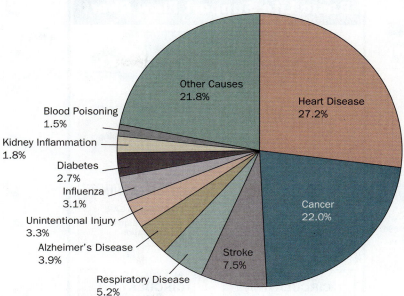

Source: U.S. Department of Health and Human Services, Women's Health 2007

Flowcharts can be found in a variety of other forms, such as organization charts or circuit diagrams. An organization chart illustrates the hierarchy of decision making in an organization. In a circuit diagram, a flowchart is used to chart the path of electricity.

Using Pictures and Drawings

Increasingly, computers give you the ability to include pictures, drawings, and video in documents. Even if you are not artistic, you can quickly use a digital camera or smartphone, a drawing program, a scanner, or a video camera to add life to your documents.

The purpose of a picture, drawing, or video is to show what something looks like. These kinds of visuals are especially helpful when your readers may not be familiar with something, like an animal or a piece of equipment. They are also helpful for showing the condition of something, like a building under construction or damage to a car.

A Flowchart

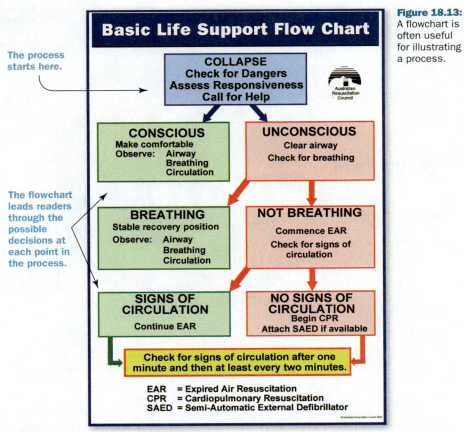

The process starts here.

The flowchart leads readers through the possible decisions at each point in the process.

Basic Life Support Flow Chart

COLLAPSE
Check for Dangers
Assess Responsiveness
Call for Help

Australian Resuscitation Council

CONSCIOUS
Make comfortable
Observe: Airway
Breathing
Circulation

UNCONSCIOUS
Clear airway
Check for breathing

BREATHING
Stable recovery position
Observe: Airway
Breathing
Circulation

NOT BREATHING
Commence EAR
Check for signs of circulation

SIGNS OF CIRCULATION
Continue EAR

NO SIGNS OF CIRCULATION
Begin CPR
Attach SAED if available

Check for signs of circulation after one minute and then at least every two minutes.

EAR = Expired Air Resuscitation
CPR = Cardiopulmonary Resuscitation
SAED = Semi-Automatic External Defibrillator

Figure 18.13: A flowchart is often useful for illustrating a process.

Source: Courtesy Australian Resuscitation Council, http://www.resus.org.au/public/bls_flow_chart.pdf

Photographs

Digital cameras and scanners are making the placement of photographs in technical documents easier than ever. A good first step is to ask what *story* you want the photograph to tell. Then, set up a shot that tells that story.

PHOTOGRAPHING PEOPLE   If you need to include a picture of a person or a group of people standing still, take them outside and photograph them against a simple but scenic background. Photographs taken in the office tend to look dark, depressing, and dreary. Photographs taken outdoors, on the other hand, imply a sense of openness and freethinking. When photographing people working, a good strategy is to show people doing what they *actually* do (Figure 18.14).

A Photograph of a Person in Action

Figure 18.14: Try to capture people in action, close up.

The focal points divide the photograph into thirds, following the "rule of thirds."

If you need to photograph people inside, put as much light as possible on the subjects. If your subjects will allow it, use facial powder to reduce the glare off their cheeks, noses, and foreheads. Then, take their picture against a simple backdrop to reduce background clutter.

If you are photographing an individual, take a picture of his or her head and shoulders. People tend to look uncomfortable in full-body pictures.

One general photography guideline that works well in most situations, especially when photographing people, is the "Rule of Thirds." The Rule of Thirds means the focal point of a picture (e.g., a subject's eyes, the key feature of an object) will appear where the top or bottom third of the picture begins. For example, in Figure 18.14, the welder's goggles and the sparks, which are the two focal points of this picture, appear where the top and bottom thirds of the picture meet the middle third. Similarly, in Figure 18.15, notice how the focal point of the pottery (the design and bulge) is where the top third of the picture starts.

PHOTOGRAPHING OBJECTS   When taking pictures of objects, try to capture a close-up shot while minimizing any clutter in the background (Figure 18.15). It is often a good idea to put a white drop cloth behind the object to block out the other items and people in the background. Make sure you put as much lighting as possible on the object so it will show up clearly in your document.

A Photograph of an Object

Note the plain background behind the subject of the photograph.

Figure 18.15: When photographing objects, try to reduce the amount of clutter around your subject.

Focal point

When photographing machines or equipment, try to capture them close up and in action. After all, a picture of equipment sitting idle on the factory floor is rather boring. But if you show the machine being used or focus on the moving parts, you will have a much more dynamic picture.

PHOTOGRAPHING PLACES   Places are especially difficult to photograph. When you are at the place itself, snapping a picture seems simple enough. But the pictures often come out flat and uninteresting. Moreover, unless people are in the picture, the scale of the place being photographed is difficult to determine.

When photographing places, focus on people doing something in that place. For example, if you need to photograph a factory floor, you should show people doing their jobs. If you are photographing an archaeological site, include someone working on the site. The addition of people will add a sense of action and scale to your photograph.

Inserting Photographs and Other Images

A digital camera will usually allow you to save your photographs in a variety of memory sizes. High-resolution photographs (lots of pixels) require a lot of memory in the camera and in your computer. They are usually saved in formats called .tiff or .png files. Lower-resolution photographs (fewer pixels) are saved as .gif or .jpg files. Usually, .gif and .jpg files are fine for print and online documents. However, if the photograph needs to be of high quality, a .tiff or .png file might be the best choice.

Once you have downloaded an image to your computer, you can work with it using software programs like Microsoft Paint or Adobe Photoshop. These programs will allow you to touch up the photographs or, if you want, completely alter them.

When you have finished touching up or altering the image, you can then insert it into your document or presentation. Most word-processing programs have an Insert Picture command. To insert the picture, put your cursor where you want the image to appear in the document. Then, select "Insert Picture." A box will open that allows you to locate the image on your computer's hard drive. Find and select the image you want to insert.

At this point, your computer will insert the image into your document. Usually, you can then do a few simple alterations to the file, like cropping, with the Picture toolbar in your word processor.

Illustrations

Illustrations are often better than photographs at depicting buildings, equipment, maps, and schematic designs. Whereas photographs usually include more detail than needed, a good illustration highlights only the most important features of the subject.

LINE DRAWINGS AND DIAGRAMS   A line drawing or diagram is a semirealistic illustration of the subject being described. You can create simple drawings and diagrams with the Draw function of most word-processing programs. As the drawings grow more complex, however, most writers will hire professional artists to transform rough sketches into finished artwork.

Line drawings offer several advantages. They can provide a close-up view of important features or parts. They can also be easily labeled, allowing you to point out important features to the readers.

In some ways, however, drawings and diagrams are less than realistic. For example, the diagram of the rabies virus in Figure 18.16 does not look exactly like the actual virus. Instead, it shows only how the larger parts of the virus are interconnected and work together.

A Diagram

Labels are added to identify features.

Explanatory text can be added to clarify the meaning of the diagram.

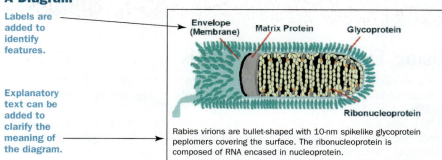

Envelope (Membrane)   Matrix Protein   Glycoprotein

Ribonucleoprotein

Rabies virions are bullet-shaped with 10-nm spikelike glycoprotein peplomers covering the surface. The ribonucleoprotein is composed of RNA encased in nucleoprotein.

Figure 18.16: A drawing is only partially realistic. It concentrates on relationships instead of showing exactly what the subject looks like.

Source: Centers for Disease Control and Prevention, http://www.cdc.gov/rabies/transmission/virus.html

Common Icons

Sources: *Centers for Disease Control and Prevention, http://www.cdc.gov/diabetes/pubs/images /balance.gif, and International Association for Food Protection, http://www.foodprotection.org, and Centers for Disease Control and Prevention, http://www.cdc.gov/diabetes/pubs /images/suneagle.gif*

Figure 18.17:
Icons are widely available on the Internet. The person in the middle is supposed to be sneezing, but, as with many icons, it could convey an unintentional meaning.

Link

For more information on copyright law, go to Chapter 4, page 76.

ICONS AND CLIP ART   Icons play an important role in technical documentation. In some documents, they are used as warning symbols. They can also serve as sign-posts in a text to help readers quickly locate important information (Figure 18.17). If you need to use an icon, standard sets of symbols are available on the Internet for purchase or for free.

Clip art drawings are commercially produced illustrations that can be purchased or used for free. Usually, when you purchase a collection of clip art, you are also purchasing the rights to use that clip art in your own documents.

It is tempting to advise you not to use clip art at all. When desktop publishing first came into the workplace, clip art was an original way to enhance the message and tone of a document. But now, most readers are tired of those little pictures of people shaking hands, pointing at whiteboards, and climbing ladders. In some cases, clip art becomes decorative fluff that takes readers' attention away from the document's message. Use it sparingly and only when it *truly* contributes to your message.

Using Transcultural Symbols

Symbols often translate among cultures better than words. They can also be more memorable and enhance understanding for second-language readers (Horton, 1993).

Symbols, however, don't always translate exactly across cultures, so you need to check your use of symbols in documents and websites with readers from other cultures. Otherwise, your symbols might lead to unintended consequences. For example, international dockworkers have been known to roughly toss boxes labeled with the broken wine glass symbol (meaning "fragile"), because they assumed the boxes contained broken glass.

The Old Versus the New Skull-and-Crossbones Symbols

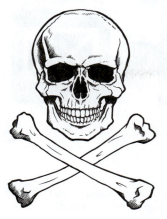

Figure 18.18: The old skull-and-cross-bones poison symbol shown on the left was problematic because children associated it with sports teams and fictional pirates. The newer poison symbol shown on the right is interpreted as negative across cultures.

In another case, the green and black "Mr. Yuk" poison symbol has had mixed results in its bid to replace the traditional skull-and-crossbones symbol shown on the left in Figure 18.18. One problem is that "Yuk" is a common name in Asia, especially Korea. Meanwhile, the use of "Mr." suggests elder status to many Asian children, implying the face deserves added respect. In a research study, a majority of international children did not understand the Mr. Yuk image or see it as negative, and a few thought the symbol meant the product was good to eat (Smith-Jackson & Essuman-Johnson, 2002).

Recently, poisonous products have begun using the European Union's skull-and-crossbones symbol shown on the right in Figure 18.18. This new symbol for poison is viewed as negative by children of almost all cultures.

To avoid misunderstandings, designers have developed collections of symbols that are intended to cross cultures. The American Institute of Graphic Arts (AIGA) created the symbol system that is familiar to North Americans and is used globally (Figure 18.19). The European Union and International Standards Organization (ISO) have also created sets of international symbols that are widely used.

Here are a few helpful guidelines for using symbols transculturally:

Keep human icons simple—Icons of humans should be simple pictographs. Distinctive clothing or facial features might lead to unintended interpretations or confusion. Smiles, frowns, winks, or smirks can have very different meanings across cultures, so symbols that use faces are particularly problematic.

International Symbols

Figure 18.19: The AIGA, European Union, and International Standards Organization (ISO) have created a set of symbols that work internationally.

Use hand signals carefully—Just about any hand signal is considered offensive in some cultures, including the thumbs-up signal, "OK" sign, V-symbol, a pointing finger, and even the palm out "halt" signal. If you can imagine an entire user's manual that uses an extended middle finger to point to things, you will get the idea about why hand signals can be problematic.

Avoid culture-specific icons—Mailboxes, phone booths, and eating utensils, among other items, can look very different in other cultures, so symbols representing them might not translate. The typical North American mailbox on a street corner, for example, looks nothing like the canister mailboxes in England, while some cultures don't have public mailboxes at all. In another case, much of the world uses chopsticks for eating, so a fork would not properly symbolize "eat" or "food" to many readers.

Avoid religious symbols—Using crosses, crescents, stars, wings, candles, yin and yang, and other religious symbols can be interpreted very differently in other cultures. The symbol for the Red Cross, for example, is the Red Crescent in Islamic cultures, and the Red Crystal is used in Israel.

Avoid animal symbols and mascots—Animals can mean very different things in other cultures. In Western societies, the owl symbolizes wisdom, but in Southeast Asia, owls are considered unintelligent and vicious. Rats are considered clever and intelligent in many Asian countries, while in Western countries they are thought to be diseased and threatening. In some Islamic cultures, dogs are considered "unclean," making them particularly bad cartoon mascots for products. Meanwhile, the word *mouse* is not associated with computers in some cultures, so using a mouse symbol to represent a computer's pointing device would be confusing.

Link

For more information on cross-cultural readers, go to Chapter 2, page 24.

Symbols can be very helpful in technical documents because they enhance translation and comprehension. Your best approach is to use internationally accepted symbols whenever they are available and to always check your use of symbols with likely transcultural readers.

- Computers have made including graphics in technical documents easier, so readers have come to expect them.

- Graphics should: (1) tell a simple story; (2) reinforce the text, not replace it; (3) be ethical; and (4) be properly labeled and placed on the page.

- Various kinds of graphs, tables, and charts allow you to tell different stories with data or facts.

- Digital cameras and scanners are making the placement of photographs in documents easier than ever.

- Use icons and clip art only when they enhance the readability and comprehension of the document. Clip art, especially, can simply clutter a document.

- Graphics need to be carefully considered when documents need to work transculturally. Images and symbols can have very different meanings in other cultures.

EXERCISES AND PROJECTS

Individual or Team Projects

1. On the Internet, find a chart or graph that you can analyze. Using the four guidelines for graphics discussed in this chapter, critique the chart or graph by discussing its strengths and places where it might be improved. Present your findings to your class.

2. Find a set of data. Then, use different kinds of charts and graphs to illustrate trends in the data. For example, you might use a bar chart, line graph, and pie chart to illustrate the same data set. How does each type of graphic allow you to tell a different "story" with the data? What are the strengths and limitations of each kind of graphic? Which kind of chart or graph would probably be most effective for illustrating your data set?

3. Using a digital camera or the camera on your phone, practice taking pictures and inserting those pictures into documents. Take pictures of people, objects, and places. When taking pictures of people, compare pictures taken inside and outside. Take full-body pictures and head shots. When taking pictures of objects, first leave the background behind the object cluttered. Then, use a backdrop to unclutter the picture. When photographing places, try to make images that tell a story about the place.

    When you are finished, compare and contrast your photographs. Which types of photographs seem to work best in a document? What kinds of photographs tend not to work?

Collaborative Project

With a group of classmates, locate a large document that has few or no visuals. Then, do a "design makeover" in which you find ways to use visuals to support and clarify the written text. Try to include at least one visual for every two pages in the document. Use graphs, photographs, and drawings to illustrate important points in the document. Then, add icons and clip art to reinforce important points or themes in the document.

When you are finished, write a brief report to your instructor about how you made over the document. Critique the original draft of the document, showing how the lack of adequate visuals made the information in the document hard to access. Then, discuss the ways in which your revised version improves on the original. Finally, discuss some of the following issues about the amount and types of visuals used in this kind of document:

- At what point are there too many graphics?
- Do some graphics work better than others?
- How can you balance the written text with visuals to avoid making the document too text heavy or visual heavy?
- How do the needs and characteristics of the expected readers of the document shape the kinds of visuals that are used?

Your report might offer some additional guidelines, beyond the ones discussed in this chapter, for using visuals more effectively.

Visit MyWritingLab for a Post-test and more technical writing resources.

Looking Guilty

Thomas Helmann was recently promoted to sergeant with the campus police at Southwest Vermont University. One of his added responsibilities was mentoring Officer Sharon Brand, who had been hired a couple of weeks ago. Newly hired officers were usually given the "paperwork jobs" that the other officers didn't want to do.

One of those jobs was putting together the "Campus Crime Statistics Report" for the Executive Committee.

So, it wasn't a surprise when the captain of the campus police gave Sharon the job of collecting all the statistics and writing the report. At their weekly mentoring session, Thomas advised Sharon, "Just look at last year's report and include the same kinds of facts and figures. The secretary can give you statistics from this year."

A couple of weeks later, Sharon submitted the report to Thomas. He didn't have time to read the report closely, but the figures all looked accurate, and it covered the same issues as last year.

Sharon also inserted several photographs to add some life and color to the report. Most of the photos showed places where petty crimes had happened, including dorms, bike racks, and parking lots. A couple of pictures showed students drinking beer at a football tailgate party.

There were also pictures of students, whom Sharon recruited, pretending to steal bikes, deal drugs, tag walls, and take computers out of dorm rooms. Thomas thought the photos were silly, but he didn't think they were a problem.

He sent a dozen copies to the Executive Committee.

A few days later, Thomas was called into the captain's office. She was really angry. "Sergeant, we have a big problem with the Crime Statistics Report."

A bit surprised, Thomas asked her what the problem was.

"Well, a member of the University's Executive Committee pointed out that all the staged pictures of criminal activities used African Americans and Hispanics as models."

She handed the report to Thomas. Sure enough, all the people pretending to wheel off bicycles, deal drugs, steal computers, and spray paint walls were minorities. Meanwhile, the students drinking at the football tailgater were white. He was shocked he hadn't noticed the racist tone of the photographs, but now the problem was glaringly obvious.

Stunned, he tried to offer an apology. The captain snapped back, "I'm not the person you should be apologizing to, though my butt is in the fire, too. This report makes the campus police look like a bunch of racists."

How do you think Thomas should respond to this issue? What should he tell Sharon? Whom should he and/or Sharon apologize to? What else do you think should happen at this point?

CHAPTER

19

Revising and Editing for Usability

Levels of Edit *499*

Level 1 Editing: Revising *499*

Level 2 Editing: Substantive Editing *501*

Level 3 Editing: Copyediting *503*

Level 4 Editing: Proofreading *505*

Using Copyediting Symbols *509*

Lost In Translation: Transcultural Editing *509*

Document Cycling and Usability Testing *512*

What You Need to Know *516*

Exercises and Projects *516*

Case Study: A Machine by Any Other Name *518*

In this chapter, you will learn:

- How to use revising and editing as a form of quality control.
- How to apply the four levels of editing to your text.
- How to use copyediting symbols.
- Strategies for revising your draft by reviewing its rhetorical situation (subject, purpose, readers, and context of use).
- Strategies for reviewing the content, organization, and design of your document.
- How to revise your sentences, paragraphs, headings, and graphics.
- How to proofread for grammar, punctuation, and word usage.
- Strategies for making your documents appropriate for transcultural readers.
- Strategies for document cycling and usability testing.

Link

For more information on quality control, turn to Chapter 3, page 54.

Revising and editing are forms of *quality control* in a document. Of course, you want to get things right, but your documents should also reflect the quality standards that are held by your company (or they should reflect an even higher quality standard). The revising and editing phase is where your documents will go from "adequate" to "excellent."

Levels of Edit

Professional editors use a tool called the "levels of edit," which is illustrated in Figure 19.1, to assess how much editing a document needs before the deadline:

> *Level 1: Revising*—revises the document as a whole, which is why this level of edit is often called "global editing." Revision pays attention to the document's subject, purpose, readers, and context of use.

> *Level 2: Substantive editing*—pays special attention to the content, organization, and design of the document.

> *Level 3: Copyediting*—concentrates on revising the style for clarity, persuasion, and consistency, especially at the sentence and paragraph levels.

> *Level 4: Proofreading*—catches only the grammar mistakes, misspellings, and usage problems.

Which level of edit is appropriate for your document? The answer to this question depends on two factors: (a) how much time you have and (b) the quality needed in the document. Given enough time, you should ideally go through all four levels, beginning with revising (Level 1) and ending with proofreading (Level 4). In reality, though, the time devoted to revising and editing often depends on how much time is left before the deadline.

So, as you begin the revising and editing phase, start out by determining what level of editing is possible and/or needed to produce the desired quality of document (Figure 19.1). Then, begin reworking the document at that level.

Level 1 Editing: Revising

While you were drafting the document, you revised as you wrote. You paused to sharpen your ideas, reconsider your purpose, and adjust the design. Now that the document is drafted, you can start revising it as a whole.

Revision is a process of "re-visioning" the document. In other words, you are trying to see your document from a variety of perspectives, looking for ways to improve it.

To revise (re-vision) your document, look back at your initial decisions about the rhetorical situation at the beginning of your writing process.

The Levels of Editing

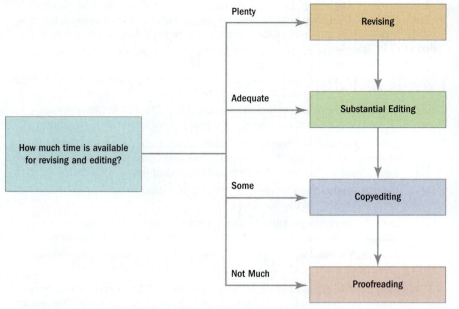

Figure 19.1: Ideally, writers would always go through all four levels of edit, from revision to proofreading. Sometimes, though, limited time determines what level is appropriate to finish a document.

SUBJECT   Determine whether your subject needs to be narrowed or broadened.

- How has your subject changed or evolved?
- In what ways did you limit or expand the scope of your subject while drafting?
- Where has your document strayed from the subject? If it has, should the additional content be removed, or do other parts of the document need to be adjusted to fit the new aspects of the subject?

PURPOSE   Make sure the document is achieving its purpose.

- Where exactly does the document actually achieve your original purpose?
- Has your purpose become more specific or has it broadened?
- If the purpose has shifted, what kinds of adjustments to the document are needed?

READERS   Looking back at your original profile of your readers, think about the characteristics of the primary readers and other possible readers.

- What additional need-to-know information should be added to help the primary readers make a decision?
- Where have you not fully anticipated your readers' values and attitudes?
- How can you better address the needs of the secondary, tertiary, and gatekeeper readers?

Link

For more information on defining the rhetorical situation, go to Chapter 1, page 4.

CONTEXT OF USE   Consider the contexts in which your document might be read or used.

- Where can you make changes that anticipate the physical places in which your readers will use the document?
- How does your better understanding of the readers' economic, political, and ethical issues change the document?
- How can you better respond to the personal, corporate, and industry-related issues that will shape your readers' understanding of your argument?

AT A GLANCE

Guidelines for Revising (Level 1)

- Subject—Is the subject too narrow or too broad?
- Purpose—Does the document achieve its stated purpose?
- Readers—Is the document appropriate for the readers?
- Context of use—Is the document appropriate for its context of use?

Once you have reconsidered the document's rhetorical situation, you can read through the text to see if it stays focused on the subject and achieves its purpose (Figure 19.2).

Revision at this global level requires some courage. You may discover that parts of your document need to be completely rewritten. In some cases, the whole document may need to be reconceived. But it is better to be honest with yourself at this point and make those changes. After all, a document that fails to achieve its purpose is a waste of your and your team's time.

Level 2 Editing: Substantive Editing

While doing substantive editing, you should concentrate on the content, organization, and design of the document (Figure 19.3). A good approach to substantive editing is to review the document from three different perspectives.

CONTENT   Look for any gaps or digressions in the content.

- What kinds of facts, data, examples, proofs, or graphics would help you fill in gaps in your argument?
- Where should you do more research to support your points?
- Where have you included information that the readers do not need to know to make a decision or take action?

ORGANIZATION   A document should conform to a recognizable genre, and it should have an identifiable introduction, body, and conclusion.

- Where have you deviated from the organizational pattern of the genre you are following? Are these deviations helpful toward achieving your purpose? Or, should you reorganize the document to suit the genre?
- Does the introduction clearly identify the subject, while stating your purpose and your main point? Should the introduction include more background information or stress the importance of the subject?
- Does the conclusion restate your main point, re-emphasize the importance of the subject, and look to the future?

Revising the Document

When revising, look back at your original notes about the rhetorical situation.

Do you need to sharpen your purpose statement?

Do you have a better understanding of the readers?

Has the context of use changed?

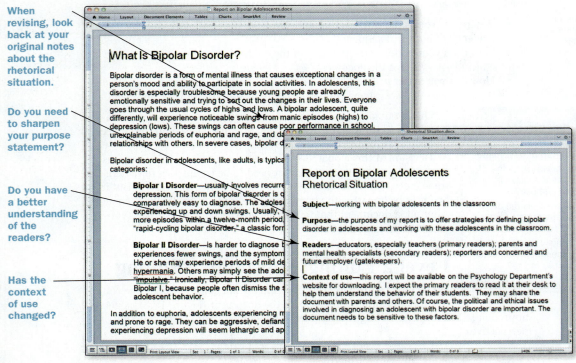

Figure 19.2:
Look back at your original notes about the rhetorical situation. Have any of these elements changed or evolved? Does your document reflect these original decisions? If not, does the document need to change or does your understanding of the rhetorical situation need to change?

Link

For more information about organization, see Chapter 15, page 399.

DESIGN The document should be designed for its readers and the contexts in which it will be used.

- How can the text be made more readable for the situations and places where people will use it?
- In what ways could the design better reflect your readers' values and attitudes?
- In what ways does the design properly use principles of balance, alignment, grouping, consistency, and contrast? Where does it stray from those principles?
- How can the titles and subheads better signal the purpose and structure of the document?
- Do the graphics support the text, and do they clarify difficult points?

AT A GLANCE

Guidelines for Substantive Editing (Level 2)

- Content—Are there any digressions or gaps in content?
- Organization—Does the document conform to a recognizable genre or pattern?
- Design—Do the page layout and graphics enhance the readability of the document?

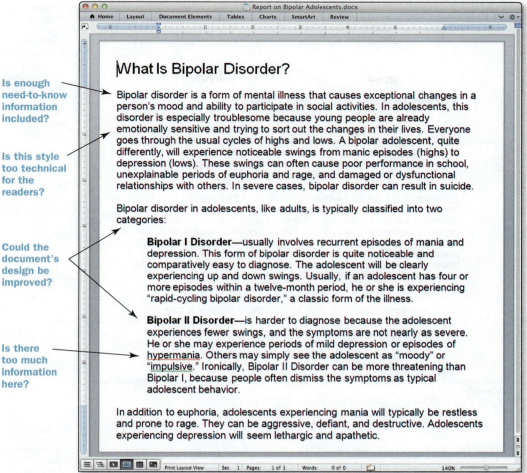

Is enough need-to-know information included?

Is this style too technical for the readers?

Could the document's design be improved?

Is there too much information here?

Figure 19.3: Substantive editing urges you to ask questions about the appropriateness of the content, style, and design of your document. When answering these questions, think about the needs of your readers.

Link

For more document design strategies, see Chapter 17, page 447.

Level 3 Editing: Copyediting

When you are copyediting, you should concentrate on improving style and consistency, especially at the sentence and paragraph levels. You should also look over the headings and graphics to make sure they are appropriate and accurate.

While copyediting, you might find the Track Changes feature of your word processor especially helpful (Figure 19.4). It will show places where changes were made to the text. Later, you can decide whether you want to keep those changes. This feature is especially helpful if you are working with a team on a document. That way, any changes are recorded for the others in the group to approve.

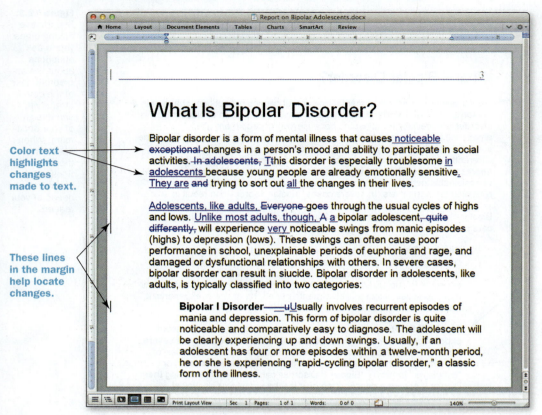

Figure 19.4: With the Track Changes function, your word processor can keep track of the changes you (or others) make to the document.

Color text highlights changes made to text.

These lines in the margin help locate changes.

SENTENCES   Look over the sentences to make sure they are clear and concise.

- Are the subjects of the sentences easy to locate?
- Do the verbs express the actions of the sentences?
- Can you eliminate any unnecessary prepositional phrases?
- Which sentences go beyond breathing length? Should they be trimmed down or divided?

Link

For help on improving style at the sentence level, go to Chapter 16, page 422.

PARAGRAPHS   Make sure the paragraphs support specific claims. Rework the sentences in the paragraphs to improve the flow of the text.

- Does each paragraph have a clear topic sentence (a claim) and enough support to back it up?
- Would any paragraphs be stronger if you included a transition sentence at the beginning or a point sentence at the end?

Link

For more information on using headings, see Chapter 17, page 457.

Link

For more help using graphics, turn to Chapter 18, page 477.

AT A GLANCE

Guidelines for Copyediting (Level 3)

- Sentences—Are the sentences clear and concise?
- Paragraphs—Do the paragraphs have a clear topic sentence and support?
- Headings—Do the headings help the readers scan for important information?
- Graphics—Do the graphics support the written text?

- Are the subjects in the paragraph aligned, or could you use given/new strategies to smooth out the text?
- Would transitions or transitional phrases help bridge any gaps between sentences?

HEADINGS   The headings should be easy to understand and consistently used.

- Do the headings in the document properly reflect the information that follows them?
- Do the headings make the document scannable, highlighting places where important information can be found?
- Are there clear levels of headings that help readers identify the structure of the document and the importance of each part of the document?

GRAPHICS   Look over the graphics in the document to make sure they support the written text. Check the graphics for accuracy.

- Does each graphic tell a simple story?
- Does each graphic support the written text without replacing it?
- Are the graphics clearly titled and referred to by number in the written text?

Level 4 Editing: Proofreading

Proofreading begins when the document is complete in almost every way. While proofreading, you need to focus only on the mechanical details of the document, like the grammar, spelling, punctuation, and word usage. While proofreading, you should focus on marking "errors" and making only minor stylistic changes to the text.

Grammar

In technical documents, grammar errors are a sign of low quality. Most readers can figure out the meaning of a document even when it contains some grammar errors. The real problem with grammar errors is that they will cause your readers to doubt the quality or soundness of the document and the information it contains.

Most word-processing programs have a grammar checker, but these checkers are notoriously unreliable. So you should be cautious when following any advice from the grammar checker. Your computer will often miss obvious errors, while flagging grammatically correct sentences.

There is no substitute for mastering grammar rules yourself. Figure 19.5 describes some of the more common grammatical errors. In the Grammar and Punctuation Guide (Appendix A), you will find examples of and remedies for these common errors.

Punctuation

Punctuation reflects the way we speak. For example, a *period* is supposed to reflect the amount of time (a period) that it takes to say one sentence. If you were to read a

Common Grammatical Errors

Error	Explanation
comma splice	Two or more distinct sentences are joined only by a comma.
run-on sentence	The sentence is composed of two or more distinct sentences.
fragment	The sentence is incomplete, usually missing a subject or verb.
dangling modifier	A modifier (usually an introductory phrase) implies a different subject than the one in the sentence's subject slot.
subject-verb disagreement	A singular or plural subject does not agree with the verb form.
misused apostrophe	An apostrophe is used where it doesn't belong (usually confusing *it's* and *its*).
misused comma	A comma signals an unnecessary pause in a sentence.
pronoun-antecedent disagreement	A pronoun does not agree with a noun used earlier in the sentence.
faulty parallelism	A list of items in a sentence is not parallel in structure.
pronoun case error	The case of a pronoun is incorrect (usually due to confusion about when to use *I* or *me*).
shifted tense	Sentences inconsistently use past, present, and future tenses.
vague pronoun	It is unclear what the pronoun refers to.

Figure 19.5: Here are the usual grammatical error culprits. If you avoid these simple errors, your document will have almost no grammatical problems.

document out loud, the periods would signal places to breathe. Similarly, commas are used to signal pauses. When you come across a comma in a sentence, you pause slightly.

By understanding the physical characteristics of punctuation, you can learn how to use the marks properly (Figure 19.6). The Grammar and Punctuation Guide (Appendix A) includes a more detailed explanation of punctuation usage.

Link

For more on grammar rules, go to Appendix A, page A-1.

Spelling and Typos

Spelling errors and typos can be jarring for readers. One or two in a document may be forgivable, but several errors will cause your readers to seriously question your commitment to quality. Here are some ways to avoid those errors.

Use the spell check feature on your computer—Most word-processing programs come with a spelling checker that is rather reliable. Even if you are a good speller, the spelling checker will often catch those annoying typos that inevitably find their way into texts (Figure 19.7).

However, a spelling checker is not perfect, so you will still need to pay careful attention to spelling in your documents. Here is a sentence, for example, that has no errors according to a spelling checker:

> Eye sad, they're our many places four us to sea friends and by good she's stakes in Philadelphia.

Link

For a more detailed discussion of punctuation, go to Appendix A, page A-8.

Physical Characteristics of Punctuation

Punctuation Mark	Physical Characteristic
capitalization	signals a raised voice to indicate the beginning of a sentence or a proper name
period [.]	signals a complete stop after a statement
question mark [?]	signals a complete stop after a question
exclamation mark [!]	signals a complete stop after an outcry or objection
comma [,]	signals a pause in a sentence
semicolon [;]	signals a longer pause in a sentence and connects two related, complete statements
colon [:]	signals a complete stop but joins two equal statements; or, it indicates the beginning of a list
hyphen [-]	connects two or more words into a compound word
dash [—]	sets off a comment by the author that is an aside or interjection
apostrophe [']	signals possession, or the contraction of two words
quotation marks [" "]	signal a quotation, or when a word or phrase is being used in a "unique way"
parentheses [( )]	enclose supplemental information like an example or definition

Figure 19.6: Punctuation mirrors the physical characteristics of speech.

Running the Spelling Checker

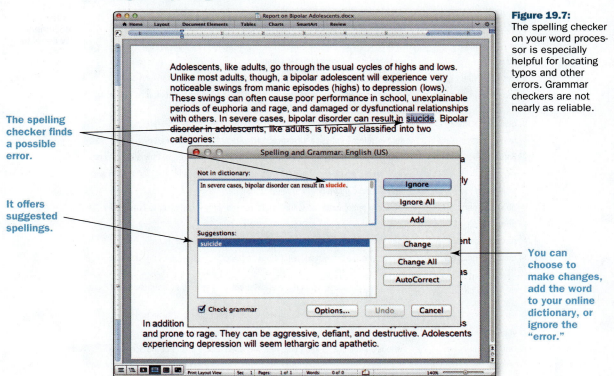

The spelling checker finds a possible error.

It offers suggested spellings.

You can choose to make changes, add the word to your online dictionary, or ignore the "error."

Figure 19.7: The spelling checker on your word processor is especially helpful for locating typos and other errors. Grammar checkers are not nearly as reliable.

AT A GLANCE

**Guidelines for Proof-
reading (Level 4)**

- Grammar—Are all the
  sentences grammati-
  cally correct?
- Punctuation—Are the
  sentences properly
  punctuated?
- Spelling and typos—
  Are there any spelling
  errors or typos?
- Word usage—Are all
  the words used
  properly?

To avoid these embarrassing errors, don't rely exclusively on the spelling checker.

Check the dictionary—You should regularly consult online or print dictionaries for spellings of words. Keep in mind that technical documents often use terms and jargon that are not in your computer's spelling checker. On the Internet, you may be able to find dictionaries that define specialized words in your field.

Word Usage

In English, many words seem the same, but they have subtle differences in usage that you should know (Figure 19.8). To help you sort out these subtle differences, you should check online or print usage guides.

Common Usage Problems in Technical Documents

Figure 19.8:
You can avoid some of the most common usage problems in technical documents by consulting this list.

Confused Words	Explanation of Usage
accept, except	*accept* means to receive or agree to; *except* means to leave out
affect, effect	*affect* is usually used as a verb; *effect* is usually used as a noun
anyone, any one	*anyone* is a pronoun that refers to a person; *any one* means any one of a set
between, among	*between* is used for two entities; *among* is used for more than two entities
capitol, capital	*capitol* is the seat of a government; *capital* is money or goods
criterion, criteria	*criterion* is singular; *criteria* is plural
ensure, insure	*ensure* means to make certain; *insure* means to protect with insurance
complement, compliment	to *complement* is to complete something else or make it whole; a *compliment* is a kind word or encouragement
discreet, discrete	*discreet* means showing good judgment; *discrete* means separate
farther, further	*farther* refers to physical distance; *further* refers to time or degree
imply, infer	*imply* means to suggest indirectly; *infer* means to interpret or draw a conclusion
its, it's	*its* is always possessive; *it's* is always a contraction that means "it is"; *its'* is not a word
less, fewer	*less* refers to quantity; *fewer* refers to number
personal, personnel	*personal* refers to an individual characteristic; *personnel* refers to employees
phenomenon, phenomena	*phenomenon* is singular; *phenomena* is plural
precede, proceed	*precede* means to come before; *proceed* means to move forward
principle, principal	a *principle* is a firmly held belief or law; a *principal* is someone who runs a school or it's the something that is "first in order of importance"
their, there, they're	*their* is a possessive pronoun; *there* is a place; *they're* is a contraction that means "they are"
whose, who's	*whose* is a possessive pronoun; *who's* is the contraction of "who is"
your, you're	*your* is a possessive pronoun; *you're* is a contraction that means "you are"
who, whom	*who* is a subject of a sentence; *whom* is used as the object of the sentence

Using Copyediting Symbols

While editing, you might find it helpful to use the same editing symbols that professional editors use. To mark any stylistic changes and inconsistencies, editors have developed a somewhat universal set of copyediting marks (Figure 19.9). They are easy to use and widely understood. See Figure 19.10 for examples of how they are used.

Editing Symbols and Their Uses

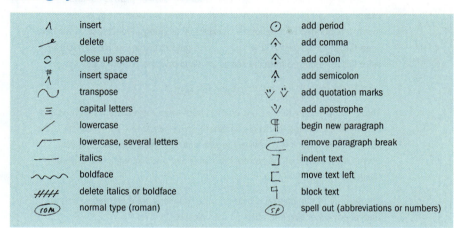

Lost In Translation: Transcultural Editing

Today, translation software programs like Babylon, Power Translator, and Promt are about 90 percent accurate. Free online translators like Google Translate and Bing Translator, among others, are about 80 percent accurate. That's good, but it also means 10 to 20 percent of any "machine-translated" document might be flawed or confusing.

When working with transcultural documents, you need to put extra effort into the revising and editing process. Several companies have experienced some classic gaffes when they have not taken the extra time to edit their texts from their readers' cultural point of view. For example, the baby food brand name Gerber means "vomit" in French. Also, when Gerber began introducing their jars of baby food in Africa, they kept its familiar design with a plump, happy baby on the front of the jar. In parts of Africa, though, where many are illiterate, customers assume that the label shows what kind of food is inside.

Meanwhile, the Germanic word for travel is "Fahrt," which causes some classic problems with travel-related products that are sold in both Central Europe and English-speaking countries. For example, the Swedish furniture maker IKEA once sold a mobile workbench called the "Fartfull" in the United States and Europe.

Figure 19.10: Copyediting marks can be used to identify changes in the text.

Eruption History of Kilauea

Can you be more specific here? Are more accurate estimates available?

When Kilauea began to form is not known, but various estimates are 300,000–600,000 years ago. The volcano had been active ever since, with no prolonged periods of quiescence known. geologic studies of surface exposures and examination of drillhole samples show that Kilauea is made mostly of lava flows locally interbedded with deposites of explosive eruptions. Probably what we have seen hapen in the past 200 years is a good guide to what has happened ever since Kilauea emerged from the sea as an island perhaps 50,000–100,000 years ago.

Lava Erupts from Kilauea's Summit and Rift Zones

Define the jargon in this paragraph.

Throughout its history Kilauea has erupted from three main areas: its summit and two rift zones. Geologists debate whether Kilauea has Always had a caldera at the summit or whether it is a relatively recent feature of the past few thousand years. It seems most likely that the caldera has come and gnoe throughout the life of Kilauea.

The summit of the volcano is high because eruptions are more frequent there than at any other single location on the volcano.

It's hard to figure out what you're describing here. A diagram would help.

However, more eruptions actually occur on the long rift zones than in the summit area, but they are not localized instead eruptions construct ridges of lower elevation than the summit. Eruptions along the east and southwest rift zones have build ridges reaching outward from the summit some 125 KM and 35 KM, respectively.

Most eruption are relatively gentle, sending lava flows downslope from fountains a few meters to a few hundred meters high. OVER and over again these eruptions occur, gradually building up the volcano and giving it a gentle, shield-like form. Every few decades to centuries, however powerful explosions spread ejecta across the landscape. Such explosions can be lethal, as the one in 1790 that killed scores of people in a war party near the summitting of Kilauea. Such explosions can take place from either the bridging summit or the upper rift zones.

Source: U.S. Geological Survey, http://hvo.wr.usgs.gov/kilauea/history/main.html. Errors in the text were added and did not appear in the original.

Moreover, slogans often don't translate well. In 1996, Japanese designers at Panasonic created a web browser that used Woody Woodpecker as a mascot. Japanese executives were horrified to learn that the English meaning of their slogan "Touch Woody—The Internet Pecker" was not exactly what they had intended (Yoshida, 1996).

International business specialists Carol Leininger and Rue Yuan (1998) offer the following advice for creating and editing transcultural documents:

Use short, direct sentences that follow subject, verb, object order—Second-language readers and translation software will be more successful if they can easily locate the subjects and verbs of sentences. Longer sentences should be cut into shorter sentences.

Use positive sentences and minimize negative sentences—Negative sentences sometimes translate more harshly than originally intended. A negative sentence that offers a simple caution to the reader can translate into one that makes dire predictions of harm or death.

Use a limited set of words—Most international companies, such as Caterpillar and IBM, have developed standard language guides of English words to be used in international documents. Documents that use these words are easier for people and translation software to translate.

Avoid humor or jokes—Jokes are highly culture-specific and situational, so they rarely translate well into other cultures and languages. Usually, they are just confusing, but sometimes they are insulting to the reader.

Minimize jargon and slang—Jargon words and slang phrases are also culturally dependent and difficult to translate. These terms should be translated into their common meanings even though they might lose some of their original flair.

Check any sayings, clichés, or idioms—These turns of phrase often do not translate well. For example, in North America people "cross their fingers" for luck, but in Germany, people "hold their thumbs."

Avoid obvious metaphors—Metaphors cannot be completely avoided, but obvious ones should be removed. For example, sports metaphors like, "She hit a home run" or "He just punted" will be confusing to most transcultural readers. Metaphors that use body parts (e.g., "I'll keep an eye on the project") or animals (e.g., "He's a workhorse") can have very different and disturbing meanings when translated.

Check slogans—Slogans usually rely on a cultural twist of words, so they are particularly risky when translated. In Taiwan, Pepsi's slogan "Come alive with the Pepsi Generation" translated into, "Pepsi will bring your ancestors back from the dead" (Pendergrast, 1994).

Check product names—Names of products can also translate in embarrassing ways. Products like the Pinto, Puffs, Waterpik, and latte, among others, have sexually suggestive meanings in other languages. The Chevy Nova didn't sell well in Mexico and Latin America because "no va" means "It doesn't go" in Spanish.

To ensure that your documents will work across cultures, your best strategy is to user-test your documents with readers from likely target cultures. Translation software will rarely catch the subtleties of language. Also keep in mind that your translation software or online translator probably won't include insulting phrases or sexually suggestive slang. A test reader from the target culture can help you identify those embarrassing places in your document.

Document Cycling and Usability Testing

When you are completing your document, it is important that you gain an outside perspective. Often, while drafting, we become too close to our documents. Consequently, we can no longer edit or assess our own work objectively. Two ways to gain that outside perspective are *document cycling* and *usability testing*.

Document Cycling

Document cycling is a method for letting others at your company look over your draft. When you *cycle* a document, you pass it among your co-workers and supervisors to obtain feedback (Figure 19.11).

Computers give you the ability to quickly send your document around to others for suggestions for improvement. You can send it as an e-mail attachment or share it through file-sharing services like Google Drive or Dropbox. Then, your supervisors, colleagues, and even your primary readers can look it over and offer suggestions for improvement.

When revising and editing your documents, it is important to let others look over your work. Document cycling is an important part of a *quality feedback loop,* a central principle of quality management. If you rely on yourself alone to edit your work, the quality of your document might suffer.

Usability Testing

Usability testing means trying out your document on real readers. This kind of authentic testing can be informal or formal, depending on the importance of your document and the time you have to test it (Figure 19.12).

Document Cycling in the Workplace

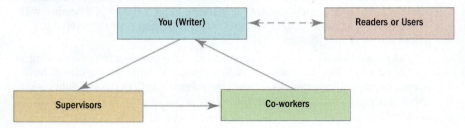

Figure 19.11: Document cycling gathers feedback by letting others look over the document.

Types of Usability Testing

	Usability Test	How It Is Conducted
informal testing	document markup	Readers are asked to read through a document, marking places where they stumble or fail to understand.
	read and locate test	Readers are asked to locate specific kinds of information in a document. They are timed and videotaped.
	summary test	Readers are asked to summarize the important information in a document.
	protocols	Readers are asked to talk out loud as they are using the text. Their comments are taped and transcribed.
	journal or tape recording	Readers are asked to keep a written or taped journal at their workplace to record their experiences with the document.
	surveying	Readers are given a questionnaire after they use the document, asking them about their experience.
	interviewing	Readers are interviewed about their experiences using a document.
	focus groups	Groups of readers look over a document and discuss their reactions to the work.
formal testing	laboratory testing	Through cameras and a one-way mirror, readers are carefully observed using a text.

Figure 19.12:
A variety of methods are available to user-test a document.

Most usability testing is designed to answer four questions:

Can they find it? — *Read-and-locate tests* are used to determine whether users can locate important parts of the document and how quickly they can do so. Often, the users are videotaped and timed while using the document.

Can they understand it? — *Understandability tests* are used to determine if the users retain important concepts and remember key terms. Users are often asked to summarize parts of the document or define concepts.

Can they do it? — *Performance tests* are used to determine whether users can perform the actions the document describes. These tests are often used with instructions and procedures.

Is it safe? — *Safety tests* are used to study whether the activities described in the document, especially in instructions or user's manuals, are safe. These tests carefully watch for possible safety problems by having sample readers use the product documentation.

As you devise a usability test or series of usability tests, you should set quantifiable objectives that will allow you to measure *normal* and *minimal* user performance with the document.

READ-AND-LOCATE TESTS: CAN THEY FIND IT?   To run a read-and-locate test, list five to seven important pieces of information that you want readers to locate in the document. Then, while timing and/or videotaping them, see how long it takes them to find that information.

Videotaping your subjects is especially helpful, because you can observe how readers go about accessing the information in your document. Do they go right to the beginning or the middle? Do they flip through the text looking at the headings or graphics? Do they look at the table of contents or index (if these features exist)?

After your subjects locate the major pieces of information you asked them to look for, have them tell you about these major points orally or in writing. Then, check their answers against your original list. If they successfully found four or five items from your list of most important pieces of information, your document is likely well written and well designed. If, however, they struggled to find even a few of your major points, you probably need to revise your document to ensure that the important information is easy to locate.

UNDERSTANDABILITY TESTS: CAN THEY UNDERSTAND IT? When running an understandability test, you want to determine how well the users of your document grasped its meaning. Before running the test, write down your document's purpose and main point. Then, write down three important concepts or points that anyone should retain after reading the document.

Give your readers a limited amount of time to read through the document or use it to perform a task. Then, have them put the document away so they cannot use it. Verbally or in writing, ask them:

- What is the purpose of this document?
- What is the document's main point?
- Can you tell me three major points that are made in the document?

If their answers to these questions are similar to the ones you wrote down, your document is likely understandable. If, however, your readers struggle to answer these questions, or get them wrong, you should think seriously about revising the document to highlight the information you intended your readers to retain.

PERFORMANCE TESTS: CAN THEY DO IT? Almost all technical documents are written to help readers take some kind of action. A set of instructions, obviously, asks readers to follow a procedure. A report might make some recommendations for change.

To do a performance test, have the users perform the procedure the document describes. Or, ask them to react to your recommendations. Here again, videotaping the users is a good way to keep a record of what happened. Did they seem to find the document easy to use? Where did they stumble or show frustration? When did they react positively or negatively to the tasks or ideas described in the document?

Ultimately, performance tests are designed to find out whether the users can do what the document asks of them. But it is also important to determine their attitude toward performing these tasks. You want to ensure not only that they *can* do it, but also that they *will* do it.

SAFETY TESTS: IS IT SAFE? Above all, you want your documentation and products to be safe. It is impossible to reduce all risk of injury, but you should try to reduce the risk as much as possible. Today, it is common for companies to be sued when their documentation or products are shown to be inadequate. Often, in product liability

Usability Testing a Document

To test the usability of a document, you can run experiments with people who represent real readers.

lawsuits, documents like instructions and user's manuals are used to prove or deny a company's negligence for an injury.

Without putting test subjects at risk themselves, safety tests are usually designed to locate places where users may make potentially injurious mistakes. They also ask readers about the warnings and cautions in the document to determine whether the reader observed and understood these notices.

SETTING OBJECTIVES AND MEASURING RESULTS   The challenge to effective usability testing is to first identify some objectives for the document. These objectives could refer to (1) how well the users can find information, (2) how well they understand important ideas, and (3) how well they perform tasks described in the document. Then, measure the results of your usability testing against these objectives.

It's often quite sobering to watch people fumble around with your document, misunderstand its meaning, and not follow its directions. But, the results of your tests should help you revise the document to improve its usability.

No form of usability testing will ensure that your document is a success. However, feedback from users is usually the best way to gain new insights into your document and to solicit suggestions for improvement.

- Revising and editing are forms of quality control that should be a regular part of your writing process.

- Documents and presentations can be edited at four different levels: revising, substantive editing, copyediting, and proofreading.

- Editorial tools such as copyediting marks are helpful even for nonprofessional editors.

- Readers from other cultures may respond differently than you expect to common metaphors, cultural references, and images. You should edit for any cultural references that may be confusing or offensive to readers from the target culture.

- Document cycling is a process of circulating your text among colleagues and your supervisor. You can use e-mail attachments or file-sharing services like Google Drive or Dropbox to send your work out for review by others.

- Usability testing can involve informal or formal methods to test the effectiveness of your document. You might ask sample readers to test documents that will be used by a broad readership.

Individual or Team Projects

1. Find a document on campus or at your workplace that needs editing. Edit the document by working backward from a level 4 edit (proofreading) to a level 1 edit (revising). As you apply each level of edit to the document, pay attention to the different kinds of actions and decisions you make at each level. How is the document evolving as you edit it?

2. Exchange a text with a member of your class. Then, do a level 2 edit (substantive editing) of the draft, using copyediting symbols to reflect the changes you think should be made to the document. Write a cover letter to the author in which you explain the changes you want made. Hand in a copy of this documentation to your instructor.

3. Find a text on the Internet that needs to be edited. Do a level 3 edit (copyediting) of the text, using the copyediting marks shown in this chapter. Write a memo to your instructor in which you discuss how you edited the text. Discuss some of the places where you struggled to mark the changes you wanted to make.

4. Find a text that needs editing and use the online editing strategies discussed in this chapter to edit it. In an e-mail to your instructor (with the edited version attached), discuss some of the differences and difficulties between paper-based and online editing. Discuss which form of editing you prefer and why.

Collaborative Project

With your group, locate a longer document on the Internet that needs editing. The document might be a report or proposal, or perhaps even a website. Then, do a level 2 edit (substantive editing) on the document, including the two levels of editing below it (copyediting and proofreading).

As you are editing, set up a document cycling routine that allows you to distribute your document among your group members. You can cycle the document in a paper version or use online editorial strategies to keep track of versions and changes in the document.

When your group has finished editing the document, revise it into a final form. Conduct usability tests on the document, using other members of your class as subjects.

In a memo to your instructor, discuss the evolution of the document at each stage of the editorial process. Tell your instructor (1) how you used substantive editing to improve the document, (2) how you cycled the document among your team members, and (3) how you used usability testing to identify places where the document might be improved.

Visit MyWritingLab for a Post-test and more technical writing resources.

A Machine by Any Other Name

Brad Hennings is a sales engineer who works for a medical equipment supplier called NilesTech. Recently, his company has begun exporting medical equipment to hospitals in Indonesia. As an engineer who works with the sales team, Brad's main responsibility is offering technical consultation for installing larger machines, like x-ray machines, proton radiotherapy machines, ultrasound scanners, electron microscopes, and CT scanners.

Last week, Brad was called to a sales meeting. The Vice President of Sales, Jane Martin, said she was generally pleased with their efforts, but she was concerned that NilesTech's most popular line of machines, the Kontol X-Ray System, was not selling at all in Indonesia.

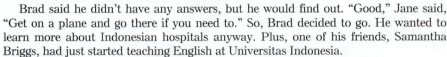

"It makes no sense." Jane said, "We sell these machines everywhere except Indonesia. We're selling these things in India, China, Europe. Nothing in Indonesia. Something has to be wrong."

One of the sales managers, Brad Hammonds, spoke up, "Maybe they just don't need these kinds of machines."

"That's just not possible." Jane shot back, "Every hospital deals with broken bones, tumors, and those kinds of procedures. Plus, we know our competitors are selling x-ray machines in Indonesia. We've missed out on millions of dollars of sales."

Brad said he didn't have any answers, but he would find out. "Good," Jane said, "Get on a plane and go there if you need to." So, Brad decided to go. He wanted to learn more about Indonesian hospitals anyway. Plus, one of his friends, Samantha Briggs, had just started teaching English at Universitas Indonesia.

He set up a few appointments with hospital administrators, collected print materials for all NilesTech's machines, and caught a flight to Jakarta.

As he visited with hospital administrators, he watched each of them look closely at the materials for all other machines and then pass quickly over the materials for the x-ray machines. Finally, after this happened at a fifth hospital, Brad decided to ask the administrator politely why he wasn't considering the Kontol x-ray machine.

The administrator seemed embarrassed and looked away. He was clearly hesitant to talk about it. Finally, the man complimented the x-ray machine and moved on. Brad decided not to push the issue.

That night, Brad was having dinner with his friend, Samantha, and two of her new Indonesian colleagues, Aulia and Ridho. The colleagues were friendly, so Brad asked them if they could help him with a perplexing cross-cultural problem. They agreed.

He showed them the materials for the x-ray machine. One of them gasped, and then they both started laughing. Samantha looked confused.

After they stopped laughing, Brad asked them why the materials were so funny.

"Well," Aulia began, "the name of your machine is a slang word in the Indonesian language." Ridho leaned over and whispered what the word means to Brad.

Brad was shocked and embarrassed. Now that he knew what the word meant, he was dismayed to see it all over the promotional materials. Some of the sentences were awkward and even funny when the meaning of this word was inserted.

Meanwhile, the name was printed in large letters on the x-ray machines themselves. It was no wonder Indonesian hospitals were not buying the machines.

Of course, changing the name of the x-ray machines would be easy. But Brad wanted to learn from this experience. How should he handle this problem in Indonesia and other countries? What do you think his company should do to avoid these kinds of transcultural embarrassments in the future?

CHAPTER

20

Preparing and Giving Presentations

Planning and Researching Your Presentation *521*

Choosing the Right Presentation Technology *526*

Organizing the Content of Your Presentation *529*

Help: Giving Presentations with Your Mobile Phone or Tablet *534*

Choosing Your Presentation Style *540*

Creating Visuals *542*

Delivering the Presentation *545*

Rehearsing *548*

Working Across Cultures with Translators *548*

What You Need to Know *554*

Exercises and Projects *554*

Case Study: The Coward *556*

In this chapter, you will learn:

- The importance of being able to prepare and deliver public presentations.

- How to define the rhetorical situation (subject, purpose, audience, and context of use) for your presentation.

- Strategies for organizing the content of presentations.

- How to create an effective presenting style.

- How to create and use visuals in presentations.

- The importance of practice and rehearsal.

- How to work effectively with translators in transcultural situations.

I f you don't like giving public presentations, you are not alone. Each year, surveys show that people fear speaking in public more than anything else—even more than death.

Yet giving public presentations is an essential part of most technical careers. More than likely, you will find yourself regularly giving presentations to clients, supervisors, and colleagues. Presenting information in public is a crucial skill in today's technical workplace.

Public Speaking Is More Important Than Ever

Public presentations are easier than ever with computers. You will find, though, that audiences now expect polished, professional presentations with plenty of graphics and visual appeal.

Planning and Researching Your Presentation

The preparation of a public presentation should follow a process, just like preparing written documents (Figure 20.1). Before getting up in front of an audience, you will need to:

- plan and research your subject
- organize your ideas
- choose an appropriate presentation style
- create graphics and slides
- practice and rehearse your presentation

The Preparation Process for a Presentation

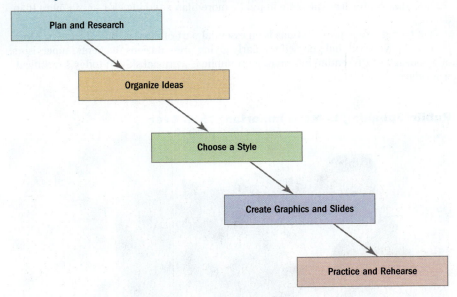

Figure 20.1:
Just as with written documents, you should follow a process as you prepare a presentation.

Even if you are already an accomplished public speaker, it is important that you spend significant time on each stage of the process. After all, a presentation cannot succeed on content alone. You need to pay attention to issues of organization, style, design, and delivery.

As you begin planning your talk, remember that presentations can be either formal or informal:

> **Formal presentations**—These presentations often include the use of a podium, speaking notes, and slides made with presentation software. Formal presentations include speeches, workshops, trainings, briefings, demonstrations, and panel discussions. They are made to clients, management, and colleagues.

> **Informal presentations**—Most presentations at work are informal. At monthly meetings, you will be asked to report on your team's progress. If you have a new idea, you will need to pitch it to your boss. And, if your supervisor stops by and says, "Hey, in 10 minutes, could you come by my office to tell the regional manager how the project is going?" you are about to make an informal public presentation.

In both formal and informal presentations, solid planning is the key to success. A good way to start the planning phase is by analyzing the rhetorical situation of your presentation. Begin by asking some strategic questions about your subject, purpose, and audience and the context in which you will be giving your talk.

The Five-W and How Questions give you a good place to start.

Who will be in my audience?

What kind of information do the audience members need or want?

Where will I be presenting?

When will I need to give my talk?

Why am I presenting this information to this audience?

How should I present this information?

Your answers to these questions should help you start crafting your materials into something that will be interesting and informative to the audience.

Defining the Rhetorical Situation

Now that you have considered the Five-W and How Questions, you can think a little more deeply about the situation in which you will be speaking (Figure 20.2). Consider closely your subject, purpose, audience, and the context of use.

SUBJECT   Identify what the audience needs to know, putting emphasis on information they require to take action or make a decision. You might also ask yourself what the audience does *not* need to know. That way, you can keep your presentation concise and to the point.

Asking Questions About the Rhetorical Situation

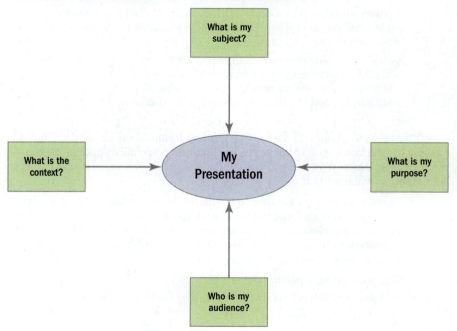

Figure 20.2: Asking questions about the subject, purpose, audience, and context will help you anticipate the information you need and how that information should be presented.

PURPOSE You need to know exactly what you want to achieve in your presentation. Try to state your purpose in one sentence.

My goal is to persuade elected officials that climate change is a looming problem for our state.

We need to demonstrate the G290 Robot Workstation to the CEO of Geocom Industries, showing her how it can be used to clean up toxic spills.

I need to motivate our technical staff to improve quality so we can meet the standards demanded by our new client.

If you need more than one sentence to express your purpose, you are probably trying to do too much in your presentation.

Link

For more help defining your purpose, go to Chapter 1, page 5.

AUDIENCE Members of your audience will come to your presentation with various needs, values, and attitudes. You should anticipate these characteristics and shape your presentation to meet their specific requirements and interests.

Primary audience (action takers)—For most presentations, the primary audience is the most important, because it is made up of people who will be making a decision or taking action.

Secondary audience (advisors)—These members of the audience might advise the primary audience on what actions to take. They might be experts in your field or people who have information or opinions on your subject.

Tertiary audience (evaluators)—Others in the audience may have an interest in what you are saying. They might be journalists, lawyers, activists, or concerned citizens.

Gatekeepers (supervisors)—Your supervisors and others at your company will often need to see your presentation before you give it to an audience. They will be looking for accuracy and checking whether you are achieving your purpose and fulfilling the mission of the company.

Link

For more audience analysis techniques, go to Chapter 2, page 20.

CONTEXT OF USE Context is always important in technical communication, but it is especially important in public presentations. You need to be fully aware of the physical, economic, ethical, and political factors that will shape your presentation and how your audience will react to it.

Physical context—Take time to familiarize yourself with the room in which you will be speaking and the equipment you will be using. You will need to adjust your presentation, including your visuals, to the size, shape, and arrangement of the room. Also, find out what kind of furniture and equipment you will have available.

Will you be using a podium or lectern?

Will you be sitting behind a table or standing out in the open?

Will there be a microphone?

Will a projector be available, and will you be able to use it?

Will you need to bring your own projector and computer?

Will other visual aids like whiteboards, flip charts, and large notepads be available?

Will the audience be eating, and will drinks be available?

When will the audience need breaks?

It is astonishing how many presentations fail because speakers are not prepared for the physical characteristics of the room. They show up with slides that can't be read because the room is too large, or they try to talk to a large audience with no public address system.

These sorts of problems might be someone else's fault, but it's your presentation. You will be the person who looks unprepared. Proper preparation for the physical context will help you avoid these problems.

Economic context—As always, money will be a central concern for your audience members. So, consider the microeconomic and macroeconomic factors that will influence how they will receive your presentation. Microeconomic issues might include budgetary concerns or constraints. Macroeconomic issues might include your audience's economic status, economic trends in the industry, or the state of the local or national economy.

Ethical context—Presentations almost always touch on ethical issues in one way or another. As you prepare, identify and consider any rights, laws, or issues of common concern that might shape your presentation.

Political context—Politics also play a role in presentations. In some cases, politics might simply involve the usual office politics that shape how people react to you and your subject. In other situations, larger political issues may come into play. National issues (energy policies, conservation, gun rights, privacy, security, etc.) will evoke different political responses among members of your audience.

Link

For more information on ethics, go to Chapter 4, page 61.

Link

To learn more about analyzing context of use, go to Chapter 2, page 21.

Allotting Your Time

As the speaker, you have an unstated "contract" with the audience. According to this contract, your audience is allowing you a specific number of minutes. It's your responsibility to fill that time productively—*and not go over that amount of time.* Few things annoy an audience as much as a speaker who runs past the time allotted.

So, as you are planning your presentation, first determine how much total time you have to speak. Then, *scale* your presentation to fit the allotted time. Figure 20.3 shows how a few common time periods might be properly budgeted.

Of course, if you have fewer or more than four topics, you should make adjustments to the times allowed for each. Also, you might need to spend more time on one topic than another. If so, adjust your times accordingly.

There are two things you should notice about the times listed in Figure 20.3.

- Longer presentations do not necessarily allow you to include substantially longer introductions and conclusions. No matter how long your presentation is scheduled to run, keep your introductions and conclusions concise.

	15-Minute Presentation	**30-Minute Presentation**	**45-Minute Presentation**	**One-Hour Presentation**
Introduction	1 minute	1–2 minutes	2 minutes	2–3 minutes
Topic 1	2 minutes	5 minutes	8 minutes	10 minutes
Topic 2	2 minutes	5 minutes	8 minutes	10 minutes
Topic 3	2 minutes	5 minutes	8 minutes	10 minutes
Topic 4	2 minutes	5 minutes	8 minutes	10 minutes
Conclusion	1 minute	1–2 minutes	2 minutes	2 minutes
Questions	2 minutes	5 minutes	5 minutes	10 minutes

Figure 20.3: When planning your presentation, carve up your time carefully to avoid going over the total allotted time.

- You should not budget all the time available. Always leave yourself some extra time in case something happens during your talk or you are interrupted.

In the end, the unstated contract with your audience is that you will finish within the time scheduled. If you finish a few minutes early, you won't hear any complaints. However, if you run late, your audience will not be pleased.

Choosing the Right Presentation Technology

As you plan your presentation, it is a good idea to think about what presentation technology you will use for your talk. Will you use presentation software with a digital projector? Are you going to use a whiteboard? Are you going to make transparencies for an overhead projector? The kind of presentation technology you need depends on the type of presentation you will be making (Figure 20.4).

Fortunately, presentation software like PowerPoint, Presentations, and Keynote makes it easy to create slides and use graphics. These programs will help you create visually interesting presentations for a variety of situations.

Each kind of visual aid offers specific advantages and disadvantages. Here are some pros and cons of the more common types of visuals:

> **Digital projector with a computer**—Most companies have a digital projector available for your use. The projector can display the slides from your computer screen onto a large screen. The advantages of digital projectors are their ease of use and their ability to create highly attractive, colorful presentations. The disadvantage is that the projected slides often dominate the room because the lights need to be turned down. As a result, the audience can become fixated on the slides and stop listening to what you are saying.

> **Overhead projector with transparencies**—The overhead projector is the tried-and-true method for giving presentations. You can use an overhead projector

Presentation Technologies

Type of presentation	Visuals
Presentation to a group of more than 10 people	Digital projector with computer
	Overhead projector with transparencies
	35-mm slide projector
	Whiteboard or chalkboard
Presentation to a group of fewer than 10 people	Digital projector with computer
	Overhead projector with transparencies
	35-mm slide projector
	Flip charts
	Large notepads
	Digital video on TV monitor (DVD or CD-ROM)
	Posters
	Handouts
	Computer screen
	Whiteboard or chalkboard

Figure 20.4: There are many different ways to present materials. You should choose the one that best fits your subject and audience.

to project slides onto a large screen. Transparencies for the projector can be made on a paper copier. The advantages of overhead projectors are that they are commonly available in workplaces and they are more reliable than digital projectors. Plus, you can use a marker to write on transparencies as you interact with the audience. The disadvantage is that presentations using overheads often seem more static and lifeless than ones made with digital projectors. The colors are not as sharp, and the pictures can be blurry.

Whiteboard, chalkboard, or large notepad—People often forget about the possibility of using a whiteboard, chalkboard, or large notepad in a room. But if you are giving a presentation that requires interaction with the audience, you can use these items to make visuals on the fly. The advantage is that you can create your visuals in front of the audience. Your listeners won't feel that they are receiving a canned presentation in which they have little input. The disadvantage is that you need to think on your feet. You need to find ways to translate your and the audience's comments into visuals on the board.

Flip charts—For small, more personal presentations, a flip chart is a helpful tool. As the speaker talks, he or she flips a new page forward or behind with each new topic. The advantage of flip charts is their closeness to the audience. You can give a flip chart presentation to a small group. The disadvantage of flip charts is that they are too small to be seen from a distance. If you have more than a handful of people in the audience, a flip chart won't work.

Using a Digital Projector

Digital projectors are increasingly common. They project your computer screen onto a large screen.

Posters—In some cases, you might be asked to present a poster. A poster usually includes about five to seven slides that describe a product or show a procedure. The slides are often used to summarize an experiment. The advantage of a poster is that everything covered in the talk is visually available to the audience. In some cases, the poster might be left alone on a display or a wall so viewers can inspect it on their own time. Posters, however, have the same disadvantage as flip charts. They can be used only in presentations to a handful of people. They are too hard to see from a distance.

Handouts—Handouts can be helpful in some cases, giving the audience something to take away from the presentation for review. When used properly, they can reinforce points made in your presentation or provide data that won't be visible with a projector. Also, handouts made with presentation software can be formatted to leave room for note taking. Handouts, though, can also be very distracting. In a large room, handouts can take a few minutes to be passed around, causing the speaker to lose momentum. Meanwhile, the audience might be distracted by the handout, reading it instead of listening to the presentation.

Using a Flip Chart

Flip charts are low tech, but they are especially effective in presentations to a few people.

These kinds of technology decisions are best made up front—while you are planning—because your choice of technology will often shape your decisions about the content, organization, style, and design/delivery of your information.

Organizing the Content of Your Presentation

One problem with organizing public presentations is that you usually end up collecting more information than you can talk about in the time allowed. Of course, you cannot tell the audience everything, so you need to make some hard decisions about what they need to know and how you should organize that information.

Keep your purpose and audience foremost in your mind as you make decisions about what kind of content you will put in the presentation. You want to include only need-to-know information and cut out any want-to-tell information that is not relevant to your purpose or audience. As you make decisions about what to include or cut, you should keep the following in mind: *The more you say, the more they will forget.*

Always keep your audience in mind. Most audiences prefer a concise, to-the-point presentation.

Building the Presentation

There is an old adage about public presentations: *Tell them what you're going to tell them. Tell them. Tell them what you told them.* In other words, like any document, your presentation should have a beginning (introduction), a middle (body), and an end (conclusion) (Figure 20.5).

The Introduction: Tell Them What You're Going to Tell Them

The beginning of your presentation is absolutely crucial. If you don't catch the audience's attention in the first few minutes, there is a good chance they will tune out and not listen to the rest of your presentation. Your introduction slide(s) should provide at least the subject, purpose, and main point of your presentation (one slide). As shown in Figure 20.6, you might also use a second slide to forecast the structure of the talk.

Basic Pattern for a Presentation

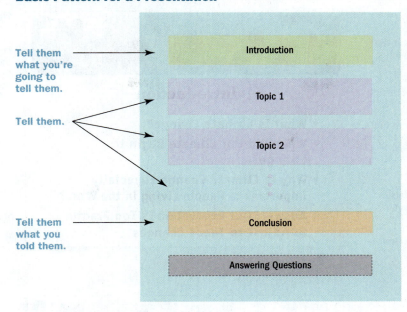

Figure 20.5:
A presentation has a beginning, a middle, and an end. Usually, time is left for questions at the end.

Like the introduction to a document, your presentation should begin by making up to six moves:

MOVE 1: DEFINE THE SUBJECT   Make sure the audience clearly understands the subject of your presentation. You might want to use a *grabber* to introduce your subject. A grabber states something interesting or challenging to capture the audience's attention. Some effective grabbers include the following:

> **A rhetorical question**—"Have you ever thought about changing your career and becoming a professional chef?"

> **A startling statistic**—"A recent survey shows that 73 percent of children aged fifteen to eighteen in the Braynard area have tried marijuana. Almost a third of Braynard teens are regular users of drugs."

> **A compelling statement**—"Unless we begin to do something about climate change soon, we will see dramatic changes in our ecosystem within a couple of decades."

> **An anecdote**—"A few years ago, I walked into a computer store, only to find the place empty. I looked around and didn't find a salesperson anywhere. Now, I've always been an honest person, but it did occur to me that I could pocket thousands of dollars of merchandise without being caught."

> **A quotation**—"William James, the famous American philosopher, once said, 'Many people believe they are thinking, but they are merely rearranging their prejudices.'"

Introduction Slides for a Presentation

Define the
subject.

Offer
background
information.

Stress the
importance of
the subject to
the audience.

State the
purpose
and main
point of the
presentation.

Introduction

• What Is Climate Change?
• When Did Our Climate Begin to
  Change?
• Why Is Climate Change Especially
  Important to People Living in the West?
• Answer: Our Ecosystem Is Too Fragile
  to Adjust to These Changes

Figure 20.6:
An introduc-
tion builds a
context for
the body of
the presenta-
tion.

Forecast the
structure
of the
presentation.

Today's Presentation

• Causes of Climate Change
• Effects of Climate Change in the West
• Solutions to This Problem
• Recommendations

A show of hands—"How many of you think children watch too much violent television? Raise your hands." Follow this question with an interesting, startling statistic or compelling statement.

But where do you find grabbers? The Internet is a source of endless material for creating grabbers. There are plenty of reference websites like Bartleby.com or Infoplease.com that will help you find quotations, statistics, and anecdotes.

Otherwise, you can use search engines like Google.com, Ask.com, or Yahoo.com to find interesting information for grabbers. Type in your subject and a keyword or phrase that sets a specific tone that you want your grabber to establish. The search engine will locate stories, quotes, statistics, and other information that you can use to create an interesting grabber.

MOVE 2: STATE THE PURPOSE OF YOUR PRESENTATION   In public presentations, you can be as blunt as you like about what you are trying to achieve. Simply tell the audience your purpose up front.

> The purpose of this presentation is to prove to you that climate change is real, and it is having a serious impact on Nevada's ecosystem.

> In this demonstration, our aim is to show you that the G290 Robot is ideal for cleaning up toxic spills.

MOVE 3: STATE YOUR MAIN POINT   Before moving into the body of your presentation, you should also state your main point. Your main point holds the presentation together, because it is the one major idea that you want the audience to take away from your talk.

> Climate change is a serious problem for our state, and it is growing worse quickly. By switching to nonpolluting forms of energy, we can do our part to minimize the damage to our ecosystem.

> The G290 Robot gives you a way to clean up toxic spills without exposing your hazmat team to dangerous chemical or nuclear materials.

MOVE 4: STRESS THE IMPORTANCE OF THE SUBJECT TO THE AUDIENCE   At the beginning of any presentation, each of the audience members wants to know, "Why is this important to me?" Tell them up front why your subject is important.

> Scientists predict that the earth's overall temperature will minimally rise a few degrees in the next 30 years. It might even rise 10 degrees. If they are correct, we are likely to see major ecological change on this planet. Oceans will rise a foot as the polar ice caps melt. We will also see an increase in the severity of storms like hurricanes and tornadoes. Here in Nevada, we will watch our deserts simply die and blow away.

> OSHA regulations require minimal human contact with hazardous materials. This is especially true with toxic spills. As you know, OSHA has aggressively gone after companies that expose their employees to toxic spills. To avoid these lawsuits and penalties, many companies are letting robot workstations do the dirty work.

Giving Presentations with Your Mobile Phone or Tablet

One major hassle about giving presentations with digital projectors is lugging along the laptop that holds your presentation. Even if a laptop is provided in the classroom it's always risky to show up with only a flash drive or DVD that holds your presentation. If something doesn't work, you're in trouble.

The solution? Why not use your mobile phone or tablet to store and give your presentation? Your phone or tablet is portable (you were taking it anyway, right?), and you can hold it in your hand while you're talking. Also, depending on your device you can add background music and video to your presentation and play it right through the projector (Figure A).

Using Your Mobile Phone or Tablet to Give a Presentation

Figure A:
Your tablet or phone is a lightweight way to transport your presentation. It also eliminates some of the problems of connecting laptops to projectors or televisions.

An added advantage is that you can review and practice your presentation any time without firing up that laptop or even bringing it along to campus or on your trip.

How can you turn your phone or tablet into a presentation tool? You will need an AV cable that can be plugged into the projector. This kind of cable usually plugs into the place where your phone's or tablet's charger cord plugs in.

Create your presentation in PowerPoint, Keynote, or any other presentation software. Then, download an app that will allow you to turn it into a presentation that can be viewed on the screen of your phone or tablet. Keynote is a good one for iPhones and iPads. Apps for Android phones include Mighty Meeting and Presentation Remote.

When you are ready to give your presentation, plug your AV cord into the projector. Your presentation should appear on the screen. You can navigate your presentation with the app you downloaded.

Opening Moves in a Presentation

AT A GLANCE

- Define the subject.
- State the purpose of your presentation.
- State your main point.
- Stress the importance of the subject to the audience.
- Offer background information on the subject.
- Forecast the structure of the presentation.

MOVE 5: OFFER BACKGROUND INFORMATION ON THE SUBJECT
Providing background information on your subject is a good way to build a framework for the audience to understand what you are going to say. You can give the audience a little history on the subject or perhaps tell about your relationship with it.

MOVE 6: FORECAST THE STRUCTURE OF THE PRESENTATION   In your introduction, tell the audience how you have organized the rest of the presentation. If you are going to cover four topics, say something like,

> In this presentation, I will be going over four issues. First, I will discuss . . . . Second, I will take a look at . . . . Third, I will identify some key objectives that . . . . And, finally, I will offer some recommendations for . . . .

Forecasting gives your audience a mental framework to follow your presentation. A major advantage to forecasting is that it helps the audience pay attention. If you say up front that you will be discussing four topics, the audience will always know where you are in the presentation.

The Body: Tell Them

The body of your presentation is where you are going to do the heavy lifting. Start out by dividing your subject into two to five major topics that you want to discuss.

Experience and research show that people can usually remember only five to seven items comfortably. So, if a presentation goes beyond five topics, the audience will start feeling overwhelmed or restless. If you have more than five topics, try to consolidate smaller topics into larger ones.

If you have already written a document, you might follow its organizational structure. If you are starting from scratch, you can follow some of the basic organizational patterns listed below.

PROBLEM, NEED, SOLUTION   This pattern is most effective for proposing new ideas. After your introduction, offer a clear definition of the problem or opportunity you are discussing. Then, specify what is needed to solve the problem or take advantage of the opportunity. Finally, offer a solution/plan that achieves the objective.

CHRONOLOGICAL   When organizing material chronologically, divide the subject into two to five major time periods. Then, lead the audience through these time periods, discussing the relevant issues involved in each. In some cases, a three-part *past-present-future* pattern is a good way to organize a presentation.

SPATIAL   You might be asked to explain or demonstrate visual spaces, like building plans, organizational structures, or diagrams. In these cases, divide the subject

Presenting the Content

Keep your presentation to two to five major points. You risk losing the audience if you try to cover more than five points.

into two to five zones. Then, walk audience through these zones, showing each zone individually and discussing how it relates to the zones around it.

NARRATIVE   Audiences always like stories, so you might organize your presentation around the narrative pattern. Narratives typically (1) set a scene, (2) introduce a complication, (3) evaluate the complication, (4) resolve the complication, and (5) explain what was learned from the experience.

Link

For more information on presenting research, go to Chapter 10, page 285.

METHODS, RESULTS, DISCUSSION   This pattern is commonly used to present the results of research. This pattern (1) describes the research plan or methodology, (2) presents the results of the study, (3) discusses and interprets the results, and (4) makes recommendations.

CAUSES AND EFFECTS   This pattern is common for problem solving. Begin the body of the presentation by discussing the causes for the current situation. Then, later in the body, discuss the effects of these causes and their likely outcomes. You can also alternate between causes and effects. In other words, discuss a cause and its effect together. Then, discuss another cause and its effect, and so on.

Link

To learn more about describing products or processes, turn to Chapter 6, page 135.

DESCRIPTION BY FEATURES OR FUNCTIONS   If you are demonstrating a product or process, divide your subject into its two to five major features or functions. Then, as you discuss each of these major features/functions, you can discuss the minor features/functions that are related to them.

Common Patterns for Public Presentations

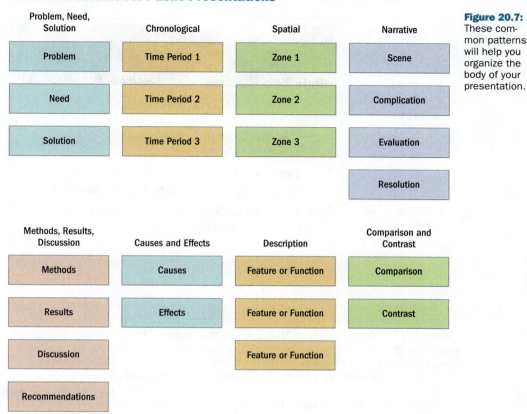

Figure 20.7: These common patterns will help you organize the body of your presentation.

Problem, Need, Solution
- Problem
- Need
- Solution

Chronological
- Time Period 1
- Time Period 2
- Time Period 3

Spatial
- Zone 1
- Zone 2
- Zone 3

Narrative
- Scene
- Complication
- Evaluation
- Resolution

Methods, Results, Discussion
- Methods
- Results
- Discussion
- Recommendations

Causes and Effects
- Causes
- Effects

Description
- Feature or Function
- Feature or Function
- Feature or Function

Comparison and Contrast
- Comparison
- Contrast

COMPARISON AND CONTRAST   Usually this pattern is followed when the speaker is comparing something new or unfamiliar with something that the audience knows well. Choose two to five major points on which these two things can be compared and contrasted. Then, compare and contrast them point by point.

There are countless patterns available for organizing the body of your presentation. The ones shown in Figure 20.7 are some of the most common in technical communication. These patterns are not formulas to be followed in lockstep. Rather, they can be manipulated to fit a variety of speaking situations.

The Conclusion: Tell Them What You Told Them

The conclusion is often the most important part of any presentation, and yet speakers consistently make mistakes at the end of their talks. They often end the presentation by shrugging their shoulders and saying, "Well, that's all I have to say. Any questions?"

Conclusion Slide for a Presentation

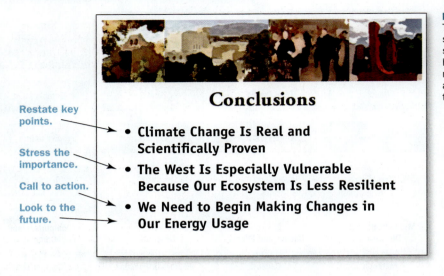

Figure 20.8: The conclusion slide should drive home your main points and look to the future.

Restate key points.

Stress the importance.

Call to action.

Look to the future.

Conclusions

- **Climate Change Is Real and Scientifically Proven**
- **The West Is Especially Vulnerable Because Our Ecosystem Is Less Resilient**
- **We Need to Begin Making Changes in Our Energy Usage**

Your conclusion needs to do much more. Specifically, you want to summarize your key points, while leaving the people in your audience in a position to say *yes* to your ideas. But you don't have much time to do all these things. Once you signal that you are concluding, you probably have about one to three minutes to make your final points. If you go beyond a few minutes, your audience will become agitated and frustrated.

Like the introduction, a conclusion should make some standard moves.

MOVE 1: SIGNAL CLEARLY THAT YOU ARE CONCLUDING   When you begin your conclusion, use an obvious transition such as, "In conclusion," "Finally," "To summarize my main points," or "Let me wrap up now." When you signal your conclusion, your audience will sit up and pay attention because they know you are going to tell them your main points.

Concluding Moves in a Presentation

- Signal that you are concluding.
- Restate your key points.
- Reemphasize the importance of the subject.
- Call the audience to action.
- Look to the future.
- Say thank you.
- Ask for questions.

AT A GLANCE

MOVE 2: RESTATE YOUR KEY POINTS   Summarize your key points for the audience, including your overall main point (Figure 20.8). Minimally, you can simply list them and go over them one last time. That way, if your audience remembers anything about your presentation, it will be these most important items.

MOVE 3: REEMPHASIZE THE IMPORTANCE OF YOUR SUBJECT TO THE AUDIENCE Tell the people in your audience again why they should care about this subject. Don't tell them why it is important to you—that's assumed. Instead, answer the audience's "What's in it for me?" questions.

MOVE 4: CALL THE AUDIENCE TO ACTION   If you want people in the audience to do something, here is the time to tell them. Be specific about what action they should take.

MOVE 5: LOOK TO THE FUTURE   Briefly, offer a vision of the future, usually a positive one, that will result if they agree with your ideas.

MOVE 6: SAY THANK YOU   At the end of your presentation, don't forget to thank the audience. Saying "Thank you" signals that you are really finished. Often, it will also signal the audience to applaud, which is always a nice way for a presentation to end.

MOVE 7: ASK FOR QUESTIONS   Once the audience has stopped applauding, you can ask for questions.

Preparing to Answer Questions

While preparing and researching your presentation, you should spend some time anticipating the kinds of questions you might be asked. Questions are an opportunity to interact with the audience and clarify your ideas. You will generally be asked three types of questions: elaboration, hostile, and heckling.

THE ELABORATION OR CLARIFICATION QUESTION   Members of the audience might ask you to expand on your ideas or explain some of your concepts. These questions offer you an opportunity to reinforce some of your key points. You should not feel defensive or threatened by these questions. The person asking the question is really giving you a chance to restate some of your main points or views.

When you receive one of these kinds of questions, start out by rephrasing the question for the audience. For example, "The question is whether climate change will have an impact that we can actually observe with our own eyes." Your rephrasing of the question will allow you to shift the question into your own words, making it easier to answer.

Then, offer more information or reinforce a main point. For instance, "The answer is 'yes.' Long-time desert residents are already reporting that desert plants and animals are beginning to die off. One example is the desert willow. . . ."

THE HOSTILE QUESTION   Occasionally, an audience member will ask you a question that calls your ideas into doubt. For example, "I don't trust your results. Do you really expect us to believe that you achieved a precision of .0012 millimeters?"

Here is a good three-step method for deflecting these kinds of questions:

1. **Rephrase the question**—"The questioner is asking whether it is possible that we achieved a precision of .0012 millimeters."

2. **Validate the question**—"That's a good question, and I must admit that we were initially surprised that our experiment gave us this level of precision."

3. **Elaborate and move forward**—"We achieved this level of precision because . . . ."

You should allow a hostile questioner only one follow-up remark or question. After giving the hostile questioner this second opportunity, do not look at that person. If you look elsewhere in the room, someone else in the audience will usually raise his or her hand and ask about a different topic.

Answering Questions

Prepare in advance for the kinds of questions you might be asked after your presentation.

THE HECKLING QUESTION   In rare cases, a member of the audience will be there only to heckle you. He or she will ask rude questions or make blunt statements like, "I think this is the stupidest idea we've heard in twenty years."

In these situations, you need to recognize that the heckler is *trying* to sabotage your presentation and cause you to lose your cool. Don't let the heckler do that to you. You simply need to say something like, "I'm sorry you feel that way. Perhaps we can meet after the presentation to talk about your concerns." Usually, at this point, others in the audience will step forward to ask more constructive questions.

It is rare that a heckler will actually come to talk to you later. That's not why he or she was there in the first place. If a heckler does manage to dominate the question-and-answer period, simply end your presentation. Say something like,

> Well, we are out of time. Thank you for your time and attention. I will stick around in the room for more questions.

Then, step back from the podium or microphone and walk away. Find someone to shake hands with. Others who have questions can approach you one-on-one.

Choosing Your Presentation Style

Your speaking style is very important. In a presentation, you can use style to add flair to your information while gaining the audience's trust. A flat or dull style, on the other hand, can bore the audience, annoy them, and even turn them against you.

There are many ways to create an appropriate style for your presentation, but four techniques seem to work best for technical presentations. Each of these techniques will help you project a particular tone in your speaking.

DEVELOP A PERSONA   In ancient Greek, the word *persona* meant "mask." So, as you consider your presentation style, think about the mask you want to wear in front of the audience. Then, step into this character. Put on the mask. You will find that choosing a persona will make you feel more comfortable, because you are playing a role, much like an actor plays a role. The people in the audience aren't seeing and judging *you*. They are seeing the mask you have chosen to wear for the presentation.

SET A THEME   A theme is a consistent tone you want to establish in your presentation. The best way to set a theme is to decide which one word best characterizes how you want the audience to *feel* about your subject. Then, use logical mapping to find words and phrases associated with that feeling (Figure 20.9).

As you prepare your talk, use these words regularly. When you give your presentation, the audience will naturally pick up on your theme. For example, let's say you want your audience to be "concerned." Map out words and phrases related to this feeling. Then, as you prepare your presentation, weave these words and phrases into your speech. If you do it properly, your audience will feel your concern.

A Theme in a Presentation

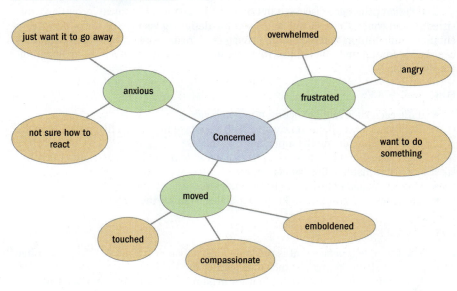

Figure 20.9: By mapping around a key term and seeding your speech with related words, you can set a theme that creates a specific feeling in your audience.

Creating Your Presentation Style

AT A GLANCE

- Develop a persona.
- Set a theme.
- Show enthusiasm.
- KISS: Keep It Simple (Stupid).

SHOW ENTHUSIASM   If you're not enthusiastic about your subject, your audience won't be either. So, get excited about what you have to say. Be intense. Get pumped up. Show that you are enthusiastic about this subject (even if you aren't), and the audience members will be, too.

KISS: KEEP IT SIMPLE (STUPID)   The KISS principle is always something to keep in mind when you are presenting, especially when it comes to style. Speak in plain, simple terms. Don't get bogged down in complex details and concepts.

In the end, good style is a choice. You may have come to believe that some people just have good style and others don't. That's not true. In reality, people with good style are just more conscious of the style they want to project.

Creating Visuals

In this visual age, you are really taking a risk if you try to present information without visuals. People not only want visuals but also *need* them to fully understand your ideas (Munter & Russell, 2011).

Designing Visual Aids

One of the better ways to design visual aids is to use the presentation software (PowerPoint, Keynote, or Presentations) that probably came bundled with your word-processing software. These programs are rather simple to use, and they can help you quickly create the visuals for a presentation. They also generally ensure that your slides will be well designed and readable from a distance.

The design principles discussed in Chapter 17 (balance, alignment, grouping, consistency, and contrast) work well when you are designing visual aids for public presentations. In addition to these design principles, here are some special considerations concerning format and font choices that you should keep in mind as you are creating your visuals.

FORMAT CHOICES

- Title each slide with an action-oriented heading.
- Put five or fewer items on each slide. If you have more than five points to make about a topic, divide the topic into two slides.
- Use left-justified text in most cases. Centered text should be used infrequently and right-justified text, almost never.
- Use lists instead of paragraphs or sentences.
- Use icons and graphics to keep your slides fresh for the audience.

FONT CHOICES

- Use a simple typeface that is readable from a distance. Sans serif fonts are often more readable from a distance than serif fonts.
- Use a minimum of a 36-point font for headings and a minimum of a 24-point font for body text.

Sample Slides from a Presentation

Cover Slide

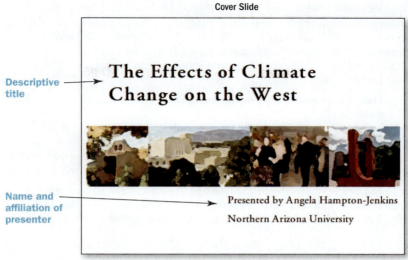

Descriptive title →

The Effects of Climate Change on the West

Name and affiliation of presenter →

Presented by Angela Hampton-Jenkins

Northern Arizona University

Figure 20.10: These two slides show good balance, simplicity, and consistency. Keep your slides simple so that the audience doesn't have to work too hard to read them.

Slide from Body of Presentation

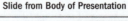
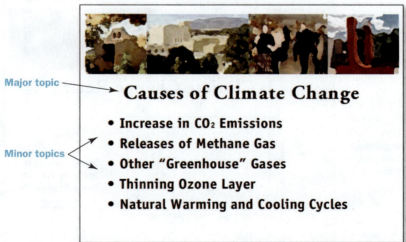

Major topic →

Causes of Climate Change

Minor topics

- **Increase in CO_2 Emissions**
- **Releases of Methane Gas**
- **Other "Greenhouse" Gases**
- **Thinning Ozone Layer**
- **Natural Warming and Cooling Cycles**

- Use color to keep slides interesting and to improve retention.
- Do not use ALL UPPERCASE letters because they are hard to read from a distance.

Overall, it is best to keep your slides as simple as possible (Figure 20.10). After all, if your audience needs to puzzle through your complex slides, they probably won't be listening to you.

Using Graphics

Graphics are also helpful, especially when you are trying to describe something to the audience. An appropriate graph, chart, diagram, picture, or even a movie will help support your argument (Figure 20.11). Chapter 18 discusses the use of graphics in documents. Most of those same guidelines apply to presentations.

Here are some guidelines that pertain specifically to using graphics in a presentation:

Link

For more information on creating and using graphics, go to Chapter 14, page 374.

- Make sure words or figures in the graphic are large enough to be read from a distance.
- Label each graphic with a title.
- Keep graphics uncomplicated and limited to simple points.
- Keep tables small and simple. Large tables full of data do not work well as visuals because the audience will not be able to read them—nor will they want to.
- Use clip art or photos to add life to your slides.

Graphics, including clip art and photos, should never be used merely to decorate your slides. They should reinforce the content, organization, and style of your presentation.

Using a Graphic on a Presentation Slide

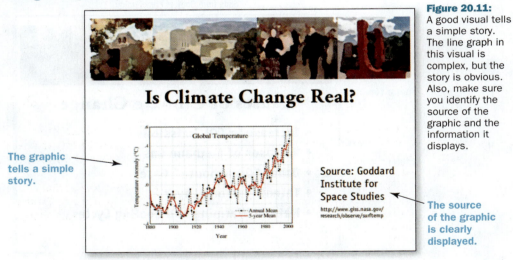

The graphic tells a simple story.

Source: Goddard Institute for Space Studies
http://www.giss.nasa.gov/research/observe/surftemp

The source of the graphic is clearly displayed.

Figure 20.11: A good visual tells a simple story. The line graph in this visual is complex, but the story is obvious. Also, make sure you identify the source of the graphic and the information it displays.

Slides to Avoid

All of us have been to a presentation in which the speaker used ineffective slides. He or she put up a transparency with a 12-point type font and minimal design (Figure 20.12). Or, the speaker put up a table or graph that was completely indecipherable because the font was too small or the graphic was too complex.

These kinds of slides are nothing short of painful. The only thing the audience wants from such a slide is for the speaker to remove it—as soon as possible. Always

An Ineffective Slide

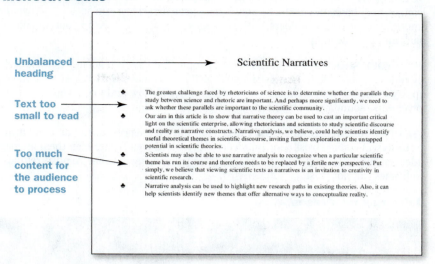

Figure 20.12:
An ineffective slide often says a great deal—if the audience can read it.

remember that we live in a visual culture. People are sensitive to bad design. So take the time to properly create slides that enhance your presentation, not detract from it.

Delivering the Presentation

Why do people go to presentations, especially if a printed or screen version of the talk is available?

People attend presentations because they want to see you perform the material. They want to see how you act and interact with them. They want you to put a human face on the material. You should pay close attention to your delivery so that the audience receives a satisfying performance.

The usual advice is to "be yourself" when you are presenting. Of course, that's good advice if you are comfortable talking to an audience. Better advice is to "be the person the audience expects." In other words, like an actor, play the role that seems to fit your material and your audience.

Body Language

The audience will pay close attention to your body language. So use your body to reflect and highlight the content of your talk.

DRESS APPROPRIATELY   Your clothing should reflect the content and importance of your presentation. A good rule of thumb is to dress a level better than how you expect your audience to dress. For example, if the audience will be in casual attire, dress a little more formally. A female speaker might wear a blouse and dress pants or a nice skirt. A male speaker might wear a shirt, tie, and dress pants. If the audience will be wearing suits and "power" dresses, you will need to wear an even *nicer* suit or an even *better* power dress.

STAND UP STRAIGHT When people are nervous, they have a tendency to slouch, lean, or rock back and forth. To avoid these problems when you speak, keep your feet squarely under your shoulders, with your knees slightly bent. Keep your shoulders back and your head up.

DROP YOUR SHOULDERS Under stress, people also have a tendency to raise their shoulders. Raised shoulders restrict your airflow and make the pitch of your voice go up. By dropping your shoulders, you will improve airflow and lower your voice. A lower voice sounds more authoritative.

USE OPEN HAND AND ARM GESTURES For most audiences, open hand and arm gestures will convey trust and confidence. If you fold your arms, keep them at your sides, or put both hands in your pockets, you will convey a defensive posture that audiences will not trust.

Delivering the Presentation

You can use your body and hands to highlight important parts of your presentation.

MAKE EYE CONTACT Everyone in the audience should believe that you made eye contact with him or her at least once during your presentation. As you are presenting, make it a point to look at all parts of the room at least once. If you are nervous about making eye contact, look at audience members' foreheads instead. They will think you are looking them directly in the eye.

There are exceptions to these generally accepted guidelines about gestures and eye contact. In some cultures, like some Native American cultures, open gestures and eye contact might be considered rude and even threatening. If you are speaking to an unfamiliar audience, find out which gestures and forms of eye contact are appropriate for that audience.

MOVE AROUND THE STAGE   If possible, when you make important points, step toward the audience. When you make transitions in your presentation from one topic to the next, move to the left or right on the stage. Your movement across the stage will highlight the transition.

POSITION YOUR HANDS APPROPRIATELY   Nervous speakers often strike a defensive pose by using their hands to cover specific parts of their bodies (perhaps you can guess which parts). Keep your hands away from these areas.

Voice, Rhythm, and Tone

A good rule of thumb about voice, rhythm, and tone is to *speak lower and slower than you think you should.*

Why lower and slower? When you are presenting, you need to speak louder than normal. As your volume goes up, the pitch of your voice will go up. So your voice will seem unnaturally high (even shrill) to the audience. By consciously lowering your voice, you should sound just about right to the audience.

Meanwhile, nervousness usually causes you to speak faster than you normally would. By consciously slowing down, you will sound more comfortable and more like yourself.

USE PAUSES TO HIGHLIGHT MAIN POINTS   When you make an important point, pause for a moment. Your pause will signal to audience members that you just made an important point that you want them to consider and retain.

USE PAUSES TO ELIMINATE VERBAL TICS   Verbal tics like "um," "ah," "like," "you know," "OK?" and "See what I mean?" are simply nervous habits that are intended to fill gaps between thoughts. If you have problems with a verbal tic (who doesn't?), train yourself to pause when you feel like using one of these sounds or phrases. Before long, you will find them disappearing from your speech altogether.

Using Your Notes

The best presentations are the ones that don't require notes. Notes on paper or index cards are fine, but you need to be careful not to keep looking at them. Nervousness will often lead you to keep glancing at them instead of looking at the audience. Some speakers even get stuck looking at their notes, glancing up only rarely at the audience. Looking down at your notes makes it difficult for the audience to hear you. You want to keep your head up at all times.

The following are some guidelines for making and using notes.

USE YOUR SLIDES AS MEMORY TOOLS   You should know your subject inside out. So you likely don't need notes at all. Practice rehearsing your presentation with your slides alone. Eventually, you will be able to completely dispense with your written notes and work solely off your visual aids while you are speaking.

TALK TO THE AUDIENCE, NOT TO YOUR NOTES OR THE SCREEN   Make sure you are always talking to the audience. It is sometimes tempting to begin looking at your notes while talking. Or, in some cases, presenters end up talking to the screen. You should only steal quick glances at your notes or the screen. Look at the audience instead.

PUT WRITTEN NOTES IN A LARGE FONT   If you need to use notes, print them in a large font on the top half of a piece of paper. That way, you can quickly find needed information without effort. Putting the notes on the top half of the paper means you won't need to glance at the bottom of the piece of paper, restricting airflow and taking your eyes away from the audience.

USE THE NOTES VIEW FEATURE IN YOUR PRESENTATION SOFTWARE   Presentation software usually includes a Notes View feature that allows you to type notes under or to the side of slides (Figure 20.13). These notes can be helpful, but be wary of using them too much. First, they force you to look at the bottom of a sheet of paper, restricting your airflow. Second, if you are nervous, you may be distracted by these notes or start reading them to the audience.

IF SOMETHING BREAKS, KEEP GOING   If your overhead projector dies, your computer freezes, or you drop your notes all over the front row, don't stop your presentation to fumble around trying to fix the situation. Keep going. You need only acknowledge the problem: "Well, it looks like some gremlins have decided to sabotage my projector. So, I will move forward without it." Then do so.

Rehearsing

For some presentations, you might want to rehearse your presentation in front of a test audience. At your workplace, you can draft people into listening to your talk. These practice audiences might be able to give you some advice about improving your presentation. If nothing else, though, they will help you anticipate how the audience will react to your materials. Groups like Toastmasters can also provide a test audience (Figure 20.14). At Toastmasters meetings, people give presentations and work on improving their public speaking skills.

The more you rehearse, the more comfortable you are going to feel with your materials and the audience. Practicing will help you find the errors in your presentation, but rehearsal will help you put the whole package together into an effective presentation.

Evaluating Your Performance

Evaluation is an important way to receive feedback on your presentation. In some speaking situations, the audience will expect to evaluate your presentation. If an evaluation form is not provided, audience members will expect you to hand one out so they can give you and supervisors feedback on your performance. Figure 20.15 shows a typical evaluation form that could be used for a variety of presentations.

The "Notes View" Feature

The copy of the slide is up here.

The notes appear down here.

Causes of Climate Change

- Increase in CO$_2$ Emissions
- Releases of Methane Gas
- Other "Greenhouse" Gases
- Thinning Ozone Layer
- Natural Warming and Cooling Cycles

Causes of Climate Change

Increase in CO$_2$ Emissions—Scientists at the Hanson Laboratories report that carbon dioxide emissions, especially from cars, are on the rise. We have seen an increase of 15 percent in emissions.

Releases of Methane Gas—Methane is naturally occurring. Cows, for example, belch methane gas. The problem is with larger and larger releases of methane gas due to industrialization.

Other Greenhouse Gases—A variety of other greenhouse gases, like nitrous oxide and halocarbons, need to be controlled.

Thinning Ozone Layer—The thinning has slowed, but it still continues. As developing countries become more industrialized, they are using more chemicals that thin the ozone layer.

Natural Warming and Cooling Cycles—The earth does naturally warm and cool, creating "ice ages" and "hot periods." These changes are very gradual, though, and could only minimally account for the climate change we are experiencing now.

5

Figure 20.13: The Notes View feature in your presentation software allows you to put notes below or to the side of a slide. Your audience won't be able to see them, but you can print out each slide with your notes so that you don't need to keep looking up at your slides.

Places to Improve Your Presentation Skills

Figure 20.14: Toastmasters is a group that helps people practice and improve their public speaking skills. Local groups can be found in almost any large town.

Working Across Cultures with Translators

When speaking to an audience from a different culture, you may need the services of a translator. A translator does more than simply convert one language into another. He or she will also modify your words to better capture your intent and adjust them to the cultural expectations of your audience. An effective translator will help you better express any subtle points while avoiding cultural taboos and gaffes.

Here are some strategies to help you work more effectively with a translator. These strategies can also be helpful when speaking in any transcultural situation.

KEEP YOUR SPEECH SIMPLE The words and sentences in your speech should be as plain and simple as possible. Figures of speech, clichés, or complex sentences will be difficult to translate, especially when the audience is right in front of you.

AVOID JOKES Translators cringe when speakers decide to tell jokes, because jokes that are funny in one culture are often not funny in another. Meanwhile, jokes often rely on turns of phrase or puns that are impossible to translate. Translators have been known to tell the audience, "The speaker is now telling a joke that doesn't translate into our language. I will tell you when to laugh." Then, as the speaker finishes the joke, the translator signals that the audience should laugh.

SPEAK SLOWLY A translator will struggle to keep up with someone who is speaking at a faster-than-normal pace, leading to errors in translation. Meanwhile, the structure of some languages (e.g., German) can cause translation to take a little longer.

An Evaluation Form for Presentations

Presentation Evaluation Form

Please answer these questions with one or more sentences.

Content

Did the speaker include more information than you needed to know? If so, where?

Where did the speaker not include enough need-to-know information?

What kinds of other facts, figures, or examples would you like to see included in the presentation?

Organization

In the introduction, was the speaker clear about the subject, purpose, and main point of the presentation?

In the introduction, did the speaker grab your attention effectively?

In the body, was the presentation divided into obvious topics? Were the transitions among these topics obvious to you?

In the conclusion, did the speaker restate the presentation's main point clearly?

Did the speaker leave enough time for questions?

Style and Delivery

Did the speaker speak clearly and loudly enough?

Figure 20.15: An evaluation form is a good way to receive feedback on your presentation. Have your audience comment on your presentation's content, organization, style, and delivery.

(continued)

Did the speaker move effectively, using hands and body language to highlight important points?

Did the speaker have any verbal tics (uh, um, ah, you know)?

Did the speaker look around the room and make eye contact?

Was the speaker relaxed and positive during the presentation?

Visuals

Did the visuals effectively highlight the speaker's points in the presentation?

Did the speaker use the visuals effectively, or did they seem to be a distraction?

Did the speaker use notes effectively? Was the speaker distracted by his or her notes?

Concluding Remarks

List five things you learned during this presentation.

What did you like about this presentation?

What did you not like about this presentation?

What suggestions can you offer to make this presentation better?

MINIMIZE SLANG, JARGON, AND SAYINGS   These words and phrases rarely translate easily into other languages, because they are culturally dependent. For example, if the speaker says, "Instead of doing another kickoff meeting, we just need to sit down and hammer out an agreement," the translator would struggle to translate three concepts in this sentence: "doing" a meeting, "kicking off" that meeting, and "hammering out" an agreement. The meanings of these words are dependent on the culture of the speaker and might have little meaning to the audience.

Working with a Translator

Translators are becoming increasingly important as technology and manufacturing become more international.

AVOID RELIGIOUS REFERENCES   In most cases, it is risky to include religious themes or terms in transcultural speeches. Even seemingly harmless phrases like "God help us" or "Let's pray that doesn't happen" can translate in unexpected ways. Meanwhile, attempts to incorporate the sayings of a religious figure or scripture can be potentially insulting and even sacrilegious.

KNOW YOUR TRANSLATOR   Whenever possible, check your translator's level of fluency and understanding of your subject matter. One of your bilingual colleagues may be able to help you determine your translator's abilities. Also, you should hire a translator from your audience's specific culture. Just because a translator knows Spanish doesn't mean he or she can handle the dialects and colloquialisms in all Spanish-speaking cultures.

PROVIDE YOUR SPEECH, VISUALS, AND HANDOUTS IN ADVANCE   Giving your translator your speech ahead of time will greatly improve the accuracy of the translation, because he or she will have time to become familiar with the topic and anticipate ideas that are difficult to translate.

STAND WHERE YOUR TRANSLATOR CAN SEE YOUR FACE   A translator may have trouble hearing you correctly if you are turned away from him or her. Also, translators sometimes read lips or facial expressions to help them figure out difficult words or concepts.

For now, English speakers are fortunate that their language has become an international language of business and technology. Consequently, many people in your audience will be able to understand your speech without the help of a translator. Before too long, though, people from other cultures will expect business to be conducted in their languages, too. At that point, translators will become even more critical in technical fields.

- Public presentations are an essential part of communicating effectively in technical workplaces.

- Planning is the key to successful public presentations. You need a firm understanding of the subject, purpose, audience, and context of your presentation.

- A well-organized presentation "tells them what you're going to tell them, tells them, and tells them what you told them."

- Visual aids are essential in presentations. Software programs are available to help you make these aids.

- People come to presentations because they want to see you *perform* the material.

- Good delivery means paying attention to your body language, appearance, voice, rhythm, tone, and use of notes.

- Practice is important, but so is rehearsal. Practice to iron out the rough spots in the presentation, and then rehearse, rehearse, rehearse.

- Translators can help you appropriately present your message to an audience from a different culture. Keeping your words simple and speaking at a normal pace will help translators more accurately reflect your intended meaning.

Individual or Team Projects

1. Attend a public presentation at your campus or workplace. Instead of listening to the content of the presentation, pay close attention to the speaker's use of organization, style, and delivery. In a memo to your instructor, discuss some of the speaker's strengths and suggest places where he or she might have improved the presentation.

2. Using presentation software, turn a document you have written for this class into a short presentation with slides. Your document might be a set of instructions, a report, a proposal, or any other document. Your task is to make the presentation interesting and informative to the audience.

3. Pick a campus or workplace problem that you think should be solved. Then, write a three-minute oral presentation in which you (a) identify the problem, (b) discuss what is needed to solve the problem, and (c) offer a solution. As you develop your presentation, think about the strategies you might use to persuade the audience to accept your point of view and solution.

4. Interview one of your classmates for ten minutes about his or her hometown. Then, from your notes alone, make an impromptu presentation to your class in which you introduce your classmate's hometown to the rest of the class. In your presentation, you should try to persuade the audience members that they should visit this town.

Collaborative Projects

Group presentations are an important part of the technical workplace because projects are often team efforts. Therefore, a whole team of people often needs to make the presentation, with each person speaking about his or her part of the project.

Turn one of the collaborative projects you have completed in this class into a group presentation. Some of the issues you should keep in mind are:

- Who will introduce the project, and who will conclude it?
- How will each speaker "hand off" to the next speaker?
- Where will each presenter stand while presenting?
- Where will the other team members stand or sit while someone else is presenting?
- How can you create a consistent set of visuals that will hold the presentation together?
- How will questions and answers be handled during and after the presentation?
- How can the group create a coherent, seamless presentation that doesn't seem to change style when a new speaker steps forward?

Something to keep in mind with team presentations is that members of the audience are often less interested in the content of the presentation than they are in meeting your team. So, think about some ways in which you can convey that personal touch in your team presentation while still talking effectively about your subject.

Visit **My**Writing**Lab** for a Post-test and more technical writing resources.

The Coward

Jennifer Sandman is an architect who works for a small firm in Kansas City. The firm is completing its largest project ever, designing a building for a GrandMart superstore. Jennifer and her boss, a lead architect, Bill Voss, are in charge of the project.

At an upcoming city council meeting, they will need to give a public presentation on their plans for the new GrandMart. At the meeting, the mayor and city council will look over the plans and listen to comments from people in the audience. Failure to persuade the audience might mean the loss of the project as well as future business with GrandMart, an important client.

Everyone knows that the meeting will be contentious, with many angry residents arguing against the plans. And yet, GrandMart's surveys have shown that a silent majority would welcome the new store in the neighborhood. Meanwhile, GrandMart's marketing specialists are certain that the store would be profitable, because there are no competitors within ten miles.

Jennifer has one problem—her boss is a coward. He scheduled a business trip to coincide with the meeting, and he promptly delegated the presentation to her. As her boss walked out the door, he said, "It will be a good growth opportunity for you. Just don't make the firm look bad."

For Jennifer, giving presentations isn't a problem. She is a whiz with PowerPoint, and she has given enough presentations to feel comfortable in front of people. Her concern, though, is the potentially hostile audience. There might even be some hecklers. These hostile people will never accept the idea that a GrandMart should be built in their neighborhood. Others in the audience, though, will be undecided. So she wants to devise ways in her presentation to soften and deflect some of the hostile criticisms, while gaining the support of people in the community who want the store built.

If you were Jennifer, how would you craft your presentation to fit these difficult conditions? How would you prepare for the hostile and heckling questions? How would you design and deliver your presentation to avoid being seen as defensive?

CHAPTER

21

Writing for the Web

Writing for Websites *558*

Using Social Networking in the Workplace *565*

Creating Blogs and Microblogs *568*

Making Internet Videos and Podcasts *569*

Writing Articles for Wikis *571*

What You Need to Know *572*

Exercises and Projects *572*

Case Study: My Boss Might Not "Like" This *574*

In this chapter, you will learn:

- The basic features of websites.
- How to use style to make a website more readable.
- How design principles are used to create an effective website interface.
- How to start a social networking site.
- How to create your own blog.
- How to post a video or podcast.
- How to add an article to a wiki.

In the technical workplace, electronic communication is the norm. People are constantly communicating with each other through texting, e-mail, video chatting, Twitter feeds, blogs, and social networking. They organize and share information through websites, wikis, and databases. In many ways, the web, or the Internet, has become the central nervous system of the technical workplace.

Today, people entering high-tech fields are expected to know how to use electronic networks and write for the web. Fortunately, the communication skills you have developed already work well in these electronic environments. This chapter will give you some additional strategies for succeeding in electronic environments.

Writing for Websites

The first thing you should remember about websites is that *they are documents*. They may look different from paper-based documents and they may function differently, but they are still *written texts* with words and images. As a result, you can use many of the communication strategies you already know to write for websites.

In the workplace, you will usually need to write material for an existing corporate website. In these situations, the company's webmaster will usually give you guidelines about length, format, and use of images.

If you want to develop a website on your own, you have many options. Adobe's Dreamweaver is still the most commonly used website development software. It's similar to a word processor. Online website building sites like Wix.com and Web.com are easy to use at little or no cost. Meanwhile, Wordpress, a blogging site, is becoming sophisticated enough to create a fully functioning website that isn't just a blog.

Basic Features of a Website

One important difference between websites and paper documents is that people tend to read websites visually and spatially, scanning from one block of information to another block of information. People rarely read websites sentence-by-sentence and paragraph-by-paragraph. Instead, they hop from one block of information to another, searching for the information they need. They *navigate* within the website by jumping from one page to another.

To help readers navigate, websites usually contain a few kinds of pages:

> **Home page**—The home page is usually the main page of the site. It identifies the subject and purpose of the website, while forecasting its overall structure. In many ways, the home page is like an introduction and a table of contents of the website (Figure 21.1).
>
> **Node pages**—The home page will typically have links to a number of node pages. Node pages divide the website's content into larger topic areas. For example, a university's home page will have links that go to node pages like *Colleges and Departments, Libraries, Students,* and *Faculty and Staff.* These are all nodes in the website.
>
> **Pages**—Individual pages contain the facts, details, images, and other information that readers are seeking.
>
> **Navigation pages**—Navigation pages help readers find the information they are seeking. They might include a search engine or a site map that lists the content of the site.

A Home Page

Navigation bar offers links to other parts (nodes) of the website.

Source: U.S. Forestry Service, http://www.fs.fed.us.

Splash page—A splash page, when used, comes before the home page. Splash pages often use an image or animation to welcome readers to the site. Today, they are primarily used for advertising, directing users to appropriate language versions of the website, and requiring users to register before accessing the site.

As shown in Figure 21.2, websites generally use spatial (or nonlinear) organizational patterns. Keep in mind that websites come in many shapes and sizes, and they are usually not as symmetrical as the diagram shown in Figure 21.2.

How many levels should a website have? Professional website designers use the following guidelines to determine the number of levels needed in a website:

- a maximum of three links for the most important information.
- a maximum of five links for 80 percent of all information.
- a maximum of seven links for all information.

These guidelines are helpful but they aren't absolute rules, so you can include as many levels as you need. However, if you force your readers, especially customers, to

Basic Pattern for a Website

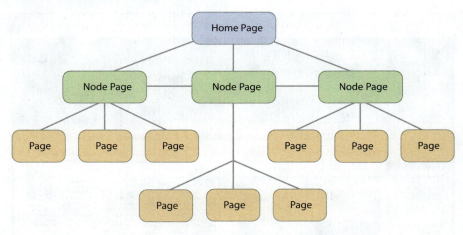

Figure 21.2: Websites are spatial rather than linear. They allow readers to move in a variety of different directions. In this example, readers can go directly to any of three pages from a node page without going through other pages.

wade through too many pages, you risk losing them. If you make them work too hard, they will grow frustrated and give up.

Step 1: Develop the Content

When you write for the web, you should start out by clearly defining your message's *subject, purpose, readers,* and the *context.* You want to be especially clear about the boundaries of your subject and the purpose you want to achieve.

> **Subject and Purpose:** We want to create a website that explains the paleontology research being pursued at Dinosaur National Monument and allows paleontologists to network with each other.

> **Subject and Purpose:** This webpage will offer biographical information on the Nobel Physicist Richard Feynman.

Keep in mind that you need to focus on your subject and get to the point. You may feel like you have unlimited space on a website or webpage, but always remember that online readers are impatient. They will jump to something else as soon as your webpage or website becomes unfocused.

To help you generate new ideas and content, you can use invention strategies like logical mapping, freewriting, brainstorming, and the Five-W and How questions to determine what will go on each page. Then, do research with electronic, print, and empirical sources to collect facts, observations, and data about your subject.

Step 2: Organize and Draft Your Webpage or Website

As you begin organizing and drafting your material, you should concentrate on including only the information your readers need to know. Space may seem unlimited in a website but your readers will quickly grow impatient if you aren't giving them what they need.

A typical webpage will have an opening and a body.

> **Opening**—Each page should begin with a brief opening paragraph, typically one to three sentences, that clearly identifies the subject, purpose, and main point of the page.

> **Body**—The body of the webpage will usually include only about two to five paragraphs. A good guideline is to keep the complete content of each page below one and a half screens. In other words, readers should not need to scroll down more than half a screen to read all the information on the page.

Occasionally, webpages will include a closing paragraph or conclusion that restates the main point of the page. However, webpages written for technical workplaces often don't have closing paragraphs. The page ends when the need-to-know information has been provided.

Adding links is a good way to keep webpages focused and brief. Instead of explaining at length an idea or concept, you can create a link to a webpage where you offer more information. Likewise, instead of providing longer examples to illustrate your ideas, use a link to take your readers to other pages or outside websites that offer those examples.

Step 3: Choose the Style and Design of Your Webpage or Website

Always remember that readers of websites are "raiding" for information. So, the style needs to help them quickly access the information they need. Here are some strategies for improving the style of your website.

> **Keep sentences short**—On average, sentences in websites should be shorter than sentences in paper-based documents.

> **Keep paragraphs short**—Paragraphs should be kept to a few sentences. That way, readers can scan each paragraph in a glance.

> **Links should reflect titles**—When readers click on a link, the title of the selected page should be the same as the link they clicked.

> **Create a consistent tone**—The tone of the webpage should reflect the subject you are discussing. Ideas that are exciting should be presented with an excited tone, while serious material should use a serious tone. As described in Chapter 16 on "Using Plain and Persuasive Style," you can use logical mapping and other stylistic strategies to create specific tones or themes in your writing.

Design is also an important component to help people find the information they are looking for. The *interface* of your website concerns how the pages look on the screen and how readers will navigate the site.

> **Balance information on the screen**—Each webpage should look balanced. Items on the left side of the screen should be balanced with items on the right.

> **Alignment**—Aligned items on each webpage will help readers identify different levels of information in the interface.

> **Grouping**—Items that are near each other on the screen will be seen as "grouped." So, if items are related, put them near each other. If they are not related, separate them.

Consistency—Each page in the website should look similar to the others, so readers can quickly locate the new information on each page.

Contrast—Contrast is helpful for sharpening the boundaries between images and text, headings and text, and text and the background.

The interface shown in Figure 21.3, for example, demonstrates all of these principles successfully. Notice how the text is balanced from side to side. Information is also aligned in clear vertical lines, and you can see where specific information has been grouped into larger blocks. Meanwhile, consistency and contrast are used to make the interface interesting but consistent.

These five design principles should be used to develop a consistent interface, called a template, for your webpages. The template will give your website a standardized, predictable design, allowing your readers to quickly locate the information they are seeking.

Link

For more information on designing interfaces, see Chapter 17, page 451.

A Well-Designed Interface

Good contrast, making the text easy to read

Good grouping putting related information together in blocks

Figure 21.3: This home page uses all the design principles successfully. Notice how the interface uses balance, alignment, grouping, consistency, and contrast to create an attractive and functional page.

Good balance, using design features in ways that offset each other on the screen

Good alignment, creating a vertical line of items

Good consistency, with similar items designed the same

Source: National Oceanic and Atmospheric Administration (NOAA), http://www.noaa.gov.

Step 4: Add Images

Websites are visual documents, so you should look for opportunities to use photos, graphs, and charts to help explain or illustrate important concepts.

Images for your website can be saved as separate files on your computer and on the server. These files can include any pictures, graphs, or drawings you might want to include on your webpage. They also include elements of the interface, such as banners on the screens, corporate logos, and icons. Images can be saved in a variety of *file formats*. The two formats most commonly used for websites are *jpeg* and *gif* formats (Figure 21.4).

> **jpeg (joint photographic experts group)** — The jpeg file format is widely used for photographs and illustrations with many colors. Images in jpeg format can use millions of different colors, allowing them to better capture the subtleties of photographs.
>
> **gif (graphic interchange format)** — The gif format is primarily used for illustrations, logos, and simple graphics. Gif images can use a maximum of only 256 colors, making them less useful for photographs.

You can tell the difference between jpeg and gif files by the extensions on their file names. A jpeg file will have the extension ".jpg" added to it (e.g., cougarpic.jpg), and a gif file will have the extension ".gif" added (e.g., cougarpic.gif).

Step 5: Anticipate the Needs of Transcultural Readers

On the web, your information will be available worldwide. Of course, you can't anticipate the needs of all potential readers around the world, but you can make your website more usable in a few important ways.

Two Major Types of Screen-Based Images

Figure 21.4: Most images on websites use either the jpeg or the gif format. The image of Hurricane Katrina on the left is a jpeg. The Purdue logo on the right is a gif.

Sources: NASA, http://rapidfire.sci.gsfc.nasa.gov/gallery/?search=katrina, and Purdue University.

Use common words—Try to use words that are commonly defined in English. The meanings of slang and jargon words change quickly, sometimes leaving international readers confused.

Avoid clichés and colloquialisms—Informal American English includes phrases like "piece of cake" or "miss the boat" that might be meaningless to people from other cultures. Also, sports metaphors like "kickoff meeting" or "hit a home run" sound very odd to people who are not familiar with American football and baseball.

Avoid cultural icons—Symbols, especially religious symbols, should be avoided where possible and carefully used where necessary.

Minimize humor—Humor does not translate well across cultures because most jokes or funny sayings are culturally dependent. So, attempts to be funny on your website might be offensive or just confusing.

Translate the website—If your company regularly does business with people from a specific country or culture, you should translate your website into the readers' language. Otherwise, transcultural readers can use Google Translate or Bing Translator to convert your website into their own languages (Figure 21.5).

Chapter 2 discusses writing for transcultural audiences in more depth. In most cases, these guidelines for writing for transcultural readers are applicable to websites also.

Link

For more information on writing for international and transcultural readers, go to Chapter 2, page 24.

Translating a Website

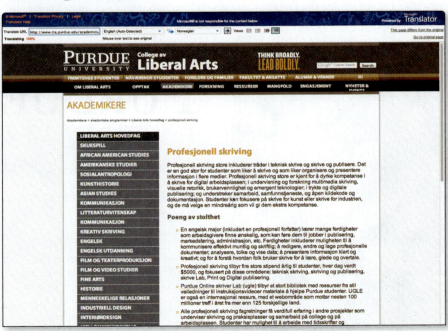

Figure 21.5: Here is a Norwegian translation of a webpage about the Professional Writing program at Purdue. This translation was made by Bing Translator.

Source: Free Online Translation Tool: Bing screenshot, Bing Translator 291.eda896321. Microsoft Corporation. Copyright 2014. http://www.bing.com/translator

Uploading the Website

Files from the original computer start here.

The files are moved to the server in this window.

Figure 21.6: An FTP program copies files from your computer's hard drive to a server. The server is connected to the Internet.

Source: SmartFTP, http://www.smartftp.com

Step 6: Upload Your Website

To make your website available to the public, you need to upload it to a server—a large computer that connects your computer to the Internet. Before uploading to the server, most writers of websites prefer to complete the website on their computer's hard drive. Then they use a file transfer protocol (FTP) software program to copy the whole website to the server at once (Figure 21.6).

Increasingly, universities and corporations are making this process easier by creating a special WWW folder for each person or division on a server. To upload your website, you only need to move the files from your hard drive to the WWW folder.

When you copy your webpage files, don't forget to also copy your image files at the same time. If the image files are not included with the webpage files, the pictures, illustrations, graphs, and other images you want placed on your website will not appear.

Using Social Networking in the Workplace

Until recently, people debated whether companies should allow employees to use social networking sites at work. Managers were concerned that their employees would be distracted by their Facebook accounts or Twitter feeds. Today, companies have figured out that these social networking tools are useful for developing new clients and building customer loyalty.

You should have two social networking sites. Your personal site, such as Facebook or Instagram, should be for staying in touch with your friends. Your professional site, such as LinkedIn, should be used exclusively for your professional life.

Your company or team may also keep one or more corporate Facebook or Twitter sites that you can use to collaborate with co-workers or communicate with clients.

Step 1: Create Your Social Networking Accounts

Starting a social networking site is easy. When you have decided which ones would work best for you, go to their websites and select "Sign up for an Account" or a similar option. For example, Figure 21.7 shows the homepage for LinkedIn, which is a social networking site for professionals.

To start an account, you will need to enter some basic information. The site will then lead you through the set-up process.

Step 2: Choose Your Friends (Wisely)

If you already have a social networking site, you probably have a long list of friends, including people you may or may not know personally. As you start your professional life, you should be more selective about who has access to your site. You want to remove any people you don't know or individuals who might cause a future or present employer to question your judgment.

A Social Networking Site

Figure 21.7: LinkedIn is a popular social networking site. LinkedIn is similar to Facebook, except it's for professional networking.

Source: LinkedIn, http://www.LinkedIn.com.

Step 3: Maintain Your Site

You should check your social networking site regularly to keep it clean and up to date. You should never assume that your personal website is a "safe place" from recruiters and supervisors. Today, recruiters are finding ways to access personal sites as they do background checks on possible employees. Meanwhile, it's easy for someone to forward something from your social networking site to one of your supervisors. So you don't want to say anything or post something that might cause them to question your judgment.

Link

To learn more about collaborating with co-workers, turn to Chapter 3, page 40.

Step 4: Collaborate with Others, But Carefully

You can collaborate with your coworkers through Facebook and other social networking sites, but you need to be extra careful about posting anything that might be proprietary information. Any proprietary information should be handled through a more secure medium, like print or secure forms of e-mail.

Step 5: Communicate with Your Company's "Fans"

Your company may also have an official presence on sites like Facebook or Twitter. If you are asked or allowed to contribute to the corporate site, you need to first understand why the company has created the site. Many companies see social networking as a way to enhance their brand and build customer loyalty. So they are generally looking for ways to improve their image and perhaps counter negative images from other social networking accounts.

Or, your company may be looking for ways to interact with its customers, especially ones who choose to sign up as "fans." Loyal customers can be a good source of feedback and suggestions for improvement. Plus, they can be among the first indicators if there is a problem with the company's products or services.

To keep these fans happy, you should do three things regularly.

KEEP ADDING FRESH MATERIAL TO THE SITE   The fans on a corporate site need fresh material to keep them coming back. If a site goes cold for even a few days, they will stop visiting it. So, on a daily or weekly basis, try to give them product news, chances to do polls, and questions they can respond to.

ANSWER POSTS FROM FANS   People who take the time to visit a corporate social networking site and leave comments want to be acknowledged. If they offer a compliment, respond with a thank you or some additional information about the product or service. If they have a complaint, try to explain how the company is handling the situation and perhaps improving it.

SHOW FANS HOW THEIR COMMENTS ARE BEING USED   Sometimes fans have good ideas for improving the product or service. Where possible, mention how ideas submitted by fans are being used by people at the company.

Creating Blogs and Microblogs

Blogs are websites that contain a series of posts written by a person or a team of people. Usually, they include written entries, but there are also an increasing number of photo blogs, video blogs, and audio blogs on the Internet.

Blogs are usually more secure than social networking sites, so supervisors and coworkers often use them for making announcements, soliciting new ideas, updating colleagues on projects, and gathering feedback about new ideas and proposed changes in policies.

Microblogs, like Twitter, are similar to regular blogs, except they limit posts to a specific character amount, like 140 characters. In technical workplaces, microblogs are especially useful because they allow colleagues, clients, and customers to "follow" you, your team, or your company, receiving updates when things happen. You can also follow others. Managers are increasingly using microblogs to send out workplace announcements, set up meetings, or alter schedules.

Both blogs and microblogs can be used for collaborating with your team on a project. Here are some tips for setting up and using blogging and microblogging sites.

Step 1: Choose Your Blog's Host Site

You shouldn't need to pay for a blogging site. Some popular free blogging host sites include Blogger, WordPress, Blogsome, and Moveable Type (Figure 21.8). Each one has its strengths and weaknesses, so you might look at them all to determine which one will fit your needs and reach the people you want to speak to.

Creating Your Blog

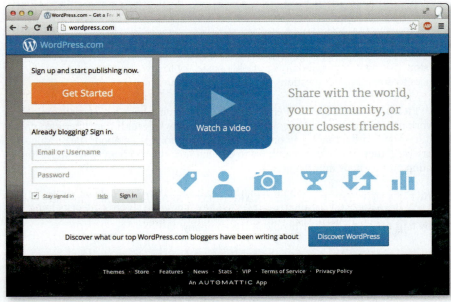

Figure 21.8: Starting a blog is simple. Choose the blog host site that best fits you. Then, sign up for an account. Here is the sign-up page from WordPress, one of the more common blog host sites.

Source: WordPress.com (Automattic, Inc.), http://www.wordpress.com.

Twitter is still the dominant microblogging site, but there are others like App.net, Tumblr, and Plurk that you might consider trying out. These sites do basically the same things as Twitter, though some offer more capability with images, sound, and video than others.

Step 2: Write and Maintain Your Blog

On your blogging site, look for the buttons on the screen that allow you to "compose," "edit," and "publish" what you write. You can also personalize your blog by adding photographs, profiles, polls, newsreels, icons, and other gadgets.

Your blog or microblog should be regularly maintained, just like your personal networking site. You can use it to share your ideas and comment on what is happening around you. Keep in mind, though, that a blog can be a public site. If you want to blog about things happening at work, be careful about any information you share or opinions you express. You don't want to say or reveal anything that will cause problems for you, your co-workers, and your supervisors. Also, you don't want to share information that might give your company's competitors proprietary information or some other kind of advantage.

Your blog and microblog are not places to share gossip or complain about people at work. Your unkind comments can be forwarded to people you didn't intend to offend.

Step 3: Let Others Join the Conversation

The initial settings for your blogging site will give you strict control over the content of your blog. You and you alone will be able to post comments on the site. As you grow more comfortable, though, you might want to loosen up your settings to allow others to add comments. If so, you should first decide what kinds of people should be able to make comments on your blog. Then, in your settings, identify the "registered users" whom you give permission to comment on your blog. Never open your settings to allow "anyone" to comment, because trolls and spammers will contribute posts that annoy or embarrass you.

Making Internet Videos and Podcasts

Until recently, Internet video sites like YouTube and podcasting sites like Podcast Alley were mainly for posting funny home videos and amateur music. Now, these sites are widely used by corporations to communicate with clients, customers, and the press.

Some of the more popular video sites include YouTube, MySpace Videos, MSN Video, Yahoo! Vimeo, Veoh, Dailymotion, Google Video, Hulu, Metacafe, and blip.tv. Some popular podcasting sites include Podcast Alley, iTunes, LibSyn, PodOmatic, Amazon S3, and Buzzsprout.

More than likely, your company's marketing team will be responsible for putting videos and podcasts on the Internet, but you may find yourself creating or helping to make these kinds of broadcasts yourself. Here's how to do it.

Link

For more information on creating a presentation, turn to Chapter 20, page 521.

Step 1: Write the Script

Before making a video or podcast, especially for workplace purposes, you need to do some careful preparation. Recording a video or podcast requires more than just setting up a camera or microphone. Instead, you should first think about your topic, purpose, readers, and the contexts of use for your video or podcast. Then, research the content and draft out a script. You should also make some strategic decisions about where your video will be filmed and what kinds of background scenery you will need.

As you draft your script, keep it as concise as possible. Long, rambling videos and audios tend to bore the audience. Keep the message brief and to the point. Avoid writing or doing anything that will put you or your company in a bad light. Trying to be funny can be risky, especially in corporate videos and podcasts. You also want to avoid broadcasting something that might help your company's competitors or give them information to use against you or your company.

Step 2: Shoot the Video or Record the Podcast

Recording a quality video or podcast is rarely something you can do in one try. Instead, you should record a few or even several versions of your video or podcast. Then, afterward, you can splice together the best parts of each recording.

If you are recording other people, you should explain ahead of time what you want them to do. In other words, be a director of the film. Explain what each scene, perhaps each line, is intended to accomplish. Then, walk them through the script a couple times, so they know their parts.

Above all, keep your video as brief as possible. As soon as you or your speakers start to ramble, you will lose the audience. Focus on the need-to-know information for the product, issue, or problem you are addressing. Trim away any extra information.

Step 3: Edit Your Video or Podcast

One major difference between an amateurish effort and a professional product is the editing of the video and audio. Some good video editing software packages include Corel VideoStudio, MS Movie Maker, Adobe Premiere, Final Cut, and iMovie. The most common sound editing software packages for podcasts include Adobe Audition, Audacity, GarageBand, and Ableton Live (Figure 21.9). One or more of these editing tools may have already been preloaded onto your computer, so look for them in your applications before you buy something new. Otherwise, there are free versions of audio editors widely available on the web.

Editing software will allow you to cut and paste segments of your broadcast to eliminate parts that you don't want to include in the final product. You can also add titles and transitions, while eliminating any background hiss.

Step 4: Upload Your Video or Podcast

When you have finished editing your video or podcast, go to the host website, like YouTube or Podcast Alley, where you want it to appear. The site will ask you to create an account, and it will ask for some basic information.

Once your account is created, click the "upload" button on the screen. The site will lead you through the process. More than likely, it will ask you for a title and description of your video or podcast. You will also have an opportunity to include some keywords or "tags" that will help people find your video.

Editing Your Podcast

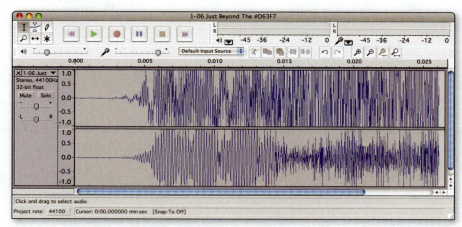

Source: Audacity, http://audacity.sourceforge.net.

Figure 21.9: You might already have video and editing software installed on your computer. Here is the editing screen from Audacity, which is a good podcast editing tool.

Writing Articles for Wikis

Wikis are websites that let users add and modify the content. You probably know some of the popular wikis, like Wikipedia, WikiHow, and Wikicars. In the technical workplace, wikis are becoming important tools for keeping documentation and specifications up to date and doing customer service. In fact, user-generated wikis are often better than corporate-run websites for troubleshooting.

Step 1: Write the Text

There isn't anything special about writing a wiki article. You should begin by identifying your subject, purpose, readers, and the contexts in which your article would be used. Research your subject thoroughly and draft the article. Add any graphics or videos. Below your article, you should also create a reference list of your sources and identify any "external links" that readers might want to explore on your topic. Then, edit and proofread your work carefully.

In most cases, you should compose and edit your article completely in a word processor. It is possible to compose in the wiki itself, but the interface is often not as flexible as your word processor, making the work much harder.

Step 2: Post Your Article

On most wiki homepages, you can find a button that says something like "Create an Article" or "Start the X Article." When you are ready to upload your contribution, click on that button. Then, cut and paste your article into the window provided. Before saving your article in the wiki, edit and proofread one more time. It's easier to catch and correct problems at this point, rather than trying to fix them after the article is posted.

Step 3: Return to Edit Your Articles

Other people will have the ability to rewrite and edit your wiki article. That's what wikis are all about. So you should regularly return to your articles, especially ones on contentious issues, to make sure no one has added anything inaccurate. The nice thing about wikis is that other people will add to and refine what you wrote. You might be pleasantly surprised by what other information people have provided.

WHAT YOU
NEED TO KNOW

- The ability to write for the web is often an expectation of new hires at technical companies.

- The basic features of a website are a home page, node pages, basic pages, and navigational pages.

- Choose a consistent style to make your website easier to scan and interpret.

- The design of the website should follow the five principles of design: balance, alignment, grouping, consistency, and contrast.

- Corporate social networking sites need to stay fresh and interactive with their "fans."

- Blogs and microblogs are websites that allow you to make regular commentaries about issues that interest you.

- You can create videos and podcasts with a variety of software products, including ones that are probably already loaded on your computer.

- A wiki is a website that lets users add articles and modify the existing content.

EXERCISES
AND PROJECTS

Individual or Team Projects

1. On paper or a whiteboard, map out the contents of a website you find on the Internet. Identify its home page, node pages, basic pages, and navigational pages. Then, in a presentation to your class, discuss the organization of the website. Show its strengths and identify any places where the website's organization might be improved.

2. Set up a blog or microblog of your own. Go to one of the free blogging sites, like Blogger, Blogspot, or Wordpress. Sign up for an account. Then, each day for a week, post at least one comment related to your major or future career. Your posts can be comments about things that are happening in your field, including comments about news articles or companies you have found on the Internet. Send the blog address to your instructor.

3. Find a website at your college or workplace that is ineffective. Write a report to a specific reader in which you discuss the shortcomings of the site and make recommendations for improvement (you don't need to send the report). In your report, consider the content, organization, style, and design of the site. In your recommendations, show your sample reader pages and organizational schemes that would improve the site.

Collaborative Project

Imagine that your group has been hired to create or renovate the Facebook site for your college or university. Start out by first exploring the rhetorical situation that shapes how this site works and how people use it (subject, purpose, readers, context of use). What are its current strengths? What are its weaknesses?

Now, rethink the rhetorical situation to sharpen the focus of the site. What kind of content do you think would be appropriate for the readers of this site? What do you think the site should try to achieve? How can the site be improved to attract the kinds of readers it seeks? How could the site get these readers involved and keep them coming back?

Write a two-page proposal to your university's public relations department in which you describe how the Facebook site could be improved. Describe the problems with the current site, show how the site could be improved, and explain why making these changes would make the site more effective.

To make this collaborative project more challenging, try to accomplish all this work through Skype or Facetime and a file-sharing service like Google Drive or Dropbox.

Visit **My**Writing**Lab** for a Post-test and more technical writing resources.

My Boss Might Not "Like" This

Henry Blackburg was a biomedical engineer for a manufacturer of CAT scan machines in Stamford, Connecticut. For the most part, he was good at keeping his professional and personal lives separate. People at work didn't even know he was gay, and he liked it that way. Frankly, it was none of their business. When they asked about whether he was seeing anyone or whether they could fix him up with a female date, he would tell them he was dating someone in New York, which was true. He went to New York often because it was a place where he could "be himself."

Henry's boss, John Hamilton, occasionally made negative comments about gays, and he was not particularly open-minded about most social issues. However, Henry didn't think he would be fired or held back if his boss found out about his sexual orientation, but he didn't want to take any chances.

Facebook was Henry's lifeline to the gay community in New York. It was how he stayed in touch and found out where social events were going to happen. His friends would also post photos from weekend parties. They were tame by most standards, but it was obvious that these weren't heterosexual events.

Until last week, all was well. Henry's boss knew about Facebook, but he didn't have an account. The company, however, encouraged everyone to get on Facebook to see the new corporate fansite. So Henry's boss signed up and went a little Facebook crazy. Facebook began prompting him to friend people from his high school, university, and, yes, his workplace. So, Henry received a friend request from his boss.

Henry didn't know what to do. He wasn't embarrassed about being gay, but he wanted to keep that aspect of his personal life separate from his work life. Plus, he didn't want to "straighten up" his Facebook site to keep his boss from figuring out he was gay. There was no way he could be a friend with his boss and continue to stay connected with his real friends.

Henry ignored his boss's friend request, hoping it was just a passing thing. A few days later in a meeting, though, his boss announced that he would be sending work-related updates over Facebook, so if anyone hadn't responded to his friend request, they should do so right away.

Other people in the room looked uneasy. Henry realized he wasn't the only person who didn't want to be a "friend" with the boss on Facebook.

How do you think Henry should handle this situation?

Grammar and Punctuation Guide

This guide is a reference tool to help you handle mechanical issues in writing. The guide has two parts: (1) The Top Ten Grammar Mistakes, and (2) a Punctuation Refresher. The Top Ten Grammar Mistakes will show you how to avoid the ten most common grammar mistakes. The Punctuation Refresher will update you on punctuation rules, showing you how to use punctuation marks properly.

Consistent correct grammar and punctuation are essential if you are going to clearly express yourself, especially in technical documents and presentations. Any grammar and punctuation mistakes in your writing will undermine even your best ideas. Moreover, readers will make judgments about you and your work based on your grammar and punctuation. If you send a document littered with grammatical errors to your supervisor or your company's clients, they will question your attention to quality, your commitment to the project, and even your intelligence.

Mastering basic grammar and punctuation does not take long. If you haven't worked on improving your grammar since high school, take some time to refresh these rules in your mind.

The Top Ten Grammar Mistakes

Don't be one of those people who is always apologizing with statements like, "I'm not good at grammar." These kinds of statements do not excuse your grammatical problems; they only indicate that you have not taken the time to learn basic grammar rules. If you are one of those grammar apologists, commit to spending the little time necessary to master the rules. An hour or two of study will make grammatical problems disappear.

Comma Splice

A significant percentage of grammar errors are comma splices. A comma splice occurs when two complete sentences are joined together with a comma.

Incorrect

The machine kept running, we pulled the plug.

We moved the telescope just a little to the left, the new nova immediately came into view.

In these examples, notice how the parts before and after the commas could stand alone as sentences. The comma is *splicing* these sentences together.

How can you fix these comma splices? There are a few options.

Correct

The machine kept running, so we pulled the plug.

We moved the telescope just a little to the left, and the new nova immediately came into focus.

(Add a conjunction [so, and, but, yet] after the comma.)

Correct

The machine kept running; we pulled the plug.

We moved the telescope just a little to the left; the new nova immediately came into focus.

> (Replace the comma with a semicolon.)

The machine kept running. We pulled the plug.

We moved the telescope just a little to the left. The new nova immediately came into focus.

> (Replace the comma with a period and create two grammatically correct sentences.)

The machine kept running; therefore, we pulled the plug.

We moved the telescope just a little to the left; consequently, the new nova immediately came into view.

> (Replace the comma with a semicolon and add a conjunctive adverb [*therefore, consequently, however, thus*].)

Since the machine kept running, we pulled the plug.

Because we moved the telescope just a little to the left, the new nova immediately came into view.

> (Insert a subordinating conjunction [*since, because*] at the beginning of the sentence.)

Run-On Sentence

The run-on sentence error is a close cousin of the comma splice. In a run-on sentence, two or more sentences have been crammed into one.

Incorrect

The computer suddenly crashed it had a virus.

The Orion nebula lies about 1500 light-years from the sun the nebula is a blister on the side of the Orion molecular cloud that is closest to us.

Run-on sentences are corrected the same way comma splices are corrected. You can use conjunctions (*and, but, or, nor, for, because, yet, however, furthermore, hence, moreover, therefore*) to fix them. Or, you can divide the sentences with a semicolon or period.

Correct

The computer suddenly crashed because it had a virus.

The computer suddenly crashed; we guessed it had a virus.

The computer suddenly crashed. It had a virus.

The Orion nebula lies about 1500 light-years from the sun. The nebula is a blister on the side of the Orion molecular cloud that is closest to us.

The Orion nebula lies about 1500 light-years from the sun; moreover, the nebula is a blister on the side of the Orion molecular cloud that is closest to us.

In most cases, run-on sentences are best fixed by adding a period, thus separating the two sentences completely.

Fragment

A fragment, as the name suggests, is an incomplete sentence. A fragment typically occurs when the sentence is missing a subject or a verb, or it lacks a complete thought:

Incorrect

Because the new motherboard was not working.

> (This fragment contains a subject and verb but does not express a complete thought.)

The report missing important data.

> (This fragment contains a subject but no verb.)

The first fragment can be corrected in the following ways:

Correct

The new motherboard was not working.

> (Remove the conjunction [*because*].)

Because the new motherboard was not working, we returned it to the manufacturer.

> (Join the fragment to a complete sentence [an independent clause].)

The second fragment can be corrected in the following ways:

Correct

The report was missing important data.

> (Insert a verb [*was*].)

The report, missing important data, was corrected immediately.

> (Insert a verb [*was corrected*] and an adverb [*immediately*].)

Sometimes writers, especially creative writers, will use fragments for the purpose of jarring their readers. In technical writing, you don't want to jar your readers. Leave the creative uses of fragments to creative writers.

Dangling Modifier

A dangling modifier occurs when a phrase does not properly explain the subject.

Incorrect

While eating lunch, the acid boiled over and destroyed Lisa's testing apparatus.

> (The acid is apparently eating lunch while it does damage to the testing apparatus. That's some acid!)

After driving to Cleveland, our faithful cat was a welcome sight.

(The cat apparently drove the car to Cleveland. Bad kitty!)

These kinds of errors are common—and often funny. To avoid them (and your readers' grins), make sure that the introductory phrase is modifying the subject of the sentence. Here are corrections of these sentences:

Correct

While Lisa was eating lunch, the acid boiled over and destroyed her testing apparatus.

After driving to Cleveland, we were glad to see our faithful cat.

Notice how the information before the comma modifies the subject of the sentence, which immediately follows the comma.

Subject-Verb Disagreement

svd

Subject-verb disagreements occur when the subject of the sentence does not match the verb. Singular subjects should go with singular verbs, while plural subjects should have plural verbs. Here are a few sentences with subject-verb disagreement:

Incorrect

The windows, we discovered after some investigation, was the reason for heat loss in the house.

(The singular verb *was* does not match the plural subject *windows*.)

The robin, unlike sparrows and cardinals, do not like sunflower seeds.

(The subject *robin* is singular, while the verb phrase *do not like* is plural.)

Either my DVD player or my stereo were blowing the fuse.

(The subject *DVD player or my stereo* is singular, while the verb *were* is plural.)

Here are the correct sentences:

Correct

The windows, we discovered after some investigation, were the reason for heat loss in the house.

Robins, unlike sparrows and cardinals, do not like sunflower seeds.

Either my DVD player or my stereo was blowing the fuse.

When *or* is used in the subject, as it is in the third example, the verb needs to agree with the noun that follows *or*. In this sentence, the use of *or* means we are treating the DVD player and the stereo separately. So a singular verb is needed.

This third example brings up an interesting question: What if one or both of the words flanking the *or* is plural? Again, the answer is that the verb will agree with the noun that comes after the *or*.

The speeding cars or the reckless motorcyclist was responsible for the accident.

Either the falling branches or the high winds were responsible for the damage.

Collective nouns (*crowd, network, group*) that name a group as a whole take a singular verb:

The group uses a detailed questionnaire to obtain useful feedback.

Pronoun-Antecedent Disagreement

Pronoun-antecedent disagreement usually occurs when a writer forgets whether the subject is plural or singular.

Incorrect

Anyone who thinks Wii is better than Sony PlayStation should have their head examined.

Like the scientists, we were sure the rocket was going to blast off, but it wasn't long before you knew it was a dud.

In these cases, words later in the sentence do not agree with pronouns earlier in the sentence. In the first sentence, *anyone* is singular while *their* is plural. In the second sentence, *we* is a first-person noun while *you* is a second-person pronoun. Here are a couple of ways to correct these sentences:

Correct

People who think Wii is better than Sony PlayStation should have their heads examined.

(The subject is made plural [*people*] and an s is added to *head* to make it plural.)

Anyone who thinks Wii is better than Sony PlayStation should have his or her head examined.

(The subject [*anyone*] is kept singular, and the plural *their* is changed to the singular *his or her*.)

Like the scientists, we were sure the rocket was going to blast off, but it wasn't long before I knew it was a dud.

(The *you* was changed to *I,* keeping the whole sentence in first person.)

Like the scientists, we were sure the rocket was going to blast off, but it wasn't long before we knew it was a dud.

(The *you* was changed to *we,* again keeping the whole sentence in first person.)

In most cases, the secret to avoiding these subtle errors is to check whether the pronouns later in the sentence match the subject earlier in the sentence.

Faulty Parallelism

Lists can be difficult to manage in sentences. A good rule of thumb is to remember that each part of the list needs to be parallel in structure to every other part of the list.

Incorrect After the interview, we went out for dinner, had a few drinks, and a few jokes were told.

> (In this sentence, the third part of the list, *jokes were told,* is not parallel to the first two parts, *went out for dinner* and *had a few drinks.*)

Our survey shows that people want peace, want to own a home, and that many are worried about their jobs.

> (In this sentence, the second item in the list, *want to own a home,* is not parallel to the first and third items.)

To correct these sentences, make the items in the list parallel.

Correct After the interview, we went out for dinner, had a few drinks, and told a few jokes.

Our survey shows that people want peace, most want to own a home, and many are worried about their jobs.

To avoid faulty parallelism, pay special attention to any lists you write. Check whether the items are parallel in phrasing.

pc Pronoun Case Error (*I* and *Me, We* and *Us*)

Often, people are confused about when to use *I* or *me* and *we* or *us.* Here is a simple way to make the right decision about which one to use: If you are using the word as the subject of the sentence or phrase, use *I* or *we.* Anywhere else, use *me* or *us.*

Incorrect Jones's team and me went down to the factory floor to see how things were going.

> (The word *me* is misused here because it is part of the subject of the sentence. In this case, *I* should have been used.)

When the roof fell in, the manager asked Fred and I to start developing a plan for cleaning up the mess.

> (The word *I* is misused in this sentence because the phrase *Fred and I* is not the subject. In this case, the phrase *Fred and me* should have been used.)

Things were getting pretty ugly in there, so us unimportant people slipped out the back door.

> (The phrase *us unimportant people* is the subject of the clause that follows the comma. Therefore, the phrase *we unimportant people* should have been used.)

Remember, if the word is being used as the subject of a phrase or sentence, use *I* or *we.* Anywhere else, use *me* or *us.* Here are the correct versions of these sentences:

Correct Jones's team and I went down to the factory floor to see how things were going.

When the roof fell in, the manager asked Fred and me to start developing a plan for cleaning up the mess.

Things were getting pretty ugly in there, so we unimportant people slipped out the back door.

Shifted Tense

Sentences can be written in past, present, or future tense. In most cases, neighboring sentences should reflect the same tense. Shifting tenses can make readers feel like they are hopping back and forth in time.

Incorrect

Few countries possess nuclear weapons, but many countries tried to build them.

(Here, *possess* is in present tense, while *tried* is in past tense.)

Parts flew everywhere on the factory floor as the robot finally breaks down.

(Here, *flew* is in past tense, while *breaks* is in present tense.)

The advances in microchip technology allowed electronics to become much smaller, which leads to today's tiny electronic devices.

(The word *allowed* is in past tense, while *leads* is in present tense.)

We found ourselves staring in disbelief. The excavation site is vandalized by people who wanted to have a campfire.

(Here, *found* is in past tense, while *is vandalized* is in present tense.)

To revise these sentences, make the tenses consistent.

Correct

Few countries possess nuclear weapons, but many countries are trying to build them.

Parts flew everywhere on the factory floor as the robot finally broke down.

The advances in microchip technology allowed electronics to become much smaller, which led to today's tiny electronic devices.

We found ourselves staring in disbelief. The excavation site had been vandalized by people who wanted to have a campfire.

Tense shifts are not always wrong. Sometimes a sentence or phrase needs to be in a different tense than those around it. When checking sentences for unnecessary tense shifts, look for places where tense shifts cause more confusion than clarity.

Vague Pronoun

Occasionally, a writer uses a pronoun, seeming to know exactly who or what the pronoun refers to, while readers are left scratching their heads, trying to figure out what the writer means.

Incorrect   Fred and Javier went to the store, and then he went home.

(Whom does *he* refer to, Fred or Javier?)

They realized that the inspection of the building was not going well. It was fundamentally unsound.

(In this sentence, *It* could refer to the inspection or the building.)

We really had a great week. Our program review went well, and we made huge strides toward finishing the project. This is why we are taking all of you to lunch.

(What does *This* refer to? The great week? The program review? The huge strides? All of them?)

The camera captured the explosion as it ripped apart the car. It was an amazing experience.

(In these sentences, the multiple uses of *it* are confusing. In the first sentence, *it* might refer to the camera or the explosion. In the second sentence, *It* might refer to the taking of the picture or the explosion. Or, the final *It* might just be a weak subject for the second sentence and doesn't refer directly to anything in the previous sentence.)

Correcting these sentences mostly involves rewording them to avoid the vague pronoun.

Correct   Fred and Javier went to the store, and then Javier went home.

They realized that the inspection of the building was not going well. The inspection process was fundamentally unsound.

We really had a great week. Our program review went well, and we made huge strides toward finishing the project. For these reasons, we are taking all of you to lunch.

The camera captured the explosion as it ripped apart the car. Seeing the explosion was an amazing experience.

A common cause of vague pronoun use is the overuse of "It is . . . " and "This is . . . " to begin sentences. These kinds of sentences force readers to look back at the previous sentence to figure out what *It* or *This* refers to. In some cases, two or three possibilities might exist.

To avoid these problems, train yourself to avoid using "It is . . . " and "This is . . . " sentences. Occasionally, these sentences are fine, but some writers rely on them too much. You are better off minimizing their use in your writing.

Punctuation Refresher

More than likely, you already have a good sense of the punctuation rules. However, there are quirks and exceptions that you need to learn as your writing skills advance to a new level. So spend a little time here refreshing your memory on punctuation rules.

Period, Exclamation Point, Question Mark

Let's start with the most basic marks—the period, exclamation point, and question mark. These punctuation marks signal the end of a sentence, or a full stop.

> We need to test the T6 Robot on the assembly line.
>
> The acid leaked and burned through the metal plate beneath it!
>
> Where can we cut costs to bring this project under budget?

The period signals the end of a standard sentence. The exclamation point signals surprise or strong feelings. The question mark signals a query.

Periods can also be used with abbreviations and numbers.

> C.E.
>
> Feb.
>
> Fig. 8
>
> Dr. Valerie Hanks
>
> 56.21 cm

Question marks can also be used in a series.

> How will global warming affect this country? Will it flood coastal cities? Create drought in the southwest? Damage fragile ecosystems?

Using periods, exclamation points, and question marks with quotes

A common mistake with periods, exclamation points, and question marks is their misuse with quotation marks. In almost all cases, these punctuation marks are placed inside the quotation marks.

Incorrect   He said, "The audit team reported that we are in compliance".

We asked him, "Do you really think we are going to finish the project on time"?

Correct   He said, "The audit team reported that we are in compliance."

We asked him, "Do you really think we are going to finish the project on time?"

The one exception to this rule is when a quoted statement is placed within a question.

> Did he really say, "The company will be closing the Chicago office"?

Commas

In the English language, commas are the most flexible, useful, and therefore problematic punctuation mark. In most cases, a comma signals a pause in the flow of a sentence.

When he hiked in the mountains east of Ft. Collins, he always took along his compass and map to avoid getting lost.

> (This comma signals that an introductory clause is finished.)

My smartphone is a helpful organizing tool, and it makes a great paperweight too.

> (This comma signals that two independent clauses are joined with a conjunction [*and, yet, but, so, because*].)

Our company's CEO, the engineering genius, is scheduled to meet with us tomorrow.

> (These commas set off information that is not essential to understanding the sentence.)

We are, however, having some luck locating new sources of silicon on the open market.

> (These commas set off a conjunctive adverb [*therefore, however, furthermore, nevertheless, moreover*].)

The archaeological dig yielded pottery shards, scraping tools, and a cornmeal grinding stone.

> (These commas separate items in a series.)

Using commas with quotation marks

Using commas with quotation marks can be problematic. Just remember that commas almost always go before, not after, the quotation mark.

Albert Einstein said, "God does not play dice."

> (Here the comma sets off a speaker tag. Notice that the comma is placed before the quotation mark.)

"I'm having trouble hearing you," she said, "so I'm switching over to a new phone."

> (Again, the commas in this sentence offset the speaker tag. Note that both commas come before the quotation marks.)

Using commas in numbers, dates, and place names

Commas are also used with numbers, dates, and place names.

Reporters estimated that the rally drew nearly 10,000 people.

We first noticed the problem on January 10, 2009.

For great pizza you need to go to Uncle Pete's in Naperville, Illinois.

Removing excess commas

There is some flexibility in the use of commas. Many editors recommend an "open" punctuation style that eliminates commas where they do not help comprehension. For example, the following sentences are both correct:

> In minutes, she whipped up the most amazing apple pie.

> In minutes she whipped up the most amazing apple pie.

Here, the comma after *minutes* is not aiding understanding, so it can be removed. Be careful, though. Sometimes the lack of a comma can cause some confusion.

Confusing	Soon after leaving the airplane needed to turn back for mechanical reasons.
Not Confusing	Soon after leaving, the airplane needed to turn back for mechanical reasons.

Semicolon and Colon

Semicolons and colons are less common than periods and commas, but they can be helpful in some situations. In a sentence, semicolons and colons signal a partial stop.

The trick to using these marks properly is to remember this simple rule: In most cases, the phrase on either side of a semicolon or colon should be able to stand alone as a separate sentence (an independent clause).

> We were not pleased with the results of the study; however, we did find some interesting results that gave us ideas for new research.

> > (The semicolon joins two independent clauses. The second clause [the part starting with *however*] supports the first clause.)

> Commuting to work by car requires nerves of steel: Each mile brings you into contact with people who have no respect for the rules of the road.

> > (Here, the colon also divides two independent clauses. In this example, though, the colon signals that the two parts of the sentence are equivalent to each other.)

How do you know when to use a semicolon or a colon? It depends on whether the part of the sentence following the mark is *lesser than* or *equal to* the first part. If lesser, use the semicolon. If equal, use the colon.

If you want to avoid problems, use semicolons and colons only when necessary. When considering these punctuation marks in a sentence, you should ask yourself whether a period or a conjunction (*and, but, so, yet*) would make the sentence easier to understand. After all, joining sentences together with semicolons and colons can often create long, difficult-to-read sentences.

As with most punctuation rules, there are exceptions to the rule that semicolons and colons are used with independent clauses.

Using semicolons in a series

Semicolons can be used to punctuate complicated lists in a sentence.

> We have offices in Boston, Massachusetts; Freetown, New York; and Sedona, Arizona.

Using colons to lead off lists

Colons can be used to signal a list.

> Four steps are required to complete the process: (1) preparing the workspace, (2) assembling the model, (3) painting the model, and (4) checking quality.

> Keep in mind the following issues when searching for a job:
>
> - You can't get the job if you don't apply.
> - Jobs don't always go to the people with the most experience.
> - What makes you different makes you interesting.

Using colons in titles, numbers, and greetings

Colons are commonly used in titles of books and articles, in numbers, and in greetings in letters and memos.

> *The Awakening: The Irish Renaissance in Nineteenth-Century Boston*
>
> Genesis 2:18
>
> 11:45 A.M.
>
> They won by a 3:1 ratio.
>
> Dear Mr. Franklin:

Using semicolons and colons with quotation marks

Unlike commas and periods, semicolons and colons should appear after the quotation mark in a sentence.

> Land Commissioner George Hampton claimed, "The frogs will survive the draining of the lake"; but he was clearly wrong.

> One of my favorite chapters in Leopold's *A Sand County Almanac* is "Thinking Like a Mountain": This essay is his best work.

Whenever possible, though, you should avoid these kinds of situations. In both examples, the sentences could be rearranged or repunctuated to avoid awkward, though correct, uses of the semicolon or colon.

Misusing the colon

A common misuse of the colon is with an incomplete sentence.

Incorrect   The reasons for our dissatisfaction are: low quality, late work, and slow response.

> (The colon is misused because the phrase before the colon cannot stand alone as a sentence.)

For example:

> (Again, the phrase before the colon cannot stand alone as a sentence. In this case, a dash or comma should be used. Or, turn the phrase *For example* into a complete sentence.)

In his report, Bill Trimble claims: "We have a golden opportunity to enter the Japanese market."

> (Yet again, the information before the colon is not a sentence. In this case, a comma should have been used instead of the colon.)

As a rule, the information before the colon should *always* be able to stand alone as a complete sentence. Here are the correct versions of these sentences:

Correct

The reasons for our dissatisfaction are the following: low quality, late work, and slow response.

For example, consider these interesting situations:

In his report, Bill Trimble makes this important statement: "We have a golden opportunity to enter the Japanese market."

Notice how all three examples have independent clauses (full sentences) before the colon.

Apostrophe

The apostrophe has two important jobs in the English language: (1) to signal contractions and (2) to signal possession.

Using an apostrophe to signal a contraction

An apostrophe that signals a contraction identifies the place where two words have been fused and letters removed.

They're going to the store today.

He really isn't interested in the project.

They shouldn't have taken that road.

Contractions should be used only in informal writing. They signal a familiarity with the readers that could seem too informal in some situations. Some other common contractions include *won't, it's, I'm, you've, wouldn't,* and *couldn't.*

Using an apostrophe to signal possession

An apostrophe is also used to signal possession. With a singular noun, an *'s* is added to signal possession. Joint possession is usually signaled with an *s'*.

We have decided to take Anna's car to the convention.

The players' bats were missing before the game.

When plural nouns do not end in an *s,* you should use an *'s* to create the plural.

> We rode the children's bikes.

> The men's briefcases were left near the door.

When singular nouns end in an *s,* you should add an *'s* to show possession.

> They met in Mary Jones's office.

> Charles's computer was shorting out.

Using apostrophes to show possession with two or more nouns

When you are showing possession with multiple nouns, your use of the apostrophe depends on your meaning. If two nouns are acting as one unit, only the last noun needs an apostrophe to signal possession.

> We decided to accept Grim and Nether's proposal.

But if you are signaling possession for several separate nouns, each needs an apostrophe.

> I found it difficult to buy meaningful gifts for Jane's, Valerie's, and Charles's birthdays.

Using apostrophes to signal plurals of numbers, acronyms, and symbols

You can use apostrophes to signal plurals of numbers, acronyms, and symbols, but do so sparingly. Here are a couple of situations where apostrophes would be appropriate:

> The *a*'s just kept appearing when I typed *x*'s.

> Is it necessary to put ©'s on all copyrighted documents?

In most cases, though, do not include apostrophes to show a plural if they do not aid the meaning of the text.

> The police discovered a warehouse full of stolen TVs.

> The 1870s were a tough time for immigrants.

> In the basement, a crate of dead CPUs sat unnoticed.

Quotation Marks

Quotation marks signal that you are using someone else's words. Quotation marks should not be used to highlight words. If you need to highlight words, use italics.

Using quotation marks to signal a quote

Quotation marks are used to frame an exact quotation from another person.

> In *The Panda's Thumb,* Gould states, "The world, unfortunately, rarely matches our hopes and consistently refuses to behave in a reasonable manner."

"Not true" was her only response to my comment.

He asked me, "Are you really working on that project?"

Use quotation marks only when you are copying someone else's exact words. If you are only paraphrasing what someone else said, do not use quotation marks.

In *The Panda's Thumb,* Gould argues that nature often does not meet our expectations, nor does it operate in predictable ways.

She rejected my comment as untrue.

He asked me whether I was working on the project.

Also, when paraphrasing, avoid the temptation to highlight words with quotation marks.

Using quotation marks to signal titles

Titles of works that are part of larger works, like articles, songs, or documents, should be set off with quotation marks.

Time published an article called "The Silicon Valley Reborn."

A classic blues tune covered by the Yardbirds was "I'm a Man."

The report, "Locating Evidence of Ancient Nomads in Egypt," is available online.

Titles of books and other full works should not be set in quotation marks. They should be italicized.

Taking the Quantum Leap, by Fred Wolf, is a very helpful book.

Revolver is one of the Beatles' best albums.

Using single quotation marks to signal a quote or title within another quote

When quoting something within another quote, you should use single quotation marks to set off the inner quotation.

Tim Berra shows the weakness of the creationist argument by quoting one of its strongest advocates: "Morris wrote 'the only way we can determine the true age of the earth is for God to tell us what it is.'"

One of the physicists at the conference remarked, "I cannot believe that Einstein's 1916 theory of general relativity is already a century old."

Using quotation marks to signal irony

Quotation marks are often used incorrectly to highlight words and slang terms.

Incorrect   One problem with "free-trade policies" is that the laborers who work for developing countries work almost for free.

> I found working with her to be "wonderful," because she is so "attentive" and "understanding."

The sentences above do not need quotation marks to set off these words. If you do need to highlight words that are not direct quotes, use italics.

You can, however, use quotation marks to signal irony by quoting another person's misuse of a term or phrase.

> Conservation is more than former Vice President Cheney's notion of a "personal virtue."

> *The Matrix* is an entertaining film, but it's hard to accept the "biblical significance" that Clarke and others claim for this highly violent movie.

Using quotation marks with in-text citations

One of the exceptions to placing periods inside quotation marks is when quotation marks are used with in-text citations.

> In his article on ancient dams, Abbas points out that "water-driven power systems have been around for thousands of years" (p. 67).

Here, note that the period comes after the in-text citation, not within the closing quotation mark.

Dashes and Hyphens

The uses of dashes and hyphens follow some rather specific rules. There are actually two types of dashes, the "em dash" and the "en dash." The em dash is the longer of the two (the width of an *m*), and it is the more widely used dash. The en dash is a bit shorter (the width of an *n*), and it is less widely used. Hyphens are shorter than the two dashes.

Using em dashes to highlight asides from the author or the continuation of a thought

An em dash is typically used to insert comments from the author that are asides to the readers.

> At the meeting, Hammons and Jenkins—this is the ironic part—ended up yelling at each other, even though they both intended to be peacemakers.

> We must recognize the continuing influence of Lamarckism in order to understand much social theory of the recent past—ideas that become incomprehensible if forced into the Darwinian framework we often assume for them.

An em dash can be made with two hyphens (--). Most word processors will automatically change two dashes into an em dash. Otherwise, a series of keystrokes (usually, shift-command-hyphen) will create this longer dash (—).

Using en dashes in numbers and dates

It might seem trivial, but there is a difference between en dashes and em dashes. An en dash is almost always used with numbers and dates.

> Copernicus (1473–1543) was the first European to make a cogent argument that the earth goes around the sun rather than the sun going around the earth.

> Young and Chavez argue conclusively that Valles Bonita is really a dormant sunken volcano, called a *caldera* (pp. 543–567).

As you can see in these examples, the en dash is slightly shorter than the em dash.

Using the hyphen to connect prefixes and make compound words

The hyphen is mainly used to connect prefixes with words or to connect two or more words to form compound words.

> neo-Platonists

> one-to-one relationship

> trisomy-21

> four-volume set of books

One thing you should notice is how hyphens are used to create compound adjectives but not compound nouns. You can write "four-volume set of books," where *four-volume* is an adjective. But you would need to write "the four volumes of books," because the word *volumes* is being used as a noun. Hyphens are generally used to make compound adjectives, but not compound nouns.

Parentheses and Brackets

Parentheses and brackets are handy for setting off additional information, like examples, definitions, references, lists, and asides to the readers.

Using parentheses to include additional information

Parentheses are often used to include additional information or refer readers to a graphic.

> When hiking through the Blanca Mountains, you will be surprised by the wide range of animals you will see (e.g., elk, deer, hawks, eagles, and the occasional coyote).

> The data we collected show a sharp decline in alcohol use when teens become involved in constructive, nontelevision activities (see Figure 3).

> These unicellular organisms show some plant-like features (many are photosynthetic) and others show more animal-like features.

Using parentheses to clarify a list

Parentheses can be used to clarify the elements of a long list.

> When meeting up with a bear in the wild, (1) do not run, (2) raise your arms to make yourself look bigger, (3) make loud noises, and (4) do not approach the animal.

> Only three things could explain the mechanical failure: (1) the piston cracked, (2) one of the pushrods came loose, or (3) the head gasket blew.

Using brackets to include editorial comments or to replace a pronoun

Brackets are less common than parentheses, but they can be helpful for inserting editorial comments or replacing a pronoun in a quote.

> Though pictures of the moon are often spectacular, *any view of the moon from earth is slightly blurred* [emphasis mine].

> Shea points out, "Whether he intended it or not, [Planck] was the originator of the quantum theory."

In this second example, the second *he* was replaced with *Planck* to make the meaning of the quote clear.

Ellipses

Ellipses are used to show that information in a quote was removed or to indicate the trailing off of a thought. An ellipsis is made with three dots, with spaces between each dot (. . .), not (...).

Using an ellipsis to signal that information in a quote has been removed

Sometimes a passage, especially a longer one, includes more information than you want to quote. In those cases, ellipses can be used to trim out the excess.

> As historian Holton writes, "What Bohr had done in 1927. . . was to develop a point of view that allowed him to accept the wave-particle duality as an irreducible fact" (117).

Using ellipses to show that a thought is trailing off

At the end of a sentence, you might use an ellipsis to urge the reader to continue the thought.

> For those who don't want to attend the orientation, we can find much less pleasant ways for you to spend your day . . . .

When an ellipsis ends a sentence, use an additional dot to make four (. . . .). The extra dot, after the last word, is the period that signals the end of the sentence.

B English as a Second Language Guide

The English language is a composite of many languages. As a result, English has many maddening exceptions and inconsistencies in spelling, syntax, and usage. If English is not your native language, you should pay special attention to these irregularities so that your writing and speaking will be consistent with the writing and speaking of fluent speakers.

This English as a Second Language (ESL) guide will not help you learn English. Instead, this guide concentrates on three major sources of irregularities in technical English: use of articles, word order of adjectives and adverbs, and verb tenses. As you master the English language, you should first concentrate on understanding these three sources of irregularities. Then, you can turn to other ESL resources to help you refine your use of English.

Using Articles Properly

Perhaps the most significant source of ESL problems is the use of articles (*a, an, the*) in English. For example, the sentences "The computer broke down" and "A computer broke down" have significantly different meanings in English. The use of *the* suggests that a specific computer broke down. The use of *a* suggests that one computer— among many computers—broke down.

Using *the* to refer to specific items

If you are referring to a specific item, use *the* to signal the noun.

> The planet Saturn has been bright during the last week.

> The car stalled, so we started walking to the nearest service station.

> The professor asked us to work harder on the next assignment.

Using *a* to refer to nonspecific items

If you are referring to a nonspecific item, use *a* to signal the noun.

> A planet was found circling a star in the Orion system.

> A car stalled in the road, so we needed to drive around it.

> A professor asked us to attend the party.

Using articles only with countable things

Articles should be used only with things that can be counted, like *the eight cars, the five bikes,* or *an orange.* When items are not counted or cannot be counted, do not use an article.

He surfaced for air.

They decided to have tea with dinner.

Rice grown in Asia tastes better than rice grown in North America.

Putting Adjectives and Adverbs in the Correct Order

Compared to some languages, English is flexible in its syntax. Nevertheless, word order in sentences is important for expressing the meaning you intend. In this section, we will go over the two major sources of word-order problems for ESL writers: adjectives and adverbs.

Using adjectives in the proper order

In English, adjectives should be placed in the proper order.

Improper   The red beautiful sailboat came into the bay.

Proper   The beautiful red sailboat came into the bay.

Fluent speakers of English will still understand the improper sentence, but it will sound odd to them. To properly order adjectives, you can use the following hierarchy of adjectives, which has been modified from *The New Century Handbook*, 5th edition, by Hult and Huckin (© 2011, Pearson). Hult and Huckin offer a more comprehensive approach.

1. article, determiner, or possessive (*a, an, the, this, that, those, my, our, their, Lisa's*)
2. ordinal (*first, second, third, final, next*)
3. quantity (*one, two, three, more, some, many*)
4. size and shape (*big, tiny, large, circular, square, round*)
5. appearance (*beautiful, filthy, clean, damaged, old, young, ancient*)
6. color (*red, yellow, black, green*)
7. substance (*wool, copper, wood, plastic*)

When properly ordered, adjectives can be strung together indefinitely in a sentence.

A third, large, beautiful, ancient, red, wooden sailboat came into the bay.

Keep in mind, though, that you should not string together too many adjectives. More than three or four adjectives strung together can be difficult to understand.

Using adverbs in proper places

Adverbs usually modify verbs in clauses. Adverbs can be used in a variety of places in the clause. Three guidelines are especially helpful for placing adverbs.

GUIDELINE 1: *Adverbs involving time and place usually go after the verb.*

The cat went *outside* when the children came over.

She arrived *late* to the lecture.

He went *promptly* to his professor's office for help.

GUIDELINE 2: *Adverbs that show frequency usually go before the verb.*

The cat *typically* runs outside when the children come over.

She *usually* arrives late to the lecture.

He *always* goes to his professor's office for help.

GUIDELINE 3: *Do not put an adverb between the verb and the object of a clause.*

Improper   Maria drives *recklessly* her car on the interstate.

Kim eats *quickly* his breakfast before he goes to class.

Proper   Maria drives her car *recklessly* on the interstate.

Kim eats his breakfast *quickly* before he goes to class.

Using Verb Tenses Appropriately

Proper use of verbs and verb phrases can be difficult in English, even for fluent speakers. So, learn them as best you can, and be patient while you are mastering the numerous English tenses.

To use tenses appropriately, remember that English, like most languages, has *past, present,* and *future* tenses. Each of these tenses also has four verbal aspects, which are called *simple, progressive, perfect,* and *perfect progressive.*

Simple—indicates whether the event happened, is happening, or will happen.

Progressive—indicates that the event was, is, or will be in progress at a specific time.

Perfect—indicates that the event was, is, or will be completed by a specific point in time.

Perfect progressive—indicates whether the event was, is, or will be progressing until a specific point in time.

Altogether, English has twelve tenses that need to be learned. Let's consider them separately.

Past Tense

Past tense refers to events that have already happened.

Simple Past Tense

Victor walked to the store yesterday.

Past Progressive Tense

Victor was walking to the store yesterday, when he was nearly hit by a car.

Past Perfect Tense

Before going to class, Victor had walked to the store.

Past Perfect Progressive Tense

Victor had been walking to the store before class.

Present Tense

Present tense refers to events that are happening at the moment.

Simple Present Tense

I enjoy talking with my friends.

Present Progressive Tense

I am enjoying talking with my friends this evening.

Present Perfect Tense

I have enjoyed talking with my friends this evening.

Present Perfect Progressive Tense

I have been enjoying talking with my friends this evening.

Future Tense

Future tense refers to events that will happen.

Simple Future Tense

The movie will start at 6:00 this evening.

Future Progressive Tense

The movie will be starting at 6:00 this evening.

Future Perfect Tense

By 6:10, the movie will have started.

Future Perfect Progressive Tense

By 6:10, the movie will have been playing for nearly 10 minutes.

When learning English, you should begin by mastering the simple past, present, and future forms of verbs. Then, as you grow more comfortable with the language, you can begin using the progressive, perfect, and perfect progressive tenses.

When you are unsure about whether to use progressive, perfect, or perfect progressive, just revert to the simple form. In most cases, simple sentences will be correct, though perhaps a bit awkward sounding to fluent speakers of English.

APPENDIX C

Documentation Guide

Documenting sources is an important part of doing research. As you collect information on your subject, you need to keep track of the sources from which you drew quotes and ideas. Then cite these sources in your text and use them to create a list of references at the end of your document.

When should you cite and document a source? The best way to determine the necessary level of documentation is to consider your readers' needs. How much citing and documenting will they need to feel confident in your work?

Some commonly documented materials include the following:

Quotes or ideas taken from someone else's work—If others wrote it or thought it before you did, you must cite them as the owners of their words and ideas. Otherwise, you might be accused of lifting their work.

Materials that support your ideas—You can build the credibility of your work by showing that others have discussed the topic before.

Sources of any data or facts—Any numbers or facts that you did not generate yourself need to be carefully cited and documented. That way, readers can check your sources for accuracy.

Materials that refer to your subject—By citing sources, including those with which you disagree, you show that you have a comprehensive understanding of the issues involved.

Historical sources on your subject—To build a background for readers to understand your subject, include any sources that might help them understand its history.

Graphics taken from online or print sources—Sometimes you will need permission to use nonprint and online sources. Minimally, though, you must cite the sources from which you obtained them.

In this appendix, we will review the three common documentation styles in technical communication:

- The **APA documentation style** from the American Psychological Association is widely used in engineering, human sciences, and physical sciences.
- The **CSE documentation style** from the Council of Science Editors is used primarily in biological and medical sciences, though it is gaining popularity in other scientific fields.
- The **MLA documentation style** from the Modern Language Association is used in English and the humanities. Although this style is not commonly used in engineering and science, it is sometimes used when scholars approach technical issues from cultural, historical, rhetorical, or philosophical perspectives.

Other documentation styles are available, so find out which documentation style is used in the organization or company for which you work.

If you want to use footnotes or endnotes, consult the style guide you are using. Footnotes and endnotes will not be covered here because they are rarely used in technical documents.

We will discuss the most common in-text citations and full-entry patterns. If one of the following models does not fit your needs, you should consult the style guide (APA, CSE, or MLA) that you are following.

APA Documentation Style

APA documentation style is most common in the natural and human sciences, except in fields related to biology and medicine. The official source for this style is the *Publication Manual of the American Psychological Association,* sixth edition (2010).

When using APA style, you will need to include in-text citations and a list of alphabetically arranged references at the end of your document.

APA In-Text Citations

APA style follows an author-year system for in-text citations, meaning the author and year are usually cited within the text.

Individual Authors

Individual authors are cited using their last name and the date of the article.

> One study reports a significant rise in HIV cases in South Africa in one year (Brindle, 2011).

> One study reported a 12.2% rise in HIV cases in only one year (Brindle, 2011, p. 843).

> Brindle (2011) reports a significant rise in HIV cases in South Africa in one year.

> Brindle (2011) reports a 12.2% rise in HIV cases in South Africa in one year (p. 843).

In most cases, only the author and year need to be noted, as shown in the first example. If you are reporting a specific fact or number, however, you should cite the page from which it was taken.

Multiple Authors

If an article has two authors, you should use the ampersand symbol (&) to replace the word *and* in the in-text citation. The word *and* should be used in the sentence itself, however.

> (Thomas & Linter, 2013)

> According to Thomas and Linter (2013) . . .

Technical documents often have more than two authors. If the work has less than six authors, cite all the names the first time the work is referenced. After that, use the last name of the first author followed by "et al."

First Citation of Work

(Wu, Gyno, Young, & Reims, 2014)

As reported by Wu, Gyno, Young, and Reims (2014) . . .

Subsequent Citations of Work

(Wu et al., 2013)

As reported by Wu et al. (2013) . . .

If the work has six or more authors, only the first author's last name should be included, followed by "et al." This approach should be used with all citations of the work, including the first in-text citation.

Corporate or Unknown Authors

When the author of the document is a corporation or is unknown, the in-text citation uses the name of the corporation or the first prominent word in the title of the document.

First Citation of Work

(National Science Foundation [NSF], 2014)

("Results," 2012)

(*Silent,* 2002)

Subsequent Citations of Work

(NSF, 2014)

("Results," 2012)

(*Silent,* 2002)

Notice in these examples that the first word of a journal article title should be put in quotation marks, while the first word of a book title should be put in italics.

Paraphrased Materials

When citing paraphrased materials, usually only the year and page number are needed because the authors' names are typically mentioned in the sentence. In many cases, only the year is needed.

Franks and Roberts report that aptitude for visual thinking runs in families (2013, p. 76).

The instinct for survival, according to Ramos (2014), is strong in the Mexican wolf.

Jones (2011) argues that finding a stand of dead trees near an industrial plant is a good indicator that something is seriously wrong (pp. 87–88).

Two or More Works in Same Parentheses

In some cases, several documents will state similar information. If so, you should cite them all and separate the works with semicolons. The sources should be listed in alphabetical order.

> Studies have shown remarkable progress toward reviving the penguin population on Vostov Island (Hinson & Kim, 2004; Johnson & Smith, 2010; Tamili, 2012).

Personal Communication and Correspondence

APA style discourages putting any forms of personal communication—conversations, e-mails, letters, even interviews—in the References list. So, in-text citations are the only citations for these sources in a document.

> Bathers (personal communication, December 5, 2013) pointed out to me that . . .

These sources are not listed in the References list because they are not retrievable by readers.

The References List for APA Style

When using APA style, your references should be listed in alphabetical order at the back of the document. List only the items that you actually cited in your document. After all, if a document is important enough to list in your references, it should be important enough to cite in the text itself.

In most cases, the reference list is identified by the centered heading "References." Entries should be double-spaced. Also, each reference should use a hanging indent style (i.e., the second line and subsequent lines should be indented). The first line should be flush with the left margin.

The following list includes examples of APA style, but it is not comprehensive. If you do not find a model here for a document you are adding to your references list, you should check the *Publication Manual of the American Psychological Association,* sixth edition (2010).

1. **Website or Webpage, Author Known**

   Loris, N. (2014). EPA proposes next step of regulatory cap-and-trade. *Heritage Foundation.* Retrieved from http://heritage.org/research /reports/2014/06/epa-proposes-next-step-of-regulatory-cap-and-trade

2. **Website or Webpage, Corporate Author**

   National Wildlife Service. (2002). *Managing forest on your land.* Retrieved from http://www.nws.gov/manageyourforest.htm

3. **Webpage, Author Unknown**

   Skin cancer treatments debated. (2004, January 1). CNN.com. Retrieved from http://www.cnn.com/2004/HEALTH/conditions/01/19 /skincancer.treatment.ap/index.html

4. Book, One Author

Jones, S. (2001). *Darwin's ghost: The origin of species updated*. New York, NY: Ballantine.

5. Book, More Than One Author

Pauling, L., & Wilson, E. B. (1935). *Introduction to quantum mechanics*. New York, NY: Dover.

6. Book, Corporate or Organization Author

American Psychiatric Association. (2013). *Diagnostic and statistical manual of mental disorders* (5th ed.). Arlington, VA: American Psychiatric Publishing.

7. Book, Edited Collection

Mueller-Vollmer, K. (Ed.). (1990). *The hermeneutics reader*. New York, NY: Continuum.

8. Book, Translated

Habermas, J. (1979). *Communication and the evolution of society* (T. McCarthy, Trans.). Boston, MA: Beacon Press.

9. Book, Author Unknown

Usborne complete book of the microscope. (2006). Tulsa, OK: Educational Development Corp.

10. Book, Second Edition or Beyond

Williams, R., & Tollet, J. (2008). *The non-designer's design book* (3rd ed.). Berkeley, CA: Peachpit.

11. Book, Dissertation or Thesis

Simms, L. (2002). *The Hampton effect in fringe desert environments: An ecosystem under stress* (Unpublished doctoral dissertation). University of New Mexico, Albuquerque, NM.

12. Book, Electronic

Darwin, C. (1862). *On the various contrivances by which British and foreign orchids are fertilised by insects*. Retrieved from http://pages .britishlibrary.net/charles.darwin3/orchids/orchids_fm.htm

13. Document, Government Publication

Greene, L. W. (1985). *Exile in paradise: The isolation of Hawaii's leprosy victims and development of Kalaupapa settlement, 1865 to present*. Washington, DC: U.S. Department of the Interior, National Park Service.

14. Document, Pamphlet

The Colorado Health Network. (2002). *Exploring high altitude areas*. Denver, CO: Author.

15. Film or Video Recording

Jackson, P. (Director), & Osborne, B., Walsh, F., & Sanders, T. (Producers). (2002). *The lord of the rings: The fellowship of the ring* [Motion picture]. Hollywood, CA: New Line.

16. **Article, Journal with Continuous Pagination**

    Katz, A. & Te'eni, D. (2014). The role of communication complexity in adaptive contextualization. *IEEE Transactions on Professional Communication,* 57, 98-112. doi:1109/TPC.2014.2312454

17. **Article, Journal without Continuous Pagination**

    Lenhoff, R., & Huber, L. (2000). Young children make maps! *Young Children, 55*(5), 6–12.

18. **Article, Journal with Digital Object Identifier (DOI)**

    Satomura, T., Wedel, M. & Picters, R. (2014). Copy alert: A method and metric to detect visual copycat brands. *Journal of Marketing Research, 51*(i), 1–13. doi.org/10.1509/jmr.11.046

19. **Article, Edited Book**

    Katz, S. B., & Miller, C. R. (1996). The low-level radioactive waste siting controversy in North Carolina: Toward a rhetorical model of risk communication. In G. Herndl & S. C. Brown (Eds.), *Green culture: Environmental rhetoric in contemporary America* (pp. 111–140). Madison: University of Wisconsin Press.

20. **Article, Magazine**

    Appenzeller, T. (2004, February). The case of the missing carbon. *National Geographic,* 88–118.

21. **Article, Online Magazine**

    Oremus, W. (2014, June 6). Silicon Valley uber alles. Retrieved from http://www.slate.com/articles/technology/technology/2014/06/uber_17_billion_valuation_it_s_now_worth_nearly_as_much_as_hertz_and_avis.html

22. **Article, Newspaper**

    Hall, C. (2002, November 18). Shortage of human capital envisioned, Monster's Taylor sees worker need. *The Chicago Tribune,* p. E7.

23. **Article, Author Unknown**

    The big chill leaves bruises. (2004, January 17). *Albuquerque Tribune,* p. A4.

24. **Article, CD-ROM**

    Hanford, P. (2001). Locating the right job for you. *The electronic job finder* [CD-ROM]. San Francisco, CA: Career Masters.

25. **Blog Posting**

    Katie. (2007, 17 September). 30 days and tech writing [Blog post]. Retrieved from http://techwriterscrum.blogspot.com

26. **Podcast**

    DMN Communications (Producer). (2008, May 18). Talking wikis with Stewart Mader [Audio podcast]. *Communications from DMN.* Retrieved from http://dmn.podbean.com/2008/05

27. **Song or Recording**

    Myer, L. (1993). Sometimes alone. *Flatlands* [CD]. Ames, IA: People's Productions.

28. **Television or Radio Program**

Harris, R. (2003, January 6). *Destination: The south pole.* Washington, DC: National Public Radio. Retrieved from http://discover.npr.org/features /feature.jhtml?wfld=904848

29. **Personal Correspondence, E-Mail, or Interview**

This result was confirmed by J. Baca (personal communication, March 4, 2014). (In APA style a personal correspondence is not included in the References list. Instead, the source of the information should appear in the in-text citation.)

Creating the APA References List

In APA style, the References list is placed at the end of the document on a separate page or in an appendix. The sources cited in the document should be listed alphabetically by author's last name.

References

Assel, R., Cronk, K., & Norton, D. (2003). Recent trends in Laurentian Great Lakes ice cover. *Climatic Change, 57,* 185–204.

Hoffmann, A., & Blows, M. (1993). Evolutionary genetics and climate change: Will animals adapt to global warming? In P. M. Kareiva, J. G. Kingsolver, & R. B. Huey (Eds.), *Biotic interactions and global change* (pp. 13–29). Sunderland, MA: Sinauer.

Jamieson, D. (2014). *Reason in a dark time: Why the struggle against climate change failed—and what it means to our future.* New York, NY: Oxford University Press.

Kishbaugh, S. (2014). My poor little lake. *New York State Conservationist, 68*(5), 24-27.

Nicks, D. (2014). *Your breakfast is under assault from climate change.* Time.com. Retrieved from http://time.com/105459/breakfast-cereal-climate-change-oxfam

CSE Documentation Style (Citation-Sequence)

CSE documentation is most commonly used in the biological and medical fields, though it is gaining popularity in other scientific fields. The official source for this style is *Scientific Style and Format: The CSE Manual for Authors, Editors, and Publishers,* eighth edition (2014).

The *CSE Manual* describes three citation methods. The first method, called the *author-year* system, is very similar to APA style, so it will not be discussed here. If you need to use the CSE author-year system, you can consult the *CSE Manual.* The second method, called the *citation-sequence* system, will be discussed here because it offers a good alternative to APA style. (The third method, *citation-name,* differs from citation-sequence in the way it orders the References list.)

In the citation-sequence system, sources are referred to by number within the text, usually with a superscript number similar to a footnote.

> This bacteria has been shown[1] to grow at a significant rate when exposed to black light.

When referring to multiple sources, a dash or a hyphen is used to signal the range of sources.

> Several studies[3-8, 10] have illustrated this relationship.

In some situations, editors will ask for the citations to use numbers in parentheses or brackets instead of superscript numbers:

> This relationship between the virus and various illnesses has been demonstrated in numerous studies (3, 12–15).

> Franklin and Chou argued this point in their influential research on HIV mutation [3], in which they explained its tendency to seek out new paths for replication.

In the References list at the end of the document, the sources are numbered and listed in the order in which they were cited in the text. Then, other references to that source in the document will use the same number.

The advantage of the citation-sequence system is that readers feel less disruption than with the author-year system, because the superscript numbers are less intrusive. However, a disadvantage is that readers need to flip back to the list of references to see author names for any sources of information.

The References List for CSE Citation-Sequence Style

The following list includes examples of CSE citation-sequence style. This list is not comprehensive. If you do not find a model here for a document you are adding to your references, you should check *Scientific Style and Format: The CSE Manual for Authors, Editors, and Publishers,* eighth edition.

The format of the list of references for CSE citation-sequence style is somewhat different from that of reference lists following APA or MLA style:

- Sources are numbered (1, 2, 3, and so on) to reflect the order in which they were cited.
- The items in the References list begin with a number at the left; subsequent lines align below the word that follows that number.
- When a citation refers to a specific page or set of pages in a stand-alone document, the full text reference includes the page number(s) after a *p.* (e.g., *p. 23* or *p. 123–36*). If the citation is referring to the whole work, the page numbers are not needed.

Items in the References list should be single-spaced.

1. **Website or Webpage, Author Known**

   12. Prindle J. Albert Einstein site online. Santa Monica (CA): Albert Einstein Website Online; 2012 [accessed 2014 Jun 5]. http://www.alberteinsteinsite.com

2. **Website or Webpage, Corporate Author**

   34. National Wildlife Service. Managing forest on your land. Washington: NWS; c2003 [accessed 2004 Sep 8]. http://www.nws.gov/manageyourforest.htm

3. **Webpage, Author Unknown**

   3. Skin cancer treatments debated. Atlanta (GA): CNN.com; c2004 [accessed 2004 Jan 1]. http://www.cnn.com/2004/HEALTH/conditions/01/19/skincancer.treatment.ap/index.html

4. **Webpage, Online Periodical**

   7. Grinspoon D. Is Mars ours? Slate Magazine. 2004 Jan 7 [accessed 2004 Jan 19]. http://slate.msn.com/id/2093579

5. **Book, One Author**

   23. Jones S. Darwin's ghost: the origin of species updated. New York: Balantine Books; 2001. p. 86–92.

6. **Book, More Than One Author**

   2. Pauling L, Wilson EB. Introduction to quantum mechanics. New York: Dover Publications; 1935. p. 38.

7. **Book, Corporate or Organization Author**

   11. American Psychiatric Association. Diagnostic and statistical manual of mental disorders. 5th ed. Arlington (VA): American Psychiatric Publishing; 2013.

8. **Book, Edited Collection**

   22. Mueller-Vollmer K, editor. The hermeneutics reader. New York: Continuum; 1990. p. 203–12.

9. **Book, Translated**

   14. Habermas J. Communication and the evolution of society. McCarthy T, translator. Boston (MA): Beacon Press; 1979. p. 156.

10. **Book, Author Unknown**

    13. The Usborne complete book of the microscope. Tulsa (OK): Educational Development Corp; 2006.

11. **Book, Second Edition or Beyond**

    21. Williams R, Tollet J. The non-designer's design book. 3rd ed. Berkeley (CA): Peachpit; 2008. p. 123–27.

12. **Book, Dissertation or Thesis**

    18. Simms L. The Hampton effect in fringe desert environments: an ecosystem under stress [dissertation]. [Albuquerque (NM)]: University of New Mexico; 2002.

13. Book, Electronic

13. Darwin C. On the various contrivances by which British and foreign orchids are fertilised by insects London: John Murray; c1862 [accessed 2002 Sep 5]. http://pages.britishlibrary.net/charles.darwin3/orchids /orchids_fm.htm

14. Document, Government Publication

6. Greene LW. Exile in paradise: the isolation of Hawaii's leprosy victims and development of Kalaupapa settlement, 1865 to present. Washington: Department of Interior (US), National Park Service; 1985.

15. Document, Pamphlet

23. Colorado Health Network. Exploring high altitude areas. Denver (CO); 2002.

16. Film or Video Recording

16. The lord of the rings: the fellowship of the ring [DVD]. Jackson P, director. Osborne B, Walsh F, Sanders T, producers. Hollywood (CA): New Line Productions; 2002.

17. CD-ROM

7. Geritch T. Masters of renaissance art [CD-ROM]. Chicago: Revival Productions; 2000. 2 CD-ROMs: sound, color, 4¾ in.

18. Article, Journal with Continuous Pagination

Katz A, Te'eni D. The role of communication complexity in adaptive contextualization. IEEE Trans on Prof Comm. 2014;57:98-112. doi:1109/TPC.2014.2312454.

19. Article, Journal Without Continuous Pagination

32. Lenhoff R, Huber L. Young children make maps! Young Children. 2000; 55(5):6–12.

20. Article, Edited Book

1. Katz SB, Miller CR. The low-level radioactive waste siting controversy in North Carolina: toward a rhetorical model of risk communication. In: Herndl G, Brown SC, editors. Green culture: environmental rhetoric in contemporary America. Madison: University of Wisconsin Press; 1996. p. 111–40.

21. Article, Magazine

12. Appenzeller T. The case of the missing carbon. National Geographic. 2004 Feb: 88–118.

22. Article, Online Publication

12. Oremus W. Silicon Valley uber alles. Washington (DC); Slate.com; 2014 [accessed 2014 Jun 6]. http://www.slate.com/articles/technology/technology/2014/06/uber_17_billion_valuation_it_s_now_worth_nearly_as_much_as_hertz_and_avis.html.

23. Article, Newspaper

6. Hall C. Shortage of human capital envisioned, Monster's Taylor sees worker need. Chicago Tribune. 2002 Nov 18;Sect E:7(col 2).

24. **Article, Author Unknown**

   3. The big chill leaves bruises. Albuquerque Tribune. 2004 Jan 17;Sect A:4(col 1).

25. **Article, CD-ROM**

   21. Hanford P. Locating the right job for you. The electronic job finder [CD-ROM]. San Francisco: Career Masters; 2001. CD-ROM: sound, color, 4¾ in.

26. **Song or Recording**

   12. Myer L. Sometimes alone. Flatlands [CD]. Ames (IA): People's Productions; 1993.

27. **Television or Radio Program**

   4. Harris R. Destination: the south pole [recording]. Washington: National Public Radio; 2003 Jan 6 [accessed 2004 Jan 19]. http://discover.npr .org/features/feature.jhtml?wfId=904848

28. **Personal Correspondence, E-Mail, or Interview**

   These complications seem to have been resolved (2014 e-mail from FH Smith to me) while others seem to have emerged.

(References that refer to personal correspondences or personal interviews should be placed within the text and not in the References list.)

Creating the CSE References List (Citation-Sequence Style)

In CSE style, the References list is placed at the end of the document or in an appendix. The sources are listed by number in the order in which they were first referenced in the text.

References

1. Hoffmann A, Blows M. Evolutionary genetics and climate change: will animals adapt to global warming? In: Kareiva P, Kingsolver J, Huey R, editors. Biotic interactions and global change. Sunderland (MA): Sinauer; 1993. p. 13–29.
2. Nicks D. Your breakfast is under assault from climate change. Washington (DC): Time.com; 2014 [accessed 2014 Jul 21]. http://time.com/105459/breakfast-cereal-climate-change-oxfam.
3. Assel R, Cronk K, Norton D. Recent trends in Laurentian Great Lakes ice cover. Climatic Change. 2003;57:185–204.
4. Kishbaugh S. My poor little lake. New York State Conservationist. 2014;68(5):24-27.
5. Jamieson D. Reason in a dark time: why the struggle against climate change failed—and what it means to our future. New York (NY): Oxford University Press; 2014. p 15.

MLA Documentation Style

The MLA documentation style is not commonly used in technical or scientific fields; it is most commonly used in the arts and humanities. Nevertheless, there are occasions where MLA style is requested because it is widely used for documentation. The official source for this style is the *MLA Handbook for Writers of Research Papers*, seventh edition (2009).

When using MLA style, you will need to use in-text citations and a list of alphabetically arranged references, called "Works Cited," at the end of your document.

MLA In-Text Citations

MLA style follows an *author-page number* system for in-text citations, meaning the author and the page number are usually cited within the text.

Individual Authors

Individual authors are cited using their last name and the page number(s) from which the information was drawn. If the year is significant, put it after the author's name in parentheses.

> One study reports a significant rise in HIV cases in South Africa in one year (Brindle 834).

> One study reported a 12.2% rise in HIV cases in only one year (Brindle 834).

> Brindle (2014) reports a significant rise in HIV cases in South Africa in one year.

> Brindle (2014) reports a 12.2% rise in HIV cases in South Africa in one year (834).

In most cases, only the author and page number need to be cited, as shown in the first example above. In MLA style, the year of publication is not usually a concern, so include the year only when necessary.

Multiple Authors

If an article has two or more authors, use the word *and* to connect the authors' last names.

> (Thomas and Linter 130)

> According to Thomas and Linter (2013), the number of mammals in this area was dramatically reduced during the Ice Age (130).

Technical documents often have more than two authors. In these cases, cite all the names the first time the work is referenced. Afterward, you can repeat all the names or use the last name of the first author followed by "et al."

First Citation of Work

> (Wu, Gyno, Young, and Reims 924)

Subsequent Citations of Work

> (Wu et al. 924)
>
> As reported by Wu et al., the Permian Age . . .

Corporate or Unknown Authors

When the author of the document is a corporation or is unknown, the in-text citation uses the name of the corporation or the first prominent word in the title of the document.

> (National Science Foundation 76)
>
> ("Results" 91)
>
> (*Silent* 239)

As shown here, if the source is an article, put the first prominent word in quotes. If it is a book, put it in italics.

Paraphrased Material

Because the authors' names are typically mentioned in the sentence, citing paraphrased material usually requires only a mention of the page number.

> Franks and Roberts report that aptitude for visual thinking runs in families (76).
>
> The instinct for survival, according to Ramos, is strong in the Mexican wolf (198-201).
>
> Jones argues that finding a stand of dead trees near an industrial plant is a good indicator that something is seriously wrong (87-88).

Two or More Works in One Citation

In some cases, several documents will state similar information. In such cases, you should cite them all and separate them with semicolons.

> Studies have shown remarkable progress toward reviving the penguin population on Vostov Island (Hinson and Kim 330; Johnson and Smith 87; Tamili 102).

The Works Cited List for MLA Style

When using MLA style, your Works Cited list should be in alphabetical order at the back of the document. In your list, you should include only the items that you actually cited in your document. Leave any documents that you consulted but did not cite out of the list of works cited. After all, if a document is important enough to include in your Works Cited, it should be important enough to cite in the text itself.

In most cases, the list is identified by the centered heading "Works Cited." Entries should be double-spaced. Also, each reference should use a hanging indent style (i.e., the second line and subsequent lines should be indented). The first line should be flush with the left margin.

The following list includes examples of MLA style. This list is not comprehensive. If you do not find a model here for a source you are adding to your Works Cited, you should check the *MLA Handbook for Writers of Research Papers*, seventh edition.

1. **Website or Webpage, Author Known**

   Prindle, Joseph. *Albert Einstein Site Online*. 2012. Web. 6 Jun. 2014.

2. **Website or Webpage, Corporate Author**

   Managing Forest on Your Land. National Wildlife Service. 8 Sept. 2002. Web. 10 Oct. 2008.

3. **Webpage, Author Unknown**

   "Skin Cancer Treatments Debated." CNN.com. 1 Jan. 2004. Web. 9 Aug. 2008.

4. **Webpage, Online Periodical**

   Oremus, W. "Silicon Valley Uber Alles." *Slate Magazine*. 6 Jun. 2014. Web. 9 Jul. 2014.

5. **Book, One Author**

   Jones, Steve. *Darwin's Ghost: The Origin of Species Updated*. New York: Ballantine, 2001. Print.

6. **Book, More Than One Author**

   Pauling, Linus, and E. Bright Wilson. *Introduction to Quantum Mechanics*. New York: Dover, 1935. Print.

7. **Book, Corporate or Organization Author**

   American Psychiatric Association. *Diagnostic and Statistical Manual of Mental Disorders*. 5th ed. Arlington, VA: American Psychiatric Publishing 2013. Print.

8. **Book, Edited Collection**

   Mueller-Vollmer, Kurt, ed. *The Hermeneutics Reader*. New York: Continuum, 1990. Print.

9. **Book, Translated**

   Habermas, Jurgen. *Communication and the Evolution of Society*. Trans. Thomas McCarthy. Boston: Beacon Press, 1979. Print.

10. **Book, Author Unknown**

    Usborne Complete Book of the Microscope. Tulsa: Educational Development Corporation, 2006. Print.

11. **Book, Second Edition or Beyond**

    Williams, Robin, and John Tollet. *The Non-Designer's Design Book*. 3rd ed. Berkeley: Peachpit, 2008. Print.

12. **Book, Dissertation or Thesis**

    Simms, Laura. "The Hampton Effect in Fringe Desert Environments: An Ecosystem under Stress." Diss. U of New Mexico, 2002. Print.

13. **Book, Electronic**

    Darwin, Charles. *On the Various Contrivances by Which British and Foreign Orchids Are Fertilised by Insects*. London: John Murray, 1862. Web. 1 Jan. 2008.

14. Document, Government Publication

Greene, Linda W. *Exile in Paradise: The Isolation of Hawaii's Leprosy Victims and Development of Kalaupapa Settlement, 1865 to Present.* Washington: US Department of the Interior, National Park Service, 1985. Print.

15. Document, Pamphlet

Exploring High Altitude Areas. Denver: TCHN, 2002. Print.

16. Film or Video Recording

The Lord of the Rings: The Fellowship of the Ring. Dir. Peter Jackson. Prod. Barrie Osborne, Peter Jackson, Fran Walsh, and Tim Sanders. New Line, 2002. Film.

17. CD-ROM

Geritch, Thomas. *Masters of Renaissance Art.* CD-ROM. Chicago: Revival Productions, 2000.

18. Article, Journal with Continuous Pagination

Katz, Adi, and Dov Te'eni. "The Role of Communication Complexity in Adaptive Contextualization." *IEEE Transactions on Professional Communication 57* (2014): 98-112. Print.

19. Article, Journal without Continuous Pagination

Lenhoff, Rosalyn, and Lynn Huber. "Young Children Make Maps!" *Young Children* 55.5 (2000): 6-12. Print.

20. Article, Edited Book

Katz, Steven B., and Carolyn R. Miller. "The Low-Level Radioactive Waste Siting Controversy in North Carolina: Toward a Rhetorical Model of Risk Communication." *Green Culture: Environmental Rhetoric in Contemporary America.* Ed. Carl G. Herndl and Stuart C. Brown. Madison: U of Wisconsin P, 1996. 111-40. Print.

21. Article, Magazine

Appenzeller, Tim. "The Case of the Missing Carbon." *National Geographic* Feb. 2004: 88-118. Print.

22. Article, Newspaper

Hall, Cheryl. "Shortage of Human Capital Envisioned, Monster's Taylor Sees Worker Need." *Chicago Tribune* 18 Nov. 2002: E7. Print.

23. Article, Author Unknown

"The Big Chill Leaves Bruises." *Albuquerque Tribune* 17 Jan. 2004: A4. Print.

24. Article, CD-ROM

Hanford, Peter. "Locating the Right Job for You." *The Electronic Job Finder.* CD-ROM. San Francisco: Career Masters, 2001.

25. Song or Recording

Myer, Larry. "Sometimes Alone." *Flatlands.* Ames: People's Productions, 1993. CD.

26. **Television or Radio Program**
    "Destination: The South Pole." Narr. Richard Harris. *All Things Considered.*
        National Public Radio. 6 Jan. 2003. Web. 4 Feb. 2004.

27. **Personal Correspondence, E-Mail, or Interview**
    Baca, James. Personal interview. 4 Mar. 2014.

Creating the MLA Works Cited List

In MLA style, the Works Cited list is placed at the end of the document on a separate page. The sources referenced in the document should be listed alphabetically, and each entry should be double-spaced.

Works Cited

Assel, Robert, Kevin Cronk, and David Norton. "Recent Trends in
    Laurentian Great Lakes Ice Cover." *Climatic Change* 57 (2003): 185-204. Print.

Hoffmann, Amber, and Marlin Blows. "Evolutionary Genetics and Climate
    Change: Will Animals Adapt to Global Warming?" *Biotic Interactions and
    Global Change.* Ed. Paul M. Kareiva, John G. Kingsolver, and Renee B. Huey.
    Sunderland: Sinauer, 1993. 13-29. Print.

Houghton, James. *Global Warming: The Complete Briefing.* 2nd ed.
    Cambridge, MA: Cambridge UP, 1997. Print.

Kishbaugh, Scott. "My Poor Little Lake." *New York State Conservationist*
    68.1 (2014): 24-27. Print.

Nicks, Denver. "Your Breakfast is Under Assault from Climate Change."
    Time 21 May 2014. Web. 8 Jul. 2014.

References

AIGA. (2014). Symbol signs. Retrieved from http://www.aiga.org/symbol-signs

American Diabetes Association [ADA]. (n.d.) *Where do I begin? Living with type 2 diabetes.* Alexandria, VA: American Diabetes Association.

American Psychological Association. (2010). *Publication manual of the American Psychological Association* (6th ed.). Washington, DC: Author.

American Red Cross. (2014). Home page. Retrieved from http://www.redcross.org

American Society of Civil Engineers. (2008). *Welcome to the ASCE online research library.* Retrieved from http://ascelibrary.org

Arnheim, R. (1969). *Visual thinking.* Berkeley: University of California Press.

Australian Resuscitation Council. (2002). *Basic life support flowchart.* Retrieved from http://www.resus.org.au/public/bls_flow_chart.pdf

Aversa, A. (2003). *Galaxy simulations.* Retrieved from http://www.u.arizona.edu/~aversa/galaxysims.pdf

Bed bug control for homes. (n.d.). Trenton, NJ: New Jersey Department of Health and Senior Services.

Bernhardt, S. (1986). Seeing the text [Survey]. *College Composition and Communication, 30,* 66–78.

Bjelopera, J. P. (2013). *The domestic terrorist threat: Background and issues for Congress.* Washington, DC: U.S. Congressional Research Service.

Bledsoe, L., & Sar, B. K. (2001). *Campus survey report: Safety perception and experiences of violence.* Retrieved from http://www.louisville.edu

Boisjoly, R. (1985). SRM o-ring erosion/potential failure criticality. In *Report of the Presidential Commission on the Space Shuttle* Challenger *Accident.* Retrieved from http://science.ksc.nasa.gov/shuttle/missions/51-l/docs/rogers-commission/table-of-contents.html

Boor, S., & Russo, P. (1993). How fluent is your interface? Designing for international users. *Proceedings of INTERCHI '93,* 342–347.

CBS News (2008). *Are we retreating in the war on cancer?* Retrieved from www.cbsnews.com/stories/2008/05/20/eveningnews

Chaney, L., & Martin, J. (2004). *Intercultural business communication* (3rd ed.). Upper Saddle River, NJ: Pearson Prentice Hall.

Clark, R. (1971). *Einstein: His life and times.* New York, NY: World Publishing.

Council of Science Editors. (2014). *The CSE manual for authors, editors, and publishers* (8th ed.). Reston, VA: Author.

Davis, D. (2007, Nov. 4). Off target in the war on cancer. *Washington Post.* Retrieved from http://www.washingtonpost.com/wp-dyn/content/article/2007/11/02/AR2007110201648.html

Deming, W. E. (2000). *Out of crisis.* Cambridge, MA: MIT Press.

Dragga, S. (1996). A question of ethics: Lessons from technical communicators on the job. *Technical Communication Quarterly, 6,* 161–178.

Dropbox. (2014). How do I share folders with other people? Retrieved from https://www.dropbox.com/help/19/en

Einstein, A. (1939). *August 2, 1939, letter to Franklin Roosevelt* [Letter]. Retrieved from http://www.anl.gov/OPA/frontiers96arch/aetofdr.html

Facebook. (2014). *Community standards.* Retrieved from https://www.facebook.com/communitystandards

Fermi National Accelerator Laboratory. (2014). *Fermilab.* Retrieved from http://www.fermilab.gov

Field Museum. (2014). Home page. Retrieved from http://www.fieldmuseum.org

Gibaldi, J. (2009). *MLA handbook for writers of research papers* (7th ed.). New York, NY: Modern Language Association.

Google. (2008). *Google.* Retrieved from http://www.google.com

Google Chrome. (2008). *Google Chrome Internet browser* [Manual]. Retrieved from http://www.google.com/chrome

Google Drive. (2014). *Google Drive interface.* Retrieved from http://drive.google.com

Haneda, S., & Shima, H. (1983). Japanese communication behavior as reflected in letter writing. *Journal of Business Communication, 19,* 19–32.

Hoft, N. (1995). *International technical communication.* New York, NY: Wiley.

Horton, W. (1993). The almost universal language: Graphics for international documents. *Technical Communication, 40,* 682–683.

Husqvarna. (2002). *Working with a chainsaw* [Manual]. Åsbro, Sweden: Electrolux.

Indiana Department of Transportation. (2007). *Dry flow testing of flowable backfill materials* [Fact sheet]. Retrieved from http://www.in.gov/indot

Institute of Electrical and Electronics Engineers. (2006). *IEEE code of ethics.* Retrieved from http://www.ieee.org/portal/pages/iportals/aboutus/ethics/code.html

Institute for Social and Economic Research. (2007). *British household panel survey* [Survey]. New Policy Institute. Retrieved from http://www.poverty.org.uk

International Association for Food Protection. (2008). *Sneezing icon* [Graphic]. Retrieved from http://www.foodprotection.org/aboutIAFP/iconmania.asp

International Energy Agency. (2008, May 13). *Oil market report,* 26–27.

International Organization for Standardization. (2008). *ISO 9000 and ISO 14000.* Retrieved from http://www.iso.org

Johnson-Sheehan, R. (2002). *Writing proposals: A rhetoric for managing change.* New York, NY: Longman.

Johnson-Sheehan, R., & Baehr, C. (2001). Visual-spatial thinking: Thinking differently about hypertexts. *Technical Communication, 48,* 37–57.

Koffka, K. (1935). *Principles of gestalt psychology.* New York, NY: Harcourt.

Kostelnick, C., & Roberts, D. (1998). *Designing visual language.* Boston, MA: Allyn & Bacon.

Lakoff, G. (2004). *Don't think of an elephant.* White River Junction, VT: Chelsea Green.

Lawrence Livermore National Laboratory. (2014). *Counterterrorism.* Livermore, CA: Lawrence Livermore National Laboratory. Retrieved from https://missions.llnl.gov/?q=counterterrorism

Leininger, C., & Yuan, R. (1998). Aligning international editing efforts with global business strategies. *IEEE Transactions on Professional Communication, 41,* 16–23.

Leopold, A. (1986). *A Sand County almanac.* New York, NY: Ballantine.

LinkedIn. (2014). *Get started.* http://www.LinkedIn.com

Logitech. (2010). *Surround Sound Speakers Z906 user's guide.* Newwark, CA: Logitech.

Manitoba Conservation Wildlife and Ecosystem Protection Branch. (2004). *Manitoba's species at risk: Ferruginous hawk* [Brochure].

Mathes, J., & Stevenson, D. (1976). *Designing technical reports.* Indianapolis, IN: Bobbs-Merrill.

MacLeod, H. (2009). *Ignore everybody: 39 other keys to creativity.* New York: Penguin.

Medline Plus. (2014). Home page. Retrieved from http://www.medlineplus.gov

Meyer, M. (2014). *Portfolio.* Retrieved from https://sites.google.com/a/g.clemson.edu/melissameyer/Home

Microsoft. (2013). Middle Eastern web page. Retrieved from www.microsoft.com/middleeast

Microsoft. (2007). *Project Standard 2007 overview* [Software]. Retrieved from http://www.office.microsoft.com/en-us/project/HA101656381033.aspx

MLA. (2008). *Style manual and guide to scholarly publishing.* (3rd ed.). New York, NY: Modern Language Association of America.

Moore, P. (2007, December 12). Going nuclear over global warming. *Sacramento Bee.* Retrieved from http://www.sacbee.com/110/story/560569.html

MotionRC. (2010). *RocHobby instruction manual.* Lake Barrington, IL: MotionRC.

Mozilla Firefox. (2006). *Help.* Retrieved from www.mozilla.com

Munter, M. & Russell, L. (2011) *Guide to presentations* (3rd ed) Upper Saddle River, NJ: Prentice Hall.

National Aeronautics and Space Administration. (2004). *Mars Exploration Rover* [Press release]. Retrieved from http://www.jpl.nasa.gov/news/presskits/merlandings.pdf

National Aeronautics and Space Administration. (2005). *Hurricane Katrina approaching the gulf coast* [Graphic]. Washington, DC. Retrieved from http://rapidfiresco.gsfc.nasa.gov/gallery/?search=Katrina

National Aeronautics and Space Administration. (2008). *Why the moon?* [Poster]. Retrieved from http://www.nasa.gov/pdf/163561main_why_moon2.pdf

National Aeronautics and Space Agency [NASA]. (2012). *Mars science laboratory landing: Press kit.* Washington, DC: NASA.

National Aeronautics and Space Agency [NASA]. (2014). *Hubble Space Telescope.* Retreived from http://www.nasa.gov/mission_pages/hubble/story/index.html#.U5sLio1dWAQ

National Aeronautics and Space Agency [NASA]. (2014). *Match stick rocket.* Retrieved from http://www.grc.nasa.gov/WWW/k-12/TRC/Rockets/match_rocket.html

National Commission on Writing. (2004). *A ticket to work . . . or a ticket out: A survey of business leaders.* New York: College Board.

National Human Genome Research Institute. (2014). Home page. Retrieved from http://www.genome.gov

National Library of Medicine. (2003). *Medline Plus.* Retrieved from http://www.nlm.nih.gov/medlineplus/medlineplus.html

National Oceanic and Atmospheric Administration. (2014). Home page. Retrieved from http://www.noaa.gov

National Ocean Service. (2005). *National Ocean Service Accomplishments.* Washington, DC: National Ocean Service.

National Science Foundation. (2014). Home page. Retrieved from http://www.nsf.gov

National Survey on Drug Use and Health. (2009). *Users of tobacco products.* Substance Abuse and Mental Health Services Administration.

National Weather Service Weather Forecast Office. (2012). *Solar and lunar eclipse page.* Retrieved from http://www.crh.noaa.gov/fsd/?n=suneclipse

New York Metropolitan Transportation Authority [MTA]. (n.d.) *Onboard train emergency instructions.* Retrieved from http://web.mta.info/lirr/safety/bilevel3.htm

Nikon. (2014). *The Nikon D5100 user manual.* [Manual]. Tokyo, Japan: Nikon.

Nova. (2010). *Terrestrial and Jovian planets.* Boston, MA: WGBH Educational Foundation. Retrieved from http://www.pbs.org/wgbh/nova/education/activities/3113_origins_07.html

Obesity update. (2012). Paris: Organisation for Economic Cooperation and Development.

Occupational Safety and Health Administration. (2007). *Fact sheet, flood cleanup* [Fact sheet]. Retrieved from http://www.osha.gov/OshDoc/data_Hurricane_Facts/floodcleanup.pdf

Office of Applied Studies, Substance Abuse and Mental Health Services Administration. (2009). *Nonmedical use of Adderall® among full-time college students* [Survey]. Washington, DC: Author.

Online Ethics Center for Engineering and Science. (2014). Home page. Retrieved from http://www.onlineethics.org

Pakiser, L., & Shedlock, K. (1997). *Earthquakes* [Fact sheet]. Retrieved from http://pubs.usgs.gov/gip/earthq1/earthqkgip.html

Parallax. (2004). *Crawler kit for the Boe-Bot robot.* Rocklin, CA: Parallax.

Peckham, G. (2003). Safety symbols. *Compliance engineering* [Graphic]. Retrieved from http://www.ce-mag.com/archive/02/03/peckham.html

Pendergrast, M. (1994). *For god, country, and Coca-Cola.* New York: Collier.

Pew Research Center. (2014). *Reports.* Retrieved from http://www.pewinternet.org/reports.asp

Plotnik, A. (1982). *The elements of editing.* New York, NY: Macmillan.

Pyle, R.M. (1981). *The National Audubon Society field guide to North America.* New York: Knopf.

Researchers create hips that function better and last longer. (2012, Winter). *Materials science and engineering* [Northwestern University], 1.

Restoring v-site: Birthplace of the gadget. (2007). *Nuclear Weapons Journal, 1,* p. 13.

Reynolds, S., & Valentine, D. (2004). *Guide to cross-cultural communication.* Upper Saddle River, NJ: Pearson Prentice Hall.

Robert Wood Johnson Foundation. (2012). *Influence of competitive food and beverage policies on children's diets and childhood obesity.* Princeton, NJ: Robert Wood Johnson Foundation.

Ryobi. (2000). *510r 4-cycle garden cultivator operator's manual* [Manual]. Chandler, AZ: Ryobi.

Safetyline Institute. (1998). *Gas laws* [Fact sheet]. Retrieved from http://www.safetyline.wa.gov.au/institute/level2/course16/lecture47/l47_02.asp

Shapiro, G. (1998, March). The ABCs of asthma. *Discover, 35,* 30–33.

Smith-Jackson, T.S. & Essuman-Johnson, A.E. (2002). Cultural ergonomics in Ghana, West Africa: A descriptive survey of industry and trade workers' interpretations of safety symbols. *International Journal of Occupational Safety and Ergonomics,* 8.1, 37-50.

Smith-Jackson, T., Essuman-Johnson, A., & Leonard, S. D. (2002) Symbol printes: Cross-cultural comparison of symbol representation. *Proceedings of the 15th Triennial Congress of the International Ergonomics Association,* Seoul, Korea.

Solarworld. (2014). *Sunmodule SW 255 mono/2.5 frame.* Hillsboro, OR: Solarworld.

Sunsmart Victoria. (2011). *Skin type chart.* Melbourne: Cancer Council Victoria. Retrieved from http://www.sunsmart.com.au

TiVo. (2002). *Start here* [Manual]. Tokyo: TiVo and Pioneer Corporation.

Toastmasters International. (2013). Home page. Retrieved from http://www.toastmasters.org

Tuckman, B. W. (1965). Development sequence in small groups. *Psychological Bulletin, 63,* 384–399.

University of Chicago Press. (2010). *Chicago manual of style* (16th ed.). Chicago, IL: Author.

University of Minnesota Libraries. (2014). Home page. Retrieved from http://www.lib.umn.edu

U.S. Census Bureau. (2014). Home page. Retrieved from http://www.census.gov

U.S. Centers for Disease Control. (2003). *Fight the bite* [Fact sheet]. Retrieved from http://www.cdc.gov/ncidod/dvbid/westnile/index.htm

U.S. Centers for Disease Control. (2003). *The rabies virus* [Fact sheet]. Retrieved from http://www.cdc.gov/rabies/virus.htm

U.S. Centers for Disease Control. (2003). *West Nile Virus (WNV) infection: Information for clinicians* [Fact sheet]. Retrieved from http://www.cdc.gov/ncidod/dvbid/westnile/index.htm

U.S. Centers for Disease Control. (2007). *Balance scale.* Retrieved from http://www.cdc.gov/diabetes/pubs/images/balance.gif

U.S. Centers for Disease Control. (2013). *West Nile Virus (WNV) fact sheet.* Washington, DC.

U.S. Centers for Disease Control. (2013). *West Nile Virus: Diagnosis & reporting.* Retrieved from http://www.cdc.gov/westnile/healthCareProviders/healthCareProviders-ClinLabEval.html

U.S. Centers for Disease Control and Prevention [CDC]. (2014). *Social media: Zombie apocalypse.* Retrieved from http://emergency.cdc.gov/socialmedia/zombies.asp

U.S. Copyright Office. (2014). Home page. Retrieved from http://www.loc.gov/copyright

U.S. Department of Agriculture Rural Development. (2008). *How to write a grant proposal.* Washington, DC: USDA.

U.S. Department of Agriculture [USDA]. (2012). *Bioenergy science white paper.* Washington, DC: USDA.

U.S. Department of Energy. (2014). *How fuel cells work.* Retrieved from http://www.fueleconomy.gov/feg/fcv_PEM.shtml

U.S. Department of Health and Human Services. (2007). *Women's health* [Fact sheet]. Retrieved from http://www.cdc.gov/lcod.htm

U.S. Environmental Protection Agency. (2002). *Global warming impacts: Forests.* Retrieved from http://yosemite.epa.gov/oar/globalwarming.nsf/content/ImpactsForests.html

U.S. Environmental Protection Agency [EPA]. (2013). *Climate impacts on forests.* Washington, DC: U.S. Environmental Protection Agency. Retrieved from http://www.epa.gov/climatechange/impacts-adaptation/forests.html

U.S. Forestry Service. (2014). *National news.* Retrieved from http://www.fs.fed.us

U.S. Geological Survey. (1997). *Predicting earthquakes* [Fact sheet]. Retrieved from http://pubs/usgs/gov/gip/earthq1/predict.html

U.S. Geological Survey. (2002). *Eruption history of Kilauea* [Fact sheet]. Retrieved from http://hvo.wr.usgs.gov/kilauea history/main.html

U.S. Geological Survey. (2003). *A proposal for upgrading the national-scale soil geochemical database for the United States.* Washington, DC: Author.

U.S. National Center for Education Statistics. (2010). *Indicators of school crime and safety.* Retrieved from http://nces.ed.gov/programs/crimeindicators/crimeindicators2010/figures/figure_13_1.asp

U.S. Office of Energy Policy and New Uses. (2011). *Renewable power opportunities for rural communities.* Washington, DC: U.S. Department of Agriculture.

Velasquez, M.G. (2002). *Business ethics: Concepts and cases* (5th ed.). Upper Saddle River, NJ: Prentice Hall.

Vucetich, J. (2003). *Population data from the wolves and moose of Isle Royale* [Data file]. Retrieved from http://www.isleroyalewolf.org

Washington State Department of Ecology. (2003). *North Creek water cleanup plan* [Fact sheet]. Retrieved from http://www.ecy.wa.gov/programs/wq/tmdl/watershed/north-creek/solution.html

West Virginia Office of Emergency Medical Services. (2007). *EMT-paramedic treatment protocol 4202* [Manual]. Morgantown, WV: Trauma and Emergency Care System, NOROP Center.

Wordpress. (2014). Wordpress.com. Retrieved from http://www.wordpress.com

Yoshida, J. (1996, October 7). A suggestive Woody has Japanese touchy. *Electronic Engineering Times.*

Credits

Text Credits

Chapter 1 Page 7 © 2003 by TiVo Inc. and Pioneer Corporation. Reprinted by permission of TiVo Inc. and Pioneer Corporation (Tokyo). TiVo's trademarks and copyrighted material are used by Pearson Education, Inc. under license. VCR Plus+ is a registered trademark of Gemstar Development Corp., reprinted with permission of Rovi Corporation. The DVD logos are trademarks of DVD FLLC. Other trademarks are the properties of their respective owners. Page 9 The American Red Cross name and emblem are used with its permission, which in no way constitutes an endorsement, express or implied, of any product, service, company, opinion or political position. The American Red Cross logo is a registered trademark owned by the American Red Cross. For more information, please visit www.redcross.org. Page 11 Courtesy: National Human Genome Research Institute. www.genome.gov. Page 13 National Ocean Service / 2005. Used by permission. Page 14 National Commission on Writing Report 2004, Used by permission.

Chapter 2 Pages 25–26; 27–28 United States Centers for Disease Control and Prevention. www.cdc.gov. Page 35 LEGO and the LEGO Logo are trademarks of the LEGO Group of Companies, used here by permission. © 2014 The LEGO Group.

Chapter 3 Page 43 © Copyright 2014 AtTask, Inc. All rights reserved. Page 55 Copyright © 2014 SmartSoft Ltd. Used with permission.

Chapter 4 Page 61 Ronald W. Clark, *The Life and Times of Einstein*. William Morrow; 1st edition (April 10, 2007). Pages 62–63 Argonne National Laboratory. Page 68 Aldo Leopold, "The Land Ethic" from *A Sand County Almanac*. Oxford University Press, 1949. Page 71 Code of Ethics from the Institute of Electrical and Electronics Engineers. Copyright 2006 IEEE. Reprinted with permission of the IEEE. Page 73 The Online Ethics Center at the National Academy of Engineering, http://www.onlineethics.org. Copyright 2003–2013 National Academy of Sciences. All rights reserved. Used with permission. Page 73 Facebook. See https://www.facebook.com/communitystandards for full listing. Page 79 US Copyright Office, http://www.copyright.gov/.

Chapter 6 Pages 122–124 Courtesy NASA. Page 126 The International Organization for Standardization, Used by permission. Pages 129–130 Courtesy NASA. Pages 132–134 National Weather Service Weather Forecast Office, NOAA .gov. Page 136 U.S. Office of Transportation & Air Quality. Pages 141–142 Specification for SolarWorld Sunmodule SW 255 mono / 2.5 Frame, SW 01-6001US 03-2013. Copyright 2013. Used by permission of SolarWorld. Page 143 Scott McCloud/Google. Page 145 chem.answers.com/definitions/the-definition-of-ionic-compounds. Pages 148–149 U.S. Department of Labor, Occupational Safety & Health Administration. www.OSHA.gov.

Chapter 7 Page 156 Centers for Disease Control and Prevention, Used by permission. Pages 158–160 West Virginia Office of Emergency Medical Services. EMT-Paramedic Treatment Protocol 4202. Copyright 2007. Used with permission. Pages 161–164 Indiana Department of Transportation. Page 169 Crawler Kit for the Boe-Bot (Registered TM Symbol) Robot (#30055). Copyright Parallax, Inc. 2004. Used by permission of Parallax, Inc. Page 172 Nikon D5100 User Manual, pages 10 and 11. © 2014 Nikon Corporation Used by permission. Pages 174–175 "Chain Saws—Safety, Operation, Tree Felling Techniques," by Eric Ward, Kansas Forest Service. Published by Kansas State University, Manhattan, KS, April 2011, MF2013Rev. Page 177 Peckham, Geoffrey. "Safety Symbols," originally appearing in *Compliance Engineering Magazine*. Used with permission, Clarion Safety Systems, LLC. Page 178 Placement of Hazard Statements: RYOBI. "RYOBI" is a registered trademark of Ryobi Limited. Used with permission. Pages 180–181 NASA, Glenn Research Center. Page 182 Troubleshooting Guide from Motion RC. Reprinted with permission of Motion RC. www.motionrc.com. Page 183 Mozilla.org. Pages 186–187 How do I share folders with other people? Used by permission of Dropbox. Page 190 Courtesy of the Metropolitan Transportation Authority, reprinted with permission.

Chapter 8 Page 201 The National Science Foundation, www.nsf.gov/. Pages 204–205 Rural Development, USDA. Page 221 U.S. Department of the Interior, U.S. Geological Survey, http://www.usgs.gov. Pages 224–225 © 2014 AirDroids, Inc. Used by permission.

Chapter 9 Page 234 Bioenergy Science White Paper, US Department of Agriculture Research, Research and Economics, Office of the Chief Scientist, July 24, 2012. Pages 244–247 Congressional Research Service, Library of Congress. http://www.loc.gov/crsinfo/.

Chapter 10 Pages 256–258 Office of Applied Studies, Substance Abuse & Mental Health Services Administration, http://www.samhsa.gov/. Page 263 U.S. Census Bureau, www.census.gov/. Page 264 The National Science Foundation, www.nsf.gov/. Page 277 ©2014 Google. Used with permission. Pages 281–283 USDA, www.usda.gov. Page 288 Patterns in sea otter resource selection in Kachemak Bay, Alaska by Nathan Lord Stewart. Used with permission of the author.

Chapter 11 Page 296 Monster.com. Reprinted by permission. Page 320 Melissa Meyer. Used with permission. Page 325 Welch Architecture, http://www.welcharchitecture.com. Used by permission of Cliff Welch.

Chapter 12 Page 333 Mozilla.org. Page 335 Logical Mapping Software. Diagram created in Inspiration® by Inspiration Software®, Inc. Used with permission of Inspiration Software.

Chapter 13 Pages 345–348 © 2001–2014 Robert Wood Johnson Foundation. All Rights Reserved. Used with permission. Pages 354–355 Copyright 2014 American Diabetes Association, reprinted with permission. Page 358 Courtesy NASA.

Chapter 14 Page 372 American Society of Civil Engineers, http://www.ascelibrary.org. Page 373 University of Minnesota Libraries screenshot. Regents of the University of Minnesota. Copyright 2014. All rights reserved. Pages 376–377 Bledsoe; Sar, Pearson Education Inc. Page 380 U.S. Department of the Interior, US Geological Survey, www.usgs.gov/. Page 382 U.S. Department of the Interior, US Geological Survey, www.usgs.gov/. Page 386 Zotero.org. Zotero is a project of the Roy Rosenzweig Center for History and New Media, and was initially funded by the Andrew W. Mellon Foundation, the Institute of Museum and Library Services, and the Alfred P. Sloan Foundation. Used with permission.

Chapter 15 Page 398 Roger Boisjoly. Page 398 Microsoft Corporation. Pages 405–406 Sunmoni, Mobolaji. "Flooding: Causes and Effects" from "The Environmentalist." http://ecoremediation.blogspot.com/2012/07/flooding-causes-and-effects.html. Used by permission of the author. Page 407 "Terrestrial and Jovian Planets" from NOVA, "Origins:

Where are the Aliens" website (http://www.pbs.org/wgbh/nova/education/activities/3113_origins_07.html) © 2010 WGBH Educational Foundation. Page 409 United States Environmental Protection Agency, www.epa.gov/. Page 410 Alan G. Aversa. Pages 412–414 Copyright © Washington State Department of Ecology.

Chapter 16 Page 427 Lawrence Livermore National Laboratory. Page 438 "What is Cloning?" from The Genetic Science Learning Center at The University of Utah. Copyright 2012. http://learn.genetics.utah.edu. Page 439 Chickscope, Imaging Technology Group, Beckman Institute for Advanced Science and Technology, University of Illinois at Urbana-Champaign. Used with permission. Page 440 Devra Davis/The Washington Post. Page 440 ©2014 CBS Interactive. All rights reserved. Page 441 Patrick Moore, A Persuasive Argument, Going Nuclear Over Global Warming, Sacramento Bee, December 12, 2007, http://www.sacbee.com/110/story/560569.html.

Chapter 17 Page 449 Manitoba Conservation Wildlife and Ecosystem Protection Branch. Page 450 Nuclear Weapons Journal, p. 13. Page 451 Fermi National Accelerator Laboratory, http://www.fnal.gov/. Page 454 Materials Science and Engineering, Winter 2012. Northwestern University Engineering, Robert R. McCormick School of Engineering and Applied Science. Copyright 2012. Used by permission of Northwestern University. Page 458 The Field Museum, Chicago, Illinois, http://www.fieldmuseum.org. Pages 462–463 Jabra BT160 Bluetooth User Manual, pp. 2–5. GN Netcom, Inc. Used by permission of GN Netcom, Inc. Page 466 Oil Market Report, May 13, 2008, International Energy Agency. Page 467 Microsoft Corporation. Page 469 Patricia Russo and Stephen Boor. 1993. How fluent is your interface?: designing for international users. In Proceedings of the INTERACT '93 and CHI '93 Conference on Human Factors in Computing Systems (CHI '93). ACM, New York, NY, USA, 342–347, Table 1. © 1993 Association for Computing Machinery, Inc. Reprinted by permission. DOI=10.1145/169059.169274 http://doi.acm.org/10.1145/169059.169274. Page 470 Microsoft Corporation. Page 474 State of New Jersey Department of Health and Senior Services, http://www.state.nj.us/health/.

Chapter 18 Page 478 'Policy Brief: Obesity update 2012 http://www.oecd.org/health/49716427.pdf ' originally presented in ' OECD (2010), Obesity and the Economics of Prevention: Fit not Fat, OECD Publishing. http://dx.doi.org/10.1787/9789264084865-en. Page 479 National Center for Education Statistics. Page 481 Labeling of a Graphic from British Household Survey Panel, The Poverty Site (www.poverty.org.uk). Used by permission of Guy Palmer. Page 482 Wolves and Moose of Isles Royale, www.isleroyalewolf.org. Used with permission. Page 483 Worksafe Department of Commerce, Used with Permission. Page 485 Substance Abuse & Mental Health Services Administration (SAMHSA). Page 486 Skin Type table adapted by SunSmart Victoria (2011) using Fitzpatrick scale (1975). Images courtesy Cancer Research UK. Page 487 US Dept. of Health and Human Services. Page 488 Australian Resuscitation Council. Page 491 United States Centers for Disease Control and Prevention. www.cdc.gov. Page 492 United States Centers for Disease Control and Prevention. www.cdc.gov. Page 494 International Symbols from AIGA.

Chapter 19 Page 510 U.S. Department of the Interior, U.S. Geological Survey, http://www.usgs.gov.

Chapter 20 Page 534 National Weather Service Weather Forecast Office, NOAA .gov. Page 550 © 2014 Toastmasters International. All rights reserved. Used with permission.

Chapter 21 Page 559 U.S. Forestry Service, http://www.fs.fed.us. Page 562 National Oceanic and Atmospheric Administration (NOAA), http://www.noaa.gov. Page 564 Microsoft Corporation. Free Online Translation Tool: Bing screenshot, Bing Translator 291.eda896321. Microsoft Corporation. Copyright 2014. http://www.bing.com/translator. Page 565 SmartFTP, http://wwwsmartftp.com. and Microsoft Corporation. Page 566 LinkedInCorporation. Page 568 Creating Your Blog from Wordpress.com, WordPress (Automattic, Inc.), http://www.wordpress.com. Page 570 Audacity, used with permission.

Photo Credits

Page 1 Moodboard/Alamy. Page 2 Fancy Collection/Superstock. Page 12 The Star-Ledger/Ed Murray/The Image Works. Page 15 Paul Conklin/PhotoEdit. Page 18 Hero Images/Digital Vision/Getty Images. Page 19 Bikeriderlondon/Shutterstock. Page 29 Anton Vengo/Superstock. Page 30 Mary Knox Merril/The Image Works. Page 34 LEGO and the LEGO Logo are trademarks of the LEGO Group of Companies, used here by permission. © 2014 The LEGO Group Page 35 Michaeljung/Fotolia. Page 39 John Fedele/Blend Images/Getty Images. Page 53 John Fedele/Blend Images/Getty Images. Page 59 Pete Leonard/Corbis. Page 60 Exactostock/Superstock. Page 64 Time & Life Pictures/Getty Images. Page 68 Aldo Leopold Foundation, Inc. Page 77 Hans Engbers/Alamy. Page 82 S. Dashkevych/Shutterstock. Page 83 Comstock Images/Getty Images. Page 84 Blend Images/ColorBlind Images/Getty Images. Page 104 More Images/Shutterstock. Page 119 PRISMA Visual & Written/The Image Works. Page 129 Courtesy NASA. Page 138 Jennifer Richards/Fotolia. Page 150 Helen King/Corbis. Page 152 Peter Chen/The Image Works. Page 155 Bob Daemmrich/PhotoEdit, Inc. Page 156 Centers for Diseases Control. Page 195 Roger Bamber/Alamy. Page 229 Auremar/Fotolia. Page 230 Norbert Schwerin/The Image Works. Page 252 Getty Images. Page 253 Age Fotostock/Shutterstock. Page 292 Laurence Mouton/Corbis. Page 293 Exactostock/Shutterstock. Page 318 Dorling Kindersley Limited. Page 321 Kayte Deioma/PhotoEdit, Inc. Page 328 Klaus Tiedge/Corbis. Page 329 corbisrffancy/Fotolia. Page 342 StocklLite/Shutterstock. Page 343 racon/shutterstock. Page 359 Dave and Les Jacobs/ Alamy. Page 363 © Jenoche/Fotolia. Page 364 David M. Grossman/The Image Works. Page 365 Fotostock. Page 375 David M. Grossman/The Image Works. Page 393 Jeff Greenberg/The Image Works. Page 394 Andrey_Popov/Shutterstock. Page 420 bikeriderlondon/Shutterstock. Page 421 racorn/Shutterstock. Page 445 auremar/Shutterstock. Page 446 Dotshock/Shutterstock. Page 473 StockLite/Shutterstock. Page 476 Erik Isakson/Getty Images. Page 478 Nada's Images/Fotolia. Page 489 Nikkytok/Fotolia. Page 490 Newark Museum/Art Resource. Page 492 Centers for Disease Control. Page 493 left Noedelhap/Getty Images. Page 493 right iStock/360/Getty Images. Page 494 AIGA Journal of Graphic Design. Page 497 Bob Daemmrich/The Image Works. Page 498 imtmphoto/Shutterstock. Page 515 Serge Bertasius Photography/Shutterstock. Page 518 Tyler Olson/Fotolia. Page 520 Flying Colours Ltd/Getty Images. Page 521 Stockbyte/Corbis. Page 528 Doug Martin/Photo Researchers, Inc. Page 529 Dorling Kindersley. Page 530 Exactostock/SuperStock. Page 534 goodween123/Fotolia. Page 536 Dmitriy Shironosov/Alamy. Page 540 Cultura RM/Alamy. Page 546 Bob Daemmrich/PhotoEdit, Inc. Page 553 Hossein Fatemi/Newscom. Page 556 Ralf Schultheiss/Corbis. Page 557 Monkey Business/Fotolia. Page 563 left Nasa.gov. Page 563 left NASA. Page 563 right Purdue University. Page 574 RTimages/Alamy.

Index

a, use of article, A-19
Abandonment/Acceptance, of hypothesis, 390
Ableton Live, 570
Abstract, in analytical report, 278–280
Acceptance/Abandonment, of hypothesis, 390
Access points
　in document design, 447
　headings as, 459
Acronyms
　apostrophe use with, A-14
　in transcultural documents, 429
Action verbs. *See also* Verbs
　in activity reports, 239
　in analytical report, 259
　in describing purpose, 6, 6*f*
　in instructions and documentation, 155
　in letters, memos, and e-mail, 89
　in proposals, 201
　in résumé, 306
　in technical descriptions and specifications, 124
Active voice
　in analytical reports, 285
　in application letters, 316
　passive voice and, 316, 435–437
Activity journal, 236
Activity reports, 231–249
　briefings as, 231
　conclusion in, 241
　context of use, 239
　features of, 232
　incident reports, 232, 235*f*
　introduction in, 240, 240*f*
　laboratory reports, 236, 237*f*–238*f*
　medium for, 243
　organizing and drafting of, 239–241
　planning and researching of, 236, 239
　progress reports, 231, 233*f*, 242*f*
　purpose of, 231, 239
　readers of, 239
　status reports, 249–250, 250*f*
　style and design of, 241, 243–247
　subject of, 239
　types of, 231–236
　white papers as, 231, 234*f*
Address, on envelope, 109, 109*f*
Adjectives, order of, A-20
Adjustment letters and memos, 93, 96, 97*f*
Adobe Audition, 570
Adobe Dreamweaver, 184
Adobe InDesign, 460
Adobe Photoshop, 491
Adobe Premiere, 570
Advantages. *See* Better and worse statements
Adverbs
　order of, A-20–A-21
　proper placement of, A-20–A-21
Advertisements, classified, 297
Agenda, for meeting, 48, 49*f*
　recap of items on, 50

Agreement
　pronoun-antecedent disagreement, A-5
　subject-verb, A-4–A-5
Alignment
　centering and, 456, 457*f*
　as design element, 447, 455–456
　in résumé, 308
　of sentence subjects in paragraph, 433–434
Amazon Prime, 371
Amazon S3, 569
American Institute of Aeronautics and Astronautics (AIAA), survey by, 14
American Institute of Graphic Arts (AIGA), symbols created by, 493, 494*f*
Analogies, 439
　in technical descriptions, 137
Analysis charts
　Context Analysis Chart, 23, 23*f*
　Reader Analysis Chart, 22, 22*f*
　Team Performance Review, 56*f*
　Writer-Centered, reader identification and, 20–21, 20*f*
Analytical reports, 254–288
　conclusions and recommendations in, 267
　designing, 286, 286*f*
　drafting front and back matter for, 278–284
　feasibility reports, 253, 268*f*–276*f*
　features of, 255
　as genre, 2
　graphics in, 286
　IMRaD pattern for, 254, 255
　methodology section of, 266
　nature of, 3*f*
　organizing and drafting of, 265–276
　planning of, 259–260
　poster presentation as, 287, 288*f*
　purpose of, 254, 259
　researching, 260–265
　results section of, 266–267
　style of, 285–286
　types of, 255
　virtual teaming and, 277–278, 277*f*
Android phones, giving presentations with, 534
Anecdotes, in presentation introduction, 531
Angle, of research, 368
Animal symbols and mascots, 494
Antecedent, pronoun-antecedent disagreement and, A-5
APA documentation style, 384–385, A-24
　in-text citations, A-25–A-27
　reference list for, 384*f*, 385, A-27–A-30
Apostrophe, 507*f*, A-13–A-14
　possession signaled by, A-13–A-14
　using with plurals of numbers, acronyms, and symbols, A-14
Appendixes, in analytical report, 284
Application letters, 310, 313–319

　content and organization of, 310, 310*f*, 315
　education emphasized in, 314*f*
　features of, 295
　revising and proofreading, 317
　style of, 316–317
　work experience emphasized in, 315*f*
Argumentativeness, high-context cultures and, 359
Arm gestures, in presentation, 546
Articles (grammar), for ESL, A-19–A-20
Articles (publication)
　in APA documentation style, A-29
　in CSE documentation style, A-33
　in journals and newspapers, 374
　in MLA documentation style, A-38
　for wikis, 571–572
Asia, direction of reading in, 31, 31*f*, 569
Asides, using em dashes to set off, A-16
Ask.com, 371, 534
Attachments, to e-mail, 85, 88*f*, 112
AtTask, 42, 43*f*
Attire
　for interview, 320
　for presentation, 545
Attitudes
　in application letters, 316
　nature of, 22
　persuasion through, 356
　of readers, 22
Audacity, 570
Audience. *See also* Readers
　for presentation, 524, 530, 538
　test, for presentation, 548, 550*f*
　transcultural, presentations for, 548, 550, 552–553
Audio, presentations and, 534
Author-year system, in CSE documentation style, A-30, A-31
Authoritative tone, mapping of, 438, 439*f*
Authors
　in APA documentation style, A-25–A-30
　in CSE documentation style, A-31–A-34
　in MLA documentation style, A-35–A-36
Awards and activities
　in portfolio, 318
　in résumé, 307

Babylon, 429, 509
Back matter, drafting, 284
Back translation, 429
Background color, in design, 467
Background information
　for e-mail, 99, 111
　for instructions and documentation, 165
　in introduction, 400
　for letter or memo, 99, 100*f*
　for presentation, 535
　for proposals, 202
　for technical description, 125
Backward-planning project calendar, 42, 44*f*
"Bad news" letters, 96, 98*f*

Balance, as design element, 447–455, 492 (fig.)
  in résumé, 308
  on website, 561, 562, 562*f*
Banners
  in interface, 451*f*, 456, 458*f*
  rules and, 460
Bar charts, 483–484, 484*f*
  ethical and unethical, 477, 478*f*
"bcc" line, 85
Because, in persuasion process, 349
  online, 352
Beliefs, in online persuasion strategy, 352
Better and worse statements, 350, 404
Bias
  personal, 388
  of sources, 387–388
Binder, portfolio in, 318*f*, 319
Bing, 371, 429
Bing Translator, 430*f*, 509, 564, 564*f*
Bio, 324–325
blip.tv, 569
Block format, for message in letter, 108
Blogger (software), 568
Blogs, 78
  in APA documentation style, A-29
  creating, 568–569, 568*f*
  as research source, 371
Blogsome, 568
Body
  of activity reports, 241
  of application letter, 313
  of current situation section (proposals), 208, 209*f*
  of document, 395, 396*f*, 397*f*
  of document section, 402, 402*f*, 403
  of e-mail, 85, 88*f*, 100*f*, 101
  of letter or memo, 85, 100*f*, 101
  of methodology section of analytical report, 266
  organizing and drafting, 402–410
  of presentation, 535–537
  of project plan (proposals), 211
  sections of, 402–403, 402*f*
  of webpage, 561
Body language, during presentation, 545–546
Boisjoly, Roger, 395, 397*f*
Books
  in APA documentation style, A-28
  in CSE documentation style, A-32
  in MLA documentation style, A-37
  as research source, 373
Borders, in design, 460, 461*f*
Boxing, 337
  in drafting process, 338*f*
Brackets, A-18
Brainstorming. *See also* Logical mapping
  in creating tone, 105–106
  for e-mail, 105–106
  idea generation through, 336
  for letter or memo, 105–106
  for website content, 560
Briefings, 231
Bureaucratic phrasing, 106, 316
Buzzsprout, 569

© (copyright symbol), 80
Calculations, in analytical report, 284
Calendar(s)
  groupware for, 54, 55*f*, 333–334
  online, planning with, 333–334
  project, 42, 43*f*, 44*f*, 333–334, 333*f*
"Calling the question," consensus and, 50
Care, in social ethics, 66, 66*f*
Career objective, in résumé, 299, 300
Career summary, in résumé, 300
Careers, 294–325
  application letters, 295, 310, 313–319
  goals for, setting, 294
  interviewing strategies, 320–324
  networking for, 296–297
  planning for, 294–298
  professional bio, 324–325
  professional portfolio, 317–320
  résumé for, 295, 298–309
  sources for job search, 294–298
Case studies, in research, 264, 375
The Catalog of U.S. Government Publications, 374
Cause and effect
  as document pattern of arrangement, 403–404, 405*f*–406*f*
  as presentation pattern, 536, 537*f*
  in proposals, 203
  statements of, 349
Caution statements, in instructions, 176, 177*f*
"cc" line, 85, 111
CD-ROMs
  in APA documentation style, A-29
  in CSE documentation style, A-33
  in MLA documentation style, A-38
CDs
  online documentation on, 183, 184
  for research, 371
Centered text, alignment problems with, 456, 457*f*
Chalkboard, for presentations, 527
Change
  creativity and, 334
  in instructions and documentation, 166
  technical descriptions and, 126
Charts
  bar charts, 483–484, 484*f*
  flowcharts, 486–487, 488*f*
  Gantt chart defined, 482
  pie charts, 485–486, 487*f*
"Checkpoints," 332
Chrome (browser), 140, 371
Chronological order
  as document pattern of arrangement, 408
  in presentation, 535, 537*f*
Chronological résumé, 298, 299–307
  examples of, 301*f*–305*f*
Citation manager, 385–386, 386*f*
Citation-sequence system, in CSE documentation style, A-30–A-34
Claim letters and memos, 93, 95*f*
Clarification questions, 539
Clarizen, 42
Classified advertisements, job search in, 297

Clichés
  in e-mail, 112
  in transcultural documents, 511
  on websites, 564
Client satisfaction, 55
Clip art, 492
Closed-ended questions, 375
Closing, of document
  letter, 107*f*, 108–109
  memo, 110*f*, 111
  project plan (proposals), 211
Closing, of document section
  in body of document, 402, 402*f*, 403
  in current situation section (proposals), 208
  in methodology section of analytical report, 266
Clothing
  for interview, 320
  for presentation, 545
Code of ethics
  of IEEE, 71*f*
  sample of, 71*f*
Collaboration. *See* Teaming
College placement office, 297
Colloquialisms, on websites, 564
Colons, 507*f*, A-11–A-12, A-11–A-13
  to lead off lists, A-12
  misuse of, A-12–A-13
  in titles, numbers, and greetings, A-12
  using with quotation marks, A-12
Color
  in design, 467
  in highlighting of text, 467
  in other cultures, 31, 468, 469*f*
Comma splice, A-1–A-2
Command voice, for instructions and documentation, 171, 190
Commas, 507*f*, A-9–A-11
  in numbers, dates, and place names, A-10
  with quotation marks, A-10
  removing excess, A-11
Commentary, in research process, 383
Comments
  about subject of sentence, 423
  instructional steps with, 173
  in social networking, 567
Common knowledge, citing sources for, 389
Communication. *See also specific type of communication*
  transcultural. *See* Transcultural communication
  in virtual teaming, 52–53
Comparison and contrast
  as document pattern of arrangement, 404, 407*f*
  as presentation pattern, 537, 537*f*
Compelling statement, in presentation introduction, 531
Complaint letters and memos, 93, 95*f*
Completion reports, 254
Compound words, hyphens with, A-17
Computers. *See also* Internet; Software; Word processors
  clip art and, 492
  in collaboration process, 10, 11

cookies and, 77
for cultural research, 32
cyberbullying and, 74–75
and digital projector, for presentations, 526, 528f
electronic networks, 52, 54, 77
ethics of using electronic files, 78–80
global and transcultural communication and, 24
keeping notes on, 379, 379f
on-screen documentation, 183–184
plain sentences created with, 427–428
in research process, 6
spelling and grammar checker on, 429, 505, 506, 507f, 508
virtual teaming with, 52–53, 54–55, 277–278, 277f
Concept map, in research, 367, 367f
Conciseness
in instructions and documentation, 171
reader desire for, 20
Conclusion
in activity reports, 241, 242f
in analytical reports, 267
in application letter, 313
closing moves in, 411, 414
in document, 395, 396f, 397f, 415f
in e-mail, 85, 88f, 101
indirect approach to, in transcultural communication, 415–416, 417f
in instructions and documentation, 177, 179
in letter or memo, 85, 101, 101f
main point restated in, 102–103
organizing and drafting, 411, 414
in presentation, 537–539
in proposals, 218, 219f
in technical descriptions, 137
in webpage, 561
Conclusion slides, for presentation, 538f
Conditions required, in instructions, 170
Conflict
handling, in forming stage of teaming, 43–44
managing, in storming phase of teaming, 44, 48–51
mediating, in meetings, 50–51, 51f
Conflict mediation methods, 50–51, 51f
Consensus, reaching in meetings, 50
in high-context cultures, 359
Conservation ethics, 64, 65f, 67–69
ethical dilemma and, 69, 70f
Consistency
as design element, 447, 459, 461–466, 462f–463f, 562
in language use, 429, 459
in layouts, 462f–463f
in résumé, 308
Constitution (U.S.), 76–77, 78
Constitutional rights, in social ethics, 65
Consultation with colleagues, resolving ethical dilemmas and, 72
Contact information
in analytical reports, 267
in conclusion, 414

in proposals, 218, 219f
in résumé, 299
Content
of application letter, 310, 310f, 313
cultural differences in, 24, 28–29
editing for, 501
generating through mapping, 100, 100f
organizing, 395, 396
of presentations, organizing, 529–540
Context
of subject, in technical description, 126
of use. See Context of use
Context Analysis Chart, 23, 23f, 24
Context of use
for activity reports, 239
for analytical reports, 260
for e-mail, 90
in editing process, 501
in forming stage of teaming, 41
identifying, 22–24
for instructions and documentation, 165
for letters and memos, 90
page layout fitting, 139
for presentations, 524–525
for proposals, 202
reader profiles and, 24, 25f–28f
in rhetorical situation, 5, 5f, 90
for technical descriptions, 125
for websites, 560
Contextual cues, in transcultural communication, 24, 357, 359–360
Continuous Quality Improvement (CQI), 55
Contractions, apostrophes with, A-13
Contrast
as design element, 447, 466–467, 562
in résumé, 308
in webpage, 467f
Cookies, computer, 77
Coordinator (team role), 42
Copyediting, 8, 499, 503–505
symbols for, 509, 509f, 510f
Track Changes feature and, 503, 504f
Copyright law, 76, 78–80, 79f
avoiding problems with, 79–80, 265
copyrighting one's own work, 80
plagiarism and, 80
Copyright symbol (©), 80
Corel VideoStudio, 570
Corporate authors
in APA documentation style, A-26, A-28
in CSE documentation style, A-32
in MLA documentation style, A-36, A-37
Corporate codes, resolving ethical dilemma and, 70
Corporate policies, social ethics and, 65
Correspondence. See also E-mail; Letters; Memos
in APA documentation style, A-27, A-30
in CSE documentation style, A-34
in MLA documentation style, A-38
Costs and benefits
as document pattern of arrangement, 404, 406
as proposal section, 218, 219f
statements of, 350
Coursework, in résumé, 300

Cover letters and memos, 90, 93, 94f
Cover sheet, for portfolio, 318
Creativity
generating new ideas, 336–341
in strategic planning, 336–341
Cropping, digital photography and, 138–139
Cross-cultural communication. See Transcultural communication
CSE (citation-sequence) documentation style, A-30–A-34, A-24
Cues, contextual, in transcultural communication, 357, 359–360
Culturally deep documents, 468
Culturally shallow documents, 468
design considerations for, 468–469
Culture. See also Transcultural communication
design and, 468–470
design considerations and, 31–32, 31f
high-context, 357, 359–360
low-context, 414
Customers, interacting with, social networking sites and, 567
Cyberbullying, 74–75

Dailymotion, 569
Danger statements, in instructions, 176
Dangling modifier, A-3–A-4
Dashes, 507f, A-16–A-17
em dashes, A-16
en dashes in numbers and dates, A-17
Data
in graphs, tables, and charts, 481–487
persuasion with, 351
Databases, research, 371, 372f
Dates
commas in, A-10
dashes in, A-17
Decisions
how readers make, 22
recording in meetings, 50
Deliverables, in forming stage of teaming, 41
Delivery, of presentation, 545–548
Deming, W. Edwards, 55
Description by features/functions, in presentation, 536, 537f
Design, 447–470. See also Design elements
of activity reports, 243, 244f–247f
of analytical reports, 286, 286f
cultural differences in, 31–32, 31f, 468–470
editing for, 502
importance of, 10f, 13f, 20
of instructions and documentation, 184–188
of letters and memos, 106–109
of presentation visuals, 542–543
principles of, 447. See also specific principles
of proposals, 218, 220–222
of résumé, 308
of technical descriptions, 139–143
for transcultural communication, 189
of websites, 561–562, 562f
in writing process, 3, 4f, 8, 10f, 106–109

Design elements
    alignment as, 447, 455–456, 561–562
    balance as, 447–455, 561–562
    borders and rules as, 460, 461f
    consistency as, 447, 459, 461–466, 462f–463f, 562
    contrast as, 447, 466–467, 562
    grouping as, 447, 456–461, 561
    typefaces as, 461, 464, 464f
Designer (team role), 42
Diagrams, 491, 491f
Dictionary
    online, 508
    for spelling, 508
Digital photographs, in technical description, 138–139
Digital projector, for presentations, 526, 528f
Direction of reading, 31, 31f, 469, 470f
Disadvantages. See Better and worse statements
Discussion lists, 54
Discussion section, in analytical report, 267
Dissent, in meetings, 50
Document cycling, 512, 512f
Document design. See Design
Document Map, drafting in, 337, 337f
Documentation. See also Instructions and documentation
    categories of, 153
    features of, 154
    on-screen, 183–184
Documentation of sources, 383–388, A-24–A-39
    APA documentation style, 384–385, A-24, A-25–A-30
    to avoid plagiarism or copyright problems, 79–80, 265, 389
    CSE documentation style (citation-sequence), A-24, A-30–A-31
    footnotes/endnotes, A-25
    MLA documentation style, A-24, A-34–A-39
Documents
    commenting on, 54
    comparison with website, 559, 560f
    culturally deep/culturally shallow, 468–469
    designing. See Design
    for general public vs. experts, 25f–28f
    groupware for posting, 54
    improving quality of, strategies for, 512
    outlining of, 337, 337f, 395–396, 398f, 399
    patterns of arrangement for, 254, 255, 403–412
    posting of, 54
    reason-based/values-based statements in, 344f
    reasoning used in, 345f–348f
    revising, 499–501
    substantive editing of, 8, 501–503, 503f
    transcultural. See Transcultural documents
    word usage problems in, 508, 508f
Drafting, 399–414
    of activity reports, 239–241
    of analytical reports, 265–276

of basic webpages, 560–561
of body, 402–410
of conclusion, 411, 414
front and back matter for analytical reports, 278–284
of instructions and documentation, 167–182
of introduction, 399–401, 400, 401f
of navigational pages, 559–560
outlining and, 337, 337f, 395–396
of proposals, 203–218
of technical descriptions, 128, 131–137
in writing process, 4f, 6
Dragga, S., 86
Drawings, using, 487–492
Dress
    for interviews, 320
    for presentation, 545
Dropbox, sharing documents via, 11, 78, 243, 512
DVDs
    online documentation on, 183, 184
    for research, 371

E-mail
    in APA documentation style, A-30
    attachments to, 85, 88f, 112
    claim, 93
    complaint, 93
    conclusion in, 102
    context of use and, 90
    in CSE documentation style, A-34
    described, 85
    face-to-face communication vs., 352
    features of, 85, 88f
    formatting of, 85–86, 88f
    graphics in, 112
    header for, 85
    of inquiry, 90
    introduction in, 85, 96, 99, 101, 101f
    message area of, 88f
    in MLA documentation style, A-38
    netiquette for, in transcultural communication, 111–112
    organizing and drafting, 96, 99–103
    planning and researching, 88–90
    of refusal, 96
    of response, 90
    sharing documents via, 11
    signature file for, 112
    signature in, 88f
    status report, 249–250, 250f
    style of, 105–106
    subject line in, 85
    thank you, 324
    transcultural communication and, 111–112
    transmittal, 90, 93
    types of, 90–97
Economic context of use, 23
    for analytical reports, 260
    for presentation, 525
    for proposals, 202
Ecosystem, as ethical issue, 67–69
Editing
    copyediting. See Copyediting

levels of, 499–508, 500f
of podcasts, 570, 571f
proofreading and. See Proofreading
revising. See Revising
spelling and grammar checkers and, 429, 505, 506, 507f, 508
substantive, 8, 499, 501–503, 503f
in transcultural communication, 509, 511–512
of videos, 570
in writing process, 3, 4f, 8–9
Editor (team role), 42
Editorial comments, using brackets for, A-18
Educational background
    in application letter, 314f
    in portfolio, 318
    in résumé, 300
Einstein, Albert, 61–64, 64f
    letter to Roosevelt, 62f–63f
Either... or, as document pattern of arrangement, 349, 408, 410f
Elaboration questions, 539
Electronic networks
    as intranets, 52
    local area, 54
    surveillance in, 77
Electronic portfolio, 319, 320f
Electronic sources, in research, 371, 372f
Elevator pitch, as proposal, 223–225
Ellipses, A-18
    to show thought is trailing off, A-18
    to signal information removal from quote, A-18
Em dashes, A-16
Emergency instructions, 189–191
Emotional tone, mapping of, 184, 185f, 220f, 437, 438f
Empirical research, 365, 366, 366f, 374–378
    reports on, 254
    sources in, 371
En dashes, A-17
EndNote, 385
English as a Second Language (ESL), grammar guide for, A-19–A-23
English language, in instructions for transcultural markets, 188
Enthusiasm, in presentation, 542
Envelopes, 109, 109f
Environment, conservation ethics and, 64, 65f, 67–69
Error(s)
    admitting, in online persuasion strategy, 352
    of grammar. See Grammar, common errors in
Ethical codes
    of IEEE, 71f
    sample of, 71f
Ethical context of use, 24
    for analytical reports, 260
    for presentation, 525
Ethical dilemma(s)
    balancing different issues in, 69–70, 70f
    categories of, 66–67

defined, 61
nature of, 61
resolving, 61, 69–73
Ethics, 61–80
balancing different issues in, 69–70, 70f
conflicts between individual and
company, 72–73
conservation, 64, 65f, 67–69, 70f
copyright law and, 76
defined, 61
dilemmas in, 61
of graphics, 479, 480f
personal, 64–65, 65f, 69, 70f
in proposals, 202
resolving dilemmas and, 69–73
safety information and, 190
social, 64, 65–67, 65f, 69, 70f
sources of, 64–69, 65f
in technical communication, 12
in technical workplace, 76–78
Ethnographies, in research, 375
Etiquette, for e-mail in transcultural
communication, 111–112
European Union, symbols created by, 493,
493f, 494f
Evaluation of presentation, 548, 551f–552f
form for, 551f–552f
Evidence, reasoning with, 344, 344f,
350–351
Examples
as document pattern of arrangement, 408
instructional steps with, 173
reasoning with, 344, 344f, 350
Excel, 485
Exclamation point, 507f, A-9
Executive summary, in analytical report,
278–280, 281f–283f
Expenses, in activity reports, 241
Experiences, persuasion with, 350–351
Experiments, in research, 264, 374
Experts. See also Subject matter experts
(SMEs)
documents prepared for general public
vs., 25f–28f
quoting in persuasive argument, 351
Extended definitions, 144, 145
External proposals, 196, 203
Eye contact
cultural differences, 321
during presentation, 546
transcultural communication and, 32
with translator of presentation, 553

Face-to-face communication, e-mail vs., 352
Facebook, 75, 566, 567
anti-harassment and cyberbullying poli-
cies, 74, 74f
Facilitator, for meeting, 48
Facts, persuasion with, 351
in high-context cultures, 359
Fair use, of copyrighted material, 78, 79–80
Faulty parallelism, A-5–A-6
Feasibility reports, 254, 268f–276f
Features, partitioning subject by, 127
Feedback
in instructions, 176

for presentation, 548, 551f–552f
quality feedback loop, 55, 512
Field notes
and observations, in research, 374
purpose of, 120
File transfer protocol (FTP), uploading
website and, 564, 564f
Films
in APA documentation style, A-28
in CSE documentation style, A-33
in MLA documentation style, A-38
Final Cut, 570
Firefox (browser), 184, 371
citation management and, 385, 386f
First Amendment, on trademarked items,
76–77
First-level headings, 458, 459f
Five-W and How Questions
for activity reports, 236
for analytical reports, 259
for career goals, 294
in defining rhetorical situation, 4, 5f
for drafting introductions, 399
idea generation through, 338–339
for instructions and documentation, 155
for letters and memos, 88
for presentations, 523
for proposals, 196
for technical descriptions, 120
for website, 560
Flip charts, for presentations, 527, 529
Flowcharts, 486–487, 488f
Fonts
in presentation visuals, 542–543, 543f
serif and sans serif, 461, 464, 464f
size of, 467
Footers, inserting, 466, 466f
Forecasting
in analytical report introduction, 265,
270f
in conclusions, 102, 267, 411, 539
of content in introduction, 400
presentation's structure, 535
Formal presentations, 522
Formal usability testing, 512, 513f
Formality, in high-context cultures, 360
Formatting
of e-mail, 85–86, 88f
of envelopes, 109, 109f
of letters, 85–86, 86f, 106–109, 107f
of memos, 85–86, 87f, 109–111, 110f
of presentation visuals, 542
Forming stage of teaming, 40–44, 40f
Fourth-level headings, 458, 459f
Fragments, A-3
Frames, in persuasion, 351
Framing
logical mapping for, 357f
from reader's perspective, 356
reframing and, 356, 358f
Fraud, ethics and, 78
Freewriting, idea generation through,
336f, 337
for website content, 560
Friends, on social networking sites, 566
Front matter, drafting, 278–284

Functional résumé, 298, 307–308, 309f
Functions, partitioning subject by, 127
Future, looking to, in conclusion, 102, 267,
411, 539
Future tenses, A-22
perfect, A-22
perfect progressive, A-22
progressive, A-22

Gantt chart, defined, 482
GarageBand, 570
Gatekeepers (supervisors), 20f, 21
of analytical reports, 260
of e-mail, 89
of instructions and documentation,
165
for letters and memos, 89
for presentations, 524
of proposals, 202
of technical descriptions, 125
Gender
in personal titles, 108, 111
transcultural communication and, 31
Genius Project, 42
Genre set, 3
Genres
choosing, 395
examples of, 3f
nature of, 2–3
organization by, 395–396, 398f, 399
technical writing process and, 3–9
Gif (graphic interchange format) files, 563,
563f
Given/new method of writing, for paragraphs, 434–435
Global communication, strategies for, 32.
See also Transcultural communication
"Global editing," 499
Global market, 14, 15f
Glossary
in analytical report, 284
of technical definitions, 144
Goals
for career, 294
and needs compared, 353
in persuasion, 351
Goldstein, Noah, 352
Good Collaboration Suite, 52
Google, 333, 371, 387
Google Drive, sharing documents via, 11,
52, 54, 78, 277–278, 277f, 512
Google Translate, 509, 564
Google Video, 569
Google.com, 534
Government publications
in APA documentation style, A-28
in CSE documentation style, A-33
in MLA documentation style, A-37
as research source, 374
Grabbers, for presentation, 533
Grammar
in e-mails, transcultural communication
and, 111
ESL guide to. See Grammar guide, for
ESL
and punctuation guide, A-1–A-8

Grammar, common errors in, 506*f*
  comma splice, A-1–A-2
  dangling modifier, A-3–A-4
  faulty parallelism, A-5–A-6
  fragments, A-3
  pronoun-antecedent disagreement, A-5
  proofreading for, 505, 506*f*
  run-on sentences, A-2–A-3
  shifted tense and, A-7
  subject-verb disagreement, A-4–A-5
  vague pronoun, A-7–A-8
Grammar checkers, 505, 507*f*
Grammar guide, for ESL, A-19–A-23
  adjective order, A-20
  adverb order, A-20–A-21
  articles, A-19–A-20
  verb tenses, A-21–A-23
Grand style, 422
Grant proposals, 196
Graphics, 477–496. *See also* Visuals
  in analytical reports, 286
  bar charts as, 483–484, 484*f*
  choosing, 481, 482*f*
  clip art as, 492
  copyediting, 505
  data display with, 481–487
  in e-mail, 112
  ethical use of, 479, 480*f*
  flowcharts as, 486–487, 488*f*
  Gantt chart defined, 482
  guidelines for using, 477–481
  on home page, 559*f*
  illustrations as, 491–492
  for instructions and documentation, 186,
    186*f*–187*f*
  labeling and placement of, 464, 479–480,
    481*f*
  line drawings and diagrams, 491, 491*f*
  line graphs as, 481–483, 482*f*–483*f*
  photographs as. *See* Photographs
  pie charts as, 485–486, 487*f*
  in presentations, 544, 544*f*
  in proposals, 220, 221*f*, 222
  storytelling with, 477, 478*f*
  tables as, 484–485, 485*f*, 486*f*
  for technical descriptions, 127, 140, 143*f*
  in transcultural communication, 32,
    468–469, 492–494
  written text complemented by, 477, 478*f*,
    479*f*, 486*f*
Graphs
  data display with, 481–483, 482*f*–483*f*
  storytelling with, 477, 479, 479*f*
"Green Century," 69
Greetings
  colons in, A-12
  interview, 321
  in letter, 107*f*, 108
Grids
  for interfaces, 455*f*
  for page layout, 451–455, 452*f*–453*f*,
    454*f*
Grouping
  as design element, 447, 456–461, 561
  as online persuasion strategy, 352
  in résumé, 308

Groupware, 52
  using for project scheduling, 54, 55*f*,
    333–334
  for virtual teams, 277–278, 277*f*
Hand gestures/signals
  in presentations, 546, 547
  transcultural communication and, 31, 32,
    189, 469, 494
Handouts, for presentations, 528, 553
Harassment
  computer, 74–75
  through questions, 539–540
Hazard statements, in instructions, 177,
    177*f*
  placement of, 178*f*
Headers
  in e-mail, 85
  inserting, 466, 466*f*
  of memo, 109, 110*f*
Headings
  as access points, 459
  consistency in, 459
  copyediting, 505
  levels of, 458, 459*f*
Heckling questions, 540
Help, asking for, as online persuasion
    strategy, 352
Help & Manual, 183
Helpinator, 183
Hierarchy, in high-context cultures, 360
High-context cultures, 357, 359–360
  organization of document for, 414–417
"High-context" linguistic strategies, 24
Highlighting of text, 467
Historical records, resolving ethical di-
    lemma and, 72
Home page, 558, 559*f*
Horizontal alignment, 455
Hostile questions, 539
Hulu, 569
Hulu Plus, 569
Human icons, 493–494
Human rights, in social ethics, 65
Humor
  in e-mail, 112
  in transcultural communication, 32, 511
  in transcultural presentation, 550
  on websites, 564
Hyphens, 507*f*, A-16–A-17
  in compound words, A-17
  to connect prefixes, A-17
Hypothesis
  abandoning/accepting, 390
  in analytical reports, 261, 265
  in research, 366*f*, 368, 390
  revising, 265, 390

I and *me,* pronoun case error with, A-6–A-7
Icons
  common, 492*f*
  cultural, on websites, 564
  culture-specific, 494
  in emergency instructions, 190
  as graphics, 492*f*
  human, 493–494

  in instructions for transcultural markets,
    189
  for safety information, 177, 177*f*
Ideals, in persuasion, 351
Idioms, in transcultural documents, 511
IEC symbols, 177*f*
If . . . then, as document pattern of arrange-
    ment, 349, 408, 409*f*
IHMC Concept Mapping Software, 336
Illustrations, 491–492
Images
  animal, 494
  human icons, 493–494
  inserting, 490–491
  in other cultures, 468–469
  in photography, 488–491, 489*f*, 490*f*
iMovie, 570
Importance of task, in instructions, 167
IMRaD pattern, for analytical reports, 254,
    255
In-text citations, 380, 383
  in APA documentation style, 384, A-
    25–A-27
  in MLA documentation style,
    A-35–A-36
  using quotation marks with, A-16
Incident reports, 232, 235*f*
Indexes, to research sources, 374
Indirect approach, to introductions and
    conclusions, in transcultural communi-
    cation, 415–416, 417*f*
Informal presentations, 522
Informal usability testing, 512, 513*f*
Information
  for analytical report, 263–265,
    263*f*–264*f*
  appraising sources of, 387–390
  balanced on screen, 561
  collection methods, in research, 263–265
  documenting sources of, A-24–A-39
  need-to-know. *See* Need-to-know
    information
  proprietary, ethics and, 77–78
  sharing, ethics of, 76, 77, 78. *See also*
    Groupware
  want-to-tell, in research, 378
Information management, 6, 365, 378–388,
    395
Informative documents, purpose of, action
    verbs defining, 6, 6*f*
Innovation, 55
Inquiry, letter/memo/e-mail of, 90, 91*f*
Insert Picture command, 491
Inside address, 107*f*, 108
Inspiration (software), 335*f*
Instant messaging (IM), 54
Instructions and documentation
  danger statements in, 176
  design of, 184–188
  drafting, 167–182
  emergency instructions, 189–191
  examples of, 156*f*–157*f*
  features of, 153, 154
  as genre, 7, 7*f*
  graphics in, 176, 177, 177*f*, 186,
    186*f*–187*f*, 190

as learning tool, 179, 180f–181f
online, 183–184
organizing, 167–182
parts, tools, and conditions required in, 168–170
planning, 155, 164–165
researching, 165–166, 166f
safety information and symbols in, 176–177, 177f, 189–191
sequentially ordered steps in, 170–176, 170f, 172f
style of, 184–188
for transcultural readers, 188–189
troubleshooting in, 179, 182f
user-testing of, 179
Interactivity, computers for, 10, 11f
Interfaces
alignment of, 458f
balanced, 451f, 454f
design of, 561–562, 562f
grids for, 455f
grouping in, 458f
right-to-left design, 469, 470f
stable, 456, 458f
Internal proposals, 196, 198f–200f
International communication. See Transcultural communication
International Organization for Standardization (ISO)
9000/14000 standards, 125, 126f, 138
symbols approved by, 177
symbols created by, 493, 494f
website, 125, 126f
International symbols, 177, 493, 493f, 494f
Internet. See also E-mail; Search engines; Social networking; Webpages; Websites
fraud on, 78
job search process on, 294, 296, 296f
obtaining information from, 263, 263f–264f
online documentation on, 184
online persuasion strategies, 352
sources for technical definitions on, 508
Interpretation of text, reader responsibility for, 19
Interviews
in APA documentation style, A-30
in CSE documentation style, A-34
in job search process, 320–324
in MLA documentation style, A-38
in research process, 264, 374
strategies for, 320–324
Intranets, 52
Introduction
in activity reports, 240, 240f
in analytical reports, 265
in application letter, 313
to document, 395, 396f, 397f, 399–401
in e-mail, 85, 96, 99, 102
home page as, 558, 559f
indirect approach to, in transcultural communication, 415–416, 417f
in instructions and documentation, 167
in letter or memo, 85, 96, 99–101, 100f–101f

opening moves in, 399–400, 401f
organizing and drafting, 399–401
to presentation, 530–535, 532
in proposals, 206, 207f
in technical descriptions, 131, 135
versions of, 400, 401f
Invention techniques, 335–341
iPad, giving presentations with, 534
iPhone, giving presentations with, 534
Irony, quotation marks signaling, A-15–A-16
ISO. See International Organization for Standardization (ISO)
iTunes, 569

Jargon, 285
in transcultural communication, 511, 552
in transcultural documents, 429
Job search process
application letter in, 295, 310, 313–319
Internet in, 294, 296, 296f
interviews in, 320–324
job-searching cycle and, 298f
planning, 294–298
professional bio in, 324–325
professional portfolio in, 317–320
résumé in, 295, 298–309, 317
Jokes. See Humor
Journalist's questions. See Five-W and How Questions
Journals
in APA documentation style, A-29
in CSE documentation style, A-33
in MLA documentation style, A-38
as research source, 373
Jpeg (joint photographic experts group) files, 563
Justice, in social ethics, 65, 66–67, 66f
tension between ethical stances and, 69, 70

Keynote
for activity reports, 243
for organizing content, 396
for presentations, 534
for proposals, 222
for technical descriptions, 140
KISS (Keep It Simple Stupid) principle, using in presentations, 542, 550

Labeling, of graphics, 464, 479–480, 481f
Laboratory reports, 236, 237f–238f
Land ethic, 68, 68f
Language other than English, in résumé, 307
Laws
copyright, 76, 78–80, 79f
resolving ethical dilemma and, 70
Layouts. See Page layouts
Learning tool, instructions as, 179, 180f–181f
Legal issues
ethical, 70, 72
in social ethics, 66
in technical communication, 12
Leininger, Carol, 37, 511
Leopold, Aldo, 68, 68f
Letterhead, 106, 107, 107f
Letters

adjustment, 93, 96, 97f
claim, 93, 95f
complaint, 93, 95f
conclusion in, 102
context of use and, 90
described, 84
features of, 85, 86f, 106–109, 107f
formatting of, 85–86, 86f, 106–109, 107f
of inquiry, 90, 91f
introduction in, 96, 99, 100f, 101
organizing and drafting, 96, 99–103
planning and researching, 88–90
of reference, in portfolio, 319
of refusal, 96, 98f
with reports, 278
of response, 90, 92f
style of, 105–106
thank you, 322–324, 323f
tone in, 116–117
transmittal, 90, 93, 278
types of, 90–97
Libel, ethics and, 78
Library research, 264, 371–374
Library search engine, 373f
LibSyn, 569
Limited use, of copyrighted material, 80
Line drawings, 491
Line graphs, 481–483
showing a trend, 482f
showing relationship between variables, 483f
LinkedIn, 565, 566, 566f
Links
in e-mail, 88f
to webpages, 88f, 560
Listening, in transcultural communication, 32
Lists
colons in, A-12
idea generation through, 336
parentheses clarifying, A-18
sequential and nonsequential, 464–466, 465f
Listservs, 371
Literature review, of sources, 388
Local area networks (LANs), 54
Logic, reasoning with, 344, 344f, 349–350
Logical mapping
of authoritative tone, 438, 439f
of current situation (proposals), 206, 208, 208f
to develop a research methodology, 262, 262f
of emotional tone, 184, 185f, 220f, 437, 438f
for framing, 357f
to generate content, 100, 100f
for generating ideas, 335–336, 335f, 367, 367f
to identify steps in instructions, 170–171, 170f
for instructions and documentation, 165, 166f
for letter or memo, 101, 102f
partitioning of subject with, 127–128, 128f
of plan, 331, 332f

Logical mapping (*continued*)
of project plan, 210, 210*f*
for proposals, 202, 203*f*, 206, 208*f*, 220*f*
of research methodology, 369–370, 369*f*
software in, 335–336, 335*f*
use by researchers, 367, 367*f*, 369–370, 369*f*
for websites, 560, 561
Low-context cultures, 414

Magazines
in APA documentation style, A-29
in CSE documentation style, A-33
in MLA documentation style, A-38
as research sources, 374
Main point
of analytical report, 265, 267
in conclusion, 102
of e-mail, 96, 99, 102
of home page, 561
in introduction, 400
of letter or memo, 96, 99, 102
of presentation, 533
restating in conclusion, 102, 411, 538
of technical description, 131
Maps/Mapping
to generate content, 100, 100*f*
logical. *See* Logical mapping
website, 558
Mars Curiosity Rover, technical description of, 127, 129*f*–130*f*
Martin, Steve, 352
Mascots, graphic uses of, 494
McCloud, Scott, 140
Me and *I*, pronoun case error with, A-6–A-7
Measurements, technical description and, 126
Measuring results, in usability testing, 515
Mediation
of conflict in meetings, 50–51, 51*f*
in ethical conflict with company, 72
Mediator, of meeting conflict, 50
Medium
for activity reports, 243
for instructions and documentation, 188
for proposals, 222
for technical descriptions, 140
Meeting facilitator, 48
Meetings
agenda for, 48, 49*f*, 50
avoiding texting/tweeting during, 103
effective, strategies for conducting, 48–50
mediating conflict during, 56–57, 57*f*
next, deciding upon, 50
recording decisions in, 50
scheduling in task list, 333
Memo to file, in ethical conflict with company, 72
Memos
adjustment, 93, 96
body of, 87*f*, 100*f*
claim, 93
complaint, 93
conclusion in, 100*f*, 102
context of use for, 90
described, 84

design of, 106
features of, 85, 87*f*, 109–111, 110*f*
formatting of, 85–86, 87*f*, 109–111, 110*f*
of inquiry, 90
introduction in, 96, 99, 101, 101*f*
organizing and drafting, 96, 99–103
planning and researching, 88–90
of refusal, 96
with reports, 278
of response, 90
style of, 105–106
tone in, 105–106
transmittal, 90, 93, 94*f*, 278
types of, 90–97
Mendeley, 385
Message
in letter, 107*f*, 108
in memo, 110*f*, 111
Message area, in e-mail, 88*f*
Metacafe, 569
Metaphors, 439–440
in technical descriptions, 137
in transcultural documents, 511
Methodology, research, 368–371
for analytical report, 262–263, 262*f*
describing, 370, 370*f*
logical mapping of, 367*f*, 369–370, 369*f*
outlining, 370*f*
revising, 370–371
using, 370–371
Methodology section, in analytical report, 266
Methods/results/discussion pattern, in presentation, 536, 537*f*
Metrics, 55
Microblogs, 78, 568–569
Microform/microfiche, as research source, 374
Microsoft Exchange, 54
Microsoft Explorer, 184
Microsoft Expression Web, 184
Microsoft Movie Maker, 570
Microsoft Outlook, 52, 54
Microsoft Paint, 491
Microsoft Project, 42
Middle East, direction of reading in, 31*f*, 469, 570*f*
Mighty Meeting (app), 534
MindManager, 336
Mission statement, in forming stage of teaming, 41
MLA documentation style, A-24, A-34–A-39
for in-text citations, A-35–A-36
for works cited list, A-36–A-39
Mobile devices
giving presentations with, 534
global and transcultural communication and, 24
Modifier, dangling, A-3–A-4
Moral guidance, resolving ethical dilemma and, 72
Motion
in instruction and documentation, 166
technical description and, 126
Motivation, providing in instructions, 168

Moveable Type, 568
MP3 players, 371
MSN Videos, 569
Music
in APA documentation style, A-29
copyright law and, 78
in CSE documentation style, A-33
in MLA documentation style, A-38
MySpace, 75
MySpace Videos, 569

Name
meanings in transcultural markets, 188
in résumé, 299
Narrative pattern, in presentation, 536, 537*f*
NASA
reframing of issues by, 356, 358*f*
technical description of Mars Curiosity Rover, 127, 129*f*–130*f*
National Commission on Writing, 14
National Science Foundation (NSF) website, 196, 201*f*
Navigation pages, 558
Need-to-know information, 20
in letters, memos, and e-mails, 101, 102*f*
in research, 378
Needs. *See also* Problem/needs/solution pattern
and goals compared, 353
nature of, 22
of readers, 21
Negative information, avoiding "you" style with, 105
Netflix, 371
Netiquette, for e-mail in transcultural communication, 111–112
Networking. *See also* Social networking
electronic networks, 52, 54
personal, 297
professional, 297
surveillance and, 77
Newspapers
in APA documentation style, A-29
in CSE documentation style, A-33
in MLA documentation style, A-38
as research sources, 374
"No," in transcultural communication, 24, 360
Node pages, 558
Nominalizations, eliminating, 425
from analytical report, 285
Nonbureaucratic phrasing, 106
Nonsequential lists, designing, 464–466, 465*f*
Noodle, 52
Norming stage of teaming, 40*f*, 52–54
Note taking
paraphrasing as, 380–381
for quotations, 379–380
in research process, 379–384
Notepad, for presentations, 527
Notes. *See also* Field notes
instructional steps with, 173
using during presentation, 547–548

Notes View feature, in presentation software, 548, 549, 549f
Nouns, apostrophe use with, A-14
Numbered steps
in instructions and documentation, 172–173
paragraph style instructions and, 173, 174–175f
Numbers
apostrophe use with, A-14
colons in, A-12
commas and, A-10
dashes in, A-17

Object of sentence, in transcultural documents, 511
Objectives
in forming stage of teaming, 41
of meeting, 48, 49f
in norming stage of teaming, 51
revising, 52
in strategic planning process, 330–331
for usability testing, 515
Objects, photographing, 489–490, 490f
Observations
field notes and, in research, 374
for instruction research, 165
persuasion with, 350–351
purpose of, 120
reasoning with, 350–351
in research, 264
"OK" hand signal, 469
On-screen documentation, 183–184. See also Instructions and documentation
Online calendars, 333–334, 333f
Online Ethics Center, National Academy of Engineering, 73, 73f
Online Help features, 183, 183f
Online persuasion strategies, 352
Online sources, for technical definitions, 508
Open-ended questions, 375
Opening
of current situation section (proposals), 208
of document section, 402, 402f
of methodology section of analytical report, 266
of project plan (proposals), 211
of webpage, 561
Oppenheimer, Robert, 64f
Options, reducing, as online persuasion strategy, 352
Organization, 395–417
of activity reports, 239–241
of analytical reports, 265–276
for any document, 395, 396f
of application letter, 310, 310f, 313, 316f
cultural differences in, 29–30
and drafting of body, 402–410
and drafting of conclusion, 411, 414
and drafting of introduction, 399–401
of e-mail, 96, 99–103
editing for, 501
by genre, 395–396, 398f, 399
of instructions and documentation, 167–182

of letters and memos, 84, 96, 99–103
outline and, 395–396, 398f, 399
of portfolio, 318–319
of presentation content, 529–540
presentation software for, 548
of proposals, 203–218
role of genres in, 2–3, 3f, 395–396, 398f, 399
of technical descriptions, 128, 131–137
of transcultural documents, 414–417
of websites, 560–561
in writing process, 3, 4f, 6
Outcomes
in forming stage of teaming, 41
in norming stage of teaming, 52
Outline mode/view, in word processor, 337, 337f, 398f
Outlining
of document, 337, 337f, 395–396, 398f, 399
in drafting process, 337
of research methodology, 370, 370f
using genres for, 395–396, 398f, 399
Overhead projector, 526–527

Page layouts
for analytical report, 286f
balance in, 448f, 449f, 450f, 451–455
consistency in, 462f–463f
grids for, 451–455
for instructions and documentation, 185, 186f–187f
for proposals, 220, 221f, 222
for technical description, 139–140
weighting, 448, 451
Pamphlets
in APA documentation style, A-28
in CSE documentation style, A-33
in MLA documentation style, A-38
Paragraph, sentence types in, 431f
Paragraphs
in active and passive voice, 435–437
aligning sentence subjects in, 433–434
copyediting, 504–505
elements of, 430–432
given/new method of writing, 434–435
paragraph style instructions, 173, 174–175f
in plain writing style, 243, 430–435
using sentence types in, 432–433
on websites, 561
Parallelism, faulty, A-5–A-6
Paraphrased materials
APA documentation style for, A-26
in executive summary, 280, 281f–283f
MLA documentation style for, A-36
recording, 380–381
Parentheses, 507f, A-17–A-18
Parenthetical citations
in APA documentation style, A-27
in MLA documentation style, A-36
Partitioning of subject
with logical mapping, 127–128, 128f
in technical description, 127–128, 128f
Parts list, in instructions, 168, 169f
Parts of a sentence, 423

Passion, creativity and, 335
Passive voice
in analytical reports, 285
in application letter, 316
decision to use, 435–437
Past tenses, A-21–A-22
perfect, A-22
perfect progressive, A-22
progressive, A-22
Patchwriting, 80, 389
Patents
ethics and, 77
purpose of, 120
Patience, persuasion and, 359
Patterns of arrangement
for documents, 254, 255, 403–412
for presentations, 535–537, 537f
Pauses, in presentation, 547
PDF (Portable Document Format) files, 84
for activity reports, 243
for instructions and documentation, 184
for technical descriptions, 140
People
photographing, 488–489, 489f
use of images in transcultural texts, 468
Perfect tenses, A-21
progressive, A-21
Performance tests, in usability testing, 514
Performing stage of teaming, 40f
Period, 507f, A-9
Periodical index, 374
Permission
copyright and, 79–80
for using source material, 389
Persona, presentation style and, 541
Personal communication. See Correspondence
Personal ethics, 64–65, 65f
in ethical dilemma, balancing, 70f
Personal networking, 297
Persuasion, 344–360
in analytical reports, 285–286
in ethical conflict with company, 72
in high-context cultures, 357, 359–360
online strategies for, 352
reasoning-based, 344–351
types of, 344f
values-based, 344f, 351, 353–357, 354f–355f, 357f
Persuasive documents, purpose of, action verbs defining, 6, 6f
Persuasive style, 8, 422
balance between plain style and, 442
for proposals, 220
sample persuasive argument, 441f
techniques for, 344f, 437–442
uses of, 437–442
Pew Charitable Trust website, 264f
Pew Research Center, archive of, 264f
Phone, mobile, giving presentations with, 534
Photographs, 488–491, 489f, 490f
digital, 138–139
in e-mail, 112
inserting into documents, 490–491
storytelling with, 477, 478f
in technical descriptions, 138–139

Phrasing
  bureaucratic vs. nonbureaucratic, 106
  rhyming, use of, 352
Physical context of use, 22, 23
  for analytical reports, 260
  for presentation, 524–525
  for proposals, 202
Pictures, using, 487–492
Pie charts, 485–486, 487f
Place names, commas in, A-10
Places, photographing, 490
Plagiarism
  avoiding, 79–80, 265, 388–389
  defined, 80, 389
Plain sentences, 243
  creating with computer, 427–428
  writing, 422–428, 427f
Plain style, 8, 422
  for activity reports, 243
  for analytical reports, 285–286
  balance between persuasive style and, 442
  for instructions and documentation, 184–185
  paragraphs in, 430–435
  for proposals, 220
  sentences in. See Plain sentences
  for technical description, 139
PlanetIntra's Noodle, 52
Planning. See also Strategic planning
  for activity reports, 236, 239
  for analytical reports, 259–260
  for career, 294–298
  for e-mail, 88–90
  for instructions and documentation, 155, 164–165
  for letters and memos, 88–90
  with online calendars, 333–334, 333f
  for presentations, 521–526
  for proposals, 196, 201–202
  for technical descriptions, 120–125
  timeline in, 332
  in writing process, 4–6, 4f
Plurals, apostrophe use with, A-14
Podcast Alley, 569, 570
Podcasts/Podcasting, 569–570, 571f
  in APA documentation style, A-29
  editing, 570, 571f
  recording, 570
  as research source, 371
  uploading, 570
PodOmatic, 569
Point sentences, 432–433
  in paragraph, 433
Politeness, transcultural communication and, 32
Political context of use, 23
  for analytical reports, 260
  for presentation, 525
  for proposals, 202
Political dimensions, in technical communication, 12
Portfolio
  assembling in binder, 319
  electronic, 319, 320f
  organizing, 318–319

professional, 317–320, 322
  using in interview, 322
Possession, apostrophe signaling, A-13–A-14
Posters
  NASA example, 356, 358f
  presentations using, 287, 288f, 528
Posture, for presentation, 546
Power Translator, 429, 509
PowerPoint
  for activity reports, 243
  for organizing content, 396, 398f
  for presentations, 534
  for proposals, 222
  for technical descriptions, 140
Prefixes, hyphens with, A-17
Prepositional phrases, eliminating excessive, 426
Present tenses, A-22
  perfect, A-22
  perfect progressive, A-22
  progressive, A-22
Presentation Remote (app), 534
Presentation software, 548. See also individually named software
  apps for mobile phone or tablet, 534
  Notes View feature in, 548, 549, 549f
  as outlining tool, 396, 398f, 399
Presentation style, 540–542
  enthusiasm and, 542
  persona and, 541
  theme and, 541, 541f
Presentations, 521–553
  answering questions during/after, 539
  audience for, 524, 530, 538
  body of, 535–537
  conclusion in, 537–539
  delivering, 545–548
  evaluation of, 548, 551f–552f
  grabbers for, 533
  introduction in, 530–535
  organizing content of, 529–540
  pattern of arrangement for, 531f, 535–537, 537f
  planning and researching, 521–526
  practice and rehearsal for, 548
  preparation process for, 522f
  rehearsing, 548
  slides for, 532, 538f, 543f, 544–545, 545f, 547
  structure of, 530, 531f
  subject of, 523, 531–533, 538
  technology for, 526–529, 527f
  test audience for, 549
  time management in, 525–526, 526f
  for transcultural audience, translators and, 548, 550, 552–553
  visuals for, 542–545, 553
Prezi
  for activity reports, 243
  for technical descriptions, 140
Primary audience (action takers), for presentations, 524
Primary readers (action takers), 20–21, 20f, 21
  of analytical reports, 259

of e-mail, 89
  of instructions and documentation, 165
  of letters, memos, and e-mail, 89
  of proposals, 202
  of technical descriptions, 125
Primary research, 365, 366, 366f, 374–378
Print sources
  forms of, 373–374
  in research, 371, 372–374, 373f
Prioritization, of issues in meeting, 50
Privacy issues, 77, 77f
Problem/needs/solution pattern
  as document pattern of arrangement, 408, 412f–414f
  for presentations, 535, 537f
Procedures/Protocols. See also Instructions and documentation
  example of, 158f–160f
  features of, 154
  nature of, 153
  organizing by genre, 395–396, 398f, 399
Process, stages of, partitioning subject in technical descriptions, 127
Product names, in transcultural documents, 511
Production, 55
Professional codes, resolving ethical dilemma and, 70
Professional networking, 297
Professional portfolio, 317–320
  using in interview, 322
Profiling, of readers, 19–24
Progress reports, 231, 233f, 242f
Progressive tenses, A-22
Project calendar, 42, 43f, 44f, 333–334, 333f
Project planning
  logical mapping for, 210, 210f, 331, 332f
  software for, 42, 43f
Prompt, 509
Pronouns
  brackets to replace, A-18
  case error (I and me, we and us), A-6–A-7
  pronoun-antecedent disagreement, A-5
  vague, A-7–A-8
Proofreading, 8, 499, 505–508
  of application letter, 317
  Track Changes feature and, 501f, 503
Proposals, 196–225
  categories of, 196
  conclusion in, 218, 219f
  context of use, 202
  costs and benefits section of, 218, 219f
  current situation in, describing, 206, 208
  design of, 218, 220–222
  elevator pitch, 223–225
  features of, 197
  grant, 196
  graphics in, 220, 221f, 222
  legal and ethical issues and, 202
  logical mapping for, 202, 203f, 206, 208f, 220f
  medium for, 222
  organizing and drafting of, 203–218
  planning of, 196, 201–202

project plan for, 208, 210–211, 212f–215f
purpose of, 201–202
qualifications section of, describing, 211, 216f–217f
researching, 202–203
solicited, 196, 198f–200f
style of, 220
tone in, 220, 221f
unsolicited, 196
Proprietary information, ethics and, 77–78
Protocols. See Procedures/Protocols
Public speaking, 521. See also Presentations
Publication Manual of the American Psychological Association, 384
Punctuation
copyediting, 505–506
guide to, A-8–A-18
physical characteristics of, 507f
Puns, in transcultural documents, 430
Purpose
action verbs defining, 6, 6f
of activity reports, 239
of analytical reports, 254, 259
defining, 5–6, 6f
of e-mail, 89, 96, 99
in editing process, 500
as element of rhetorical situation, 89
in forming stage of teaming, 41
of home page, 560
of instructions and documentation, 155, 167
in introduction, 399
for letters and memos, 89, 96, 99
of presentations, 524, 533
of proposals, 201–202
in rhetorical situation, 5, 5f, 89
of technical descriptions, 124–125, 131
of website, 560

Qualifications section, of proposals, 211, 216f–217f
Qualitative research, 374
Quality control, editing as, 499
Quality feedback loops, 55, 512
Quality improvement, 55
Quality of document, improvement strategies, 512
Quantitative research, 374
QuarkXPress, 460
Quattro Pro, 485
Question mark, 507f, A-9
Questionnaires, for research, 375, 376f–377f
Questions. See also Five-W and How Questions
answering during/after presentation, 539
for appraising sources, 387f
closed-ended/open-ended, 375
in interview, 321–322
research. See Hypothesis
survey, 264, 375, 376f–377f
in usability testing, 513–515
Quotation marks, 507f, A-9, A-14–A-16
commas with, A-10
with in-text citations, A-16
for quotations, A-14–A-15

within quotations, 379
signaling irony, A-15–A-16
for title within a quote, A-15
using colons and semicolons with, A-12
using periods, exclamation points, and question marks with, A-9
Quotations/Quotes, A-9
documenting, A-24
from experts, 351
in presentation introduction, 531
quotation marks for, A-14–A-15
quotation marks within, 379
recording, 379–380
using ellipses with, A-18

Radio programs
in APA documentation style, A-30
in CSE documentation style, A-34
in MLA documentation style, A-38
as research source, 371
Read-and-locate tests, 513–514
Reader Analysis Chart, 22, 22f, 24
Reader profile(s)
contexts of use and, 24, 25f–28f
creating, 19–24
Readers. See also Audience; Gatekeepers (supervisors); Primary readers (action takers); Secondary readers (advisors); Tertiary readers (evaluators)
of activity reports, 239
of analytical reports, 259–260
of e-mail, 89
in editing process, 500
in forming stage of teaming, 41
general public vs. experts as, 25f–28f
identifying, 20–21
of instructions and documentation, 164–165, 168
for letters and memos, 89
making decisions, 22
needs, values, and attitudes of, 21–22
of proposals, 202
as "raiders" for information, 8, 19
in rhetorical situation, 5, 5f, 89
of technical communication, 10–11, 89
of technical descriptions, 125
transcultural, instructions and documentation for, 188–189
types of, 20–21, 20f
of website, 560
Reader's Guide to Periodical Literature, 374
Reading, direction of, 31, 31f, 469, 470f
Reasoning
document using, 345f–348f
with examples and evidence, 344, 344f, 350–351
in high-context cultures, 359
with logic, 344, 344f, 349–350
persuading with, 344–351
Recipient address, on envelope, 109, 109f
Recommendation reports, 254
Recordings
in APA documentation style, A-29
in CSE documentation style, A-33
in MLA documentation style, A-38
Redundancy in sentence, eliminating, 426

Reference list, 383
in APA documentation style, 384f, 385, A-27–A-30
in CSE documentation style, A-31–A-34
MLA works cited list and, A-36–A-39
Reference materials, as research source, 374
References (personal)
in portfolio, 319
in résumé, 307
Reframing of issues, 356, 358f
Refusal, letters/memos/e-mail of, 96, 98f
RefWorks, 385
Rehearsal, of presentation, 548
Relationships
building in high-context cultures, 357, 359
between variables, line graphs for, 481, 483f
Reliability, of sources, 365, 366, 366f, 374, 387–388, 489
Religious references and symbols, 494, 553
Reply text, in e-mail, 88f
Reports. See individually named report types, e.g. Activity reports
Research, 365–390, 378–388
for activity reports, 236, 239
for analytical reports, 260–265
beginning, 365–366, 366f
bias in, 387–388
defining subject for, 366–368, 367f
for e-mail, 88–90
electronic sources for, 371, 372f
empirical (primary), 365, 366, 366f, 374–378
hypothesis for. See Hypothesis
information appraisal in, 387–390
information collection methods, 263–265
information management in, 365, 395
for instructions and documentation, 165–166, 166f
interviews for, 374
for letters and memos, 88–90
methodology for, 262–263, 262f, 368–371, 369f
narrowing subject of, 367–368
need-to-know information in, 20, 378
note taking in, 379–384
plagiarism and, 80, 265, 388–389
for presentations, 521–526
print sources for, 373–374
process of, 366f
for proposals, 202–203
quantitative and qualitative, 374
question. See Hypothesis
questionnaires, 375, 376f–377f
secondary, 366, 366f
source materials in, 366, 366f, 371–375
for technical descriptions, 125–127
for transcultural communication, 32
triangulating materials in, 366f, 375, 378, 378f
want-to-tell information in, 378
in writing process, 6
Research angle, 368

Research databases, 371, 372*f*
Research question. *See* Hypothesis
Research reports, 254, 256*f*–258*f*
Research subject, 366–368, 367*f*
Research triangle, 378*f*
Researcher(s)
 logical mapping used by, 367, 367*f*
 as team role, 42
Resignation, in ethical conflict with company, 73
Resolution, in digital photography, 138
Respect, in virtual teaming, 53
Response, letter/memo/e-mail of, 90, 92*f*
Results, in usability testing, 515
Résumé, 298–309
 chronological, 298, 299–307, 301*f*–305*f*
 design of, 308
 features of, 295
 functional, 298, 307–308, 309*f*
 revising and proofreading, 317
 scannable/searchable, 311, 312*f*
Retouching, digital photography, 139
Return address, on envelope, 109, 109*f*
Return on investment (ROI), 55
Revising, 499–501
 of application letter, 317
 of document, 502*f*
 of research hypothesis, 265, 390
 of research methodology, 371–372
 of résumé, 317
 in writing process, 3, 4*f*, 8–9
Rhetorical question, in introduction, 531
Rhetorical situation
 in activity reports, 236, 239
 in analytical reports, 259–260
 defining, 4–5, 5*f*, 41
 in e-mail, 88–90
 for editing, 500–501
 elements of, 5, 5*f*
 in letters and memos, 89–90
 for presentations, 523–525, 523*f*
 proposal writing and, 201–202
Rhyme phrases, use of, 352
Rhythm, of presentation, 547
Rights, in social ethics, 65, 66–67, 66*f*
 tension between ethical stances and, 69
RoboHelp, 183
Roles, in teams, 42
 redefining, 54
Roosevelt, Franklin D., 61
 Einstein's letter to, 62*f*–63*f*
Rules, in design, 460
Run-on sentences, A-2–A-3

Safari (browser), 184, 371
Safety information
 in instructions and documentation, 176–177, 189–191
 in usability testing, 514–515
Sans serif typefaces, 461, 464, 464*f*
Sayings, in transcultural communication, 429, 511, 552
Scannable résumé, 311, 312*f*
Scanning pages
 by culture, 469, 470*f*
 transcultural communication and, 31, 31*f*

Scarcity, creating impression of, 352
Scheduling, in groupware, 54, 55*f*, 333–334
Screen-based documents
 design balance in, 447–455, 448–451
 types of images in, 563
Search engines, 371, 373*f*, 533
 for jobs, 296, 296*f*
 for research, 387
Searchable résumé, 311, 312*f*
Searches, Internet, 263
Second-level headings, 458, 459*f*
Secondary audience (advisors), for presentations, 524
Secondary readers (advisors), 20*f*, 21
 of analytical reports, 260
 of e-mail, 89
 of instructions and documentation, 165
 of letters, memos, and e-mail, 89
 of proposals, 202
 of technical descriptions, 125
Secondary sources, 365, 366
Security clearance, 78
Semicolons, 507*f*, A-11–A-12
 in a series, A-12
 using with quotation marks, A-12
Senses
 instructions and documentation and, 166
 technical description and, 126, 136
Sentences. *See also* Subject of sentence
 in active and passive voice, 435–437
 aligning subjects in paragraphs, 433–434
 basic parts of, 423
 copyediting, 504
 definitions, 144, 145
 faulty parallelism, A-5–A-6
 fragment, A-3
 guidelines for writing, 422–428
 length of, 220, 285, 426–427, 429, 440, 442, 561
 in paragraph, 430–435
 in plain writing style. *See* Plain sentences
 run-on, A-2–A-3
 subject-verb agreement, A-4–A-5
 transition, 430–431, 432–433
 types in paragraph, 431*f*
 on websites, 561
Sequential lists, 464–466, 465*f*
Sequentially ordered steps, in instructions, 170–176, 170*f*, 172*f*
Series, semicolons in a, A-12
Serif typefaces, 461, 464, 464*f*
Set of instructions. *See* Instructions and documentation
Shading, in design, 467
Shared values, 353, 358*f*
Sharing information, ethics of, 76, 77, 78
Shifted tense, A-7
Shoulders, relaxing during presentation, 546
Show of hands, in presentation introduction, 533
Shutter speed, digital photography and, 138
Sidebars, for design balance, 460
Signal, for conclusion of presentation, 538
Signatures

in e-mail, 88*f*
 for letters, 107*f*, 108
 signature file, for e-mail, 112
Similes, 438
 in technical descriptions, 136–137
Simple tenses, A-21
 future, A-22
 past, A-21
 present, A-22
Site maps, 558
Skills
 in application letter, 315*f*
 in portfolio, 318
 in professional bio, 324–325
 in résumé, 306–307
Slander, ethics and, 78
Slang, in transcultural communication, 511, 552
Slide sorter, content organization and, 396
Slides, for presentation, 532, 538*f*, 543*f*, 545*f*
 ineffective, 544–545
 as memory tool, 547
Slogans
 meanings in transcultural markets, 188–189
 in transcultural documents, 511
Social ethics, 64, 65–67, 65*f*
 in ethical dilemma, balancing, 70*f*
Social harmony, persuasion and, 359
Social networking, 75, 296–297, 565–569
 blogs, 78, 371, 568–569, 568*f*, A-29
 collaboration and, 567
 company interaction with customers via, 567
 maintaining site for, 567
 microblogs, 568–569
 for personal use, 565–566
 for professional use, 565–566
 texting and tweeting, 103–104
 in workplace, 565–567
Software. *See also* Word processors
 for boxing, 338*f*
 citation manager, 385–386
 grammar checker, 505, 507*f*
 groupware, 52, 54–55, 55*f*, 277–278, 277*f*
 for handling graphics, 491
 Help-authoring, 183
 for logical mapping, 335–336, 335*f*
 presentation. *See* Presentation software
 project planning, 42, 43*f*
 sound editing, 570
 spelling checker, 429, 506, 507*f*, 508
 spreadsheet programs, 485
 translation, 429–430, 509, 564, 564*f*
 video editing, 570
Solicited proposals, 196, 198*f*–200*f*
Songs
 in APA documentation style, A-29
 in CSE documentation style, A-33
 in MLA documentation style, A-38
Spatial organization, in presentation, 535–536, 537*f*
Specialized terms, 285–286

Specifications. *See also* Instructions and
documentation; Technical descriptions
example, 141*f*–142*f*, 161*f*–164*f*
features of, 154
as genre, 2
nature of, 3*f*, 153
purpose of, 120
Speed of speech, during presentation, 550
Spelling checkers, 429, 506, 507*f*, 508
Splash page, on website, 559
Spreadsheet programs, 485
Stages of process, technical description by, 135, 136*f*
partitioning of subject in, 127
Start-up research, in writing process, 6
Statistics, startling, in presentation intro- duction, 531
Status reports, 248–249, 249*f*
Steps, in instructions
adding comments, notes, or examples to, 173
command voice for, 171
feedback on, 176
numbering the steps, 172–173
one action per step, 171, 172*f*
paragraph style, 173, 174*f*–175*f*
referring to graphics in, 176
sequentially ordered, 170–176, 170*f*, 172*f*
Storming stage of teaming, 40*f*, 44, 48–51
Storytelling, with graphics, 477, 478*f*
Strategic planning, 330–339. *See also* Planning
in forming stage of teaming, 40–44
generating new ideas, 336–341
objectives in, 330–331
online calendars in, 333–334, 333*f*
steps in, 330–332, 330*f*
task list for, 331–332
using, 330–332
Style, 422–442
of activity reports, 243
of analytical reports, 285–286
of application letters, 316–317
cultural differences in, 30–31
defined, 422
of e-mail, 105–106
grand, 422
of instructions and documentation, 184–188
of letters and memos, 105–106
persuasive, 422, 437–442
plain. *See* Plain style
of presentation, 540–542
of proposals, 220
of technical descriptions, 139–143
of website, 561
in writing process, 3, 4*f*, 8
Subject
of activity reports, 236
of analytical reports, 259, 261*f*
of e-mail, 85, 88*f*, 89, 96, 99
in editing process, 500
in forming stage of teaming, 41
of home page, 560
of instructions and documentation, 155

in introduction, 399, 400, 531–533
for letters and memos, 85, 87*f*, 89, 96, 99, 100*f*, 101
partitioning, in technical descriptions, 127–128
of presentation, 523, 531–533, 538
of presentations, 523, 531–533, 538
of proposals, 201
re-emphasizing, in conclusion, 411
of research, 366–368, 367*f*
researching and managing, 6
in rhetorical situation, 5, 5*f*, 89
of sentence. *See* Subject of sentence
of technical descriptions, 124, 131, 135
of website, 560
Subject line, of memo, 100*f*, 109, 110*f*, 111
Subject matter experts (SMEs)
on campus, 374
identifying, 22
for instructions and documentation, 166
journal articles by, 373
for proposals, 202
for technical descriptions, 127
Subject of sentence, 423–425
"doer" as, 424
position of, 424–425
in transcultural documents, 511
Subject-verb disagreement, A-4–A-5
Substantive editing, 8, 499, 501–503, 503*f*
Summary
in analytical report, 266, 278–280
recording from research sources, 381, 382*f*–383*f*
Supervisors. *See* Gatekeepers (supervisors)
Support sentences, in paragraph, 431–432
Surveillance, in electronic networks, 77, 77*f*
Surveillance cameras, 77, 77*f*
Surveys, in research, 264, 375, 376*f*–377*f*
Sustainability, and conservation ethics, 69
Symbols
animal, 494
apostrophe use with, A-14
for copyediting, 509, 509*f*, 510*f*
in instructions for transcultural markets, 189
in other cultures, 469
religious, 494
safety, 177
transcultural, 492–494

Table of contents, in analytical report, 284
Tables, 484–485, 486*f*
parts of, 485*f*
Tablet device, giving presentations with, 534
Targeting, of companies, in job search, 297
Task list
for strategic planning, 331–332
task dates in, 332
Team members
assigning responsibilities to, 42
firing, 51
Team Performance Review, 55, 56*f*
Teaming, 10, 11, 40–57
advantages and disadvantages of, 57
firing team member and, 51
forming stage of, 40–44

keys to, 57
member responsibilities in, 42
norming stage of, 40*f*, 52–54
performing stage of, 40*f*, 54–55
project calendar and, 42, 43*f*, 44*f*, 333–334, 333*f*
roles in, 42, 54
stages of, 40, 40*f*
storming stage of, 40*f*, 44–51
in technical communication, 10, 12*f*
through social networking sites, 567
virtual, 52–53, 54–55, 277–278, 277*f*
writing work plan and, 42–43, 45*f*–47*f*
Teamwork. *See* Teaming
Technical ability, describing in instruc- tions, 167–168
Technical communication, 9–15
defined, 9
genre-based approach to, 3–9
genres in, 3–9
importance of, 14–15
overview of, 2–15
qualities of, 9, 10–14, 10*f*
Technical definitions, 144–145
online sources for, 508
writing, 144–145
Technical descriptions
context of use and, 125
designing, 139–143
digital photography in, 138–139
examples, 122*f*–124*f*, 129*f*–130*f*
by features, functions, or stages in pro- cess, 127, 135, 136*f*, 536, 537*f*
features of, 121, 122*f*–124*f*, 128, 131–137
ISO 9000/ISO 14000 standards and, 125, 126*f*, 138
medium for, 140
organizing and drafting, 128, 131–137
partitioning subject for, 127–128
planning of, 120–125
purpose of, 120
researching of, 125–127
by senses, similes, analogies, and meta- phors, 136–137
style of, 139–143
Technology, for presentations, 526–529, 527*f*
Telecommuting/teleworking, 52–53
Teleconferences, 53, 53*f*
Television programs
in APA documentation style, A-30
in CSE documentation style, A-34
in MLA documentation style, A-38
as research source, 371
Tenses
shifted, A-7
verb, A-21–A-23
Tertiary audience (evaluators), for presentations, 524
Tertiary readers (evaluators), 20*f*, 21
of analytical reports, 260
of instructions and documentation, 165
of letters and memos, 89
of proposals, 202
of technical descriptions, 125

Text
  graphics complementing, 477, 479, 479f
  highlighting of, 467
Texting, in workplace, 103–104
Thank you
  in analytical reports, 267
  in conclusion, 95f, 101f, 102, 414, 539
  in proposal conclusion, 218, 219f
  in transcultural communication, 30
Thank-you letters
  after interviews, 322–324, 323f
  via e-mail, 324
the, use of article, A-19
Themes
  in application letters, 316–317
  setting in presentation, 541f
Third-level headings, 458, 459f
Time, required for completion, in instructions, 168
Time management. See also Calendar(s)
  in meetings, 48
  in planning process, 332
  in presentations, 525–526, 526f
  in teaming, 53, 54, 55f, 333–334
Title page, in analytical reports, 278, 279f
Titles, personal, 108, 111
Titles of works
  colons in, A-12
  in instructions and documentation, 167, 189, 190f
  quotation marks with, A-15
  in technical descriptions, 131
  title page of analytical report, 278
Toastmasters International, 549, 550f
Tone
  in activity reports, 243
  in application letters, 316
  elevating, for persuasive style, 437–438
  in email, 105–106
  in instructions and documentation, 185
  in letters and memos, 105–106
  mapping of, 220f, 437–438, 438f, 439f
  persuasive, for proposals, 220, 220f, 221f
  of presentation, 547
  in transcultural communication, 511
  of websites, 561
  word mapping of, 184, 185f
Tools list, in instructions, 168
Topic sentence, 432–433
  in paragraph, 431
Total Quality Management (TQM), 55
Track Changes, 503, 504f
Trademarks, ethics and, 76–77
Transcultural communication, 14. See also Transcultural documents
  computers and, 24
  content and, 24, 28–30
  customs in, 24–32, 111–112
  design and, 31–32, 31f, 468–470
  design considerations in, 189
  e-mail and, 111–112
  editing in, 509, 511–512
  graphics in, 32, 468–469, 542–543
  in high-context cultures, 357, 359–360, 414–417
  listening in, 32

presentations for international audience, 548, 550, 552–553
  scanning page and, 570f
  strategies for, 32
  style and, 30–31
  symbols and, 542–543
  translators and, 548, 550, 552–553
  verbal considerations in, 188–189
  websites for, 563–564
Transcultural documents
  editing of, 509, 511–512
  organizing, considerations for, 29–30, 414–417, 417f
  scanning pages in, 569
Transition, in conclusion, 411
Transition sentences, 430–431, 432–433
Translation, 429–430
Translation software, 429–430, 509, 564, 564f
Translations
  in CSE documentation style, A-32
  of instructions and documentation, 188
  in MLA documentation style, A-37
  for transcultural communication, 509, 511–512512
  for transcultural presentations, 548, 550, 552–553
  website, 564, 564f
Transmittal documents, 90, 93, 94f, 278. See also E-mail; Letters; Memos
Transparencies, for overhead projector, 526–527
Trends, line graphs for, 481, 482f
Triangulation, of research materials, 366, 366f, 375, 378, 378f
Troubleshooting guide, 179, 182f
Trust, in virtual teaming, 53
Tuckman, Bruce, 40
Tweeting, in workplace, 103–104
Twitter, 78, 566, 567, 568, 569
Type size, as design element, 467
Typeface, as design element, 461, 464, 464f

Uncountable things, misusing article with, A-19–A-20
Understandability tests, in usability testing, 514
Unsolicited proposals, 196
URL of source material, recording, 379
U.S. Census Bureau website, 263f
U.S. Copyright Office, 76, 78, 80
  website, 79f
U.S. Patent and Trademark Office, 76
Us and we, pronoun case error with, A-6–A-7
Usability, revising and editing for, 499–515
Usability testing, 512–515
  for instructions and documentation, 179
  questions in, 513–515
  types of, 513f
Usage
  common problems in technical documents, 508f
  proofreading for, 508, 508f
User performance, setting objectives for, 513, 515

User-testing, of instructions and documentation, 179
Utility, in social ethics, 66–67, 66f
  tension between ethical stances and, 69

Vague pronoun, A-7–A-8
Values. See also Ethics
  appealing to, 344f, 353, 354f–355f
  nature of, 22
  in personal ethics, 65
  of readers, 21
  reframing of, 356, 358f
  shared, 353, 354f–355f, 358f
Values-based persuasion, 344, 344f, 351, 353–357, 354f–355f, 357f
Velasquez, Manuel, 65
Veoh, 569
Verbal information, in tables, 485, 486f
Verbs. See also Action verbs
  for action of "doer," 424
  in sentence, 424
  as sentence part, 423
  shifted tense, A-7
  subject-verb disagreement, A-4–A-5
  tenses of, A-21–A-23
  in transcultural documents, 511
Verification, in research process, 388
Vertical alignment, 455, 456f
Videoconferences, 53
Videos
  in APA documentation style, A-28
  in CSE documentation style, A-33
  editing, 570
  Internet, 569–570, 571f
  in MLA documentation style, A-38
  presentations and, 534
  as research source, 371
  shooting, 570
  uploading, 570
  in usability testing, 514
Virtual Office, 52
Virtual teaming, 52–53, 54–55, 277–278, 277f
Visio, 336
Visual cues, in technical communication, 12, 13f
Visuals. See also Graphics
  adding to websites, 563, 563f
  in instructions and documentation, 166
  in presentations, 542–545, 553
  in proposals, 203
  for transcultural markets, 189, 492–494
  transcultural symbols as, 492–494
  using, 487–492
Voice
  in application letter, 316
  passive and active, 316, 435–437
  in presentations, 547

Want-to-tell information, in research, 378
Warning statements, in instructions, 176, 177f
We and us, pronoun case error with, A-6–A-7
Webcasting, 78

Weblogs. *See* Blogs
Webpages, 558–559
  in APA documentation style, A-27
  contrast in, 467*f*
  in CSE documentation style,
    A-31–A-32
  drafting of, 560–561
  interactivity and, 10, 11*f*
  in MLA documentation style,
    A-36–A-37
  navigation, 558
  node, 558
Websites, 558–572
  in APA documentation style, A-27
  basic pattern for, 560*f*
  comparison with other documents, 559,
    560*f*
  in CSE documentation style,
    A-31–A-32
  design of, 561–562, 562*f*
  documentation (user's manuals) on, 184
  drafting, 560–561
  ethical case studies on, 73, 73*f*
  features of, 558–560, 559*f*
  images on, 563, 563*f*
  interactivity and, 10, 11*f*
  for international and transcultural read-
    ers, 563–564
  levels of, 561
  in MLA documentation style,
    A-36–A-37
  for NSF grant information, 196, 201*f*
  plain writing style in, 427*f*
  for research, 371
  style of, 561

uploading, 565, 565*f*
  writing for, 558–565
Whistle-blowing, 73
White papers, 231, 234*f*
  template example for, 244*f*–247*f*
White space, using, 457. *See also* Grouping
Whiteboard, for presentations, 527
Wikis, writing articles for, 571–572
Women. *See* Gender
Word processors
  aligning of sentences in paragraph, 433
  grammar checker and, 505, 507*f*
  Insert Picture command, 491
  keeping notes on, 379, 379*f*
  Outline mode/view in, 337, 337*f*, 398*f*
  spelling checker and, 429, 506, 507*f*, 508
  Track Changes feature and, 503, 504*f*
Word usage. *See* Usage
Wordpress, 568, 568*f*
Work experience
  in application letter, 315*f*
  in résumé, 300, 306
Work log, 236
Work plan
  revising, 52
  virtual teaming and, 52
  writing, 42–43, 45*f*–47*f*
Workforce Solutions Group, 2013 survey
  findings, 14
Workload, redistribution within team, 54
Workplace
  developing writing process in, 2–3
  document cycling in, 512*f*
  ethics in, 76–78
  texting and tweeting in, 103–104

Works cited list, for MLA documentation
  style, A-36–A-39
Writer-Centered Analysis Chart, 20–21, 20*f*
Writing
  for websites, 558–565
  for wikis, 571–572
Writing process, 3–9, 4*f*
  designing the document, 106–109
  genres and, 3–9, 4*f*
  stages in, 3–9, 4*f*. *See also individually
    named stages, e.g.* Planning
  stages of, 3
  team member responsibilities
    for, 42
  for work plan, 42–43, 45*f*–47*f*
  in workplace, developing, 2–3
Written text, graphics complementing, 477,
  478*f*, 479, 479*f*, 486*f*

Yahoo!, 333, 371, 387
Yahoo! Vimeo, 569
Yahoo.com, 534
"Yes," in transcultural communication,
  24, 360
"You" style
  in application letter, 316
  in e-mail, 105
  in instructions and documentation, 173
  in letters and memos, 105
  in online persuasion, 352
YouTube, 371, 569, 570
Yuan, Rue, 511

Zimbra, 54, 55*f*
Zotero, 286*f*, 385

SAMPLE DOCUMENTS

Memos

Agenda   *49*
Memos   *87, 100–101, 110, 115–116, 118*
Memo of Transmittal   *94*
"Smoking Gun" Memo   *397*
Work Plan   *45–47*

Letters

Adjustment Letter   *97*
Claim Letter   *95*
Envelope Formatting   *109*
Indirect Approach Letter   *417*
Letter   *86*
Letter of Application Emphasizing Education   *314*
Letter of Application Emphasizing Work Experience   *315*
Letter to F. D. Roosevelt About the Atom Bomb   *62–63*
Letter Formatting   *107*
Letter of Inquiry   *91*
Letter That Uses Reasoning   *345–348*
Professional Biography   *325*
Refusal Letter   *98*
Response Letter   *92*
Thank You Letter   *323*

Brochures and Booklets

Booklet That Appeals to Values   *354*
Brochure with a Balanced Design   *449*
Brochure with Good Design   *13*

Technical Definitions

Extended Definition: Print   *145*
Specification   *141–142*

Webpages

Blog Host Site   *568*
Electronic Portfolio: Welcome Page   *320*
Google Drive Interface   *277*
Home Pages   *201, 559*
Home Page with a Balanced Interface   *451*
Home Page with a Good Design   *9*
Home Page That Uses Alignment and Grouping Well   *458*
Home Page That Uses Contrast   *467*
Library Search Engine   *373*
Model Webpage   *11*
Online Translation Tool   *430*
Research Database   *372*
Social Networking Home Page   *566*
Translating a Website with Bing Translator   *564*
Webpage That Uses Plain Language   *427*
Webpage That Uses Right-to-Left Interface Design   *470*
Well-Designed Interface   *562*

Evaluations

Evaluation Form for Presentations   *551–552*
Team Performance Review   *56*

Résumés

Chronological Résumés   *301, 302, 303*
Chronological Résumé: Student Who Returned to College   *304–305*
Functional Résumé   *309*
Searchable Résumé   *311*